process, any event on the timeline could be placed in more than one category. Some scholars cla̶... ...e̶n̶ happening for a long time, and others say it has only been happening for a relatively short time. As you read through this timelin̶... ...your social world are part of this larger process of global change.

1989 Fall of the Berlin Wall

1991 End of the USSR

1940–1945 WWII

1932 Saudi Arabia is established

1973 Oil crisis follows the 1973 Yom Kippur War

1945 Start of the Cold War

1954 Racial segregation in U.S. schools outlawed by Supreme Court

1992 Creation of the European Union (EU)

1993 UN establishes High Commissioner for Human Rights

1919 League of Nations established

1961 Soviet cosmonaut Yuri Gagarin is the first human to orbit the earth

1997 UK returns Hong Kong to China

2000 Supreme Court decides U.S. presidential election

Early 1930s Great Depression

1995 Foundation of the World Trade Organization (WTO)

1996 NATO forces deployed to the former Yugoslavia

1987 Stock market crash

Rapid growth of Chinese and Indian economies

1947 General Agreement on Tariffs and Trade (GATT) signed

2005 Chinese bid for Unocal

1960 Creation of the Organization of the Petroleum Exporting Countries (OPEC)

1929 Discovery of penicillin

1961 First live televised political news conference (John F. Kennedy) broadcasts

1976 First direct broadcast satellite

1977 First commercial use of fiber-optic cables

2005 Pope John Paul II dies

1930 World's population reaches 2 billion

1955 First McDonald's restaurant opens

1973 First mobile phone

1969 World's first global media event: U.S. astronauts land on the moon

1950 World's urban population reaches 30%

1971 Invention of the microchip by Intel

1969 Construction of the Concorde

1901 Nobel Prizes established

1966 Anti-Vietnam War protests

1997 Bird flu in humans

1962 Concept of the "Galactic Network"

1999 Seattle Anti-Globalization Movement

2002 Severe acute respiratory syndrome (SARS) is recognized

2005–2006 Danish cartoons of Mohammed spark fury

1918 Spanish flu kills between 20 and 40 million people

1960 Marshall McLuhan coins the term "global village"

1945 First atomic bombs dropped on Hiroshima and Nagasaki

1961 Bay of Pigs invasion

1962 First communications satellite launched

1957 Advent of the intercontinental ballistic missile

2005 London Transport bombings

1962 Cuban Missile Crisis

1998 India and Pakistan test nuclear weapons

2003 Iraq War begins

1954–1975 Second Indochina War, the Vietnam War

1967 World Health Organization (WHO) launches global smallpox eradication program

1986 Chernobyl nuclear accident

1980 HIV/AIDS identified in the United States

2006 Iran demands right to develop nuclear power

1944–1947 Bretton Woods and foundation of the United Nations, International Monetary Fund, and the World Bank

2004 Colin Powell declares genocide in Sudan

1949 North Atlantic Treaty Organization (NATO)

2001 September 11 Attack on the World Trade Center and launch of the War on Terror

2006 North Korea tests a nuclear weapon

1950–1953 Korean War

1967 Six Day War

1942–1946 Manhattan Project, the development of a nuclear bomb and the U.S. Atomic Energy Commission

2000 Human Genome Project completed

1996 First sucessful cloning of a mammal, Dolly the Sheep

1946 First digital computer

1969 First Boeing 747

1969 ARPANET, precursor to the Internet

1999 First hybrid car in United States

1942 Invention of the computer

1979 Three Mile Island nuclear power accident

1927 Development of the television

1973 Global positioning system (GPS)

1934–1937 Dust Bowl in the United States

1971 Greenpeace is founded

1987 Hole in the ozone layer is discovered

1972 Publication of *The Limits to Growth* for the Club of Rome

1979 First World Climate Conference of the World Meteorological Organization

2004 Asian tsunami

1972 First UN Global Conference on the Environment

1992 Earth Summit in Rio de Janeiro

2005 Hurricane Katrina devastates Gulf Coast

1962 Rachel Carson writes *Silent Spring*, which helps start the environmental movement

1970 First Earth Day

1997 Kyoto Protocol to the UN

| 1950 | 1960 | 1970 | 1980 | 1990 | 2000 | 2001 | 2002 | 2003 | 2004 | 2005 | 2006 |

MODERN ERA

SECOND EDITION

OUR SOCIAL WORLD
Introduction to Sociology

Jeanne H. Ballantine | Keith A. Roberts

To the Student

Improve Your Grade With These Student Study Tools!

Our praised student study site at **www.pineforge.com/ballantine2study** features

- Updated and revised audio episodes of National Public Radio's *This American Life*
- New video links for YouTube and for PBS's *Frontline*
- New Global Lab Manual with student exercises
- Updated chapter quizzes, e-flashcards, and Internet exercises
- Updated "Learning From SAGE Journal Articles" features for each chapter with related discussion questions
- New recommended readings
- and much more!

Chapter-opening visual representations of the **Social World Model** display visually the micro, meso, and macro levels for that chapter's topic, with "Think About It" questions to focus your thinking on key ideas.

Thinking Sociologically features throughout the text challenge your understanding of core concepts and ask you to apply the material to your own life.

Color bars within each chapter break down analysis of important subjects by micro, meso, or macro level.

Chapter-ending review material includes "So What?" chapter summaries and "Key Points: What Have We Learned?" features to ensure mastery of the chapter's core material.

Thinking Sociologically

Do you think technology and the spread of pop culture are bringing the world closer together as communication and ideas are shared globally, or might it cause tensions as societies attempt to protect their citizens against fraud, pornography, and misuse of technology?

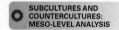

SUBCULTURES AND COUNTERCULTURES: MESO-LEVEL ANALYSIS

So What?

Human beings are not born to be noble savages or depraved beasts. As a species, we are remarkable in how many aspects of our lives are shaped by learning—by socialization. Human socialization is pervasive, extensive, and lifelong. We cannot understand what it means to be human without comprehending the impact of a specific culture on us, the influence of our close associates, and the complex interplay of pressures from micro, meso, and macro levels. Indeed, without social interaction, there would not even be a self. We humans are, in our most essential ...

Contributing to Our Social World: What Can We Do?

At the Local Level: Every community has shelters for homeless people and soup kitchens where very poor people can get a free meal. These organizations often need volunteer help or interns. In fact, student groups on many campuses regularly provide such services. If you know of such a group on your campus, consider working with it, as you will benefit from the experiences of others who are familiar with the situation. Also, if you or your friends sponsor events or meetings ... als, see if you can arrange for the ... be donated to a shelter.

commitment, but most who have done it agree that it was worth the effort. And there are few more effective ways to apply sociology in a global context. The Peace Corps is an independent agency of the U.S. government, founded in 1961. Volunteers work in foreign countries throughout the world, helping local people improve their economic conditions, health, and education. The Peace Corps Web site (www.peacecorps.gov) provides information on the history of the organization, volunteer opportunities and ... present volunteers.

Key Points
What Have We Learned?

- Human beings must work with their biological makeup, but most of what makes us uniquely human has to do with things we learn from our culture and society—our socialization. Humans who are not socialized and live in isolation from others are tragic—barely human—creatures. (See pp. 100–102.)
- The self consists of the interaction of the *I*—the basic impulsive human with drives, needs, and feelings—and the *Me*—the reflected self one develops by role-taking to see how others might see one. (See pp. 102–105.)
- The self is profoundly shaped by others, but it also has ... is an initiator of action and the maker of ... 105–107.)

- Although the self is somewhat elastic in adjusting to different settings and circumstances, there is also a core self that is often vested in meso-level organizations and institutions of which the self participates. (See p. 109.)
- The self is modified as it moves through life stages, and some of those stages require major resocialization—shedding old roles and taking on new ones as one enters new statuses in life. (See pp. 109–113.)
- A number of agents of socialization are at work on each of us, communicating messages that are relevant at the micro, the meso, or the macro level of social life. At the meso level, for ... messages about what

Excerpt From Review in *Teaching Sociology*

"It is exciting to see a new offering such as Our Social World *that is innovative in its pedagogical choices. It is an exceptionally well-organized and well-written text, and as such is an exciting new option for any introductory sociology class. This text strikes us as particularly effective at engaging students. It becomes quite evident that these two award-winning coauthors understand where students are coming from and which questions are most likely to engage them and push them to think analytically."*

—Reviewed by Catherine Fobes and Laura von Wallmenich,
Alma College, in *Teaching Sociology,* Vol. 36, 2008 (April: 161–184)

Student Praise for *Our Social World*

"It's been one of my favorite textbooks to read!"

"I felt the text was speaking 'my language.'"

"I liked that it explains what careers come from sociology. I love the real-life examples to explain key words. This really helped me understand how sociology applies to life."

"I really enjoyed how it stated off with a story as an example of what sociology is . . . I formed a picture in my mind that stayed there throughout the chapter."

"The charts/diagrams are very helpful in understanding the topics."

"It helped me relate my life and personal experiences to the concepts in sociology. . . . It made me concentrate on what was happening to others instead of worrying whether I could get through all the reading. I stayed focused."

"The chapters provide a good overview of the concepts of sociology."

"The 'Thinking Sociologically' questions are a great way to stop and reflect because you remember what you read so much better when you have a chance to make it personal."

"It made me become more aware of why people are the way they are and do the things they do. It taught me to view the world with a different outlook. . . . By being aware of the various social groups out there, I can become a better person."

"Overall, I found this to be one of the most interesting things I have ever been forced to read, and I mean that in a good *forced* way."

"I really enjoy the book. It is clear to understand, funny at times, and has great examples!"

"I enjoyed how a real person's story was told at the opening of the chapters. It made sociology seem pertinent to real life."

To the Instructor

A New Intro Text for a New Generation of Students . . .
Incredibly Successful in Its First Edition and Even Better in Its Second!

Written by two award-winning sociology instructors who are passionate about excellence in teaching, this textbook has already been adopted at a variety of community colleges, four-year colleges, and comprehensive research universities, and these schools have used it in traditional as well as online Introduction to Sociology courses. Some of the many schools that have adopted the book include

- The Ohio State University
- Florida Community College at Jacksonville
- University of Albany
- Ferrum College
- University of North Carolina, Wilmington
- Trinity Christian College
- University of Colorado
- Ithaca College
- Corning Community College

- St. Louis University
- University of Central Florida
- University of Cincinnati
- Manhattanville College
- Kutztown University
- Houston Community College
- John Jay College of Criminal Justice
- University of Miami

. . . . and many, many more! We would like to say **THANK YOU** to our loyal adopters who chose **Our Social World** as a new first edition text and made it such an overwhelming success. We hope you find the **Second Edition** even more exciting, as we do.

Instructor Praise for *Our Social World*

"Unlike most textbooks that I have read, **the breadth and depth of coverage . . . is very impressive**. This text forces the students deep into the topics covered and challenges them to see the interconnectedness of them."
—Keith Kerr, *Texas A&M University*

"**I love the global emphasis, the applied material, and the emphasis on solutions** to social problems."
—Gina Carreno, *Florida Atlantic University*

"So often students ask, 'What can I do with sociology?' Having this **applied information interspersed in the text** allows them to get answers to that question over and over again."

"Finally, **a text that brings sociology to life!** . . . This is so well written that I'm not sure the students will even realize they are learning theory!"
—Martha Shockey, *St. Louis University*

"After extensive review, this book was my choice sight unseen thanks to your **terrific Web site**."
—Michelle Ronda, *Marymount Manhattan College*

Finally, here is a text that engages students. In the widely praised **Our Social World, Second Edition,** the focus is on developing sociological skills of analysis rather than emphasizing memorization of basic ideas.

The text is both personal and global. It introduces sociology clearly, with the Social World Model providing a cohesive framework that lends integration and clarity to the course. With the theme of globalization critically intertwined throughout the text, an emphasis on the applied side of sociology, and an emphasis on deep learning and critical thinking, **Our Social World, Second Edition,** inspires critical thinking as well as community participation. This edition also offers multiple new boxed features written by guest authors who are leaders in the teaching sociology and applied sociology movements—resulting in a unique, dynamic, incredibly valuable learning experience!

Teaches Students the Basics of Sociology via the Clearly Structured, Visually Compelling "Social World Model"

The model, which visually introduces each chapter, illustrates the level of analysis of each topic from micro to meso to macro, as well as how each topic is related. This simple and clear model of the social world is the organizing framework for the text, and the **Second Edition** clarifies the difference between the meso level and other levels of society.

Introduces a Global Perspective Throughout, Asking Students to Be Citizens of the World and to Develop the Ability to Role-Take

This text uniquely weaves a truly global perspective into each part of the book, challenging students to think of themselves as global citizens rather than as local citizens looking out at others in the world. "Sociology Around the World" features introduce fascinating historical or global examples of key concepts.

Think About It . . .

- Micro: How does political power penetrate my own life, even in the privacy of my own home?
- Micro: How do people in my local community exercise power in constructive or destructive ways?
- Meso: How does the political institution interact with the economic institution?
- Macro: Who holds power in my government, and why?
- Macro: Why do power relations often devolve into war and terrorism?

Macro: Global Community
Macro: Society
Meso: National Organizations, Institutions, and Ethnic Subcultures
Micro: Local Organizations and Community
Micro: Me (and My Political and Workplace Allies)
Micro: Fraternities/sororities, civil clubs, family life
Meso: State/provincial government; state Supreme Court, political parties
Macro: Federal government; national Supreme Court
Macro: Cross-national political or economic organizations such as the United Nations; global programs to address human rights or poverty at international level (such as Amnesty International)

A Chinese family sits outside on the ground enjoying a home-cooked meal.

In Calcutta's red-light district, more than 7,000 women and girls work as prostitutes. Only one group has a lower standing: their children. Zana Briski first began photographing prostitutes in Calcutta in 1998. Living in the brothels for months at a time, she quickly developed a relationship with many of the kids who, often terrorized and abused, were drawn to the rare human companionship she offered. Because the children were fascinated by her camera, Zana thought it would be great to see the world through their eyes. It was at that moment that she had the idea of teaching photography to the children of prostitutes. A film she produced based on her work won the Oscar for Best Documentary in 2006. It led to a crusade to keep these children of prostitutes, pictured here, out of a life of prostitution. Learn more about her organization, Kids with Cameras, at www.kids-with-cameras.org.

The residents of Thimpu, Bhutan, visit the vegetable market. Although this is a large, impersonal market, people form primary groups among both the vendors and the shoppers. Shoppers may find their favorite vendors and develop close relationships.

Sociology Around the World

Evolutionary Cuisine

Early Humans' Salad Bar

This menu comes from early hominids who lived in the savannahs of eastern and southern Africa from roughly 1.5 to 5 million years ago. Everything was served raw. Cooking with fire had not been discovered.

Main Course: Nuts, birds' eggs, roots, tubers, beans, leaves, gum, sap, greens, insects, worms, grubs, termites, and seasonal berries and fruits. (90 percent of the diet.)

Raw Meat Appetizer Tray: Opportunist and gathered delicacies include small mammals, birds, reptiles, fish, shellfish, slow game, dead or dying animals, and infants of species such as antelope, pig, giraffe, or baboons when available. Bone marrow or the contents of animal heads and stomachs are delicious additions to this menu. Season with honey, rock salt, or puree of worms and insects. (10 percent of the diet.)

Ancestral Potluck Dinner

The first members of our own genus, *Homo erectus,* used these recipes from about 100,000 to 1.5 million years ago in the tropical and temperate zones of Africa and Eurasia. New technologies in fire making, advanced scavenging, and simple hunting as well as social advances in cooperation, sharing, and the gender division of labor provided some very tasty and nourishing meals for our ancestors.

Main Courses: Stew or soup made with vegetables, bird bones, roots, nuts, and foods from the Salad Bar and Raw Meat Appetizer Tray plus other gathered foods as available. Add leftovers and herbal seasonings. (80 percent of the diet.)

Outdoor Barbecue: Sizzling deer haunch, roasted rabbit, shellfish, wild boar, ox, or cattle ribs. (20 percent of the diet.)

Encourages Deep Learning and Critical Thinking With Uniquely Effective Pedagogy

"Thinking Sociologically" activities, "So What" plus "Key Points: What Have We Learned?" end-of-chapter summaries, and "Sociology in Your Social World" features encourage critical thought, challenging students to reflect on how the material is relevant and applicable to their lives.

Thinking Sociologically

Do you think technology and the spread of pop culture are bringing the world closer together as communication and ideas are shared globally, or might it cause tensions as societies attempt to protect their citizens against fraud, pornography, and misuse of technology?

So What?

Human beings are not born to be noble savages or depraved beasts. As a species, we are remarkable in how many aspects of our lives are shaped by learning—by socialization. Human socialization is pervasive, extensive, and lifelong. We cannot understand what it means to be human without comprehending the impact of a specific culture on us, the influence of our close associates, and the complex interplay of pressures from micro, meso, and macro levels. Indeed, without social interaction, there would not even be a self. We humans are, in our most essential natures, social beings. This has been the purpose of this chapter—to open our eyes to the ways in which we become the individuals we are.

Most of the influences that shape us occur in our interactions with others—through networks, groups, organizations, and even bureaucracies. In the next chapter, we turn to an analysis of these aspects of our social world.

Sociology in Your Social World

Bowling Alone Versus Contributing to Your Social World

To join or not to join—that is a question many college students must decide. They are torn between spending time with their computers and video games and joining groups, even doing volunteer work in the community or working on a political campaign. Research on joining organized groups versus engaging in individual activities gives us some insight into choices and consequences of these choices.

According to one study of group activities, bowling leagues have experienced significant declines in membership in recent years. Yet, more people in the United States bowl than vote, often enjoying the sport as individuals rather than in organized groups. For sociologists, this pattern points to a broad trend—those who once participated in group activities are turning inward and not joining organized groups (Putnam 1995, 2001). Does this reflect a breakdown of the U.S. community? Parent-Teacher Associations (PTAs), Red Cross, and other civic groups were all down in the 1990s. The result is that peo...

In a separate study, a team of sociologists from the University of California, Berkeley, also analyzed the relationship between individualism and sense of community. They concluded that individualism is problematic for Americans living in an interdependent world (Bellah et al. 1996). As individuals lose contact with others, they face private problems alone. What the United States needs, according to the authors of this study, is a greater sense of community to give individuals a feeling of belonging and to link the micro and macro levels of the social world (Bellah et al. 1996). In other words, individuals should think about "bowling together" or find other ways to connect and build a sense of community through group affiliation or involvement.

More recently, there is evidence that different types of groups and affiliations, some based on new technologies, some based on volunteering, are emerging to replace bowling leagues and similar organizations (Putnam...). From college...

Key Points

What Have We Learned?

- Human beings must work with their biological makeup, but most of what makes us uniquely human has to do with things we learn from our culture and society—our socialization. Humans who are not socialized and live in isolation from others are tragic—barely human—creatures. (See pp. 100–102.)

- The self consists of the interaction of the I—the basic impulsive human with drives, needs, and feelings—and the Me—the reflected self one develops by role-taking to see how others might see one. (See pp. 102–105.)

- The self is profoundly shaped by others, but it also has agency—it is an initiator of action and the maker of meaning. (See pp. 105–107.)

- The self develops through stages, from mimicking others (the play stage) to more intellectually sophisticated abilities to role-take and to see how various roles fit together—the game stage. (See pp. 107–109.)

- Although the self is somewhat elastic in adjusting to different settings and circumstances, there is also a core self that is often vested in meso-level organizations and institutions of which the self participates. (See p. 109.)

- The self is modified as it moves through life stages, and some of those stages require major resocialization—shedding old roles and taking on new ones as one enters new statuses in life. (See pp. 109–113.)

- A number of agents of socialization are at work on each of us, communicating messages that are relevant at the micro, the meso, or the macro level of social life. At the meso level, for example, we may receive different messages about what it means to be a "good" person depending on our ethnic, religious, or social class subculture. (See pp. 113–122.)

- Some of these messages may be in conflict with each other, as when global messages about tolerance for those who differ conflict with a nation's desire to have absolute loyalty and sense of superiority. (See p. 122.)

Contributing to Our Social World: What Can We Do?

At the Local Level: Every community has shelters for homeless people and soup kitchens where very poor people can get a free meal. These organizations often need volunteer help or interns. In fact, student groups on many campuses regularly provide such services. If you know of such a group on your campus, consider working with it, as you will benefit from the experiences of others who are familiar with the situation. Also, if you or your friends sponsor events or meetings that include meals, see if you can arrange for the food that is prepared but not eaten to be donated to a shelter. Remember to tip generously when you are being served by people in minimum-wage jobs—housekeeping maids who have cleaned your room, breakfast servers at the continental breakfast, and employees at fast-food restaurants. If you have never had such a job, consider taking one on a part-time basis. You may learn more than you ever wanted to know about life at the bottom of the stratification system.

At the Organizational or Institutional Level: One of the most successful volunteer organizations that assist people in need is the faith-based Habitat for Humanity. Participants work with current and prospective home owners in repairing or constructing housing for little or no cost. Habitat projects are under way or planned for many communities in the United States and around the world. See the organization's Web site for more details at www.habitat.org. After graduation, consider doing one year of service with AmeriCorps. Founded in the early 1990s, more than 200,000 volunteers have served in a wide range of jobs, including teaching and community service. The pay is not good, but the experience and contribution to those in need provide other rewards. See the AmeriCorps Web site at www.americorps.org.

At the National and Global Levels: You or some of your friends may have already considered joining the Peace Corps after graduation. Doing so involves a serious, long-term

commitment, but most who have done it agree that it was worth the effort. And there are few more effective ways to apply sociology in a global context. The Peace Corps is an independent agency of the U.S. government, founded in 1961. Volunteers work in foreign countries throughout the world, helping local people improve their economic conditions, health, and education. The Peace Corps Web site (www.peacecorps.gov) provides information on the history of the organization, volunteer opportunities, and reports of former and present volunteers.

For a shorter-term global commitment, consider doing a paid internship sponsored by Sociologists without Borders (or *Sociólogos sin Fronteras;* www.sociologistswithoutborders.org). This organization promotes human rights globally. It advocates that sociologists participate, democratically, with others to set standards for human well-being and devote energies to understanding how to achieve these standards. Grameen Bank (www.grameen-info.org/bank or www.grameenfoundation.org) was started in Bangladesh by Professor Muhammad Yunus, winner of the 2006 Nobel Prize for Peace. It makes small business loans to people who live in impoverished regions of the world and who have no collateral for a loan. The default rate on these loans is one of the lowest of any bank anywhere. Rather than collateral, the promise to repay is based on social ties to others in one's community, who will not receive loans unless the first party pays regularly on his or her loan. Consider doing a local fundraiser with friends for the Grameen Bank or other micro-credit organizations, such as Finca and Care International.

Visit **www.pineforge.com/ballantine2study** for online activities, sample tests, and other helpful information. Select "Chapter 7: Stratification" for chapter-specific activities.

Inspires an Active Engagement in Sociology via Motivating Chapter Features

"Contributing to Our Social World: What Can We Do?" suggestions include work and volunteer opportunities in which students can apply their newfound sociological knowledge right away. "The Applied Sociologist at Work" boxes introduce students to a variety of people with sociology degrees, illuminating post-degree career options.

Ancillaries

Compatible With Blackboard and Other Course Management Systems

To facilitate the use of **Our Social World, Second Edition,** with Blackboard and other course management platforms, SAGE and Pine Forge provide the following tools to ensure your success:

- *Instructors' Resources on CD-ROM (IRCD):* The **IRCD** includes a "Course Management HELP" document that contains instructions for loading content from the **Instructors' Resources on CD-ROM** and **Student Study Site** to various platforms.
- *Brownstone Test Bank on the Instructors' Resources on CD-ROM:* This test bank has been formatted to be compatible with various course management platforms.

Instructors' Resources on CD-ROM

The **IRCD** features a variety of praised effective teaching aids, including

- An updated and revised test bank, including multiple-choice, true/false, short-answer, and essay questions, with page numbers and answers provided
- Updated and revised PowerPoint slides
- Updated chapter overviews and lecture outlines
- Updated classroom exercises and worksheets
- Suggestions, teaching tips, and resources for using the Social World Model
- Teaching tips for teaching online and traditional courses
- Sample syllabi
- Updated Web resources
- Templates for photo essay projects
- "Learning From SAGE Journal Articles" writing assignments
- Suggested video resources

Test Bank

The computerized test bank, compatible with both PC and Mac computers, comes on the **IRCD** and allows for easy question sorting and exam creation. In keeping with the deep learning focus of this book, the test questions feature more emphasis on *application skills* rather than merely offering rote memorization questions—the latter a too-common characteristic of many intro test banks.

PowerPoint Slides

Because visuals are important additions to classroom lectures, PowerPoint slides that include lecture outlines and relevant maps, tables, diagrams, photos, and short quotes are included on the **IRCD** for instructors to use in the classroom.

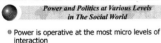

Power and Politics at Various Levels in The Social World

- Power is operative at the most micro levels of interaction

- Politics also operates at the meso level
  - Cities, countries, states/provinces
  - Large bureaucratic organizations and corporations have hierarchies of power

- At the macro level, global systems of power include international organizations such as the United Nations

© Pine Forge Press, an Imprint of SAGE Publications, Inc., 2009.

Teaching Tips

- Teaching Tips for traditional and online Introduction to Sociology courses
- Teaching Tips for teaching the Social World Model

These Teaching Tips are all available to adopters of **Our Social World, Second Edition,** to help make teaching from this text easier and even more effective and enjoyable for the instructor. Contact Customer Care at 1-800-818-SAGE (7243).

Free online access to Bryant's *21st Century Sociology: A Reference Handbook* (SAGE, ©2007), is available to adopters to help make teaching globally even more impactful. Contact Customer Care at 1-800-818-SAGE (7243) for more information on this highly praised teaching aid.

Student Study Site at www.pineforge.com/ballantine2study
(See p. ii for details on what is included on the study site.)

To further enhance students' understanding of and interest in the course material, we have created a Student Study Site, which includes

- Updated and revised audio episodes of National Public Radio's *This American Life*
- New video links for YouTube and for PBS's *Frontline*
- New Global Lab Manual with student exercises
- Updated chapter quizzes, e-flashcards, and Internet exercises
- Updated "Learning From SAGE Journal Articles" features for each chapter with related discussion questions
- New recommended readings
- and much more!

SAGE and Pine Forge Press Teaching Innovations and Professional Development Awards Fund

Partly inspired by the authors of **Our Social World**, SAGE and its sociology imprint, Pine Forge Press, have created this awards fund to help graduate students and pre-tenure faculty attend the annual American Sociological Association pre-conference, hosted by the Section on Teaching and Learning in Sociology, with grants of approximately $500 per recipient. In its first year, there were 13 award recipients; in 2008 (the second year of the award), out of a pool of 104 applicants, 19 awards were granted. In 2008, the ASA's Section on Teaching and Learning in Sociology awarded SAGE and Pine Forge Press with a glass plaque to honor the publisher and its participating authors and editors—including the authors of **Our Social World**—for their commitment to excellence in teaching.

About the Authors

Jeanne H. Ballantine (bottom center) is Professor of Sociology at Wright State University, a state university of about 17,000 students in Ohio. She has also taught at several four-year colleges, including an "alternative" college and a traditionally black college, and at international programs in universities abroad. Jeanne has been teaching introductory sociology for more than 30 years with a mission to introduce the uninitiated to the field and to help students see the usefulness and value in sociology. Jeanne has been active in the teaching movement, shaping curriculum, writing and presenting research on teaching, and offering workshops and consulting in regional, national, and international forums. She is a Fulbright Senior Scholar and serves as a Departmental Resources Group consultant and evaluator.

Jeanne has written several textbooks, all with the goal of reaching the student audience. As the original director of the Center for Teaching and Learning at Wright State University, she scoured the literature on student learning and served as a mentor to teachers in a wide variety of disciplines. Local, regional, and national organizations have honored her for her teaching and for her contributions to helping others become effective teachers. In 1986, the American Sociological Association's Section on Undergraduate Education (now called the Section on Teaching and Learning in Sociology) recognized her with the Hans O. Mauksch Award for Distinguished Contributions to Teaching of Sociology. In 2004, she was honored by the American Sociological Association with its Distinguished Contributions to Teaching Award.

Keith A. Roberts (center) is Professor of Sociology at Hanover College, a private liberal arts college of about 1,100 students in Indiana. He has been teaching introductory sociology for more than 30 years with a passion for active learning strategies and a focus on "deep learning" by students that transforms the way students see the world. Prior to teaching at Hanover, he taught at a two-year regional campus of a large university. Between them, these authors have taught many types of students at different types of schools.

Keith has been active in the teaching movement, writing on teaching and serving as a consultant to sociology departments across the country in his capacity as a member of the ASA Departmental Resources Group. He has written a very popular textbook in the sociology of religion, has coauthored a book on writing in the undergraduate curriculum, and annually runs workshops for high school sociology teachers. He has been honored for his teaching and teaching-related work at local, state, regional, and national levels. The American Sociological Association's Section on Teaching and Learning awarded him the Hans O. Mauksch Award for Distinguished Contributions to Teaching of Sociology in 2000.

2004 AMERICAN SOCIOLOGICAL ASSOCIATION

DISTINGUISHED CONTRIBUTIONS TO TEACHING AWARD

2000 AMERICAN SOCIOLOGICAL ASSOCIATION
Section on Teaching and Learning

HANS O. MAUKSCH AWARD FOR DISTINGUISHED CONTRIBUTIONS TO TEACHING SOCIOLOGY

Visit www.pineforge.com for valuable
Intro to Sociology supplemental texts
1-800-818-SAGE (7243)
www.pineforge.com

Writing this book has been a labor of love,

for we are both passionate about sociology and about teaching sociology.

Still, this labor of love has sometimes come at a steep price to others we love.

Thus, we dedicate this book to two saints of patience, support, and understanding,

Hardy Ballantine

and

Judy Roberts,

our supportive and beloved spouses,

and to our children, who have shared their educational trials and triumphs,

giving us food for thought as we wrote.

SECOND EDITION

OUR SOCIAL WORLD
WORLD
Introduction to Sociology

Jeanne H. Ballantine | Keith A. Roberts
Wright State University   Hanover College

PINE FORGE PRESS
An Imprint of SAGE Publications, Inc.
Los Angeles • London • New Delhi • Singapore • Washington DC

For information:

Pine Forge Press
An Imprint of SAGE Publications, Inc.
2455 Teller Road
Thousand Oaks, California 91320
E-mail: order@sagepub.com

SAGE Publications Ltd.
1 Oliver's Yard
55 City Road
London EC1Y 1SP
United Kingdom

SAGE Publications India Pvt. Ltd.
B 1/I 1 Mohan Cooperative Industrial Area
Mathura Road, New Delhi 110 044
India

SAGE Publications Asia-Pacific Pte. Ltd.
33 Pekin Street #02-01
Far East Square
Singapore 048763

Printed in Canada

Library of Congress Cataloging-in-Publication Data

Ballantine, Jeanne H.
Our social world : introduction to sociology / Jeanne H. Ballantine, Keith A. Roberts.—2nd ed.
    p. cm.
Includes bibliographical references and index.
ISBN 978-1-4129-6818-8 (pbk.)
  1. Sociology. 2. Sociology—Cross-cultural studies. I. Roberts, Keith A. II. Title.

HM586.B35 2009
301—dc22   2008036189

This book is printed on acid-free paper.

08 09 10 11 12   10 9 8 7 6 5 4 3 2 1

Acquisitions Editor:	Jerry Westby
Editorial Assistant:	Nancy Scrofano
Production Editor:	Laureen A. Gleason
Copy Editor:	Jacqueline Tasch
Typesetter:	C&M Digitals (P) Ltd.
Proofreader:	Theresa Kay
Indexer:	Molly Hall
Cover Designer:	Janet Foulger
Marketing Manager:	Jennifer Reed Banando

Brief Contents

Detailed Contents

Chapter 8 • Race and Ethnic Group Stratification: Beyond "We" and "They" 232

Chapter 9 • Gender Stratification: She/He—Who Goes First? 270

Preface

To Our Readers

This book asks you to think outside the box. Why? The best way to become a more interesting person, to grow beyond the old familiar thoughts and behaviors, and to make life exciting is to explore new ways to view things. The world in which we live is intensely personal and individual in nature, with much of our social interaction occurring in intimate groups of friends and family. Our most intense emotions and most meaningful links to others are at this "micro" level of social life.

However, these intimate micro-level links in our lives are influenced by larger social structures and global trends. At the beginning of the 21st century, technological advances make it possible to connect with the farthest corners of the world. Multinational corporations cross national boundaries, form new economic and political unions, and change job opportunities of people everywhere. Some groups embrace the changes, while others try to protect their members from the rapid changes that threaten to disrupt their traditional lives. Even our most personal relationships or what we eat tonight may be shaped by events on the other side of the continent or the globe. From the news headlines to family and peer interactions, we confront sociological issues daily. The task of this book and of your instructor is to help you see world events and your personal lives from a sociological perspective. Unless you learn how to look at our social world with an analytical lens, many of its most intriguing features will be missed.

The social world you face in the job markets of the 21st century is influenced by changes and forces that are easy to miss. Like the wind, which can do damage even if the air is unseen, social structures are themselves so taken for granted that it is easy to miss seeing them. However, their effects can be readily identified. No wonder increasing numbers of undergraduate students are taking introductory sociology classes each year, courses that provide a framework for understanding the social environment that shapes our lives. Sociology provides new perspectives, helping students to understand their families, their work lives, their leisure, and their place in a diverse and changing world.

A few of you will probably become sociology majors. Others will find the subject matter of this course relevant to your personal and professional lives. Some of the reasons the authors of this book and your own professor chose to study sociology many years ago are the factors that inspire undergraduates today to choose a major in sociology: learning about the social world from a new perspective; working with people and groups; developing knowledge, inquiry, and interpersonal skills; and learning about social life, from small groups to global social systems. As the broadest of the social sciences, sociology has a never-ending array of fascinating subjects to study. This book touches only the surface of what the field has to offer and the exciting things you can do with this knowledge. These same considerations motivated us and gave us direction in writing this introductory book.

Where This Book Is Headed

Like an effective essay, a well-constructed course needs to be organized around a central question, one that spawns other subsidiary questions and intrigues the participants. The problem with introductory courses in many disciplines is that there is no central question and thus no coherence to the course. They have more of a flavor-of-the-week approach (a different topic each week), with no attempt at integration. We have tried to correct that problem in this text.

The Social World Model

For you to understand sociology as an integrated whole rather than a set of separate chapters in a book, we have organized the chapters in this book around the *social world model*: a conceptual model that demonstrates the relationships between individuals (micro level); organizations, institutions, and subcultures (meso level); and societies and global structures (macro levels of analysis). At the beginning of each chapter, a visual diagram of the model will illustrate this idea as it relates to the topic of that chapter, including how issues related to the topic have implications at various levels of analysis in the social world. For example, the family is explored in Chapter 10 as a part of the whole social world, interrelating with other parts of society. No part exists in a vacuum. On the other hand, this model does not assume that everyone always gets along or that relationships are always harmonious or supportive. Sometimes, different parts of the society are in competition for resources, and intense conflict and hostility may be generated.

This micro- to macro-level analysis is a central concept in the discipline of sociology. Many instructors seek first and foremost to help students develop a *sociological imagination*, an ability to see the complex links between various levels of the social system. This is a key goal of this book. Within a few months, you may not remember all of the specific concepts or terms that have been introduced, but if the way you see the world has been transformed during this course, a key element of deep learning has been accomplished. Learning to see things from alternative perspectives is a precondition for critical thinking. This entire book attempts to help you recognize connections between your personal experiences and problems and larger social forces of society. You will be learning to take a new perspective on the social world in which you live.

A key element of that social world is diversity. We live in societies in which there are people who differ in a host of ways: ethnicity, socioeconomic status, religious background, political persuasion, gender, sexual orientation, and so forth. Diversity is a blessing in many ways to a society because the most productive and creative organizations and societies are those that are highly diverse. Why? People with different backgrounds solve problems in very different ways. When people with such divergences come together, the outcome of their problem solving can create new solutions to vexing problems. However, diversity often creates challenges as well. Misunderstanding and "we" versus "they" thinking can divide people. These issues will be explored throughout this book. We now live in a global village, and in this book, you will learn something about how people on the other side of the village live and view the world.

We hope you enjoy the book and get as enthralled with sociology as we are. It genuinely is a fascinating field of study.

Jeanne H. Ballantine
Wright State University

Keith A. Roberts
Hanover College

Instructors

How to Make This Book Work for You

Special features woven throughout each chapter support the theme of the book. These will help students comprehend and apply the material and make the material more understandable and interesting. These features are also designed to facilitate deep learning, to help students move beyond rote memorization and increase their ability to analyze and evaluate information.

For students to understand both the comparative global theme and sociology as an integrated whole rather than as a set of separate chapters in a book, we have organized the chapters in this book around the *social world model*: a conceptual model that demonstrates the relationships between individuals (micro level), organizations, institutions, and subcultures (meso level), and societies and global structures (macro levels of analysis). At the beginning of each chapter, a visual diagram of the model will illustrate this idea as it relates to the topic of that chapter, including how issues related to the topic have implications at various levels of analysis in the social world.

"Think About It"

So that students can become curious, active readers, we have posed questions as part of the introductory figure that we hope are relevant to everyday life, but that are also tied to the micro–meso–macro levels of analysis that serve as the theme of the book. The purpose is to transform students from passive readers who run their eyes across the words into curious active readers who read to answer a question and to be reflective. Active or deep reading is key to comprehension and retention of reading material. Instructors can also use this feature to encourage students to think critically about the implications of what they have read. Instructors might want to ask students to write a paragraph about one of these questions before coming to class each day. These questions might also provide the basis for in-class discussions.

Students should be encouraged to start each chapter by reading and thinking about these questions, looking at the topics in the chapter, and asking some questions of their own. This will mean they are more likely to stay focused, remember the material long-term, and be able to apply it to their own lives.

A Global Perspective and the Social World Model

We are part of an ever-shrinking world, a global village. What happens in distant countries is not only news the same day but also affects relatives living in other countries, the cost of goods, work and travel possibilities, and the balance of power in the world. Instead of simply including cross-cultural examples of strange and different peoples, this book incorporates a global perspective throughout. This is done so students can see how others live different but rewarding lives and so they can see the connections between others' lives and their own. Students will need to think and relate to the world globally in future roles as workers, travelers, and global citizens. Our analysis illustrates the interconnections of the world's societies and their political and economic systems and demonstrates that what happens in one part of the world affects others. For instance, if a major company in the area moves much of its operations to another country with cheaper labor, jobs are lost, and the local economy is hurt.

This approach attempts to instill interest, understanding, and respect for different groups of people and their lifestyles. Race, class, and gender are an integral part of understanding the diverse social world, and these features of social life have global implications. The comparative global theme is carried throughout the book in headings and written text, in examples, and in boxes and selection of photos. As students read this book, they should continually think about how the experiences in their private world are influenced by and may influence events at other levels: the community, organizations and institutions, the nation, and the world.

Opening Vignettes

Chapters typically open with an illustration relevant to the chapter content. For instance, in Chapter 2, "Examining the Social World," the case of Hector, a Brazilian teenager living in poverty in a *favela*, is used to illustrate research methods and theory throughout the chapter. Chapter 3, "Society and

Culture," begins with scenarios of mealtime scenes from around the world to illustrate the variations in human cultures. In Chapter 4, "Socialization," the case of an immigrant child attending school in his new society and facing a new learning environment is discussed. These vignettes are meant to interest students in the upcoming subject matter by helping them relate to a personalized story. In several cases, the vignettes serve as illustrations throughout the chapters.

"Thinking Sociologically" Questions

Following major topics, students will find questions that ask them to think critically and apply the material just read to some aspect of their lives or the social world. The purpose of this feature is to encourage students to apply the ideas and concepts in the text to their lives. These questions can be the basis for in-class discussions and can be assigned as questions to start interesting conversations with friends and families to learn how the topics relate to their own lives. Some of these questions have a miniature icon—a small version of the chapter-opening model—signifying that these questions reinforce the theme of micro, meso, and macro levels of social influence.

Key Concepts, Examples, and Writing Style

Key terms that are defined and illustrated within the running narrative appear in bold. Other terms that are defined but are of less significance are italicized. The text is rich in examples that bring sociological concepts to life for student readers. Each chapter has been student tested for readability. Both students and reviewers describe the writing style as reader friendly, often fascinating, and accessible, but not watered down.

Special Features

Although there are numerous examples throughout the book, boxed inserts provide more in-depth illustrations of the usefulness of the sociological perspective to understand world situations or events with direct relevance to a student's life. There are four kinds of boxed material. "Sociology in Your Social World" features focus on a sociological issue or story, often with policy implications. In "Sociology Around the World" features, we take readers to another part of the globe to explore how things are different (or how they are the same) from what they might experience in their own lives. "The Applied Sociologist at Work" features examine profiles of contemporary sociologists

who are working in the field so that students can learn what sociologists actually study and do. "How Do We Know?" features describe well-known sociological studies and are included to help students learn how sociologists know what they know. These summaries are a way to reinforce the point that sociology is a social science rooted in empirical methods of gathering data and testing theories. Students need to understand what is—and what is not—*evidence* for a social scientist.

Technology and Society

Nearly every chapter examines issues of technology as they would be relevant to that chapter. We have especially sought out materials that have to do with the Internet and with communications technology.

Social Policy and Becoming an Active Citizen

Most chapters include discussion of some social policy issues: an effort to address the concerns about public sociology and the relevance of sociological findings to current social debates. Finally, because students sometimes feel helpless to know what to do about social issues that concern them at macro and meso levels, we have concluded each chapter with a few ideas about how they might become involved as active citizens, even as undergraduate students. Suggestions in the "Contributing to Your Social World: What Can We Do?" section may be assigned as service learning or term projects or simply used as suggestions for ways students can get involved on their own time.

Summary Sections

Each chapter ends with review material: a "So What?" feature to encourage critical thought and a "Key Points: What Have We Learned?" summary to ensure mastery of the chapter's core material.

A Little (Teaching) Help From Our Friends

Whether the instructor is new to teaching or an experienced professor, there are some valuable ideas that can help invigorate and energize the classroom. A substantial literature on teaching methodology tells us that student involvement is key to the learning process. Built into this book are discussion questions and projects that students can report on in class. In addition, there are a number of suggestions in the supplements and teaching aids for active learning in large or small classes.

Instructors' Resources on CD-ROM (IRCD)

The IRCD contains a number of helpful teaching aids, from goals and objectives for chapters to classroom lecture ideas, active learning projects, collaborative learning suggestions, and options for evaluating students. Suggestions for the use of visual materials—videos, transparencies, and multimedia—are also included. A listing of helpful sources on teaching, including American Sociological Association Teaching Resources Center publications, is part of the IRCD.

Test Banks

Compatible with both PC and Mac computers, the computerized test bank allows for easy question sorting and exam creation. It includes multiple-choice, true/false, short-answer, and essay questions with the page number(s) or section of the book from which the question is taken. In keeping with the deep learning thrust of this book, however, the test questions will have more emphasis on application skills rather than rote memorization questions—the latter a too common characteristic of test banks.

PowerPoint Slides

Because visuals are an important addition to classroom lectures, recognizing the varying learning styles of students, PowerPoint slides that include lecture outlines and relevant tables, maps, diagrams, pictures, and short quotes are included in the IRCD for instructors to use in the classroom.

Companion Study Site

To further enhance students' understanding of and interest in the material, we have created a student Web site to accompany the text. This Web site includes the following:

- **Flashcards** that allow for easy reviewing of key terms and concepts;
- **Self-quizzes** that can be used to check their understanding of the material or can be sent in to the professor for a grade;
- **Web exercises** that direct students to various sites on the Web and ask them to apply their knowledge to a particular topic;
- *This American Life* radio segments that illustrate each chapter's concepts;
- **"Learning From Journal Articles"** features that include original research from SAGE journal articles and teach students how to read and analyze a journal article;
- A list of **recommend Web sites** that students can explore for research or their own edification;
- Information on how to create **video and photo essays**;
- and much more!

Visit **www.pineforge.com/ballantine2study** to view the site.

What Is New in the Revised Edition?

One important change is a response to requests for more on politics, especially in the year following the presidential election in the United States. This new chapter (Chapter 13—Politics: Penetrating Power) has extensive analysis of the interconnections of micro, meso, and macro levels of the political system. The subtitle, "Penetrating Power," focuses both on how power penetrates our lives and on how a sociological lens can help us penetrate the meanings and consequences of power. The chapter focuses on politics, but it also connects to the economic systems of privilege and power. Like all other chapters, this one reinforces the central purpose of the book—development of a sociological imagination that extends to global understanding.

We have also made hundreds of other changes—adding new information, updating data, and in some cases changing topics within chapters. We have tried to be more explicit about the meso level in this book because instructors told us that was the hardest level for students to grasp. We have also added questions throughout the book that reinforce the theme. Even the chapter-opening model helps raise questions at each level of the social system. The second edition is filled with new examples, new and updated boxed features, a thorough review of the photographic program by someone skilled in visual sociology, and new data in every chapter. We also added a summary to the end of each chapter: the "Key Points: What Have We Learned?" feature. Finally, although we had been told that the writing was extraordinarily readable, we have tried to simplify sentence structure in a number of places. In short, we have tried to respond to what we heard from all of you (both students and instructors) to make this book more engaging and more accessible.

A Personal Note to the Instructor

We probably share many of the same reasons for choosing sociology as our careers. Our students also share these reasons for finding sociology a fascinating and useful subject: learning about the social world from a new perspective; working with people and groups; developing a range of knowledge, inquiry, and interpersonal skills; and learning the broad and interesting subject matter of sociology, from small groups to societies. In this book, we try to share our own enthusiasm for the subject with students. The following explains what we believe to be unique features of this book and some of our goals and methods for sharing sociology. We hope you share our ideas and find this book helps you meet your teaching and learning goals.

What Is Distinctive About This Book?

What is truly distinctive about this book? This is a text that tries to break the mold of the typical textbook synthesis, the cross between an encyclopedia and a dictionary. *Our Social World* is a unique course text that is **a coherent essay on the sociological imagination—understood globally**. We attempt to radically change the feel of the introductory book by emphasizing coherence, an integrating theme, and current knowledge about learning and teaching, but we also present much traditional content. Instructors will not have to throw out the well-honed syllabus and begin from scratch, but they can refocus each unit so it stresses understanding of micro-level personal troubles within the macro-level public issues framework. Indeed, in this book, we make clear that the public issues must be understood as global in nature.

Here is a text that engages students. *They* say so! From class testing, we know that the structure of chapters and sections, the "Thinking Sociologically" features, the wealth of examples, and other pedagogical aids help students to stay focused, think about the material, and apply it to their lives. It neither bores them nor insults their intelligence. It focuses on deep learning rather than memorization. It develops sociological skills of analysis rather than emphasizing memorization of vocabulary. Key concepts and terms are introduced but only in the service of a larger focus on the sociological imagination. The text is both personal and global. It speaks to sociology as a science as well as addressing applied aspects of sociology. It has a theme that provides integration of topics as it introduces the discipline. This text is an analytical essay, not a disconnected encyclopedia.

As one of our reviewers noted,

> Unlike most textbooks I have read, the breadth and depth of coverage in this one is very impressive. It challenges the student with college-level reading. Too many textbooks seem to write on a high-school level and give only passing treatment to most of the topics, writing in nugget-sized blocks. More than a single definition and a few sentences of support, the text forces the student deep into the topics covered and challenges them to see interconnections.

Normally, the global-perspective angle within textbooks, which seemed to grow in popularity in the mid- to late-1990s, was implemented by using brief and exotic examples to show differences between societies—a purely comparative approach rather than a globalization treatment. They gave, and still give to a large extent, a token nod to diversity. This textbook, however, forces the student to take a broader look at social institutions and functions operating in all cultures and societies.

So our focus in this book is on deep learning: (1) expansion of student's ability to role-take or "perspective-take" and (2) deeper sophistication in their epistemology. Deep learning goes beyond the content of concepts and terms and cultivates the habits of thinking that allow one to think critically. Being able to see things from the perspective of others is essential to doing sociology, but it is also indispensible to seeing weaknesses in various theories or recognizing blind spots in a point of view. Using the sociological imagination is one dimension of role-taking because it requires a step back from the typical micro-level understanding of life's events and fosters a new comprehension of how meso- and macro-level forces—even global ones—can shape the individual's life. Enhancement of role-taking ability is at the core of this book because it is a *prerequisite* for deep learning in sociology. Second, how can students become more critical thinkers if they do not know *how we know* when we claim to know something? Developing a more informed understanding of what is (and what is not) considered evidence is at the core of critical thought.

We have made some strategic decisions based on these principles of learning and teaching. We have focused much of the book on higher order thinking skills rather than memorization and regurgitation. We want students to learn to think sociologically: to apply, analyze, synthesize, evaluate, and comprehend the interconnections of the world through a globally informed sociological imagination. However, we think it is also essential to do this with an understanding of how students learn.

Many introductory-level books offer several theories and then provide a critique of the theory. The idea is to teach critical thinking. We have purposefully refrained from extensive critique of theory (although some does occur) for several reasons. First, providing critique to beginning-level students does not really teach critical thinking. It trains them to memorize someone else's critique. Furthermore, it simply confuses many of them, leaving students with the feeling that sociology is really just contradictory ideas, and the discipline really does not have anything firm to offer. Teaching critical thinking needs to be done in stages, and it needs to take into account the building steps that occur before effective critique is possible. That is why we focus on the concept of deep learning. We are working toward building the foundations that are necessary for sophisticated critical thought at upper levels in the curriculum.

Therefore, in this beginning-level text, we have attempted to focus on a central higher order or deep learning skill—synthesis. Undergraduate students need to grasp this before they can fully engage in evaluation. Deep learning involves understanding of complexity, and some aspects of complexity need to be taught at advanced levels. While students at the introductory level are often capable of synthesis, complex evaluation requires some foundational skills. Thus, we offer contrasting theories in this text, and rather than telling what is wrong with each one, we encourage students through "Thinking Sociologically" features to analyze the use of each and to focus on honing synthesis and comparison skills.

Finally, research tells us that learning becomes embedded in memory and becomes long-lasting only if it is related to something that learners already know. If they memorize terms but have no unifying framework to which they can attach those ideas, the memory will not last until the end of the course, let alone until the next higher level course. In this text, each chapter is tied to the social world model that is core to sociological thinking. At the end of a course using this book, we believe that students will be able to explain coherently what sociology is and construct an effective essay about what they have learned from the course as a whole. Learning to develop and defend a thesis, with supporting logic and evidence, is another component of deep learning. A text that is mostly a dictionary does not enhance that kind of cognitive skill.

Organization and Coverage

Reminiscent of some packaged international tours, in which the travelers figure that "it is Day 7, so this must be Paris," many introductory courses seem to operate on the principle that it is Week 4 so this must be deviance week. Students do not sense any integration, and at the end of the course, they have trouble remembering specific topics. This book is different. A major goal of the book is to show the integration between topics in sociology and between parts of the social world. The idea is for students to grasp the concept of the interrelated world. A change in one part of the social world affects all others, sometimes in ways that are mutually supportive and sometimes in ways that create intense conflict.

Although the topics are familiar, the textbook is organized around levels of analysis, explained through the social world model. This perspective leads naturally to a comparative approach and discussions of diversity and inequality. Each chapter represents a part of the social world structure (society, organizations and groups, and institutions) or a process in the social world (socialization, stratification, and change).

Chapter order and links between chapters clarify this idea. Part I (Chapters 1 and 2) introduces the student to the sociological perspective and tools of the sociologist: theory and methods. Part II examines "Social Structure, Processes, and Control," exploring especially processes such as socialization, interaction, and networks. Part III covers the core issue of inequality in society, with emphasis on class, race or ethnicity, and gender. Part IV turns to the structural dimensions of society, as represented in institutions. Rather than trying to be all-encompassing, we examine family, education, religion, politics, and medicine to help students understand how structures affect their lives. We do not cover sports, science, or economics in separate chapters, although economics is woven into many chapters and is extensively explored in meso-level connections with each of the other institutions—especially politics. It was a painful decision to leave any institution out, but attention to length and cost required hard choices. Part V turns to social dynamics: how societies change. Population patterns, urbanization, social movements, technology, and other aspects of change are included.

As instructors and authors, we value books that provide students with a well-rounded overview of approaches to the field. Therefore, this book takes an eclectic theoretical approach, drawing on the best insights of various theories and stressing that multiple perspectives enrich our understanding. We give attention to most major theoretical perspectives in sociology: structural-functional and conflict theories at the meso and macro levels of analysis and symbolic interaction and rational choice theories at the micro to meso levels of analysis. Feminist, postmodern, and ecological theories are discussed where relevant to specific topics. Each of these is integrated into the broad social world model, which stresses development of a sociological imagination.

The book includes 16 chapters plus additional online materials, written to fit into a semester or quarter system. It allows instructors to use the chapters in order, or to alter the order, because each chapter is tied into others through the social world model. We strongly recommend that Chapter 1 be used early in the course because it introduces the integrating model and explains the theme. Otherwise, the book has been designed for flexible use. Instructors may also want to supplement the core book with other materials, such as those suggested in the Instructors' Resources on CD-ROM. While covering all of the key topics in introductory sociology, the cost and size of a midsized book allows for this flexibility. Indeed, for a colorful introductory-level text, the cost of this book is remarkably low—roughly half the cost of some other very popular introductory texts.

A Unique Program Supporting Teaching of Sociology

There is one more way in which *Our Social World* has been unique among introductory sociology textbooks. In 2007, the authors teamed with SAGE/Pine Forge Press to start a new program to benefit the entire discipline. Using royalties from *Our Social World*, there is a new award program called the SAGE/Pine Forge Teaching Innovations & Professional Development Award. It is designed to prepare a new generation of scholars within the teaching movement in sociology. People in their early career stages (graduate students, assistant professors, newer PhDs) can be reimbursed $500 each for expenses entailed while attending the day-long American Sociological Association (ASA) Section on Teaching and Learning's pre-conference workshop. The workshop is the day before ASA meetings. In 2007, 13 students received this award and benefited from an extraordinary workshop on learning and teaching. Joined by other SAGE/Pine Forge authors and by the publisher, in 2008, 19 people were able to attend because of donations from royalties.

We hope you find this book engaging. If you have questions or comments, please contact us.

Jeanne H. Ballantine
Wright State University

Keith A. Roberts
Hanover College

Acknowledgments

Knowledge is improved through careful, systematic, and constructive criticism. The same is true of all writing. This book is of much greater quality because we had such outstanding critics and reviewers. We, therefore, wish to honor and recognize the outstanding scholars who served in this capacity. These scholars are listed on this page and the next.

We also had people who served in a variety of other capacities: drafting language for us for special features, doing library and Internet research to find the most recent facts and figures, and reading or critiquing early manuscripts. Khanh Nguyen deserves special mention as an amazing research assistant. Other contributors include Kate Ballantine, Jessica Hoover, Kelly Joyce, Justin Roberts, Kent Roberts, Susan Schultheis, Vanessa M. Simpson, and members of an introductory sociology class at Wright State University in the fall of 2005. Authors of short sections within the book include Helen Berger, Jeffrey Breese, Leslie Elrod, Robert Horton-Rosten, Melanie Hughes, Kichiro Iwamoto, Jeffrey Lashbrook, Laura McCloud, Ruth Meizen-Dick, Wendy Ng, Amy Orr, Lynette Osborne, Tony Pickard, Daryl Poole, Lynn Richey, Elise Roberts, Roland Robertson, Susan St. John, and Jay Weinstein. Susan Alexander provided a critique of the visual messages in the first edition and helped select photos for the second edition. Scholars who helped with early drafts of some chapters include James W. Burfiend, Timothy Buzzell, Dora Lodwick, and Gregory Weiss. Thanks also to designer Bruce Stiver.

Both of us are experienced authors, and we have worked with some excellent people at other publishing houses. However, the team at Pine Forge/SAGE Publications was truly exceptional in support, thoroughness, and commitment to this project. Our planning meetings have been fun, intelligent, and provocative. Ben Penner, former Pine Forge acquisitions editor, provided excellent advice and support, and Jerry Westby has been a sustaining member of the team as executive editor. Elise Caffee, developmental editor, coordinated the work of many people and even managed to keep her sometimes cranky authors in line and in good humor. Other folks who have meant so much to the quality production of this book include Nancy Scrofano, editorial assistant; Laureen Gleason, production editor supervisor; Jacqueline Tasch, copy editor; Sheri Gilbert, permissions editor; Jennifer Reed Banando, senior marketing manager; Claudia Hoffman, managing editor; Scott Hooper, manufacturing manager; Ravi Balasuriya, art director; Steven Martin, vice president—production; Michele Sordi, vice president and editorial director—books acquisitions; Helen Salmon, director—books marketing; David Horwitz, vice president—sales; Tom Taylor, vice president—marketing and sales; and Blaise Simqu, president and chief executive officer. We have become friends and colleagues with the staff at Pine Forge/SAGE Publications. They are all greatly appreciated.

Thanks to the following reviewers:

Sabrina Alimahomed
University of California, Riverside

Fred Beck
Illinois State University

David L. Briscoe
University of Arkansas at Little Rock

Jamie M. Dolan
Carroll College (MT)

Obi N. I. Ebbe
The University of Tennessee at Chattanooga

Stephanie Funk
Hanover College

Loyd R. Ganey, Jr.
Western International University

Mary Grigsby
University of Missouri–Columbia

Keith Kerr
Blinn College

Elaine Leeder
Sonoma State University

Stephen Lilley
Sacred Heart University

David A. Lopez
California State University, Northridge

Add Akbar Madhi
Ohio Wesleyan University

Gerardo Marti
Davidson College

Laura McCloud
The Ohio State University

Meeta Mehrotra
Roanoke College

Melinda S. Miceli
University of Hartford

Leah A. Moore
University of Central Florida

R. Marlene Powell
University of North Carolina at Pembroke

Martha L. Shockey-Eckles
Saint Louis University

Toni Sims
University of Louisiana–Lafayette

Frank S. Stanford
Blinn College

Tracy Steele
Wright State University

Rachel Stehle
Cuyahoga Community College

John Stone
Boston University

Stephen Sweet
Ithaca College

Tim Ulrich
Seattle Pacific University

Thomas L. Van Valey
Western Michigan University

Chaim I. Waxman
Rutgers University

Deborah J. White
Collin County Community College

Jake B. Wilson
University of California, Riverside

John Zipp
University of Akron

PART I

Understanding Our Social World

The Scientific Study of Society

hy are we studying what seems to be common sense? Why would anyone want to study how friends and family get along, how groups work, and where a society fits into the global system? What can we learn from scientifically studying our everyday lives? What exactly does it mean to see the world sociologically? Can sociology make our lives any better as the study of biology or chemistry does through new medications?

Studying sociology takes us on a trip to a deeper level of understanding of ourselves and our social world. The first chapter of this book helps answer two questions: What is sociology, and why study it? The second chapter addresses how sociology began and how sociologists know what they know. Like your sociology professor, this book will argue that sociology is valuable because it gives us new perspectives on our personal and professional lives and because sociological insights and skills can help all of us make the world a better place.

When sociologists make a statement about the social world, how do they know it is true? What perspective or lens might sociologists employ to make sense of their information? For example, when sociologists find that education does not treat all children equally, what can be done about it? What evidence would be considered reliable, valid, dependable, and persuasive to support this statement? By the time you finish reading the first two chapters, you should have an initial sense of what sociology is, how it can help you understand your social world, why the field is worth taking your time to explore, and how sociologists know what they know. We invite you to take a seat and come on a trip through the fascinating field of sociology, our social world.

CHAPTER 1

Sociology

A Unique Way to View the World

Sociology involves a transformation in the way one sees the world—learning to recognize the complex connections of our intimate personal lives with large organizations and institutions and with national and global structures and events.

Think About It . . .

Micro: How can sociology help me understand my own life and my sense of self?

Micro: How can sociology help me to be a more responsible and effective citizen in my local community?

Meso: What do sociologists *do* to help us understand organizations and institutions? How can they help us understand and even improve our lives in families, educational systems, or health care?

Macro: How do national loyalty or policies within my country influence my life?

Macro: How might global events affect my life?

Global Community

Society

National Organizations, Institutions, and Ethnic Subcultures

Local Organizations and Community

Me (and My Inner Circle)

Micro examples: Community civic organizations; local religious congregations; scout troops; athletic teams

Meso examples: A nation's education or health care system; an ethnic community within the larger society

Macro examples: Canada; Brazil; India; Great Britain; Australia

Macro examples: United Nations; World Court; World Bank; Google; NATO; the Roman Catholic Church; multinational corporations

What do we mean by "our social world"? Consider the following: Several years ago, a man was determined to set a record by sailing across the Atlantic in a tiny, one-person craft powered only by the wind. The man designed and constructed his sailing vessel, which was so small that there was no room for anything other than food and water. He took no radio or other communication device, and he knew he would be out of contact with other people for the duration of the voyage.

The man embarked alone on this perilous journey, departing from the east coast of the United States, and for 2 months, he sailed in solitude. Although some feared he was lost at sea when he was not seen or heard from for many weeks, fortune was with him. His craft was spotted off the Irish coast—his destination. As he sailed into port, the media had been alerted to his arrival and awaited him. When the man disembarked to end this remarkable and sometimes painfully lonely journey, a reporter asked him what he had learned on his solitary voyage. The intrepid sailor thought for a moment and calmly replied, "I learned a lot about people."

By being so totally alone for so long, this sailor learned how completely social we humans really are. He learned that even when he was alone, he spent much of his time reflecting on people. He also learned how painful and disorienting it can be to live without human contact. In short, his experiences taught him a basic sociological insight: Humans are fundamentally social beings.

Strange as it may seem, the social world is not merely something that exists outside of us. As this story illustrates,

A man at sea alone for two months says he learned a lot about people. We humans are fundamentally social beings.

the social world is also something we carry inside of us. We are part of it, we reflect on it, and we are influenced by it, even when we are alone. The patterns of the social world engulf us in ways both subtle and obvious, with profound implications for how we create order and meaning in our lives.

Sometimes it takes a dramatic and shocking event for us to realize just how deeply embedded we are in a social world that we take for granted. "It couldn't happen in the United States," read typical world newspaper accounts, "This is something you see in Bosnia, Kosovo, the Middle East, Central Africa, and other war-torn areas . . . It's hard to imagine this happening in the economic center of the United States." Yet on September 11, 2001, shortly after 9 a.m., a commercial airliner crashed into a New York City skyscraper, followed a short while later by another pummeling into the paired tower, causing this mighty symbol of financial wealth—the World Trade Center—to collapse. After the dust settled and the rescue crews finished their gruesome work, nearly 3,000 people were dead or unaccounted for. The world as we knew it changed forever that day. This event taught U.S. citizens how integrally connected they are with the international community.

Following the events of September 11, the United States launched its highly publicized War on Terror, and many terrorist strongholds and training camps were destroyed. Still, troubling questions remain unanswered. Why did this extremist act occur? How can such actions be deterred in the future? How do the survivors recover from such a horrific event? Why was this event so completely disorienting to Americans and to the world community? These terrorist acts horrified people because they were unpredicted and unexpected in a normally predictable world. They violated the rules that foster our connections to one another. They also brought attention to the discontent and disconnectedness that lie under the surface in many societies—discontent that expressed itself in hateful violence.

Terrorist acts represent a rejection of modern civil society (Smith 1994). The terrorists themselves see their acts as justifiable, but few outside their inner circle can understand the behavior. When terrorist acts occur, we struggle to fit such events into our mental picture of a just, safe, comfortable, and predictable social world. The events of September 11 forced U.S. citizens to realize that, although they may see a great diversity among themselves, people in other parts of the world view them as all the same. U.S. citizens may also be despised for what they represent, as perceived by others. In other words, terrorists view U.S. citizens as intimately connected. For many U.S. citizens, their sense of loyalty to the nation was deeply stirred by the events of 9/11. Patriotism abounded. So, in fact, the nation's people became more connected as a reaction to an act against the United States.

Most of the time, we live with social patterns that we take for granted as routine, ordinary, and expected.

These signs were put up right after the September 11th attacks on the World Trade Center by people looking for missing loved ones. The experience of New Yorkers was alarm, fear, grief, and confusion—precisely the emotions that the terrorists sought to create. Terrorism disrupts normal social life and daily routines and undermines security.

These social patterns, or social facts, characterize social groups. They are external to us (unlike motivations, drives, or instincts) but guide (or constrain) our behaviors and thoughts. Without shared expectations between humans about proper patterns of behavior, life would be chaotic. Connections require some basic rules of interaction, and these rules create routine and safe normality in everyday interaction. For the people in and around the World Trade Center, the social rules governing everyday life broke down that awful day. How could anyone live in society if there were no rules?

This first chapter examines the social ties that make up our social world, as well as sociology's focus on those ties. We will learn what sociology is and why it is valuable to study it; how sociologists view the social world and what they do; how studying sociology can help us in our everyday life; and how the social world model is used to present the topics we will study throughout this book.

What Is Sociology?

In a fast-food restaurant or cafeteria at school, at a party or in our residence hall, at work or within our home, we interact with other people. Such interactions are the foundation of social life, and they are the subject of interest to sociologists. According to the American Sociological Association (2002),

> **Sociology** is the scientific study of social life, social change, and the social causes and consequences of human behavior. Since all human behavior is social, the subject matter of sociology ranges from the intimate family to the hostile mob; from organized crime to religious cults; from the divisions of race, gender, and social class to the shared beliefs of a common culture; and from the sociology of work to the sociology of sports. (p. 1)

As we shall see, sociology is relevant and applicable to our lives in many ways. Sociologists conduct scientific research on social relationships and problems that range from tiny groups of two people to national societies and global social networks.

Unlike the discipline of psychology, which focuses on attributes, motivations, and behaviors of individuals, sociology tends to focus on group patterns. Whereas a psychologist might try to explain behavior by examining the personality traits of individuals, a sociologist would examine the position of different people within the group and how positions influence what people do. Sociologists seek to analyze and explain why people interact with others and belong to groups, how groups work, who has power and who does not, how decisions are made, and how groups deal with conflict and change. From its early beginnings (discussed in Chapter 2), sociologists have asked questions about the rules that govern group behavior; about the causes of social problems, such as child abuse, crime, or poverty; and about why nations declare war and kill each other's citizens.

Two-person interactions—dyads—are the smallest units sociologists study. Examples of dyads include roommates discussing their classes, a professor and student going over an assignment, a husband and wife negotiating their budget, and two children playing. Next in size are small groups consisting of three or more interacting people—a family, a neighborhood group, a classroom, a work group, or a street gang. Then come increasingly larger groups—organizations such as sports or scouting clubs, neighborhood associations, and local religious congregations. Among the largest groups contained within nations are ethnic groups and national organizations or institutions, including economic, educational, religious, health, and political systems. Nations themselves are still larger and can sometimes involve hundreds of millions of people. In the past several decades, social scientists have also pointed to globalization, the process by which the entire world is becoming a single interdependent entity. Of particular interest to sociologists are how these various groups are organized, how they function, why they conflict, and how they influence one another.

Thinking Sociologically

Identify several dyads, small groups, and large organizations to which you belong. Did you choose to belong, or were you born into membership in the group? How does each group influence decisions you make?

An athletic team teaches members to interact, cooperate, develop awareness of the power of others, and deal with conflict. Here, children experience ordered interaction in the competitive environment of a football game. What values, skills, attitudes, and assumptions about life and social interaction do you think these young boys are learning?

Assumptions Underlying Sociology

Sociology is based on a few important beliefs or assumptions that sociologists tend to take for granted about the social world. These ideas about humans and social life are supported by considerable evidence, but they are assumptions, in that they are no longer matters of debate or controversy. Understanding these core assumptions helps us see how sociologists approach the study of people in groups.

People are social by nature. This means that humans seek contact with other humans, interact with each other, and influence and are influenced by the behaviors of one another. Furthermore, humans need groups to survive. Although a few individuals may become socially isolated as adults, they could not have reached adulthood without sustained interactions with others. The central point here is that we become who we are because other people and groups constantly influence us.

People live much of their lives belonging to social groups. It is in social groups that we interact, learn to share goals and to cooperate, develop identities, obtain power, and have conflicts. Our individual beliefs and behaviors, our experiences, our observations, and the problems we face are derived from connections to our social groups.

Interaction between the individual and the group is a two-way process in which each influences the other. Individuals can influence the shape and direction of groups; groups provide the rules and the expected behaviors for individuals.

Recurrent social patterns, ordered behavior, shared expectations, and common understandings among people characterize groups. A degree of continuity and recurrent behavior is present in human interactions, whether in small groups, large organizations, or society.

The processes of conflict and change are natural and inevitable features of groups and societies. No group can remain stagnant and hope to perpetuate itself. To survive, groups must adapt to changes in the social and physical environment. In the past half century, for example, Asian societies such as China, Korea, and Thailand have evolved from agricultural societies to complex, technologically based world economic powers. Yet, such rapid change often comes at a price. It can lead to conflict within a society—between traditional and new ideas and between groups that have vested interests in particular ways of doing things.

Rapid change can give rise to protest activities, as in the case of riots over the assassination of a famous Pakistani political leader and presidential candidate, Benazir Bhutto. Moreover, changing in a controversial direction or failing to change fast enough can spark conflict, including revolution. Historical examples such as the Russian revolution come to mind, where the aristocracy seemed unable to understand or respond to the needs of a starving and war-torn nation. The elites were violently overthrown. More recently, the collapse of Soviet domination of Eastern Europe and the violence of citizens against what some saw as a corrupt election in Kenya illustrate the demand for change that can spring from citizens' discontent with corrupt or authoritarian rule.

As you read this book, keep in mind these basic assumptions that form the foundation of sociological ideas: People are social; they live and carry out activities largely in groups; interaction influences both individual and group behavior; people share common behavior patterns and expectations; and processes such as change and conflict are always present. In several important ways, sociological understandings differ from our everyday views of the social world and provide new lenses for looking at our social world.

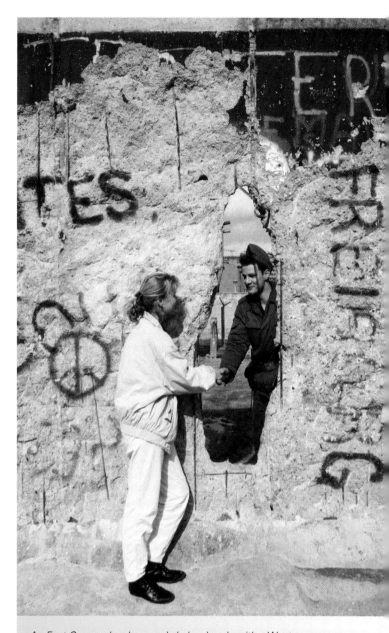

An East German border guard shakes hands with a West German woman through a hole in the Berlin Wall. Although their governments were hostile to one another, the people themselves often had very different sentiments toward those on the other side of the divide.

Sociology Versus Common Sense

Human tragedy can result from inaccurate commonsense beliefs. For example, the Nazi genocide and the existence of slavery both have their roots in false beliefs about racial superiority. Consider for a moment some events that have captured media attention, and ask yourself questions about

these events: Why do some families remain poor generation after generation? Are kids from certain kinds of neighborhoods more likely to get into trouble with the law than kids from other neighborhoods? Why do political, religious, and ethnic conflicts exist in the Congo, Rwanda, Sudan, the Middle East, and other areas? Why do some families experience high levels of violence in the home? Why are fewer women than men employed in careers as scientists and

One society in Niger in sub-Saharan Africa illustrates that our notions of masculinity and femininity—which common sense tells us are innate and universal—are actually socially defined, variable, and learned. Wodaabe men are known for their heavy use of makeup to be attractive to women.

mathematicians? Why is the homicide rate in the United States so much higher than that of other developed nations? Why do some people join religious cults? Our answers to such questions reflect our beliefs and assumptions about the social world. These assumptions often are based on our experiences, our judgments about what our friends and family believe, what we have read or viewed on television, and common stereotypes, which are rigid beliefs, often untested and unfounded, about a group or a category of people.

Common sense refers to ideas that are so completely taken for granted that they have never been seriously questioned and seem to be sensible to any reasonable person. Sociologists assume human behavior can be studied scientifically; they use scientific methods to test the accuracy of commonsense beliefs and ideas about human behavior and the social world. Commonsense interpretations based on personal experience are an important means of processing information and deciding on a course of action. Although all of us hold such ideas and assumptions, that does not mean they are accurate. Would our commonsense notions about the social world be reinforced or rejected if examined with scientifically gathered information?

The difference between common sense and sociology is that sociologists test their beliefs by gathering information and analyzing the evidence in a planned, objective, systematic, and replicable (repeatable) scientific way. Indeed, they set up studies to see if they can disprove what they think is true. This is the way science is done. Consider the following examples of commonsense beliefs about the social world and some research findings about these beliefs.

Commonsense Beliefs and Social Science Findings

Belief: Most of the differences in the behaviors of women and men are based on "human nature"; men and women are just plain different from each other. Research shows that biological factors certainly play a part in the behaviors of men and women, but the culture (beliefs, values, rules, and way of life) that people learn as they grow up determines how biological tendencies are played out. A unique example illustrates this: In the Wodaabe tribe in Africa, women do most of the heavy work while men adorn themselves with makeup, sip tea, and gossip (Beckwith 1983). Variations in behavior of men and women around the world are so great that it is impossible to attribute behavior to biology or human nature alone.

Belief: As developing countries modernize, the lives of their female citizens improve. This is generally false. In fact, the status of women in many developed and developing countries is getting worse. Women make up roughly 51% of the world's more than 6.7 billion people and account for two thirds of the world's hours-at-work. However, in no country for which data are available do they earn what men earn, and sometimes, the figures show women earning less than 50% of men's earnings for similar work. Women hold many unpaid jobs in agriculture, and they own only 1% of the world's property. Furthermore, of the world's 1 billion illiterate adults, two thirds are women (World Factbook 2007a). Only 77% of the world's women over age 15 can read and write compared to 87% of men. Illiteracy rates for women in South Asia, sub-Saharan Africa, and the Middle East are highest in the world, implying lack of access to education. These are only a few examples of the continuing poor status of women in many countries (Institute for Statistics 2006a; World Factbook 2007a; youthxchange 2007).

Belief: Young people in modern industrial societies who join cults are duped through brainwashing or other techniques into changing their beliefs and values; therefore, the key to combating cults is debunking the outrageous beliefs that are passed on to new converts. Extensive research using firsthand observation of new religious movements has been nearly unanimous in its conclusions: Change in a sense of belonging to a group comes before change of beliefs and values. Most recruits to religious movements are recruited through friendship networks or friendship-making strategies (Bromley and Shupe 1981; Lofland and Skonovd 1981; Richardson 1985; Roberts 2004). Once the people in the religious community become a group to which the person wants to belong and wants to conform, the person begins to modify beliefs in line with the group. Change of beliefs and values is a late stage in the conversion process, not the first step. Indeed, the same may be true for members of conventional religious organizations. As sociologist and Roman

Catholic priest Andrew Greeley (1972) puts it, "We might say that instead of Americans belonging to churches because they believe in religion, they believe in religion because they belong to churches" (p. 115). Therefore, trying to persuade individuals who join an unconventional religious movement that there is an error in their beliefs has little effect.

Belief: Given high divorce rates in the United States and Canada, marriages are in serious trouble. Although the divorce rate in North America is high, the rate of marriage is also one of the highest in the world (Coontz 2005). If the fear-of-commitment hypothesis were true, it is unlikely the marriage rate would be so high. Moreover, even those who have been divorced tend to remarry. Despite all the talk about decline and despite genuine concern about high levels of marital failure, Americans now spend more years of their lives in marriage than at any other time in history. Divorce appears to be seen as rejection of a particular partnership rather than as a rejection of marriage itself (Coontz 2005; Wallerstein and Blakeslee 1996). The divorce rate reached a peak in the United States in 1982 and has declined modestly since that time (Newman and Grauerholz 2002).

As these examples illustrate, many of our commonsense beliefs are challenged by social scientific evidence. On examination, the social world is often more complex than our commonsense understanding of events, which is based on limited evidence. Throughout history, there are examples of beliefs that seemed obvious at one time but have been shown to be mistaken through scientific study. Social scientific research may also confirm some common notions about the social world. For example, the unemployment rate among African Americans in the United States is higher than that of most other groups; women with similar education and jobs earn less income than men with the same education and jobs; excessive consumption of alcohol is associated with high levels of domestic violence; people tend to marry others who are of a similar social class. The point is that the discipline of sociology provides a method to assess the accuracy of our commonsense assumptions about the social world.

To improve lives of individuals in societies around the world, decision makers must rely on an accurate understanding of the society. Accurate information gleaned from sociological research can be the basis for more rational and just social policies—policies that better meet the needs of all groups in the social world. The sociological perspective, discussed below, helps us gain reliable understanding.

Thinking Sociologically

What are some commonsense beliefs you hold about your social world such as those mentioned above? How did you develop your beliefs?

Literacy is a major issue for societies around the globe. These Chinese children are learning to read, but in many developing countries, boys have more access to formal education than girls have. The commonsense notion is that most children in the world, boys and girls, have equal access to education, yet many children, especially girls, do not gain literacy.

The Sociological Perspective and the Sociological Imagination

What happens in the social world affects our individual lives. If we are unemployed or lack funds for our college education, we may say this is a personal problem when often broader social issues are at the root of our situation. The sociological perspective holds that we can best understand our personal experiences and problems by examining their broader social context—by looking at the big picture.

As sociologist C. Wright Mills (1959) explains, individual problems or private troubles are rooted in social or public issues, what is happening in the social world outside of one's personal control. This relationship between individual experiences and public issues is the **sociological imagination**. For Mills, many personal experiences can and should be interpreted in the context of large-scale forces in the wider society.

Consider, for example, the personal trauma caused by being laid off of a job. The unemployed person often experiences feelings of inadequacy or lack of worth. This, in turn, may produce stress in a marriage or even result in divorce. These conditions not only are deeply troubling to the person most directly affected but also are related to wider political and economic forces in society. The unemployment may be due to corporate downsizing or to a corporation taking operations to another country where labor costs are cheaper and where there are fewer environmental regulations on companies. People may blame themselves or each other for personal troubles such as unemployment or a failed marriage, believing that they did not try hard enough. Often, they do not see the connection between their private lives and larger economic forces beyond their control. They fail to recognize the public issues that create private troubles.

Families also experience stress as partners have, over time, assumed increasing responsibility for their mate's and their children's emotional and physical needs. Until the second half of the 20th century, the community and the extended family unit—aunts, uncles, grandparents, and cousins—assumed more of that burden. Extended families continue to exist in countries where children settle near their parents, but in modern urban societies, both the sense of community and the connection to the extended family are greatly diminished. There are fewer intimate ties to call on for help and support. Divorce is a very personal condition for those affected, but it can be understood far more clearly when considered in conjunction with the broader social context of economics, urbanization, changing gender roles, lack of external support, and legislated family policies.

As we learn about sociology, we will come to understand how social forces shape individual lives, and this will help us to understand aspects of everyday life we take for granted. In this book, we will investigate how group life influences our behaviors and interactions, and why some individuals follow the rules of society and others do not. A major goal is to help us incorporate the sociological perspective into our way of looking at the social world and our place in it. Indeed, the notion of sociological imagination—connecting events from the global and national level to the personal and intimate level of our own lives—is the core organizing theme of this book.

Thinking Sociologically

How does poverty, a war, or a recession cause personal troubles for someone you know? Why is trying to explain the causes of these personal troubles by examining only the personal characteristics of those affected not adequate?

Some sociologists study issues and problems and present their results for others to use. Others become involved in solving the very problems they study. The following feature, "Sociology in Your Social World," provides an extension on the sociological imagination, illustrating how some use their sociological knowledge to become involved in their communities or the larger world; these students of sociology advocate an active role in bringing about change.

Questions Sociologists Ask—and Don't Ask

Sociologists ask questions about human behavior in social groups and organizations—questions that can be studied scientifically. Sociologists, like other scientists, cannot answer certain questions—philosophical questions about the existence of God, the meaning of life, the ethical implications of stem cell research, or the morality of physician-assisted suicide. What sociologists do ask, however, is this: What effect does holding certain ideas or adhering to certain ethical standards have on the behavior and attitudes of people? For example, are people more likely to obey rules if they believe that there are consequences for their actions in an afterlife? What are the consequences—positive and negative—of allowing suicide for terminally ill patients who are in pain? Although sociologists may study philosophical or religious beliefs held by groups, they do not make judgments about what beliefs are right or wrong or about moral issues involving philosophy, religion, values, or opinion. Rather, they focus on issues that can be studied objectively and scientifically, rather than those that are judgmental or value based.

Applied sociologists, those who carry out research to help organizations solve problems, agree that the research itself should be as objective as possible. After the research is completed, then the applied sociologists might use the research findings to explore policy implications and make recommendations for change.

Consider the following examples of questions sociologists might ask:

- Who gets an abortion, why do they do so, and how does society as a whole view abortion? These are matters of fact that a social scientist can explore. However, sociologists avoid making ethical judgments about whether abortion is right or wrong. Such a judgment is a question of values, not one that can be answered through scientific analysis. The question about the morality of abortion is very important to many people, but it is based on philosophical or theological rationale, not on sociological findings.
- Who is most beautiful? Cultural standards of beauty impact individual popularity and social interaction, and this analytical issue interests some social scientists. However, the sociologist would not judge which individuals are more or less attractive. Such questions are matters of aesthetics, a field of philosophy and art.
- What are the circumstances around individuals becoming drunk and drunken behavior? This question is often tied more to social environment than to alcohol itself. Note that a person might be very intoxicated at a fraternity party but behave differently at a wedding reception, where the expectations for behavior are very different. The researcher does not make judgments about whether use of alcohol is

Sociology in Your Social World

How Will You Spend the 21st Century?

By Peter Dreier

Today, Americans enjoy more rights, better working conditions, better living conditions, and more protection from disease in childhood and old age than anyone could have imagined 100 years ago . . . But that doesn't let you off the hook! There are still many problems and much work to do. Like all agents for social change, . . . social reformers [such as] Frances Perkins and Martin Luther King Jr. [both sociology majors] understood the basic point of sociology, that is, to look for the connections between people's everyday personal problems and the larger trends in society.

Things that we experience as personal matters—a woman facing domestic violence, or a low-wage worker who cannot afford housing, or middle-class people stuck in daily traffic jams—are really about how our institutions function. Sociologists hold a mirror up to our society and help us see our society objectively. One way to do this is by comparing our own society to others. This sometimes makes us uncomfortable—because we take so much about our society for granted. Conditions that we may consider "normal," other societies may consider serious problems. For example, if we compare the United States to other advanced industrial countries such as Canada, Germany, France, Sweden, Australia, Holland, and Belgium, we find some troubling things:

- The United States has the highest per capita income among those countries. At the same time, the United States has, by far, the widest gap between the rich and the poor.
- Almost 30 percent of American workers work full-time, year-round, for poverty-level wages.
- The United States has the highest overall rate of poverty. More than 33 million Americans live in poverty.
- Over 12 million of these Americans are children. In fact, one out of six American children is poor. They live in slums and trailer parks, eat cold cereal for dinner, share a bed or a cot with their siblings, and sometimes with their parents, and are often one disaster away from becoming homeless . . .
- Only three out of five children eligible for the Head Start program are enrolled because of the lack of funding . . .
- The United States has the highest infant mortality rate among the major industrial nations . . .
- The United States is the only one of these nations without universal health insurance. More than 43 million Americans—including 11 million children—have no health insurance.
- Americans spend more hours stuck in traffic jams than people of any of these other countries. This leads to more pollution, more auto accidents, and less time spent with families.
- Finally, the United States has a much higher proportion of our citizens in prison than any of these societies . . .

. . . What would you like *your* grandchildren to think about how *you* spent the 21st century? . . . No matter what career you pursue, you have choices about how you will live your lives. As citizens, you can sit on the sidelines and merely be *involved* in your society, or you can decide to become really *committed* to making this a better world.

Today, there are hundreds of thousands of patriotic Americans committed to making our country live up to its ideals . . . They are asking the same questions that earlier generations of active citizens asked: Why can't our society do a better job of providing equal opportunity, a clean environment, and a decent education for all? They know there are many barriers and obstacles to change, but they want to figure out how to overcome these barriers, and to help build a better society.

So ask yourselves: What are some of the things that *we* take for granted today that need to be changed? What are some ideas for changing things that today might seem "outrageous," but that—25 or 50 or 100 years from now—will be considered common sense?

. . . A record number of college students today are involved in a wide variety of "community service" activities—such as mentoring young kids in school, volunteering in a homeless shelter, or working in an AIDS hospice. As a result of this student activism, more than 100 colleges and universities have adopted "anti-sweatshop" codes of conduct for the manufacturers of clothing that bear the names and logos of their institutions.

Positive change *is* possible, but it is *not* inevitable . . . I am optimistic that your generation will follow a lifelong commitment to positive change.

I know you will *not* be among those who simply "see things the way they are and ask: why?" Instead, you will "dream things that never were and ask: why not?" [Robert Kennedy].

What is acceptable or unacceptable drinking behavior varies according to the social setting—a wedding reception versus a fraternity party. Binge drinking, losing consciousness, vomiting, or engaging in sexual acts while drunk may be a source of storytelling at a college party but be offensive at a wedding reception.

Thinking Sociologically

Why would you or would you not become involved in change? How might the "sociological imagination" influence your decision?

good or bad, right or wrong, and avoids—as much as possible—opinions regarding responsibility or irresponsibility. The sociologist does, however, observe variations in the use of alcohol in social situations, and resulting behaviors. An applied sociologist researching alcohol use on campus for a college or for a national fraternity may, following the research, offer advice based on that research about how to reduce the number of alcohol-related deaths or sexual assault incidents on college campuses (Sweet 2001).

Sociologists learn techniques to avoid letting their values influence their research designs, data gathering, and analysis. Still, complete objectivity is difficult at best, and what one chooses to study may be influenced by one's interests and concerns about injustice in society. The fact that sociologists know they will be held accountable by other scientists for the objectivity of their research is a major factor in encouraging them to be objective when they do their research.

Thinking Sociologically

From the information you have just read, what are some questions sociologists might ask about divorce or cohabitation or same-sex unions? What are some questions sociologists *would not* ask about these topics, at least while in their roles as researchers?

The Social Sciences: A Comparison

Not so long ago, our views of people and social relationships were based on stereotypes, intuition, superstitions, supernatural explanations, and traditions passed on from one generation to the next. Natural sciences first used the scientific method, a model later adopted by social sciences. Social scientists, including anthropologists, economists, cultural geographers, historians, and political scientists, apply the scientific method to study social relationships, to correct misleading and harmful misconceptions about human behaviors, and to guide policy decisions. Consider the following examples of specific studies a social scientist might conduct. This is followed by a brief description of the focus of the discipline.

An anthropologist works as a cocktail waitress in a bar to study the subculture of that environment and to uncover subtle ways in which gender roles are reinforced. Anthropology is closely related to sociology. In fact, the two areas have common historical roots. *Anthropology* is the study of humanity in its broadest context. There are four subfields within anthropology: physical anthropology (which is related to biology), archaeology, linguistics, and cultural anthropology (sometimes called *ethnology*). This last field has the most in common with sociology. Cultural anthropology focuses on the culture, or way of life, of the society being studied and uses methods appropriate to understanding culture.

A psychologist wires research subjects to a machine that measures their physiological reaction to a violent film clip, then asks them questions about what they were feeling. *Psychology* is the study of individual behavior and mental processes (e.g., sensation, perception, memory, and thought processes). It differs from sociology in that it focuses on individuals, rather than on groups, institutions, and societies as sociology does. Although there are different branches of psychology, most psychologists are concerned with what motivates individual behavior, personality attributes, attitudes, beliefs, and perceptions. Psychologists also explore abnormal behavior, the mental disorders of individuals, and stages of normal human development (Wallerstein 1996; Wallerstein and Blakeslee 2004).

A political scientist studies opinion poll results to predict who will win the next election or how elected officials will vote on proposed legislation. *Political science* is concerned with government systems and power—how they work, how they are organized, forms of government, relations between governments, who holds power and how they obtain it, how power is used, and who is politically active. For instance, governments oversee many aspects of individuals' lives. In China, they have established laws for how many children a family may have. Political science overlaps with sociology, particularly in the study of political theory and the nature and the uses of power.

An economist studies the latest stock market trends and tries to predict its movement and its impact on banking practices. *Economists* analyze economic conditions and explore how people organize, produce, and distribute material goods. They are interested in supply and demand, inflation and taxes, prices and manufacturing output, labor organization, employment levels, and comparisons of industrial and nonindustrial nations.

What all of these social sciences—sociology, anthropology, psychology, economics, political science, cultural geography, and history—have in common is that they study

Urban Chinese families are allowed to have only one child. Having more than one would result in penalties. Thus, families pay a great deal of attention to their single child.

aspects of human behavioral and social life. Social sciences share many common topics, methods, concepts, research findings, and theories, but each has a different focus or perspective on the social world. Each of these social sciences relates to topics studied by sociologists, but sociologists focus on human interaction, groups, and social structure, providing the broadest overview of the social world.

Thinking Sociologically

Consider other issues such as the condition of poverty in developing countries or homelessness in North America. What question(s) might different social sciences ask about these problems?

Why Study Sociology . . . and What Do Sociologists Do?

Did you ever wonder why some families are close and others are estranged? Why some work groups are very productive while others are not? Why some people are rich and others remain impoverished? Why some people engage in criminal behaviors and others conform rigidly to rules? Although sociologists do not have all the answers to such questions, they do have the perspective and methods to search for a deeper understanding of these and other patterns of human interaction.

Two ingredients are essential to the study of our social world: a keen ability to observe what is happening in the social world and a desire to find answers to the question of why it is happening. The value of sociology is that it affords us a unique perspective from which to examine the social world, and it provides the methods to study systematically important questions about human interaction, group behavior, and social structure. The practical significance of the sociological perspective is that it

- fosters greater self-awareness, which can lead to opportunities to improve one's life;
- encourages a more complete understanding of social situations by looking beyond individual explanations to include group analyses of behavior;
- helps people to understand and evaluate problems by enabling them to view the world systematically and objectively rather than in strictly emotional or personal terms;
- cultivates an understanding of the many diverse cultural perspectives and how cultural differences are related to behavioral patterns;
- provides a means to assess the impact of social policies;
- reveals the complexities of social life and provides methods of inquiry to study them; and
- provides useful skills in interpersonal relations, critical thinking, data collection and analysis, problem solving, and decision making.

This unique perspective has practical value as we carry out our roles as workers, friends, family members, and citizens. For example, an employee who has studied sociology may better understand how to work with groups and how the structure of the workplace affects individual behavior, how to approach problem solving, and how to collect and analyze data. Likewise, a school teacher trained in sociology may have a better understanding of classroom management, student motivation, causes of poor student learning that have roots outside the school, and other variables that shape the professional life of teachers and academic success of students. Consider the example in the "How Do We Know?" feature, which explores how high school groups such as "jocks" and "burnouts" behave and why each clique's behavior might be quite logical in certain circumstances. *Burnouts and Jocks in a Public High School* explores a social environment very familiar to most of us, the social cliques in a high school.

What Sociologists Do

Sociologists are employed in a variety of settings. Although students may first encounter them as teachers and researchers in higher education, sociologists also hold nonacademic,

applied sociology jobs in social agencies, government, and business. The amount of study completed in sociology, plus the sociologists' areas of specialization, help determine the types of positions they hold. The three typical sociology degrees are bachelor of arts or bachelor of science (BA or BS), master of arts (MA), and doctorate (PhD).

Many sociologists with a bachelor's degree work in the social service sector (such as criminal justice or family services), in government positions, or in business personnel offices. With a master's or a doctorate degree, graduates usually become college teachers, researchers, clinicians, and consultants.

Consider your professor. The duties of professors vary depending on the type of institution and the level of courses offered. Classroom time fills only a portion of the professor's working days. Other activities include preparing for classes, preparing and grading exams and assignments, advising students, serving on committees, keeping abreast of new research in the field, and conducting research studies and having them published. This "publish or perish" task is deemed the most important activity for faculty in some major universities.

Most sociologists are employed in colleges and universities, but as Table 1.1 illustrates, a significant portion of sociologists work in business, government, and social service agencies (American Sociological Association 2006; Dotzler and Koppel 1999).

In businesses, applied sociologists use their knowledge and research skills in human resources or to address organizational needs or problems. In government jobs, they provide data such as population projections for education and health care planning. In social service agencies, such as police departments, they help to address deviant behavior, and in health agencies, they may be concerned with doctor-patient interactions. Applied sociology is an important aspect of the field; each chapter includes boxed inserts discussing the work of an applied sociologist. These examples will provide a picture of what you can do with a sociology degree. In addition, you will find a section discussing policy examples and implications at the end of chapters, related to that chapter topic. Figure 1.1 provides some ideas of career paths for graduates with a degree in sociology.

Table 1.1 **Where Sociologists Are Employed**	
Places of Employment	*Percentage Employed*
College or university	75.5
Government (all positions)	7.1
Private, for-profit business	6.2
Not-for-profit public service organizations	7.6
Self-employed	0.4

Source: American Sociological Association 2006.

How Do We Know?

Burnouts and Jocks in a Public High School

High schools are big organizations made up of smaller friendship networks and cliques; a careful examination can give us insight into the tensions that exist as the groups struggle for resources and power in the school.

Sociologist Penelope Eckert (1989) focused on two categories of students that exist in many high schools in North America: "burnouts" and "jocks." The burnouts defied authorities, smoked in the restrooms, refused to use their lockers, made a public display of not eating in the school cafeteria, and wore their jackets all day. Their open and public defiance of authority infuriated the jocks—the college prep students who participated in choir, band, student council, and athletics and who held class offices. The burnouts were disgusted with the jocks. In their view, by constantly sucking up to the authorities, the jocks received special privileges, and by playing the goody-two-shoes role, they made life much more difficult for the burnouts.

Despite their animosity toward one another, the goal of both groups was to gain more autonomy from the adult authorities who constantly bossed students around. As the burnouts saw things, if the jocks would have even a slight bit of backbone and stand up for the dignity of students as adults, life would be better for everyone. The burnouts believed that school officials should earn their obedience. The burnouts maintained their dignity by affirming that they did not recognize bossy adults as authorities. Wearing coats all day was another way to emphasize the idea that "I'm just a visitor in this school."

The jocks, for their part, became irritated at the burnouts when they caused trouble and were belligerent with authorities; then the administration would crack down on everyone, and no one had any freedom. Jocks found that if they did what the adults told them to do—at least while the adults were around—they got a lot more freedom. When the burnouts got defiant, however, the principal got mad and removed everyone's privileges.

Sociologist Eckert (1989) found that the behavior of both groups was quite logical for their circumstances and ambitions. Expending energy as a class officer or participating in extracurricular activities is a rational behavior for college preparatory students because those leadership roles help students get into their college of choice.

However, those activities do not help one get a better job in a factory in town. In fact, hanging out at the bowling alley makes far more sense. For the burnouts, having friendship networks and acquaintances in the right places is more important to achieving their goals than a class office listed on their resume.

Eckert's (1989) method of gathering information was effective in showing how the internal dynamics of schools—conflicts between student groups—were influenced by outside factors such as working- and upper middle-class status. Recent research upholds Eckert's findings on the importance cliques play in shaping school behavior. Like Eckert, Bonnie Barber and colleagues (2001) followed various friendship cliques starting in 10th grade in a Michigan high school. In their research, they support what Eckert suggests: The jocks in their study were the most integrated to mainstream society in adult life. The burnouts (or criminals, as they are labeled in Barber's research) were most likely to have been arrested or incarcerated, showing that the propensity to defy authority figures may carry on into adult life.

In addition, sociologist Dana Haynie (2001), finds that it is not just the clique that someone is in, but the properties of that clique that influence teen behavior. Haynie shows that cliques with more reciprocal friendships have members who act more alike. The underlying rationale is that when our friends are friends with one another, we are more likely to do the same things, including being delinquent. These studies show that sociological analysis can help us understand some ways that connections between groups—regardless of whether they are in conflict or harmony—shape the perceptions, attitudes, and behaviors of people living in this complex social world.

Business or Management	Human Services	Education
Market researcher	Social worker	Teacher
Sales manager	Criminologist	Academic research
Customer relations	Gerontologist	Administration
Manufacturing representative	Hospital administrator	School counselor
Banking or loan officer	Charities administrator	Policy analyst
Data processor	Community advocate or organizer	College professor
Attorney		Dean of student life

Research	Government	Public Relations
Population analyst	Policy advisor or administrator	Publisher
Surveyor	Labor relations	Mass communications
Market researcher	Legislator	Advertising
Economic analyst	Census worker	Writer or commentator
Public opinion pollster	International agency representative	Journalist
Interviewer	City planning officer	
Policy researcher	Prison administrator	
Telecommunications researcher	Law enforcement	
	FBI agent	
	Customs agent	

Figure 1.1 What Can You Do With a Sociology Degree?

Note: Surveys of college alumni with undergraduate majors in sociology indicate that this field of study prepares people for a broad range of occupations. Notice that some of these jobs require graduate or professional training. For further information, contact your department chair or the American Sociological Association in Washington, D.C., for a copy of *Careers in Sociology,* 6th edition.

Thinking Sociologically

From what you have read so far, how might interaction skills and knowledge of how groups work be useful to you in your anticipated major and career?

What Employers Want and What Sociology Majors Bring to a Career

Sociologists and other social scientists have studied what job skills and competencies employers seek in new employees, in addition to subject matter expertise. As we will discover, sociology majors learn many of these skills (Ballantine 1991; Hansen and Hansen 2003). Note that learning the following skills and competencies is part of most sociological training:

1. Communication skills (listening, verbal and written communication, working with peers, and effective interaction in group situations);

2. Analytical and research skills (research skills);

3. Computer and technical literacy (basic understanding of computer hardware and software programs);

4. Flexibility, adaptability, and multitasking (ability to set priorities, manage multiple tasks, adapt to changing situations, and handle pressure);

5. Interpersonal skills (working with coworkers);

6. Effective leadership skills (ability to take charge and make decisions);

7. Sensitivity to diversity in the workplace and with clients;

8. Organizing thoughts and information and planning effectively (ability to design, plan, organize, and implement projects and to be self-motivated);

9. Ability to conceptualize and solve problems and be creative (working toward meeting the organization's goals);

10. Working with others (ability to work toward a common goal);

11. Personal values (honesty, flexibility, work ethic, dependability, loyalty, positive attitude, professionalism, self-confidence, willingness to learn) (Hansen and Hansen 2003).

These competencies reflect skills stressed in the sociology curriculum: an ability to understand and work with others, research and computer skills, planning and organizing skills, oral and written communication skills, critical thinking skills (WorldWideLearn 2007). Keep these skills in mind as you proceed through this book.

We now have a general idea of what sociology is and what sociologists do. It should be apparent that sociology is a broad field of interest; sociologists study all aspects of human social behavior. The next section of this chapter shows how the parts of the social world that sociologists study relate to each other, and it outlines the model you will follow as you continue to learn about sociology.

Thinking Sociologically

What are some advantages of mayors, legislators, police chiefs, or government officials making decisions based on information gathered and verified by sociological research rather than on their own intuition or assumptions?

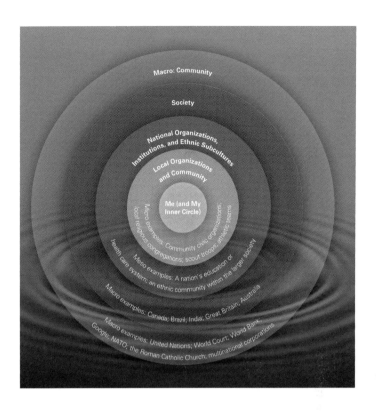

The Social World Model

Think about the different groups you depend on and interact with on a daily basis. You wake up to greet members of your family or your roommate. You go to a larger group—a class—that exists within an even larger organization—the college or university. Understanding sociology and comprehending the approach of this book requires a grasp of **levels of analysis**, social groups from the smallest to the largest. It may be relatively easy to picture small groups, such as a family, a sports team, or a sorority or fraternity. It is more difficult to visualize large groups, such as corporations—The Gap, Abercrombie and Fitch, Eddie Bauer, General Motors Corporation, or Starbucks—or organizations such as local or state governments. The largest groups include nations or international organizations, such as the sprawling networks of the United Nations or the World Trade Organization. Groups of various sizes shape our lives. Sociological analysis requires that we understand these groups at various levels of analysis.

The **social world model** helps us picture the levels of analysis in our social surroundings as an interconnected series of small groups, organizations, institutions, and societies. Sometimes, these groups are connected by mutual support and cooperation, but sometimes, there are conflicts and power struggles over access to resources. What we are asking you to do here and throughout this book is to develop a sociological imagination—the basic lens used by sociologists. Picture the social world as a linked system made up of increasingly larger circles. To understand the units or parts in each circle of the social world model, look at the social world model shown here:

This social world model will be used throughout our book to illustrate how each topic fits into the big picture, our social world. No social unit of our social world can stand alone. All units affect each other, either because they serve needs of other units in the system or because of intense conflict and tension affecting different units. The social world is organized into two parts—structures and processes. Now, let us take a trip through our social world.

Social Structures

The social world model is made up of a number of **social units**, interconnected parts of the social world. These range from interaction in dyads and small groups to negotiating or warring societies. All these units combine into a system to form the **social structure** that holds societies together and brings order to our lives by regulating the way the units work in combination. Compare this to a picture of our body's skeleton, which governs how our limbs are attached to the torso and how they move.

Sometimes, the interconnections in the social structure conflict, however, due to divergent beliefs or self-interests of units. For example, a religion that teaches that it is wrong to have blood transfusions may conflict with the health care system regarding how to save the life of a child. Business executives want to produce products at the lowest possible cost, but this may mean paying workers low wages and causing damage to the environment. All levels of analysis are linked. Some links are supportive; others are in conflict.

Social institutions are found in every society—family, education, religion, politics, economics, science, sports, and

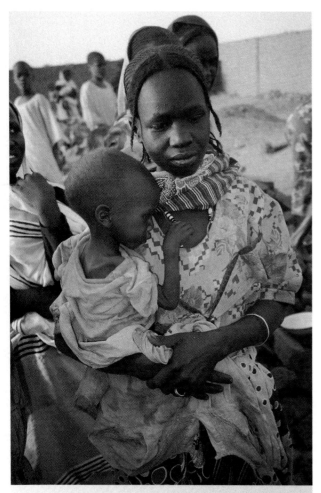

This Darfur refugee mother and child represent the smallest social unit, a dyad. In this case, they are trying to survive with help from larger groups such as the United Nations.

The **national society**, one of the largest social units in our model, includes a population of people, usually living within a specified geographic area, who are connected by common ideas and are subject to a particular political authority; it also features a social structure with groups and institutions. Although a national society is one of the largest social units, it is still a subsystem of the interdependent global system. France, Kenya, Brazil, and Laos are all national societies on separate continents, but they are linked as part of the global system of nations. Each national society has its own distinct, relatively permanent geographic and political boundaries, language, and way of life. In most cases, national societies involve countries or large regions where the inhabitants share a common identity as members. In certain other instances, such as contemporary Great Britain, a single national society may include several groups of people who consider themselves distinct nationalities (Welsh, English, Scottish, and Irish within the United Kingdom). Such multicultural societies may or may not be harmonious.

Thinking Sociologically

Think about a significant social conflict or change and how it influences any one of the following social institutions— family, education, religion, politics, economics, science, sports, or health care. How might a significant change in one institution affect stability or change in another institution?

Social Processes

Picture **social processes** as the actions taken by people in social units. Processes keep the social world working, much as the beating heart keeps the body working. Consider the processes of socialization, stratification, conflict, and change. The process of socialization teaches individuals how to become productive members of society. It takes place through actions of families, educational systems, religious organizations, and other social units. Socialization is essential for the continuation of any society. Similarly, our social positions in society are the result of stratification, the process of layering people into social strata based on such factors as birth, income, occupation, and education. Conflict occurs between individuals or groups over money, jobs, and other needed resources. The process of change is also a continuous pattern in every social unit; change in one unit affects other units of the social world, often in a chain reaction. For instance, change in the quality of health care can impact the workforce; a beleaguered workforce can impact the economy; instability in the economy can affect families, as breadwinners lose jobs; and family economic woes can impact religious communities because devastated families cannot afford to give money to the churches, mosques, or temples.

health care. They provide the rules, roles, and relationships to meet human needs and guide human behavior. They are the parts of the social structure in societies through which organized social activities take place, and they provide the setting for activities essential to human and societal survival. For example, we cannot survive without an economic institution to provide guidelines and a structure for meeting our basic needs of food, shelter, and clothing. Likewise, we would never make it to adulthood as functioning members of society without the family, the most basic of all institutions.

Like the system of organs that make up our bodies—heart, lungs, kidneys, bladder—all social institutions are interrelated. Just as a change in one part of the body affects all others, a change in one institution affects the others. When governments pass laws providing money to schools for children's lunches, requiring standardized testing, or limiting extracurricular activities due to lack of funds, it affects both families and schools. Likewise, if many people are unable to afford medical treatment, the society is less healthy, and there are consequences for families, schools, and society as a whole.

Sociologists generally do not judge these social processes as good or bad. Rather, sociologists try to identify and explain processes that take place within social units. Picture these processes as overlaying and penetrating our whole social world, from small groups to societies. Social units would be lifeless without the action brought about by social processes, just as body parts would be lifeless without the processes of electrical impulses shooting from the brain to each organ or the oxygen transmitted by blood coursing through our arteries to sustain each organ.

The Environment

Surrounding each social unit is an **environment**. It includes everything that influences the social unit, such as its physical and organizational surroundings and technological innovations. The environment is part of our social world. Each unit has its own environment to which it must adjust, just as each individual has a unique social world, including family, friends, and other social units that make up the immediate environment. Some parts of the environment are more important to the social unit than others. Your local church, synagogue, or mosque is located in a community environment. That religious organization may seem autonomous and independent, but it depends on its national organization for guidelines and support, the local police force to protect the building from vandalism, and the local economy to provide jobs to members so that the members, in turn, can support the organization. If the religious education program is going to train children to understand the scriptures, the local schools are needed to teach the children to read. A religious group may also be affected by other religious bodies, competing with one another for potential members from the community. These religious groups may work cooperatively—organizing a summer program for children or jointly sponsoring a holy-day celebration—or they may define one another as evil, each trying to stigmatize the other. Moreover, one local religious group may be composed primarily of professional and business people, and another group mostly of laboring people. The religious groups may experience conflict in part because they each serve a different socioeconomic constituency.

The point is that to understand a social unit or the human body, we must consider the structure and processes within the unit, as well as the interaction with the surrounding environment. No matter what social unit the sociologist studies, the unit cannot be understood without considering the interaction of that unit with its unique environment.

Perfect relationships or complete harmony between the social units is unusual. Social units are often motivated by self-interests and self-preservation, with the result that they compete with other groups and units for resources (time, money, skills, energy of members). Therefore, social units within the society are often in conflict. Whether groups are in conflict or mutually supportive does not change their interrelatedness; units are interdependent. The nature of that interdependence is likely to change over time and can be studied using the scientific method.

Studying the Social World: Levels of Analysis

Picture for a moment your sociology class as a social unit in your social world. Students (individuals) make up the class, the class (small group) is offered by the sociology department, the sociology department (a large group) is part of the college or university, the university (an organization) is located in a community and follows the practices approved by the social institution (education) of which it is a part, and education is an institution located within a nation. The practices the university follows are determined by a larger accrediting unit that provides guidelines and oversight for institutions. The national society, represented by the national government, is shaped by global events—technological and economic competition between nations, natural disasters, global warming, wars, and terrorist attacks. Such events influence national policies and goals, including policies for the educational system. Thus, global tensions and conflicts may shape the curriculum that the individual experiences in the sociology classroom.

Each of these social units—from the smallest (the individual student) to the largest (society and the global system)—is referred to as a level of analysis (Table 1.2). These levels are illustrated in the social world model at the beginning of each chapter, and relation to that chapter's content is shown through examples in the model.

 MICRO-LEVEL ANALYSIS

Sometimes, sociologists ask questions about face-to-face interactions in dyads or small groups. A focus on individual or small-group interaction entails **micro-level analysis**. Micro-level analysis is important because face-to-face interaction forms the basic foundation of all social groups and organizations to which we belong, from families, to corporations, to societies. We are members of many groups at the micro level.

To illustrate micro-level analysis, consider the problem of spousal abuse. Why does a person remain in an abusive relationship, knowing that each year thousands of people are killed by their lovers or mates, and millions more are severely and repeatedly battered? To answer this, several possible micro-level explanations can be considered. One view is that the abusive partner has convinced this person that she is powerless in the relationship or that she "deserves" the abuse. Therefore, she gives up in despair of ever being able to alter the situation. The abuse is viewed as part of the interaction—of action and reaction—and the partners come to see abuse as what comprises "normal" interaction.

Another explanation for remaining in the abusive relationship is that the person may have been brought up in a family situation where battering was an everyday part of life. However unpleasant and unnatural this may seem to

Table 1.2 **The Structure of Society and Levels of Analysis**

	Level	Parts of Education
Micro-level analysis	Interpersonal	Sociology class; study group cramming for an exam
	Local organizations	University; sociology department
Meso-level analysis	Organizations and institutions	State boards of education; National Education Association
	Ethnic groups within a nation	Islamic madrassas or Jewish yeshiva school systems
Macro-level analysis	Nations	Policy and laws governing education
	Global community	World literacy programs

outsiders, it may be seen by the abuser or by the abused as a "normal" and acceptable part of intimate relationships.

Another possibility is that an abused woman may fear that her children would be harmed or that she would be harshly judged by her family or church if she "abandoned" her mate. She may have few resources to make leaving the abusive situation possible. To study each of these possible explanations involves analysis at the micro level because each focuses on interpersonal interaction factors rather than on society-wide trends or forces. Meso-level concerns lead to quite different explanations for abuse.

 MESO-LEVEL ANALYSIS

Analysis of intermediate-size social units, called **meso-level analysis**, involves looking at units smaller than the nation but larger than the local community or even the region. This level includes national institutions (such as the economy of a country, the national educational system, or the political system within a country); nationwide organizations (such as a political party, a soccer league, or a national women's rights organization); nationwide corporations (such as Ford Motor Company or IBM); and ethnic groups that have an identity as a group (such as Jews, Mexican Americans, or the Lakota-Sioux in the United States). Organizations, institutions, and ethnic communities are smaller than the nation or global social forces, but they are still beyond the everyday personal experience and control of individuals, unless those individuals organize to collectively change these structures. They are intermediate in the sense of being too large to know everyone in the group, but they are not nation-states at the macro level. Consider the fact that a state in the United States, or province in Canada, or a prefecture in Japan is more accessible and easier to change than the national bureaucracies of countries.

Using meso-level analysis to examine changes in women's status, for example, could include study of women's legal, educational, religious, economic, political, scientific, and sports-related opportunities in society. However, meso-level changes that create new opportunities for women may also cause conflicts and even abuse within individual families at the micro level as women take advantage of expanding opportunities outside the home (Newman and Grauerholz 2002).

In discussing micro-level analysis, we used the example of domestic violence. The micro-level explanations of abuse discussed above are sometimes criticized because they "blame the victim"—in this case, the abused person—for getting into an abusive relationship and for failing to act in ways that stop the abuse. To avoid blaming victims for their own suffering, many social scientists look for broader explanations of spousal abuse, such as the social conditions at the meso level of society that cause the problem (Straus and Gelles 1990). When a pattern of behavior in society occurs with increasing frequency, it cannot be understood solely from the point of view of individual cases or micro-level causes. For instance, sociological findings show that fluctuations in spousal or child abuse are related to levels of unemployment. Frustration resulting in abuse erupts within families when poor economic conditions make it nearly impossible for people to find stable and reliable means of supporting themselves and their families. Economic issues must be addressed if violence in the home is to be lessened.

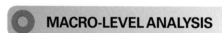 **MACRO-LEVEL ANALYSIS**

Studying the largest social units in the social world, called **macro-level analysis**, involves looking at entire nations, global forces, and international social trends. Macro-level analysis is essential to our understanding of how larger social forces, such as global events, shape our everyday lives. A natural disaster such as the 2005 tsunami in Indonesia, or the heat waves of summer 2006 in Europe, or floods in the United States in the summer of 2008, or frequent earthquakes around the world may change the foods we are able to put on our family dinner table because much of our cuisine is now imported from other parts of the world. Map 1.1 shows some of the most deadly natural disasters of the past few years. Likewise, a political conflict on the other side of the planet can lead to war, which means that a member of

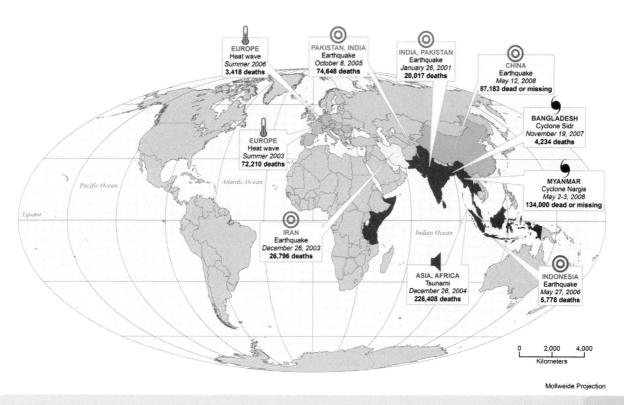

Map 1.1 The Ten Most Deadly Natural Disasters From January 2001 to May 2008

Source: EM-DAT Emergency Events Database, Centre for Research on the Epidemiology of Disasters. Map by Anna Versluis.

your family may be called up to active duty and sent into harm's way more than 7,000 miles from your home. Each member of the family may experience individual stress, have trouble concentrating, and feel ill with worry. The entire globe has become an interdependent social unit. If we are to prosper and thrive in the 21st century, we need to understand connections that go beyond our local communities.

Even patterns such as domestic violence, considered as micro- and meso-level issues above, can be examined at the macro level. Worldwide patterns may tell us something about a social problem and offer new lenses for understanding variables that contribute to a problem. A study of 95 societies around the world found that violence against women (especially rape) occurs at very different rates in different societies, with some societies being completely free of rape (Benderly 1982) and others having a "culture of rape." The most consistent predictor of violence against women was a macho conception of masculine roles and personality. Societies that did not define masculinity in terms of dominance and control were virtually free of rape. Some sociologists believe that the same pattern holds for domestic violence: A society or subgroup within society that teaches males that the finest expression of their masculinity is physical strength and domination is very likely to have battered women (Burn 2005). The point is that understanding individual human behavior often requires investigation of larger societal beliefs that support that behavior.

Let us reconsider the following question: Why is it important to understand different levels of analysis? Sociologists employ different theories and methods to explain human behavior, depending on the level of analysis. Therefore, it is important to know the level of analysis in any sociological research. Recognizing the level at which a problem exists helps sociologists to determine appropriate research methods to study sociological questions (keeping in mind that the other levels of analysis will lend depth to the understanding of any topic). All three levels of analysis are discussed throughout this book. Micro-level analysis is most pertinent when discussing face-to-face interaction, small groups, and the process of socialization—learning to become a member of society. Meso-level analysis is necessary to study processes such as inequality within the society and to analyze and understand institutions such as politics, religion, and education. Macro-level analysis explores issues for people as members of nations and for nations as they interact in the international arena.

Thinking Sociologically

Placing yourself at the center of your social world, describe the social units—including small groups, organizations, institutions, and the nation—of which you are a part. Now describe your environment.

This photo depicts the damage following the tsunami in Indonesia in 2005. This event not only changed the lives of people living in the countries where it struck but had ripple effects on economic exchange, relief efforts around the globe, and international trade that can affect the cost of oil or the foods that are available to put on your table.

Distinctions between each level are not sharply delineated. The micro level shades into the meso level, and the lines between the meso level and the macro level are blurry. Still, it is clear that in some micro-level social units, you know everyone, or at least every member of the social unit is only two degrees of relatedness away. Every person in the social unit knows someone whom you also know. We also all participate in meso-level social units that are smaller than the nation but that can be huge. Millions of people may belong to the same religious denomination or the same political party. We have connections with those people, and our lives are affected by people we do not even know. Consider political activities in the United States and other countries that take place on the Internet. In political campaigns,

millions of individuals join organizations such as Moveon .org and True Majority, participate in dialogue online, and contribute money. People living thousands of miles from one another united financially and in spirit to support Obama-Biden or McCain-Palin in the 2008 election. Thus, the meso level is different from the micro level, but both influence us. The macro level is even more removed from the individual, but its impact can change our lives.

The social world model presented in the chapter opening illustrates the interplay of micro-, meso-, and macro-level forces, and Figure 1.2 illustrates that this micro-to-macro model should be seen as a continuum. In the next "Sociology Around the World," we examine a village in Tunisia to see how macro-level forces influence a meso-level local community and individual micro-level lives.

Micro social units   Meso social units   Macro social units

Figure 1.2 The Micro-to-Macro Continuum

Sociology Around the World

Tunisian Village Meets the Modern World

This is a story of change as macro-level innovations enter a small traditional village. It illustrates how the social units of the social world model and the three levels of analysis enter into sociological analysis. As you read, try to identify both the units and levels of analysis being discussed and the impact of globalization on a community that cannot know what these changes will bring.

The workday began at dawn as usual in the small fishing village on the coast of Tunisia, North Africa. Men prepared their nets and boats for the day, while women prepared breakfast and dressed the young children for school. About 10 a.m., it began—the event that would change this picturesque village forever. Bulldozers arrived first, followed by trench diggers and cement mixers, to begin their overhaul of the village.

Villagers had suspected something was afoot when important-looking officials arrived 2 months earlier with foreign businessmen, followed by two teams of surveyors. Without their approval, the government had sold land that the village had held communally for generations to the foreigners so they could build a multimillion-dollar hotel and casino. When concerned citizens asked what was happening in their village, they were assured that their way of life would not change. The contractor from the capital city of Tunis said they would still have access to the beach and ocean for fishing. He also promised them many benefits from the hotel project— jobs, help from the government to improve roads and housing, and a higher standard of living.

The contractor had set up camp in a trailer on the beach, and word soon got around that he would be hiring some men for higher hourly wages than they could make in a day or even month of fishing. Rivalries soon developed between friends over who should apply for the limited number of jobs.

As the bulldozers moved in, residents had mixed opinions about the changes taking place in their village and their lives. Some saw the changes as exciting opportunities for new jobs and recognition of their beautiful village; others viewed the changes as destroying a lifestyle that was all they and generations before them had known.

Today, the village is dwarfed by the huge hotel, and the locals are looked on as quaint curiosities by the European tourists. Fishing has become a secondary source of employment to working in the hotel and casino or selling local crafts and trinkets to souvenir-seeking visitors. Many women are now employed outside the home by the hotel, creating new family structures as grandparents, unemployed men, and other relations take over childrearing responsibilities.

To understand the changes in this one small village and other communities facing similar change, a sociologist uses the sociological imagination. This involves understanding the global political and economic trends that are affecting this village and its inhabitants (macro-level analysis). It requires comprehension of transformation of social institutions within the nation (meso-level analysis). Finally, sociological investigation explores how change impacts the individual Tunisian villagers (micro-level analysis).

To sociologically analyze the process of change, it is important to understand what is going on in this situation. The government officials and the international business representatives negotiated a lucrative deal to benefit both Tunisia and the business corporation. The community and its powerless residents presented few obstacles to the project from the point of view of the government, and in fact, government officials reasoned that villagers could benefit from new jobs. However, economic and family roles of the villagers—how they earned a living and how they raised their children— changed dramatically with the disruption to their traditional ways. The process of change began with the demand of people far from Tunisia for vacation spots in the sun. Ultimately, this process reached the village's local environment, profoundly affecting the village and everyone in it. For this Tunisian village, the old ways are gone forever.

Building and staffing of this resort in Tunisia—which is patronized by affluent people from other continents (global)—changed the economy, the culture, the social structure (meso-level), and individual lives (micro-level) in the local community.

Thinking Sociologically

Place the groups to which you belong in a hierarchy from micro, to meso, to macro levels. Note how each social unit and its subunits exist within a larger unit until you reach the level of the entire global community.

The Social World Model and This Book

Throughout this book, the social world model will be used as the framework for understanding the social units, processes, and surrounding environment. Each social unit and process is taken out, examined, and returned to its place in the interconnected social world model so that you can comprehend the whole social world and its parts. Look for the model at the beginning of every chapter. You can also expect the micro-, meso-, and macro-level dimensions of issues to be explored throughout the text.

The social world engulfs each of us from the moment of our birth until we die. Throughout our lives, each of us is part of a set of social relationships that provide guidelines for how we interact with others and how we see ourselves. This does not mean that human behavior is strictly determined by our links to the social world. Humans are more than mere puppets whose behavior is programmed by social structure. It does mean, however, that influence between the individual and the larger social world is reciprocal. We are influenced by and we have influence on our social environment. The social world is a human creation, and we can and do change that which we create. It acts on us, and we act on it. In this sense, social units are not static but are constantly emerging and changing in the course of human interaction.

The difficulty for most of us is that we are so caught up in our daily concerns that we fail to see and understand the social forces that are at work in our personal environments.

What we need are the conceptual and methodological tools to help us gain a more complete and accurate perspective on the social world. The concepts, theories, methods, and levels of analysis employed by sociologists are the very tools that will help give us that perspective. To use an analogy, each different lens of a camera gives the photographer a unique view of the world. Wide-angle lenses, close-up lenses, telephoto lenses, and special filters each serves a purpose in creating a distinctive picture or frame of the world. No one lens will provide the complete picture. Yet, the combination of images produced by various lenses allows us to examine in detail aspects of the world we might ordinarily overlook. That is what the sociological perspective gives us: a unique set of tools to see the social world with more penetrating clarity. In seeing the social world from a sociological perspective, we are better able to use that knowledge constructively, and we are better able to understand who we are as social beings.

So What ?

Why study sociology? Of what use might it be? We live in a complex social world with many layers of interaction. If we really want to understand our own lives, we need to comprehend the various levels of analysis that affect our lives and the dynamic connections between those levels. Moreover, as citizens of democracies, we need to understand how to influence our social environments, from city councils, school boards, and state legislatures, to congressional, presidential, and other organizations with major policymakers. To do so wisely, we need both objective lenses for viewing this complex social world and accurate, valid information (facts) about the society. As the science of society, sociology can provide both tested empirical data and a broad, analytical perspective.

The next issue, then, is how one gathers these accurate data that inform how we understand and influence the social world. When we say we know something about society, how is it that we know? What is considered evidence in sociology, and what lens (theory) do we use to interpret the data? These are the central issues of the next chapter.

Key Points

What Have We Learned?

- Humans are, at their very core, social animals—more akin to pack or herd animals than to individualistic cats. (See pp. 5–7.)

- A core concept in sociology is the sociological imagination. It requires that we see how our individual lives and personal troubles are shaped by historical and structural events outside of our everyday lives. It also prods us to see how we can influence our society. (See pp. 9–10.)

- Sociology is a social science and, therefore, uses the tools of the sciences to establish credible evidence to understand our social world. (See pp. 10–12.)

- Sociology as a science asks questions that help us analyze and explain our social world. Sociology is scientific and objective rather than value laden. (See pp. 12–13.)

- Sociology provides information that can help policymakers make better decisions and help students develop skills that are essential for the job market and life. (See pp. 13–17.)

- Sociology focuses on social units or groups, on social structures such as institutions, on social processes that give a social unit its dynamic character, and on their environments. (See pp. 17–19.)

- The social world model is the organizing theme of this book. Using the sociological imagination, we can understand our social world best by clarifying the interconnections between micro, meso, and macro levels of the social system. Each chapter of this book will examine society at these three levels of analysis. (See pp. 19–25.)

Contributing to Our Social World: What Can We Do?

At the end of this and all subsequent chapters, you will find suggestions for work and volunteering that encourage you to apply the concepts, principles, and ideas discussed in the chapter in practical contexts.

At the Local Level: Many sociology departments have student organizations or clubs through which you can meet other students interested in sociology, get to know faculty members, and attend presentations by guest speakers. If such an organization exists on your campus, visit a meeting and consider joining. If not, consider forming one with the help of a faculty member. Sociologists also have an undergraduate honors society, Alpha Kappa Delta (AKΔ). Visit the AKΔ Web site at www.alpha-kappa-delta.org and learn more about it and what it takes to form a chapter.

At the Regional and National Levels: The American Sociological Association (ASA) is the leading professional organization of sociologists in the United States. It has several programs and initiatives of special interest to students. Visit the ASA Web site at www.asanet.org and click on the "Students" link at the top of the page. Read the items and follow the links to additional material on the advantages of studying sociology. Most sociologists also participate in a major state or regional association. These groups are especially student friendly and feature publications and sessions at their annual meetings specifically for undergraduates. The organizations and Web site addresses are listed by the ASA, with direct links to their home pages at http://www2.asanet.org/governance/aligned.html.

Visit **www.pineforge.com/ballantine2study** for online activities, sample tests, and other helpful information. Select "Chapter 1: Sociology" for chapter-specific activities.

Examining the Social World

How Do We Know?

Science is about knowing through empirical investigation. Pictured here are scientists: archaeologists, a sociologist, a geologist, an astronaut, a geneticist, and a chemist. Sociology is a social science because of the way we gather scientific evidence.

Think About It . . .

Micro: When you say that you know something, how do you know?

Micro: When you are trying to convince neighbors or people in your community of your opinion, why is *evidence* important?

Meso: How do sociologists go about gathering dependable facts, statistics, and other data about families, educational institutions, or ethnic groups?

Macro: What does it mean to study national societal patterns *scientifically*?

Macro: How can theories about social interaction between global units help us understand forces affecting our own lives?

Global Community

Society

National Organizations, Institutions, and Ethnic Subcultures

Local Organizations and Community

Me (and My Closest Friends and Family)

Micro Level

Meso Level

Macro Level

Macro Level

Hector is a 16-year-old boy living in a *favela* (slum) on the outskirts of São Paulo, Brazil. He is a polite, bright boy, but his chances of getting an education and steady job in his world are limited. Like millions of other children around the world, he comes from a poor family that migrated to the urban area in search of a better life. However, his family ended up in a crowded slum with only a shared spigot for water and one string of electric lights along the dirt road going up the hill on which they live. The sanitary conditions in his community are appalling—open sewers, no garbage collection, disease. His family is relatively fortunate, perhaps, for they have cement walls and wood flooring, although no water or electricity. Many adjacent dwellings are little more than cardboard walls with corrugated metal roofs and dirt floors.

Hector wanted to stay in school but was forced to drop out to help support his family. Since leaving school, he has picked up odd jobs—deliveries, trash pick-up, janitorial work, gardening—to help pay the few centavos for the family's dwelling and to buy food to support his parents and six

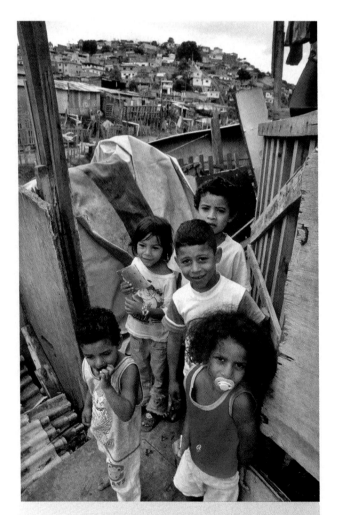

Slum dwellers of São Paulo, Brazil. Hector lives in a neighborhood with shelters made of available materials such as boxes, no electricity or running water, and poor sanitation.

siblings. Even when he was in school, Hector's experience was discouraging. He was not a bad student, and some teachers encouraged him to continue, but other students from the city teased the *favela* kids and made them feel unwelcome. Most of his friends dropped out before he did. Hector often missed school because of other obligations—opportunities for part-time work, a sick relative, or a younger sibling who needed care. The immediate need to put food on the table outweighed the long-term value of staying in school. What is the bottom line for Hector and millions like him? Because of his limited education and work skills, obligations to his family, and limited opportunities, he most likely will continue to live in poverty.

Sociologists are interested in the factors that influence the social world of children like Hector: family, friends, school, community, and the place of one's nation in the global political and economic structural systems. To understand how sociologists study poverty and many other social issues, consider the theories and methods they use to do their work. Understanding the *how* helps us to see that sociology is more than guesswork or opinion. Rather, it involves the use of scientific methods based on a systematic process for expanding knowledge of the social world.

Whatever our area of study or job interests, we are likely to find ourselves asking sociological questions. Consider some examples: Why is there binge drinking on college campuses? Do sexually explicit videos and magazines reinforce sexist stereotypes or encourage sexual violence? Do tough laws and longer prison sentences deter people from engaging in criminal conduct? Are workers more productive and more satisfied when they are given a share of company profits? How do we develop our religious and political beliefs? Do classroom teachers treat children from different social classes, races, or ethnic groups the same? Why do people join zealous religious groups that require tremendous self-sacrifice? How are the Internet and other technologies affecting everyday life for people around the world? Is there a digital divide, with technology making inequality in the world even more pronounced than previously? How do people in countries with great poverty view national debates in affluent countries about limiting immigration? How are people's cultures affected by the globalization of commerce and production?

This chapter will introduce you to the basic tools used to plan studies and gather dependable information on topics of interest. It will help you understand how sociology approaches research questions. To this end, we will consider the development of sociology as a science; the relationship between sociological theories and research methods; how sociologists study the social world using the process and tools of research methods; ethics involved in conducting sociological research; and contemporary sociological theories. We start with some background on the origins of sociology to provide a better understanding of how sociology developed.

The Development of Sociology as a Science

Throughout recorded history, humans have been curious about how and why people form groups. That should not be surprising because the groups we belong to are so central to human existence and to a sense of satisfaction in life.

Early Sociological Thought

Religion played a major part in influencing the way individuals thought about the world and their social relationships. Christianity dominated European thought systems during the Middle Ages, from the end of the Roman Empire to the 1500s, while Islamic beliefs ruled in much of the Middle East and parts of Africa. North African Islamic scholar Ibn Khaldun (1332–1406) was probably the first to suggest a systematic approach to explain the social world.

Khaldun was particularly interested in understanding the feelings of solidarity that held tribal groups together during his day, a time of great conflict and wars. These issues interested philosophers and theologians, but they did not use scientific methods to gather data and test their theories, processes that now allow us to get closer to the truth. They speculated and used pure reason to generalize about human behavior and group solidarity.

Sociology has its modern roots in the ideas of 19th-century social, political, and religious philosophers, mostly European, who laid the groundwork for the scientific study of society. Although it seems likely that humans have always thought about their place in the world, it was not until the 19th century that a modern scientific discipline to study society began to emerge.

THE TAKING of the BASTILLE,
By the Citizens of Paris, headed by the National Guards, the 14 July, 1789. This Fortress was begun to be built in 1369, in the Reign of Charles 5. Hugues Aubrist, at that time Provost of Paris, laid the first stone, it was not completely finished till 1383. He was a Native of DIJON and was the first imprisoned there on a Charge of Heresy.

The Bastille, a state prison in Paris, France, and symbol of oppression, was seized by the common people in the French Revolution, an upheaval in society that forced social analysts to think differently about society and social stability.

Until the 19th century, social philosophers provided the primary approach to understanding society, one that invariably had a strong moral tone. Their opinions were derived not from scientific evidence but from thinking—abstract reflection—about how the social world works. Often, they advocated forms of government that they believed would be just and good, denouncing those they considered inhumane or evil. For instance, Plato's *Republic*, written around 400 BCE, outlines plans for an ideal state—complete with government, family, economic systems, class structure, and education—designed to achieve social justice. Even today, people still debate the ideal communities proposed by Plato, Aristotle, Machiavelli, Thomas More, and other philosophers from the past.

Conditions Leading to Modern Sociology

Several conditions in the 19th century gave rise to the emergence of sociology. First, European nations were imperial powers that were establishing oppressive colonies in other cultures (see Map 2.1). This exposure to other cultures encouraged at least some Europeans to learn more about the people that had been conquered. Equally important, the social upheaval of revolutions, along with sweeping changes brought about by the Industrial Revolution, demanded a deeper understanding of social change. Finally, advances in the natural sciences demonstrated the value of the scientific

method as a tool for examining the physical world. Applying this scientific method to understand the social world was a logical step.

The social backdrop for the earliest European sociologists was the Industrial Revolution (which began around the middle of the 1700s) and the French Revolution (1789–1799). No one had clear, systematic explanations for why the old social structure, which had lasted since the early Middle Ages, was collapsing or why cities were exploding with migrants from rural areas. French society was in turmoil. Members of the nobility were being executed, and new rules of justice were taking hold. Churches were subordinated to the state, equal rights were established for citizens under the law, and democratic rule emerged. These dramatic changes marked the end of the traditional monarchy and the beginning of a new social order. With no methods to collect information on the dramatic changes taking place, leaders in France had to rely on the social philosophies of the time to react to the problems that surrounded them. Some of those philosophies were not informed by facts about social life.

It was in this setting that the scientific study of society emerged. Two social thinkers, Henri Saint-Simon (1760–1825) and Auguste Comte (1798–1857), decried the lack of systematic data collection or objective analysis in social thought. These Frenchmen are considered the first to suggest that a science of society could help people understand and perhaps control the rapid changes and unsettling revolutions taking place.

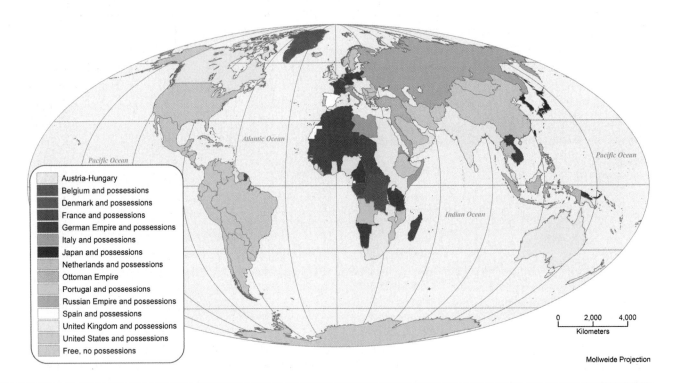

Austria-Hungary
Belgium and possessions
Denmark and possessions
France and possessions
German Empire and possessions
Italy and possessions
Japan and possessions
Netherlands and possessions
Ottoman Empire
Portugal and possessions
Russian Empire and possessions
Spain and possessions
United Kingdom and possessions
United States and possessions
Free, no possessions

Mollweide Projection

Map 2.1   Colonial Possessions in 1914

Source: Barraclough 1986:100–01; O'Brien 1999:206; Shepherd 1964:166–67; Stone 1991:243. Map by Anna Versluis.

Comte officially coined the term *sociology* in 1838. His basic premise was that religious or philosophical speculation about society did not provide an adequate understanding of how to solve society's problems. Just as the natural sciences provided basic facts about the physical world, so too there was a need to gather scientific knowledge about the social world. Only then could leaders systematically apply this scientific knowledge to improve social conditions.

Comte wanted to use scientific methods to address two basic questions that continue to interest sociologists to this day: What holds society together and gives rise to a stable order rather than anarchy, and why is there change in society? To answer these basic questions, Comte conceptualized society as divided into two parts. *Social statics* referred to aspects of society that give rise to order, stability, and harmony. *Social dynamics* referred to change and evolution in the parts of society and in society itself over time. Simply stated, Comte was concerned with what contemporary sociologists and the social world model in this book refer to as *structure* (social statics) and *process* (social dynamics). By understanding these aspects of the social world, Comte felt leaders could strengthen the society and could respond appropriately to change. His optimistic belief was that sociology would be the "queen of sciences," guiding leaders to construct a better social order.

Although he helped to found a new discipline, Comte had some ideas that are not above reproach. While advocating the use of science, Comte still maintained strong philosophical biases toward order and stability, even though the outcomes of that order might reinforce inequality and oppression. Nevertheless, the two main contributions of Comte stand the test of time: The social world can and should be studied scientifically, and the knowledge gained from the scientific study of society can and should be used to improve the human condition.

Sociology continued its evolution as scholars contemplated further changes brought about by the Industrial Revolution. In the 18th and 19th centuries, scenes of urban squalor were common in Great Britain and other industrializing European nations. Machines replaced both agricultural workers and cottage (home) industries because they produced an abundance of goods faster, better, and cheaper. Peasants were pushed off the land by the new technology and migrated to urban areas to find work at the same time that a powerful new social class of capitalists was emerging.

These massive social and economic changes brought about restructuring and sometimes the demise of political monarchies, aristocracies, and feudal lords. Industrialization brought the need for a new skilled class of laborers, which in turn placed increasing demands on what had been an education system serving only the elite. Families were no longer self-sufficient in agriculture or cottage industries but depended on wages from their labor in the industrial sector to stay alive. Thus, even from the very beginnings of the discipline, sociologists focused on the relationship between micro-, meso-, and macro-level processes.

Harriet Martineau (1802–1876) wrote Society in America, *a critique of America's failure to live up to its democratic principles, especially as they related to women. Published in 1837, 11 years before Karl Marx's most famous work, the book was one of many social analyses she published in her lifetime. Her work is a precursor to current feminist work and to conflict theory.*

These changes stimulated other social scientists to study society and its problems. Writings of Émile Durkheim, Karl Marx, Harriet Martineau, Max Weber, W. E. B. Du Bois, and many other early sociologists set the stage for development of sociological theories—statements or explanations of how two or more facts about the social world are related to each other. Accompanying the development of sociological theory was the utilization of the scientific method—systematic gathering and recording of reliable and accurate data to test ideas. First let us examine assumptions that underlie the scientific method.

Assumptions of Science

Throughout most of human history, people came to "know" the world by traditions being passed down from one generation to the next. Things were so because authoritative people in the culture said they were so. Often, there was reliance on magical or religious explanations of the forces in nature, and these explanations also became part of tradition. People were interested in the natural world and observed it carefully, but with advances in the natural sciences, observations of cause-and-effect processes became more systematic and controlled.

Lightning has been understood as a form of electricity rather than a message from an angry god only since 1752, thanks to an experiment by Benjamin Franklin. We still have much to learn about the social world, using empirical methods, which is why being a social scientist is so exciting.

As the way of knowing about the world shifted, tradition and magic as primary means to understand the world were challenged. It was only a little more than 200 years ago that people thought lightning storms were a sign of an angry god, not electricity caused by meteorological forces.

The scientific approach is based on several core assumptions. The first assumption is that there is a real physical and social world that can be studied scientifically. Second, there is a certain order to the world, and this order results from a series of causes and effects. In other words, there are identifiable patterns that can be understood and predicted by examining the sequences that produce them. The world is not merely a collection of unrelated random events but rather events that are causally related and patterned. Third, the way to gain knowledge of the world is to subject it to empirical testing. **Empirical knowledge** means that the facts have been objectively (without opinion or bias) observed and carefully measured and that the reality of what is being measured is the same for all people who observe it.

For knowledge to be scientific, therefore, it must come from phenomena that can be observed and measured. Phenomena that some people presume to exist but that can never be subject to measurement are not within the realm of scientific inquiry. The existence of God, the devil, heaven, hell, and the soul cannot be observed and measured and therefore cannot be examined scientifically. Note that while certain religious notions cannot themselves be subjects of scientific inquiry, religion can be studied in terms of the role it plays in society: its impact on our values and behavior (the sociology of religion), the historical development of specific religious traditions (history of religion), or the emotional comfort and stability it brings to people (psychology of religion).

Finally, science is rooted in **objectivity**, using methods that limit the impact of the researcher's personal opinions or biases on the study being planned, data collection, and analysis of evidence about the social world. **Evidence** refers to facts and information that are confirmed through systematic testing using the five senses and sometimes enhanced with research tools. Moreover, scientists are obliged not to distort their research findings so as to promote a particular point of view. Scientific research is judged first on whether it passes the test of being conducted objectively, without bias.

One way to evaluate evidence is to see whether the research does or does not support what the researcher thinks is true. The failure to disprove one's ideas offers evidence to support the findings. For example, if we wish to study whether gender is a major factor in a person being altruistic, then we must plan the research study so that we can either support or disprove our hypothesis (educated guess or prediction).

A failure to meet these standards—empirical knowledge, objectivity, and scientific evidence—means that a study is not scientific. Someone's ideas can seem plausible and logical but still not be supported by the facts. This is why evidence is so important. Sociology is concerned with having accurate evidence, and it is important to know what is or is not considered accurate, dependable evidence. You have probably seen one of the *CSI (Crime Scene Investigation)* series on television; the shows in this series depict the importance of careful collection of data and commitment to objective analysis. Sociologists deal with different issues, but the same sort of concern for accuracy in gathering data guides their work.

Systematic, objective observation proved to be a powerful tool for understanding the natural world and also defined the new approach to understanding the social world. For example, the 18th-century English scholar Thomas Malthus was one of the early social scientists who used systematic methods to gather data for analysis of population patterns and growth. Some of his formulae are still used today. However, he was also influenced by philosophical biases of his time. He made judgments about groups of people in his social commentaries, such as "the poor breed like rabbits," showing the tenuous and sometimes biased beginnings of social science.

Sociologists have come a long way from the early explanations of the social world that were based on the moralizing of the 18th- and 19th-century social philosophers and the guesswork of social planners. Part of the excitement of sociology today comes from the challenge to improve the scientific procedures applied to the study of humans and social behavior and to base policy on carefully collected data.

Thinking Sociologically

Imagine that you want to understand why people join new religious movements and commit their lives to charismatic cult leaders. Why are scientifically gathered data on why people join preferable to explanations based on anecdotes told by former (now disgruntled) members of these groups?

Empirical Research and Social Theory

We all have beliefs about how our social world works. We tend to take these beliefs, developed throughout our lives, for granted. They serve to define how we see our social world and justify our actions. Social researchers use the scientific method to examine these views of society. They assume that (1) there are predictable social relations in the world, (2) social situations will recur in certain patterns, and (3) social situations have causes that can be understood. If the social world were totally chaotic, little would be gained by scientific study.

From these assumptions, sociologists develop preferences for different social theories, just as individuals develop preferences for different religious or political beliefs that guide their lives. The main difference between individual beliefs and social theories is that the latter are subject to ongoing, systematic empirical testing.

Theories are statements or explanations of how two or more facts about the social world are related to each other. Theories try to explain social interactions, behaviors, and problems; a good theory should allow the scientist to make predictions about the social world. Different theories are useful at each level of analysis in the social world; which theory a sociologist uses to study the social world depends on the level of analysis to be studied, from the micro-level individual in a small group to macro-level societies in the global system, as illustrated in the following model.

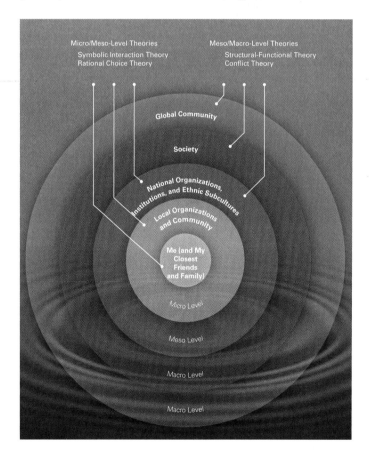

Each of the major theoretical perspectives discussed in this chapter—symbolic interactionism, rational choice theory, functionalism, and conflict theory—gives a perspective on the way the social world works. To study Hector's life

What factors—individual, group, institutional, national, and global—cause poverty in the developing world? This grocery store in Nairobi, Kenya, is a visual representation of the poverty in parts of Africa, Latin America, and Asia.

in Brazil, researchers might focus on the micro-level interactions between Hector and his family members, peers, teachers, and employers as factors that contribute to his situation. For example, why does Hector find some activities (working) more realistic or immediately rewarding than others (attending school)? A meso-level focus might examine the organizations and institutions—such as the business world, the schools, and the religious communities in Brazil—to see how they shape the forces that affect Hector's life. Alternatively, the focus might be on macro-level analysis—the class structure (rich to poor) of the society and the global forces such as trade relations between Brazil and other countries that influence opportunities for the Brazilian poor.

The poverty Hector experiences can be considered from any of these levels of analysis. Sociologists look beyond individual explanations, focusing instead on group or societal explanations to understand issues such as the poverty that haunts Hector's life. Different research methods to collect data are appropriate depending on the level of analysis, the theory being used, and the question being researched.

Scientists, including sociologists, often use theories to predict why things happen and under what conditions they are likely to happen. Although theories provide explanations about the relationships between social variables, these relationships need to be tested by collecting data. This is where research methods—the procedures one uses to gather data—are relevant. Theory and research are used together and are mutually dependent.

Research methods provide guidelines to help us gather the facts to formulate and test the theory. If a theory—for example, an explanation related to Hector's situation—is not supported by the data, it must be reformulated or discarded in favor of a theory that is consistent with the facts that have been uncovered using research methods. The facts (data) collected must be carefully assessed, as described in the next section.

Three Sociological Traditions

Three long-standing traditions in sociology speak to the relationship between empirical research and social theory (Buechler 2008). All three traditions have been around for as long as the discipline has existed. The founders of sociology tended to combine them, especially the first and third traditions.

One tradition, strongly influenced by the ideas of Auguste Comte, Émile Durkheim, and others, stresses scientific sociology. The thrust is on objectivity and on modeling the discipline after the natural sciences. For these scholars, the net result of sociological work is pure, unbiased analysis for the purposes of scientific understanding. As they saw it, others would be left to decide how to use the facts and findings in the social world. Sociology was to stick to fact finding and testing hypotheses.

A second tradition is called humanistic sociology: "When scientific sociologists do science, they emphasize the word *science*, linking it to other sciences. When humanistic sociologists do social science, they emphasize the word *social*, separating it from other sciences" (Buechler 2008). This tradition puts much more emphasis on the unique capacity of humans to create meaning, and it recognizes the subjective nature of meaning. However, when one is studying meaning, it is virtually impossible to produce objective quantitative data that are often the standard of the natural sciences. Humanistic sociologists argue that studying humans is qualitatively different and that focusing only on the standards of objectivity causes researchers to miss some of the most interesting and important dimensions of human social behavior. Studies should be relevant to humans by improving society and the quality of human life, they assert.

A third tradition sees the role of the discipline as improving society. This often takes two forms. One approach is to help us to think more critically about the society in which we live, with special focus on issues of social justice; this is known as critical sociology. Critical sociology was the focus of Karl Marx, and many in this tradition call for rather drastic changes in the society if fairness is to be a possibility for all citizens.

Another strand of the "social improvement" emphasis of sociology is applied sociology. **Applied sociology** is concerned with pragmatic ways to improve the society, sometimes with major reorganization of the society and sometimes with modest policy proposals that will make modern organizations operate more smoothly. Some applied sociologists are interested in working within the current system to fine-tune it rather than overhaul it. In any case, practical applications of the field and concern for justice for women and other "second-class citizens" has been a central focus of the field all the way back to the first president of the American Sociology Association, Lester Ward.

Whether the concern is justice (the passion of Marx) or compassion and humane treatment of all people (a focus of many in applied sociology or "sociological practice"), the common concern is with practical uses of sociology in formulating social policy.

All three of these traditions will be given attention in this book, for they are all part of mainstream sociology today.

Scientific Inquiry: Deductive and Inductive Reasoning

Like other scientists, sociologists conduct their investigations using one of two main lines of reasoning. **Deductive reasoning** begins with broad general ideas, or theories, of human social behavior. From these ideas, more specific patterns are identified or "deduced" using logical reasoning. These educated guesses—which still do not have data to support them—are called **hypotheses**.

Consider the following example: Suppose we wish to study how self-help groups work to aid those with problems; alcohol, weight, or mild psychological disorders are examples. We would begin by determining the level of analysis of the problem. In this case, micro-level individual problems are being addressed in small groups such as Alcoholics Anonymous or Weight Watchers. A micro-level theory would be our choice to help understand this problem. Previous research has indicated that self-help groups take people through a process of redefining their lives. They develop a different script for interpreting their behavior. Therefore, our hypothesis (educated guess) to test might be the following:

> During meetings of self-help groups, one redefines one's identity. This takes place as one listens to other people give testimonies; one learns to identify one's problem, applying the solutions to one's own life. This is done by conforming to certain rules of interaction in the group and learning to apply a script about one's wayward ways, followed by testimonies using the script that bring acceptance and support by the group.

We could then gather data by attending meetings of self-help groups to see whether this pattern was common to these groups. Then, we would compare our data findings with the hypothesis to see if the statement is supported by the evidence.

Inductive reasoning, on the other hand, begins with specific facts (data) or evidence and tries to find or develop a theory—a more generalized set of concepts—to explain the facts. First, the researcher collects facts and then attempts to explain the relationship between these facts. In so doing, the researcher is building up to a generalization, moving from the concrete facts to the abstract theory. The specific facts give rise to a theory, and that theory can be tested again in the future using new data. A researcher interested in the consequences of involvement in a self-help group might interview family members and employers of group members (after gaining permission of the members, of course) to see how the group influenced the individual. The researcher would then develop a theory from the data collected to explain the pattern. The study does not begin with a theory about causal relationships, but the data are used to create

Figure 2.1 Inductive and Deductive Reasoning

an explanation of causality, consequences of involvement in a self-help group.

The next step is that a generalization—a theory—would emerge from the data. In this case, the research begins with research questions (but not a hypothesis as in deductive reasoning). Figure 2.1 illustrates the relationship of inductive and deductive reasoning to theory and facts.

In summary, social scientists use both inductive and deductive reasoning in their work. Deductive reasoning tests the theory, using scientific research methods to obtain facts (data) relevant to that theory. Inductive reasoning connects scientifically collected facts to social theory. It tries to find or create a general theory to explain the facts. Research data may confirm a theory, force its modification, require the scientist to abandon it altogether, or lead to an entirely new theory. Whatever the case, theory and methods work together and cannot be separated in the research process. The following section illustrates inductive and deductive approaches by discussing how sociologists plan research studies to test theories.

Thinking Sociologically

Imagine that a sociologist collects facts by interviewing Hector and other children from his *favela* to learn about their family lives, educational histories, and work experiences. How would a sociologist approach the problem of poverty in Hector's life using a deductive approach? How would it be different using an inductive approach?

How Sociologists Study the Social World

Since the origins of the discipline, sociologists have designed and refined scientific tools for studying sociological questions. What is presented here is a skeleton of the research process that sociologists and other social scientists spend years studying and perfecting. This section will begin to provide a sense of how sociologists study issues and know what they know. If you study more sociology, you will learn more

about the research process. It is exciting to collect accurate information and learn answers to important, meaningful questions that can make a difference to people's lives.

To use the scientific method to study the social world, a researcher follows a number of logically related steps.

   I.   Planning a Research Study

       Step 1: Define a topic or problem that can be investigated scientifically.

       Step 2: Review existing relevant research studies and theory to refine the topic and define variables.

       Step 3: Formulate hypotheses or research questions and operationalize variables.

   II. Designing the Research Method and Collecting the Data

       Step 4: Design the research method that specifies how the data will be gathered.

       Step 5: Select a sample of people or groups to study from the population.

       Step 6: Collect the data using appropriate research methods.

   III. Making Sense of the Data

       Step 7: Analyze the data, figuring out exactly what the study says about the research question(s).

       Step 8: Draw conclusions and present the final report, including suggestions for future research.

Each of these steps is very important, whether you become a professional sociologist or do a study for a local organization or your workplace. To introduce the research process, we provide a quick summary: planning a research study, designing the research, doing the analysis, and drawing conclusions.

Planning a Research Study

Planning a research study involves four initial steps: define the topic or problem clearly, find out what is already known about the topic, formulate hypotheses, and operationalize definitions of variables.

Step 1, the most important step, is to define a topic or problem that can be investigated scientifically. Without a clear problem, the research will go nowhere. Using poverty as an example of a broad topic area, sociologists could focus on a number of issues—for example, rates of poverty in different countries, poverty and levels of education, race and poverty, gender and poverty, or the relationship between poverty and drug or alcohol abuse. These broad topic areas are a good start, but they must be more specific and defined before they become suitable topics for systematic research. One must clarify specifically what one wants to know about the topic.

Specific research topics, ones that can be measured and tested, are usually posed in the form of questions: Why is it that, in some countries, large segments of the population live in poverty? What causes some students—especially those in poor families—to drop out of school? Why are there disproportionate numbers of women and people of color living in poverty? Are people who are poor more vulnerable to excessive drug or alcohol use? The research question must be asked in a precise way. Otherwise, it cannot be tested empirically. Asking good research questions is extremely important in sound scientific research.

Thinking Sociologically

Pick a topic of interest to you. Now, write a research question based on your topic.

Step 2 in planning the research is reviewing existing relevant research studies and theory to determine what other researchers have already learned about the topic. One needs to know how the previous research was done, how terms were defined, and the strengths and limitations of that research. Social scientists can then know what has been done and link their study to existing findings to build the knowledge base. This step usually involves combing through scholarly journals and books on the topic. In the case of Hector, researchers would need to identify what previous studies said about why impoverished young people drop out of school.

In Step 3, based on the review of the literature on the topic, social scientists often formulate hypotheses—reasonable, educated guesses about the relationship between variables based on the knowledge researchers have gained on the topic. A hypothesis predicts the relationship between two or more variables and ways in which variables are related to each other (such as poverty and education). "Poverty leads teenagers to drop out of school for opportunities to earn money" is a testable hypothesis that predicts future at-risk young people. Another hypothesis could predict the opposite—that dropping out of school leads to poverty. A hypothesis to study Hector's situation might be as follows: "Poverty is a major cause of teenagers in the *favela* dropping out of school because they need to earn money for the family." Again, a hypothesis provides a statement to be tested.

Researchers then identify the key concepts, or ideas, in the hypothesis (e.g., poverty and dropping out of school). These concepts can be measured by collecting facts or data. This process of determining how to measure concepts is called operationalizing variables. **Variables** are concepts (ideas) that can vary in frequency of occurrence from one time, place, or person to another. Examples include levels of

poverty, percentage of people living in poverty, or number of years of formal education. Variables can then be measured by collecting data to test hypothesized relationships between variables.

To operationalize variables, researchers link social concepts such as poverty to specific measurement indicators. Using the hypothesis above, concepts such as dropouts and poverty can be measured by determining the number of times they occur. Dropouts, for instance, might be defined by the number of days of school missed in a designated period of time according to school records. Poverty could be defined as having an annual income that is less than half of the average income for that size of family in Brazil. Measurement of poverty could also include family assets such as ownership of property or other tangible goods such as cattle, automobiles, and indoor plumbing, as well as access to medical care, education, transportation, and other services available to citizens. It is important to be clear, precise, and consistent about how one measures poverty. This is essential so that those reading the study are clear on what has been done and those doing a follow-up study can critique and improve on the study. Background research—including examination of previous studies of poverty—provides guidelines or examples for how to operationalize variables.

Thinking Sociologically

Considering your research question, what are your variables, and how could you operationalize them?

Underlying this discussion about defining the problem is the ability to plan a study that accurately measures the predicted relationship between concepts. The following key research terms are important in understanding how two variables (concepts that vary in frequency and can be measured) are related:

- **Correlation** refers to a relationship between variables in which change in one variable is associated with change in another. The hypothesis above predicts that poverty and teenagers dropping out of school vary together.
- **Cause-and-effect relationships** help establish the relationship between two variables. Once we have determined that there is probably a correlation—the fact that the two variables such as poverty and dropping out of school both occur in the same situation—we need to take the next step of testing for a causal relationship between variables. The **independent variable** is hypothesized to cause the change; in terms of time sequence, it comes first and affects the

dependent variable. If we hypothesize that poverty causes Hector and others to drop out of school, *poverty* is the independent variable in this hypothesis, and *dropping out of school* is the dependent variable, dependent on the poverty. In determining cause and effect, the independent variable must always precede the dependent variable in time sequence if we are to say one variable causes another.

- **Spurious relationships** occur when there is no causal relationship between the independent and dependent variables, but they vary together, often due to a third variable working on both of them. For example, if the quantity of ice cream consumed is highest during those weeks of the year when the most swimming pool drownings occur, these two events are correlated. However, eating ice cream did not cause the increase in pool deaths. Indeed, hot weather may have caused more people both to purchase ice cream and to go swimming, thus resulting in more chance of drowning incidents—a spurious relationship. **Controls** are used by researchers to eliminate all spurious variables, leaving only those related to the hypothesis. Using controls helps ensure the relationship is not spurious.

Designing the Research Method and Collecting the Data

After the researcher has carefully planned the study, Step 4 is to select appropriate data collection methods. These depend on the levels of analysis of the research question (micro, meso, and macro) the researcher is asking. If researchers want to answer a macro-level research question, such as the effect of poverty on school success nationwide, they are likely to focus on large-scale social and economic problems in society. To learn about micro-level issues such as the influence of peers on an individual's decision to drop out of school, researchers will focus on small group interactions. Figure 2.2 illustrates different levels of analysis.

Different data collection techniques will be appropriate for research questions and hypotheses at different levels of analysis in the social world. The method selected is one of the most important decisions in research because the quality of the data collected is directly related to the value of the study findings. Accuracy in planning can mean the difference between a fruitful scientific study and data that have little meaning.

The primary methods used to collect data for research studies include surveys (both interviews and questionnaires), observation studies, controlled experiments, and use of existing materials. Our discussion cannot go into detail about how researchers use these techniques, but a brief explanation gives an idea of why they use these primary methods.

The **survey method** is used when sociologists want to gather information directly from a number of people regarding how they think or feel or what they do. Two forms of surveys are common: the interview and the questionnaire. Both involve a series of questions asked of respondents.

Interviews are conducted by talking directly with people and asking questions in person or by telephone. Questionnaires are written questions to which respondents reply in writing. In both cases, questions may be open-ended, allowing the respondent to say or write whatever comes to mind, or closed-ended, requiring the respondent to chose from a set of possible answers.

One method to study school dropouts is to survey teenagers about what caused them to leave school. The researcher would have to evaluate whether an interview

Micro Level

Individual	Hector
Small group	Hector's family and close friends
Local community	The *favela*; Hector's local school, church, neighborhood organizations

Meso Level

Organizations	Brazilian corporations, Catholic Church, and local school system in Brazil
Institutions	Family; education; political, economic, and health systems in the region or nation of Brazil
Ethnic subcultures	Native peoples, African-Brazilians

Macro Level

| National society | Social policies, trends, and programs in Brazil |
| Global community of nations | Status of Brazil in global economy; trade relations with other countries; programs of international organizations or corporations |

Figure 2.2   The Social World Model and Levels of Analysis

or questionnaire would provide the best information. Interviews are more time consuming and labor intensive than questionnaires but are better for gathering in-depth information. However, if the researcher wants information from a large number of teenagers, questionnaires are often more practical and less costly.

Thinking Sociologically

How would you word questions in a survey about the effects of peer influence on dropping out of school? How could you find out whether your questions are good ones?

Field studies (also called observational methods) are used when systematic, planned observation of interaction is needed to obtain data. Observation—the systematic viewing and recording of behavior or interaction in the natural settings where behavior takes place—can take several forms. One form, detached or nonparticipant observation, involves the researcher observing as an outsider, without being involved in the activities of the group. For instance, the researcher may observe or videotape a classroom that Hector and his friends attend to study the group dynamics. The individuals or groups may never be aware of the researcher's presence, especially if it takes place behind a one-way mirror.

Participant observation occurs when the researcher actually participates in the activities of the group being studied. The researcher, for instance, might hang out with Hector and his friends or join Alcoholics Anonymous to observe group processes as they occur naturally. Participation is particularly useful when studying illegal or deviant activities, where it might be impossible to gain scientifically useful information any other way.

The results from observation studies are referred to as *qualitative* rather than *quantitative* research. They provide valuable information that is rich in detail about the context of the situation, such as the *favela* or Hector's classroom, rather than providing hard data such as percentages or other numbers that can be illustrated in neat tables.

A problem for participant-observers is that they may alter group functioning and interaction by their presence—a process called *research effects*. Another problem is that they may become involved in the group to such a degree that objectivity becomes difficult. This is much less of a problem in large public settings such as attending religious meetings or watching children on a playground to observe gender segregation. However, in a smaller group, the very presence of the researcher may change things. Furthermore, the researcher must be aware that interpretation of the social scene is especially subject to bias. Despite these potential problems, observation remains a useful way of obtaining information.

One example of a survey is the census, done in the United States and many other countries every 10 years. Sometimes it is difficult to gather accurate data on the entire population, as in the situation with this census worker, who is counting homeless people in Penn Station in New York City.

Ethnography (also called ethnographic research) is a form of field study involving some unique strategies of inquiry and methods of analysis. Ethnographers use self-reflection as the research progresses. The researcher pursues any ideas that may shed light on the research problem. Often, the research takes place on site in a natural setting (home, office, playground) and involves using several different data collection techniques, such as interviewing and observing, with recorded systematic field notes about the observations. Thus, ethnography relies on the researcher pursuing all relevant data. Flexibility of the researcher to pursue all leads using the scientific method to answer research questions (often without formal hypotheses) is key to the success of the study. The research evolves in response to what the researcher learns as the research progresses. Unlike research driven by hypotheses to be tested, this method allows the researcher to respond to new ideas that come up during the research (Creswell 2003).

In **controlled experiments,** all variables except the one being studied are held constant. In this way, researchers can study the effects of a particular variable. A controlled experiment usually requires an **experimental group**, in which people are exposed to the variable being studied to test its effect, and a **control group**, in which the subjects are not exposed to the variable the experimenter wants to test.

The control group provides a baseline to which the experimental group can be compared. By separating the sample into experimental and control groups, the researcher can see if the study's independent variable makes a difference in the behavior of people who are exposed to that variable. For example, researchers may want to determine whether viewing violence on television makes children behave more aggressively. The control group is exposed to television programming with nonviolent content, and the experimental group is provided with a program involving high levels of violence. The aggression levels of the two groups of children after watching the different shows can then be compared to determine if television violence affected the children's behavior.

Controlled experiments are powerful because they are the most accurate test of cause and effect. Despite the advantages of controlled experiments, there are some drawbacks, and they cannot be used to study many sociological research questions. First, many sociological questions cannot be studied in controlled settings because they deal with meso- and macro-level organizations and social forces and cannot be placed in a controlled situation. For example, Hector's situation in the *favela* cannot be studied in a laboratory setting. Second, the mere fact of being in a laboratory setting and knowing one is in an experiment may affect the research results—another form of research effects. Third, because of ethical constraints, social scientists cannot do studies that might harm people. Thus, there are many variables that social scientists cannot introduce in the laboratory.

Research using **existing sources** involves sources of material that already exist are being employed in a new way or to understand a new relationship. There are two approaches to using existing sources: secondary analysis and content analysis.

Secondary analysis uses existing data, that is, information that has already been collected in other studies. Often, large data-collecting organizations such as the United Nations or a country's census bureau, national education department, or a private research organization will make data available for use by researchers. Consider the question of the dropout rate in Brazil. Researchers can learn a great deal about patterns of school dropouts from analysis of information gathered by ministries or departments of education. Likewise, if we want to compare modern dropout rates with those of an earlier time, we may find data from previous decades to be invaluable. Sometimes, secondary analysis is the sole method of data collection, and sometimes, it is used along with other methods.

Despite its usefulness, secondary analysis cannot be used in some research studies, and it has several potential weaknesses. First, not all data sets are representative of the total population the researcher is studying. This is especially true in comparing data sets from countries using different definitions of variables (such as levels of poverty) and different data gathering techniques. Second, secondary analysis does not touch the "human side" of research questions in the way interviews or observation can. Secondary analysis involves no direct observation of the behavior in question or contact with those involved. School dropouts, for example, have individual stories and problems that

are not told by large, impersonal data sets. Third, the data sets available for secondary analysis are gathered for purposes other than the research questions to which they are now being applied. They may not directly answer the researcher's questions. Finally, any problems or biases that exist in the original data are carried over to the secondary analysis. Despite such limitations, however, secondary analysis can be an excellent way to do meso- or macro-level studies that reveal large-scale patterns in the social world.

Content analysis involves systematic categorizing and recording of information from written or recorded sources. With content analysis (a common method in historical research and study of organizations), sociologists can gather the data they need from printed materials—books, magazines, video recordings, newspapers, laws, letters, memos, and sometimes even artworks. A researcher studying variations in levels of concern about child abuse could do a content analysis of popular magazines to see how many pages or stories were devoted to child abuse in 1965, 1975, 1985, 1995, and 2005. Content analysis has the advantage of being relatively inexpensive and easy to do. It is also unobtrusive, meaning that the researcher does not influence the subject being investigated by having direct contact. The written or visual record to be examined is already available. Furthermore, using materials in historical sequence can be effective in recognizing patterns over time—what comes before and what comes after. However, accuracy of the study relies on what content is available.

Thinking Sociologically

What methods would be appropriate to collect data on your research question?

An example of historical research using existing materials to examine social patterns is illustrated in "How Do We Know?" In this case, the researcher, Virginia Kemp Fish, studied records and writings to discover the contributions of early women sociologists in Chicago to sociology and to the betterment of society.

Triangulation, or multiple methods of social research, combines two or more methods of data collection to enhance the accuracy of the findings. To study Hector's situation, a research study could use macro-level data on poverty in Brazil and micro-level interviews with Hector and his peers to determine their goals and views. Thus, if all findings point to the same conclusion, the researcher can feel much more confident about the study results. Data collection techniques—survey, field study, controlled experimentation, and analysis of existing sources—represent the dominant methods used to collect data for sociological research.

Step 5 involves selecting a sample. It would be impossible to study the reasons for poverty or for dropping out

How Do We Know?

The Hull House Circle: Historical Content Analysis in Sociology

Historical research can be an important source of data for sociological analysis, for history can demonstrate causal events vividly. Historical circumstances provide context for understanding why things evolved to the present state of affairs. One fascinating historical study focuses on the contribution of the Hull House women to developing the science of sociology. Hull House was a settlement house, one of several residences established in urban immigrant neighborhoods. Settlement houses created a sense of community for residents and offered a multitude of services to help residents negotiate poverty.

Hull House in Chicago was the location for a group of women social researchers, reformers, and activists, and Jane Addams was one of them. These women had obtained college degrees in some of the few fields then open to women (political science, law, economics), and because they were often excluded from full-time careers in these fields, they used their education and skills to help others and to do research on social conditions. Until recently, women sociologists, such as the members of the Hull House Circle, have not received much attention for their contributions to the science of sociology.

Some of the earliest social survey research was conducted by the women connected with Hull House, sometimes employing the Hull House residents to help collect data. These women led the first systematic attempt to describe an immigrant community in an American city, a study found in *Hull House Maps and Papers* (Residents of Hull House [c. 1895] 1970).

Jane Addams, social researcher, critic, and reformer.

Virginia Kemp Fish (1986), who originated the designation *Hull House Circle,* researched historical literature to learn more about the lives and contributions of these women and their place in the sociological literature. She examined records, letters, biographies, and other historical sources to piece together their stories.

By studying their writings and their activist work, Fish showed how they supported each other's work and scholarship and provided emotional encouragement and intellectual stimulation rather than interacting in terms of an unequal power distribution.

Fish also made an interesting observation about these women's professional styles as compared with those of men. While men often received their training and support from a mentor (an older, established, and respected man in the field), the women of Hull House operated within a network of egalitarian relationships and interactions.

According to Fish's research, data and documents collected by leader Jane Addams and other Hull House women provide baseline information that has been used as a starting point or comparison for later studies—for social researchers in the fields of immigration, ethnic relations, poverty, health care, housing, unemployment, work and occupations, delinquency and crime, war, and social movements (Fish 1986).

Sociologist Viviana Zelizer (1985) followed in Fish's footsteps, using historical documents to enrich our sociological understanding of the modern world. Zelizer's work focused on how money is socially defined. In *The Social Meaning of Money,* Zelizer (1994) looked at charities like Hull House to understand how society comes to define the poor. Zelizer argued that social workers like Addams and policymakers define the worth of the poor by the amount and type of aid we offer them. By looking to the past, we can enrich our understanding of the future.

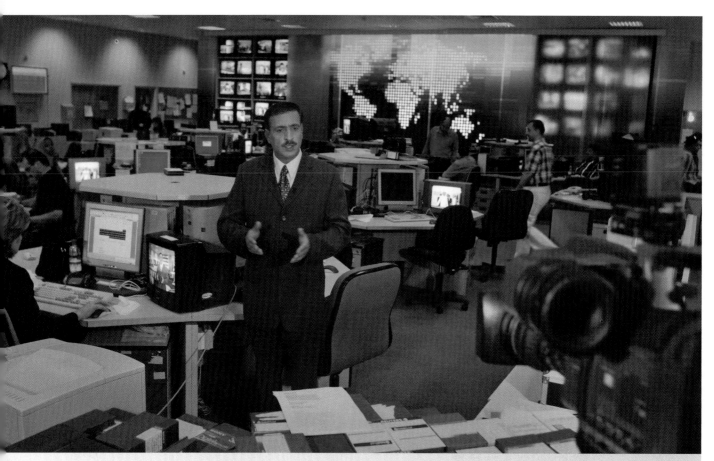

Social scientists aren't the only professionals who use triangulation. Journalists also consult a variety of sources including social scientists to put together news broadcasts.

of school for every teenager in Brazil. Researchers must select a representative group to study that will help us understand the larger group. A part of the research design is determining how to make sure the study includes people who are typical of the total group. When the research study involves a survey or field observation, sociologists need to decide who will be observed or questioned to provide a group representative of the whole. This involves careful selection of a **sample**, a small and more manageable group of people to study, systematically chosen to accurately represent the characteristics of the entire group (or population) being studied.

Researchers use many types of samples. A common one, the representative sample, attempts to accurately reflect the group being studied so that the sample results can be generalized or applied to the larger population. In the case of Hector's *favela,* a sample for a study could be drawn from all 13- to 16-year-olds in his region or city of Brazil. We have all experienced polling before elections, either by being participants in the polls or reading about them. The

recent U.S. election provided us with frequent updates on the standings of candidates.

The most common form of representative sample is the *random sample*. People from every walk of life and every group within the population have an equal chance of being selected for the study. By observing or talking with this smaller group selected from the total population under study, the researcher can get an accurate picture of the total population and have confidence that the findings apply to the larger group. Drawing a representative sample is not always simple. In the case of Brazil, people constantly move in and out of the *favela*. Those who have just arrived may not have the same characteristics as those who have been living there a long time. Thus, developing an effective sampling technique is often a complex process.

It is important to have a sample that represents the group being studied. If researchers wanted to know attitudes of Brazilian teenagers toward school, they would not question people who live in Quebec, Canada, or all people from the city of São Paulo, Brazil, for they do not represent the group of concern. In another example, if researchers wanted to understand the views of all Christians in Canada about the recently passed legislation on gay marriage, they would not ask questions only of those who are affiliated with the conservative Christian Coalition. Christians hold many other points of view, and most in Canada are not evangelical; the social ideas of the full range of Christians would need to be included. Otherwise, the sample would be unrepresentative.

Step 6 involves collecting the data. Now that the appropriate research method for collecting data and the sample to study have been selected, the researcher's next step is to collect the data, then analyze those data and see what they say about the research questions and hypotheses. Researchers study many techniques to ensure accurate data collection.

Making Sense of the Data

Once data are gathered, Step 7 is to analyze the data and decide what they mean. Now that we have, say, 500 questionnaires or a notebook full of field observation notes, what do we do with them? Social researchers use multiple techniques to analyze data. The general idea is to evaluate the data to determine the relationship of variables to each other. For instance, if dropout rates are high among Hector's friends, was their school achievement low? What other factors are present? This analysis can become quite complex, but the purpose is the same—to determine the relationship between the variables being examined. After stating the initial research question or hypotheses to test, sociology is not guesswork or speculation. It involves careful, objective analysis of specific data.

Interpretation of data involves judgment and opinion, often based on the theory guiding the research. As such, it can be challenged by other researchers, who might interpret the results differently or challenge the methods used to collect and analyze the data. Discussion and criticism are an important part of science and make possible more accurate findings, new ideas and interpretations, and more sophisticated methodological approaches to problems. Sociologists grow through these critiques, as does the field of sociology itself. Because every research study should be replicable—capable of being repeated—enough information must be given to ensure that another researcher could repeat the study and compare results.

Step 8 involves discussion of results and drawing conclusions for the analysis. A report is developed, outlining the research project and analysis of the data collected. The final section of the report presents a discussion of results, draws conclusions as to whether or not the hypotheses were supported, interprets the results, and makes recommendations from the researcher's point of view, if appropriate. As part of the presentation and discussion of results, the report may contain tables or figures presenting summaries of data that are useful in understanding the data. "How to Read a

Research Table" provides useful tips on reading research tables found in journal articles and newspapers.

Given that social science research focuses on humans and humans are changeable, it is difficult to say that any single study has definitively proven the hypothesis or answered a research question with finality. Indeed, the word *prove* is never used to describe the interpretation of findings in the social and behavioral sciences. Rather, social scientists say that findings tend to support or reject hypotheses.

So, why bother doing social science research if findings can be challenged and nothing is absolute? Systematic, scientific research brings us closer to the reality of the social world than guesswork and opinions. Having supportive findings from numerous studies, not just one, builds a stronger case to support a theory. The search for truth is ongoing—a kind of mission in life for those of us who are scholars. Furthermore, as we get closer to accurate understanding of society, our social policies can be based on the most accurate knowledge available. Most sciences are cautious about claiming that they have the absolute truth.

Applied Sociology

You may have asked yourself, "What can I do with sociology and sociological methods?" Chapter 1 discussed some careers held by sociologists, providing a partial answer to the question. We add to that the application of sociological theory and research by applied sociologists to answer questions raised by agencies, organizations, or government. Applied sociology (also known as sociological practice) refers to "any use (often client-centered) of the sociological perspective and/or its tools in the understanding of, intervention in, and/or enhancement of human social life" (Steele and Price 2004:4).

Since the founding of sociology, especially in the United States, some sociologists have had a problem-solving or social-reform orientation to the discipline, always asking about the practical implications of sociological findings (Mauksch 1993; Pickard and Poole 2007). The following discussion outlines the beginnings of applied sociology.

Today, sociologists engaged in applied research use the theories and data collection techniques discussed in this chapter, applying them to address questions and problems of clients in organizations. Table 2.2 on page 48 outlines key differences between basic (pure) and applied sociology.

In each chapter, you will find a feature called "The Applied Sociologist at Work," which describes a sociologist with a bachelor's, master's, or doctoral degree working in the topic area being discussed. In the "Applied Sociologist at Work" feature that appears on page 48, Ruth Pickard and Daryl Poole, professional applied sociologists, provide further background on the emergence of sociological practice as a scholarly field and a career field.

Sociology in Your Social World

How to Read a Research Table

A statistical table is a researcher's labor-saving device. Quantitative data presented in tabular form are more clear and concise than the same information presented in several written paragraphs.

A good table has clear signposts to help the reader and avoid confusion. For instance, the table below shows many of the main features of a table, and the list that follows explains how to read each feature.*

Table 2.1   Educational Attainment by Selected Characteristic: 2006, for Persons 25 Years Old and Over Reported in Thousands (191,884 represents 191,884,000)

		Percent of Population—Highest Level				
Characteristic	*Population (1,000)*	*Not a High School Graduate*	*High School Graduate*	*Some College, but No Degree*	*Associate's Degree[1]*	*Bachelor's Degree*	*Advanced Degree*
Total persons	191,884	14.5	31.7	17.0	8.7	18.3	9.7
Age:							
25 to 34 yrs old	39,480	13.0	28.6	19.1	9.3	21.8	8.1
35 to 44 yrs old	43,121	11.9	30.5	16.8	9.8	21.1	10.0
45 to 54 yrs old	42,797	11.4	31.5	17.4	10.3	19.0	10.4
55 to 64 yrs old	30,981	12.7	32.0	17.6	8.5	16.7	12.4
65 to 74 yrs old	18,554	21.1	37.3	14.7	5.7	12.5	8.8
75 yrs old or over	16,951	28.9	36.1	12.9	4.5	10.8	6.7
Sex:							
Male	92,233	15.0	31.9	16.3	7.7	18.5	10.7
Female	99,651	14.1	31.6	17.7	9.71	8.1	8.8
Race:							
White[2]	157,566	13.9	31.8	16.9	9.0	18.6	9.8
Black[2]	21,600	19.3	35.6	19.0	7.7	12.6	5.8
Other	12,718	14.7	23.9	14.2	7.6	24.6	14.9
Hispanic origin:							
Hispanic	23,499	40.7	28.4	12.7	5.9	8.8	3.6
Non-Hispanic	168,385	10.9	32.2	17.6	9.1	19.6	10.5
Region:							
Northeast	36,282	13.0	33.9	12.9	7.7	19.8	12.7
Midwest	42,603	10.9	35.0	17.7	9.7	17.8	8.9
South	69,458	16.9	32.1	16.8	8.5	17.2	8.6
West	43,541	15.7	26.1	20.0	9.1	19.5	9.6

Source: U.S. Census Bureau, 2008 Current Population Survey.

1. Includes vocational degrees.

2. For persons who selected this race group only.

*Features of the table adapted from Broom and Selznick 1963.

TITLE: The title provides information on the major topic and variables in the table.

"Educational Attainment by Selected Characteristic for 2006"

HEADNOTE (or Subtitle): Many tables will have a headnote or subtitle under the title, giving information relevant to understanding the table or units in the table.

For this table, the reader is informed that this includes all persons over the age of 25, and they will be reported in thousands.

HEADINGS AND STUBS: Tables generally have one or two levels of headings under the title and headnotes. These instruct the reader about what is in the columns below.

In this table the headings indicate the level of education achieved so the reader can identify the percentage with a specified level of education.

The table also has a stub: the far-left column. This lists the items that are being compared according to the categories found in the headings. In this case, the stub indicates population of various characteristics: age, sex, race, Hispanic origin, and region.

MARGINAL TABS: In examining the numbers in the table, try working from the outside in. The marginals, the figures at the margins of the table, often provide summary information.

In this table, the first column of numbers is headed "Population (1,000)," indicating (by thousands) the total number of people in each category who were part of the database. The columns to the right indicate—by percentages—the level of educational attainment for each category.

CELLS: To make more detailed comparisons, examine specific cells in the body of the table. These are the boxes that hold the numbers or percentages.

In this table, the cells contain data on age, sex, racial/ethnic (white, black, Hispanic), and regional differences in education.

UNITS: Units refer to how the data are reported. It could be in percentages or in number per 100 or 1,000, or in other units.

In this table the data are reported first in raw number in thousands and then in percentages.

FACTS FROM THE TABLE: After reviewing all of the above information, the reader is ready to make some interpretations about what the data mean.

In this table the reader might note that young adults are more likely to have a college education than older citizens. Likewise, African Americans and Hispanics are less likely than whites to have college or graduate degrees, but "Other" is even higher than whites, probably because it includes Asian Americans. People in the Northeast have the highest levels of education, followed by those in the West. What other interesting patterns do you see?

FOOTNOTES: Some tables have footnotes, usually indicating something unusual about the data or where to find more complete data.

In this table, two footnotes are provided so the reader does not make mistakes in interpretation.

SOURCE: The source note, found under the table, points out the origin of the data. It is usually identified by the label "source."

Ethical Issues in Social Research

Sociologists and other scientists are bound by ethical codes of conduct governing research. This is to protect any human subjects used in research from being harmed by the research. The American Sociological Association (ASA) code of ethical conduct outlines standards that researchers are expected to observe when doing research, teaching, and publishing. They include points such as being objective, reporting findings and sources fully, making no promises to respondents that cannot be honored, accepting no support that requires violation of these principles, completing contracted work, and delineating responsibilities in works with multiple authors. Related to these standards are the following key ethical issues for sociologists, each a part of the ASA code of ethics:

- How will the findings from the research be used? Will it hurt individuals, communities, or nations if it gets into the hands of "enemies"? Can it be used to aggravate hostilities? In whose interest is the research being carried out? To illustrate the relevance of these questions, in 1964, a number of U.S. social researchers began a study called Project Camelot. The goal was to predict when revolutions would occur in Latin America and to show how governments could stop them. However, the $6 million project was canceled when social scientists complained that it would be unethical for research findings to be used so that the United States could intervene in the internal affairs of other countries, especially when such interference might short-circuit movements for human rights.
- How can the researcher protect the privacy and identities of respondents and informants? Is the risk

Table 2.2 **Basic Versus Applied Sociology**

	Basic Sociology	Applied Sociology
Orientation	Theory building, hypothesis testing	Program effects, focus on consequences of practices
Goal	Knowledge production	Knowledge utilization, problem solving
Source	Self- or discipline-generated	Client-generated

Source: Adapted with permission from the NTL Institute (DeMartini 1982).

The Applied Sociologist at Work— Ruth Pickard and Daryl Poole

The Study of Society and the Practice of Sociology

The scientific study of social issues and the use of study findings to change society are closely woven together in the history of sociology. Auguste Comte, often considered the father of sociology, and his 18th-century contemporaries were intrigued with the idea of applying the new methods of science to social issues. They believed the resulting knowledge could lead to social betterment. Since that early period, the relationship between sociology and its application has remained central to sociology but has taken various forms over time.

During its emergence in the United States in the late 19th and early 20th centuries, sociology had a strong social reform base. Many early sociologists were concerned with the growing disorganization of family and work life that accompanied rapid urbanization and industrialization. They believed that scientific sociology could be used to control such processes and, thus, improve the conditions they considered undesirable. This notion was exemplified by Lester F. Ward, the first president of the American Sociological Society, who in 1906 wrote that the purpose of applied sociology was social improvement.

The early reformist sociology carried the seeds of an internal tension within sociology in the very methods it developed. Surveys and other techniques used by the reformers to gather data soon became the tools of sociologists in universities whose focus turned increasingly toward more academically accepted scientific scholarly work. Establishing credibility in academia meant defining sociology as a quantitatively sophisticated, objective, and value-free science. This concern for pure scientific analysis and reformist sociology goals—using sociological findings to change society—existed side by side and sometimes created conflict between sociologists. At the University of Chicago, which then had the leading sociology program in the nation, an original concern with real-world problems and reform, known as the "Chicago School," gave way in the 1930s to a research emphasis that dominated both the Chicago program and the discipline of sociology for much of the next four decades. Despite this shift toward abstract, theoretical science, however, there continued to be some sociologists interested in putting sociological findings to use.

In the late 1920s and during the Great Depression of the 1930s, a large number of sociologists were employed by the government to analyze and address the United States' escalating economic and social distress. With the coming of World War II, the research skills of many of these applied sociologists were directed toward finding ways to boost the morale of the country's armed forces, mobilize civilian support, and demoralize the enemy. After the war, issues such as racism, crime, and illiteracy drew the attention of the action-oriented sociologists. This emphasis became a major subdiscipline of sociology with the establishment in 1951 of a new professional organization, the Society for the Study of Social Problems.

The economic good times of the late 1950s, 1960s, and early 1970s supported and even encouraged applied research with social policy implications. During this period, sociology evolved along two lines: those sociologists who emphasized social action and those who pushed for increasingly sophisticated methodological and theoretical purity. Throughout this period, some prominent thinkers advocated the fusion of these scientific and action orientations.

In more recent years, applied sociology has received increased attention due in part to declining opportunities for university employment. Today, sociologists can be found in a wide variety of work situations, and depending on the focus, they may be known as sociological practitioners, applied sociologists, clinical sociologists, policy analysts, program planners, or evaluation researchers, among other titles. This role expansion is generating a vigorous new area of employment but also raising the old debate about the role of sociologists.

to subjects justified by an anticipated outcome of improved social conditions? For example, in several instances, courts have subpoenaed journalists and social scientists, forcing them to reveal confidential sources and information. Some researchers have spent time in jail to protect the confidentiality of their respondents (Comarow 1993; Scarce 1999).

- Is there informed consent among the people being studied? How much can and should the researcher tell subjects about the purpose of the research without completely biasing the outcome? Does informed consent mean only signing a release form at the beginning of a study? This issue relates to the harm or danger faced by respondents as well as the question of deception by social scientists. Is it acceptable to lie or to mislead participants so they do not change their behavior when they are responding to the situations that the researcher has created? If the public learns that social scientists actively deceive them, what will be the consequences for trusting researchers at a later time when a different study is being conducted?

- Will there be any harm to the participants— including injury to self-esteem or feelings of guilt and self-doubt? Philip Zimbardo and colleagues (1973) conducted a well-known social psychological experiment in which he designed a mock prison and assigned students to roles of prisoners and guards. The purpose of the study was to gauge the degree to which social roles affect attitudes and behaviors. However, the students took the roles so seriously that they no longer distinguished reality from the artificial situation, and some "guards" became violent and abusive toward the "prisoners." Given these negative reactions, the experiment was discontinued, and students were informed about the purpose of the study. Is a research project unethical if it negatively affects a subject's self-esteem? Most social scientists would say yes, such research is beyond the boundaries of ethical conduct.

- How much invasion of privacy is legitimate in the name of research? How much disclosure of confidential information, even in disguised form, is acceptable? For example, a researcher who studies sexual behavior and attitudes may collect data about the most intimate of relationships. How this confidential information is handled to protect respondents is of utmost importance in research ethics.

Codes of ethics cannot answer all ethical dilemmas that arise for researchers, but they do provide general guidelines. In addition, most universities and organizations where research is common have human subjects review boards whose function is to ensure that human participants are not harmed by the research.

Thinking Sociologically

Consider some ethical issues in conducting research. Why is informed consent important? Is it ethical to talk to people when they do not know you are recording their words? Is it ethical to be a researcher in a setting or situation but not inform the group of your research study or that you are studying them? Why?

Research methods work in tandem with sociological theories. The theories suggest how social life is organized and help to shape the questions sociologists ask by suggesting which variables are most important. Knowing this information helps determine appropriate methods to use in a study. The next section summarizes four main sociological theories. Other theories will be discussed when relevant to chapter topics.

Sociology's Major Theoretical Perspectives

Let us return to our opening example of Hector. Sociologists have several perspectives that can help us understand the poverty Hector experiences in São Paulo, Brazil. Hector's interactions with family, peers, school teachers, employers, and religious leaders can be studied at the micro level of analysis.

Hector's motivation to find work versus going to school can be understood by studying interpersonal interactions with significant others. A micro analysis would stress the small groups and neighborhood of which he is a part. By contrast, meso-level analysis focuses on institutions, large organizations, and ethnic communities. For instance, forces or trends in Brazilian institutions affect the health and vitality of the economy. Likewise, migration from rural areas into the big city of São Paulo, where there are few employment opportunities for those with low skills, make it harder for all poor people living in *favelas* to find jobs.

Macro-level analysis considers the larger social context— national and global—within which Hector and his family live. From this perspective, Hector's position in society is part of a total system in which the poor in Brazil and other countries constitute a reserve labor force, available to work in unskilled jobs as needed. International trade, or a change in the Brazilian economy, could have an influence on Hector's job prospects quite independent of his individual motivation to work. Macro-level theories would consider questions related to Brazilian policies as a nation and the position of Brazil in the world system.

Sociologists draw on major theoretical perspectives at each level of analysis to guide their research and to help them understand social interactions and social organizations. A **theoretical perspective** is a basic view of society

Micro-level interactions occur in classrooms every day, both among peers and between teacher and students.

that guides sociologists' ideas and research. Theoretical perspectives are the broadest theories in sociology, providing overall approaches to understanding the social world and social problems. These perspectives help sociologists to develop explanations of social patterns and to see relationships between patterns.

Recall the description of the social world model presented in Chapter 1. It stresses the levels of analysis—smaller units existing within larger social systems. We have mentioned that some methods of data collection are more conducive to analysis of micro-level processes of interaction (e.g., participant observation), whereas other methods work more effectively to understand macro-level social systems (e.g., secondary data analysis). The same is true of theoretical perspectives. Some are especially effective in understanding micro-level interactions, and others illuminate macro-level structures, although the distinctions are not absolute. Either type of theory—those most useful at the micro or macro levels—can be used at the meso level, depending on the research question being asked. To illustrate how a social problem is approached differently by these four major theoretical perspectives, we will further delve into our examination of Hector's circumstances (Ashley and Orenstein 2009; Turner 2003). Keep in mind that sociologists use many theories, some of which will be introduced where relevant in future chapters.

Micro- to Meso-Level Theories

Symbolic Interaction

Symbolic interaction theory (also called social construction or interpretative theory) is concerned with how people create shared meanings regarding symbols and events and then interact on the basis of those meanings. For example, Hector interacts with his family and friends in the *favela* in ways that he has learned are necessary for survival there. In Hector's world of poverty, the informal interactions of the street and the more formal interactions of the school carry different sets of meanings that guide Hector's behavior.

Symbolic interaction theory assumes that groups form around interacting individuals. Through these interactions, people learn to share common understandings and to learn what to expect from others. They make use of symbols such as language, or verbal and nonverbal communication (words and gestures), to interpret interactions with others. Symbolic communication (for example, language) helps people construct a meaningful world. This implies that humans are not merely passive agents responding to their environments. Instead, they are actively engaged in creating their own meaningful social world based on their constructions and interpretations of the social world. In some cases, people may passively accept the social definitions and interpretations of others. This saves them the effort of making sense of the stimuli around them and of figuring out interpretations (Blumer 1969; Fine 1990). Still, more than any other theory in the social sciences, symbolic interactionism stresses human agency—the active role of individuals—in creating their social environment.

George Herbert Mead (1863–1931) is prominently identified with the symbolic interaction perspective through his influential work, *Mind, Self, and Society* (Mead [1934] 1962). Mead linked the human mind, the social self, and the structure of society to the process of interaction. He believed that humans have the ability to decide how to act based on their perceptions of the social world, or what sociologists refer to as their definition of the situation. Mead explored the mental processes associated with how humans define situations. He placed special emphasis on human interpretations of gestures and symbols (including language) and the meanings we attach to our actions. He also examined how we learn our social roles in society such as mother, teacher, and friend and how we learn to carry out these roles. Indeed, as we will see in Chapter 4, he insisted that our notion of who we are—our self—emerges from social experience and interaction with others. These ideas of how we construct our individual social worlds and have some control over them come from a perspective known as the Chicago School.

Another symbolic interaction approach—the Iowa School (named after scholars from the University of Iowa)—makes a more explicit link to the meso level of the social system. Manford Kuhn (1964) of the Iowa School sees individual identities connected to roles and positions within organizations. If we hold several positions—honors student, club president, daughter, sister, student, athlete, thespian, middle-class person—those positions form a relatively stable core self. We will interpret new situations in light of our social positions, some of which are very important and anchor how we see the social world. Once a core self is established, it guides and shapes the way we interact with people in many situations—even new social settings. Thus, if you are president of an organization and have the responsibility for overseeing the organization, part of your self-esteem, your view of responsible citizenship, and your attitude toward life will be shaped by that position. Thus, the Iowa School of symbolic interactionism places a bit less emphasis on individual choice, but it does a better job of recognizing the link between the micro, meso, and macro levels of the society (Carrothers and Benson 2003; Stryker 1980).

The following principles summarize the modern symbolic interaction perspective and how individual action results in groups, institutions, and societies (Ritzer 2004b):

- Humans are endowed with the capacity for thought, shaped by social interaction.
- In social interaction, people learn the meanings and symbols that allow them to exercise thought and participate in human action.
- People modify the meanings and symbols as they struggle to make sense of their situations and the events they experience.
- Interpreting the situation involves seeing things from more than one perspective, examining possible courses of action, assessing the advantages and disadvantages of each, and then choosing one course of action.
- These patterns of action and interaction make up the interactive relations that we call groups, institutions, and societies.
- Our positions or memberships in these groups, organizations, and societies may profoundly influence the way we define our selves and may lead to fairly stable patterns of interpretation of our experiences and of social life.

To summarize, the modern symbolic interaction perspective emphasizes the process each individual goes through in creating and altering his or her social reality and identity within a social setting. Without a system of shared symbols, humans could not coordinate their actions with one another, and hence society as we understand it would not be possible.

Critique of the Symbolic Interaction Perspective. Although widely used today, symbolic interactionism (especially the Chicago School) is often criticized for neglecting the macro-level structures of society that affect human behavior. By focusing on interpersonal interactions, large-scale social forces such as an economic depression or political revolution that shape human destinies are given less consideration.

With the focus on individual agency and the ability of each individual to create meaning, symbolic interaction has often been less attuned to issues of social class position, social power, historical circumstances, or international conflict between societies. Yet, these are important issues (Meltzer, Petras, and Reynolds 1975). In addition, critics point out the difficulty in studying ambiguous ideas such as the development of the self or how the mind works.

Despite these limitations, theorists from the symbolic interaction perspective have made significant contributions to understanding the development of social identities and interactions as the basis for groups, organizations, and societies. Many of these studies will be discussed in chapters throughout the book.

Rational Choice Theory

Women may decide whether to stay in abusive relationships based on the balance of rewards versus costs. In considering a divorce, do the rewards of escaping a conflicted, abusive marriage outweigh the costs of daily economic and emotional stresses related to going it alone? For a lesbian couple, there are potential costs of coming out of the closet to friends, family, and employers. There may also be significant benefits: When applying for health insurance, coverage is often denied to unrecognized partners, and acknowledged lesbians no longer live in hiding with constant fear of being exposed. These cost and benefit decisions are the types of questions addressed by rational choice theorists.

A central premise of micro-level rational choice theory is that human behavior involves choices. On what basis do people make their choices? As the term implies, **rational choice** approaches assume that people chart a course of action on the basis of rational decisions. From this perspective, people are expected to act in ways that maximize their rewards and minimize their costs. Where the balance lies determines our behavior.

Rational choice, also called exchange theory, has its roots in several disciplines—economics, behavioral psychology, anthropology, and philosophy (Cook, O'Brien, and Kollock 1990). Social behavior is seen as an exchange activity—a transaction in which resources are given and received (Blau 1964; Homans 1974). Every interaction involves an exchange of something valued—money, time, material goods, attention, sex, allegiance. People stay in relationships because they get something from the exchange, and they leave relationships that cost them without providing adequate benefits. Simply stated, people are more likely to act if they see some reward or success coming from their behavior. The implication is that self-interest for the individual is the guiding element in human interaction.

Applying the rational choice theory to Hector's situation, we could examine how he evaluates his life options. What are the costs and rewards for staying in school versus those associated with dropping out and earning money from temporary jobs? For Hector, the immediate benefit of earning a meager

People make critical decisions about resource allocation at the micro (local community) level and are often eager to increase access to resources provided by development institutions at the meso or the macro level of the social system. The village elders in this photo continue to have authority to make decisions about the traditional irrigation canals that are being improved in their village in Tanzania, but their expanded water supply is possible in part because of international financial support.

income to put food on his family's table comes at a cost—the loss of a more hopeful and prosperous future. When hungry, the reward of being paid for odd jobs may outweigh the cost of leaving school and losing long-term opportunities.

Critique of the Rational Choice Perspective. Rational choice theorists give little attention to macro-level analysis and internal mental processes. They see human conduct as self-centered, with rational behavior implying that people seek to maximize rewards and minimize costs. Charitable, unselfish, or altruistic behavior is not easily explained by this view. Why would a soldier sacrifice his or her life to save a comrade? Why would a starving person in a Nazi concentration camp share a crust of bread with another? Proponents of rational choice counter the criticism by arguing that if a person feels good about helping another, that in itself is a benefit that compensates for the cost.

Another critique is that humans often do not behave in ways that maximize their own self-interest. In Ohio, some residents voted against public school levies because they did not want to pay the extra hundred dollars or so per year in taxes. Yet, the same voters are dismayed when trying to sell their house, only to find that their property value has dropped by as much as $15,000 because they live in a district that does not support education (Roberts 2003). In short, acting in our own self-interest requires an accurate definition of the situation and implications of various acts.

Some theorists (Denzin 1992; Fiske 1991) have attempted a synthesis between the interaction level of analysis and macro-level theories. For instance, studies of friendships, employee-employer contracts, relations in families,

and consumer-salesperson transactions can all be represented as exchange relationships. By combining the millions of exchange relationships, these researchers contend that we can study macro-level patterns in the social world (Fiske 1991).

Thinking Sociologically

How can symbolic interaction and rational choice perspectives help explain dating behavior? For example, what might a good-night kiss versus sexual intercourse mean to females versus males? How does one learn the cues that indicate attraction to a person of the same or opposite sex? Why are these micro-level questions?

Meso- and Macro-Level Theories

Meso- and macro-level theories consider larger units in the social world such as organizations, institutions (such as education, politics, or economics), societies, or global systems. For example, Hector lives in a modernizing country, Brazil, which is struggling to raise the standard of living of its people and compete in the world market. The decisions that are made by his government at a national and international level affect his life in a variety of ways. As Brazil industrializes, the nature of jobs and modes of communication change. Local village cultures modify as the entire nation gains more uniformity of values, beliefs, and norms. Similarly, resources such as access to clean water in Tanzania may be allotted at the local level, but local communities need national and sometimes international support, as illustrated in the photo. We can begin to understand how the process of modernization influences Hector, this village in Tanzania, and other people around the globe by looking at two major macro-level approaches: structural-functional and conflict perspectives. Recall that sociological theories provide possible explanations to help us understand the social world.

Structural-Functional Theory

The structural-functional perspective, also called **functional theory**, assumes that all parts of the social structure (including groups, organizations, and institutions), the culture (values and beliefs), and social processes (for example, social change or socialization—learning to be a member of society) work together to make the whole society run smoothly and harmoniously. To understand the social world from this perspective, we must look at how the parts of society (structure) fit together and how each part contributes (functions) toward the maintenance of society. For instance, two functions of the family include reproducing children and teaching them to be members of society. These and other functions help perpetuate society, for without reproducing and teaching new members to fit in, societies would collapse.

Structural-functional theory traces its roots to the French Revolution. To Auguste Comte, the question of how to bring about order and harmony out of the chaos of the French Revolution was paramount. He argued that by gaining scientific knowledge about society, leaders could create a better social order. Comte borrowed concepts from the biological sciences, including an analogy between social and biological organisms. This idea held that societies, like biological organisms, develop and become more complex and interdependent. As parts of society grow and change, so do the functions or purposes they serve. To understand why a structure exists, we must understand the needs it meets in society. These ideas are basic to functionalists.

Émile Durkheim (1858–1917) further developed functionalism by theorizing that society is made up of necessary parts that fit together into a working whole. Durkheim (1947) felt that individuals conform to the rules of societies because of a collective conscience—the shared beliefs in the values of a group. People grow up sharing the same values, beliefs, and rules of behavior as those around them. Gradually, these shared beliefs and rules are internalized. A person's behavior is, in a sense, governed from within because it feels right and proper to behave in accordance with what is expected. As such, the functionalist perspective of Durkheim and subsequent theorists places emphasis on societal consensus, which gives rise to stable and predictable patterns of order in society. Because people need groups for survival, they adhere to the group's rules so that they fit in. This means that most societies run in an orderly manner with most individuals fitting into their positions in society.

Since the 1950s, functionalism has been dominated by several influential U.S. theorists including Talcott Parsons (1951b) and Robert Merton (1968b). Parsons (1951a) developed a grand theory of society, so grand that it encompasses all the major parts of society—family, education, religion, politics, economics, and health. Underlying his theory is the assumption that all the parts of the social system are interrelated, and each performs some task or function necessary for a society's survival. The whole is a highly integrated system, cemented together by value consensus, agreement on right and proper actions among individuals who make up the system.

Functions can be manifest or latent. **Manifest functions** are the planned outcomes of social organization or institutions. The function of the microwave oven, for instance, has been to allow people to prepare meals quickly and easily, facilitating life in overworked and stressed modern families. **Latent functions** are often unplanned or unintended consequences (Merton 1938). The unplanned consequences of the microwave oven were creation of a host of new jobs and stimulation of the economy as people wrote new cookbooks and as businesses were formed to produce microwavable cookware and prepared foods for the microwave.

Dysfunctions (Merton 1938) are those actions that undermine the stability or equilibrium of society. By allowing people to cook meals without using a convection oven,

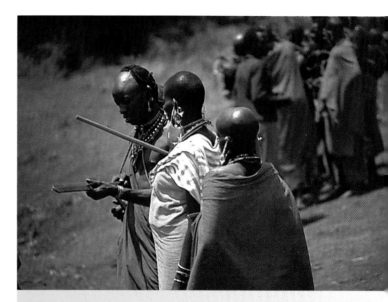

A Masai family works together as a unit, and in so doing, they enhance the stability and continuity of their entire society.

the microwave oven has contributed to some young people having no idea how to cook, thus making them highly dependent on expensive technology and processed foods.

Processed foods as a regular diet are not very good for one's body, potentially causing health problems, and the higher cost of processed food makes it increasingly important for families to have rather substantial incomes to survive. The requirement of substantial incomes may limit families from making other kinds of choices (vacations may be limited, cultural opportunities may be curtailed, decisions to allow only one person to work or to job-share may not be an option, and so forth). From a functionalist perspective, it is important to examine the possible functional and dysfunctional aspects of the different parts of society in terms of the maintenance and harmony of society as a whole.

Critique of the Structural-Functional Perspective. Because sociologist Talcott Parsons was a leading scholar and proponent of structural-functional theory, much criticism is directed toward his ideas. His grand theory has been criticized because it is so abstract that it is difficult to test empirically. Moreover, functionalism does not explain social changes in society, such as conflict and revolution. As we try to understand the many societal upheavals in the world, from suicide bombings in Iraq to the democracy and economic privatization movements in China, it is clear that dramatic social change is possible. The functionalist assumption is that if a system is running smoothly, it must be working well because it is free from conflict. It assumes that conflict is harmful, even though we know that stability sometimes comes from ruthless dictators suppressing the population.

Feminist sociologists criticize functionalism's support of the status quo. If the family or economic system of society seems to be functioning smoothly, this does not mean

Karl Marx was a social analyst who is often identified as the founder of conflict theory.

that these systems are fair and equitable or that women and minorities are content with their roles in them. A paradigm that assumes so is making false assumptions, according to feminist theorists. Feminists and others reject the implicit idea of functionalism that orderly society is always positive. The point is that a stable system is not the same thing as a healthy system.

Functionalism has had a profound impact on social science analysis. Still, functionalism in the 21st century fails to explain many contemporary social situations, according to proponents of a rival macro-level perspective, conflict theory.

Thinking Sociologically

Are existing social arrangements in a society necessarily desirable, and is dramatic change necessarily dysfunctional as suggested by functional theory?

Conflict Theory

Conflict in any group or society is inevitable. To support this view, conflict theorists advance the following key ideas:

- Conflict and the potential for conflict underlie all social relations.
- Social change is desirable, particularly changes that bring about a greater degree of social equality.
- The existing social order reflects powerful people imposing their values and beliefs upon the weak.

The conflict perspective claims that inequality and injustice are the source of conflicts that permeate society. Because resources and power are distributed unequally in society, some members have more money, goods, and prestige than others. The rich protect their positions by using the power they have accumulated to keep those less fortunate in their places. From the perspective of poor people such as Hector, it seems the rich get all the breaks. Because most of us want more of the resources in society (money, good jobs, nice houses, and cars), conflict erupts between the haves and the have-nots. Sometimes, the conflict brings about a change in the society.

Modern conflict theory has its origins in the works of Karl Marx (1818–1883), a German social philosopher who lived in England during the height of 19th-century industrial expansion. He recognized the plight of exploited underclass workers in the new industrial states of Europe and viewed the ruling elites and the wealthy industrial owners as exploiters of the working class. Marx wrote about the new working class crowded in urban slums, working long hours every day, not earning enough money for decent housing and food, and living and working in conditions that were appalling. Few of the protections enjoyed by workers today—such as retirement benefits, health coverage, sick leave, the 40-hour workweek, and restrictions against child labor—existed in Marx's time.

Capitalism emerged as the dominant economic system in Europe. Capitalism is an economic system in which (1) the equipment and property for producing goods is owned privately by wealthy individuals, who have the right to use these resources however they want; and (2) the market system (supply and demand) determines the distribution of resources and the levels of income (including wages, rents, and profits). Although there are various forms of capitalism, the core principles involve private ownership of industries and nonintervention by government (Heilbroner and Milberg 2007).

Marx believed that two classes, the capitalists (also referred to as bourgeoisie or "haves") who owned the **means of production** (property, machinery, and cash) and the workers (also referred to as proletariat or "have-nots"), would continue to live in conflict until the workers shared more equally in the profits of their labor. The more workers came to understand their plight, the more awareness they would have of the unfairness of the situation. Eventually, Marx believed that workers would rise up and overthrow capitalism, forming a new classless society. Collective ownership—shared ownership of the means of production—would be the new economic order (Marx and Engels [1848] 1969).

The idea of the bourgeoisie (the capitalist exploiters who own the factories) and the proletariat (the exploited workers who sell their labor) has carried over into analysis of modern-day conflicts between labor and management, between women's and men's interests, and between warring factions within countries such as the Congo, Rwanda, Darfur, Indonesia, and countries in the Middle East. From a conflict perspective, Hector in Brazil and millions like him in other countries are part of the reserve labor force—a cheap labor pool that can be called on when labor is needed or disregarded when demand is low, thus meeting the changing labor needs of industry and capitalism. This pattern results in permanent economic insecurity and poverty for Hector and those like him.

Many branches of the conflict perspective have grown from the original ideas of Marx. Here, we mention two contributions to conflict theory, those of American sociologists W. E. B. Du Bois ([1899] 1967) and Ralf Dahrendorf (1959). As you can see, social conflict has been a major focus of sociological investigation for more than a century.

One of the very first American conflict theorists was W. E. B. Du Bois, the first African American to receive a doctorate from Harvard University. Du Bois felt that sociology should be active in bettering society, that although research should be scientifically rigorous and fair-minded, the ultimate goal of sociological work was social improvement—not just human insight. He saw the conflict between haves and have-nots as being based largely on race in the United States, not just social class.

Du Bois ([1899] 1967) not only wrote on these issues but also acted on them. He was one of the cofounders of the National Association for the Advancement of Colored People (NAACP). He stressed the need for minority ethnic groups to become advocates for their rights, to create conflict where destructive harmony exists, and to change the society toward greater equality and participation. He was—and continues to be—an inspiration to many sociologists who believe that their findings should have real applications and should be used to create a more humane social world (Mills 1956). He was well ahead of his time in recognizing the conflicting nature of American society and the way privilege and self-interest blinded people to the inequities.

A half-century later, Dahrendorf (1959) argued that society is always in the process of change and affected by forces that bring about change. Dahrendorf refined Marx's ideas in several ways. First, he pointed out that Marx's predicted overthrow of capitalism had not come about because of changes in conditions for workers (employee organizations, unions). Instead, a middle class developed, some workers became part owners, stockholders dispersed the concentration of wealth, and a higher standard of living was achieved for workers. Second, he proposed that class conflict occurs between the haves and the have-nots by adding several new categories of people: quasi-groups, interest groups, and conflict groups.

Quasi-groups include individuals who have similar social positions and interests but do not belong to an organized

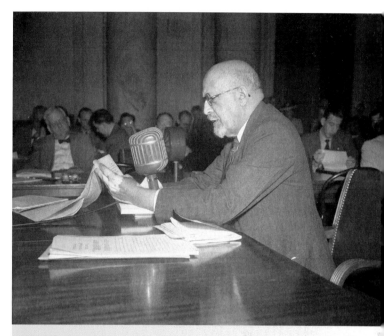

W. E. B. Du Bois was an outstanding contributor to the development of conflict theory and was among the first to apply that theory to American society.

group. They therefore have little power. For example, residents who live in poverty like Hector but live in different *favelas* surrounding São Paulo are a quasi-group. People in quasi-groups are vulnerable precisely because they lack a social power base.

Interest groups, such as members of Hector's *favela*, emerge from the quasi-groups as a way to seek the power to solve problems. They share interests, such as a desire for sanitation, running water, electricity, and a higher standard of living. From within these more organized interest groups, conflict groups arise to fight for changes. There is always potential for conflict when those without power realize their common position and form interest groups. How much change or violence is brought about depends on how organized those groups become.

Dahrendorf's major contribution is the recognition that class struggle goes beyond Marx's idea of economic self-interests; control of the means of production by the elite; and distributions of power, authority, and prestige. A split society—haves and have-nots—becomes sliced in many directions. Thus, conflict over resources results not just in a conflict between proletariat and bourgeoisie but in a multitude of divisions including old people versus young people, rich versus poor, one region of the country versus another, Christians versus non-Christians, men versus women, African Americans versus Jews or Hispanics, and so forth. This acknowledges multiple rifts in the society based in interest groups. The notion that men and women can be seen as interest groups, each looking out for its own self-interests, has resulted in one particular version of conflict theory, feminist theory (discussed below).

Whereas Marx emphasized the divisive nature of conflict, other theorists have offered a modified theory. His contemporary, Georg Simmel (1858–1918), looked at how conflict could help to hold together groups in society. This idea was also discussed by American theorist Lewis Coser (1956), who took a very different approach to conflict from that of Marx, arguing that it can strengthen societies and organizations within them. According to Coser, problems in a society or group lead to complaints or conflicts—a warning message to the group that all is not well. Resolution of the conflicts shows that the group is adaptable in meeting needs of its members, thereby creating greater loyalty to the group. Thus, conflict provides the message of what is not working to meet people's needs, and the system adapts to the needs for change because of the conflict (Coser 1956; Simmel 1955).

Critique of the Conflict Perspective. First, many conflict theorists focus on the macro-level analysis and lose sight of the individuals involved in conflict situations, such as Hector and his family. Second, empirical research to test conflict propositions is limited. The conflict perspective often paints a picture with rather broad brushstrokes. Research to test the picture involves interpretations of broad spans of history and is more difficult to claim as scientific. Third, conflict theorists tend to focus on social stress, power plays, and disharmony. Conflict theory is not as effective in explaining social cohesion and cooperation. Fourth, many theorists are not convinced that self-interest is the ultimate motivator of behavior or that altruism and cooperation are uncommon.

Thinking Sociologically

Imagine you are a legislator. You have to decide whether to cut funding for a senior citizens program or slash a scholarship program for college students. You want to be reelected, and you know that approximately 90% of senior citizens are registered, and most do actually vote. You also know that less than half of college-age people are likely to vote. These constituencies are about the same size. What would you do, and how would you justify your decision? How does this example illustrate conflict theory? Why are these meso-level questions?

Feminist Sociological Theory

Feminists argue that sociology has been dominated by a male perspective and that the male perspective does not give a complete view of the social world. Feminist analysis critiques the hierarchical power structures, which feminists argue treat women and other minorities unequally (Cancian 1992). Much of feminist theory, then, has foundations in the conflict perspective. Women are viewed as disadvantaged by the hierarchical way that society is arranged, whereas men experience privilege because of those arrangements. Men become an interest group intent on preserving its privileges.

Some branches of feminist theory, however, are not based on Marx's writings. Instead, their ideas come from interaction perspectives, emphasizing the way gender cues and symbols shape the nature of much human interaction. Thus, feminist theory moves from meso- and macro-level analysis (e.g., looking at national and global situations that give privileges to men) to micro-level analysis (e.g., inequality between husbands and wives in marriage). In particular, feminist theory points to the importance of gender as a variable influencing social patterns.

Feminists contend that there is a disparity between what actually goes on in women's lives and many accounts by social scientists of social relations between males and females. Men's explanations of gender relations often have not presented women's lives in a way that is authentic for women themselves. The ideas, work opportunities, and life experiences of women of color are even less understood by traditional sociology (Collins 2000). Thus, many studies and writing about women are far removed from women's own experiences, and the reality for women becomes distorted.

In general, feminists point out, women's experiences in social relations involve interdependence with others whereas males have been taught to be competitive and individualistic in sports, business competition, and many other social arenas. Males learn early in their lives that vulnerability must be avoided so that one is not exploited by others. This, according to feminist theorists, influences the way men think about society. For example, rational choice theory maintains that each individual is out to protect self-interests and to make choices that benefit only the self. This theory is based on a male view of society. Men are also more likely to view hierarchical social arrangements as normal, contributing to their difficulty in recognizing how patriarchal our society is. Also, some feminists claim that we are blind to the fact that gender roles are socially created, not biologically determined. As a result of these differences in experience and in socialization, women's views on issues of justice, morality, and society lend a different interpretation of society (Brettell and Sargent 2001; Kramer 2005) and can present a more inclusive view of the world (Burn 2005; Lengermann and Niebrugge-Brantley 1990).

It is interesting that many women today will begin a sentence with the disclaimer, "I am not a feminist, but . . ." This seems to be because some feminists have had a rather strident style and often focused on men as the cause of problems. Not all feminists are strident or focus on men as oppressors. Indeed, many men call themselves feminists, for a feminist is someone who believes that men and women should be given equal standing and equal opportunities in the society. Feminists have opened the door to understanding how social structures can bind and inhibit the freedom of both men and women. They also recognize that males have generally had more privileges than females in societies around the world. To study sociological questions, feminist methodology puts emphasis on qualitative methods that involve empathetic role-taking with respondents in interviews and trying to understand the world from the female or male respondents' point of view.

Critique of the Feminist Sociological Perspective. Feminists are not the only group with concerns about being fairly and accurately represented in theory and research. Race and ethnic groups and social class groups are also affected. Thus, some theorists argue that theory should represent the intersection between race, class, and gender. When trying to understand minority women in minimum-wage jobs or factors affecting homelessness, this intersection can provide a more complete view.

Multi-Level Analysis: Max Weber's Contributions

Max Weber (1864–1920), a German-born social scientist, has had a lasting effect on sociology and other social sciences. He cannot be pigeonholed easily into one of the theoretical categories, for his contributions include both micro- and macro-level analyses. His emphasis on **verstehen** (meaning deep empathetic understanding) gives him a place in micro-level theory, and his discussions of Karl Marx and of bureaucracies give him a place in meso- and macro-level theory (Weber 1946).

Verstehen stems from the interpretations or meanings individuals give to parts of their social worlds, to their subjective interpretations or understandings of the social world. Actions that occur outside of individual lives affect these interpretations and our actions. Sociologists try to understand both people's behaviors and the meanings that they attach to their behaviors and their experiences.

The goal-oriented, efficient new organizational form called bureaucracy was the focus of much of Weber's writing at the meso level. This form was based not on tradition but on rationality. In other words, decisions were based on what would best accomplish the organization's goals, not individual benefit. Hiring and promotion on the basis of individual merit (getting the most qualified person rather than hiring a friend or relative) is one example of this rational decision making. This is a principle we take for granted now, but it was not always so. The entire society becomes transformed through a change in how individuals make decisions on behalf of a bureaucratic organization.

Opportunities for jobs were changed, the culture became more geared to merit as a basis for decisions, and organizational life became more governed by rules and routines. All of this came from a redefinition of appropriate ways to make decisions. Weber's conceptualizations of society at the meso level have laid the groundwork for theoretical understanding of modern organizations.

Weber also attempted to understand macro-level processes. For instance, he asked how capitalists understood the world around them, resulting in his famous book, *The Protestant Ethic and the Spirit of Capitalism* (Weber [1904–1905] 1958). His work was influenced by Marx's writings and the idea of conflict between groups in society. Whereas Marx focused on economic conditions as the key factor shaping history and power relations, Weber argued that

Coretta Scott King speaks here in Houston at a rally for women's rights that also addressed the needs of minority women. A resolution, approved by the National Women's Conference, declared that minority women suffered a double discrimination—based on race and gender. The women depicted here are unapologetic about believing that men and women should be treated equally or about being called feminist.

Marx's focus was too narrow and that politics, economics, religion, psychology, and the military all help explain the social world, power relationships, and conflict. In short, Weber thought that the society was more complex than Karl Marx's core notion that two groups—the haves and the have-nots—are in conflict over economic resources.

Thinking Sociologically

To what extent are human beings free agents who can create their own social world and come up with their own definitions about life? To what extent are our lives determined or profoundly shaped by our culture, by the social systems around us, and by our positions of power or powerlessness in the economic and political system?

Using Different Theoretical Perspectives

Each of the theoretical perspectives described in this chapter begins from a set of assumptions about humans. Each makes a contribution to our understanding, but each has limitations or blind spots, such as not taking into account the other levels of analysis (Ritzer 2004a). Figure 2.3 provides a summary of cooperative versus competitive perspectives to illustrate how the theories differ.

	Macro analysis	Micro analysis
Humans viewed as cooperative (people interact with others on the basis of shared meanings and common symbols)	*Structural-Functional Theory*	*Symbolic Interactionism Theory*
Humans viewed as competitive (behavior governed by self-interest)	*Conflict Theory* (group interests)	*Rational Choice Theory* (individual interests)

Figure 2.3   Cooperative Versus Competitive Perspectives

It is important to understand that there are different and viable perspectives to explain society. None of these is right or wrong. Rather, a particular theory may be more or less useful when studying some level of analysis or aspect of society. It is also important to learn about the major theoretical perspectives and how each can be used to provide a framework and viewpoint to guide research. The micro-, meso-, and macro-level social world model used in this book does not imply that one of these theories is better than another. The strength of a theory depends on its ability to explain and predict behavior accurately. Each theoretical perspective focuses on a different aspect of society and level of analysis and gives us a different lens through which to view our social world. The social world model helps us picture the whole system and determine which theory or synthesis of theories best suits our needs in analyzing a specific social process or structure.

Thinking Sociologically

Consider the issue of homelessness in cities around the world. How could each of the theories discussed in this chapter be used to help understand the problem of homelessness?

So What ?

What makes a discipline scientific is not the subject matter. It is how we conduct our research and what we consider valid evidence. The core features of a science are (1) commitment to empirically validated evidence, facts, and information that are confirmed through systematic processes of testing using the five senses; (2) an effort to disprove whatever it is we think is true, allowing us to be convinced by the evidence rather than by our preconceived ideas; (3) absolute integrity and objectivity in reporting and in conducting research; and (4) continual openness to how our findings are reexamined and new interpretations proposed.

It is the fourth feature that causes us to invite and be open to criticism and alternative interpretations. To have credible findings, we always consider the possibility that we have overlooked alternative explanations of the data and alternative ways to view the problem. This is one of the hardest principles to grasp, but it is one of the most important in reaching the truth. Science—including social science—is not facts to be memorized. Science is a process that is made possible by a social exchange of ideas, a clash of opinions, and a continual search for truth. Knowledge in the sciences is created by vigorous debate. Rather than just memorizing concepts in this book to take a test, we hope you will engage in the creation of knowledge by entering into these debates.

Theories serve as lenses to help us make sense of the data that we gather with various research strategies. However, the data themselves can be used to test the theories, so there is an ongoing reciprocal relationship between theory (the lens for making sense of the data) and the research (the evidence used to test the theories). The most important ideas in this chapter are what sociology considers evidence and how sociology operates as a science. In each chapter of this book, we include a study to address the question "How do we know?"

So far, we have focused on what sociology is and how sociologists know what they know. The rest of the book examines what the social world is like. The next chapter explores the relationships between culture and society at various levels in our social world.

Key Points

What Have We Learned?

- Attempts to understand society have existed for at least two and a half millennia, but gathering of scientific evidence to test hypotheses and validate claims is a rather modern idea. (See pp. 31–35.)

- Science of society employs both deductive reasoning (beginning with general theoretical ideas and moving to specifics) and inductive reasoning (beginning with facts and moving to theory). (See pp. 35–38.)

- As a science, sociology uses eight systematic steps to gather data and test theories about the social world. (See pp. 38–47.)

- In most cases, planning a research study requires that we identify causes (independent variables) and effects (dependent variables) and that we make sure correlations of variables are not spurious; the simultaneous occurrence of two variables can be accidental or noncausal. (See pp. 39–40.)

- Major methods for gathering data in sociology include surveys (for example, interviews and questionnaires), field studies (direct observation of a natural setting), controlled experiments, and analysis of existing sources (through secondary sources or through content analyses). (See pp. 40–42.)

- Use of multiple methods—triangulation—increases confidence in the findings. (See p. 42.)

- Scientific confidence in results also requires representative samples, usually drawn randomly. (See p. 44.)

- Sociology has three strong traditions: One stresses the objective posture of science; another emphasizes the uniquely human qualities such as humans making meaning and argues that complete objectivity is never fully attained; and a third stresses practical applications of research to make a more humane, just, and compassionate society. Each of these has a long tradition within sociology and each will be given attention in this book. (See pp. 47–49.)

- Theories are especially important to science because they raise questions for research, and they explain relationships between facts. Sociology has four primary overriding theoretical perspectives or paradigms: symbolic interactionism, rational choice theory, functionalism, and conflict theory. Other perspectives, such as feminist theory, serve as correctives to the main paradigms. Most of these theories are more applicable at the micro to meso level or at the meso to macro level. (See pp. 49–58.)

Contributing to Our Social World: What Can We Do?

At the Local Level: Every community has one or more local service organizations that work to provide for unmet needs of community members: housing, legal aid, medical care, elder care, and so on. Identify and contact one of these organizations (faculty members often have good contacts, and the United Way works with most of them). Volunteer to work with the organization in its needs assessment research and learn more about the sociological principles and research methods that are used.

At the National and Global Levels: Although the U.S. Bureau of the Census is best known for its decennial (every 10 year) enumeration of the population, its work continues each year as it prepares special reports, population estimates, and regular publications (including *Current Population Reports*). Visit the Bureau's Web site at www .census.gov and explore the valuable and extensive amount of quantitative data and other information available. You

can also arrange to visit your local Census Bureau office to discuss volunteer work. As a branch of the U.S. Department of Commerce, the Census Bureau houses many of its local offices in regional federal buildings. Through your sociology club or informal group of students and faculty members, you can invite a representative of the bureau to your campus to discuss the census operations and how you can get involved as a volunteer or paid staff member in their work.

Visit **www.pineforge.com/ballantine2study** for online activities, sample tests, and other helpful information. Select "Chapter 2: Examining the Social World" for chapter-specific activities.

PART II

Social Structure, Processes, and Control

Picture a house. First there is the wood frame, then the walls and roof. This provides the framework or structure. Within that structure, activities or processes take place—electricity to turn on lights and appliances, water to wash in and drink, and people to carry out these processes. If something goes wrong in the house, we take steps to control the damage and repair it.

Our social world is constructed in a similar way: Social structure is the framework of society with its organizations, and social processes are the dynamic activities of the society. This section begins with a discussion of the structure of society, followed by the processes of culture and socialization through which individuals are taught cultural rules—how to function and live effectively within their society. Although socialization takes place primarily at the micro level, we will explore its implications at the meso and macro levels as well.

If we break the social structure into parts, like the wood frame, walls, and roof of a house, it is the groups and organizations (including bureaucracies) that make up the structure. To work smoothly, these organizations depend on people's loyalty so that they do what society and its groups need to survive. However, smooth functioning does not always happen. Things break down. This means those in control of societies try to control disruptions and deviant individuals in order to maintain control and function smoothly.

As we explore the next chapters, we will continue to examine social life at the micro, meso, and macro levels, for each of us as individuals is profoundly shaped by social processes and structures at larger and more abstract levels, all the way to the global level.

CHAPTER 3

Society and Culture

Hardware and Software of Our Social World

What we consider food is influenced by the structure of society, including the organization of food production, distribution, and technology, and by the culture—the ideas about what is edible. Families in various parts of the world gather here around the things they would typically eat.

Think About It . . .

Micro: Could you be human without culture?

Micro: How do microcultures—the values and beliefs in your fraternity, choir, or athletic team—affect you?

Meso: How do subcultures and counter cultures shape the character of the nation and influence your own life?

Macro: How do social structures at the national level impact you and how can you influence those national structures?

Macro: Why do people live so differently in various parts of the world, and how can those differences be relevant to your own people?

Macro: Global Community

Macro: Society

Meso: National Organizations, Institutions, and Ethnic Subcultures

Micro: Local Organizations and Community

Me (and My Closest Associates)

Microculture: Your family; a college sorority chapter; a local Boy Scout troop; a high school baseball team

National Institutions: Education; state governments

Organizations: Red Cross; Ford Motor Company; political party

Subcultures: Ethnic groups; distinctive religious communities (e.g., Mormons)

National Society: United States; Canadian society

National Culture: American culture; Canadian culture

Global Societies: Multinational organizations (United Nations, World Bank, World Health)

Global Culture: Standards of human rights that cross national borders

What do people around the world eat? To answer this question, researchers asked families to buy food supplies for a week. They then took pictures of families with their weekly diets laid out. The differences in these foods and what each family paid to eat give us an insight into differences in one aspect of cultures around the world.

Mrs. Ukita, the mom in the Ukita family, rises early to prepare a breakfast of miso soup and a raw egg on rice. The father and two daughters eat quickly and rush out to catch their early morning trains to work and school in Kodaira City, Japan. The mother cares for the house, does the shopping, and prepares a typical evening meal of fish, vegetables, and rice for the family.

The Ahmed family lives in a large apartment building in Cairo, Egypt. The 12 members of the extended family include the women who shop for and cook the food—vegetables including peppers, greens, potatoes, squash, tomatoes, garlic, spices, and rice along with pita bread and often fish or meat. The adult men work in shops in one of the many bazaars while the school-aged children attend school, then help with the chores.

The nine members of the Ayme family live in Tingo, Equador, high in the Andes mountains, where the main occupation of Indian families is herding and growing potatoes and other crops suited to the high altitude and cool climate. Their diet consists of foods that are readily available in the market: plantains, potatoes, onions, carrots, and grains.

In the Breidjing refugee camp in Chad, many Sudanese refugees eat what relief agencies can get to them—and that food source is not always reliable. Typical for the Aboubakar family, a mother and five children, is rice or other grain, oil for cooking, occasionally some root plants or squash that keep longer than fresh fruits and vegetables, dried legumes, and a

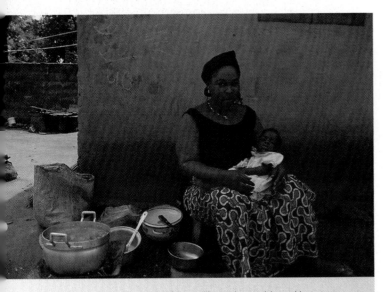

Meal preparation in many African villages is outside and is a communal affair.

few spices. The girls and women go into the desert to fetch firewood for cooking and to get water from whatever source has water at the time. This is a dangerous trip as they may be attacked and raped or even killed outside of the camps.

In Sicily, the Manzo family—mother, father, and three young boys—enjoy fresh bread from the baker for breakfast and often have pasta with sauce and vegetables and fish or meat for dinner. Typically, the father works in the family orchard while the mother takes care of the house and the boys go to school, helping with chores after school.

Although most diets include some form of grain and starch, locally available fruits and vegetables, and perhaps meat or fish, broad variations in food consumption exist even within one society. Yet all of these differences have something in common: Each represents a society that has a unique culture that includes what people eat. **Culture** consists of ideas and "things" that are passed on from one generation to the next in a society—the knowledge, beliefs, values, rules or laws, language, customs, symbols, and material products (such as food, houses, and transportation) that help meet human needs. Culture provides guidelines for living. Learning our culture helps us to get a "fix" on the world and where we fit within it, to put our social world in an understandable framework, and to provide a tool kit with a variety of "tools" we can draw on to help us construct the meaning of our world and who we are within that world (Bruner 1996; Nagel 1994).

A **society** consists of individuals who live together in a specific geographic area, who interact more with each other than they do with outsiders and cooperate for the attainment of common goals. Each society includes key institutions—such as family, education, religion, politics, economics, and health—that meet basic human needs. Members of a society share a common culture over time. The way people think and behave in any society is largely prescribed by its culture, which is reshaped, learned, and transmitted from generation to generation. All activities in the society, whether educating young members, preparing and eating dinner, selecting leaders for the group, finding a mate, or negotiating with other societies, are guided by cultural rules and expectations. In each society, culture provides the social rules for how individuals carry out necessary tasks, just as software provides the rules for computer applications.

While culture provides the "software" for the way people live, society represents the "hardware"—the structure that gives organization and stability to group life. Society—organized groups of people—and culture—their way of life—are interdependent. The two are not the same thing, but they cannot exist without each other, just as computer hardware and software are each useless without the other.

This chapter explores the ideas of society and culture and discusses how they relate to each other. We will look at what society is and how it is organized, how it influences and is influenced by culture, what culture is, how and why culture develops, the components that make up culture, cultural theories, and policy issues. After reading this chapter we will have a better idea of how we as individuals fit into society and learn our culture.

Society: The Hardware

All societies have geographical boundaries or borders and individuals who live together in families and communities and who share a culture. The structures that make up society include the interdependent positions we hold (parents, workers), the groups to which we belong (family, work group, clubs), and the institutions in which we participate. This "hardware" (structure) of our social world provides the framework for "software" (culture) to function.

Societies also exist in place and time and change over time. Human societies have become more complex over time, but people have been hunters and gatherers for 99% of human existence. A few groups remain hunter-gatherers today. As Table 3.1 illustrates, if all of human history were compressed into the lifetime of an 80-year-old person, humans would have started cultivating crops and herding animals for food supply only a few months ago. Note the incredible rate of change that has occurred just in the past two centuries.

Thinking Sociologically

What major changes took place in your grandparents' lifetimes that affect the way you and your family live today? You may want to look at the timeline inside the cover of this book.

Societies are organized in particular patterns that this chapter explores, patterns that are shaped by a range of factors including the way people procure food, availability of resources, contact with other societies, and cultural beliefs. For example, people can change from herding to farming only if they have the knowledge, skills, and desire to do so and only in environments that will support agriculture. As societies develop, changes take place in the social structures and relationships between people that characterize each type of society. For example, in industrialized societies, relationships between people typically must become more formal because people must interact with strangers and not just relatives. It is important to note that not all societies go through all stages. Some are jolted into the future by political events or changes in the global system, and some resist pressures to become modernized and continue to live in simpler social systems.

A Chinese family sits outside on the ground enjoying a home-cooked meal.

Increasingly in the United States, where both parents work, dinner is a fast-food takeout or ready-to-cook packaged meal—a quick dash for nourishment in front of the TV rather than a communal event.

Evolution of Societies

The Saharan desert life for the Taureg tribe is pretty much as it has been for centuries. In simple traditional societies, individuals are assigned to comparatively few social positions or statuses. Today, however, few societies are isolated from global impact. Even the Taureg are called on to escort adventurous tourists through the desert for a currency unknown to them and unneeded until recently.

Table 3.1   One Million Years of Human History Compressed Into One 80-Year Lifetime

Year	Age	Event
2,500,000 years ago	Birth	*Homo habilis* is born—the first ancestor to make/use tools and have culture. Evidence of sharing food, congregating, and probably sharing housing.
2 million years ago	2 years old	*Homo erectus* shows early evidence of family structures. Findings of longer life spans and three generations alive simultaneously.
15,000 years ago	79 years old	6 months ago: North America settled by early humans, hunters and gatherers.
11,000 years ago	79 years old	5 months ago: In the Middle East, first agricultural communities indicating food cultivation.
10,000 years ago	79 years old	20 weeks ago: The last ice age is over. Humans spread more widely over the planet.
5,000 years ago	79 years old	10 weeks ago: Humans began to cast and use metals and built the pyramids.
2,000 years ago	79 years old	7 weeks ago: Beginning of the Common Era (under the Holy Roman Empire).
220 years ago	79 years old	2½ weeks ago: The United States began a new experiment with democracy.
100 years ago	79 years old	Yesterday morning: The airplane was invented.
30 years ago	79 years old	Yesterday afternoon: Humans first set foot on the moon. After dinner, we broke the DNA (genetic) code.
12 AM today	80th birthday	The 21st century with new technologies. Futurists predict that this century will see stem-cell breakthroughs, worldwide use of cell phones, nanotechnology, alternative energy sources (especially wind and solar), brain computer interfaces for disabled, travel to the moon, and much more . . . stay tuned!

Source: Data from Relethford 2008.

In such traditional societies, men teach their sons everything they need to know, for all men do much the same jobs, depending on where they live—hunting, fishing, or farming and protecting the community from danger. Likewise, girls learn their jobs from their mothers—such as child care, fetching water, food preparation, farming, weaving, and perhaps house building. By contrast, more complex societies, such as industrial or "modern" societies, have thousands of interdependent statuses based on complex divisions of labor with designated tasks. The interesting question is how traditional societies change into new types of societies.

Émile Durkheim (1893–1947), an early French sociologist, pictured a continuum between simple and complex societies. He described simple premodern societies as held together by *mechanical solidarity*—common beliefs, values, and emotional ties. Furthermore, the division of labor is based largely on male/female distinctions and age groupings. Members of premodern societies tend to think the same way on important matters, and everyone fulfills his or her expected social positions. This provides the glue that holds the society together. The entire society may involve only a few hundred people, with no meso-level institutions, organizations, and subcultures. Prior to the emergence of nation-states, there was no macro level either—only tribal groupings.

According to Durkheim, as societies transformed, they became more complex through increasingly complex divisions of labor and changes in the ways people carried out necessary tasks for survival. Societies in which social positions are specialized and interdependent are held together by *organic solidarity*. Prior to the factory system, for example, individual cobblers made shoes to order. With the Industrial Revolution, factories took over the process, with many individuals carrying out interdependent tasks. The division of labor is critical because it leads to new forms of social cohesion based on interdependence, not emotional ties. Changes from mechanical (traditional) to organic (modern) society also involve harnessing new forms of energy and finding more efficient ways to use them (Nolan and Lenski 2008). For example, the use of steam engines and coal for fuel triggered the Industrial Revolution, leading to the development of industrial societies.

Also, as societies changed, they developed more levels, and the meso level—institutions and large bureaucratic organizations—became more influential. Still, as recently as 200 years ago, even large societies had little global interdependence, and life for the typical citizen was influenced mostly by events at the micro and meso levels. Keep in mind that it was just over 200 years ago when American colonies selected representatives to form a loosely federated government that came to be called the United States.

As you read about each of the following types of societies, from the simplest to most complex, notice the presence of these variables: division of labor, interdependence of

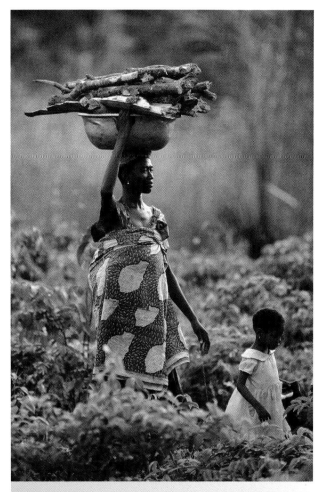

A mother in Côte d'Ivoire (West Africa), carrying her load on her head, returns to the village with her daughter after gathering wood. Carrying wood and water is typically women's work. In this society, the primary social cohesion is mechanical solidarity.

people's positions, increasingly advanced technologies, and new forms and uses of energy. Although none of these variables appears *sufficient* to trigger evolution to a new type of society, they may all be *necessary* for a transition to occur.

According to Durkheim, then, in traditional societies with mechanical solidarity, interpersonal interaction and community life at the micro level were the most important aspects of social life. Meso and macro-level societies developed as a result of changes toward more organic solidarity. As societies become more complex, meso- and macro-level institutions become more important and have more profound impacts on the lives of individuals.

Hunter-Gatherer Societies

From the beginning of human experience until recently, hunting and gathering (or foraging) were the sole means of sustaining life. Other types of societies emerged only

Masai men in Kenya herd their cattle, leading them to water or better grazing. The strategy of domesticating cattle rather than hunting game has been a survival strategy for the Masai, but it also affects the culture in many other ways.

recently (Nolan and Lenski 2008), and today, only a handful of societies still rely on hunting and gathering.

In the Kalahari Desert of Southwest Africa live hunter-gatherers known as the !Kung. (The ! is pronounced with a click of the tongue.) The !Kung live a nomadic life, moving from one place to another as food supplies become available or are used up. As a result, they carry few personal possessions and live in temporary huts, settling around water holes for a few months at a time. Settlements are small, rarely more than 20 to 50 people, for food supplies are not great enough to support large, permanent populations (Lee 1984). !Kung women gather groundnuts and other edible plant matter, while !Kung men hunt. Beyond division of labor by gender and age, however, there are few differences in roles or status.

Life is organized around kinship ties and reciprocity for the well-being of the whole community. When a large animal is killed, people gather from a wide area to share in the bounty, and great care is taken to ensure that the meat is distributed fairly. Resources are shared among the people, but sharing is regulated by a complex system of mutual obligations. A visitor who eats food at another's hearth is expected to repay that hospitality in the future.

The !Kung are a typical **hunter-gatherer society**, in which people rely directly on plants and animals in their habitat to live. People make their clothing, shelter, and tools from available materials and through trade with other nearby groups. People migrate seasonally to new food sources. Population size remains small as the number of births and deaths are balanced.

Today, the hunter-gatherer lifestyle is becoming extinct. For example, much of the wild game on which the !Kung subsisted has been overhunted or is now protected on game preserves. The governments of South Africa and Botswana have attempted to settle the groups on reservations, and contacts with the macro-level societies, by choice and by force, have forever changed the !Kung way of life and that of other hunting and gathering societies.

Herding and Horticultural Societies

The Masai inhabit the grasslands of Kenya and Tanzania, depending on their herds for survival. Their cattle and goats provide meat, milk, blood (which they drink), and hides. A seminomadic herding society, the Masai move camp to find grazing land for their animals and set up semipermanent shelters for the few months they will remain in one area. Settlements consist of huts constructed in a circle with a perimeter fence surrounding the compound. At the more permanent settlements, the Masai grow short-term crops to supplement their diet. The Masai are under some pressure to become agriculturalists, however, as the government of Kenya—a relatively new macro-level influence in their lives—now restricts their territory and herding practices that encroach on wild animal refuges. Tourism also greatly influences their economy.

Herding societies have food-producing strategies based on keeping herds of domesticated animals, whose care is the central focus of their activities. Domesticating animals has replaced hunting them. In addition to providing food and other products, cattle, sheep, goats, pigs, horses, and camels represent forms of wealth on which further changes in roles and status may be built.

Horticultural societies keep domesticated animals but focus on primitive agriculture or gardening. Horticulturalists use digging sticks and wooden hoes to cultivate tree crops, such as date palms or bananas, and to plant and maintain produce in garden plots, such as yams, beans, taro, squash, or corn. This is more efficient than gathering wild vegetables and fruits.

Both herding and horticultural societies differ from hunter-gatherer societies in that they make their living by cultivating food and have some control over its production (Ward and Edelstein 2006).

The ability to control food sources was a major turning point in human history. Societies became more settled and built surpluses of food, which led to increases in population size. A community could contain as many as 3,000 individuals. More people, surplus food, and greater accumulation of possessions encouraged the development of private property and created new status differences between individuals and families. Forms of social inequality became even more pronounced in agricultural societies.

The end of the horticultural stage saw advances in irrigation systems, fertilization of land, and crop rotation. The Neolithic Revolution, occurring as early as 14,500 years ago in Egypt, 10,000 years ago in Melanesia, and 9,000 to 7,000 years ago in the Middle East Fertile Crescent and many parts of Asia, was characterized by more permanent settlements, land ownership, human modification of the natural environment, higher population density (cities), changes in diets to more vegetables and cereals, and power hierarchies. However, the technological breakthrough that moved many societies into the agricultural stage was the plow, introduced more than 6,000 years ago. It marked the beginning of the agricultural revolution in Europe, the Middle East, and other parts of the world, and it brought massive changes in social structures to many societies.

Agricultural Societies

Pedro and Lydia Ramirez, their four young children, and Lydia's parents live as an extended family in a small farming village in Nicaragua. They rise early, and while Pedro heads for the fields to do some work before breakfast, Lydia prepares his breakfast and lunch and sees that their eldest son is up and ready to go to school, while Lydia's mother looks after the younger children. After school, the boy also helps in the fields. Most of the land in the area is owned by a large company that grows coffee, but the Ramirez family is fortunate to have a small garden plot of its own where they grow some vegetables for themselves. At harvest time, all hands help, including young children. The families receive cash for the crops they have grown, minus rent for the land. The land is plowed with the help of strong animals such as horses and oxen, and fertilizers are used. Little irrigation is attempted, although the garden plots may be watered by hand in the dry season.

The Ramirez's way of life is typical of that in an agricultural society. Like horticulturalists, agrarian farmers rely primarily on raising crops for food. However, **agricultural societies** are more efficient than horticulture: Technological advances such as the plow, irrigation, use of animals, and fertilization allow intensive and continuous cultivation of the same land, thus permitting permanent settlements and greater food surpluses. Through time, as increasingly sophisticated agricultural technology resulted in surplus food, the size of population centers increased to as much as a million or more.

As surpluses accumulated, land in some societies became concentrated in the hands of a few individuals. Wealthy landowners built armies and expanded their empires. During these periods, controlling land took precedence over technological advance. War was prevalent, and societies were divided increasingly into rich and poor classes. Those who held the land and wealth could control the labor sources and acquire serfs or slaves. Thus, the feudal system was born. Serfs (the peasant class) were forced to work the land for their survival. Food surpluses also allowed some individuals to leave the land and to trade goods or services in exchange for food. For the first time, social inequality became extensive enough that we can refer to social classes. At this point, religion, political

A fair trade coffee farmer ("fair trade" means no slavery was used in the production, and workers were paid a fair price) picks organic coffee beans in Central America. Producing a crop for cash exchange, rather than growing something to eat locally, is the normal pattern in an agricultural society.

power, a standing army, and other meso-level institutions and organizations came to be independent of the family. The meso-level became well established.

As technology advanced, goods were manufactured in cities and peasants moved from farming communities where land could not support the population, to rapidly growing urban areas, where the demand for labor was great. It was not until the mid-1700s in England that the next major transformation of society took place, resulting largely from technological advances and harnessing of energy.

Industrial Societies

The Industrial Revolution brought the harnessing of steam power and gasoline engines, permitting machines to replace human and animal power; a tractor can plow far more land in a week than a horse, and an electric pump can irrigate more acres than an ox-driven pump. As a result of the new technologies, raw mineral products, such as ores, raw plant products, such as rubber, and raw animal products, such

Industrialization brought major changes in social organization and in culture as production was removed from families to companies with highly organized processes controlled by capitalists.

as hides, could be transformed into mass-produced consumer goods. The Industrial Revolution brought enormous changes in products and social structures.

Industrial societies rely primarily on mechanized production for subsistence, resulting in greater division of labor based on expertise. Economic resources were distributed more widely among individuals in industrial societies, but inequities between owners and laborers persisted. Wage earning gradually replaced slavery and serfdom, and highly skilled workers earned higher wages, leading to the rise of a middle class. Farm workers moved from rural areas to cities to find work in factories, which produced consumer goods such as cars and washing machines. Cities come to be populated by millions of people.

Family and kinship patterns at the micro level also changed. Agricultural societies need large, land-based extended family units to do the work of farming (recall how the Ramirez parents, grandparents, and children in Nicaragua all help out at harvest time), but industrial societies need individuals with specific skills and smaller families to support. Family roles changed. For example, children are an asset in agrarian societies and begin farm work at an early age. In an industrial society, however, children become a liability because they contribute less to the finances of the family and ultimately compete with their parents for jobs.

Meso- and macro-level dimensions of social life expand in industrializing societies and become more influential in the lives of individuals. National institutions and multinational organizations develop. Today, for example, global organizations such as the World Bank, the World Court, the United Nations, and the World Health Organization address social problems and sometimes even make decisions that

change national boundaries or national policies. Medical organizations such as Doctors Without Borders work cross-nationally; corporations become multinational; and voluntary associations such as Amnesty International lobby for human rights around the globe.

Perhaps the most notable characteristic of the industrial age is the rapid rate of change compared to other stages of societal development. The beginning of industrialization in Europe was gradual, based on years of population movement, urbanization, technological development, and other factors in modernization. Today, however, societal change occurs so rapidly that societies at all levels of development are being drawn together into a new age—the postindustrial era.

Postindustrial or Information Societies

The difference between India and the United States is "night and day"—literally. As Keith and Jeanne finished chapters for this book, they were sent to India in the evening and returned typeset by morning, a feat made possible by the time differences. Efficiency of overnight delivery and cost of production have led many publishing companies to turn to businesses halfway around the world for much of the book production process. As India and other developing countries increase their trained, skilled labor force, they are being called on by national and multinational companies to carry out global manufacturing processes. India has some of the world's best technical training institutes and the most modern **technology**—that is, knowledge and tools used to extend human abilities. Although many people in India live in poverty, a relatively new middle class is rapidly emerging in major business centers around the country.

After World War II, starting in the 1950s, the transition from industrial to postindustrial society began in the United States, Western Europe (especially Germany), and Japan. This shift was characterized by movement from human labor to automated production and from a predominance of manufacturing jobs to a growth in service jobs, such as computer operators, bankers, scientists, teachers, public relations workers, stockbrokers, and salespeople. More than two thirds of all jobs in the United States now reside in organizations that produce and transmit information, thus the reference to an "information age." Daniel Bell (1973) describes this transformation of work, information, and communication as "the third technological revolution" after industrialization based on steam (what he calls the first technological revolution) and the invention of electricity (the second technological revolution). According to Bell, the third technological revolution was the development of the computer, which has led to this Postindustrial or Information Age.

As in the other types of society, **postindustrial societies** are undergoing significant structural changes. For example, postindustrial societies require workers with high levels of technical and professional education, such as those in India. Those without technical education are less likely to find rewarding employment in the technological revolution

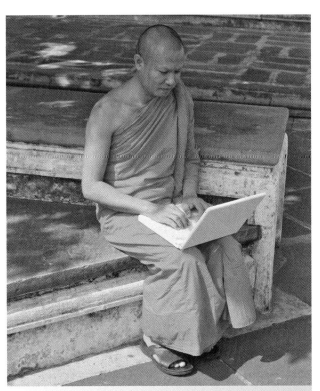

This Buddhist monk uses modern technology, including a laptop that can connect him with colleagues on the other side of the globe.

Hybrid buses have been adopted in some cities and in national parks because of the effects of pollution on the globe and its occupants.

(Tapscott 1998). This results in new class lines being drawn, based in part on skills and education in new technologies. Inequalities in access to education and technology will create or perpetuate social inequalities. In 2003, for example, 62% of households in the United States had one or more computers, and 88% of computer users had Internet access (U.S. Census Bureau 2005b). Use of computers in 2004 by adults ages 18 to 27 was 85%, ages 28 to 39 was 87%, ages 40 to 49 was 84%, ages 50 to 58 was 76%, 59 to 68 was 57%, and age 69 and older was 24%. Note the decline in use with end of work years and among earlier generations, who had less—or no—access to computers when they were growing up. Women and men are about equal among users, at 73%. Among English-speaking Hispanics, 75% use computers, whites 73%, and blacks 62%. Computer usage grows as household incomes and education become greater, with more than 90% of households above $50,000 using computers (Pew Internet and American Life Project 2004).

Postindustrial societies rely on new sources of power such as atomic, wind, and solar energy and new uses of computer automation, such as computer-controlled robots, which eliminate the need for human labor other than highly skilled technicians. In an age of global climate change, there is also a lot of concern about technologies that reduce pollution, as the photo of the hybrid bus illustrates. The core issue in a postindustrial society is this: Control of information and ability to develop technologies or provide services rather than control of money or capital become most important.

Values of 21st-century postindustrial societies favor scientific and creative approaches to problem solving, research, and development, along with attitudes that support the globalization of world economies. Satellites, cell phones, fiber optics, and especially the Internet are further transforming postindustrial societies of the Information Age.

One sociologist is studying the relationship of creativity to local cultural climate and to economic prosperity. His research has important applied dimensions. "The Applied Sociologist at Work" explores this fascinating research and explains why it is important to policymakers in local communities. As Richard Florida's research makes clear, the organization of the society and the means of providing the necessities of life have a profound impact on values, beliefs, lifestyle, and other aspects of culture.

Thinking Sociologically

What are likely to be the growth areas for jobs in your society? What competencies and skills will be essential in the future for you to find employment and be successful on the job?

What will the future bring? Futurologists predict new trends based on current activities, predictions of new advances and technologies, and inventions on the horizon. Among the many ideas for the future, technological advances dominate the field. Predictions include use of cell phones, connecting the poorest corners of the globe with

The Applied Sociologist at Work— Richard Florida

Creativity, Community, and Applied Sociology

Like the transformations of societies from the hunter-gatherer to the horticultural stage or from the agricultural to the industrial stage, our own current transformation seems to have created a good deal of "cultural wobble" in the society. How does one identify the elements or the defining features of a new age while the transformation is still in process? This was one of the questions that intrigued sociologist Richard Florida, who studied U.S. communities.

Dr. Florida (2002) combined several methods. First, he traveled around the country to communities that were especially prosperous and seemed to be on the cutting edge of change in U.S. society. In these communities, he did both individual interviews and focus-group interviews. Focus-group interviews are semistructured group interviews with seven or eight people where ideas can be generated from the group by asking open-ended questions. Professor Florida recorded the discussion and analyzed the transcript of the discussion. The collected data helped Professor Florida identify the factors that caused people to choose the place where they decided to live. His informants discussed quality of life and the way they make decisions. As certain themes and patterns emerged, he tested the ideas by comparing statistical data for regions that were vibrant, had growing economies, and seemed to be integrated into the emerging information economy. He used another method to compare communities and regions of the country— analyzing already existing archival data collected by various U.S. government agencies, especially the U.S. Bureau of Labor Statistics and the U.S. Census Bureau.

Florida argues that the economy of the 21st century is largely driven by creativity, and creative people often decide where to live based on certain features of the society. Currently, more than one third of the jobs in the United States—and almost all of the extremely well-paid professional positions—require creative thinking. These include not just the creative arts but scientific research, computer and mathematical occupations, educational and library science positions, and many media, legal, and managerial careers. People in this "creative class" are given an enormous amount of autonomy; in their work, they have problems to solve and freedom to figure out how to do so. Florida found that modern businesses flourish when they hire highly creative people. Thus, growing businesses tend to seek out places where creative people locate.

Through his research, Florida identified regions and urban areas that are especially attractive to the creative class. Florida's research led him to collaborate with Gary Gates, a scholar who was doing research on communities that are open and hospitable to gays and lesbians. Gates and Florida were amazed to find that their lists were nearly identical. Florida found that creative people thrive on diversity—ethnic, gender, religious, and otherwise—for when creative people are around others who think differently, it tends to spawn new avenues of thinking and problem solving. Tolerance of difference and even the enjoyment of individual idiosyncrasies is a hallmark of thriving communities. Interestingly, Florida is now very much in demand as a consultant to mayors and urban-planning teams, and his books have become required reading for city council members. Some elected officials have decided that fostering an environment conducive to creativity that attracts creative people leads to prosperity because business will follow. Key elements for creative communities are local music and art festivals, the presence of organic food grocery stores, legislation that encourages interesting mom–and-pop stores (and keeps out large "box stores" that crush such small and unique endeavors), encouragement of quaint locally owned bookstores and distinctive coffee shops, provisions for bike and walking paths throughout the town, and ordinances that establish an environment of tolerance for people who are "different."

Note: Richard Florida heads the Prosperity Institute at the Rotman School of Management at the University of Toronto. He also runs a private Creative Class Institute. He earned his bachelor's degree from Rutgers College and his doctorate in Urban Planning from Columbia University.

the rest of the world. One billion mobile phone users are predicted for China by 2020, with 80% of the population having phones. Alternative energy sources from wind and solar power to hydrogen will replace gasoline. One million hydrogen-fueled cars are predicted for the United States. Rechargeable batteries that will run for 40 hours without recharging will run most home appliances by 2030. Those who are paralyzed will find help from Brain Computer Interfaces, giving them ability to control their environments. Many advances will occur in space travel; a hotel may open on the moon by 2025, with transport to the moon. Medical advances will result in stem-cell breakthroughs that can develop into various types of body tissue (Future for All 2008; News of Future 2007). These are just a few of the many predictions that will affect societies and alter some human interactions. The point is that rapid change is inevitable, and the future looks exciting.

In much of this book, we focus on complex, multilevel society, for this is the type of system in which most of us reading this book now live. We turn next to a discussion of the social software that complements the hardware of our society.

Culture: The Software

I sleep on a bed. Perhaps you sleep on a tatami mat. I brush my teeth with a toothbrush and toothpaste. Perhaps you chew on a special stick to clean your teeth. I speak English, along with 514 million native English speakers. You may speak one of the many other languages in the world, as do over one billion Mandarin Chinese speakers, 495 million Hindustani speakers, or 425 million Spanish speakers (Information Please 2008). I like meat and veggies. Perhaps you like tofu and grasshoppers. I wear jeans and a T-shirt. Perhaps you wear a sari or burqa. In the United States, proper greetings include a handshake, a wave, or saying "hello" or "hi." The greeting ceremony in Japan includes bowing, with the depth of the bow defined by the relative status of each individual. To know the proper bowing behavior, Japanese business people who are strangers exchange business cards on introduction. Their titles, as printed on their cards, disclose each person's status and thus provide clues as to how deeply each should bow. The proper greeting behavior in many European countries calls for men as well as women to kiss acquaintances on both cheeks.

The point of these examples is to show that the culture—the ideas and "things" that are passed on from one generation to the next in a society, including their knowledge, beliefs, values, rules and laws, language, customs, symbols, and material products—varies greatly as we travel the globe. Each social unit of cooperating and interdependent people, whether at the micro, meso, or macro level, develops a unique way of life. This culture provides guidelines for the actions and interaction of individuals and groups within the society. The cultural guidelines that people follow when they greet another person are examples.

As you can see, the sociological definition of culture refers to far more than "high culture"—such as fine art, classical music, opera, literature, ballet, or theater, and also far more than "popular culture"—such as heavy metal, reality TV, professional wrestling, YouTube, and other mass entertainment. In fact, much of pop culture has been shaped by technology, as is illustrated in the next "Sociology in Your Social World." The sociological definition of culture includes both high culture and pop culture and has a much broader meaning besides.

Thinking Sociologically

Do you think technology and the spread of pop culture are bringing the world closer together as communication and ideas are shared globally, or might it cause tensions as societies attempt to protect their citizens against fraud, pornography, and misuse of technology?

Everyone shares a culture with others, although there may be different views within and between cultures about what rules and behaviors are most important. No one could survive without culture, for without culture, there would be no guidelines or rules of behavior. Societies would be chaotic masses of individuals. Culture provides the routines, patterns, and expectations for carrying out daily rituals and interactions. Within a society, the process of learning how to act is called socialization (discussed in detail in Chapter 4). From birth, we learn the patterns of behavior approved in our society.

Culture evolves over time and is adaptive. What is normal, proper, and good behavior in hunter-gatherer societies, where cooperation and communal loyalty is critical to the hunt, differs from appropriate behavior in an information age, where individualism and competition may be encouraged and enhance one's well-being.

The creation of culture is ongoing and cumulative because individuals and societies continually build on existing culture to adapt to new challenges and opportunities. The behaviors, values, and institutions that seem natural to you are actually shaped by your culture. Culture is so much a part of life that you may not even notice behaviors that outsiders find unusual or even abhorrent. You may not think about touching someone on the head, putting a baby in a crib, or picking up food with your left hand, but in some other cultures, such acts may be defined as inappropriate or morally wrong.

The transmission of culture is the feature that most separates humans from other animals. Some societies of higher primates have shared cultures but do not systematically enculturate (teach a way of life to) the next generation. Primate cultures focus on behaviors relating to food getting, use of territory, and social status. Human cultures have significantly more content and are mediated by language. Humans are the only mammals with cultures that enable them to adapt to and even modify their environments so they can survive on the equator, in the Arctic, or even beyond the planet.

Sociology in Your Social World

Pop Culture and Technology

How surprising to think that digital telephones, high-speed lines for computers, digitized print media, and the World Wide Web have all occurred within about the past half century. Vinyl records, dial telephones, and VHS videos have been surpassed by CDs, high-speed cell phones, and DVDs. Slim laptops and hand-held computers are rapidly replacing bulky desktop computers. The following timeline shows the rapid advances of Internet and World Wide Web in recent years; the point of this timeline is to illustrate the rapid advance of technology and the place it holds in our lives. Technology is now a primary conveyer of pop culture.

An Internet and World Wide Web Timeline

1844:	The telegraph constitutes a data network forerunner.
1866:	Transoceanic telegraph service begins.
1876:	The telephone is introduced.
1915:	The first transcontinental phone call is made.
1946:	ENIAC, the first general-purpose computer, is developed for military purposes.
1951:	UNIVAC becomes the first civilian computer.
1962:	The first communications satellite and the first digital phone networks are introduced.
1965:	A highly usable computer language, BASIC, is developed.
1969:	The U.S. Department of Defense launches Arpanet, the first communications network.
1971:	Microprocessors are developed, making possible personal computer technology.
1972:	First video game, *Pong*, is introduced. E-mail is developed on Arpanet for military use.
1975:	The first personal computer, Altair, is launched.
1977:	The first fiber optic network is created.
1978:	Cellular phone service begins.
1980s:	Hypertext is developed in the mid-1980s, making possible the eventual creation of the World Wide Web.
1982:	The National Science Foundation sponsors a high-speed communications network, leading to the Internet.
1983:	Modifications of Arpanet make possible the launching of the Internet.
1984:	Apple Macintosh introduces the first PC with graphics.

1989:	A new company called AOL (America Online)—the first successful Internet service provider—is formed.
1990:	The first Internet search engine, Archie, is developed.
1991:	The Internet opens to commercial uses, HTML is developed, and the Web is finally launched.
1993:	The first point-and-click Web browser, Mosaic, is introduced.
1994:	The first Internet cafes open. Jeff Bezos launches Amazon.com.
1995:	Digital cellular phones are introduced. The first online auction house, eBay, is launched.
1996:	Google makes its debut.
2000:	Cookies technology allows for information profiles to be created, enabling data mining.
2001:	Instant messaging services expand to allow exchanges between different service providers.
2002:	Broadband technology is developed in South Korea.
Mid-2000s and continuing:	The Internet converges with previous media (radio, television, etc.) to produce online versions of all media forms. It also becomes a source of new forms of communication, including Web sites such as MySpace, Facebook, and YouTube.

The continuing rapid advances in technology have paralleled development of shared pop culture in the United States and around the world, culture that is accessible to everyone, not just the elite. Music groups from Africa, Asia, the Middle East, and Europe have gained audiences in the United States and vice versa. New musical groups can become instant success stories through YouTube. Push technology or Webcasting allows audio and video presentations on demand, and streaming allows for people around the world to listen to broadcasts on the Internet. The spread of pop culture—music, mass art, fashion, books, you name it—has been made possible by advances in technology.

We know that "there is no turning back the clock once an innovation is introduced that makes communication more rapid, cheap, efficient, and broadly accessible" (Danesi 2008:21). The question is how these rapid changes will affect cultures and what they will mean for our futures.

Thinking Sociologically

Try playing a game of cards with four people in which each player thinks a different suit is trump. (Trump is a rule that any card from the trump suit wins over any card from a different suit.) In this game, one person believes hearts is trump, another assumes spades is trump, and so forth. What would happen? How would the result be similar to a society with no common culture?

Real and Ideal Culture

Culture is manifested in two ways. **Ideal culture** consists of practices, beliefs, and values that are regarded as most desirable and are consciously taught to children. Not everyone, however, follows the approved cultural patterns. **Real culture** refers to the way things in society are actually done. For the most part, we hardly question these practices and beliefs that we see around us. Rather like animals who have always lived in a rain forest and cannot imagine a treeless desert, we often fail to notice how our culture helps us to make sense of things. Because of this, we do not recognize the gap between what we tell ourselves about ourselves and what we actually do.

For example, the ideal in many societies is to ban extramarital sex. Sex outside marriage can raise questions of paternity and inheritance, besides leading to spousal jealousy and family conflict. Historically, prohibitions against extramarital sex are commonly found in societies where women are viewed as the sexual property of men. In reality, however, extramarital sex occurs to some extent in all societies. In the United States, about one fourth of all married men and one in seven married women report that they have had at least one extramarital affair (Newman and Grauerholz 2002). So while we claim that we believe in marital fidelity and this is at the core of family morality, actual behavior is frequently a bit different.

Ethnocentrism and Cultural Relativity

As scientists, sociologists must rely on careful use of the scientific method to understand behavior. The scientific method calls for objectivity, the practice of considering observed behavior independently of one's own beliefs and values. The study of social behavior thus requires both sensitivity to a wide variety of human social patterns and a perspective that reduces bias. This is more difficult than it sounds because sociologists themselves are products of society and culture. All of us are raised in a particular culture that we view as normal or natural. Yet, not every culture views the same things as "normal."

The Arapesh of New Guinea, a traditional and stable society, encourage premarital sex. It is a way for a girl to

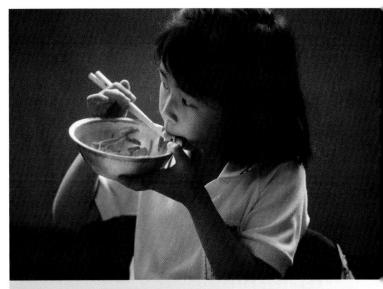

This Japanese schoolgirl might think that eating with a fork or spoon is quite strange. She has been well socialized to know that polite eating involves competent use of chopsticks.

prove her fertility, which makes her more attractive as a potential marriage partner (Mead [1935] 1963). Any babies born out of wedlock are simply absorbed into the girl's extended family. The baby's care, support, belonging, and lineage are not major issues for the Arapesh. The babies are simply accepted and welcomed as new members of the mother's family because the structure is able to absorb them. For the Arapesh, sexual behavior outside of marriage is not a moral issue. Other societies, such as the Bontoc of the Philippines, have similar views.

From studies of 154 societies documented in the *Human Relations Area Files* (Ford 1970; a source of comparative information on many traditional societies around the world), scientists have found that about 42% of the 154 included societies encourage premarital sex, whereas 29% forbid such behavior and punish those who disobey this rule. The remainder fall in between. As you can see, social values, beliefs, and behaviors can vary dramatically from one society to the next. Differences can be threatening and even offensive because most people judge others according to their own perspectives, experiences, and values.

The tendency to view one's own group and its cultural expectations as right, proper, and superior to others is called **ethnocentrism.** If you were brought up in a society that forbids premarital or extramarital sex, for instance, you might judge the Arapesh—or many Americans—to be immoral. In a few Muslim societies, people who violate this taboo may be severely punished, or even executed, because premarital sex is seen as an offense against the faith and the family and as a weakening of social bonds. In turn, the Arapesh would find rules of abstinence to be strange and even wrong.

Societies instill some degree of ethnocentrism in their members because ethnocentric beliefs hold groups together

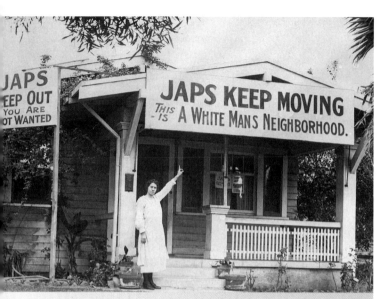

In 1923, the Hollywood Association started a campaign to expel the Japanese from their community. Signs like these were prominent throughout Hollywood and other California communities. They illustrate ethnocentrism.

and help members feel that they belong to the group. Ethnocentrism promotes loyalty, unity, high morale, and conformity to the rules of society. Fighting for one's country, for instance, requires some degree of belief in the rightness of one's own society and its causes. Ethnocentric attitudes also help to protect societies from rapid, disintegrating change. If most people in a society did not believe in the rules and values of their own culture, the result could be widespread dissent, deviance, or crime.

Ethnocentrism can take many forms (see, for example, how you react to Map 3.1). Unfortunately, ethnocentrism often leads to misunderstandings between people of different cultures. In addition, the same ethnocentric attitudes that strengthen societies may also encourage hostility, racism, war, and even genocide against others—even others within the society—who are different. Virtually all societies tend to "demonize" their adversary—in movies, the news, and political speeches—while the conflict is most intense. Dehumanizing another group with labels makes it easier to torture or kill them or to perform acts of discrimination and brutality. We see this in current conflicts in Iraq in which both sides in the conflict feel hatred for the other combatants.

Map 3.1   "Southside Up" Global Map

Source: Map by Anna Versluis.

Note: This map illustrates geographic ethnocentrism. Americans tend to assume it is natural that the north should always be "on top." The fact that this upside-down map of the world, where south is "up," looks incorrect or disturbing is a consequence of an ethnocentric view of the world. Most peoples think of their countries or regions as occupying a more central and larger part of the world.

However, as we become a part of a global social world, it becomes increasingly important to accept those who are "different." Bigotry and attitudes of superiority do not enhance cross-national cooperation and trade—which is what the global village and globalization entail.

Ethnocentrism can lead to misunderstandings between members of different cultures. Consider the American businesspeople who go to Japan to negotiate deals and sign contracts. The Japanese way of doing business takes time. It involves getting to know the other party by socializing over drinks in the evening. It is important not to rush the deal. To the Japanese, the Americans seem pushy, too concerned about contract details rather than trust, and in too much of a hurry. Many an international business arrangement has fallen through because of such cultural misunderstandings.

U.S. foreign relations also illustrate how ethnocentrism can produce hostility. Many U.S. citizens are surprised to learn that the United States—great democracy, world power, and disseminator of food, medicine, and technological assistance to developing nations—is despised in many countries. One cause is the political dominance of the United States and the threat it poses to other people's way of life (Hertsgaard 2003). U.S. citizens are regarded by some as thinking ethnocentrically and only about their own welfare as their country exploits weaker nations. U.S. tourists are often seen as loudmouthed ignoramuses whose ethnocentric attitudes prevent them from seeing value in other cultures or from learning other languages.

Anti-U.S. demonstrations in South America, the Middle East, and Asia have brought this reality to life through television. Indeed, politicians in several Latin American and European countries have run for office on platforms aimed at reducing U.S. influence. Thus, U.S. ethnocentrism may foster anti-American ethnocentrism by people from other countries. Note that even referring to citizens of the United States as "Americans"—as though people from Canada, Mexico, or South America do not really count as Americans—is seen as ethnocentric by many people from these other countries. *America* and the *United States* are not the same thing, but many people in the United States, including some presidents, fail to make the distinction, much to the dismay of other North and South Americans.

In contrast to ethnocentrism, **cultural relativism** is a view that requires setting aside cultural and personal beliefs and prejudices to understand another group or society through the eyes of a member of that group. Instead of judging cultural practices and social behavior as good or bad according to one's own cultural practices, the goal is to be impartial in learning the purposes and consequences of practices and behaviors in the group under study. Just as we may have preferences for certain software programs to do word processing, we can recognize that other software programs are quite good, may have some features that are better than the one we use, and are ingeniously designed.

Yet, being tolerant and understanding is not always easy, and even for the most careful observer, the subtleties of other cultures can be elusive. The idea of being "on time," which is so much a part of the cultures of the United States, Canada, Japan, and parts of Europe, is a rather bizarre concept in many societies. Among many Native American people, such as the Dineh (Apache and Navajo), it is ludicrous for people to let a timepiece that one wears on one's arm—a piece of machinery—govern the way one constructs and lives life. The Dineh orientation to time—that one should do things according to a natural rhythm of the body and not according to an artificial ticking mechanism—is difficult for

In the United States, dogs are family members and are highly cherished, with dog care becoming a growth industry. In Nanking, China, dogs are valued more as a culinary delicacy and a good source of protein. If you feel a twinge of disgust, that is part of the ethnocentrism we may experience as our perspectives conflict with those elsewhere in the world.

Sociology Around the World

Evolutionary Cuisine

Early Humans' Salad Bar

This menu comes from early hominids who lived in the savannahs of eastern and southern Africa from roughly 1.5 to 5 million years ago. Everything was served raw. Cooking with fire had not been discovered.

Main Course: Nuts, birds' eggs, roots, tubers, beans, leaves, gum, sap, greens, insects, worms, grubs, termites, and seasonal berries and fruits. (90 percent of the diet.)

Raw Meat Appetizer Tray: Opportunist and gathered delicacies include small mammals, birds, reptiles, fish, shellfish, slow game, dead or dying animals, and infants of species such as antelope, pig, giraffe, or baboons when available. Bone marrow or the contents of animal heads and stomachs are delicious additions to this menu. Season with honey, rock salt, or puree of worms and insects. (10 percent of the diet.)

Ancestral Potluck Dinner

The first members of our own genus, *Homo erectus*, used these recipes from about 100,000 to 1.5 million years ago in the tropical and temperate zones of Africa and Eurasia. New technologies in fire making, advanced scavenging, and simple hunting as well as social advances in cooperation, sharing, and the gender division of labor provided some very tasty and nourishing meals for our ancestors.

Main Courses: Stew or soup made with vegetables, bird bones, roots, nuts, and foods from the Salad Bar and Raw Meat Appetizer Tray plus other gathered foods as available. Add leftovers and herbal seasonings. (80 percent of the diet.)

Outdoor Barbecue: Sizzling deer haunch, roasted rabbit, shellfish, wild boar, ox, or cattle ribs. (20 percent of the diet.)

---

many North Americans to grasp. Misunderstandings occur when those of European heritage think "Indians are always late" and jump to an erroneous conclusion that "Indians" are undependable. Native Americans, on the other hand, think whites are neurotic about letting some instrument control them (Basso 1979; Farrer 1996; Hall 1959, 1983).

An example of ethnocentrism is making judgments about what is proper food to eat and what is just not edible. While food is necessary for survival, there are widespread cultural differences in what people eat, where and how they obtain food, and how they prepare and consume it. The French revere truffles, whereas a New Guinea tribe savors grasshoppers; Europeans and Russians relish raw fish eggs (caviar); Eskimo children find seal eyeballs a treat; some Indonesians eat dog; and some Nigerians prize termites. Whether it is from another time period or another society, variations in food can be shocking to us, making it hard to understand other people and other times, as the essay above on "Sociology Around the World" illustrates. Cultural relativism requires that we shrug our shoulders and admit, "Well, they are getting vitamins, proteins, and other nutrients, and it seems to work for them."

Cultural relativism does not require that social scientists accept or agree with all the beliefs and behaviors of the societies or groups they study. Certain behaviors, such as infanticide, cannibalism, head-hunting, slavery, female genital mutilation

(removal of the clitoris), forced marriage, terrorism, or genocide may be regarded as unacceptable by almost all social scientists. Yet, it is still important to try to understand those practices in the social and cultural contexts in which they occur. Many social scientists take strong stands against violations of human rights, environmental destruction, and other social policies. They base their judgments on the concept of universal human rights and the potential for harm to human beings and to the world community. Yet, note that most Western democracies are adaptations to systems that thrive on values of extreme individualism, differentiation, and competition, consistent with very complex society. Other societies do not always think our ideas of "universal rights" are universal.

Thinking Sociologically

Small, tightly knit societies with no meso or macro level often stress cooperation, conformity, and personal sacrifice for the sake of the community. Complex societies with established meso- and macro-level linkages are more frequently individualistic, stressing personal uniqueness, individual creativity, and critical thinking. Why might this be so?

Society, Culture, and Our Social World

Whether their people are eating termite eggs, fish eggs, or chicken eggs, societies always have a culture, and culture is always linked to a society. Culture provides guidelines for each level of society, from the global system to the individual family. The social world model at the beginning of the chapter, with its concentric circles, represents the micro to macro levels of society. Smaller social units such as a school operate within larger social units such as the community, which is also part of a region of the country. What takes place in each of these units is determined by the culture. There is a social unit—a structural "hardware"—and a culture or "software" at each level.

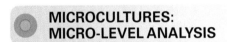

MICROCULTURES: MICRO-LEVEL ANALYSIS

Micro-level analysis focuses on social interactions in small-group or organizational settings. To apply this idea to culture, we look at microcultures. Groups and organizations such as a Girl Scout troop, or a local chapter of the Rotary Club, or participants in a Facebook chat room involve a small number of people. These organizations influence only a portion of members' lives. When the culture affects only a small segment of one's life, affecting a portion of one's week or influencing a limited time period in one's life, it is called a **microculture** (Gordon 1970). Other classic examples from sociology include a street gang, a college sorority, a business office, or a summer camp group. In fact, workplaces have been studied in some detail to explore the climate of these microcultures that we inhabit daily, as we see in the next "How Do We Know?"

Hospitals are social units with microcultures. People in different-colored uniforms scurry around carrying out their designated tasks as part of the organizational culture. Hospital workers interact among themselves to attain goals of patient care. They have a common in-group vocabulary, a shared set of values, a hierarchy of positions with roles and behaviors for each position, and a guiding system of regulations for the organization—all of which shape interactions during the hours that each member works in the hospital. Yet, the hospital culture may have little relevance to the rest of the employees' everyday lives. Microcultures may survive over time, with individuals coming in and going out from the group, but in a complex society no one lives his or her entire life within a microculture. The values, rules, and specialized language used by the hospital staff continue as one shift ends and other medical personnel enter and sustain that microculture.

When these people work together in a hospital, they share a common culture: shared terminology, rules of interaction, and values regarding objectifying human body parts so they are not sexualized. However, the hospital microculture only affects a part of each day and each week for the hospital personnel.

Every organization, club, and association has an organizational microculture—its own set of rules and expectations. Schools develop their own unique cultures with cliques and traditions; as students graduate and move out of that microculture, others move into it. Organizational microcultures may last for some time. In contrast, some microcultures exist for a limited period of time or for a special purpose. A summer camp microculture may develop but exists only for that summer. The following summer, a very different culture may evolve because of new counselors and campers. A girls' softball team may develop its own cheers, jokes, insider slang, and values regarding competition or what it means to be a good sport, but next year, the girls may be realigned into different teams, and the transitory culture of the previous year changes. In contrast to microcultures, subcultures continue across a person's life span.

SUBCULTURES AND COUNTERCULTURES: MESO-LEVEL ANALYSIS

A **subculture** is a way of life in a social unit or group that is smaller than the nation but large enough to sustain people throughout the life span. A subculture is in some ways unique to that group yet at the same time shares the culture of the dominant society (Arnold 1970; Gordon 1970). For example, one can be African Canadian, Chinese Canadian, or Hispanic Canadian, living within an ethnic community

How Do We Know?

Culture in Workplaces Around the World

By Lynn Ritchey

Think for a moment about your work environments. Some probably have been enjoyable, and some miserable. In the workplace that was most enjoyable, you might have been working for someone who valued your insights. In the miserable workplace, you may have worked for a tyrant who dictated everything and allowed no flexibility. The workplace is an environment in which most of us will have sustained interactions with people of different cultural backgrounds. With this in mind, it becomes important for us to understand the rules of how work is to be done. Professor Geert Hofstede is a social scientist who understands the impact of the culture of the workplace and also recognizes that different countries have different values when it comes to the workplace.

Between 1967 and 1973, IBM (International Business Machines) surveyed employees in 70 countries about their preferences within and outside the workplace. Surveys provide researchers with information, generally from large samples, to answer research questions. For example, the survey questionnaire used in the IBM study asked whether the employees want a job that provides sufficient time for personal life. This survey has been updated, most recently in January 2008, and administered more broadly, including airline pilots, students, and wealthy consumers. Hofstede analyzed the survey data and identified cultural dimensions and value orientations relative to the workplace in different countries. The dimensions include power distance, individualism, masculinity, and uncertainty avoidance.

The Power Distance Index (PDI) measures the degree to which less powerful people in an organization accept the unequal distribution of power in the organization. In countries with a high score on the "power distance" index, the "followers" expect that the more powerful people in the organizations will dictate what everyone else does in the workplace. The powerful do not seek input from followers. The United States has a low Power Distance Index score. This means most workers in the United States expect that they will have input into decisions about their workplace and tasks that they perform.

The Individualism Index (IDV) compares countries on whether they are more individualist or collectivist in value orientation. This dimension assesses the degree of interrelatedness between individuals. Countries scoring high on individualism, like the United States, have looser connections with groups, and the employees are working mostly for their own personal benefit. Countries with low scores on individualism are more collectivist or group oriented and work for the success of the entire group, whether it be the extended family, school community, or work group.

The Masculinity Index (MAS) measures the degree that "masculine" traits are valued in the country more than "feminine" ones. Countries scoring low in the Masculinity Index value modesty, caring, group cohesion, personal relationships, and overall quality of life. Competition is not especially valued in low masculinity countries. The United States has a high Masculinity Index score because competition and assertiveness are rewarded. We strive for success with little concern about group cohesion or personal relationships. Only the strong survive; dog eat dog.

The Uncertainty Avoidance Index (UAI) measures the degree to which a society socializes it members to feel comfortable in ambiguous settings. Countries with a high score on the Uncertainty Avoidance Index have very strict laws and rules governing most areas of life. Everyone knows what is expected, and very little is left to chance. Countries with low scores on the Uncertainty Avoidance Index, like the United States, are more accepting of ambiguous situations. There is more flexibility, creativity, and acceptance of diverse points of view.

Understanding these value orientations is important because many of us will come into contact with people from other cultures in the workplace. When we are aware of our own value orientations and the value orientations of those with whom we work, we can become more successful in our interactions and reduce the frustration and confusion we might experience when we interact with culturally different people. For example, instead of thinking your boss is a tyrant, you might come to understand that your boss is from a high power-distance country. To explore the scores for different countries, visit http://www.geert-hofstede.com/.

This type of understanding is possible because of extensive surveys that have revealed patterned differences across societies and across workplace settings.

that provides food, worship, and many other resources, and still be a good Canadian citizen. One can also be a Mormon and live almost all of one's life in Utah, interacting entirely with other Mormons, and still be a good American citizen.

Many groups have their own subcommunities within the larger society and their own subcultures within the dominant culture. Subcultures add their own set of conventions and expectations to the general standards of the dominant culture. Subcultures are suitable for meso-level analysis because the social unit plays a more continuous role in the life of members. (Table 3.2 illustrates the connection between the social unit at each level and the type of culture at that level.) One can be born, work, marry, and die in that social unit. Members maintain a feeling of "we" (belonging to the group) versus "they" (those outside the group). Members also maintain a belief in the rightness of their customs, rituals, religious practices, dress, food, or whatever else distinguishes them as a subculture.

Note that many categories into which we group people are not subcultures. For example, redheads, left-handed people, tall people, individuals who read *Wired* magazine, people who are single, visitors to Graceland, and DVD watchers do not make up subcultures because they do not interact as social units or share a common way of life. A motorcycle gang, a college fraternity, and a summer camp are also not subcultures because they affect only a segment of one's life (Gordon 1970; Yablonski 1959). A subculture, on the other hand, influences a person's life every day in pervasive ways throughout the person's life.

In the United States, subcultures include ethnic groups, such as Mexican American and Korean American; closed religious groups, such as the Mennonites in Ohio and Orthodox Jews in New York City; and social class groups, including the exclusive subculture of the elite upper-class on the East and West coasts of the United States. The super-wealthy have networks, exclusive clubs, and the Social Register, which lists names and phone numbers of the elite, so they can maintain contact with one another. They have a culture of opulence that differs from middle-class culture, and this culture is part of their experience throughout their lives.

Another example is Hasidic Jews, who adhere to the same laws as other Americans but follow additional rules specific to their religion. Clothing and hairstyles follow

A young Orthodox Jewish boy prepares to pray according to Jewish law by wrapping the leather strap of his Tefillin around his arm and a Tallit (prayer shawl) around his shoulders. He is part of a subgroup of the larger society, the Jewish faith community. This community will affect his values throughout life—from infancy to death. It is a subculture.

strict rules; men wear beards and temple-locks (*payos*), and married women wear wigs. Their religious holidays are different from those of the dominant Christian culture. Hasidic Jews observe dietary restrictions such as avoiding pork and shellfish, and they observe the Sabbath from sunset Friday to sunset Saturday. Hasidic Jews are members of a subculture in the larger society of which they are citizens. In today's world, this is a global subculture maintained through Web sites of, by, and for Hasidic Jews. Again, one can live one's entire life under the influence of the values and rules of the subculture, and this is certainly true of the Hasidic Jews.

A give-and-take exists between subcultures and the dominant culture, with each contributing to and influencing the other. Hispanic Americans have brought many foods to American cuisine, for example, including tacos, burritos, and salsa.

Table 3.2   Correlation of Social Units of Society With Levels of Culture

Social Unit (the people who interact and feel they belong)	Culture (the way of life of that social unit)
Dyads; small groups; local community	Microculture
Ethnic community or social class community	Subculture
National society	Culture of a nation
Global system	Global culture

A counterculture, such as the Amish, rejects important aspects of the mainstream or dominant culture such as technology and consumerism, replacing it with biblical principles calling for a simple lifestyle.

Subcultural practices can be the source of tensions with the dominant group, which has the power to determine cultural expectations in society. In direct conflict with the law, a very small faction of Mormons in the United States believe in and practice polygamy. Having more than one wife (polygyny) violates federal laws and state laws in Utah, where many live, but some hold to the old teachings of founder Joseph Smith and cling to this practice as sanctioned by God.

When conflict with the larger culture becomes serious, and laws of the dominant society are violated, a different type of culture emerges. A **counterculture** is a group with expectations and values that contrast sharply with the dominant values of a particular society (Yinger 1960).

One type of counterculture is represented by the Old Order Amish of Pennsylvania and Ohio. The Amish drive horse-drawn buggies and seldom use electricity or modern machines. They reject many mainstream notions of success and replace them with their own work values and goals. Conflicts between federal and state laws and Amish religious beliefs have produced shaky compromises by the Amish on issues of educating children, using farm machinery, and transportation. The Old Order Amish prefer to educate their children in their own communities, insisting that their children not go beyond an eighth-grade education in the public school curriculum. They also do not use automobiles or conventional tractors. The Amish are pacifists and will not serve as soldiers in the national military.

Other types of countercultures seek to withdraw from society or to operate outside its economic and legal systems or even to bring about the downfall of the larger society. Examples are survivalist groups such as racist militia and skinheads, who reject the principles of democratic pluralism. Organized crime families and prison gangs are countercultures as well.

Countercultures of all types have existed throughout history. The "old believers" of 17th-century Russia committed group suicide rather than submit to the authority of the czar of Russia on matters of faith and lifestyle (Crummey 1970). There are now Russian old believer communities in Oregon, northern Alberta, and the Kenai Peninsula of Alaska. Some of their villages are so isolated that they are virtually inaccessible by car, and visitors are greeted with "no trespassing" signs. The Ranters—a group that arose in 16th-century England with its strict puritan attitudes toward sensuality and sex—flaunted their opposition to those attitudes by running naked through the streets and having sex in village squares (Ellens 1971; Hill 1991).

These contrary groups can operate at the meso or the micro level. Some countercultures continue over time and can sustain members throughout their life cycle—such as the Amish. They are like subcultures in that they operate at the meso level, but they strongly reject the mainstream culture. However, most countercultural groups, such as punk rock groups or violent and deviant teenage gangs, are short-lived or are relevant to people only at a certain age—operating only at the micro level.

Members of countercultures do not necessarily reject all of the dominant culture, and in some cases, parts of their culture may eventually come to be accepted by the dominant culture. During the Vietnam War, for instance, some antiwar protestors focused their lives on protesting the U.S. involvement in Southeast Asia (and related political and economic issues). By the early 1970s, opposition to the war had become widespread in society, so antiwar protesters were no longer outside of the mainstream. They were less likely to be labeled as unpatriotic or anti-American for their beliefs. Following the war, many counterculture antiwar hippies became active in the mainstream culture and developed conventional careers in the society. Thus, ideas, protest songs, emblems, longer hair for men, and the peace symbol from the 1960s civil rights and antiwar movements in the United States were absorbed into the larger culture.

Countercultures are not necessarily bad for society. According to the conflict perspective, which was introduced in Chapter 2, the existence of counterculture groups is clear evidence that there are contradictions or tensions within a society that need to be addressed. Countercultures often challenge unfair treatment of groups in society that do not hold power and sometimes develop into social organizations or protest groups. Extremist religious and political groups, whether Christian, Islamic, Hindu, or other, may best be understood as countercultures against Western or global influences that they perceive as threatening to their way of life. Figure 3.1 graphically illustrates the types of cultures in the social world and the relationship of countercultures

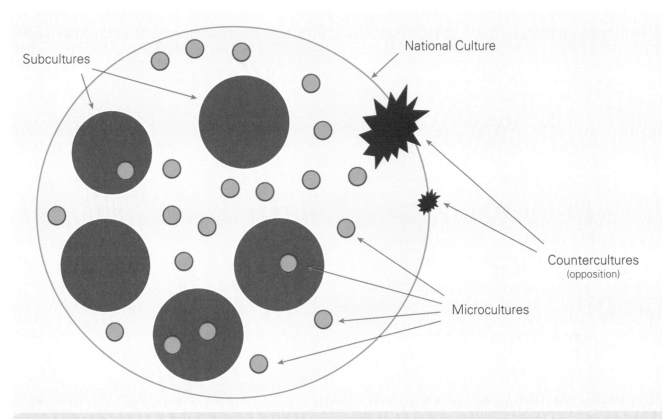

Figure 3.1   Cultures at Various Levels in the Social World

to their national culture. Countercultures, as depicted, view themselves and are viewed by others as "fringe" groups—partial outsiders within a nation.

Thinking Sociologically

Describe a counterculture group whose goals are at odds with those of the dominant culture. Do you see evidence that the group is influencing behavioral expectations and values in the larger society? What effect, if any, do they have on your life?

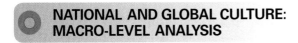 **NATIONAL AND GLOBAL CULTURE: MACRO-LEVEL ANALYSIS**

Canada is a national society, geographically bounded by the mainland United States on the south, the Pacific Ocean and Alaska on the west, the Atlantic Ocean on the east, and the Arctic on the north. The government in Ottawa passes laws that regulate activities in all provinces (which are similar to states or prefectures), and each province passes its own laws. These geographic boundaries and political structures make up the national society of Canada.

National Society and Culture

The national society is made up of a group of people who interact more with each other than with outsiders and who cooperate for the attainment of certain goals. Within the nation, there may be smaller groups, such as ethnic, regional, or tribal subcultures made up of people who identify closely with each other. Along with subcultures, most nations have a **national culture** of common values and beliefs that tie citizens together. The national culture affects the everyday lives of all its citizens to some extent. Within some countries of Africa and the Middle East that became self-governing nations during the 20th century, local ethnic or religious loyalties are much stronger than any sense of national culture. Subcultural differences divide many nations. Consider, for example, the loyalties of Shiites, Sunnis, and Kurds in Iraq, where the national culture struggles for influence over its citizens through laws, traditions, and military force.

In colonial America, people thought of themselves as Virginians or Rhode Islanders rather than as U.S. citizens. Even during the "war between the states" of the 1860s, the battalions were organized by states and often carried their state banners into battle. The fact that some southern states still call it the War Between the States rather than the Civil War communicates the struggle over whether to recognize the nation or states as the primary social unit of loyalty and identity. People in the United States today are increasingly likely to think of themselves as U.S. citizens (rather than as Iowans or Floridians), yet, the national culture determines only a few of the specific guidelines for everyday life. Still, the sense of nation has grown stronger in most industrialized societies over the past century, and primary identity is likely to be "American" or "Canadian."

Global Society and Culture

Several centuries ago, it would have been impossible to discuss a global culture, but with expanding travel, economic interdependence of different countries, international political linkages, global environmental concerns, and technology allowing for communication throughout the world, people now interact across continents in seconds. **Globalization** refers to the process by which the entire world is becoming a single interdependent entity—more uniform, more integrated, and more interdependent (Pieterse 2004; Robertson 1997; Robertson and Khondker 1998; Stutz and Warf 2005). Globalization is not a product or an object, but a process of increased connectedness and interdependency that affects people across the planet (Eitzen and Zinn 2006).

Western political and economic structures dominate in the development of this global society, largely as a result of the domination of Western (Europe and U.S.) worldviews, and Western control over resources. For example, the very idea of governing a geographic region with a bureaucratic structure known as a nation-state is a fairly new notion. Formerly, many small bands and tribal groupings dominated areas of the globe. However, with globalization, nation-states now exist in every region of the world.

Global culture refers to behavioral standards, symbols, values, and material objects that have become common across the globe. For example, beliefs that monogamy is normal; that marriage should be based on romantic love; that people have a right to life, liberty, and the pursuit of happiness; that people should be free to choose their leaders; that women should have rights such as voting; that wildlife and fragile environments should be protected; and that everyone should have a television set are spreading across the globe (Leslie and Korman 1989; Newman and Grauerholz 2002). During the 20th century, the idea of the primacy of individual rights, civil liberties, and human rights spread around the world, creating conflicts in nations that traditionally lack democratic institutions and processes. Backlashes against these and other Western ideas also can be seen in acts of groups that have embraced terrorism (Eitzen and Zinn 2006; Misztal and Shupe 1998; Turner 1991a, 1991b). Still, these trends are aspects of the emerging global culture. Even 100 years ago, notions of global cooperation and competition would have seemed quite bizarre (Lechner and Boli 2005). However, in nations all over the globe, people who travel by plane know they must stand in line (at least most see this as the norm), purchase a ticket, negotiate airport security, squeeze their bodies into confined spaces, and stay seated until they are told they can get up

(Lechner and Boli 2005). Regardless of nationality, we know how to behave in any airport in the world, and for the most part, we conform to common norms that shape our travel.

Nations are accepted as primary units of social control, and use of coercion is perfectly normal if it is done by the government. We compete in Olympic Games as citizens of nations, and the winner stands on the platform while her or his national anthem is played. Across the globe this seems "normal," yet only a few centuries ago, notions of nations would have seemed very strange (Lechner and Boli 2005). Global culture probably has fairly minimal impact on the everyday interactions and lives of the average person, yet it affects nations, which in turn affect our lives. For example, many of the rules governing airline travel are established by global organizations and apply to the global community.

As the world community becomes more interdependent and addresses issues that can only be dealt with at the global level (such as global warming or international terrorism), the idea of a common "software" of beliefs, social rules, and common interests takes on importance. Common ideas for making decisions allow for shared solutions to conflicts that previously would have resulted in war and massive killing of people. Global culture at the macro level will increasingly be a reality in the third millennium.

However, global culture is not the only pattern that is new. Today, we are seeing a counterculture at the global level. Stateless terrorist networks reject the values of the World Court, the Geneva Convention, and other international systems designed to resolve disputes. Terrorists do not recognize the sovereignty of nations and do not acknowledge many values of respect for life or for civil discourse. This counterculture at the global level is a more serious threat than those at the micro and meso levels.

Much of this book focuses on social interaction and social structures, including interpersonal networking, the growth of bureaucratic structures, social inequality within the structure, and the core institutions necessary to meet the needs of individuals and society. In short, "hardware"—society—is the focus of many subsequent chapters. The remainder of this chapter will focus on the "software" dimension (culture) and how we study it.

Thinking Sociologically

Make a list of social units of which you are a part. Place these groups into microculture, subculture, national culture, or global culture categories. Consider which of them affects only a portion of your day or week (like your place of work) or only a very limited time in your entire life span. Consider which groups are smaller than the nation, but which will likely influence you over much of your life. To what cross-national (global) groups do you belong? Do you belong to fewer groups at the national culture and global culture level? If so, why do you suppose that is the case?

The Components of Culture

Things and thoughts—these make up much of our culture. From our things—**material culture**—to our thoughts (feelings, beliefs, values, attitudes)—**nonmaterial culture**—culture provides the guidelines for our lives.

Material Culture: The Artifacts of Life

Material culture includes all the objects we can see or touch, all the artifacts of a group of people—their grindstones for grinding cassava root, microwave ovens for cooking, bricks of mud or clay for building shelters, hides or woven cloth for making clothing, books or computers for conveying information, tools for reshaping their environments, vessels for carrying and sharing food, and weapons for dominating and subduing others. Material culture includes anything you can touch that is made by humans.

Some material culture is of local, micro-level origins. The kinds of materials with which homes are constructed and the materials used for clothing often reflect the geography and resources of the local area. Likewise, types of jewelry, pottery, musical instruments, or clothing reflect tastes that emerge at the micro and meso levels of family, community, and subculture. At a more macro level, national and international corporations interested in making profits work hard to establish trends in fashion and style that may cross continents and oceans.

Material culture in many ways drives the globalization process. Many of our clothes are now made in Asia or Central American countries. Our shoes may well have been produced in the Philippines. The oil used to make plastic water bottles and devices in our kitchens likely came from the Middle East. Even food is imported year-round from around the planet. That romantic diamond engagement ring—a symbol that represents the most intimate tie—may well be imported from a South African mine using low-paid or even slave labor. Our cars are assembled from parts produced on nearly every continent. Moreover, we spend many hours in front of a piece of material culture—our computers—surfing the World Wide Web. Material culture is not just for local homebodies anymore.

Thinking Sociologically

Think of examples of material culture that you use daily: stove, automobile, cell phone, refrigerator, clock, money, and so forth. How do these material objects influence your way of life and the way you interact with others? How would your behavior be different if these material objects, say watches or cars, did not exist?

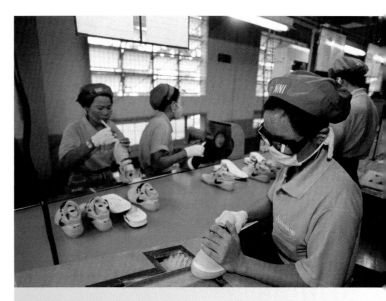

Multinational corporations know no national barriers. With some 50,000 employees, Nike is Vietnam's largest private employer, exporting 22 million pairs of shoes annually. Thousands of products you use every day were likely made or assembled on the other side of the globe.

Nonmaterial Culture: Beliefs, Values, Rules, and Language

Nonmaterial culture refers to invisible and intangible parts of culture; they are of equal or even greater importance than material culture for they involve the society's rules of behavior, ideas, and beliefs that shape how people interact with others and with their environment. Although we cannot touch the nonmaterial components of our culture, they pervade our life and are instrumental in determining how we think, feel, and behave. Nonmaterial culture is complex, comprising four main elements: beliefs, values, norms or rules, and language.

Beliefs are ideas we hold about life, about the way the society works, and about where we fit into the world. Beliefs come from traditions established over time, religious teachings, experiences people have had, and lessons given by parents and teachers or other individuals in authority. Beliefs influence the choices we make. Many Hindus, for example, believe that fulfilling behavioral expectations of one's own social caste will be rewarded in one's next incarnation. In the next life, good people will be born to a higher social status. By contrast, some Christians believe that one's fate in the afterlife depends on whether one believes in certain ideas—for instance, that Jesus Christ is one's personal savior.

Values are shared judgments about what is desirable or undesirable, right or wrong, good or bad. They express the basic ideals of any culture. In industrial societies, for instance, a good education is highly valued. Gunnar Myrdal (1964), a Swedish sociologist and observer of U.S. culture, referred to the U.S. value system as the "American creed."

Sociology Around the World

Life and Death in a Guatemalan Village

In her four decades of life, Rigoberta Menchú Tum experienced the closeness of family and cooperation in village life. These values are very important in Chimel, the Guatemalan hamlet where she lives. She also experienced great pain and suffering with the loss of her family and community. A Quiche Indian, Menchú became famous throughout the world in 1992 when she received the Nobel Peace Prize for her work to improve the conditions for Indian peoples.

Guatemalans of Spanish origin hold the power and have used Indians almost as slaves. Some of the natives were cut off from food, water, and other necessities, but people in the hamlet helped to support each other and taught children survival techniques. Most people had no schooling. Menchú's work life in the sugar cane fields began at age 5. At 14, she traveled to the city to work as a domestic servant. While there, she learned Spanish, which helped her to be more effective in defending the rights of the indigenous population in Guatemala. Her political coming of age occurred at age 16 when she witnessed her brother's assassination by a group trying to expel her people from their native lands.

Her father started a group to fight repression of the indigenous and poor, and at 20, Menchú joined the movement, *Comite de Unidad Campesina* (CUC), which the government claimed was communist inspired. Her father was murdered during a military assault, and her mother was tortured and killed. Menchú moved to Mexico with many other exiles to continue the nonviolent fight for rights and democracy.

The values of the native population represented by Menchú focus on respect for and a profound spiritual relationship with the environment, equality of all people, freedom from economic oppression, the dignity of her culture, and the benefits of cooperation over competition. The landowners tended to stress freedom of people to pursue their individual self-interests (even if inequality resulted), the value of competition, and the right to own property and to do whatever one desired to exploit that property for economic gain. Individual property rights were thought to be more important than preservation of indigenous cultures. Economic growth and profits were held in higher regard than religious connectedness to the earth.

The values of the native population and landowners are in conflict. Only time will tell if the work of Indian activists such as Rigoberta Menchú Tum and her family will make a difference in the lives of this indigenous population.

Values become a creed when they are so much a part of the way of life that they acquire the power of religious doctrine. We tend to take our core values for granted, including freedom, equality, individualism, democracy, efficiency, progress, achievement, material comfort, and patriotic duty (Macionis 2007; Williams 1970).

At the macro level, conflicts may arise between groups in society because of differing value systems. For example, there are major differences between the values of various Native American groups and the dominant culture—whether that dominant culture is in North, Central, or South America (Lake 1990; Sharp 1991). Consider the story in "Sociology Around the World" about Rigoberta Menchú Tum and the experiences of Native American populations living in Guatemala.

The conflict in values described in the story of Rigoberta Menchú Tum is not unlike conflicts between Native American meso-level subcultures and national cultures of Canada and the United States. Cooperation is a cultural value that has been passed on through generations of Native Americans because group survival depends on group cooperation in the hunt, in war, and in daily life. This value may have led to unwarranted trust in others. As a result, some people believe that Native Americans have received the worst terms in many treaties and other agreements with governments. Native populations unintentionally gave up rights to lands that had once been their domain. The value of cooperation can place native children at a disadvantage in North American schools that emphasize competition. Native American and Canadian First Nation children experience more success in classrooms that stress cooperation and sociability over competition and individuality (Lake 1990; Mehan 1992).

Another Native American value is the appreciation of and respect for nature. Conservation of resources and protection of the natural environment—Mother Earth—have always been important because of the people's dependence on nature for survival. Today, we witness disputes between native tribes and governments of Canada, the United States, Mexico, Guatemala, Brazil, and other countries over raw resources found on native reservations. While many other North and South Americans also value cooperation and respect for the environment, these values do not govern decision making in most communities (Brown 2001; Marger 2006). The values honored by governments and corporations are those held by the people with power, prestige, and wealth.

Thinking Sociologically

How are different cultural values a source of major problems for native peoples or for other groups with which you are familiar?

Norms are rules of behavior shared by members of a society and rooted in the value system. Norms range from religious warnings such as "thou shalt not kill" to the expectation that young people will complete their high school education. Sometimes, the origins of particular norms are quite clear. Few people wonder, for instance, why there is a norm to stop and look both ways at a stop sign. Other norms, such as the rule in many societies that women should wear skirts but men should not, have been passed on through the generations and become unconsciously accepted patterns and a part of tradition. Sometimes, we may not know how norms originated or even be aware of norms until they are violated.

Norms are generally classified into three categories—folkways, mores, and laws—based largely on how important the norms are in the society and people's response to the breach of those norms. *Folkways* are customs or desirable behaviors, but they are not strictly enforced: Some examples are responding appropriately and politely when introduced to someone, speaking quietly in a library, not scratching your genitals in public, using proper table manners, or covering your mouth when you cough. Violation of these norms causes people to think you are weird or even uncouth but not necessarily immoral or criminal.

Mores are norms that most members observe because they have great moral significance in a society. Conforming to mores is a matter of right and wrong, and violations of many mores are treated very seriously. The person who deviates from mores is considered immoral or bordering on criminal. Being honest, not cheating on exams, and being faithful in a marriage are all mores. Table 3.3 provides examples of folkways and mores.

Taboos are the strongest form of mores. They concern actions considered unthinkable or unspeakable in the culture. For example, most societies have taboos that forbid incest (sexual relations with a close relative) and prohibit defacing or eating a human corpse. Taboos are most common and numerous in societies that do not have centralized governments to establish formal laws and to maintain jails.

Taboos and other moral codes may be of the utmost importance to a group, yet behaviors that are taboo in one situation may be acceptable at another time and place. The incest taboo is an example found in all cultures, yet application of the incest taboo varies greatly across cultures (Brown 1991). In medieval Europe, if a man and woman were within seven degrees of relatedness and wanted to marry, the marriage could be denied by the priest as incestuous. (Your first cousin is a third degree of relatedness from you.) On the other hand, the Balinese permit twins to marry because it is believed they have already been intimately bonded together in the womb (Leslie and Korman 1989). In some African and Native American societies, one cannot marry a sibling but might be expected to marry a first cousin. As Table 3.4 illustrates, the definition of what is and what is not incest varies even from state to state in the United States.

Laws are norms that have been formally encoded by those holding political power in society, such as laws against stealing property or killing another person. The violator of a law is likely to be perceived not just as a weird or immoral person but as a criminal who deserves formal punishment.

Table 3.3 **Types of Norms**	
Folkways: Conventional Behaviors *Proper, polite: violators are "weird"*	*Mores: Morally Significant Behaviors* *Right and wrong: violators are "immoral"*
Swearing in house of worship	Lying or being unfaithful to a spouse
Wearing blue jeans to the prom	Buying cigarettes or liquor for young teens
Using poor table manners	Having sex with a professor as a way to increase one's grade
Picking one's nose in public	Parking in handicap spaces when one is in good physical condition

Table 3.4	**Incest Taboos in the United States: States That Allow First-Cousin Marriage**		
Alabama	Connecticut	Maryland	Rhode Island
Alaska	District of Columbia	Massachusetts	South Carolina
California	Florida	New Jersey	Tennessee
Colorado	Georgia	New Mexico	Vermont
Hawaii	New York	North Carolina	Virginia

States that allow only under certain conditions: The following states also allow first-cousin marriage but only under certain conditions such as marriage after a *certain age or inability to bear children:* Arizona, Illinois, Indiana, Utah, and Wisconsin.

Marriage of half cousins: Kansas, Maine, Montana, Nebraska, Nevada, and Oklahoma.

Marriage of adopted cousins: Louisiana, Mississippi, Oregon, and West Virginia.

States that do not allow first-cousin marriage: All other U.S. states disallow marriages to first cousins within the state: Arkansas, Delaware, Idaho, Iowa, Kentucky, Michigan, Minnesota, Missouri, New Hampshire, North Dakota, Ohio, Pennsylvania, South Dakota, Texas, Washington, and Wyoming.

Historically, in the United States, incest laws forbid in-law marriages far more than first-cousin marriages.

Source: "Cousin Marriage Laws in the U.S." 2008.

Many mores are passed into law, and some folkways are also made into law. Formal punishments are imposed. Spitting on the sidewalk is not a behavior that has high levels of moral contempt, yet it is illegal in some cities, with fines to punish violators. Furthermore, behaviors may be folkways in one situation and mores in another. For example, nudity or various stages of near nudity may be only mildly questionable in some social settings (the beach or certain fraternity parties) but would be quite offensive in others (a four-star restaurant or a house of worship) and against the law in others, incurring a penalty.

Sanctions reinforce norms through rewards and penalties. **Formal sanctions** to enforce the most important norms are implemented by official action. Fines for parking illegally, lowered grades on an assignment for plagiarism, or expulsion for bringing drugs or weapons to school for fighting are formal negative sanctions your school might impose. Honors and awards are formal positive sanctions. **Informal sanctions** are unofficial rewards or punishments. A private word of praise by your professor after class about how well you did on your exam would be an informal positive sanction; gossip or ostracism by other students because of clothes you are wearing would be informal negative sanctions. Sanctions vary with the importance of the norm and can range from a parent frowning at a child who fails to use proper table manners (a micro-level setting) to a prison term or death sentence. Similarly, when we obey norms, we are rewarded, sometimes with simple acts such as smiles and jokes and pats on the back that indicate solidarity with others. Most often, adherence to norms is ingrained so deeply that our reward is simply "fitting in." Your reward for polite social behavior—for asking about someone's interests and activities, for not being overly shy or pushy in conversation—is friendship

Nudity may be considered a violation of law, or mores, or folkways, or it may simply be accepted as normal, as in the case of this nude beach.

and fitting into the group. Folkways and many mores are enforced through informal sanctions, yet sometimes penalties for deviant behavior can be severe.

Norms concerning sexual behaviors are often very strong and carry powerful sanctions, sometimes even imposed by national governments. A woman who becomes pregnant outside of marriage in societies that strongly condemn premarital and nonmarital sex is likely to be ostracized and her child labeled illegitimate. Such children may be stigmatized for life, living as outcasts in poverty on the streets, begging for food. This was the case in Vietnam during the French colonial period and during the U.S.-Vietnam War, when many biracial children were excluded from participation in society. "Half-breed" children bore the stigma, fueled by xenophobia and nationalism, because they were reminders of interaction with the country's colonial and wartime past (Lawson 1991; Nguyen 2005).

When a society faces change, especially from war, rapid urbanization, industrialization, and modernization, traditional norms that have worked for the society for centuries are challenged. In the past few decades, examples have been seen in many Islamic countries in which modernization has met with a resurgence of religious fundamentalism. A case in point is Iran. The rapid modernization and social changes that took place in the post–World War II era under the Shah of Iran, Mohammed Reza Pahlavi, were met by a backlash from religious fundamentalists. When the shah was ousted in 1979, Ayatollah Ruhollah Khomeini restored traditional Islamic rule. Radio music and drinking of alcoholic beverages were banned, and women were required to again wear the veil, as in previous times. Afghanistan and other Muslim nations are currently struggling with the conflicts between traditional religious and cultural values and those related to pressures from the social environment, in this case Western nations, for change and modernization. Strict Muslim laws and swift, often severe punishments are meted out to offenders.

At the global level, there are newly emerging norms to deal with some areas of technology, such as fraud and theft on the Internet and the World Wide Web. Without norms, there are no guidelines for interactions between individuals and groups. E-mail has been in existence for civilians only since 1994, thus allowing social scientists to watch the emergence of norms in this new social environment.

Communication is often mediated and enhanced through nonverbal indicators such as tone of voice, inflection, facial expressions, or other gestures that communicate emotion. In e-mail, the words are just words without context. To establish norms, many listservs now have rules for polite communication to avoid "flaming" someone—insulting them with insensitive words by a faceless person. The development of smileys and emoticons add combinations of characters that represent the emotional context of the message. Norms of Internet communication are still emerging, and you probably have experienced times when messages have been misunderstood because the norms of communication are ambiguous.

Thinking Sociologically

One of the problems of Internet communication has been that many norms of civil discourse are ignored, and new norms emerge. What do you see as the current rules for Internet communication? A related problem is that some young people then think these new norms are appropriate in other communication situations—such as communicating with a professor or an employer. What problems might occur when applying Internet norms to communication in other social situations?

Language is the foundation of every culture. The mini-drama between infant and adult is played out every day around the world as millions of infants learn the language of the adults who care for them. In the process, they acquire an important part of culture. Although many animals can communicate with a limited repertoire of sounds, the ability to speak a language is unique to humans. Human infants have the potential for developing language because the human voice box, tongue, and brain make speech biologically possible. In their early months, babies make many sounds—squealing, growling, "raspberries," cooing, tongue clicks. These become more recognizable as syllables in the second six months of life (Oller 2006). At about one year of age, most infants begin to pronounce recognizable words in the language of their culture. The human infant is capable of making roughly 1,000 sounds, but any given society considers only about 40 or 50 of these to be language sounds. The baby soon learns that some of those sounds elicit enthusiastic responses from the adult caretakers, reinforcing their use.

Transport a baby from France to the Arapesh tribe in New Guinea and another baby from New Guinea to France, and each will learn to speak the language and adhere to the culture in which it is brought up. The reason is that language, like other components of culture, is learned. Language conveys verbal and nonverbal messages among members of society. Simply put, without language there would be little, if any, culture. Through the use of language, members of culture can pass on essential knowledge to children and can share ideas with other members of their society. Work can be organized; the society can build on its experiences and plan its future. Through language, members express their ideas, values, beliefs, and knowledge, a key ingredient in the ability of humans to sustain social life as we know it.

Language takes three primary forms: spoken, written, and nonverbal. Spoken language allows individuals to produce a set of sounds that symbolize an object or idea. That sound combination is learned by all who share a culture, and it generally holds similar meaning for all members. Written language enables humans to store ideas for future generations, accelerating the accumulation of ideas on which to build. It also makes possible communication over

福 | Поздравляю! | Θεος | לחם שר בא | -십 시요 | العربية | राम

Figure 3.2   Societies Use Various Symbols to Communicate Their Written Language

distances. Members of a society learn to read these shared symbols, some of which are displayed in Figure 3.2.

Nonverbal language consists of gestures, facial expressions, and body postures. This mode of communication may carry as much as 90% of the meaning of the message (Samovar and Porter 2003). Every culture uses nonverbal language to communicate, and just like verbal language, those cues may differ widely among cultures. For instance, an A-OK gesture or a hand wave that is positive in one culture may have a negative, even obscene, meaning in another.

The power to communicate nonverbally is illustrated in American Sign Language, designed for the hearing challenged and the mute. Complex ideas can be transmitted without vocalizing a word. Indeed, one can argue that the deaf have a distinctive culture of their own rooted in large part in the unique language that serves them. In addition, technology has aided communication among the hearing-impaired through text messaging.

Misunderstandings occur between ethnic groups because of cultural differences regarding communication. The Apache Indians in the American Southwest tell "white-man jokes"—ridiculing white people because they engage in such grossly unacceptable actions as calling one another by name even when they do not know each other intimately, asking about one another's health, complementing one another's clothing, and greeting others who walk into a room. Because so many white U.S. citizens do not understand that these behaviors are viewed as offensive, they may violate expectations and create difficulties for themselves in dealing with Apaches. They may act in ways that are considered ill-mannered and rude (Basso 1979).

Misinterpretation of nonverbal signals can also occur between male and female microcultures in Western societies. When women nod their heads in response to a person who is talking, they often are encouraging the speaker to continue, signaling that they are listening and that they want the speaker to carry on with clarification and explanation. It does not signal agreement. When men nod their heads when another person is speaking, they typically assume the message is "I agree with what you are saying." This can lead to awkward, confusing, and even embarrassing miscues when men and women talk to one another, with a man mistakenly confident that the woman agrees with his ideas (Stringer 2006).

Language also plays a critical role in perception and in thought organization. The linguistic relativity theory (Sapir 1929, 1949; Whorf 1956) posits that the people who speak a specific language make interpretations of their reality—they notice certain things and may fail to notice certain other things. "A person's 'picture of the universe' or 'view of the world' differs as a function of the particular language or languages that person knows" (Kodish 2003:384). Children in each different culture will learn about the world within the framework provided by their language. Scientists continue to debate the extent to which language can influence thought, but most agree that while language may contribute to certain ways of thinking, it does not totally determine human thinking (Gumpers and Levinson 1991). Although this theory is controversial and aspects have been misinterpreted, the idea of language, culture, consciousness, and behavior affecting each other is influential when studying the role of language.

Consider how language impacts planning of our day: Many nonindustrial peoples in Asia, Africa, Australia, and South and North America do not keep time in the kinds of exact units used in the industrial world—seconds, minutes, hours. The smallest units might be sunrise, morning, midday, late afternoon, dusk, and night (Hall 1983). Meeting someone for an appointment requires great patience, for there are no words for what we call seconds, minutes, or even hours. Think about how this would change your life and the pace of everything around you. If you showed up at a predesignated location, your friend might appear three hours later but would be on time because the unit of time would include a four- or five-hour time period. In such a culture, one would eat when food is prepared or when one is hungry. One gets up when one is rested. Time-based words cause most of us to organize our days in particular ways and even to become irritated with others who do not adhere to these expectations (Bertman 1998).

To use another example, in the English language, people tend to associate certain colors with certain qualities in a way that may add to the problem of racist attitudes. In *Webster's Unabridged English Dictionary,* the definition of the word *black* includes "dismal," "boding ill," "hostile," "harmful," "inexcusable," "without goodness," "evil," "wicked," "disgrace," and "without moral light." The word *white*, on the other hand, is defined as "honest," "dependable," "morally pure," "innocent," and "without malice." If the linguistic relativity thesis is correct, it is more than coincidence that bad things are associated with the "black sheep" of the family, the "blacklist," or "Black Tuesday" (when the stock market dropped dramatically).

Language development is extremely important to becoming fully human, and it happens very rapidly from about the first year of life. Still, babies learn to communicate in a variety of other ways. Note how these infants communicate emotions nonverbally. What does each of them seem to be communicating?

This association of blackness with negative images and meanings is not true of all languages. The societies that have negative images for black and positive images for white are the same societies that associate negative qualities with people of darker skin. The use of *white* as a synonym for "good" or "innocent"—as in reference to a "white noise machine" or a "white lie"—may contribute to a cultural climate that devalues people of color. In essence, English may influence our perception of color in a manner that contributes to racism. Interestingly, there is empirical evidence supporting this

claim of color symbolism. Athletic teams that wear black uniforms have more penalties called on them than teams with lighter colored uniforms (Frank and Gilovich 1988).

One thing is clear: Different language evolves in different settings in the social world. In a prison where inmates are closed off from the larger world, a whole lingo evolves that is incomprehensible to outsiders but essential to survival within the prison: *kites, rats, store, punks, wolves, cops,* and *ballbuster* are examples of prison terms. Even within your own college, there are probably terms used to refer

Table 3.5 Material and Nonmaterial Cultural Components in Western Courtship

Material objects	Rings, flowers, candy, and similar tokens of caring are given or displayed.
Nonmaterial cultural components	
Beliefs	Young people date before marriage; marriage is based on romantic love.
Values	Courtship is needed to provide a period for getting to know the partner, for falling in love; couples that are getting close to permanent commitment ought to be exclusive in their romantic and sexual relationships.
Rules	Couple must be officially sanctioned to make the bond permanent.
Language or symbols	Couple expresses their feelings verbally and nonverbally; special names are used: *significant other, boyfriend, fiancée, soul mate.*
	Couple shows affection through gift giving, exchanging meaningful objects such as a diamond engagement ring.

Language varies from one social setting to another, and one must learn the language to survive. The prison is a society separated from the larger society, and it develops its own microculture. In prison, one must learn the lingo and the associated values that are applied to "kites," "rats," "store," "punks," "wolves," "cops," and "ballbusters." Inmates, such as these men in the yard of San Quentin State Prison, develop their own insider lingo.

and other processes that are meaningful in that context but may be utterly confusing to those not in that microculture.

When grouped together, material and nonmaterial components form cultural patterns. People's lives are organized around these patterns. For example, family life includes patterns of courtship, marriage, child rearing, and care of the elderly. Table 3.5 illustrates some of the more prominent material and nonmaterial cultural components involved in one pattern of Western society, the ritual of courtship.

We have seen that material artifacts and nonmaterial beliefs, values, norms, and language are the basic components of culture. Next, we explore theoretical explanations for culture.

Thinking Sociologically

The words *bachelor* and *spinster* are supposedly synonymous terms, referring to unmarried adult males and females, respectively. Generate a list of adjectives that describe each of these words and that you frequently hear associated with them (e.g., eligible, swinging, old, unattractive). Are the associated words positive or negative in each case? How are these related to the position of the unmarried in societies?

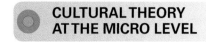 **CULTURAL THEORY AT THE MICRO LEVEL**

When students first read about sociology or other social sciences, the underlying message may seem to be that humans are shaped by the larger society in which they live. External

to course sequences, majors, or Greek houses that people at other universities would find bewildering. At the Massachusetts Institute of Technology, for example, students often respond to the question "What is your major?" with the number from the catalog: "I'm majoring in 23." That would be a truly bizarre response at some other campuses. Within the meso-level medical profession, people may discuss MRIs, brain scans, heart catheterizations, PSA tests, forces do shape us in many ways, but that is not the whole story, as we see when we examine the **symbolic interaction** approach to culture.

Symbolic Interaction Theory

How amazing it is that babies learn to share the ideas and meanings of complex cultures with others in those cultures. Symbolic interaction theory considers how we learn to share meanings of symbols, whether material or nonmaterial. Culture is about symbols, such as rings, flags, and words that stand for or represent something. A ring means love and commitment. A flag represents national identity and is intended to evoke patriotism and love of country. A phrase such as *middle class* conjures up images and expectations of what the phrase means, and we share this meaning with others with whom we interact. Together in our groups and societies, we define what is real, normal, and good.

Symbolic interaction theory maintains that our humanness comes from the impact we have on each other through these shared understandings of symbols that humans have created. When people create symbols, such as a new greeting ("give me five") or a symbolic shield for a fraternity or sorority, symbols come to have an existence and importance for a group. This is Step 1: The symbol is created. Who designed the Star of David and gave it meaning as a symbol of the Jewish people? Who initiated the sign of the cross for Catholics to use before prayer? Who designed the fraternity's or sorority's shield? Who determined that an eagle should symbolize the United States? Most people do not know the answers to these questions, but they do know what the symbol stands for. They share with others the meaning of a particular object. Step 2: The symbol is objectified, assuming a reality independent of the creator. In fact, people may feel intense loyalty to the symbol itself. An entire history of a people may be recalled and a set of values rekindled when the symbol is displayed. Step 3: The group has internalized the symbol. This may be the case whether the symbol is part of material culture or a nonmaterial gesture. Members of a culture absorb the ideas or symbols of the larger culture—which were originally created by some individual or small group.

Symbolic interaction theory pictures humans as consciously and deliberately creating their personal and collective histories. The theory emphasizes the part that verbal and nonverbal language and gestures play in the shared symbols of individuals and smooth operation of society. More than any other theory in the social sciences, symbolic interaction stresses the active decision-making role of individuals—the ability of individuals to do more than conform to the larger forces of the society.

This notion that individuals shape culture and that culture influences individuals is at the core of symbolic interaction theory. Other social theories tend to focus at the meso and macro levels.

Thinking Sociologically

Recall some of the local "insider" symbols that you used as a teenager—such as friendship bracelets. Some individual started each idea, and it spread rapidly from one school to another and one community to another. How are the three steps in the creation of symbols illustrated by a symbol you and your friends used?

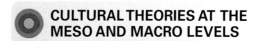

CULTURAL THEORIES AT THE MESO AND MACRO LEVELS

How can we explain such diverse world practices as eating grubs and worshipping cows? Why have some societies allowed men to have four wives whereas others—such as the Shakers—prohibited sex between men and women entirely? Why do some groups worship their ancestors while others have many gods or believe in a single divine being? How can societies adapt to extremes of climate and geographical terrain—hot, cold, dry, wet, mountainous, flat? Humankind has evolved practices so diverse that it would be hard to find a practice that has not been adopted in some society at some time in history.

To explain cultural differences, we will examine two perspectives that have made important contributions to understanding culture at the meso and macro levels: structural-functional and conflict theories.

Structural-Functional Theory

Structural-functional theory seeks to explain why members of an ethnic subculture or a society engage in certain practices. To answer, structural-functionalists look at how those practices meet social needs or contribute to the survival or social solidarity of the group or society as a whole. A classic example is the reverence for cattle in India. The "sacred cow" is protected and treated with respect and is not slaughtered for food. The reasons relate to India's ancient development into an agricultural society that required sacrifices (Harris 1989). Cattle were needed to pull plows, and their dried dung was the only source of fuel. To this day, cows are symbols of sacrifice. Cows gained religious significance because of their importance for the survival of early agricultural communities. They must, therefore, be protected from hungry people for the long-term survival of the group.

Functionalists view societies as composed of interdependent parts, each fulfilling certain necessary functions or purposes for the total society (Radcliffe-Brown 1935).

Conflict theorists believe that society is composed of groups, each acting to meet its own self-interests, and those groups struggle to make their own cultural values supreme in the society. The recent 2006 conflict over immigration laws is illustrated by the thousands of protesters who expressed their opinions in New York as Democrats and Republicans remained divided over plans to overhaul immigration laws.

Shared norms, values, and beliefs, for instance, serve the function of holding a society—or a subculture—together. At a global macro level, functionalists see the world moving in the direction of having a common culture, potentially reducing "we" versus "they" thinking and promoting unity across boundaries. Synthesis of cultures and even the loss of some cultures are viewed as a natural result of movement into a postindustrial world.

Although most cultural practices serve positive functions for the maintenance and stability of the society, some practices, such as slavery or child abuse, may be dysfunctional for minority groups or individual members of society. The fact is that some societies have faded and died out, which would suggest that their way of life is not always functional in the long run. The functionalist perspective has been criticized because it fails to consider how much dysfunction a society has, how much conflict a society can tolerate, and how much unity is necessary for a society to survive. Some critics argue that functional theory overemphasizes the need for consensus and integration among different parts of society, thus ignoring conflicts that may point to problems in societies (Dahrendorf 1959).

Conflict Theory

Whereas functionalists assume consensus because all people in society have learned the same cultural values, rules, and expectations, conflict theorists do not view culture as having this uniting effect. Conflict theorists describe societies as composed of groups—class, ethnic, religious, and political groups at the meso level—vying for power. Each group protects its own self-interests and struggles to make its own cultural ways dominant in the society. Instead of consensus, the dominant groups may impose their cultural beliefs on minorities and other subcultural groups, thus laying the groundwork for conflict. Conflict theorists identify tension between meso and macro levels, whereas functionalists tend to focus on harmony and smooth integration between those levels.

Actually, conflict may contribute to a smoother-running society in the long run. The German sociologist Georg Simmel (1955) believed that some conflict could serve a positive purpose by alerting societal leaders to problem areas that need attention. This view is illustrated by the political changes that followed the women's movement or by the organic food industry that has arisen in response to corporate agribusiness, genetically modified foods, and massive use of pesticides.

Conflict theorists argue that the people with privilege and power in society manipulate institutions such as religion and education. In this way, people learn the values, beliefs, and norms of the privileged group and foster beliefs that justify the dominant group's self-interests, power, and advantage. The needs of the privileged are likely to be met, and their status will be secured. For instance, schools that serve lower-class children usually teach obedience to authority, punctuality, and respect for superiors—behaviors that make for good laborers. The children of the affluent, meanwhile, are more likely to attend schools stressing divergent thinking, creativity, and leadership, attributes that prepare them to occupy the most professional, prestigious, and well-rewarded positions in the society. Conflict theorists point to this control of the education process by those with privilege as part of the overall pattern by which the society benefits the rich.

Conflict theory can also help us to understand global dynamics. Poor nations feel that the global system protects the self-interests of the richest nations and that those rich nations impose their own culture, including their ideas about economics, politics, and religion, on the less affluent.

Some scholars believe there is great richness in local customs that is lost when homogenized by the cultural domination in the macro-level trends of globalization (Ritzer 2004a). Conflict theory is useful for analyzing relationships between societies (macro level) and between subcultures (meso level) within complex societies. It also helps illuminate tensions in a society when local (micro level) cultural values clash with national (macro level) trends. Conflict theory is not as successful, however, in explaining simple, well-integrated societies in which change is slow to come about and cooperation is an organizing principle.

Social Policy and Cultural Change

Technology is bringing change to societies around the world, often with unanticipated consequences. While technology (an example of material culture) advances rapidly, the nonmaterial culture lags behind, resulting in social disruption. Sociologist William Ogburn (1950) used the term **cultural lag** for this change that occurs unequally between material culture (tangible objects) and nonmaterial culture (ideas, beliefs, and values). Rapid change is opposed by people whose lifestyle is threatened and who wish to preserve their native cultures. Should policymakers respect these differences and reduce the impact of change? That is the policy dilemma.

Imagine living in a remote village on Borneo that, due to its location in the East Indies, has remained largely isolated from the outside world for hundreds of years. Traditions are well established, and members seldom question how things are done. Then television comes to the village—one set located in a central meeting hut. Initially, it is used for educational programs, but the village TV receives its share of Western movies and reruns of American sitcoms (situation comedies). The advertisements also expose people to new consumer products. This village in Borneo will never be the same again. Villagers develop a desire for goods hitherto unknown, and young people leave for cities and new opportunities. Refrigerators, dishwashers, and fancy autos become known commodities. People learn that modern medicines can relieve suffering, cure some illnesses, and extend life, making for a higher quality and longer life for many people. Change also challenges the old traditions. Without new norms to take their place, disorganization can occur.

For societies to remain isolated in the global system is rare. Most are drawn into the dynamics of the 21st century, even if they are not full participants. Societies interact constantly through negotiation, trade, alliances, competition, compromise, conflict, and war. External forces bring about change in political and economic ideologies and make available raw materials, new products, and growing markets.

The social costs of rapid change can be great. During the period of early industrialization, newly arrived peasants lived in an urban squalor hard to imagine today. Even today, these problems exist as people in impoverished regions of the world leave their villages to seek employment in overcrowded urban areas. New technologies have the potential to save lives and to make life less harsh, if they are distributed to those who need them, but introduction of Western technology can also disrupt and even destroy indigenous cultures. This destruction of a culture—called *ethnocide*—can be extremely disorienting to the people (Lemkin 1933). A contributing factor to terrorism is the challenge and threat to traditional cultures and values.

Policymakers cannot stop change, but they can determine how to introduce change for the most beneficial and positive results.

Thinking Sociologically

Is it appropriate to try to change the politics or religion of another culture? Why or why not? Do individual human rights always have supremacy over the rights of a group to determine their own culture? These are tough questions that trouble many people who work in the area of human rights policy.

The Fit Between Hardware and Software

Computer software cannot work with incompatible machines. Some documents cannot be easily transferred to another piece of hardware, although sometimes a transfer can be accomplished with significant modification in the formatting of the document. The same is true with the hardware of society and the software of culture. For instance, having large extended families, typically valued in agricultural societies, does not work well in industrial and postindustrial societies. Other values such as rewarding people based on individual merit, emphasizing the idea that humans are motivated primarily by their own self-interests, or believing that change in cultures is inevitable and equals progress are not particularly compatible with the hardware (structure) of traditional horticultural or herding societies. Values and beliefs ("software") can be transferred to another type of society ("hardware"). However, there are limits to what can be transferred and the change of "formatting" may mean the new beliefs are barely recognizable.

Attempts to transport U.S.-style "software" (culture)—individualism, capitalism, freedom of religion, and democracy—to other parts of the world illustrate that these ideas are not always successful in other settings. The hardware of other societies may be able to handle more than one type of software or set of beliefs, but there are limits to the adaptability. Thus, we should not be surprised when our ideas are transformed into something quite different when they are imported to another social system. If we are to understand the world in which we live and if we want to improve it, we must first fully understand these societies and cultures.

Each society relies on the process of socialization to teach the culture to its members. The next chapter discusses the ways in which we learn to become members of society.

Thinking Sociologically

Some anthropologists argue that *team sports*, groups playing each other in coordinated competition, were learned by Europeans from certain Native American groups. How has the diffusion of team sports into U.S. culture influenced the nature of U.S. society and culture? How might society be different if we had only individual sports?

So What?

Individuals and small groups cannot live without the support of a larger society, the hardware of the social world. Without the software—culture—there could be no society for there would be no norms to guide our interactions with others in society. Humans are inherently social and learn their culture from others. Furthermore, as society has evolved into more complex and multileveled social systems, humans have learned to live in and negotiate conflicts between multiple cultures, including those at micro (microcultures), meso (subcultures), and macro (global cultures) levels. Life in an information age society demands adaptability to different sociocultural contexts and tolerance of different cultures and subcultures. This is a challenge to a species that has always had tendencies toward ethnocentrism.

Because there is such variation between societies and cultures in what they see as normal, how do any of us ever adjust to our society's expectations? The answer is addressed in the next chapter. Human life is a lifelong process of socialization to social and cultural expectations.

Key Points

What Have We Learned?

- Society consists of individuals who live together in a specific geographic area, interact with each other more than with outsiders, cooperate to attain goals, and share common culture over time. Each society has a culture, ideas and "things" that are passed on from one generation to the next in a society; the culture has both material and nonmaterial components. (See p. 65.)

- Societies evolve from very simple societies to more complex ones, from the simple hunting-gathering society to the information societies of the postindustrial world. (See pp. 65–73.)

- The study of culture requires that we try to avoid ethnocentrism (judging other cultures by the standards of our culture), taking a stance of cultural relativity instead so that the culture can be understood from the standpoint of those inside it. (See pp. 75–78.)

- Just as social units exist at various levels of our social world, from small groups to global systems, cultures exist within different levels of the social system—microcultures, subcultures, national cultures, and global cultures. Some social units at the micro or meso level stand in opposition to the dominant national culture, and they are called countercultures. (See pp. 79–92.)

- Various theories offer different lenses for understanding culture. While symbolic interaction illuminates the way humans bring meaning to events (thus generating culture), the functionalist and conflict paradigms examine cultural harmony/seamless fit and conflict between cultures, respectively. (See pp. 92–95.)

- The metaphor of hardware (society's structure) and software (culture) describes their interdependent relationship, and as with computers, there must be some compatibility between the structure and the culture. If there is none, either the cultural elements that are transported into another society will be rejected, or the culture will be "reformatted" to fit the society. (See p. 96.)

Contributing to Our Social World: What Can We Do?

At the Local and National Level: Most large (and many smaller) communities have organizations and clubs that focus on the interests of specific ethnic groups: Arabic Americans, Chinese Americans, Italian Americans, Polish Americans, and so on. Select and contact one of these groups (of your own background or, even more interesting, of a background that differs from your own). Arrange to visit one of the group's meetings and learn about the activities in which members are involved. Many ethnically oriented organizations assist recent immigrants in dealing with adjustment to American life, especially those from Mexico and other Spanish-speaking countries, Arabic-speaking countries of the Middle East, and Eastern and South Asian countries such as China, Vietnam, The Philippines, Korea, and India. Contact one of these groups and explore the possibility of volunteering or serving as an intern.

At the Global Level: As the process of globalization accelerates, the cultures, languages, and basic rights of indigenous people are under increasing threat. We have experienced this in North America in relation to Native American and Inuit populations, but it is occurring throughout the world. The United Nations has a program known as the UN Permanent Forum on Indigenous Issues that is intended to assist the affected groups in facing these challenges. Visit their Web site at www.un.org/esa/socdev/unpfii, and contact them about the possibility of volunteering. You might also contact a leading nongovernmental organization engaged in similar, action-oriented programs: Cultural Survival at www.cs.org. According to its statement of purpose, Cultural Survival partners with indigenous peoples to

- secure their rights in international and national law;

- promote respect for their right to self-determination;

- ensure their right to full and effective participation in the political, economic, and social life of the country in which they live; and

- enjoy their rights to their lands, resources, languages, and cultures.

Visit **www.pineforge.com/ballantine2study** for online activities, sample tests, and other helpful information. Select "Chapter 3: Society and Culture" for chapter-specific activities.

CHAPTER 4

Socialization

Becoming Human and Humane

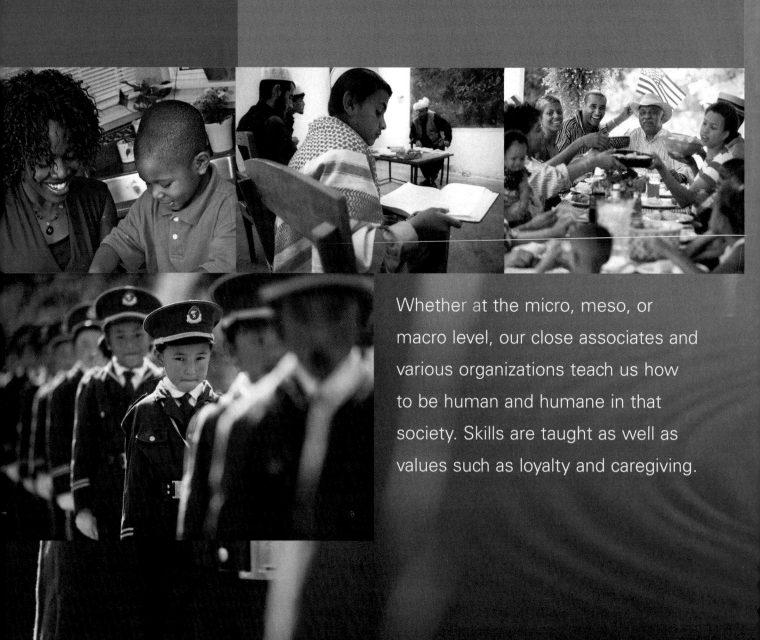

Whether at the micro, meso, or macro level, our close associates and various organizations teach us how to be human and humane in that society. Skills are taught as well as values such as loyalty and caregiving.

Think About It . . .

Micro: What does it mean to have a "self"? How might you be different if you had been raised in complete isolation from other people?

Micro: What groups in your community have shaped your values and beliefs?

Meso: How do various subcultures or organizations of which you are a member (your political party, your religious affiliation) influence your position in the social world?

Macro: What would you be like if you had been raised in a different country? How does your sense of national identity influence the way you see things?

Macro: How might globalization or other macro-level events impact you and your sense of self?

Macro: Global Community

Macro: Society

Meso: National Organizations, Institutions, and Ethnic Subcultures

Micro: Local Organizations and Community

Micro: Me (and My Significant Others)

Micro: Networks of friends; religious congregations; civic clubs; the local PTA; local Little League organization

Meso: Political parties; religious denominations; nationwide corporations with a "corporate culture"

Macro: Socialization for loyalty to the nation (patriotism or nationalism)

Macro: Socialization across borders; Internet norms; learning tolerance and respect for others

Ram, a first grader from India, had been in school in Iowa for only a couple of weeks. The teacher was giving the first test. Ram did not know much about what a test meant, but he rather liked school, and the red-haired girl next to him had become a friend. He was catching on to reading a bit faster than she, but she was better at the number exercises. They often helped each other learn while the teacher was busy with a small group in the front of the class.

The teacher gave each child the test, and Ram saw that it had to do with numbers. He began to do what the teacher instructed the children to do with the worksheet, but after a while, he became confused. He leaned over to look at the page Elyse was working on. She hid her sheet from him, an unexpected response. The teacher looked up and asked what was going on. Elyse said that Ram was "cheating." Ram was not quite sure what that meant, but it did not sound good. The teacher's scolding of Ram left him baffled, confused, and entirely humiliated.

This incident was Ram's first lesson in the individualism and competitiveness that govern Western-style schools. He was being socialized into a new set of values. In his parents' culture, competitiveness was discouraged, and individualism was equated with selfishness and rejection of community. Athletic events were designed to end in a tie so that no one would feel rejected. Indeed, a well-socialized person would rather lose in a competition than cause someone else to feel bad because they lost.

Socialization is the lifelong process of learning to become a member of the social world, beginning at birth and continuing until death. It is a major part of what the family, education, religion, and other institutions do to prepare individuals to be members of their social world. Like Ram, each of us learns the values and beliefs of our culture. In Ram's case, he literally moved from one cultural group to another and had to adjust to more than one culture within his social world.

Have you ever interacted with a newborn human baby? Infants are interactive, ready to develop into members of the social world. As they cry, coo, or smile, they gradually learn that their behaviors elicit responses from other humans. This exchange of messages—this **interaction**—is the basic building block of socialization. Out of this process of interaction, a child learns its culture and becomes a member of society. This process of interaction shapes the infant into a human being with a social self—perceptions we have of who we are.

Human biological potential, culture, and individual experiences all provide the framework for socialization. Babies enter this world unsocialized, born totally dependent on others to meet their needs, and completely lacking in social awareness and an understanding of the rules of their society. Despite this complete vulnerability, they have the potential to learn the language, norms, values, and skills needed in their society. They gradually learn who they are and what is expected of them. Socialization is necessary not only for the survival of the individual but also for the survival of society and its groups. The process continues in various forms throughout our lives as we enter and exit various positions—from school to work to retirement to death.

In this chapter, we will explore the nature of socialization and how individuals become socialized. We consider why socialization is important. We also look at development of the self, socialization through the life cycle, agents of socialization, macro-level issues, and a policy example illustrating socialization. First, we briefly examine an ongoing debate: Which is more influential in determining who we are—our genes (nature) or our socialization into the social world (nurture)?

Nature and Nurture

What is it that most makes us who we are? Is it our biological makeup or the environment in which we are raised that guides our behavior and the development of our self? One side of the contemporary debate regarding nature versus nurture seeks to explain the development of the self and human social behaviors—violence, crime, academic performance, mate selection, economic success, gender roles, and other behaviors too numerous to mention here—by examining biological or genetic factors (Harris 1998; Winkler 1991). Sociologists call this sociobiology, and psychologists refer to it as evolutionary psychology. The theory claims that our human genetic makeup wires us for social behaviors (Wilson et al. 1978). For example, according to this theory,

Babies interact intensively with their parents, observing and absorbing everything around them and learning what kinds of sounds or actions elicit response from the adults. Socialization starts at the beginning of life.

altruism—the inclination to share and to cooperate—is genetically determined, at least in part.

We perpetuate our own biological family lines and the human species through various social behaviors. Human groups develop power structures, are territorial, and protect their kin. A mother ignoring her own safety to help a child, soldiers dying in battle for their comrades and countries, communities feeling hostility toward outsiders or foreigners, and neighbors defending property lines against intrusion by neighbors are all examples of behaviors that sociobiologists claim are rooted in genetic makeup of the species. Sociobiologists would say these behaviors continue because they result in an increased chance of survival of the species as a whole (Lerner 1992; Lumsden and Wilson 1981; Wilson 1980, 1987).

Most sociologists believe that sociobiology and evolutionary psychology explanations have flaws. Sociobiology is a *reductionist* theory; that is, it reduces complex social behaviors to a single factor—in this case an inherited trait. There is no evidence for the existence of an altruism gene, an aggression gene, or any other behavioral gene. There are great variations in the way members of different societies and groups behave. People born in one culture and raised in another adopt social behaviors common to the culture in which they are raised (Gould 1997), as Ram in the opening example is doing. If social behavior is genetically programmed, then it should manifest itself regardless of the culture in which humans are raised. The key is that what makes humans unique is not our biological heritage but our ability to learn the complex social arrangements of our culture. We learn what it means to be human in our individual social worlds, and we learn how to behave through our interaction with other people. Still, the nature-versus-nurture controversies continue.

Most sociologists recognize that individuals are influenced by biology, which limits the range of human responses and creates certain needs and drives, but they believe that nurture is far more important as the central force in shaping human behavior through the socialization process. Some sociologists propose theories that consider both nature and nurture. Alice Rossi, former president of the American Sociological Association, argues that we need to build both biological and social theories—or biosocial theories—into explanations of social processes such as parenting. Rather than biology shaping human culture, each society's culture shapes biology to meet its needs (Freese, Powell, and Steelman 1999; Rossi 1984). Socialization is key in this process.

The Importance of Socialization

If you have lived on a farm, watched animals in the wild, or seen television nature shows, you probably have noticed that many animal young become independent shortly after birth.

Intense interaction by infants and their caregiver, usually a parent, occurs in all cultures and is essential to becoming a part of the society and to becoming fully human. This African father shares a tender moment with his son.

Horses are on their feet in a matter of hours, and their parents are long gone by the time turtles hatch from eggs. Many species in the animal kingdom do not require contact with adults to survive because their behaviors are inborn and instinctual. Generally speaking, the more intelligent the species, the longer the period of gestation and of nutritional and social dependence on the mother and family. Humans clearly take the longest time to socialize their young. Even among primates, human infants have the longest gestation and dependency period. Table 4.1 compares human infants and other primate babies. This extended dependency period for humans—what some have referred to as the *long childhood*—allows each human being time to learn the complexities of culture. This suggests that biology and social processes work together.

Normal human development involves learning to sit, crawl, stand, walk, think, talk, and participate in social interactions. Ideally, the long period of dependence allows children the opportunity to learn necessary skills, knowledge, and social roles through affectionate and tolerant interaction with people who care about them. Yet, what happens if children are deprived of adequate care or even human contact? The following section illustrates the importance of socialization by showing the effect of deprivation and isolation on normal socialization.

Table 4.1   **Dependence on Adults Among the Primates**

Primate Form	Pregnancy Period	Period of Absolute Nutritional Dependency on Mother or Mother-Surrogate	Nursing Period	Social Independence
Human	266 days	1 year or more	1–2 years	6–8 years
Ape: chimpanzee	235 days	3–6 months	2–3 months	12–28 months
Monkey: rhesus	166 days	1–3 weeks	2–4 weeks	2–4 months
Lemur	111–145 days	1–3 days	2–14 days	2–3 weeks

Note: Lemurs and monkeys, among the less complex members of the primate order, depend on adults for food for a much shorter time than do apes and humans. The period of dependence affords human infants time to absorb the extensive knowledge important to the survival of the species.

Isolated and Abused Children

Have you ever wondered what children would be like if they grew up without human contact? Among the most striking examples are cases of severely abused and neglected children whose parents kept them isolated in cellars or attics for years without providing even minimal attention and nurturing. When these isolated children were discovered, typically, they suffered from profound developmental disorders that endured throughout their lives (Curtiss 1977). Most experience great difficulty in adjusting to a social world guided by complex rules of interaction learned from infancy onward.

In case studies comparing two girls, Anna and Isabelle, who experienced extreme isolation in early childhood, Kingsley Davis (1947) found that even minimal human contact made some difference in their socialization. Both "illegitimate" girls were kept locked up by relatives who wanted to keep their existence a secret. Both were discovered at about age six and moved to institutions where they received intensive training. Yet, the cases were different in one significant respect: Prior to her discovery by those outside her immediate family, Anna experienced virtually no human contact. She saw other individuals only when they left food for her. Isabelle lived in a darkened room with her deaf-mute mother, who provided some human contact. Anna could not sit, walk, or talk, and learned little in the special school in which she was placed. When she died from jaundice at age 11, she had learned the language and skills of a two- or three-year-old. Isabelle, on the other hand, did progress. She learned to talk and played with her peers. After two years, she reached an intellectual level approaching normal for her age but remained about two years behind her classmates in performance levels (Davis 1940, 1947).

Less extreme than the cases of isolation but equally illustrative are the cases of children who come from war-torn countries (Povik 1994), live in orphanages, or are neglected or abused. Although not totally isolated, these children also experience problems and disruptions in the socialization process. These neglected children's situations have been referred to as abusive, violent, and dead-end environments that are socially toxic because of their harmful developmental consequences for children.

What is the message? These cases illustrate the devastating effects of isolation, neglect, and abuse early in life on normal socialization. Humans need more from their environments than food and shelter. They need positive contact, a sense of belonging, affection, safety, and someone to teach them knowledge and skills. This is children's socialization into the world through which they develop a self. Before we examine the development of the self in depth, however, we consider the complexity of socialization in the multilayered social world.

Socialization and the Social World

Sociologists are interested in how individuals become members of their society and learn the culture to which they belong. Through the socialization process, individuals learn what is expected in their society. At the micro level, most parents teach children proper behaviors to be successful in life, and peers influence children to "fit in" and have fun. Psychologists focus on the individual: the origins of identity and stages in development of reasoning (Piaget 1989; Piaget and Inhelder 1999), morality (Gilligan 1982; Kohlberg 1971), or personality (Erikson 1950). However, most recognize that individual development and behavior occur in social settings.

In fact, the process of socialization in groups allows the self to develop as individuals learn to interact with others in their culture. Interaction theory, focusing on the micro level, forms the basis of this chapter, as you will see.

At the meso level, religious denominations espouse their versions of the Truth, and schools teach the knowledge and skills necessary for functioning in society. At the nationwide macro level, television ads encourage viewers to buy products that will make them better and happier people, or they encourage people to join the military. From interactions with our significant others to dealing with government bureaucracy, most activities are part of the socialization experience that teaches us how to function in our society.

The social world model at the start of the chapter illustrates the levels of analysis in the social world. The process of socialization takes place at each level, linking the parts. Small micro-level groups include families, **peer groups** (who are roughly equal in some status within the society, such as the same age or the same occupation), and voluntary groups such as civic clubs. Examples of meso-level institutions are education and political parties, while an important macro-level unit is the federal government. All of these have a stake in how we are socialized because they all need trained and loyal group members to survive. Organizations need citizens who have been socialized to devote time, energy, and resources that these groups need to survive and meet their goals. For example, charitable organizations cannot thrive unless people are willing to volunteer their energy, time, skills, and money. Lack of adequate socialization increases the likelihood of individuals becoming misfits or social deviants.

Most perspectives on socialization focus on the micro level, as we shall see when we explore development of the self. An influential microsociologist, Erving Goffman (1922–1982), developed what he referred to as "dramaturgy." Influenced by symbolic interaction, he explored the importance of symbols and ritual in everyday life, using participant observation. His book, *Presentation of Self in Everyday Life* ([1959] 2001) analyzes social life as drama, with our on-stage behavior played out for an audience, and our backstage behavior involving only significant others. Goffman focused on understanding our ritual behavior, what we do in the presence of others, as part of understanding our interactions. We learn to manage the impressions we present to others through the roles we play, much as actors do in a theatrical production. Although Goffman's theory is unique and appealing, he was scientifically unsystematic in his research, so among sociologists who stress sociology as science, there is less enthusiasm for his approach.

Meso- and macro-level theories add to our understanding of how socialization prepares individuals for their roles in the larger social world. For example, structural-functionalist perspectives of socialization tend to see different levels of the social world operating to support each other. According to this perspective, scouting groups socialize girls and boys by stressing national values and instilling patriotism, thereby enhancing a commitment to the nation and willingness to sacrifice for it. Sports teams often instill values of competition, strategic thinking, and aggression. Education in many Western societies reinforces individualism and an achievement ethic. Families often organize holidays around patriotic themes, such as a national independence day, or around religious celebrations. These activities are believed to strengthen family members' commitment to the nation and to buttress the moral values emphasized in churches, temples, and mosques. All these values are compatible with preparing individuals to support national political and economic systems.

Socialization can also be understood from the conflict perspective, with the linkages between various parts of the social world based on competition with or even direct opposition to another part. Consider the following examples. Socialization into a nation's military forces stresses patriotism and ethnocentrism, sometimes generating conflict and hostility toward other groups and countries. Demands from organizations for our resources (time, money, and energy devoted to the Little League, the Rotary Club, and library associations) may leave nothing to give to our religious communities or even our families, setting up a conflict. Each organization and unit competes to gain our loyalty in order to claim some of our resources.

At the meso level, the purposes and values of organizations or institutions are sometimes in direct contrast with one another or are in conflict with the messages at other levels of the social system. Businesses and educational institutions try to socialize their workers and students to be serious, hardworking, sober, and conscientious, with lifestyles focused on the future. By contrast, many fraternal organizations and barroom microcultures favor lifestyles that celebrate frivolity, playfulness, and living for the moment. This creates conflicting values in the socialization process.

Conflict can occur in the global community as well. For example, religious groups often socialize their members to identify with humanity as a whole ("the family of God") or at least with other members of their religion (e.g., all Christians). However, in some cases, nations do not want their citizens socialized to identify with those beyond their borders. They may seek to persuade Christians to kill other Christians or Jews or Muslims who are defined as "the enemy," as in the case of Nazi Germany's efforts to exterminate Jews during World War II in Europe. If religion teaches that all people are "brothers and sisters" and if religious people object to killing, the nation may have trouble mobilizing its people to arms when the leaders call for war.

Conflict theorists believe that those who have power and privilege use socialization to manipulate individuals in the social world to support the power structure and the self-interests of the elite. Individuals compete to meet their own needs. Those who have power and privilege are in the best position to get what they need, and they also have significant influence on the socialization of others through schools and political institutions. Most individuals have little power

Having considered the multiple levels of analysis and the issues that make socialization complicated, let us focus specifically on the micro level: Where does the sense of self originate?

Thinking Sociologically

Although the socialization process occurs primarily at the micro level, it is influenced by events at each level of analysis shown in the social world model. Give examples of family, community, subcultural, national, or global events that might influence how you were socialized or how you would socialize your child.

DEVELOPMENT OF THE SELF: MICRO-LEVEL ANALYSIS

The central product of the socialization process is the self. Fundamentally, **self** refers to the perceptions we have of who we are. Throughout the socialization process, our self is derived from our perceptions of the way others are responding to us. The development of the self allows individuals to interact with other people and to learn to function at each level of the social world.

Humans are not born with a sense of self. It develops gradually, beginning in infancy and continuing throughout adulthood. Selfhood emerges through interaction with others. Individual biology, culture, and social experiences all play a part in shaping the self. The hereditary blueprint each person brings into the world provides broad biological outlines, including particular physical attributes, temperament, and a maturational schedule. However, nature is only part of the picture, as shown in our earlier discussion of nature versus nurture. Each person is also born into a family that lives within a particular culture. This hereditary blueprint, in interaction with family and culture, helps to create each unique person, different from any other person yet sharing the types of interactions, resulting in socialization, by which the self is formed.

Most sociologists, although not all (Irvine 2004), believe that we humans are distinct from other animals in our ability to develop a self and to be aware of ourselves as individuals or objects. Consider how we refer to ourselves in the first person—*I* am hungry, *I* feel foolish, *I* am having fun, *I* am good at basketball. We hold attitudes and feelings toward ourselves. We have a conception of who we are, how we relate to others, and how we differ from and are separate from others in our abilities and limitations. We have

Our sense of self is often shaped by how others see us and what is reflected back to us by the interactions of others. Operating somewhat like a mirror, Cooley called this process the "looking-glass self."

to control and decide their futures. For example, parents decide how they would like to raise their children and what values they want to instill in their children, but as soon as the school enters into socialization, parents must share the socialization process. One reason some parents choose to home-school their children is to control external influences on the socialization process.

Each theoretical explanation has merit for explaining some situations. Whether we stress harmony in the socialization process or conflict rooted in power differences, the development of a sense of self through the process of socialization is an ongoing, lifelong process. Individuals make choices that help to construct their reality in a complex social system.

1. We imagine how we want to appear to others.
2. Others make judgments and respond.
3. We experience feelings and react based on our interpretations.

Figure 4.1 The Looking-Glass Process of Self-Development

an awareness of the characteristics, values, feelings, and attitudes that give us our unique sense of self (James [1890] 1934; Mead [1934] 1962).

Thinking Sociologically

Write a character sketch that describes your talents. Who are some of the people who have been most significant in shaping your *self*? How have their actions and responses helped to shape your self conception as musically talented, or athletic, or intelligent, or kind, or assertive, or any of the other hundreds of traits that make up your *self*?

The Looking-Glass Self and Taking the Role of the Other

The theoretical tradition of symbolic interaction, with particular emphasis on the major contributions of Charles H. Cooley ([1909] 1983) and George Herbert Mead ([1934] 1962), offers important insights into how individuals develop the self. Cooley believed the self is a social product, shaped by interactions with others from the time of birth. He likened interaction processes to looking in a mirror wherein each person reflects an image of the other.

Each to each a looking-glass

Reflects the other that doth pass. (Cooley 1983:184)

For Cooley ([1909] 1983), the **looking-glass self** is a reflective process based on our interpretations of the reactions of others. In this process, Cooley believed that there are three principal elements: (1) we imagine how we appear to others,

(2) others judge our appearance and respond to us, and (3) we react to that feedback. We experience feelings such as pride or shame based on this imagined judgment and respond based on our interpretation. Moreover, throughout this process, we actively try to manipulate other people's view of us to serve our needs and interests. (See Figure 4.1.) This is one of the many ways we learn to be boys or girls—the image that is reflected back to us lets us know whether we have behaved in ways that are socially acceptable according to gender expectations. The issue of gender socialization in particular will be discussed in some detail in Chapter 9.

Of course, this does not mean our interpretation of the other person's response is correct, but our interpretation does determine how we respond. Our self is influenced by the many "others" with whom we interact, and each of our interpretations of their reactions feeds into our self-concept. Recall that the isolated children failed to develop this sense of self precisely because they lacked interaction with others. The next "Sociology in Your Social World" illustrates the looking-glass self process for African American males. This situation experienced by Brent Staples vividly illustrates the impact of the reflection of others on us.

Taking the looking-glass self idea a step further, Mead ([1934] 1962) explained that individuals take others into account by imagining themselves in the position of the other, a process called **role-taking**. When children play mommy and daddy, doctor and patient, or fireperson, they are imagining themselves in another's shoes. Role-taking allows humans to view themselves from the standpoint of others. This requires mentally stepping out of our own experience to imagine how others experience and view the social world. Through role-taking, we begin to see who we are from the standpoint of others. In short, role-taking allows humans to view themselves as objects, as though they were looking at themselves from outside themselves. For Mead, role-taking is a uniquely human behavior and is the foundation for the self and for most interaction in our social world.

Sociology in Your Social World

Black Men and Public Space

By Brent Staples

Many stereotypes—rigid images of members of a particular group—surround the young African American male in the United States. How these images influence these young men and their social world is the subject of this feature. Think about the human cost of stereotypes and their effect on the socialization process as you read the following essay. If your sense of self is profoundly influenced by the ways others respond to you, how might the identity of a young African American boy be affected by public images of black males?

My first victim was a woman—white, well dressed, probably in her early-twenties. I came upon her late one evening on a deserted street in Hyde Park, a relatively affluent neighborhood in an otherwise mean, impoverished section of Chicago. As I swung onto the avenue behind her . . . she cast back a worried glance. To her, the youngish black man—broad, six-feet two-inches tall, with a beard and billowing hair, both hands shoved into the pockets of a bulky military jacket—seemed menacingly close. After a few more quick glimpses, she picked up her pace and was running in earnest. Within seconds, she disappeared into a cross street.

That was more than a decade ago. I was 22 years old, a graduate student newly arrived at the University of Chicago. It was in the echo of that terrified woman's footfalls that I first began to know the unwieldy inheritance I'd come into. . . . It was clear that she thought herself the quarry of a mugger, a rapist, or worse. Suffering a bout of insomnia, however, I was stalking sleep, not defenseless wayfarers. . . . I was surprised, embarrassed, and dismayed all at once. Her flight . . . made it clear that I was indistinguishable from the muggers who occasionally seeped into the area from the surrounding ghetto. That first encounter, and those that followed, signified that a vast, unnerving gulf lay between night-time pedestrians—particularly women—and me. And I soon gathered that being perceived as dangerous is a hazard in itself. I only needed to turn a corner into a dicey situation, or crowd some frightened, armed person in a foyer somewhere, or make an errant move after being pulled over by a policeman. Where fear and weapons meet—and they often do in urban America—there is always the possibility of death.

In that first year, my first away from my hometown, I was to become thoroughly familiar with the language of fear. At dark, shadowy intersections, I could cross in front of a car stopped at a traffic light and elicit the thunk, thunk, thunk, thunk of the driver—black, white, male,

or female—hammering down the door locks. On less-traveled streets after dark, I grew accustomed to but never comfortable with people crossing to the other side of the street rather than pass me. Then there was the standard unpleasantness with policemen, doormen, bouncers, cabdrivers, and those whose business it is to screen out troublesome individuals before there is any nastiness.

After dark, on the warren-like streets of Brooklyn where I live, I often see women who fear the worst from me. They seem to have set their faces on neutral, and with their purse straps strung across their chests bandolier-style, they forge ahead as though bracing themselves against being tackled. I understand, of course, that . . . women are particularly vulnerable to street violence, and young black males are drastically overrepresented among the perpetrators of that violence. Yet these truths are no solace against the kind of alienation that comes of being ever the suspect. . . .

Over the years, I learned to smother the rage I felt at so often being taken for a criminal. Not to do so would surely have led to madness. I now take precautions to make myself less threatening. I move about with care, particularly late in the evening. I give a wide berth to nervous people on the subway platforms during the wee hours. . . . I have been calm and extremely congenial on those rare occasions when I've been pulled over by the police.

And on late-evening constitutionals, I employ what have proved to be excellent tension-reducing measures: I whistle melodies from Beethoven and Vivaldi and the more popular classical composers. Even steely New Yorkers hunching toward nighttime destinations seem to relax, and occasionally they even join in the tune. Virtually everybody seems to sense that a mugger wouldn't be warbling bright, sunny selections from Vivaldi's Four Seasons. It is my equivalent of the cowbell that hikers wear when they know they are in bear country.

Mead also argued that role-taking is possible because humans have a unique ability to use and respond to **symbols**. Symbols, discussed in Chapter 3 on culture, are human creations such as language and gestures that are used to represent objects or actions; they carry specific meaning for members of a culture. Symbols such as language allow us to give names to objects in the environment and to infuse those objects with meanings. Once the person learns to symbolically recognize objects in the environment, the self can be seen as one of those objects. In the most rudimentary sense, this starts with possessing a name that allows us to see our self as separate from other objects. Note that the connection of symbol and object are arbitrary, such as the name Al Gore and a specific human being. When we say that name, most listeners would immediately think of the same person, former U.S. vice president, congressman and senator, 2000 presidential nominee, environmental activist, and Nobel Peace Prize winner.

Most sociologists think other mammals do not use symbols to communicate, with the exception of a few human-trained chimps and gorillas learning sign language or computer usage. Chimps rely on physical gestures or signs rather than symbolic meaning to communicate. A sign indicates some physical object or event that is close at hand—a cue or stimulus that leads the animal to an unreflecting, instant response. A dog growling and baring its teeth is a warning or sign that it is prepared to attack.

At the micro level, the symbolic interaction theory further helps us understand the self. In the process of symbolic interaction, we take the actions of others and ourselves into account. Individuals may blame, encourage, praise, punish, or reward themselves. An example would be a basketball player missing the basket because the shot was poorly executed and thinking, "What did I do to miss that shot? I'm better than that!" Reflexive behavior, being able to look at oneself and one's behaviors as though from the outside, includes the simple act of taking mental notes or mentally talking to one's self. Two important ideas are that the self can be both a passive object shaped by the way we think others see us and an active object that can initiate action. The self has *agency*—it is an initiator of action and a maker of meaning. Moreover, to fully comprehend the self, it is necessary to understand that the self develops in stages and is composed of distinct but related parts.

Thinking Sociologically

Brent Staples goes out of his way to reassure others that he is safe and harmless. What might be some other responses to this experience of having others assume one is dangerous and untrustworthy? How might one's sense of self be influenced by these responses of others? How is the looking-glass self at work in this scenario?

Parts of the Self

According to the symbolic interaction perspective, the self is composed of two distinct but related parts—dynamic parts in interplay with one another (Mead [1934] 1962). The most basic element of the self is what George Herbert Mead refers to as the *I*, the spontaneous, unpredictable, impulsive, and largely unorganized aspect of the self. These spontaneous, undirected impulses of the *I* initiate or give propulsion to behavior without considering the possible social consequences. We can see this at work in the "I want it now" behavior of a newborn baby or even a toddler. Cookie Monster on the children's television program *Sesame Street* illustrates the *I* in every child, gobbling cookies at every chance.

The *I* continues as part of the self throughout life, tempered by the social expectations that surround individuals. In stages, humans become increasingly influenced by interactions with others who instill society's rules. Children develop the ability to see the self as others see them and critique the behavior of the *I*. Mead called this reflective capacity of the self the *Me*. The *Me* has learned the rules of society through socialization and interaction, and it controls the *I* and its desires. Just as the *I* initiates the act, the *Me* gives direction to the act. In a sense, the *Me* channels the impulses of the *I* in an acceptable manner according to societal rules and restraints, yet meets the needs of the *I* as best it can. When we stop ourselves just before saying something and think to ourselves, "I'd better not say that," it is our *Me* monitoring and controlling the *I*. Notice that the *Me* requires the ability to take the role of the other, to anticipate the other's reaction.

Stages in the Development of the Self

The process of developing a social self occurs gradually and in stages. Mead identified three critical stages: imitation stage, the play stage, and the game stage, each of which requires the unique human ability to engage in role-taking. In the **imitation stage,** the child under three years old is preparing for role-taking by observing others and imitating their behaviors, sounds, and gestures.

The **play stage** involves a kind of play-acting in which the child is actually "playing at" a role. Listen to children who are three to five years old play together. You will notice that they spend most of their time telling each other what to do. One of them will say something like, "You be the mommy, and Jose can be the daddy, and Julie, you be the dog. Now you say 'good morning dear,' and I'll say, 'How did you sleep?' and Julie, you scratch at the door like you want out." They will talk about their little skit for 15 minutes and then enact it, with the actual enactment taking perhaps one minute. Small children mimic or imitate role-taking based on what they have seen.

By imitating roles she has seen, this child is learning both adult roles and empathy with others. This kind of role enactment is an important prerequisite to the more complex interaction of playing a game with others.

A child who is playing mommy or daddy with a doll is playing at taking the role of parent. The child is directing activity toward the doll in a manner imitative of how the parents direct activity toward the child. The child is trying to act another role, although the child often does not know what to do when playing the role of a parent "going off to work." Children can play only roles they have seen or are familiar with, and they do not know what the absent parent does when not in their presence. The point is that this "play" is actually extremely important "work" for children because they need to observe and imitate the relationships between roles to form the adult self (Handel, Cahill, and Elkin 2007).

Society and its rules are initially represented by **significant others**—parents, guardians, relatives, or siblings, whose primary and sustained interactions with the child are especially influential. That is why much of the play stage involves role-taking based on these significant people in the child's life. The child does not yet understand the complex relations and multiple role players in the social world outside the immediate family. Children may have a sense of how Mommy or Daddy sees them, but children are not yet able to comprehend how they are seen by the larger social world. Lack of role-taking ability is apparent when children say inappropriate things such as "Why are you so fat?"

In the **game stage**, the child learns to take the role of multiple others concurrently. Have you ever watched a team of young children play "tee ball" (a pre–Little League baseball game in which the children hit the ball from an upright rubber device that holds the ball), or have you observed a

soccer league made up of six-year-olds? If so, you have seen Mead's point illustrated vividly. In soccer (or football), five- or six-year-old children will not play their positions despite constant urging and cajoling by coaches. They all run after the ball, with little sense of their interdependent positions. Likewise, a child in a game of tee ball may pick up a ball that has been hit, turn to the coach, and say, "Now what do I do with it?" Most still do not quite grasp throwing it to first base, and the first-base player may actually have left the base to run for the ball. It can be hilarious for everyone except the coach, as a hit that goes seven feet turns into a home run because everyone is scrambling for the ball.

Still, the lesson of incomplete role-taking is clear. Prior to the game stage, the vision of the whole is not possible. When the children enter the game stage at about age seven or eight, they will be developmentally able to play the roles of various positions and enjoy a complex game. Each child learns what is expected and the interdependence of roles because they are then able to respond to the expectations of several people simultaneously (Hewitt 2007; Meltzer 1978). This allows the individual to coordinate his or her activity with others.

In moving from the play stage to the game stage, children's worlds expand from family and day care to neighborhood playmates, school, and other organizations. This process gradually builds up a composite of societal expectations—what Mead refers to as the **generalized other**. The child learns to internalize the expectations of society—the generalized other—over and above the expectations of any "significant others." Behavior comes to be governed by abstract rules ("no running outside of the baseline" or "no touching the soccer ball with your hands unless you are the goalie") rather than guidance from and emotional ties to a "significant other." Children become capable of moving into new social arenas such as school, organized sports, and (eventually) the workplace and to function with others in both routine and novel interactions. Sociologists see individuals as active in shaping their social contexts, the self, and the choices they make about the future.

An illustration of internalizing the generalized other into one's conception of self is the common human experience of feeling embarrassed. Blushing, a physiological response to feeling embarrassed, may occur when one has violated a social norm and is taking into account how others view that behavior. Making an inappropriate remark at a party or having another call undue attention to one's appearance can cause embarrassment. According to this role-taking view, we see ourselves as objects from the standpoint of others, and we judge ourselves accordingly. Very young children, however, do not feel embarrassment when they do such things as soil their pants or make inappropriate comments because they have not incorporated the generalized other. They have not yet learned the perspective of others. The capacity to feel embarrassed is not only an indicator of having internalized the generalized other but also a uniquely human outcome of our role-taking ability (Hewitt 2007).

As we grow, we identify with new in-groups such as a neighborhood, college sorority, or the military. We learn new ideas and expand our understanding. Some individuals ultimately come to think of themselves as part of the global human community. Thus, for many individuals, the social world expands through socialization. However, some individuals never develop this expanded worldview, remaining narrowly confined and drawing lines between themselves and others who are different. Such narrow boundaries often result in prejudice against others.

Thinking Sociologically

Who are you? Write down 15 or 20 roles or attributes that describe who you are. How many of these items are characteristics associated with the *Me*—nouns such as *son*, *mother*, *student*, *employee*? Which of the items are traits or attributes—adjectives such as *shy*, *sensitive*, *lonely*, *selfish*, *vulnerable*? How do you think each of these was learned or incorporated into your conception of your *self*?

Very young children who play soccer do not understand the role requirements of games. They all—including the goalie—want to chase after the ball. Learning to play positions is a critical step in socialization, for it requires a higher level of role-taking than children can do at the play stage.

The Self and Connections to the Meso Level

Much of the discussion thus far has focused on the Chicago School of symbolic interaction. That perspective emphasizes the role of the *I* and focuses on the active agency of individuals in their own development. The Iowa School of symbolic interaction places more emphasis on the *Me*—on the role of others and the external social environment in shaping us (Carrothers and Benson 2003).

In the "Thinking Sociologically" exercise above, we asked you to think about how you see yourself and what words you might use to portray yourself. If you were describing yourself for a group of people you did not know, we suspect that you would use mostly nouns describing a status—a social position within the society: student, employee, athlete, violinist, daughter, sister, Canadian, Lutheran, and so forth. To a large extent, our sense of who we are is rooted in social positions that are part of organizations and institutions in the society (Kuhn 1964; Stryker 1980). This is a key point made by the Iowa School of symbolic interaction: Selfhood is relatively stable because we develop a core self—a stable inner sense of who we are regardless of the immediate setting in which we find ourselves. This core often centers on the most important social positions we hold in the larger structure of society. You may think of yourself as politically or religiously conservative or liberal, and that may influence the way you conduct yourself in a wide range of situations and social settings. It may shape your sexual behavior, the honesty with which you

conduct business with others, and whether you are willing to cheat on an exam—even though you may not be around other people of your moral or political persuasion at the time (Turner 2003).

The Iowa School stresses that our identities are linked to institutions, organizations, and nations. Because of that, we have a vested interest in the stability of the society and the survival of those organizations that mean a lot to us—whether it is the college where we are a student, the Greek house that we join, the faith community with which we affiliate, or the nation of which we are a citizen. We will voluntarily give up our resources—time, energy, money, or even our lives—to preserve our beliefs, way of life, institutions, or our nation. So the selfhood is not just a function of an individual's identity. Individuals create organizations and institutions, and those social structures take on an independent existence that affects individual actions and thoughts. Thus, the self and meso-level structures are linked (Kuhn 1964; Stryker 1980, 2000; Stryker and Stratham 1985; Turner 2003).

Socialization Throughout the Life Cycle

Markers in many societies point to movement from one stage to the next in the socialization process: birth; naming

Children learn many things in school, but one of the first is to master rules such as standing in lines.

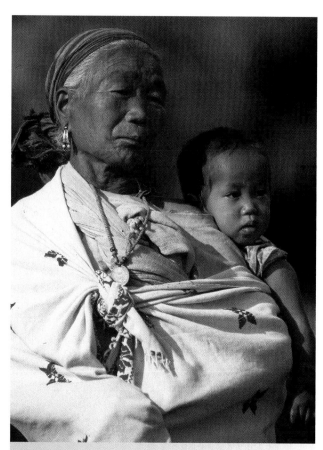

An elder Noctes woman with a grandchild strapped to her back watches traditional dances in her village. The Noctes live in extended family longhouses, so babies and children live under the supervision and care of the elder family members, who are greatly revered.

ceremonies or christenings; starting school at age five or six; rites of passage to mark puberty; obtaining a drivers license at about age 16; becoming eligible for military draft; being able to vote at age 18; retirement. Most social scientists emphasize the importance of rites of passage—celebrations or public recognitions when individuals shift from one status to another. The importance of this shift resides in how others come to perceive the individual differently, the different expectations that others hold for the person, and changes in how the person sees him- or herself.

Socialization is a lifelong process with many small and large passages. Infants begin the socialization process at birth. In childhood, one rite of passage is a child's first day at school—entrance into a meso-level institution. This turning point marks a child's entry into the larger world. The standards of performance are now defined by the child's teachers, peers, friends, and others outside the home. Adolescence is an important stage in Western industrial and postindustrial societies, but this stage is far from universal. Indeed, it is largely an invention of complex societies over the past two centuries, characterized by extensive periods of formal education and dependency on parents (Papalia, Olds, and Feldman 2006). Adolescence is, in a sense, a structurally produced mass identity crisis because Western societies lack clear rites of passage for adolescents. Teens come to view

themselves as a separate and distinct group with their own culture, slang vocabulary, clothing styles, and opinions about appropriate sexual behavior and forms of recreation.

Most of our adult years are spent in work and home life, including marriage and parenting roles. It is not surprising, then, that graduation from one's final alma mater (whether it be high school, college, or graduate school), marriage, and acceptance of one's first full-time job are rites of passage into adulthood in modern societies. Media hype about the aging of the baby boomer generation increases as the number of citizens in the United States older than 65 grows (now more than 12%) (U.S. Census Bureau 2005i). The average life expectancy in 1929 was 57 years. Today, it is roughly 79 years (Center for Disease Control and Prevention 2006a). This leaves time for new transitions into aging roles. Even the retired and elderly members of society are constantly undergoing socialization and resocialization and developing their sense of self. The type of society influences the socialization experience of the elderly and how they carry out their roles, as well as their status in society. Consider the changes that have taken place in the lifetimes of one group of elders, described in the following excerpt:

> *If you were born before 1945*: We were born before television, before polio shots, frozen foods, Xerox, plastic contact lenses, Frisbees and the Pill. We were born before credit cards, split atoms, laser beams and ballpoint pens; before pantyhose, dishwashers, clothes dryers, electric blankets, air conditioners in our homes, drip-dry clothes and before man walked on the moon. . . . We were before house husbands, gay rights, computer dating, dual careers and commuter marriages. We were before day care centers, group therapy and nursing homes. We never heard of FM radio, tape decks, electric typewriters, artificial hearts, word processors, yogurt, and guys wearing earrings. For us time sharing means togetherness—not computers and condominiums. A chip meant a piece of wood, hardware meant hardware and software wasn't even a word . . . smoking was fashionable, grass was mowed, coke was a cold drink and pot was something you cooked in. And we were the last generation that was so dumb as to think that you needed a husband to have a baby.
>
> Oh my, how the world has changed! (Grandpa Junior 2006)

A body is placed on a pyre at a cremation site next to the Ganges River in India. Cremation is a ritual designed to do much more than dispose of the body. It is intended to release the soul from its earthly existence. Hindus believe that cremation is most spiritually beneficial to the departed soul. The closest relative of the deceased takes charge of the final rite and lights the funeral pyre.

Thinking Sociologically

What are the rites of passage from adolescence into adulthood in your country? Is there ambiguity? Why do adolescents engage in defiant acts against adults? To establish independence? To demonstrate their standing as emerging adults?

The elderly are vitally important to the ongoing group in more settled agricultural societies. They are the founts of wisdom and carry group knowledge, experiences, and traditions that are valued in societies where little change takes place. In industrial and postindustrial countries, the number of elderly is growing rapidly as medical science keeps people alive longer, diets improve, and diseases are brought under control. Yet, in modern systems, social participation by the elderly often drops after retirement. Retirement is a rite of passage to a new status, like that of marriage or parenthood, for which there is little preparation. As a result, retired people sometimes feel a sense of uselessness when they abruptly lose their occupational status. Yet, retirees in Western societies generally have 20 or more years of life yet to live. Many retirees develop hobbies, enjoy sports, or have new jobs they can pursue.

Dying is the final stage of life (Kübler-Ross 1997). Death holds different meanings in different cultures: passing into another life, a time of judgment, a waiting for rebirth, or a void and nothingness. In some religious groups, people

In the Muslim tradition, the dead are washed and wrapped before burial. In the cemetery in Najaf, Iraq, parlors specializing in the washing of the dead prepare as many as 30 bodies for burial a day. Najaf is regarded as one of the holiest sites in Iraq for people to be buried. With many bodies, some mutilated from the war, these parlors are hard-pressed to keep up with demand for their services.

work hard or do good deeds because they believe they will be rewarded in an afterlife or with rebirth to a better status in the next life on Earth. Thus, beliefs about the meaning of death can affect how people live their lives and how they cope with dying and death.

U.S. Honor Guards carry a casket bearing the remains of U.S. Air Force personnel at Arlington National Cemetery outside Washington, D.C.

the society, the social world perpetuates itself and outlives the individuals who populate it.

Thinking Sociologically

How were you socialized to view death and dying? What have you learned in your family about how to cope with death?

The Process of Resocialization

If you have experienced life in the military, a boarding school, a convent, a mental facility, or a prison or had a major transition in your life such as divorce or the death of a spouse or child, you have experienced **resocialization**. Resocialization is the process of shedding one or more positions and taking on others. It involves changing from established patterns learned earlier in life to new ones suitable to the newly acquired status (Goffman 1961). Resocialization may take place in a **total institution** in which a group of people are bureaucratically processed, physically isolated from the outside world, and scheduled for all activities. These include prisons, mental hospitals, monasteries, concentration camps, boarding schools, and military barracks. Bureaucratic regimentation and the manipulation of residents for the convenience of the staff is part of the routine (Goffman 1961).

We often associate resocialization with major changes in adult life—divorce, retirement, and widowhood. One must adjust to raising children alone, living alone, loneliness, and possible financial problems. One divorcee of three years told the author: "There are many things to commend the single life, but I still have not adjusted to eating alone and cooking for myself. But worse than that are Sunday afternoons. That is the loneliest time."

Sometimes, resocialization describes individuals' attempts to adjust to new statuses and roles, such as widowhood. In other cases, individuals are forced into resocialization to correct or reform behaviors that are defined as undesirable or deviant. Prison rehabilitation programs provide one example. However, research suggests the difficulty in resocializing prisoners is rooted in the nature of the prison environment itself. Prisons are often coercive and violent environments, which may not provide the social supports necessary for bringing about change in a person's attitudes and behaviors.

Although resocialization is the goal of self-help groups such as Alcoholics Anonymous, Gamblers Anonymous, Parents Anonymous, drug rehabilitation groups, and weight-loss groups, relapse is a common problem among participants. These groups aim to substitute new behaviors and norms for old undesirable ones, but the process of undoing socialization and achieving resocialization is difficult. Some applied sociologists work on projects to resocialize clients, as shown in the next "Applied Sociologist at Work" feature.

A policy issue being debated in many countries is physician-assisted suicide, sometimes called euthanasia, or "good death" (Batavia 2000). Currently, the Netherlands permits the practice, but with many safeguards. Most U.S. states prohibit the practice under specific physician-assisted suicide laws or general homicide laws (Darr 2007; Nightingale Alliance 2007), although the citizens of Oregon voted in 1994 on measures to allow euthanasia and voted again to uphold this law (Lee and Werth 2000; Nightingale Alliance 2007). These measures are being challenged in courts, but at this time, the law still stands. So how you die—certainly an intensely personal experience—may be decided by a medical facility, an agency, or decision-making body of the federal government. Even death involves decisions by macro-level social structures.

Each stage of the life cycle involves socialization into new roles in the social world. Many social scientists have studied these developmental stages and contributed insights into what happens at each stage (Clausen 1986; Erikson 1950; Freud [1923] 1960; Gilligan 1982; Handel et al. 2007; Kohlberg 1971; Papalia et al. 2006; Piaget 1989). Although examination of these valuable theories is beyond the scope of this chapter, developmental theorists have detailed stages in the growth process.

Death ends the lifelong process of socialization, a process of learning social rules and roles and adjusting to them. When the individual is gone, society continues. New members are born, are socialized into the social world, pass through roles once held by others, and eventually give up those roles to younger members. Cultures provide guidelines for each new generation to follow, and except for the changes each generation brings to

The Applied Sociologist at Work— Jeffrey Breese

Role Exit and Socialization: Researching Adults in the Midst of Change

By Jeffrey Breese

Individuals constantly wrestle with unique situations and life events that force them to think and rethink how they define themselves. Sociologists who focus on life transitions for adults offer to other colleagues an understanding of the process of making role changes and how socialization is a lifelong process. My own research on adult nontraditional women students in the midst of career and personal transitions serves to assist counselors who work with these individuals. In fact, counselors are becoming increasingly interested in life role counseling as a means of assisting clients to cope with changes.

Role exit theory is the sociological construct that helps sociologists explain events and changes in adult life. These "exits" can be the result of an act of nature (such as death of a spouse), expulsion by a group (being excommunicated by your church), involuntary action (termination from a job), or voluntary (a chosen career change or divorce). Often, a combination of factors and events leads to someone undergoing a role exit. The social significance of this process is that you literally "exit" a role, yet that past part of your identity continues on into the present and could continue to impact decisions you make, how you approach daily work, and how others perceive and interact with you.

Helen Rose Ebaugh's book (1988), *Becoming an Ex: The Process of Role Exit,* laid the foundation for research into this process by examining groups of individuals undergoing key life-changing events. She considered doctors, teachers, and air traffic controllers who made career changes; widowers, divorcees, and mothers without custody, each wrestling with family life transitions; and ex-nuns who decided to leave their religious lifestyle. Ebaugh's research demonstrates that studying something as significant as a role exit has informative elements (for the field of sociology) as well as applied aspects (the research assists professionals in related helping professions).

Sociologists who study and research socialization issues appreciate the complexity of life transitions and role exits. As an example, adult women students now have more options when it comes to selecting a major for study. Although some traditional perceptions of "women's work" remain, many of our society's preconceived notions of what women can do and should do have been washed away. Clinical sociologists, who often partner with social workers and professional counselors, offer the data and expertise to share with their colleagues. They can offer professional guidance to individuals making life changes. The sociologists who study socialization processes inform others by offering insights into the complex nature of such transitions. Does the individual have the support of others with this life transition? Is the event a voluntary or involuntary change? Is an individual undergoing the change alone (fired from a job) or as part of a much larger group (the entire factory was shut down)? Adult life transitions, while experienced by an individual, must be understood in the larger cultural context. Sociologists studying career changes, divorce trends, and educational issues are also informing professionals in other fields who are assisting the individuals exiting roles that are central to their identity.

I have been working with those making role transitions and exits and studying these transitions for many years. My work provides guidance for counselors and others working with adult or non-traditional women.

Note: Jeffrey Breese is an associate professor of sociology and associate dean of the School of Education and Human Services at Marymount University. He received his bachelor's degree from Youngstown University, his master's from Ohio University, and his doctorate from The University of Akron. In addition to researching in the areas of qualitative methods, race and ethnic relations, and the teaching of sociology, he teaches courses at Marymount University.

Jeffrey Breese's work focuses on role transitions and exits for adults.

There are multiple individuals, groups, and institutions involved in the socialization process. These socialization forces are referred to as agents of socialization.

AGENTS OF SOCIALIZATION: THE MICRO-MESO CONNECTION

Agents of socialization are the transmitters of culture— the people, organizations, and institutions that teach us how to thrive in our social world. Agents are the mechanism by which the self learns the values, beliefs, and behaviors of the culture. Agents of socialization help new members find their place, just as they prepare older members for new responsibilities in society. At the micro level, one's family, the peer group, and local groups and organizations help people to know what is expected of them. At the meso level, formal sources of learning—education, religion, politics, economics, health—and other informal sources of learning such as the media and books are all agents that contribute to socialization. They transmit information to children and to adults throughout our lives.

Thinking Sociologically

As you read this section, make a list of the socializing agents discussed in these pages. When you are done making the list, list two or three central messages that you think each agent of socialization tries to instill in people. Consider which agents are micro, which are meso, and which are macro agents. Are there different kinds of messages at each level? Do any of them conflict? Why do you think they conflict? Does the conflict cause any problems?

In early childhood, the family acts as the primary agent of socialization, passing on messages about respect for property, authority, and neatness, for example (Handel et al. 2007). Peer groups are also important, especially during the teenage years. Some writers even argue that the peer group is most important in the socialization process of children and teens (Aseltine 1995; Harris 1998). Each agent has its own functions or purposes and is important at different stages of the life cycle, but meso-level institutions play a more active role as one matures. For example, schools and religious bodies become more involved in socialization as children become six years old compared to when they were preschool age. For us, the authors of this book, other members of the American Sociological Association serve as "significant others" and shape our sense of appropriate behavior for sociologists and professors.

"How Do We Know?" discusses how we know about socialization in schools by exploring an important and widely cited research project. Note what kind of data is viewed as legitimate evidence for understanding gender socialization.

Lessons from one agent generally complement those of other agents. Parents work at home to support what school and religion teach. However, at times agents provide conflicting lessons. For example, family and faith communities often give teens messages that conflict with those of peer groups regarding sexual activity and drug use. This is an instance of mixed messages given by formal and informal agents.

For **formal agents**, socialization is the stated goal. Formal agents usually have some official or legal responsibility for instructing individuals. A primary goal of families is to teach children to speak and to learn proper behavior. In addition, school teachers educate by giving formal instruction, and religious training provides moral instruction. (These formal agents of socialization will be discussed in Chapters 10, 11, and 12.)

Informal agents do not have the express purpose of socialization, but they function as unofficial forces that shape values, beliefs, and behaviors. For example, the media, books, the Internet, and advertisements bring us continuous messages even though their primary purpose is not socialization but entertainment or selling products. Children watch countless advertisements on television, many with messages about what is good and fun to eat and how to be more attractive, more appealing, smarter, and a better person through the consumption of products. This bombardment is a particularly influential part of socialization at young ages.

This distinction between formal, intentional socialization and informal, unplanned socialization has important implications for the kinds of messages that are presented and for how such messages are received.

Thinking Sociologically

What dilemmas do you think might be created for children when the formal and informal agents of socialization provide different messages about values or acceptable behaviors? Is this contradiction something that we should be concerned about? Why or why not?

Families: Micro-Level Socializing Agents

One way in which families teach children what is right and wrong is through rewards and punishments, called sanctions. Children who steal cookies from the cookie jar may receive a verbal reprimand or a slap on the hand, be sent to their rooms, have "time out," or receive a beating, depending on differences in child-rearing patterns. These are examples of negative sanctions. Conversely, children may be rewarded for good behavior with a smile, praise, a cookie, or a special

The primary socialization unit for young children is the family, but as they become teenagers, the reference group becomes increasingly important in shaping the norms, values, and attitudes. Young Kurdish men play network games and socialize in Erbil, Iraq.

How Do We Know?

Gender Socialization in American Public Schools

Pause for a moment as you pass a school yard, and observe the children at play. Children's behavior on the school playground translates into a powerful agent of gender socialization in a world that is very complex. Consider the evidence reported in the ethnographic study of Barrie Thorne, recounted in her award-winning book, *Gender Play*.

Many people assume that gender differences are natural and that we are born that way. By contrast, Thorne provides evidence that gender differences are social constructions, influenced by the setting, the players involved in the situation, and the control people have over the situation.

As an astute observer and researcher, Thorne suspected that girls and boys have complex relations that play out in the classroom and school yard. She chose the playground as the focus of her observation on the separate worlds of girls and boys. As her research strategy, she points out that "when adults seek to learn about and from children, the challenge is to take the closely familiar and to render it strange" (Thorne 1993:12).

To test her idea about gender socialization, Thorne used the methodology of participant observation and then wrote an ethnography, a systematic observation of social contexts. Kids and adults play an active role in defining and shaping gender expectations through the collective practices of forming lines, choosing seats, teasing, gossiping, and participating in selected activities, as she observed.

Thorne (1993) used two schools for her research. One school was in a small city on the coast of California and the other on the outskirts of a large city in Michigan. Both schools had about 400 students, mostly from working-class backgrounds. Most students were white, with 12% to 14% Latino and 5% African American. Ethnographer Thorne entered the world of the children, sometimes sitting apart on the playground taking notes, sometimes participating in their activities such as eating and talking with them in the lunchroom.

In each setting, she recorded her observations and experiences in the process of observation and interpretation. For example, she noted what children call themselves and how they think of themselves. She was intrigued by the reference to the opposite sex—a term that stresses difference and opposition rather than similarity and sense of "we." Thorne was struck by the active meaning-construction of children as they gained a notion of "normal" gender behavior. The real focus of her work is in taking seriously how children themselves make sense of sex differences—and how they sometimes ignore any difference as irrelevant to their activities.

Previous studies concluded that boys tend to interact in larger, more age-heterogeneous groups, in more rough and tumble play and physical fighting. Thorne also found that boys' play involves a much larger portion of the playgrounds, and their play space was generally further from the building, making them less subject to monitoring and sanctioning. Girls played close to the buildings in much smaller areas and rarely ventured into the boys' area. By contrast, boys used the entire playground and would often run "sneak invasions" into the girls' space to take things belonging to the girls. Many boys felt they had a right to the geographical space that was occupied by females.

Girls' play tended to be characterized by cooperation and turn-taking. They had more intense and exclusive friendships, which took shape around keeping and telling secrets, shifting alliances, and indirect ways of expressing disagreement. Instead of direct commands, girls more often used words like "let's" or "we gotta" (Thorne 1993). However, Thorne found that these notions of "separate girls' and boys' worlds" used in most previous studies miss the subtleties in the situation—race, class, and other factors.

Valerie Ann Moore (2001) updated Thorne's study by examining children at a summer day camp. Like Thorne, she watched the children play and interact with one another. Moore found that the children also use play to construct meaning of race and age. All of the "little men" in the camp showed their age by defying the adults' rules, which unified them across racial and age boundaries. The "little women" at the camp, on the other hand, were much more likely to separate by age and race when interacting with other campers.

Moore (2001) found that boys and girls come together and that romance and narratives of romance were most likely to break the physical boundaries among older campers. These romances, however, emphasize gender differences. The camp counselors reinforced this difference by constantly creating and maintaining gender boundaries to prohibit romances from forming between the teens.

The major contribution of these two studies is to alert us to the complexity of the gender socialization process, helping us see the extent to which children are active agents who are creating their own definitions of social relations, not just short automatons who enact adult notions of what gender means.

Japanese fathers and their sons eat lunch during a festival. While mothers are the key agents of socialization in Japan, fathers also have a role, especially during special events in the life of the child.

A Japanese mother helps her son at Heian Shinto Shrine during Shichi-go-san Matsuri, also called 7–5–3 Festival, a celebration with prayers of long life for children aged three to seven.

event. These are examples of positive sanctions. The number and types of sanctions dispensed in the family shape the socialization process, including development of the self and the perceptions we have of who we are. Note that family influence varies from one culture to another.

In Japan, the mother is the key agent in the process of turning a newborn into a member of the group, passing on the strong group standards and expectations of family, neighbors, community, and society through the use of language with emotional meaning. The child learns the importance of depending on the group and therefore fears being cast out. The need to belong creates pressure to conform to expectations, and the use of threats and fear of shame helps socialize children into Japanese ways (Hendry 1987; White 1987).

Nonconformity is a source of shame in Japan. The resulting ridicule is a powerful means of social control. In some cases, the outcast is physically punished by peers. Thus, to bring shame on oneself or the family is to be avoided. In the most extreme cases, young people have committed suicide because they did not conform to group expectations and felt profoundly ashamed as a result. The interaction of family and formal education in Japan is explored in more detail in the next "Sociology Around the World."

In the United States, most parents value friendliness, cooperation, orientation toward achievement, social competence, responsibility, and independence as qualities their children should learn, in contrast to values of conformity and fitting into the group espoused in Japan. However, subcultural values and socialization practices may differ within the diverse groups in the U.S. population. Conceptions of what makes a "good person" or a "good citizen" and different goals of socialization bring about differences in the process of socialization around the world.

In addition, the number of children in a family and the placement of each child in the family structure can influence the unique socialization experience of the child. In large families, parents typically have less time with each additional child. Where the child falls in the hierarchy of siblings can also influence the development of the self. In fact, birth order is a better predictor of social attitudes than race, class, or gender, according to some studies (Benokraitis 2004; Freese et al. 1999), and firstborns are typically the highest achievers ("First Born" 2008; Paulhus, Trapnell, and Chen 1999). Younger children may be socialized by older siblings as much as by parents, and older siblings often serve as models that younger children want to emulate.

Social Class: Meso-Level Socialization

Our educational level, our occupation, the house we live in, what we choose to do in our leisure time, the foods we eat, and what we believe in terms of religion and politics are just a few aspects of our lives that are affected by socialization.

Sociology Around the World

Socialization in Japan: The Family and Early Schooling

By Wendy Ng

Each of our families prepares us through the socialization process for the culture we are entering. How families carry out this process differs around the world, just as the cultures for which they are preparing their children differ. Here we consider the family and early schooling in Japanese socialization.

The family is one of the most important socializing influences in Japan. The basis of the family unit in Japan is called the *ie* (pronounced ee-ay). Traditionally, it is made up of blood relatives who reside in the same household, as well as ancestors and descendents not yet born. Thus, family in Japan goes beyond those who belong to the immediate nuclear grouping and includes a broader array of individuals. Compared with the past, the modern *ie* in Japan relies more on the nuclear and living extended family and serves as the major reference group that socializes individuals within the family. Thus, family members within the *ie* are responsible for teaching individuals their family roles, values, and norms within the culture.

A unique feature of interdependence that is found within the family structure is that of *amac* (ah-may), which roughly translated means passive love but is often referred to as an emotional bond usually held between mother and child. Through this relationship, children are socialized to understand that they are an important part of the family, and they also learn that parents are to be respected and obeyed as the adults within the family. Although this appears hierarchical, the emotional bond of *amae* sets up a relationship of interdependency between child and parent for their lifetime. As children grow into adulthood, they will take care of their parents in the way that they were taken care of as children. This bond of loyalty between parent and child within the family structure is translated into other social structures outside the family. For example, in a business organization, there is a similar expectation of group loyalty.

In terms of early childhood socialization, Japanese children learn the distinction between two related, yet distinct concepts: *uchi* and *soto*. Roughly translated these mean "inside" and "outside" and can apply to material distinctions of clean and unclean spaces. In behavior, this means taking one's shoes off outside the house because the inside is clean and the outside is unclean. In Japanese households, the bathroom has similar clean and unclean designations. The bath is "clean" and the toilet, used to dispose of bodily wastes, is "unclean." Thus, one would never wear the same shoes or slippers in the toilet room as the bathroom because that would be mixing clean and unclean elements.

Within the family, immediate members are "insiders" and other people are "outsiders." Children learn that the family is a safe and secure environment where the emphasis is on harmony among the various family members. Interactions between individuals stress cooperation, and interpersonal disputes are avoided. If a disagreement happens, children are taught to apologize to one another. Reciprocity is yet another behavior that is emphasized within the family. Children are taught to put themselves in the role of the other person and to think of the consequences of their behavior before acting out. This type of role behavior suggests that harmony between and among family members is important and sets the foundation for the child's educational socialization.

Whereas the family serves as the central socializing force when children are very young, as they grow, the educational system continues to socialize children through group interaction and learning. When children enter kindergarten they become familiar with participating in a social group with peers. The Japanese kindergarten system emphasizes group equality among children and thus socializes children to be loyal to their classmates and group. Other children now form their new *uchi* or "inside" associations and friendships. The emphasis on group over individual identities is accomplished through wearing identical uniforms or smocks, having similar educational tools for all students, and having children take turns in different duties in the classroom. For example, the responsibility of passing out paper in the classroom, or food at lunchtime, are rotated among all the children in the classroom. Thus, cooperation and group participation becomes an important defining feature of kindergarten socialization.

At first glance, the emphasis on equality among individuals in the kindergarten classroom setting might seem to conflict with the emphasis on hierarchical authority present in much of Japanese society. In fact, the emphasis on group socializing helps to encourage a sense of belonging and group identity that works well within hierarchical authority structures. By learning these behaviors at a young age, the children learn that they are individuals within a larger group, and that their actions reflect not only on themselves but also on their family, school, or whatever social group they belong to as adults.

This father passes on a love for the piano to his young son. Because of the social class of this father, his son is likely to receive many messages about creativity, curiosity, and self-direction.

Applying what we know from sociological research, the evidence strongly suggests that socialization varies by **social class**, or the wealth, power, and prestige rankings that individuals hold in society (Ellison, Bartkowski, and Segal 1996). Meso-level patterns of distribution of resources affect who we become. For example, upper-middle-class and middle-class parents in the United States usually have above average education and managerial or professional jobs. They tend to pass on to their children skills and values necessary to succeed in this social class subculture. Autonomy, creativity, and self-direction (the ability to make decisions and take initiative), responsibility, curiosity, and consideration of others are especially important for middle-class success (Kohn 1989). If the child misbehaves, for example, middle-class parents typically analyze the child's reasons for misbehaving, and punishment is related to these reasons. Sanctions often involve instilling guilt and denying privileges.

Working-class parents tend to pass on to children their cultural values of respect for authority and conformity to rules, lessons that will be useful if the children also have blue-collar jobs (Kohn 1989). Immediate punishment with no questions asked if a rule is violated functions to prepare children for

positions in which obedience to rules is important to success. They are expected to be neat, clean, well-mannered, honest, and obedient students (MacLeod 1995). Socialization experiences for boys and girls are often different, following traditional gender-role expectations. Moreover, these differences in behavior across social classes and parenting styles are apparent cross-culturally as well (Leung, Lau, and Lam 1998).

What conclusions can we draw from these studies? Members of each class are socializing their children to be successful in their social class and to meet expectations for adults of that class. Schools, like families, participate in this process. Although the extent to which schools create or limit opportunities for class mobility is debated, what is clear is that children's social class position on entering school has an effect on the socialization experiences they have in school (Ballantine and Hammack 2009). Families and schools socialize children to adapt to the settings in which they grow up and are likely to live.

Electronic Media: Meso-Level Agents Within the Home

Television and computers are important informal agents of socialization. In developed countries, there is scarcely a home without a television set, and many homes have computers and Internet access. About 51% of households in the United States have one or more computers, and 9 out of 10 children have computer access (U.S. Census Bureau 2001b). Researchers have collected nearly five decades of information on how television has become a way of life in homes.

By the time an average child in the United States reaches age 18, he or she will have spent more time watching television than any other single activity besides sleeping. On average, children between ages 8 and 18 spend three hours a day watching television, one hour and 11 minutes watching videos or DVDs, one hour and 44 minutes with audio media, one hour using computers, and 49 minutes playing video games, with a total media exposure in a typical day of eight hours and 33 minutes. Table 4.2 shows total media exposure of children by several variables (Kaiser Family Foundation 2005).

Thinking Sociologically

Considering the data in Table 4.2, how would you describe television-watching patterns among different groups? How might television watching affect other aspects of socialization of children?

Between the ages of 2 and 18, children in the United States spend an average of half an hour a day using computers, including computer use at school. Children ages 8

Table 4.2	**Total Media Exposure (average hours per day)**	
		Hours per Day
Age	8 to 10 years old	8:05
	11 to 14 years old	8:41
	15 to 18 years old	8:44
Gender	Boys	8:38
	Girls	8:27
Race	White	7:58
	Black	10:10
	Hispanic	8:52
Parent education	High school or less	8:30
	Some college	8:02
	College graduate	8:55
Income	Under $35,000	8:40
	$35,000–$50,000	8:28
	Over $50,000	8:34

Source: Kaiser Family Foundation 2005.

Elderly people learn how to use computers in Shanghai, China. Keeping up with the rapid pace of change—especially in technology— is sometimes a challenge for seniors in post-industrial societies. Their grandchildren may know more than they about technology.

and older spend more than an hour and a half each day on computers: 22% of this time is doing schoolwork; 33% is spent on the Internet chatting, surfing the Web, or sending e-mail; and 26% is spent playing games (National Parent Information Network 2000). This means that the moguls of mass media—a meso-level social system—are able to influence socialization within the most intimate of environments. "Children [in the U.S.] use computers at very young ages—21 percent of children 2 years and younger, 58 percent of 3- to 4-year-olds, and 77 percent of 5- to 6-year-olds" (National Science Foundation 2005:1).

A serious concern related to socialization centers around the messages children receive from television and computer games, along with the behavioral effects of these messages. There is ample evidence that children are affected in negative ways from excessive television viewing, especially television violence (National Science Foundation 2005), but a direct causal link between television viewing and behavior is difficult to establish. Researchers know, however, that parents who play an active role in helping children understand the content of television shows can have a powerful effect on mitigating television's negative impacts and enhancing the positive aspects of television shows. The television-viewing habits of parents—length of viewing time, types of shows watched, times of day—can also influence how their children respond to television.

Perhaps the most important aspect of television and computers is something that we do not fully understand but that has frightening potential. For the first time in human history, we have powerful agents of socialization in the home from a child's birth onward. Time spent attending to television or

computer games means less time spent engaging in interaction with caregivers and peers. Intimate family bonds formed of affection and meaningful interaction are being altered by the dominant presence of electronic media in the home. Television and computer games augment, and potentially compete with, the family as a socializing agent. Those who control the flood of mass media messages received by children may have interests and concerns that are very much at odds with those of parents.

We can conclude that part of the socialization process occurs with the assistance of electronic equipment that shares the home with parents and siblings and that commands a significant portion of a child's time and attention. The next "Sociology in Your Social World" compares socialization in schools, television, and the Internet.

Most formal institutions in modern societies (education, political systems, family, health care, and religion) socialize people to identify with values and behaviors acceptable in their local and national groups. With globalization, global knowledge and understanding also become important parts of school curricula and media coverage. We move next to a discussion of some of the national and global processes that impact socialization.

Thinking Sociologically

What other agents of socialization in addition to family, social class, and electronic media are important in teaching us our roles, norms, values, and beliefs? What is the impact, for example, of friendship networks or peer groups?

Sociology in Your Social World

Formal and Informal Agents of Socialization: A Comparison of Schooling, Television, and the Internet

By Alan McEvoy and Laurie McCloud

Schooling, television, and the Internet share a basic characteristic: All are purveyors of messages to young people. Despite this similarity, however, there are also many differences. Schools are formal agents of socialization with the expressed purpose of socializing the young. Television and the Internet are informal agents of socialization because their goals are entertaining, selling products, and increasing consumerism. Socialization is a secondary result.

Schools	Television	Internet
Schooling is formal and bureaucratic; it takes place in specially designed buildings.	TV viewing generally takes place in the informal setting of one's home.	The majority of Internet users have home access (Pew Internet and American Life Project 2007), but others use the Internet in institutional settings such as work and school. Internet access requires a service fee and computer ownership for home use.
Acquisition of information requires obeying certain rules (e.g., no eating, no talking, no running around).	There are often no rules for watching TV, although parents may put limits on how much time can be spent viewing or what shows can be watched.	There are no rules for Internet viewing, except those imposed by parents. Listserv applications and blogs sometimes develop and impose their own rules of civility. The issue of rules for civil use is an emerging one in this new medium, especially with e-mail.
School is structured around a sequential, age-appropriate curriculum that intends to inform and to build on skills.	TV has no structured curriculum but a random content (channel surfing), which is usually designed to entertain. Watching TV requires no special skills.	The Internet has random content, and it can be user-provided, which means a large variety of information and opinions is represented.
Students are a captive audience, required to attend school for specified periods (usually 8 a.m. to 3 p.m., excluding weekends and certain holidays).	Watching TV is voluntary, and programs are available 24 hours per day throughout the year.	Internet use is voluntary. Web sites are available 24 hours a day throughout the year.
There is a power imbalance between teachers and students; students have a role imposed on them and have little control over the requirements of that role. Students do not directly control the flow of information from teachers.	There are no role requirements imposed on the viewer from the TV. The viewer has power to control the flow of information with the on/off switch and choice of channels.	Many Web sites are interactive or have user content. Most users passively view content. Users can close Web browsers and change pages at will.

Schools	Television	Internet
Schools do not provide information to students for commercial purposes (no profit motive).	TV messages are generally provided to viewers for commercial purposes (excepting public TV).	Commercial Web site messages are generally provided to viewers to generate profit.
Students are grouped in classes by age or ability, and groups of students (15 to 30) together receive the message.	Viewers watch TV individually or in small groups, and millions may receive the same message.	Internet users typically do so individually, though they may be communicating with people geographically very distant from themselves.
Face-to-face interaction defines the relationship between students and teachers and among students, as each takes the other into account throughout the interaction. Face-to-face interaction allows for mutual influence.	Vicarious interaction with an electronic image (rather than a live person) defines the relationship between viewers and media personalities. Viewers are not able to interact directly with the millions of other people receiving the same messages, hence no mutual influence.	Web sites vary in the ability to interact with the content provider. No face-to-face interaction occurs. Some sites allow users to post comments or edit content. Many sites allow only passive viewing of shared information.
Influence of schooling starts when the child begins school (about age 5).	The influence of TV begins in infancy when children become new members of the family, and the impact of TV is significant even before a child has entered school.	Individuals are introduced to the Internet at a young age, and the Web appears to have a growing influence throughout the life course.

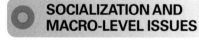

SOCIALIZATION AND MACRO-LEVEL ISSUES

Heterogeneous Societies and Sense of Self Versus "Other"

Immigration patterns and ethnic conflicts around the world have resulted in a fairly new phenomenon: transnationalism. **Transnationalism** involves an individual or a family that has national loyalty to more than one country (Levitt 2001). Often, it occurs after migration of war refugees, when one's roots lie in the country of origin and many of one's close family members continue to live there. Consider children raised in war-torn countries. In the Palestinian territories, especially Gaza, and in Israeli settlements along the border, children grow up with fear and hatred, major influences on their socialization. Some war refugees spend childhoods in refugee camps and may never return to their countries.

For people experiencing transnationalism, there are conflicting messages about culturally appropriate behaviors and the obligations of loyalty to family and nation. However, one need not migrate to another country to experience global pressures. The Internet and cell phones have increasingly created a sense of connectedness to other parts of the world and an awareness of global interdependencies (Brier 2004; Roach 2004). Some commentators have even suggested that the Internet is a threat to the nation-state as it allows individuals to maintain traditions and loyalties to relatives and friends in more than one country (Drori 2006). Ideas of social justice or progress in many parts of the world are shaped not just by the government that rules the country but by international human rights organizations and ideas that are obtained from media that cross borders, such as the World Wide Web.

Access to international information and friendships across borders and boundaries are increasingly possible as more people have access to the Internet. Map 4.1, on Internet use around the world, illustrates variability of access but also how widespread this access is becoming. One interesting question is how access or lack of access will influence the strength of "we" versus "they" feelings.

At a time when people lived in isolated rural communities and did not interact with those unlike themselves, there was little price to pay for being bigoted or chauvinistic toward those who were different. However, we now live in a global village where we or our businesses will likely interact with very different people in a competitive environment. If we hold people in low regard because they are unlike us or because we think they are destined for hell because of their spiritual beliefs, there may be

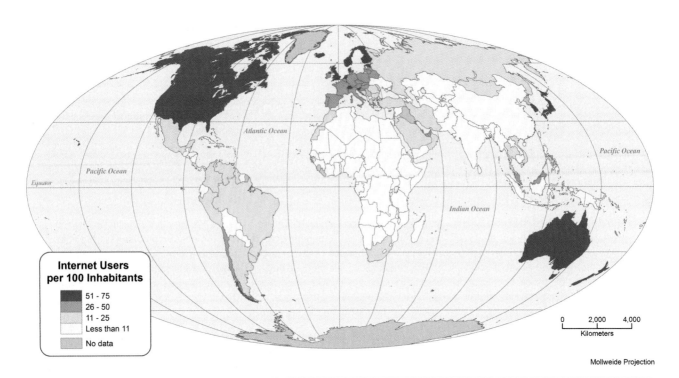

Map 4.1   Internet Users per 100 People in 2005

Source: World Bank.

a high cost for this alienation toward those who are not like us. Among other problems, terrorism is fermented where people feel alienated. Therefore, diversity training and cultural sensitivity to those "others" has become an economic and political issue.

The reality is that children in the 21st century are being socialized to live in a globalized world. Increasingly, children around the world are learning multiple languages to enhance their ability to communicate with others. Some college campuses are requiring experiences abroad as part of the standard curriculum because faculty members and administrators feel that a global perspective is essential in our world today and part of a college education. Socialization to global sensitivity and tolerance of those who were once considered "alien" has become a core element of our day (Robertson 1992; Schaeffer 2003; Snarr and Snarr 2002).

Global Events and Personal Identity

Sometimes, global events can cause a different turn: away from tolerance and toward defensive isolation. When 19 young men from Saudi Arabia and other Middle Eastern countries crashed planes into the World Trade Center in New York City and into the Pentagon in Washington, D.C., the United States was shocked and became mobilized to defend itself and its borders. The messages within schools and from the government suddenly took a more patriotic turn. Then-U.S. Secretary of Defense Donald Rumsfeld stated that the problem with America is that citizens

do not have a strong enough sense of "we" versus "they." So this event and other terrorist acts, clearly tragedies rooted in global political conflicts, can intensify boundaries between people and loyalty to the nation-state. Global forces are themselves complex and do not always result in more tolerance.

Indeed, the only thing we can predict with considerable certainty is that in this age of sharing a small planet, the socialization of our citizens will be influenced by events at the macro level, whether national or global.

Policy and Practice

Should preschoolers living in poverty be socialized in day care settings? Should adolescents work while going to school? Should new parents be required to take child-rearing classes? How should job-training programs be structured? How can communities use the talents and knowledge of retirees? Can the death process be made easier for the dying person and the family? Should we place emphasis in high school and college on in-group loyalty and patriotism or on developing a sense of global citizenship mobilized around common human issues such as global climate change? These are all policy questions—issues of how to establish governing principles that will enhance our common life.

These policy questions rely on an understanding of socialization—how we learn our beliefs and our positions in society. For example, making decisions about how to provide positive early childhood education experiences at a time when young children are learning the ways of their culture relies on understanding the socialization they receive at home and at school. The quality of child care we provide for young children will affect not only how effective our future workforce is but also whether kids turn out to be productive citizens or a drain on society.

Some sociologists do research to try to help policymakers have accurate data and make good interpretations of the data so they can make wise decisions. Others are more activist, working in the field as applied sociologists trying to solve the problems through private foundations, consulting firms, or state agencies. An example of someone working in the field, using sociology to solve problems, is Joyce Miller, as revealed in the account of her work in the following "The Applied Sociologist at Work."

The Applied Sociologist at Work— Joyce Miller

Evaluating Socialization for Young Children

The state of Pennsylvania evaluates early child-care facilities (as do most states) to ensure that they are meeting standards set by the state. Part of sociologist Joyce Miller's responsibilities as president of Keystone University Research Corporation is to help plan and oversee the evaluations and training of child care workers. As an applied sociologist, Dr. Miller works with clients such as the state to develop policy, evaluate programs to determine if standards are being met, and recommend interventions to improve child care.

Miller and her colleagues work as a team to design, implement, and evaluate programs in child care training aimed at improving skills of early childhood teachers, and they set up training opportunities for professional development. To evaluate how well child care teachers and facilities are serving children, Keystone collects data on the child care centers, analyzes those data, and makes reports with policy recommendations available to the centers and the state. For instance, Keystone staff members administer an environmental rating scale used in observing child care centers.

Miller's training for her position involved both skill areas of applied research and several content areas of her work: child care, gerontology, juvenile justice, and sex equity. Her PhD degree from Kent State University was in applied sociology, social evaluation research, and social policy. While her content and skill areas are essential to her work, she feels that sociological knowledge of how organizational systems work has proved most important. Another necessary skill for her work is knowledge of computer statistical packages for analysis of data.

As Miller points out, sociologists are ideally suited to do applied research because of their understanding of data and how to work with them. They also know how to use measuring and analyzing programs and turn their findings into recommendations for change or new initiatives. Miller has a useful, satisfying, and fun role. As she says, "there is never a dull day, and no two days are alike." She moves in different contexts and has opportunities to work with a variety of people, from child care teachers to legislators.

So What ?

Human beings are not born to be noble savages or depraved beasts. As a species, we are remarkable in how many aspects of our lives are shaped by learning—by socialization. Human socialization is pervasive, extensive, and lifelong. We cannot understand what it means to be human without comprehending the impact of a specific culture on us, the influence of our close associates, and the complex interplay of pressures from micro, meso, and macro levels. Indeed, without social interaction, there would not even be a self. We humans are, in our most essential natures, social beings. This has been the purpose of this chapter—to open our eyes to the ways in which we become the individuals we are.

Most of the influences that shape us occur in our interactions with others—through networks, groups, organizations, and even bureaucracies. In the next chapter, we turn to an analysis of these aspects of our social world.

Key Points

What Have We Learned?

- Human beings must work with their biological makeup, but most of what makes us uniquely human has to do with things we learn from our culture and society—our socialization. Humans who are not socialized and live in isolation from others are tragic—barely human—creatures. (See pp. 100–102.)

- The self consists of the interaction of the *I*—the basic impulsive human with drives, needs, and feelings—and the *Me*—the reflected self one develops by role-taking to see how others might see one. (See pp. 102–105.)

- The self is profoundly shaped by others, but it also has agency—it is an initiator of action and the maker of meaning. (See pp. 105–107.)

- The self develops through stages, from mimicking others (the play stage) to more intellectually sophisticated abilities to role-take and to see how various roles fit together—the game stage. (See pp. 107–109.)

- Although the self is somewhat elastic in adjusting to different settings and circumstances, there is also a core self that is often vested in meso-level organizations and institutions of which the self participates. (See p. 109.)

- The self is modified as it moves through life stages, and some of those stages require major resocialization—shedding old roles and taking on new ones as one enters new statuses in life. (See pp. 109–113.)

- A number of agents of socialization are at work on each of us, communicating messages that are relevant at the micro, the meso, or the macro level of social life. At the meso level, for example, we may receive different messages about what it means to be a "good" person depending on our ethnic, religious, or social class subculture. (See pp. 113–122.)

- Some of these messages may be in conflict with each other, as when global messages about tolerance for those who are different conflict with a nation's desire to have absolute loyalty and sense of superiority. (See pp. 122.)

Contributing to Our Social World: What Can We Do?

At the Local Level: In every community, numerous opportunities exist for volunteer work in helping children from economically and otherwise disadvantaged backgrounds to succeed in school. If your college or university has a program in early childhood education, contact a faculty member about working as a tutor or mentor in the local schools. Head Start centers for poor preschool children often need volunteers. The National Head Start Association maintains a Web site at www.nhsa.org. Local Boys and Girls Clubs provide socialization experiences for children through their teens. They also need volunteers and frequently provide sites for internships. Care facilities and hospices for people who are ill or dying help reduce loneliness and provide positive interaction for individuals in these facilities. Check for volunteer opportunities or part-time work opportunities. All of these activities provide excellent opportunities for Academic Service Learning (ASL) credit in which course assignments include such community work under the supervision of the instructor. Find out about ASL programs on your campus.

At the National and Global Levels: Literacy, one of the most vital components of socialization, remains an unmet need in many parts of the world, especially in the less-developed countries of Africa and Asia. More than 30 countries have adult literacy rates below 50%, including Niger, Afghanistan, Pakistan, Angola, and India. One of the leading organizations dedicated to bringing reading skills to children (and adults) is World Education. Visit this group's Web site at www.worlded.org to learn about its wide variety of projects and how you can participate in these activities. Care International and Save the Children are among the other international organizations that provide funding for families to send children to school and to receive specialized training. Opportunities exist for fundraising, internships, or eventually jobs with these organizations.

Visit **www.pineforge.com/ballantine2study** for online activities, sample tests, and other helpful information. Select "Chapter 4: Socialization" for chapter-specific activities.

CHAPTER 5

Interaction, Groups, and Organizations

Connections That Work

Human interaction results in connections—networks—that work to make life more fulfilling and that make our economic efforts more productive. These connections are critical in our social world—from small micro groups to large bureaucratic organizations.

Think About It . . .

Micro: Are you likely to meet your perfect mate over the Internet?

Micro: How does interaction with others affect who you are and what you believe?

Meso: Is bureaucratic "red tape" really necessary?

Macro: How do national trends—such as the spread of fast food chains and huge "box stores"—influence your quality of life?

Macro: How are you connected through networks to people across the globe?

Macro: Global Community

Macro: Society

Meso: National Organizations, Institutions, and Ethnic Subcultures

Micro: Local Organizations and Community

Micro: Me (and My Network of Close Friends)

Micro: Networks of school alumni; local religious congregations; scout groups; civic clubs

Meso: Participation in ethnic organizations; political parties; religious denominations

Macro: Connection between citizens of a nation

Macro: Global networks; United Nations; international laws or courts; transnational corporations

Today, cyberspace is linking the world. In seconds, business people can transact multimillion-dollar deals with geographically distant clients who have contracts with multinational corporations. There is no need to wait for the mail or even talk on the phone. The information superhighway is opening new communication routes and networking individuals with common interests. Yet only a few decades ago, we read about cyberspace in science fiction novels written by authors with a little science background and a lot of imagination. Indeed, the word *cyberspace* was coined in 1984 by science fiction writer William Gibson (Brasher 2004).

The implications of the rapidly expanding links in cyberspace are staggering. We cannot even anticipate some of them because change is so rapid. For entertainment, we can talk with friends on listservs or with people we have "met" through cyber social groups. Some of these acquaintances have never left their own country, which is on the other side of the planet. All of this takes place in the comfort of our homes. Face-to-face communication may or may not ever occur.

Universities now communicate with students and employees by computer. You may be able to register for class by "talking" to the computer. Computers track your registration and grades, and they may even write you letters about your status. They also monitor employee productivity. For doing certain types of research, library books are becoming secondary to the World Wide Web.

Jeanne, one of the coauthors of this book, took a leave of absence in the mid-1980s to do some research in Japan. A benefit of that leave was that she escaped the distractions of ringing phones and could concentrate. Fax was almost unknown, and e-mail did not exist for the civilian population. In 2007, she took a leave of absence to teach on Semester at Sea. Even in the middle of the ocean, she was in instant contact with her office and publisher over the international e-mail superhighway. She could insert earphones into her laptop computer and have a Skype conversation by voice, or pick up a mobile phone and call her family or coauthor. What a change in less than 25 years! Technology is creating a smaller world where time zones are the only thing separating us, but it also may be making the world more impersonal because there is less need to meet face-to-face.

One of our students recently reported that she was ecstatic about having met the perfect man—over the Internet. She expressed reservations about meeting her perfect man in person because it might change this "perfect" relationship. Dating services have sprung up to introduce people via the Internet, and people put pictures and biographies, like home pages, on the Internet. Whether cyberspace is limiting face-to-face contacts is a subject of much debate, but individuals do interact, whether through cyberspace or face-to-face, and form networks linking them to the social world.

This chapter continues the discussion of how individuals fit into the social world, exploring the link between the individual and the social structure. Socialization prepares individuals to be part of the social world, and individuals interact with others to form groups and organizations. Interacting face-to-face and belonging to groups and organizations are the primary focus in the following pages. First, we consider how networks and connections link individuals and groups to different levels of analysis. Then, we focus on micro-level interactions, meso-level groups, and meso- and macro-level organizations and bureaucracies. Finally, we consider macro-level national and global networks.

All students at Seton Hall University are issued laptop computers their first year as part of their tuition. Many colleges are now wi-fi connected so that the students can access the Internet wireless from any location on campus.

Networks and Connections in Our Social World

Try imagining yourself at the center of a web, as in a spider's web. Attach the threads that spread from the center first to family members and close friends, on out in the web to peers, then friends of friends. Some thread connections are close and direct. Others are more distant but connect more and more people in an ever-expanding web. Now imagine trying to send a letter to someone you do not know. A researcher actually tried this experiment to discover how people are networked and how far removed citizens are from one another within the United States. The "How Do We Know?" feature will explain the empirical evidence behind the film, *Six Degrees of Separation,* and will also give you a sense of another way to gather empirical evidence to test a hypothesis.

How Do We Know?

Studying Degrees of Separation

It is not often that a commercial film is made with a theme based on an empirical research project, but *Six Degrees of Separation* is such a film. Perhaps you have heard it said that every American is only six steps (or degrees) from any other person in the country. This assertion is rooted in a study with evidence to support it, although the film's conclusion is oversimplified.

Stanley Milgram and his associates (Korte and Milgram 1970; Milgram 1967; Travers and Milgram 1969) studied social networks by selecting several target people in different cities, just common people that the researcher happened to know. Then they identified "starting persons" in cities more than 1,000 miles away. Each starter person was given a booklet with instructions and the target person's name, address, occupation, and a few other facts. The starter person was instructed to pass the booklet to someone he or she knew on a first-name basis who lived closer to or might have more direct networks with the target person than the sender had. Although many packages never arrived at their destinations, one third did. The researchers were interested in how many steps were involved in the delivery of the packages that did arrive. The number of links in the chain to complete delivery ranged from 2 to 10, with most having five to seven intermediaries. This is the source of the reference to "six degrees of separation."

Watts has been replicating what he dubs the "Small World" Study for over 30 years now. Most recently, working with Peter Sheridan Dodds and Roby Muhamed (Dodds, Muhamed, and Watts 2003), Watts replicated the study with a global sample. Dodds and colleagues found that most "starting persons" find their "target persons" within 5 to 7 intermediaries. The only difference between the U.S. and the international sample is that more people dropped out of the global sample. The researchers suggest this may be due to the mechanism used to find the "target," a forwarded e-mail.

Despite the fact that we interact daily with a fairly small number of people, most Americans actually have a pool of 500 to 2,500 acquaintances. If you were to pick one of those who lived in the general direction of the target person and that person picked one of his or her 1,000 or 2,000 acquaintances who lived even closer, the numbers multiply very quickly. The numbers of his or indirect contacts through networks expand geometrically. Clearly, networks are powerful linkages and create a truly small world.

Our **social network** refers to individuals linked together by one or more social relationships, forming a social network. These networks connect us to the larger society, as Milgram's research in the feature above makes clear. Networking refers to using our social network to get jobs or favors, often from people who are not very far removed from us in the web. Networks begin with micro-level contacts and exchanges between individuals in private interactions and expand to small groups, then to large (even global) organizations (Granovetter 2007; Hall 2002:28; Marsden 1987). The stronger people's networks, the more influential they can be in the person's life. However, types of networks differ. For example, women's networks for both getting jobs and promotions and succeeding in careers are broader (more extensive), but also weaker than men's in helping with promotions. This is because men's networks are more "instrumental," that is, focused on the task at hand (Burt 1992; Rothbard and Brett 2000). The network web in Figure 5.1 illustrates that individuals are linked to other people, groups, organizations, and nations in the social world through networks.

Although network links can be casual and personal rather than based on official positions and channels, they place a person within the larger social structure, and it is from these networks that group ties emerge. People in networks talk to each other about common interests. This communication process creates linkages between clusters of people. For example, cyber networks on the Internet bring together people with common interests.

Family and Friends: Micro-Level Networks

At the most micro level, you develop close friends in college—bonds that may continue for the rest of your life. You introduce your friends from theater to your roommate's friends from the soccer team, and the network expands. These acquaintances from the soccer team may have useful information about which professors to avoid, how to make contacts to study abroad, and how to get a job in your field. Membership in food cooperatives,

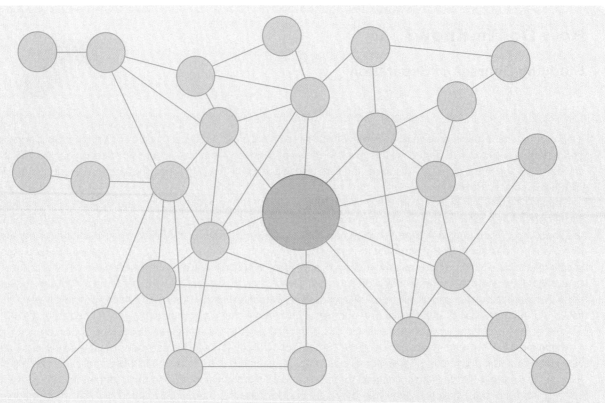

Picture yourself as the circle in the middle. Some of your friends know each other, but others do not. Friends from high school may not know those you meet at college, and neither will know people you meet on the job. Each of these friends has connections, creating a web of networks in which you "have a friend who has a friend." Some of these may be important connections for you someday. Note that poor people have fewer friends who are connected to those with resources and influence, reducing their networking capabilities.

Figure 5.1   Networks: A Web of Connections

self-help groups such as Alcoholics Anonymous and Weight Watchers, and computer-user groups are examples of networks that connect individuals with common interests (Powell 1990).

All of you—if you are successful at your university— will eventually become part of the university's alumni association, and this may become important to you for social contacts, business connections, or help with settling in a new location. When people refer to the Old Boy network, they are talking about contacts made through general association with people such as alumni. Men have used networks quite successfully in the past, and networks of working women—New Girl networks—are expanding rapidly. One of the reasons for persistent inequality in our society is that members of certain groups may not have access to these privilege-enhancing networks.

Thinking Sociologically

Map your social network web. What advantages do you get from your network? What economic benefits might your connections have for you?

Meso- and Macro-Level Networks

Network links create new types of organizational forms, such as those in the opening example of cyberspace and the Internet. These networks cross societal, racial, ethnic, religious, and other lines that divide people. Networks also link groups at different levels of analysis. In fact, you are linked through networks to (1) local civic, sports, and religious organizations; (2) formal complex organizations such as a political party or national fraternity and ethnic or social class subcultures; (3) the nation of which you are a citizen and to which you have formal obligations (such as the requirement that you go to war as a draftee if the government so decides); and (4) global entities such as the United Nations, which use some of your taxes or donate resources to help impoverished people, tsunami victims, and earthquake survivors elsewhere in the world. These networks may open opportunities, but they also may create obligations that limit your freedom to make your own choices. As we move from micro-level interactions to larger meso- and macro-level organizations, interactions tend to become more formal. Formal organizations will be explored in the latter half of this chapter.

One of the most interesting developments at the beginning of the 21st century is the way Internet technology is influencing networking, linking individuals to people around the globe. Internet users have redefined networking through the creation of blogs, chat rooms, message boards, listservs, newsgroups, and dozens of Web sites devoted to online networking ("Five Rules" 2005). Web sites such as LinkedIn.com and WorldWIT.org offer business and professional networking, whereas other sites such as Myspace .com, Tribe.net, Xanga.com, Classmates.com, and Facebook .com focus on personal and social networking.

LinkedIn.com has more than 4 million registered users, who can use the site to connect with colleagues and clients, list job openings, and reconnect with previous coworkers (www.linkedin.com/static?key=tour_flash). Ryze.com has 250,000 members and allows users to post free networking-oriented home pages and create or join more than 1,000 networks based on industry, interests, or location (www.ryze .com/faq.php). WorldWIT, an online networking organization for women in business, has more than 30,000 members and, according to its communications director, Kristen Hughes, allows members to find everything "from realtors to dog walkers to employees and new jobs" ("Five Rules" 2005).

Web sites dedicated to social networking focus on sharing mutually interesting information, finding and keeping up with friends, uploading photos and videos, finding activity partners, publishing notes, or establishing professional contacts. One of the largest and most popular, with well over 60 million participants, is Facebook (www.facebook.com), which launched in February 2004 at Harvard University. It is now used by university students around the world and has spread to high school students and companies. Like many other social networking sites, it allows users to post a profile and pictures, offer testimonials about others, create and join groups, and link to the profiles of "friends"—often a mixture of friends, colleagues, relatives, and acquaintances of varying levels and from various periods of life. Users can view the profiles of anyone within four degrees of separation—friends of friends of friends of friends—and search the network for people with the same friends, location, hometown, occupation, schools attended, interests, hobbies, or taste in movies, books, or television shows. In many cases, users link to dozens of friends and can access thousands of profiles around the world without reaching beyond the friends-of-friends level of connectivity.

Through online social and business networking, users have been able to expand personal networks at unprecedented levels. Users can discover who in their town attended the same college, link college friends to high school friends, search for people with overlapping "friends" and interests in a town where they plan to move or visit, or reconnect with lost friends. Even life partners may be found using the Internet, as the illustration from eHarmony suggests. The networks and their potential uses are virtually unlimited and will continue to reshape networking for the foreseeable future. The point here is that these networks create connections for individuals that can span the globe.

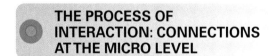

eHarmony is an online matchmaking agency that uses computers and the Internet to help people find a mate, or at least a good date.

Thinking Sociologically

How have you or friends used the Internet to expand social or professional networks? How have these networks influenced you or your friends?

THE PROCESS OF INTERACTION: CONNECTIONS AT THE MICRO LEVEL

Each morning as you rouse yourself and prepare for the challenges ahead, you consider what the day might bring, what activities and obligations are on your calendar, and who you will talk to. As you lift your limp, listless body from a horizontal to upright position and blood begins coursing through your veins, thoughts of the day's events begin to penetrate your semiconscious state. A cup of caffeine, cold water on the face, and a mouth-freshening brush bring you to the next stage of awareness. You evaluate what is in store for you, what roles you will play during the day, and with whom you are likely to interact.

Should you wear the ragged but comfortable jeans and T-shirt? No, not today. There is that class trip to the courthouse. Something a bit less casual is in order. Then,

The same words, "let's have a drink," may have very different meanings in different social interaction contexts. Humans must learn not only the language but also how to read interactional settings.

you are meeting with your English professor to discuss the last essay you wrote. What approach should you take? You could act insulted that she failed to think of you as a future J. K. Rowling. Maybe a meek, mild "please tell me what I did wrong, I tried so hard" approach would work. She seems a nice, sympathetic sort. After class, there is a group

of students who chat in the hall. It would be nice to meet them. What strategy should you use? Try to enter the conversation? Tell a joke? Make small talk? Talk to the students individually so you can get to know each before engaging the whole group? Each of these responses is a strategy for interaction, and each might elicit various reactions.

The Elements of Social Interaction

"Let's have a drink!" Such a simple comment might have many different meanings. We could imagine two children playing together, men going to a bar after work, a couple of friends getting together to celebrate an event, fraternity brothers at a party, or a couple on a date. In all these cases, **social interaction** consists of two or more individuals purposefully relating to each other.

"Having a drink," like all interaction, involves action on the part of two or more individuals, is directed toward a goal that people hope to achieve, and takes place in a social context that includes cultural norms and rules governing the situation, the setting, and other factors shaping the way people perceive the circumstances. The action, goal, and social context help us interpret the meaning of statements such as "Let's have a drink."

The norms governing the particular social context tell what is right and proper behavior. Recall from Chapter 3 that norms are rules that guide human interactions. People assume that others will share their interpretation of a situation. These shared assumptions about proper behavior provide the cues for your own behavior that become a part of your social self. You look for cues to proper behavior and rehearse in your mind your actions and reactions. In the "let's have a drink" scenario, you assume that the purpose of the interaction is understood. What dress, mannerisms, speech, and actions you consider appropriate depends on expectations from your socialization and past experience in similar situations (Parsons 1951b), for in modern societies, a range of behaviors and responses is possible in any social situation.

Although most people assume that talking, or verbal communication, is the primary means of communication between individuals, words themselves are actually only a part of the message. In most contexts, they make up less than 35% of the emotional content of the message (Birdwhistell 1970). **Nonverbal communication**—interactions using facial expressions, the head, eye contact, body posture, gestures, touch, walk, status symbols, and personal space— make up the rest (Drafke and Kossen 2002). These important elements of communication are learned through socialization as we grow up. Although you may master another written and verbal language, it is much more difficult to learn the nonverbal language.

People who travel to a country other than their own often use gestures to be understood. Like spoken language, nonverbal gestures vary from culture to culture, as illustrated in the Photo Essay. Communicating with others in one's own

Photo Essay
Gestures Around the World

Gestures are symbolic forms of interaction. However, these gestures can have entirely different meanings in different cultures. A friendly gesture in one culture may be obscene in the next. In some regions in China, the gesture at the top right means you want four of something. If you held up four fingers in China, people might have no idea what you want.

Friends interact at a different distance—1 ½ to 4 feet. In different cultures, distances may seem inappropriately intrusive or cold and removed, and the other person may take offense.

A more formal setting calls for a distance of 4 to 10 feet. In a formal context, if one party comes closer than 4 feet, the other party may feel crowded and even offended. If the distance is quite large, the situation can feel very formal and very intimidating. What is the message at this meeting?

language can be difficult enough. Add to this the complication of individuals with different language, cultural expectations, and personalities using different nonverbal messages, and misunderstandings are likely. Nonverbal messages are the hardest part of another language to master because they are specific to a culture and learned through socialization.

Consider the following example: You are about to wrap up a major business deal. You are pleased with the results of your negotiations so you give your hosts the thumb-and-finger A-OK sign. In Brazil, you have just grossly insulted your hosts—it is like giving them "the finger" in the United States. In Japan, you have asked for a small bribe. In the south of France, you have indicated the deal is worthless. Although your spoken Portuguese, Japanese, or French may have been splendid, your nonverbal language did not cut the deal. Intercultural understanding is more than being polite and knowing the language.

Consider another example of nonverbal language: personal space. Most people have experienced social situations, such as parties, where someone gets too close. One person backs away, the other moves in again, the first backs away again—into a corner or a table with nowhere else to go. Perhaps, the person approaching was aggressive or rude, but it is also possible that the person held different cultural norms or expectations in relation to personal space.

The amount of personal space an individual needs to be comfortable or proper varies with the cultural setting, gender, status, and social context of the interaction. Individuals from Arab countries are comfortable at very close range. However, people from Scandinavia or the United States need a great deal of personal space. Consider the following four categories of social distance and social space based on a study of U.S. middle-class people. Each category applies to particular types of activity (Hall and Hall 1992):

1. *Intimate distance*: from zero distance (touching, embracing, kissing) to 18 inches. Children may play together in such close proximity, and adults and children may maintain this distance, but between adults, this intimate contact is reserved for private and affectionate relationships.

2. *Personal distance*: from 18 inches to 4 feet. This is the public distance for most friends and for informal interactions with acquaintances.

3. *Social distance*: from 4 feet to 12 feet. This is the distance for impersonal business relations, such as a job interview or class discussions between students and a professor. This distance implies a more formal interaction or a significant difference in the status of the two people.

4. *Public distance*: 12 feet and beyond. This is the distance most public figures use for addressing others, especially in formal settings and in situations in which the speaker has very high status.

Personal space also communicates one's position in relation to others. The higher the position, the greater the control of space. In social situations, individuals with higher positions spread out, prop their feet up, put their arms out, and use more sweeping gestures (Knapp and Hall 1997). Women and men differ with regard to personal space and other forms of nonverbal language. For instance, women are more sensitive to subtle cues such as status differences and the use of personal space (Henley, Hamilton, and Thorne 2000).

Sociologists study interactions, including verbal and nonverbal communication, to explain this very basic link between humans and the group. The following theoretical perspectives focus on the micro level of analysis in attempting to explain interactions.

Thinking Sociologically

What are some complications that you or your friends have had in interactions involving cross-cultural contacts or male-female miscommunication? What might help clarify communication in these cases?

Theoretical Perspectives on the Interaction Process

How many people do you interact with each day, and what happens in each of these interactions? You probably have not given the question much thought or analysis, but that process is exactly what fascinates interaction theorists. Why do two people interact in the first place? What determines whether the interaction will continue or stop? How do two people know how to behave and what to say around each other? What other processes are taking place as they "talk" to each other? Why do people interact differently with different people? What governs the way they make sense of messages and how they respond to them? These questions interest sociologists because they address the basic interaction processes that result in group formation, ranging in size from dyads (two people) to large organizations.

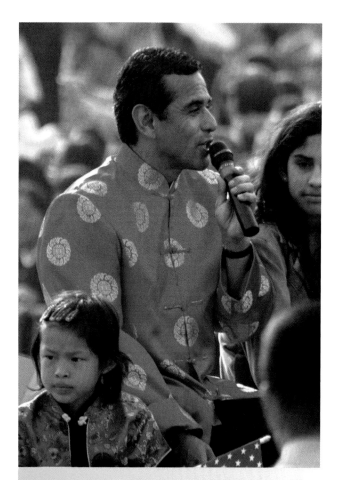

When a respected person speaks in a public setting, listeners would be expected to keep themselves at a greater distance. Los Angeles Mayor Antonio R. Villaraigosa speaks here in a formal setting with appropriate public distance.

Rational Choice Theory

Exchange (or rational choice) theorists look at why relationships continue, considering the rewards and costs of interaction to the individual. If the benefits of the interaction are high and if the costs are low, the interaction will be valued and sustained. Every interaction involves calculations of self-interest, expectations of reciprocity (a mutual exchange of favors), and decisions to act in ways that have current or eventual payoff for the individual.

Symbolic Interaction Theory

Symbolic interaction theory focuses instead on how individuals interpret situations, such as "let's have a drink," and how this, in turn, affects their actions. Two theories that are variations on symbolic interaction theory—ethnomethodology and dramaturgy—explain aspects of symbolic interaction that are part of interpreting situations or manipulating how people perceive interactions.

Ethnomethodology

Suppose an acquaintance greets you with a friendly, "Hi, how ya' doin'?" and you respond with "Rotten, I want to die!" or "Oh, shut up!" rather than the perfunctory "Fine, how's it goin'?" You may have had a really bad day, but you would get a strong reaction because you would be breaching norms related to casual greetings. Similarly, if you violate elevator behavior by singing in the elevator, trying to sell a product to others in the elevator, sniffing the person next to you, or staring at other occupants rather than at the floor numbers, you are breaching elevator norms. These norms are generally understood, even among strangers. Most people take for granted the underlying interaction rules—norms that govern the expected behaviors and the verbal or nonverbal exchanges. However, ethnomethodologists do not take these norms for granted.

Norm-breaking behavior, such as singing in the elevator, is one tool used by ethnomethodologists to study the formation of ground rules underlying social interaction and people's responses to violation of norms (Riehl 2001). This is often done by violating norms to see how strongly others in the social setting respond to the improper behavior. These researchers use empirical methods to study how people develop shared meanings and consider how common ground rules originated. They question even the most basic aspects of social interactions such as spatial relations, one example of shared assumptions that can be violated, especially if you enter a different culture.

Thinking Sociologically

Try an experiment: Violate rules of elevator behavior or of a game such as checkers or basketball, and observe the reactions. How can you explain the reactions to this situation? Keep in mind that the level of emotion in the response is an indicator of how important the rule is in that setting and to others in the group.

Dramaturgy

Dramaturgy theorists analyze life as a play or drama on a stage, with scripts and props and scenes to be played. The play we put on creates an impression for our audience. In everyday life, individuals learn new lines to add to their scripts through the socialization process, including influence from family, friends, films, and television. They perform these scripts for social audiences in order to maintain certain images, much like the actors in a play.

Every day in high schools, thousands of teenagers go on stage—in the classroom or the hallway with friends and peers and with adult authorities who may later be giving grades or writing letters of reference. The props these students use include their clothing, a backpack with paper and pen, and a smile or "cool" look. The set is the classroom, the cafeteria, and perhaps the athletic field. The script is shaped by the actors, with teachers establishing an authoritarian relationship; with classmates engaging in competition for grades; or with peers seeking social status among companions. The actors include hundreds of teens struggling with issues of identity, changing bodies, and attempts to avoid humiliation. Each individual works to assert and maintain an image through behavior, clothing, language, and friends.

As individuals perform according to society's script for the situation, they take into consideration how their actions will influence others. By carefully managing the impression they wish the acquaintance to receive—a process called impression management—people hope to create an impression that works to their advantage. In other words, the actor is trying to manipulate how others define the situation, especially as it relates to their opinion of the actor.

Most of the time, we engage in front-stage behavior, the behavior safest with casual acquaintances because it is scripted and acted for the public and it presents a definition of self we hope others will accept as the "real me." A poor or unacceptable performance will be embarrassing both for us and our audience. People develop strategies to cover up their weaknesses or failures such as laughing at a joke even though they do not understand it.

Each part or character an individual plays and each audience requires a different script. For example, interacting with peers at a bar differs from meeting a professor in her office. We learn to avoid those performance activities that are likely to result in humiliation or failure or that contradict the image we have worked to create. At home or with close friends with whom we are more intimate, we engage in backstage behavior, letting our feelings show and behaving in ways that might be unacceptable for other audiences (Goffman [1959] 2001, 1967). Dramaturgical analysis can be a useful approach to broadening our understanding of interactions.

Thinking Sociologically

What are some ways your life feels like a dramatic production—with a front stage presentation and backstage preparation?

Social Status: The Link to Groups

Recall the network web you drew. Now add to that web your **social statuses**, positions you hold in the social world. An individual's social status defines how, for example, we interact with others and how others react to us in a specific situation. We interact differently when in the daughter status with our parents, in a student status with our professor, or in friend status with our peers. Each individual holds many statuses, and this combination held by any individual is called a status set: daughter, mother, worker, teammate, student.

Each individual's unique status set is the product of family relationships and groups that the individual joins (a university or club) or into which she or he is born (an ethnic group or gender). Many statuses change with each new stage of life, such as work, student status, or marital status. Statuses at each stage of life and the interactions that result from those statuses form each person's unique social world.

Statuses affect the type of interactions individuals have. In some interactions (as with classmates), people are equals. In other situations, individuals have interchanges with people who hold superior or inferior statuses. If you are promoted to supervisor, your interaction with subordinates will change. Consider the possible interactions shown in Figure 5.2, in

Figure 5.2 Types of Status Relationships You May Experience

which the first relationship is between equals and the others are between those with unequal statuses.

When individuals are in dominant or subordinate positions, power or deference affects interactions. With a friend, these status relationships are constantly being negotiated and bargained: "I'll do what you want tonight, but tomorrow I choose." Studies of interaction between males and females find that in addition to gender, power and hierarchical relationships are important in determining interaction patterns. The more powerful person, such as one who has more wealth or privilege, can interrupt in a conversation with his or her partner and show less deference in the interaction (Kollock, Blumstein, and Schwartz 1985).

People have no control over certain statuses they hold. These **ascribed statuses** are often assigned at birth and do not change during an individual's lifetime. Some examples are gender and race or ethnicity. Ascribed statuses are assigned to a person without regard for personal desires, talents, or choices. In some societies, one's caste, or the social position into which one is born (e.g., a slave), is an ascribed status because it is usually impossible to change.

Achieved status, on the other hand, is chosen or earned by decisions one makes and sometimes by personal ability. Attaining a higher education, for example, improves an individual's occupational opportunities and hence his or her achieved status. Being a guitarist in a band is an achieved status and so is being a prisoner in jail, for both are earned positions based on the person's own decisions and actions.

At a particular time in life or under certain circumstances, one of an individual's statuses may become most important and take precedence over others. Sociologists call this a **master status**. Whether it is an occupation, parental status, or something else, it dominates and shapes much of an individual's life, activities, self-concept, and position in the community for a period of time. For a person who is very ill, for instance, that illness may occupy a master status needing constant attention from doctors, influencing social relationships, and determining what that person can do in family, work, or community activities.

Thinking Sociologically

What are your statuses? Which ones are ascribed, and which are achieved statuses? Do you have a master status? How do these statuses affect the way you interact with others in your network of relationships?

The Relationship Between Status and Role

Every status (position) in your network includes certain behaviors and obligations as you carry out the expected behaviors, rights, and obligations of the status—referred to as **roles**. Roles are the dynamic, action part of statuses in a society. They define how each individual in an interaction is expected to act (Linton 1937). The role of a college student includes behaviors and obligations such as attending classes, studying, taking tests, writing papers, and interacting with professors and other students. Individuals enter most statuses with some knowledge of how to carry out the roles dictated by their culture. Through the process of socialization, individuals learn roles by observing others, watching television and films, reading, and being taught how to carry out the status. Both statuses (positions) and roles (behavioral obligations of the status) form the link with other people in the social world because they must be carried out in relationships with others. A father has certain obligations (or roles) toward his children and their mother. The position of father does not exist on its own but in relationship to significant others who have reciprocal ties.

Your status of student requires certain behaviors and expectations, depending on whether you are interacting with a dean, a professor, an adviser, a classmate, or a prospective employer. This is because the role expectations of the status of student vary as one interacts with specific

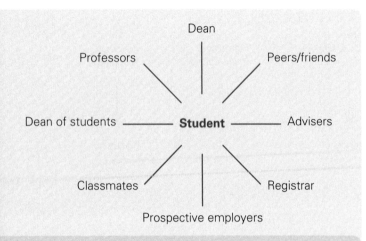

Figure 5.3 Types of Interactions Students Have With Reciprocal Status Holders

people in other statuses. In Figure 5.3, the student is the subject, and the others are those with whom the student interacts in the status of student.

Within a group, individuals may hold both formal and informal statuses. One illustration is the formal status of high school students, each of whom plays a number of informal roles in cliques that are not part of the formal school structure. They may be known as jock, nerd, loner, goth, clown, prep, outcast, or life-of-the-party. Each of these roles takes place in a status relationship with others: teacher-student, peer-peer, coach-athlete. The connections between statuses, roles, and environment are illustrated in Table 5.1.

Social networks, discussed in the beginning of the chapter, link individuals through their statuses to social groups in the social world. In other words, our statuses connect us and make us integral parts of meso- and macro-level organizations. Sometimes, the link is through a status in a family group such as son or daughter, sometimes through an employer, and sometimes through our status as citizen of a nation. Social networks may be based on ascribed characteristics such as age, race, ethnicity, and gender, or on achieved status such as education, occupation, or common interests (House 1994). These links, in turn, form the basis for social interactions and group structures (Hall 2002). However, at times, individuals cannot carry out their roles as others expect them to, creating role strain or conflict.

Thinking Sociologically

In your web, detail your network from close family and friends to distant acquaintances. Include your statuses and roles in each part of the network with family members, friends, and school and work acquaintances. What do you notice about your network?

Role Strain and Role Conflict

Every status carries role expectations, the way the status is supposed to be carried out according to generally accepted societal or group norms. Most people have faced times in their lives when they simply could not carry out all the

Table 5.1 **The Relationship Between Statuses and Roles**

Status (position in structure)	Role (behavior, rights, obligations)	Setting and Relationship With Others (environment)
Student	*Formal* Study, attend class, turn in assignments *Informal* Be a jock, clown, cut-up; abuse alcohol on weekends	Setting: school Others: teachers, students, roommates
Parent	*Formal* Provide financial support, child care *Informal* Be a playmate, lead family activities	Setting: home and community Others: child, spouse, relatives
Employee	*Formal* Work responsibilities: punctuality, doing one's tasks *Informal* Befriend coworkers, join lunch group, represent company in bowling league	Setting: workplace Others: employer, other clients

Photo Essay

Work Status and Roles Around the World

Positions people carry out in different cultures depend on tasks important in that culture. Upper left: The two women from Ghana carry yams, a staple food, from the fields. Upper right: Formal social control in societies falls to police officers in many societies. Middle left: Preparing cloth in a traditional method is a man's task in Ghanaian culture. Middle right: The market for these Asian women is on the water. Lower left: Men in China use traditional methods to keep the roads open. Lower middle: The Asian farmer works long hours in the field planting, sowing, weeding, and harvesting. Lower right: Fishermen in India pull in a catch for their livelihood.

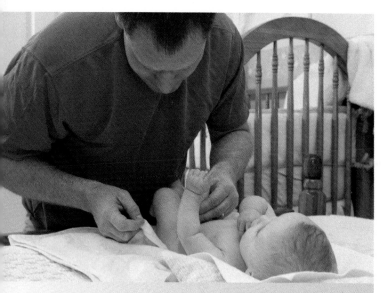

Parenting roles often need to be negotiated. In some traditional families in the past, the status had more explicit role expectations and fathers were rarely expected to change diapers.

obligations of a status such as student—write two papers, study adequately for two exams, complete the portfolio for the studio art class, finish the reading assignments for five classes, and memorize lines for the oral interpretation class, all in the same week. In these cases, individuals face **role strain**, tension between roles *within* one of the statuses.

Role strain causes the individual to be pulled in many directions by various obligations of the single status, as in the above example regarding the status of "student." Another such strain is often experienced by first-time fathers as they attempt to reconcile their role expectations of fathering with ideas held by their wives.

To resolve role strain, individuals cope in one of several ways: pass the problem off lightly (and thus not do well in classes), consider the dilemma humorous, become highly focused and pull a couple of all-nighters to get everything done, or become stressed, tense, fretful, and immobilized because of the strain. Most often, individuals set priorities based on their values and make decisions accordingly: "I'll work hard in the class for my major and let another slide."

Role conflict differs from role strain in that conflict is *between* the roles of two or more statuses. The conflict can come from within an individual or be imposed from outside. College athletes face role conflicts from competing demands on their time (Adler and Adler 1991, 2004). They must complete their studies on time, attend practices and be prepared for games, perhaps attend meetings of a Greek house to which they belong, and get home for a little brother's birthday. Similarly, a student may be going to school, holding down a part-time job to help make ends meet, and raising a family. If the student's child gets sick, the status of parent comes into conflict with that of student and worker. In the case of role conflict, the person may choose—or be informed by others—which status is the master status. Figure 5.4 visually illustrates the difference between role conflict and role strain.

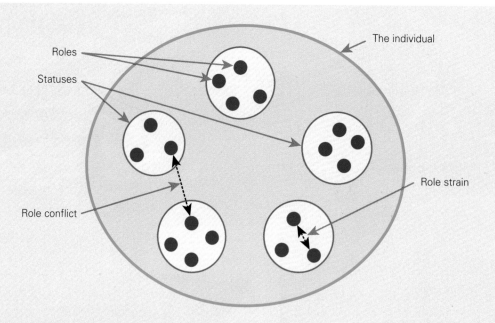

Figure 5.4 Role Strain and Role Conflict

Note: Each individual has many statuses: his or her status set. Each status has many roles: a role set. A conflict between two roles of the same status is a role strain. A conflict between the roles of two different statuses is a role conflict.

Thinking Sociologically

Using Figure 5.4, fill in the statuses you hold in your social world and roles you perform in these statuses. Then, list three examples of role conflicts and three examples of role strains that you experience.

Statuses and the accompanying roles come and go. You will not always be a student, and someday, you may be a parent and hold a professional job. Certainly, you will retire from your job. For instance, as people grow older, they disengage from some earlier statuses in groups and engage in new and different statuses and roles.

Our place within the social world is guaranteed, even obligatory, because of statuses we hold at each level of society—within small groups (family and peers), in larger groups and organizations (school and work organizations), in institutions (political parties or religious denominations), and ultimately as citizen of the society and the world (workers in global corporations). Each of these statuses connects us to a group setting.

Groups in Our Social World: The Micro-Meso Connection

When Jeanne, one of the coauthors of this book, was a child, the town she lived in had a hermit. He lived in a house on stilts in the bay. He made a big impression on all the kids in the neighborhood. They were fascinated! How does he live? How does he get food? Is he lonely all by himself? Does he get cold without heat? How can he survive without all the conveniences of modern life? One day, Jeanne was lucky enough to see him rowing to the shore. He was a bearded old man, dressed in a torn plaid shirt and jeans. Although he looked quite harmless and gentle, she remembers feeling a little afraid. Anyone who would choose to live alone, without others, must be very strange indeed, she thought.

Few of us could survive as this hermit did—without others. Most of us constantly interact with the people around us. We are born into a family group. Our socialization occurs in groups. We depend on the group for survival. Even hermits depend on others to meet certain needs; no hermit is completely isolated. Groups are necessary for protection, to obtain food, to manufacture goods, to get jobs done. Groups meet our social needs for belonging and acceptance, support us throughout our lives, and place restrictions on us. Groups can be small, intimate environments—micro-level interactions such as a group of friends—or they can become quite large as they morph into meso-level organizations. In any

case, it is through our group memberships that the micro and meso levels are linked.

Groups are two or more people who interact with each other because of shared common interests, goals, experiences, and needs (Drafke and Kossen 2002). The members feel they belong to the group and are seen by others as thinking, feeling, and behaving with a common goal. Members consider each other's behavior and engage in structured interaction patterns. Groups have defined memberships and ways to take in new members. They also have rules that guide behavior of members. In this section, we look at several questions: What are groups, and how do they vary? How is interaction affected by small groups? What is the importance of groups for individuals?

Not all collections of individuals are groups, however. For instance, your family is a group, but people shopping at a mall or waiting for a bus are not a group because they do not interact or acknowledge shared common interests.

Groups form through a series of succeeding steps. Consider people in a village. First step is initial interaction. If membership is rewarding and meets individuals' needs, the individuals will attempt to maintain the benefits the group provides (Mills 1984). A group of people live near each other and interact to form this village. In the second step, a collective goal emerges. For example, villagers may work together to build an irrigation system or a school. Groups establish their own goals and pursue them, trying to be free from external controls or constraints. In the third and final step, the group attempts to expand its collective goals by building on the former steps and by pursuing new goals. For example, the irrigation system may improve crop production, so the villagers decide to sell the extra produce at the town vegetable market to earn money for the school.

The Importance of Groups for the Individual

Groups are essential parts of human life (micro level) and of organizational structures (meso and macro levels). They establish our place in the social world, providing us with support and a sense of belonging. Few individuals can survive without groups. This becomes clear when we consider two problems: anomie and suicide.

Anomie and Suicide

With the rapid changes and continued breakdown of institutional structures in Afghanistan as rival warlords vie for power over territory, and in Iraq as religious groups vie for political and economic power, horrific problems abound. Civil disorder, conflicts for power, suicide bombings, murder of police officers, and looting are frequent occurrences. Social controls (police and military forces) are strained, and leaders struggle to cope. The result of this breakdown in norms is **anomie**, the state of normlessness; the rules for

This monk committed suicide—setting himself on fire—as a public statement against war. He was tightly integrated into his community and his people, and his own death seemed a worthy sacrifice if it would end the suffering that the war brought to his nation. This illustrates altruistic suicide.

imagination, micro-level social interaction shaped by events and forces at other levels in the social system.

Durkheim found that Protestants committed suicide more often than Catholics, urban folks more often than people living in small communities, people in highly developed and complex societies more frequently than those in simple societies, and people who lived alone more than those situated in families. The key variable linking these findings was the degree to which an individual was integrated into the group, that is, the degree of social bond with others. During war, for instance, people generally felt a sense of common cause and belonging to their country. Thus, suicide rates were greater during peacetime because it offered less cause for feeling that bond.

Durkheim then went on to describe three distinct types of suicide. *Egoistic suicide* occurs when the individual feels little social bond to the group or society and lacks ties such as family or friends that might prevent suicide. Egoistic suicide is a result of personal despair and involves the kind of motive most people associate with suicide. This is what we often think of when we hear about a suicide.

Anomic suicide occurs when a society or one of its parts is in disorder or turmoil and lacks clear norms and guidelines for social behavior. This situation is likely during major social change or economic problems such as a severe depression. The recent suicides of an Enron executive, Clifford Baxter, and member of a U.S. president's inner circle, Vincent Foster, were related to economic problems and scandal during organizational turmoil.

Altruistic suicide differs from the others in that it involves such a strong bond and group obligation that the individual is willing to die for the group. Self-survival becomes less important than group survival (Durkheim 1897/1964). Examples of altruistic suicide include the young Arab Muslims who hijacked commercial airlines to fly into the World Trade Center and Pentagon, Muslims in Iraq committing suicide missions against American military forces and Iraqi police forces, Palestinian suicide bombers in Israel, Buddhist monks who burned themselves to protest the Vietnam War, Japanese Kamikaze pilots who dive-bombed targets during World War II, and Irish Republican Army members who starved themselves to death. These are suicides rooted in extraordinarily high integration into a group—usually occurring in societies or religious groups that have very clear norms and high levels of consensus about values from their religious or political commitments.

Durkheim's analysis provides an excellent example of the importance of the group for individuals. Following Durkheim's lead, many sociologists have studied suicide, confirming the importance of group ties for individuals in religious, educational, and social group networks that provide integration of individuals into the society (Hall 2002; Pescosolido and Georgianna 1989).

No individual is an island. Even a hermit needs the language he learned in childhood to think and organize his

behavior in society break down under extreme stress from rapid social change or conflict (Merton 1968a). Consider the example of suicide.

Suicide seems like an individual act, committed because of personal problems. However, early sociologist Émile Durkheim took a unique approach. In his volume, *Suicide* (Durkheim [1897] 1964), he discussed the social factors contributing to suicide. Using existing statistical data to determine suicide rates in European populations, Durkheim looked at such variables as sex, age, religion, nationality, and the season in which suicide was committed. His findings were surprising to many, and they demonstrate that individual problems cannot be understood without also understanding the group context in which they occur—the sociological

life. Without the cultural categories and skills learned earlier in life, cultural guidelines are lacking. The importance
of groups is an underlying theme throughout this text.
Groups are essential to human life, but to understand them
more fully, we must understand the various kinds of groups
in which humans participate.

Types of Groups

Each of us belongs to several types of groups. Some groups
provide intimacy and close relationships, whereas others do
not. Some are required affiliations, and others are voluntary.
Some provide personal satisfaction, and others are obligatory or necessary for survival. The following discussion
points out several types of groups and reasons individuals
belong to them.

Primary groups are characterized by close contacts
and lasting personal relationships—the most micro level.
Your family members and best friends, school classmates
and close work associates, and clubs whose members are
close friends are all of primary importance in your everyday life. Primary groups provide a sense of belonging and
shared identity. Group members care about you, and you
care about the other group members, creating a sense of
loyalty. Approval and disapproval from the primary group
influence the activities you choose to pursue. Belonging
rather than accomplishing a task is the main reason for
membership. The group is of intrinsic value—enjoyed for
its own sake—rather than for some utilitarian value such as
making money.

For individuals, primary groups provide an anchor
point in society. You were born into a primary group—your
family. You play a variety of roles in primary relationships—
those of spouse, parent, child, sibling, relative, close friend.
You meet with other members face-to-face or keep in touch
on a regular basis and know a great deal about their lives.
What makes them happy or angry? What are sensitive
issues? In primary groups you share values, say what you
think, let down your hair, dress as you like, and share
your concerns and emotions, your successes and failures
(Goffman [1959] 2001, 1967). Charles H. Cooley ([1909]
1983), who first discussed the term *primary group*, saw
these relationships as the source of close human feelings
and emotions—love, cooperation, and concern.

Secondary groups are those with formal, impersonal,
businesslike relationships. In the modern world, people
cannot always live under the protective wing of primary
group relationships. Secondary groups are usually large and
task oriented because they have a specific purpose to achieve
and focus on accomplishing a goal. As children grow, they
move from the security and acceptance of primary groups—
the home and neighborhood peer group—to the large school
classroom, where each child is one of many students vying for
the teacher's approval and competing for rewards. Similarly,
the job world requires formal relations and procedures:

Even Buddhist monks and nuns, who spend much of their lives devoted
to private meditation, need the support and solidarity of a group.

Members of this Chinese family—a primary group—enjoy one
another's company as they play a game of Mahjong. They will not be
richer or have more prestige because of the time they spend at this
game. The connections are valued for intrinsic reasons.

applications, interviews, contracts. Employment is based on
specific skills, training, and job knowledge, and there may
be a trial period. In Western cultures, we assume that people
should not be hired because of personal friendship or nepo-
tism, but rather for their competence to carry out the role
expectations in the position.

Because each individual in secondary groups carries out
a specialized task, communication between members is often

The residents of Thimpu, Bhutan, visit the vegetable market. Although this is a large, impersonal market, people form primary groups among both the vendors and the shoppers. Shoppers may find their favorite vendors and develop close relationships.

the courses you are taking this term. Secondary groups operate at the meso and macro levels of our social world, but they affect individuals at the micro level.

As societies modernize, they evolve from small towns and close, primary relationships to predominantly urban areas with more formal, secondary relationships. In the postindustrial world, as family members are scattered across countries and around the world, secondary relationships have come to play ever greater roles in people's lives. Large work organizations may provide day care, health clinics, financial planning, courses to upgrade skills, and sports leagues.

The small micro- and large macro-level groups often occur together. Behind most successful secondary groups are primary groups. Consider the small work group that eats together or goes out for a beer Friday afternoons. These relationships help individuals feel a part of larger organizations, just as residents of large urban areas have small groups of neighborhood friends. Megachurches began in the 1950s. They have more than 10,000 members, with the largest church in the world (in Korea) having 830,000 members. About half of these churches are nondenominational Protestant, and the rest are related to evangelical or Pentecostal groups. The focus of programming is on creating small support groups (primary groups) within the huge congregation ("O Come All Ye Faithful" 2007; Sargeant 2000; Thumma and Travis 2007). In a formal setting such as a university or corporation, primary groups can play a major role in making people feel they belong. For instance, many students live with roommates at the university, study with a small group, go out Friday night with friends, and regularly have meals with close friends. Table 5.2 summarizes some of the dimensions of primary and secondary groups.

Problems in primary groups can affect performance in secondary groups. Consider the problems of a student who has an argument with a significant other or roommate or experiences a failure of his or her family support system due to divorce or other problems. Self-concepts and social skills diminish during times of family stress and affect group

specialized as well. Contacts with doctors, store clerks, and even professors are generally formal and impersonal parts of organizational life. Sometimes, associations with secondary groups are long lasting, sometimes of short duration—as in

Table 5.2 **Primary and Secondary Group Characteristics**

	Primary Group	Secondary Group
Quality of relationships	Personal orientation	Goal orientation
Duration of relationships	Usually long-term	Variable, often short-term
Breadth of activities	Broad, usually involving many activities	Narrow, usually involving few largely goal-directed activities
Subjective perception of relationships	As an end in itself (friendship, belonging)	As a means to an end (to accomplish a task, earn money)
Typical examples	Families, close friendships	Coworkers, political organizations

relationships in other parts of one's life (Drafke and Kossen 2002; Parish and Parish 1991).

Thinking Sociologically

In the past, raising children was considered a family task, done by the primary group. Today, many children are in child care settings, often run by secondary groups. Can a secondary group provide care comparable to a family? Can the secondary group provide better care than abusive families? Is this an issue that policymakers should consider?

Reference groups are composed of members who act as role models and establish standards against which all members measure their conduct. Individuals look to reference groups to set guidelines for behavior and decision making. The term is often used to refer to models in one's chosen career field. Students in premed, nursing, computer science, business, or sociology programs watch the behavior patterns of those who have become professionals in their chosen career. When people make the transition from student to professional, they adopt clothing, time schedules, salary expectations, and other characteristics of the new role. They emulate those who epitomize success in the field. Professional organizations such as the American Bar Association or American Sociological Association set standards for behavior and achievements. People who already belong to a reference group, such as practicing lawyers, look up to leaders within the field. However, it is possible to be an attorney or an athlete and not aspire to be like others in the group if they are unethical or abuse substances such as steroids. Instead, a person might be shaped by the values of a church group or a political group with which he or she identifies. Not every group one belongs to is a reference group. It must provide a standard by which you evaluate your behavior for it to be a reference group.

Ethnic groups provide some adolescents with strong reference group standards by which to judge themselves. The stronger the ethnic pride and identification, the more some teens may separate themselves from contact with members of other ethnic groups (Schaefer and Kunz 2007). This can be functional or dysfunctional for the teens, as shown in the next section on in-groups and out-groups.

One group can serve several purposes for an individual, for example, as a primary group, a peer group, and a reference group. These different terms refer to different features of a group. For instance, a peer group, people who share similar age or social status, could also be a reference group. The cross-country team may be Jared's peer group, but his everyday decisions may be based on standards of a religious group or professional society. Note also that someone may have a reference group but not actually be a member. The volleyball team or the American Medical Association may be Raluca's reference group, even though she has not yet attained membership in either one. However, if the standards and judgments of members of those groups to which she aspires influence her own decisions and give her direction, they are reference groups for her.

An **in-group** is one to which an individual feels a sense of loyalty and belonging. It also may serve as a reference group. An **out-group** is one to which an individual does not belong, but more than that, it is a group that is often in competition or in opposition to an in-group.

Membership in an in-group may be based on sex, race, ethnic group, social class, religion, political affiliation, the school one attends, an interest group such as the fraternity or sorority one joins, or the area where one lives. People tend to judge others according to their own in-group identity. Members of the in-group—for example, supporters of a high school team—often feel hostility toward or reject out-group members, boosters of the rival team. The perceived outside threat or hostility is often exaggerated, but it does help create the in-group members' feelings of solidarity. Sometimes, even one's declared major is the source of in-group loyalties, as students from biology ridicule psychology, or history majors bash sociology. Unfortunately, these feelings can result in prejudice and ethnocentrism, overlooking the individual differences of group members. Teen groups or gangs such as the Bloods and the Crips are examples of in-groups and out-groups in action, as are the ethnic and religious conflicts between Sunni and Shiite Muslims in Iraq; Serbs, Bosnian, and Albanian Muslims in the former Yugoslavia; Israeli Jews and Palestinians; Hutus and Tutsis in Rwanda; and Catholics and Protestants in Northern Ireland. In each case, the group loyalty is enhanced by hostility toward the out-group, resulting in gang conflicts and war.

Bloods gang members in Los Angeles use their in-group hand signal to identify one another.

Thinking Sociologically

What are some examples of your own group affiliations: Primary groups? Secondary groups? Peer groups? Reference groups? In-groups and out-groups?

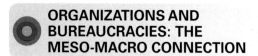

ORGANIZATIONS AND BUREAUCRACIES: THE MESO-MACRO CONNECTION

Our days are filled with activities that involve us with complex organizations: from the doctor's appointment to the college classes; from the political rally for the issue we are supporting to Sabbath worship in our church, temple, or mosque; from paying state sales tax for our toothpaste to buying a sandwich at a fast-food franchise. Figure 5.5 shows institutions of society, each made up of thousands of organizations (your medical organization, educational organization, religious group, economic corporations, political movements, the government itself) and each following the cultural norms of our society. We have statuses and roles in each group, and these link us to networks and the larger social world.

How did these organizational forms develop? Let us consider briefly the transformations of organizations into their modern forms and the characteristics of meso-level organizations today.

The Evolution of Modern Organizations

Empires around the world have risen and fallen since the dawn of civilization. Some economic, political, and religious systems have flourished. Others such as monarchies and fascism have withered. We cannot understand our social world at any historical or modern time without comprehending the organizational structures and processes present at that time. Recall the discussion of types of societies, from hunter-gatherer to postindustrial, in Chapter 3. Each type of society entails different organizational structures, from early cities and feudal manors to craft guilds, heavy industries, and Web-based companies (Blau 1956; Nolan and Lenski 2008).

The development of modern organizations and bureaucracies began with industrialization in the 1700s and was becoming the dominant form of industrial organizations by the 1800s. **Rationality**, the attempt to reach maximum

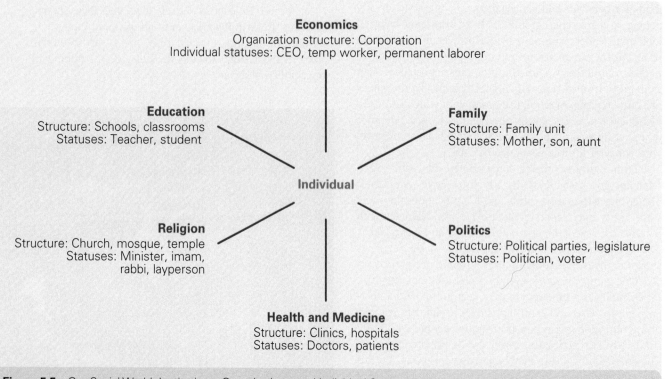

Figure 5.5   Our Social World: Institutions, Organizations, and Individual Status

efficiency, became the trend in managing organizations and was thought to be the best way to run organizations—efficiently and with rules that are rationally designed to accomplish goals (Weber 1947). People were expected to behave in purposeful, coordinated ways to reach goals efficiently. No longer were decisions made by tradition, custom, or the whim of a despot. Instead, trained leaders planned policies to achieve organizational efficiency. Tasks became more specialized, and some manual jobs were taken over by machines.

Standardization of products allowed for greater productivity, precision, and speed. These modern rational organizations, called **formal organizations**, are complex secondary groups deliberately formed to pursue and achieve certain goals. The Red Cross, General Motors Corporation, Blue Cross/Blue Shield insurance, and your university are all formal organizations.

Bureaucracies are specific types of very large formal organizations that have the purpose of maximizing efficiency. They are characterized by formal relations between participants, clearly laid-out procedures and rules, and pursuit of stated goals. Bureaucracies evolved as the most efficient way of producing products economically for mass markets (Ritzer 2004a). An example of rational bureaucracy is found in the fast-food empires springing up around the world. The next "Sociology Around the World" describes the trend toward the "McDonaldization of society"—Ritzer's pop-culture term for rationalization.

As societies became dominated by large organizations, fewer people worked the family farm or owned a cottage industry in their homes, and the number of small shopkeepers diminished. Today, some countries are organizational societies in which a majority of the members work in organizations. Many other societies around the world are moving in this direction.

Societies making the transition between traditional and modern organizational structures often have a blend of the two, and in many industrializing countries, traditional organizational systems mix with newer forms (Nolan and Lenski 2008). Bribery, corruption, and favoritism govern some nations as they move toward modern bureaucracies. People in government jobs are promoted based on whom they are connected to in their family tree, not on the basis of their competence as assessed by formal training, examinations, or criteria derived from the needs of the position and organization. Breaking down old systems can create disruption, even anomie, in societies undergoing these transitions.

Postindustrial societies feature high dependence on technology and information-sharing. Few people live and work on farms. In the United States today, only 2.5% of the civilian labor force, that is 3.5 million people, are working in agriculture, forestry, and fisheries out of a total civilian labor force of 141 million. This is compared to 11.6% in farm-related occupations in 1950 and 63.7% in 1850 (Europa World Year Book 2005).

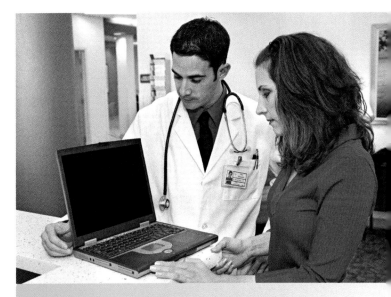

The hospital setting is an example of a modern formal organization that not only is governed by formal rules and impersonal relations, but also increasingly involves extensive communication via computers.

Thinking Sociologically

Make a list of your activities in a typical day. Which of these activities are, and which are not, associated with large (meso-level) formal organizations?

Characteristics of Modern Organizations

Organizations and modern life are almost synonymous. Live in one, and you belong to the other. In this section, we consider some characteristics of bureaucracy, and some processes and problems that occur in organizations.

Think about the many organizations that regularly affect your life: the legal system that passes laws, your college, your workplace, and voluntary organizations to which you belong. Individuals require organizations for human interaction and to meet their needs, and organizations need humans to hold positions and carry out tasks or roles. Some organizations, such as the local chapter of the Rotary Club or a chapter of a sorority, function at the micro level. Everyone is in a face-to-face relationship with every other member of the organization. However, those local chapters are part of a nationwide organization that is actually a meso-level corporation. At another level in terms of size, the federal government is a very complex organization that influences the lives of every citizen, and some transnational corporations are global in their reach. Both operate at the macro level.

Sociology Around the World

The McDonaldization of Society

The process of rationalization described by Max Weber—the attempt to reach maximum bureaucratic efficiency—comes in a new modern version, expanded and streamlined, as exemplified by the fast-food restaurant business and the chain "box" stores found around the world. Efficient, rational, predictable sameness is sweeping the world—from diet centers such as NutriSystem to 7-Eleven and from Wal-Mart to Gap clothing stores with their look-alike layouts. Most major world cities feature McDonald's or Kentucky Fried Chicken in the traditional main plazas or train stations for the flustered foreigners and curious native consumers.

The McDonaldization of society, as George Ritzer (2004b) calls it, refers to several trends: First, *efficiency* is maximized by the sameness—same store plans, same mass-produced items, same procedures. Second is *predictability,* the knowledge that each hamburger or piece of chicken will be the same, leaving nothing to chance. Third, everything is *calculated* so that the organization can assure that everything fits a standard—every burger is cooked the same number of seconds on each side. Fourth, there is *increased control* over employees and customers so there are fewer variables to consider—including substitution of technology for human labor as a way to ensure predictability and efficiency.

What is the result of this efficient, predictable, planned, automated new world? According to Ritzer, the world is becoming more dehumanized, and the efficiency is taking over individual creativity and human interactions. The mom-and-pop grocery, bed and breakfasts, and local craft or clothing shops are rapidly becoming a thing of the past, giving way to the McClones. This process of the McDonaldization of society, meaning principles of efficiency and rationalization exemplified by fast-food chains, is coming to dominate more and more sectors of our social world (Ritzer 1998, 2004a, 2004b). While there is aspects of this predictability that we all like, there is also a loss of uniqueness and local flavor that individual entrepreneurs bring to a community.

To try to re-create this culture, Ritzer suggests, there is a movement toward "Starbuckization." Starbucks is unique because of its aesthetic contribution. Starbucks makes customers feel like they are purchasing a cultural product along with their coffee. This culture, however, is as controlled as any other McDonaldized endeavor, making Starbucks as much a McClone as its predecessors.

McDonaldization is so widespread and influential that many modern universities are McDonaldized. A large lecture hall is a very efficient way of teaching sociology or biology to many students at once. Similarly, distance learning, PowerPoint presentations, multiple choice exams, and limited textbooks increase the predictability of course offerings. Grade point averages and credit hours completed are very calculated ways to view students. Moreover, universities control students by deciding what courses are offered, when they are offered, and what professors will teach them.

Some organizations provide us work necessary for survival. Others are forced on us—prisons, mental hospitals, military draft systems, even education to a certain age. Still others are organizations we believe in and voluntarily join—scouts, environmental protest groups, sports leagues (Etzioni 1975). Membership in voluntary organizations is higher in the United States than in many other countries (Johnson and Johnson 2006), yet in recent years, membership in many voluntary organizations has dropped, a factor discussed in the next "Sociology in Your Social World." Some analysts argue that new types of affiliations and interactions, including the Internet, are replacing some older affiliations.

Sociology in Your Social World

Bowling Alone Versus Contributing to Your Social World

To join or not to join—that is a question many college students must decide. They are torn between spending time with their computers and video games and joining groups, even doing volunteer work in the community or working on a political campaign. Research on joining organized groups versus engaging in individual activities gives us some insight into choices and consequences of these choices.

According to one study of group activities, bowling leagues have experienced significant declines in membership in recent years. Yet, more people in the United States bowl than vote, often enjoying the sport as individuals rather than in organized groups. For sociologists, this pattern points to a broad trend—those who once participated in group activities are turning inward and not joining organized groups (Putnam 1995, 2001).

Does this reflect a breakdown of the U.S. community? Parent-Teacher Associations (PTAs), Red Cross, bowling leagues, and other civic groups were all down in numbers in the mid-1990s. The result is that people got together less often. The U.S. enthusiasm for organizational participation that de Tocqueville observed some 200 years ago appeared to be dampening. Robert Putnam, the researcher, speculated that loss of faith in institutions and the existence of television and computers, what some call "technological individualizing," in many homes kept people from connecting with others. Staying home and watching TV or surfing the net replaced a night out with friends or joining organized groups.

In a separate study, a team of sociologists from the University of California, Berkeley, also analyzed the relationship between individualism and sense of community. They concluded that individualism is problematic for Americans living in an interdependent world (Bellah et al. 1996). As individuals lose contact with others, they face private problems alone. What the United States needs, according to the authors of this study, is a greater sense of community to give individuals a feeling of belonging and to link the micro and macro levels of the social world (Bellah et al. 1996). In other words, individuals should think about "bowling together" or find other ways to connect and build a sense of community through group affiliation or involvement.

More recently, there is evidence that different types of groups and affiliations, some based on new technologies, some based on volunteering, are emerging to replace bowling leagues and similar organizations (Putnam 2001; Thoits and Hewitt 2001). From college students involved in the 2008 political campaigns to volunteer work on Habitat for Humanity and other work projects, volunteerism has increased in the past decade (Cillizza and Murray 2008). Consequences for those who join groups and volunteer are increased physical and psychological well-being, happiness, greater life satisfaction, higher self-esteem, more sense of control over life, better physical health, and less depression. Thus, contributing to your social world may have many benefits for both you as an individual and for those you are helping.

Thinking Sociologically

Think about your friends and their activities. Are they involved in social activities or volunteer work? What differences do you see between your friends based on their involvement? Is lack of involvement a real threat to a local community?

Characteristics of Bureaucracy

Bureaucracies are a particular form of modern organization, characterized by trained officials who carry out procedures and tasks in an efficient way. You need groceries. You probably expect to go into the store, see clearly marked prices on items, even broken down by price-per-unit for comparative purposes. You expect to go to the cashier and pay the set price that is established by the bureaucratic system. Yet, if

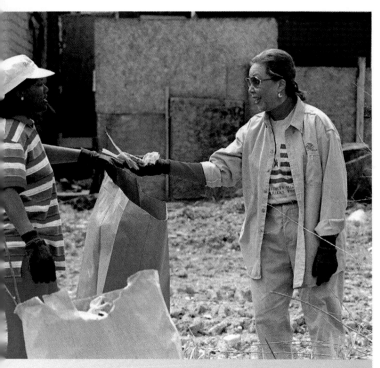

In Philadelphia, people come together for the voluntary civic action of cleaning up the community.

you have been to a Caribbean, African, Asian, or Middle Eastern market, you know that the bartering system is used to settle on a mutually agreeable price. This system is more personal and involves intense interaction between the seller and buyer, but it also takes more time, is less efficient, and can be frustrating to the uninitiated visitor accustomed to the relative efficiency and predictability of bureaucracy. As societies transition, they tend to adopt bureaucratic forms of organization.

To get a drivers' license, pay school fees, or buy tickets for a popular concert or game, you may have to stand in a long line. Finally, after waiting in line, you discover that you have forgotten your social security number, or they do not take a credit card. The rules and red tape are irksome. Yet, what is the alternative? Some institutions have adopted telephone and online registration or ticket purchases, but even with this automated system, problems can occur. Frustrations with bureaucracy are part of modern life, but the alternatives (such as bartering) are less efficient and sometimes more frustrating or bewildering to those who are used to bureaucratic efficiency.

Most organizations in modern society—hospitals, schools, churches, government agencies, industries, banks, even large clubs—are bureaucracies. Therefore, understanding these modern organizations is critical to understanding the modern social world in which we live.

At the beginning of the 20th century, Max Weber (1864–1920) looked for reasons behind the massive changes taking place in societies that were causing the transition from traditional society to bureaucratic, capitalistic society. He wanted to understand why the rate of change was more rapid in some parts of Europe than others and why bureaucracy came to dominate forms of organization in some countries. Whereas traditional society looked to the past for guidance, bureaucratic industrial society required a new form of thinking and behavior, a change in attitude toward rationality. Weber observed that leadership in business and government was moving from traditional forms with powerful families and charismatic leaders toward more efficient and less personal bureaucracy.

Weber's (1947) term, **ideal-type bureaucracy**, refers to the dominant and essential characteristics of organizations that are designed for reliability and efficiency. It describes not a good or perfect organization but merely an organization with a particular set of traits. Any particular bureaucracy is unlikely to have all of the characteristics in the ideal type, but the degree of bureaucratization is measured by how closely an organization resembles the core characteristics of the ideal type. The following characteristics of Weber's ideal type bureaucracy provide an example of how these characteristics relate to schools:

1. *Division of labor* based on technical competence: Administrators lead but do not teach, and instructors teach only in areas of their certification; staff are assigned positions for which credentials make them most qualified, and recruitment and promotion are governed by formal policies.

2. *Administrative hierarchy*: There is a specified chain of command and designated channels of communication, from school board to superintendent to principal to teacher.

3. *Formal rules and regulations*: Written procedures and rules—perhaps published in an administrative manual—spell out systemwide requirements, including discipline practices, testing procedures, curricula, sick days for teachers, penalties for student tardiness, field trip policies, and other matters.

4. *Impersonal relationships*: Formal relationships tend to prevail between teachers and students and between teachers and administrative staff (superintendents, principals, counselors); written records and formal communication provide a paper trail for all decisions.

5. *Emphasis on rationality and efficiency to reach goals*: Established processes are used, based on the best interests of the school. Efficiency is defined in terms of lowest overall cost to the organization in reaching a goal, not in terms of personal consequences.

6. *Provision of life-long careers*: Employees may spend their entire careers working for the same organization, working their way up the hierarchy through promotions.

Although the list of characteristics makes bureaucracies sound formal and rigid, informal structures allow organizational members to deviate from rules both to meet goals of the organization more efficiently and to humanize an otherwise uncaring and sterile workplace. The **informal structure** includes the unwritten norms and the interpersonal networks that people use within an organization to carry out roles. Likewise, although bylaws, constitutions, or contracts spell out the way things are supposed to be done, people often develop unwritten shortcuts to accomplish goals. The U.S. Postal Service has rules specifying that letter carriers are not supposed to walk across people's lawns, yet, if they did not find shortcuts, it would take many more hours before people's mail was delivered.

Informal norms are not always compatible with those of the formal organization. Consider the following example from a famous classical study. In the Western Electric plant near Chicago, the study found that new workers were quickly socialized to do "a fair day's work," and those who did more or less than the established norm—what the work group thought was fair—were considered "rate busters" or "chiselers" and experienced pressure from the group to conform. These informal mechanisms gave informal groups of workers a degree of power in the organization (Roethlisberger and Dickson 1939).

Thinking Sociologically

How closely does each of Weber's characteristics of ideal-type bureaucracy describe your college or your work setting? Is your college highly bureaucratized, with many rules and regulations? Are decisions based on efficiency and cost effectiveness, educational quality, or both? To what extent is your work setting characterized by hierarchy, formal rules governing your work time, and impersonality?

Individuals in Bureaucracies

Lindi England, a young woman from a small town in West Virginia looking for opportunity and adventure, joined the military. Instead, she became a victim and a scapegoat. The bureaucracy was the U.S. military; the setting was the Abu Ghraib prison in Iraq; the group pressure was to conform and fit in under stressful conditions by "going along with the guards" who were abusing and humiliating prisoners (Zimbardo 2004). Caring and humane military officers may allow abuse of prisoners or order bombing strikes even though they know that some innocent people will be killed or maimed. In the military command in a war, a cold, impersonal cost-benefit analysis takes priority. In bureaucracies, self-preservation is the core value, and rational choice is often effective in explaining interactions in these contexts.

Humans can be moral, altruistic, and self-sacrificing for the good of others, but nations and other extremely large organizations (such as corporations or government) are inherently driven by a cost-benefit ratio (Niebuhr 1932). As one moves toward larger and more impersonal bureaucracies, the nature of interaction often changes.

Professionals in bureaucracies include doctors, lawyers, engineers, professors, and others who have certain special attributes: advanced education, knowledge and competency in a field, high levels of autonomy to make decisions based on their expertise, strong commitment to their field, a service orientation and commitment to the needs of the client, standards and regulations set by the profession, and a sense of intrinsic satisfaction from the work (rather than motivation rooted in external rewards, such as salary). Professionals also claim authority, power, and control in their work area because of their mastery or expertise in a field (Hall 2002). Professionals may face conflicting loyalties to their profession and to the bureaucratic organization in which they are employed. A scientist hired by a tobacco company faced a dilemma when his research findings did not support the company position that nicotine is not addictive. They wanted him to falsify his research, which would be a violation of professional ethics. Should he be a whistle-blower and publicly challenge the organization? Several professionals have done so but lost their jobs as a result.

Bureaucracy, some argue, is the number one enemy of professionalism, for it reduces autonomy. First, bureaucrats insist that authority rests in the person who holds an organizational status or title in the hierarchy rather than the person with the most expertise. Second, bureaucrats tend to reward people with external rewards such as bonuses rather than internal motivations. Third, bureaucrats focus on the needs of the organization as primary rather than on the needs of the client or professional. The potential clash between professionals and bureaucracy raises key concerns as universities, hospitals, and other large organizations are governed increasingly by bureaucratic principles (Roberts and Donahue 2000). Alienation among professionals occurs when they are highly regulated rather than when they have some decision-making authority and are granted some autonomy (Hall 2002). For example, high-tech companies that depend on engineering designers find that hierarchical structures undermine productivity, whereas factors such as intrinsic satisfaction, flexible hours, and relaxed work environments are central to creative productivity (Florida 2002; Friedman 2005; Molotch 2003).

Thinking Sociologically

When you shop or eat, is it at McClones fast-food chain or at individually owned stores? Can anything be done to protect the non-McClones, or are they destined to be eliminated by the competition?

Women in many countries have low-paid, dead-end jobs that make them feel uninvolved and unconnected. The jobs result in alienation, but these women need the work, and they have little choice but to accept dead-end jobs.

Minorities in bureaucracies may come up against barriers that keep women and minority group members from reaching high levels of management. The result is that individuals from these groups are found disproportionately in midlevel positions with little authority and less pay than others with similar skills and credentials. (Chaffins, Forbes, and Fuqua 1995). When employees have little chance for promotion, they have less ambition and loyalty to the organization (Kanter 1977).

Research indicates that women executives bring valuable alternative perspectives to organizational leadership. They share information readily, give employees greater autonomy, and stress interconnectedness between parts of the organization, resulting in a more democratic type of leadership (Helgesen 1995; Kramer 2005). The more women in an organization's senior positions, the more likely newcomers are to find support.

The interaction of people who see things differently because of religious beliefs, ethnic backgrounds, and gender experiences increases productivity in many organizations. Having a wide range of perspectives can lead to better problem solving (Florida 2004; Molotch 2003). Because diversity actually increases productivity and problem-solving, the barriers to promotion have been irrational and dysfunctional to the organization.

Problems in Bureaucracies

Bureaucratic inefficiency and red tape are legendary and have been the theme for many classic novels, from Charles Dickens's *Bleak House*, which describes the legal system in England in the 1800s, to George Orwell's *1984*, which depicts a sterile, controlled environment. Yet, bureaucracies are likely to stay, for they are the most efficient form of modern organization yet devised. Nonetheless, several individual and organizational problems created by bureaucratic structures are important to understand.

Alienation, feeling uninvolved, uncommitted, unappreciated, and unconnected, occurs when workers experience routine, boring tasks or dead-end jobs with no possibility of advancement. Marx believed that alienation is a structural feature of capitalism with serious consequences: Workers lose their sense of purpose and seem to become dehumanized and objectified in their work, creating a product that they often do not see completed and for which they do not get the profits (Marx [1844] 1964).

Dissatisfaction comes from low pay and poor benefits; routine, repetitive, and fragmented tasks; lack of challenge and autonomy, leading to boredom; and poor working conditions. Workers who see possibilities for advancement put more energy into the organization, but those stuck in their positions are less involved and put more energy into activities outside the workplace (Kanter 1977).

Workers' productive behavior is not solely a result of rational factors such as pay and working conditions but is influenced by emotions, beliefs, and norms (Roethlisberger and Dickson 1939). To address these factors, many organizations have moved toward workplace democracy, employee participation in decision making, and employee ownership plans.

Thinking Sociologically

How might participation in decision making and increased autonomy for workers enhance commitment and productivity in your place of work or in your college? What might be some risks or downsides to such worker input and freedom?

Oligarchy, the concentration of power in the hands of a small group, is a common occurrence in organizations. In the early 1900s, Robert Michels, a French sociologist, wrote about the **iron law of oligarchy,** the idea that power becomes concentrated in the hands of a small group of leaders in political, business, voluntary, or other organizations. Initially, organizational needs, more than the motivation for power, cause these few stable leaders to emerge. As organizations grow, a division of labor emerges so that only a few leaders have access to information, resources, and the overall picture. This, in turn, causes leaders who enjoy their elite positions of power to become entrenched (Michels [1911] 1967). An example is the Enron Corporation scandal, in which Enron executives hid information about financial problems from workers and investors.

Goal displacement occurs when the original motives or goals of the organization are displaced by new secondary goals. Organizations form to meet specific goals. Religious organizations are founded to worship a deity and serve humanity on behalf of that deity, schools are founded to educate children, and social work agencies are organized to serve the needs of citizens who seem to have fallen between the cracks. Yet, over time, original goals may be met or become less important as other motivations and interests emerge (Merton 1968b; Whyte 1956).

Parkinson's law, which states that in a bureaucracy work expands to fill the time and space available for its completion, is an example of inefficiency (Parkinson 1957). If we build a new room on our house, we are likely to fill it to capacity. If classes are canceled for a day, our free day gets filled up with other activities. If we have two tests to study for, each takes half a day, but if we have one, it may still take most of the day. Despite the expansion of space or time, we still do not seem to have enough time or room. Organizations work similarly. Parkinson's point is that organizations grow automatically, sometimes beyond efficiency or effectiveness.

Policymakers have explored possibilities of other ways of organizing society. Alternative organization structures refer to recent approaches that have developed to deal with some of the problems discussed previously. Employee-owned companies are owned in part or in full by employees, who are given or can buy shares. Profit sharing is generally part of the deal. If the company does well, all workers benefit. Studies show that this increases production and improves dedication, but the decision-making process is slower, and there is increased risk for the individual employees. However, the idea is that employees have a stake in their company and the job they do (Blasi, Kruse, and Bernstein 2003). Other companies, democratic-collective organizations, rely on cooperation, place authority and decision making in the collective group, and use personal appeals to ensure that everyone participates in problem solving. The rules, hierarchy, and status distinctions are minimized, and hiring is often based on shared values and friendships (Deming 2000). Members believe these organizations are more humane, and workers feel connected to the purpose and the product. The hope is that these new forms of organization—nonbureaucratic forms—may actually be a more effective way to organize a postindustrial corporation.

Although we may fantasize about escaping from the rat-race world, about isolating ourselves on an island or living as a hermit in a house on stilts, groups and bureaucracies are a part of modern life that few can escape. These are only a few examples of problems in bureaucracies.

Thinking Sociologically

In what areas of your college or workplace do you see goal displacement? That is, where do you see decisions being driven by goals other than the original purpose of the university, which was to educate a new generation and expand human knowledge?

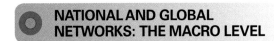

NATIONAL AND GLOBAL NETWORKS: THE MACRO LEVEL

In one sense, learning to understand people who are unlike us, to network with people who have different cultures, and to make allowances for alternative ideas about society and human behavior have become core competencies in our globalizing social world. Increasingly, colleges have study-abroad programs, jobs open up for teaching English as a second language, and corporations seek employees who are multilingual and culturally competent in diverse settings. One rather recent college graduate with a sociology degree found that she could use her sociology skills in leading groups of college-age students in international travel experiences. She explains this applied use of sociology in the next "The Applied Sociologist at Work."

With modern communication and transportation systems and the ability to transfer ideas and money with a touch of the keyboard, global networks are superseding national boundaries. Multinational corporations now employ citizens from around the world and can make their own rules because there is no oversight body. National systems and international organizations, from the United Nations to the World Bank to multinational corporations, are typically governed through rational bureaucratic systems.

One complicating factor at the national and global levels is multilingualism, the reality that many languages are used to communicate. Although Spanish, Chinese, and Arabic are widely used in homes across the globe, English has become the language of commerce. This is because much of the political and economic power and control over the expansion of technology has been located in English-speaking countries.

Technology has some interesting implications for human interaction. E-mail, Web pages, chat rooms, and blogs have made it possible for people around the world to talk with each other, exchange ideas, and even develop friendships. When Keith, one of the coauthors, was conducting research in Wales, he was able to use the Internet to set up interviews before leaving the United States. In other parts of the world, dictators can no longer keep the citizenry from knowing what people outside their country think. In China, as fast as officials censor information on the World Wide Web, computer experts find ways around

The Applied Sociologist at Work— Elise Roberts

Using Sociology in International Travel and Intercultural Education

By Elise Roberts

After graduating from college with a bachelor's degree in sociology, I left the country to backpack through Mexico and Central America. My studies helped me to be more objective and aware as I experienced other societies. My international travel helped me examine my own societal assumptions and further understand how society creates so much of one's experience and view of the world. Eventually, I found a job leading groups of teenagers on alternative-education trips abroad. I was excited to get the job, but I was soon to learn that leading groups of teenagers in other countries is actually very hard work.

What struck me on meeting my first group was that I had very few students who initially understood this sociological perspective that I took for granted and that was so insightful in dealing with others. At times, my students would make fun of the way things were done in other countries, calling them "weird" or "stupid." They would mock the local traditions, until we discussed comparable traditions in American culture. These students were not mean or unintelligent. In fact, they loved the places we were seeing and the people we were meeting. They just thought everything was factually, officially weird. They had been socialized to understand their own society's ways as "right" and "normal." They were fully absorbed in the U.S. society, and they had never questioned it before.

It was interesting to think about how to teach the concepts of social constructionism in such an applied environment, and it was rewarding to apply concepts from my textbooks in the real world. My coleaders and I learned to have fun while encouraging our students to become more socially conscious and analytical about their travel experience. We sent the groups out on scavenger hunts, and they would inevitably come back proudly announcing what they had paid for a rickshaw ride—only to learn that they had paid 10 times the local price. We would use this experience to talk about the role of foreigners, the assumptions that the local population made due to our skin color, and the culture of bartering. They had to learn to understand "odd" gestures, like pointing with the lips or side-to-side nodding. We would use these experiences to discuss nonverbal communication and gestures that we take for granted in U.S. culture.

We would encourage our novice travelers to interact with the people around them, which helped them understand the struggles facing immigrants and non-English speakers in the United States. We would force them to have conversations while standing toe-to-toe with each other, and they would finish with backaches from leaning away from one another. We would not allow them to explain their behavior with "because it's creepy to stand so close together," even though this was the consensus. "Why do you feel uncomfortable?" we would ask. "Why is this weird?" The answer has to do with social constructions of what is "normal" in any society.

Of course, while traveling internationally, one is surrounded by various other sociological issues, such as different racial or ethnic conflicts, gender roles, or class hierarchies, and learning about these issues was a part of our program as well. Without realizing it, many group conversations and meetings began to remind me of some of my favorite Macalester classes. "Study sociology!" I would say, plugging my major to the most interested students.

I have always thought that travel was an incredibly useful means not only to learn about the society and culture one is visiting but also to learn much about oneself and one's home society. For teenagers who otherwise might never step back to think about the role of being a foreigner or the traditions and social patterns they take for granted, it is even more important. Traveling abroad on my own and leading programs abroad were such extremely rich and rewarding experiences not only due to the cross-cultural exchanges and the intense personal examination that I saw in my students but also because it was fascinating and rewarding to be able to use my sociology degree every day on my job.

Note: Elise Roberts graduated from Macalester College with a major in sociology. Her recent travels took her through Central America, the South Pacific, and many parts of Asia. She is currently at graduate student at Columbia University in international social work.

Around the world, two thirds of the poorest adults are women, even though women produce more than two thirds of food supplies in the world. A Laotian woman works in the field (left), and an Indian woman transports goods to market (right).

the restrictions. Officials in Myanmar try to block satellite communication to restrict access to the information highway. Despite efforts by some nations to limit access, the process of change is occurring so rapidly that we cannot know what technology will mean for the global world, but it is almost certain that the processes of interaction across national lines will continue despite some efforts to curb communication. The World Wide Web was not invented until 1989, and e-mail has been available to most citizens—even in affluent countries—only since the early 1990s (Brasher 2004). Countries are still struggling with what this means for change.

Within nations, people with common interests, be it organic food or peace, can contact one another. Hate groups also set up Web pages and mobilize others with their view of the world, and terrorists use the Internet to communicate around the world. Clearly, ability to communicate around the globe is transforming the world and our nations in ways that affect local communities and private individuals. Indeed, the Internet has become a major outlet for sellers and source for consumers. A wide range of products can be obtained through Internet orders from Web sites that have no geographical home base. In some cases, there are no actual warehouses or manufacturing plants, and there might not be a home office. Some businesses are global and exist in the Ethernet, not in any specific nation (Ritzer 2004b). This reality makes one rethink national and global loyalties and realities.

From the discussion of rationalization and the McDonaldization of society in the previous section, we see

some results: Family loyalties are considered less important than needs of the corporation. Feelings are subordinated to thought processes. Efficiency and calculability are highly prized in the social system. However, as these Western notions of how public life should operate are exported to other countries, a severe backlash has occurred. In many Middle Eastern Islamic countries, for example, these values clash with Muslim loyalties and priorities. The result has been high levels of anger at the United States and Western Europe. Many scholars believe that Middle Eastern anger at the United States is based not on opposition to freedom and democracy, as our politicians sometimes say, but on what some Middle Easterners see as crass utilitarianism and impersonal organizational structures we try to import into their micro- and meso-level worlds. They feel that their very culture is threatened. Radical fundamentalist movements—groups that are fueled by social, economic, and religious environmental stressors and that cope by rejecting all ambiguity—are mostly anti-modernization movements turned militant (Antoun 2001; Davidman 1990; Heilman 2000; Marty 2001; Marty and Appleby 1992, 2004; Ontario Consultants on Religious Tolerance, 2004; Shupe and Hadden 1989). They have emerged in Christianity, Judaism, Islam, Sikh, and other groups, largely as a response to a perceived crisis (Armstrong 2000). Some aspects of global terrorism and international conflict are based in the way the Western world organizes its social life and exports it to other parts of the world. These conflicts, in turn, have resulted in mobilization of the military in the United States. The result is that members of your own family might be serving abroad even as you read these pages.

Thinking Sociologically

How do you think global interaction will be transformed through Internet technology? How will individual connections between people be affected by these transformations at the macro levels of our social world?

Policy Issues: Women and Globalization

Women around the world are viewed as second-class citizens, the most economically, politically, and socially marginalized people on the planet, caught in expectations of religion, patriarchy, and roles needed to sustain life (Schneider and Silverman 2006). To help their children survive, women do whatever their situation allows to make money: street-selling, low-paying factory assembly line work, piecework (e.g., sewing clothing in their homes), prostitution and sex work, and domestic service. Women also produce 75% to 90% of the food crops in the world, run households, and are often the main support for children in poor countries. Yet, due to

the "feminization of poverty," two out of three poor adults are women (Enloe 2006; Robbins 2005). Causes of the many problems facing women are found at each level of analysis and will be discussed throughout the book.

One macro-level organization with policies to help raise the status of women through development is the United Nations. Each decade since the 1960s, this global organization has set forth plans to improve conditions in poor countries. Early plans to help poor countries were driven by interests of capitalist countries in the first world. This left women out of the equation and planning. Women suffered more under some of these plans because their positions and responsibilities did not change. Conditions got worse as development money went to large corporations with the idea that profits would trickle down to the local level, an idea that did not materialize in most countries (Boulding and Dye 2002).

More recently, the United Nations has sponsored conferences on the status of women. The United Nations' Division for the Advancement of Women and other organizations are now developing policies to help educate local women in health, nutrition, basic first aid, and business methods. Many projects have been spawned, including micro-lending organizations (Grameen Bank, SEWA, Finca, Care), allowing individuals and groups of women to borrow money to start cooperatives and other small-business ventures. These organizations can have very beneficial effects if they are used wisely by policymakers who care about the people rather than just about their own benefits. In the next few chapters, we will learn about some of the factors that cause some individuals and countries to be poorer than others.

So What?

Our social lives are lived in small groups and personal networks. The scope of those networks has broadened with increased complexity and includes the global social world. Indeed, it is easy not to recognize how extensively our networks reach, even to the global level. Although bureaucracies existed in previous eras such as the Roman Empire, the modern world is primarily a phenomenon of the past three centuries. The intimate experiences of our personal lives are far more extensively linked to meso- and macro-level events and to people and places on the other side of the globe than was true for our parents' generation. If we hope to understand our lives, we must understand this broad context. Although humans have always depended on groups for survival, it may have been possible to live without global connections and bureaucratic systems several centuries ago. However, these networks are intricately woven into our lifestyles and our economic systems today. The question is whether we control these networks or they control us.

Our networks set norms and curb our behaviors, usually inclining us to conform to the social expectations of our associates. This, of course, contributes to stability of the entire social system because deviation can threaten the existence of "normal" patterns.

Key Points

What Have We Learned?

- People in the modern world are connected through one acquaintance to another in a chain of links, referred to as networks. (See pp. 128–131.)

- Increasingly our electronic technology is creating networks that span the globe, but this same impersonal technology is used to enhance friendship networks and to meet a romantic life-partner. (See pp. 130–131.)

- Interpersonal interactions at the micro level are affected by unspoken assumptions that are understood due to context, by nonverbal communication, and by the symbolism of space between people. (See pp. 131–136.)

- Many of our behaviors are shaped by the statuses (social positions) we hold and the roles (expectations associated with a status) we play. However, our multiple status occupancy can create role conflicts (between the roles of two statuses) and role strains (between the role expectations of a single status). (See pp. 136–141.)

- When the norms of behavior are unclear, we may experience anomie (normlessness), and this ambiguity compromises our sense of belonging and is linked to reasons for individuals performing one of the most personal of acts—suicide. (See pp. 141–143.)

- Various types of groups affect our behavior—from primary and secondary groups to peer groups and reference groups. (See pp. 143–145.)

- At the meso level, we find that formal organizations in the contemporary modern world are ruled by rational calculation of the organization's goals rather than by tradition or emotional ties. These modern formal organizations expand, are governed by impersonal formal rules, and stress efficiency and rational decision making. They have come to be called bureaucracies. (See pp. 146–151.)

- Bureaucracies often involve certain problems for individuals, and they may actually develop certain problems that make them inefficient or destructive. (See pp. 151–153.)

- While bureaucratization emerged at the meso level as the defining element of the modern world, it is also found at the national and global levels where people do not know each other on a face-to-face basis. (See pp. 153–156.)

- Some scholars think that this impersonal mode of organizing social life—so common in the West for several centuries now—is a critical factor in anti-American and anti-Western resistance movements. (See pp. 155–156.)

Contributing to Our Social World: What Can We Do?

At the Local Level: One of the most powerful concepts to emerge in the study of social interaction in recent years is social capital. This refers to the stock of personal contacts, networks, and organizations that an individual can draw on in coping with difficult situations. It is frequently the case that people who have trouble dealing with life's daily challenges lack adequate social capital, whereas people who are generally successful have a substantial base of contacts to support them. Most campuses have programs that are designed to help students who are struggling with their studies. If your campus has one or more of these, contact its office and arrange to observe and/or volunteer in its work. Examine the extent to which the social capital theory applies to the students in need and, if appropriate, work to improve the stock of social capital to which they have access.

At the Organizational or Institutional Level: The social capital theory can also be applied to meso-level community organizations, including those that work to reduce conflict or improve intergroup relations such as the Anti-Defamation League, the Arab Anti-Defamation League, and the National Association for the Advancement of Colored People. These organizations often use volunteers or interns and can provide you with the opportunity to learn about the extent to which social contacts and networks play a role in managing social conflict.

Visit **www.pineforge.com/ballantine2study** for online activities, sample tests, and other helpful information. Select "Chapter 5: Interaction, Groups, and Organizations" for chapter-specific activities.

CHAPTER 6

Deviance and Social Control

Sickos, Perverts, Freaks, and Folks Like Us

Deviants are often thought of as perverts and rule breakers without consciences. We often contrast them to people like us, but the reality is that the line between deviants and conformists is frequently vague, and we may be surprised to learn that often "deviants are us."

Think About It . . .

Micro: Are you deviant? Who says?

Micro: Why do some people in your community become deviant?

Meso: What are the implications of organized crime or occupational crime in large bureaucratic organizations?

Macro: What are the costs—and the benefits—of deviance for a nation?

Macro: How can a global perspective on crime enhance our understanding of international criminal activities?

Macro: Global Community

Macro: Society

Meso: National Organizations, Institutions, and Ethnic Subcultures

Micro: Local Organizations and Community

Micro: Me (and My Peers)

Micro: Violations of local ordinances; problems with neighbors; theft, burglary, local corruption

Meso: Violations of state laws; white collar crimes within corporations and crimes by corporations; cover-ups of religious clergy sex crimes

Macro: Individual federal crimes (treason, tax fraud, infringement of copyright laws); crimes committed by the state, including domestic terrorism against its own citizens; Internet fraud

Macro: Global environmental destruction; international terrorism; human rights violations such as genocide; violations of international treaties about treatment of prisoners

Wafa grew up as other girls do, but she was destined to make world headlines on January 27, 2002—the first female suicide bomber in the Palestinian-Israeli conflict. She was the age of most university students reading this book, but she never had an opportunity to attend. Her story sounds simple: She was to take explosives across the Israeli border for the intended bomber, her brother. Instead, she blew up herself and an Israeli soldier. She was declared a martyr, a *sahida*, by the Al-Aqsa Martyrs Brigade, and they took credit for the attack. Her act was given approval by the group's political leadership, opening the way for other women to follow. Why did this happen? What motivated her to commit suicide and take other lives in the process? Was she driven by ideology to participate in the Palestinian-Israeli struggle? Were there sociological and social structural factors that affected her decision? Most important, was she deviant in carrying out this act, and according to whom?

Wafa Idris grew up in Palestine. She was married at a young age but could not have children. Because this leaves a woman with no role to play in Palestinian society, her husband divorced her and remarried. She had no future, for who would want a barren, divorced woman in a society that values women for their purity and their child-bearing ability? She was a burden to her family. Her way out of an impossible and desperate situation was to commit suicide, bringing honor and wealth to her family and redeeming herself in the process. Other women who followed Wafa have similar stories: Most share an inability to control their own lives in the patriarchal society (Handwerk 2004; Victor 2003).

Ironically, terrorist cells in Palestine saw this as an opportunity to recruit other women. Most who joined the cause were vulnerable, broken, with no way out of untenable situations, and felt they had nothing to lose. For most, this was a way to escape problems in their lives, but also to bring honor to their families in the process. It is not a measure of equality that women, too, commit suicide bombings. This development results from a structure of inequality, according to Barbara Victor, who analyzed the lives of these women.

Our question is this: Are these women deviant criminal terrorists, or are they martyrs to be honored for their acts? Who says so? Both views are held depending on who is judging the situation. Are they victims of their situations, powerless and lacking status in a patriarchal society? From this opening example, we can begin to see several complexities that arise when considering deviance, and some of these ideas may encourage new ways of looking at what is deviant. In this chapter, we will consider who is deviant, under what circumstances, and in whose eyes. We will find that most people around the world conform to social norms of their societies most of the time, and we will explore why some turn to deviance.

Most people conform to the expected norms of their society most of the time. Occasionally, they may violate a norm, and depending on its importance and on the severity of the violation, the violator may or may not be seen as deviant. Wearing strange clothes may be seen as amusing and nonconformist once in a while, but it is labeled deviant if it becomes a regular occurrence. Adorning oneself with tattoos and rings to be distinctive and individualistic may result in widespread adoption of these behaviors so that they become accepted rather than deviant.

In this chapter, we discuss **deviance**—the violation of social norms—and the social control mechanisms that keep most people from becoming deviant. We also explore crime, the form of deviance on which formal penalties are imposed by the society. The content of this chapter may challenge some of your deeply held assumptions about human behavior and defy some conceptions about deviance. In fact, it may convince you that we are all deviant at some times and in some places. The self-test in the next "Sociology in Your Social World" illustrates this point. Try taking it to see whether you are deviant.

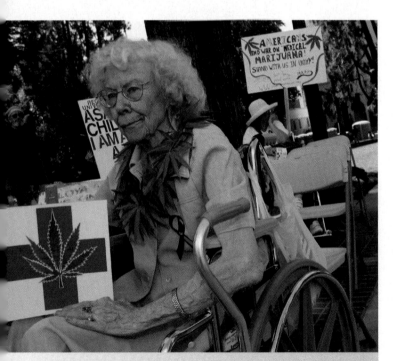

Medical marijuana patient Kay Mitchell, 82, of Sonoma, joined more than 1,000 people protesting outside the California state capitol against the Justice Department's arrests at state-approved and licensed medical marijuana dispensaries in California, which serve mostly terminally ill patients suffering from cancer, AIDS, and other ailments. Although the federal government views marijuana use as criminal, this woman thinks it is humane and compassionate to allow it.

Thinking Sociologically

First, read and answer the questions in "Sociology in Your Social World." Do you think of yourself as being deviant? Why or why not? Are deviants really only those who get caught? For instance, if someone steals your car but avoids being caught, is he or she deviant?

Sociology in Your Social World

Who Is Deviant?

Please jot down your answers to the following self-test questions. No need to share your responses with others.
Have you ever engaged in any of the following acts?

1. stolen anything, even if its value was under $10
2. used an illegal drug
3. misused a prescription drug
4. run away from home prior to age 18
5. used tobacco prior to age 18
6. drunk alcohol prior to age 21
7. engaged in a fist fight
8. carried a knife or gun
9. used a car without the owner's permission
10. driven a car after drinking alcohol
11. (boys) forced a girl to have sexual relations against her will
12. offered sex for money
13. damaged property worth more than $10
14. been truant from school
15. arrived home after your curfew
16. been disrespectful to someone in authority
17. accepted or transported property that you had reason to believe might be stolen
18. taken a towel from a hotel room after renting the room for a night

All of the above are delinquent acts (violations of legal standards), and most young people are guilty of at least one infraction. However, few teenagers are given the label of *delinquent*. If you have answered yes to any of the preceding questions, you have committed a crime in the state of Ohio and in many other states. Your penalty or sanction for the infraction could range from a stiff fine to several years in prison—*if* you got caught!

What Is Deviance?

Deviance refers to violation of the society's norms, which then evokes negative reactions from others. The definition is somewhat imprecise because of constantly changing ideas and laws about what acts are considered deviant. Some acts are deviant in most societies most of the time: murder, assault, robbery, and rape. Most societies impose severe penalties on these forms of deviance, and if the government imposes severe formal penalties, then the deviant actions become **crimes**. Occasionally, deviant acts may be overlooked or even viewed as understandable, as in the case of looting by citizens following the fall of the Iraqi government in 2003 or following Hurricane Katrina along the Gulf Coast in August 2005. The killing of innocent people, looting, and burning of houses during a civil or tribal war, which occurred in the aftermath of the 2008 presidential election in Kenya, also may have seemed reasonable to those committing the atrocities. Other acts of deviance are considered serious offenses

in one society but tolerated in another. Examples include prostitution, premarital or extramarital sex, gambling, corruption, and bribery. Even within a single society, different groups may define deviance and conformity quite differently. The state legislature may officially define alcohol consumption by 19-year-olds as deviant, but on a Saturday night at the fraternity party, the 19-year-old "brother" who does not drink may be viewed as deviant by his peers. What do these cases tell us about what deviance is?

Deviance is socially constructed. This means that members of groups in societies define what is deviant. Consider the phenomenon of today's young people getting tattoos, tongue studs, and rings anyplace on the body one can place a ring. Is this deviant? It depends on who is judging. Are tattoos and rings symbols of independence and rebellion, a "cool" and unique look? What if many people begin to adopt the behavior? Is it still a sign of independence, or does it become conformity to a group? Do such "deviant" acts then become a symbol of conformity? When the Beatles started the long hair

Photo Essay

Social Construction of Deviance

Are any of these people deviant? Why or why not?

rage in the 1960s, this was deviant behavior to many. Today, we pay no special attention to men with long hair.

Some acts are deviant at one time and place and not at others. Stem cell research has been viewed as unacceptable and a violation of U.S. law because of ethical concerns about using or destroying human cells. Yet, in many other countries, there are no moral restrictions, and scientists are proceeding with such research.

An individual's status or group may be defined as deviant. Some individuals have a higher likelihood of being labeled deviant because of the group into which they were born, such as a particular ethnic group, or because of a distinguishing mark or characteristic, such as a deformity. Others may escape being considered deviant because of their dominant status in society. The higher one's status, the less likely one is to be suspected of violating norms and the less likely any violations will be characterized as "criminal." Who would suspect that a respectable white-collar husband and father is embezzling funds or was once in a mental hospital? The Société General French bank scandal of 2008 involved massive fraud and attracted extraordinary attention because it was an "impossible" white-collar crime. The "crook" was a bank employee and beyond suspicion.

Even the looting that happened following Hurricane Katrina was addressed differently when it was done by whites rather than African Americans. (An image of a looter in New Orleans appears in the lower left corner of the Photo Essay on page 162.) The media showed photos of black "looters" who "stole food," but the same media described whites who "broke into grocery stores" in search of food as "resourceful." Likewise, gays and lesbians are often said to be deviant and accused of flaunting their sexuality. Heterosexuals are rarely accused of "flaunting" their sexuality, regardless of how overtly flirtatious they are. So one's group membership or ascribed traits may make a difference in whether or not one is defined as deviant.

Deviance can be problematic or functional for society. It represents a breakdown in norms. However, according to structural-functional theory, deviance serves vital functions by setting examples of what is considered unacceptable behavior, providing guidelines for behavior that is necessary to maintain the social order, and bonding people together through their common rejection of the deviant behavior. Deviance is also functional because it provides jobs for those who deal with deviants—police, judges, social workers, and so forth (Gans 2007). Furthermore, deviance can signal problems in society that need to be addressed and can therefore stimulate positive change. Sometimes, deviant individuals break the model of conventional thinking, thereby opening the society to new and creative paths of thinking. Scientists, inventors, and artists have often been rejected in their time but have been honored later for accomplishments that positively affected society. Vincent Van Gogh, for example, lived in poverty and mental turmoil during his life, but

Some sociologists point out that crime can be "functional" because it creates jobs for people like these above, and it unifies the society against the nonconformists.

he became recognized as a renowned painter after his death, his paintings selling for millions of dollars.

Our tasks in this chapter are to understand what deviance is, what causes it, and where it fits in the social world. We look at theoretical perspectives that help explain deviance, how some deviant acts become crimes, and what policies might be effective in controlling or reducing crime.

Thinking Sociologically

What would be the results in a heterogeneous society if everyone conformed, and no one ever deviated from social standards? In other words, what might be some negative consequences of *total* social conformity?

Misconceptions About Deviance

Many common beliefs about deviance are, in fact, misperceptions. Using scientifically collected data, the sociological perspective helps dispel false beliefs, as in the examples below.

Popular belief: Some acts are inherently deviant. Fact: Deviance is relative to time, place, and status of the individual. At some place or time, almost any behavior you can mention has been defined as deviant, just as most acts have been legal or even the typical behavior in other times and places. For example, homosexual liaisons were normal for men in ancient Greece and have been acceptable in various societies throughout time. Deviance is not inherent in certain behaviors but is defined by people and their governments (Erikson 1987).

Those in power have great influence over what is defined as deviant and can often determine punishment for deviant behavior. Some individuals are defined as deviant because they do not fit into the dominant system of values and norms. They may be seen as disruptive, a liability, or a threat to the system. In the military dictatorship of Myanmar (Burma) in Asia, political indoctrination controls many aspects of the citizens' lives. The rate of deviance is low because of threats against those who do not conform. Those who commit deviant acts are severely punished. However, ongoing protests against the military by Buddhist monks and dissidents show that not all agree with the norms of the powerful military government. Within dissident groups, anti-government protests are heroic rather than deviant.

Famous individuals remembered in history books were often considered deviant in their time. In the Middle Ages, for example, anyone who questioned the concept of a flat Earth at the center of the universe (with sun and stars circling it) was a deviant and a religious heretic. In the early 17th century, Galileo, following Copernicus's lead, wrote a treatise based on empirical observations that upheld the concept of the Earth revolving around the sun. He was tried by the Inquisition, a Roman Catholic church court, in Rome and condemned for heresy because of his theory.

Definitions of deviance also vary depending on the social situation or context in which the behavior occurs (Clinard and Meier 2004; McCaghy et al. 2006). If we take the same behavior and place it in a different social context, perceptions of whether the behavior is deviant may well change. In Greece, Spain, and other Mediterranean countries, the clothing norms on beaches are very different from those in most of North America. Topless sunbathing by women is not at all uncommon, even on beaches designated as family beaches. The norms vary, however, even within a few feet of the beach. Women will sunbathe topless, lying only 10 feet from the boardwalk where concessionaires sell beverages, snacks, and tourist items. If these women become thirsty, they cover up, walk the 15 feet to purchase a cola, and return to their beach blankets, where they again remove their tops. To walk onto the boardwalk topless would be highly deviant, yet, to be topless on the sand is acceptable. Likewise, drunken behavior on spring break or at Mardi Gras in New Orleans may be acceptable, but conducting oneself in the same manner while sipping champagne at a wedding reception would be cause for disgust. The same behavior can be conventional or deviant depending on where it occurs.

Popular belief: Those who deviate are socially identified and recognized. Fact: Most of us deviate from some norm at some time, as you saw when completing the questionnaire on deviance. (See the preceding "Sociology in Your Social World.") However, most behaviors that violate a norm are never socially recognized as deviant. Only about one third of all crime that is reported to the police in the United States ever leads to an arrest. This means that two thirds is never officially handled through the formal, legal structure, and the perpetrators escape being labeled deviant.

Popular belief: Deviants purposely and knowingly break the law. Fact: Although it is a popular notion that those who engage in deviant behavior make a conscious choice to do so, much deviance is driven by emotion, encouraged by friends, caused by disagreements over norms (as in the case of whether marijuana use should be criminalized), or is a result of conditions in the immediate situation (as in cases of teens spontaneously engaging in a behavior in response to boredom or a struggle for prestige among peers) (McCaghy et al. 2006).

Popular belief: Deviance occurs because there is a dishonest, selfish element to human nature. Fact: While surveys show many of us believe this, most people who commit deviant acts do not attribute their own deviance to basic dishonesty or other negative personality factors. These misperceptions imply that most people believe they have clear understandings of what deviance is and that deviant individuals know when they are being deviant and plan their actions. Yet, there is little empirical evidence to support these beliefs, as the research reported in this chapter shows.

Thinking Sociologically

Think of examples in your life that illustrate the relative nature of deviance. For instance, are some of your behaviors deviant in one setting but not in another, or were they deviant when you were younger but not deviant now?

Clearly there are many misconceptions about deviance in our society. Sociologists use a variety of methods to test the veracity of popular ideas, employing various empirical methods. The next "How Do We Know?" box shows how notions about pornography and deviance have recently been tested using experiments.

Crime: Deviance That Violates the Law

When the criminal justice system gets involved and formal penalties are imposed by society, we refer to deviance as crime— deviance that violates criminal law. Laws reflect opinions of what is considered right and wrong or good and bad at a particular time and place in a society. Like all other norms, laws change over time, reflecting changing public opinion based on social conditions or specific events. Still, there are formal sanctions—punishments—that the government imposes for violation of laws, and the stigma associated with these deviant acts results in being identified as "criminal."

At the end of the 1920s, 42 of the 48 U.S. states had laws forbidding interracial marriages (Coontz 2005). Legislatures in half of these states removed those restrictions by the 1960s, but the rest of these laws became unconstitutional only after a U.S. Supreme Court ruling in 1968. Today, this legal bar on interracial marriage has been eliminated completely, illustrating that most laws change to reflect the times and sentiments of the majority of people. This pattern is illustrated in Map 6.1 (page 167).

When members of society are in general agreement about the seriousness of deviant acts, these are referred to as **consensus crimes** (Brym and Lie 2007; Goodman and Brenner 2002; Hagan, Silva, and Simpson 1977). Predatory crimes (premeditated murder, forcible rape, and kidnapping for ransom) are consensus crimes that are considered wrong in and of themselves in most nations.

In the United States, up until 1968, this couple would have been violating the law in roughly half of the states, and their family would be "illegitimate." Interracial marriages were illegal until the Supreme Court decided otherwise. Change in definitions of what is illegal has been common in the past 50 years.

By contrast, **conflict crimes** occur when one group passes a law over which there is disagreement or that disadvantages another group (Hagan 1993, 1994). Examples include laws concerning public disorder, chemical (drug and alcohol) offenses, prostitution, gambling, property offenses, and political disenfranchisement (denying voting rights only to some citizens—females, particular ethnic groups, or those without property). Public opinion about the seriousness of these crimes is often divided, based on people's different social class, status, and interests. The severity of societal response also varies, with high disagreement over the harmfulness of conflict crimes. Consensus or conflict about whether the behavior is harmful has implications for the punishment or support experienced by the person who is accused.

Crimes are often thought to be the most threatening forms of deviance, but it is important to recognize that they are still just one type of deviant behavior. We will discuss crime further at a later point in this chapter. Be aware that as we discuss theories in the next section, the theories explain a range of deviant acts, including (but not limited to) crimes.

What Causes Deviant Behavior? Theoretical Perspectives

Helena is a delinquent. Her father deserted the family when Helena was 10, and before that, he had abused Helena and her mother. Now, her mother has all she can cope with; she is just trying to survive financially and keep her three children in line. Helena gets little attention and little support or encouragement in her school activities. Her grades have fallen steadily. As a young teen, she sought attention from boys, and in the process, she became pregnant. Now, the only kids who have anything to do with her are others who have also been in trouble, and her friends are other

How Do We Know?

Research on Deviance: What Turns You On?

By Michael Norris

Pornography is often considered a form of deviance, but is it really deviance? Consider the following information: Adult videos generate more revenue than Hollywood box office cinema; more people visit porn sites on the Internet than prominent news sites; 70% of those who visit porn sites admit doing so at work; and college students have more legal access to pornography than alcohol. On the other hand, pornography has been linked with prostitution as an exploitive industry, and violent pornography has been linked to violent behavior.

New research by Meredith Chivers of the Centre for Addiction and Mental Health at the University of Toronto considers gender differences in reaction to the actors and activity in sexual videos. She used a mixed method approach in which research subjects were hooked to medical devices to measure genital arousal, and subjects also gave their subjective impressions of how excited they were by viewing sexual material.

Chivers and her colleagues (Chivers, Seto, and Blanchard 2007) found that for women, sexual activity in videos was more influential in sexual arousal, whereas men tended to be influenced more by the gender of the actors in the videos. Women were aroused by sexual activity regardless of whether the target actor was their preferred gender, and even if the actors were nonhuman primates. It seems that women can be genitally aroused just by cues of sexual activity. Heterosexual men were aroused by videos of nude women engaged in nonsexual activities such as exercise, while similar videos of nude males were no more arousing to heterosexual women than "control" videos of the Himalayan mountain range (Newman 2008).

Chivers and her colleagues (2007) also discovered gender differences in whether physically measured arousal was correlated with self-reported (subjective) arousal. Based on quantitative data, the researchers concluded that these two measures had higher correlation for men, regardless of self-reported sexual orientation. This gender difference has been verified in previous research, which suggests that genital arousal may be more "automatic" in women—that is, biological reactions precede subjective awareness of arousal. Biological arousal happens within seconds of presenting a sexual stimulus and may even occur without any self-reported or subjective arousal at all.

The researchers caution against drawing broad conclusions from their data because subjects were recruited from one Canadian university, and fewer than 100 subjects participated. An additional limitation is that volunteers for this type of research tend to be more sexually active, with more permissive sexual attitudes, more experience, and higher levels of interest in sexually explicit materials than the general population.

This research adds to a growing body of literature suggesting greater flexibility of women's sexuality in terms of sexual identity, same-sex attraction, and same-sex behavior. Women's greater sexual flexibility may result from a tendency to identify with both male and female targets of sexual activity and greater same-sex emotional attachments than men.

This study also helps explain the fact that for heterosexuals viewing mainstream, commercially available pornography, watching two women having sex is more socially acceptable than watching two men having sex. A popular cultural myth, reinforced by comedians, is that men particularly enjoy "lesbian action" in adult videos. Research by Chivers and others suggests that this is not the case. In fact, the adult video industry may include these vignettes to more effectively market their product to women.

The use of experiments—controlling variables to examine variations in biological and subjective experience of arousal—in order to gain knowledge about normal and deviant reactions to pornography, helps answer "how do we know" about human sexual behavior.

Note: Michael Norris is based at Wright State University, where he teaches and does research in sociology and criminal justice.

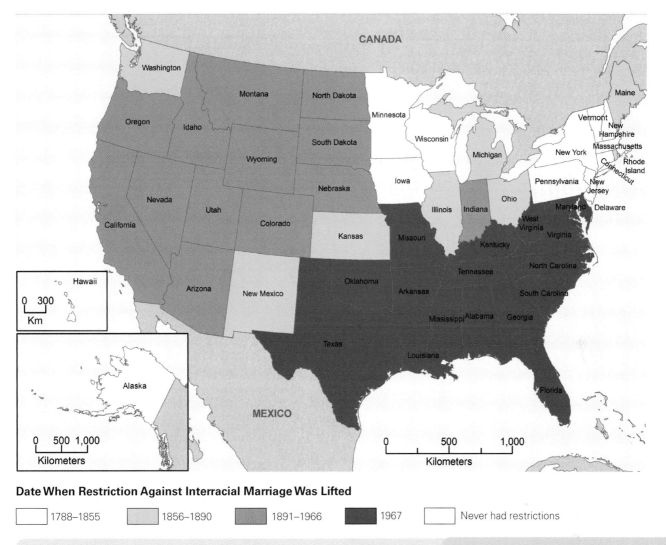

Date When Restriction Against Interracial Marriage Was Lifted

| | 1788–1855 | | 1856–1890 | | 1891–1966 | | 1967 | | Never had restrictions |

Map 6.1 Historical Restrictions on Interracial Marriage in the United States

Source: Wallenstein 2002:253–54. Map by Anna Versluis.

young people who have been labeled delinquent. Helena's schoolmates, teachers, and mother see her as a delinquent troublemaker, and it would be hard for Helena to change their views and her status.

How did this happen? Was Helena born with a biological propensity toward deviance? Does she have psychological problems? Is the problem in her social environment? Helena's situation is, of course, only one unique case. Sociologists cannot generalize from Helena to other cases, but they do know from their studies that there are thousands of teens with problems like Helena's.

Throughout history, people have proposed explanations for why some members of society "turn bad"—from biological explanations of imbalances in hormones and claims of innate personality defects to social conditions within individual families or in the larger social structure. Biological and psychological approaches focus on personality

disorders or abnormalities in the body or psyche of individuals, but they generally do not consider the social context in which deviance occurs.

Social scientists attempt to study questions of deviance scientifically. They examine why certain acts are defined as deviant, why some people engage in deviant behavior, and how other people in the society react to deviance. Sociologists place emphasis on understanding the interactions, social structure, and social processes that lead to deviant behavior, rather than on individual characteristics. They consider the socialization process and interpersonal relationships, group and social class differences, cultural and subcultural norms, and power structures that influence individuals to conform or deviate from societal expectations (Liska 1999). Theoretical explanations about why people are deviant are important because the interpretations influence social policy decisions about what to do with deviants.

This section explores several approaches to understanding deviance and crime. Some theories explain particular categories of crime better than others, and some illuminate micro-, meso-, or macro-level processes better than others. Taken together—as complementary perspectives on a complex dimension of human behavior—these theories help us understand a wide range of deviant and criminal behaviors.

Micro-Level Explanations of Deviance: Rational Choice and Interaction Theories

No one is born deviant. Individuals learn to be law-abiding citizens or to be deviant through the process of socialization. Thus, behavior is acquired during the processes of interaction and socialization as people develop their social relationships. Why do some people learn to become deviant and others learn to follow the norms of society? A rational choice explanation focuses on cost-benefit analysis of one's choices. Another approach, based in symbolic interaction theory, is that people are exposed to the opportunity to commit delinquent acts through their social relationships with peers and family members, and they come to be labeled deviant. Rational choice and symbolic interaction theories focus primarily on micro-level issues.

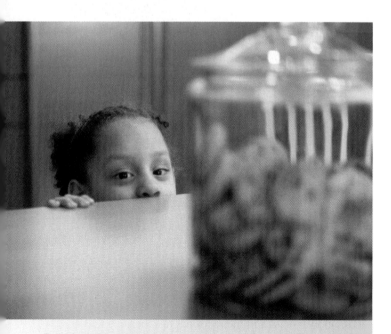

Rational choice theories hold that people weigh the possible negative consequences against the benefits, and if the benefits outweigh the costs, then violating official rules or expectations may be worth it. This would suggest that the cost must be increased to deter deviance. This little girl is weighing the costs and benefits of taking cookies, and the benefits are looking pretty sweet!

Social Control Theory and Rational Choice

One of sociology's central concepts is social control (Gibbs 1989; Hagan 2002). Control theory focuses on why most people conform most of the time and do not commit deviant acts. If human beings were truly free to do whatever they wanted, they would likely commit more deviant acts. Yet, to live near others and with others requires individuals to control their behaviors based on social standards and sanctions—in short, social control.

A perpetual question in sociology is the following: How is order possible in the context of rapidly changing society? A very general answer is that social control results from social norms that promote order and predictability in the social world. When people fail to adhere to these norms, or when the norms are unclear, the stability and continuance of the entire social system may be threatened.

People are bonded to society by four powerful factors:

1. *Attachment* to other people who respect the values and rules of the society. Individuals do not want to be rejected by those to whom they are close or whom they admire.

2. *Commitment* to conventional activities (such as school and jobs) that they do not want to jeopardize.

3. *Involvement* in activities that keep them so busy with conventional roles and expectations that they do not have time for mischief.

4. *Belief* in the social rules of their culture, which they accept because of childhood socialization and indoctrination into conventional beliefs.

Should these variables be weakened, there is an increased possibility that the person could commit deviant acts (Hirschi [1969] 2002).

Two primary factors shape our tendency to conform. The first is internal controls, those voices within us that tell us when a behavior is acceptable or unacceptable, right or wrong. The second is external controls, society's formal or informal controls against deviant behavior. Informal external controls include smiles, frowns, hugs, and ridicule from close acquaintances (Gottfredson and Hirschi 1990). Formal external controls come from the legal system through police, judges, juries, and social workers. In both cases, the cost-benefit ratios shift, making either conformity or deviance a rational choice.

The basic idea in rational choice approaches is that when individuals make decisions, they calculate the costs and benefits to themselves. Humans seek to maximize pleasure (benefit) and to minimize pain (costs), and the decision regarding whether to conform or deviate from social norms is determined by the individual's assessment and rational decision of the pleasure-pain ratio from their mental calculations in a given situation. Social control comes from shifting the balance toward more pain and fewer benefits for those who deviate from norms.

The shift in this cost-benefit ratio may mean change in the sanctions provided by society for certain behaviors. Positive sanctions reward those behaviors approved by society. This is the reason schools have honor ceremonies, companies reward their top salespeople, and communities recognize civic leadership with "citizen of the year" awards. All of these actions enhance the rewards for conventional behavior. Negative sanctions (or punishments) increase the cost to those who have deviated from the norm. They range from fines for traffic violations to prison sentences for serious crimes and even death for acts considered most dangerous to society. If one belongs to a subculture or group whose norms conflict with those of the dominant society, conformity to the subculture may take precedence over conformity to the larger society.

Deterring deviance can be accomplished by increasing the costs (tougher penalties in the courts), by increasing awareness of the costs that are already in place, by reducing the benefits of being deviant (lessening social benefits like admiration), or by changing perception of the cost-benefit balance.

Thinking Sociologically

Think of a time when you committed a deviant act or avoided doing so despite tempting opportunity. What factors influenced whether you conformed to societal norms or to deviant norms?

Shooting drugs as a way of spending time and money is a way of life for some young people. Yet some teens would not know the technique for preparing and injecting illegal drugs, nor would they have learned from associates that this is a fun or acceptable way to spend one's time.

Differential Association Theory

If someone offered you some heroin, what would determine whether you took it? First, would you define sticking a needle in your arm and injecting heroin as a good way to spend your afternoon? Second, do you typically hang around with others who engage in this type of behavior, and define it as "the thing to do"? Third, would you know the routine—how to cook the heroin to extract the liquid—if you had never seen it done? You likely would not know the proper technique for how to prepare the drug or how to inject it. Why? This depends on whether you have associated with drug users and whether your family and friends define drug use as acceptable or deviant.

Differential association or *reinforcement theory* refers to two processes that can result in individuals learning to engage in crime. First, association with others who share criminal values and commit crimes results in learning how to carry out a criminal act (Sutherland, Cressey, and Luckenbil 1992). Second, social learning also results in reinforcement of criminal behavior (Akers 1992, 1998; Burgess and Akers 1966; Lee, Akers, and Borg 2004). This approach links the learning process with the criminal behavior.

Differential association theory focuses on the process of learning deviance from family, peers, fellow employees, political organizations, neighborhood groups such as gangs, and other groups in one's surroundings (Akers 1992; Akers et al. 1979; Sutherland et al. 1992). This theory is a symbolic interaction approach because the emphasis is on how others shape one's definition of what is normal and acceptable. Helena, for example, came to be surrounded by people who made dropping out of school and other delinquent acts seem normal. If her close friends and siblings were sexually active as teens, her teen pregnancy might not be remarkable and might even be a source of some prestige with her group of peers.

According to differential association theory, the possibility of becoming deviant depends on four factors: the duration, intensity, priority, and frequency of time spent with the deviant group (Sutherland et al. 1992). If deviant behavior exists in people's social context and if they are exposed to deviance regularly and frequently (duration and intensity), especially if they are in close association with a group that accepts criminal behavior, they are more likely to learn deviant ways. Furthermore, individuals learn motives, drives, rationalizations, and attitudes, and they develop techniques that influence behavior and cause them to commit a deviant act.

Early studies using differential association theory focused on the idea that youths of lower socioeconomic status are more likely than their higher status counterparts to engage in violent delinquency because they have learned in their social setting to be more accepting of the use of force, coercion, and violence to solve problems.

Some theorists contend that lower class life constitutes a distinctive subculture in which delinquent behavior patterns are transmitted through socialization. The values, beliefs, norms, and practices that have evolved in lower class communities over time can often lead to violation of laws. These values and norms have been defined by those in power as deviant. Just as upper class youth seem to be expected and destined to succeed, lower class youth may learn other behaviors that those with privilege have defined

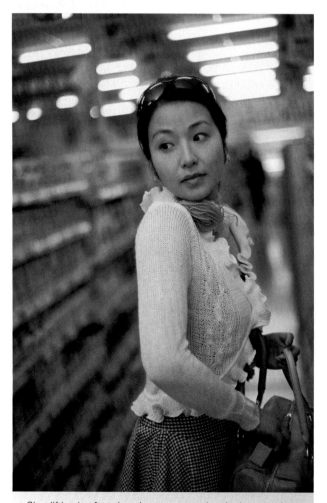

Shoplifting is often done by young people who have not been arrested for anything—a form of primary deviance.

as delinquent and criminal (Bettie 2003; Chambliss 1973). For instance, in a recent study, Bettie (2003) found that race, class, and gender intersect in important ways to increase the labeling (discussed next) and decrease the opportunities for lower class and minority high school girls. For some inner-city youth, the local norms are to be tough and disrespectful of authority, to live for today, to seek excitement, and to be "cool"—these are survival techniques. With time, these attitudes and behaviors become valued in and of themselves by their peer group.

Today, we know that members of all social classes commit crimes, and no socioeconomic class has a monopoly on violence, graft, corruption, or dishonesty. Elijah Anderson's (2000) book, *Code of the Street*, describes two types of groups that coexist in poor neighborhoods: "decent people" and "street people." The code of the street often involves norms that are opposed to those of mainstream society, yet many children are socialized in areas where this code provides the dominant norms. "Street-oriented people" hang with peers on streets and adopt a certain look with their clothes and jewelry—an image expected by the group. Peers become more important than society's social control agents. "Decent families" accept mainstream values and often find support systems in church communities or other organizations. Lower status youth are more likely to be suspected, watched, and caught for deviant behavior than higher status youth. Thus, reported delinquency rates may be higher for this group, even if the incidence of violence is not greater (Anderson 2000). The next theoretical approach, labeling, explains why.

Labeling Theory

Labeling theory is also related to the symbolic interaction perspective, for labels (such as "juvenile delinquent") are symbols that have meanings that affect the self. Labeling theory focuses on how people define deviance—what is or is not "normal"—which is a core issue in the symbolic interactionist paradigm. The basic assumption underlying labeling theory is that no behavior or individual is intrinsically deviant. Behavior is deviant because individuals in society label it deviant.

The basic social process of labeling someone is as follows: Members of society create deviance by defining certain behaviors as deviant—smoking pot, wearing long hair, holding hands in public, or whatever is seen as inappropriate at a particular time and place. They then react to the deviance by rejecting the miscreant or by imposing penalties.

Labeling theorists define two stages in the process of becoming a deviant. **Primary deviance** is a violation of a norm that may be an isolated act, such as a young teenager shoplifting something on a dare by friends. Most people commit acts of primary deviance. However, few of us are initially labeled deviant as a result of these primary acts. Remember how you marked the deviant behavior test that you took at the beginning of this chapter? If you engaged in deviant acts, you were probably not labeled deviant for the offense. If you had been labeled, you might not be in college.

If an individual continues to violate a norm and begins to take on a deviant identity, this is referred to as **secondary deviance**. Secondary deviance becomes publicly recognized and the individual is identified as deviant, beginning a deviant career. If a teenager such as Helena in the opening example is caught, her act becomes known, perhaps publicized in the newspaper. She may spend time in a juvenile detention center, and parents of other teens may not want their children associating with her. Employers and store managers may refuse to hire her. Soon, there are few options open to her, and others expect her to be delinquent. The teen may continue the deviant acts and delinquent acquaintances. Society's reaction, then, is what defines a deviant person (Lemert 1951, 1972).

The process of labeling individuals and behaviors takes place at each level of analysis, from individual to society. If community or societal norms define a behavior as deviant, individuals are likely to believe it is deviant. Sanctions for juvenile delinquents can have the effect of reinforcing the deviant behavior by (1) increasing alienation from the social world, (2) forcing increased interaction with deviant peers, and (3) motivating juvenile delinquents to positively value and identify with the deviant status (Kaplan and Johnson 1991).

The self-fulfilling prophesy refers to a belief that becomes reality. Individuals may come to see themselves as deviant because of harassment, ridicule, rejection by friends and family, and negative sanctions. James is eight years old and already sees himself as a failure because his parents, teachers, and peers tell him he is "dumb." In keeping with the idea of self-fulfilling prophesy, James accepts the label and acts accordingly. Unless someone—such as an insightful teacher—steps in to give him another image of himself, the label is unlikely to change. Again, labeling theory focuses on the micro level: the individual and the formation of the self.

Thinking Sociologically

What labels do you carry, and how do they affect your self-concept?

Another explanation of why certain individuals and groups are labeled deviant has to do with their status and power in society. Those who are on the fringes, away from power and nonparticipants in the mainstream, are more likely to be labeled deviants—the poor, minorities, members of new religious movements, or those who in some way do not fit into the dominant system. Because the powerful

have the influence to define what is acceptable, they protect themselves from being defined as deviants. People from different subcultures, social classes, or religious groups may be accorded deviant labels.

A study by Chambliss (1973) illustrates the process of labeling in communities and groups. Perhaps during your high school years you witnessed situations similar to that described in his study. Chambliss looked at the behavior of two small peer groups of boys and at the reactions of community members to their behavior. The Saints, boys from "good" families, were some of the most delinquent boys at Hanibal High School. Although the Saints were constantly occupied with truancy, drinking, wild driving, petty theft, and vandalism, none was officially arrested for any misdeed during the two-year study, partly because they had cars and could go out of town for their pranks. The Roughnecks were constantly in trouble with police and community residents, even though their rate of delinquency was about equal to that of the Saints. Chambliss found that poor kids, the Roughnecks, may be involved in deviant behavior because the dominant cultural goals seem distant and unattainable. On the other hand, rich kids, the Saints, indulge in delinquent activities to cope with boredom, to rebel, or to seek visibility among peers.

What was the cause of the disparity between these two groups? Community members, police, and teachers alike labeled the boys based on their perceptions of the boys' family backgrounds and social class. The Saints came from stable, white, upper middle-class families, were active in school affairs, and were precollege students whom everyone expected to become professionals. The general community feeling was that the Roughnecks would amount to nothing. They carried around a label that was hard to change, and that label was realized. The Saints almost all became professionals, whereas none of the Roughnecks did. Two Roughnecks ended up in prison, two became coaches, and little is known of the others. For these groups of boys, the prophecy became self-fulfilling (Chambliss 1973). The belief that the Roughnecks would "amount to nothing" came true because that was what was expected by the community, their opportunities were affected by their labels, and the boys came to expect nothing for themselves.

A theory that blends labeling and differential association theories, the general learning theory of crime and deviance, combines elements of both theories. It argues that "labeling effects are mediated by associations with ones peer group, including delinquent peers" (Schmalleger 2006:256; see also Adams 1996). So someone may be labeled, and whether or not the label sticks to that person may have to do with how his peer group responds to that label—perhaps even by claiming the "deviant" designation with some pride.

Still, labels are powerful and can stigmatize – branding the target as disgraceful or reprehensible. This process can be extended to a number of issues, including fatness, as the next "Sociology in Your Social World" illustrates.

Sociology in Your Social World

Stigmatizing Fatness

By Leslie Elrod

America is now the fattest country in the world. The Centers for Disease Control and Prevention has found that more than 60% of American adults are classified as overweight or obese, and 25% of children are classified as obese. Deviation from the idealized image of physical thinness allows others to judge and condemn individual behavior, resulting in embarrassment, severe isolation, or alienation. According to Cooley's theory of the looking-glass self, because we tend to define ourselves by the attitudes of and interaction with others, the obese may suffer lower self-esteem and have negative self-images, thus creating heightened levels of psychological distress. When a physical attribute is assigned social significance, norm-violators such as the obese are likely to endure negative labeling because of perceived physical imperfections. The obese, labeled as self-indulgent, gluttonous, lazy, sloppy, and mean, experience social condemnation. Obese women tend to experience greater discrimination than obese men.

Women are taught that their physical appearance is a valuable commodity, both in the public and private spheres. Ascertaining the degree to which they fit the media image models of female perfection, women attempt to adapt their appearance to reach this standard of beauty. Holding up an image of female perfection, such as slenderness, daintiness, or being demure, the media insinuates that the woman herself somehow falls short of that perfection. This is exemplified in print ads, magazines, television programming, and movies as well as merchandising directed toward females of all ages. The "feminine failing" not only jeopardizes her happiness but also challenges her femininity. The appearance discrepancy is based on the fact that over the course of the past century, as real women grew heavier, models and "beautiful" women were portrayed as increasingly thinner. An example of the change in media imagery is that of the White Rock mineral girl, portrayed as 5 feet 4 inches tall and 140 pounds in 1950. More recently, she is 5 feet 10 inches tall, weighing 110 pounds (Phipher 1994).

While much of the research on women's obsession with weight assumes that all women and girls are affected by the culture of thinness, there is some evidence to suggest that not all women are affected equally. Obesity rates are highest among minorities, the poor, and the disenfranchised. Yet Powell and Kahn (1995) have noted that "few black women seem to have eating disorders . . . and less emphasis [is placed] on eating and weight in general among black college students compared to white students" (p. 190). When compared to black females, white women are under significantly greater social pressure to be thin. Hesse-Biber (2007) finds that eating disorders, an outcome of body mass dissatisfaction, are no longer confined to upper-class white females, indicating that the effects of body mass on self-esteem may be changing.

This is not to suggest that people of color are not concerned about body image; rather, it suggests that the messages disseminated through the majority culture are mediated in various ways through the experiences and expectations that are associated with distinct social locations. Moreover, since media portrayals are still predominantly white, whether through the use of white or white-featured models—thin lips, thin hips, straight hair, and light complexion—there is less pressure on minorities to relate and compare themselves to the given images because these images do not represent their reference groups.

Because they are victims of prejudice and discrimination resulting from social norm violation, the obese are less likely than their non-obese counterparts to be involved in various organizational and social activities such as extracurricular participation for fear of social rejection. Olson, Schumaker, and Yawn (1994) found that weight-based embarrassment was indicated as a reason that obese people shied away from social obligations. Several clinical studies have documented that obese women delay seeking medical care and participating in preventative medical techniques.

Some obese persons reject the stigmatizing "fat identity," using a variety of coping mechanisms such as avoidance of others who stigmatize them or coping through immersion in supportive subcultures. Those who suffer from low self-esteem may actively seek out activities and relationships that have the capacity to improve their self-esteem. While not all obese persons experience and internalize fat stigmatization, a statistically significant number of overweight and obese juveniles do indicate poor body image and diminished self-esteem. Many experts suggest that individuals should take a proactive approach by seeking medical or psychological help, joining support groups, and dealing with the problem if it is impairing their activities.

Why do certain behaviors come to be defined as deviant? Again, a majority of individuals agree that some acts are deviant. In other cases, powerful members of society can label certain behaviors as deviant. While labeling theory is mostly based on symbolic interactionism (a micro-level theory), labeling theorists also point to the role of macro-level social forces—social inequality or lack of access to power—in shaping whether people are labeled or whether they can avoid being labeled. Thus, labeling theory is also sometimes used by conflict theorists. When members of the dominant group in society see certain behaviors as potentially threatening or disruptive to the society or to the interests of those who have privileged statuses, the group in power reinforces its position by creating an impossible situation for minority group members. The minority's non-acceptance of the rules becomes deviant. For instance, dissidents opposed to government restrictions or human rights violations in China, Myanmar (Burma), and other countries have been thrown in jail because their protests were labeled deviant by those in power.

Chinese soldiers tried in vain to stop student protesters in China as the students demanded more freedom to make choices. The students were defined by the government as deviant, many were arrested, and some were shot in Tiananmen Square, the main square in Beijing.

Thinking Sociologically

You have a friend who is getting into drugs. From what you know about the above theories, what might this tell you about why this is happening and about what, if anything, you could do for your friend?

Meso- and Macro-Level Explanations of Deviance: Structural-Functional and Conflict Theories

While interpersonal interaction processes can result in deviance, many sociologists believe that meso- and macro-level analysis creates greater understanding of the societal factors leading to deviance. Meso-level analysis focuses on ethnic subcultures and national organizations and institutions inside a nation. Macro-level theories focus on societies and global social systems. However, when it comes to deviance and conformity, the same theories tend to operate at meso and macro levels. We look first at structural-functional theories of deviance, those with the longest history in sociology. They include two themes: (1) anomie, the breakdown of the norms guiding behavior, which leads to social disorganization, and (2) strain created by the difference between definitions of success (goals) and the means available to achieve those goals.

Anomie and Social Disorganization

Villagers from industrializing countries in Africa, Asia, and Latin America were pushed off marginally productive rural lands and were pulled by the lure of the city: new opportunities, excitement, and a chance to change their lives. They flocked to population centers with industrial opportunities, but when they arrived, they were often disappointed. Poor, unskilled, and homeless, they moved into crowded apartments or shantytowns of temporary shacks and tried to adjust to the new style of life that often included unemployment. This description could apply to immigrants from 9 months ago to 90 years ago.

Many industrializing countries face structural changes as their economies move from agriculture to industry or service economies. Young men in particular leave behind strong bonds and a common value system that exist in the countryside. In cities, individuals melt into the crowd and live anonymously. Old village norms that provided the guidelines for proper behavior crumble, sometimes without clear expectations emerging to take their places. The lack of clear norms in the rapidly changing urban environment leads to high levels of social disorganization and deviant behavior.

Sociologists use the term *anomie*, or normlessness, to describe the breakdown of norms caused by the lack of shared, achievable goals and lack of socially approved means to achieve goals (Merton 1968a). When norms are absent or conflicting, deviance increases as the previous example illustrates. Émile Durkheim (1858–1917) first described this normlessness as a condition of weak, conflicting, or absent norms and values that arise when societies are disorganized. This situation is typical in rapidly urbanizing, industrializing societies, at times of sudden prosperity or depression, during rapid technological change, or when a government is overthrown. Anomie affects urban areas first but may eventually affect the whole society. Thus, macro-level events, such as economic recessions or wars, show how important social solidarity is to an individual's core sense of values.

This general idea of anomie led a group of Chicago sociologists to study the social conditions of that city that are correlated with deviance. The Chicago School, as the research team is known, linked life in transitional slum areas to high incidence of crime. Certain neighborhoods or zones in the Chicago area—generally inner-city transitional zones with recent settlers—have always had high delinquency rates, regardless of the group that occupied the area. Low economic status, ethnic heterogeneity, residential mobility, family disruption, and competing value systems (because of the constant transitions) led to community disorganization. Although new immigrant groups have replaced older groups over time, the delinquency rate has remained high because each generation of newcomers experienced anomie (Shaw and McKay 1929). The high in-migration and out-migration in these communities in itself explains the lack of stability in primary families. Peer group norms became influential, and models of nondeviant behavior were scarce for many teenagers and adults (Anderson 2000).

Strain Theory

Most people in a society share similar values and goals, but those with poor education and few resources have less opportunity to achieve those shared goals than others. When legitimate routes to success are cut off, frustration and anger result, and deviant methods may be used to achieve goals. Strain theory focuses on contradictions and tensions between the shared values and goals on the one hand and the opportunity structures of the society on the other.

Strain theory (Merton 1968b) suggests that the difference between the society's definitions of goals and legitimate means, or ways, of attaining the goals can lead to strain in the society. Individuals may agree with society's definition and goals for success (say, financial affluence) but not be able to achieve it using the socially prescribed means of achieving that success. The strain that is created can lead to deviance. Merton uses U.S. society as an example because it places a heavy emphasis on success, measured by wealth and social standing. He outlines five ways individuals adapt to the strain. Figure 6.1 shows these five types and their relationship to goals and means. To illustrate these, we trace a lower class student who realizes the value of an education, who knows it is necessary to get ahead, but who has problems financing education and competing in the middle class–dominated school setting.

1. *Conformity* means embracing the society's definition of success and adhering to the established and approved means of achieving success. The student works hard despite the academic and financial obstacles, trying to do well in school to achieve success and a good job placement. She uses legitimate, approved means—education and hard work—to reach goals that the society views as worthy.

2. *Innovation* refers to use of illicit means to reach approved goals. Our student uses illegitimate means to achieve her education goals. She may cheat on exams or get papers from Internet sources. Success in school is all that matters, not how she gets there.

3. *Ritualism* involves strict adherence to the culturally prescribed rules, even though individuals give up on the goals they hoped to achieve. The student may give up the idea of getting good grades and graduating from college but, as a matter of pride and self-image, she continues to try hard and to take classes. She conforms to expectations, for example, but with no sense of purpose. She just does what she is told.

4. *Retreatism* refers to giving up on both the goals and the means. A student either bides her time, not doing well, or drops out, giving up on future job goals. She abandons or retreats from the goals of a professional position in society and on the means to get there. She may even turn to a different lifestyle—for example, a user of drugs and alcohol—as part of the retreat.

5. *Rebellion* entails rejecting the socially approved ideas of success and the means of attaining that success. It replaces those with alternative definitions of success and alternative strategies for attaining the new goals. Rebelling against the dominant cultural goals and means, a student may join a radical political group or a commune, intent on developing new ideas of how society should be organized and what a "truly educated" person should be.

Deviant behavior results from retreatism, rebellion, and innovation. According to Merton, the reasons individuals resort to these behaviors lie in the social conditions that lead to different levels of access to success, not in their individual biological or psychological makeup.

Anomie and strain theories fall under the structural-functional umbrella of theories. They help explain deviance from a social structural point of view, focusing on what happens if deviance disrupts the ongoing social order. They explore what causes deviance, how to prevent disruptions, how to keep change slow and nondisruptive, and how deviance can be useful to the ongoing society. However, anomie and strain theories fail to account for class conflicts, inequities, and poverty, which conflict theorists argue cause deviance.

Conflict Theory

In Kenya, thousands of citizens protested what they felt was the corrupt 2008 election process for a new president. As a result, many Kenyans were killed in tribal fighting.

Figure 6.1 Merton's Strain Theory

Greenpeace, an environmental activist group, confronted Japanese whaling vessels in the Southern Ocean Whale Sanctuary in January 2008, preventing them from killing whales in the area. From 2002 to the present, protests have been held in many major cities around the world by antiwar protestors against the war in Iraq, and protestors in Venezuela blocked oil shipments in attempts to overthrow the government. Some Canadian and American peace advocates went to Baghdad as "human shields" so the Bush administration would not begin the war with Iraq. Are these protesters deviants and criminals, or are they brave heroes? The response depends on who answers the question.

Conflict theorists assume that conflict between groups is inevitable. Because many societies today are pluralistic, heterogeneous groupings of people, the differences (goals, resources, norms, and values) between interest groups and groups in power often cause conflict. Conflict theory focuses on macro-level analysis of deviance, looking at deviance as a result of social inequality or of the struggle between groups for power.

Deviance is often related to social class status, interest groups, or cultural conflict between the dominant group and ethnic, religious, political, regional, or gender groups. Wealthy and powerful elites want to maintain their control and their high positions (Domhoff 1998). They have the power to pass laws and define what is deviant, sometimes by effectively eliminating opposition groups. The greater the cultural difference between the dominant group and other groups in society, the more the possibility of conflict. This is because minority groups and subcultures challenge the norms of the dominant groups and threaten the consensus in a society (Huizinga, Loeber, and Thornberry 1994).

Some conflict theorists blame capitalist systems for unjust administration of law and argue that the ruling class uses the legal system to further the capitalist enterprise (Quinney 2002). The dominant class defines deviance, applies laws to protect its interests, represses any conflict or protest, and, in effect, forces those in subordinate classes

to carry out actions defined as deviant. These actions, in turn, support the ideology that works against subordinate classes. Activities that threaten the interests and well-being of the wealthy capitalist class become defined as deviant. By subordinating certain groups and then defining them as deviant or criminal, the dominant group consolidates its powerful position. Because the dominant class is usually of one ethnic group and those of other races or ethnicities tend to be in the subordinate class, conflict often has racial and ethnic implications as well as social class dimensions.

The fact that, for the same offenses, subordinate class or race members are arrested and prosecuted more often than

Members of Rainbow Warrior, part of the Greenpeace environmental group, stage a sit-down protest in front of the U.S. embassy in Manila. The group wants the U.S. military to clean up toxic wastes around Clark and Subic Bay, a former U.S. naval base north of Manila. Greenpeace believes that confrontation with the existing powers is necessary to bring change.

Ishraht Abullah is comforted by her mother in a Pakistani hospital after her husband threw sulfuric acid over her during a domestic dispute. She has burns inflicted to more than 30% of her body. Her husband and mother-in-law repeatedly berate her, but also plead that she not press charges. Such instances are not unusual in parts of South Asia, and they are a concern of feminist scholars.

Feminist Theory

The goal of most feminist theorists is to understand and improve women's status, including their treatment by men and those in power. Feminists argue that traditional theories do not give an adequate picture or understanding of women's situations. Although there are several branches of feminist theory, most see the macro-level causes of abuses suffered by women as rooted in the capitalist patriarchal system. They include the following ideas: (1) women are faced with a division of labor resulting from their sex, (2) separation between public (work) and private (home) spheres of social activity create "we" versus "they" thinking between men and women, and (3) socialization of children into gender-specific adult roles has implications for how males and females perceive and relate to each other.

One result of women's status is that they are often victims of crime. The type of victimization varies around the globe, from sex trafficking to rape (Bales 2004; Mohanty 1988). Women are less often in a position to commit crimes. In fact, deviant acts by women have traditionally fallen into the categories of shoplifting, credit card or welfare fraud, writing bad checks (in developed societies), prostitution, and in some countries adultery or inappropriate attire. Many Western feminist theorists contend that until women around the world are on an equal footing with men, crimes against women and definitions of various behaviors of women as deviant are likely to continue.

Consider the case of intimate partner violence, including rape. Until recent years, there have been few serious consequences for the offenders in many countries (especially during times of anomie or war), and women often were blamed or blamed themselves for "letting it happen" (Boy and Kulczycki 2008). The next "Sociology Around the World" feature illustrates this pattern.

Cultural attitudes toward intimate partner violence differ depending on the status of women in society. For example, where women are held to high standards of virtue and women's sexuality is subject to strict controls, deviation may be dealt with severely, at least as judged by Western standards. In some cultures, women fear reporting violence and may blame themselves for the beating or rape. Yet, from limited studies, we know that 16% to 52% of married women in the Middle East were assaulted in one year, compared to 1.3% to 12% in Europe and North America (Krug et al. 2002).

Feminist theorists look for explanations in gender relations and societal structures for violence against women and the secondary status of most women. Feminist theorists have attempted to explain this situation in cultural contexts. They argue that we learn our gender roles, part of which is men learning to be aggressive. Women's status in society results in their being treated as sex objects, to be used for men's pleasure. Women's race and class identification become relevant in the exploitation of poor ethnically distinct women from developing countries as they become victims of human trafficking. Powerless poor women rightly fear becoming sex slaves.

dominant class or race members is provided as evidence to support this contention by conflict theorists (Quinney 2002). The result may be that subordinate groups find illegal methods to survive. Moreover, when people feel they are not treated fairly by the society, they have less loyalty to the society and to its rules, resulting in activities considered deviant by those in power.

To reduce deviance and crime, conflict theorists agree that we must change the structure of society. For instance, laws in many countries claim to support equal and fair treatment for all, but when one looks at the law in action, another picture emerges. Recall the example of the Saints and Roughnecks; the students from powerful families and higher social classes received favored treatment. Unequal treatment of groups that differ from the dominant group—the poor, laboring class, and racial or ethnic minorities in particular—are rooted in the legal, political, and occupational structures of societies.

If the structure of society were changed and there were no dominant group exploiting subordinate groups, would crime disappear? To answer this, we can look to patterns of crime in societies that have attempted to develop a communist economic classless structure. The rate of crime in China and Cuba, for instance, is lower than that in many Western democracies, in part because of less dramatic inequality and strict social controls on behavior. On the other hand, deviance is still present in noncapitalist societies. So although capitalistic inequality contributes to deviance, it is only one of many variables at work.

Sociology Around the World

Blaming the Victim: An Extreme Case

Every woman fears being raped—forced into having sex against her will. In most countries, rape is considered a deviant behavior on the part of the perpetrator, a crime punishable by imprisonment. The woman is provided medical help and counseling, yet only a small percentage of estimated rapes are reported. In a few countries or regions in countries, the legal system is based on strict interpretations of religious books by those who practice fundamentalist interpretations of the religion in attempts to guard against loss of the woman's virtue, shame, and illegitimate children. Some would also argue these laws maintain patriarchal control. Although the following examples are rare, they show the extremes to which communities can go to protect the "virtue" of women and the family. In the first case, excerpted from *The New York Times,* a woman was blamed for sex outside marriage even though she was raped.

The evidence of guilt was there for all to see: a newborn baby in the arms of its mother, a village woman named Zafran Bibi.

Her crime: she had been raped. Her sentence: death by stoning.

Now Ms. Zafran, who is about 26, is in solitary confinement in a death-row cell in Kohat, a nearby town. The only visitor she is allowed is her baby daughter, now a year old and being cared for by a prison nurse. In photographs, Ms. Zafran is a tall woman with striking green eyes—a peasant woman of the hot and barren hills of Pakistan's northwest frontier country. . . .

Thumping a fat red statute book, the white-bearded judge who convicted her, Anwar Ali Khan, said he had simply followed the letter of the Koran-based law, known as *hudood,* that mandates punishments. "The illegitimate child is not disowned by her and therefore is proof of *zina,*" he said, referring to laws that forbid any sexual contact outside marriage. Furthermore, he said, in accusing her brother-in-law of raping her, Ms. Zafran had confessed to her crime.

"The lady stated before this court that, yes, she had committed sexual intercourse, but with the brother of her husband," Judge Khan said. "This left no option to the court but to impose the highest penalty."

Although legal fine points do exist, little distinction is made in court between forced and consensual sex.

When *hudood* was enacted 23 years ago, the laws were formally described as measures to ban "all forms of adultery, whether the offense is committed with or without the consent of the parties," but it is almost always the women who are punished, whatever the facts. (Mydans 2002:A3)

Bibi appealed the decision, and was subsequently released from prison. She still fears, however, that she will be the victim of violence because she became a public figure through the press her case received, and individuals who opposed her acquittal know where she lives and what she looks like.

In a second case, covered extensively by American and European news, a young Pakistani woman, Mukhtar Mai, was ordered to be raped as punishment for her brother being seen with a woman from another, more powerful tribe. In 2004, Pakistani governments (mostly those of small towns and villages) ordered about 400 rapes as punishment for both sexual and nonsexual offenses. Higher policing groups do occasionally arrest the rapists in these cases for sexual violation, but this is not uniform. For Mai, 6 of her 14 rapists have been charged with rape, and Mai has asked that the men not be acquitted (BBC News 2005).

One thing is certain: Women who have been victimized need help from family and loved ones to feel in control again (McEvoy and Brookings 2008), but some are unjustly blamed for the rape. Keep in mind that each cultural practice evolved for a reason in each society. The meaning of these standards needs to be understood through the eyes of that culture so that we can effectively deal with human rights abuses. Western values make it difficult to understand the reason for certain practices.

According to feminist theory, women's work in the private sphere—housework, child care, and sexual satisfaction of their husbands—is undervalued, as are the women who carry out these roles. In some societies, women are the property of their husbands, with men's strength and physical force the ultimate means of control over women. Thus, some branches of feminist theory argue that men exploit women's labor power and sexuality to continue their dominance. The system is reproduced through new generations that are socialized to maintain the patriarchy and to view inequality between the sexes as "normal" and "natural." Women who deviate from the cultural expectations of "normal" behavior are condemned.

No one theory of why deviance occurs can explain all deviance. Some theories consider micro-level processes that shape one's values and self-identity. These approaches examine why certain behaviors and certain individuals are defined as deviant, and they explore the consequences of being labeled deviant. Meso- and macro-level theories attempt to explain structural factors at the community, national, or even the global level that result in deviance being more common among certain groups, in certain areas, or at certain times. Thus, depending on the level of analysis of the questions sociologists wish to study (micro, meso, or macro), they select the theory that best fits the data they find.

In the following sections, we explore in more detail the micro-meso-macro connections as they apply to one manifestation of deviance—crime. This illustrates how the sociological imagination can be applied to deviance at each level in the social system.

Thinking Sociologically

Deviance can be encouraged by interactions with friends or neighbors or by personal calculations of benefits over anticipated costs. However, meso- and macro-level social forces may be even more powerful in explaining deviance. What might be factors that contribute to deviance at the meso and macro levels?

Pick a recent example of deviance from your newspaper or television news. Which sociological theories help explain this deviance?

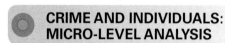

CRIME AND INDIVIDUALS: MICRO-LEVEL ANALYSIS

In this and the following two sections, we will be looking at one type of deviance—crime—at various levels in the social system (micro, meso, and macro). You will recall that crime is deviance that (if one is caught) involves formal sanctions from the government. A criminal justice system or court becomes involved in reinforcing conformity. Notice how this varies at the micro, meso, and macro levels of the social system.

Crimes that affect the individual or primary group seem most threatening to us and receive the most attention in the press and from politicians. Yet, these micro-level crimes are only a portion of the total crime picture and, except for hate crimes, are not the most dysfunctional or dangerous crimes. In the United States, more than 2,800 acts are listed as federal crimes. These acts fall into several types of crime, some of which are discussed below. They may be caused by meso- and macro-level factors but involve individuals (micro level) as the primary actors and victims. First, we consider how crime rates are measured.

How Much Crime Is There?

How do sociologists and law enforcement officials know how much crime there is, especially because not all crime is reported to the police? Each country has methods of keeping crime records. For instance, the official record of crime in the United States is found in the FBI's (Federal Bureau of Investigation's) *Uniform Crime Reports* (UCR). The FBI relies on information submitted voluntarily by law enforcement agencies and divides crimes into two categories: Type I and Type II offenses. Type I offenses, also known as *FBI index crimes*, include murder, forcible rape, robbery, aggravated assault, burglary, larceny theft, motor vehicle theft, and arson. There are hundreds of Type II offenses, including fraud, simple assault, vandalism, driving under the influence of alcohol or drugs, and running away from home. The Crime Clock in Figure 6.2 summarizes UCR crime records on Type I offenses.

To examine trends in crime, criminologists calculate a rate of crime, usually per 100,000 individuals. Recent data indicate that the rate of violent crime in the United States dropped since the mid-1990s, but it has begun to inch up

Every 3.2 seconds	1 property crime
Every 4.8 seconds	1 larceny, theft
Every 14.4 seconds	1 burglary
Every 26.4 seconds	1 motor vehicle theft
Every 22.2 seconds	1 violent crime
Every 36.6 seconds	1 aggravated assault
Every 1.2 minutes	1 robbery
Every 5.7 minutes	1 forcible rape
Every 30.9 minutes	1 murder

Figure 6.2   Crime Clock

Source: U.S. Federal Bureau of Investigation 2006c.

Table 6.1 **Index of Violent Crime, United States**	
Year	Violent Crime Rate (per 100,000 residents)
1985	558.1
1990	729.6
1995	684.5
2000	506.5
2001	504.5
2002	494.4
2003	475.8
2004	465.5
2005	469.0
2006	473.5

Source: U.S.Federal Bureau of Investigation 2006d.

Note: The number of violent crime offenses in the United States in 2006 was 1,417,745.

again. Table 6.1 indicates changes in the rate of Index Crimes from 1985 to 2006 (Federal Bureau of Investigation 2006d).

Although the UCR data provide a picture of how much crime gets reported to the police and leads to arrest, it does not provide information on how much crime there is in the United States. Sometimes, a crime that is reported to the police does not lead to an arrest, or an arrest is made but the case is never prosecuted in court, or a prosecutor will initiate prosecution but the case never comes to trial. Instead, it is plea-bargained—a suspect agrees to plead guilty in exchange for being given a lesser charge, perhaps because the suspect feels guilt or because the person does not have the resources to fight the charges with a good attorney or because the suspect is willing to exchange information for a lighter sentence. The reduction in the number of cases at each level of the criminal justice system is just one of the problems of attempting to determine accurate crime rates.

Changes in the UCR to eliminate some of its problems have led to a new measurement, the *National Incident-Based Reporting System* (NIBRS). In this measure, the reporting is incident-driven, meaning that the FBI gathers not only information on the crime but also more detailed information on victim and offender characteristics and often more detailed categories. Reports include the type of offense, whether a weapon was used, location, whether drugs were a factor, and any motivations related to race, religion, or gender. Ultimately, this system will provide more detailed and accurate crime statistics.

Another technique to assess crime rates is self-reporting surveys—asking individuals what criminal acts they have committed. Criminal participation surveys typically focus on adolescents and their involvement in delinquency.

Yet another way to assess crime rates is victimization surveys—surveys that ask people how much crime they have experienced. The most extensively gathered victimization survey in the United States is the National Crime Victimization Survey, conducted by the Bureau of Justice Statistics. According to these records, the tendency to report crime to the police varies by the type of crime, with violent victimizations having the highest reporting rate. The victimization survey corroborates the findings of the Index of Crime, showing that violent crime rates have declined since 1994, although the trend has recently reversed slightly.

How crime is measured affects what and how much crime is reported. Although differences in crime reports are often difficult to reconcile, each measurement instrument provides a different portion of the total picture of crime. By using several data-gathering techniques (triangulation), a more accurate picture of crime begins to emerge. Most of the crimes that concern average citizens of countries around the world are violent crimes committed by individuals or small groups. The following are some examples of these micro-level crimes.

Thinking Sociologically

Which source of data discussed above do you think best tells us what the crime rates are? Why might there be a benefit to having more than one method? Why are FBI reports usually given attention by the press?

Predatory or Street Crimes

Crimes committed against individuals or property are called predatory crimes by law enforcement agencies and are considered the most serious crimes by the public. In the United States, the Uniform Crime Report lists eight serious index crimes used to track crime rates. These index crimes are predatory acts against people (murder, robbery, assault, and rape) and property (burglary, arson, theft, and auto theft).

Citizens in the United States are increasingly afraid of violent predatory crime, especially by strangers. Surveys show that citizens feel they cannot trust others. Some people keep guns. Others, especially women, African Americans, older Americans, and low-income individuals, are afraid to go out near their homes at night (U.S. Bureau of Justice Statistics 2001). Because one's property and bodily safety are at stake, the public fixates on these crimes as the most feared and serious. However, the percentage of U.S. households experiencing one or more crimes dropped from 25% in 1994 to 14% in 2005 (Klaus 2007). Most criminologists feel there are more serious crimes to be discussed under meso- and macro-level deviance.

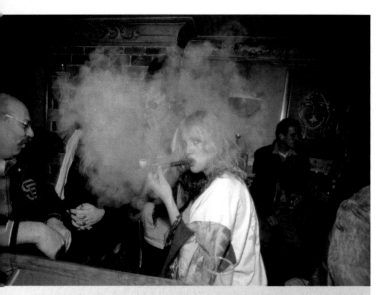

A woman smokes a marijuana pipe in Amsterdam, Netherlands, where smoking pot is legal. The Dutch do not think there is any victim, and therefore there should be no prohibition of the behavior.

Crimes Without Victims

Acts committed by or between consenting adults are known as **victimless** or **public order crimes**. Depending on the laws of countries, these can include prostitution, homosexual acts, gambling, smoking marijuana and using drugs, drunkenness, and some forms of white-collar crime. Participants involved do not consider themselves to be victims, but the offense is mostly an affront to someone else's morals. The behaviors labeled deviant by law fall into the category of conflict crime. These illegal acts may be tolerated as long as they do not become highly visible. Some prostitution is overlooked in major cities of the world, but if it becomes visible or is seen as a public nuisance, authorities crack down, and it is controlled. Even though these acts are called victimless, there is controversy over whether individuals are victims even when consenting to the act, and whether others such as family members are victims dealing with the consequences of the illegal activities.

Thinking Sociologically

Can a person be victimized by drugs even if he willingly uses them? Many prostitutes only consent to sex acts because poverty leaves them with few other options and because, like many women without resources, they are vulnerable to domination by men. Are they victims?

Societies respond to victimless crimes such as using and selling drugs with a variety of policies, from execution in Iran and hanging in Malaysia to legalization in Holland. Long prison terms in the United States mean that 3 out of every 10 prison cells are now reserved for the user, the addict, and the drug seller—yet the problem has not diminished (Goode 1997, 2005). Proposals to legalize drugs, gambling, prostitution, and other victimless crimes meet with strong opinions both for and against. Although in many countries current policies and programs toward drugs are not working by almost any measure of success, the various consequences of alternative proposals are also uncertain.

Hate Crimes

Ethnic violence around the world results in reports of hate crimes in communities, at workplaces, and on college campuses. Hate crimes are criminal offenses committed against a person, property, or group that are motivated by the offender's bias against a religion, ethnic or racial group, national origin, gender, or sexual orientation. The Uniform Crime Reports in the United States indicate that hate crimes account for 11.5% of total criminal offenses. Most hate crimes are directed against property (84.4%) and involve destruction, damage, or vandalism; 31.3% include direct intimidation, totaling 9,035 hate crimes involving 9,528 victims (Federal Bureau of Investigation 2005; U.S. Bureau of Justice Statistics 2005).

Research suggests that most hate crimes are spontaneous incidents, often a case of the victim being in the wrong place at the wrong time. Consider the case of Matthew Shepard, the gay college student who was robbed, tied to a fence post, beaten, and left to die in the cold Wyoming night. Nearly 16% of hate crimes are against those with different sexual orientations. Victims often form supportive in-groups to protect them from others who create a "culture of hate" (Jenness and Broad 1997; Levin and McDevitt 2003).

Hate crimes are often vicious and brutal because the perpetrators feel rage against the victim as a representative of a group they despise. The crimes are committed by individuals or small vigilante groups. The targets are usually individuals who happen to have certain traits or are part of a particular community. In the case of some white supremacy movements, philosophical, political, and even religious principles guide their group beliefs (Blee 2008).

The examples above represent only three of the many micro-level crimes, characterized by individual or small group actions. We now turn to crime in organizations and institutions. Not only is crime rooted in complex organizations at the meso level, but crimes themselves are committed within or by organizations.

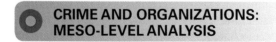

CRIME AND ORGANIZATIONS: MESO-LEVEL ANALYSIS

Understanding criminal behavior is especially important if we wish to understand complex modern societies. First, as

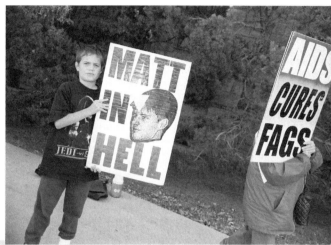

Advocates of a hate-free America express their support for the gay and lesbian community immediately before production of a play about the tragic murder of Matthew Shepard, a gay student who was beaten and left to die in a hate crime in Wyoming. Others (right) express their sentiment that Shepard was a deviant who had no moral standing or, seemingly, even the right to live.

societies modernize, there is an almost universal tendency for crime rates to increase dramatically due to anomie that new migrants and the poor experience in urban areas as old norms are no longer relevant (Merton 1968a). Second, as societies modernize, they become more reliant on formal or bureaucratic mechanisms of control—in other words, development of a criminal justice system at the meso level of our social world.

Crimes Involving Organizations and Institutions

Some crimes are committed by highly organized, hierarchically structured syndicates that are formed for the purpose of achieving their economic objectives in any way possible. These groups intentionally flout the law. On the other hand, some crime is done by legitimate corporations that cross the line. Their crimes are very serious, but the purpose and the public image of the organization are not criminal. We will look first at organized criminal organizations and then at crime committed by people within their legitimate occupations.

Organized Crime

Organized crime, ongoing criminal enterprises, have the ultimate purpose of personal economic gain through illegitimate means (Siegel 2006). Organized criminals use business enterprises for illegal profit. They engage in violence and corruption to gain and maintain power and profit (Adler et al. 2004). Our image of this type of crime is sometimes glamorized, coming from stereotypes in films such as *No Country for Old Men, The Godfather, The Last Dawn,*

Casino, Bugsy, Carlito's Way, Analyze This, Gangs of New York, The Departed, Pulp Fiction, Mystic River, Road to Perdition, and *A History of Violence.* Of course on television, *The Sopranos* is the ultimate media "mob" depiction. Despite the alluring view of these idealized stories, organized crime is a serious problem in many countries. It is essentially a counterculture with a hierarchical structure, from the boss down to underlings. The organization relies on power, control, fear, violence, and corruption. This type of crime is a particular problem when societies experience anomie and social controls break down.

Marginalized ethnic groups that face discrimination may become involved in a quest to get ahead through organized crime. Early in U.S. history, Italians were especially prominent in organized crime, but today, many groups are involved. Organized crime around the world has gained strong footholds in countries in transition (Siegel and Nelen 2008). For example, in Russia, the transition from a socialist economy to a market economy has provided many opportunities for criminal activity. The *Mafiya* is estimated to be 100,000 people strong, and some estimate members control 70% to 80% of all private business and 40% of the nation's wealth in Russia (Lindberg and Markovic n.d.; Schmalleger 2006). Organized crime usually takes one of three forms: (1) the sale of illegal goods and services, including gambling, loan-sharking, trafficking in drugs and people, selling stolen goods, and prostitution; (2) infiltrating legitimate businesses and unions through threat and intimidation, and using bankruptcy and fraud to exploit and devastate a legitimate company; and (3) racketeering, the extortion of funds in exchange for protection (i.e., not being hurt). Activities such as running a casino or trash collection service often appear to be legitimate endeavors on the surface but may be cover operations for highly organized illegal crime rings.

Although the exact cost of organized crime in the United States is impossible to determine exactly, estimates of the annual gross income from organized crime activity is at least $50 billion, more than 1% of the gross national product. Some scholars estimate earnings at $90 billion per year (Siegel 2000).

Transnational organized crime takes place across national boundaries, using sophisticated electronic communications and transportation technologies. Experts identify several major crime clans in the world: (1) Hong Kong–based triads, (2) South American cocaine cartels, (3) Italian mafia, (4) Japanese Yakuza, (5) Russian Mafiya, and (6) West African crime groups. Each operates across borders. Organized crime is responsible for thousands of deaths a year through drug traffic and murders, and it contributes to a climate of violence in many cities (Siegel 2006). The value of the global illicit drug market, for example, is estimated at more than $13 billion at the production level, $94 billion at the wholesale level, and $322 billion at the retail level (based on retail prices and taking seizures and other losses into account). The largest market is cannabis, followed by cocaine, the opiates, and other markets (methamphetamine, amphetamine, and ecstasy) (Common Sense for Drug Policy 2006; United Nations Development Programme 2005b). Many people survive off of the drug trade, from the poppy farmers in Afghanistan, who grow more than 75% of the world's poppies, to the street drug dealers. In 2007, the acreage devoted to growing poppies was the highest ever, especially in southern Afghanistan. This problem is not likely to end soon because farmers are in debt to the Taliban and are therefore forced to continue growing poppies. The Taliban profit from the sales by more than $100 million per year, helping to keep them in power. Thus, Westerners who use opium drugs help to financially sustain this group (National Public Radio 2008).

Add other types of crimes (transporting migrants, trafficking in women and children for the sex industry, and sales of weapons and nuclear material) and the estimates of profits for international crime cartels are from $750 billion to more than $1.5 trillion a year (United Nations Development Programme 2005b).

Occupational Crime

The Arthur Andersen accounting firm employee working with Enron shredded documents, covering a trail of shady dealings. This was illegal. The Enron and Arthur Andersen scandal became the largest fraud in American business history, and the taint spread to other companies (Shore 2008).

A violation of the law committed by an individual or group in the course of a legitimate, respected occupation or financial activity is called white-collar or occupational crime (Coleman 2006; Hagan 2002). Occupational crime can be committed by individuals from virtually any social class, and it can occur at any organizational level. However, most often this refers to white-collar crimes, in the United States, "estimated to be ten times greater than all the annual losses from all the crimes reported to the police" (Coleman 2006:43). Collapse of the savings and loan industry cost the public billions of dollars. Antitrust violations cost $250 billion. Tax fraud costs $150 billion, and health care industry fraud costs $100 billion. Employee theft adds 2% to the retail purchase price of products we buy (Coleman 2006). Occupational crime receives less attention than violent crimes because it is less visible and because it is frequently committed by people in positions of substantial authority and prestige, as opposed to reports of violent crimes that appear on the television news each night. Yet, it is far more costly in currency, health, and lives.

Occupational crime is less publicized because it does not always cause obvious physical injury to identifiable people. It occurs in the less visible arena of the meso-level social structure. However, occupational crime can cause death and injuries from lack of safety precautions or malfunctioning machines, as seen in cases of mining safety. The cost is tremendous, running into hundreds of billions of dollars a year, far more than violent predatory crimes. Victims of financial scams who have lost their life savings are well aware of this.

In addition to occupational crimes such as embezzlement, pilfering, bribery, tax evasion, price fixing, obstruction of justice, and various forms of fraud, computer crime is adding to the losses of businesses and government. Identity theft, embezzlement, international illegal transfers of money, illegal stock trades, sales of illegal or inferior products, creation of computer viruses, computer hackers— this list is long and will become longer. "As technology advances, it facilitates new forms of behavior . . . new and as yet unimaginable opportunities for criminals positioned to take advantage of it and the power such technology will afford" (Schmalleger 2006:473). Sociologists divide occupational crimes into four major categories: crimes against the company, against the employees, against customers, and against the general public (Hagan 2002).

Crimes against the company include pilfering (using company resources such as the photocopy machine for personal business) and employee theft ("borrowing company property," taking from the till, and embezzlement). Most employees are otherwise upstanding citizens, but those who commit occupational crimes say they do so for several reasons. First, they feel little or no loyalty to the organization, especially if it is large and impersonal. It is like stealing from nobody, they say. Second, workers feel exploited and resentful toward the company. Stealing is getting back at the company. Third, the theft is seen as a "fringe benefit" or "informal compensation" that they deserve. Making personal long-distance calls on company phones or taking paper and pens are examples. Fourth, workers may steal because of the challenge. It makes the job more interesting if they can get away with it. It is important to note that these people do not see themselves as criminals, especially compared with "street" criminals (Altheide et al.1978).

The next three types of corporate crime are often done on behalf of the company, and the victims are employees or members of the larger society. Crimes against employees refer to corporate neglect of worker safety. In the United States, the Occupational Safety and Health Act was passed in 1970 to help enforce regulations to protect workers, but there are still many problems. Government agencies estimate that the death rate each year from job-related illness and injuries is fivefold the number of all deaths from street crimes. For example, one out of every five cancer cases have been traced to pollutants in workplaces, and many of these cases were preventable (Simon 2006). Neglect of worker safety is a serious problem in some developing or peripheral countries trying to attract corporations with low taxes, cheap labor, and few regulations.

Why does corporate crime and negligence occur? Several theories of crime are helpful in explaining this pattern. Organizational crimes by executives take place in environments where profits are expected by investors and by one's coworkers (as explained by differential association theory) and where the benefits of such behavior seem, at the time, to outweigh the costs (which illustrates rational choice theory). The micro-level environment within the larger corporation shapes the decision-making process in a way that fosters crime.

Strain theory points out that goals of corporations are to make the greatest short-term profits. In fact, it is illegal for a U.S. corporation to do anything contrary to the interests of the stockholders. Thus, to install expensive equipment or safety devices cuts those profits, and many employers are concerned with the bottom line, not long-term consequences. Although government agencies in many countries are responsible for reducing environmental hazards and workplace dangers, they do not have sufficient staff to police companies for adherence to laws. Internationally, there is little oversight. When agencies do step in, it is usually after the fact—when complaints are lodged because of serious health and safety problems. Multinational corporations generally look for the cheapest labor costs and lowest environmental regulations to maximize their profits, and governments of poor countries try to attract foreign corporations to keep the poor populace employed, regardless of the environmental or workplace consequences.

Thinking Sociologically

How might conflict theory explain corporate crime?

Crimes against customers involve acts such as selling dangerous foods or unsafe products, consumer fraud, deceptive advertising, and price-fixing (setting prices in

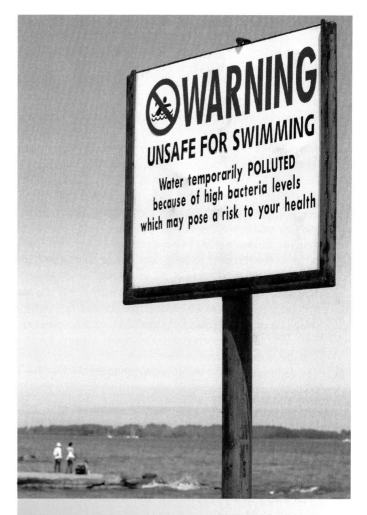

Some beaches in the United States, even in beautiful resort communities, have been closed due to unsafe water, and in some communities, children cannot play outside during the warm months due to risk of injury to their lungs. The U.S. Environmental Protection Agency has documented many cases in which industries violate pollution control laws, and it is the citizenry who suffer. This illustrates corporate crimes against citizens, but it is still not considered a "major" crime in the FBI index crimes or by most journalists.

collusion with another producer). The purpose of advertising is to convince customers, by whatever means, to buy the product—appealing to vanity, sexual interests, or competition to keep up with neighbors. Sometimes, these techniques cross the line between honesty and deception. The result can be customers purchasing products that are defective and even highly dangerous—all with the full knowledge of company officials.

Crimes against the public include acts by companies that negatively affect large groups of people. One example is hospitals or medical offices that overbill Medicare, which costs U.S. taxpayers an estimated $100 billion a year. The FBI estimates that 3% to 10% of total health care expenditures, both public and private, are fraudulent (Federal

Bureau of Investigation 2006b). Surreptitiously dumping pollutants into landfills, streams, or the air is another crime against the public. Proper disposal of contaminants can be costly and time consuming for a company, but shortcuts can cause long-term effects for the public. One example is Love Canal, New York, the illegal dumping ground for toxic chemicals from the Hooker Chemical Corporation. Years after the dumping, the chemicals injured children and others. Hooker eventually paid $227 million in damages, but cleanup cost taxpayers another $280 million (Coleman 2006). Pollutants from industrial wastes have caused high rates of miscarriages, birth defects, and diseases among residents. These cases demonstrate how lethal crimes against the public can be. The film *Erin Brockovich* illustrated the fight of families against chemical polluters. Other films that provide popular culture images of corporate malfeasance are *A Civil Action, The Insider, Silkwood,* and *Thunderheart.*

After reviewing the evidence, Coleman (2006) draws the conclusion that white-collar crime committed by company executives is by far our most serious crime problem. The economic cost of white-collar crime is vastly greater than the economic cost of street crime. White-collar criminals kill considerably more people than all violent street criminals put together (Coleman 2006).

Thinking Sociologically

Why are meso-level crimes considered more dangerous and more costly to the public than micro-level crimes? Why do they get so much less attention?

 NATIONAL AND GLOBAL CRIME: MACRO-LEVEL ANALYSIS

Terrorism refers to "premeditated, politically motivated violence perpetrated against noncombatant targets by subnational groups or clandestine agents, usually intended to influence an audience" (U.S. State Department 2002b). Add to that international terrorism, terrorism practiced in a foreign country, and terrorism can be seen to be a worldwide problem. The number of international terrorist attacks in 2004 increased dramatically in one year from 175 in 2003 to 655 in 2004, perhaps because there was more surveillance (Glasser 2005). Terrorist groups can be religious, state-sponsored, left- or right-wing, or nationalist. Table 6.2 shows types of terrorist groups (Schmalleger 2006:347).

Crime is a national and global issue as illustrated by *state organized crime.* Overlooked by the public and by social scientists, this form of crime includes acts defined by law as criminal but committed by state or government officials in the pursuit of their jobs. For example, a government might be complicit in smuggling, assassination, or torture, acting as an accessory to crime that is then justified in terms of "national defense." Government offices may also violate laws that restrict or limit government activities such as eavesdropping. In some countries, including the United States, political prisoners are held without charges, access to lawyers, and trials for long periods, or they are tortured, violating both national and international laws. Some countries have also violated their own laws, but it is difficult to cast blame when the guilty party is the government. In places such as North Korea and Iraq under Saddam Hussein, the government terrorized the citizenry into conformity and passivity.

Bribery and corruption are the way of life in many governments and businesses. Table 6.3 shows comparative corruption rankings as measured by bribes paid to obtain services (Transparency International 2007).

Thinking Sociologically

Sometimes, government officials and even heads of state are the perpetrators of crimes. Is there a difference in crime if it is done by an official and justified as necessary for national defense? Why or why not? Is it ever justified for a military or intelligence agency to violate its own country's laws?

Table 6.2 **Types of Terrorist Groups**

Nationalist	Irish Republican Army, Basque Fatherland and Liberty, Kurdistan Workers' Party
Religious	Al-Qaeda, HAMAS, Hezbollah, Aum Shinrikyo (Japan)
State-sponsored	Hezbollah (backed by Iran), Abu Nidal Organization (Syria, Libya), Japanese Red Army (Libya)
Left-wing	Red Brigades (Italy), Baader-Meinhof Gang (Germany), Japanese Red Army
Right-wing	Neo-Nazis, skinheads, white supremacists
Anarchist	Some contemporary antiglobalization groups

Table 6.3	Percentage of Respondents Who Said They Had Paid a Bribe to Obtain Services
Africa	**42%**
Cameroon	79%
Nigeria	40%
South Africa	3%
Asia Pacific	**22%**
Cambodia	72%
Hong Kong	3%
India	25%
Indonesia	31%
Japan	1%
Korea, South	1%
Malaysia	6%
Pakistan	44%
Philippines	32%
Vietnam	14%
Latin America	**13%**
Argentina	5%
Bolivia	27%
Panama	13%
Peru	18%
Venezuela	12%
Newly Independent	**21%**
Russia	17%
Ukraine	30%
European Union	**5%**
Austria	1%
Bulgaria	7%
Denmark	2%
Finland	2%
France	1%
Greece	27%
Iceland	1%
Ireland	2%
Netherlands	2%
Portugal	2%
Romania	33%
Spain	3%
Sweden	1%
Switzerland	1%
United Kingdom	2%
Southeast Europe	**12%**
Albania	71%
Croatia	8%
Kosovo	67%
Macedonia	44%
Serbia	21%
Turkey	6%
North America	**2%**
Canada	1%
United States	2%

Source: Reprinted from *Transparency International Global Corruption Barometer, 2007.* Copyright © 2007 Transparency International: The Global Coalition against Corruption. Used with permission. For more information, visit http://www .transparency.org.

Detainees sit in a holding area at the naval base in Guantanamo Bay, Cuba, during in-processing to the "temporary" detention facility. Four years later, most of these men were still being held without trial. In several U.S. Supreme Court rulings (2006 and 2008), the verdict was that the rights of these people have been violated by the U.S. administration. However, little has changed.

Cross-National Comparison of Crimes

The vending machine was on the corner near the Ballantines' house in Japan. The usual cola, candy, and sundries were displayed, along with cigarettes, beer, whiskey, sake, and pornographic magazines. Out of curiosity, Jeanne and her husband watched to see who purchased what from the machines, and not once did they see teenagers sneaking the beer, cigarettes, or porn. It turns out the Ballantines were not the only ones watching! The neighbors also kept an eye on who did what, the neighborhood watch being an effective form of social control in Japan. Because of the **stigma**, the disapproval attached to disobeying the expected norms, teens understand the limits, and vigilant neighbors help to keep the overall amount of deviance low. The neighborhood watch sends a signal that deviant behavior is unacceptable and provides social control on behaviors of those who might be tempted to commit crimes.

Japan and the United States are both modern, urban, industrial countries, but their crime rates and the way they deal with deviant behavior and crime are quite different. Japan has 21 violent crimes for every 100,000 individuals (including one homicide, two rapes, five robberies). That means in a population of 127 million, Japan had 1,391 homicides in 2005. Compare that to the rate in the United States, 637 for every 100,000 individuals (including six homicides, 32 rapes, 149 robberies)—a rate 30 times greater (Greimel 2007; Interpol 2003). Yet, the overall crime rate in Japan has increased to 2.27 million cases in 2005, compared to 1.81 million in 1996. The Japanese are concerned with the increase, although compared to the number of homicides in the United States, 16,692 in a population of about 300 million, their rate is still low (Greimel 2007).

How can these differences in crime rates be explained? Researchers look at cultural differences: Japan's low violent crime rate is due in part to Japan's homogeneous society—inequality between citizens is not great. Moreover, the definition of success in Japan is not as focused on material possessions and consumption. Japanese people are loyal to a historic tradition of cooperation that provides a sense of moral order, a network of group relations, strong commitment to social norms, and respect for law and order (Westermann and Burfeind 1991). The example about vending machines in Japan illustrates this idea.

Although Japan's crime rate is roughly one third that of the United States, it is not attained through harsher penalties. The government actually spends far less of its gross national product on police, courts, and prisons, and police in Japan want to be thought of as kind and caring rather than strict in their enforcement of the law (Bayley 1991). For many crimes in Japan, the offender may simply be asked to write a letter of apology. This is frequently sufficient sanction to deter the person from further violation of the law. The humiliation of writing an apology and the fear of shame and embarrassing one's family are strong enough to curb deviant behavior.

Criminologists consider the causes of economic inequality in different countries. If minority status prevents certain individuals and groups from fitting into the dominant society and getting ahead, this helps explain higher levels of deviance among the disfranchised groups. The overall health of a country's economy—as measured by job opportunities, unemployment, and inflation—also affects the crime rate. When the economy is poor, the crime rates rise. Research shows that the incidence of homicide is higher in countries with greater income inequality.

Although comparing cross-national data on crime is difficult because there are variations in the definitions of crime and measurements used, comparisons do give us insight into what types of crimes are committed, under what circumstances, and how often. Two sources of international data are Interpol (the International Criminal Police Organization) and the United Nations. Although these organizations collect and present data, they have no way to check accuracy of the data they receive from countries.

Table 6.4 provides information on crimes in selected countries. Note the differences in crime rates (Interpol 2007). As discussed above, these differences are due in part to the much higher disparity in income between rich and poor and the heterogeneity of populations.

Thinking Sociologically

Look at the data in Table 6.4. What can you tell about countries from studying their crime rates? Do the rape rates, especially, tell us anything significant? If so, what?

Global Crimes

Increasingly, crimes are global in nature. Some crimes are committed by transnational conglomerates and may involve organized crime and the smuggling of illegal goods and humans. Other crimes are committed by countries that violate international laws, treaties, and agreements. Consider international agreements regarding protection of the environment that some countries and transnational corporations ignore when these agreements act against their own self-interests. Yet, these violations of agreements may affect the entire global ecological system. The international community has the capacity to try people, organizations, and countries for violation of human rights or international laws, but the process is difficult and politically charged.

Some scholars use a world systems perspective, arguing that the cause of global crime lies in the global economy, inequalities between countries, and competition between countries for resources and wealth. As a result of the capitalist mode of production, an unequal relationship has arisen between core nations (developed, wealthy ones in the Global North) and periphery nations (in the Global South) that results in inequality. Core nations often take unfair advantage of peripheral nations. Peripheral nations, in turn, must find ways to survive in this global system, and they sometime turn to surreptitious methods to achieve their goals (Chase-Dunn and Anderson 2006). Some nations with lots of resources are semiperiphery nations. Benefiting from extensive trade, they are less vulnerable than the poorest nations. Map 6.2 (page 188) helps you see where some of these core, peripheral, and semi-peripheral nations are located.

As you look at this map, note that the developed or affluent countries are almost all located in the northern hemisphere. Although some poor countries are north of the equator, the pattern is obvious. Furthermore, the phrase "gone south" is often a colloquialism for an economy that is not strong. To avoid some misleading implications of the words *developed* and *developing*, some scholars prefer the term Global South to refer to less affluent nations. If you see or hear the phrase "Global South," this map should help you see why it refers to developing or poor countries (see Map 6.2, page 188).

The forms of global corruption are too extensive to catalog here, so we will settle for an illustration of one of the newest manifestations of global crime against people and property: computer crimes. Internet deviance or cyberspace crime is growing faster than a cybergeek can move a mouse.

Table 6.4   **Crime Incidents in Selected Countries**

Country	Murders	Rapes	Assaults	Burglaries	Auto Thefts
Australia	302	15,630	141,124	436,865	139,094
Bulgaria	332	593	3,084	293,416	11,281
Canada	489	24,049	233,517	23,065	160,268
Chile	235	1,250	53,133	13,375	Not available
Colombia	26,539	1,861	25,219	74,231	33,135
Czech Republic	174	500	21,998	99,568	23,839
Denmark	58	497	9,796	1,297	32,203
Finland	148	579	27,820	370,993	16,391
France	1,051	8,458	106,484	1,885	301,539
Germany	960	7,499	116,912	Not available	83,063
Greece	81	114	3,322	8,969	8,486
Hungary	205	589	11,161	2,407	10,024
India	37,170	15,468	236,313	23,042	Not available
Ireland	38	218	9,921	2,426	14,851
Italy	746	2,336	29,068	Not available	243,890
Japan	637	2,260	43,229	3,027	309,638
Korea, South	955	6,139	14,925	9,871	Not available
Mexico	13,829	13,061	255,179	3,984	158,801
Netherlands	183	1,648	44,129	91,146	38,320
New Zealand	45	861	30,177	65,675	21,992
Norway	49	555	14,727	5,297	23,339
Poland	2,170	2,399	32,792	364,786	68,062
Portugal	247	385	37,979	47,328	26,428
Saudi Arabia	105	87	4,705	11	5,573
South Africa	21,995	53,008	535,461	394,557	99,963
Spain	494	5,664	90,453	23,856	134,584
Switzerland	69	404	Not available	60,384	9,349
Thailand	5,140	4,020	20,125	13,222	3,276
Tunisia	113	334	40,558	7,680	1,176
United Kingdom	850	8,593	450,865	836,027	338,796
United States	12,658	89,110	2,238,480	2,099,700	1,147,300
Zimbabwe	912	5,567	93,062	55,280	1,342

Source: Interpol Data 2007.

This new world of crime ranges from online identity theft and gambling, to cybersex and pornography, to hate sites and stalking, to hacking into files and terrorism (Thio 2007).

As one team of researchers reports, the Internet "is where crime is rampant and every twisted urge can be satisfied. . . . Fraudsters can tap into an international audience from anyplace in the world" (Sager et al. 2006:261). The illegal "underground web" of businesses such as arms-dealing was estimated at more than $36 billion in 2002. Compare that to legitimate business consumers in the United States spending just over $39 billion on the Internet the same

year. Of the fraud complaints received by the U.S. government, more than 70% involved the Internet. Financial fraud costs consumers $22 billion annually according to *Business Week*, and identity theft is running $22 billion annually, according to the Identity Theft Resource Center (Sager et al. 2006). "The Underground Web, if unchecked, has the potential to undermine the values of society. It enables—even encourages—ordinary citizens to break the law" (Sager et al. 2006:262).

Even legitimate businesses such as Google, Yahoo!, or eBay can unwittingly support crime by connecting people

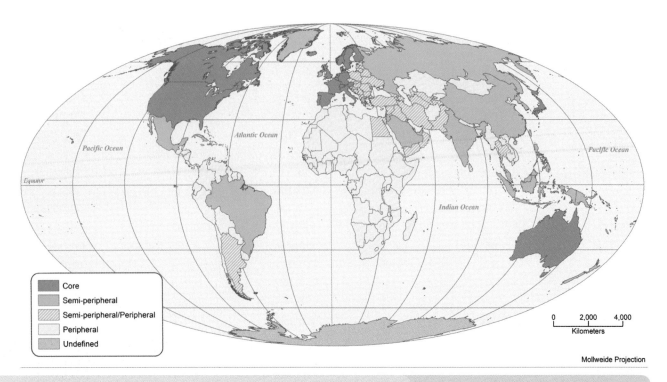

Map 6.2 Core, Semiperipheral, and Peripheral Countries of the World

Source: Map by Anna Versluis.

Note: Some countries are left undefined (in gray).

to illegal operations. Drug traffic is one of the most common forms of scam. For example, people purchase body-building drugs that are life threatening, find recipes for making illegal methamphetamines, or purchase the date rape drug GHB. Another venue of illegal Internet usage is music and video downloading and sales (Friedman 2005).

Other crimes have also become easier to commit: The FBI reported an increase of 1,789% in online child porn cases opened between 1996 and 2006. The arrests and summons during the same time period increased from 68 in 1996 to 1,546 in 2006, a 2,174% increase, and the increase in convictions and pretrial diversions was from 68 to 1018 (Federal Bureau of Investigation 2006a). One policy difficulty is that law enforcement gets gridlocked in both national and international jurisdictional confusion. As many as five different federal U.S. agencies can be involved in preventing financial fraud on the Internet, not to mention the state and local agencies that might play a role. If the fraud involves international cybercrime, the customs services and other branches of governments also may enter the investigation. The resulting confusion and lack of clear authority regarding who should prosecute can play into the hands of lawbreakers. Few local authorities feel that identity theft is within their jurisdiction, but government officials may not have the personnel or the interest to pursue these cases (Sager et al. 2006).

Controlling Crime: Social Policy Considerations

When people are afraid to walk the streets because they might be assaulted and when a significant number of individuals are dropping out of society and taking up deviant lifestyles, deviance becomes a topic of great concern. Most governments pass laws and make policies to keep deviance from disrupting the smooth functioning of society. This section discusses mechanisms used by societies to control the amount of deviance.

Dealing With Crime: The Criminal Justice Process

Every society has a process for dealing with criminals. Sometimes, the ground rules and processes of justice respect human rights and represent blind justice, meaning that all people are treated equally, but often, they do not.

Structural-functionalists see the justice system as important to maintaining order in society. Some conflict theorists argue that the criminal justice system depicts the threat of crime as a threat from poor people and minorities, which creates fear of victimization in members of society. It is in the interests of those in power to maintain the image that crime is primarily the work of outsiders and the poor. This deflects discontent and hostility from the powerful and helps them retain their positions (Reiman 1998). Conflict theorists point out that there will always be a certain percentage of crime in society because the powerful will make sure that something is labeled deviant. So policy might focus on how to deter deviant acts, or it could focus on the injustices of the system and ways in which the criminal justice system protects and sustains the power structure. In either case, prisons and jails—penal institutions—are currently a primary means of controlling individual criminal behavior.

Prisons and Jails

Protection from offenders often means locking criminals in prisons, a form of total institution that completely controls the prisoners' lives and regulates all of their activities. Inmates' lives are drastically changed through the processes of degradation, which marks the individual as deviant, and mortification, which breaks down the individual's original self as the inmate experiences resocialization (Goffman 1961; Irwin 1985). The inmate is allowed no personal property. There is little communication, and verbal abuse of inmates by guards is common. Heterosexual activity is prohibited, uniforms and standard buzz cuts are required, and the inmates' schedules are totally controlled.

Social systems that develop within the prison often involve rigid roles, norms, and privileges. In a famous study that simulated a prison situation, Zimbardo et al. (1973) illustrated the social organization that develops and the roles that individuals play within the prison system. Students were assigned to roles as prisoners or prison guards. Within a short time, the individuals in the study were acting out their roles. The students playing the role of "guard" became cruel and sadistic, causing Zimbardo to end the experiment prematurely to prevent problems. Participants had taken their roles so seriously that abuse was beginning to have alarming consequences (Zimbardo et al. 1973). The recent abuse of prisoners in Iraq and at Guantanamo prison in Cuba parallel the findings from Zimbardo's earlier study about roles that develop in these social situations (Zimbardo 2009).

Jails in local communities have been called catchall asylums for poor people. Most people in jails are there for their "rabble existence"—including petty hustlers, derelicts, junkies, "crazies," and outlaws—but mostly disorganized and economically marginal members of society (Irwin 1985). Jails in Europe and the United States house disproportionate numbers of immigrants (especially those with non-European features and skin tones), young men, and members of the poorest class of the citizenry. In the

Jails or prisons are often the formal sanctions applied to enforce the rules passed by legitimate officials. This woman is being arrested for a legal infraction that is fairly serious.

United States, whites make up only 34% of the incarcerated population. Their percentage of the U.S. population is about 66.4%. African Americans make up 38% of all inmates and about 12.8% of total population, and Hispanics 21% of all inmates and about 14.8% of the total population (Federal Bureau of Investigation 2006c; U.S. Census Bureau 2006g). Among women, the number of African Americans incarcerated declined as white women increased from 33 to 48 per 100,000 between 2000 and 2006. Table 6.5 (page 190) breaks down the incarcerated population by race/ethnicity and sex.

Overall, the number of incarcerated individuals has increased rather dramatically in the United States. From 2005 to 2006, the increase was 2.8% nationwide, and the average annual growth rate of the prison population from 2000 to 2005 was 1.9% (Sabol 2007). The reasons for the increase in incarceration rates in the United States have to do with get-tough-on-crime policies, preventative detention policies that lock people up for minor offenses, and the "war on drugs," which increases the number of people put in jails and prisons. The increase in inmates in the United States has meant more jails being built and more people hired to work in the legal system.

Table 6.5	**U.S. State and Federal Sentenced Prisoners by Gender, Race, and Hispanic Origin, 2000 and 2006**			
	2000		*2006*	
	Number	*%*	*Number*	*%*
Male	1,237,500	93.7%	1,502,200	93.1%
White	398,800	30.2%	1,399,100	31.8%
African American	528,300	40.0%		
Hispanic/Latino	240,700	18.2%		
Female	83,700	6.3%	103,100	6.9%
White	33,300	2.5%	49,100	3.3%
African American	32,000	2.4%	28,600	1.9%
Hispanic/Latino	13,000	1.0%	17,500	1.2%
Total	1,321,100	100%	1,502,200	100%

Source: Sabol 2007.

Thinking Sociologically

From what you have learned so far in this chapter, why are the people who get sent to jail disproportionately young, poor, immigrants, or racial and ethnic minorities?

The Functions and Effectiveness of Prisons

Prisons serve several functions for society. The desire for revenge or retribution leads to harsh penalties such as death or life imprisonment. Removing dangerous people from society is also seen as a way to protect the public by incapacitating those we think are a threat. Deterrence serves the purpose of preventing an individual from future deviance and deterring others from becoming deviant. Finally, rehabilitation efforts are reflected in counseling, education, and work training programs inside prisons (Johnson 2002).

Criminals in prison are exposed to more criminal and antisocial behavior, so rehabilitation and deterrence goals are often undermined by the nature of prisons. Consider the case of rape behind bars (Banbury 2004). Of more than 2.2 million inmates crowded into U.S. facilities, nearly 300,000 males are sexually assaulted in U.S. prisons every year (about one in five), often in gang rapes. Threats of sexual violence and displays of power are a more common occurrence than actual rape. Domination of others to prove manhood prevails in situations in which one cannot otherwise fulfill masculine role expectations (Hanser 2002). This ongoing problem of assault, rape, and threat of violence in prison so brutalizes inmates that it becomes difficult for them to reenter society as well-adjusted citizens ready to conform to the conventional society they feel has brutalized them (Hensley, Koscheski, and Tewksbury 2005).

Although estimates indicate that only 3% of known criminals go to prison, there has been a tremendous increase in incarceration rates in the United States. By the end of 2006, the federal and state prison and local jail population reached more than 2.26 million prisoners (U.S. Bureau of Justice Statistics 2006). Incarceration rates were 751 of every 100,000 U.S. residents (International Centre for Prison Studies 2006). Figure 6.3 illustrates the increase in the prison population since 1925 (Harrison and Karberg 2003).

One in eight African American males between the ages of 25 and 29 (12.6%) are in prison today. Likewise, 3.6% of the Hispanic population is imprisoned, compared to 1.7% of whites. In some areas such as Washington, D.C., the rate is much higher (The Sentencing Project 2006).

At 751 per 100,000, the U.S. rate of locking up citizens is the highest in the world, and five to eight times higher than that in other industrial nations (International Centre for Prison Studies 2006; The Sentencing Project 2006). Table 6.6 shows the countries with the highest incarceration rates and compares rates of incarceration in industrial countries.

The disturbing reality is that, despite the high rates of incarceration in the United States, **recidivism rates**—the likelihood that someone who is arrested, convicted, and imprisoned will later be a repeat offender—are also very high in the United States. Three out of four men who do time in prison will be confined again for a crime. This means that as a specific deterrent or for rehabilitation, imprisonment does not work very well (National Center for Policy Analysis 2001). What options does government have? In the following sections, we discuss the death penalty and alternatives to prisons.

The Death Penalty

All modern societies provide some means of protecting individuals from criminals, especially those considered

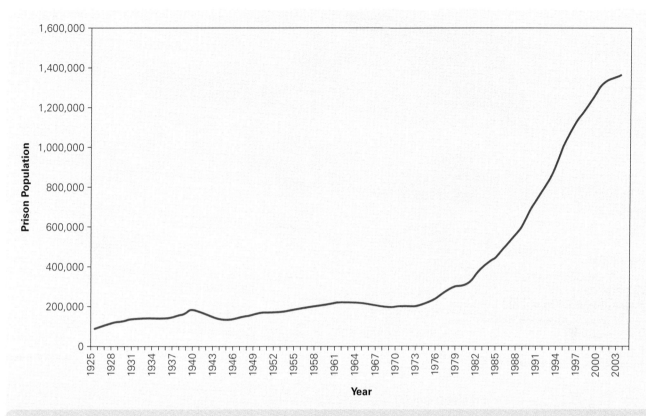

Figure 6.3   State and Federal Prisoners in the United States, 1925–2003

Table 6.6   **World Rates of Incarceration (rates per 100,000 people)**

Top 10 Countries		Other Industrialized Countries	
United States	724	United Kingdom: England and Wales	144
Russian Federation	594	Spain	143
St. Kitts and Nevis	536	Netherlands	127
Bermuda	532	Australia	126
Virgin Islands (U.S.)	521	Portugal	123
Turkmenistan	489	Austria	108
Cuba	487	Canada	107
Palau	478	Germany	97
Belize	470	Italy	97
Bahamas	462	France	88
		Switzerland	83
		Sweden, Denmark, Finland	78–75
		Japan	62

Source: International Centre for Prison Studies 2006.

dangerous. Crimes of murder, assault, robbery, and rape usually receive severe penalties. The most controversial (and irreversible) method of control is for the state to put the person to death. The most common argument for using the death penalty, more formally known as capital punishment, is to deter people from crime. The idea is that not only the person who has killed but also others will be deterred because they know this is a possibility. Although most developed countries

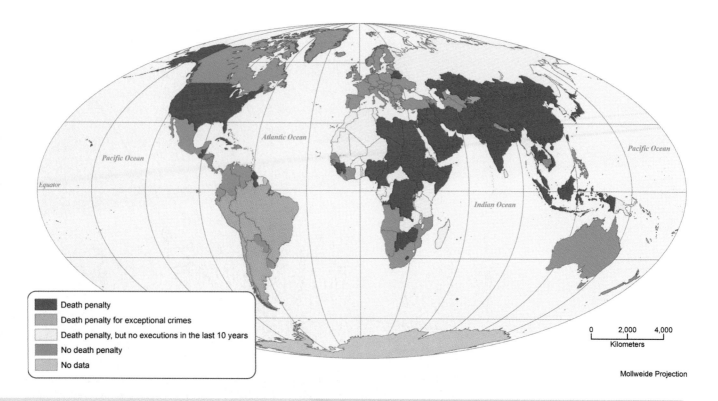

Map 6.3 Global Status of the Death Penalty in 2008

Source: Amnesty International. Map by Anna Versluis.

do not use the death penalty, the United States still does. In fact, as you can see from Map 6.3, the United States is one of the few countries in North or South America with the death penalty. Capital punishment is most common in Asia, the Middle East, and parts of Africa.

By 2007, 133 of the 192 United Nations member states (July 2006) had abolished the death penalty in law or in practice, declaring it cruel and unusual punishment. In 2006, 86 countries had laws against the death penalty, 11 more forbid it except for exceptional crimes (such as war crimes), and 27 additional countries had not executed anyone in 10 or more years, although they had no laws forbidding capital punishment. That means 133 countries do not actively employ the death penalty. Other countries retain the right to use the death penalty in extraordinary cases, although many of those countries actually do not follow through with the sentence (Amnesty International 2006).

In 2006, there were 1,591 known executions in the world, a drop of 25% from 2,148 executions in 2005. About 91% of those executions occurred in six countries: China, Iran, Iraq, Pakistan, Sudan, and the United States (Amnesty International 2007). Methods of killing included beheading, electrocution, hanging, lethal injection, shooting, and stoning to death. Research has not shown that the death penalty deters crime, although it serves as retribution (punishment for a crime) (Hood 2002).

U.S. states with the death penalty assume that those contemplating crimes will be deterred by severe penalties, and those who have committed crimes will be justly punished. However, studies on the deterrent effects of capital punishment do not support the first assumption. Fewer than 25% of inmates questioned believe the death penalty to be a deterrent to violent crime (Steele and Wilcox 2003). Those who had committed three or more violent crimes indicated that their crimes were not planned, they "just happened," "things went wrong," and they were not thinking or caring about the possible penalty when committing their crimes (Wilcox and Steele 2003). In 2004, the average murder rate per 100,000 people in states with the death penalty was 5.1, and the murder rate was much less—2.9—in states that do not have the death penalty (Death Penalty Information Center 2006; Hood 2002). So murder is more likely to happen in states with the death penalty, which is not very good evidence that this penalty has been a deterrent.

Thinking Sociologically

How can you explain higher murder rates in U.S. states that do have the death penalty?

Is the death penalty fairly administered? There is evidence that the death penalty is race and class biased. In most U.S. states with capital punishment, a disproportionate number of minority and lower class individuals are put to death. African Americans make up 42% of the death sentence inmates (Bonczar and Snell 2005). In some jurisdictions, African Americans receive the death penalty at a rate 38% higher than all other groups. Since 1976, 35% of all those executed have been African American, a disproportionate number when considering that they make up less than 13% of the population (Amnesty International 2005; Sarat 2001; Siegel 2006).

Furthermore, the death penalty is usually imposed if a white person has been murdered. Homicides in which African Americans, Latinos and Latinas, Native Americans, and Asian Americans are killed are much less likely to result in a death penalty for the murderer, implying that people in society view their loss of life as less serious (Amnesty International 2006). In addition, mistakes are made. Since 1973, 123 prisoners have been released from death row because they were found innocent. DNA tests are acquitting other death row prisoners and have exonerated people who have already been executed.

A perhaps unexpected fact is that it cost more to put someone to death in most cases than to sentence them to life in prison, largely because of the tremendous cost to taxpayers for legal fees. This combines with the facts that the death penalty sometimes kills innocent people, that it is often racially discriminatory, and that it is not an effective deterrent. These realities have led to a search for alternative means to deter crime and has spurred policy analysts to rethink assumptions about what factors are effective in controlling human behavior.

Alternative Forms of Social Control

Based on the assumptions that most criminal behavior is learned through socialization, that criminals can be resocialized, and that tax dollars can be saved, several sociological theories of crime suggest methods of treatment other than incarceration without rehabilitation. The goal is to reduce both the number of individuals who go to prison and the number who are rearrested after being released—the recidivism rate. Improving social capital of potential offenders is one approach based in theory.

Social capital refers to social networks, shared norms, values, and understanding that facilitate cooperation within or among groups and access to important resources (Flavin 2004). Social capital encompasses relationships, support systems and services, and access to community resources (Jarrett, Sullivan, and Watkins 2005). Increasing an individual's social capital by increasing educational attainment, job skills, and ability to take advantage of available resources can reduce the chances of that person going to prison in the first place and of recidivism, or repeat offenses and incarceration (Faulkner 2006). Consider the case study in "The Applied Sociologist at Work" on the next page.

The tendency to think that the way to control human behavior is through more severe punishments is based on a rational choice theory. If the cost is high enough for deviant acts, so the idea goes, people will conform. Yet, despite severe punishments, crime rates generally remain higher in the United States than in other countries.

What works in one country cannot necessarily be imported directly into another country. Deterrence is complex. It is influenced by dozens of variables including cultural values and meanings attached to specific behaviors. Not many people think that the apology technique used in Japan would work as a deterrent to crimes in the United States. On the other hand, there is a wide range of options available for dealing with crime other than harsh (and expensive) punishments. Seeing how crime is controlled in other countries may challenge assumptions in one's own country, causing authorities to come up with creative new solutions that do work. For example, many criminologists argue that the United States should concentrate on the serious criminals and reduce the number of minor offenders in jails. They also suggest a number of alternatives to sending offenders to jail and prisons such as community service, work release, and educational training programs.

Thinking Sociologically

Do you think changing the "cost-benefit" ratio so the costs of crime to the criminal are higher will deter crime, or are other policies or methods more effective in enticing people to be responsible, contributing members of society?

Prison reforms, rehabilitation, training programs, shock probation, work release, halfway houses, and other alternative programs are intended to integrate the less serious offenders into the community in a productive way and help them regain social capital. If we can integrate the potential criminal into the community, reduce discrimination, and teach at-risk youth acceptable behavior patterns, we may reduce crime and gain productive citizens.

If ex-prisoners can turn to alternative behaviors other than crime, if they have educational or job skills, and if they have families to return to, they are less likely to commit further crimes. Therefore, some state penal systems provide education from basic skills to college courses and allow conjugal and family stays to help keep families together. More than one in three prisoners in state correctional facilities around the United States were enrolled in academic programs from adult basic education to college, another third

The Applied Sociologist at Work—James Faulkner **Reducing Recidivism by Increasing Social Capital**

By James Faulkner

James Faulkner is a police department detective. Part of his work is with adults and juveniles, trying to increase their chances of leading productive lives and staying out of prison by increasing their social capital. The following is a case study by Detective Faulkner, at the time a school resource officer, describing his work with one young man.

Ray was a 20-year-old male, African American college student who started life with absolutely no social capital and continues to struggle to increase his chances for success. He was the type of offender who continually violated the law. Ray's father left when he was seven years old, and his mother died when he was eight. The father's whereabouts were no longer known. With no information and no parents, this was a prime example of someone with limited resources.

As a school resource officer, I was approached by a school official who was concerned for Ray's long-term future, due to the complexities of his life. As a member of law enforcement and through my personal experiences and observations, I knew Ray was stealing frequently to eat and live. Ray was living with a disabled aunt in deplorable conditions with no food in the house. When I picked him up to help him move in with yet another relative, there was no electricity, water, or phone.

We used my phone as a light as we gathered his items, and I helped him pack what few clothes he had. I began taking Ray food with the assistance of others, a concept not known to Ray.

With his high school graduation approaching, Ray asked me to help him find a job. A simple endeavor proved to be very difficult. It began with a potential employer's request for his social security card. Not only did Ray not have one, but he had no idea how to get one. Initially thinking that this would be relatively simple to solve, I asked him to bring his birth certificate, and we would go apply for his social security card. It was then that he asked me how one goes about "getting one of those birth certificate things."

After graduation and the following summer, and with the aid of the assistant school superintendent, who took Ray under her wing, we set out to increase Ray's level of social capital. I felt motivated to help Ray because he had been so motivated to try to help himself, yet he had met failure after failure. He continually fell, got back up, and tried something else. This encouraged me to invest in Ray. Small increases in his level of social capital and resources helped Ray establish a network of support for a more successful future. It is my belief that these small increases in Ray's resources will have significant impact on his future lifestyle and reduce his chances for a life of crime. Among other things, we taught him how to apply for loans to get financial help.

With the help of government loans and grants, Ray was admitted and entered college that fall. We helped supply him with housing, toiletries, and clothing. We did our best not to do these things for him but rather show him how to do them himself. There was no family or celebration after his high school graduation, so some school officials and I took Ray to a local steakhouse to celebrate his graduation and entering college, a step he had once perceived as unobtainable. By investing a small amount of social capital in the form of relationships and resources, we were able to steer Ray in the direction of accumulating additional social capital in the form of education.

This could be his ticket out of his previous way of life.

Note: James Faulkner has a master's degree in Applied Social Science/Criminal Justice.

were involved in vocational training, 13% were engaged in counseling or therapy programs, and 8% received drug and alcohol counseling (U.S. Bureau of Justice Statistics 2003).

Other programs included shock probation (releasing a first-time offender early in the hope that the shock of prison life would deter them), community service to help develop citizenship and pay restitution for the offense, and day treatment and halfway houses to help inmates readjust to community life and find jobs. The programs can relieve overcrowded prisons and save money by reducing the cost of incarceration. There is some evidence that they reduce recidivism as well.

Work release programs build social capital by placing primarily nonviolent offenders in positions to earn wages and help support their families rather than accumulate debt while in prison. They also provide work experience and keep offenders away from hardened criminals in prison, thus helping to reintegrate the offender into the community.

A key to the success of such programs is adequate supervision. Transmitters are often used to track offenders and protect concerned community members (The Urban Institute 2004).

Restitution puts the offender in the position of "making it right" with the victim. The offender renders money or service to the victim or community under supervised parole to compensate the victim. This is a positive way of teaching juvenile offenders lessons in responsibility without imprisonment and exposure to more criminal behavior. Restitution is less costly than long incarceration, and victims are often satisfied with this type of program. The likelihood of repeated offense at a later time is also lower in restitution programs than for those who are sent to prison.

Another current trend is toward privatization of prisons in an attempt to run them in a more businesslike, cost-effective way. This trend is unlikely to improve the rehabilitation aspects in this age of overcrowded prisons and cost cutting, but several states are experimenting with private facilities, and some federal agencies such as the Immigration and Naturalization Service have contracted with private operators to run facilities. Because sociologists and criminologists study prison programs, make recommendations to improve the correction programs, and help find solutions to deviance, they are highly skeptical of privatization. There are many problems in having any public service administered by people whose primary and perhaps only goal is to make a profit. The current trend seems to be to "warehouse prisoners," with little effort to rehabilitate them or to help them reenter society as productive citizens (Irwin 2005).

At the beginning of the chapter, we said that some of the material presented in this chapter might surprise you, some commonly held assumptions about deviance might be challenged, and a different way of looking at deviance might emerge.

Thinking Sociologically

Considering what you have read, how has this affected some of your ideas about deviance, crime, and the criminal justice system?

So What?

Perhaps the answers to some of the chapter's opening questions—what is deviance, why do people become deviant, and what should we do about deviance—have now taken on new dimensions. Deviance as defined by society, communities, and even religion or subcultural groups has many possible explanations, and there are multiple interpretations about how it should be handled. Deviance and crime are issues for any society, for unless most of the people obey the rules most of the time, there can be real threats to stability, safety, and sense of fairness that undermine the social structure. The criminal justice system tends to be a conservative force in society because of its focus on ensuring social conformity.

Regardless of its role, to make the society run more smoothly, we must understand why deviance and crime happen. Good policy must be based on accurate information and careful analysis of the information. We must also understand that deviance and conformity operate at various levels in the social world: micro, meso, and macro. In addition, it is important to understand that there may be positive aspects of deviance for any society, from uniting society against deviants to providing creative new ways to solve problems.

One of the dominant characteristics of modern society is social inequality, and as we have seen, that inequality is often an issue in criminal activity. Indeed, many of our social problems are rooted in issues of inequality. Extreme inequality may even be a threat to the deeper values and dreams of the society, especially one that stresses individualism and achievement. In the following three chapters, we look at three types of inequality: socioeconomic, ethnic or racial, and gender-based inequity.

Key Points

What Have We Learned?

- Deviance—the violation of social norms, including those that are formal laws—is a complex behavior that has both positive and negative consequences for individuals and for society. (See pp. 160–161.)

- Deviance is often misunderstood because of simplistic and popular misconceptions. (See pp. 161–165.)

- Many theories try to explain deviance—rational choice, differential association, and labeling theories at the micro level, along with structural explanations including anomie and disorganization, strain theory, conflict theory, and feminist theory. (See pp. 165–178.)

- Many of the formal organizations concerned with crime (like the FBI and the media) focus on crimes involving individuals—predatory crimes, crimes without victims, and hate crimes—but the focus on these crimes may blind us to crimes that actually are more harmful and more costly. (See pp. 178–180.)

- At the meso level, organized and occupational crimes may cost billions of dollars and create great risk to thousands of lives. Occupation crime may be against the company, employees, customers, or the public. (See pp. 180–184.)

- At the macro level, national governments sometimes commit state-organized crimes, sometimes in violation of their own laws or in violation of international laws. These crimes may be directed against their own citizens (usually minorities) or people from other countries. (See pp. 184–186.)

- Also at the macro level, some crimes are facilitated by global networks and by global inequities of power and wealth. (See pp. 186–188.)

- Controlling crime has generated many policy debates, from the use of prisons to the death penalty and even to alternative approaches to control of deviance. (See pp. 188–195.)

Contributing to Our Social World: What Can We Do?

At the Local Level: Gender identity/orientation that differs from the traditional heterosexual norms has typically been studied as a form of social deviancy. Yet, many college students have confronted these issues in themselves and among their friends. College campuses throughout the country have support groups for students who are lesbian, gay, bisexual, and/or transgender (often abbreviated as "LGBT"). The Consortium of Higher Education LGBT Resource Professionals, a national organization of such campus groups, maintains a Web site at http://www.lgbtcampus.org.Regardless of your identity/orientation, consider contacting your campus LGBT group, attending meetings, and participating in its support and public education activities.

At the Organizational or Institutional Level: The U.S. criminal justice system is an extensive and rapidly growing institution. Every community has numerous organizations that work in this area. Some focus on crime prevention, some on law enforcement, some on corrections, and some on rehabilitation. Identify the aspect of the system that interests you most and, using faculty and community contacts, select an appropriate organization for volunteer work or an internship. The criminal courts are central actors in the administration of criminal justice, and trials are often open to the public. Attending a trial and/or contacting a judge or magistrate could provide a good introduction to a longer term relationship. Some of you may have participated in a prevention program such as DARE in high school. These are administered by local law enforcement agencies such as departments of police and might provide opportunities for volunteer work and for observing how the system works "from the inside." Other possibilities in the corrections and rehabilitation area include Boys and Girls Clubs or halfway houses for teens in trouble. These groups provide work one-on-one with juveniles in afterschool or weekend programs to provide positive role models and increase their social capital. Battered women's shelters are among the many community programs that provide safe houses, counseling, and practical help for women and children in abusive situations. The Date Rape Project provides information and research on date rape on college campuses and in other locations. Working with any of these organizations will allow you to learn about how our social world operates while you contribute to making it a better world.

At the National and Global Levels: One of the most serious forms of global organized crime is trafficking in human beings. This often involves kidnapping, slavery, sexual exploitation of children and adults, and even torture and murder. The international organization Human Trafficking is engaged in research and action programs intended to end such crimes. Its Web site, at http://www.humantrafficking.org, discusses several programs in which you can participate, including a special section on activities at academic institutions. A similar organization, The Polaris Project (www.polarisproject.org), works to reduce global trafficking in women and children. Volunteers participate in letter-writing campaigns, support anti-trafficking legislation, and conduct research on the problem.

Visit **www.pineforge.com/ballantine2study** for online activities, sample tests, and other helpful information. Select "Chapter 6: Deviance and Social Control" for chapter-specific activities.

PART III

Inequality

The underlying question in the next three chapters is why some people rise to the top of society with wealth, power, and prestige at their fingertips, and others languish near the bottom. Why are some individuals and countries rich and others poor? The focus of these chapters is inequality, the process of stratification through which some people "make it" and others do not. At the very bottom of the human hierarchy are those starving and diseased world citizens who have no hope of survival for themselves or their families. This compares with corporate executives and some world politicians or royalty who have billions of dollars at their disposal.

Social inequality is one of the most important processes in modern societies, and the implications extend all the way to the global social network. Sometimes, the inequality is based on socioeconomic status, but the basis of differential treatment is often other characteristics: race, ethnicity, gender, sexual orientation, religion, or age. These differences often result in strong "we" versus "they" thinking. One factor runs throughout these patterns of inequality: They have implications for social interaction at the micro, meso, and macro levels of analysis. In this section, we do not try to cover all forms of inequality; rather, we illustrate the patterns by exploring issues of social class, race or ethnicity, and gender.

CHAPTER 7

Stratification

Rich and Famous— or Rags and Famine?

In rich countries, such as the United States, Canada, Japan, and Western European nations, we assume there are many economic opportunities, and we like to believe that anyone can become rich and famous. The reality, however, is that our social world is very brutal for many people, and what they experience is rags and famine.

Think About It . . .

Micro: Why do you buy what you buy, believe what you believe, and live where you live?

Micro: Why are some people in your community rich and others poor?

Meso: How do institutions—such as education, the economy, religion, and family—help to keep people in the status they were born into?

Macro: Why are some nations affluent and others impoverished?

Macro: How does the fact that we live in a global environment affect you and your social position?

Macro: Global Community

Macro: Society

Meso: National Organizations, Institutions, and Ethnic Subcultures

Micro: Local Organizations and Community

Micro: Me (and My Rags or Riches)

Micro: Prestige and power determined by access to resources; respect based on leadership and self-confidence

Meso: Institutions support elites and stabilize the stratification system; members of ethnic subcultures often disadvantaged

Macro: The rich, famous, and powerful control resources, tax breaks, health care, religious ideology; stock markets respond to their needs

Macro: Position of countries and companies in the international system reflects power and access to resources

Prince Harry of England, second in line to the British throne, was in Afghanistan in 2008 fighting along with the regular grunts, hoping not to be discovered, but when his cover was blown he was pulled out immediately. Because of his royal status, British leaders thought he would be a target for the enemy and a danger to those around him.

Not just anyone can belong to a royal family. One must be born as royalty or marry into it. Members of royal families—such as Prince William and Prince Harry of Britain—grow up in a world of the privileged: wealth, prestige, all doors open to them, or so it appears. Their lifestyles include formal receptions, horse races, polo games, royal hunts, state visits, and other social and state functions. The family has several elegant residences at its disposal. However, like most royalty, William and Harry also live within the confines of their elite status, with its strict expectations and limitations. They cannot show up for a beer at the local pub or associate freely with commoners, and their problems or casual antics are subject matter for front pages of tabloids. In today's world, some royalty are figureheads with little political power; others—such as the Ashanti chiefs in West Africa, King Bhumibol Adulyadej of Thailand, King Sihanok of Cambodia, and Emperor Akihito in Japan—have great influence in state affairs.

In Newport, Rhode Island, spacious mansions are nestled along the coast, with tall-masted sailboats at the docks. These are the summer homes of the U.S. aristocracy. They do not hold royal titles, but their positions allow for a life of comfort similar to that of royalty. Members of this class have an elegant social life, engage in elite sports such as fencing and polo, patronize the arts, and are influential behind the scenes in business and politics.

Hidden from the public eye in each country are people with no known names and no swank addresses; some have no address at all. We catch glimpses of their plight through vivid media portrayals, such as those of refugees in Darfur, Sudan, and of impoverished victims of Hurricane Katrina in 2005 along the Gulf of Mexico coast. They are the poor; many of them live in squalor. Economic hard times have pushed some of them from their rural homes to cities in hopes of finding jobs. However, with few jobs for unskilled and semiskilled workers in today's postindustrial service economies, many of the poor are left behind and homeless. They live in abandoned buildings or sleep in unlocked autos, on park benches, under bridges, on beaches, or anywhere they can stretch out and hope not to be attacked or harassed. Beggars stake out spots on sidewalks, hoping citizens and tourists will give them a handout. In the United States, cities such as Houston, Los Angeles, Washington DC, and New York try to cope with the homeless by setting up sanitary facilities and temporary shelters, especially in bad weather; cities rely on religious and civic organizations such as churches and the Salvation Army to run soup kitchens.

In some areas of the world, such as sub-Saharan Africa and India, the situation is much more desperate, and many families are starving. At daybreak, a cattle cart traverses the city of Calcutta, India, picking up bodies of diseased and starved homeless people who have died on the streets during the night. Mother Teresa, who won the Nobel Peace Prize for her work with those in dire poverty, established a home in India where these people could die with dignity; she also founded an orphanage for children who would otherwise wander the streets begging or die.

Survival, just maintaining life, is a daily struggle for the 37 million people (up 1.1 million from 2003) who live in poverty-stricken parts of the world (U.S. Census Bureau 2005e). These humans are at the bottom of the stratification hierarchy.

This raises the following question: Why do some people live like royalty and others live in desperate poverty? Most of us live between these extremes. We study and work hard for what we have, but we also live comfortably, knowing that starvation is not pounding at our door. This chapter discusses (1) why stratification is important, (2) why people are rich or poor (stratification systems), (3) the importance and consequences of social rankings for individuals, (4) whether one can change social class positions (social mobility), (5) characteristics of major stratification systems, (6) poverty and social policies to address problems, and (7) the global digital divide (patterns of stability and change).

The Importance of Social Stratification

Social stratification refers to how individuals and groups are layered or ranked in society according to how many valued resources they possess. Stratification is an ongoing process of sorting people into different levels of access to resources, with the sorting legitimated by cultural beliefs about why the inequality is justifiable. This chapter focuses on socioeconomic stratification, and subsequent chapters examine ethnic and gender stratification.

Three main assumptions underlie the concept of stratification: (1) people are divided into ranked categories; (2) there is an unequal distribution of desired resources, meaning that some members of society possess more of what is valued and others possess less; and (3) each society determines what it considers to be valued resources. In an agricultural society, members are ranked according to how much land or how many animals they own. In an industrial society, occupational position and income are two of the criteria for ranking. Most Japanese associate old age with high rank, whereas Americans admire and offer high status to some people for their youthful vigor and beauty.

What members of each society value and the criteria they use to rank other members depend on events in the society's history, its geographic location, its level of development in the world, the society's political philosophy, and the decisions of those in power. Powerful individuals are more likely to get the best positions, most desirable mates, and the greatest opportunities. They may have power because of birth status, personality characteristics, age, physical attractiveness, education, intelligence, wealth, race, family background, occupation, religion, or ethnic group—whatever the basis for power is in that particular society. Those with power have advantages that perpetuate their power, and they try to hold onto those advantages through laws, custom, power, or ideology.

Consider your own social ranking. You were born into a family that holds a position in society—upper, middle, or lower class, for instance. The position of your family influences the neighborhood in which you live and where you shop, go to school, and attend religious services. Most likely, you and your family carry out the tasks of daily living in your community with others of similar position. Your position in the stratification system affects the opportunities available to you and the choices you make in life. The social world model at the beginning of the chapter provides a visual image of the social world and socioeconomic stratification. The stratification process affects everything from individuals' social rankings at the micro level of analysis to positions of countries in the global system at the macro level.

Micro-Level Prestige and Influence

Remember how some of your peers on the playground were given more respect than others? Their high regard may have come from belonging to a prestigious family, having a dynamic or domineering personality, or owning symbols that distinguished them—"cool" clothing, a desirable bicycle, expensive toys, or a fancy car. This is stratification at its beginning stage.

Wealth, power, and prestige are accorded to those individuals who have *cultural capital* (knowledge and access to important information in the society) and *social capital* (networks with others who have influence). Individual qualities such as leadership, personality, sense of humor, self-confidence, quick-wittedness, physical attractiveness, or ascribed characteristics—such as the most powerful gender or ethnic group—influence cultural and social capital.

Meso-Level Access to Resources

Often, our individual status in the society is shaped by our access to resources available through organizations and institutions. Our status is learned and reinforced in the family through the socialization process. We learn grammar and manners that affect our success in school, for example. Educational organizations treat children differently according

Prince William and Prince Harry of the United Kingdom live lives of extraordinary privilege, but their status may also limit their understanding of common people and enjoyment of some everyday pleasures of group camaraderie and friendship. This is in sharp contrast to everyday lives of hard labor of many people in the world—whose standard of wealth may be ownership of a single horse. The young men below travel to their village in Afghanistan by horse.

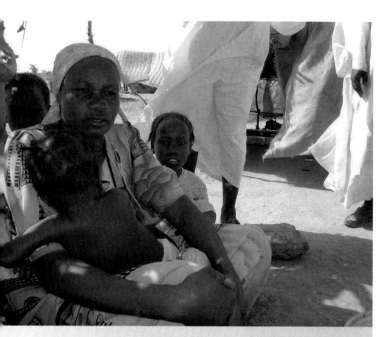

A displaced woman and her children sit beneath a temporary shelter at a refugee camp in South Darfur. A disproportionate number of displaced civilians in the camps are women and children. Although such refugees are clean and tidy people, their disrupted lives often result in illness and famine.

Even in affluent North America, some people are homeless and spend nights on sidewalks, in parks, or in homeless shelters that are often dangerous and very noisy and have no privacy. Sleeping on a sidewalk actually offers more safety than being in an isolated area.

to their social status, and our religious affiliation is likely to reflect our social status. Political systems, including laws, the courts, and police, reinforce the stratification system. Access to health care often depends on one's position in the stratification system. Our position and connections in organizations have a profound impact on how we experience life and how we interact with other individuals and groups.

Macro-Level Factors Influencing Stratification

The economic system, which includes the occupational structure, level of technology, and distribution of wealth in a society, is often the basis for stratification. (See Map 7.1.) Haiti, located on the island of Hispanola, is the poorest country in the Western hemisphere and one of the poorest countries in the world, with little technology, few resources, and an occupational structure based largely on subsistence farming. Even its forest resources are almost gone as desperately poor people cut down the last trees for firewood and shelters, leaving the land to erode (Diamond 2005). The economy is collapsing, leaving many already poor people still more destitute and on the lowest rungs of the world's stratification system.

The economic position and geographic location of nations such as Haiti affect the opportunities available to individuals in those societies. If the economy is robust and diverse, people have more opportunity to raise their status than they would have in poor or stagnant economies. There are simply no opportunities for Haitians to get ahead. Thus, macro-level factors can shape the opportunity structure and distribution of resources.

One problem for Haiti is that it has few of the resources that many other countries in the global system take for granted—a strong educational system, well-paying jobs in a vibrant economy, productive land, an ample supply of water, money to pay workers, and access to the most efficient and powerful technology. Almost all societies stratify members, and societies themselves are stratified in the world system, so that each individual and nation experiences the world in unique ways. Stratification is one of the most powerful forces that we experience, but we are seldom conscious of how it works or how pervasive it is in our lives. This is the driving question sociologists ask when developing theories of stratification: How does it work?

Thinking Sociologically

Place yourself in the center of the social world model. Working outward from micro-level interactions toward the macro-level institutions, indicate what has influenced where you fall in the stratification system.

Theoretical Explanations of Stratification

Why do some people have more money, possessions, power, and prestige than others? We all have opinions about this

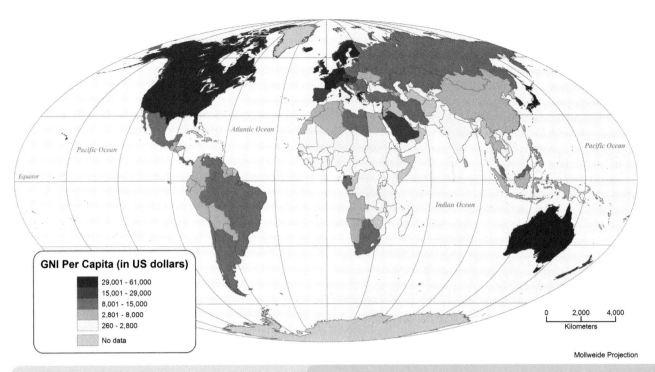

Map 7.1   Gross National Income per Capita in 2006

Source: World Bank. Map by Anna Versluis.

question. Sociologists also have developed explanations—theories that help explain stratification. Recall that theories provide a framework for asking questions to be studied. Just as your interpretation of a question may differ from your friends' ideas, sociologists have developed different explanations for stratification and tested these with research data. These explanations of social rankings range from individual micro-level to national and global macro-level theories.

Micro-Level Theory

Symbolic Interaction

Most of us have been at a social gathering, perhaps at a swank country club or in a local bar, where we felt out of place. Each social group has norms that members learn through the socialization process. These norms are recognized within that group and can make clueless outsiders feel like space aliens. People learn what is expected in their groups—family, peer group, social class—through interaction with others. For instance, children are rewarded or punished for behaviors appropriate or inappropriate to their social position. This process transmits and perpetuates social rankings. Learning our social position means learning values, speech patterns, consumption habits, appropriate group memberships (including religious affiliation), and even our self-concept.

Consider the example of different school socialization experiences of children. Students bring their language patterns,

values, experiences, and knowledge they have learned at home with them to school. These attributes are referred to as their *cultural capital*. Schools place children into courses and academic groups based in part on the labels they receive due to their cultural capital. Home environments can help children by expanding vocabularies; developing good grammar; experiencing concerts, art, and theater; visiting historical sites; providing reading materials; and modeling adults who like to read. The parents of higher class families tend to stress thinking skills as opposed to simply learning to obey authority figures. The result of this learning at home is that members of the middle and upper classes or higher castes get the best education, setting them up to be future leaders with better life chances (Ballantine and Hammack 2009). In this way, children's home experiences and education help reproduce the social class systems.

Symbols often represent social positions. Clothing, for example, sets up some people as special and privileged. In the 1960s, wearing blue jeans was a radical act by college students to reject status differences. It represented a solidarity with laborers and a rejection of the prestige and status games in our society. Today, the situation has changed, as young people wear expensive designer jeans that low-income people cannot afford. Drinking wine rather than beer, driving a Jaguar rather than a simpler mode of transportation, and living in a home that has six or eight bedrooms and 5,000 square feet is an expression of *conspicuous consumption*—displaying goods in a way that others will notice and that will presumably earn the owner respect (Veblen 1902). Thus, purchased products become symbols that are intended to define the person as someone of high status.

In India, many people must bathe every day in public in whatever water supply they can find. Homeless people must bathe this way, but here in Calcutta, even some people with homes would not have their own water supply.

Interaction theories help us understand how individuals learn and live their positions in society. Next, we consider theories that examine the larger social structures, processes, and forces that affect stratification and inequality: structural-functional and various forms of conflict theory.

Meso- and Macro-Level Theories

Structural-Functional Theory

Structural-functionalists (sometimes simply called functionalists) view stratification within societies as an inevitable—and probably necessary—part of the social world. The stratification system provides each individual a place or position in the social world and motivates individuals to carry out their roles. Societies survive by having an organized system into which each individual is born, where each is raised and where each contributes some part to the maintenance of the society.

The basic elements of the structural-functional theory of stratification were explained by Kingsley Davis and Wilbert Moore (1945), and their work still provides the main ideas of the theory today. Focusing on stratification by considering different occupations and how they are rewarded, Davis and Moore argue the following:

1. Positions in society are neither equally valued nor equally pleasant to perform. Some positions—such as physicians—are more highly valued because people feel they are very important to society. Therefore, societies must motivate talented individuals to prepare for and occupy the most important and difficult positions, such as being physicians.

2. Preparation requires talent, time, and money. To motivate talented individuals to make the sacrifices necessary to prepare for and assume difficult positions such as becoming a physician, differential rewards of income, prestige, power, or other valued goods must be offered. Thus, a doctor receives high income, prestige, and power as incentives.

3. The differences in rewards in turn lead to the unequal distribution of resources for occupations in society. Therefore, stratification is inevitable. The unequal distribution of status and wealth in society provides societies with individuals to fill necessary positions—such as willingness to undertake the stress of being chief executive officer of a corporation in a highly competitive field.

In the mid-20th century, functional theory provided sociologists with a valuable framework for studying stratification (Tumin 1953), but things do change. In the 21st century, new criteria such as controlling information and access to information systems have become important for determining wealth and status, making scientists and technicians a new class of elites. The society also experiences conflict over distribution of resources that functionalism does not fully explain.

Conflict Theory

Conflict theorists see stratification as the outcome of struggles for dominance and scarce resources, with some individuals in society taking advantage of others. Individuals and groups act in their own self-interest by trying to exploit others, leading inevitably to a struggle between those who have advantages and want to keep them and those who want a larger share of the pie.

Conflict theory developed in a time of massive economic transformation. With the end of the feudal system, economic displacement of peasants, and the rise of urban factories as major employers, a tremendous gap between the rich and the poor evolved. This prompted theorists to ask several basic questions related to stratification: (1) How do societies produce necessities—food, clothing, housing? (2) How are relationships between rich and poor people shaped by this process? and (3) How do many people become alienated in their routine, dull jobs in which they have little involvement and no investment in the end product?

Karl Marx (1818–1883), considered the father of conflict theory, lived during this time of industrial transformation. Marx described four possible ways to distribute wealth, according to (1) what each person needs, (2) what each person wants, (3) what each person earns, or (4) what each person can take. It was this fourth way, Marx believed, that was dominant in competitive capitalist societies (Cuzzort and King 2002; Marx and Engels 1955).

Marx viewed the stratification structure as composed of two major economically based social classes: the haves and the have-nots. The haves consisted of the capitalist bourgeoisie, whereas the have-nots were made up of the working class proletariat. Individuals in the same social class had similar lifestyles, shared ideologies, and held common outlooks on social life. The struggle over resources between haves and have-nots was the cause of conflict (Hurst 2006).

The haves control what Marx called the means of production—money, materials, and factories (Marx [1844] 1964). The haves dominate because the lower class have-nots cannot earn enough money to change their positions. The norms and values of the haves dominate the society because of their power and make the distribution of resources seem "fair" and justified. Social control mechanisms including laws, religious beliefs, educational systems, political structures and policies, and police or military force ensure continued control by the haves.

The unorganized lower classes can be exploited as long as they do not develop a class consciousness—a shared awareness of their poor status in relation to the means of production (control of the production process). Marx contended that, with the help of intellectuals who believed in the injustice of the exploited poor, the working class would develop a class consciousness, rise up, and overthrow the haves, culminating in a classless society in which wealth would be shared (Marx and Engels 1955).

Unlike the structural-functionalists, then, conflict theorists maintain that money and other rewards are not necessarily given to those in the most important positions in the society. Can we argue that a rock star or baseball player is more necessary for the survival of society than a teacher or police officer? Yet, the pay differential is tremendous. Conflict theorists are not convinced that our social reward system (levels of payment) is rooted in enticing people to make sacrifices to perform the "most important" tasks in the society. These high prestige positions often go to sons and daughters of elites.

Not all of the predictions of Karl Marx have come true. No truly classless societies have developed, but some developments have moved in that direction. Labor unions arose to unite and represent the working class and put them in a more powerful position vis-à-vis the capitalists, manager and technician positions emerged to create a large middle class, some companies moved to employee ownership, and workers gained legal protection from government legislative bodies in most industrial countries (Dahrendorf 1959).

Even societies that claim to be classless, such as China, have privileged classes and poor peasants. In recent years, the Chinese government has allowed more private ownership of shops, businesses, and other entrepreneurial efforts, motivating many Chinese citizens to work long hours at

Celebrity Oprah Winfrey (top) is paid millions of dollars each year to entertain the public, while the public school teacher in the bottom photo would take 30 years of teaching hundreds of children to read before her total cumulative income for her entire career would add up to one million dollars.

their private businesses to "get ahead." The only classless societies are a few small hunter-gatherer groups that lack extra resources allowing some to accumulate wealth.

Some theorists criticize Marx for his focus on only the economic system, pointing out that noneconomic factors enter into the stratification struggle as well. Max Weber (1864–1920), an influential theorist, amended Marx's theory by considering other elements in addition to economic forces. He agreed with Marx that group conflict is inevitable, that economics is one of the key factors in stratification systems, and that those in power try to perpetuate their positions. However, he added two other influential factors that he argued determine stratification in modern industrial societies: power and prestige, discussed later in this chapter. Sometimes, these are identified as the "three Ps": property, power, and prestige.

Recent theorists suggest that using three Ps, we can identify five classes—capitalists, managers, the petty bourgeoisie, workers, and the underclass—rather than just haves and have-nots. *Capitalists* own the means of production, and they purchase and control the labor of others. *Managers* sell their labor to capitalists and manage the labor of others for the capitalists. The *petty bourgeoisie*, such as small shop or business owners, own some means of production but control little labor of others; nevertheless, they have modest prestige, power, and property (Sernau 2005). *Workers* sell their labor to capitalists and are low in all three Ps. The *underclass* has virtually no property, power, or prestige.

In the modern world, as businesses become international and managerial occupations continue to grow, conflict theorists argue that workers are still exploited but in different ways. Owners get more income than is warranted by their responsibilities—for example, the CEO of Office Depot received $12 million in 2007 (Porter 2007)—and better educated and skilled people get more income than is warranted by the differential in education (Wright 2000). Moreover, the labor that produces our clothes, cell phones, digital cameras, televisions, and other products is increasingly provided by impoverished people around the world working for low wages at multinational corporations (Bonacich and Wilson 2005). In rich countries, service providers receive low wages at fast-food chains and box stores such as Wal-Mart (Ehrenreich 2001, 2005). One controversial question is whether multinational corporations are bringing opportunity to poor countries or exploiting them, as many conflict theorists contend (Wallerstein 2004).

Thinking Sociologically

Is it possible for a society to be truly "classless" with shared wealth? Why or why not? What empirical evidence might support your position?

The Evolutionary Theory of Stratification: A Synthesis

Evolutionary theory (Lenski 1966; Nolan and Lenski 2008) borrows assumptions from both structural-functional and conflict theories in an attempt to determine how scarce resources are distributed and how that distribution results in stratification. The basic ideas are as follows: (1) to survive, people must cooperate; (2) despite this, conflicts of interest occur over important decisions that benefit one individual or group over another; (3) valued items such as money and status are always in demand and in short supply; (4) there is likely to be a struggle over these scarce goods; and (5) customs or traditions in a society often prevail over rational criteria in determining distribution of scarce resources. After the minimum survival needs of both individuals and the society are met, power determines who gets the surplus: prestige, luxury living, the best health care, and so forth. Lenski believes that privileges (including wealth) flow from having power, and prestige usually results from having access to both power and privilege (Hurst 2006).

Lenski (1966; Nolan and Lenski 2008) tested his theory by studying societies at different levels of technological development, ranging from simple to complex. He found that the degree of inequality increases with technology until it reaches the advanced industrial stage. For instance, in subsistence-level hunting and gathering societies, little surplus is available, and everyone's needs are met to the extent possible. As surplus accumulates in agrarian societies, those who acquire power also control surpluses, and they use this to benefit their friends and relations. However, even if laws are made by those in power, the powerful must share some of the wealth or fear being overthrown. Interestingly, when societies finally reach the advanced industrial stage, inequality is moderated. This happens because people in various social classes enjoy greater political participation and because more resources are available to be shared in the society.

Lenski's (1966; Nolan and Lenski 2008) theory explains many different types of societies by synthesizing elements of both structural-functional and conflict theory. For instance, evolutionary theory takes into consideration the structural-functional idea that talented individuals need to be motivated to make sacrifices by allowing private ownership to motivate them. Individuals will attempt to control as much wealth, power, and prestige as possible, according to this view, resulting in potential conflict as some accumulate more wealth than others (Nolan and Lenski 2008). The theory also recognizes exploitation leading to inequality, a factor that conflict theorists find in capitalist systems of stratification. The reality is that while some inequality may be useful in highly complex societies, there is far more stratification in the United States than seems necessary. Indeed, extraordinary amounts of differential access to resources may even undermine productivity by making upward mobility so impossible that the most talented people are not always those in the most demanding and responsible jobs.

The amount of inequality differs in societies, according to evolutionary theorists, because of different levels of technological development. Because industrialization brings surplus wealth, a division of labor, advanced technology, and interdependence among members of a society, no one individual can control all the important knowledge, skills, or capital resources. Therefore, this eliminates the two extremes of haves and have-nots because resources are more evenly distributed.

The symbolic interaction, structural-functional, conflict, and evolutionary theories provide different explanations for understanding stratification in modern societies. These theories are the basis for micro- and macro-level discussions of stratification. Our next step is to look at some factors that influence an individual's position in a stratification system and the ability to change that position.

Thinking Sociologically

According to the theories discussed above, what are some reasons for *your* position in the stratification system?

 INDIVIDUALS' SOCIAL STATUS: THE MICRO LEVEL

You are among the world's elite. Only about 3% of the world's population ever enters the halls of academia, and fewer than 1% have a college degree. However, that number is expanding rapidly as countries such as China provide higher education opportunities to more students to support their growing economies. In 2005, 16 million Chinese students were enrolled, surpassing the U.S. enrollment. By 2010, the worldwide enrollment in higher education is likely to be 120 million, up from 100 million a few years ago (Daniel, Kanwar, and Uvalic-Trumbic 2006).

Yet, being able to afford the time and money for college is a luxury. It is beyond the financial or personal resources of 99% of people in the world. Spending time and money now to improve life in the future has little relevance to those struggling to survive each day. Considered in this global perspective, college students learn professional skills and have advantages that billions of other world citizens will never know or even imagine.

In the United States, access to higher education is greater than in many other countries because there are more levels of entry—technical and community colleges, large state universities, and private four-year colleges, to name a few. However, with limited government help, most

students must have financial resources to help pay tuition and the cost of living. Many students do not realize that the prestige of the college they choose makes a difference in their future opportunities. Those students born into wealth can afford better preparation for entrance exams as well as tutors or courses to increase SAT scores. They often attend private prep schools and gain acceptance to prestigious colleges that open opportunities not available to those attending the typical state university or non-elite colleges (Persell 2005).

Ascribed characteristics, such as gender, can also affect one's chances for success in life. In Japan and a number of other countries, the imbedded gender stratification system makes it difficult for women to rise in the occupational hierarchy. Many Japanese women earn college degrees but often leave employment after getting married and having children (Japan Institute of Labor 2002). Of 2,396 companies surveyed, the number with women directors was just 72 (less than 3%). Furthermore, Japanese women hold only 2% of all corporate board seats, and few are on boards of directors (Globe Women's Business Network 2006). Issues of gender stratification will be examined in more depth in Chapter 9, but they intersect with socioeconomic class and must be viewed as part of a larger pattern of inequality in the social world.

Individual Life Chances

Life chances refer to your opportunities, depending on your achieved and ascribed status in society. That you are in college, probably have health insurance and access to health care, and are likely to live into your late 70s or 80s are factors directly related to your life chances. Let us consider several examples of how placement in organizations at the meso level affects individual experiences and has global ramifications.

Education

Although education is valued by most individuals, the cost of books, clothing, shoes, transportation, child care, and time taken from income-producing work may be insurmountable barriers to attendance from grade school through college. Economically disadvantaged students in most countries are more likely to attend less prestigious and less expensive institutions if they attend high school or university at all.

One's level of education affects many aspects of life, including political, religious, and marital attitudes and behavior. Generally speaking, the higher the education level, the more active individuals are in political life, the more mainstream or conventional their religious affiliation, the more likely they are to marry into a family with both economic and social capital, the more stable the marriage, and the more likely they are to have good health.

Health, Social Conditions, and Life Expectancy

Pictures on the news of children starving and dying dramatically illustrate global inequalities. The poorest countries in the world are in sub-Saharan Africa, where most individuals eat poorly, are susceptible to diseases, have great stress in their daily lives just trying to survive, and die at young ages compared to the developed world. (See Table 7.1.)

If you have a sore throat, you can usually get an appointment to see your doctor. Yet, many people in the world will never see a doctor. Access to health care requires doctors and medical facilities, money for transportation and treatment, access to child care, and released time from other tasks to get to a medical facility. The poor sometimes do not have these luxuries. By contrast, the affluent eat better food, are less exposed to polluted water and unhygienic conditions, and are able to pay for medical care and drugs when they do have ailing health. Even causes of death illustrate the differences between people at different places in the stratification hierarchy. For example, in the poor Global South, shorter life expectancies and deaths, especially among children, are due to controllable infectious diseases such as cholera, typhoid, tuberculosis, and other respiratory ailments. By contrast, in affluent countries, heart disease and cancer are the most common causes of death, and most deaths are of people over the age of 65. (See Tables 14.6 and 14.7 on page 488.) So whether considered locally or globally, access to health care resources makes a difference in life chances. To an extent, the chance to have a long and healthy life is a privilege of the elite. Again, globally speaking, if you are reading this book as part of a college course, you are part of the elite. The impact of social conditions on life expectancy is especially evident if we compare cross-national data. Countries with the shortest life expectancy at birth illustrate the pattern. These countries lack adequate health care, immunizations, and sanitation; have crises of war and displacement of population resulting in refugees; and experience illnesses, epidemics, and famine. Even a drought has more tragic impact when no other aid resources are available to help families cope. By studying Table 7.1, you can compare life expectancy with two other measures of life quality for the poorest and richest countries: the gross national product (GNP) per capita income—the average amount of money each person has per year—and the infant mortality rates (death rates for babies).

Thinking Sociologically

What questions do the data in Table 7.1 raise regarding mortality and life expectancy rates?

Note that average life expectancy in poor countries is as low as 39 years, income as low as $220 a year (many of the people in these populations are subsistence farmers), and infant mortality is as high as 184 deaths in the first year of life for every 1,000 births (World Bank 2006). Numbers for the richest countries are dramatically different.

The United States has much larger gaps between rich and poor people than most other wealthy countries, resulting in higher poverty rates (more people at the bottom rungs of the stratification ladder). This is, in turn, reflected in health statistics, with infant mortality rates of 6.4 deaths in the first year of

Table 7.1	**Life Expectancy, per Capita Income, and Infant Mortality for Richest and Poorest Countries**						
Poorest Countries	Life Expectancy, 2007 (in years)	Per Capita GNP ($) 2005	Infant Mortality 2007	Richest Countries	Life Expectancy, 2007 (in years)	Per Capita GNP ($) 2005	Infant Mortality 2007
Swaziland	39.6	1,934	71	Japan	82.6	38,980	2.8
Mozambique	42.1	310	110	Hong Kong	82.2	27,670	2.9
Zambia	42.4	490	101	Iceland	81.8	46,320	3.3
Sierre Leone	42.6	220	158	Switzerland	81.7	54,930	4.3
Lesotho	42.6	960	80	Australia	81.2	32,220	4.6
Angola	42.7	1,350	184	Spain	80.9	25,360	4.3
Zimbabwe	43.5	340	51	Sweden	80.9	41,060	2.8
Afghanistan	43.8	N/A	157	United States	78.2*	43,740	6.4

Source: World Fact Book 2008 for life expectancy; Swivel 2007 for infant mortality; World Bank 2006 for per capita income.

Note: Infant mortality is per 1,000 live births.

*United States is number 38 in life expectancy.

life per 1,000 births. Sweden and Japan have the lowest infant mortality rates in the world, a measure of their health standards (World Fact Book 2007). Deaths of children under 5 are highest in Sierre Leone (270 per 1,000), Angola (260), and Afghanistan (257). More than 26,000 children under five years old die each day on average. The world average infant mortality is 43.5 per 1,000 (Swivel 2007). This evidence supports the assertion that health, illness, and death rates are closely tied to socioeconomic stratification. Race and gender interact with social class in ways that often have negative results.

Thinking Sociologically

What are some factors at the micro, meso, and macro levels that affect your life expectancy and that of your family?

Family Life and Child-Rearing Patterns

In many countries, higher social class correlates with later marriage and lower divorce rates. Members of lower classes tend to marry earlier and have more children. Because of tensions from life stresses including money problems, they often have less stable marriages and more instances of divorce and single parenthood.

Child-rearing patterns are also affected by social rankings and serve to reinforce one's social class status. For instance, lower class families in the United States tend to use more physical punishment to discipline children than middle-class parents, who use guilt, reasoning, time-outs, and other non-physical sanctions to control children's behavior.

Individual Lifestyles

An individual's **lifestyle** includes attitudes, values, beliefs, behavior patterns, and other aspects of one's place in the social world, which are shaped through the socialization process. As individuals grow up, the behaviors and attitudes consistent with their culture and family's status in society become internalized through the process of socialization. Lifestyle is not a simple matter of having money. Acquiring money—say, by winning a lottery—cannot buy a completely new lifestyle (Bourdieu and Passeron 1977). This is because values and behaviors are ingrained in our self-concept from childhood. You may have material possessions at your disposal, but that does not mean you have the lifestyle of the upper-class rich and famous. Consider some examples of factors related to your individual lifestyle: attitudes toward achievement, political involvement, and religious membership.

Attitudes Toward Achievement

These differ by social status and are generally closely correlated with life chances. Motivation to get ahead and beliefs

The poor around the world often get health care at clinics or emergency rooms, if they have access to care, where they wait for hours to see a health care provider. This is true in the United States as well as in this mother-child health clinic in Kisumu, Kenya. On the other hand, those with resources may have an entire team of physicians working on their case.

about what you can achieve are in part products of your upbringing and what opportunities you think are available. Even tolerance for those different from yourself is influenced by your social status.

Religious Membership

Religion also correlates with social status variables of education, occupation, and income. For instance, in the United States, upper-class citizens are found disproportionately in Episcopalian, Unitarian, and Jewish religious groups,

Clothing not only covers our bodies but also acts as a symbol of our social status and reflects our lifestyles. These children attend a private school in England.

whereas lower class citizens are attracted to Nazarene, Southern Baptist, Jehovah's Witnesses, and other holiness and fundamentalist sects. Each religious group attracts members predominantly from one social class, as will be illustrated in Chapter 12 on religion (Kosmin and Lackman 1993; Roberts 2004).

Political Behavior

What political preferences one holds and how one votes are also affected by social status. Around the world, upper-middle classes are most supportive of elite or pro-capitalist agendas because these agendas support their way of life; lower working-class members are least supportive (Wright 2000). Generally, the lower the social class, the more likely people are to vote for liberal parties (Kerbo 2008), and the higher the social status, the more likely people are to vote conservative on economic issues consistent with protecting wealth (Brooks and Manza 1997).

In the United States, members of the lower class tend to vote liberal on economic issues, favoring government intervention to improve economic conditions. However, those with lower levels of education and income vote conservatively on many social issues relating to minorities and civil liberties (e.g., rights for homosexuals, gay marriage, and abortion) (Gilbert and Kahl 2003; Jennings 1992; Kerbo 2008). In the 2008 election, especially regarding congressional and Senate races, many of these voters had to make choices about economic policies they liked and whether those policies were more important than their preferences on some of the social issues.

The reality is that some people experience high status on one trait, especially a trait that is ascribed, but may experience low status in another area. For example, a professor may have high status but low income. Max Weber called this unevenness in one's social standing *status inconsistency*. Individuals who experience such status inconsistency, especially if they are treated as if their lowest ascribed status is the most important one, are likely to be very liberal and to experience discontent with the current system (Weber 1946).

People tend to associate with others like themselves, perpetuating and reinforcing lifestyles. In fact, people often avoid contact with others whose lifestyles are outside their familiar and comfortable patterns. Life chances and lifestyles are deeply shaped by the type of stratification system that is prevalent in the nation. Such life experiences as hunger, the unnecessary early death of family members, or the pain of seeing one's child denied opportunities are all experienced at the micro level, but their causes are usually rooted in events and actions at other levels of the social world. This brings us to our next question: Can an individual change positions in a stratification system?

Thinking Sociologically

Describe your own lifestyle and life chances. How do these relate to your socialization experience and your family's position in the stratification system? What difference do they make in your life?

SOCIAL MOBILITY: THE MICRO-MESO CONNECTION

The Kobe Bryants and Peyton Mannings of the world make millions of dollars—at least for the duration of their playing careers. Each hoop or touchdown throw is worth thousands of dollars. These riches give hope to those in rags that if they "play hard" on their local hoops, they too may be on the field or court making millions. Problem is that the chances of making it big are so small that such hopes are some of the cruelest hoaxes faced by young African Americans and others in the lower or working class. Therefore, it is a false promise to think of sports as the road to opportunity (Dufur and Feinberg 2007; Edwards 2000). The chances of success or even of moving up a little in the social stratification system through sports are very small.

Those few minority athletes who do "make it big" and become models for young people experience "stacking," holding certain limited positions in a sport. When retired from playing, few black athletes rise in the administrative hierarchy of the sports of football and baseball, although basketball has a better record of hiring black coaches and managers. Thus, when young people put their hopes and energies into developing their muscles and physical skills, they may lose the possibility of moving up in the social class system, which requires developing their minds and their technical skills. Misplaced focus thwarts their dreams of upward social mobility. Of course, systematic discrimination, discussed in the next chapter, also makes upward mobility—even in the world of sports—a difficult prospect.

The whole idea of changing one's social position is called social mobility. **Social mobility** refers to the "extent to which people move up or down in the class system, especially from one generation to the next" (Gilbert 2008:123). What is the likelihood that your status will be different from that of your parents over your lifetime? Will you start a successful business? Marry into wealth? Win the lottery? Experience downward mobility due to loss of a job, illness, or inability to complete your education? What factors at different levels of analysis might influence your chances of mobility? These are some of the questions addressed in this section and the next.

Four issues dominate the analysis of mobility: (1) types of social mobility, (2) methods of measuring social mobility, (3) factors that affect social mobility, and (4) whether there is a "land of opportunity."

Types of Social Mobility

Most people believe that they can improve their social class ranking with hard work and good education. *Intergenerational mobility* refers to change in status compared to one's parents' status, usually resulting from education and occupational attainment. If you are the first to go to college in your family and you become a computer

programmer, this would represent intergenerational mobility. The amount of intergenerational mobility in a society measures the degree to which a society has an **open class system**—one that allows movement between classes.

Intragenerational mobility (not to be confused with *intergenerational mobility*) refers to the change in position in a single individual's life. For instance, if you begin your career as a teacher's aide and end it as a school superintendent, that is intragenerational mobility. However, mobility is not always up. *Vertical mobility* refers to movement up or down in the hierarchy and sometimes involves changing social classes. You may start your career as a waitress, go to college part-time, get a degree in engineering, and get a more prestigious and higher paying job, resulting in upward mobility. Alternatively, you could lose a job and take one at a lower status, a reality for many when the economy is doing poorly.

How Much Mobility Is There? Measures of Social Mobility

Can one move up in the class system? One traditional method of measuring mobility is to compare fathers and sons. Surveys ask men about their occupations and those of their fathers or sons. Table 7.2 reflects questions asked of U.S. fathers about their son's mobility. Several conclusions can be derived from this table (Gilbert 2008):

1. There is a high level of occupational inheritance—sons following fathers into jobs at the very same occupational level.

Table 7.2 **Outflow From Father's Occupation to Son's Occupation**

	Son's Occupation (in percent)					
	Upper-White Collar	Lower-White Collar	Upper Manual	Lower Manual	Farm	Total
Father's Occupation						
Upper-White Collar	42	31	12	15	1	100
Lower-White Collar	34	33	13	19	1	100
Upper Manual	20	20	29	29	1	100
Lower Manual	20	22	20	36	2	100
Farm	16	18	19	35	12	100
Total (N = 3,398)	27	25	19	27	3	100

Summary of mobility:

Up	Stable	Down	Total
41	33	26	100

Source: Gilbert 2008:124.

Note: Rows but not columns add to 100%. For example, read across the row that begins with "lower manual" on far left to trace the sons of fathers who held unskilled "lower manual jobs." While 20% rose to upper-white collar (professional or managerial) positions, the largest group (36%) followed their fathers into unskilled manual jobs.

2. The higher the father's occupation level, the better the son's chances for occupational achievement.

3. There is also considerable movement up and down the occupational ladder from one generation to the next.

4. By a considerable margin, sons are more likely to move up than down. (Gilbert 2008:124–25)

Determining the mobility of women is more difficult because they often have lower level positions and their mothers may not have worked full-time. However, Table 7.3 presents a comparison of fathers' and daughters' occupations similar to that of men above. One conclusion that can be drawn is that both women's and men's occupational attainment is powerfully influenced by class origins.

Factors Affecting an Individual's Mobility

Why are some people successful at moving up the ladder while others lag behind? Mobility is driven by many factors, from your family's *cultural capital* to global economic variables. One's chances to move up depend on micro-level factors—one's family background, socialization, personal characteristics, and education—and macro-level factors such as the occupational structure and economic status of countries, population changes, the numbers of people vying for similar positions, discrimination based on gender or ethnicity, and the global economic situation.

The study of mobility is complicated because these key variables are interrelated: The macro-level forces (such as

the economy, opportunity, and occupational structure in a country) are related to meso-level factors (such as access to education and opportunities) and micro-level factors (such as socialization and family background) (Blau and Duncan 1967). An individual's background accounts for nearly half of the factors affecting occupational attainment (Jencks 1979). Numerous models and studies have attempted to refine measures of mobility. Consider a few of the variables that can make a difference in your chances for mobility.

Socialization

In industrial societies, change of jobs is most likely to occur at the same socioeconomic level because our socialization and training prepare us for certain jobs (Sernau 2005). Our family background socializes us into certain behavior patterns and expectations most relevant to particular occupations.

Education, Skills, and Social Ties

College is one key to upward mobility. Although not all those with a college degree are successful, few have a chance to be successful without a college degree (Lareau 2003). We can see from Table 7.4 that most students with high ability from high-status families go to college, while high ability, low-status high school graduates do so less often (83% versus 51%). Note that a student with top cognitive ability but from the lowest income families is less likely to enroll in college than someone from the third quartile of cognitive ability but the top socioeconomic quartile of society (51% versus 57%).

When we look at actual college degrees, the pattern is more extreme, with diplomas going disproportionately to

Table 7.3   **Outflow From Father's Occupation to Daughter's Occupation**

	Daughter's Occupation (in percent)					
	Professional and Managerial	Sales and Clerical	Service	Blue Collar	Farm	Total
Father's Occupation						
Upper-White Collar	54	33	9	3	1	100
Lower-White Collar	49	34	11	6	*	100
Upper Manual	35	37	18	8	1	100
Lower Manual	32	39	19	9	1	100
Farm	34	28	22	14	2	100
Total (*N* = 3,398)	27	25	19	27	3	100

Source: Gilbert 2008:127.

Note: Rows but not columns add to 100%. For example, read across the row that begins with "upper-white collar" on far left to trace the daughters of fathers who held upper white-collar jobs. The largest group (54%) followed their fathers into upper-white collar jobs, and only 3% ended up in blue-collar occupations.

* Under .5%

These men may both be good fathers—caring, supportive, and offering their children the wisdom and skills they know can help their children in the working world. One of these fathers, however, is likely to offer more cultural capital and more opportunities because of his education, family background, and networks with others in positions of influence.

Table 7.4 **College Attendance by Social Class and Cognitive Ability (percent in college)**

Cognitive Ability Quartile	Family Socioeconomic Status Quartile			
	Top	3rd	2nd	Lowest
Top	83	74	63	51
Second	69	51	42	33
Third	57	40	24	23
Lowest	35	20	13	13
Total (N = 3,398)	69	48	33	24

Source: Gilbert 2008:142.

students in the top status groups (50%), compared to only 10% of students from the bottom half of income levels. If American society was truly a meritocracy, as is so often claimed, one would expect cognitive ability to be the most important variable (Gilbert 2008).

Many poor people lack education and skills such as interviewing and getting recommendations needed to get or change jobs in the postindustrial occupational structure (Ehrenreich 2001, 2005; McLeod 2004). Isolated from social networks in organizations, they lack contacts to help in the job search. The type of education system one attends also affects mobility. In Germany, Britain, France, and some other European countries, children are "streamed" (tracked) into either college preparatory courses or more general curricula, and the rest of their occupational experience reflects this early placement decision in school. In the United States, educational opportunities remain more open to those who can afford them.

Occupational Structure and Economic Vitality

The global structure, a country's position as a rich or poor country in the world system, affects the chances for individual mobility. As agricultural work is decreasing and technology jobs increasing (Hurst 2006), these changes in the composition and structure of occupations affect individual opportunity. The health of a country's economy in the global system shapes employment chances of individuals.

Poverty on the Hopi reservation in Arizona is such that much of this town looks like it is part of a country in the Global South.

Table 7.5 Median Annual Earnings by Race/Ethnicity and Sex		
Race/Gender	*Earnings*	*Wage Ratio*
White men	$47,814	100.0%
White women	35,151	73.5
Black men	34,480	72.1
Black women	30,398	63.6
Hispanic men	27,490	57.5
Hispanic women	24,738	51.7
All men	$42,210	
All women	$32,649	
Wage gap		77.4%

Source: U.S. Census Bureau (2007).

Population Trends

The fertility rates, or number of children born at a given time, influence the number of people who will be looking for jobs. The U.S. nationwide baby boom that occurred following World War II resulted in a flood of job applicants and downward intergenerational mobility for the many who could not find work comparable to their social class at birth. By contrast, the smaller group following the baby boomer generation had fewer competitors for entry-level jobs. Baby boomers hold many of the executive and leadership positions today, so promotion has been hard for the next cohort. As baby boomers retire, opportunities will open up, and mobility should increase.

Gender and Ethnicity

Many women and ethnic minority groups, locked in a cycle of poverty, dependence, and debt, have little chance of changing their status. Women in the U.S. workforce, for instance, are more likely than men to be in dead-end clerical and service positions with no opportunity for advancement. In the past three decades, the wage gap between women and men has narrowed, and women now earn 73.5% of what men earn for similar jobs (U.S. Census Bureau 2007a), compared to 60% in 1980 (U.S. Department of Labor 2005). African American men make 72.1% and African American women 63.6% of white men's earnings for comparable jobs. Table 7.5 shows the earnings for white males and the percentage of those earnings for other gender and ethnic groups.

The competition for jobs among baby boomers is more intense because more women have been looking for jobs. In most cases, the economy has adjusted to the larger workforce. Special circumstances such as war have often allowed women and others who were denied access to good jobs to get a "foot in the door" and actually enhance their upward mobility. Another factor affecting career success by women is that more females than males are earning college degrees.

Some people experience *privilege* (e.g., white, European-born, native-speaking males who are in the middle class or higher), whereas some experience *disprivilege* due to socioeconomic status, ethnicity, gender, or a combination of these. Be aware that various forms of inequality intersect in U.S. society in highly complex ways.

The Interdependent Global Market and International Events

If the Asian stock market hiccups, it sends ripples through world markets. If high-tech industries in Japan or Europe falter, North American companies in Silicon Valley, California, may go out of business, costing many professionals their lucrative positions. In ways such as these, the interdependent global economies affect national and local economies, and that affects individual families.

Whether individuals move from "rags to riches" is not determined solely by their personal ambition and work ethic. Mobility for the individual, a micro-level event, is linked to a variety of events at other levels of the social world.

Thinking Sociologically

Do you know individuals who have lost jobs because of economic slowdowns at the meso or macro level or who have gotten jobs because of economic booms and opening opportunities? What changes have occurred in their mobility and social class?

Is There a "Land of Opportunity"? Cross-Cultural Mobility

Television shows bombard us with images of rich bachelors and the desirability of marrying a millionaire to improve one's status in life. By playing a game of trivia on TV, we too might "strike it rich" by answering correctly and thus become rich and famous. Alternatively, we might win the lottery by buying a ticket at our local grocery. Although we may know someone who has this good fortune, in reality, these quick fixes and easy get-rich-fast plans are unrealistic, and the chances of us profiting are slim indeed.

The question for this section is whether you have a better chance to improve your status in England, Japan, the United States, or some other country. However, the answer is not simple. If there is a land of opportunity where individuals can be assured of improving their economic and social position, it is not easy to identify, as many variables affect the opportunity structure. Countless immigrants have sought better opportunities in new locations. Perhaps, your parents or ancestors did just this. The reality of the "land of opportunity" depends on the historical period and economic conditions, social events, and political attitudes toward foreigners when the immigrants came, their personal skills, and their ability to blend into the new society.

During economic growth periods, many immigrants have found great opportunities for mobility in the United States and Europe. Early industrial tycoons in railroads, automobiles, steel, and other industries are examples of success stories. Today, fortunes are being made in the high-tech industries of China, India, and other countries and in energy resources in Russia. The number of millionaires and billionaires in the world is increasing dramatically, yet, this is still a very small percentage of the world's population. In 2007, there were 946 billionaires globally, and 95,000 individuals had more than $30 million in 2006, 38,400 of those in North America (Merrill Lynch and Capgemini 2007). Such wealth eludes most people who immigrate and must work multiple low-paying jobs just to feed their families and stay out of poverty.

Opportunities for upward mobility have changed significantly with globalization. Many manufacturing jobs in the global economy have moved from the Global North to the Global South with cheap labor, reducing the number of unskilled and low-skilled jobs available in Global North countries. Since the 1970s, the earnings differential between high school graduates and college graduates has widened, leaving high school graduates struggling to find work that will support a family. Multinational corporations look for the cheapest sources of labor, mostly in the Global South, which features low taxes, no labor unions, few regulations, and many workers needing jobs, thus draining away low-skilled jobs from the United States.

Why the changes in the job structure? First, there are fewer demands for manufacturing jobs as service-producing jobs requiring higher education expand. Second, the increase in international trade results in demand for high-tech products from the United States, but fewer manufacturing products. New technologies and automation leave low-skilled workers in advanced countries without jobs. Third, the minimum-wage and low-wage jobs are all that is available to lower skilled workers, and labor unions have less influence on the wages and working conditions of these workers today (Gilbert 2008). High-tech positions are good news for those with college degrees and technical skills, but the replacement of laboring positions with service jobs in fast-food and box store chains (e.g., Wal-Mart, K-Mart, Home Depot, Lowe's) means a severe loss of genuine opportunity for living wages.

Although the new multinational industries springing up in Global South countries such as Malaysia, Thailand, and the Philippines provide opportunities for mobility to those of modest origins, much of the upward mobility in the world is taking place among those who come from small, highly educated families with individualistic achievement-oriented values and people who see education as a route to upward mobility (Blau and Duncan 1967; Featherman and Hauser 1978; Jencks 1979; Rothman 2005). They are positioned to take advantage of the changing occupational structure and high-tech jobs. As the gap between rich and poor individuals and countries widens, more individuals in the United States begin to move down rather than up in the stratification system.

What Are Your Chances for Mobility?

College education is the most important factor for high-income status in Global North countries. In fact, the economic rewards of a college degree have increased. Those with degrees become richer, and those without become poorer. This is because of *changes in occupational structures*, creating new types of jobs and a new social class with skills for the computer information age. These "social-cultural specialists" who work with ideas, knowledge, and technology contrast with the old middle class of technocrats, manufacturers, business owners, and executives (Florida 2002; Hurst 2006).

With the rapid growth of postindustrial economies and computer technologies, fewer unskilled workers are needed, resulting in underemployment or unemployment for this group. They will continue to live at the margins in information societies, forming the lower class. Do you know individuals who are being nickel-and-dimed in today's economic environment? The next "Sociology in Your Social World" discusses this situation.

Thinking Sociologically

What social factors in your society limit or enhance the likelihood of upward social mobility for you and your generation? Explain.

Sociology in Your Social World

Nickel-and-Dimed

Have you or has someone you know held a minimum-wage job? Did you have to support yourself and maybe other family members on that wage, or was it just pocket money? Millions in the United States live in this world of unskilled laborers, getting from $5.15 to $7 an hour for their work, and most rely on these wages to support themselves and their families.

Author Barbara Ehrenreich (2001) asked how individuals and families survive on these wages. To find out, she tried it herself. Living in several cities—Key West, Florida; Portland, Maine; and Minneapolis, Minnesota—she held jobs as a waitress, retail clerk at Wal-Mart, hotel housekeeper, and nursing home aide. Each job was physically and mentally demanding.

After describing the details of each job and the lives of her coworkers, Ehrenreich concludes that people are earning far less than they need to live. Her coworkers struggled to meet minimum housing costs (sometimes living in hotels or cars), bought cheap food, and shopped at thrift stores. They were also consistently struggling with transportation, child care, and health care. Many were also managing large debts.

The number of "working poor" is growing. Many states added work requirements for mothers to remain eligible for welfare benefits. These reforms became federal law when President Bill Clinton replaced Aid to Families with Dependent Children (AFDC) with Temporary Aid to Needy Families (TANF). Beyond work requirements, TANF also added time limits for welfare eligibility and eliminated increased benefits for families that grew while receiving assistance.

"The Economic Policy Institute recently reviewed dozens of studies of what constitutes a living wage and came up with an average figure of $30,000 a year for a family of one adult and two children, which amounts to a wage of $14 an hour" (Ehrenreich 2001:214). This budget includes health insurance, a telephone, and child care, but no extras, and it is more than most minimum-wage workers have. Upward mobility for this large group in the population is difficult if not impossible. Ehrenreich's research makes it clear: To be a society of at least minimal opportunity for all, we must reconsider economic policies to better address underpaid workers as well as the unemployed. Although many states have raised the minimum wage since *Nickel and Dimed* was published—and federal minimum wage is incrementally increasing to $7.25 by July 24, 2009—no state currently has a minimum wage that meets minimum living wage requirements by the Economic Policy Institute's calculation. Add to that the increases in costs of gas and food, and many U.S. citizens are struggling to make ends meet.

MAJOR STRATIFICATION SYSTEMS: MACRO-LEVEL ANALYSIS

Mansa's family works on a plantation in Mozambique. He tries in vain to pay off the debts left by his father's family. However hard he and his wife and children work, they will always be in debt because they cannot pay the total amount due for their hut or food from the owner's store. Basically, they are slaves—they do not have control over their own labor. They were born into this status, and there they will stay.

Imagine being born into a society in which you have no choices or options in life because of your family background, age, sex, and ethnic group. You cannot select an occupation that interests you, cannot choose your mate, cannot live in the part of town you favor. You see wealthy aristocrats parading their advantages and realize that this will never be possible for you. You can never own land or receive the education of your choice.

This situation is reality for millions of people in the world— they are born this way and will spend their lives in this plight. In **ascribed stratification systems**, such characteristics determine one's position in society. In contrast, **achieved stratification systems** allow individuals to earn positions through their ability and effort. For instance, in a class system, it is sometimes possible to achieve a higher ranking by working hard, obtaining education, gaining power, or doing other things that are highly valued in that culture.

Ascribed Status: Caste and Estate Systems

Caste systems, the most rigid ascribed systems, are maintained by cultural norms and social control mechanisms that are deeply imbedded in religious, political, and economic institutions. Individuals born into caste systems have predetermined occupational positions, marriage partners, residences, social associations, and prestige levels. A person's caste is easily recognized through clothing, speech patterns, family name and identity, skin color, or other distinguishing characteristics. From their earliest years, individuals learn their place in society through the process of socialization. To behave counter to caste prescriptions would be to go against religion and social custom and to risk not fitting into society. Religious ideas dictate that one's status after death (in Christian denominations) or one's next *reincarnation* or rebirth (in the Hindu tradition) also might be in jeopardy. Stability is maintained by the belief that people can be reborn into a higher status in the next life if they fulfill expectations in their ascribed position in this life. Thus, believers in both religions work hard in hopes of attaining a better life next time around. The institution of religion works together with the family, education, and economic and political institutions to shape (and sometimes reduce) both expectations and aspirations and to keep people in their prescribed places in caste systems.

The clearest example of a caste system is found in India. The Hindu religion holds that individuals are born into one of four *varna,* broad caste positions, or into a fifth group below the caste system, the *outcaste* group. The first and highest varna, called Brahmans, originally was made up of priests and scholars but now includes many leaders in society. The second varna, Kshatriyas or Rajputs, includes the original prince and warrior varna and now embraces much of the army and civil service. The Vaishyas, or merchants, are the third varna. The fourth varna, the Sudras, include peasants, artisans, and laborers.

The final layer, below the caste system, encompasses profoundly oppressed and broken people—"a people put aside"—referred to as untouchables, outcastes, *Chandalas* (a Hindu term), and *Dalits* (the name preferred by many "untouchables" themselves). Although the Indian Constitution of 1950 granted full social status to these citizens, and a law passed in 1955 made discrimination against them punishable, deeply rooted traditions are difficult to change. Caste distinctions are still very prevalent, especially in rural areas, as seen in the discussion in "Sociology Around the World."

Just as the position of individuals in caste systems is ascribed, estate systems are similarly rigid in stratifying individuals. **Estate systems** are characterized by the

These Aboriginal boys in Australia seem to be having fun as children, but their futures are determined by their place and family of birth. It is highly unlikely they will ever experience much affluence. Still, they may have rewarding lives surrounded by family if they are not absorbed into the larger world system that makes them dependent on a cash income. That is often what makes families vulnerable and forced to trade their children into slavery.

concentration of economic and political power in the hands of a small minority of political-military elite, with the peasantry tied to the land (Rothman 2005). During the Middle Ages, knights defended the realms and the religion of the nobles. Behind every knight in shining armor were peasants, sweating in the fields and paying for the knights' food, armor, and campaigns. For farming the land owned by the nobility, peasants received protection against invading armies and enough of the produce to survive. Their life was often miserable. If the crops were poor, they ate little. In a good year, they might save enough to buy a small parcel of land. A very few were able to become independent in this fashion.

Estate systems are based on ownership of land, the position one is born into, or military strength. An individual's

Sociology Around the World

The Outcastes of India

The Dalits—sometimes called "untouchables"—are the most impoverished people in India and some of the most impoverished in the world. While they live in incredible hardship, they are beginning to mobilize and demand rights as citizens of India and the world.

The village south of Madras in the state of Tamil Nadu was on an isolated dirt road, one kilometer from the nearest town. It consisted of a group of mud and stick huts with banana leaf–thatched roofs. As our group of students arrived, the Dalit villagers lined the streets to greet us—and stare. Many had never seen Westerners. They played drums and danced for us and threw flower petals at our feet in traditional welcome.

Through our translator, we learned something of their way of life. The adults work in the fields long hours each day, plowing and planting with primitive implements, earning about eight cents from the landowner, often not enough to pay for their daily bowl of rice. Occasionally, they catch a frog or bird to supplement their meal. In the morning, they drink rice gruel, and in the evening, they eat a bowl of rice with some spices. Women and children walk more than a kilometer to the water well—but the water is polluted during the dry season. There are no privies but the fields. As a result of poor sanitation, inadequate diet, and lack of health care, many people become ill and die from health problems that are easily cured in Western societies. For instance, lack of vitamin A, found in many fruits and vegetables to which they have little access, causes blindness in many village residents. Although the children have the right to go to the school in the closest village, many cannot

do so because they have no transportation, shoes, or money for paper, pencils, and books. Also, the families need them to work in the fields alongside their parents or help care for younger siblings. Many taboos rooted in tradition separate the Dalit from other Indians. For instance, they are forbidden to draw water from the village well, enter the village temple, or eat from dishes that might be used later by people of higher castes. The latter prohibition eliminates most dining at public establishments. About 95% are landless and earn a living below subsistence level.

Dalits who question these practices have been attacked and their houses burned. In one instance, 20 houses were burned on the birthday of Dr. Ambedkar, a leader in the Dalit rights movement. Official records distributed by the Human Rights Education Movement of India state that every hour, two Dalits are assaulted, three Dalit women are raped, two Dalits are murdered, and two Dalit houses are burned (*Dalit Liberation Education Trust* 1995; Thiagaraj 2006; Wilson 1993). This group on the bottom rung of the stratification system has a long fight ahead to gain the rights that many of us take for granted.

A few Dalit have migrated to cities, where they blend in, and some of these have become educated and are now leading the fight for the rights and respect guaranteed by law. Recently, unions and interest groups have been representing the Dalit, and some members turn to religious and political groups that are more sympathetic to their plight, such as Buddhists, Christians, or Communists.

One social activist, Henry Thiagaraj, has committed his life to improving conditions for the Dalit. Thiagaraj works on a micro, meso, and macro level. On the micro level, he suggests that those in power form Dalit youth and women *sangams* (activist groups) and organize the people who live in Dalit slums. At the meso level, Thiagaraj and other Dalit activists work to initiate micro lending to the Dalit and improve their education and labor training. On the macro level, Dr. Thiagarj works with non-government organizations (NGOs) to increase support for Dalit interests. He also works to improve media coverage of the Dalit to raise awareness of their experiences. Dr. Thiagaraj's (2007) book, *Human Rights from the Dalits' Perspective*, provides an outstanding retrospective of how India has addressed caste discrimination since the 1980s.

rank and legal rights are clearly spelled out, and arranged marriages and religion bolster the system. Estate systems existed in ancient Egypt, the Incan and Mayan civilizations, Europe, China, and Japan. Today, similar systems exist in some Central and South American, Asian, and African countries with large banana, coffee, and sugar plantations, as exemplified in the description of Mansa's life in Mozambique, which opened this chapter. Over time, development of a mercantile economy resulted in modifications in the estate system. Now, peasants often work the land in exchange for the right to live there and receive a portion of the produce.

Achieved Status: Social Class Systems

Social class systems of stratification are based on achieved status. Members of the same social class have similar income, wealth, and economic position. They also share comparable styles of living, levels of education, cultural similarities, and patterns of social interaction. Most of us are members of class-based stratification systems, and we take advantage of opportunities available to our social class. Our families, rich or poor, educated or unskilled, provide us with an initial social ranking and socialization experience. We tend to feel a kinship and sense of belonging with those in the same social class—our neighborhood and work group, our peers and friends. We think alike, share interests, and probably look up to the same people as a reference group. Our social class position is based on the three main factors determining positions in the stratification system: property, power, and prestige.

Compared with systems based on ascribed status, achieved status systems maintain that everyone is born with common legal status; everyone is equal before the law. In principle, all individuals can own property and choose their own occupations. However, in practice, most class systems pass privilege or poverty from one generation to the next. Individual upward or downward mobility is more difficult than the ideology invites people to believe.

Property, Power, and Prestige

This is the trio that, according to Max Weber, determines where individuals rank in relation to each other (Weber 1946, 1947). Positions in social stratification systems, according to Weber, are determined by these three elements and the opportunities the individual has to gain these. By **property (wealth)**, Weber refers to owning or controlling the means of production. **Power**, the ability to control others, includes not only the means of production but also the position one holds. **Prestige** involves the esteem and recognition one receives, based on wealth, position, or accomplishments. Table 7.6 gives examples of households in the upper and lower social classes; it illustrates the variables that determine a person's standing in the three areas listed above.

Table 7.6 **Basic Dimensions of Social Stratification**

	Class Variables (Economic)	Prestige Variables	Power Variables (Political-Legal)
	Income Wealth Occupation Education Family stability Education of children	Occupational prestige Respect in community Consumption Participation in group life Evaluations of race, religion, ethnicity	Political participation Political attitudes Legislation and governmental benefits Distribution of justice
Households in the upper social class	Affluence: economic security and power, control over material and human investment Income from work but mostly from property	More integrated personalities, more consistent attitudes, and greater psychic fulfillment due to deference, valued associations, and consumption	Power to determine public policy and its implementation by the state, thus giving control over the nature and distribution of social values
Households in the lower social class	Destitution: worthlessness on economic markets	Unintegrated personalities, inconsistent attitudes, sense of isolation and despair; sleazy social interaction	Political powerlessness, lack of legal recourse or rights, socially induced apathy

Source: Rossides 1997:15.

Note: Contains examples of values in the top and bottom classes within each dimension and examples of subdimensions. For expository purposes, religious and ethnic or racial rankings are omitted.

Although these three dimensions of stratification are often found together, this is not always so. Recall the idea of status inconsistency: An individual can have a great deal of prestige yet not command much wealth (Weber 1946). Consider winners of the prestigious Nobel Peace Prize such as Wangari Maathai of Kenya, Rigoberta Menchu of Guatemala, or Betty Williams and Mairead Corrigan of Northern Ireland. None of them is rich, but each has made contributions to the world that have gained them universal prestige. Likewise, some people gain enormous wealth through crime or gambling, but this wealth may not be accompanied by respect or prestige.

The Property Factor

One's income, property, and total assets comprise one's **wealth**. These lie at the heart of class differences. The contrast between the splendor enjoyed by Britain's princes and other royalty and the daily struggle for survival of those in poverty is an example of the differences extreme wealth creates. Another example is shown in the income distribution in the United States by quintiles (see Table 7.7). Note that there has been minimal movement between the groups over the years.

Although income distribution in the United States has not changed dramatically over time, there has been an increase in overall inequality, as the middle class has decreased by more than 8% since 1969. A majority of the 8% have experienced a downward movement, although a few have moved up in the stratification system (Rose 2000).

The Power Factor

Power refers to the ability to control or influence others, to get them to do what you want them to do. Positions of power are gained through family inheritance, family connections, political appointments, education, hard work, or friendship networks. Two theories dominate the explanations of power—power elite and pluralist theories.

We discussed previously the conflict theorists' view that those who hold power are those who control the economic capital and the means of production in society (Ashley and Orenstein 2009). Consistent with Marx, many recent conflict theorists have focused on a *power elite*—individuals with powerful positions in political, business, and military arenas (Domhoff 2001; Mills 1956). These people interact with each other and have a kind of conspiracy to ensure that their power is not threatened. Each tends to protect the power of the other. The idea is that those who are not in this interlocking elite group do not hold real power (Dye 2002).

Power pluralism theorists argue that power is not held exclusively by an elite group but is shared among many power centers, each of which has its own self-interests to protect (Ritzer and Goodman 2004). They contend that well-financed special interest groups (e.g., dairy farmers or truckers' trade unions) and professional associations (e.g., the American Medical Association) have considerable power through collective action. Officials who hold political power are vulnerable to pressure from influential interest groups, and each interest group competes for power with others. Creating and maintaining this power through networks and pressure on legislators is the job of lobbyists. For example, in the ongoing U.S. debate over health care legislation, interest groups from the medical community, insurance lobbies, and citizens' groups wield their power to influence the outcome, but because these major interests conflict and no one group has the most power, no resolution has been reached.

The Prestige Factor

Prestige refers to an individual's social recognition, esteem, and respect commanded from others. An individual's prestige ranking is closely correlated with the value system of society. Chances of being granted high prestige improve if one's patterns of behavior, occupation, and lifestyle match those that are valued in the society. Among high-ranked occupations across nations are scientists, physicians, military officers, lawyers, and college professors. Table 7.8 shows selected occupational prestige rankings in the United States. A 2005 Harris Poll adds some occupations to the list in Table 7.8. Note the correlation between recent events such as 9/11 and the increased rankings of occupations in which people have been portrayed as "heroes" in the United States. For example, 63% of the U.S. population sees fire fighters as having "very great prestige," even though their incomes do not reflect this (Schienberg 2006). Being a hero, obtaining material possessions, or increasing one's educational level can boost prestige but in themselves cannot change class standing.

Table 7.7	**Share of Household Income in Quintiles**			
	1995	2000	2003	2004
Lowest quintile	3.7	3.6	3.4	3.4
Second quintile	9.0	8.9	8.7	8.7
Third quintile	15.0	14.9	14.7	14.8
Fourth quintile	23.3	23.0	23.2	23.4
Highest quintile	49.0	49.7	50.1	49.8
Ratio of highest fifth to lowest fifth	13.2	13.8	14.7	14.6

Source: U.S.Census Bureau 2000, 2005f.

Thinking Sociologically

Describe your own wealth, power, and prestige in society. Does your family have one factor but not others? What difference does each of the factors make in your life?

Occupations (Base: All Adults)	Very Great Prestige	Considerable Prestige	Some Prestige	Hardly Any Prestige at All	Not Sure/ Refused
Scientist	51	25	20	2	3
Doctor	50	30	17	1	2
Military officer	47	27	21	3	2
Teacher	47	23	20	7	2
Police officer	40	32	20	7	1
Priest/minister/clergyman	36	25	24	11	3
Engineer	34	32	28	4	2
Architect	27	34	31	4	4
Member of Congress	27	30	29	11	3
Athlete	21	24	37	15	3
Entertainer	19	29	34	15	3
Journalist	19	25	41	12	4
Business executive	18	29	36	13	4
Lawyer	15	25	38	20	2
Banker	15	29	44	10	2
Union leader	14	22	37	23	5
Accountant	13	23	42	17	4

Table 7.8 **Prestige Rankings of 17 Professions and Occupations (percents)**

Source: Taylor 2002.

Social Classes in the United States

When asked about their social class, most people in the United States identify themselves as middle class, whereas two thirds of the British population identify themselves as "working class" (Cashell 2007). In the current U.S. economic structure, most people are middle class, but the middle class is shrinking. There is slight movement to the upper class and somewhat more movement to the lower class. As noted previously, the U.S. system allows for mobility within the middle class, but there is little movement at the very top and very bottom of the social ladder. People in the top rung often use the power and wealth to insulate themselves and protect their elite status, and the bottom group is isolated because of vicious cycles of poverty that are hard to break (Gilbert and Kahl 2003). Figure 7.1 illustrates the social class structure in the United States (Gilbert-Kahl Model of Social Class in Gilbert 2008:13).

The middle class, as defined by sociologists, makes up about 30% of the population in the United States, depending on what economic criteria are used. Most people identify themselves as middle class, but the whole social class structure has been affected by transformations in the global economy. What we know is that since the 1970s, wealth has become increasingly concentrated in the hands of the richest 1% of households. The income gap between the top 5% and bottom 40% of the U.S. population is increasing, and the number of full-time workers in poverty is rising. There has been no reduction in poverty since the 1970s,

yet the proportion of families exceeding $100,000 in annual income has been growing (Gilbert 2008).

Wages and salaries in the middle classes have declined since the 1980s, but those of the upper classes have risen. Reasons for middle-class decline include downsizing and layoffs of workers, global shifts in production, technological innovations that displace laborers, competition, trade deficits between countries, and deregulation. All of these are macro-level economic forces that mean lower incomes for middle-class workers. The top 20% of income earners increased their percentage of the total income available in the United States by almost 6% between 1977 and 2005, with the top 5% receiving 22% of all income. Changes in class groups are due largely to structural changes in society. The upward movement among the few who have received huge gains in earning power is causing wages and earnings to become more unequal.

Upper middle-class families typically have high income, high education, high occupational level (in terms of prestige and other satisfactions), and high participation in political life and voluntary associations. Families enjoy a stable life, stressing companionship, privacy, pleasant surroundings in safe neighborhoods, property ownership, and stimulating associations. They stress internalization of moral standards of right and wrong, taking responsibility for one's own actions, learning to make one's own decisions, and training for future leadership positions.

The *lower middle class* includes small business-people and farmers, semiprofessionals (teachers, local elected

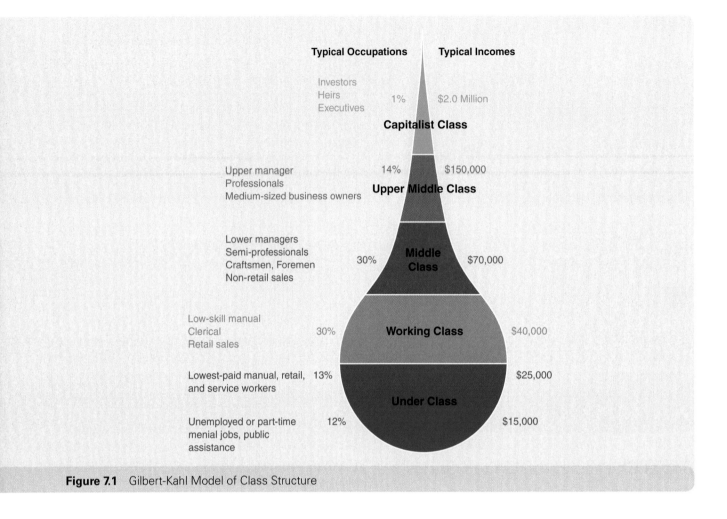

Figure 7.1   Gilbert-Kahl Model of Class Structure

officials, social workers, nurses, police officers, firefighters), middle-management personnel, both private and public, and sales and clerical workers in comfortable office settings. Families in this class are relatively stable. They participate in community life, and although they are less active in political life than the upper classes, they are more politically involved than those in classes below them. Children are raised to work hard and obey authority. Therefore, childrearing patterns more often involve swift physical punishment for misbehavior than talk and reasoning, which is typical of the upper middle class.

Thinking Sociologically

How does today's popular culture on TV and in films, magazines, and popular music reflect interests of different social classes? How are poor people depicted, and who is responsible for their poverty? Do any of these depictions question the U.S. class system? What kinds of music are class based?

Poverty: Multilevel Determinants and Social Policy

Stories about hunger and famine in Third World countries fill the newspapers. Around the world, 800 million people go to bed hungry every night, and one third of all deaths—18 million people each year or 50,000 per day—are due to poverty-related causes (UN Millennium Project 2007; World Health Organization 1999). One hardly expects to see hunger in rich countries, and indeed, 88% of U.S. households had enough food for the family in 2004. About 13.5 million U.S. households (11.9% of all households), however, did not have enough food at some time during the year due to lack of money or other resources (U.S. Department of Agriculture 2005b).

The poor come from disenfranchised groups such as the homeless, unemployed, single parents, disabled, elderly, and migrant workers. With downturns in employment, low

This little boy sits at the feet of an aid worker. How much power do you imagine this little African boy's parents have to make sure their child's needs are met? This boy and his family have personal troubles because the meso and macro systems of his society have failed to work effectively. Compare his circumstances to that of the little girl with her cell phone in a limousine.

wages, and reduced aid to poor families, hunger and poor health in the United States are likely to continue. In the next "How Do We Know?" box, we explore the different experiences of children who grow up in families from different social classes. Consider where your family fits into the social class hierarchy and how this affects your life.

The poor have no property-based income and no permanent or stable work, only casual or intermittent earnings in the labor market. They are often dependent on help from government agencies or private organizations to survive. In short, they have personal troubles in large part because they have been unable to establish linkages and networks in the meso- and macro-level organizations of our social world. They have no collective power and, thus, little representation of their interests and needs in the political system.

Thinking Sociologically

Explain how your family's ability to provide food for its members is largely a function of connectedness to the meso and macro levels of society.

Sociologists recognize two basic types of poverty: absolute poverty and relative poverty. **Absolute poverty**, not having resources to meet basic needs, means no prestige, no access to power, no accumulated wealth, and insufficient means to survive. Whereas absolute poverty in the United States is quite limited, the Dalit of India, described earlier in "The Outcastes of India," provide an example. They often die of diseases that might be easily cured in other people because their bodies are weakened by chronic and persistent hunger and almost total lack of medical attention.

Relative poverty refers to those whose income falls below the poverty line, resulting in an inadequate standard of living relative to others in a given country. In most industrial countries, relative poverty means shortened life expectancy, higher infant mortality, and poorer health, but not many people die of starvation or easily curable diseases, such as influenza.

The *feminization of poverty* refers to the trend in which single females, increasingly younger and with children, make up a growing proportion of those in poverty. Vicki's situation provides one example. After her parents divorced, she quit high school to take odd jobs to help her mother pay the bills. At 18, she was pregnant, and the baby's father was out of the picture, so Vicki lived on government aid because without a high school degree, she could not get a job that paid enough

How Do We Know?

Social Class Differences in Family Life

By Jeffrey Lashbrook

When you were growing up, were your afterschool hours, weekends, and summers filled with adult-organized activities (e.g., formal lessons, youth sports)? Perhaps instead you were pretty much free to play on your own, watch TV, and/or hang out with friends or extended family.

Do all kids grow up the same? Sociologist Annette Lareau, author of *Unequal Childhoods: Class, Race, and Family Life*, reports that families' social class locations shape "the daily rhythms of family life" (Lareau 2003:8). Because she was interested in families' "daily rhythms," she needed in-depth, up-close portraits of families from different social classes. Recall from Chapter 2 that field research, consisting of observation and informal interviewing, is well-suited for accomplishing this aim. Her field research is an *ethnography* of family life. She observed and interacted with family members in a variety of family-related *natural* settings (e.g., in the home, on the way to the doctor's office, at parent-teacher meetings).

Studying families so intensively is not easy. Picture yourself sitting on the couch in the home of someone who is essentially a stranger, asking him or her to go about daily business paying no mind to you. Indeed, Lareau said she wanted to be treated like "the family dog . . . step over and ignore us, but allow us to hang out with [you]" (Lareau 2003:9). A key to doing this type of research is establishing *rapport*. Lareau, in fact, already had interviewed many of the parents because they were part of a larger study of 88 children exploring connections between families and schools, so they were familiar with her and her interests. In addition, such seemingly minor gestures as bringing a pie to their house and later sending a thank-you note for their earlier cooperation helped build this rapport.

For the observation phase of the research, Lareau targeted 19 families with a particular mix of social class, race, and family characteristics in mind. She sent letters to them, followed up with phone calls, and then made an initial visit to their homes to further explain the study, secure their written permission to be observed (*informed consent*), and schedule initial visits. As an added incentive, families were offered $350 to participate. Although she notes that the money likely made some difference, especially among those families financially hard-pressed, more important in her mind was that "the children were strong allies" (p. 266) because they had already had a chance to develop some rapport with Lareau based on the prior school observations. Twelve of the 19 families agreed to participate.

Field research is very labor intensive, and even though the sample is only 12 families, it typically requires more than one person. Thus, six graduate students also helped Lareau observe. Home visits typically lasted two to three hours, were broken up to capture different times and days, and also included other family-related events. The researchers even tried to arrange an overnight stay with each family. Illustrating Chapter 2's description of the ethnographic process, she and her team recorded their observations in field notes, and they met periodically to discuss and reflect on what they were finding.

Recall from Chapter 2 that one relevant problem for observational studies is *research effects*, which refer to the possibility that the researcher's presence alters the subjects' behavior and therefore the accuracy of the findings. Lareau (2003) admits that the "first few visits were awkward" (p. 269), but as is typical with this kind of research, families did eventually grow accustomed to their presence. One sign that families were acting "naturally" relates to another discussion from Chapter 2—ethical issues in sociological research. Should the researchers intervene if it looked like there might be some harm done to a research participant? Members of one particularly hard-stressed family exhibited behaviors that some may find objectionable. Yet, to criticize would corrode the rapport and possibly alter the family dynamics so they are no longer "natural." There is no automatic formula to guide researchers when confronting these issues. Researchers typically have to make judgment calls as they go. Lareau's rule-of-thumb was "not to intervene unless there was blood or an imminent threat of serious danger" (Lareau 2003: 271).

From her study, Lareau concluded that middle-class parents engage in the "concerted cultivation" (p. 238) of their kids. They scheduled their kids in multiple activities, engaged in more elaborate verbal communication with them, and "intervened on their behalf" with school and other authorities (p. 238). Working-class parents, other than providing daily essentials, tended to be more hands-off, an approach that Lareau labeled the "accomplishment of natural growth" (p. 238). These kids engaged in more casual play rather than having their time dominated by adult-organized activities, had fewer linguistic opportunities, and were at the mercy of school and other authorities to a greater degree than middle-class kids. Overall, while Lareau takes pains to point out the advantages and disadvantages of each pattern, she concludes that they are consequential because they lead to the "transmission of differential advantages to children" (p. 5). Middle-class children are enabled to navigate the educational and, later, occupational worlds more successfully than are working-class children, thus influencing the social class destinations of each group.

This study is important because of its in-depth exploration of social class differences in families. Moreover, these patterns are consequential because they lead to the "transmission of differential advantages to children" (Lareau 2003:5). Sociologists will continue to do intensive field research to uncover the often-hidden dynamics of our social lives.

to support herself and her baby and certainly not enough to pay for health insurance. She eventually could not pay her rent and lived out of her car, which did not run because she lacked the money to repair it. Her life spiraled out of control, and her daughter has now been placed in foster care.

We do not like to admit that this can happen in the affluent North American and European countries, and we try to blame the victim (why did Vicki not finish high school, not get pregnant, have an abortion). Still, people do what they must to survive. This problem is heightened as many middle-class women are pushed into poverty through divorce. Some of them sacrificed their own careers for husbands and family so their earning power is reduced, yet many are unable to collect child support from the fathers. The numbers in poverty are highest in and around large central cities such as Paris, France; Mexico City, Mexico; Sao Paulo, Brazil; and Caracas, Venezuela. In the United States, numbers are highest in cities such as New York, Chicago, Detroit, Cleveland, and Los Angeles, where the percentage of poor African American families headed by females reaches close to 50% in some cities. Girls who grow up in female-headed households or foster homes, without a stable family model, are more likely to become single teen mothers and to live in poverty, causing disruption in their schooling and setting limits on their employment possibilities and marital opportunities. Conflict theorists argue that poor women, especially women of color, in capitalistic economic systems are used as a reserve labor force that can be called on when labor is needed and dismissed when not needed (Ehrenreich 2001). They are an easily exploited group.

Why does poverty persist? The elite groups in each culture define what it means to be a success. One major way that success is defined is via popular entertainment, which is run and financed by wealthy companies and individuals (Aguirre and Baker 2007). Those who cannot live up to these media-created expectations are labeled "failures" and blamed for their misfortune. They live under constant stress, which can cause mental or physical breakdowns and humiliating alienation from the social system. Some turn to alcohol or drugs to escape the pressure and failure or to crime to get money to pay the bills. Poor physical and mental health, inadequate nutrition, higher mortality rates, obesity, low self-esteem, feelings of hopelessness, daily struggle to survive, and dependence on others are a few of the individual consequences of poverty within our social world. Costs to the larger society are great:

- It loses the talents and abilities that these people could contribute.
- It must expend tax dollars to address their needs or to regulate their lives with social workers and police.
- People live with a contradiction of cultural values: The United States claims that all citizens "are created equal" and are worthy of respect, yet not all can "make it" in U.S. society.

Welfare programs in affluent countries are only one of a number of kinds of government assistance programs. In the United States, such programs are often thought of as unearned giveaways for the poor; however, there are massive programs of government support for people at all levels of the social system. Universal health care is provided in most affluent countries. University students pay nothing to attend college in some countries, and in a number of others, they pay roughly one third of the cost of their education (taxpayers picking up the rest of the cost). This kind of educational support is clearly not just for the poor. In addition, grants and subsidies provide a safety net to farmers, oil companies, and financial institutions. The question is whether affluence and prosperity are viewed as collectively created and shared, rather than as individual achievements.

Thinking Sociologically

Why is it that programs to help the poor are often stigmatized in the United States as unearned giveaway programs?

Those working with people in poverty generally argue that the elimination of poverty takes money and requires choices by policymakers to *do* something about poverty. Some argue that poverty will never be eliminated because poor people are needed in society. Consider the position put forth in the next "Sociology in Your Social World."

Eliminating Poverty: Some Policy Considerations

Some policymakers suggest attacking the problem of poverty institution by institution, offering incentives for family stability, for students to finish high school, and for job training. The Joint Center for Poverty Research, among other think tanks, has set forth policies to reduce poverty based on research (Poverty Research News 2002). Yet all these programs, public and private, require either massive commitment of funds or remodeling of our social institutions. For instance, government programs in the United States and other countries are designed to help individuals through difficult times during economic downturns. The stated goal of most welfare programs is to eliminate poverty by changing the factors that perpetuate poverty, but this requires money and jobs. Can welfare reform plans "end welfare as we know it" as policymakers claim?

Welfare and Other Aid Programs

For most societies, poverty means loss of labor, a drain on other members in society to support the poor, and

Sociology in Your Social World

The Functions of Poverty

Surely wealthy countries such as the United States have the means to eliminate poverty if they chose to do so. Its persistence invites debate. Some sociologists argue that poverty serves certain purposes or *functions* for society (Gans 1971, 1995), and these make it difficult to address the problem directly and systematically. Some people actually benefit from having poor people kept poor. Consider the following points:

1. The fact that some people are in poverty provides us with a convenient scapegoat for societal problems. We have individuals to blame for poverty—the poor individuals themselves—and can ignore meso- and macro-level causes of poverty that would be expensive to resolve.

2. Having poor people creates many jobs for those who are not poor, including "helping" professions such as social workers, as well as law enforcement jobs such as police, judges, and prison workers.

3. The poor provide an easily available group of laborers to do work, and they serve as surplus workers to hire for undesirable jobs.

4. The poor serve to reinforce and legitimate our own lives and institutions. Their existence allows the rest of us to feel superior to someone, enhancing our self-esteem.

5. Their violation of mainstream values helps to remind us of those values, thereby constantly reaffirming the values among the affluent.

This perspective can be extended to poverty on the global scale.

1. Just as poor U.S. laborers can be hired for undesirable jobs, the global poor work at very low wages to provide consumers in wealthy nations with low-cost goods.

2. The gifted and talented individuals in poor societies often migrate to wealthier nations, creating a brain drain that removes human capital from poor states and increases it in wealthy states.

3. The poor of the world are blamed for macro-level social problems such as overpopulation and terrorism. As with our local poor, their existence allows us to overlook the macro-level causes of poverty.

From this perspective, the poor serve a role in the structure of society. Therefore, some groups of people, be it individuals or nations, will always be at the bottom of the stratification ladder.

---

extensive health care and crime prevention systems. Most Global North countries provide assistance to citizens who need help when unemployed, sick, or elderly. Some of the U.S. Great Society programs of the 1960s and 1970s were successful in reducing poverty by attacking the root causes. The Women, Infants, and Children Program provides nutritional help, and Head Start provides early childhood education. Both programs have received good grades for helping poor women and children, but funding to some of these programs has been cut back due to other funding priorities, and as a result, their effectiveness has diminished (which will surely lead to criticism of its ineffectiveness). Other programs—Aid to Families with Dependent Children, Medicaid, Medicare, food stamps—helped many who had short-term problems but were

criticized as creating dependence of families on aid (Blank 2002; Corbett 1994/1995; Haskins 2006).

Britain, France, the United States, and other countries have instituted work incentive programs such as *workfare* that encourage or require recipients of aid to work or attend job training, and in order to qualify to receive food stamps. In the United States, able-bodied unemployed or underemployed adults must work 20 to 30 hours a week, be receiving on-the-job training, or be getting education in basic skills or college work to qualify for assistance for up to five years. Since 1996, when welfare reform was legislated, the number of people on welfare has dropped 57% in the United States. Child poverty rates have also dropped, although they are still high compared to other countries (MacDougal 2005).

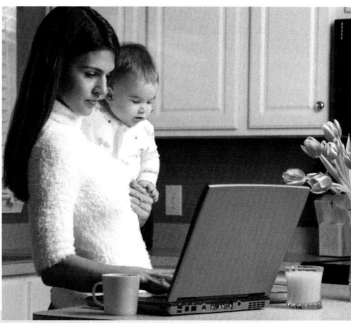

In rural villages in Laos where people live in grass houses such as this one, there is no reliable electricity or other support systems for Internet technology. Few people in such communities have ever been online or even know about the resources made available through the World Wide Web. That contrasts sharply with homes like the second one, where access to computers is taken for granted.

Work incentive programs have gained adherents who argue that many welfare recipients would work if provided support and motivation. In addition to micro-level incentives and work training, success in helping people out of poverty depends on meso-level economic conditions: Are there jobs available at living wages? Are taxpayers, many of whom are attracted to politicians who cut taxes, willing to provide money for social programs to help the "invisible" poor out of poverty as well as subsidies to other groups? In fact, institutions such as prisons absorb public funds that could go to poverty reduction, yet crime is often a result of people feeling that they have no other options for survival.

Information needed by policymakers to establish sound policies is often provided by social research centers. Data collected on social problems such as poverty, drug problems, and welfare affect governmental decisions about how to deal most effectively with problems. The next "Applied Sociologist at Work" provides an example of one sociology major who became an activist in the welfare rights movement, attempting to influence policymakers.

Thinking Sociologically

Recalling what you have learned about poverty, how would you develop a plan to attack the problem of poverty within your community or country taking into account factors at the different levels—micro, meso, and macro? Is it a matter of job training, family values, breaking the cycle, welfare support, or something else?

NATIONAL AND GLOBAL DIGITAL DIVIDE: MACRO-LEVEL STRATIFICATION

Two of Jeanne's African student friends, Mamadou from Niger and Eric from Ghana, answer their cell phones to the sound of chimes from London's Big Ben clock tower and a Bob Marley song. One speaks in Kanuri and French and the other in Twi to friends thousands of miles away. They are the future generation of elites from the Global South, fluent in the languages of several countries, of computers, and of the digital age. Many of their fellow citizens in Niger and Ghana are not so fortunate. They live subsistence lives and have little contact with the digital world swirling overhead through satellite connections. This represents the *digital divide*, the gap between those with access to information technology and those without it. The lines of the divide are drawn by socioeconomic status, minority group, and urban versus rural residence (Mehra et al. 2004).

The global social world is increasingly based on producing and transmitting information through digital technology. Few tools are more important in this process than the computer, Internet, and cell phones. In nearly every salaried and professional position, computer knowledge and ability to navigate the Internet are critical employment skills. Therefore, individuals with insufficient access to computers and lack of technical skills face barriers to many professions and opportunities. Because computer skills are important for personal success, this is an important micro-level issue. The digital divide is breaking down for some young and elite

The Applied Sociologist at Work— Karen Schaumann
The Struggle for Welfare Rights in Michigan

By Jay Weinstein

Karen Schaumann received her BA and MA degrees in sociology from Eastern Michigan University (EMU) in Ypsilanti. She went on to serve as a lecturer in sociology at EMU and is currently on the faculty of nearby Schoolcraft College. As a graduate student, she took a leadership role in creating a local welfare rights union. Later, she became its faculty sponsor and began a campaign that continues to this day to organize and educate welfare recipients about how the welfare system operates. For Karen, "Being able to help generation after generation of low-income EMU students (and staff!) achieve a college degree is one of the most rewarding things I've done professionally," she said in an interview.

Drawing on a long history of welfare rights activism at the national, state, and even local levels, Karen's involvement in the movement at EMU began when she returned to school as a recently divorced, low-income single parent. Prior to returning to school, she had looked for employment and was unable to find a job that would even cover daycare expenses for her then 3- and 1-year-old daughters. She notes that "returning to school was the best decision I'd made in some time. However, it was really a struggle dealing with the welfare bureaucracy. If you didn't know your rights, you pretty much had none."

Karen and others in a similar position learned from some strong, bright women in the leadership of Michigan Welfare Rights that there was power in their numbers, that they could form their own union and advocate for each other with the state welfare department. They encountered an obvious social class bias at the department. In particular, they found that some agency personnel devalued them and displayed a lack of respect for recipients, stereotyped them and their children, and generally felt that they were doing the recipients a personal favor by doing their job. The women banded together in self-defense and to help ensure the survival of their children.

The union organization's main achievement on the micro level was family survival, along with the ability to help members navigate the confusing bureaucracy. Many of those in the core group were able to finish college, although it took them longer than most students. As Karen points out, "That is a fierce victory to achieve during the era of 'welfare reform.'"

At the macro level, the union helped to create a Michigan Department of Human Services/Family Independence Agency advisory board, and it worked with legal services to create training for recipients and agencies. In cooperation with the Poverty Law Program at the University of Michigan, the group successfully challenged policies that endangered the lives of women escaping domestic violence. The union helped to create a viable advocating force. Members traveled to Washington, D.C., with the National Organization for Women to lobby against welfare reform. Members set up tent cities in Detroit, Ann Arbor, Flint, and Lansing to protest the elimination of general assistance in the cold winter of 1991. These tent cities were a symbol of the homelessness being forced on low-income single adults in Michigan, but they were also a practical waystation for hundreds if not thousands of ex-recipients who had been evicted from the single-room occupancy "welfare hotels" (SROs) into the snowy Michigan winter.

Karen recalls that "we saw people who were locked out without coats, boots, or identification. You name it, we saw it. I personally remember a man named Jesse in the Detroit tent city, confined to a wheelchair by the time he reached us. He had lost his feet from frostbite." Ultimately the union was not able to halt welfare reform.

One victory does stand out—winning an administrative law case for a functionally illiterate woman with a severe learning disability. The judge found that the local human services agency violated her rights by not assisting her with meeting program requirements.

Karen continues to help interested college students, faculty members, and community members organize for mutual survival. Karen's work exemplifies applied sociology in that it requires a sociological imagination—the ability to connect private troubles with public issues. Once people realize that they are not alone in their struggle, they have taken an important first step. In this work, the sociologist is close to the ground, so to speak, and is well aware of where the problems are. The job is to help to solve those problems, on both the micro and macro levels. It requires serious critical thinking skills. When policymakers and legislators claim that welfare reform is a "success," the sociologist is able to point to measures of child well-being and statistics that show that merely declaring a case closed does not mean that a family has moved out of poverty.

Karen invites sociology teachers and students who are interested in doing something similar to send an e-mail message to kschauman@emich.edu. The union will send you a packet called *How to Start a Welfare Rights Union*. "Don't Agonize, Organize!"

Note: Jay Weinstein, professor of sociology, received his doctorate and bachelor's degrees from University of Illinois-Urbana and his master's from Washington University-St. Louis. He currently holds the position of editor-in-chief of *Applied Social Science Journal*.

members of developing societies such as Mamadou and Eric, but few individuals and countries have sufficient technology and educated population to participate in this new economy (Drori 2006; Nakamura 2004).

The recent growth in both the development and use of technology has taken place mostly in affluent Global North countries, especially among young, well-educated elite (Horrigan and Smith 2007). The number of Internet users around the globe increased from 16 million in 1995 to 500 million in 2001 to 1.3 billion in 2007 (Drori 2006; Miniwatts Marketing Group 2008). For most users, English is the language, although it is the second spoken language of more than 200 million users. Chinese is the next most popular language on the Internet, and its use is increasing at a high rate. Access to the Internet is not equal around the world (Gibson 1999). In the United States, one of the most wired countries in the world, many poor people do not have access to computers or mentors to teach them how to use computers. This digital divide is beginning to close, but it still creates barriers for many (Nakamura 2004; Shade 2004).

Comparing countries cross-nationally, only 5% of the total world population is online, but 50% of residents in North America and Scandinavia (Sweden, Norway, Finland, Denmark, and Iceland) are connected. About 79% of the online population lives in nations that belong to the Organization for Economic and Cooperative Development—countries that hold 14% of the people on the planet. By contrast, in sub-Saharan Africa and in India, only 4 out of every 1,000 citizens use the Internet (Drori 2006). About 97% of Internet hosts are in the Global North (which has only 16% of the world's population), and 66% of income from royalties and licensing fees goes to two countries: The United States receives 54% and Japan 12%. In some countries, the monthly access fee for hooking up to the Internet is stunningly high compared to average monthly income: in Bangladesh, 191%; in Nepal, 278%; and in Madagascar, 614%. This may be why 35 of the poorest countries in the world have less than 1% of the Internet users (Drori 2006).

An additional difficulty is that most Web sites and e-mail services use English, computer keyboards are designed with a Western alphabet, and some of the digital systems in computers are established on the basis of English symbols and logic. It is difficult to use the Internet in other languages—a fact that many of us may not think about as we use the system (Drori 2006). For people who are struggling for the very survival of their culture, the dominance of English may feel like a threat, one more example of Western dominance. So resistance to the use of computers and the Internet is more than a matter of finances or technology. There may be cultural objections as well.

Policy decisions at the international level affect the status of the Global South. The United Nations, the International Monetary Fund, and other international organizations have pressured countries to develop their Internet capacities. Indeed, this is sometimes used as a criterion for ranking countries in terms of their "level of modernization" (Drori 2006). Countries that have not been able to get "in the game" of Internet technology cannot keep pace with a rapidly evolving global economy.

Internet technology has created a digital divide, but it also has had some beneficial economic impact, stimulating jobs in poor countries. In 1999, computer component parts were a substantial percentage of production in some poor countries: 52% of Malaysia's exports, 44% of Costa Rica's, and 28% of Mexico's. The high-tech revenue for India increased from 150 million U.S. dollars in 1990 to 4 billion dollars in 1999. On the less positive side, e-waste from electronic equipment is extremely toxic, and it is almost always shipped to poor countries, where extremely poor people must deal with the consequences of toxic pollution (Drori 2006).

Digital technology is an example of one important force changing the micro- and macro-level global stratification system—a spectrum of people and countries from the rich and elite to those that are poor and desperate.

Thinking Sociologically

What evidence of the digital divide do you see in your family, community, nation, and world? For instance, can your grandparents program their VCR? Do they know how to work a cell phone or navigate the Internet? Could they create their own Facebook page if asked to do so?

The Global "Digital Divide" and Social Policy

"In India, access to private cable television has promoted female autonomy, decreased . . . wife beating, and reduced . . . preferences for sons over daughters . . . (also the study finds) increases in female school enrollment and decreases in fertility" (Jensen and Oster 2007:2). Village access to television programming has increased dramatically, with 30 million Indian households adding cable service between 2001 and 2006. As more women are exposed to images of lifestyles in urban areas and other countries, including stories of women working outside the home, controlling money, and attaining high levels of education, new possibilities are opened. Technology is bringing the world to remote villages around the world, opening new horizons and changing lifestyles.

As poor countries become part of the electronic age, some are making policies that facilitate rapid modernization. They are passing over developmental stages that rich countries went through. As an illustration, consider the telephone. In 2002, 90% of all telephones in the world were cell phones, many using satellite connections. Some countries never did get completely wired for land lines, thus eliminating one phase of phone technology. With satellite technology in place, some computer and Internet options will be available without expensive intermediate steps (Drori 2006).

In less than 20 years, cell phones that originated for the business elite have become a personal item. Use in poor countries has quadrupled in the last decade, giving people access to health care and other services ("Cell phone use . . ." 2007).

Engineers in India, working through an organization called Simputer Trust, have been designing a simple computer (a "simputer") that will be less expensive and will have more multilingual capacities than the PC. Such efforts will enhance access of poor countries to the computer and Internet and will provide the means for children in poor countries to become part of the competitive global stratification system. Technology is leveling the world playing field (Drori 2006; Friedman 2005).

The changing global economic landscape is affecting nations' internal economic competition as well. Bangalore is home to India's booming digital industries, which are successfully competing in the global high-tech market. Yet, many villages and cities in India provide examples of the contrasts between the caste system and the emerging class system. In rural agricultural areas, change is extremely slow despite laws forbidding differential treatment of outcastes and mandating change. In urban industrial areas, new opportunities are changing the traditional caste structures, as intercaste and intracaste competition for wealth and power is increasing with the changes in economic, political, and other institutional structures. The higher castes were the first to receive the education and lifestyle that create industrial leaders. Now, shopkeepers, wealthy peasants, teachers, and others are vying for power. Within the world system, India is generally economically poor but developing certain economic sectors rapidly. Thus, India is in transition both internally and in the global world system.

A small percentage of societies control most world resources. Because of this, the gap between the rich and poor countries is large and in most cases growing. Competition over unequal distribution of power, wealth, and resources creates tensions between countries. These tensions can stimulate development or cause bitter conflicts and hostilities that include terrorism, civil wars, revolution, and other forms of hostility and protest. For instance, Middle Eastern countries have a key world resource at their core—oil. This creates the possibility of conflicts both between Middle Eastern countries and in the world, as exemplified by the 1989 Gulf War between Iraq and Kuwait and the current Middle Eastern conflicts involving Iraq, the United States, and other countries.

So What?

Perhaps your understanding of why you are rich or poor—and what effect your socioeconomic status has on what you buy, what you believe, and where you live—has taken on new dimensions. Perhaps you have gained some insight into what factors affect your ability to move up in the social class system. The issue of social stratification calls into question the widely held belief in the fairness of our economic system. By studying this issue, we better understand why some individuals are able to experience prestige (respect) and to control power and wealth at the micro, meso, and macro levels of the social system, while others have little access to those resources. Few social forces affect your personal life at the micro level as much as stratification. That includes the decisions you make about what you wish to do with your life or who you might marry. Indeed, stratification influenced the fact that you are reading this book.

We leave this discussion of stratification systems, including class systems, with a partial answer to the question posed in the beginning of this chapter: Why are some people rich and others poor? In the next two chapters, we expand the discussion to include other variables in stratification systems—race and ethnicity and gender. By the end of these chapters, the answer to the opening questions should be even clearer.

Key Points

What Have We Learned?

- Stratification—the layering or ranking of people within society—is one of the most important factors shaping the life chances of individuals. This ranking is influenced by micro, meso, and macro forces and resources. (See pp. 200–202.)

- Various theories of stratification disagree on whether inequality is functional or destructive to society and its members. The evolutionary perspective suggests ways stratification can be positive, but much of the inequality currently experienced creates problems for individuals and societies. (See pp. 202–207.)

- For individuals, personal respect (prestige) is experienced as highly personal, but it is influenced by the way the social system works at the meso and macro level—from access to education and the problems created by gender and ethnic discrimination to population trends and the vitality of the global economy. (See pp. 207–210.)

• People without adequate connections to the meso and macro levels are likely to experience less power, wealth, and prestige. (See pp. 210–216.)

• Some macro systems stress ascribed status (assigned to one, often at birth, without consideration of one's individual choices, talents, or intelligence). Other systems purport to be open and based on achieved status (dependent upon one's contributions to the society and one's personal abilities and decisions). Unlike the caste system, the class system tends to stress achieved status, although it does not always perform openly. (See pp. 216–219.)

• The elements of stratification are complex, with property, power, and prestige having somewhat independent influences on the system of inequality and on one's standing. (See pp. 219–222.)

• Poverty itself is a difficult problem, one that can be costly to a society as a whole. But various solutions at the micro, meso, or macro levels have had mixed results, partially, perhaps, because it is in the interests of those with privilege to have an underclass to do the unpleasant jobs. (See pp. 222–227.)

• Technology is both a contributor and possible remedy to inequality, as the digital divide creates problems for the poor, but electronic innovations may create new opportunities in the social structure for networking and connections to the meso and macro levels—even for those in the Global South—the poor regions of the world. (See pp. 227–230.)

Contributing to Our Social World: What Can We Do?

At the Local Level: Every community has shelters for homeless people and soup kitchens where very poor people can get a free meal. These organizations often need volunteer help or interns. In fact, student groups on many campuses regularly provide such services. If you know of such a group on your campus, consider working with it, as you will benefit from the experiences of others who are familiar with the situation. Also, if you or your friends sponsor events or meetings that include meals, see if you can arrange for the food that is prepared but not eaten to be donated to a shelter. Remember to tip generously when you are being served by people in minimum-wage jobs—housekeeping maids who have cleaned your room, breakfast servers at the continental breakfast, and employees at fast-food restaurants. If you have never had such a job, consider taking one on a part-time basis. You may learn more than you ever wanted to know about life at the bottom of the stratification system.

At the Organizational or Institutional Level: One of the most successful volunteer organizations that assist people in need is the faith-based Habitat for Humanity. Participants work with current and prospective home owners in repairing or constructing housing for little or no cost. Habitat projects are under way or planned for many communities in the United States and around the world. See the organization's Web site for more details at www.habitat.org. After graduation, consider doing one year of service with AmeriCorps. Founded in the early 1990s, more than 200,000 volunteers have served in a wide range of jobs, including teaching and community service. The pay is not good, but the experience and contribution to those in need provide other rewards. See the AmeriCorps Web site at www.americorps.org.

At the National and Global Levels: You or some of your friends may have already considered joining the Peace Corps after graduation. Doing so involves a serious, long-term commitment, but most who have done it agree that it was worth the effort. And there are few more effective ways to apply sociology in a global context. The Peace Corps is an independent agency of the U.S. government, founded in 1961. Volunteers work in foreign countries throughout the world, helping local people improve their economic conditions, health, and education. The Peace Corps Web site (www.peacecorps.gov) provides information on the history of the organization, volunteer opportunities, and reports of former and present volunteers.

For a shorter-term global commitment, consider doing a paid internship sponsored by Sociologists without Borders (or *Sociólogos sin Fronteras;* www.sociologistswithoutborders.org). This organization promotes human rights globally. It advocates that sociologists participate, democratically, with others to set standards for human well-being and devote energies to understanding how to achieve these standards. Grameen Bank (www.grameen-info.org/bank or www.grameenfoundation.org) was started in Bangladesh by Professor Muhammad Yunus, winner of the 2006 Nobel Prize for Peace. It makes small business loans to people who live in impoverished regions of the world and who have no collateral for a loan. The default rate on these loans is one of the lowest of any bank anywhere. Rather than collateral, the promise to repay is based on social ties to others in one's community, who will not receive loans unless the first party pays regularly on his or her loan. Consider doing a local fundraiser with friends for the Grameen Bank or other micro-credit organizations, such as Finca and Care International.

Visit **www.pineforge.com/ballantine2study** for online activities, sample tests, and other helpful information. Select "Chapter 7: Stratification" for chapter-specific activities.

CHAPTER 8

Race and Ethnic Group Stratification

Beyond "We" and "They"

As we travel around our social world, the people we encounter gradually change appearance. As human beings, we are all part of "we," but there is a tendency to define those who look different as "they."

Think About It . . .

Micro: Why do you look different from those around you? What relevance do these differences have for your life?

Micro: Why do people in the local community "categorize" others into ethnic groups?

Meso: How are privilege and disprivilege embedded in institutions—so that they operate independently of personal bias or prejudice?

Macro: Why are minority group members in most countries economically poorer than dominant group members?

Macro: In what ways might ethnicity or race shape international negotiations and global problem solving? What can you do to make the world a better place for *all* people?

Macro: Global Community

Macro: Society

Meso: National Organizations, Institutions, and Ethnic Subcultures

Micro: Local Organizations and Community

Micro: Me (and My Minority Friends)

Micro: Local reference groups; deliberate exclusion of ethnic group members

Meso: Laws that intentionally or unintentionally discriminate; educational testing biases

Macro: Laws or court rulings that set policy for state and local levels

Macro: Racial and ethnic hostilities at the national and global levels result in wars, genocide, or ethnic cleansing

When Siri wakes, it is about noon. In the instant of waking, she knows exactly who and what she has become . . . the soreness in her genitals reminds her of the 15 men she had sex with the night before. Siri is 15 years old. Sold by her impoverished parents a year ago, she finds that her resistance and her desire to escape the brothel are breaking down and acceptance and resignation are taking their place. . . . Siri is very frightened that she will get AIDS . . . as many girls from her village return home to die from AIDS after being sold into the brothels. (Bales 2002:207–09)

Siri is a sex slave, just like millions of other young women around the world. Slavery is not limited to poor countries: Dora was enslaved in a home in Washington, D.C., and domestic slaves have been discovered in London, Chicago, New York, and Los Angeles. The Central Intelligence Agency (CIA) reports thousands of women and children are smuggled into the United States each year as sex and domestic slaves or locked away in sweat shops (Bales 2004). International agencies estimate that more than one million children in Southeast Asia have been sold into bondage, mostly into the booming sex trade.

It may be surprising to know that slavery is alive and flourishing around the world (Free the Slaves 2005). An estimated 27 million people, mostly women and children from poor families in poor countries, are slaves, auctioned off or lured into slavery each year by kidnap gangs, pimps, and cross-border syndicates (Bales 2004; Kyle and Koslowski 2001).

As a global phenomenon, human trafficking in slaves from such places as Ukraine, Myanmar (Burma), Laos, Nepal, and the Philippines, mostly for commercial sex industry, is so profitable that criminal business people invest in involuntary brothels much as they would in a mining operation. (Kyle and Koslowski 2001:1)

International events such as the Olympics and major soccer matches bring new markets for the sex trade. Young foreign girls are brought in from other countries—chosen for sex slaves because they are exotic, free of AIDS, and cannot escape due to insufficient money and knowledge of the language or the country to which they are exported (Moritz 2001). Sometimes, poor families sell their daughters for the promise of high wages and perhaps money sent home. As a result, girls as young as six are held captive as prostitutes or as domestic workers. Child labor, a problem in many parts of the world, requires poor young children to do heavy labor for long hours in agriculture as well as brick-making, match-making, and carpet factories. Although they earn little, their income helps families pay debts. Many argue that this is slavery, although others say such transactions are necessary for the families' survival. The children dare not complain, for the sanctions may involve severe injury or death. Much of the cacao (used to make chocolate) and coffee (unless they are Fair Trade Certified products) that we buy also supports slavery. Chocolate especially is grown and harvested at slave camps where young boys are given a choice of unpaid hard labor (with beatings for any disobedience) or death by starvation or shooting (Bales 2000, 2004). Very little chocolate is produced *without* slave labor.

Debt bondage is another form of modern-day slavery. Extremely poor families—often people with differences in appearance or culture from those with power—work in exchange for housing and meager food. Severe debt, passing from generation to generation, may also result when farmers borrow money because they face drought or need cash to keep their families from starving. The only collateral they have on the loan is themselves—put up for bondage until they can pay off the loan. No one but the wealthy landowner keeps accounting records, which results in there being no accountability. The poor families may find themselves enslaved. The lack of credit available to marginal people contributes to slavery. Because those in slavery have

In Calcutta's red-light district, more than 7,000 women and girls work as prostitutes. Only one group has a lower standing: their children. Zana Briski first began photographing prostitutes in Calcutta in 1998. Living in the brothels for months at a time, she quickly developed a relationship with many of the kids who, often terrorized and abused, were drawn to the rare human companionship she offered. Because the children were fascinated by her camera, Zana thought it would be great to see the world through their eyes. It was at that moment that she had the idea of teaching photography to the children of prostitutes. A film she produced based on her work won the Oscar for Best Documentary in 2006. It led to a crusade to keep these children of prostitutes, pictured here, out of a life of prostitution. Learn more about her organization, Kids with Cameras, at www.kids-with-cameras.org.

little voice and no rights, the world community hears little about this tragedy (Bales 2004). A recent successful international movement in impoverished areas provides women very small loans—called *micro credit*—to help them start small businesses and move out of desperate poverty and slavery. We will read more about this in future chapters.

In the slavery of the 19th century, slaves were expensive, and there was at least some economic incentive to care about their health and survival. In the new slavery, humans are cheap and replaceable. There is little concern about working them to death, especially if they are located in remote cacao or coffee plantations (Bales 2000). By current dollars, a slave in the southern United States would have cost as much as $40,000, but contemporary slaves are cheap. They can be procured from poor countries for an average of $90 (Bales 2004). The cost is $40 in Mali for a young male and $1,000 in Thailand for an HIV-free female (Free the Slaves 2008). Slaves produce an estimated $1.4 billion in produce and profits for their owners each year. Employers can legally exploit and abuse them with long hours and without legal interference because the slaves owe money.

What is the point of slavery for our discussion of race and ethnic group stratification? What all of these human bondage situations have in common is that poor minority groups are victimized. Because many slaves are members of ethnic, racial, religious, tribal, gender, age, caste, or other minority groups and have obvious physical or cultural distinctions from the people who exploit them, they are at a distinct disadvantage in the stratification system. Although all humans have the same basic characteristics, few people have a choice about being born into a minority group, and it is difficult to change that minority status. Visible barriers include physical appearance, names, dress, language, or other distinguishing characteristics. Historical conditions and conflicts rooted in religious, social, political, and historical events set the stage for dominant or minority status, and people are socialized into their dominant or subservient group.

Minority or dominant group status affects most aspects of people's experiences in the social world. These include status in the community, socialization experience, where they can live, opportunities for success and achievement in education and occupation, the religious group to which they belong, and the health care they receive. In fact, it is impossible to separate minority status from position in the stratification system (Aguirre and Turner 2006; Farley 2005; Rothenberg 2007).

In this chapter, we explore characteristics of race and ethnic groups that lead to differential placement in stratification systems, including problems at the micro, meso, and macro levels—prejudice, racism, discrimination, group contact, effects of these problems, and related policies. The next chapter considers ascribed status based on gender. The topics in this chapter and the next continue the discussion of stratification: who is singled out for differential treatment, why they are singled out, results for both the individuals and the society, and some actions or policies that deal with differential treatment.

In India, many slaves are used to extract slate from mines, and the slate then is used to make cheap pencils that can be exported around the world. The key to slavery is powerless humans exploited by those who need cheap labor. Young children who have no family are often sucked into slavery, as these children were. The law prohibits the employment of children under 14, and the authorities are perfectly aware that large numbers of 4- to 11-year-olds are used in these mines.

The Fair Trade Certified symbol signifies that products such as coffee, tea, and chocolate (made from cacao) meet sustainable development goals, help support family farmers at fair prices, and are not produced by slave labor. Much of the work on cacao plantations is done by child slaves smuggled from poor countries.

Thinking Sociologically

Poor people around the world often lose control over their lives. What situations can lead to this condition, and what are the results for these people?

What Characterizes Racial and Ethnic Groups?

Migration, war and conquest, trade, and intermarriage have left virtually every geographical area of the world populated by groups of people with varying ethnicities. In this section, we consider characteristics that set groups apart, especially groups that fall at the lower end of the stratification system.

Minority Groups

Several factors characterize **minority groups** and their relations with dominant groups in society (Dworkin and Dworkin 1999):

1. Minority groups are distinguishable from dominant groups due to factors that make them different from the group that holds power.

2. Minority groups are excluded or denied full participation at the meso level of society in economic, political, educational, religious, health, and recreational institutions.

3. Minority groups have less access to power and resources within the nation and are evaluated less favorably based on their characteristics as minority group members.

4. Minority groups are stereotyped, ridiculed, condemned, or otherwise defamed, allowing dominant group members to justify and not feel guilty about unequal and poor treatment.

5. Minority groups develop collective identities among members to insulate themselves from the unaccepting world; this in turn perpetuates their group identity by creating ethnic or racial enclaves, intragroup marriages, and segregated group institutions such as churches.

Thinking Sociologically

Look again at the list of minority group characteristics above. How might people be affected at the micro, the meso, and the macro levels of society, depending on their membership in dominant or minority groups?

Because minority status is determined by history and ideology, the minority group could be the dominant group in a different time or society. Throughout England's history, wars and assassinations changed the ruling group from Catholic to Protestant and back several times. In Iraq,

Shiite Muslims are dominant in numbers and now also in power, but they were a minority under Saddam Hussein's Sunni rule. Map 8.1 indicates the location of major minority groups in the United States today, although you should be aware that the density of groups in a particular location changes over time.

Dominant groups are not always a numerical majority. In the case of South Africa, advanced European weapons placed the native African Bantu population under the rule of a small percentage of white British and Dutch descendants in what became a complex system of planned discrimination called *apartheid*. Until recently, each major group—white, mixed colored, and black—had its own living area, and members carried identification cards showing the "race" to which they belonged. In this case, racial classification and privilege were defined by the laws of the dominant group.

The Concept of Race

Racial minority is one of the two types of minority groups most common in the social world. A **race** is a group identified by a society because of certain biologically inherited physical characteristics. However, in practice, it is impossible to accurately identify racial types. Most attempts at racial classifications have been based on combinations of appearance, such as skin color and shade, stature, facial features, hair color and texture, head form, nose shape, eye color and shape, height, and blood or gene type. Our discussion of race focuses on three issues: (1) origins of the concept of race, (2) the social construction of race, and (3) the significance of race versus class.

Origins of the Concept of Race

In the 18th and 19th centuries, scientists attempted to divide humans into four major groupings—Mongoloid, Caucasoid, Negroid, and Australoid—and then into more than 30 racial subcategories. In reality, few individuals fit clearly into any of these types. The "Sociology in Your Social World" on page 238 provides insight into the origins of racial categories that have had a major impact on history and form the basis for many conflicts today.

From the earliest origins in East Africa more than 7 million years ago, humans slowly spread around the globe, south through Africa, north to Europe, and across Asia. Many scholars believe humans crossed the Bering Straits from Asia to North America around 20,000 BCE and continued to populate North and South America (Diamond 1999). Physical adaptations of isolated groups to their environments originally resulted in some differences in physical appearance—skin color, stature, hair type—but mixing of peoples over the centuries has left few if any isolated "pure" races, only gradations as one moves around the world. Thus, the way societies choose to define race has come

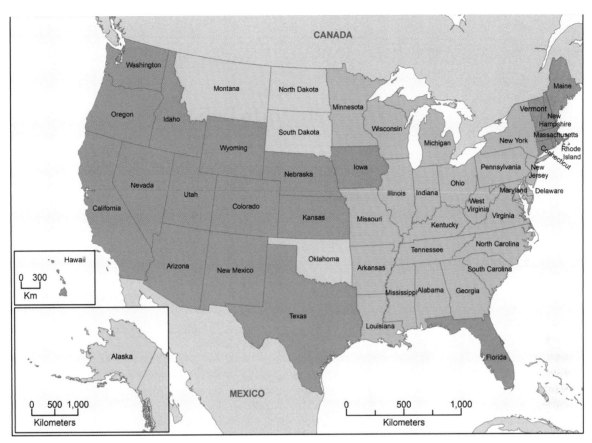

Minority Group With Highest Percent of State Population

Excluding the category "White, not Hispanic"

Asian   Black   Hispanic   Native American   Two or more ethnic groups, not Hispanic

Map 8.1 Prevalence of Minority Ethnic Groups in the United States

Source: U.S. Census Bureau 2000. Map by Anna Versluis.

about largely through what is culturally convenient for the dominant group.

In the 1970s, the United Nations, concerned about racial conflicts and discrimination, issued a "Statement on Race" prepared by a group of eminent scientists from around the world. This and similar statements by scientific groups point out the harmful effects of racist arguments, doctrines, and policies. The conclusion of their document upheld that (1) all people are born free and equal both in dignity and in rights, (2) racism stultifies personal development, (3) conflicts (based on race) cost nations money and resources, and (4) racism foments international conflict. Racist doctrines lack any scientific basis, as all people belong to the same species and have descended from the same origin. In summary, problems arising from race relations are social, not biological, in origin; differential treatments of groups based on "race" falsely claim a scientific basis for classifying humans. Biologically speaking, a "race" exists in any life form when the two groups cannot interbreed, and if they do, the offspring are infertile/sterile. This

is not true of any group of human beings. So what is the problem?

Social Construction of Race: Symbolic Interaction Analysis

Why are sociologists concerned about a concept that has little scientific accuracy and is ill defined? The answer is its social significance. The social reality is that people are defined or define themselves as belonging to a group based in part on physical appearance. As individuals try to make meaning of the social world, they may learn from others that some traits—eye or nose shape, hair texture, or skin color—are distinguishing traits that make people different. Jean Piaget, famous cognitive psychologist, described the human tendency to classify objects as one of our most basic cognitive tools (Piaget and Inhelder [1955] 1999). This inclination has often been linked to classifying "racial" groups. Once in place, racial categories provide individuals with an identity based on ancestry—"my kind of people have these traits."

Sociology in Your Social World

Historical Attempts to Define Race

Throughout history, political and religious leaders, philosophers, and even scientists have struggled with the meaning and significance of race. The first systematic classification of all living phenomena was published in 1735 by Carl von Linne (Linnaeus). His hierarchy of species was actually quite complex, including monkeys, elephants, and angels. His work was based on the study of fossil remains of various species, implying evolution of the species over time. Then, in 1758, he published *Systema Naturae,* in which he suggested four human types: Americanus (Native Americans), Asiaticus, Africanus, and Europeanus (Cashmore and Troyna 1990). Other scientists proposed other divisions. Johann Blumenbach was the first to use the word *race* in his 1775 classification system: Caucasian, Mongolian, Ethiopian, American, and Malay.

By the 19th century, race began to take on a biological meaning and to signify inherent physical qualities in humans (Goldberg 1990). From there, it was a short step to theorizing about inherent inequalities between races. For instance, Joseph Arthur, Comte de Gobineau (1816–1882), questioned why once great societies had declined and fallen. He argued that each race has specific characteristics, and he attributed the demise of societies to the inequality of races. His book, *Essay on Inequality of the Human Races*, published in 1853–55, earned him the title "father of modern racism." A major event in theories of race was the publication of Charles Darwin's *The Origin of Species* ([1858] 1909). Among his many ideas was that human races *might* represent stages or branches of a tree of evolution.

This idea implied that those groups of humans who were biologically best suited to the environment would survive. He argued that "natural selection," or "survival of the fittest," was true of all races in the human species, not of individuals within a species. However, from Darwin's ideas emerged the concepts of *survival of the fittest* and *ever-improving races.*

These two late 19th-century concepts were taken out of context and became the foundation for a number of theories of superior races. For instance, in 1899, the Brit-turned-German Houston Stewart Chamberlain published an aristocratic, anti-Semitic work in which he argued that northern and western European populations, Teutonic in particular, were superior. He argued for racial purity, a theme the Nazis of the 1930s and 1940s adopted. Gustaf Kossina introduced the idea of *Volk* in his writings, claiming a commonality of traits among Germans that, he felt, qualified the German people to become the "ruling elite" (Cashmore and Troyna 1990).

Mein Kampf (1939) was Adolf Hitler's contribution to the concept of a superior race. In it, he conceptualized two races, the Aryans and Others. He focused attention on several groups, in particular the Jews. German economic and social problems were blamed on the Jews.

What followed in the name of German purity was the extermination of millions of Jews, Poles, Catholics, Gypsies, homosexuals, and other groups and individuals who were deemed "less human" or who opposed the Nazis. The extent to which Hitler succeeded exemplifies what can happen when one group needs to feel superior to others, blames other groups for its shortcomings, and has the power to act against those minorities. More recent attempts to classify groups have been based not on external characteristics but on blood or gene type, even though blood types or genome do not always correlate with other traits.

As applied to mammals, the term *race* has biological significance only when it refers to closely inbred groups in which all family lines are alike—as in pure breeds of domesticated animals. These conditions are never realized in humans and are impossible in large populations of any species (Witzig 1996). Many groups have been mislabeled "races" when differences are actually cultural. Jews, Poles, Irish, and Italians have all erroneously been called "races." In short, when it comes to humans, scientists do not agree about how many races there are in the biological sense of that word or whether race is a biological reality at all.

Symbolic interaction theory contends that if people believe something is real, it may be real in its consequences. It does not matter whether scientists say that attempts to classify people into races are inaccurate and that the word is biologically meaningless. People on the streets of your hometown think *they* know what the word *race* means. Moreover, people do look different as we traverse the globe. That people *think* there are differences has consequences. As a social concept, race has not only referred to physical features and inherited genes but has carried over to presumed psychological and moral characteristics, thus justifying discriminatory treatment. The following examples illustrate the complex problems in trying to classify people into "races."

With the enactment of apartheid laws in 1948, the white government in South Africa institutionalized differential laws based on their definitions of racial groups and specified the privileges and restrictions allotted to each group (Marger 2006). Bantu populations—the native Africans—and Coloreds—those of mixed blood—were restricted to separate living areas and types of work. Asians—descendants of immigrants from India and other Asian countries—received higher salaries than the Bantu groups but less than whites, while whites of European descent, primarily Dutch and English, had the highest living standard and best residential locations. Under the apartheid system, race was determined by tracing ancestry back for 14 generations. A single ancestor who was not Dutch or English might cause an individual to be considered "colored" rather than white. Physical features mattered little. Individuals carried a card indicating their race based on genealogy. Although this system began to break down in the 1990s due to international pressure and under the leadership of the first black president (Nelson Mandela, elected in 1994), vestiges of these notions of "reality" will take generations to change.

By contrast, in Brazil, an individual's race is based on physical features—skin tone, hair texture, facial features, eye color, and so forth—rather than on the "one drop of blood" rule in South Africa. Brothers and sisters who have the same parents and ancestors may be classified as belonging to different races. The idea of race is based on nearly opposite criteria in Brazil and South Africa, illustrating the arbitrary nature of racial classification attempts (Keith and Herring 1991; Walker and Karas 1993).

Before civil rights laws were passed in the United States in the 1960s, a number of states had laws that spelled out differential treatment for racial groups. These were commonly referred to as Jim Crow laws. States in the South passed laws defining who was African American or Native American. In many cases, it was difficult to determine to which category an individual belonged. For instance, African Americans in Georgia were defined as people with any ascertainable trace of "Negro" blood in their veins. In Missouri, one-eighth or more Negro blood was sufficient, whereas in Louisiana, one-thirty-second Negro blood defined one as black. Differential treatment was spelled out

in other states as well. In Texas, for example, the father's race determined the race of the child. In Vermont, newborn babies of racially mixed parentage were listed as "mixed" on the birth certificate. In West Virginia, a newborn was classified as "black" if either parent was considered black. Until recently, several U.S. states still attempted to classify the race of newborns by the percentage of black blood or parentage (Lopez 1996). Federal law now prohibits discrimination on the basis of "racial" classifications, and most explicitly racial state laws have been challenged and dropped.

The Significance of Race Versus Class

From the time of slavery in the Americas until the late 20th century, race has been the determining factor in social stratification and opportunity for people of African descent in the United States, the Caribbean, and Brazil. Whether this is changing in the 21st century is a question that has occupied sociologists, politicians, educators, and other scientists in recent years. Some scholars argue that race is a primary cause of different placement in the stratification system, whereas others insist that race and social class are both at work, with socioeconomic factors (social class) more important than race.

An influential participant in the debate, sociologist William Julius Wilson, states that the racial oppression that characterized the African American experience throughout the 19th century was caused first by slavery and then by a lingering caste structure that severely restricted upward mobility for African Americans. However, the breakdown of the plantation economy and the rise of industrialism created more opportunities for African Americans to participate in the economy (Wilson 1978, 1993a, 1993b).

Wilson (1978) argues that after World War II, an African American class structure developed with characteristics similar to those of the white class structure. Occupation and income took on ever greater significance in social position, especially for the African American middle class. However, as black middle-class professionals moved up in the stratification structure, lower-class African American ghetto residents became more isolated and less mobile. Limited unskilled job opportunities for the lower class have resulted in poverty and stagnation so severe that some families are almost outside of the functioning economic system. Wilson (1978, 1984, 1993a) calls this group the *underclass*.

Some researchers assert that the United States cannot escape poverty because well-paid, unskilled jobs requiring few skills and little education are disappearing from the economy and because the poor are concentrated in segregated urban areas (Massey 2007; Massey and Denton 1998). Poorly educated African American teenagers and young adults from the inner city see their job prospects limited to the low-wage sector (e.g., fast-food work paying minimum wage), and they experience record levels of unemployment (Wilson 1987). Movement out of poverty becomes almost impossible.

The house in the Chicago slums was not atypical of the quality of homes in segregated America in the 1940s.

Wilson's point is illustrated by the following: More than two in five African Americans are now middle-class, compared to one in twenty in 1940. Thus, there is an ever-widening gap between poor African Americans and their middle-class counterparts. On the other hand, most adults in many inner-city ghetto neighborhoods are not employed in a typical week. Thus, children in these neighborhoods may grow up without ever seeing someone go to work (Wilson 1996). The new global economic system is a contributing factor as unskilled jobs go abroad to cheaper labor (Friedman 2005; Massey 2007). Without addressing these structural causes of poverty, we cannot expect to reduce the number of people in the underclass—whether they are white, black, or other minority.

A big debate among scholars surrounds the following question: Has race declined in significance and class become more important in determining placement in the stratification system? Tests of Wilson's thesis present us with mixed results (Jencks 1992). For instance, African Americans'

average education level (12.4 years in school) is almost the same as whites' (12.7 years), suggesting they have comparable qualifications for employment. However, this equity stops at the high school level; 27.6% of whites are college graduates, compared to 17.3% of blacks (U.S. Census Bureau 2005h). More important, African Americans earn less than whites in the same occupational categories. As Tables 8.1a and 8.1b make clear, income levels for African Americans and whites are not even close to being equal. Unemployment and poverty affect a higher percentage of black families than white ones, so economics alone does not seem a complete answer to who is in the underclass.

Although racial bias has decreased at the micro (interpersonal) level, it is still a significant determinant in the lives of African Americans, especially those in the lower class. The data are complex, but we can conclude that for upwardly mobile African Americans, class may be more important than race. Still, physical traits such as skin color cannot be dismissed. They can be crippling for the underclass.

Table 8.1a Race and Family Income

	Median Family Annual Income
White	$55,768
Black	$34,369 (62% of white-family income)
Hispanic	$34,272 (61% of white-family income)

Source: U.S. Census Bureau 2006e:Table 679. Figures are for 2003.

Table 8.1b Income (in dollars) by Educational Level and Race/Ethnicity

Education	White	Black	Hispanic
Not a high school graduate	19,110	16,201	18,349
High school graduate	28,708	23,777	23,472
Some college, no degree	30,316	25,616	27,586
College graduate	52,259	42,968	43,676
Master's degree	62,981	57,449	56,486
Professional degree	119,712	87,713	78,190

Source: U.S. Census Bureau 2006e:Table 217. Figures are for 2003.

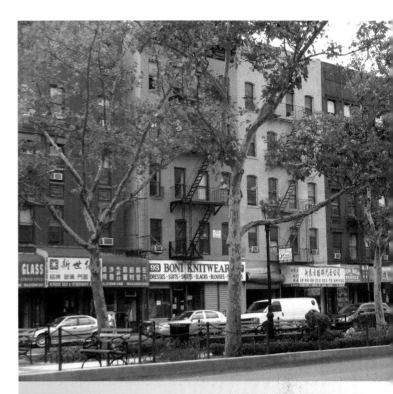

Ethnic enclaves have a strong sense of local community, holding festivals from the old country and developing networks in the new country. Such areas are called "ghettos" and are not necessarily impoverished. The photo depicts a street on the Lower East Side of New York, which was once a transition station and ghetto for recent immigrants.

Thinking Sociologically

Look around you. On what bases do you classify people into social groups? How do you describe someone to another person? Why do you describe them this way? Do you use racial terms only for people of color? Why? Are people who are white "just normal"? If so, what does that say?

Ethnic Groups

The second major type of minority group—the **ethnic group**—is based on cultural factors: language, religion, dress, foods, customs, beliefs, values, norms, a shared group identity or feeling, and sometimes loyalty to a homeland, monarch, or religious leader. Members are grouped together because they share a common cultural heritage, often connected with a national or geographical identity. Some social scientists prefer to call racial groups "ethnic groups" because the term *ethnic* encompasses most minorities and avoids problems with the term *race* (Aguirre and Turner 2006).

Visits to ethnic enclaves in large cities around the world give a picture of ethnicity. Little Italy, Chinatown, Greek Town, and Polish neighborhoods may have non-English street signs and newspapers, ethnic restaurants, culture-specific houses of worship, and clothing styles that reflect the ethnic subculture. Occasionally, an ethnic group shares power in pluralistic societies, but most often they hold a minority status with little power.

How is ethnicity constructed or defined? Many very different ethnic groups have been combined in government categories, such as censuses conducted by countries, yet they speak different languages and often have very different religions. For example, in North America, ethnic group members do not view themselves as "Indian" or "Native American." Instead, they use 600 independent tribal nation names to define themselves, including the Ojibwa (Chippewa), Dineh (also called the Navajo), Lakota (also called the Sioux), and many others (see Map 8.2). Likewise, in the U.S. census, Koreans, Filipinos, Chinese, Japanese, and Malaysians come from very different cultures but are identified as *Asian Americans* in the census. People from Brazil, Mexico, and Cuba are grouped together in a category called *Hispanics* or *Latinos*. When federal funds for social services were made

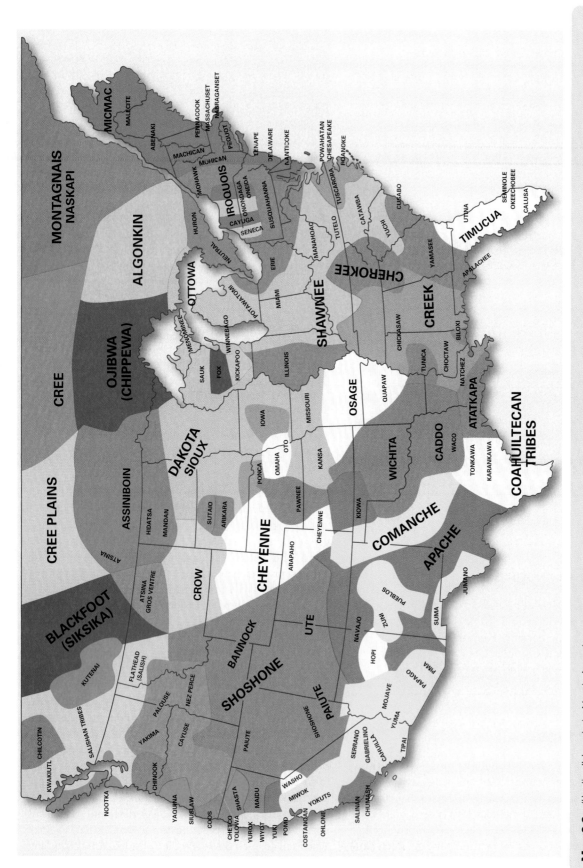

Map 8.2 "Indian" Lands in North America

Source: Adapted from Smith 1989. Courtesy of Cherokee Publications, P.O. Box 430, Cherokee, NC 28719, phone (828) 488-8856.

Note: Long before "white people" set foot in the Americas, many thriving societies lived in groups on the North and South American continents. Each group developed a lifestyle compatible with the geographical area and material goods available to it. Many different cultures, languages, religions, value systems, economies, and political systems emerged. Thus, the terms *Native American* and *First Nations* refer to many different societies, each with its own identity.

available to Asian Americans or American Indians, these diverse people began to think of themselves as part of a larger grouping for political purposes (Esperitu 1992). The federal government essentially created an ethnic group by naming and providing funding to that group. If people wanted services (health care, legal rights, and so forth), they had to become a part of a particular group. This process of merging many ethnic groups into one broader category emphasizes that ethnic identity is itself socially shaped and created.

Biracial and Multiracial Populations: Immigration, Intermarriage, and Personal Identification

Our racial and ethnic identities are becoming more complex as migration around the world brings to distant shores new immigrants in search of safety and a new start. Keep in mind that our racial and ethnic identities come largely from external labels placed on us by governments and our associates but reinforced by our own self-identification. The important point is this: *Race is a social construct that can change with conditions in a country.*

Many European countries are now host to immigrants from their former colonies, making them multiracial. France hosts many North and West Africans, and Great Britain hosts large populations from Africa, India, and Pakistan. The resulting mix of peoples has blurred racial lines and created many multiracial individuals. Original migration patterns are shown in Map 8.3. These patterns illustrate that "push" factors drive people from some countries and pull them to other countries. The most common push-pull factors are job opportunities, living conditions, desire for security, political or religious fear of persecution, and promise of individual liberties, availability of medical care, and educational opportunities. The target countries of migrants are most often in North America, Australia, or Western Europe, and the highest emigration rates are from Africa, Eastern Europe, Central Asia, and South and Central America.

The United States was once considered a biracial country, black and white (which of course, disregarded the Native American population). However, the nation currently accepts more new immigrants than any other country. Immigration from every continent has led to a more diverse population, with up to 16% of the U.S. population in any year being foreign born. With new immigration, increasing rates of intermarriage, and many more individuals claiming multiracial identification, the picture is much more complex today, and the color lines have been redrawn (DaCosta 2007; Lee and Bean 2004, 2007). One in forty individuals

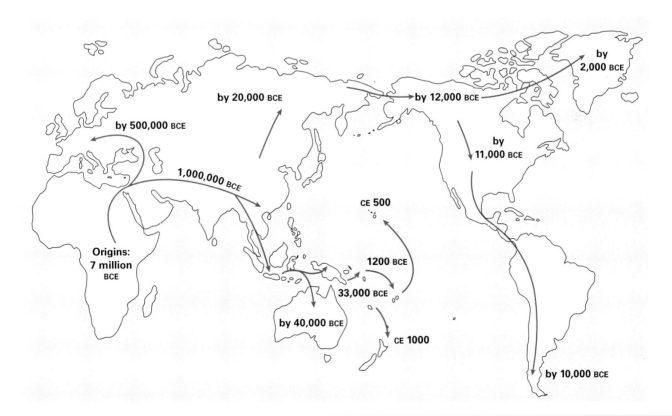

Map 8.3 The Spread of Humans Around the World

Source: Diamond 1999:37.

claims multiracial status today, and estimates are that one in five will do so by 2050 (Lee and Bean 2004).

Most immigrants enter through several border states, with California, New York, and Texas receiving the largest share. In turn, population redistribution takes place within the United States, largely to the South and Midwest. Asians have the largest number of interstate movers, followed by Mexicans and other Latin Americans (Parrillo 2005).

Census data are used in countries to determine many characteristics of populations. In the United States, questions about race and ethnic classification have changed with each 10-year study. The important point is that government-determined categories thereafter define the racial and ethnic composition of a country. In the 2000 census, citizens were for the first time given the option of picking more than one racial category. Seven million people or 2.3% of the U.S. population selected two or more racial categories, with white/American Indian being the most common mixed category (Schaefer 2008).

Hispanics, some of whom prefer the term *Latinos*, made up 12.5% of the population in the 2000 U.S. Census, 35.3 million of the total census of 281.4 million. This is an increase of more than 50% since the 1990 census. As of January 21, 2003, Hispanics are the largest and fastest-growing minority group, up 4.7% in one year (2000–2001) and accounting for 37 million people, or 13% of the population. Blacks follow with 36 million and 12.7% of the population. Whites make up 70% and Asians 4% of the total U.S. population (CBS News 2003).

Of Latinos in the census, Mexicans made up 58.5%, Puerto Ricans 9.6%, Cubans 3.5%, Central Americans 4.8%, and South Americans 3.8% (U.S. Census Bureau 2001c). About 5.3 million, or 15.1%, of all Latinos identified themselves as *panethnic,* that is, not identifying with one Latino ethnic group but as Latino in general (McConnell and Delgado-Romero 2004).

One controversy in the U.S. Congress and in the 2008 presidential election was illegal immigration. Immigrants seeking opportunities come by ship, in cargo containers, across borders. Border crossings between the United States and Mexico cause the most controversy. At 2,000 miles (3,200 kilometers) long, it has proven difficult to patrol. Proposals to curb illegal immigration include criminalizing illegal immigration, creating a guest worker program, and building the fence that is in progress along parts of the border. No law has yet been passed and the debate continues.

Arbitrary socially constructed classifications such as those in the examples above are frequently used as justification for treating individuals differently despite the lack of scientific basis for such distinctions (Williams 1996). The legacy of "race" remains even in countries where discrimination based on race is illegal. Poverty and discrimination justify and reinforce differential treatment in poor schools, employment, and other areas of life, thus resulting in a cycle of more poverty and discrimination. The question remains: Why is a multiracial baby with any African, Native American, or other minority heritage classified by the minority status?

Thinking Sociologically

Identify one dominant and one minority group in your community or on campus. Where do that group's members fall in the stratification system? Does this placement reflect a similar racial, ethnic, or other minority group status in the nation as a whole? How are the life chances of individuals in these groups influenced by factors beyond their control?

PREJUDICE AND RACISM: MICRO-LEVEL ANALYSIS

Have you ever found yourself in a situation in which you were viewed as different, strange, undesirable, or "less than human"? Perhaps you have felt the sting of rejection, based not on judgment of you as a person but solely because of the ethnic group into which you were born. Then again, you may have been insulated from this type of rejection if you grew up in a homogeneous community or in a privileged group; you may have even learned some negative attitudes about those different from yourself. It is sobering to think that where and when in history you were born determine how you are treated, your life chances, and many of your experiences.

Racial and ethnic minorities experience disproportionate prejudice and racism. Several processes act to keep minority groups among the have-nots of society. Consider the following factors:

Process	Result
Stratification	Minority status
Prejudice	Poor self-concept, negative relations with others
Discrimination	Poor jobs, income, education, housing
Racism	Systems that limit access to resources
Negative contact	Hostilities, war, conflict between groups

Prejudice

When minority groups are present within a society, prejudice influences dominant-minority group relations. **Prejudice** refers to attitudes that prejudge a group, usually negatively and not based on facts. Prejudiced individuals lump together people with certain characteristics as an undifferentiated group without considering individual differences. Although prejudice can refer to positive attitudes and exaggerations (as when a mother is prejudiced in thinking her own child is gifted), in this chapter, we refer to the negative aspects of prejudice. We also focus on the adverse effects brought on minority group members by prejudice. While prejudice can be stimulated by events such as conflicts at the institutional level and war at the societal level, attitudes are held by individuals and can be best understood as a micro-level phenomenon.

When prejudiced attitudes are manifested in actions, they are referred to as **discrimination**, differential treatment and harmful actions against minorities. These actions at the micro level might include refusal to sell someone a house because of the religion, race, or ethnicity of the buyer or employment practices that treat groups differently based on minority status (Feagin and Feagin 2007). Both prejudice and discrimination affect the lives of both discriminators and those discriminated against. Discrimination, such as laws that deny opportunities or resources to members of a particular group, operates largely at the meso or macro level, discussed later in the chapter.

The Nature of Prejudice

Prejudice is an understandable response of humans to their social environment. To survive, every social group or unit—a sorority, a sports team, a civic club, or a nation—needs to mobilize the loyalty of its members. Each organization needs to convince people to voluntarily commit energy, skills, time, and resources so the organization can meet its needs. Furthermore, as people commit themselves to a group, they invest a portion of themselves and feel loyalty to the group.

Individual commitment to a group influences one's perception and loyalties, creating preference or even bias for the group. This commitment is often based on stressing distinctions from other groups and deep preference for one's own group. However, these loyalties may be dysfunctional for out-group members and the victims of prejudice.

One reason people hold prejudices is that it is easier to pigeonhole the vast amount of information and stimuli coming at us in today's complex societies, and to sort information into neat unquestioned categories, than to evaluate each piece of information separately for its accuracy. Prejudiced individuals often categorize large numbers of people and attribute to them personal qualities based on their dress, language, skin color, or other identifying racial or ethnic features. This process is called **stereotyping**.

Stereotypes, or the pictures in our heads, are often distorted, oversimplified, or exaggerated ideas passed down over generations through cultures. They are applied to all members of a group, regardless of individual differences, and used to justify prejudice, discrimination, and unequal distribution of power, wealth, and opportunities. Often, the result is unfair and inaccurate judgments about individuals who are members of the stereotyped groups. The problem is that both those stereotyping and those being stereotyped come to believe the "pictures" and act accordingly.

Prejudice is difficult to change because it is rooted in traditions and cultural beliefs and is based on culturally imbedded stereotypes of groups. Individuals grow up learning these ingrained beliefs, which often go unchallenged. Yet when studied scientifically, stereotypes seldom correspond to facts.

Social scientists know, for instance, that prejudice is related to the history and to the political and economic climate in a region or country, part of the macro-level cultural and social environment. For instance, in some southern U.S. states where African Americans constitute a majority of the population, there is evidence that white racial attitudes are more antagonistic due to perceived or real economic and political competition for jobs and power (Farley 2005; Glaser 1994).

In wartime, the adversary may be the victim of racial slurs, or members of the opponent society may be depicted in films or other media as villains. During World War II, American films often showed negative stereotypes of Japanese and German people, stereotypes that likely reinforced the decision to intern more than 110,000 Japanese Americans, the majority of whom were U.S. citizens, in detention camps following the bombing of Pearl Harbor (see the photo essay on page 246). Similar issues and stereotypes have arisen for American citizens with Middle Eastern ancestry since the attacks on the New York World Trade Center on September 11, 2001.

Sometimes, minority group members incorporate prejudiced views about themselves into their behavior. This process, an example of a *self-fulfilling prophesy*, involves the adoption of stereotypical behaviors. (See Chapter 4.) No group is born dumb, lazy, dirty, or money hungry, but its members can be conditioned to believe such depictions of themselves or be forced into acting out certain behaviors based on expectations of the dominant group.

Thinking Sociologically

Watch the Oscar-winning movie *Crash*. In what ways does this video raise issues of majority-minority stereotypes? How does it highlight labeling done by each group?

Explanations of Prejudice

We have all met them—the people who express hostility toward others. They tell jokes about minorities, curse them, and even threaten action against them. Why do these individuals do this? The following theories have attempted to explain the prejudiced individual.

Photo Essay

Prejudice and Discrimination Against Japanese Americans

On December 7, 1941, Japan bombed Pearl Harbor in Hawaii. Fear of a Japanese invasion and of subversive acts by Japanese Americans prompted President Franklin D. Roosevelt to sign Executive Order 9066 on February 19, 1942. The order designated the West Coast as a military zone from which "any or all persons may be excluded." Although not specified in the order, Japanese Americans were singled out for evacuation. More than 110,000 people of Japanese ancestry were removed from California, southern Arizona, and western Washington and Oregon and sent to 10 relocation camps. Those forcibly removed from their homes, businesses, and possessions included Japanese immigrants who were legally forbidden to become U.S. citizens (Issei), the American born (Nisei), and children of the American born (Sansei).

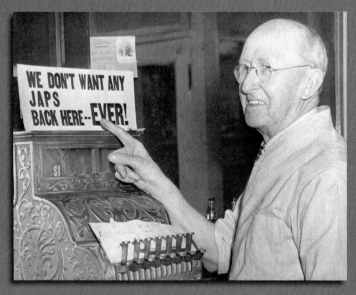

After the internment of Japanese Americans from the Seattle region, barber G. S. Hante points proudly to his bigoted sign that reads, We Don't Want Any Japs Back Here . . . EVER!

Evacuees of Japanese ancestry were interned at Santa Anita, California, among other places, for the duration of the Second World War.

Anxious to show their loyalty to their country, Japanese American citizens on their way to an internment camp flash "victory" signs, and one young boy waves an American flag.

Frustration-aggression theory. In Greensboro, North Carolina, in 1978, a group of civil rights activists and African American adults and children listened as a guitarist sang freedom songs. A nine-car cavalcade of white Ku Klux Klan (KKK) and American Nazi Party members arrived. The intruders unloaded weapons from the backs of their cars, approached the rally, and opened fire for 88 seconds, then, they left as calmly as they had arrived. Four white men and a black woman were dead (Greensboro Justice Fund 2005). According to frustration-aggression theory, many of the perpetrators of this and other heinous acts feel angry and frustrated because they cannot achieve their work or other goals. They blame any vulnerable minority group—religious, ethnic, sexual orientation—and members of that group become targets of their anger. Frustration-aggression theory focuses largely on poorly adjusted people who displace their frustration with aggressive attacks on others. Hate groups evolve from like-minded individuals, often because of prejudice and frustration (see Map 8.4 on page 248).

Scapegoating. When it is impossible to vent frustration toward the real target—one's boss, teachers, the economic system—frustration can take the form of aggressive action against minority group members who are vulnerable because of their low status. They become the scapegoats. The word *scapegoat* comes from the Bible, Leviticus 16:5–22. Once a year, a goat (which was obviously innocent) was laden with parchments on which people had written their sins. The goat was then sent out to the desert to die. This was part of a ritual of purification, and the creature took the blame for others.

Scapegoating occurs when a minority group is blamed for others' failures or shortcomings. It is difficult to look at oneself to seek reasons for failure but easy to transfer the cause for one's failure to others. Individuals who feel they are failures in their jobs or other aspects of their lives may blame minority groups. From within such a prejudiced mind-set, even violence toward the out-group becomes acceptable. One example is the hostility represented in a notice distributed to a college campus's mailboxes: "Earth's Most Endangered Species: The White Male. Help Preserve It." The notice expressed frustration with the "plight" of white males and blamed policies favoring minorities for their perceived problems.

Today, jobs and promotions are harder for young adults to obtain than they were for the baby boom generation, but the reason is mostly demographic. The baby boom of the 1940s and 1950s resulted in a bulge in the population. There are so many people in the workforce at each successive step on the ladder that it will be another few years before those baby boomers retire in large numbers. Until that happens, there will be a good deal of frustration about apparent occupational stagnation. It is easier—and safer—to blame minorities or affirmative action programs than to vent frustration at the next-oldest segment of the

Klansmen in traditional white robes demonstrate in front of a courthouse in New York City in 1999. They carried a flag sewn together from parts of American and Confederate flags, a symbol of their blended loyalties.

population or at one's grandparents for having a large family. Blacks, Hispanics, other minorities, and policies such as affirmative action become easy scapegoats.

Although this theory helps explain some situations, it does not predict when frustration will lead to aggression, why only some people who experience frustration vent their feelings on the vulnerable, and why some groups become targets (Marger 2006).

Racism

Racism is any attitude, belief, or institutional arrangement that favors one racial group over another, and this favoritism may result in intentional or unintentional consequences for minority groups (Farley 2005). Racism is often embedded in institutions of society and supported by people who are not aware of the social consequence of their actions. Many people without social science training see racism as a micro-level issue—one involving individual initiative and individual bigotry—whereas most social scientists see the problem as occurring at the meso and macro levels. Still, issues at the micro level continue to be real. *Ideological racism* is an attempt to justify racism on the basis of a pseudo-scientific set of ideas. It involves the belief that humans are divided into innately different groups, some of which are biologically inferior. Those who hold these views see biological differences as the cause of most cultural and social differences, as Hitler's actions against the Jews and other groups illustrate (Marger 2006). (This is illustrated in the discussion of "Historical Attempts to Define Race" in "Sociology in Your Social World" on page 238.)

Number of Hate Groups

| 51–80 | 26–50 | 11–25 | 0–10 |

Map 8.4 Active Hate Groups in 2007

Source: Reprinted by permission of the Southern Poverty Law Center. Map by Anna Versluis.

In *symbolic racism,* people insist that they are not prejudiced or racist—that they are color-blind and committed to equality—but at the same time, they oppose any social policies that would eliminate racism and make true equality of opportunity possible (Farley 2005). Symbolic racists claim to reject race and racism but also fail to correct any problems that are created because it still is embedded in our social system.

Institutional racism involves discrimination that is hidden within the system, and symbolic racism allows it to remain in place. Symbolic racists reject ideological racism as blatant, crude, and ignorant but fail to recognize that their actions may perpetuate institutional inequalities. This will be discussed under meso-level analysis below.

Racism has psychological and social costs, both to those on the receiving end and to the perpetrators. There is a waste of talent and energy of both minorities and those who justify and carry out discriminatory actions. In the 1990s, individual membership in white supremacy groups in Europe and North America grew, as did attacks on blacks, Jews, immigrants, and those whose religious and cultural practices were different from those of the majority. For instance, in the United States, racism resulted in a rash of African American church bombings in 1996 (Feagin, Vera, and Batur 2001; Sack 1996), and in 2006 alone, there were 1,554 anti-Semitic incidents involving vandalism, assaults, or threats directed at Jewish citizens or Jewish establishments (Anti-Defamation League 2007; Stephen Roth Institute 2006). Unfortunately, until there are better economic opportunities for more people, individual racism is likely to be one result of economic competition for jobs (Feagin et al. 2001).

Although social-psychological theories shed light on the most extreme cases of individual or small-group prejudice and racism, there is much these theories do not explain. They say little about the everyday hostility and reinforcement of prejudice that most of us experience or engage in, and they fail to deal with institutional discrimination.

DISCRIMINATION: MESO-LEVEL ANALYSIS

Dear Teacher, I would like to introduce you to my son, Wind-Wolf. He is probably what you would consider a typical Indian kid. He was born and raised on the reservation. He has black hair, dark brown eyes, and an olive complexion. And, like so many Indian children his age, he is shy and quiet in the classroom. He is 5 years old, in kindergarten, and I can't understand why you have already labeled him a "slow learner." He has already been through quite an education compared with his peers in Western society. He was bonded to his mother and to the Mother Earth in a traditional native childbirth ceremony. And he has been continuously cared for by his mother, father, sisters, cousins, aunts, uncles, grandparents, and extended tribal family since this ceremony. . . .

Wind-Wolf was strapped (in his baby basket like a turtle shell) snugly with a deliberate restriction on his arms and legs. Although Western society may argue this hinders motor-skill development and abstract reasoning, we believe it forces the child to first develop his intuitive faculties, rational intellect, symbolic thinking, and five senses. Wind-Wolf was with his mother constantly, closely bonded physically, as she carried him on her back or held him while breast-feeding. She carried him everywhere she went, and every night he slept with both parents. Because of this, Wind-Wolf's educational setting was not only a "secure" environment, but it was also very colorful, complicated, sensitive, and diverse.

As he grew older, Wind-Wolf began to crawl out of the baby basket, develop his motor skills, and explore the world around him. When frightened or sleepy, he could always return to the basket, as a turtle withdraws into its shell. Such an inward journey allows one to reflect in privacy on what he has learned and to carry the new knowledge deeply into the unconscious and the soul. Shapes, sizes, colors, texture, sound, smell, feeling, taste, and the learning process are therefore functionally integrated—the physical and spiritual, matter and energy, and conscious and unconscious, individual and social.

It takes a long time to absorb and reflect on these kinds of experiences, so maybe that is why you think my Indian child is a slow learner. His aunts and grandmothers taught him to count and to know his numbers while they sorted materials for making abstract designs in native baskets. And he was taught to learn mathematics by counting the sticks we use in our traditional native hand game. So he may be slow in grasping the methods and tools you use in your classroom, ones quite familiar to his white peers, but I hope you will be patient with him. It takes time to adjust to a new cultural system and learn new things. He is not culturally "disadvantaged," but he is culturally different. (Lake 1990:48–53)*

This letter expresses the frustration of a father who sees his son being labeled and discriminated against by the school system without being given a chance. *Discrimination* refers to actions taken against members of a minority group. It can occur at individual and small-group levels but is particularly problematic at the organizational and institutional levels—the meso level of analysis.

Thinking Sociologically

How might the schools unintentionally misunderstand Wind-Wolf (discussed in the letter at the left) in such a way that this has negative consequences for his success?

Discrimination is based on race, ethnicity, age, sex, sexual orientation, nationality, social class, religion, or whatever other category members of a society choose to make significant (Feagin and Feagin 2007; McLemore, Romo, and Baker 2001). **Individual discrimination**, actions taken against minority group members by individuals, can take many forms, from avoiding contact by excluding individuals from one's club, neighborhood, or even country, to physical violence against minorities as seen in hate crime attacks on Asian Americans perceived to be taking jobs from white Americans.

Institutional discrimination, or meso-level discrimination, is often a normal or routine part of the way an organization operates. It includes both intentional actions, such as laws restricting minorities, and unintentional actions, which have consequences that restrict minorities. Institutional discrimination is built into organizations and cultural expectations in the social world. Even nonprejudiced people can participate in institutional racism quite unintentionally. For example, many schools track students into classes based on standardized test results. Minority children end up disproportionately in lower tracks for a number of reasons (see Chapter 11). Thus, a policy that is meant to give all children an equal chance ends up legitimizing the channeling of some minorities into the lower-achieving classroom groupings.

Purposeful discrimination is built into the law or is part of the explicit policies of an organization. It is sometimes called *de jure* discrimination—meaning discrimination by law. Jim Crow laws, passed in the late 1800s in the United States, and laws that barred Jewish people in Germany from living, working, or investing in certain places are examples. By contrast, unintentional discrimination results from policies that have the unanticipated consequence of favoring one group and disadvantaging another. This is sometimes called *de facto* discrimination, for there is discrimination "in fact" even if not in intent. It can be more damaging than discrimination by individuals because it is often done by people who are not the least bit prejudiced and may not recognize the effects of their actions (Merton 1949a).

---

*Reprinted by permission of Medicine Grizzly Bear Lake, www.nativehealer.net.

Jim Crow laws played out in a Pensacola, Florida, movie house in the 1930s: This was the rear entrance for African Americans.

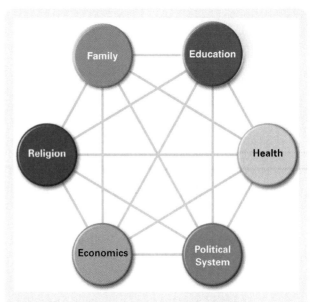

Each circle represents a different institution—family, education, religion, health, political-legal system, and economics. These meso-level systems are interdependent, using information or resources from the others. If discrimination occurs in one institution, the second institution may unintentionally borrow information that results in discrimination. In this way, discrimination occurs at the meso level without awareness by individuals at the micro level.

Figure 8.1   Side-Effect Discrimination

Unintentional discrimination usually occurs through one of two processes: side-effect discrimination or past-in-present discrimination (Feagin and Feagin 2007). **Side-effect discrimination** refers to practices in one institutional area that have a negative impact because they are linked to practices in another institutional area. Figure 8.1 illustrates this idea. Each institution uses information from the other institutions to make decisions. Thus, discrimination in the criminal justice system, which has in fact been well documented, may influence discrimination in education or health care systems.

Consider the following examples of side-effect discrimination. The first is in the criminal justice and employment systems. In a 1999 interview conducted by one of the authors, a probation officer in a moderate-size city in Ohio said that he had never seen an African American in his county get a not-guilty verdict and that he was not sure it was possible. He had known of cases in which minorities had pleaded guilty to a lesser charge even though they were

innocent because they did not think they could receive a fair verdict in that city. When people apply for jobs, however, they are required to report the conviction on the application form. By using information about someone's criminal record, employers who clearly do not intend to discriminate end up doing so whether or not the individual was guilty. The side-effect discrimination is unintentional discrimination; the criminal justice system has reached an unjust verdict, and the potential employer is swayed unfairly.

Thinking Sociologically

Think of the information that is used in one organization (such as a business that is hiring people) and has been provided by another institution or organization (say, the criminal justice system). How might some of that information be a source of unintended side-effect discrimination for a minority group member?

The second example of side-effect discrimination shows that the Internet also plays a role in institutional discrimination and privilege. For example, in Alaska, 15.6% of the population is Native, but Natives hold only 5% of state jobs (U.S. Census Bureau 2003a). Consider that the State of Alaska uses the Internet as its primary means of advertising and accepting applications for state jobs (State of Alaska 2006). No affordable Internet access is available in 164 predominantly Native villages in Alaska (Denali Commission 2001). Other options for application include requesting applications by mail, if a person knows about the opening. The usefulness of this process is limited, however, by the reliability and speed of mail service to remote villages and the often-short application periods for state jobs. State officials may not intentionally use the mechanism to prevent Aleuts, Inupiats, Athabaskans, or other Alaska Natives from gaining access to state jobs, but the effect can be institutionalized discrimination. Here, Internet access plays a role in participation of minorities in the social world (Nakamura 2004).

The point is that whites, especially affluent whites, benefit from privileges not available to low-income minorities. The privileged members may not purposely disadvantage others and may not be prejudiced, but the playing field is not level, even though discrimination may be completely unintentional (Rothenberg 2008). Put yourself in the position of a person who does not have these privileges, identified by Peggy McIntosh (2002:97–101):

I can avoid spending time with people who mistrust people of my color.

I can protect my children most of the time from people who might not like them.

I can criticize our government and talk about how I fear its policies and behavior without being seen as a cultural "outsider."

I can easily buy posters, postcards, picture books, greeting cards, dolls, toys, and children's magazines featuring people of my race.

I can arrange my activities so that I will never have to experience feelings of rejection owing to my race.

Past-in-present discrimination refers to practices from the past that may no longer be allowed but that continue to affect people today. In Mississippi between 1951 and 1952, the average state expenditure to educate a white child was $147 per pupil, whereas the average was $34 per black pupil in segregated schools (Luhman and Gilman 1980). Such blatant segregation and inequality in use of tax dollars is no longer legal. This may seem like ancient history, yet some African Americans who were in school in the 1950s and 1960s are now trying to support a family and pay for their children's college expenses. To those who received a

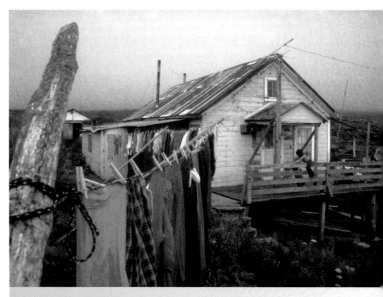

Children play on the porch of their rustic home with no plumbing in the rural Alaska village of Akhiok, among the Aleutian Islands. Finding jobs through the Internet is not an option from this location.

substandard education and did not have an opportunity for college, it is not ancient history because it affects their opportunities today.

Stanley Lieberson (1980) asked a difficult question: Why do some minority groups do better than others? He used multiple methods of gathering data to test various explanations. His study and conclusion are explained in the next "How Do We Know?" As you read it, think about the special structural circumstances that made things different for African Americans than for many other minority groups. How are side-effect discrimination and past-in-present discrimination at work?

Some countries have attempted to make amends for past institutional discrimination by passing laws that prohibit differential treatment on the basis of race, age, sex, or sexual preference. India has legal protections and education quotas for outcaste members, forbids discrimination on the basis of caste, and encourages the hiring of lower and outcaste members. However, tradition and unintentional discrimination make change a slow process.

Remember that prejudice is an attitude, discrimination an action. If neighbors do not wish to have minority group members move onto their block, that is prejudice. If they try to organize other neighbors against the newcomers or make the situation unpleasant once the minority family has moved in, that is discrimination. If minorities cannot afford to live in the neighborhood because of discrimination in the marketplace, that is institutional discrimination. Discrimination can cause prejudice and vice versa, but they are most often found working together, reinforcing one another (Merton 1949a; Myers 2003).

How Do We Know?

A Piece of the Pie

Why did new immigrant groups from south, central, and eastern Europe fare so much better than African Americans in the United States? Frequently heard explanations point out that the handicaps faced by blacks were more severe than those faced by whites, that blacks could not shed their skin color, making them more recognizable as "different" and more subject to discrimination. Yet, Japanese and Chinese people have fared well. They, too, have faced discrimination and can be singled out because of their physical features. To address these difficult questions, Stanley Lieberson (1980) consulted an array of historical writings about immigrants, slavery, and the economic and educational systems of the 1800s. He studied secondary data, mostly collected from census data, and analyzed explanations by other social scientists, thus developing an overview of the economic and social circumstances that have affected different groups in the United States.

Lieberson (1980) concludes that the new immigrants and blacks who were arriving in the North did not differ greatly in their aspirations to get an education and good jobs. Just after slavery, the prospects for blacks looked promising. In fact, while many immigrants favored jobs over pursuit of education, blacks were initially fairly successful in narrowing the gap in education. So what caused African Americans to fall behind? Just before World War II, discrimination against blacks was intense. In the hierarchy of respect, blacks were lower than Asian or European immigrants, probably as a result of unfavorable attitudes during the slave period—another case of the past-in-present influence. Immigrants were preferred over blacks for jobs, especially in those positions that required minimal skills. Immigrants received more of the jobs in manufacturing that had possibilities for future mobility, while blacks could get only service jobs such as sweeping floors, where promotions were nonexistent. Asian groups also experienced periods of severe discrimination, but their groups were limited in number due to immigration laws, and they posed little economic threat. Meanwhile, labor unions discriminated against African Americans, and Realtors enforced segregation in housing. Moreover, African Americans migrated to the North much faster than other ethnic groups. Unlike members of smaller ethnic groups, who can more easily assimilate into occupational niches, black migrants flooded the job market and became marginalized as a result.

Another factor identified by Lieberson (1980) was the context of intergroup contact. Slaves and Native Americans were forced into contact with whites, whereas immigrants came voluntarily, usually for economic betterment. Voluntary immigrants perceived the economic conditions to be better because they chose to come. They started out with better economic prospects and more "cultural capital"—education, useful language skills, knowledge of how the social system works, and established kinship or friendship networks.

The use of secondary analysis, that is, the analysis of existing data from historical sources, findings from U.S. Census surveys, and other previously existing materials, can provide rich data for understanding trends and patterns over time.

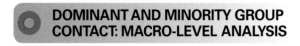

Thinking Sociologically

Think of some events in history that have an effect on attitudes toward particular groups today. Why might the events cause inter-group hostility? How does discrimination, as discussed above, help us to understand world conflicts such as the intense hostility between Palestinians and Jews in Israel?

DOMINANT AND MINORITY GROUP CONTACT: MACRO-LEVEL ANALYSIS

Economic hard times hit Germany in the 1930s, following that nation's loss in World War I. To distract citizens from the nation's problems, a scapegoat was found—the Jewish population. The German states began restricting Jewish activities and investments. Gradually, hate rhetoric intensified, but even then, most Jews had little idea about the fate that awaited them. Millions perished in gas chambers because the ruling Nazi party defined them as an undesirable race (although being Jewish is actually a religious or ethnic identification, not biological).

Japanese policies have resulted in a relatively homogeneous population over time, but one group, the Burakumin, have been treated as outcasts because their ancestors were relegated to performing work considered ritually unclean—butchering animals, tanning skins, digging graves, and handling corpses. Today, discrimination is officially against the law, but customs persist. Ostracized and kept within certain occupations and neighborhoods (Alldritt 2000; Kristof 1995), the Burakumin rarely intermarry or even socialize with other Japanese. They remain a minority.

Mexico, Guatemala, and other Central American governments face protests by their Indian populations, descendants of Aztecs, Maya, and Inca, who have distinguishing features and are generally relegated to servant positions. These native groups have been protesting against government policies and their poor conditions—usurping of their land, inability to own land, absentee land ownership, poor pay, and discrimination by the government (DePalma 1995).

These examples illustrate contact between governments and minority groups. The Jews in Germany faced genocide; Burakumin in Japan, segregation; and Native Americans, population transfer. The form these relations take depends on the following:

1. Which group has more power

2. The needs of the dominant group for labor or other resources (such as land) that could be provided by the minority group

3. The cultural norms of each group, including level of tolerance of out-groups

4. The social histories of the groups, including their religious, political, racial, and ethnic differences

5. Physical and cultural identifiers that distinguish the groups

6. The times and circumstances (wars, economic strains, recessions)

Where power between groups in society is unequal, the potential for differential treatment is always present. Yet, some groups live in harmony whether their power is equal or unequal (Kitano, Aqbayani, and de Anda 2005). The Pygmies of the Ituri rainforest have traded regularly with nearby local African settlements by leaving goods in an agreed place in exchange for other needed goods. There is often only minimal direct contact between these groups.

Whether totally accepting or prone to conflict, dominant-minority relations depend on time, place, and circumstances. Figure 8.2 indicates the range of dominant-minority relationships and policies.

Genocide is the systematic effort of a dominant group to destroy a minority group. Christians were thrown to the lions in ancient Rome. Hitler sent Jews and other non-Aryan groups into concentration camps to be gassed. Turks slaughtered Armenians in 1915. Iraqis used deadly chemical weapons against the Kurdish people within their own country. Members of the Serbian army massacred Bosnian civilians to rid towns of Bosnian Muslims, an action referred to as ethnic cleansing (Cushman and Mestrovic 1996). From 1975 to 1979, two million Cambodians, almost 25% of the population, suffered genocide as a result of leaders instituting new political philosophies. In Rwanda, people of the Tutsi and Hutu tribes carried out mass killings against each other in the late 1990s. In Darfur, a section of western Sudan in Africa, massive genocide is occurring while powerful nations of the world do little to stop it. The United Nations estimates that two million Sudanese people have died, disappeared, or become refugees in other countries (Smith 2005). Recently, villagers in Kenya, who had lived peacefully alongside their neighbors of different tribes, began killing each other after what was declared a rigged election. Genocide has existed at many points in history, and it still exists today. These examples illustrate the lethal consequences of racism, one group systematically killing off another, often a minority, to gain control and power.

Subjugation refers to the subordination of one group to another that holds power and authority. Haiti and the Dominican Republic are two countries sharing the island of Hispaniola in the Caribbean. Because many Haitians are poor, they are lured by promises of jobs in the sugar cane fields of the Dominican Republic. However, they are forced to work long hours for little pay and are not allowed to leave until they have paid for housing and food, which may be impossible to do on their low wages.

Slavery is one form of subjugation that has existed throughout history. When the Roman empire defeated other lands, captives became slaves. This included ancient Greeks, who also kept slaves at various times in their history. African tribes enslaved members of neighboring tribes, sometimes selling them to slave traders, and slavery has existed in Middle Eastern countries such as Saudi Arabia. As mentioned in the opening story for this chapter, slavery is flourishing today (Bales 2000, 2004).

Segregation, another form of subjugation, keeps minorities powerless by formally separating them from the dominant group and depriving them of access to the dominant institutions. Jim Crow laws, instituted in the southern United States after the Civil War, legislated separation between groups—separate facilities, schools, neighborhoods

Figure 8.2 Types of Dominant-Minority Group Relations

The Rwandan genocide began in April 1994 when the Rwandan president's plane was shot down. In the next 100 days, more than 800,000 Rwandans were slaughtered in the ethnic fighting between the Hutu and Tutsi tribes, and the genocide continued for the next several years. Tens of thousands of refugees fled into neighboring Tanzania, Burundi, and Zaire. The United Nations and the world stood by, not able to agree on a strategy or funding to support troops. Many argue the same thing is happening in the Darfur region of Sudan, where the international community has not been effective in stopping the slaughter.

(Bobo and Smith 1998; Feagin and Feagin 2007; Massey and Denton 1998). Around the world, barrios, reservations, squatters' quarters, *favela,* and even regions (e.g., Tibet) are sometimes maintained by the dominant group, usually unofficially but sometimes officially, and serve to isolate minorities in poor or overcrowded areas.

Domestic colonialism refers to exploitation of minority groups within a country (Blauner 1972; Kitano et al. 2005). African Brazilians and Native Americans in the United States and Canada have been "domestically colonized groups"—managed and manipulated by dominant group members.

Population transfer refers to the removal, often forced, of a minority group from a region or country. Generally, the dominant group wants land, resources, or political and economic power held by the minority. In 1972, Uganda's leader, General Idi Amin, gave the 45,000 Asians in that country, mostly of Indian origin, 36 hours to pack their bags and leave under threat that they would be arrested or killed. Many found homes in England, while others went to India. Yet, for the thousands who were born and raised in Uganda, this expulsion was a cruel act, barring them from their homeland. Because the Asian population had great economic power, the primary motivation for their expulsion was to regain economic power for Africans. Their departure, however, left the country in economic chaos with a void in the business class.

Examples of other population transfers are numerous: Native Americans in the United States were removed to reservations. The Cherokee people were forced to walk from Georgia and North Carolina to new lands west of the Mississippi—a "Trail of Tears" along which about 40% of the people perished. During World War II, Japanese Americans were forcibly moved to "relocation centers" and had their land and property confiscated. Many Chinese were forced to flee from Vietnam on small boats in the 1970s. Homeless and even nation-less people, they were dubbed "the boat people" by the press. In 2001, many Afghani people fled to Pakistan to escape U.S. bombing, and others departed earlier to escape oppression by the ruling Taliban. Today, civilians in the tense border region of Pakistan and Afghanistan still suffer displacement.

Movements of people across borders can result in **transnationalism**, people who fully participate in and have loyalty to two nations and cultures and often hold dual citizenship. An increasing number of naturalized U.S. citizens are also tax-paying members of their countries of origin, and they return often to help families and neighbors with financial needs or immigration plans (Levitt 2001). Yet, dual citizenship can create dilemmas of identity and sense of belonging.

Assimilation refers to the structural and cultural merging of minority and majority groups, a process by which minority members may lose their original identity. It occurs when ethnic groups in a region disregard distinctions between groups. Interaction among racial and ethnic groups occurs in housing, schooling, employment, political circles, family groups, friendship, and social relationships (Kitano et al. 2005). Forced assimilation occurs when a minority group is forced to suppress its identity. This happened in Spain around the time of World War II, when the Basque people were forbidden by the central government to speak or study the Basque language. For several centuries—ending only a few decades ago—the British government tried to stamp out the Welsh language from Wales. However, assimilation is often a voluntary process in which a minority group such as immigrants chooses to adopt the values, norms, and institutions of the dominant group.

Assimilation is more likely to occur when the minority group is culturally similar to the dominant group. For instance, in the United States, the closer a group is to being white, English speaking, and Protestant, or what is referred to as WASP (white Anglo-Saxon Protestant), the faster its members will be assimilated into the society, adopting the culture and blending in biologically through intermarriage.

Pluralism occurs when each ethnic or racial group in a country maintains its own culture and separate set of institutions but has recognized equity in the society. For example, Switzerland has three dominant cultural language groups: French, German, and Italian. Three official languages are spoken in the government and taught in the schools. Laws are written in three languages. Each group respects the rights of the other groups to maintain a distinctive way of life. In Malaysia, three groups share power—Malays, Chinese, and Indians. Although the balance is not completely stable because Chinese and Indians hold more political and economic power than the native Malays, there is a desire to maintain a pluralistic society. While tensions do exist, both Switzerland and Malaysia represent examples of pluralist societies. Legal protection of smaller or less powerful groups is often necessary to have pluralism.

Many individuals in the world face disruptions during their lifetimes that change their position in the social structure. The dominant-minority continuum illustrates the range of relations with dominant groups that can affect people's lives as transitions take place.

Thinking Sociologically

Think of examples from current news stories of positive and harmful intercultural contact. Where do your examples fit on the continuum from genocide to pluralism? What policies might address issues raised in your examples?

Theoretical Explanations of Dominant-Minority Group Relations

Are human beings innately cruel, inhumane, greedy, aggressive, territorial, or warlike? Some people think so, but the evidence is not very substantial. To understand prejudice in individuals or small groups, psychological and social-psychological theories are most relevant. To understand institutional discrimination, studying meso-level organizations is helpful, and to understand the pervasive nature of prejudice and stereotypes over time in various societies, cultural explanations are useful. Although aspects of macro-level theories relate to micro- and meso-level analysis, their major emphasis is on understanding the national and global systems of group relations.

Conflict Theory

In the 1840s, as the United States set out to build a railroad, large numbers of laborers immigrated from China to do the hard manual work. When the railroad was completed and competition for jobs became tight, the once-welcomed Chinese became targets of bitter prejudice, discrimination, and sometimes violence. Between 1850 and 1890, whites in California protested against Chinese, Japanese, and Chicano workers. Members of these minority groups banded together in towns or cities for protection, founding the Chinatowns we know today (Kitano 2001). Non-Chinese Asian groups suffered discrimination as well because the prejudiced generalizations were applied to all Asians (Son 1992; Winders 2004).

In 1988, people in horse-drawn covered wagons and on horseback reenacted the Trail of Tears, the 1,000-mile journey that Cherokees traveled 150 years earlier.

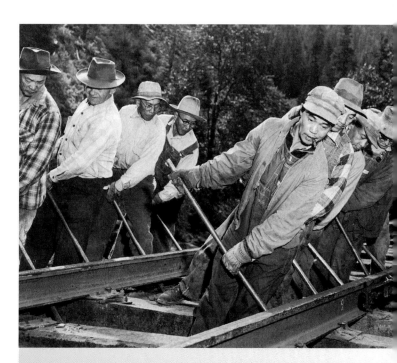

Chinese men were invited and encouraged to come to North America to help build railroads. However, prejudice was extremely prevalent, especially once the railroads were completed and the immigrants began to settle into various jobs in the U.S. economy.

Why does discrimination occur? Conflict theorists argue that creating a "lesser" group protects the dominant group's advantages. Because privileges and resources are usually limited, those who have them want to keep them.

One strategy used by privileged people, according to conflict theory, is to perpetrate prejudice and discrimination against minority group members. A case in point is the *gastarbeiter* (guest workers) in Germany and other Western European countries, who immigrate from Eastern Europe, the Middle East, and Africa to fill positions in European economies. They are easily recognized because of cultural and physical differences and are therefore ready targets for prejudice and discrimination, especially in times of economic competition and slowing economies. This helps to keep many of them in low-level positions.

Karl Marx argued that exploitation of the lower classes is built into capitalism because it benefits the ruling class. Unemployment creates a ready pool of labor to fill the marginal jobs, with the pool often made up of identifiable minority groups. This pool protects those in higher level positions from others moving up in the stratification system.

Three critical factors contribute to hostility over resources, according to one conflict theorist (Noel 1968): First, if two groups of people are identifiably different in appearance, clothing, or language, then we-versus-they thinking may develop. However, this by itself does not establish long-term hostility between the groups. Second, if the two groups come into conflict over scarce resources that both groups want for themselves, hostilities are very likely to arise. The resources might be the best land, the highest-paying jobs, access to the best schools for one's children, or positions of prestige and power. Conflict over resources is likely to create stereotypes and animosity. If the third element is added to the mix—one group having much more power than the other—then intense dislike between the two groups and misrepresentation of each group by the other is virtually inescapable. What happens is that the group with more power uses that power to ensure that they (and their offspring) get the most valued resources. However, because they do not want to see themselves as unfair and brutish people, they develop stereotypes and derogatory characterizations of "those other people" so the lack of access provided to "them" seems reasonable and justified. Discrimination comes first, and prejudiced ideology comes later to excuse the discrimination (Noel 1968). Thus, macro- and meso-level conflicts can lead to micro-level attitudes.

Split labor market theory, a branch of conflict theory, characterizes the labor market as having two levels: The primary market involves clean jobs, largely in supervisory roles, and provides high salaries and good advancement possibilities, whereas the secondary market involves undesirable, hard, and dirty work, compensated with low hourly wages and few benefits or career opportunities. Minorities, especially those from the urban underclass, are most likely to find dead-end jobs in the secondary market. For instance, when Mexicans work for little income picking crops as migrant laborers, they encounter negative stereotypes because they are poor and take jobs for low wages. Prejudice and discrimination build against the new, cheaper workers who threaten the next level of workers as the migrant workers seek to move up in the economic hierarchy. Thus, competition for lesser jobs pits minorities against each other and low-income whites against minorities. By encouraging division and focusing antagonism between worker groups, employers reduce threats to their dominance and get cheaper labor in the process. Workers do not organize against employers who use this dual system because they are distracted by the antagonisms that build up between workers—hence, the split labor market (Bonacich 1972, 1976). This theory maintains that competition, prejudice, and ethnic animosity serve the interests of capitalists because that atmosphere keeps laboring classes from uniting.

Conflict theory has also been used to illuminate issues of ethnic hostility on other continents, for this theory has broad application. Kichiro Iwamoto, who does sociological work on race relations issues in Africa and elsewhere, discusses the conflicts in Africa in the next "Sociology Around the World."

Conflict theory has taught us a great deal about racial and ethnic stratification. However, conflict theorists often focus on people with power quite intentionally oppressing others to protect their own self-interests. They depict the dominant group as made up of nasty, power-hungry people. As we have seen in the meso-level discussion of side-effect discrimination and past-in-present discrimination, discrimination and privilege are often subtle and unconscious, which means they can continue even without prejudice or ill will among those who are in the dominant group. Their privilege has been institutionalized. Conflict theorists sometimes miss this important point.

Structural-Functional Theory

From the structural-functional perspective, maintaining a cheap pool of laborers who are in and out of work serves several purposes for society. Low-paying and undesirable jobs for which no special training is needed—busboys, janitors, nurse's aides, street sweepers, and fast-food service workers—are often filled by minority group members of societies, including immigrant populations seeking to improve their opportunities.

Not only does this cheap pool of labor function to provide a ready labor force for dirty work or the menial unskilled jobs, but these individuals also serve other functions for society. They make possible occupations that service the poor, such as social work, public health, criminology, and the justice and legal systems. They buy goods others do not want—day-old bread, old fruits and vegetables, secondhand clothes. They set examples for others of what not to be, and they allow others to feel good about giving to charity (Gans 1971, 1994).

Sociologist Thomas Sowell (1994) contends that history and the situation into which one is born create the major differences in the social status of minority groups. Minority individuals must work hard to make up for their

Sociology Around the World

Violence in Kenya

By Kichi Iwamoto

In January 2008, violence gripped Kenya as rival political leaders representing different ethnic groups fought for control of the country in a contested election. Former Secretary General of the United Nations Kofi Annan said, while visiting western Kenya during the unrest, "What we saw was heart-wrenching. We saw houses burning, grandmothers and children being pushed out of their homes, and people suffering everywhere." He told the rival political leaders to resolve the political conflict as the violence was out of control in the country (UPI 2008).

At a small Assembly of God church in Kiambaa, Kenya, armed men trapped Kikuyu women, children, and elderly people inside, barricaded all the doors, and burned the building down, killing an estimated 50 people. The attackers were reported to be members of a rival tribe, the Kalenjin (Gettleman 2008). The skeptical eye of sociology can identify the key variables in this complex, tragic event.

Political conflicts over power can incite age-old rivalries and erupt into genocide, systematic killing of "others." These ethnic differences between the tribal groups can generate prejudice and negative contact, with the Kalenjin and Kikuyu attacking each other. Tribalism leads to discrimination against other tribes that are viewed as economic and power rivals, "different," and often inferior, and then resentments result in reprisals. The violence is perpetuated in a vicious cycle of "we" versus "they" animosity.

What are some meso- and macro-level sociological factors that could be contributing to this massacre? As in most ethnic conflicts, economic and political factors contribute to a violent racial or ethnic event. In Kenya, the mob violence and social chaos may have been advantageous for those in high political positions as the "reign of terror" kept frightened people from protesting the controversial national election of December 2007. "President Mwai Kibaki's electoral victory, seen by the opposition as fraudulent, triggered days of ugly tribal violence," one report said (Los Angeles Times 2008). The tribal violence kept the population fragmented, weakening any opposition and challenge to the current political structure. The situation was also exacerbated by roads that are too dangerous to use, tremendous food scarcity in many parts of the country, and many citizens struggling for survival rather than focusing on immediate political justice.

Some argue that the roots of these (Kenyan) conflicts are not tribal. "A *tribe* in Africa is a particular (social) identity construction created by colonial powers in an effort to more easily dominate the population. Ethnicity is a group of people who share a common identity, rituals, and most commonly, language. There are ethnic differences in Kenya, however constructed, but they are commonly trumped by kinship, class, labor, religion and even geographic identities" (Marcus 2008). Still, it is clear that the horrific violence is rooted in conflicts over scarce resources and defense of the self-interests of one group against another.

---

disadvantages. Sowell's contentions are controversial in part because of the implication that institutional discrimination can be overcome by hard work. Conflict theorists counter his argument by saying that discrimination that reduces opportunities is built into institutional and organizational structures and must be dealt with through structural change. They argue that hard work is necessary, but not sufficient, for minorities to get ahead.

Prejudice, racism, and discrimination are dysfunctional for society, resulting in loss of human resources, costs to societies due to poverty and crime, hostilities between groups, and disrespect for those in power (Schaefer 2008).

Thinking Sociologically

What are some micro-, meso-, and macro-level factors that enhance the chances that minority persons can move up the social ladder to better jobs?

This Japanese worker tends the gardens at the Golden Temple in Kyoto, Japan. Many Japanese have created niche markets in other countries in gardening.

The Effects of Prejudice, Racism, and Discrimination

Pictures of starving orphans from Sudan and Ethiopia and broken families from war-torn Bosnia remind us of the human toll resulting from prejudice and discrimination. This section discusses the results of prejudice, racism, and discrimination for minority groups and for societies.

The Costs of Racism

Individual victims of racism suffer from the destruction of their lives, health, and property, especially in societies where racism leads to poverty, enslavement, conflict, or war. Poor self-concept and low self-esteem result from constant reminders of a devalued status in society.

Prejudice and discrimination result in costs to organizations and communities as well as to individuals. First, they lose the talents of individuals who could be productive and contributing members. Because of poor education, substandard housing, and inferior medical care, these citizens cannot use their full potential to contribute to society. In 2005, 46.6 million or 15.9% of U.S. citizens did not have health insurance. This number has grown by 5.4 million since the recession year of 2001 and increased 1.3 million since 2004. The number of uninsured children is 8.3 million and growing (Center on Budget and Policy Priorities 2006). Yet the United States spends 16% of its gross domestic product (GDP) on health care, the highest expenditure in the world. Table 8.2 shows the differences in health care for ethnic groups in the United States.

Table 8.2 **Health Care in the United States**

	White	Black	Hispanic
U.S. Citizens Not Covered by Health Care (a)	11.3%	19.6%	32.7%
Average Expenditure per Customer for Health Care in the United States (b)	$2,490	$1,339	$1,366

Source: (a) Center on Budget and Policy Priorities 2006; (b) U.S. Census Bureau (2005i, Table 125).

Thinking Sociologically

How might lack of health care and insurance affect other aspects of a person's life (work, family life, education)?

Cultural explanations point out that prejudice and discrimination are passed on from generation to generation through cultural transmission. Stereotypes about groups limit our perceptions of what these groups can do and thereby limit the opportunities available to minority group members. Cultural beliefs are passed on through micro-level socialization processes and macro-level institutional structure, aided by media stereotypes. Even when we see cases of minorities who do not conform to the prevalent images, selective perception reinforces stereotypes, prejudices, and labels we have learned.

Cultural beliefs help to explain why racism remains in place and why inequality is sustained over a long period of time. From this perspective, cultural beliefs serve to stabilize inequality once it is created in a society, but beliefs alone do not cause inequality to form in the first place. The phenomenon of symbolic racism in contemporary North America is a good example: The assertion that the society is already fair prevents an honest look at institutional discrimination, which operates so subtly and so pervasively at the meso and macro levels of a society.

Second, government subsidies cost millions in the form of welfare, food stamps, and imprisonment, but they are made necessary in part by the lack of opportunities for minority individuals. Representation of ethnic groups in the U.S. political system can provide a voice for concerns of groups. Table 8.3 shows the representation of ethnic groups in Congress.

Continued attempts to justify racism by stereotyping and labeling groups have cultural costs, too. There are many talented African American athletes who are stars on college sports teams, but very few of them have been able to break into the ranks of coaches and managers, although there has been more opportunity in basketball than in other sports (Edwards 1994; Eitzen and Sage 2003; Sage 2005). The number of African American and Mexican American actors and artists has increased, but the numbers of black playwrights and screenwriters who can get their works produced or who have become directors remains limited. African American musicians have found it much more difficult to earn royalties and therefore cannot compose full-time (Alexander 2003). Because these artists must create and perform their art "as a sideline," they are less able to contribute their talents to society. The rest of us in the society are the poorer for it.

Sudanese children: Young victims of famine wait in line to receive food in the Sudanese camp of Narus. A worldwide study released May 2, 2006, by UNICEF reveals that some 5.6 million children die every year in part because they do not consume enough of the right nutrients, and 146 million children are at risk of dying early because they are underweight. Consider the cost to these countries and the world.

Thinking Sociologically

How might one's self-interests be underrepresented in policy decisions if there is low representation of one's ethnicity in Congress?

Minority Reactions to Prejudice, Discrimination, and Racism

How have minority groups dealt with their status? Five different reactions are common: assimilation, acceptance, avoidance, aggression, and change-oriented actions directed at the social structure. The first four are micro-level responses. They do not address the meso- and macro-level issues.

Assimilation is an accommodation to prejudice and discrimination. Some minority group members attempt to pass or assimilate as members of the dominant group so as to avoid bigotry and discrimination. Although this option is not open to many because of their distinguishing physical characteristics, this strategy usually involves abandoning their own culture and turning their back on family roots and ties, a costly strategy in terms of self-esteem and sense of identity. People who select this coping strategy are forced to deny who they are as defined by their roots and to live their lives in constant anxiety, feeling as though they must hide something about themselves.

In the 1960s, popular items advertised in African American magazines included "whitening creams" or "skin bleaches." Light-colored people with African ancestry would bleach their skin to pass as white. Skin-whitening creams can still be found today on pharmacy shelves in many countries. Dissatisfaction with one's body has an impact on one's self-concept.

Table 8.3 **Representation in Congress, 2006**

	Native American	Asian	Black	Hispanic
Senate	0	2 (2%)	1 (1%)	2 (2%)
House	1 (0.2%)	5 (1%)	42 (9.6%)	22 (5%)
Percentage of Population	1.5%	3.8%	12.7%	12.8%

Source: U.S. Census Bureau (2006e).

Passing also has been a common response of gays and lesbians, who are afraid to come out. Homosexuals experience the costly impact on self-esteem and the constant fear that they may be discovered. Likewise, assimilated Jews have changed their religion and their names to be accepted. Despite the wrenching from their personal history, passing has allowed some individuals to become absorbed into the mainstream and to lose the stigma of being defined as a minority. To these people, it is worth the high cost.

Acceptance is another common reaction to minority status. Some minority groups have learned to live with their minority status with little overt challenge to the system. They may or may not hold deep-seated hostility, but they ultimately conclude that change in the society is not very likely, and acceptance may be the rational means to survive within the existing system.

There are many possible explanations for this seeming indifference. For example, religious beliefs allow poor Hindus in India to believe that if they accept their lot in life, they will be reincarnated in a higher life-form. If they rebel, they can expect to be reincarnated into a lower life-form. Their religion is a form of social control.

Unfortunately, many children are socialized to believe that they are inferior or superior because minority group members are expected by the dominant group to behave in certain ways and often live up to that expectation because of the self-fulfilling prophesy (Farley 2005). Evidence to support stereotypes is easily found in individual cases—"inferior" kids live in shabby houses, dress less well, speak a different dialect. At school and on the job, minority position is reaffirmed by these characteristics.

Avoidance means shunning all contact with the dominant group. This can involve an active and organized attempt to leave the culture or live separately as some political exiles have done. In the United States, Marcus Garvey organized a Back-to-Africa movement in the 1920s, encouraging blacks to give up on any hope of justice in American society and to return to Africa. Native Americans continually moved west in the 19th century—trying to or being forced to get away from white Anglo settlers who brought alcohol and deadly diseases. In some cases, withdrawal may mean dropping out of the society as an individual—escaping by obliterating consciousness in drugs or alcohol. The escape from oppression and low self-concept is one reason why drug use is higher in minority ghettos and alcohol abuse is rampant on Native American reservations.

Aggression resulting from anger and resentment over minority status and from subjugation may lead to retaliation or violence. Because the dominant group holds significant power, a direct route such as voting against the dominant group or defeating oppressors in war is not always possible. Indeed, direct confrontation can be very costly to those lacking political or economic power. Suicide bombers from Palestine represent the many Palestinians who are frustrated and angry over their situation in relation to Israel.

Aggression usually takes one of two forms, indirect aggression and displaced aggression. Indirect aggression includes biting assertiveness in the arts—literature, art, racial and ethnic humor, and music—and in job-related actions such as inefficiency and slowdowns by workers. Displaced aggression, on the other hand, involves hostilities directed toward individuals or groups other than the dominant group, as happens when youth gangs attack other ethnic gangs in nearby neighborhoods. They substitute aggression against the dominant group by acting against the other minority group to protest their frustrating circumstances.

The four responses discussed thus far address the angst and humiliation that individual minorities feel. Each strategy allows an individual person to try to cope, but none addresses the structural causes of discrimination. The final strategy is change-oriented action: Minority groups pursue social change in the meso- and macro-level structures of society.

Nonviolent Resistance: Institutional and Societal Policy for Change

Another technique for bringing about change at the institutional and societal level is nonviolent resistance by minority groups. The model for this technique comes from India where, in the 1950s, Mahatma Gandhi led the struggle for independence from Britain. Although Britain clearly had superior weapons and armies, boycotts, sit-ins, and other forms of resistance eventually led to British withdrawal as the ruling colonial power. Jesse Jackson, a U.S. presidential candidate in 1984 and 1988, led his Chicago-based organization, PUSH, in economic boycotts against companies such as Coca-Cola to force them to hire and promote blacks, and Cesar Chavez led boycotts against grape growers to improve the working conditions of migrant workers. This strategy has been used successfully by workers and students to bring about change in many parts of the world.

In the United States, Martin Luther King Jr. followed in the nonviolent resistance tradition of India's Gandhi, who sought to change India's laws so minorities could have equal opportunities within the society. King's strategy involved nonviolent popular protests, economic boycotts, and challenges to the current norms of the society. The National Association for the Advancement of Colored People (NAACP) sought to bring about similar kinds of change at the legislative level through lawsuits that create new legal precedents on behalf of racial equality. Often, these lawsuits address side-effect discrimination—a meso-level problem. Many other associations for minorities—including the Anti-Defamation League (founded by Jews) and La Raza Unida (a Chicano organization) also seek to address problems both within organizations and institutions (meso level) and in the nation as a whole (macro level).

Like King, who had an undergraduate degree in sociology, many sociologists have used their training to address the issues of discrimination and disprivilege through empowerment and change. One example of a person with a BA in sociology who has used his knowledge to try to improve the society is Robert Animikii Horton, a member of the Anishinaabe "First Nation" (the preferred term in Canada for Native Americans). His work is discussed in the next "Applied Sociologist at Work."

Minority groups in some countries embrace violent tactics as a means to bring about change—riots, insurrections, hijackings, and terrorist bombings aimed at the dominant group. Their hope is either to destroy the dominant power structure or to threaten the stability of the current macro-level system

The Applied Sociologist at Work— Bebaamoyaash (Robert Animikii Horton)
Protecting the Rights and Preserving the Culture of First Nations

Bebaamoyaash (Robert Animikii Horton), a member of Rainy River First Nations, is choosing to follow the footsteps set before him by family—a long history of indigenous leadership, responsibility to his people, and community involvement. To that long family tradition, he brings something new: a degree in sociology. Losing a young cousin in a school shooting in Minnesota and witnessing inequality from a very young age helped Horton develop a sociological imagination: "Our conditions on a social level reach us on a personal level, and it happens every day." Intertwining sociological skills with commitment to cultural and clan responsibilities, Horton has been very involved with First Nations (Native) communities in Canada and the United States.

His interest in using social sciences for the benefit of his people stems from his childhood, when he became conscious of social and economic stratification between the communities where his family lives (native communities in Minnesota, Ontario, and Manitoba) and his friends' communities "off-reserve." Even at the young age of seven, he recalls "feeling something was unjust" as many resources, services, and privileges seemed nonexistent in his community. From this root of youthful observation, he continued to study social stratification in college and graduate school, especially ways in which privileges are unevenly distributed. As a result, Horton is dedicated to assisting First Nations with progress and cultural revitalization, applying sociological skills and experience to help his own people feel agency and empowerment ("social consciousness") and to address political realities at the meso level through action research.

Horton is currently conducting research on the educational needs and concerns of the Rainy River First Nations. Acknowledging significant gaps in educational success and high school completion, Horton has given voice to community members from the Rainy River District. He has interviewed students, alumni, educators, and administrators on the struggles that young people face in school. He says, "I feel that when we are young, our voices are minimized by policymakers and educators, with little consultation of what we feel, need, or believe. Our people have faced a history of this . . . and even our elders are left with hushed voices."

Horton has previously done analysis of other forms of social, economic, and political disprivilege of Rainy River First Nations. During his time as the group's social policy analyst, Horton assisted with a consultation regarding the governance and policy of the schools in his community. He has designed a First Nation curriculum for the Rainy River District School Board, which emphasizes a cultural core and regional history around Manitou Rapids. "Through an applied social lens, our youth must be given the tools to survive in the world," he says, "but just as importantly, the means to continue who we are as Anishinaabe people." As a member of the Minnesota Indian Education Association Board of Directors, he learned that "dedicated involvement and remembering who we are as a People is the key to progressive change, but the first step is becoming socially conscious of the conditions outside our front doors as well as those within ourselves."

Horton says, "I firmly believe that applied sociology, social science, and social analysis (if done properly) can bring positive results to our sovereign nations, but can also hinder progress if it is done improperly." He believes that sociological methods and theories in the hands of native peoples can bring constructive change. As he puts it: "I began my career in sociology with a desire and commitment to assist our people, our communities, and seven generations forward. I saw the field of sociology as offering skills and methods to fine-tune critical thought and offer insights on how to influence positive change in our society. . . . My work, from social analysis projects to curriculum development to educational research, is rooted in applied sociology. It can be time consuming, but knowing that giving up a portion of my youth so our First Nations young people will have opportunities [is] a more than rewarding outcome. . . . What do I wish to stress to our youth? Be the change which you wish to see. Defy convention. Dream. Hope. Imagine. Inspire."

Note: Robert Animikii Horton ("Bebaamoyaash") did his honors undergraduate work at St. Cloud State University and is completing his masters at Lakehead University in Thunder Bay, Ontario. He intends to earn his doctorate in indigenous governance or aboriginal education.

Mahatma Gandhi, leader of the Indian civil disobedience revolt, marched to the shore to collect salt, a clear violation of the law, one that he felt was inhumane and unjust. On the right is a woman lieutenant in his nonviolent resistance movement.

such that the group in power is willing to make some changes. Sometimes, minority reactions result in assimilation, but often, the goal is to create a pluralistic society in which cultures can be different yet have economic opportunities open to all.

Thinking Sociologically

The discussion above presents five types of responses by minorities to the experience of discrimination and rejection. Four of these are at the micro level and only one at the meso and macro level. Why do you suppose most of the coping strategies of minorities are at the micro level?

Policies Governing Minority and Dominant Group Relations

Civilians, mostly women, children, and elderly people, are fleeing the Darfur region of Sudan in great numbers, trying to find a degree of safety, food, and shelter after people in their villages have been penetrated by bullets and machetes. Towns have been pillaged and bombed, and planting fields have been burned (Polgreen 2008). Most of the 45,000 survivors are seeking refuge in camps in eastern Chad, places already crowded with more than 300,000 survivors (UNHCR Statistical Yearbook 2006). The conflicts are complex and represent different ethnic and religious groups fighting for power, land, and resources. For our purposes, the important point is that the refugees come from minority groups in the country, civilians caught in a conflict they cannot control. About 17 countries have policies to host or accept refugees from war-torn countries as new citizens. Refugees who cannot return home may end up in a new country, perhaps a new continent.

Darfur, Sudan, is only one recent site of war resulting in refugees. Kenya is also experiencing internal refugee displacement as a result of conflicts over their recent elections. In the 1990s, residents fled from Albania, Bosnia, Cuba, Haiti, Rwanda, Zaire, and other nations. In the 1980s, refugees from war-torn countries such as Afghanistan, Lebanon, Cambodia, and El Salvador sought political asylum in the United States, Canada, Australia, France, Norway, and several Latin American countries (Omi and Winant 1989). These movements, brought about by war, famine, and economic dislocation, force families to seek new locations where they can survive and perhaps improve their circumstances. The degree of acceptance children and their families find in their newly adopted countries varies depending on the government's policies, the group's background, and economic conditions in the host country (Rumbaut and Portes 2001). Some formerly refugee-friendly countries are closing their doors to immigration because of the strain on their economy and threats of terrorism. In this section, we consider the policies that emerge as dominant and minority groups come into contact and interact.

Policies to Reduce Prejudice, Racism, and Discrimination

In the preceding pages, we considered some of the costs to individuals, groups, societies, and the global community inflicted by discriminatory behavior and policies. Discrimination's influence is widespread, from slavery and subjugation to unequal educational and work opportunities, to legal and political arenas, and to every other part of the social world. If one accepts the premise that discrimination is destructive to both individuals and societies, then ways must be found to address the root problems effectively. However, solutions to ethnic tensions around the world have many experts baffled. Consider ethnic strife in Bosnia and Croatia; conflicts between Palestinians and Israelis; conflicts between Shiites and Sunni Muslims in Iraq; tribal genocide in Kenya, Sudan, and Rwanda; and conflicts between religious groups in Northern Ireland. In places such as these, each new generation is socialized into the prejudice and antagonisms that perpetuate the animosity and violence. Social scientists and policymakers have made little progress in resolving conflicts that rest on century-old hostilities.

From our social world perspective, we know that no problem can be solved by working at only one level of analysis. A successful strategy must bring about change at every level of the social world—individual attitudes, organizational discrimination, cultural stereotypes, societal stratification systems, and national and international structures. However, most current strategies focus on only one level of analysis. Figure 8.3 shows some of the programs enacted to combat prejudice, racism, and discrimination at the individual, group, societal, and global levels.

Individual or Small-Group Solutions

Programs to address prejudice, racism, and stereotypes through human relations workshops, group encounters, and therapy can achieve goals with small numbers of people. For instance, African American and white children who are placed in interracial classrooms in schools are more likely to develop close interracial friendships (Ellison and Powers 1994). Also, the higher the people's education level, the more likely they are to respect and like others and to appreciate and enjoy differences. Education gives a broader, more universal outlook, reduces misconceptions and prejudices, shows that many issues do not have clear answers, and encourages multicultural understanding and focus on individuals, not judging groups.

Two groups with strong multicultural education programs are the Anti-Defamation League and the Southern Poverty Law Center's Teaching Tolerance Program. Both groups provide schools and community organizations with their literature, videos, and other materials aimed at combating intolerance and discrimination toward others.

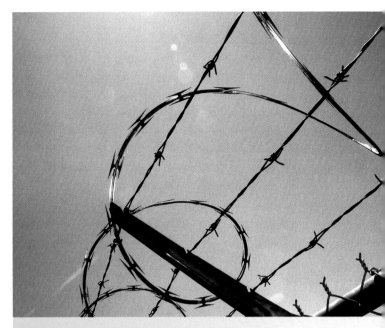

There has been a great deal of controversy about the fence along the U.S. border with Mexico. This section of fencing includes both barbed wire and razor wire. Some people feel it is the only way to enforce immigration laws and to control the growth rate of the country. Others think walls of this sort foster we-they thinking, are a waste of money, and do not lead to permanent solutions. Many Mexican Americans think such a wall is insulting to Mexican American people. Do you think such a wall is a step in the right direction or not?

However, these strategies do not address the social conditions underlying the problems because they reach only a few people: those who are exposed through school or other programs, who voluntarily seek help, or who are required to participate in prejudice reduction programs. Thus, this approach alone achieves only limited results. It also does not begin to address dilemmas that are rooted in meso- and macro-level discrimination. Micro-level solutions are often blind to the structural causes of problems.

Group Contact

Many social scientists advocate organized group contact between dominant and minority group members to improve relations

Types of Problems at Each Level	Types of Solutions or Programs
Individual level: stereotypes and prejudice	Therapy, tolerance-education programs
Group level: negative group interaction	Positive contact, awareness by majority of their many privileges
Societal level: institutional discrimination	Education, media, legal-system revisions
Global level: deprivation of human rights	Human rights movements, international political pressures

Figure 8.3 Problems and Solutions

An AmeriCorps volunteer supervises construction on a Habitat for Humanity building in St. Tammany Parish, Louisiana, for people displaced by Hurricane Katrina—many of them minorities. The solution proposed by some Non-Governmental Organizations (NGOs) such as Habitat is to address problems and suffering with volunteer labor and donations. Do you agree?

all were needed to solve the problem. The groups not only worked together, but their established stereotypes eventually began to fade away. Such a situation in the larger society might arise from efforts to get a candidate elected, a bill passed, or a neighborhood improved.

Programs involving group contact to improve conditions for minorities have been tried in many areas of social life, including integrated housing projects, job programs to promote minority hiring, and busing children to schools to achieve a higher level of racial and socioeconomic integration. For instance, the Chicago Housing Authority opened a refurbished mixed-income housing experiment with resident participation in decision making. Although many predicted failure, the project thrived, with long waiting lists of families wanting to participate (McCormick 1992). Positive contact experiences tend to improve relations in groups on a micro level by breaking down stereotypes, but to solidify gains, we must also address institutionalized inequalities.

Institutional and Societal Strategies to Improve Group Relations

Sociologists contend that institutional and societal approaches to reduce discrimination get closer to the core of the problems and affect larger numbers of people than do micro-level strategies. For instance, voluntary advocacy organizations pursue political change through lobbying, watchdog monitoring, educational information dissemination, canvassing, protest marches, rallies, and boycotts (Minkoff 1995). Groups like the NAACP have filed lawsuits and lobbied legislators for changes in laws that they believed were discriminatory.

The Civil Rights Commission, Fair Employment Practices Commission, and Equal Employment Opportunity Commission are government organizations that protect rights and work toward equality for all citizens. These agencies oversee practices and hear complaints relating to racial, sexual, age, and other forms of discrimination. Legislation, too, can modify behaviors. Laws requiring equal treatment of minorities have resulted in increased tolerance of those who are "different" and have opened doors that previously were closed to minorities.

In the United States, executive action to end discrimination has been taken by a number of presidents. In 1948, Harry Truman moved to successfully end military segregation, and subsequent presidents have urged passage of civil rights legislation and equal employment opportunity legislation. Affirmative action laws, first implemented during Lyndon Johnson's administration, have been used to fight pervasive institutional racism (Crosby 2004; Farley 2005).

Affirmative Action

One of the most contentious policies in the United States has been affirmative action. The following discussion addresses the intentions and forms of the policy (Gallagher 2004). A societal policy for change, affirmative action actually involves

and break down stereotypes and fears. Although not all contact reduces prejudice, many studies have shown the benefits of contact, from school desegregation (Fishbein 1996) to housing projects. Some essential conditions for success are equal status of participants, noncompetitive and nonthreatening contact, and projects or goals on which to cooperate (Farley 2005).

In a classic study of group contact, social psychologists Muzafer Sherif and Caroline Sherif (1953) and their colleagues ran summer camps for boys ages 11 and 12 and studied how groups were established and reestablished. On arrival, the boys were divided into two groups that competed periodically. The more fierce the competition, the more hostile the two cabins of boys became toward each other. The experimenters tried several methods to resolve the conflicts and tensions:

1. Appealing to higher values (be nice to your neighbors). This proved of limited value.

2. Talking with natural leaders of the groups (compromises between group leaders). Group leaders agreed, but their followers did not go along.

3. Bringing groups together in a pleasant situation (a mutually rewarding situation). This did not reduce competition; if anything, it increased it.

4. Introducing a superordinate goal that could be achieved only if everyone cooperated. This technique worked. The boys were presented with a dilemma: The water system had broken, or a fire needed to be put out, and

three different policies. Its simplest and original form, which we call *strict affirmative action*, involves affirmative or positive steps to make sure that unintentional discrimination does not occur. It requires, for example, that an employer who receives federal monies must advertise a position widely and not just through internal or friendship networks. If the job requires an employee with a college education, then by federal law, employers must recruit through minority and women's colleges as well as state and private colleges in the region. If employers are hiring in the suburbs, they are obliged to contact unemployment agencies in poor and minority communities as well as those in the affluent neighborhoods. After taking these required extra steps, employers are expected to hire the most qualified candidate who applies, regardless of race, ethnicity, sex, religion, or other external characteristics. The focus is on providing opportunities for the best qualified people. For many people, this is the meaning of affirmative action, and it is inconceivable that this could be characterized as reverse discrimination, for members of the dominant group will be hired if they are in fact the most qualified. These policies do not overcome the problem that qualified people who have been marginalized may be competent but do not have the traditional paper credentials that document their qualifications.

The second policy is a quota system, a requirement that employers *must* hire a certain percentage of minorities. For the most part, quotas are now unconstitutional. They apply only in cases in which a court has found a company to have a substantial and sustained history of discrimination against minorities and in which the employment position does not have many requirements (if the job entails sweeping floors and cleaning toilets, there would not be an expectation of a specific academic degree or a particular grade point average).

The third policy and the one that has created the most controversy among opponents of affirmative action is preference policies. Preference policies are based on the concept of equity, the belief that sometimes people must be treated differently in order to treat them fairly. This policy was enacted to level the playing field, which was not rewarding highly competent people because of institutional racism.

The objectives of preference policies are to (1) eliminate qualifications that are not substantially related to the job but that unwittingly favor members of the dominant group and (2) foster achievement of objectives of the organization that are only possible through enhanced diversity. To overcome these inequalities and achieve certain objectives, employers and educational institutions take account of race or sex by making special efforts to hire and retain workers or accept students from groups that have been underrepresented because of race. In many cases, these individuals bring qualifications others do not possess. Consider the following examples.

A goal of the medical community is to provide access to medical care for underserved populations. There is an extreme shortage of physicians on the Navajo reservation. Thus, a Navajo applicant for medical school might be accepted, even if her scores are slightly lower than another candidate, because she speaks Navajo and understands the culture. One could argue that she is more qualified to be a physician on the reservation than someone who knows nothing about Navajo society but has a slightly higher grade point average or test score. Some argue that tests should not be the only measure to determine successful applicants.

Likewise, an African American police officer may have more credibility in a minority neighborhood and may be able to defuse a delicate conflict more effectively than a white officer who scored slightly higher on a paper-and-pencil placement test. Sometimes, being a member of a particular ethnic group can actually make one more qualified for a position.

A 1996 proposition in California to eliminate affirmative action programs in the state passed in a popular referendum. The result was that colleges in California are allowed to offer preference based on state residency, athletic competency, musical skill, having had a parent graduate from the school, and many other factors—but not race. Many colleges and universities admit students because they need an outstanding point guard on the basketball team, an extraordinary soprano for the college choir, or a student from a distant state for geographic diversity. These students were shown preference by being admitted with lower test scores than some other applicants.

A lawsuit filed in a Detroit district court in 1997 alleged that the University of Michigan gave unlawful preference to minorities in undergraduate admissions and in law school admissions. In this controversial case, the court ruled that undergraduate admissions were discriminatory because they used numbers rather than individualized judgments to make the determination (University of Michigan Documents Center 2003). Consider "Sociology in Your Social World," and decide whether you think the policy was unfair and whether only race and ethnicity should have been deleted from the preferences allowed.

The question remains, should preferences be given to accomplish diversity? Some people feel that programs involving any sort of preference are reverse discrimination. Others believe such programs have encouraged employers, educational institutions, and government to look carefully at hiring policies and minority candidates and that many more competent minority group members are working in the public sector as a result of these policies.

Thinking Sociologically

First, read the boxed feature on the next page. Should colleges consider an applicant's state of origin, urban or rural background, ethnicity, musical or athletic ability, alumni parent, or other factors in admitting students if it helps the college achieve its goals? Should men with lower scores be admitted because the college wants to have balanced gender enrollment? Is ethnic diversity so central to the learning environment that it must be an admissions criterion? Why?

Sociology in Your Social World

Preference Policies at the University of Michigan

To enhance diversity on the campus—a practice that many argue makes a university a better learning environment and enhances the academic reputation of the school—many colleges have preference policies in admissions. However, the University of Michigan was sued by applicants who felt they were not admitted because others replaced them on the roster due to their racial or ethnic background.

The University of Michigan is a huge university where a numbering system is needed to handle the volume (tens of thousands) of applicants; they cannot make a decision based on personal knowledge of each candidate. Thus, they give points for each quality they deem desirable in the student body. A maximum of 150 points is possible, and a score of a 100 would pretty much ensure admission. The university felt that any combination of points accumulated according to the following formula would result in a highly qualified and diverse student body.

For academics, up to 110 points possible:

- 80 points for grades (a particular grade point average in high school resulted in a set number of points; a 4.0 resulted in 80 points; a 2.8 resulted in 56 points)
- 12 points for standardized test scores (ACT or SAT)
- 10 points for the academic rigor of high school (so all students who went to tougher high schools earned points)
- 8 points for the difficulty of the curriculum (e.g., points for honors curriculum vs. keyboarding courses)

For especially desired qualities, including diversity, up to 40 points possible of any combination of the following (but no more than 40 in this "desired qualities" category):

- Geographical distribution (10 for Michigan resident; an additional 6 for underrepresented Michigan county)
- Legacy—a relative had attended Michigan (4 pts for a parent; 1 pt for grandparent or sibling)
- Quality of submitted essay (3 points)
- Personal achievement—a special accomplishment that was noteworthy (up to 5 points)
- Leadership and service (5 points each)
- Miscellaneous (only one of these could be used):
  o Socioeconomic disadvantage (20 points)
  o Racial or ethnic minority (20 points; disallowed by the court ruling)
  o Men in nursing (5 points)
  o Scholarship athlete (20 points)
  o Provost's discretion (20 points; usually the son or daughter of a large financial donor or of a politician)

In addition to ethnicity being given preference, athleticism, musical talent, having a relative who is an alum, or being the child of someone who is noteworthy to the university were also considered. Some schools also give points for being a military veteran or for coming from a distant state. The legal challenge to this admissions system was based only on the racial and ethnic preference given to some candidates, not to the other items that are preferred.

Does this process seem reasonable as a way to get a diverse and highly talented incoming class of students?

Global Movements for Human Rights

A unique coalition of world nations has emerged from a recent international event—the terrorist attack of September 11, 2001. In this attack on the World Trade Center in New York City, a center housing national and international businesses and workers, citizens from 90 countries were killed when two hijacked commercial jetliners flew into the towers. In addition to the world condemnation, many countries' governments have pledged to fight against terrorism. Yet, why did such a heinous act occur? Many social scientists attempting to identify a cause point to the disparities between rich and poor peoples of the world.

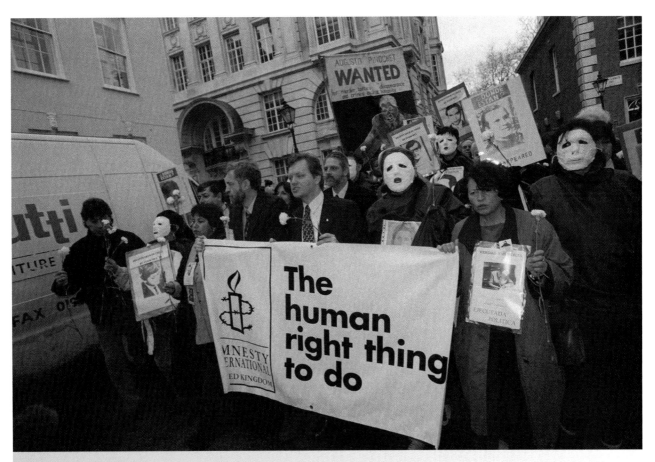

Some civil rights or human rights movements have justice issues in other countries as their focal point. Amnesty International is one such movement, which has strong support at many college campuses.

The perpetrators likely felt that Muslims were treated as inconsequential players in the global world, and they struck out to make a dramatic impact on the world community and the United States. The point is that global issues and ethnic conflicts in the social world are interrelated.

The rights granted to citizens of any nation used to be considered the business of each sovereign nation, but after the Nazi holocaust, German officers were tried at the Nuremberg trials, and the United Nations passed the Universal Declaration of Human Rights. Since that time, many international organizations have been established, often under the auspices of the United Nations, to deal with health issues, world poverty and debt, trade, security, and many other issues affecting world citizens—World Health Organization, World Bank, World Trade Organization, and numerous regional trade and security organizations.

Probably more than any other U.S. president, Jimmy Carter made human rights the centerpiece of his foreign policy. In addition, the United Nations, several national governments (Britain, France, and Canada), and privately funded advocacy groups speak up for international human rights as a principle that transcends national boundaries. The most widely recognized private group is Amnesty International, a watchdog group that does lobbying on behalf of human rights and supports political prisoners and ethnic group spokespersons When Amnesty International was awarded the Nobel Peace Prize in 1997, the group's visibility was dramatically increased. Even some activist sociologists have formed Sociologists Without Borders, or SSF (*Sociólogos sin Fronteras*; http://www.sociologistswithout borders.org), a transnational organization committed to the idea that "all people have equal rights to political and legal protections, to socioeconomic security, to self-determination, and to their personality."

Everyone can make a positive difference in the world, and one place to start is in our community (see "Contributing to Your Social World"). We can counter prejudice, racism, and discrimination in our own groups by teaching children to see beyond "we" and "they" and by speaking out for fairness and against stereotypes and discrimination.

So What ?

Why are minority group members in most countries poorer than dominant group members? This and other chapter-opening questions can be answered in part by considering individual causes of prejudice and racism, physical and cultural differences that distinguish groups of people, and the fact that human beings have a tendency to create "we" and "they" categories and to treat those who are different as somehow less human. The categories can be based on physical appearance, cultural differences, religious differences, or anything the community or society defines as important. Once people notice differences, they are more inclined to hurt "them" or to harbor advantages for "us" if there is competition over resources that both groups want. Even within a nation, where people are supposedly all "us," there can be sharp differences and intense hostilities.

Indeed, "we" and "they" thinking can invade some of the most intimate settings. Inequality is not limited to social classes, race or ethnic groups, or religious communities. It can infect relations between men and women in everything from the home to the boardroom and from the governance of nations to the decisions of global agencies. We will explore this in the next chapter: "Gender Stratification."

Key Points

What Have We Learned?

- Although the concept of race has no real meaning biologically, race is a social construction because people *believe* it is real. (See pp. 234–236.)

- Minority group status—having less power and less access to resources—may occur because of racial status or because of ethnic (cultural) factors. (See pp. 236–244.)

- Prejudice operates at the micro level of society and is closest to people's own lives, but it has much less impact on minorities than discrimination. Symbolic racism has become more of a problem—the denial of overt prejudice but the rejection of any policies that might correct inequities. (See pp. 244–248.)

- At the meso level, institutional discrimination operates through two processes: side effect and past-in-present. These forms of discrimination are unintended and unconscious—operating quite separate from any prejudice of individuals in the society. (See pp. 249–252.)

- When very large ethnic groups or even nations collide, some people are typically displaced and find themselves in minority status. (See pp. 252–253.)

- The policies of the dominant group may include genocide, subjugation, population transfer, assimilation, or pluralism. (See pp. 253–258.)

- The costs of racism to the society are high, including loss of human talent and resources, and the costs make life more difficult for the minority group members. (See pp. 258–259.)

- Coping devices used by minorities include five strategies, only one of which addresses the meso and macro causes. These strategies are assimilation, acceptance, avoidance, aggression, and organizing for societal change. (See pp. 259–262.)

- Policies to address problems of prejudice and discrimination range from individual and small-group efforts at the micro level to institutional, societal, and even global social movements. (See pp. 262–264.)

- Affirmative action policies are one approach, but the broad term "affirmative action" includes three different sets of policies that are quite distinct and have different outcomes. (See pp. 262–264.)

Contributing to Our Social World: What Can We Do?

At the Local Level: Most campuses have student organizations dedicated to fighting racism and promoting the rights of racial minorities. These include African-American Student Associations, Arab-American Student Associations, and Native-American Student Associations. Identify one of these groups on your campus and arrange to attend a meeting. If appropriate, volunteer to help with its work.

At the Organizational or Institutional Level: The Leadership Conference on Civil Rights/Leadership Conference on Civil Rights Education Fund is a national coalition dedicated to combating racism and its effects. It maintains a Web site that includes a directory of more than 100 local chapters, listed by state (www.civilrights.org/action_center/national_directory). Using this directory, find a chapter in your area, and explore ways in which you can participate in its programs. Teaching Tolerance (www.splcenter.org/center/tt/teach.jsp) is a program of the Southern Poverty Law Center, which has curriculum materials for teaching about diversity and a program for enhancing cross-ethnic cooperation and dialogue in schools. Contact faculty members on your campus who supervise internships in local primary and secondary schools and explore with them ways in which the Teaching for Tolerance approach can be incorporated into the curricula.

At the National and Global Levels: Native Americans have often been considered a "forgotten minority," in part because of the relatively small size of the group and in part because of decades of segregation from the general population. Yet, Native Americans are among the most historically and culturally significant minorities in the United States and have been subject to some of the most extreme and dehumanizing

forms of racism. A leading, highly activist, organization, the American Indian Movement (AIM), has worked for many years to bring the plight of Native Americans to the attention of the public and the government and to promote the civil/human rights of community members. Visit the AIM Web site at http://www.aimovement.org and explore ways in which you can learn more about Native Americans and assist in the community's educational and legislative initiatives. At the end of Chapter 3, we discussed the plight of indigenous people and noted two organizations involved in assisting these groups, Cultural Survival and the UN Permanent Forum on Indigenous Issues (www.cs.orgwww and un.org/esa/socdev/unpfii). Generally speaking, these people are viewed as racial minorities in their native countries. Thus, organizations such as these also provide opportunities for combating racism globally. You should also consider purchasing only coffee and—especially—chocolate that are Fair Trade products (packages are clearly marked as such). Among other things, this will ensure that you are not supporting slavery someplace around the globe with your purchases. Amnesty International (www.amnestyusa.org or www.amnesty.org) is a worldwide movement of people who campaign for internationally recognized human rights. It relies heavily on volunteer workers.

Visit **www.pineforge.com/ballantine2study** for online activities, sample tests, and other helpful information. Select "Chapter 8: Race and Ethnic Group Stratification" for chapter-specific activities.

CHAPTER 9

Gender Stratification

She/He—Who Goes First?

Social inequality is especially evident in gender relations, and although in some societies women are treated with deference, they are rarely given first access to positions of significant power or financial reward. While they may hold many work roles, they often carry the load of child care by themselves, causing more role strains. The photos presented here focus on women.

Think About It . . .

Micro: How does being female or male affect your thoughts and behaviors?

Micro: Why do some people face violence in their homes and communities because of their sexuality?

Meso: Can anything be done in our organizations and institutions to make men and women more equal?

Macro: Why do women have second-class status in your society? Other societies?

Macro: How is gender inequality an issue in this new age of globalization?

Macro: Global Community

Macro: Society

Meso: National Organizations, Institutions, and Ethnic Subcultures

Micro: Local Organizations and Community

Micro: Me (and My Gendered Groups)

Micro: Peers, neighbors, teachers, coaches, and religious education instructors socialize children into gender roles

Meso: Leadership positions limited in institutions for women; segregation of boys and girls or men and women that limits access to resources

Macro: National policies provide sex-based privileges

Macro: Women across the globe often have lower status as determined by institutions of society, laws, and power structures

Women in some parts of the world are treated in ways that might be unthinkable to you. Some women are considered unclean during menstruation and are segregated in special huts. Other women are thought to have extra powers during menstruation. Some men trade sisters or cousins to obtain wives. Some women must be completely covered when in public; women elsewhere are expected to wear next to nothing at the beach. Historically, some women bound their feet to keep them small and attractive to men. Other women's clitorises are removed so they will not have sexual urges or be temptresses to men. Some wives burned themselves on the funeral pyres of their dead husbands (*sati,* "virtuous" women being burned alive with their dead husbands), and other women are burned alive in their kitchens for lack of sufficient dowry (marriage payment) from their families. Some girls are killed at birth so they will not be an economic burden to their families. While a few women are elected to premier leadership roles, such as prime minister or president of the nation, others are kept isolated from the world outside of their homes. Some societies believe women should shave their armpits and legs. If they do not, they are thought to be unattractive. In other societies, hair is natural and considered desirable, even beautiful.

All of these beliefs and practices are cultural creations affecting the lives of individual females in various societies around the world. Some practices of your own society may seem very strange to women and men in another society, just as some practices above repulse you. Although gender identities and roles change slowly, they do change over time, reflecting the economic, political, and social realities of the society and the influence of other societies. For instance, women in today's India seldom commit *sati* (suicide) on their husband's funeral pyre, but before the practice of *sati* was outlawed, it was common as a way to deal with widows who no longer had a role in society or a means of support. A woman who refused to comply might be stigmatized and dishonored as a bad or unfaithful wife (Weitz 1995).

In this chapter, we will explore the concept of gender and the implications of one's sexuality and one's sex, combined with race and class in the stratification system. At the micro level, we consider gender socialization, and at the meso and macro levels, gender stratification, or placement in the society's stratification system. The costs and consequences of gender stratification plus policy implications will end the chapter.

Sex, Gender, and the Stratification System

You name it, and some society has probably done it! Gender relations are no exception. The social roles we play and identities we create for ourselves are influenced by our societies.

Variations around the world show that most roles and identities are not biological but rather socially constructed. In Chapter 7, we discussed factors that stratify individuals into social groups (castes and classes), and in Chapter 8, we discussed the roles race and ethnicity play in stratification. Add the concepts of sex and gender, and we have a more complex picture of how class, race and ethnicity, and gender together influence who we are and our positions in society. Consider the following examples from societies that illustrate some unusual human social constructions based on sex and gender. These examples illustrate that gender roles are created by humans to meet needs of their societies. We will then move to more familiar societies.

Men of the Wodaabe society in Niger, Africa, are nomadic cattle herders and traders who would be defined as effeminate by most Western standards because of their behavior patterns. The men are like birds, showing their colorful feathers to attract women. They take great care in doing their hair, applying makeup, and dressing to attract women. They also gossip with each other while sipping their tea. What are the women doing? They are cooking meals, caring for the children, cleaning, tending to the animals, planting small gardens, and preparing for the next move of this nomadic group (Beckwith 1993; Zimmer 1992). These patterns have developed as a way for the group to meet its basic human needs and survive.

People in industrial societies might seem unacceptably aggressive and competitive to people of the Arapesh tribe in New Guinea, where gentleness and nonaggression are the rule for both women and men. Yet nearby, women of the Tchambuli people are assertive, businesslike, and the primary economic providers. Men of the Tchambuli exhibit expressive, nurturing, and gossipy behavior. The Mbuti and !Kung peoples of Africa value gender equality in their division of labor and treatment of women and men, and among the Agta of the Philippines, women do the hunting. In West African societies such as the Ashanti and Yoruba kingdoms, women control much of the market system (Dahlberg 1981; Mead 1935/1963; Turnbull 1962). Each tradition has evolved over time to meet certain needs of society.

Under the Taliban in Afghanistan, women cannot be seen in public without total body covering that meets strict requirements. Anyone not obeying could be stoned to death. Women could not hold public positions or work outside their homes. If they became ill, women could not be examined by a physician because all doctors are male. Instead, they had to describe their symptoms to a doctor through a screen (Makhmalbaf 2003). Again, ask yourself why these practices evolved and what purpose these rules serve for society.

Obligations of the youngest daughter in some Mexican households require that she forgo marriage, stay at home, and care for her mother as she ages (Esquivel 2001). In China, women and men work in the factories and fields. Children are cared for in state-run child care settings and schools. Equality between the sexes is the goal, although many women claim they serve in the public work arena in addition to doing a disproportionate amount in the private home setting.

Why did groups in different corners of the globe develop such radically different ways of organizing their gender roles? Certain tasks must be carried out by individuals and organizations in each society for members to survive. Someone must be responsible for raising children, someone must provide people with the basic necessities (food, clothing, shelter), someone needs to lead, someone must defend the society, and someone must help resolve conflicts. One's sex and age are often used to determine who holds what positions and who carries out what tasks. Each society develops its own way to meet all of the needs, and this results in a wide range of gender role expectations from one society to the next.

Defining Terms

At birth, when doctors say, "It's a . . . ," they are referring to the distinguishing primary characteristics that determine **sex**, the penis or vagina. **Sex** is a biological term referring to ascribed genetic, anatomical, and hormonal differences between males and females. Right? Partly. Sex is also "a determination made through the application of socially agreed upon biological criteria for classifying persons as females or males" (West and Zimmerman 1987:127). In other words, sometimes this binary male-female categorization by biological criteria is not clear. Occasionally, people are born with ambiguous genitalia, not fitting the typical definitions of male or female (the *intersexed*). About 1.7% of babies are born with "anomalies of sex chromosomes, internal procreative organs, and external genitalia in a variety of combinations" (Fausto-Sterling 2000:50–54). These babies often undergo surgeries to clarify their gender, with hormonal treatments and possible further surgery at adolescence, although there is controversy about what the surgeries try to accomplish (Chase 2000). Whether male, female, or intersexed, anatomical differences at birth or chromosomal typing before birth result in cultural attempts to clearly categorize sex.

In many societies, great lengths are taken to assign a sex. Why is this an issue? The reality is that sex constitutes a major organizing principle in most societies. People's roles and statuses and society's expectations guiding their behavior are largely determined by their sex. Our attraction to others is expressed by our sexuality and our sexual identity. Most people fall into the category of heterosexual (other sex), homosexual (same sex), bisexual (both sexes), or "varied." The term *heteronormativity* defines the cultural expectations held in most societies that a "normal" girl or boy will be sexually attracted to and eventually have sex with someone of the other sex (Lorber and Moore 2007). The point is that sex is not always a straightforward distinction.

In adolescence, secondary characteristics further distinguish the sexes, with females developing breasts and hips,

Wodaabe men in Niger (Africa) go to great pains with makeup, hair, and jewelry to ensure that they are highly attractive, a pattern that is thought by many people in North America to be associated with females.

and males developing body hair, muscle mass, and deep voices. Individuals are then expected to adopt the behaviors appropriate to their anatomical features as defined by society. In addition to the physical sex differences between males and females, a few other physical conditions are commonly believed to be sex linked, such as a prevalence of colorblindness, baldness, learning disabilities, autism, and hemophilia in males. Yet, some traits that members of society commonly link to sex are actually learned through socialization. There is little evidence, for instance, that emotions, personality traits, or ability to fulfill most social statuses are determined by inborn physical sex differences.

Although the terms *sex, gender,* and *sexuality* are often used interchangeably, it is useful to understand the technical difference. A person's sex—male, female, or other—is a

Muslim girls in some parts of the world—including sections of India—cover their faces when in public. The display of bodies, even in a college classroom, would be immoral to many Muslims. However, this is far from a universal pattern, and in many countries, such coverings would be unusual.

2007), and individuals are expected to act appropriately for their sex category. **Gender roles** are those commonly assigned tasks or expected behaviors linked to an individual's sex category. Expectations and tasks vary greatly, as illustrated in the opening examples of this section (Lips 2005). Members of each society learn the psychological, social, and cultural guidelines expected of each gender. In many societies, these distinctions are the way they are because beliefs have developed that "men are men and women are women—a division perceived to be natural and rooted in biology" (West and Zimmerman 1987:128). However, constructed gender identities vary greatly across cultures, with each different culture defining what is right and wrong. Our gender identity, then, is constructed within our culture's framework for gender. There is not some global absolute truth governing gender roles and identities.

Sexuality refers to how cultures shape the meanings of sexuality and the act of sex and how we experience our own bodies and our bodies in relation to others. Strange as it may seem, sexuality is *socially constructed.* A sex act is a "social enterprise," with cultural norms defining what is normal and acceptable in each society, how we should feel, and hidden assumptions about what the act means (Steele 2005). Even what we find attractive is culturally defined. For a period in China, men found tiny feet a sexual turn-on—hence, bound feet in women. In some cultures, legs are the attraction, and in others, men are attracted by breasts.

Consider the ideal male body as depicted in popular magazines in contemporary Western cultures: "over 6 feet tall, 180 to 200 pounds, muscular, agile, with straight white teeth, a washboard stomach, six-pack abs, long legs, a full head of hair, a large penis (discreetly shown by a bulge), broad shoulders and chest, strong muscular back, clean shaven, healthy, and slightly tanned if White, or a lightish brown if Black or Hispanic" (Lorber and Moore 2007:114). We grow up learning what is appealing.

In the 19th century, medical science began to study sexuality and sexual behavior. Most often, sexuality was defined in binary terms (Colligan 2004), and behaviors falling outside heterosexual boundaries were often defined as perverse. In the 20th century, researchers such as Kinsey (Kinsey, Pomeroy, and Martin 1948; Kinsey et al. 1953) and Masters and Johnson (1966, 1970) conducted studies that uncovered actual sexual behaviors, not just those that had been defined as normal. These studies considered a range of sexual practices, from premarital sex and homosexuality to orgasm and masturbation (Lindsey 2005).

The struggles that individuals have with their sexual identity are reflected in the studies of *transgender:* when intersexed individuals do not fit clearly into female or male sex classifications (Leeder 2004). Transgender refers to "identification as someone who is challenging, questioning, or changing gender from that assigned at birth to a chosen gender—male-to-female, female-to-male, transitioning between genders, or gender 'queer' (challenging gender

basis for stratification around the globe, used in every society to assign positions and roles to individuals. However, what is defined as normal behavior for a male, female, or intersexed person in one society could get one killed in another.

Gender identity is learned and created. It refers to a society's notions of masculinity and femininity—socially constructed meanings associated with male or female—and how individuals construct their gender identity within these constraints. The examples in the opening of the chapter and at the beginning of this section illustrate some differences in how cultures are structured around gender.

These gender meanings determine proper behaviors and placement in the stratification system (Rothenberg norms)" (Lorber and Moore 2007:6). Transgendered individuals are of interest to sociologists studying sex and gender because of their ambiguous life, living on the boundaries. Due to the pressure to fit in, most transgendered people change themselves, sometimes through surgery, to fit into their chosen gender. They may "pass" as one sex or engage in social interaction as both men and women.

In summary, although the terms *sex, gender,* and *sexuality* are often used interchangeably, they do have distinct meanings. The distinctions between these terms are not always as clear-cut as the definitions would imply. One can be a masculine heterosexual female, a masculine homosexual male, or any of a number of possible combinations. Individuals are continually negotiating the meanings attached to gender and sexuality, that is, they are *doing gender,* a concept discussed later in this chapter (West and Zimmerman 1987).

Sex, Gender, and Sexuality: The Micro Level

"It's a boy!" brings varying cultural responses. In many Western countries, that exclamation results in blue blankets, toys associated with males (such as footballs, soccer balls, and trucks), roughhousing, and gender socialization messages. In some Asian societies, boys are sources for great rejoicing whereas girls may be seen as a burden. In China and India, *female infanticide* (killing of newborn girl babies) is sometimes practiced, in part because of the cost to poor families of raising a girl and the diminished value of girls. In China, the male preference system is exacerbated by the government's edict that a couple may have just one child.

Beginning at birth, each individual passes through many stages. At each, there are messages that reinforce appropriate gender behavior in that society. Although gender socialization differs in each society, proper roles are established by the culture and learned from birth. These gender expectations are inculcated into children by parents, siblings, grandparents, neighbors, peers, and even daycare providers. If we fail to respond to the expectations of these significant people in our lives, we may experience negative sanctions: teasing, isolation and exclusion, harsh words, and stigma. To avoid these informal sanctions, which can be extremely uncomfortable, children usually learn to conform, at least in their public behavior.

The lifelong process of gender socialization continues once we reach *school-age* and become more involved in activities separate from our parents. Other people in the community—teachers, religious leaders, coaches—also begin to influence us. We are grouped by sex in many of these social settings, and we come to think of ourselves as like *this* group and unlike *that* group: boys versus girls, we versus they. Even if our parents are not highly traditional in their gender expectations, we still experience many influences at the micro level to conform to traditional gender notions.

With adulthood, differential treatment and stratification of the sexes take new forms. Men traditionally have more networks and statuses, as well as greater access to resources outside of the home. This has resulted in women having less power because they are more dependent on husbands or fathers for resources. Even spousal abuse is related to imbalance of power in relationships. Lack of connections to the larger social system makes it difficult for women to remove themselves from abusive relationships.

The subtitle of this chapter asks, Who goes first? When it comes to the question of who walks through a door first, the answer is that in many Western societies, *she* does—or at least, formal etiquette would suggest this is proper. The strong man steps back and defers to the weaker female, graciously holding the door for her (Walum 1974). Yet, when it comes to who walks through the metaphorical door to the professions, it is the man who goes first. Women are served first at restaurants and at other micro-level settings, but this seems little compensation for the fact that doors are often closed to them at the meso and macro levels of social intercourse.

Some scholars argue that language is powerful in shaping the behavior and perceptions of people, as discussed in the chapter on culture. Women often end sentences with tag questions, a pattern that involves ending a declarative statement with a short tag that turns it into a question: "That was a good idea, don't you think?" This pattern may cause male business colleagues to think women are insecure or uncertain about themselves. The women themselves may view it as an invitation to collaboration and dialogue. Yet, a perception of insecurity may prevent a woman from getting the job or the promotion. On the flip side, when women stop using these "softening" devices, they may be perceived by men as strident, harsh, or "bitchy" (Wood and Reich 2006).

Other aspects of language may also be important. The same adverb or adjective, when preceded by a male or female pronoun, can take on very different meanings. When one says, "He's easy" or "He's loose," it does not generally mean the same thing as when someone says, "She's easy" or "She's loose." Likewise, there are words such as *slut* for women for which there is no equivalent for men. There is no female equivalent for *cuckold,* the term describing a man whose wife is making a fool of him by having an affair. Why is that? To use another example, the word *spinster* is supposed to be the female synonym for *bachelor,* yet it has very different connotations. Even the more newly coined *bachelorette* is not usually used to describe a highly appealing, perhaps lifelong role. What might be the implications of these differences?

Those who invoke the biological argument that women are limited by pregnancy, childbirth, or breast-feeding from participating in public affairs and politics ignore the fact that in most societies, these biological roles are time limited and that women play a variety of roles in addition to keeping the home and hearth. They also ignore those societies in which males are deeply involved in nonaggressive and nurturing activities such as child rearing.

Many women today are in major leadership positions. India's newly elected President Pratibha Patil (top right) is the first woman to hold the post in her country, and she won the election with about twice the votes of the opposition candidate. Michelle Bachelet (top left), the president of Chile, won almost 54% of the popular vote in 2006. Songul Chapouk, trained engineer, teacher, and women's activist (bottom left), and Dr. Raja Habib al-Khuzaai, southern tribal leader (bottom right), are members of the 25-member Governing Council of Iraq, composed of the nation's most prominent leaders.

Thinking Sociologically

Some people always write *he* first when writing "he and she." Others sometimes put *she* first. Does this influence gender roles, or is this just fussiness about insignificant matters? Explain.

Sex, Gender, and Sexuality: The Meso Level

By whatever age is defined as adulthood in our society, we are expected to assume leadership roles and responsibilities in the institutions of society—carrying out family roles, educating the young, providing health care, teaching principles of our faith, providing for support through the economic institution, and participating in government. The roles we play in these institutions often differ depending on our sex or gender, which determine our placements and many of our experiences in the social world (Brettell and Sargent 2005).

In most societies, sex and age stipulate when and how we experience rites of passage, rituals and formal processes that acknowledge a change of status. These include any ceremonies or recognitions that admit one to adult duties and privileges. Rites of passage are institutionalized in various ways: religious rituals such as bar mitzvah or bat mitzvah ceremonies, which are a bit different for males and females; educational celebrations such as graduation ceremonies, which often involve caps and gowns of gender-specific colors or place females on one side of the room and males on the other; and different ages at which men and women are permitted to marry.

Other institutions segregate us by sex as well. Traditional Greek Orthodox Christian churches and Orthodox Jewish synagogues, for example, do not have families seated together. Men sit on one side of the sanctuary, and women on the other. Many institutions, including religious, political, and economic organizations, have historically allowed only males to have leadership roles. Only men are to teach the scriptures to the young among traditional Jews, but few men fill that role in contemporary Christian congregations.

Often, women's reduced access to power in microlevel settings has to do with a lack of power and status in meso-level organizations and institutions. This is one reason why policymakers concerned about gender equality have focused so much on inclusion of women in social institutions. For example, micro-credit organizations around the world make small financial loans, primarily to women, to start small businesses to support their families. One of these organizations is described in the next "Sociology Around the World."

Men and women are segregated in many social settings, including rituals of various sorts. Here, we see only men attending a funeral service in Cairo, Egypt.

Thinking Sociologically

How might women's lack of positions of authority in organizations and institutions—the meso level of society—influence females at the micro level? How might it influence their involvements at the macro level?

Sex, Gender, and Sexuality: The Macro Level

Going to school, driving a car, voting, working—people around the world engage in these necessary activities. Yet, in some parts of the world, these activities are forbidden for women. When we turn to the national and global level, we again witness inequality between the sexes that is quite separate from any form of personal prejudice or animosity toward women. Patterns of social action that are imbedded in the entire social system may influence women and men, providing unrecognized privileges or disadvantages (McIntosh 1992). This is called *institutionalized privilege* or *disprivilege*.

In hunter-gatherer and agricultural societies, women increase their power relative to men as they age and as people gain respect for their wisdom. Especially within a clan or a household, women become masters over their domains. Men move from active roles outside the home to passive roles after retirement, whereas women often do the opposite.

Sociology Around the World

Micro Credits and Empowerment of Women

The 30 village women gather regularly to discuss issues of health, crops, their herds, the predicted rains, goals for their children, and how to make ends meet. They are from a subsistence farming village in southern Niger on the edge of the Sahara desert. Recently, a micro-credit organization was established with a small grant of $1,500 from abroad. With training from Care International, an international nongovernmental organization (NGO), the women selected a board of directors to oversee the loans. Groups of five or six women have joined together to explain their projects to the board and request small loans. Each woman is responsible for paying back a small amount on the loan each week, once the project is established and bringing in money.

The women are enthusiastic. In the past they had no funds, and banks charged enormous interest rates on loans.

A loan of between $20 and $50 from the micro-credit organization is a tremendous sum considering that for many of these women, it is equivalent to six months' earnings. Strong social norms are instituted to encourage repayment. Women who repay their loans promptly often decide who is eligible for future loans. Participation in the program often encourages women and grants them economic and social capital otherwise unavailable to them.

With the new possibilities for their lives, they have big plans: For instance, one group plans to buy a press to make peanut oil, a staple for cooking in the region. Currently, people pay a great deal for oil imported from Nigeria. Another group will buy baby lambs, fatten them, and sell them for future festivals at a great profit. Yet another group plans to set up a small bakery. Women are also discussing the possibility of making local craft products to sell to foreign fair-trade organizations such as *10,000 Villages* (a fair-trade organization that markets products made by villagers and returns the profits to the villagers).

Some economists and social policymakers claim that grassroots organizations like micro credits may be the way out of poverty for millions of poor families and that women are motivated to be small entrepreneurs to help support their families and buy education and health care for their children (KBYU-TV 2005). Indeed, in 2006, Muhammad Yunus, who founded Grameen Bank—a micro-credit lender for the very poor—received the Nobel Prize for Peace.

Micro-credit lenders build significant social capital for their participants, but critics suggest that there is an underresearched downside to micro lending. As they see it, despite its success, the solution is a micro-level attempt to address a macro-level problem. Macro economists such as Linda Mayoux (2002, 2008) question whether or not the program will address the gender inequalities in the developing nations they target. Most economists agree that micro-lending works best alongside macro-level initiatives seeking to address similar problems.

The winds of change are influencing the roles of women in many parts of the world, as is seen in governing structures. Although women are still denied the right to vote in a few countries, voting is a right in most. In the United States, women have voted for a little more than 80 years. Yet, in the entire history of the United States, only 34 women have served in the U.S. Senate. As of 2008, the number is at an all-time high, with 16 out of 100 senators being women. Still, the United States is far behind many other countries in women's representation in governing bodies. The nation with the highest percentage of women in the national parliament or congress is Rwanda (sub-Saharan Africa) at 48.8%. The other countries in the top 10, with women constituting at least 35% or more of members in the national legislature, are Sweden (47%), Cuba (43%), Finland (42%), Argentina (40%), Netherlands (39%), Denmark (38%), Costa Rica (37%), Spain (37%), Norway (36%), and Belgium and Mozambique (35% each). Canada is 58th among nations at 21%, and the United States ranks 84th at just under 17%, ranked between Bolivia and El

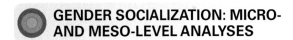

Map 9.1 Percentage of Seats in National Parliaments Held by Women in 2008

Source: Inter-Parliamentary Union. Map by Anna Versluis.

Salvador and well below Afghanistan, Ethiopia, Sudan, and Uzbekistan (Inter-Parliamentary Union 2008).

Several factors have been especially effective in increasing women's positions in national parliaments in Africa: the existence of a matriarchal culture (where women may have increased authority and power in decision making), political systems that stress proportional representation, and the adoption of gender quotas for government positions (Yoon 2004). Yet, democratization of governmental systems is sometimes linked to a *decrease* in representation by women, a sad reality for those committed to establishing democracy around the world (Yoon 2001, 2005). Globally, women's access to power and prestige is highly variable, with northern European countries having a position of leadership when it comes to gender equity in government. (See Map 9.1, Table 9.1.)

Cross-cultural analyses confirm that gender roles either evolve over centuries or are transformed by sweeping reform laws such as voting rights. The fact that women in China generally work outside the home whereas women in some Muslim societies hardly venture from their homes is due to differences in cultural norms about gender roles that are dictated by governments or tradition and learned through the socialization process.

GENDER SOCIALIZATION: MICRO- AND MESO-LEVEL ANALYSES

The old adage says, "Sugar and spice and everything nice—that's what little girls are made of. Snips and snails and puppy dog tails—that's what little boys are made of." As the verse implies, different views of little girls and little boys start at birth, based on gender and stereotypes about what is biologically natural. Behavioral expectations stem from cultural beliefs about the nature of men and women, and these expectations guide socialization from the earliest ages and in intimate primary group settings.

Socialization into gender is the process by which people learn the cultural norms, attitudes, and behaviors appropriate to their gender. That is, they learn how to think and act as boys or girls, women or men. Socialization reinforces the "proper" gender behaviors and punishes the improper behaviors. This process, in turn, reinforces gender stereotypes. In many societies, traits of gentleness, passivity, and dependence are associated with femininity, whereas boldness, aggression, strength, and independence are identified with masculinity. For instance, in most Western societies, aggression in women is considered unfeminine, if not inappropriate or disturbed.

Table 9.1 **Women in National Governments (Selected Countries)**

Rank	Country	Lower or Single House			Upper House or Senate		
		Seats	Women	% W	Seats	Women	% W
1	Rwanda	80	39	48.8	26	9	34.6
2	Sweden	349	164	47.0	—	—	—
3	Cuba	614	265	43.2	—	—	—
4	Finland	200	83	41.5	—	—	—
5	Argentina	255	102	40.0	72	28	38.9
6	Netherlands	150	59	39.3	75	26	34.7
7	Denmark	179	68	38.0	—	—	—
8	Costa Rica	57	21	36.8	—	—	—
9	Spain	350	128	36.6	259	60	23.2
10	Norway	169	61	36.1	—	—	—
11	Belgium	150	53	35.3	71	27	38.0
12	Mozambique	250	87	34.8	—	—	—
13	Iceland	63	21	33.0	—	—	—
14	New Zealand	121	40	33.1	—	—	—
15	South Africa	400	132	33.0	54	22	40.7
16	Austria	183	60	32.8	61	15	24.6
17	Germany	613	194	31.6	69	15	21.7
18	Uganda	332	102	30.7	—	—	—
19	Burundi	118	36	30.5	49	17	34.7
20	United Rep. of Tanzania	319	97	30.4	—	—	—
21	Peru	120	35	29.2	—	—	—
26	Switzerland	200	57	28.5	46	10	21.7
28	Afghanistan	242	67	27.7	102	22	21.6
32	Grenada	15	4	26.7	13	4	30.8
33	Viet Nam	493	127	25.8	—	—	—
35	Iraq	275	70	25.5	—	—	—
45	Honduras	128	30	23.4	—	—	—
47	Mexico	500	116	23.2	128	23	18.0
50	Pakistan	338	76	22.5	100	17	17.0
51	United Arab Emirates	40	9	22.5	—	—	—
55	Ethiopia	529	116	21.9	112	21	18.8
57	Bulgaria	240	52	21.7	—	—	—
58	Canada	305	65	21.3	93	32	34.5
61	China	2963	611	20.6	—	—	—
62	Philippines	239	49	20.5	23	4	17.4
65	Dem. People's Rep. of Korea	687	138	20.1	—	—	—
69	United Kingdom	646	126	19.5	750	148	19.7
72	Venezuela	167	31	18.6	—	—	—
73	Nicaragua	92	17	18.5	—	—	—
74	France	577	105	18.2	330	60	18.2
77	Sudan	443	80	18.1	50	3	6.0
78	Tajikistan	63	11	17.5	34	8	23.5
79	Uzbekistan	120	21	17.5	100	15	15.0
80	Italy	630	109	17.3	322	45	14.0
81	Nepal	329	57	17.3	—	—	—
83	Bolivia	130	22	16.9	27	1	3.7
84	United States of America	435	73	16.8	100	16	16.0
85	El Salvador	84	14	16.7	—	—	—
87	Panama	78	13	16.7	—	—	—
89	Turkmenistan	50	8	16.0	—	—	—
90	Zimbabwe	150	24	16.7	66	24	34.4

Source: Inter-Parliamentary Union 2008. Reprinted with permission of the Inter-Parliamentary Union.

Note: To examine the involvement of women in other countries or to see even more recent figures, go to www.ipu.org/wmn-e/classif.htm.

Likewise, the gentle, unassertive male is often looked on with scorn or pity, stigmatized as a "wimp." Expectations related to these stereotypes are rigid in many societies (Pollack 1999).

Stages in Gender Socialization

Bounce that rough and tumble baby boy and cuddle that precious delicate little girl. Thus begins gender socialization, starting at birth and taking place through a series of life stages, discussed in Chapter 4 on socialization. Examples from infancy and childhood show how socialization into gender roles takes place.

Infancy

Learning how to carry out gender roles begins at birth. Parents in the United States describe their newborn daughters as soft, delicate, fine-featured, little, beautiful, pretty, cute, awkward, and resembling their mothers. They depict their sons as strong, firm, alert, and well-coordinated (Lindsey 2005; Rubin 1974). Clothing, room decor, and toys also reflect notions of gender. For instance, in Spain, parents and grandparents dress babies and their carriages in pink or blue depending on gender, proudly showing off the little ones to friends as they promenade in the evenings. Although gender stereotypes have declined in recent years, they continue to affect the way we handle and treat male and female infants (Karraker 1995).

Childhood

Once out of infancy, research shows that many boys are encouraged to be more independent and exploratory whereas girls are protected from situations that might prove harmful. More pressure is put on boys to behave in "gender appropriate" ways. Boys are socialized into "the boy code" that provides rigid guidelines (see "How Do We Know?"). Cross-cultural studies show boys often get more attention than girls because of their behavior, with an emphasis on achievement, autonomy, and aggression for boys (Kimmel and Messner 2004).

Thinking Sociologically

First, read about "The Boy Code" on page 282. What evidence do you see of the Boy Code when you observe your friends and relatives? What is the impact of the Boy Code? Is there a similar code for girls?

Stereotypes for girls in a majority of societies label feminine behaviors as soft, nonaggressive, and noncompetitive and favor diminutive women. Consider that boys act out their aggressive feelings, but girls are socialized to be nice, nurturing, and not aggressive. In a study about how school girls express aggression, Simmons (2002) finds that girls express "relational aggression," that is, aggression that affects girls' social contacts indirectly through rumors, name-calling, giggling, ignoring, backbiting, exclusion, and manipulation of victims. Friendship and needing to belong are the weapons rather than sticks and stones. This form of bullying is subtle and hard to detect, but it can have long-lasting effects on girls (Simmons 2002).

Names for children also reflect stereotypes about gender. Boys are more often given strong, hard names that end in consonants. The top 10 boys' names in 2006 include Jacob, Michael, Joshua, Ethan, Matthew, Daniel, Christopher, Andrew, Anthony, and William. Girls are more likely to be given soft pretty names with vowel endings such as most of the top 10: Emily, Emma, Madison, Isabella, Ava, Abigail, Olivia, Hannah, Sophia, and Samantha (Social Security Online 2008). Alternatively, girls may be given feminized versions of boys' names—Roberta, Jessica, Josephine, Nicole, Michelle, or Donna. Sometimes, boys' names are given to girls without first feminizing them. Names such as Lynn, Stacey, Tracey, Faye, Dana, Jody, Lindsay, Robin, and Carmen used to be names exclusively for men, but within a decade or two after they were applied to girls, parents stopped using them for boys. So a common name for males may for a time be given to either sex, but then it is given to girls only. The pattern rarely goes the other direction. Once feminized, the names seem to have become tainted (Lieberson, Dumais, and Bauman 2000).

In the early childhood years, children become aware of their own gender identity. As they reach school age, they learn that their sex is permanent, and they begin to categorize behaviors that are appropriate for their sex. As children are rewarded for performing proper gender roles, these roles are reinforced. That reinforcement solidifies gender roles, setting the stage for gender-related interactions, behaviors, and choices in later life.

Meso-Level Agents of Gender Socialization

Clues to proper gender roles surround children in materials produced by corporations (books, toys, games), in mass media images, in educational settings, and in religious organizations and beliefs. In Chapter 4 on socialization, we learned about agents of socialization. Those agents play a major role in teaching children proper gender roles. The following examples demonstrate how organizations and institutions in our society teach and reinforce gender assumptions and roles.

Corporations

Corporations have produced materials that help socialize children into proper conduct. Publishers, for example, produce books that present images of expected gender behavior. Language and pictures in preschool picture books, elementary children's books, and school textbooks are steeped in gender role messages reflecting society's expectations and stereotypes. In a classic study of award-winning children's

How Do We Know?

The Boy Code

Boys and girls begin to conform to gender expectations even more once they are old enough to understand that their sex is rather permanent, that boys are not capable of becoming "mommies." They become even more conscious of adhering to norms of others in their gender category.

In Chapter 5, we mentioned the Old Boy network in American society—a system that favors adult men through networks. This system actually starts with "the boy code," the rules about boys' proper behavior. Young boys learn "the code" from parents, siblings, peers, teachers, and society in general.

They are praised for adhering to the code and punished for violating its dictates. William Pollack (1999) writes that boys learn several stereotyped behavior models exemplifying the boy code:

1. "The sturdy oak": Men should be stoic, stable, and independent; a man never shows weakness.

2. "Give 'em hell": From athletic coaches and movie heroes, the consistent theme is extreme daring, bravado, and attraction to violence.

3. "The 'big wheel'": Men and boys should achieve status, dominance, and power; they should avoid shame, wear the mask of coolness, and act as though everything is under control.

4. "No sissy stuff": Boys are discouraged from expressing feelings or urges perceived as feminine—dependence, warmth, empathy.

The boy code is ingrained in society; by five or six years of age, boys are less likely than girls to express hurt or distress. They have learned to be ashamed of showing feelings and of being weak. This gender straitjacket, according to Pollack, causes boys to conceal feelings in order to fit in and be accepted and loved. As a result, some boys, especially in adolescence, become silent, covering any vulnerability and masking their true feelings. This affects boys' relationships, performance in school, and ability to connect with others. It also causes young males to put on what Jackson Katz (2006) calls the "tough guise", when young men and boys emphasize aggression and violence to display masculinity.

Pollack (1999) suggests that we can help boys reconnect to non-gendered norms by

1. giving some undivided attention each day just listening to boys;

2. encouraging a range of emotions;

3. avoiding language that taunts, teases, or shames;

4. looking behind the veneer of "coolness" for signs of problems;

5. expressing love and empathy;

6. dispelling the "sturdy oak" image; and

7. advocating a broad, inclusive model of masculinity.

To obtain information for his study, reported in *Real Boys*, Pollack (1999) relied on several data collection methods. He used his notes from more than 20 years of working with men and boys as codirector of the Center for Men at McLean Hospital and Harvard Medical School. This provided data and professional notes on the lives of hundreds of young and adolescent boys. In addition, he observed boys in various situations from homes to sports fields, and he interviewed parents of boys.

His questions to boys evoked candid responses on questions about home life, school, friends, and emotional lives. Pollack's involvement in the project, Listening to Boys' Voices, provided information that spurred him to find more information about boy's lives. For instance, boys are two times as likely as girls to be labeled "learning disabled" and as having attention deficit disorder (ADD). In addition, 67% of students in special education classes are boys. The complexity of the issues related to studying boys led Pollack to use multiple methods to study and write about boys' lives.

With the women's movement and shifts in gender expectations have come new patterns of male behavior. Some men are forming more supportive and less competitive relationships with other men, and there are likely to be continued changes in and broadening of "appropriate" behavior for men (Kimmel and Messner 2004; Nardi 1992; Stoltenberg 1993).

books from the United States that have sold more than 3 million copies, Weitzman (Weitzman et al. 1972) made several observations: (1) Males appear more often in stories as central characters; (2) activities of male and female characters in books differ, with boys playing active roles and girls being passive or simply helping brothers, fathers, or husbands; and (3) adult women are pictured as more passive and dependent, whereas males are depicted as carrying out a range of activities and jobs.

Although more recent books show some expansion in the roles book characters play, studies confirm a continuing pattern of gender role segregation in children's books (Anderson and Hamilton 2005; Diekman and Murmen 2004). Whether Peter Rabbit, Curious George the Monkey, or Babar the Elephant, the male animal characters in children's books outnumber females; studies show that males of any species most often are portrayed as adventurous, brave, competent, clever, and fun, whereas female counterparts may be depicted as incompetent, fearful, and dependent on others (Purcell and Stewart 1990). Moreover, even though authors and publishers have begun producing books presenting unbiased gender roles and strong girls and women, the tens of thousands of older, classic, books in public and school libraries mean that a parent or child picking a book off of the shelf is still likely to select a book that has these stereotypical views of boys and girls.

Producers of toys and games also contributed to traditional messages about gender. Store-bought toys fill rooms in homes of children in the Western world, and it is usually quite clear which are boys' rooms and which are girls.' Boys' rooms are filled with sports equipment, army toys, building and technical toys, and cars and trucks. Girls' rooms have fewer toys, and most are related to dolls and domestic roles. Boys have more experience manipulating blocks, Tinker Toys, Legos, and Erector sets—toys paralleling masculinized activities outside the home in the public domain, from constructing and building trades to military roles and sports. Girls prepare for domestic roles with toys relating to domestic activities. Barbie dolls stress physical appearance, consumerism, and glamour. Only a few Barbies are in occupational roles. By contrast, the Ken dolls that Mattel

Girls and boys quickly pick up messages—from parents, from other children, and from the media—about what kinds of toys are appropriate for someone of their sex. Many toys—and games like "Pretty Pretty Princess"—have very explicit messages.

designed to match Barbie (and have now discontinued) were often doctors or other professionals. In 2000, Mattel produced two computers. The Barbie model was designed with girls as the target market, and a Hot Wheels model was developed for boys. These models differed in more than simple appearance. The two computers had different software installed in them, including different educational programs. The contrast in what they teach children is illustrated in Table 9.2. The Mattel Corporation claimed that the popular Barbie software, involving "accessories" for Barbie, consumed too much space on the Barbie model computer to include the educational software that was on the Hot Wheels computer. Although these computerized toys are no longer being produced, there was a recent generation of children exposed to this different socialization.

Table 9.2 **Toys That Teach Gendered Lessons**

Only Barbie Computer Has	Only Hot Wheels Computer Has	Both Models Have
Fashion designer	Cluefinders math 9–12	A 3D world atlas
Detective Barbie	Compton's complete reference collection	Math workshop
Miscellaneous Barbie accessories	Kid pix studio	Typing tutorial
	Logical journey	National Geographic: The 90s
	Zoombinis (thinking game)	Writing and creativity center
	A human anatomy and 3D visualization program	

Source: Headlam 2000; Kramer 2005.

At the left, a young girl picks out the Barbie dolls she wants. Mattel's Barbie dolls have been heavily criticized for extremely traditional and highly sexualized images of young women. The boy at the right is in the "blue" aisle—which sometimes has even more army fatigue colors. He is getting different messages than the girl at the left.

Each toy or game prepares children through anticipatory socialization for future gender roles. Toys that require building, manipulating, and technical skills provide experiences for later life. Choices ranging from college major and occupational choice to activities that depend on visual-spatial and mathematical interests and abilities appear to be affected by these early choices and childhood learning experiences (Tavris and Wade 1984).

Consider the example of "Dungeons and Dragons," a popular game primarily among adolescent boys in Europe, Japan, and North America. The participants role-play their way through scenarios full of demons and dragons, using a vast array of dungeons, weapons, and magical spells. The boys develop characters that they impersonate throughout the game as they negotiate, bargain, create, imitate, and develop a variety of other social or cognitive skills. They must calculate complex mathematical formulae and use logic and imagination—all skills that will aid them in coping with the adult public world. Although more girls are taking up gaming activities, the packaging of this product makes it clear it is a boys' activity.

Mass Media

Have you ever noticed the media coverage of female celebrities who have made poor choices? The men who get into trouble, like radio talk show host Don Imus and actor Mel Gibson, are slapped on the hand. "Boys will be boys," after all. However, actresses such as Paris Hilton, Lindsey Lohan, and Britney Spears experience intense scrutiny and hostility. Is this because of their class, their gender, or their nontraditional roles and nonconforming behavior? Whatever variables affect the reactions to these women, they are subjects of mass media frenzy.

Mass media in their many forms—magazines, ads, films, music videos, Internet sites—are major agents of socialization into gender roles. Young men and women, desiring to fit in, are influenced by messages from the media. For instance, the epidemic of steroid use among boys and dieting among girls is a health concern in the United States (Taub and McLorg 2007), driven by ads. Yet, manufacturers advertise such products with promises to remake teens into more attractive people.

Video games that dehumanize women teach and perpetuate stereotypes about women. A scandal arose in 2003 over a video game, "Hunting for Bambi," and subsequent claims that the game was being played "in reality." This video game featured men hunting in a forest for naked women and shooting them with paintballs. Critics condemned it as violent, degrading, and voyeuristic—a dehumanizing of women. Women in such videos become objects to be exploited. Would society allow videos called "Hunting Italian Americans," "Hunting African Americans," or "Hunting Jewish Americans" (Glass 2003)? The goal of another controversial video game, "Custer's Revenge," was to seek out and rape a bound Native American woman. This game was criticized as promoting rape and racism. Still other games feature women as objects: "Xtreme Beach Volleyball" is not as much about the sport as about displaying breasts (Gallaway 2003; GameSpy 2002). A few recent games depict more positive and realistic images of girls and women.

Some action films produced within the past decade include adventurous and competent girls and women, helping to counter images like the ones in the video described above. Hermione in *Harry Potter* is intelligent and creative. Queen of Naboo and Senator Amidala in *Star Wars* and Lyra

Olsen twins Mary-Kate and Ashley (left) pose together in front of their new star on the Walk of Fame in Hollywood. Like most glamour stars, they must conform to the image of very thin, shapely femininity. Kirstie Alley appears at Showtime's Fat Actress *premiere (right). When Kirstie gained weight, her range of acting options suddenly became very slim.*

Belacqua in *The Golden Compass* are strong, brave, intelligent (and beautiful). Lara Croft in *Tomb Raider* holds her own against evil. However, videos depicting highly competent females are few, and most of those few women are unrealistically thin and highly attractive with large breasts.

Television is another powerful socializing agent. By the time they start school, typical English, Canadian, and U.S. children will have spent more time in front of a television than they will in classrooms in the coming 12 years of school, a behavior that contributes to obesity in the United States (Randerson 2008). Television presents a simple, stereotyped view of life, from advertisements to situation comedies to soap operas. Women in soap operas and ads, especially those working outside the home, are often depicted as having problems in carrying out their role responsibilities (Benokraitis and Feagin 1995). Even the extraordinary powers of superheroes on Saturday morning television depict the female characters as having gender-stereotyped skills such as super-intuition. Notice the next

time you are in a video game room that the fighting characters are typically male and often in armor. When fighting women do appear, they are usually clad in skin-revealing bikini-style attire—odd clothing in which to do battle!

Films and television series in the United States seldom feature average-size or older women (although more variety of ages and body types is seen in the British Broadcasting Company productions). Movie stars are attractive and thin, presenting an often unattainable model for young women, making many feel inadequate and feeding the diet frenzy (Kramer 2005; Taub and McLorg 2007). Women who are quite large are almost entirely depicted as comic figures in U.S. television.

How do social scientists know that television affects gender role socialization? Studies have shown that the more television children watch, the more gender stereotypes they hold. From cartoons to advertisements, television in many countries provides enticing images of a world in which youth is glorified, age is scorned, and female and male roles are stereotyped and/or unattainable (Kilbourne 2000; Tuchman 1996).

Thinking Sociologically

Think of recent mass media examples that you have seen. How do they depict women and men? How might the depictions affect young men and women, if at all?

Educational Systems

Even centers of learning bolster sex-specific expectations and limitations. Educational systems are socialization agents of children through textbooks, classroom activities, playground games, and teachers' attitudes. For example, boys are encouraged to join competitive team sports and girls to support them (Gilligan 1982; Kramer 2005). These simulate hierarchical adult roles of boss/secretary and physician/nurse. Furthermore, the team sports that the boys learn teach them strategic thinking—a critical skill that involves anticipating the moves of the opponent and countering with one's own strategy. This is a very useful skill in the business world and is not explicitly taught in other places in the school curriculum. Girls' games rarely teach this skill.

Children's experiences in grade and middle school reinforce boundaries of "us" and "them" in classroom seating and activities, in the lunchroom, and in playground activities, as girls and boys are seated, lined up, and given assignments by sex (Sadker and Sadker 2005). Those who go outside the boundaries, especially boys, are ridiculed by peers and sometimes teachers, reinforcing stereotypes and separate gender role socialization (Sadker and Sadker 2005; Thorne 1993).

Boys act out and receive more attention in school classrooms than girls do, even though it may be negative attention. Boys are called on more often to do physical chores such as erasing the boards and emptying the trash. Teachers reward girls for being passive and obedient. Boys begin at young ages to work and play together as teams. Girls also join team sports, but their play more frequently involves one-on-one activities. In contrast to girls, boys learn the skills of competition, negotiating, bargaining, aggressiveness, good sportsmanship, and strategic thinking.

Part of the issue of male-female inequality in schools is tied to the issue of popularity, which it seems has less to do with being liked than with being known. For a girl, if everyone knows her name, she is popular (Eder, Evans, and Parker 1995). At the middle-school level, there are more ways that boys can become known. Even when there are both boys' and girls' basketball teams, many spectators come to the boys' contests and very few to the girls' games. Thus, few people know the female athletes' names. In fact, a far more visible position is cheerleader—standing on the sidelines cheering for the boys—because those girls are at least visible (Eder et al. 1995). The other major way in which girls are visible or known is physical appearance, a major standard of popularity and esteem (Eder et al. 1995). Generally, there are far more visible positions for the boys than for girls in middle school.

Title IX of the U.S. Educational Amendments Act of 1972 was a major legislative attempt to level the educational and sports playing field. Passed to bar gender discrimination in schools receiving federal funds, this legislation mandates equal opportunity for participation in school-sponsored programs (Lindsey 2005). The law has reduced or eliminated blatant discrimination in admissions, health care, counseling, housing, sex-segregated programs, financial aid, dress codes, and other areas that were of concern. However, the biggest impact of Title IX legislation has been in athletics.

Partly aided by Title IX, the number of women's athletic programs and scholarship opportunities grew in the late 1990s but has slowed since 2000 and still lags behind men's levels. From 1995 to 2005, the number of women in college sports at 738 NCAA schools surveyed grew by 26,000 to 205,492, while the number of men was 291,797 (Rosen 2007). Some men's sports have been cut back, but others have grown, resulting in a steady number of opportunities for men in sports. One third of high school women participate in sports compared to 45% of males. In high school performing arts, academic clubs, yearbook, and student government, about one third of girls and 20% of boys participate (National Center for Education Statistics 2004). Overall, 79% of the public supports Title IX and what it has accomplished (Women's Sports Foundation 2005). Other aspects of women in education are discussed in Chapter 11 on education.

Religious Beliefs

Religious beliefs serve as agents of socialization by defining, reinforcing, and perpetuating gender role stereotypes and cultural beliefs. Religious teachings provide explanations of birth, death, and the reason for living, so it is only natural to find notions of proper male/female roles. Although the specific teachings vary, the three major monotheistic religions that affirm that there is only one God—Christianity, Islam, and Judaism—are traditionally patriarchal, stressing separate female and male spheres (Kramer 2005). The following are examples of some of these traditional role expectations and the status of women in various religions.

Some interpretations of the Adam and Eve creation story in the Hebrew Bible (which is the Old Testament of the Christian Bible) state that because man was created first, men are superior. Because Eve, created from the rib of man, was a sinner, her sins keep women forever in an inferior, second-class position. For these reasons, in some branches of these religions, women are restricted in their roles within family and religious organizations. They cannot be priests in Catholic churches and cannot vote on business matters in some religious organizations. However, recent work by feminist scholars is challenging the notion of patriarchy in Judaic and Christian history, pointing out that women may have played a much broader role in religious development than currently recognized (Hunter College Women's Studies Collective 2005). Even *Yahweh*—the name for God in the Hebrew Bible—had both male and female connotations, and when God is referred to as a source of wisdom, feminine pronouns and references were used (Borg 1994). Increasingly, denominations are granting women greater roles in the religious hierarchies, ministries, and priesthood of major religious groups.

Women in Judaism lived for 4,000 years in a patriarchal system where men read, taught, and legislated while women followed (Lindsey 2005). Today, three of the five main branches of Judaism allow women equal participation, illustrating that religious practices do change over time. However, Hasidic and Orthodox Jews have a division of labor between men and women following old laws, with designated roles for the home and religious life.

Some Christian teachings have treated women as second-class citizens, even in the eyes of God. For this reason, some Christian denominations have excluded women from a variety of leadership roles and told them they must be subservient to their husbands. Other Christians point to the admonition by Saint Paul that theologically speaking, "There is no such thing as . . . male and female, for you are all one in Christ Jesus." This suggests that women and men are not spiritually different (Galatians 3:28).

Traditional Hindu religion painted women as seductresses, strongly erotic, and a threat to male spirituality and asceticism. To protect men from this threat, women were kept totally covered in thick garments and veils and seen only by men in their immediate families. Today, Hinduism comes in many forms, most of which honor the domestic sphere of life—mothers, wives, and homemakers—while accepting women in public roles, depending on the woman's caste position (Lindsey 2005).

Traditional Islamic beliefs also portrayed female sexuality as dangerous to men, although many women in Islamic societies today are full participants in the public and private sphere. The *Quran* (also spelled *Qur'an* or *Koran*), the Muslim sacred scripture, includes a statement that men are superior to women because of the qualities God has given men. Hammurabi's Code, written in the Middle East between 2067 and 2025 BCE, is the earliest recorded legal system. The laws about women's status were written to distinguish between decent women, belonging to one man, and indecent or public women. Some aspects of these traditional beliefs have carried over to present times. Sharia law, strict Islamic law, was recently imposed on a woman in Nigeria who had a child out of wedlock and on another woman in Pakistan who was a rape victim. Both women were sentenced to death by stoning, but their sentences

High school and college athletics are much less reliable paths for women to become known on campus because so few people come to the games. Even this professional basketball game has sparse attendance (top photo). By contrast, women in very sexy outfits are highly visible and can even become local celebrities when they perform as cheerleaders in front of 80,000 fans at men's sporting events.

have not been carried out because of protests from within and outside the countries. These women suffer social humiliation, degradation, and potential death, but they also confirm the social expectations for others who might stray from the laws (Mydans 2002).

Women in fundamentalist Muslim societies such as Algeria, Iran, Syria, and Saudi Arabia are separated from men (except for fathers and brothers) in work and worship. They generally remain covered. *Purdah,* which means curtain, refers to practices of seclusion and separate worlds for women and men in Islamic cultures. Screens in households and veils in public enforce female modesty and prevent men from seeing women where this is dictated (Ward and Edelstein 2006). Today, some women argue that the veil they wear is for modesty, cosmetic purposes, or to protect them from stares of men. Others claim that the veil is a symbol of oppression and subservience, showing that women must keep themselves in submissive positions. In Turkey, a secular Muslim society, schools and universities have long forbidden religious representation including the wearing of scarves. However, recent debates in Turkey have challenged the rulings forbidding scarves in schools, and the president has declared it legal for women to choose (BBCNews 2004; Knickmeyer 2008). The debate in Turkey, France, and other countries continues.

Religious laws often provide the justifications to keep women servile, and public shaming and threat of severe punishments reinforce the laws. Meso-level religious systems influence how different societies interpret proper gender roles and how sometimes these belief systems change with new interpretations of scriptures.

All of these agents of socialization—corporations, mass media, schools, and religious groups—reinforce "appropriate" gender roles in each society.

Thinking Sociologically

What are some books, toys, childhood games, television shows, school experiences, religious teachings, and peer interactions that influenced your gender role socialization? In what ways did they do so?

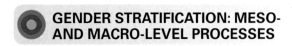
GENDER STRATIFICATION: MESO- AND MACRO-LEVEL PROCESSES

"The *glass ceiling* keeps women from reaching the highest levels of corporate and public responsibility, and the 'sticky floor' keeps the vast majority of the world's women stuck in low-paid jobs" (Hunter College Women's Studies Collective 2005:393; see also Kimmel 2003). Men, on the other hand, face the "glass escalator," especially in traditionally female

occupations. Even if they do not seek to climb in the organizational hierarchy, occupational social forces push them up the job ladder into higher echelons (Williams 1992). Women around the world do two thirds of the work, receive 10% of the world's income, and own 1% of the world's means of production (Robbins 2005). They make up more than 40% of the world's paid workforce but hold only about 20% of managerial jobs, and for those, they are often compensated at lower pay than their male counterparts. Only 5% of the top corporate jobs are held by women. However, companies with women in leadership positions do realize high profits (Adler 2001; Hunter College Women's Studies Collective 2005).

Women and Men at Work: Gendered Organizations

How can I do it all—education, social life, marriage, children, career? This is a question that women in our college classes ask. They already anticipate a delicate balancing act. Work has been central to the definition of masculinity in U.S. society, and for the past half century, women have been joining the workforce in greater numbers (Kramer 2005). Today, women's proportion of the workforce is almost equal to men in the United States and many other Western countries. Working is necessary for many women, especially single mothers, to support their families, and many women with career education and goals want to work. Among countries of the Global North, Sweden has the highest percentage of women in the labor force (82%) and lowest percentage of homemakers. Yet, even in Sweden, with its parental leave and other family-friendly policies, women feel pressures of work and family responsibilities (Eshleman and Bulcroft 2006). Dual-career and -income marriages raise questions about child rearing, power relations, and other family factors in juggling work and family.

Every workplace has a gendered configuration: ratios of female to male workers and matters of who are in the supervisory statuses and how positions are distributed. This, in turn, affects our experiences in the workplace. Consider the example of mothers who are breastfeeding their babies. Must they quit their jobs or alter their family schedules if the workplace does not provide a space for breastfeeding? Some workplaces accommodate family needs, but others do not. Yet, many women have multiple responsibilities: They try to support their families financially and in other ways, be good mothers, and be responsible employees or employers. Men do not face the same issues because most corporations assume the average worker is male.

Research shows that workers are more satisfied when the sex composition of their work group and distribution of men and women in power are balanced (Britton 2000:430). Feminists propose ideas to minimize gender differences in organizations, that is, to "degender" organizations so that all members have equal opportunities (Britton 2000).

Thinking Sociologically

If corporate structures were reversed so that women structured and organized the workplace, how might the workplace environment change?

Institutionalized Gender Discrimination

Gender stratification at the meso level—like race and ethnic stratification—can occur quite independently of any overt prejudice or ill will by others. It becomes part of the social system, and we are not even conscious of it, especially if we are one of the privileged members of society. Most of what has been discussed so far is de jure discrimination, done deliberately and justified with laws and ideological beliefs about women's inability to carry out certain tasks, beliefs that are reinforced with unbecoming cultural images of women. The more subtle process of de facto discrimination (which is not intended) also needs attention. When inequality is woven into the web of the macro-level social structure and becomes taken for granted, it is called institutional discrimination. It can include intentional actions such as bank policies requiring single women, compared with single men, to have three times as much money up-front for a house down payment to receive a homeowner's loan, but it can also include unintentional actions with consequences that disadvantage women (Feagin and Feagin 1986, 2007).

You may recall from the previous chapter that side-effect discrimination involves practices in one institution that are linked to practices in another institution. The practices in the first institution have an effect in the second one that is not anticipated or even recognized by most people in the society. For example, if roles of women in family life are determined by rigid gender expectations, as research shows, then women find it more difficult to devote themselves to gaining job promotions. In addition, as long as little girls learn through socialization to use their voices and to hold their bodies and gesture in ways that communicate deference, employers assume a lack of the self-confidence necessary for major leadership roles. If women are paid less despite the same levels of education (see Table 9.3), they are likely to have less access to expensive health care or to be able to afford a $20,000 down payment for a house unless they are married. This makes women dependent on men in a way that most men are not dependent on women.

A factor affecting differences in incomes is the type of academic degrees that men and women receive (engineering rather than education, for example). However, even when these differences are factored in, men still make considerably more on average than women with identical levels of experience and training.

Little girls learn to use their voices and to hold their bodies and gesture in ways that communicate deference. This little girl does not look very powerful or confident. When women tilt their heads—either forward or to one side—they also look like they lack confidence, and this hurts their chances of promotion in the corporate world.

Men often get defensive and angry when people talk about sexism in society because they feel they are being attacked or asked to correct injustices of the past. However, the empirical reality is that the playing field is not level for men and women. Most men do not do anything to intentionally harm women, and they may not feel prejudiced toward women, but sexism operates so that men are given privileges they never asked for and may not even recognize.

Past-in-present discrimination refers to practices from the past that may no longer be allowed but that continue to affect people today. We discussed above the problem that men and women have different pay with similar levels of education. Note that a difference in the typical number of years women have spent in their professional fields is a small part of the difference in income levels. In other words, there are fewer women senior law partners in part because women who are now in their 50s or older were often not admitted to professional graduate programs in the 1960s and '70s. A policy of the past still influences women's positions and incomes today.

Let us consider another example of the past influencing the present. At an appliance industry in the Midwest investigated by one of the authors, there is a sequence of jobs one must hold to be promoted up the line to foreman.

Table 9.3	U.S. Income by Educational Level and Sex (in dollars)	
Education	Men	Women
Not a high school graduate	23,222	14,294
High school graduate	35,248	22,208
Some college; no degree	38,768	24,086
College graduate (bachelor's)	67,980	40,684
Master's degree	86,667	49,573
Doctorate	105,163	66,411
Professional degree	139,773	82,268

Source: U.S. Census Bureau, Current Population Survey 2008a.

This requirement ensures that the foreman understands the many aspects of the production at the plant. One of the jobs involves working in a room with heavy equipment that cuts through and bends metal sheets. The machine is extremely powerful and could easily cut off a leg or hand if the operator is not careful. Because of the danger, the engineers designed the equipment so it would not operate unless three levers were activated at the same time. One lever was triggered by stepping on a pedal on the floor. The other two required reaching out with one's hands so that one's body was extended. When one was spread-eagled to activate all three levers, there was no way one could possibly have a part of one's body near the blades. It was brilliant engineering. There was one unanticipated problem: The hand-activated levers were 5 feet, 10 inches off the ground and 5 feet apart. Few women had the height and arm span to run this machine, and therefore, no women had yet made it through the sequence of positions to the higher paying position of foreman. The equipment cost millions of dollars, so it was not likely to be replaced. Neither the engineers who designed the machine nor the upper-level managers who established the sequence of jobs to become foreman had deliberately tried to exclude women. Indeed, they were perplexed when they looked at their employee figures and saw so few women moving up through the ranks. The cause of women's disadvantage was not mean-spirited men but features of the system that had unintended consequences. The barriers women face, then, are not just matters of socialization or other micro-level social processes. The nature of sexism is often subtle and pervasive in the society, operating at the meso and macro levels as institutional discrimination.

Gender Differences in Internet Use

One specific form of institutionalized difference in access to resources at the global level has to do with the Internet.

Knowledge of events in the world, job skills, awareness of job openings, networks that extend beyond national borders, and other resources are available through the Internet. Women like the human connections created by the Internet, whereas men tend to like the experience and financial options it offers. Although women are catching up to men in usage in some Global North countries, there is a larger world digital divide in gender than in other categories (Drori 2006; Fallows 2005). The difference in Internet use by women as a percentage of all users varies significantly by country: Women are roughly 45% of Internet users in Sweden and Denmark, a bit more than 40% in Israel, and about 30% in China, 17% in Senegal, and 14% in Ethiopia. In the Arab world, women account for only 4% of the online population. In Kenya, a 1999 survey in two provinces found that 99% of the women had never heard of the Internet. Several other countries are close to equal in usage by women: Mexico at 46%, South Africa and Thailand each at 49% (Drori 2006). Even in these countries, women's usage has climbed to that level only in the past few years.

However, the story is different in the United States, where women have caught up with or outpaced their male age and ethnic group peers. Of the 67% of the U.S. population that goes online, 66% are women and 68% men. Between 18 and 29 years of age, more women use the Internet than men—86% compared to 80%. However, in the 65 and older cohort, more men (34%) than women (21%) are online. In addition, more African American women (60%) than men (50%) are Web savvy. Men tend to use the Internet more often and longer and have more high-speed connections (Fallows 2005). The direction of U.S. usage parallels that of other Global North countries and may predict the future in other countries.

In Chapter 7, we explored global differences in Internet usage and found that the largest variance was based on wealth of the country and access to technology. The same principle holds for women's usage in Global North and South. Many African countries may have only half of 1% of the population online, but in none of the African countries cited by Drori (2006) do women have more than 15% of that tiny share. So of the women in most African countries, fewer than 7 out of 10,000 have used the Internet. Clearly, the majority of these women are "out of the digital loop."

Internet-related gender stratification exhibits itself not just in terms of *whether* a person uses the Internet but also in terms of *how* a person uses the Internet. Even within industrialized countries such as the United States, women tend to use mostly e-mail services, with the intent of keeping up with family and friends (Shade 2004). For men, the Internet is used to gather information and to exchange ideas and facts relevant to professional activities. Thus, "women are using the Internet to reinforce their private lives and men are using the Internet for engaging in the public sphere" (Shade 2004:63). The difference has to do with choices men and women make but also reflects differences in the professional positions men and women hold.

For men, the Internet is enhancing their careers. This is far less true for women. However, things do change very rapidly in the world of the Internet.

Thinking Sociologically

Ask several people from different generations how they use computer technology and the Internet and how they learned these skills. What do you conclude?

Gender Stratification: Micro- to Macro-Level Theories

In recent years, some biologists and psychologists have considered whether there are innate differences in the make-up of women and men. For instance, males produce more testosterone, a hormone found to be correlated with aggression. Research shows that in many situations, males tend to be more aggressive and concerned with dominance, whether the behavior is biologically programmed or learned or both. Other traits, such as nurturance, empathy, or altruism, show no clear gender difference (Fausto-Sterling 1992; Pinker 2002).

Although biological and psychological factors are part of the difference between females and males, our focus here is on the major contribution that social factors make in social statuses of males and females in human society. This section explores social theories that explain gender differences.

Symbolic Interaction Theory: Micro-Level Analysis

Symbolic interactionists look at gender as socially constructed. Sex is the biological reality of different "plumbing" in our bodies, and interactionists are interested in how those physical differences come to be symbols, resulting in different social rights and rewards. This chapter's discussions of micro-level social processes have pointed out that the meaning connected to one's sex produces notions of masculinity and femininity. The symbolic interaction perspective has been forceful in insisting that notions of proper gender behavior are not intrinsically related to a person's sex. The bottom line is that gender is a socially created or constructed idea, not one that emanates from biological traits (Mason-Schrock 1996).

In some countries, there is a huge gender digital divide. In others, nearly as many women as men use computers. However, research shows that women tend to use computers in different ways. These women in Iraq are learning computer skills.

Traditional notions of gender are hard to change. Admitting confusion over proper masculine and feminine roles creates anxiety and even anomie in a society. People want guidelines. Thus, it is easier to adhere to traditional notions of gender that are reinforced by religious dogmas, making those ideas appear sacred, absolute, and beyond human change. Absolute answers are comforting to those who find change disconcerting. Others believe the male prerogatives and privileges of the past were established by men to protect their rights. Any change in concepts of gender or of roles assigned to males and females will be hard to bring about precisely because they are rooted in the meaning system and status and power structures in the social world.

Symbolic interaction—more than any other theory—stresses the idea of human agency, the notion that humans not only are influenced by the society in which they live but actively help to create it (Charon 2007; Hewitt 2007). In a study of elementary children in classrooms and especially on playgrounds, Barrie Thorne (1993) found that while teachers influenced the children, the children themselves were active participants in creating the student culture that guided their play. As children played with one another, Thorne noticed the ways in which they created words, nicknames, distinctions between one another, and new forms of interaction. This is a very important point: Humans do not just passively adopt cultural notions about gender, they *do gender*. They create it as they behave and interact with others in ways that define "normal" male or female conduct (West and Zimmerman

Some cultures suggest that women are helpless and need the door held for them, and women's stylish attire—such as many forms of shoes and many dresses—actually does make them more vulnerable and helpless in certain situations.

1987). "Doing gender" is an everyday, recurring, and routine occurrence. It is a constant ongoing process that defines each situation, takes place in organizations and between individuals, and becomes part of institutional arrangements. Social movements such as civil rights and the women's movement challenge these arrangements and can bring about change. Understanding the process of doing gender helps us understand why we think and act as we do.

When children are in an ambiguous situation, they may spontaneously define their sex as the most relevant trait about themselves or others. Indeed, even when children act as if gender matters, they are helping to make it a reality for those around them. This process helps to make the notion of gender more concrete and real to the other children. As the next child adopts the "definition of reality" from the first, acting as if sex is more important than hair color or eye color or ear lobe attachment to the cheek, this makes gender the most prominent characteristic in the mind of the next child. Yet each child, in a sense, could choose to ignore gender and decide that something else, like nationality, is more important. The same principle applies to adults.

When a person "chooses" to recognize gender as a critical distinction between two individuals or two groups, that person is "doing gender" (Hewitt 2007; O'Brien 2006).

Through interaction, people do gender, and although this process begins at a micro level, it has implications all the way to the global level. The Iowa School of symbolic interactionism places more stress on meso-level reinforcement of social constructions of gender (Carrothers and Benson 2003; Stryker 1980), emphasizing individuals conforming to or rebelling against the messages that pervade our institutions. The next section explores meso- and macro-level forces that shape gender and stratification based on sex.

Thinking Sociologically

How do you *do gender*? How did you learn these patterns of behavior? Are they automatic responses, or do you think about "who opens the door"?

Structural-Functional and Conflict Theories: Meso- and Macro-Level Analyses

Structural-Functional Theory

From the structural-functional perspective, each sex has a role to play in the interdependent groups and institutions of society. Some early theorists argued that men and women carry out different roles and are, of necessity, unequal because of needs of societies and practices that have developed since early human history. Social relationships and practices that have proven successful in the survival of a group are likely to continue and be reinforced by society's norms and laws. Thus, relationships between women and men that are believed to support survival are maintained. In traditional hunter-gatherer, horticultural, and pastoral societies, for instance, the division of labor is based on sex and age. Social roles are clearly laid out, indicating who performs which everyday survival tasks. The females often take on the primary tasks of child care, gardening, food preparation, and other duties near the home. Men do tasks that require movements farther from home, such as hunting or fishing.

As societies industrialize, roles and relationships change due to structural changes in society. Durkheim ([1893] 1947) described a gradual move from traditional societies held together by mechanical solidarity (common values and emotional ties between members) to modern societies that hold together due to organic solidarity. The glue that holds modern society together is based less on common values and more on division of labor and the interdependence of statuses within the social world. According to early functionalists, gender division of labor exists in modern societies because it is efficient and useful to have different-but-complementary male and female roles. They believed this accomplishes essential tasks and maintains societal stability (Lindsey 2005).

More recent structural-functional theorists describe society as an integrated system of roles that work together to carry out the necessary tasks in society. They argue that two complementary types of roles are needed in the modern industrial and postindustrial family. The female plays the expressive role through childbearing, nursing, and caring for family members in the home. The male carries out the instrumental role by working outside the home to support the family (Anderson 1994; Parsons and Bales 1953).

Although this pattern was relevant during the industrial revolution and again after World War II, when men returned to take jobs women had held during the war, it currently characterizes only a small percentage of families in Western industrial and postindustrial societies and less than 10% of families in the United States (Aulette 2002). In reality, gender segregation has seldom been total because in most cultures, women's work has combined their labor in the public sphere—that is, outside the home—with their work in the private sphere—inside the home (Lopez-Garza 2002). Poor minority women in countries around the world must often work in low-paying service roles in the public sphere and carry the major burden for roles in the private sphere. Gender analysis through a structural-functional perspective stresses efficiencies that are believed to be gained by specialization of tasks (Waite and Gallagher 2000).

Conflict Theory

Conflict theorists view males as the haves—controlling the majority of power positions and most wealth—and females as the have-nots. Women have less access to power and have historically depended on males for survival. This is the case even though they raise the next generation of workers and consumers, provide unpaid domestic labor, and assure a pool of available, cheap labor during times of crisis, such as war. By keeping women in subordinate roles, males control the means of production and protect their privileged status.

A classical conflict explanation of gender stratification is found in the writings of Karl Marx's colleague, Friedrich Engels (1884/1942). In traditional societies, where size and strength were essential for survival, men were often dominant, but women's roles were respected as important and necessary to the survival of the group. Men hunted, engaged in warfare, and protected women. Over time, male physical

By contrast to the clothing and gestures that create vulnerability in women, men are encouraged to use gestures that communicate strength and self-assurance, and their clothing and shoes allow them to defend themselves or flee danger.

control was transformed into control by ideology, by the dominant belief system itself. Capitalism strengthened male dominance by making more wealth available to men and their sons. Women became dependent on men, and their roles were transformed into "taking care of the home" (Engels [1884] 1942).

Ideologies based on traditional beliefs and values have continued to be used to justify the social structure of male domination and subjugation of women. It is in the interest of the dominant group, in this case men, to maintain their position of privilege: political and economic power and greater access to resources. Conflict theorists believe it unlikely that those in power by virtue of sex, race, class, or political or religious ideology will voluntarily give up their positions as long as they are benefiting from them. By keeping women in traditional gender roles, men maintain control over institutions and resources (Collins 1971).

Men who play games or sports such as golf together or who join men's-only clubs develop networks that enhance their power and their ability to "close deals." When women are not part of the same networks, they are denied the same insider privileges. Many conflict theorists would argue this is purposeful, whereas others point to it as a reality even if it is not intentional.

Feminist Theory

Feminist theorists agree with Marx and Engels that gender stratification is based on power struggles, not biology. Yet, some feminist theorists argue that Marx and Engels failed to include a key variable in women's oppression: patriarchy. Patriarchy involves a few men dominating and holding authority over all others, including women, children, and less powerful men (Arrighi 2000; Lindsey 2005). According to feminist theory, women will continue to be oppressed by men until patriarchy is eliminated.

A distinguishing characteristic of most feminist theory is that it actively advocates change in the social order, whereas many other theories we have discussed try only to explain the social world (Anderson 2006; Lorber 1998). There is a range of feminist theories. However, all feminist theories argue for bringing about a new and equal ordering of gender relationships to eliminate the patriarchy and sexism of current gender-stratification systems (Kramer 2005).

Feminist theorists try to understand the causes of women's lower status and seek ways to change systems to provide opportunities for women in education and work, to improve the standard of living, and to give women control over their bodies and reproduction. Feminist theorists also feel that little change will occur until group consciousness is raised so that women understand the system that limits their status and do not blame themselves for their situations (Sapiro 2003).

As societies become technologically advanced and need an educated workforce, women of all social classes and ethnic groups around the world are likely to gain more equal roles. Women are entering institutions of higher education in record numbers, and evidence indicates they are needed in the world economic system and the changing labor force of most countries. Societies in which women are not integrated into the economic sphere generally lag behind other countries. Feminist theorists look at these global and national patterns, but they also note the role of patriarchy in interpersonal situations—such as domestic violence, another key topic in feminist theory. For example, women in the United States who are struggling to make ends meet for their families often face limited-time welfare benefits yet may not be able to gain stable employment. Thus, they may feel no option but to return to abusive relationships out of desperation. They often have few economic or social resources to do otherwise (Scott, London, and Myers 2002).

Violence against women perpetuates gender stratification, as is evident in the intimate environment of many homes. Because men have more power in the larger society, they often have more resources within the household as well (side-effect discrimination). Women are often dependent on the man of the house for his resources, meaning they are willing to yield on many decisions. Power differences in the meso- and macro-level social systems also contribute to power differentials and vulnerability of women in micro-level settings. In addition, poor women have fewer options when considering whether to leave an abusive relationship. Although there are risks of staying in an abusive relationship, many factors enter into a woman's decision to stay or leave. The following "Sociology in Your Social World" discusses one form of violence around the world that is perpetuated predominantly against women: rape.

Thinking Sociologically

Why do women and men stay in abusive relationships? If these behaviors are hurtful or destructive, what might be done to change the situation or what policies might be enacted to address the problems?

In summary, feminist analysis finds gender patterns imbedded in social institutions of family, education, religion, politics, economics, and health care. If the societal system is patriarchal, ruled by men, the interdependent institutions are likely to reflect and support this system. Feminist theory helps us to understand how patriarchy at the meso and macro level can influence patriarchy at the micro level and vice versa.

Sociology in Your Social World

Rape and the Victims of Rape

For many women around the world, rape is the most feared act of violence and the ultimate humiliation. Rape is a sexual act but closely tied to macho behavior. Rape is often a power play to intimidate, hurt, and dominate women (Sanday and Goodenough 1990) or the act of a hypersexual man who feels entitled to sex (Felson 2002). Rape has been used by "owners" as a method to subdue women slaves (Brown 2001), by Serbian army troops to humiliate Bosnian Muslim men who are expected to protect their women, and by prison inmates against other inmates to establish power hierarchies. Some societies are largely free from rape whereas others are prone toward rape. What is the difference?

Rape provides an example of the impact of cultural practices, beliefs, and stereotypes. When a society is relatively tolerant of interpersonal violence, holds beliefs in male dominance, and strongly incorporates ways to separate women and men, rape is more common (Sanday 1981; Sanday and Goodenough 1990; Shaw and Lee 2005). Rape is also more common when gender roles and identities are changing and norms about interaction between women and men are unclear. What does this say, then, about the United States, where women have a one in five chance of being raped during their lifetime (Burn 2005), where someone is sexually assaulted or raped every two minutes, averaging more than 2,000 rapes daily and 272,350 rapes or sexual assaults annually? Most rape victims are under 30 years of age (Shaw and Lee 2005; U.S. Department of Justice 2004). These figures are probably much lower than reality because estimates are that only 1 in 10 rapes in the United States are reported (U.S. Department of Justice 2006).

An alarming problem is rape on college campuses in the United States. Researchers report that "nearly one of every four women on college campuses has experienced sexual violence" (Shaw and Lee 2005:424). Women report being sexually assaulted whereas few males define their behavior as assault. This discrepancy points to the stereotypes and misunderstandings that can occur because of different beliefs and attitudes. Rape causes deep and lasting problems for women victims as well as for men accused of rape because of "misreading" women's signals. Groups of college men report thinking of gang rape as a form of male bonding. To them, it was no big deal. The woman was just the object and instrument. Her identity was immaterial (Martin and Hummer 1989; Sanday and Goodenough 1990). Sometimes, alcohol and roofies (date-rape drugs) are involved.

Men who hold more traditional gender roles view rape very differently than women and less traditional men. They tend to attribute more responsibility to the female victim of the rape, believe sex rather than power was the motivation for rape, and look less favorably on women who have been raped. In a strange twist of logic, one study showed that some men actually believe that women want to be forced into having involuntary sex (Szymanski et al. 1993). Researchers show that societies with widespread gender stratification report more gendered violence (Sanday 1996, 2007). However, in advanced capitalist states, Felson (2002) argues, violence is a serious social problem for both genders, and male-male violence is much more common than mixed gendered altercations. Felson also believes that the link between rape and misogyny may be overstated. Women, however, are at greater risk for sexual or serious injury in male-female violence.

Many citizens and politicians see rape as an individualized, personal act, whereas social scientists tend to see it as a structural problem that stems from negative stereotypes of women, subservient positions of women in society, and patriarchal systems of power. Until there is better understanding on the part of both men and women about gender and rape, the culture of rape is likely to continue (McEvoy and Brookings 2001). A number of sociologists and anthropologists believe that rape will not be substantially reduced unless our macho definitions of masculinity are changed (Sanday and Goodenough 1990).

When women have less power at the meso level, they may also be more vulnerable at home. This girl attends to her injured mother at a hospital in Hyderabad, Pakistan, after the woman's husband chopped off her nose with an axe and broke all her teeth. According to the Pakistan Institute of Medical Sciences, more than 90% of married women report being severely abused when husbands are dissatisfied with their cooking or cleaning or when the women give birth to a girl instead of a boy or are unable to bear a child at all.

The Interaction of Class, Race, and Gender

Zouina is Algerian, but she was born in France to her immigrant parents. She lived with them in a poor immigrant suburb of Paris in the Saint-Denis region until she was forced to return to Algeria for an arranged marriage to a man who already had one wife. That marriage ended, and she returned to her "home" in France. Since she returned to France, Zouina has been working wherever she can find work. The high unemployment and social and ethnic discrimination, especially against foreign women, makes life difficult, as shown in a film, *The Perfumed Garden* (Benguigui, 2000). In 2003, there were an estimated 70,000 forced and polygamous marriages in immigrant communities of France, considered illegal under French law.

The situation is complex. Muslim women from Tunisia, Morocco, and Algeria living in crowded slum communities outside Paris face discrimination in the workplace, within their own communities, and in French society more generally (da Silva 2004). Expected to be both good Muslim women and good family co-providers—which necessitates working in French society—they face ridicule when they wear their *hijabs* (coverings) to school or to work. However, they encounter derision in their community if they do not wear them. They are caught between two cultures, not able to express their own identity or make their own choices in either.

Because of high unemployment in the immigrant communities, many youth roam the streets. Gang rapes by North

African youth against young women have been on the rise in France and elsewhere abroad. These rapes mean that North African women are faced with rejection and disdain in both the immigrant community and at their original African communities. With the conflicting messages due to their ethnic differences (race), their poor status (class), and their sex, these women attempt to construct and manage their identities under grueling circumstances (Killian 2006).

Feminist theory seeks explanations for the conditions women face (Walby 1990). One current trend in feminist interpretation, illustrated in the example above, is to view the social world as an intersection of class, race, and gender (Glenn 1999; Smith 1999). In this way, one can look at the variety of ways that many common citizens are controlled by those who have a monopoly on power and privilege. The reality is that some women are quite privileged and wealthy. Not all women live in poverty. However, even privileged women often have less power than their husbands or other men in their lives. It is also true that some women in the world are privileged because of their race or ethnicity (Rothenberg 2007). In many respects, they have more in common with men of their own ethnicity or race than they do with women of less esteemed groups, and they may choose to identify with those statuses that enhance their privilege.

Race, class, and gender have cross-cutting lines that may modify one's subjugation in the society or may intensify it. Sexual orientation, age, nationality, and other factors may have the effect of either diminishing or increasing minority status of specific women, and theorists are paying increasing attention to these intersections (Rothenberg 2007). Chapter 8 discussed the fact that racial and class lines may be cross-cutting or parallel. In the case of gender, there are always cross-cutting lines with race and social class. However, gender will still affect one's prestige and privilege within that class or ethnic group. Thus, these three variables should be considered simultaneously (Hossfeld 2006; Kirk and Okazawa-Rey 2007).

Gender and Minority Group Status

Women as a Minority

Couples in the United States, India, China, and many other countries would like their first child to be a boy, and most couples want more boys than girls. In some societies, families are more likely to continue to have children until they have boys. People in countries around the world have found ways to cull girl babies if the family already has girls, if there is not enough food to feed the family, or the family has no sons, or if the father is absent (Ward and Edelstein 2006).

For instance, in India and China, daughters have traditionally been considered a liability because they are additional mouths to feed as children, they require the girl's family to pay a dowry in order to marry, and girls move away before they can contribute to the family when parents get feeble. Hence, many female fetuses are aborted each year, and a few girl babies are killed at birth even today. In addition, adequate nourishment or medical attention may be withheld when girls are ill in some countries, resulting in a higher death rate for daughters (Bumiller 1990; Burn 2005; Ward and Edelstein 2006).

Women make up more than 50% of the world's population, yet their experience often parallels that of other smaller minority groups. Recall that a minority group has less power and influence in the society, not necessarily fewer people. Consider the characteristics of minority groups and the similarities between the position of racial/ethnic minorities and women:

1. *Physical, cultural, or social characteristics* distinguish minority group members from the dominant group. Women are distinguished by physical (sex) characteristics, just as people of color are distinguished by physical characteristics.

2. Women's share of *desired goods, positions* (power), and *rights in society is limited* because dominant groups control these. Around the world, United Nations statistics tell the story of women and other minorities: poor education, higher mortality, and less access to health care and other valued resources. Income for men and women varies significantly depending on ethnicity within the United States, but even when ethnicity is considered, women get paid less than men (see Table 9.4 on page 298). Women and African Americans did not get voting rights until the 20th century in most countries and only after persistent struggles. Both blacks and women are underrepresented in politics, with African American women facing double jeopardy. Both groups are also disproportionately found in low-paying jobs that have little opportunity for advancement.

3. *Ideological or other justifications* are used by the dominant group to deny equal treatment. Both blacks and women have been stereotyped in books and the media—blacks as "lazy" or "inferior," women as "emotional and unstable due to imbalances in hormones." Religious, political, and pseudoscientific ideologies have been used to keep women and blacks in inferior positions, with women of color experiencing additional burdens.

4. *Collective identity* among minority group members develops to help insulate them from the discriminatory acts of the dominant group. Both women and blacks have organizations and social movements with goals

Because daughters are a financial liability in India and China, there is a long-standing preference for sons. This results in extended families in which there are far more boys than girls.

to better their position in society. Both have engaged in consciousness-raising efforts, ranging from coffee klatches and women's auxiliaries to protest movements. However, many women experience more isolation from each other than do blacks because of the nuclear family's residential patterns—isolated in apartments or suburban housing that serve to separate women in their individual homes. This reduces the possibility for consciousness raising and cohesiveness among women from different social classes or groups, a pattern that is parallel to the differences that separate people of color into lower-, middle-, and upper-class.

5. *Minority group status* is generally determined by rules of descent, with members born into a status they cannot change. Race and sex are ascribed statuses of minority groups into which individuals are born and which are with them for life. In developing countries, differences in the status of men and women are more extreme. Women rank lower than men on indicators of well-being, from education and health to employment status (United Nations 2002).

Putting these characteristics together suggests that women are indeed a "minority group," subject to stereotypes, prejudice, and discrimination. Women of color can face the triple status determinants of being poor (class) women (gender) of color (race/ethnicity).

| Table 9.4 | **Median Earnings in Past 12 Months of Workers by Race, Sex (in dollars), and Percent of Men's Earnings by Women** | | | |

Race and Ethnicity	Male	Female	Women's % of Men's Earnings
Asian American	48,693	37,792	77.6
White	46,807	34,190	74.1
African American	34,433	29,588	85.9
Hispanic (any race)	27,380	24,451	89.3

Source: U.S. Census Bureau 2007b.

Gender, Homosexuality, and Minority Status

Sex and sexuality are not binary (male-female) concepts but embrace a broader range of combinations of masculine, feminine, heterosexual, homosexual, and other variations. This range is normal in human sexuality. It is societal expectations developed over time that impose categories on human sexuality.

One group of people who face particular discrimination in some countries is homosexuals. Homosexuality has always existed and has been accepted and even required at some times and places, and rejected or outlawed in others. In some cases, homosexuals have been placed in a separate sexual category with special roles. Some societies ignore its existence; a few consider it a psychological illness or form of depraved immorality; and a very few even consider this form of sexuality a crime (as in some Muslim societies today and in most states in the United States during much of the 20th century). In each case, the government or dominant religious group determines the status of homosexuals. The reality is that deviation from a society's gender norms, such as attraction to a member of the same sex, may cause one to experience minority status.

Lesbians are women attracted to other women. Because these women do not follow traditional gendered expectations of femininity in many societies, they often experience prejudice and discrimination. Women's status is typically based on their relationship with men, and in most societies, they are economically dependent on men. Therefore, lesbians—who support themselves and each other—may go against norms of societies and are in some instances perceived as dangerous, unnatural, or a threat to men's power (Burn 2005; Ward and Edelstein 2006).

Sexism affects the lives of gay men as well. Homophobia (intense fear and hatred of homosexuality and homosexuals) is highly correlated with and perhaps a cause of traditional notions of gender and gender roles (Lehne 1995; Pharr 1997; Shaw and Lee 2005). Some homosexuals deviate from traditional notions of masculinity and femininity and therefore from significant norms of many societies. This may result in hostile reactions and stigma from the dominant group. Indeed, homosexual epitaphs are often used to reinforce gender conformity and to intimidate anyone who would dare to be different from the norm (Lehne 1995). Still, the whole issue of homophobia focuses on prejudice held and transmitted by individuals.

Heterosexism is the notion that the society reinforces heterosexuality and marginalizes anyone who does not conform to this norm. Heterosexism focuses on social processes that define homosexuality as deviant and legitimize heterosexuality as the only normal lifestyle (Oswald 2000, 2001). In short, heterosexism operates often at the meso and macro levels of society, through privileges such as rights to health care and jobs granted to people who are heterosexual and denied to those who are not.

Homosexuality has been an issue in recent political elections in the United States. As of 2007, almost all states had "Defense of Marriage Acts" or constitutional amendments prohibiting same-sex marriage. Only in Massachusetts and California are marriage licenses available to same-sex couples (Stritof and Stritof 2008). This has spawned debates about family life and whether homosexuals should be allowed to marry, to adopt or have children, or to have the same rights as heterosexuals. In short, many institutions in the social world have been influenced by this debate over sexuality and gender. The notion of allowing gays and lesbians the right to a legal marriage has been extremely controversial in the United States, and more than 30 states have passed legislation defining marriage as between a man and a woman, some even approving amendments to their constitutions to ensure that same-sex marriages will not happen in those states (Newman and Grauerholz 2002).

The point here is not to argue for or against same-sex marriage but to note that homosexuals do not have many of the rights that heterosexuals have. The discrepancy is based on sexuality characteristics. Heterosexuals in the United States have a variety of rights—ranging from insurance coverage and inheritance rights for lifelong partners, to jointly acquired property, hospital visitation rights as family, rights to claim the body of a deceased partner, and rights to have the deceased prepared for burial or cremation. The U.S. federal government confers 1,138 rights to heterosexuals that they normally take for granted, but often, these rights do not extend to same-sex partners in a life-long relationship. Most states also bestow more than 200 specific rights to persons who "marry," but because most states do not allow same-sex marriages, homosexuals do not have these same rights (U.S. General Accounting Office 2003). In Canada and many European countries, citizens do have a right to same-sex marriage, and this has reduced the number of discrepancies in the rights of homosexuals and heterosexuals.

Thinking Sociologically

The concept of *homophobia* focuses on micro-level processes, whereas the notion of *heterosexism* is attentive to meso and macro forces. Which of these concepts reveals the most about issues faced by the lesbian and gay community? Why?

Costs and Consequences of Gender Stratification

In rapidly changing modern societies, role confusion abounds. Men hesitate to offer help to women, wondering if gallantry will be appreciated or scorned. Women are torn between traditional family roles, on the one hand, and working to support the family and fulfill career goals on the other. As illustrated in the examples below, sex-based stratification limits individual development and causes problems in education, health, work, and other parts of the social world.

Psychological and Social Consequences: Micro-Level Implications

For both women and men, rigid gender stereotypes can be very constraining. Individuals who hold highly sex-typed attitudes feel compelled to behave in stereotypic ways, ways that are consistent with the pictures they have in their heads of proper gender behavior (Basow 1992, 2000). However, individuals who do not identify strongly with masculine or feminine gender types are more flexible in thoughts and behavior, tend to score higher on intelligence tests, have greater spatial ability, and have higher levels of creativity. Because they allow themselves a wider range of behaviors, they have more varied abilities and experiences and become more tolerant of others' behaviors. High masculinity in males sets up rigid standards for male behavior and has been correlated with anxiety, guilt, and neuroses, whereas less rigid

masculine expectations are associated with emotional stability, sensitivity, warmth, and enthusiasm (Bellisari 1990). Rigid stereotypes and resulting sexism affect everyone and curtail our activities, behaviors, and perspectives.

Superwoman Image

The "superwoman syndrome," a pattern by which women assume multiple roles and try to do all well, takes its toll (Faludi 1993). The resulting strain contributes to depression and certain health problems such as headaches, nervousness, and insomnia (Wood 2003). Women in many societies are expected to be beautiful, youthful, and sexually interesting and interested, while at the same time they prepare the food, care for the children, keep a clean and orderly home, and sometimes bring in money to help support the family. Some are also expected to be competent and successful in their careers. Multiple, sometimes contradictory expectations for women cause stress and even serious psychological problems.

Women who work outside the home are often expected to keep up with the domestic tasks as well. Evidence indicates that when women enter the labor force, there are not parallel changes or redistribution of responsibilities in family life. On the contrary, working generally leads to an increase in what is expected of women.

Beauty Image

Beautiful images jump out at us from billboards, magazine covers, and TV and movie screens. Some of these images are unattainable by most women because they have been created through surgeries and eating disorders—and even the use of airbrushing on photographs. Disorders including anorexia and bulimia nervosa relate to societal expectations of the ideal woman's appearance. About 1 out of every 100 U.S. women (7 million women, compared to 1 million men) suffers from these severe eating disorders, and the numbers have been growing since the 1970s. This dangerous ailment occurs most frequently in females between 12 and 18 years of age, caused by distortions in body image that are brought on by what the women, especially white middle- and upper-middle-class women, see as societal images of beauty, often images created in magazines that are unattainable in real life (ANRED 2007; Kilbourne 1999; Taub and McLorg 2007).

Thinking Sociologically

If females are expending great energy and attention on how they look—to ensure that they are physically appealing to others—how might this influence their ability to get access to positions of power and prestige?

The beauty-image obsession in North America is far more of an issue with white Anglos than with African Americans or Latinas, but especially with young white women, it results in disorders relative to eating—including the bulimia this young woman is experiencing.

coverage affects not only the women but also their children, and social divisiveness leads to alienation, if not hostility. Discrimination and violence against women, whether physical or emotional, has consequences for all institutions in a society (Pan American Health Organization 2003).

Consider how the ratio of women to men in an occupational field affects the prestige of the occupation. As more men enter predominantly female fields such as nursing and library science, the fields gain higher occupational prestige, and salaries tend to increase. It seems that men take their gender privilege with them when they enter female professions (Kramer 2005). However, the evidence indicates that as women enter male professions such as law, the status tends to become lower, making women's chances of improving their position in the stratification system limited.

Gender stratification has often meant loss of the talents and brain power of women, and that is a serious loss to modern postindustrial societies because human capital—the resources of the human population—is central to social prosperity in this type of system. Yet, resistance to expanding women's professional roles is often strong. For example, 40% of Japanese women work, but only 9% hold managerial positions. Although their education levels are generally high, Japanese women earn wages that are about 65% of their male counterparts' wages. Breaking through the glass ceiling continues to be a barrier for individual women but also a challenge for entire societies that could benefit from abilities never fully maximized (French 2003).

Changing Gender Stratification and Social Policy

Women in factories around the globe face dangerous conditions and low pay. Sweatshops exist because poor women have few other job options to support their families and because people in rich countries want to buy the cheap products that perpetuate the multinational corporate system. Just a few years ago, workers in *maquiladoras* (foreign-owned assembly plants) in Mexican border towns worked for 2,000 multinational companies that paid a minimum of $3.40 per *day* compared to $5.15 per *hour* in the United States (CorpWatch 1999). The entry-level wage for low-level jobs along the border with Mexico was about 25% of the hourly wage paid to U.S. workers, and Mexico has a 48-hour work week, reducing extra expenses for overtime work (Burn 2000; Made in Mexico, Inc. 2005). Two thirds of the workers were poor women. Consider the figures in Table 9.5 on wages in the textile industry from world countries.

In El Salvador, women employees of the Taiwanese maquiladora, Manderin, are forced to work shifts of 12 to 21 hours during which they are seldom allowed bathroom breaks. They are paid about 18 cents per shirt, which is later sold for $20. Manderin makes clothes for The Gap, J. Crew, and Eddie Bauer.

Men also suffer psychological costs of stereotyping. Some men also have eating disorders, and fitness magazines picture the "perfect" male body and advertise exercise equipment and steroids. In addition, men die earlier than women, in part due to environmental, psychological, and social factors. Problems in developed countries such as heart disease, stroke, cirrhosis, cancers, accidents, and suicides are linked in part to the male role that dictates that males should appear tough, objective, ambitious, unsentimental, and unemotional—traits that require men to assume great responsibility and suppress their feelings.

Societal Costs and Consequences: Meso- and Macro-Level Implications

Gender stratification creates costs for societies around the world in a number of ways. Poor educational achievement of female children leads to the loss of human talents and resources of half of the population. Lack of health care

| | Average Hourly Wages and Benefits | Ratio to U.S. |
Region/Country	U.S. $ (2004)	Cost (%)
North America (NAFTA)		
Canada	18.61	118
Mexico	2.19	14
United States	15.78	100
South America		
Argentina	2.86	18
Brazil	2.83	18
Colombia	1.97	13
Venezuela	2.85	18
Western Europe		
France	21.03	133
Germany	27.69	175
Greece	11.67	74
Portugal	6.87	89
Switzerland	35.33	224
United Kingdom	20.17	128
Central and Eastern Europe		
Bulgaria	1.50	10
Czech Republic	3.94	25
Poland	3.80	24
Turkey	2.88	18
Northeast Asia		
China (coastal)	0.76	5
China (inland)	0.48	3
Hong Kong	6.21	39
South Korea	7.10	45
Taiwan	7.58	48
Southeast Asia		
Indonesia	0.55	4
Malaysia	1.18	7
Thailand	1.29	8
Vietnam	0.28	2
South Asia		
Bangladesh	0.28	2
India	0.67	4
Pakistan	0.37	2
Sri Lanka	0.46	3
Middle East and Africa		
Egypt	0.82	5
Israel	9.35	59
Kenya	0.67	4
Mauritius	1.57	10
Morocco	2.56	16
South Africa	3.80	24

Table 9.5 Labor Cost Comparisons in the Textile Industry, 2004–2005

Source: Werner International Management Consultants 2005.

Women in Thailand produce shoes at extremely low rates. These jobs are better than no employment at all, but before pressures from Western societies changed their cultures, most people were able to feed their families quite adequately on farms in small villages. Changes in the entire world system have made that form of life no longer feasible, but working for multinational corporations also keeps them impoverished.

In Haiti, women sewing clothing at Disney's contract plants are paid 6 cents for every $19.99 101 Dalmatians outfit they sew. They make 33 cents an hour.

Meanwhile, Disney makes record profits and could easily pay workers a living wage for less than one half of 1% of the sales price of one outfit. In Vietnam, 90% of Nike's workers are females between the ages of 15 and 28. Nike's labor costs for a pair of basketball shoes (which retail for $149.50) are $1.50, 1% of the retail price (Burn 2000:120).

These women often earn less than half of what is needed to survive in their areas. Yet, corporations can pay low wages and, in many cases, continue poor and even dangerous working environments because these areas have high unemployment, and families have no other options.

What can be done about the abusive treatment of women around the world? This is a tough issue: Governments have passed legislation to protect workers, but governments also want the jobs that multinational corporations bring and therefore do little to enforce regulations. International labor standards are also difficult to enforce. Multinationals are so large that it is difficult to influence their practices. Trade unions have had little success attracting workers to join because companies squash their recruiting efforts immediately.

One way to begin considering fair wages and conditions for workers is to adopt practices that have worked for other groups facing discrimination in the past. Consider

The movement among gays, lesbians, bisexuals, and transsexuals for equal rights and recognition is not just a North American or European phenomenon. These Nepalese transsexuals are among hundreds from across the country who gathered in Kathmandu, the capital, to demand official recognition and political representation in Nepal. This is a global movement.

the following possibilities for bringing about change: holding nonviolent protests, sit-down strikes, and walkouts to protest unequal and unfair treatment; working together in support groups to help their children and neighborhoods; using the Internet to carry the message to others; carrying out boycotts against companies that mistreat employees; following traditions that have succeeded in the past such as using the arts, preachers, storytellers, and teachers to express frustration and resistance, educate others, and provide ideas and strategies for resistance; and building on traditions of community and religious activism (Collins 2000). Most of these strategies require organized groups.

Thinking Sociologically

Consider the strategies for change listed in the previous paragraph. Which of these do you think has a realistic chance of bringing constructive change? Which approaches would surely fail? Why do you think so?

At women's conferences around the world, policymakers debate the means to create solutions to women's problems. Most United Nations member countries have at least fledgling women's movements fighting for improved status of women and their families. The movements attempt to change laws that result in discrimination, poverty, abuse, and low levels of education and occupational status. Although the goals of eliminating differential treatment of women, especially minority women, are jointly affirmed by most women's groups, the means to improve conditions for women are debated between women's groups. For instance, some advocate working within existing institutions to bring about equal rights. Others push for complete overhauling of existing systems to bring about a new order that would ignore sex as a variable in assigning power. Whether any of these efforts will change women's individual lives and the lives of their children is unknown.

We grow up being socialized into patterns of behavior, even if those patterns include discrimination. In Western countries with relatively high wages, many young women are afraid of change and of the protests implied in being an active feminist. Familiar patterns are comfortable, even if they limit opportunities. Being an activist is risky, especially if one is living a comfortable life. Restrictions caused by gender stratification become clearer as young women enter the public sphere (Hogeland 2004).

We would be too optimistic to predict that grassroots efforts or boycotts against those who are enjoying the fruits of poor women's labor will change the system. The best hope may lie in increased opportunities for women as countries modernize and in efforts of countries like Cambodia (Kampuchia), which strive to enforce labor laws and improve conditions and wages for workers. These efforts will work only if other countries join in, if Cambodia remains a competitive labor market, and if buyers support products made in countries with fair labor practices (Better Factories Movement 2006).

Policy is informed by social science research. Some applied feminist sociologists have worked in shelters for battered women, rape response centers, and other agencies that deal with concerns of women. "The Applied Sociologist at Work" looks at the work of a sociologist who is interested in another area—understanding the progress of and barriers to women pursuing careers in science, technology, engineering, and mathematics.

The Applied Sociologist at Work— Lynette Osborne

Gender Inequality and STEM

By Lynette Osborne

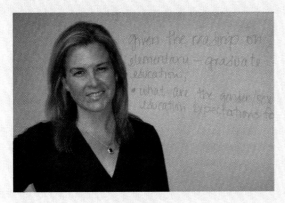

I am Dr. Lynette Osborne, a research associate at the Institute for Women's Policy Research and an adjunct assistant professor in the University Honors Program at The George Washington University. As a researcher, I am interested in gender equity in science, technology, engineering, and mathematics education (STEM) as a vehicle through which women can achieve economic security. As a professor, I teach the following honors courses: Sociology of Gender and Sexuality, Introductory Sociology, and Social Inequalities.

After completing my dissertation on the perceptions of women in engineering education, I served as an ExxonMobil Scholar-in-Residence at the National Academy of Education's Center for the Advancement of Scholarship on Engineering Education (NAE/CASEE). In this one-year appointment, I was able to contribute to several research projects that were directly related to gender and STEM, including adding to a manual for writing National Science Foundation grants to fund projects on engineering education.

My research interests are broadly concerned with the decline in women's participation in STEM education despite increased efforts to recruit and retain women in college STEM majors. More specifically, I am interested in the recruitment and retention of low-income and minority women into STEM careers through community college terminal degrees and certificate programs.

Building on my training in sociology, my first major research project utilized several types of research methods. I used questionnaires, interviews, and participant observation in my research to provide a more informed answer to the research questions. For instance, when concerned with the perceptions of women in engineering education, I triangulated the findings of a Web survey and interviews with students. In addition, to answer research questions on the types of learning-related interactions that occur in engineering classrooms, I used interviews with students and professors, a Web survey, and participant observation of engineering classes to provide a more complete picture.

In addition to participating in original empirical research, my co-researchers and I are currently working on developing a project to diffuse existing "best practices" techniques for recruiting low-income and minority women to mid-skilled STEM careers via community college training. This project allows us to synthesize a great deal of existing information from model programs and produce a dissemination method that will benefit a large number of constituents—including community college staff and policy advocates directly and the women who attend two-year programs indirectly—to contribute to women's economic independence and security.

Each project must also incorporate a theoretical framework. Because my research is concerned with gender equity, most often the guiding theoretical perspective I employ is feminist. Theories help to guide research and are integral for interpretation of results. For example, in my research on women in engineering education, the project was informed by and analyzed using feminist standpoint theory (Nancy Hartsock, Dorothy Smith, Patricia Hill Collins). The project geared toward diffusing existing information to encourage low-income and minority women to enter STEM careers is informed by Patricia Hill Collins's matrix of domination concept. Whether I am writing academic papers reporting results from empirical research or am synthesizing others' research for a diffusion project, my writing must reflect a sophisticated understanding of the issues, yet also be written in a manner that is easy to read and understand by peers and laypeople alike, if it is to be used both to contribute to a scholarly understanding and to inform policy.

In addition to research, I also teach honors undergraduates. Being in the classroom is one of the most exciting parts of my career. It is in that environment that I have the distinct privilege of bringing my excitement for sociology to life for the next generation. In addition to presenting classic and contemporary works from distinguished sociologists, I am also able to personalize sections on gender inequality in education and in labor/careers by having my students read the work that I contribute to the field. Showing students the importance and utility of sociology provides me with an immeasurable satisfaction with my contribution to the world as a sociologist.

Note: Lynette Osborne, Institute for Women's Policy Research and The George Washington University, earned her BA in psychology at California State University, Chico, followed by an MA in sociology at Old Dominion University and a PhD in sociology at Purdue University.

So What ?

In the beginning of this chapter, we asked how being born female or male affects our lives. Because sex is a primary variable on which societies are structured and stratification takes place, being born female or male affects our public and private sphere activities, our health, our ability to practice religion or participate in political life, our educational opportunities, and just about everything we do. As sociologists with a focus on empirical ways of knowing and scientific methods, we can only focus on description and analysis of what is. Other disciplines, such as philosophy and theology, may articulate what "ought" to be. Applied sociologists sometimes move from an analysis of empirical data to questions of how to improve the quality of people's lives by suggesting solutions. Likewise, policy recommendations are those that take what is known about gender relations and offer plans for changing and improving the society. Gender inequality clearly exists. What should be done to alleviate problems is a matter of debate.

Inequality based on class, race, ethnicity, and gender is a process taking place at all levels of analysis. It takes place in a social context within our social world: institutions. Institutions are the stable patterns of roles, statuses, and groups that meet the basic needs of individuals and society in an orderly way. They include family, education, religion, politics, economics, and medicine. In complex societies, there are other necessary institutions including science and technology. We turn now to a discussion of the institutions that make up our social world.

Key Points

What Have We Learned?

- Whereas sex is biological, notions of gender identity and gender roles are socially constructed and therefore variable. (See pp. 272–275.)

- Notions of gender are first taught at the micro setting—the intimacy of the home—but they are reinforced and even sacralized at the meso and macro levels. (See p. 275.)

- While "she" may go first in micro-level social encounters (served first in a restaurant or the first to enter a door), "he" goes first in meso and macro settings—with the doors open wider for men to enter leadership positions in organizations and institutions. (See pp. 277–288.)

- Greater access to resources at the meso level makes it easier to have entree to macro-level positions, but it also influences respect in micro settings. (See p. 288.)

- Much of the gender stratification today is unconscious and unintended—not caused by angry or bigoted men who purposefully oppress women. Inequality is rooted in institutionalized privilege and disprivilege. (See pp. 289–291.)

- Various social theories shed different light on the issues of sex roles and inequality. (See pp. 291–296.)

- For modern postindustrial societies, there is a high cost for treating women like a minority group—both individually for the people who experience it and for the society, which loses the intelligence, skills, and commitment of highly competent people. (See pp. 296–302.)

Contributing to Our Social World: What Can We Do?

At the Local Level: Contact the Human Resources (employment) office on your campus. Schedule an interview with the director or other staff member to learn about your school's policies regarding gender discrimination. What procedures exist to ensure that women and men have an equal opportunity to be hired for faculty and staff positions? Do women and men receive the same salaries, wages, and benefits for equal work? Have there been recent disputes or grievances over hiring, wage, or benefits discrimination? How have these disputes been negotiated and resolved? Explore the possibility of your working as a volunteer or intern in the office specifically in the area of gender equity.

At the Organizational and National Levels: The National Organization for Women (NOW) was founded in 1966 and quickly became the world's leading advocate for gender equity. Its Web site, at www.now.org, contains information and opportunities for participation (by both women and men) on issues such as abortion and reproductive rights, legislative outreach, and economic justice, as well as activities aimed at ending sex discrimination and promoting diversity. Several internship programs are listed on the site, along with contact information and state and regional affiliates. Be sure to click on the "NOW on Campus" link to learn about programs oriented to undergraduate students.

At the Global Level: MADRE is an international women's rights organization working especially in the less developed countries. Visit its Web site, at http://www.madre.org, where you will find numerous opportunities for working on issues of justice, human rights, education, and health. The site also includes several topical blogs. The home page quotes actress Susan Sarandon: "I'm proud to say that I've worked with MADRE since its founding in 1983. MADRE works tirelessly to provide women with the necessary resources to not only support themselves and their families today, but to become part of the decision-making process for a better tomorrow."

The United Nations Inter-Agency Network on Women and Gender Equality works on relevant global issues, including violence against women and women's working conditions. Its WomenWatch Web site, at www.un.org/womenwatch, contains news, information, and ideas for contributing to the worldwide campaign for women's rights.

Visit **www.pineforge.com/ballantine2study** for online activities, sample tests, and other helpful information. Select "Chapter 9: Gender Stratification" for chapter-specific activities.

PART IV Institutions

Picture a house, a structure in which you live. Within that house there are processes—the action and activities that bring the house alive. Flip a switch, and the lights go on because the house is well-wired. Adjust the thermostat, and the room becomes more comfortable as the structural features of furnace or air-conditioning systems operate. If the structural components of the plumbing and water heating systems work, you can take a hot shower when you turn the knob. These actions taken within the structure make the house livable. If something breaks down, you need to get it fixed so that everything works smoothly.

Institutions, too, provide a framework or structure of society. Processes are the action part of both institutions and society, where activities take place. These processes include the interactions between people in groups that make society work. Institutions of family, religion, education, health, politics, and economics are interdependent and mutually supportive, just as the processes in a house work together. However, breakdown in one institution or conflict over limited resources between institutions affect the whole society. The structures in any society—including institutions—are fairly stable, while the processes within society and institutions are dynamic and often lead to significant change.

Rather than trying to be all-encompassing in this book, we attempt to illustrate how various aspects of society work. The following five chapters examine five of the institutions that make up society. As you read these chapters, notice the interdependencies. Change in one institution affects others. Note that sociologists studying economics, sport, or science as institutions would raise questions similar to the ones raised as we discuss family, education, politics, religion, and medicine, at the micro, meso, and macro levels of analysis. We begin with the institution of family.

CHAPTER 10

Family

Partner Taking, People Making, and Contract Breaking

Appearing in rich variety, the family is often referred to as the "most basic" institution. In this social relationship, we take partners and "make people"—both biologically and socially speaking. In the modern world, these intimate "basic" unions often experience conflict, violence, and contract breaking as well.

Think About It . . .

Micro: Why is family important to you?

Micro: In what groups and how do people find mates?

Meso: Why is family seen as the core or basic institution of society?

Macro: What, if anything, should be done within the nation to strengthen families?

Macro: Why are families around the world so different?

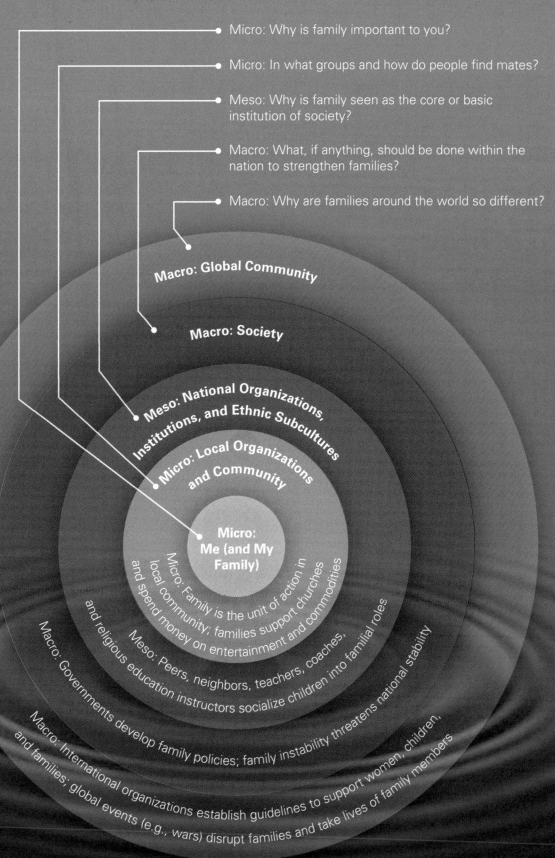

Macro: Global Community

Macro: Society

Meso: National Organizations, Institutions, and Ethnic Subcultures

Micro: Local Organizations and Community

Micro: Me (and My Family)

Micro: Family is the unit of action in local community; families support churches and spend money on entertainment and commodities

Meso: Peers, neighbors, teachers, coaches, and religious education instructors socialize children into familial roles

Macro: Governments develop family policies; family instability threatens national stability

Macro: International organizations establish guidelines to support women, children, and families; global events (e.g., wars) disrupt families and take lives of family members

In a village in Indonesia, the family is preparing for the day's chores. Chetana and Daya work with other women in the end of the long house that is used for cooking for the entire group. Other rooms along the house are designated for sleeping, greeting guests, and caring for children. Many people of all ages come and go—children, middle-aged adults, and elderly members. In this system, family units live together in an extended family, several generations of blood relatives sharing a single household.

It is morning in Sweden. Anders and Karin Karlsson are rushing to get to their offices on time. The children, a 12-year-old son and an eight-year-old daughter, are being hurried out the door to school. All will return in the evening after a full day of activities and join together for the evening meal. In this dual-career family, common in many postindustrial societies, both parents are working professionals.

The gossip at the African village water well this day is about the rich local merchant, Azi, who has just taken his fourth and last wife. She is a young, beautiful girl of 15 from a neighboring village. She is expected to help with household chores and bear children for his already extensive family unit. Several of the women at the well live in affluent households where the husband has more than one wife.

Tom and Henry recently adopted Ty into their family. The couple share custody of the five-year-old boy, attend his school events, and teach him what parents are expected to teach their children.

What do the very different scenes described at the outset of this chapter have in common? Each describes a family, yet there is controversy about what constitutes a family. Those groupings that are officially recognized as families tend to receive a number of privileges and rights,

such as health insurance and inheritance rights (Degenova and Rice 2002). In this chapter, we will discuss characteristics of families, theoretical perspectives on family, family dynamics, family as an institution, family issues, and policies regarding marriage, divorce, and social policies.

What Is a Family?

Ma, Pa, and the kids? Not always! Who defines what constitutes a family? Each individual? The government? Religious groups? Let us consider several definitions. The U.S. Census Bureau (2005d) defines the family as "a group of two or more people (one of whom is the householder) related by birth, marriage, or adoption and residing together; all such people (including related subfamily members) are considered as members of the family." Thus, a family might be composed of siblings, cousins, a grandparent and grandchild, or other groupings. Some sociologists define family as those sharing economic property, sexual access among the adults, and a sense of commitment among members (Collins and Coltrane 2001). This definition would include same-sex couples as families. Some religious groups define family as a mother, father, and their children, whereas others include several spouses and even parents and siblings living under one roof.

How do you define family? Answering the questions in the "Sociology in Your Social World" will indicate the complexity of this question.

Thinking Sociologically

First, complete the survey in "Sociology in Your Social World" on the next page. Are your answers different from a friend's or relative's? Why do you hold these particular views of "the ideal family"? Why might others in the world have answered differently?

In recent decades, the definition of family has broadened. No longer is it necessarily limited to heterosexual couples. These gay men are parents to this baby.

The family is often referred to as the most basic *institution* of any society. First, an institution is a system of norms. The place where we learn many of the norms for functioning in the larger society is the family. Second, most of us spend our lives in the security of a family. People are born and raised in families, and many will die in a family setting. Through good and bad, sickness and health, most families provide for our needs, both physical and psychological. Therefore, families meet our primary, our most basic needs. Third, major life events—marriages, births, graduations, promotions, anniversaries, religious ceremonies, holidays, funerals—take place within the family context and are celebrated with family members. In

Sociology in Your Social World

The Ideal Family

What is "the ideal family"? Does it have one adult woman and one adult man? One child or many? Grandparents living with the family? Ask a friend or relative to answer the questions below, and compare the answers with your own. Note that all of these options are found in some societies.

1. How many adults should the ideal family contain? _____

2. How many children should the ideal family contain? _____

3. What should be the sex composition of the adults in the ideal family?
   a. One female and one male
   b. Male-male or female-female
   c. Several males and several females
   d. Other (write in) _____

4. What should be the sexes of the child(ren) in the ideal family? _____

5. Who should select the marriage partner?
   a. The partners should select each other.
   b. The parents or close relatives should select the partner.
   c. A matchmaker should arrange the marriage.
   d. Other _____

6. What is the ideal number of generations living in the same household?
   a. One generation: partners and no children
   b. Two generations: partners and children
   c. Three or more generations: partners, children, grandparents, and great-grandparents
   d. Other _____

7. Where should the couple live?
   a. By themselves
   b. With parents
   c. With brothers or sisters
   d. With as many relatives as possible

8. What should the sexual arrangements be? (Check all that apply.)
   a. Partners have sex only with each other.
   b. Partners can have sex outside of marriage if it is not "disruptive" to the relationship.
   c. Partners are allowed to have sex with all other consenting adults.
   d. Male partners can have sex outside marriage.
   e. Female partners can have sex outside marriage.
   f. Other _____

9. Which person(s) in the ideal family should work to help support the family?
   a. Both partners
   b. Male only
   c. Female only
   d. Both, but the mother only after children are in school
   e. Both, but the mother only after children graduate from high school
   f. All family members including children
   g. Other _____

10. Should the couple have sex before marriage if they wish? Yes ___ No ___ Other_____

11. Should physically disabled aging parents
    a. Be cared for in a child's home?
    b. Be placed in a nursing care facility?
    c. Other _____

This Romanian family does not have much money, but the children learn many survival skills, and the most basic needs of the children, physical and psychological, are met.

Theoretical Perspectives on Family

Consider the case of Felice, a young mother locked into a marriage that provides her with little satisfaction. For the first year of marriage, Felice tried to please her husband, Tad, but gradually he seemed to drift further away. He began to spend evenings out. Sometimes, he came home drunk and yelled or hit her. Felice became pregnant shortly after their marriage and had to quit her job. This increased the financial pressure on Tad, and they fell behind in paying the bills.

Then came the baby. They were both ecstatic at first, but Tad soon reverted to his old patterns. Felice felt trapped. She was afraid and embarrassed to go to her parents. They had warned her against marrying so young without finishing school, but she was in love and had gone against their wishes. She and Tad had moved away from their hometown, so she was out of touch with her old support network and had few friends in her new neighborhood. Her religious beliefs told her she should try to stick it out, suggesting that the trouble was partly her fault for not being a "good enough wife." Lacking a job or skills to get one, she could not live on her own with a baby. She thought of marriage counseling, but Tad refused to consider this and did not seem interested in trying to work out the problems. He had his reasons for behaving the way he did, including feeling overburdened with the pressure of caring for two dependents. The web of this relationship seems difficult to untangle. Sociological theories provide us with tools to analyze such family dynamics.

Micro-Level Theories of Family and the Meso-Level Connection

Rational Choice Theory

Rational choice theory can help us understand situations like Felice's: why people seek close relationships, why they stay in abusive relationships, and why they seek quasi-family relations in foster parenting, alternative family groups, or communal living arrangements. As discussed in Chapter 2, rational choice theory evaluates the costs and rewards of engaging in interaction. We look for satisfaction of our needs—emotional, sexual, and economic—through interaction. Patterns in the family are reinforced to the extent that exchanges are beneficial to members. When the costs outweigh the rewards, the relationship is unlikely to continue. Women in abusive relationships weigh the costs of suffering abuse against the rewards of having social legitimacy, income, social acceptance, a home, and companionship. For many, not going against religious beliefs is also an issue. Many factors enter into the complex balance of the exchange. Indeed, costs and benefits of various choices are often established by meso-level organizations and institutions:

short, family is where we invest the most emotional energy and spend much of our leisure time. Fourth, the family is capable of satisfying a range of social needs—belonging to a group, economic support, education or training, religious socialization, resolution of conflicts, and so forth. One cannot conceive of the economic system providing emotional support for each individual or the political system providing socialization and personalized care for each child. Family carries out these functions. Finally, in many nonindustrialized societies and in some ethnic groups within modern cultures, the family is the key to social organization of the entire society. The institution of family is important to the survival of individuals and the society. It is the place where we confirm our partnerships as adults, and it is where we *make people*—not just biologically, but socially. In the family, we take an organism that has the potential to be fully human, and we mold this tiny bit of humanity into a caring, compassionate, productive person.

In most Western societies, individuals are born and raised in the **family of orientation**, which consists of our parent(s) and possibly sibling(s). In this family, we receive our early socialization and learn the language, norms, core values, attitudes, and behaviors of our community and society. When we find a life mate and/or have our own children, we establish our **family of procreation**. The transmission of values, beliefs, and attitudes from our family of orientation to our family of procreation preserves and stabilizes the family system. Because family involves emotional investment, we have strong feelings about what form it should take.

Whether we consider families at micro, meso, or macro levels, sociological theories can help us understand the role of families in the social world.

Photo Essay

Family Interactions

Families vary a great deal from one culture to another, but if they work well together, they provide support for members, a sense of identity, and feelings of belonging and caring.

No other institution can fulfill the functions of the family, but the family can fulfill many functions of other institutions. Here, family members in Oaxala, Mexico, work together as an economic team to produce food.

Introduction of a baby to a household changes the interpersonal dynamics, the topics of conversation, the amount of sleep people are able to get, the sense of responsibility for the future, relationships to the larger community (including schools), and many other aspects of social life.

insurance programs, health care options, and legal regulations that make partnering decisions easy or difficult.

According to rational choice theorists, even the mate selection process is shaped by a calculation of exchange. People estimate their own assets—physical, intellectual, social, and economic—and try to find the "best deal" they can make, with attention to finding someone with at least the level of resources they possess, even if those assets are in different areas. If someone marries another person with far more assets, the one with fewer assets is likely to have little power and to feel dependent on that relationship, often putting up with things that equal partners would not tolerate. Cost/benefit, according to this view, affects the forming of the relationship and the power and influence later in the relationship.

Symbolic Interaction Theory

Symbolic interaction theory also helps us to understand Felice's situation because it explains how individuals learn their particular behavior patterns and ways of thinking. Culture dictates the language we learn and how we interpret various situations. We are taught proper behavior patterns through socialization. Our role relationships are developed through interaction with others. Felice, for example, developed certain expectations and patterns of behavior by modeling her experiences on her family of orientation, observing others, and developing expectations from her initial interactions with Tad. He developed a different set of expectations.

His father had visited bars after work, had affairs with other women, and expected "his woman" at home to accept this without question. Tad modeled his role of husband after his father's behavior.

Two related concepts in symbolic interaction theory are the *social construction of reality* and the *definition of a situation*. What we define as real or as normal is shaped by what others around us accept as ordinary or acceptable. Our ideas about family, like anything else, are socially shaped by our experiences and our significant others. Children who grow up in homes where adults hit one another or shout at one another with sarcastic put-downs may come to think of this behavior as typical or a normal part of family life. They simply have known no other type of interaction. Thus, without seeing other options, they may create a similar pattern of family interaction in their own families of procreation.

Interaction with others, according to this theoretical model, is based on people's shared meanings. Concepts such as *family* or *wife* or *parenting* carry meaning to you and your siblings but may mean something very different to the person sitting beside you in class or to a potential mate.

One of the great challenges of newlyweds is meshing their ideas about division of labor, family holidays, discipline of children, spousal relations, and economic necessities, along with their assumptions about being in a committed relationship. A new couple socially constructs a new relationship, blending the models of life partnership from their own childhood homes. Of course, the couple can also create an entirely new model as they jointly define their relationship. Furthermore, the meaning of one's identity and the nature of one's obligations to others change dramatically when one becomes a parent. The mother and father have to work out what this means for each of them and for their interactions with each other. This brings us back to a central premise of symbolic interactionism: Humans are active agents who create their social structure through interaction. We not only learn family patterns, we *do family* in the sense that we create roles and relationships and pass them on to others as "normal." It is the sum total of all our actions that makes family into meso- and macro-level social patterns.

Our identities are shaped by institutional arrangements at the meso level. Family life is harder for couples when meso-level corporations, religious bodies, legal systems, and other government entities define the roles of "wife" and "husband." For example, each U.S. state actually spells out in its legal codes the duties of husbands and wives. Those who do not fulfill these duties may be in "neglect of duty." In some societies, the official state religion dictates proper roles of spouses. Our conceptions of these family roles are embedded in the larger structure in ways that many people do not realize.

Thinking Sociologically

What did you learn about spouse and parenting roles from your family of orientation? How will what you learned affect your current or future family roles?

Meso- and Macro-Level Theories of the Family

Structural-Functional Theory

Structural-functional theory points out the common purposes of families in every society. Despite great variations, most human family systems satisfy similar needs, or functions, for their members and for society. Although the families described at the beginning of this chapter vary greatly, their members have a number of common needs and problems. For instance, they all must secure food and shelter, raise children, and care for dependents.

Why do all societies have families? One answer is that families fulfill certain functions for societies and enhance their survival. Traditionally, there have been at least six

ways the family has helped stabilize the society, according to structural-functional theory:

Sexual regulation. Physically speaking, any adult human could engage in sex with any other human. However, in practice, no society allows total sexual freedom. Every society attempts to regulate the sexual behavior of its members in accordance with its own particular values, often through marriage. This regulation ensures that this strong biological drive is satisfied in an orderly way that does not create ongoing disruption, conflict, or jealousy. Certain people are "taken" and "off-limits" (Ward and Edelstein 2006).

Reproduction and replacement. Societies need children to replace members who die. Reproduction is controlled to keep family lineage and inheritance clear. Parent and caretaker roles are clearly defined and reinforced in many societies by ceremonies: baby showers, birth announcements, christenings, and naming ceremonies that welcome the child as a member of the family. In some places, such as New Guinea, procreation is so important that a young girl who has had children is more desirable because she has established her fertility capability.

Socialization. The family is the main training ground for children. In our families, we begin to learn values and norms, proper behavior, roles, and language. Later socialization in most societies is carried out by schools, religious organizations, and other institutions, but the family remains the most important initial socializing agent to prepare us for roles in society. Much of the socialization is done by parents, but siblings, grandparents, and other relatives are critical to socialization in many families and in many societies.

This woman in New Guinea became more attractive to men as a potential wife after she had proven her fertility by having children.

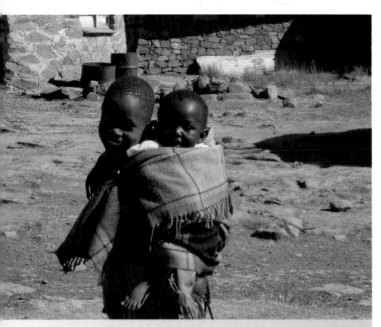

Siblings often provide some of the emotional support and part of the socialization for younger siblings. This is especially true in the poor Global South, where mothers often must work or carry water for the family from distant water sources. This sister cares for her younger sister in Soweto, South Africa.

Emotional support and protection. Families are our main source of love and belonging, giving us a sense of identity, security, protection, and safety from harm. It is one place where people may experience unqualified acceptance and feelings of being cherished. Problems of children in youth shelters and incidents of family violence and neglect are reminders that this function is not always successfully provided in families. Still, the family is the environment most capable of meeting this need if it is working well.

Status assignment. Our family of birth is the most important determinant of our social status, life chances, and lifestyles. It strongly affects our educational opportunities, access to health care, and religious and political affiliations, and values. In fact, in societies with caste systems, the ascribed position at birth is generally the position at death. Although in class societies individuals may achieve new social statuses, our birth positions and the early years of socialization have a strong impact on who and what we are.

Economic support. Historically, the family was a unit of production—running a farm or a bakery or a cobbler shop. Although this function is still predominant in many societies, the economic function carried out in individual families has pretty much disappeared in most Western families. However, the family remains an economic unit of consumption. Who

paid for your clothing, food, and other needs as you were growing up? Who helps many of you pay your college tuition and expenses? Families usually provide these necessities by buying them. Taxing agencies, advertising and commercial enterprises, workplaces, and other social institutions also treat the family as the primary economic unit.

Functional theorists ask about the consequences of what takes place in the family for other parts of the society. They are likely to recognize ways that the micro-level processes of the family (e.g., socialization of Japanese children to be cooperative and members of groups and U.S. children to be competitive and individualistic) are compatible with structural needs of society at the meso and macro levels (e.g., in the United States, the need for motivated workers who thrive on competition). At the macro level in postindustrial nations, competition may be valuable to the economy, for it stimulates the capitalistic system of production. Each part of the system, according to functionalists, works with other parts to create a functioning society.

Changing family functions. In some societies, the family is the primary unit for educating children, practicing religion, structuring leisure time activities, caring for the sick and aged, and even conducting politics. However, as societies modernize, many of these functions are transferred to other institutions.

As societies change, so do family systems. The sociohistorical perspective of family tells us that changes in intimate relationships—sexuality, marriage, and family patterns—have occurred over the centuries. Major transitions from agricultural to industrial to postindustrial societal systems change all of the institutions within those societies. Families in agricultural societies are often large and self-sufficient, producing their own food and providing their own shelter, but this is not the case in contemporary urban societies.

Industrialization and urbanization typical in 18th- and 19th-century Europe and the United States created a distinct change in roles. The wife and child became dependent on the husband who "brought home the bread." The family members became consumers rather than independent and self-supporting coworkers on a farm. This male breadwinner notion of family has not lasted long in the Western world (Coontz 2005). In addition to evolving roles, other changes in society have brought shifts to the family. Improved technology, for example, brought medical advances, new knowledge to be passed on in schools, recreation organized according to age groups, and improved transportation.

As many families moved to urban areas, tasks once carried on within the family unit moved to other institutions. The economic function has gone to the factory, store, and office. Social prestige is increasingly centered around a family member rather than the family surname. Socialization is increasingly done in schools, as teachers have become substitute parents. They do a great deal of the preparation of the child for the larger world. The traditional protection and care function has been partially replaced by police, reform schools, unemployment compensation, social security, health care systems (e.g., Medicare and Medicaid), and other types of services provided by the state. Little League baseball, industrial bowling teams, aerobic exercise groups, television, and computer games have replaced the family as the source of leisure activities and recreation. Although many would argue that the family still remains the center of the affectional life and is the only recognized place for producing children, one does not have to look far to discover that these two functions are also increasingly found outside the boundaries of the traditional family unit.

These changes have shifted the family's role in modernizing societies and made the family's functions more specialized. Still, family remains a critical institution in society. Most families still function to provide stable structures to carry out early childhood socialization and to sustain love, trust, affection, acceptance, and an escape from the impersonal world.

Thinking Sociologically

Does reduction of traditional family functions mean a decline in the importance of family or merely an adaptation of the family to changes in society? Is the modern family—based largely on emotional bonds rather than structural interdependency—a healthier system, or is it more fragile?

Conflict Theory

Conflict theorists study both individual family situations and broad societal family patterns. They argue that conflict in families is natural and inevitable. It results from the struggle for power and control in the family unit and in the society at large. As long as there is an unequal allocation of resources, conflict will arise.

Family conflicts take many forms. For instance, conflicts occur over allocation of resources, a struggle that may be rooted in conflict between men and women in the society: Who makes decisions, who gets money for clothes or a car, who does the dishes? On the macro level, family systems are a source of inequality in the general society, sustaining class inequalities by passing on wealth, income, and educational opportunities to their own members or perpetuating disadvantages such as poverty and lack of cultural capital (Benokraitis 2004).

Yet, some conflict theorists argue that conflict within the family can be important because it forces constant negotiation among individual family members and may bring about change that can strengthen the unit as a whole. Believing that conflict is both natural and inevitable, these theorists focus on root causes of conflict and how to deal with the discord. For conflict theorists, there is no assumption of a harmonious complementary family. The social world is characterized more by tension and power plays than by social accord. "Sociology Around the World" provides an example of women being used in family power relations.

Feminist Theory

The feminist approach is based on sociological studies done on, by, and for women. Because women often occupy very different places in society than men, feminist theorists argue the need for a feminist perspective to understand family dynamics. Feminist scholars begin by placing women at the center, not to suggest their superiority but to spotlight them as subjects of inquiry and as active agents in the working of society. The biases rooted in male assumptions are uncovered and examined (Eshleman and Bulcroft 2006).

One micro-level branch of feminist theory, the interpretive approach, considers women within their social contexts—the interpersonal relations and everyday reality facing women as they interact with other family members. It does not ignore economic, political, social, and historical factors but focuses on the ways women construct their reality, their opportunities, and their place in the community. According to feminist theorists, this results in a more realistic view of family and women's lives than many other theories provide. Applying this feminist approach to understand Felice's situation, the theorists would consider the way she views her social context and the way she assesses her support systems.

With roots in conflict theory, many feminist theorists argue that patterns of patriarchy and dominance lead to inequalities for women. One of the earliest conflict theorists, Friedrich Engels (Karl Marx's close associate), argued that the family was the chief source of female oppression and that until basic resources were reallocated within the family, women would continue to be oppressed. However, he said that as women become aware of their collective interests and oppression, they will insist on a redistribution of power, money, and jobs (Engels 1902).

One vivid example of how women and men can be viewed as groups with competing interests is through a feminist analysis of domestic violence. In the United States, a woman is assaulted or beaten every nine seconds (Tjaden and Thoennes 2000). Someone is sexually assaulted every two and a half minutes (U.S. Department of Justice 2002). About 60% of all married women will experience battering at some time in their lives (CALCASA, 2006). Four women are murdered each day by boyfriends or husbands (Tjaden and Thoennes 2000). In Western societies, men are under pressure to be successful. When they are not, home may be the place where they vent their frustrations. When socialization results in a hypermasculine sense of identity, and this

Sociology Around the World

Body Mutilation for Marriage

The bound foot of an elderly Chinese woman in Yunnan Province illustrates the bodily mutilation that women experienced in the interest of being considered desirable and high status.

To arrange marriage into a wealthy, high-status family, women's families around the world have done whatever it takes to make their daughters more desirable mates. We learn through socialization which parts of the body have sexual connotations. In some societies, fat is sexy, whereas in others, legs or breasts are focal points. In other societies, tattoos and piercings are marks of beauty. Consider the following two examples of body alterations to enhance the marriage prospects of women.

For centuries in China, women with tiny feet were considered sexually attractive, a prize catch for men. Besides the sexual appeal, the status for the man of having such a wife lay in the fact that women with tiny bound feet could not work in the fields or do hard labor, thus demonstrating to all that the man was wealthy. Women bound their little girls' feet starting at about age two so that the feet would not grow. Sometimes, the feet of adult women were no more than three inches long (Levy 1990; Levy, Waley, and Eberhard 1992; Yung 1995). This practice was outlawed when Communists came to power in the 1950s, and only a few elderly women remain as evidence of the practice.

To those in Western societies, one of the most abhorrent examples of altering the body for sexual purposes is the practice of clitorectomy, carried out in some African, Middle Eastern, and Asian societies. Those practicing female circumcision or excision (removal of the clitoris) believe it eliminates base sexual desire and keeps the woman from "straying," leaving only the vagina, or "source of life" (Burn 2005; "A Painful Tradition" 1999). Proponents of such practices also believe tightening the vagina increases pleasure for the male, although it can be deadly for women who hemorrhage as a result.

In some traditional societies, circumcision is a significant rite of passage in a young woman's life, accompanied by singing, dancing, and new clothes, and above all signifying her eligibility for marriage. In Guinea, for instance, women are married by age 14, sometimes given to their husbands as gifts. Some women in this society believe the female circumcision rite shows beauty and courage and is a means of achieving recognition and power. Any woman who does not go through the procedure would be an outcast and not marriageable—and marriage is a ticket to survival.

The cultural significance of female circumcision causes some anthropologists to view Western denunciation of the practice as Eurocentric. They perceive bias even in the very term most Western researchers use for the practice, *female genital mutilation* or FGM.

However, many women around the world still protest the practice as a dangerous mutilation of the body causing health and reproductive problems and violating human rights. Several cases of women trying to escape the procedure by seeking refugee status have come before foreign courts. A young Ghanaian woman who sought asylum in the United States to avoid the ritual of circumcision made front-page news in several countries. After more than two years in U.S. detention, she was granted asylum, setting a precedent for other women in similar situations (Hu 1999). Amnesty International (2006) estimates that almost two million female circumcisions occur every year, despite the Western protests of the procedures.

Many women who oppose female genital mutilation, including feminist theorists, see it as a power struggle favoring males, resulting in females' bodies becoming objects to control for the sexual attraction and pleasure of men.

is combined with an emotional dependency on a female, it is a lethal combination. Cultural messages tell men that they are to be in charge, but knowing they are emotionally and sometimes economically dependent on their wives may result in violence to regain control.

Women are most severely exploited in societies that treat them as property and in which the family is a key political unit for power and status. Where men are the heads of families and women are dependent, women may be treated as less than equal both within the family and in the labor market. Consider the practice of *sati*. Although outlawed now, it lingers in some areas of India. The widow was expected to (or was forced to) throw herself on her husband's funeral pyre because there was no structural place for her in the family after her husband's death. In some societies, a husband is expected to beat his wife if he is dissatisfied with her cooking, housekeeping, or child care. This can happen in groups such as the Masai of East Africa or in countries such as Brazil. In some cultural situations, the woman's life is valuable only as it relates to the economic situation and the needs of men. Changes in the patriarchal family structure, education and employment opportunities for women, and child care availability can lead to greater freedom of choice, equality, and autonomy for women, according to feminist theorists (Shaw and Lee 2005).

Thinking Sociologically

How do men or women mutilate their bodies in your society to be sexually appealing to others? For example, are breast implants (by which women lose feeling and perhaps the euphoria of orgasm) a similar phenomenon? Why or why not? What about the painful ritual of placing metal braces on one's teeth to pull them into different locations in order to have a better smile? Are there any painful self-mutilating rituals that men do for greater attractiveness? If so, what are those activities? If women don't perform these rituals, why not?

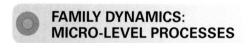

FAMILY DYNAMICS: MICRO-LEVEL PROCESSES

The Abubakar family belongs to the Hausa tribe of West Africa. They share a family compound composed of huts or houses for each family unit of one wife and her young children, plus one building for greeting guests, one for cooking, one for the older children, and one for washing. The compound is surrounded by an enclosure. Each member of the family carries out certain tasks: food preparation, washing, child care, farming, herding—whatever is needed for the group. Wives live with their husbands' families. Should there be a divorce, the children generally belong to the husband's household because the family lineage is through the father's side.

The eldest male is the leader. He makes decisions for the group. When a child is born, the eldest male within the family presides over a ceremony to name and welcome the child into the group. When the child reaches marrying age, the eldest male plays a major role in choosing a suitable mate. Upon his death, the power he has held passes to his eldest son, and his property is inherited by his sons.

However, Abubakar's eldest son has moved away from the extended family to the city, where he works in a factory to support himself. He lives in a small room with several other migrants. He has met a girl from another tribe and may marry her, although his family does not approve of his marrying outside their group, and he will do so without their blessing. He will probably have a small family because of money and space pressures in the city. His lifestyle and even values have already altered considerably. In the social world, the global trend toward the Western model of industrialization and urbanization is altering cultures around the world and changing family life.

The story indicates the extensive interdependencies of family as a micro-level social unit, a meso-level institution, and a macro-level social system. Many individual family issues that seem very intimate and personal are actually affected by norms and forces at another level (such as migration and urbanization), and decisions of individuals affect meso- and macro-level social structures (such as size of families).

Thinking Sociologically

What kinds of changes in families would you anticipate as societies change from agricultural to industrial to information economies and as individuals move from rural to urban areas? What changes has your family undergone over several generations?

Mate Selection: How Do New Families Start?

At the most micro level, two people get together to begin a new family unit. There are more than six billion people in the world, but it is highly unlikely that your mate was or will be randomly selected from the entire global population. Even in Western societies, where we think individuals are responsible for choosing their marriage partners, mate selection is seldom an entirely free choice. Indeed, mate selection is highly limited by geographical proximity, ethnicity, age, social class, and a host of other variables. So like all of the other micro-level processes we will examine here, macro-level factors also play a part. What are some factors in the mate-selection process?

Norms Governing Choice of Marriage Partners: Societal Rules and Intimate Choices

A number of norms and social constraints—meso- and macro-level expectations—govern the choice of a mate in any society. Most are unwritten, and they vary somewhat from culture to culture, but we all learn them from an early age. One of the cultural rules is **exogamy**—a norm that requires individuals to marry outside of their own immediate group. The most universal form of exogamy is the incest taboo, including restrictions against father-daughter, mother-son and brother-sister marriages. Some countries, including about half the U.S. states, forbid first cousins to marry, whereas others, such as some African groups and many Syrian villages, encourage first-cousin marriages to solidify family ties and property holdings. As we saw in Chapter 3, there is considerable cultural variation in whether first cousins are forbidden or preferred mates. On the other hand, some societies require village exogamy (marriage outside the village) because it bonds together villages and reduces the likelihood of armed conflict between them.

Anthropologists have suggested several hypotheses to explain why all societies develop norms governing, and usually prohibiting, incestuous relations. These range from intuitive recognition of the negative biological results of inbreeding to necessity for families to make ties with outside groups for survival. One clear issue is that rights to sexual access can cause jealousy that rips a social unit apart. If father and son became jealous about who was sleeping with the wife/mother/sister, relationships would be destroyed and parental authority sabotaged. Likewise, if the father was always going to the daughter for sexual satisfaction, the mother and daughter bond would be severely threatened (Davis 1960; Williams, Sawyer, and Wahlstrom 2006). No society can allow this to happen to its family system. Any society that has failed to have an incest taboo self-destructed long ago.

On the other hand, norms of **endogamy** require individuals to marry inside certain boundaries, whatever the societal members see as protecting the homogeneity of the group, encouraging group bonding and solidarity, and helping minority groups to survive in societies with different cultures. Endogamous norms may require individuals to select mates of the same race, religion, social class, ethnic background, or clan (Williams et al. 2006). For example, strictly endogamous religious groups include the Armenian-Iranians, Orthodox Jews, Old Order Amish, Jehovah's Witnesses, and the Parsi of India. The result

is less diversified groups but protection of the minority identity (Belding 2004). Whether marriages are arranged or entered into freely, both endogamy and exogamy limit the number of possible mates. In addition to marrying within a group, most people choose a mate with similar social characteristics—age, place of residence, educational background, political philosophy, moral values, and psychological traits—a practice called homogamy.

Going outside the limits in mate selection can make things tough for newlyweds who need family and community support. Few take this risk. For instance, in the United States, close to 90% marry people with similar religious values (Williams et al. 2006). About 80 to 90% of Protestants marry other Protestants, and 64 to 85% of Catholics marry within their religious faith. For Jews, the figure has been as high as 90% (Eshleman and Bulcroft 2006) but has dropped in recent decades to as low as 50% for some Jews, depending on the type of Judaism (Newman and Grauerholz 2002). In Canada, only one person in five marries across religious boundaries (Heaton 1990). However, with increased tolerance for differences, cross-denominational marriage is more likely today than a century ago. It is also higher among individuals who grew up as Catholics but are not now practicing (Sander 1993). Intermarriage between Catholics and Protestants in the United States was rare in the 1920s, but as prejudice against Catholics has declined and differences in educational levels between the groups have decreased, educational homogamy has become more important than religious endogamy.

Interracial marriages also challenge endogamous norms, yet the practice is becoming more common with every passing year. Of marriages in the United States, 5.4% involve a spouse from a different race or ethnic group. Also, one in five has a close relative in a mixed race marriage, and one half of the dating population has dated someone of a different race. The most common pattern is a white American married to someone from a different ethnic or racial group. However, among Hispanics, one in four is married to someone of another Latin ethnicity (for example, a Mexican American marrying a Cuban American). Among Hispanics, Puerto Ricans are the most likely to marry a non-Hispanic, with 21% of marriages being exogamous. Among Mexicans and Cuban Americans, roughly 12% marry non-Hispanics—usually whites. Black-white marriages, which represent the lowest intermarriage rate, usually involve black men and white women. By contrast, Asian women are more likely to marry exogamously than Asian American men (Lee and Edmonston 2005).

Each group may have different definitions of where the exogamy boundary is. For Orthodox Hasidic Jews, marriage to a Reform Jew is exogamy—strictly forbidden. For the Amish, the marriage of a Hostetler Amish woman to a Beachy Amish man is beyond consideration. Marriage of a Hopi to a Navajo has also been frowned on as marriage to an Other—even though many Anglos would think of this as an endogamous marriage of two Native Americans.

So cultural norms of societies limit individual decisions about micro-level matters such as choice of a spouse, and they do so in a way that most individuals do not even recognize. Exogamy and endogamy norms and expectations generally restrict the range of potential marriage partners, even though some of these norms are weakening. Still, the question remains: How do we settle on a life partner?

Finding a Mate

In most societies, mate selection is achieved through arranged marriages, free-choice unions, or some combination of the two. In any case, selection is shaped by cultural rules of the society.

Arranged marriages involve a pattern of mate selection in which someone other than the couple—elder males, parents, a matchmaker—selects the marital partners. This method of mate selection is most common in traditional, often patriarchal, societies. Some examples follow.

Many traditional girls in Muslim societies don a veil at puberty and wear it throughout their adult years. Custom dictates that a woman should not look into the eyes of men outside of her immediate family. Marriage for her is a matter of necessity, for her support comes from the family system. Economic arrangements and political alliances between family groups are solidified through marriage. Daughters are valuable commodities in negotiations to secure these ties between families (Burn 2005). Beauty, youth, talent, and pleasant disposition bring a high price and a good match. Should the young people like each other, it is icing on the cake. Daughters must trust that the male elders in their families will make the best possible matches for them. Clearly, the men hold the power in this vital decision.

In the Tiwi tribe of Australia, no female child is born without a husband. The father of the child-to-be betroths the unborn to an older man. Should "she" be a "he," the arrangement is cancelled. All females are married *in utero* because it is believed that the female can become pregnant at any time after birth. For a woman to have a child if she is unmarried is a serious offense. At puberty, the girl goes to live with her husband. Should the husband die, the girl is immediately transferred to another man. Although age spans between husbands and their several wives may be great, this arrangement assures everyone a home and security. It has been the tradition for the Tiwi tribe for thousands of years (Nanda and Warms 2007).

Seated front and center with the bride and groom at many Japanese weddings is the matchmaker, the person responsible for bringing the relationship into being. After both families agree to the arrangement, the couple meets over tea several times to decide whether the match suits them. Today, between 10 and 30% of marriages in Japan are still arranged this way, the rest being called "love marriages." However, some marriages are a mix, combining arrangements with "love" ("Getting Married in Japan" 2007).

Where arranged marriages are the norm, love has a special meaning. The man and woman may never have set eyes on each other before the wedding day, but respect and affection generally grow over time as the husband and wife live together. People from these societies are assured a mate and have difficulty comprehending marriage systems based on love, romance, and courtship, factors that they believe to be insufficient grounds for a lifelong relationship. They wonder why anyone would want to place themselves in a marriage market, with all of the uncertainty and rejection. Such whimsical and unsystematic methods would not work in many societies, where the structure of life is built around family systems.

Free-choice marriage, in contrast to arranged marriage, involves the partners selecting each other based primarily on romance and love. Sonnets, symphonies, rock songs, poems, and plays have been written to honor love and the psychological and physiological pain and pleasure that the mating game brings. However impractical romance may seem, marriage choice based on **romantic love** is becoming more prevalent as societies around the world become more Westernized, women gain more rights and freedoms, and families exert less control over their children's choice of mates (Eshleman and Bulcroft 2006). Industrialized societies tend to value love and individualism and tend to have high marriage rates, low fertility rates, and high divorce rates (Levine et al. 1995).

Free-choice mate selection is found in most Western societies. Couples in the United States tend to put more emphasis on romantic love and the process of attracting a mate than most other societies. Romantic love is most common in wealthy countries where individuals are emphasized over community interests (Eshleman and Bulcroft 2006). For example, 86% of U.S. college students say they would not marry without love.

The old adages about women "hooking a man" and men being "snagged or caught" are challenged by data that suggest men are more likely than women to prefer marriage over the single status for life. In a recent U.S. survey, 66% of men agreed that "it is better to get married" compared to 51% of women. In response to the statement, "it is more important for a man to spend a lot of time with his family than be successful at his career," 76% of men agreed, compared to 72% of women (Centers for Disease Control and Prevention 2006b). These sentiments are comparable in many European countries, where fewer women are marrying than in the past.

E-romance is helping to facilitate mate selection in free-choice systems. When people of all ages attempt to enter into relationships on the Internet, some find compatible mates. This facilitates what those in arranged marriage systems find bewildering about free-choice systems—How do you meet possible mates? The burgeoning business in e-romance introduces people with common interests, backgrounds, ages, and other variables. For example, eHarmony has participants fill out an extensive 436-question personality profile that it claims is a "scientifically proven" compatibility-matching system. More than nine million users hope for one or more matches from the system. The matches can then communicate electronically and may eventually decide to meet in person. A popular Asian American cyber meeting place is AsiaAvenue.com, and many other sites focus on special interests of users.

Many of the e-dating services claim that their profiles and processes are based on social science research. Pepper Schwartz, a well-known sociologist who studies relationships, helped design PerfectMatch's system. Many services have sprung up, including PerfectMatch.com, Chemistry.com, and a number of more specialized services such as Goodgenes.com and conservativematch.com.

Are these services successful in matching up potential mates? A recent study found that one in three respondents was unattached, and 7% were actively looking for partners. About 37% of those had tried online dating sites, and about half had been out on a date as a result of online services. About one third had formed long-term relationships. Because online dating is relatively new, it is unclear whether it will become a dominant form of mate selection (Gottlieb 2006). However, the number of singles in many countries is increasing. In 2000, U.S. households with people living alone outnumbered households with couples and children, resulting in a dating market of more than 100 million people (Akbar 2006).

Thinking Sociologically

Is e-dating a modern-day form of the matchmaker? Is it replacing other forms of finding a mate? Why or why not?

In this interdependent global society, the dominant Western model for finding a mate tends to infiltrate and to be adopted in other parts of the world. Once again, the social world model helps us to understand that even mate selection processes are shaped by macro-level influences that filter to the national, institutional, community, and individual family levels. A very private and personal process is becoming transformed by global forces and trends.

Starting with the assumption that eligible people are most likely to meet and be attracted to others who have similar values and backgrounds, sociologists have developed various mate selection theories, several of which view dating as a three-stage process.

1. Stimulus: We meet someone to whom we are attracted by appearance, voice, dress, similar ethnic background, sense of humor, or other factors. Something serves as a stimulus that makes us take notice. Of course, sometimes the stimulus is simply knowing the other person is interested in us.

2. Value comparison: As we learn about the other's values, we are more likely to find that person compatible

if she or he affirms our own beliefs and values toward life, politics, religion, and roles of men and women in society and marriage. If values are not compatible, the person does not pass through our filter. We look elsewhere.

3. Roles and needs stage: Another filter comes at this stage in which the couple explores roles of companion, parent, housekeeper, and lover. This might involve looking for common needs, interests, and favored activities. If roles and needs are not complementary to one's own, desire for a permanent relationship wanes.

The mate-selection process varies somewhat from person to person, but social scientists believe that a sequential series of decisions, in a pattern such as that described above, is often part of the process (Eshleman and Bulcroft 2006; Murstein 1987).

Thinking Sociologically

Conduct a small survey of dating and married couples you know. Ask them about how they became involved in their relationship and the process of deciding to get together or marry. How do their comments mesh with the three-stage process described above?

Who Holds the Power? Authority Relations in Marriage

Power relations, another micro-level issue shaped by cultural norms, affect the personal interactions and decision making in individual families. Two areas that have received particular sociological attention are decision making in marriage and work roles.

Decision Making in Marriage

Cultural traditions establish the power base in society and family: patriarchy, matriarchy, or egalitarianism. The most typical authority pattern in the world is patriarchy, or male authority. Matriarchy, female authority, is rare. Even where the lineage is traced through the mother's line, males generally dominate decision making. Some analysts have suggested reasons for male dominance: Males are physically larger, they are free from childbearing, and they are not tied to one place by homemaking and agricultural responsibilities. However, social scientists find no evidence that there are any inherent intellectual foundations for male authority as opposed to female authority (Kramer 2005; Ward and Edelstein 2006).

Egalitarian family patterns—in which power, authority, and decision making are shared between the spouses and perhaps with the children—are emerging, but they are not yet a reality in most households. For example, research indicates that in many U.S. families, decisions concerning vacation plans, car purchases, and housing are reached democratically. Still, most U.S. families are not fully egalitarian. Males generally have a disproportionate say in major decisions (Lindsey 2005).

Resource theory attempts to explain power relations by arguing that the spouse with the greater resources—education, occupational prestige, income—has the greater power. In many societies, income is the most important factor because it represents identity and power. If only one spouse brings home a paycheck, the other is usually less powerful (Tichenor 1999). In families in which the wife is a professional, other factors in addition to income such as persuasion and egalitarian values may enter into the power dynamic (Lindsey 2005; Lips 1991). Regardless of who has greater resources, men in two-earner couples tend to have more say in financial matters and less responsibility for children and household tasks.

Who Does the Housework?

The *second shift*, a term coined by Hochschild (1989), refers to the housework and child care that employed women do after their first-shift jobs. Studies over the years indicate that women take on more household responsibilities. Employment schedules also affect the amount of time each spouse contributes to household tasks. Husbands who are at home during hours when their wives are working tend to take on more tasks. Employment, education, and earnings give women more respect and independence and a power base for a more equitable division of labor across tasks (Cherlin 2002; Kramer 2005). Egalitarian shared work is most common in dual-wage families where there is agreement over an equitable division of labor.

Is there a typical division of labor in households? In many societies, couples exhibit highly sex-segregated family work patterns, even when the male contributes many hours to housework. Women take responsibility for most of the household and child care (Coltrane 2000). When men do participate, they tend to do dishes, grocery shopping, repairs, yard work, and care for the car (Bianci et al. 2000). U.S. women spend on average 11 hours a week on child care, whereas men spend 3.3 hours. Women also spend a weekly average of 19.4 hours on housework other than child care, whereas men devote 10.4 hours to such tasks (Bianci et al. 2000; Newman and Grauerholz 2002). Table 10.1 shows a typical division of household tasks for married couples.

Interestingly, husbands who do an equitable share of the household chores actually report higher levels of satisfaction with the marriage (Stevens, Kiger, and Riley 2001). The success or failure of a marriage depends in large part on

Table 10.1	**Housework and Gender: Hours per Week**	
Task	Husband	Wife
Cleaning	2.1	8.0
Cooking	1.4	5.3
Laundry	0.3	2.4
Bill paying	1.6	1.1
Outdoor work	2.1	0.8
Repairs	2.2	0.8
Pet or plant care	0.8	1.0
Total hours per week	10.4	19.4

Source: Bianci et al. 2000.

patterns that develop early in the marriage for dealing with the everyday situations including power relationships and division of labor.

Thinking Sociologically

Analyze the division of labor in your family. How did it evolve? Is it considered fair by the participants? How does it compare to Table 10.1?

While women generally are economically dependent on men, giving men the power, men are often dependent on women emotionally, for they are less likely to have same-sex friends with whom they share feelings and vulnerabilities. Men bond with one another, but they seldom develop truly intimate ties that provide support in hard times. So women are not entirely without power. It is just that their power frequently takes a different form (and results in fewer privileges) (Newman and Grauerholz 2002).

What Makes Marriages Last?

How do people reach 25 and 50 years together? Using in-depth analysis of long-lasting marriages, researchers considered how couples adjust to one another, the relationship over time, and patterns that make for lasting relationships. The study examined satisfaction in the areas of communication, sex, trust, empathy, emotional intimacy, marital conflict, and mutual decision making, and they found that marriages go through stages related to age of children. There is some long-term decline in the intensity of satisfaction with sex, although this area did improve a bit right after all the children left the home. Conflict was more intense when children entered the picture and improved after the parents had the home to themselves. Communication declined while the children were around and then improved as the couple entered the later stage. Emotional intimacy generally improved over the course of the marriage, although it did suffer while the children were in the adolescent stage. Mutual decision making, empathy, and trust all improved somewhat over the years.

The authors found that stable marriages survive for a number of reasons, including ethnic group beliefs about divorce, religious commonality, and comfortable family income. However, one predictor of lasting marriage is over-all satisfaction with the marriage. Decision making in lasting marriages was mutual and collaborative, with emphasis on equity. Communication was open and direct and became more comfortable in times of crisis as time passed. Mutual respect was maintained throughout the relationship, while trust and understanding of the other seemed to grow over the years. Although frequency of sexual intimacy declined over the years, psychological intimacy improved as success-ful couples learned to depend on each other for support. In the long run, the latter form of intimacy seemed most important. Conflicts were not a problem as long as the partners tried to solve them in ways that led to win-win resolutions (rather than rancorous win-lose contests). This conflict-resolution skill was highly related to overall satis-faction. These seemed to be the key elements of stable and fulfilling marriages (Mackey and O'Brien 1995).

⊙ THE FAMILY AS AN INSTITUTION: MESO-LEVEL ANALYSIS

We experience family life at a very personal level, but con-sider all families together and we have the family as an institution—a stable pattern of social relationships at the meso level of society.

According to the U.S. census, *households* refers to resi-dential units, whatever the family or kinship ties of the people living in that dwelling. There were 111.6 million households in 2006 (U.S. Census Bureau 2006a). About 32% of those households were nonfamily units, compared to only 10% of nonfamilies sharing households in 1950 (U.S. Census Bureau 2006a). The average number of mem-bers living in a household decreased from 3.14 persons in 1970, to 2.76 in 1980, then rose to 3.24 in 2000 and fell to 2.57 in 2005. In the year 2005, 18.2% of the households were single-parent female householders with no spouse present. The number of children living with a single parent was up to 28% in 2005 (U.S. Census Bureau 2005a). These figures give us some idea about capacity for change in the family as an institution—as a collective entity that meets needs of individuals and society as a whole. Some of the changes in this institution have resulted from—or caused—changes in other institutions.

Marriage and Family Structure: The Components of Family as an Institution

Although the family is an institution in the larger social system, it does vary in interesting ways from one society to another. How many mates does a society think a man or woman should have, for instance? Some societies believe that several wives provide more hands to do the work and establish useful political and economic alliances between family groups. They bring more children into the family unit and provide multiple family members for emotional and physical support and satisfaction. On the other hand, having one spouse per adult probably meets most individu-als' social and emotional needs very effectively, is less costly, and eliminates the possibility of conflict or jealousy among spouses. It is also easier to relocate a one-spouse family to urban areas, a necessity for many families in industrialized and postindustrial societies. Let us examine the issue of adult partners in a family.

Types of Marriages

Monogamy and polygamy are the main forms of marriage found around the world. **Monogamy**, the most familiar form to those of us in industrial and postindustrial societies, refers to marriage of two individuals. **Polygamy**, in which a man or woman has more than one spouse, is most often found in agricultural societies where multiple spouses and children mean more help with the farm work. There are two main forms of polygamy—polygyny and polyandry. Anthropologist George Murdock found that *polygyny,* a hus-band having more than one wife, was allowed (although not always practiced) in 709 of the 849 societies he cataloged in his classic *Ethnographic Atlas.* Only 16% (136 societies) were exclusively monogamous (Barash 2002).

Although many societies allow polygyny, only a small percentage of families in the world actually practice it because of the expense of maintaining a large family, high prices that men's families must pay to the bride's family in some societ-ies, and religious and political pressures from other powerful countries for monogamy. Indeed, only a limited number of men in polygynous societies can afford to support several wives. Because the numbers of men and women are usually fairly balanced in a society, there are seldom enough extra women to go around. Polygyny does increase at times of war when the number of men is reduced due to war causalities.

Polyandry, a wife having more than one husband, is practiced in less than 1% of the world's societies. Among the Todas of Southern India, brothers can share a wife, and the Marquesan Islanders allow wives to have more than one hus-band. A Tibetan practice originating in the country's system of land ownership and inheritance allows a woman to marry several men, usually brothers (O'Connel 1993). This often happens when the men are poor and must share a single plot of land to eke out a meager livelihood, so they decide to remain a single household with one wife. Murdock found only four societies in the world that practice polyandrous marriage.

Members of Western societies often find the practice of polygamy hard to understand, just as those from polygamous societies find monogamy strange. Some societies insist on strict monogamy: Marriage to one other person is lifelong, and deviation from that standard is prohibited. Yet, most Western societies practice what could be called a variation of polygamy—serial monogamy. With high divorce and remarriage rates, Western societies have developed a system of marrying several spouses, but one at a time. One has spouses in a series rather than simultaneously.

Extended and Nuclear Families

The typical ma-pa-and-kids monogamous model that is familiar in many industrialized parts of the world is not as typical as it appears. From a worldwide perspective, it is only one of several structural models of family.

Extended families include two or more adult generations that share tasks and living quarters. This may include brothers, sisters, aunts, uncles, cousins, and grandparents. In most extended family systems, the eldest male is the authority figure. This is a common pattern around the world, especially in agricultural societies. Some ethnic groups in the United States, such as Mexican Americans and some Asian Americans, live in extended monogamous families with several generations under one roof. This is financially practical and helps group members maintain their traditions and identity by remaining somewhat isolated from Anglo society.

As societies become more industrialized and fewer individuals and families engage in agriculture, the **nuclear family**, consisting of two parents and their children—or any two of the three—becomes more common. This worldwide trend toward nuclear family occurs because more individuals live in urban areas where smaller families are more practical, mate selection is based on love, couples establish independent households after marriage, marriage is less of an economic arrangement between families, fewer marriages take place between relatives such as cousins, and equality between the sexes increases (Burn 2005; Goode 1970).

The family can be found in many forms. No matter how it manifests itself structurally, a society's family institution is interdependent on each of the other major institutions. For example, if the health care system is unaffordable or not functioning well, families may not get the care they need to prevent serious illness. If the economy goes into a recession and jobs are not available, families experience stress, abuse rates increase, and marriages are more likely to become unstable. If the government fails to support families, as occurred when Hurricane Katrina hit New Orleans and southern Mississippi in the summer of 2005, families may suffer, be torn apart, and experience

Tibetan Gama Sangding (left) poses for a photo with his elder brother, La Wen (right), and their wife Cai Zhuo (center), in front of their tent in northwest China. Fraternal polyandry means that brothers share a common wife. When children are born, they call the oldest brother father *and the other brothers* uncle, *regardless of who the biological father is. Polyandry is not officially permitted by China's marriage law.*

wrenching disorientation and dislocation. Interdependence with the economy, the next topic, illustrates this point.

Thinking Sociologically

Under what social circumstances would an extended family be helpful? Under what circumstances would it be a burden?

The Economic Institution and the Family

The family is the primary economic unit of consumption, so what happens if the economy has a major impact on the structure and quality of family life? When economic times are rough, employment instability and uncertainty, economic strain, and deprivation can cause strained family relations. Low-income families, especially single-parent families headed by women, are particularly hard-hit and often have to struggle for survival (Staples 1999; Willie 2003). In some cases, families are so financially devastated that they live homeless, a difficult life, especially for children.

Poverty and Families in the United States

The poverty threshold in 2005 for a family of four was $19,806 (U.S. Census Bureau 2006e). In 2004, there were 26.5 million families (11%) that lived below the poverty level (U.S. Census Bureau 2005e). Table 10.2 shows the percentage of individuals and families in poverty. Table 10.3

Table 10.2	**Poverty Status of U.S. Families by Family Type**
Poverty Status and Family Type	*Total Percentage Below Poverty Level*
Total families	10.2
Married-couple families	5.5 (3.2 million)
Female householder, no spouse present	28.4 (4 million)

Source: U.S. Census Bureau 2005f.

a. Data include families in group quarters.

Table 10.3	**Percentage of Births to Unmarried and Married Women: United States**

Year	*Births to Unmarried Women (%)*	*Births to Married Women (%)*
2004	35.8	64.2
2000	33.2	66.8
1995	32.2	67.8
1990	8.0	72.0
1985	22.0	78.0
1980	18.4	81.6

Source: Hamilton et al. 2006, Table 4.

New York's homeless population is larger now than it was in the 1980s. The rise is mainly seen in the more than 13,000 children who spend their nights moving from shelter to shelter. Some families board a bus late at night and are taken to a city shelter. Debra Williams and her children receive conditional shelter, but they must leave the site at 6:30 a.m. for school and work. These are not conditions that make for effective parenting.

shows the increase in single-parent families between 1970 and 2004 (Hamilton et al. 2006).

The "feminization of poverty," discussed in earlier chapters, is a global problem. It occurs where single motherhood is widespread, as shown in Table 10.3, and where there are few policies to reduce poverty (Goldberg and Kremen 1990; Williams et al. 2006). Single mothers, whether in capitalist or socialist countries, have some common experiences, including dual roles as workers and mothers, lower earnings than men, irregular paternal support payments, and underrepresentation in policy-making bodies. What differ around the world are governmental policies that help mothers with child support, child care, health care, maternity leave, and family allowances. Single mothers are as prevalent in Sweden as in the United States, but U.S. single mothers are six times more likely to be poor because of fewer support systems (Casper, McLanahan, and Garfinkel 1994; Goldberg and Kremen 1990). For single teens, early motherhood, lack of education, and insufficient income lead to a multiproblem family pattern.

One reason for the increase in single-parent households among African American women is that there are 1.81 million more African American women than men (U.S. Census Bureau 2007b), due in large part to high mortality and incarceration rates of African American males. Although African Americans value family, many poor men cannot fulfill the economic role of husband and father because the number of jobs available to less-educated men is decreasing (McLeod 2004; Wilson 1987). The percentage of births to unmarried mothers varies considerably by ethnicity as shown in Figure 10.1. Although the percentage of births has increased over time, it has leveled off for African Americans in recent years.

Some argue that a culture of poverty, a set of attitudes and values including a sense of hopelessness and passivity, low aspirations, feelings of powerlessness and inferiority, and present-time orientation (concern only for the present and not planning for the future), is passed from one generation to the next (Lewis 1961, 1986). However, many sociological researchers support the argument that poverty itself causes the values and attitudes that develop in poor communities as survival mechanisms (McLeod 2004). In a field study of an African American ghetto community, Carol Stack (1998) found some creative adaptations to unhealthy environmental conditions. Relatives and intimate friends shared money, child care, food, and housing to meet each other's needs in times of crisis. In this example, the notion of family is expanded to include a network of people who provide mutual care. On the flip side, when someone does succeed in escaping the slum, close friends and relatives lean on the person for support and contacts, and the person can get drawn back into the impoverished networks. So the same networks can be both supportive and entrapping.

The issue of how poverty affects children who grow up in that environment has been studied through longitudinal studies that trace the same individuals for several decades. Some of the strategies for this type of research and some of the key findings are reported in the next "How Do We Know?" on page 328.

Figure 10.1 Percentage of All Births That Were to Unmarried Women, by Race and Hispanic Origin, Selected Years, 1960–2005*

Source: Data for 1960–1998 from National Center for Health Statistics. *Health, United States 2002 With Chartbook on Trends in the Health of Americans.* Hyattsville, MD: 2002. Table 9; Data for 2000 from Martin, J. A., Hamilton, B. E., Ventura, S. J., Menacker, F., & Park, M. M. Births: Final data for 2000. *National Vital Statistics Reports, 50*(5). Hyattsville, MD: National Center for Health Statistics. 2002. Table 17; Data for 2001 from Martin, J. A., Hamilton, B. E., Ventura, S. J., Menacker, F., Park, M. M., & Sutton, P. D. Births: Final data for 2001. *National Vital Statistics Reports, 51*(2). Hyattsville, MD: National Center for Health Statistics. 2002. Table 17; Data for 2002 from Martin, J. A., Hamilton, B. E., Sutton, P. D., Ventura, S. J., Menacker, F., & Munson, M. L. Births: Final data for 2002. *National Vital Statistics Reports, 52*(10). Hyattsville, MD: National Center for Health Statistics. 2003. Table 17; Data for 2003 from Martin, J. A., Hamilton, B. E., Sutton, P. D., et al. (2005). Births: Final data for 2003. *National Vital Statistics Reports, 54*(2). Hyattsville, MD: National Center for Health Statistics. Tables 13, 14, and 17. http://www.cdc.gov/nchs/data/nvsr/nvsr54/nvsr54_02.pdf; Data for 2004 from Martin, J. A., Hamilton, B. E., Sutton, P. D., et al. (2006). Births: Final data for 2004. *National Vital Statistics Reports, 55*(1). Hyattsville, MD: National Center for Health Statistics. Table 18. http://www.cdc.gov/nchs/data/nvsr/nvsr55/nvsr55_01.pdf; Preliminary data for 2005 from Hamilton, B. E., Martin, J. A., & Ventura, S. J. (2006). Births: Preliminary data for 2005. *National Vital Statistics Reports, 55.* Hyattsville, MD: National Center for Health Statistics. Table 1. http://ww.cdc.gov/nchs/products/pubs/pubd/hestats/prelimbirths05/prelimbirths05.htm#ref02.

*2005 estimates were based on preliminary data. The 2005 percentage for Native Americans was 58.4. For non-Hispanic blacks, data points between 1980 and 1985, 1985 and 1990, and 1990 and 1995 were estimated, which accounts for the straight trend line.

Dual-Worker Families

A different kind of economic influence can be seen in dual-career marriages. Two incomes may relieve economic strain on a household, but family life may be quite complicated. Browse through the checkout-line magazine racks next time you are in a grocery store. Note the number of articles offering advice on how to cope with stress and overload or how to budget time, cook meals in minutes, rise to the top, and "make it" together. Stress, role conflict, and work overload are common, but most couples are aware of these strains and have chosen to combine marriage, sometimes children, and the intense involvement required by a career.

With the stress found in juggling the competing homework responsibilities, some women and men are finding that work provides a haven from their hectic, sometimes unrewarding home life. Women are tending to spend more time at work, but men are not spending more time at home to balance the equation (Hochschild 1997; Schneider and Waite 2005).

In many industrialized societies, government and industry support dual-career families with various family-friendly policies: readily available child care facilities, parenting leaves for childbirth and illness, and flexible work hours or telecommuting (working from one's home). For

example, the U.S. government passed the Family and Medical Leave Act in 1993, allowing for 12 weeks of unpaid leave for the birth of a baby or care of a newborn, foster care or adoption, serious health issues in the immediate

When both parents have full-time jobs, one solution to the stress is to hire other people to do some of the familial jobs, including care of children. Many people who use child care feel it has been very good for the children, and studies confirm this—depending on the quality of the care agency.

How Do We Know?

Hitting Hard Times: Income Change and Children

By Susan St. John-Jarvis

Do brief spells of poverty put children at-risk for future unemployment? Is poverty in later childhood more, or perhaps less detrimental than in early childhood? How do family financial setbacks impact the future lives of children?

Family economic circumstances change over time. Jobs losses are common. Divorces, often costly, occur. There are illnesses or injuries that may cause temporary or long-term financial stresses for families, and at times, families move upward out of poverty. What if children with similar biographies (personal circumstances) could be tracked? Could researchers accurately identify those children most at risk?

A team of researchers tackled the challenge of developing new ways to factor in the complexities of the family as an economic unit and the children at different developmental stages. Beginning with data from a national longitudinal study (a study done over time), the Panel Study of Income Dynamics (PSID) analyzed data on a sample of 1,070 children (Wagmiller, Kuang, Aber, Lennon, and Alberti 2006).

Longitudinal study panels, such as the PSID, are great existing data sources for researchers. This panel was begun in 1968. The original PSID participants, their children, or the next closest surviving household members were followed with yearly interviews. At the time of the Michigan study, the PSID panel study maintained data on 63,453 individuals. Access to this huge database, maintained at the University of Michigan, is free, including downloadable data sets. Visit the site at http://psidonline.isr.umich.edu/.

The researchers developed a new research method that incorporates children with similar exposure and personal circumstances (such as family and economic background, race, and ethnicity) into classifications identifying children by similar family patterns and childhood experiences. This "finite mixture model" addresses the complexities of family life more completely than a snapshot of a family's socioeconomic status at the time of a single interview or assessment.

The researchers hope that children's histories of economic disadvantage will suggest timing and types of intervention that may improve high school completion rates, postsecondary academic success, and employment in early adulthood. For example, they found economic disadvantage to be more harmful in early childhood rather than later childhood. While families are "moving out of poverty" (upward mobility), younger children continue to be more at risk than children who experienced poverty only in later childhood. One possible explanation is that social networks are developed before later childhood and become social capital for future education or employment. (Surprisingly, moving into poverty may be stressful for parents, but it may be less harmful to children if it occurs in late childhood.)

The study raises many questions for future investigation. What can be learned about the length of time children experience poverty as compared to the persistent poor or the never poor? Do children in minority families experience difference outcomes, due to variations in family structure? What factors led to different experiences and outcomes for siblings in families with major financial setbacks?

In times of severely limited funding, how can agencies allocate funds to maximize improvement of high school graduation and young adult employment rates? Ideally, the family as a social institution is a collective entity that should meet both the children's needs for productive lives and society's need for productive adults. On the macro level, understanding the complexities of early and late childhood experiences could lead to community or national policies that actually improve high school completion rates and increase early adulthood employment. Finding solutions first involves accurate understanding of the problem, and longitudinal panel studies are valuable approaches to help us know how poverty actually affects children of poverty over their lives.

family, or serious medical conditions of the employee (U.S. Office of Personnel Management 2007). However, many corporations in the United States have been slow to respond to dual-career family needs. Company-sponsored day care and paternity leave are still rare. A few businesses are experimenting with family-friendly policies such as flextime, allowing individuals to schedule their own work hours within certain time frames, and job sharing, allowing individuals to split a job, with one family member working in the morning and the other in the afternoon.

Family is a diverse and complex social institution. It interacts with other institutions and in some ways reinforces them. Families prepare the next generation. Adult family members socialize children and teach national loyalty, and they mentor children on the use of money as well as reading, math, and social studies. Families pray together and talk as families about what happens after death. They provide care of disabled, infirm, or sick members. As a basic institution, the family plays a role in the vitality of the entire nation. So it should not be surprising that at the macro level, many national and global policy decisions concern how to strengthen the family.

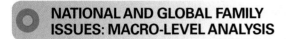

NATIONAL AND GLOBAL FAMILY ISSUES: MACRO-LEVEL ANALYSIS

The most effective way to explore macro-level issues pertaining to families is to explore policy matters that affect the family or that are intended to strengthen families. After exploring issues of national concern—teen pregnancies, cohabitation, homosexual relationships, and divorce—we look at some global trends in marriage and family life.

Teen Pregnancies and Their Consequences

Why did the news of 16-year-old Jamie Lynn Spears's pregnancy make such a splash in newspapers across the country? Perhaps because high rates of premarital sex, teenage pregnancy, and teen marriage are ongoing concerns in the United States (Luby 2007), as well as Canada and many other countries. These are national, macro-level issues because the stability of families is critical to a nation, and early pregnancy and marriage pressure governments to provide support for unstable single-parent units.

In the United States, about one third of all births in recent years have been to unmarried women. Of teenagers who become pregnant, 26% have abortions, 22% marry before childbirth, and 52% have out-of-wedlock births, resulting in single-parent families (Eshleman and Bulcroft 2006). The rate of births to teenagers in the United States is among the highest in the world at 45.9 births per 1,000 females in the 15-to-19 age group (Health in Schools 2002), but overall rates have been dropping slowly since 1991, with a 45% drop for African American teens.

Why are U.S. rates of premarital sex and teen pregnancy so high? One variable stands out: The United States is less open than most countries (excluding Muslim societies) about sexual matters, reducing the amount of information teens receive about sex. In addition, compared to other developed countries, teens in the United States have more restrictions on obtaining contraception, higher costs for contraception, and no national health care to help cover costs. High religiosity among some segments of American society results in less open discussion about sex and less contraceptive education provided in schools.

Combine these factors with explicit portrayals of sex in the media, peer pressures, sexual desire, and lack of contraception, and we have a perfect recipe for high rates of teen pregnancy. In sum, restrictive attitudes toward sex education

and an economically deprived underclass make teenage pregnancy more likely. However, education programs in some schools have helped reduce rates.

Sex outside of marriage is far less alarming to policymakers around the world than births occurring without an adequate supportive unit of care for the mother and child—usually (but not always) defined as marriage. Thus, teen pregnancy is not just a North American problem. In a study of 37 countries, those with low teenage birth rates had the following characteristics:

1. high levels of socioeconomic modernization,
2. openness about discussing sex,
3. relatively low levels of inequality in the society as measured by family income,
4. an older minimum legal age for marriage,
5. awareness of the dangers of sexually transmitted diseases, and
6. a growing economy, which makes young women more optimistic about their futures (Sommerfeld 2002).

The number of teens who are sexually active is highest among Swedish and Danish adolescents. England, France, Netherlands, and the United States have similar and somewhat lower rates. Despite this, the failure to use contraceptives is much higher among U.S. teenage girls at 20% (some reports indicate higher contraception usage; Kaiser Family Foundation 2005b), compared with 4% in Britain, 6.5% in Sweden, and 13% in Canada (Sommerfeld 2002).

Teenage parents and their children face extreme difficulties in industrial societies. Often, neither parent has finished high school or developed the skills to earn a living wage. Thus, parents cannot provide for health care, adequate nutrition, household and family stability, or other needs of their children. Births outside marriage result in less education for mother and child and less prestigious and more dead-end jobs. The resulting children often have poor test scores, grade retention, early sexual activity, and problem behaviors such as truancy and delinquency. Thus, we see that within our social world, factors at the macro level, such as contraceptive availability or cultural attitudes about discussing sex, influence pregnancy rates among teens. In turn, decisions about sexual behavior by individual teens have consequences for the macro-level systems, such as the welfare system and social services at the national, institutional, and local levels.

Because teenage families are so fragile, the result can be poorly socialized children, unhappy adults whose needs are not being met, and demands on taxpayers to provide support to these weak units and these vulnerable children. It is not surprising that policies to deter teen pregnancies are a public issue for many nations.

Counting teens and others who become pregnant, it is estimated that 60% of pregnancies are unplanned. The unprepared woman has three choices: to become a parent, to have an abortion, or to put the baby up for adoption (Heritage House

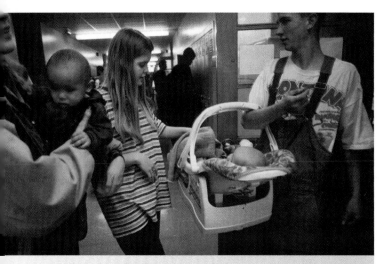

The rate of teen births in the United States is one of the highest in the world, despite more conservative attitudes toward premarital sex. At Lincoln High School, Jill Crisler hands her son, Trenton, off to the father, Luke, who is staying involved with the raising of his son. Still, trying to raise a child while still in high school is a huge challenge.

Table 10.4	**Cohabiting Households in the United States, 1980–2005**
1980	1,589,000
1985	1,983,000
1990	2,856,000
1995	3,668,000
2000	5,475,768
2006	6,235,000

Source: U.S. Census Bureau 2006a.

'76 1998). The controversy over which choice is right for which woman has resulted in heated debate, and the government has in some cases passed laws regarding abortion. The debate is usually whether to provide inexpensive birth control, allow abortion, or deter teenage pregnancy by making the costs for sexual activity very high. In the United States, there is little consensus about what the individual woman making the decision at the micro level should do, about how abortions or adoptions affect the community, or about which policies at the macro level would best strengthen families.

Thinking Sociologically

Some people think that making birth control, especially condoms, readily available will bring down teen pregnancy rates. Others argue that making birth control available would provide an enticement or an invitation to sexual experimentation at a young age and would undermine strong families. What is your view and why?

Cohabitation

Another family issue is *cohabitation*—living together in a sexual relationship without marriage. Cohabitation is a significant macro-level trend in many European and North American countries, and it has been the norm in many other countries. In the United States, the number of unmarried

couples living together doubled in the 1990s, from 2.9 million in 1990 to more than 6.2 million in 2006 (U.S. Census Bureau 2006a). The number of "unmarried households" has been rising dramatically for several decades. Between 1960 and 2000, the increase was 10-fold, with 10 million people (8% of U.S. couple households) living with a heterosexual partner. Two thirds of married couples lived together for an average of two years before marriage (Jayson 2005b).

Is cohabitation replacing dating? Some argue that a newly emerging pattern for some young adults between 25 and 34 is serial cohabitation (Harms 2000; Jayson 2005a). As Table 10.4 shows, the increases in cohabiting households (same-sex and different-sex couples) in the United States over 20 years are dramatic.

Why do heterosexual couples decide to cohabit? Cohabitors cite a number of reasons:

- rejection of the superficial dating game,
- a desire to enter more meaningful relationships with increased intimacy but with freedom to leave the union,
- emotional satisfaction and reduced loneliness,
- a chance to clarify what individuals want in a relationship and try out a relationship before permanent commitment,
- financial benefits of sharing living quarters, and
- sexual gratification (the latter cited more often by men than women) and some protection against disease by having one partner (Bumpass and Lu 2000; Lamanna and Riedmann 2003).

For some, cohabitation is part of the mate-selection process. In 1987, 33% of the adult population between the ages of 19 and 44 had cohabited at some point, and by 2000, that percentage had increased to 41%. However, at any given point in time, only about 7% of the population in the United States is cohabiting (Benokraitis 2004). Countries with the highest percentage of women between 20 and 24 years in cohabiting relationships include Sweden (77%), New Zealand (67%), Austria (64%), France (63%),

Netherlands and Norway (each 57%), and Canada (46%) (United Nations 2003). Latin American and Caribbean surveys have indicated that more than one in four women between the ages of 15 and 49 are in relationships they call consensual unions, living together without official sanction. However, such women typically have far less legal protection than European women during or after such unions. The rates of cohabitation seem to be declining in many African countries, where the rates are often below 15% of women (United Nations 2003).

Marriage versus cohabitation rates and reasons vary significantly by ethnicity. For whites in the United States, cohabitation is often a precursor to marriage. For African Americans, it may be an alternative to marriage. Financial problems encourage cohabitation in African American families because many African American men avoid marriage if they do not think they can support a family and fulfill the breadwinner role. In 2000, 68% of Hispanic families were married-couple households, compared with 83% of white households and 48% of African American households (Fields and Casper 2001). Although childbearing increases the chance of marriage, it is a much stronger impetus for white than for black cohabitors.

We might assume that cohabiting would allow couples to make more realistic decisions about entering permanent relationships. However, studies show little relationship between cohabitation and ensuing marital satisfaction, emotional closeness, sharing of roles, or amount of conflict. Some argue that this is because the relationship is not grounded in a bargain created by a marriage contract. In fact, some cohabitors experience more partner abuse, infidelity, and less family assistance should things go wrong (Waite and Gallagher 2000). Some studies from Canada, Sweden, and the United States have even found evidence of lower quality marriages, lower commitment, and greater likelihood of divorce among those who cohabited before marriage (Harms 2000; Waite and Gallagher 2000). The next "Sociology in Your Social World" discusses some reasons why cohabiting couples may have higher divorce rates than those who have not lived together prior to marriage.

Thinking Sociologically

First, read "Sociology in Your Social World." How do you evaluate the argument that cohabitation is a threat to the stability of marriages? Is reducing cohabitation an effective step to strengthening marriage?

Social analysts such as Waite and Gallagher (2000) and various scholars belonging to the conservative Council on Families in America believe that cohabitation is a threat to the stability of society. The council believes that the government should create more enticements to marry (e.g., tax breaks) and that the society should make cohabitation less acceptable and more stigmatized. This, they believe, would make for a stronger family system.

Same-Sex Relationships and Civil Unions

A hotly debated macro-level policy matter concerning the family is homosexuality. As same-sex relationships become more widely acknowledged in the Western world, many gay and lesbian couples are living together openly as families. Denmark was the first country to recognize same-sex unions in 1989 and grant legal rights to couples, and many countries have followed. The Netherlands, in 2001, was the first country to allow same-sex marriages. The 2000 U.S. Census reports 601,209 declared gay or lesbian households, but most scholars acknowledge that this is probably a substantial underreporting because of the stigma in many communities of reporting that one is homosexual (Smith and Gates 2001). Estimates are that 99.3% of all counties in the United States have same-sex couples, and about 3.1 million people live in same-sex relationships. One in three lesbian couples and one in five gay male couples are raising children (Human Rights Campaign 2003). In some places, these unions are officially recognized by state or religious organizations, but recognition is controversial at the national level. The Hawaiian Supreme Court ruled in 1993 that prohibitions against same-sex marriages are discriminatory. Alaska followed with a similar ruling a few years later. Vermont, spurred by a unanimous state Supreme Court ruling, passed a law in 2000 allowing civil unions for gays and lesbians. Other states have followed with similar contract options: Connecticut in 2005, New Jersey in 2007, and New Hampshire and Oregon in 2008 (Human Rights Campaign 2008).

However, many religious groups believe homosexuality is unacceptable, condemn it in a variety of ways, and deny the right to legal marriage (Laythe, Finkel, and Kirkpatrick 2001). More recently, the citizens of Hawaii and Alaska voted to amend their state constitutions so that marriage is limited to legal unions between a man and a woman. Furthermore, as of 2008, 44 states had passed laws to not recognize same-sex marriages or civil unions contracted in other states as legally binding, although many of those are being challenged for constitutionality. Marriage was approved for gays and lesbians in Massachusetts in 2004, although opponents have been trying to pass legislation reversing this pattern. The California legislature had come close to legalization of same-sex marriage, and then the California Supreme Court opened the door with a ruling on May 16, 2008, declaring that the state's existing ban on such marriages is unconstitutional. Even heartland

Sociology in Your Social World

Cohabiting: Facts and Fiction

It seems reasonable—and many people believe—that if a couple lives together before marriage, they are more likely to have a marriage that lasts. Yet, research shows that not all cohabiting unions are the same. Some sociologists believe that cohabitation can be a pathway to marriage, the traditional understanding (Smock 2004). Recent researchers, however, suggest that cohabitation in contemporary times has primarily become a stage of dating instead of a path to marriage (Sassler and Miller forthcoming).

Many cohabiting couples never marry. It is more common for a cohabiting couple to have a child together than it is for them to marry (Cherlin 2005). However, some cohabiting couples do choose to marry. Those who had not talked about the possibility of marriage before moving in together (cohabitation as a stage of dating) are more likely to divorce than couples who saw cohabitation as a step to marriage or couples who did not cohabit prior to marriage.

The association between cohabitation and higher risk of divorce has intrigued researchers, and several attempts have been made to explain the pattern. Linda Waite and Maggie Gallagher (2000) have offered an interesting set of data and an intriguing interpretation to explain divorce among cohabitors. They point out that marriage has many benefits. Married people have better physical and mental health, have more frequent and more satisfying sex, and are substantially better off financially by the time of retirement than single people (they have more than double the money invested per person). Interestingly, the same benefits do not accrue to people who cohabit.

Much of this is because marriage links two people together in a way that makes them responsible to each other. If one smokes or drinks excessively, the partner has the right to complain about it—to essentially nag that person into better health patterns—because one partner's health has a direct impact on the other's and vice versa. Likewise, if one partner likes to spend money freely on vacations, the more frugal person is likely to restrain the spending habits of the spendthrift.

This is acceptable because their financial futures are closely intertwined. As each person restrains the habits of the other, the couple is likely to end up with more savings. As a result, at the end of their careers, the couple is likely to have more money put away for retirement. Also, people tend to be more adjusted when they have unqualified and unambiguous emotional support from another person whose life is inextricably tied to their own.

Couples who cohabit without intending to marry are more likely to keep their finances separate and their options open. Moreover, they do not feel as if they have the right to nag the other person about health habits or finances. Their bond is emotional, but their actions toward one another do not always show that they see their futures as being intertwined. Thus, many of the advantages that come with marriage are lost. According to Waite and Gallagher (2000), when a cohabiting couple does marry, a partner may be shocked to find the other person beginning to nag them or to restrain their spending habits. The relationship is quite different, and partners are irritated by the changed behavior. So cohabitation does not always tell us what life with this other person will be like, if the intent to marry was not present from the outset.

The link between cohabitation and marriage is considerably complex. For individuals who cohabit as an alternative to marriage or as a path to marriage, relationships can be fulfilling, stable, and lifelong. However, for those who cohabit without considering marriage before moving in, relationships are less likely to result in marriage and more likely to end in divorce if they do marry. We also must consider factors that influence an individual's propensity to marry and to cohabit to make causal arguments. Older individuals, those who are religious, and those who hold traditional gender roles are all more likely to enter into marriages without cohabiting first. They are also less likely to get divorced once married. Our understanding of how dating, cohabitation, and marriage are changing will continue to be complicated as the shape of families changes.

states like Iowa (in 2007) have had court rulings that at least temporally permitted same-sex marriage, but the court battles continue (Dolan 2008; Ontario Consultants on Religious Tolerance 2008).

Despite the mixed messages on civil unions and same-sex marriages, polls in the United States show increased public acceptance of homosexuality as well as a rise in support of marriage benefits and civil rights to gay and lesbian couples. About 60% believe gay and lesbian couples should have the same rights as heterosexual married couples. The United States is evenly split on allowing gay and lesbian couples to legally form civil unions. About 52% of the public accept homosexuality as a legitimate lifestyle (Human Rights Campaign 2003), while 90% support equal opportunity for homosexuals on the job (Johnson 2005). Yet in 2003, it was still legal in 36 states to fire someone based on their sexuality (Human Rights Campaign 2003). In the mass media, inclusion of gay characters and even themes in films such as *Brokeback Mountain* (2005) and *Innocent* (2005), plus television features such as *Ellen* and *Will and Grace,* show popular culture's evolution in acceptance of portraying homosexuality.

In many other countries, same-sex couples are gaining rights that are similar to those of a heterosexual married couple. The Netherlands was the first to approve such marriages in 2001, followed shortly thereafter by Belgium. When Canada approved gay and lesbian marriages in 2005, 8 out of the 10 Canadian provinces had already approved such policies. Spain approved same-sex marriage in 2005, and South Africa followed in 2006. Denmark, France, Germany, Iceland, Norway, Sweden, and Britain offer a legal status similar to Vermont's civil unions, entailing most of the privileges of marriage, such as inheritance rights, health benefits, and family-only visitation rights in hospitals or prisons. In most of these countries, the new laws are controversial and have been challenged in court, but attitudes in Europe seem to be gradually shifting toward more acceptance of same-sex unions (Ontario Consultants on Religious Tolerance 2005).

Those who favor allowing gay and lesbian marriages claim that supportive lifelong dyadic relationships are good for individuals and good for society. They see the fact that homosexuals want stable socially sanctioned relationships as an encouraging sign about how important the family is to society and how homosexuals want to fit in. Moreover, because many societies offer tax benefits, insurance coverage, and other privileges to married couples, the denial of marriage on the basis of one's gender attraction is seen as discriminatory and may be costly to partners who are denied rights.

Those opposed insist that marriage has been a function of the church, temple, and mosque for centuries. None of the religious traditions have historically recognized

Former talk show host Rosie O'Donnell and her longtime girlfriend, Kelli Carpenter, walk down the main steps of San Francisco's City Hall after they tied the knot. This happened during a short window of time in 2004 when San Francisco allowed same-sex marriages, despite state laws to the contrary.

gay relationships as legitimate, although a few are doing so now. Some opponents appeal to biology with the assertion that marriage is a legitimate way to propagate the species. Because homosexual unions do not serve this purpose, they do not serve the society, according to this view.

Divorce—Contract Breaking

Is the family breaking down? Is it relevant in today's world? Although most cultures extol the virtues of family life, the reality is that not all partnerships work. Support is not forthcoming for the partner, trust is violated, and relationships

A security guard checks people for weapons before they board Miami-Dade County's Family Division Circuit Court bus, which was dubbed "The Divorce Bus." This mobile courtroom was the innovation of a county judge who wanted to service the needs of citizens in the area while a county courtroom was closed for several months for renovation. More than two dozen uncontested divorce cases were heard in fewer than 45 minutes. This does seem to give new meaning to the idea of divorce made convenient.

deteriorate. So we cannot discuss family life without also recognizing the often painful side of family life that results in contract breaking.

Some commentators view divorce rates as evidence that the family is deteriorating. They see enormous problems created by divorce. There are costs to adults who suffer guilt and failure, to children from divided homes, and to the society that does not have the stabilizing force of intact lifelong partnerships. Many children around the world are raised without both natural parents present. For example, nearly half of all U.S. children today live at least part of their lives in single-parent families.

Others argue that marriage is not so much breaking down as adapting to a different kind of social system. They claim that the family of the 1950s, depicted in television shows such as *Leave It to Beaver, Ozzie and Harriet,* and *Father Knows Best* as white, middle-class, and suburban, would be ill-suited to the societies we have today. Indeed, more people today express satisfaction with marriage than at any previous time period, and there are more golden (50-year) wedding anniversaries now than ever before (Gelles 1995; Kain 1990). Even late in the 19th century, the average length of a marriage

was only 13 years—mostly because life expectancy was so short. "Til death do us part" was not such a long time then as it is today, when average life expectancy is in the late 70s (Coontz 2005).

Thinking Sociologically

It is often easy to identify micro-level issues of divorce, for they may be rooted in the personalities and relationship factors of the individuals. Talk with friends and family who have divorced about micro-level factors that contributed. Now, based on the discussion above, make a list of meso-level factors (e.g., religious, economic, legal, educational) that contribute to divorce rates or reduce them.

Although some contributing factors for divorce are social, others are very personal. One reason for divorce is family violence. Domestic abuse takes many forms: emotional abuse, denial and blame, intimidation, coercion or threats, use of power, isolation, using children as pawns, and economic abuse—including withholding of funds (Mayo Clinic 2007; Straus, Gelles, and Steinmetz 2006). Children are sometimes the unwitting victims of abuse— beaten, bullied, abused, raped, targeted by predators, and neglected. The assault rate for children is over two times as high as the rate for the general population, 15.5 children per 1,000 (Finkelhor 2008). The stress on the family when violence is present means the family is not fulfilling its functions of security and belonging. Mothers may sometimes endure the pain themselves, especially if they feel they are trapped with no alternatives, but the same woman may take action when it is her child who suffers. No wonder families experiencing domestic abuse often end up with a divorce.

If we grant that not everyone is temperamentally suited to sustain a nurturing marriage for 50 years, and if we acknowledge that people do change over time, what would be an acceptable divorce rate for our society—5% of all marriages? 20%? 40%? This is difficult for governments to decide, but many people feel that the current rate, someplace between 45 and 50% of all marriages (3.6% per 1,000 people in 2005), is too high (Ahrons 2004; Divorce Magazine 2008). When people say that more than half of today's marriages will end in divorce, they are pointing out that with upward divorce trends, by the time people now in their 20s reach their 70s, the rates could be 50 to 55%. However, it is also possible that such predictions will not come true. We know that social predictions can become self-negating as people and societies change their behaviors and their policies. Still, the trend is long and strong in an upward direction (Coontz 2005).

One reason for the increases in the U.S. divorce rate in the past 35 years is a policy change: no-fault divorce laws. For centuries in North America, one had to prove that the other party was in breach of contract. Marriage was a lifelong contract that could only be severed by one party having violated the terms of the contract. Each state spelled out those acts that were so odious that they justified ending such a sacred vow. Even then, if both parties had done something wrong (he was an adulterer, but she did not clean the house and was therefore in "neglect of duty"), the judge was obligated to rule that because they both violated the contract, the divorce would be denied. This resulted in ugly and contested divorces and in people being forced to live together in unloving, non-nurturing relationships.

In 1970, the state of California was the first to initiate no-fault divorce wherein a couple could end a marriage without proving that the other person was in breach of contract. A bilateral no-fault divorce (sometimes called *dissolution*) requires both parties to agree that they want out of the marriage. If they agree to the terms of settlement (child custody, child visitation rights, split in property, and so forth), the marriage can be dissolved (Gilchrist 2003). A second form, unilateral no-fault divorce, allows one person to insist that the marriage features irreconcilable differences—the two do not have to agree. Many women feel this arrangement protects vulnerable women from staying in an unloving relationship. They do not have to give up everything to get him to sign the agreement.

All this makes divorce much easier to obtain. Some critics believe this ease has led to a *divorce culture*—a society in which people assume that marriages are fragile rather than assuming that marriages are for life (a *marriage culture*). This raises the following questions: To what extent are divorces being sought for the slightest offense? Is this a chronic problem or a highly atypical pattern? Also, is divorce really a problem? Does it have lasting consequences?

Divorce and Its Social Consequences

The highest rates of divorce in countries of the world are among young couples. Marriages that occur at later ages have lower divorce rates. In the United States, the highest rates are for women in their teens and men between 20 and 24. The rate of divorce has leveled off and even dropped since the high mark in 1981, as shown in Table 10.5.

The emotional aspects of divorce are for many the most difficult. Divorce is often seen as failure, rejection, even punishment. Moreover, a divorce often involves a splitting with family and many close friends, with one's church, mosque, or synagogue, and from other social contexts in which one is known as part of a couple (Amato 2000). No wonder divorce is so wrenching. Unlike simple societies,

Table 10.5	How the U.S. Divorce Rate in 2000 Compared With Previous Decades
Year	Divorces per 1,000 Population
1950	2.6
1960	2.2
1970	3.5
1980	5.2
1981	5.3 (highest rate)
1990	4.7
2000	4.1
2006	3.6

Source: U.S. Census Bureau 2008:Table 77.

most modern societies have no ready mechanism for absorbing people back into stable social units such as clans.

Adjustment to divorced status varies by gender: Men typically have a harder time emotionally adjusting to singlehood or divorce than women. Divorced men must often leave not only their wives but their children, and whereas many women have support networks, fewer men have developed or sustained friendships outside of marriage. Finances, on the other hand, are a bigger problem for divorced women than for men, especially if women have children to support. One major study shows that women's standard of living declined 27% one year after divorce, whereas men's increased by 10% (Peterson 1996). Almost 40% of divorced and widowed women fall into poverty during the first five years of being single (McManus and DiPrete 2001).

There are also costs for children, one million of whom experience their parents' divorce each year in the United States. These children's lives are often turned upside down: Many children move to new houses and locations, leave one parent and friends, and make adjustments to new schools. Reduced resources can have negative consequences for children. Only about 41% of custodial parents receive the full child support payments due them. One fourth receive less than the specified amount, and one third receive none at all (U.S. Census Bureau 2006e).

Adjustment depends on the age of the children and the manner in which the parents handle the divorce. Children in families with high levels of marital conflict may be better off long-term if parents divorce (Booth and Amato 2001). If the children are torn between two feuding parents or if they are the focus of a bitter custody battle, they may suffer substantial scars. Many studies indicate divorce lowers the well-being of children in the short-term, affecting school achievement, peer relationships, and behavior. However, more important may be the long-term or lasting effects on their achievement and quality of life as these children become adults (Amato and Sobolewski 2001). The studies offer quite variable findings on this. One study that followed children of divorce for 15 years showed that through adolescence and into adulthood, many children continue to feel anxious and have fears, anger, and guilt (Sun 2001; Wallerstein and Blakeslee 2004). Adults may experience depression, lower levels of life satisfaction, lower marital quality and stability, more frequent divorce, poorer relationships with parents, poorer physical health, and lower educational attainment, income, and occupational prestige (Eshleman and Bulcroft 2006). Other studies suggest that later in life, individuals whose parents divorced during their childhood have a higher probability of teen marriage, divorce, peer problems, delinquency, truancy, and depression (Chase-Lansdale, Cherlin, and Kierman 1995; Newman and Grauerholz 2002).

On the other hand, some studies find that children who are well-adjusted to begin with have an easier time with divorce, especially if they can remain in their home and in their familiar school, with both parents part of their lives, and if they maintain their friendship networks. Grandparents, too, can provide stability during these traumatic times. For instance, Ahrons (2004) found that adults whose parents were divorced are actually very well-adjusted and happy. She found no general long-term negative consequences of parental divorce in her extensive longitudinal study that traced people into their middle years. About 79% of her respondents said their parents' decision to divorce was a good one, and 78% indicated that they were not affected by the divorce. The key, she found, is the nature of the postdivorce relationships. Large numbers of divorced partners have very civil relationships and continue to cooperate and collaborate on behalf of the children. In these cases, there are few, if any, long-term wounds.

Thinking Sociologically

Would making it harder to get a divorce create stronger and healthier families? Would it create more stable but less healthy and nurturing families? If you were making divorce policies, what would you do? What are the positive and negative aspects of your policy?

Global Family Patterns and Policies

Family systems around the world are changing in similar ways, pushed by industrialization and urbanization, by migration to new countries or refugee status, by changing kinship and occupational structures, and by influences from outside the family. The most striking changes include free choice of spouse, more equal status for women, equal rights in divorce, neolocal residency (when partners in a married couple live separate from either set of parents), bilateral kinship systems (tracing lineage through both parents), and pressures for individual equality (Sado and Bayer 2001). However, countermovements in some parts of the world call for strengthening of marriage through modesty of women, separation of the sexes (in both public and private spheres), and rejection of high divorce rates and other Western practices.

Global forces, such as ethnic holocausts that create refugees, can strain and destroy families. This is a scene of refugees at a camp called Centro 24 de Julho in Mopeia Sede, Mozambique.

National policies that limit availability of birth control and knowledge about family planning affect the economic circumstances of families that are forced to raise many children. One result is an increase in out-of-wedlock births, which creates more single-parent families. Likewise, as individuals and couples around the world make decisions such as choosing a spouse based on love, rejecting multiple wives, or establishing a more egalitarian family, the collective impact may rock the foundations of the larger society. Because legislatures make policies to support families or to influence family decisions such as fertility rates, the interaction between policymakers and social scientists can lead to laws based on better information and more comprehensive analysis of possible consequences. This is part of the public contribution of applied sociology—providing accurate information and analysis for wise public policy.

Family life, which seems so personal and intimate, is actually linked to global patterns. Global aid is activated when drought, famine, or other disasters affects communities and a country is not able to provide for families. In such cases, international organizations such as the United Nations, Doctors without Borders, Oxfam, and the Red Cross mobilize to support families in crises. Support varies from feeding starving children to opposing the slavery that occurs when parents are reduced to selling their children to survive. International crises can lead to war, perhaps removing the main breadwinner from the family or taking the life of a son or daughter who was drafted to fight. Homes and cultivated fields may be destroyed and the families forced into refugee status.

Do marriage and divorce rates indicate the family is in crisis? To answer these questions, we need information on current patterns, historical trend lines, and patterns in other parts of the world. The next "Sociology Around the World" provides cross-cultural data on marriage and divorce ratios.

Marriage, Divorce, and Social Policies

In an effort to strengthen marriages and reduce divorce rates, should countries make divorce more difficult to obtain? All the 50 U.S. states now have no-fault provisions based on "irreconcilable differences" or "irreconcilable breakdown of the marriage" (Aulette 2002; Gelles 1995). The conservative U.S. organization, Council on Families in America, has argued that the United States should go back to fault divorce to make it less easy to end a marriage in this divorce culture. They argue that many couples enter marriages assuming that the marriage will probably not last. An assumption of impermanence is no way to begin a marriage, they believe, insisting that pro-family policies promote stability and are a precursor to healthy relationships (Coontz 1997; Hunter College Women's Studies Collective 2005; Popenoe, Elshtain, and Blankenhorn 1996). Other scholars think that making the divorce process more restrictive would leave many women in highly vulnerable positions in relationships with abusive men, and while such a strategy may create more marriages that stay together, it would not necessarily create healthy ones. Healthy marriages are what help the society, not unhappy ones, say the defenders of no-fault divorce.

Thinking Sociologically

Would it strengthen marriages to remove all no-fault divorce laws and return to a fault divorce where one member of the couple must prove that the other person was in breach of contract? Why or why not?

Yet another social policy proposal is to change the marriage contract itself. With the new Covenant Marriage Law implemented in Louisiana (1997), Arizona (1998), and Arkansas (2002), people can choose whether they want a standard marriage or an "upgraded" covenant marriage. If they opt for covenant marriage, premarital counseling is required before the wedding, a year of counseling is necessary before a fault divorce is permitted, and the availability of no-fault divorce is restricted by longer requirements of counseling (Laconte 1998; Nock 1999; Nock, Wright, and Sanchez 1999). Contracts mean marriages are less easily dissolved. "The Applied Sociologist at Work" discusses policies on covenant marriage.

We have been talking about a national trend (divorce rates) regarding an institution (the family) and the impact it has on individuals. Processes at the macro and meso levels affect the micro level of society, and decisions at the micro level (i.e., to dissolve a marriage) affect the community and the nation. The various levels of the social world are indeed interrelated in complex ways.

Sociology Around the World

Cross-Cultural Differences in Family Dissolution

Is the family breaking down around the world? Perhaps this is the wrong question. We may, instead, need to consider how the family copes with changing demands. Family conflict and disorganization occur when members of the family unit do not carry out roles expected of them by spouses, other family members, the community, or the society. This may be due to voluntary departure (divorce, separation, desertion), involuntary problems (illness or other catastrophe), a crisis caused by external events (death, war, depression), or failure to communicate role expectations and needs. Many of these role failures are a direct consequence of societal changes due to globalization. Once again, the social world model helps us understand macro-level trends and patterns that affect us in micro-level contexts.

Divorce is still very limited in some parts of the world, and it may be an option for only one gender. In some Arab countries, only the husband has the right to pronounce "I divorce thee" in front of a witness on three separate occasions, after which the divorce is complete. The wife returns, sometimes in disgrace, to her family of procreation, while the husband generally keeps the children in the patriarchal family and is free to take another wife. Despite this seemingly easy process, the divorce rate is comparatively low in most countries because family ties and allegiances are severely strained when divorces take place. Thus, informal pressures and cultural attitudes restrain tendencies to divorce.

Still, when family turmoil and conflict are too great to resolve or when the will to save the family disappears, the legal, civil, and religious ties of marriage may be broken. The methods for dissolving marriage ties vary, but most countries have some form of divorce. Table 10.6 compares marriage and divorce rates in selected industrial countries. Notice that while the divorce rate in the United States is quite high, the marriage rate is also high.

Table 10.6 Marriage and Divorce Ratios in Selected Countries, 1960–2002

Country	Marriages per 1,000 Persons in Population					Country	Divorces per 1,000 Persons in Population				
	1960	1970	1980	1990	2002		1960	1970	1980	1990	2002
United States	8.5	10.6	10.6	9.8	7.5	United States	2.2	3.5	5.2	4.7	3.9
Belgium	7.2	7.6	6.7	6.5	4.0	Belgium	0.5	0.7	1.5	2.0	4.0
						Canada	0.4	1.4	2.6	2.9	NA
Denmark	7.8	7.4	5.2	6.1	6.5	Denmark	1.5	1.9	2.7	2.7	6.5
France	7.0	7.8	6.2	5.1	4.6	France	0.7	0.8	1.5	1.9	4.6
Germany	9.4	7.3	5.9	6.5	4.6	Germany, Former West	0.8	1.2	1.6	1.9	4.6
Greece	7.0	7.7	6.5	5.9	5.5						
Ireland	5.5	7.0	6.4	5.1	5.1						
Italy	7.7	7.3	5.7	5.6	4.5	Italy	NA	NA	0.2	0.5	4.5
						Japan	0.7	0.9	1.2	1.3	5.8
Luxembourg	7.1	6.3	5.9	6.1	4.4	Luxembourg	0.5	0.6	1.6	2.0	4.4
Netherlands	7.8	9.5	6.4	6.4	5.0	Netherlands	0.5	0.8	1.8	1.9	5.0
Portugal	7.8	NA	7.4	7.3	5.1	Portugal	0.1	0.1	NA	0.9	5.1
Spain	7.7	7.3	5.9	5.7	5.0						
						Sweden	1.2	1.6	2.4	2.3	4.4
United Kingdom	7.5	8.5	7.4	6.5	5.1	United Kingdom	0.5	1.2	3.0	2.9	5.1

Source: United Nations 2003: Tables 23 and 25.

Note: NA = not available.

The Applied Sociologist at Work—Steven L. Nock

Covenant Marriage

Early in his career, Dr. Steven L. Nock, then professor of sociology at the University of Virginia, was interested in the impact of social stratification on American families.

His interest in families grew from a concern that family issues be incorporated into our thinking about the American class system. From this base of research, he became intrigued when several states instituted the new legislation—covenant marriages—to try to strengthen and stabilize marriages.

Nock realized that this legal innovation was the first time in history that individuals would be offered a choice regarding which system of laws would govern their marriages. He wanted to know who desires a more restrictive form of marriage—men or women, rich or poor, black or white, young or old? Furthermore, he wanted to determine whether government can predictably alter something like divorce rates through the actions of law.

Nock and his co-researchers conducted focus groups (a type of open-ended group interview) and interviews with a large number of state power brokers (legislators, governors, and other officials) about why the law was passed. They also interviewed those charged with implementing the law (court clerks, judges, clergy) and those charged with providing the mandatory counseling (marriage counselors, ministers). In addition, the researchers set up several rounds of interviews with a scientifically selected sample of covenant marriage and standard marriage couples. About 350 couples of each type were selected, and both partners in each marriage completed lengthy questionnaires at three points in the first few years of the marriage.

This policy is so new that there are virtually no data on its successes or failures. At the time of Dr. Nock's death in 2008, his colleagues were still analyzing the data and compiling results.

Writing his findings for policymakers, Nock had to understand the law and the state policies involved. Applied researchers must also be sensitive to the political and economic implications of the findings. (Will implementation require additional taxes? Will policies be acceptable to voters? Will they be possible given the existing system of laws in a state? Will they achieve the desired outcome?)

Applied research must be able to convince others that a policy or law will have a predictable consequence. The research must be understandable to the nonsociologist, and it must be done objectively, without any appearance of bias or preformed conclusions. Note that Nock had a policy agenda in his work: strengthening marriages and stabilizing families.

Because of his research, Nock was consulted by legislators and others involved in family policy decisions and passage of laws, especially when they were thinking about implementing covenant marriage in their state. While data about the policy are not yet definitive, Nock knew more about the debates and variations in covenant marriage law than perhaps anyone else in the country or world. His colleagues are working to maintain his research agenda and finish the data collection efforts he started. Nock's colleagues fully intend to release Nock's work. Thus, his impact on marriage and family research survives him. Regarding the challenges and the rewards of this work, Nock wrote this to us before he died:

I began my career in sociology with a desire to influence public policy and change social conditions. I saw the field of sociology as offering guidance to those seeking to change our society. My work on covenant marriage, and on marriage more generally, is slowly being incorporated into policy and thinking about policy. There is no doubt that people face many challenges in forming stable relationships in which to raise children. Anything that might help couples should be investigated. The work on covenant marriage takes a small step in this direction. This is one of the most rewarding aspects of my work. The other reward is the chance to collaborate with colleagues who share similar goals and objectives. Working with such valued colleagues is the most rewarding aspect of any research effort.

Note: Dr. Steven L. Nock did his undergraduate work at the University of Richmond, followed by a doctorate in sociology at the University of Massachusetts, Amherst. He worked at the University of Virginia until his death in 2008.

So What ?

Our happiest and saddest experiences are integrally intertwined with family. Family provides the foundation, the group through which individuals' needs are met. Societies depend on families as the unit through which to funnel services. It is the political, economic, health, educational, religious, and sexual base for most people. These are some of the reasons family is important to us. Despite those who lament the weakening of the family, the institution of family is here to stay. Its form may alter as it responds and adapts to societal changes, and other institutions will continue to take on functions formerly reserved for the family. Still, the family is an institution crucial to societal survival, and whatever the future holds, the family will adapt in response to changes in other parts of the social world. It is an institution that is sometimes vulnerable and needs support, but it is also a resilient institution—the way we partner and "make people" in any society.

The next three chapters continue to examine institutions and their interconnections. As children grow up and branch out from the embrace of the family, a social environment they experience is the local school. It is to education and schools that we turn next.

Key Points

What Have We Learned?

- Families are diverse entities at the micro level, having a wide range of configurations, but families also collectively serve as a core structure of society at the meso and macro levels. (See pp. 310–312.)

- The family is sometimes called the most basic unit of society, for it is a core unit of social pairing into groups (partner taking), a primary unit of procreation and socialization (people making), and so important that when it comes unglued (contract breaking), the whole social system may be threatened. (See p. 312.)

- Various theories—rational choice, symbolic interactionism, functionalism, conflict theory, and feminist theory—illuminate different aspects of family and help us understand conflicts, stressors, and functions of families. (See pp. 312–319.)

- At the micro level, people come together in partner-taking pairs, but the rules of partner taking (exogamy/endogamy, free choice/arranged marriage, polygamy/monogamy) are meso level rules. (See pp. 319–322.)

- Power within a partnership—including distribution of tasks and authority—is assigned through intimate

processes that are again largely controlled by rules imposed from another level in the social system. (See pp. 322–324.)

- "The family" is a stable pattern of social relationships and norms at the meso level. In short, it is an institution. (See pp. 324–325.)

- Like all institutions, the family is influenced by other institutions, but it is affected perhaps most obviously by the economy, as the impact on family of poverty and dual employment of partners illustrates. (See pp. 325–329.)

- At the macro level, nations and even global organizations try to establish policies that strengthen families. The issues that are of concern to at least some analysts are teen pregnancy, lack of sufficient support to single-parent and poor families, cohabitation patterns that seem a threat to family, same-sex households (including same-sex marriage), and contract breaking (divorce). (See pp. 329–337.)

- Policies to strengthen families include efforts to make divorce more difficult to obtain and the creation of new forms of marital contract (covenant marriages). (See p. 337.)

Contributing to Our Social World: What Can We Do?

At the Local Level: An ever-increasing number of undergraduate students live on or near campus with spouses, partners, and young (or even not-so-young) children. Yet, traditional college life remains oriented to the single, unattached individual student. Does your campus have a support group for married or partnered students, including those with children? If so, arrange to attend a meeting and work with members to help them meet the challenges associated with their family situation. If such a group does not exist, you might still be able to meet informally with students who are also parents and learn about their experiences and special problems.

At the Organizational or Institutional Level: Although the two-generation household remains the norm in the United States, many communities of recent immigrants live in extended family households, in which grandparents, parents, children, and possibly other relatives occupy the same home or apartment. Contact a faculty member on your campus who works with recent immigrants, or identify a local social service agency that serves such communities. Arrange an interview with a professional to discuss the challenges that these extended households face. Explore the possibility of working with a support group in these communities.

At the National and Global Levels: Select a family-related issue about which you feel strongly—pro or con: for example, covenant marriage, no-fault divorce options, or same-sex marriage policies. Find out what you can about the issue and about how it is treated in the laws of the United States or your state. Next, identify a member of the U.S. Congress, Senate, or your state legislature whose record indicates an interest in the issue. Then contact that person via letter or e-mail, stating your views and opening a dialog on the subject. International family law is a relatively new field that encompasses a wide range of global issues, including human rights, immigration policy, gender equity, adoption policies, and the rights of children. The Association of Family and Conciliation Courts is an advocacy organization specializing in international family law. Its Web site, at www.afccnet.org, includes information about the field and opportunities for volunteer work. Hofstra University maintains a resource site on international family law at http://people.hofstra.edu/lisa_a_spar/intlfam/intlfam .htm where you can learn more about the field.

Visit **www.pineforge.com/ballantine2study** for online activities, sample tests, and other helpful information. Select "Chapter 10: Family" for chapter-specific activities.

CHAPTER 11

Education

What Are We Learning?

In schools, students are learning a lot besides the three Rs, and sociologists have learned a great deal about what they are learning and the place of education within our social system. Even the settings in which learning occurs tell us something about what and how students learn.

Think About It . . .

Micro: What did you personally learn—both formally and informally—in school?

Micro: How do the role expectations of people in the schools—principals, teachers, students—affect the local climate and the learning that takes place in a school?

Meso: Do families help or hurt children's school achievement?

Macro: How is education changing in your nation?

Macro: Why is education a major concern around the world?

Macro: Global Community

Macro: Society

Meso: National Organizations, Institutions, and Ethnic Subcultures

Micro: Local Organizations and Community

Micro: Me (and My Teacher and Classmates)

Micro: Neighborhood schools; city school systems

Meso: State regulations governing education; state funding; family or economic influences on education; national teachers' lobby groups; pressure groups

Macro: National policies to improve schools (i.e., U.S. No Child Left Behind Act)

Macro: United Nations policies and programs to improve education in poor countries

Tomás is a failure. At nine years old, he cannot read, write, or get along with his peers, and out of frustration, he sometimes misbehaves. He has been a failure since he was three, but his failure started earlier than that—his parents say so. They have told Tomás over and over that he will not amount to anything if he does not shape up. His teachers have noticed that he is slow to learn and does not seem to have many friends. They, too, define him as a failure. Tomás believes his parents and teachers, for he has little evidence to contradict their judgment.

Two strikes against him are the judgments of his parents and his teachers. The third strike is Tomás's own acceptance of the label "failure." Tomás is an at-risk child, identified as having characteristics inclining him toward failure in school and society. Probably, he will not amount to anything, and he may even get in trouble with the law unless caring people intervene, encouraging him to realize that he has abilities and is not worthless.

Tomás goes to school in Toronto (Ontario), Canada, but he could live in any country. In every community, there are Tomáses. Although successful children develop a positive self-concept that helps them deal with disappointments and failures, the Tomáses internalize failures. Successful children negotiate the rules and regulations of school, and school provides them with necessary skills for future occupations. Tomás carries a label with him that will largely determine his life-chances because, next to home, schools play the biggest role in socializing children into their self-concepts and attitudes toward achievement. What factors could change educational outcomes for students like Tomás?

Children volunteer to participate during an arithmetic lesson in the village school in Lalibela, Ethiopia. This kind of overcrowding is not uncommon in poor countries.

Schooling—learning skills such as reading and math in a building via systematic instruction by a trained professional—is a luxury some children will never know. On the other hand, in most urban areas around the world and in affluent countries, formal education is necessary for success—and for survival. Education of the masses in a school setting is a modern concept that became necessary when literacy and math skills became essential to many jobs (even if just to read instructions for operating machinery). Literacy is also necessary to democratic governments, where informed citizenry elect officials and vote on public policies.

In this chapter, we will explore the state of the world's education, theoretical perspectives on education, micro-level interactions in educational organizations, what happens in schools after the school bell rings, whether education is the road to opportunity, and educational social policy issues.

State of the World's Education: An Overview

Every society educates its children. In most societies, national education systems are created for this task. Global organizations concerned with education also contribute. For the past 50 years, UNESCO (United Nations Educational, Scientific, and Cultural Organization) has become the "global center for discussion and implementation of educational ideas and organization models" (Boli 2002:307). It provides teacher training, curricular guidance, and textbook sources, and it gathers international statistics on educational achievement. Many countries have adopted UNESCO standards, including the organizational model of six years of primary school and three years apiece for intermediate and secondary school, with an emphasis on comprehensive rather than specialized training (Institute for Statistics 2006a).

Formal education—schooling that takes place in a formal setting with the goal of teaching a predetermined curriculum—has expanded dramatically in the past several decades as higher percentages of the population in many countries attend school. Although major educational gaps still exist between the elite and the poor and between females and males, these gaps are narrowing. Girls' enrollments worldwide are now close to half of students at the primary levels in most countries, and girls' secondary school enrollment rose from 32% in 1950 to 45% in the 1990s (Boli 2002:311). Women are also entering more male-dominated fields of higher education and attending university at levels equal to or exceeding men in some countries. A concern will be finding enough qualified teachers to handle the increasing global enrollments (UNESCO 2006b).

Education has become a global issue. What is considered essential knowledge to be taught in schools is based largely on a country's level of development, cultural values, political ideology, and guidelines from international standards. Leaders believe that a literate population is necessary for economic development and expansion, a thriving political system, and the well-being of the citizenry. Global trends in schooling influence education systems in Africa, Asia, Latin America, Europe, and the Middle East, regardless of political system or level of affluence. As Boli (2002) writes, "Education has become a global social process that both reflects and helps create the global society that is under formation" (p. 312). Education plays a significant role in economic growth, social stratification, and political behaviors.

The quality of education is judged in part by student-teacher ratios and literacy rates. Student-teacher ratios vary from a low of 13 to 1 in several Western European countries and 15.8 to 1 in the United States, to a high of 72 to 1 in Ethiopia and more than 60 to 1 in Chad, Congo, Malawi, Mozambique, and Rwanda. The highest numbers of students per teacher at all levels of education were in sub-Saharan Africa, with an average at all levels of education of 41 pupils per teacher, and in South and West Asia, with a ratio of 44 to 1 (Institute for Statistics 2003; National Center for Education Statistics 2002; UNESCO 2006a).

In poor Global South countries, 76% of the population is literate, including 64% of women (UNESCO 2006a).

However, there is variation among these countries: Only 38% of the women are literate in South and West Asia. Affluent countries have rates of 99% literacy for men and women (see Table 11.1). In some math and science courses, males achieve at higher levels than females, especially in countries where women's status is lower, but females often have higher achievement in language and reading.

Mass education is spreading around the world. As communication, transportation, and globalization continue to make countries more interdependent and more accessible to each other, economically developed countries influence levels and types of education worldwide. The national education curricula of many poor countries is similar to models of mass education used in colonial powers by Global North countries (Chabbott and Ramirez 2000; McEneaney and Meyer 2000). Mathematics, for instance, is taught universally, and science has been taught in most schools since World War II, although more science is taught in countries with a higher standard of living (Baker 2002). Whether this trend toward similar curricula meets the needs of individuals in all countries is a matter of debate.

Education can be studied through several different lenses or perspectives. The next section provides a summary of how various theories offer an angle for understanding education in society.

Table 11.1 **Adult Literacy Rates (age 15 and over) by Gender, 2000–2004**

	Adult Literacy Rates %		
	Total	Male	Female
World	82	87	77
Global South countries	76	83	69
Global North countries	99	99	99
Countries in transition	100	100	99
Sub-Saharan Africa	62	70	54
Arab States	62	73	51
Central Asia	99	100	99
East Asia and the Pacific	91	95	88
South and West Asia	58	71	45
Latin America and the Caribbean	89	90	88
North America and Western Europe	99	99	99
Central and Eastern Europe	97	99	96

Source: Institute for Statistics 2006a:129.

Note: Figures may not add to totals because of rounding. 2000–2004 data are derived from the March 2004 literacy assessment by the UNESCO Institute for Statistics (UIS), which uses directly reported national figures together with UIS estimates. For countries that did not report literacy data for the 2000–2004 reference period, UIS estimates for 2002 were used.

While Nicaragua shares the commitment to mass education of all young people, its resources are very meager, as we can see from this photo of an impoverished school building in a Nicaraguan village.

● EDUCATION AND INDIVIDUALS: MICRO-LEVEL THEORIES

Who were the popular kids in your school? Those who studied hard and excelled academically? Those who excelled on the sports field? Those who showed talent in the arts or a specific subject? Which kids sat together at lunch and hung out together after school? How did different individuals and student groups distinguish themselves through clothing or hairstyles, social positions that offered social visibility, or different slang? At the micro level of analysis, sociologists of education focus on questions concerning interaction in classrooms and schools between student peers, students and staff members, and students and teachers.

Social Interaction Within the Classroom: Symbolic Interaction Perspective

The symbolic interaction perspective considers how symbols affect sense of self or shape social hierarchies (Eder et al. 1995). Children actively create distinctions among individuals and groups, becoming agents in determining the social reality in which they live. Popularity, a major issue for many children, especially in middle-school years, is mostly a function of being noticed and liked and having

everyone know who you are. Students may increase their popularity by being attractive, representing the school in an athletic contest, or being seen in a leadership position. The difficulty is that there are few such positions, leading to a competition in which some individuals are going to be losers. In the United States, the losers are more likely to be children from families who cannot afford to purchase popular clothing or other status symbols or to send their children to sports training or camp. Winners have access to material and symbolic resources that give them high visibility. They are given special privileges in the school and are more likely to develop leadership skills and to feel good about themselves (Eder et al. 1995).

Research findings indicate that girls have more struggles with self-esteem than do boys, especially in middle school (American Association of University Women Educational Foundation 2001). One's sense of self—an intensely personal experience—is shaped by the micro interactions of the school. Thus, for young people from 6 to 18 years old, the extensive time spent in school means the status of student has enormous impact on how individuals see themselves. The image that is reflected back to someone—as student or as teacher, for example—can begin to mold one's sense of competence, intelligence, and likeability.

The larger school organization creates a structure that influences how individuals make sense of their reality and interact with others. The Iowa School of symbolic interaction emphasizes the link between the self and meso-level positions or statuses (Stryker 2000). Official school positions—such as president of the student council or senior class president or varsity team member—become important elements of one's self.

Thinking Sociologically

How do you think teachers affect the sense of self of students? How do you think students affect the sense of self, the confidence, and the effectiveness of each other and of teachers?

Making Choices in Educational Settings: Rational Choice Theory

Rational choice theory focuses on the cost-benefit analysis that individuals undertake in virtually everything they do. What are the costs—in terms of money, relationships, self-esteem, or other factors—and what are the benefits? If benefits outweigh costs, the individual is likely to decide to act in the specified way, whereas if costs outweigh benefits, the individual is likely to seek other courses of action. How might weighing costs and benefits influence decisions about education?

Students who are considering dropping out of school go through some analysis of costs to themselves—for example, a decision may be shaped by battered self-esteem in schools. Similarly, teachers make rational choices about staying in the teaching profession. Roughly half of new teachers in the United States leave teaching within five years, a high rate compared to other professions (Lambert 2006). Rational choice theorists explain teacher retention by looking at perception of benefits, such as rewarding professional practice working with children or adolescents, and perceived costs, such as poor salary for a college graduate; lack of respect from parents, students, and administrators; 12- to 14-hour days for nine months of the year; and lack of professionalism in treatment of teachers. Teachers compare these costs to the benefits of teaching—the feeling of making a contribution to society and helping children, time off in the summer, and enjoying many aspects of teaching, coaching, or directing. The costs today are seen by many teachers as higher than they used to be for professionals in teaching, so they leave the profession.

Thinking Sociologically

What other kinds of roles and processes within a school are influenced by costs and benefits? Do you think most behavior in schools is shaped by this kind of rational choice calculation?

○ WHY SOCIETIES HAVE EDUCATION SYSTEMS: MACRO-LEVEL THEORIES

Wherever it takes place and whatever the content, education gives individuals the information and skills that their society regards as important and prepares them to live and work in their societies. In a rural Indian village in Uttar Pradesh, children gather in a lean-to shelter for their morning lessons before going to the fields to help with the animals. The average number of years of schooling in India is eight (UNESCO 2005). In some rural areas, little more than basic literacy is considered necessary or possible, especially for girls. Village children go to the community school, tablets in hand, but when the family needs help in the fields or with child care, older children often stay at home. Even though several years of school may be mandated by law, not all people become literate. Learning to survive—how to grow crops, care for the home, treat diseases, and make clothing—are essential survival skills that come before formal education. They take most of an individual's available

Males have many ways of becoming known and respected. Male athletics draw bigger crowds than female athletics, and one can become a local celebrity based on one's skill on the field or court.

time and energy. Basic literacy is a goal, but it is sometimes limited to urban areas in the Global South where basic academic skills (literacy, mathematics, science) are essential to find employment. Mass education was not even a goal until the 1900s (Benavot, Meyer, and Kamens 1991). It was only then that it became clear that a literate citizenry is necessary for economic development and informed political participation.

The Purposes of Education: Functionalist Perspective

Functional theorists argue that formal and informal education serve certain crucial purposes in society, especially as societies

These children, who live near Inle Lake in Burma, take the only available mode of transportation to get to school, a gondola school bus.

Manifest Functions

- Socialize children to be productive members of society.
- Select and train individuals for positions in society.
- Promote social participation, change, and innovation.
- Enhance personal independence and social development.

Latent Functions

- Confine and supervise underage citizens.
- Weaken parental controls over youths.
- Provide opportunities for peer cultures to develop.
- Provide contexts for the development of friendships and mate selection.

Figure 11.1   Key Functions of Education

modernize (Boli 2002). The social functions of education as a social institution are outlined in Figure 11.1. Note that some functions are planned and formalized (manifest functions) whereas others are unintended and unorganized—informal results of the educational process (latent functions).

Latent functions may be just as important to the society as manifest functions. For example, schools give parents release time from childrearing responsibilities so they can perform other roles. Schools also keep children off the streets until they can be absorbed into productive roles in society. They provide young people with a place to congregate and interact among themselves, fostering a "youth culture" of music, fashion, slang, dances, dating, and cliques or gangs. At the ages when social relationships are being established, especially with the opposite sex, schools are the central meeting place for the young—a kind of mate selection market. Education also weakens parental control over youths, helps them begin the move toward independence, and provides experience in large, impersonal secondary groups.

In the functionalist view, the structure and processes within the educational institution remain stable only if basic functions are met. When social functions are not met adequately, an educational system becomes ripe for change. Government proposals for educational reforms are stimulated by new knowledge and technologies and by indications of poor outcomes, such as falling behind in international comparisons or experiencing high unemployment in an undertrained labor force.

Socialization: Teaching Children to Be Productive Members of Society

Societies use education to pass on essential information of a culture—especially the values, skills, and knowledge necessary for survival. Sometimes this process occurs in formal classrooms, sometimes in informal places. In West African villages, children may have several years of formal education in a village school, but they learn what is right and wrong, values, and future roles informally by observing their elders and by "playing" at the tasks they will soon undertake for survival. The girls help pound cassava root for the evening meal, while the boys build model boats and practice negotiating the waves and casting nets. In less prosperous countries, formal education beyond basic literacy is reserved mainly for the elite—the sons and daughters of the rulers and the wealthy.

In all postindustrial societies, however, elders and family members cannot teach all the skills necessary for survival. Formal schooling emerged as an institution to meet the needs of industrial and postindustrial societies, furnishing the specialized training required by rapidly growing and changing technology. Schools also teach students culture beyond what families in heterogeneous societies can provide. Diverse groups must learn rules that maintain the social order, for example (Brint, Contreras, and Matthews 2001).

Selecting and Training Individuals for Positions in Society

Students take standardized tests, receive grades at the end of the term or the year, and ask teachers to write recommendation letters. These activities are part of the selection process prevalent in competitive societies with formal educational systems. Individuals accumulate credentials—grade point averages, standardized test scores, and degrees—that determine the colleges or job opportunities available to them, the fields of study or occupations they can pursue, and ultimately their positions in society. In some societies, educational systems enact this social function through tracking, ability grouping, grade promotion and retention, high-stakes and minimum-competency testing, and pull-out programs that contribute to job training, such as vocational education and service learning.

Thus, education outfits people for making a living in their society and contributing to the economy. Individual, family, community, state, and national income and standard of living are linked to educational level. For example, Map 11.1 indicates the distribution of college degrees in the United States. How does your state rank?

Promoting Change and Innovation

Citizens expect schools to respond to constant social changes. In multicultural societies such as Israel, France, and England, schools help to assimilate immigrants by teaching them the language and customs, along with strategies for reducing intergroup tensions. In Israel, for example, many recent Jewish immigrants from Africa and Russia work hard to master Hebrew and to move successfully through the Israeli educational system. In most societies, providing educational opportunity to all groups is a

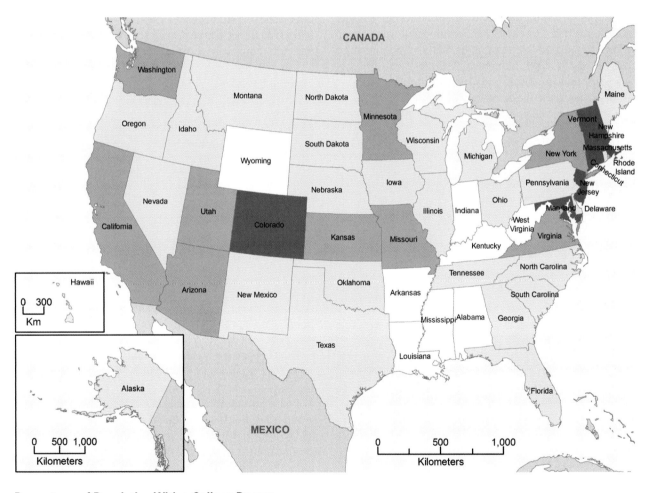

Percentage of Population With a College Degree

| 34–46 | 29–33 | 24–28 | 15–23 |

Map 11.1   Percentage of the U.S. Population Holding a Bachelor's Degree or Higher in 2004

Source: U.S. Census Bureau. Map by Anna Versluis.

challenge, but effective social participation and readiness for change require it.

Institutions of higher education are expected to generate new knowledge, technology, and ideas and to produce students with up-to-date skills and knowledge to lead industry and other key institutions in society. In our high-tech age, critical thinking and analytical skills are more essential for problem solving than rote memorization, and this fact is reflected in curriculum change.

Thus, the curriculum changes to meet the changing needs of people in new social circumstances. Familiarity with technological equipment—computers, Internet resources, electronic library searches, and so forth—become critical survival skills. Lack of training in these areas fosters further division of social classes and reduced chances for social mobility.

India has top-ranked technical institutes, and the highly skilled graduates are employed by multinational companies around the world. Companies in Europe and the United States also send information to India for processing and receive it back the next morning because of the time difference. Well-trained, efficient engineers and computer experts working in India for lower wages than workers in many highly developed countries have become an essential part of the global economy (Friedman 2005).

Enhancing Personal and Social Development

Do you remember your first day of elementary school? Perhaps it marked a transition between the intimate world of the family and an impersonal school world that emphasized discipline, knowledge and skills, responsibility, and obedience. In school, children learn that they are no longer accepted unconditionally as they typically were in their families. Rather, they must meet certain expectations and compete for attention and rewards.

In school, children develop independence and are taught social skills and ethical conduct that will enable them to function in society. For example, they learn to get along with others, resolve disputes, stay in line, follow directions, obey the rules, take turns, be kind to others, be neat, tell the truth, listen, plan ahead, work hard, meet deadlines, and so on. Children worldwide begin learning what is expected of them in preschool and kindergarten, providing the basis for schooling in the society (Neuman 2005). One scholar has compared early school socialization to military indoctrination (Gracey 1967). In the functionalist view, the prosocial values and social competencies learned in academic boot camp are necessary for social cohesion and social order.

Stratification and Education: Conflict Perspective

Critics of functionalism emphasize the role of education in a society's system of social stratification and competition between groups. Some students receive elite educations, and others do not, in part because of class, race, and gender differences (Kerckhoff 2001). Attendance at an elite school is a means of attaining high social status, for example. Graduates of British public schools, American preparatory (prep) schools, and private high schools and international schools in countries around the world attend the best universities and become leaders of government, business, and the military. Because elite schools are very expensive and highly selective, affluent members of society have the most access to them and thereby learn class privilege and advantage (Howard 2007; Persell and Cookson 1985).

Many leaders of former colonized countries have had the opportunity to study abroad, continuing Western influence in these countries. Those not born into positions of advantage have very limited chances to participate in elite education.

At a macro level, conflict theorists see institutions, including education, as tools of powerful affluent groups to ensure that their self-interests are met. Educational opportunities thus are manipulated in ways that keep the sons and daughters of the haves in positions of privilege, while lower-class children are prepared for less prestigious and less rewarding positions in society. If schools do not provide equal educational opportunities for all children in a society, as conflict theorists contend, then students cannot compete equally in the job market.

According to this view, when elites of society protect their educational advantages, the result is **reproduction of class**—socioeconomic positions of one generation passing on to the next. This process takes place in part through socialization of young people into adult work roles and compliance with the modern corporation and its needs. Schools teach students from lower socioeconomic positions to obey authority and accept the dominant ideology that justifies social inequality. If citizens believe that those with the best educations and jobs in their society personally earned them, they are not motivated to change the system. In these ways, schools serve the interests of the privileged (Bowles and Gintis 2002; Collins 2004).

The cultural values and social norms of the dominant group, such as ideas of etiquette, proper ways of speaking and writing, notions of deference to superiors, and so forth, are transmitted to all social classes and legitimated through formal schooling. Other definitions of reality from other ethnic or socioeconomic groups are marginalized. Studies comparing working-class schools with upper-middle-class schools and private schools with public schools support this view, revealing structural differences that reinforce learned differences in social class behaviors (Kozol 2005). According to conflict theorists, this process enhances power and confirms the privileges of the dominant group. The educational system is not equally beneficial to all or even to the majority of citizens in society.

Elite preparatory (prep) schools in England, Japan, the United States, and many other countries traditionally have been the training ground for the sons and daughters of the elite. In countries such as Chile, privatization of schools in the form of parental choice and vouchers was seen as a way to broaden educational opportunity, in line with Chile's transition to a market-oriented economy. After 30 years, however, inequality persists in educational opportunity and outcomes, especially in the transition to secondary schools. Advantages come to those in private-voucher and private-paid schools as opposed to public schools (Torche 2005). Proposed choice and voucher plans allowing students and parents to choose schools have been controversial in the United States, as well. Critics fear that public schools might be left with the least capable students and teachers, further stratifying an already troubled system (Chubb and Moe 1990; Witte and Thorn 1996). Private schools could also become sanctuaries for those who do not want integrated schools, perpetuating religious and racial segregation.

Having explored some lenses through which sociologists analyze educational systems, we now focus on the classrooms, corridors, local schools, and key players where the everyday drama of teaching and learning is played out.

Thinking Sociologically

Do you think education enhances upward social mobility and serves both individuals and society, or does it mostly serve the affluent, reproducing social class and training people to fulfill positions at the same level as their parents?

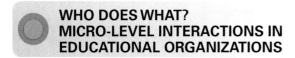

WHO DOES WHAT? MICRO-LEVEL INTERACTIONS IN EDUCATIONAL ORGANIZATIONS

Education takes place at a micro-level in the classrooms and corridors of local schools, with key players who enact the everyday drama of teaching and learning. You probably recall an important learning experience you had in which someone helped you master a skill—a scout leader, grandmother, choir director, coach, neighbor, or teacher. You know how important one-on-one mentoring can be to the learning process, how education often is an intimate exchange between two people. Education has the power to change the way people think about the world, influence their sense of competency, and affect their self-esteem and personal outlooks on self and society.

Education is also an important organization in local communities. The school is a source of pride, a unifying symbol of identity. Local communities rally around the success of their school. Moreover, in many communities, the school system is a large employer with real importance to the economic vitality of the area. At the micro level, much sociological analysis has focused on the school as a social setting and as a social organization within a community. At this level sociologists look at roles and statuses in educational settings and the informal norms and interaction patterns that evolve in those settings

Who Does What? Statuses and Roles in the Educational System

Students, teachers, staff, and administrators hold major statuses in educational systems. The roles associated with each status bring both obligations and inherent problems. When the status holders agree on expected behaviors (role expectations), schools function smoothly. When they do not agree, conflicts can arise. Let us look at several statuses and accompanying roles in schools.

Students and the Peer Culture of Schools

In some countries, going to school is a privilege. In others, it is a necessary part of life that many students resist. In either case, children understand the school system well. They know how they must behave to be considered good students or bad students, although they do not know how to change a negative label once it is in place.

Class, race, and gender are interactive, and all affect children's experiences in school and in their peer culture. In schools around the world, students are assigned a variety of social identities, often given colorful labels. These identities are part of their peer cultures, which have a major effect on their future roles in society (Waller [1932] 1965). Consider class. *Nerds* in the United States or *ear 'oles* in Britain—well-behaved, college-bound middle-class students—have an investment in the school system, whereas *burnouts* or *lads*—working-class students who often feel hostile or alienated in the school environment—may engage in behaviors that prevent them from succeeding in high school and can lead to dropping out (Jackson 1968; MacLeod 1995; Willis 1979).

In a Rwandan secondary school, class also enters in. At École des Sciences (School of Sciences) in Byimana, 45 students are crowded onto benches. They are quiet, respectful, and very hardworking. They know the norms and rules, and peer culture supports this behavior. They are in a privileged position, and many students are lined up to take their place on the bench, should they not work

Photo Essay

Student Roles

Students in schools play a variety of roles and often are identified by labels. What labels might apply to the students in these photos, and what were some of the labels applied to students in your high school?

hard and succeed. Although they have no written texts, students write down the lectures in their notebooks and memorize the material. The lessons children learn in the microculture of the classroom are supported by a peer culture. A *student peer culture* is "a stable set of activities or routines, artifacts, values, and concerns that children produce and share in interaction with peers" (Corsaro and Eder 1990:197).

Classrooms are small societies of peers that reflect the patterns and problems of the larger world (Durkheim 1956). For instance, studies indicate that girls tend to have closely knit and egalitarian friendships, sharing confidences and problems. By contrast, boys tend to have loosely knit associations, with clear status hierarchies based on dominance in a shared activity such as a sport (Wood 2005).

Interaction patterns in school also may reflect society's racial and ethnic patterns. For example, studies in the United States have found that when choosing friends, students are one sixth as likely to choose a cross-race peer as a same-race peer (Grant 2004). Racial inequalities in early schooling affect everything from preparation for jobs to college attendance (Charles, Roscigno, and Torres 2007).

While many experts acknowledge that girls and boys have different experiences in school, a recent debate in Britain and the United States focuses on whether boys or girls have a harder time in school. One response to the view that boys have a harder time is the masculinizing of schools. Masculinization involves hiring male teachers at higher pay levels than female teachers; instituting more male-dominated extracurricular activities, especially sports; and increasing practical, vocational curricula.

A current debate in the United States is whether boys and girls should be taught in separate classrooms. Those who argue for separate classrooms, especially in the middle school years, point out the different interests and learning styles of girls and boys at these early adolescent ages. Others argue that equality requires mixed gender classes. Some parochial schools have long been single-sex, and now public school districts are experimenting with single-sex classes, and research will provide more data on the effectiveness (Sax 2005; Weil 2008).

These measures may help keep boys from dropping out by making schools more "boy-friendly" (Lesko 2001). The next "Sociology in Your Social World" discusses concerns that have been raised about boys in U.S. schools.

Another gender issue in peer culture is sexual harassment. According to studies by the American Association of University Women Educational Foundation (2001), four out of five students report some type of sexual harassment in school. Compared to boys, girls experience "hostile hallways" in more physically and psychologically harmful ways. Here are some findings from a recent AAUW study of 2,064 U.S. public school students

in 8th through 11th grades and from the Gay, Lesbian, and Straight Network.

- 83% of girls and 79% of boys report having experienced harassment. More than one in four students experienced it often.
- 76% of students have experienced nonphysical harassment (taunting, rumors, graffiti, jokes, gestures), while 58% have experienced physical harassment.
- Seven in 10 students (69%) say their school has a policy on sexual harassment, compared to only 26% in 1993. Nearly all students (96%) say they know what harassment is, and boys' and girls' definitions do not differ substantially.
- 18% of students are afraid of being sexually harassed or hurt in school some or most of the time. Fewer than half (46%) report never being afraid in school.
- In 2005, slightly more than 75% (three out of four) of high school students heard derogatory sexual labels frequently or often at school, and 89% reported frequently hearing behavior or appearances described as "gay"—meaning "dumb" or "worthless."
- Nearly 4 of 10 students who identified themselves as gay, lesbian, bisexual, or transgendered experienced physical bullying at school, and half of those students had actually been assaulted because of their sexual orientation (Gay, Lesbian, and Straight Education Network 2006).

In summary, "sexual harassment is a part of everyday life for boys and girls at school . . . Parents, teachers, and administrators need to do a better job educating our children on

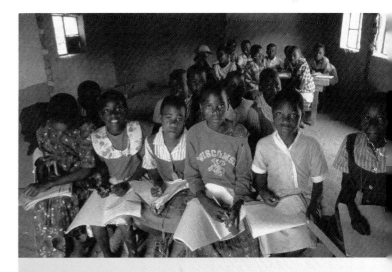

Zimbabwe once had one of the best education systems in Africa, but after severe economic crisis in the country, educational conditions have declined rapidly. Still, some children are privileged over other children, who do not get any education.

Sociology Around the World

Where the Boys Are: A Gender Gap?

The Myth of the Fragile Girl; The War Against Boys; Failing at Fairness: How America's Schools Cheat Girls; and At Colleges, Women Are Leaving Men in the Dust—these are just a few subjects in a debate about which groups have the biggest advantage or disadvantage in schools in Western societies. For many years, concern focused on factors that inhibited minorities' educational attainment in school. Recently, some authors are turning the tables and focusing their concern on dominant groups, but this is controversial, as we shall see.

Gender has been one major focus of education disparities research. Statistics indicate that the state of educational achievement varies greatly by sex, age, race or ethnicity, and socioeconomic status. Why is this so? Among the many reasons for the differences, researchers point to the incredible gains made by women and the fact that women tend to study more. In the United States, African American, Hispanic, and low-income males lag behind all other groups, including females from their own ethnic group (King 2000).

In 2003, Asian or Pacific Islanders had a higher high school completion rate (94.9%) than whites (91.9%), blacks (85%), or Hispanics (69.2%). The gap has been narrowing in recent years (Laird, DeBell, and Chapman 2006; National Center for Education Statistics 2005).

College attendance rates are shown in Table 11.2.

Table 11.2	College Attendance Rates
Race	College Attendance Rate % (2004)
White, non-Hispanic	68.8
Black	62.5
Hispanic	61.8

Source: National Center for Education Statistics 2005b: Table 181.

A study by the National Urban League (2006) indicates that one third of poorly educated young black men end up in prison, further reducing their chances for education, good jobs, and stable family life. They feel disconnected from a society that helps women with children but ignores the vulnerabilities of men (Mincy 2006). The following figures provide a partial picture:

- An estimated two to three million youth ages 16 through 24 are without postsecondary education and are disconnected—neither in school nor employed.
- Among those between ages 16 and 24 who are not enrolled in school, only about half are working, and one third are involved with the criminal justice system. Roughly three in ten will spend some time in prison or jail during their lives.
- As few as 20% of black teens are employed at any time, and education has not been a path to better jobs for neighbors and family members (Mincy 2006).

Women have surpassed men in college completion (Buchmann and DiPrete 2006), and men, regardless of race or class, get lower grades, take more time to graduate, and are less likely to get a bachelor's degree (Lewin 2006). However, men from the highest income groups attend college at a slightly higher rate than women in that group, and men from low-income families—disproportionately African American and Hispanic—are the most underrepresented in higher education.

The gender gap in favor of females has been most pronounced among low-income whites and Hispanics. The imbalance is of such concern to college admissions officers that some colleges are turning away more qualified females in favor of males (Britz 2006). Some colleges are even adding activities such as football to attract more male students (Pennington 2006).

Black women earned twice as many bachelor's degrees as black men (National Center for Education Statistics 2002); yet females who are racial or ethnic minorities lag behind white women (King 2000). Despite the sex differences, some researchers argue that the gender gap is not nearly as significant as the differences for race or ethnicity and social class. Furthermore, men still dominate math and science fields, where jobs pay more money and result in more power. Data indicate that although women do not score as high as men on achievement tests in math and science, women hold higher educational aspirations, are more likely to enroll in college, and are more likely to attain a college degree (National Center for Education Statistics 2000). Perhaps concern over boys' performance simply reflects nervousness about women's achievements (Lewin 2006).

What do we do? Girls and women face serious educational problems in many developing countries, and women in developed countries are still at a disadvantage in hiring for high-paid jobs and equal wages. Concern about boys is a relatively new twist in the equity issue. Ultimately, we hope to create an educational system that equally benefits all groups.

what is and what isn't appropriate" (American Association of University Women Educational Foundation 2001).

Student peer cultures often tolerate or ignore aggression or violence against others or against the school. Educators are deeply concerned about disruptive students, not only because they disrupt learning and make school unsafe for others, but because many are at risk of dropping out of school and becoming burdens to society. For at-risk students, some educators suggest no-fail, cooperative learning classrooms, allowing more positive peer networks and minimizing individual failure.

The environment outside the school also powerfully affects students' achievement and behavior within the school. Disorganization in the community and family is related to lack of school commitment and is reflected in delinquent behavior (Jenkins 1995; Ogbu 1998). The students at highest risk for dropping out of school in Western countries are also at higher risk for joining gangs and committing violent crimes. They often feel the system is stacked against them (Noguera 1996; Willis 1979).

Teachers: The Front Line

The degree of success students experience often depends on their role partners: teachers. You no doubt remember certain teachers with fondness and think of others with fear or anger. One scholar estimated that teachers have more than a thousand interchanges a day in their roles as classroom managers (Jackson 1968). Teachers serve as gatekeepers, controlling the flow of students, activities, resources, and privileges. They also act as timekeepers and traffic managers and spend a great deal of time in nonteaching clerical work. Many teachers complain that they are so bogged down with paperwork and forms—attendance, tardiness, student behavior, and other required reports for the state—that they have little time to address the primary objectives of the school: student learning.

Teachers are in the middle of the educational hierarchy between the micro and meso levels. They occupy the front line in implementing the goals of the school and the state. As primary socializers and role models for students, teachers are expected to set good examples. They are expected to support and encourage students and at the same time to judge their performance—giving grades and recommendations as part of the selection and allocation functions. This creates role strain, which can interfere with the task of teaching and contribute to teacher burnout (Dworkin 2007; Dworkin, Saha, and Hill 2003).

Studies in Australia and the United States show how teachers feel they are underappreciated (Saha and Dworkin 2006). Upgrading the status of teachers requires better social standing and respect for the teaching occupation (Ingersoll 2005). Teachers' status varies from society to society, depending on the value placed on their role and the pay they receive compared to other occupations.

In Japan, where education is considered extremely important for training future generations, teachers are treated with great respect and honor. They receive salaries competitive with those in industry and professions such as law and medicine (Ballantine and Hammack 2009). In Europe, many high schools are organizationally more like universities. Teachers think of themselves as akin to professors. By contrast, in the United States, high schools are under local control with the same school board as the elementary and middle schools. Teachers are part of the professional organizations that include teachers in elementary and middle schools. Therefore, secondary teachers think of themselves as more like middle-school teachers than like university professors. The reference groups of high school teachers in the United States and European schools differ (Clark 1985; Legters 2001).

Many U.S. teachers complain of feeling frustrated and dissatisfied. Morale issues are rooted in low salaries, low status of teaching as a profession, unmotivated students, problems of discipline in the classroom, lack of support from students' families and the community, criticism of schools, and interruptions of classroom work for time-consuming special programs. The public gives teachers high marks, however, and disapproves of pressures to "teach to the test" and limit curricular offerings because of government mandates, such as No Child Left Behind (Phi Delta Kappa/Gallup Poll 2001, 2005).

U.S. teachers are held accountable for students' progress as measured on standardized tests, as well as for their own competency as measured in tests to determine their knowledge and skills (Grant and Murray 1999). Thus, teachers are under pressure to prepare students for achievement and proficiency tests so they can be promoted through the grades and graduate from high school. At the same time, for teachers who are licensed and performing well, teacher competency tests seem insulting. Teachers see themselves as professionals and government-imposed standards that limit their creativity are viewed as deprofessionalizing.

Teachers are criticized for everything from their lack of skills to poor preparation to problems with motivation, yet the organizational context of teachers' work is a key source of problems. Teachers request respect from administrators, parents, and students, more autonomy, and higher salaries and benefits. To overcome poor social standing and lack of respect for the teaching occupation requires not only better recruiting and training but also upgrading the status of teachers (Ingersoll 2005). Several sociologists suggest that teachers' dissatisfactions can be addressed through organizational and structural changes, allowing teachers more autonomy and control over their environments (Dworkin 2007; Ingersoll 2005).

Still, the majority of the public and many politicians want teachers held to high standards of competence and conduct (Phi Delta Kappa/Gallup Poll 2001). The question is, who should enforce high standards: the profession itself or legislators and the public?

Photo Essay

Teacher Roles

Teachers hold the core roles in schools. Theirs is a challenging job that must delicately balance the curriculum, the needs of students, the policies of the school, the ideas of the larger community, and the concerns of parents or other constituencies.

One reason teachers' organizations tend to oppose government mandates on education is that such mandates tend to deprofessionalize teachers (Ingersoll 2004; Roberts and Donahue 2000). Most professionals have some sense of calling and commitment and are motivated not just by money but by prestige, a sense of contribution, and pride in belonging to the profession and serving others. Two key features of being a professional are autonomy on the job and self-regulation by the profession. Lawyers can be disbarred by the American Bar Association for incompetence, for example, and doctors can have their medical licenses revoked by the medical establishment. In contrast, control of teachers often comes from outside teacher organizations. When government regulates standards for teachers, quality might actually decrease as teachers—faced with lack of respect as professionals and lack of control over their work—opt instead for other occupations. This has the potential to leave schools with less capable and less committed instructors.

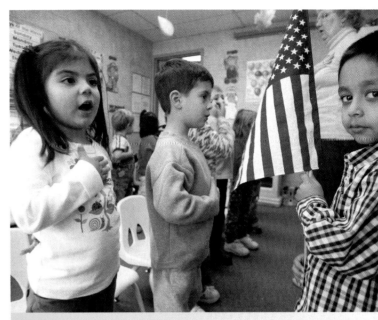

Four-year-old preschoolers recite the Pledge of Allegiance. Developing patriotism is part of the implicit and informal curriculum of schools.

Thinking Sociologically

Who should enforce high teacher standards? Who should decide what these standards are?

Administrators: The Managers of the School System

Key administrators—superintendents, assistant superintendents, principals and assistant principals, or headmasters and headmistresses—hold the top positions in the educational hierarchy of local schools. They are responsible for a long list of tasks: issuing budget reports; engaging in staff negotiations; hiring, firing, and training staff members; meeting with parents; carrying out routine approval of projects; managing public relations; preparing reports for boards of directors, local education councils, legislative bodies, and national agencies; keeping up with new regulations; making recommendations regarding the staff; and many other tasks. Some administrators specialize in overseeing discipline and acting as buffers between parents and teachers when conflicts arise. In some countries, a lay board of education oversees decisions, including hiring of administrators and expenditures.

Administrators operate one step removed from the actual educational functions of the classroom, and they mediate between the local community school and the larger bureaucracy at the state and national levels. They occupy high-profile leadership positions that may place them in conflict with the interests and goals of students, teachers, parents, or community groups.

The Informal System: What Really Happens Inside Schools?

It is the first day of class, and the teacher asks a question. Should you respond, or let someone else answer? If you respond, the teacher might be impressed, but the other students might think you are showing off or currying favor. What if you answer incorrectly and sound foolish?

The informal system of schooling includes the unspoken, unwritten, implicit norms of behavior that we learn, whether in kindergarten or college. These norms may be created or enforced by teachers or by the student peer culture. The informal system does not appear in written goal statements or course syllabi but nevertheless influences our experiences in school in important ways. Dimensions of the informal system include the hidden curriculum, the educational climate, the value climate, and power dynamics and coping strategies in the classroom.

The **hidden curriculum** refers to the implicit "rules of the game" that students learn in school (Snyder 1970). It includes everything the student learns in school that is not explicitly taught, such as unstated social and academic norms. Students have to learn and respond to these to be socially acceptable and to succeed in the education system (Snyder 1971).

Children worldwide begin learning what is expected of them in preschool and kindergarten, providing the basis for schooling in the society (Neuman 2005). For example, Gracey (1967) describes early school socialization as "academic boot camp." Kindergarten teachers teach children to follow rules, to cooperate with each other, and to accept the teacher as the boss who gives orders and controls how time is spent. All of this is part of what young children learn, lessons instilled in students even though it is not yet the formal curriculum of reading, writing, and arithmetic. These less formal messages form the hidden curriculum, examined in more detail in Table 11.3.

According to functional theorists, it is through the hidden curriculum that students learn the expectations, behaviors, and values necessary to succeed in school and society. For conflict theorists, the hidden curriculum is a social and economic agenda that maintains class differences. More is expected of elites, and they are given greater responsibility and opportunities for problem solving that result in higher achievement (Brookover and Erickson 1975), Many working-class schools stress order and discipline, teaching students to obey rules and to accept their lot as responsible, punctual workers (Willis 1979).

Educational Climate of Schools

Schools can feel comfortable and stimulating or cold and unfriendly. Some have an atmosphere of excitement about learning, with artwork and posters on the walls and excited noises coming from classrooms. Other schools have rules and warnings posted everywhere and hall guards, and uniformed students walk in columns and sit up straight in neat rows. These are aspects of school climate, a general social environment that characterizes a group, organization, or community such as a school (Brookover, Erickson, and McEvoy 1996).

The school's architecture, teachers' expectations, classroom layouts, student groupings by age and ability—all affect the climate of the school. Schools also have ceremonies and rituals that contribute to climate—logos, symbols, athletic events, pep rallies, and award ceremonies. In some countries, such as Japan, extracurricular activities are held outside school hours, often Saturday afternoons, and are sponsored by private clubs.

Classroom climates are influenced by the teachers' use of discipline and encouragement, the organization of tasks and opportunities for student interaction, the seating arrangement and classroom furnishings. These nuances can create an atmosphere that celebrates or stifles student achievement (Cohen 1997).

In addition, the friendships students make depend in part on how schools and classrooms are organized and on teachers' policies. Some schools track students on the basis of their tested ability in certain subjects, thus fostering the development of friendship groups within those tracks. Tracking systems also tend to create and maintain racial, ethnic, and social class segregation (Lucas and Berends 2002).

Teachers' responses to class, ethnicity or race, and gender differences create climates that have subtle but profound impacts on students' experiences and learning. Studies indicate that teachers give boys more attention, for example, call on them more often, and give them instructions for accomplishing tasks independently. By contrast, teachers more often do the tasks *for* the girls in the class (Sadker and Sadker 1995; Spade 2004).

Another study found that teachers unconsciously tend to groom white girls for academic attainment in a context of dependence and loyalty while encouraging African American girls to emphasize social relationships over academic work. White boys are groomed for high attainment and high-status social roles, while African American boys

Table 11.3 Syllabus for Course

Actual or Visible Curriculum	Hidden Curriculum
Instructor: Name	What should I call the instructor? (This may be formally established.)
Texts: Names	Do we really have to buy them and read them?
Course topics: Listed	What is the instructor really going to teach? What is he or she really interested in?
Requirements:	
Readings	What do I really have to do to get by?
Projects	Will it help if I speak up in class?
Exams	Will it help if I go see the instructor?
Bibliography	Am I really supposed to use this?

are trained for social conformity and are carefully monitored and controlled in the classroom (Grant 2004).

Low achievement is linked to low expectations, and bias is subtle. Do students have equal access to materials and technology? Are all students active and influential participants in the learning process? Goals of equitable teaching and learning are challenged in increasingly diverse classrooms with immigrant students from linguistically and culturally diverse backgrounds. "Different" students tend to end up in lower ability groups, guaranteeing their poorer achievement (Lucas and Berends 2002).

Table 11.4 illustrates the problems students from different backgrounds may have in schools that provide unfamiliar experiences. Even the brightest children can be failures in such circumstances.

Table 11.4 The Mismatch Between No Child Left Behind Programs and the Research Base on Native American Learning

Native American Learning Styles	No Child Left Behind (NCLB) Requirements?
Best Practices	**No Child Left Behind Programs**
Hands-on, experience-based	Abstract, "drill and kill"
Use of culturally appropriate materials	Culturally bland/generic
Informal, flexible learning environment	Highly structured, extreme inflexibility
Collaborative, teamwork	Highly individualistic, isolating
Teacher as facilitator or coach	Teacher-centered, top-down
High levels of dialogue	Scripted, unnatural interactions
Learning Styles (Preferences)	**No Child Left Behind Programs**
Holistic approach, whole-to-part	Fragmented learning, part-to-whole
Reflective meaning-making	Rote learning, memorizing
Visual learning mode, including pictures and illustrations	Heavy print emphasis
Culturally Appropriate Programs	**No Child Left Behind Programs**
Based in culture's values and beliefs	Dominant culture's values and beliefs
Both/and approach (local and global)	Dominant culture only
Begins but does not end with community	Content irrelevant to community
Environmental Conditions That Support Resiliency	**No Child Left Behind Programs**
Promotes close bonds	Not addressed in NCLB
Uses high-warmth, low-criticism style of interaction	Failure-focused
Sets and enforces clear boundaries using democratic principles	Uses top-down imposed rules
Encourages sharing of responsibilities, service to others, expectation of helpfulness	Not addressed in NCLB
Supports development of autonomy/independence	Teacher-controlled
Expresses high and realistic expectations	Expectations are low
Encourages personal goal setting and future focus	Not addressed in NCLB
Encourages development of values and life skills	Not addressed in NCLB
Encourages development of leadership, allows for decision making and other opportunities for meaningful participation	Scripted participation and decision making
Appreciates unique talents of each individual	Group-focused
Emphasizes creativity	Emphasizes conformity
Encourages development of sense of humor	Absent

Source: Starnes 2006.

Sociology in Your Social World

Sources of Teacher Expectations

We need to guard against the following factors that create lower expectations for certain groups of students (taken from Brookover et al. 1996:75–76):

- *Sex:* Boys and girls are sometimes the recipients of low academic expectations because of mistaken beliefs about boys' maturation and sex-role discrimination against girls.
- *Socioeconomic status level:* Low expectations are typically held for children from families with low-level income and education, low-status jobs, and undesirable neighborhood residence.
- *Race and ethnic identifiers:* Teachers are less likely to expect African American, Hispanic, and Native American students to succeed. They are also less likely to expect African American and Hispanic students to attend college. Asian American students receive high expectations.
- *The status of the school:* Rural and inner-city schools often have lower expectations than suburban schools. The racial, ethnic, and income level of the school is often a factor in such prejudice, with a negative "can't do anything" climate.
- *Appearance and neatness:* Lower expectations are associated with clothes and grooming that are out of style, made of cheaper material, not brand name, or purchased at thrift or discount stores, and with poor handwriting and other sloppiness in presentation.
- *Oral language patterns:* Nonstandard English is a basis for holding lower expectations for students.
- *Halo effect:* There is a tendency to label a student's current achievement based on past performance evaluations of a child. Therefore, blind grading—evaluation of student work without knowledge of who wrote the material until after it is graded—is important.
- *Seating position:* Lower expectations are typically transmitted to students who sit on the sides and in the back of a classroom.
- *Student behavior:* Students with nonacademic behaviors that are inappropriate by middle-class standards also tend to receive lower academic expectations from teachers.
- *Tracking or grouping:* Students in lower academic tracks are presumed to have been placed there for a good reason (i.e., they have limited capacities and can never be expected to learn critical knowledge and skills), yet in some cases placements may have been arbitrary or incorrect.

Value Climate of Schools

The value climate refers to students' motivations, aspirations, and achievements. Why is achievement significantly higher in some schools than in others? How much influence do the values and outlooks of peers, parents, and teachers have on students? Sociologists know that a student's home is influential in determining educational motivation. Recall the opening case of Tomás, who received only negative comments and little encouragement. Cultural components of the neighborhood racial, ethnic, and class composition also affect the value climate. Researchers have found, for example, that classrooms integrated along ethnic or class lines frequently raise the level of motivation and achievement for members of minorities (Lucas and Berends 2002). Also, students who are expected to do very well generally rise to meet these expectations (Cohen 1997; Morris 2005; Weber and Omotani 1994).

Students' and teachers' perceptions of themselves and the learning environment help shape the value climate and influence achievement. The "Sociology in Your Social World" feature (above) discusses teacher expectations. Students perform better if they feel they belong (Smerdon 2002). Students perform less well if they feel futile or hopeless or if they think the teachers do not believe in them or are obsessed with discipline. If teachers have negative expectations, students are likely to have lower aspirations and achievement levels (Rosenthal and Jacobson 1968). Others' expectations can become a self-fulfilling prophecy, affecting how children feel about their abilities, which affects their motivation to achieve and ultimately their life chances.

Taking into consideration the finding that teachers' expectations account for 5 to 10% of students' achievements (Brophy 1983), a group of researchers undertook to raise the value climate and expectations of teachers and students in a group of Chicago public schools. They based their plan on three goals for creating an effective academic learning climate: (1) schools need to be safe and orderly with no violence or disruptions, (2) schools need to be organized so that they become true academic learning communities with no ability groupings that result in large numbers of failures, and (3) schools need to be clear on what students will learn at each level in math, science, social studies, language, and technical skills such as computer literacy.

Although eliminating ability grouping (tracking) is controversial in some school districts, in Chicago the school achievement levels rose significantly with this plan (Brookover et al. 1996). Another reform plan in Chicago is Renaissance 2010, a movement to create 100 new small schools in neighborhoods across the city to relieve crowding, increase students' feelings of belonging, and bring in new leadership (Ayers and Klonsky 2006; Duncan 2006). These are only two of many plans to improve school achievement levels. Plans need to take into consideration the educational and value climates of schools in order to be successful. Whether throughout the school or in a particular classroom, the atmosphere that pervades the learning environment and expectations has an impact on students' educational achievement.

Power Dynamics and Coping Strategies in the Classroom

For teachers, getting students to obey or cooperate or take responsibility is a source of pressure. For students, winning some control from teachers or freedom from supervision is often a goal. Both students and teachers develop strategies to cope with pressures and difficult situations. Coping strategies, part of the hidden curriculum, range from complete compliance to outright rebellion. For instance, college students set priorities for studying various subjects, deciding which test is most important, and figuring out where to cut corners. Do the following five strategies sound familiar? They are taken in part from Merton's (1968a) strain theory of deviance (see Chapter 6) and represent strategies students use to cope with school pressures:

- Conformity: Acceptance of goals and means—doing the schoolwork expected.
- Innovation: Finding alternative or unapproved methods to achieve conventional goals—cheating or plagiarizing to pass a course or to win an academic contest.

Classrooms are loaded with power dynamics, and as this photo shows, it is very clear who is in charge of the classroom.

- Retreatism: Rejection of goals and means—rebelling against school establishment by not conforming or cooperating.
- Ritualism: Indifference toward goals—getting by following rules but not excelling in school.
- Rejection with replacement: Rejection of goals and means in favor of another strategy—being a discipline problem or dropping out of school to pursue other activities. (Hammersley and Turner 1980; Merton 1968b)

Teachers try to elicit cooperation and participation from students by creating a cost-benefits ratio that favors compliance. Manipulating the classroom is one effective means of control: putting students at tables or in a circle, breaking up groups of chattering friends, or leading a discussion while standing beside the most disruptive child.

Thinking Sociologically

What examples of the informal system can you see in the courses you are currently taking? How do these norms and strategies affect your learning experience?

AFTER THE SCHOOL BELL RINGS: MESO-LEVEL ANALYSIS

Schools can be like mazes, with passages to negotiate, hallways lined with pictures and lockers, and classrooms that set the scene for the educational process. Schools are mazes in a much larger sense as well. They involve complex interwoven social systems at the meso level—the state agencies above the local community that affect a school's operations. At this level, we encounter the formal organization of the school system in a more bureaucratized form.

Formal Education Systems

Formal education came into being in the Western world in 16th-century Europe. Schools were seen as a way for Catholics to indoctrinate people to religious faith and for Lutherans to teach people to read so they could interpret the Bible for themselves. The first compulsory education was in a Lutheran monastery in Germany in 1619. By the 19th century, schooling was seen as necessary to teach the European lower classes better agricultural methods, skills for the rapidly growing number of factory jobs, national loyalty, and obedience to authorities.

After 1900, national state school systems were common in Europe and its colonial outposts and former colonial empires. These systems shared many common organizational structures, curricula, and methods, as world leaders shared their ideas. The Prussian model, with strict discipline and ties to the military, became popular in Europe in the 1800s, for example, and the two-track system of education that developed—one for the rich and one for the poor—was debated worldwide.

Thus, formal education systems came into being when other social institutions required new roles, skills, and knowledge that parents did not necessarily possess. Knowledge needed by the young became too complex to be taught informally in families through example, moral lessons, and stories. Industrializing societies required workers with reading and math skills, and eventually, they would need electronic technology skills. Schooling that formerly served only the elite gradually became available to the masses, and some societies began to require schooling for basic literacy (usually third-grade level). Schools emerged as major formal organizations and eventually developed extensive bureaucracies. The postwar period from 1950 to 1992 brought about a rapid rise in education worldwide, as shown in Table 11.5.

Sometimes, differing goals for educational systems lead to conflict. What need, for example, does a subsistence farmer in Nigeria or Kenya have for Latin? Yet, Latin was often imposed as part of the standard curriculum in colonialized nations. Some countries are now revising curricula based on goals and needs of agriculturally based economies.

The Bureaucratic School Structure

The formal bureaucratic atmosphere that permeates many schools arose because it was cost-effective, efficient, and productive. Bureaucracy provided a way to document and process masses of students coming from different backgrounds. Recall Weber's bureaucratic model of groups and organizations, discussed in Chapter 5:

1. Schools have a division of labor among administrators, teachers, students, and support personnel. The roles associated with the statuses are part of the school structure. Individual teachers or students hold these roles for a limited time and are replaced by others coming into the system.

2. The administrative hierarchy incorporates a chain of command and channels of communication.

Table 11.5   **World Educational Enrollment Rates 1950–1992 and 2000–2005 (in percentages)**

Year	Primary Schooling	Secondary Schooling	Tertiary Schooling (University)
1950	36	13	1.4
1960	77	27	6.0
1970	84	36	11
1980	96	45	11
1992	98	53	14
2000–2005*	90 (M), 86 (F)	61 (M), 60 (F)	

Source: Boli 2002:309 for figures to 1992; Institute for Statistics 2006b:Table 5.

*Number of children enrolled in primary/secondary school who are of official school age, expressed as a percentage of the total number of children of official school age.

3. Specific rules and procedures in a school cover everything from course content to discipline in the classroom and use of the schoolyard.

4. Personal relationships are downplayed in favor of formalized relations among members of the system, such as placement on the basis of tests and grading.

5. Rationality governs the operations of the organization; people are hired and fired on the basis of their qualifications and how well they do their jobs.

One result of bureaucracy is that some children are not helped with personal problems or learning difficulties (Kozol 2006; Sizer 1984). Impersonal rules can lock people into rigid behavior patterns, leading to apathy and alienation. In schools, these feelings cause passivity among students, which in turn frustrates teachers. Children like Tomás in the opening example do not fit into neat cubbyholes that bureaucratic structures invariably create. These children view school not as a privilege but as a requirement imposed by an adult world. Caught between the demands of an impersonal bureaucracy and goals for their students, teachers cannot always give every child the personal help she or he needs. Thus, we see that organizational requirements of educational systems at a meso level can influence the personal student-teacher relationship at the micro level. This is another example of how the social world model helps us to understand human behavior in organizations.

The bottom line is that formal bureaucratic structures can thwart the goals of an education system. Even colleges and universities face controversies over control of decision making and direction of programs. For instance, funding of the university from business and government grants requires many professors to concentrate on research. In so doing, it takes time away from other functions of the university, such as teaching (Gamson 1998).

Education and the Social Institution of Family

Interconnections between meso-level institutions are a common refrain in this book. There are many interconnections between the institutions of family and education. When children enter kindergarten or primary school, they bring their prior experience, including socialization experiences from parents, brothers, sisters, and other relatives. Family background, according to many sociologists, is the single most important influence on children's school achievement (Jencks 1972). Children succeed in large part because of what their parents do to support them in education (MacLeod 1995; Schneider and Coleman 1993).

Most families stress the importance of education, but they do so in different ways. Middle-class parents in the

These chairs represent the bureaucracy or hierarchy of the school, with every student facing the teacher as though she or he is the only one who is expected to speak and is worthy of undivided attention. Look through other photos in this chapter, especially photos from nonindustrialized countries. What do you notice that is different about the arrangement of students that suggests differences in relationships in the school?

Global North tend to manage their children's education, visiting schools and teachers, having educational materials in the home, and holding high expectations for their children's achievement. In these families, children learn the values of hard work, good grades, and deferred gratification for reaching future goals.

In Korea, for example, parents select an academic or vocational track for their children after middle school. Some send their youngsters to private, competitive, specialized high schools that focus on foreign language, natural sciences, or the arts. At the end of high school, any student who wishes to go on to the university has only one chance to take the difficult competitive entrance exam. Koreans are concerned about the number of suicides among young people who do not pass this high-stakes exam. In Japan, students also take a high-stakes college entrance exam, but students who do not pass the first time have an additional year to retake it. In Israel, students receive either a plain or university-qualifying diploma, also based on an exam (Ayalon and Shavit 2004).

Involvement of parents from lower socioeconomic status and first-generation immigrant families can have significant impact on their children's educational outcomes (Bankston 2004; Domina 2005), yet these parents tend to look to schools as the authority. They are less involved in their children's schooling, leaving decisions to the school. Yet, children who must make educational decisions on their

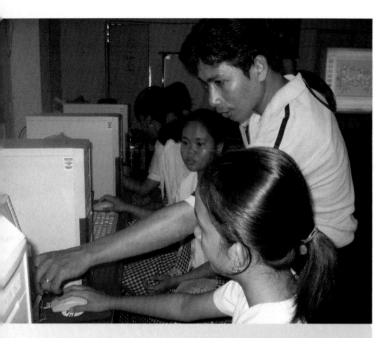

Computer skills are increasingly essential in our society and even for success in school, yet some children come from families that do not have access to computers. Children who have computers at home have a significant advantage. These students are receiving help from their teacher in the Philippines.

own are more likely to do poorly or to drop out of school (Kalmijn and Kraaykamp 1996).

Much of the disadvantage experienced by children from immigrant families, however, is rooted in the core problem—poverty. Shifts in the other institutions—family and the economy, for example—can impact educational achievement. Changes in family and work structures put parents under more stress. For example, busy single parents often have little time to help their children with school-work. People who work 60- or 70-hour weeks also find that their time being attentive to children's learning is limited.

Thinking Sociologically

How do religion, health, politics, economics, and other meso-level institutions influence education, and vice versa? What are examples of links between schools and other social institutions?

Educational Decision Making at the Meso Level

Who should have the power to make decisions about what children learn? In relatively homogeneous countries such as Japan and Sweden, where centralized goal setting and school decisions are possible, educational decision making typically causes little controversy. Centralized national ministries of education are also common in Latin American, Asian, and African countries, where educational standards and funding are controlled by the national government. By contrast, heterogeneous societies, such as Canada, Israel, and the United States, include many different racial, ethnic, regional, and religious subcultures, each with its own needs and interests. Teachers, administrators, school boards, parents, and interest groups all claim the right to influence the curriculum. Consider influences from micro and macro levels on the meso-level organization.

Local-Level Influences

At the U.S. local community level, curriculum conflicts occur routinely over the selection of reading material and sex education courses, for example, as well as any content that is thought to contain obscenity, sex, nudity, political or economic bias, profanity, slang or nonstandard English, racism or racial hatred, and antireligious or presumed anti-American sentiment (Delfattore 2004). For example, Family Friendly Libraries, an online grassroots interest group that started in Virginia, argues that the popular *Harry Potter* books should be banned from school libraries. They believe the series promotes the religion of witchcraft (DeMitchell and Carney 2005).

Banned books in the past have included *The Wizard of Oz, Rumpelstiltskin, The Diary of Anne Frank, Madame Bovary, Soul on Ice, Grapes of Wrath, Huckleberry Finn,* Shakespeare's *Hamlet,* Chaucer's *The Miller's Tale,* and Aristophanes's *Lysistrata* (Ballantine 2009). Table 11.6 shows the most frequently challenged books in 2007. Off the list this year, but on for several years past, are *Catcher in the Rye,* by J. D. Salinger, *Of Mice and Men,* by John Steinbeck, and *Beloved,* by Toni Morrison.

Decisions about sex education curricula are equally fraught with controversy. The number of sexually active teens in the United States has risen substantially since 1980, increasing the number of citizens advocating sex education. Most sexually active teens have used at least one method of birth control—98% claiming such usage in one survey (Abma et al. 2004). A growing number of large city school districts, concerned with teen pregnancy and sexually transmitted disease, including AIDS, now provide teens with sex education, information about contraception, counseling, and sometimes condoms. Many who oppose sex education in schools claim that it appears to endorse premarital sex rather than abstinence and teaches teens how to have sex. Critics also believe that sex education should be left to families and religious institutions.

National-Level Influences

Because the U.S. Constitution leaves education in the hands of each state, the involvement of the federal government has been

Table 11.6	**The 10 Most Challenged Books of 2007**

The following are the 10 books that were most often challenged in public schools in 2007 and the reasons they were being contested.

1. *And Tango Makes Three* by Justin Richardson/Peter Parnell. Reasons: Anti-Ethnic, Sexism, Homosexuality, Anti-Family, Religious Viewpoint, Unsuited to Age Group

2. *The Chocolate War* by Robert Cormier. Reasons: Sexually Explicit, Offensive Language, Violence

3. *Olive's Ocean* by Kevin Henkes. Reasons: Sexually Explicit and Offensive Language

4. *The Golden Compass* by Philip Pullman. Reasons: Religious Viewpoint

5. *The Adventures of Huckleberry Finn* by Mark Twain. Reasons: Racism

6. *The Color Purple* by Alice Walker. Reasons: Homosexuality, Sexually Explicit, Offensive Language

7. *TTYL* by Lauren Myracle. Reasons: Sexually Explicit, Offensive Language, Unsuited to Age Group

8. *I Know Why the Caged Bird Sings* by Maya Angelou. Reasons: Sexually Explicit

9. *It's Perfectly Normal* by Robie Harris. Reasons: Sex Education, Sexually Explicit

10. *The Perks of Being a Wallflower* by Stephen Chbosky. Reasons: Homosexuality, Sexually Explicit, Offensive Language, Unsuited to Age Group

Source: American Library Association 2008.

Note: For the top 100 banned books, go to www.ala.org/ala/oif/bannedbooksweek/challengedbanned/challengedbanned.htm.

more limited than in most countries. Yet, the federal government wields enormous influence through its power to make federal funds available for special programs, such as mathematics and science, reading, or special education. The government may withhold funds from schools that are not in compliance with federal laws and the U.S. Constitution. For example, the federal government, courts, and public opinion forced all-male military academies to become coeducational, despite the schools' resistance to such change. School changes as a result of the Civil Rights Act and the Americans with Disability Act are other examples of federal government influence on local schools through the enforcement of federal laws. Schools have had to accommodate people with various disabilities—people who in the past would have been left out of the system.

Thus, policy decisions by federal lawmakers influence what and how children learn. This changes with each administration, based on liberal or conservative responses to calls for school reform. Reform reports have variously called for strengthening high school graduation requirements, raising college entrance requirements, emphasizing basic skills, requiring a longer school day and school year, improving the training and status of teachers, holding educators responsible for students' performance, providing the funds necessary to improve the educational system, and holding families accountable for children's achievement.

Since 1965 and the establishment of the U.S. Department of Education, each president has put his mark on the U.S. education system. President George W. Bush's controversial

No Child Left Behind (NCLB) initiative is a prime example. President Bush tied school performance to federal funds and required annual competency testing of students. Under NCLB, schools are required to administer achievement tests for accountability—tests that focus on math and reading. Schools failing to meet guidelines are penalized. The result is that 70% of schools reduce instructional time in other subject areas. The greatest reduction is in social studies, followed by science, art, music, and physical education (Center for Education Policy 2006). Many people feel that these subject areas should not be sacrificed for numerical gains in math and reading, however, and that the tests neglect to measure other important skills, such as critical thinking. So even in the decentralized United States, where only 1 out of 14 education dollars comes from the federal government, the macro-level society has an impact on what happens in the intimate environment of classrooms.

Research on the outcomes of this policy shows mixed results. It is healthy to set high standards, constructive to expect every child to succeed, and helpful to have some consistency between school systems in a geographically mobile society. However, NCLB policy makes no provision for differences in family backgrounds, socioeconomic status, preschool education, or the community context (Bracey 2005). NCLB also ignores much of what educators and social scientists know from research about teaching and learning, overemphasizes testing, penalizes schools that have proportionally more low-income students and students with disabilities, demoralizes schools through unrealistic timetables, and does not provide the funding necessary to carry out the mandates, further disadvantaging small, rural, and poor school districts (Bracey 2005; Karen 2005). Today, 14% of U.S. adults are below the most basic level of literacy in using printed and written information to function in society and in using quantitative skills, and another 29% are at the basic level (NCES 2006a).

Thinking Sociologically

Educational needs at the micro (individual) level, the meso (institutional or ethnic group) level, or the macro (national) level can be very different. What benefits the individual may not be of benefit to the ethnic group or the system, and what helps schools as organizations may not be the highest priority for the nation. This raises the question of who makes decisions and whether individual needs or societal needs take precedence. Where do you think the primary authority for decision making should be—local, state, or national? Why?

Macro-level political and economic trends outside a country can have a significant impact on the educational system as well. External influences include international relations and events as well as new technologies and new knowledge. In the United States, for example, the terrorist attacks on the World Trade Center and Pentagon on September 11, 2001, reshaped school curricula overnight, as schools added units on terrorism, American values, and Islam.

IS EDUCATION THE ROAD TO OPPORTUNITY? STRATIFICATION AT THE MACRO LEVEL

Carlos Muñoz was born in San Diego, the only child of Rafael and Yolanda Muñoz. Both of Carlos's parents were born in Mexico, but they met and were married in the United States. They divorced several years ago, and Carlos alternates living with his mother and father. His mother has long worked as a teacher's aide in the local school district. She lives in a tidy house in a working-class, mostly Mexican area near downtown San Diego. She periodically takes Carlos on trips to Mexico.

Mrs. Muñoz graduated from a high school in the same district where she is now employed, and she is knowledgeable about the educational system here. She is happy with Carlos's high school, which is not overcrowded and understaffed as his junior high school had been, but she is worried about his school performance. She says that he lacks *ganas* (desire) and is not spending enough time or effort on his studies. "He tries to do everything fast. . . . He's getting

an F in biology and Cs in most other classes," she says. Of her career hopes for Carlos, she says, "It would be perfect for him to be a lawyer, but he needs to work harder. I don't think that he can do it." His father has now taken a more active role in Carlos's education, hoping to get him on the right track again (Portes and Rumbaut 2001:14–15).

Mrs. Muñoz and millions of other immigrant parents in countries around the world have high hopes for their children, hopes that can be realized through education. Immigrant families from around the globe view education as essential to success in their new cultures. Many groups push their children to achieve in order to improve their opportunities in the new country (Kao 2004). This section focuses on the role of education in the stratification system. Although it has implications regarding individual families' chances to succeed, the reality is that education is deeply interwoven into the macro-level inequalities of the society.

Can Schools Bring About Equality in Societies?

Equal opportunity exists when all people have an equal chance of achieving high socioeconomic status in society regardless of their class, ethnicity or race, or gender (Riordan 2004). James Coleman (1968, 1990) describes the goals of equal educational opportunity:

- to provide a common curriculum for all children regardless of background;
- to provide that children from diverse backgrounds attend the same school; and
- to provide equality within a given locality.

In the United States, equal opportunity means that children are provided with equal facilities, financing, and access to school programs (Kozol 1991). Schools in poor neighborhoods or in rural villages in the United States and around the world, however, often lack the basics—safe buildings, school supplies and books, and funds to operate. Lower class minority students who live in these areas fall disproportionately at the bottom of the educational hierarchy. Many children face what seem to be insurmountable barriers to educational success: increasing numbers of children living in poverty, lack of health care and immunizations, school absence due to illness or homelessness, or dropouts to help the family (Kozol 2005).

Two widely cited classical studies on equal educational opportunity, the Coleman Report and Jencks's study of inequality (Coleman et al. 1966; Jencks 1972), have had major impact on policy in education and stand out because of their comprehensive data collection, analysis, and contribution to the understanding of inequality. Coleman found that the differences in test scores between minority students and white students were due not only to in-school factors, but also parents' education levels and other environmental factors such as segregated schools, economic makeup of schools, and some differences in facilities. Based on these findings, Coleman recommended integration of schools to create a climate for achievement. That recommendation resulted in plans to integrate, but also in controversy and court challenges (Orfield et al. 1997). Today, busing and other methods to desegregate schools such as magnet schools and choice plans are in place. "How Do We Know?" describes a study of magnet schools.

Thinking Sociologically

In Metz's study reported on page 368, what are the advantages or disadvantages of using several different ways of gathering data?

The second major study that shaped educational policy in the 1970s (Jencks 1972) argued that schools alone cannot create equal opportunity. Even if schools reduce the educational attainment gap, economic inequality among adults continues to exist. The bottom line is that most agree schools alone cannot solve the achievement gap between students.

Who Gets Ahead and Why? The Role of Education in Stratification

Education is supposed to be a **meritocracy**, a formal system in which people are allocated to positions according to their abilities and credentials. This, of course, is consistent with the principles of a rationalized or formal bureaucratic social system, where the most qualified person is promoted and decisions are impersonal and based on "credentials" (Charles, Roscigno, and Torres 2007). Still, in societies around the world, we see evidence that middle-class and elite children, especially boys in the Global South, receive more and better education than equally qualified children. Children do not attend school on an equal footing, and in many cases, meritocracy does not exist. Why is Tomás "unlucky" while others succeed? Explanations go beyond a focus on the children's abilities to analyses of background factors, ethnic groups, the placements of their families in the stratification system, and the role of their country in the world system. Conflict theorists, in particular, maintain that education creates and perpetuates inequality. The haves hold the power to make sure that institutions, including schools, serve their own needs and protect their access to privileges (Sadovnik 2004). Elite parents have social and cultural capital—language skills, knowledge of how the social system works, and networks—to ensure that their children succeed (Kao 2004).

A country's level of education is a key indicator of quality of life and placement in the global social world. Industrialized countries want to trade with poor countries,

which provide natural resources and new pools of workers and consumers. Education helps to enable poorer countries and their citizens to participate and compete in global markets. As a consequence, international organizations such as the United Nations and transnational business communities have become more involved in educational development, especially in programs for training workers in technology.

Sources of Inequality

Three sources of inequality in schools—testing, tracking, and funding—illustrate how schools reproduce and perpetuate social stratification. They also give clues as to what might be done to minimize the repetitious pattern of poverty.

Assessing Student Achievement: Testing. Testing is one means of placing students in schools according to their achievement and merit and of determining progress being made. Critics of standardized testing argue that test questions, language differences, and testing situations are biased against lower class, minority, and immigrant students, resulting in lower scores and relegating these students to lower tracks in the educational system. In addition, in the case of IQ tests, scientists know that intelligence is complex and that paper-and-pencil tests measure only selected types of intelligence (Gardner 1987, 1999). Other scholars question whether the tests are unbiased for boys and for girls from different class and ethnic backgrounds. Critics of achievement tests point out that higher class students with better schooling and enriched backgrounds do better on the tests, even if they have not gained as much knowledge. Nonetheless, testing is the means used to evaluate student achievement locally, nationally, and internationally. Table 11.7 shows differences in ACT (American College Test) and SAT (Scholastic Assessment Test) scores depending on sex, race, and ethnic group.

Governments compare their students' educational test scores on the International Assessment of Educational Progress and the International Association for the Evaluation of Educational Achievement (IEA) with other countries' scores to determine how their students and educational systems are performing. These are tests of children around the world in literacy, mathematics, science, civic education, and foreign language. For example, recently IEA tested students in the Fourth International Mathematics and Science Study, in which more than 60 countries participated, testing children at the 4th-, 8th-, and 12th-grade levels (IEA 2007). These rankings provide information on the similarities, differences, and effects of development on education (Ballantine and Spade 2008). However, copying educational systems of successful countries is not necessarily the answer to improvement, for education occurs in different cultural contexts (Kagan and Stewart 2005; Zhao 2005).

Educational inequality among countries includes differences in achievement in different parts of the curriculum. For example, some countries rank higher in math and

How Do We Know?

Life and Learning in Magnet Schools

Mary Haywood Metz studied three magnet schools in a city school district that she identifies as Heartland, U.S.A.; the overall goal for establishing the magnet schools was to accomplish court-ordered desegregation and to stimulate innovative education. By closing some black neighborhood schools and locating magnet schools in black neighborhoods, the city achieved desegregation without mandatory reassignment of students.

Each of the three magnet schools offered a different type of program to attract students. The first offered Individually Guided Education, with special organization of the curriculum, instructional techniques, and specific roles of staff members. The second offered "open education" developed by the staff. This school offered a highly flexible curriculum that required and encouraged self-directed students. The third school—for gifted and talented students—had a policy of selective admissions and promised an enriched traditional curriculum.

Metz answered the question, "How do we know", by spending a semester in each school and three years in the district dong observation, open-ended formal and informal interviews, and analysis of documents. Ethnographic studies are useful when one wishes to learn how organizations work within their settings or environments. Metz's goal was to understand the character, atmosphere (climate), and influences shaping the lives of these three magnet schools—what really happened in these schools—and to learn about the experiences of the schools' participants. She used multiple research strategies—interviewing, participant observation, and documents—both in the schools and the school district.

> To describe and explain the character of the life of each school in a holistic way, the researcher needed to participate in that life, to observe and in some measure experience the life the adults and students led.
>
> She used open-ended interviews which allowed students, teachers, administrators, and parents to respond to questions in their own words and at length made it possible to explore their perspectives. . . .
>
> Observation was conducted in classrooms, halls, cafeterias, playgrounds, girls' bathrooms, and in teachers' lounges and dining-rooms . . . formal interviews were conducted with a small sample of students, most teachers and administrators, and a few parents. . . . Documents used for analysis included student and faculty handbooks from each school, bulletins for students and faculty, announcements of meetings, and a variety of other written statements. (Metz 1986:13–14)

In addition, Metz considered the historical context of desegregation in which the schools developed, as well as the community climate.

In her book, Metz describes aspects of the daily lives within the schools, the faculty culture, principal-teacher relations, the development of school loyalty, and other characteristics of the three magnet schools. In Heartland, the magnet school concept was only partially successful in desegregating schools. Most children bused were black, and many parents sent their children to the closest school regardless of the program offered.

The magnet schools in Heartland made desegregation palatable. Each of these three schools enjoyed some success in dealing with diverse student populations; however, many districts are struggling to understand how to integrate schools and improve student achievements. Proposed solutions include magnet schools, charter schools, and publicly owned schools.

Each solution offers promising aspects but also has bothersome limitations. This makes research like Metz's even more central to finding the right solutions for future education reforms. Metz provides researchers, school personnel, policymakers, and practitioners an understanding of daily life in these schools as experienced by the participants.

Table 11.7 ACT and SAT Scores by Sex and Race/Ethnicity

ACT Scores: 2007	Average	SAT Scores: 2008 (continued)	Average
Composite, total scores	**21.2**	**SAT Writing, all students**	**497**
Male	21.2	Male	491
Female	21.0	Female	502
Race/ethnicity		White	519
African American	17.0	Black/African American	424
American Indian	18.9	Mexican American	447
Hispanic	18.7	Puerto Rican	445
Caucasian	22.1	Other Hispanic	449
Asian American	22.6	Asian American	516
		American Indian	470
SAT Scores: 2008	Average	Other	494
SAT Critical Reading, all students	**502**	**SAT Math, all students**	**509**
Male	504	Male	527
Female	500	Female	499
White	528	White	537
Black/African American	430	Black/African American	426
Mexican American	454	Mexican American	463
Puerto Rican	456	Puerto Rican	453
Other Hispanic	455	Other Hispanic	461
Asian American	513	Asian American	591
American Indian	495	American Indian	491
Other	496	Other	512

Source: Inside Higher Ed 2007 for ACT scores; Inside Higher Ed 2008 for SAT scores.

science, but the same countries do not always rank high in reading (Baker 2002). East Asian countries routinely score highest on math and science achievement. Many educators believe that gleaning ideas and adapting methods from other successful systems will help improve scores, but cultural context determines what will be successful (Houlihan 2005; Kagan and Stewart 2005; Stewart 2005; Suarez-Orozco 2005; Zhao 2005).

Thinking Sociologically

Evaluate your testing experience on variables mentioned above. Were your scores an accurate measure of your ability or achievement? Why or why not? What other factors entered in? Have your scores affected your life chances?

Tracking. *Tracking* (sometimes called *streaming*) places students in ability groups, allowing educators to address students' individual learning needs. It also contributes to the stratification process that perpetuates inequality. Research finds that tracking levels correlate directly with factors such as the child's background and ethnic group, language skills, appearance, and other socioeconomic variables (Kilgore 1991; Oakes 1985, 1990; Rosenbaum 1999; Wells and Oakes 1996). In other words, track placement is not always a measure of a student's ability. It can be arbitrary, based on teachers' impressions or questionable test results. Even language differences between teachers and students can affect placement (Mehan 1992). Over time, differences in children's achievement become reinforced. Students from lower social classes and minority groups are clustered in the lower tracks and complete fewer years and lower levels of school (Lucas and Berends 2002; Oakes et al. 1997). School failure in early adolescence leads to other problems later on that affect employment and socioeconomic status (Chen and Kaplan 2003).

This computer class is held at a formerly failing inner-city British school, transformed by new management and increased governmental funding. Many students come from situations that present educational challenges: refugee status, children in temporary shelters, or non-English speaking homes. However, the school is highly successful and has become a "government beacon school."

School Funding. The amount of money available to fund schools and the sources providing it affect the types of programs offered, an important issue for nations that must compete in the global social and economic system. In some societies, money for education comes from central governments and, in others, from a combination of federal, state, and local government and private sources, such as religious denominations and philanthropies. In countries such as Uganda, the government runs the schools, but most funding comes from tuition paid by each student or by the student's parents.

Whatever the source, schools sometimes face budget crises and must trim programs. In the United States, unequal school spending results from reliance on local property taxes as well as state and federal funds. About 50% of the money for U.S. schools comes from state funds and most of the rest from property taxes. Spending is closely related to the racial and class composition of schools and to student achievement levels. Schools in low-income communities are particularly disadvantaged by smaller tax bases and fewer local resources (Condron and Roscigno 2003). Wealthier districts, on the other hand, can afford better education

for their children because more money is collected from property taxes. Higher class students have advantages not available in poor districts (Kozol 1991, 2005; Wenglinsky 1997). Controversies over school funding in the United States have reached the courtroom in a number of states, yet overall, the United States spends less money per student on education than most other industrialized nations.

Thinking Sociologically

Were you tracked in any subjects? What effect, if any, did this have? What effect did tracking have on friends of yours?

Public and Private Schools

In the United States, Catholic parochial schools are the most prevalent type of private schools. Other religiously affiliated schools are the next most common. Private preparatory schools are third. About 10% of U.S. students attend private schools.

Studies of low-income and minority students have found that those attending Catholic schools, especially in inner cities, perform more like white middle-class students than those attending public schools (Morgan 2001). In general, private schools are more academically demanding, more stringent, more disciplined, and more orderly. They assign more homework, and they demand more parental involvement than do public schools (Cookson and Persell 1985). They can also expel children who do not perform or are disruptive, an option the public schools often do not have.

However, much of the reason private schools have generally had higher levels of achievement is the select population they admit. A massive study released in the summer of 2006 by the U.S. Department of Education compared 7,000 public schools and 530 private schools. The study controlled for student socioeconomic backgrounds in a way that is often not done, and it found that children performed roughly on par in the two types of schools, either private or public schools, excelling slightly in either math or reading depending on grade level. The only group that lagged significantly was children attending conservative Protestant Christian schools (Schemo 2006).

Proposed choice and voucher plans allowing students and parents to choose their schools have been controversial in part because it is thought that public schools might well be left with the least capable students and teachers, further stratifying an already troubled system (Chubb and Moe 1990). Private schools could also become sanctuaries for those who do not want integrated schools and could perpetuate religious and racial segregation.

Educational Social Policy Issues

In the early 21st century, school systems around the world face dramatic changes: pressures for equal educational opportunity for all groups—classes and castes, race and ethnic groups, females and males. The need for technological training of citizenry, increased demand for more access to higher education, changes in the student composition of the classroom, and accountability and testing of students and teachers are but a few of the many issues. Because education reflects societal politics and problems, policies swing from conservative to more liberal and back again, depending on who is in power and what their agenda is for change.

Consider the current concerns about world tensions that are resulting in internationalization of the classroom (King 2006). Within our lifetimes, we are likely to experience several of these swings. For example, currently in the United States, the issues of accountability, standardized testing, and

Schoolgirls in Kenya wait for classes to begin. Children like this, whose parents can afford to send them to school, will likely grow up with enough education to have better economic prospects.

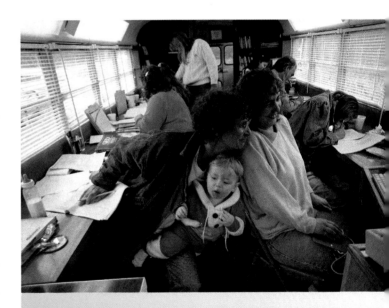

"The Little Red School Bus," sponsored by the nonprofit Christian Appalachian Project, helps residents in rural Kentucky prepare for high school equivalency certificates and a better chance of finding a job. This may be the only chance for an education these people will experience.

teaching basic skills are at the forefront, but movements toward individualization of education and developing the whole child are reappearing (Gamoran 2001). Although the past century brought some improvement in equality in education, much remains to be done to level the playing field. The greatest barrier to equal education in the 21st century, both within and between countries, may prove to be socioeconomic, with many minorities represented in lower classes.

The Applied Sociologist at Work— Carl Schmitt

Government Analyses and Planning in Education

How do local, regional, and national educational officials know about children's achievements in school? How do children in different countries compare academically? How many schools and teachers will be needed in future years? What is the effect of race, class, and gender on school experiences? Dr. Carl Schmitt has worked for the U.S. Department of Education's National Center for Education Statistics (NCES) for more than 20 years. During this time, he has used longitudinal data to research many of these questions, and his answers help officials at various levels, from the national government to local schools, plan for school children and their needs.

From 1972 to 1990, the NCES sponsored five national longitudinal studies that obtained data from students and educators through repeated surveys over time. These studies looked at the educational experiences of elementary, secondary, and postsecondary students. The first, done in 1972, focused on a cohort of high school seniors. The second, in 1980, included both high school sophomores and seniors. A third study, completed in 1988, focused on eighth graders. Then in 1990 and 1993, the agency conducted research on students' lives and successes after graduation. A sixth study in 1995 focused on early childhood kindergarten cohorts.

These studies were motivated by a number of issues in education: declining test scores, the dropout rate, increased vocational education opportunities, and access to postsecondary and vocational education. Together, they provide rich data on students' experiences and help explain why some fail. Data were collected from students and on student academic and testing records, data on school policies, teacher practices, family involvement, persistence in school, participation in postsecondary education, and information on current educational issues. These data are used by many social scientists and drive much of what we know about education.

One of Schmitt's tasks is to produce data files that can be used by others for policy formation and publications. To prepare the data, he must understand complex statistical data analyses and be able to communicate the key findings to a professional audience. One of his research projects drew insights and information from two studies to examine the institution of education as a system that has an impact on the larger society. When dealing with information about public schools, districts, and state education agencies, he looks at the data in ways that make the findings useful to others. Managing and analyzing large amounts of data are key tools for his work.

To carry out his work, Schmitt uses computers to write programs that analyze data, do graphics work, and calculate trends using statistical packages such as SPSS and SAS. Schmitt experiences some frustrations from working in a government agency because he does not always have control over what is produced from his work. However, the frustrations are easily outweighed by the rewards of providing valuable information that could make a difference in the lives of children and school officials and of making complex data accessible for large audiences.

Note: Dr. Carl Schmitt received his graduate degrees from New York University. He specialized in methodology and quantitative analysis, social stratification and inequality, and complex organizations. He learned both substantive information and methodological skills that are essential for his work.

Sociologists of education contribute to the policy discussions in their roles as researchers, consultants, policy analysts, and applied sociologists, as illustrated in "The Applied Sociologist at Work" feature at the top of this page.

Educational Policies in the United States

Today, despite numerous U.S. government policies and reports, the data on school success show a worsening picture. There are 27 million functionally illiterate U.S. citizens, with many 17–year-olds unable to write well or solve mathematical problems and lacking the basic skills needed to enter business and the military. In some major inner cities, only a quarter of students graduate from high school (CBS News 2008).

Each new presidential administration proposes educational reforms to address the same problems. Under the Bush administration plan, NCLB, schools are required to administer achievement tests for accountability—tests that focus on math and reading. Schools failing to meet guidelines are penalized. The result is that 70% of schools are reducing instructional time in other subjects to teach more reading and math. The greatest reduction is in social studies, followed by science, art, music, and physical education (Center for Education Policy 2006). Critics argue that these are extremely important fields for the 21st century and should not be shortchanged. Numerical gains based on math and reading achievement tests do not measure learning in many other areas, and they certainly do not measure ability to think critically.

Providing Early Childhood Education

Early childhood education has been touted as providing the start that many children need to be successful in school, as discussed below. In the United States, compensatory education helps to narrow the opportunity gap, and a key part is early childhood education offered by the Head Start program. Evaluations of the Head Start program in the United States, designed for three- to five-year-olds from disadvantaged backgrounds, show that it increases the likelihood that enrolled children stay in school, receive preventive health care, avoid later remedial classes, and do not become juvenile delinquents. Parental education is also part of the compensatory education program. Yet, fewer than half of the eligible children take part in the program due to fluctuations in support as political administrations change (Schweinhart 1997).

Comparing early childhood education programs, research in China, India, Brazil, Canada, and Europe demonstrate similar findings:

1. Children from birth to age five develop rapidly in linguistic and cognitive abilities, emotional development, social regulatory development, and other capacities.

2. In the child's early years, the growth trajectory in learning, health, and emotional development should not be interrupted.

3. Needs of young children are not always adequately addressed.

4. In developing countries, child survival programs that concentrate on reducing infant mortality rates, increasing immunization rates, improving nutrition, and providing clean water and sanitation services have produced long-term economic benefits (Levine 2005; UNICEF 2004).

Global Policy Issues in Education

Most societies view the education and training of young people as an economic investment in the future. Countries with capitalist economic systems are more likely to have an educational system that stresses individualism and competition, pitting students against one another for the best grades and the best opportunities. The elites often ensure that their own children get a very different education than the children of the laboring class. Socialist and traditional economic systems often encourage cooperation and collaboration among students, with the collective needs of society viewed as more important than those of individuals. The social economic values of the society are reflected in approaches to learning and in motivation of students (Rankin and Aytaç 2006).

Two young girls use the computers in a classroom during a Head Start program. The Head Start program introduces reading and writing to children who are about to enter elementary school. It is one federal effort in the United States to provide support to children from poor neighborhoods and families.

Other studies compare the curricula of nations and changes in those curricula to determine how similar and different they are. Findings generally support a convergence of curricular themes across nations, reflecting the interdependence of nations. However, many researchers question whether that convergence is good for all people in all societies, especially students from peripheral Global South countries.

Political and economic trends outside of a country can also have an impact on the educational system within the country. Examples of external influences include world educational and technological trends, new inventions, and new knowledge. Even an event like the terrorist attacks on the World Trade Center and the Pentagon on September 11, 2001, shapes the school curricula, as schools give greater weight to patriotism. In addition to loyalty, however, schools often need to teach people to accept those who are different from themselves—that is, to reduce prejudice.

Education of Girls Around the Globe

"One of the silent killers attacking the developing world is the lack of quality basic education for large numbers of the poorest children in the world's poorest countries—particularly girls" (Sperling 2005:213). In 2005, more than 110 million children—60% of them girls from ages 6 to 11—received no schooling at all. Another 150 million dropped out of primary school. About 50% of girls in sub-Saharan Africa do not complete primary school, and only 17% are in secondary school (UNESCO 2005). Of the one sixth of the world's population that is illiterate, two thirds are women (Dobriansky 2006).

Recent controversy in France has focused on Islamic girls and women wearing the traditional head covering to schools, which French officials thought was a contributor to "we" versus "they" polarization between Muslims and non-Muslims. At this school fair organized by the French League of Muslim Women, women joined in on the fun of hula-hoop challenge. Still, being "different" is alienating rather than fun, and societies work better when there is diversity and tolerance of diversity.

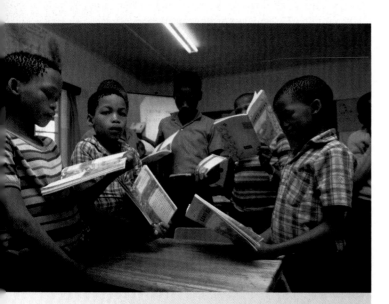

In Namibia, as elsewhere around the world, an education is increasingly necessary as the economy is globalized and skills in literacy and numeracy become critical to survival and hopes of prosperity.

In Niger, for instance, only 12% of girls in rural areas are in primary school, compared to 83% in the capital city, Niamey. In refugee camps in Africa, only 6% of children receive any secondary education due to hardships from lack of teachers as well

as AIDS and orphaned status. Even when children do receive some primary education, the quality is such that many children leave school without basic skills (UNESCO 2005).

The availability of clean drinking water is a major issue in the Global South. Because women and girls must spend as much as six hours a day carrying water to the home (26% of a woman's day in Africa), the daughters are needed to care for children. When wells are built so that usable water is more accessible, the school attendance of girls immediately increased by 15% in Bangladesh and by 12% in Tanzania (WaterAid 2004). Indeed, research by WaterAid (2008) estimates that in the Global South, 443 million school days are lost each year due to water-related diseases.

What is clear is that when girls are educated, the consequences are great: "What is striking is the breadth of benefits derived from educating girls—not only economic benefits in terms of higher wages, greater agricultural productivity, and faster economic growth, but also health benefits." Sexual activity (as well as marrying at young ages and failing to use contraception) is dramatically reduced when girls are in school and learn about AIDS. We know that girls in Uganda "with some secondary education were three times less likely to be HIV-positive, and those with some primary school were about half as likely to be HIV-positive" (Sperling 2005:214). When school fees were abolished in Uganda, Kenya, and Tanzania in East Africa, enrollments increased dramatically. Additional incentives to parents to compensate for the loss of labor of their children also increase enrollment, as shown in Bangladesh, Mexico, and Brazil. In China, better educated citizens hold more egalitarian gender attitudes (Shu 2004), and in Turkey, gender inequalities in education are lessened in metropolitan areas and in less patriarchal families (Rankin and Aytaç 2006). In Taiwan, researchers find that the social class and education level of the parents play a major role in the educational attainment of their children, especially daughters. The education of girls is raising the standards of living for them and their families (Jao and McKeever 2006).

Thinking Sociologically

How might education be important to countries competing in the world system? How might education be affected by global events, such as a war or a worldwide economic recession?

The Future of Education in the Global System

The search for the perfect model of education is never-ending. School systems around the world are under pressure to meet the diverse needs of both the societies as a whole and their individual citizens. A major concern in Global North countries as they move into the Information Age is this: What will become of those students who do not complete enough education to fit into the technological and economic needs in the 21st century (Von Holzen 2005)? In these countries, high school used to prepare most young people for a job and marriage. By the 1990s, high school was preparation for college, which was itself necessary to find a decent job in the globalizing world. In the United States, educators, corporations, wealthy individuals, and philanthropies—concerned that minority groups are falling behind—support special programs to reduce cyber-segregation of haves and have-nots (Attewell 2001), the latter composed of poor and minority families. Some companies are donating funds and computers to schools in poor countries to reduce the digital divide (Williams 2000).

Although the cyber-gap may be slowly closing, there are differences in the implementation of new innovations and ways computers are used. Electronic textbooks and materials have potential to give both the affluent Global North and the poor Global South immediate access to new knowledge and ideas that can continually be updated through e-textbooks (Rossman 2005). Video games are used by corporations, the government, and the military to educate. Advocates argue, "They let people participate in the world. They let players . . . *inhabit* roles that are otherwise inaccessible to them" (Shaffer et al. 2005:105). Much learning will take place without walls, clocks, or age segregation as students learn through distance learning and through digital technology on their own time (Lundt 2004). Classrooms of the future will incorporate technological innovations and use of information networks.

One form of technology that is having a major impact on the future is the Internet. The next "Sociology in Your Social World" discusses application of Internet and other computer technologies to higher education.

Computer and Internet skills are essential to success in college and most jobs in this globalized social world. Many courses, even degrees, can now be done online.

Thinking Sociologically

First, read the feature on distance education on page 376. How might distance education in higher education affect segments of the population—the poor, the working class, the middle class—differently? What implications does it have for equal access to education for ethnic groups? People of color? Men and women? In what ways would it be beneficial, and in what ways might it cause new problems?

The link between school completion and work, or what is referred to as the *school-to-work transition*, is clearly defined and planned by public policy in most European countries and Russia. Schools offer postsecondary options such as vocational school and associate degrees to prepare young people for skilled positions (Kerckhoff 2001), and numbers of needed engineers or dentists determine the educational slots available in these fields. However, these options are poorly defined in other countries, especially the United States (Altbach and Davis 1999).

In the process of governments developing their educational policies, we again see the interconnections of our social world. Curricula respond to global events and international markets and are also shaped by micro-level effectiveness or ineffectiveness of teachers and students in individual classrooms. The macro-level concerns and the micro-level processes come together in education, with the ultimate objective to prepare individuals in each classroom to meet the needs of the community, the state, the nation, and the world.

Sociology in Your Social World

Distance Education: Breaking Access Barriers?

Amy J. Orr

Technology has had a tremendous impact on education. Computers are used in a variety of ways in classrooms around the world for both the consumption and production of knowledge. The Internet, as well as programs such as WebCT and Blackboard, has made the distribution of education around the world much more feasible. Today, thousands of individuals worldwide can obtain a college degree while sitting in front of their computers.

According to the U.S. Department of Education, distance learning is defined as "an option for earning course credit at off-campus locations via cable television, Internet, satellite classes, videotapes, correspondence courses, or other means." In 2004–2005, about two thirds of postsecondary institutions in the United States offered distance education courses (National Center for Education Statistics 2006b), and the number continues to increase. Around the world, distance education is available in countries such as Australia, Canada, China, India, Japan, Mexico, Thailand, Turkey, and the United Kingdom.

One of the primary purposes of distance learning is to increase access by learners who might not ordinarily be able to obtain a traditional postsecondary education. For example, distance education courses are often heavily used by nontraditional students who wish to continue their education but face barriers such as family or employment. Questions arise, however, regarding the level of accessibility that is truly provided to underrepresented groups throughout the United States and the world. Does distance education provide new opportunities for these groups to attain postsecondary education? Or are new barriers created due to the increasing use of technology to deliver a college curriculum?

In an attempt to address these questions, the National Postsecondary Education Cooperative (NPEC) explored the relationship between distance learning and access to college education in the United States. In a report published in 2004, the NPEC concluded that (1) distance education increases overall access to postsecondary education, (2) a "digital divide" still remains for some groups, such as blacks and Hispanics, (3) a "dearth of germane information, literacy barriers, and limited diversity of content are significant barriers to getting lower income users online," and (4) low-income students are less likely than those with higher incomes to have opportunities to gain the skills required to use the technology (NPEC 2004).

Similar issues arise on a global level. Access to technology differs significantly by nation. Like disadvantaged students in the United States, individuals in the least developed nations may face literacy barriers or find the curriculum irrelevant. An additional concern arises with regard to diversity of cultural contexts and perspectives. Numerous studies report cross-cultural differences in student learning styles as well as diverse preferences for teaching approaches. For example, Weisenberg and Stacey (2005), on reviewing a number of cross-cultural studies, note that Asian students are accustomed to individualized learning techniques and tend to prefer "teacher-centered" teaching styles. Online pedagogies tend to emphasize collaborative learning and "student-centered" techniques. Because distance learning rests on the technological foundations of Western culture, minority cultures around the world may be further marginalized, as the dominant pedagogies may not be responsive to their cultural uniqueness (Smith and Ayers 2006).

Overall, distance education presents a dilemma with regard to the accessibility of postsecondary education. Although it provides unprecedented opportunities to expand access to education, distance education also runs the risk of creating new divides.

So What?

Educational systems are typically viewed as the channel for reduction of inequality, the source of upward mobility, the way to improve the economy, and the path for reduction of prejudice in societies. However, institutions such as education also have a vested interest in stability. Schools foster patriotism and loyalty toward the political system, families support schools and education, and education is expected to support the economic vitality of the nation. Institutions and organizations are driven by interest in their own survival, and risk-taking behaviors on behalf of change are not necessarily ones that foster survival. Taking risks may threaten those who have power, privilege, and influence. It should not be surprising, therefore, that education does more to enhance stability than to create change. Still, those who seek to improve the society see tremendous potential in education as an agent of change if its influence can be harnessed. It works largely with young minds in the socialization process—carrying out what powerful policymakers feel is important.

Another institution that socializes individuals has a meaning system that believers feel is the ultimate reality and is at the core of goodness and transformation of the world. We turn in the next chapter to a sociological perspective on religion.

Key Points

What Have We Learned?

- Education is one of the primary institutions of society, focusing on socialization of children and adults into their cultures so they become contributing members. (See pp. 344–345.)

- What we learn in schools goes far beyond the formal curriculum. Sometimes these implicit messages support the educational system, but sometimes they sabotage the formal and intended messages. (See pp. 357–361.)

- At the micro level, social theory is attentive to interaction in classrooms and local schools, using concepts of symbolic interaction or cost-benefit analysis to understand the climate of learning. (See pp. 346–347.)

- Macro-level theories focus on how education supports the social system (functionalism) or on how education serves the interests of the "haves" and reproduces social inequality (conflict theory). (See pp. 347–351.)

- At the micro level, various statuses and roles interact within a school, and classrooms develop their own cultures that may or may not enhance learning. (See pp. 351–362.)

- At the meso level, education can be understood as a formal organization that works toward certain goals (bureaucracy) but that has many of the dysfunctions of other bureaucracies. (See pp. 362–366.)

- At the macro level, national governments often try to see that their national needs are met by shaping educational policy, and their actions often create tension with those administrators and teachers at the meso and micro levels who do the actual work of teaching. (See pp. 366–373.)

- Educating is also a global concern, with a variety of questions about how to help economic development in the Global South without imposing Western models that are incompatible with the cultures of other countries. (See pp. 373–375.)

Contributing to Our Social World: What Can We Do?

At the Local Level: Many colleges and universities are faced with high rates of attrition, a measure of the extent to which students who are admitted do not complete their degrees because of poor academic performance. To counter this trend, some schools have established programs to identify and assist at-risk students at an early point in their studies. One example is the FIGS (First-Year Interest Groups) program, in which entering students identified as at-risk take special courses, receive tutoring and peer mentoring, meet together to discuss common problems, and in some cases live in the same residence hall. Is there a FIGS or similar program on your campus? If so, contact its office and learn about how it works. Find out if you can volunteer to work as a tutor or in another capacity. If not, learn more about FIGS at other schools such as the University of Wisconsin (www .lssaa.wisc.edu/figs), the University of Washington (http:// depts.washington.edu/figs/), or the University of Missouri (http://admissions.missouri.edu/housing/whatsAFIG.php). With this information, contact your school's admissions or academic advising office and explore the possibility of establishing such a program on your campus.

At the Organization or Institutional Level: Most primary schools welcome volunteers who can read to young students and tutor them in reading. Contact a faculty member on your campus who specializes in early childhood education and investigate the opportunities for such volunteer work. The faculty member may also be able to identify community learning centers that children attend after school to get help with reading. Such centers use volunteers and may even have paid, part-time job openings.

At the National and Global Levels: Teach for America is a national organization, modeled along the lines of AmeriCorps and Peace Corps, that places recent college graduates in short-term (approximately two-year) assignments teaching in economically disadvantaged neighborhood schools. According to its Web site, at www.teachforamerica.org, "Teach For America is the national corps of outstanding recent college graduates and professionals of all academic majors and career interests who commit two years to teach in urban and rural public schools and become leaders in the effort to expand educational opportunity. . . . Our mission is to build the movement to eliminate educational inequity by enlisting our nation's most promising future leaders in the effort." Visit this site and consider working for the organization as a volunteer or intern or joining the corps following graduation. At the international level, you can support educational organizations, such as UNICEF and Care International. Consider teaching English abroad through one of many organizations that sponsor teachers. Visit www.globaltesol.com, www.soyouwanna.com, www .teachabroad.com, and related Web sites.

Visit **www.pineforge.com/ballantine2study** for online activities, sample tests, and other helpful information. Select "Chapter 11: Education" for chapter-specific activities.

CHAPTER 12

Religion

The Meaning of Sacred Meaning

Religion takes many forms and is expressed in many ways—but it is always about a sense of meaning. That meaning both generates and bestows religious feeling.

Think About It . . .

Micro: How did you become committed to a faith and a church—or not become so?

Micro: How do religious congregations affect the local community?

Meso: How does religion affect your family, education, political system, social position, and other aspects of your life?

Macro: How do religions provide solidarity or conflict within your country?

Macro: How do religions help solve world problems (war, poverty, hunger, disease, bigotry) or contribute to them?

Macro: Global Community

Macro: Society

Meso: National Organizations, Institutions, and Ethnic Subcultures

Micro: Local Organizations and Community

Micro: Me (and My Faith Community)

Micro: Your local church, temple, or mosque; outreach programs that impact the local community

Meso: Churches impact the economy, family life, education, government; regional denominational divisions make church policy

Macro: Denominational positions on national policies; religiously based social movements; religious television programming influencing national culture

Macro: Cross-national religious organizations; global outreach programs to address hunger or human rights at the international level

Before going to bed, Nandi Nwankwo from Nigeria sets out a bowl of milk and some food for the ancestors who, he believes, are present outside the family's dwelling at night. Respected ancestors protect family members, but they are also a powerful and even frightening force in guiding social behavior. Children are told that they must behave or the ancestors will punish them.

Abu Salmaan, a Muslim father and shopkeeper in Syria, prays frequently in keeping with the commands of the holy book of this faith. Like his neighbors, when the call to prayer is heard, he comes to the village square, faces Mecca, and prostates himself, with his head to the ground, to honor God and to pray for peace. Doing this five times a day is a constant reminder of his ultimate loyalty to God—whom he calls Allah. As part of the larger Abrahamic religious tradition (which includes Judaism, Christianity, and Islam), he is monotheistic and accepts the Hebrew Bible and the authority of Jeremiah, Isaiah, Amos, and Jesus as prophets. He believes that God also revealed Truth in another voice—that of Muhammad. He is devoted, worshipping daily, cherishing his family as directed by his scriptures, giving generously to charities, and making business decisions based on moral standards of a God-loving Muslim.

Trevor Weaver is a Presbyterian living in Louisville, Kentucky. He attends worship and prays to God in church and in emergencies when he feels helpless. Trevor had theological studies at a church-related college, and he has a remarkably strong knowledge of the scriptures. When he makes daily decisions, he thinks about the ethical implications of his behavior as "a member of the larger family of God." He opposes prayer in schools because this would make some children feel ostracized, he values diversity and acceptance of other traditions, and he believes each person needs to "work out his own theology." He thinks of himself as a person of faith, but his evangelical neighbor thinks he is a fallen soul.

Tuneq, knowledgeable Netsilik Eskimo hunter that he is, apologizes to the soul of the seal he has just killed. He shares the meat and blubber with his fellow hunters, and he makes sure that every part of the seal is used or consumed—skin, bones, eyes, tendons, brain, and muscles. If he fails to honor the seal by using every morsel, or if he violates a rule of hunting etiquette, an invisible vapor will come from his body and sink through the ice, snow, and water. This vapor will collect in the hair of Nuliajuk, goddess of the sea. In revenge, she will call the sea mammals to her so the people living on the ice above will starve. Inuit religion provides rules that help to enforce an essential ecological ethic among these arctic hunters to preserve the delicate natural balance.

These are but a few examples from the world's many and varied religious systems. What they have in common is that each system provides directions for appropriate and expected behaviors and serves as a form of social control for individuals within that society. Whether ancestors, gods, one God, prophets, or elders are watching over us, the sanctions that encourage conformity are strong. Indeed, they are made

sacred, a realm of existence different from mundane everyday life. Religion, according to Andrew M. Greeley (1989), the well-known Catholic priest and sociologist, pervades the lives of people of faith. It cannot be separated from the rest of the social world. Members of societies believe so strongly in their religions that conquests and wars throughout history have been based on dissemination or defense of religious beliefs.

Sociologists are interested in these relationships—in the way social relationships and structures affect religion and in the consequences of religion for individuals and for society as a whole. In this chapter, we explore religion as a complex social phenomenon, one that is interrelated with other processes and institutions of society. We investigate what religion does for individuals, how individuals become religious, how religion and modern societies interact, and what social policies of religions have to say about homosexuality and other social issues.

What Does Religion Do for Us?

We began this chapter by looking at examples of daily experiences in which religion and society have enormous power over people. Why do people engage in religious practices, beliefs, and organizations? In short, they do so because religion meets certain very basic needs.

Human questions about the meaning of life, the finality of death, or whether injustice and cruelty will ever be ended cannot normally be answered by science or by everyday experience. Religion helps explain the meaning of life, death, suffering, injustice, and events beyond our control. As sociologist Émile Durkheim pointed out, humans generally view such questions as belonging to a realm of existence different from the mundane or profane world of experience. He called this separate dimension the *sacred realm*. This sacred realm elicits feelings of awe, reverence, and even fear. It is viewed as being above normal inquiry and doubt. Religious guidelines, beliefs, and values dictate "rights and wrongs," provide answers to the big questions of life, and instill moral codes and ideas about the world in members of each society or subculture. For that reason, religions are extremely important in controlling everyday behavior (Durkheim [1915] 2002).

Thus, religion is more than a set of beliefs about the supernatural. It often *sacralizes* (makes sacred and unquestionable) the culture in which we live, the class or caste position to which we belong, the attitudes we hold toward other people, and the morals to which we adhere. Religion is a part of our lifestyle, our gender roles, and our place in society. We are often willing to defend it with our lives. It is sobering to know that around the world, many different people believe quite as strongly as we do that they have found the Truth—the ultimate answers—in their religions. They, too, are willing to die for their religion, which they are convinced is "the only way."

Note various wars between Hindus and Muslims in India, Catholics and Protestants in Northern Ireland, or between two Muslim sects of Sunni and Shi'ite in the Muslim country of Iraq. Although the root causes of these wars are political and economic, religious differences help to polarize we-versus-they sentiments. Such conflicts are never exclusively about religion, but religion can convince each antagonist that God is on its side. Religion is an integral part of most societies and is important in helping individuals define reality and determine what is worth living or dying for.

Thinking Sociologically

Consider your own religious tradition. Which of the purposes or functions of religion mentioned above does your religious faith address? If you are not part of a faith community or do not hold religious beliefs, are there other beliefs or groups that fulfill these functions for you?

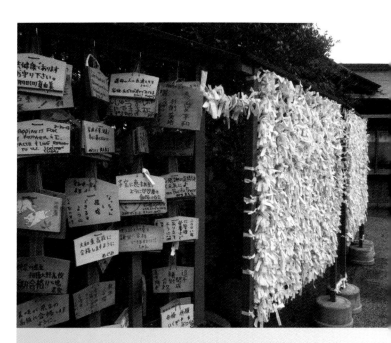

At this temple in Japan, people write their hopes and wishes on strips of paper, attaching them to ropes and trees as a form of prayer. When their life circumstances seem out of control, people will often appeal to a nonempirical or supranatural source for help, and this provides hope and some sense of meaningful action.

Components of Religion

Religion normally involves at least three components: a faith or worldview that provides a sense of meaning and purpose in life (which we will call the *meaning system*), a set of interpersonal relationships and friendship networks (which we will call the *belonging system*), and a stable pattern of roles, statuses, and organizational practices (which we will call the *structural system*) (Roberts 2004).

Meaning System

The meaning system of a religion includes the ideas and symbols it uses to provide a sense of purpose in life and to help explain why suffering, injustice, and evil exist. It provides a big picture to explain events that would otherwise seem chaotic and irrational. For example, although the loss of a family member through death may be painful, many people find comfort and hope and a larger perspective on life in the idea of life after death. Most religious people find that deep love of God gives purpose and deep satisfaction to life (discussed later in this chapter).

Because each culture has different problems to solve, the precise needs reflected in the meaning system vary. Hence, different societies have developed different ways of answering questions and meeting needs. In agricultural societies, the problems revolve around growing crops and securing the elements necessary for crops—water control, sunlight, and good soil. Meaning systems often reflect these concerns. Among the Zuni

of New Mexico and the Hopi of Arizona, water for crops is a critical concern. These Native American people typically grow corn in a climate that averages roughly 10 inches of rain per year, so it is not surprising that the central focus of the dances and the supernatural beings—*kachinas*—is to bring rain. In many societies, the death rate is so high that high fertility has been necessary to perpetuate the group. Thus, fertility goddesses take on great significance. In other societies, strong armies and brave soldiers have been essential to preserve the group from invading forces; hence, gods or rituals of war have been popular. Over time, meaning systems of religion have reflected needs of the societies in which the religion is practiced.

Belonging System

Belonging systems are profoundly important in most religious groups. Many people remain members of religious groups not so much because they accept the meaning system of the group but because that is where their belonging system—their friendship and kinship network—is found. Their religious group is a type of extended family. In fact, church membership increases as people get older and move through the family life cycle of marriage, childbearing, and childrearing (Sherkat and Ellison 1999). A prayer group may be the one area in their lives in which people can be truly open about their personal pain and feel safe to expose their vulnerabilities (Wuthnow 1994). Irrespective of the meaning

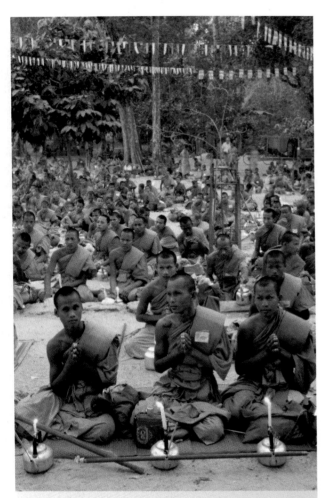

Buddhist monks pray at Bayon Temple in Angkor Thom. Their religious system of ideas gives them a sense of meaning and purpose in life.

beliefs in his or her own way and if each attaches his or her own meanings to the symbols, the meaning system becomes so individualized that *sacralization* of common values can no longer occur. Therefore, some system of control and screening of new revelations must be developed. Religious leaders in designated statuses must have the authority to interpret the theology and define the essentials of the faith. The group also needs methods of designating leaders, of raising funds to support their programs, and of ensuring continuation of the group. To teach the next generation the meaning system, members need to develop a formal structure to determine the content and form of their educational materials, and then they must produce and distribute them. In short, if the religion is to survive past the death of a charismatic leader, it must undergo institutionalization.

Religious institutions embrace several interrelated components: the meaning system, mostly operating at the micro level; the belonging system, critical at the micro level but also part of various meso-level organizations; and the structural system, which tends to have its major impact at the meso and macro levels. These may reinforce one another and work in harmony toward common goals, or there may be conflict between them. When change occurs, it usually occurs because of disruption in one of the systems.

Because religion is one institution in the larger society, it is interdependent and interrelated with the political, economic, family, education, health, and technology systems. Changes in any one of these areas can bring change to religion, and changes in religion can bring changes to other institutions of society. Consider examples of the furor that is occurring in parts of the United States over teaching of intelligent design as part of the science curriculum in public schools. The conflict is reverberating in congregations, schools, legislative chambers, courts, and scientific communities.

Although some people dislike the idea of organized religion, the fact remains that a group cannot survive in the modern world unless it undergoes *routinization of charisma.* That is, the religious organization must develop established roles, statuses, groups, and routine procedures for making decisions and obtaining resources (Weber 1947).

At the local level, too, a formal religious structure develops, with committees doing specific tasks, such as overseeing worship, maintaining the building, recruiting religious educators, and raising funds. These committees report to an administrative board that works closely with the clergy (the ordained ministers) and has much of the final responsibility for the life and continued existence of the congregation. The roles, statuses, and committees make up the structural system.

Furthermore, like any other formal organization in society, meso-level religious structures consist of individuals and committees doing specialized tasks. Contemporary Christian denominations in the United States, for example, may have national commissions on global outreach, religious

system, a person's sense of identity may be very much tied up with being a Buddhist, a Christian, or a Muslim.

In the United States, the religious groups that have grown the fastest in recent years are those that have devised ways to strengthen the sense of belonging and to foster friendship networks within the group, including emphasis on endogamy—marrying within one's group. If a person is a member of a small group in which interpersonal ties grow strong—a church bridge club, a Quran study group, or even a working committee—he or she is likely to feel a stronger commitment to the entire organization. In short, the belonging system refers to the interpersonal networks and the emotional ties that develop between adherents to a particular faith community.

Structural System

A religion involves a group of people who share a common meaning system. However, if each person interprets the

The Applied Sociologist at Work— C. Kirk Hadaway

Research for Religious Organizations

By C. Kirk Hadaway

My interest in research on and for religious institutions began when I worked with my graduate school mentor on a grant studying the growth and decline of denominations. I explored demographic change and church growth, denominational switching, and the impact of new church development on the growth of established denominations.

I am a church research officer, a position that entails everything from mundane gathering of statistics to serious social research. Our office of six persons collects membership, attendance, and giving data from all United Church of Christ (UCC) churches and analyzes those data. We do surveys among our churches, pastors, staff, and lay leaders on a wide variety of topics (issues related to congregational health, leadership, use of denominational resources, beliefs and attitudes, and so forth). I also conduct research on the state of religion/churches in modern society and on social trends that might impact our churches. This research is written up in reports and published in books that give advice to our churches and pastors. I speak to clergy groups regularly on related topics. My clients get an interpretation of data based on broader, sociologically based understanding of the religious trends.

I have studied church trends (patterns of growth and decline) using data from local congregations and studies of religious participation and religious marginality. Also, I have conducted large-scale surveys with pastors from several denominations as key informants. It is particularly gratifying to see theories confirmed with real data on real churches.

The least rewarding facets of my job are grunt work (providing routine information) and other aspects of life in a bureaucracy (forms to fill out, committee meetings, staff retreats, performance evaluations, and having one's work ignored due to other agendas).

The most rewarding aspect of my work is the ability to help church leaders see their situation from a different perspective and use that perspective and information to make a positive difference in their work.

Note: Dr. C. Kirk Hadaway received his PhD in Sociology from the University of Massachusetts, Amherst. He has worked for various boards and agencies of the Southern Baptist Convention, has been director of research at the United Church of Christ, and currently is director of research for the Episcopal Church.

education, evangelism, theological training, worship, world peace, social justice, and so forth. In addition, bishops, presbyters, or other leaders provide guidelines for the work of several hundred pastors who lead their own congregations. Religious organizations are, among other things, bureaucracies. The formal organization may be caught in some of the dysfunctions of any organization: goal displacement, the iron law of oligarchy, alienation, and other problems discussed in Chapter 5.

Just as any organization needs data on its effectiveness, religious organizations collect information to help inform policy. "The Applied Sociologist at Work" above describes the work of a sociologist who does research within such a denominational structure.

Thinking Sociologically

Outline the meaning, belonging, and structural systems of a religion with which you are familiar. Illustrate how these elements influence and are influenced by the larger social world, from individual to national and global systems.

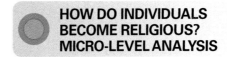

HOW DO INDIVIDUALS BECOME RELIGIOUS? MICRO-LEVEL ANALYSIS

We are not born religious, although we may be born into a religious group. We learn our religious beliefs through socialization, just as we learn our language, customs, norms, and values. Our family usually determines the religious environment in which we grow up, whether it is an all-pervasive message or a one-day-a-week aspect of socialization. We start imitating religious practices such as prayer before we understand these practices intellectually. Then, as we encounter the unexplainable events of life, religion is there to provide meaning. Gradually, religion becomes an ingrained part of many people's lives.

It is unlikely that we will adopt a religious belief that falls outside the religions of our society. For instance, if we are born in India, we will be raised in and around the Hindu, Muslim, or Sikh faiths. In most Arab countries, we will become Muslim, in South American countries, Catholic, and in many Southeast Asian countries, Buddhist. Even if we had been born into the family next door, our religion and politics might be different. Indeed, although our religious affiliation may seem normal

Kwanzaa, which means "first fruits of the harvest" in Kiswahili, was initiated in 1966 by Dr. Maulana Karenga. It is an African American celebration of the traditional African values of family, community responsibility, and self-improvement. This family celebrates Kwanzaa, which runs from December 26 to January 1. Such rituals create in children a sense of sacredness about certain values and outlooks on life.

and typical to us, none of us is part of a religion that is held by a majority of the world's people, and we may in fact be part of a rather small minority religious group when we think in terms of the global population. Map 12.1 and Table 12.1 show this vividly.

Learning the meaning system of a religious group is both a formal and an informal process. In some cultures, religious faith pervades everyday life. For the Amish, farming without machines or use of electricity is part of their Christian teachings, which affect the total lifestyle. Formal teaching in most religions takes place primarily in the temple, church, or mosque and is limited to certain holy days or special times. The formal teaching may take the form of Bar or Bat Mitzvah classes, Sunday school, or parochial school. Informal religious teaching occurs when we observe others "practicing what they preach."

One church member may be committed to the meaning system, another to the belonging system through strong friendship networks, and a third to the structural system, making large financial donations to a congregation even though he or she rarely attends services. In most cases, however, commitment to one of these systems will reinforce commitment to the others. They usually go together. (See Figure 12.1.)

Most people do not belong to a religious group because they believe. Rather, they come to believe because they want to belong and are socialized to feel they are an integral part of the group (Greeley 1972). People generally accept the

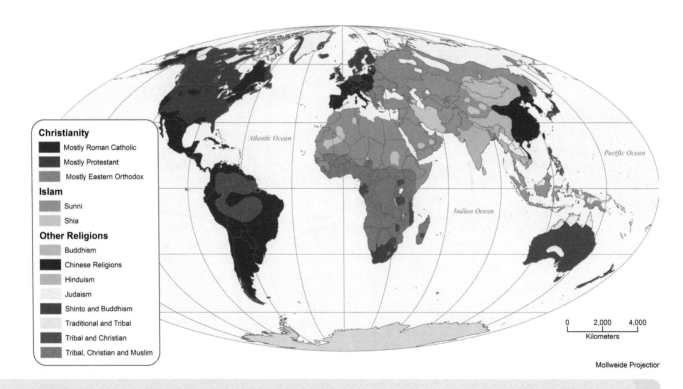

Christianity
- Mostly Roman Catholic
- Mostly Protestant
- Mostly Eastern Orthodox

Islam
- Sunni
- Shia

Other Religions
- Buddhism
- Chinese Religions
- Hinduism
- Judaism
- Shinto and Buddhism
- Traditional and Tribal
- Tribal and Christian
- Tribal, Christian and Muslim

Atlantic Ocean   *Pacific Ocean*   *Indian Ocean*

0   2,000   4,000
Kilometers

Mollweide Projection

Map 12.1   Dominant Religious Groups Around the World

Source: World Religions, 5th ed., W. Matthews, copyright © 2007. Reprinted with permission of Wadsworth, a division of Thomson. Map by Anna Versluis.

Table 12.1   **Religious Membership Around the Globe**

Religion	Membership (in millions)	Percentage of World Population	Number of Countries
Christian (Total)	2,199.8	33.3	239
Roman Catholic	1,121.5	17.0	236
Independents	433.1	6.5	222
Protestant	381.8	5.8	233
Orthodox	233.1	3.5	136
Anglican	82.6	1.2	165
Unaffiliated	19.5	1.8	232
Muslim	1,387.5	21.0	210
Hindu	875.7	13.2	126
Nonreligious	776.8	11.7	238
Universist (Chinese Folk Religion)	385.6	5.8	96
Buddhist	385.6	5.8	136
Ethnic/Tribal Religions	266.4	4.0	145
Atheist	153.4	2.3	220
New Religious Movements	106.5	1.6	107
Sikh	22.9	0.3	44
Jewish	15.0	0.2	135
Spiritist	13.5	0.2	56
Baha'i	7.7	0.1	219
Confucianism	6.4	0.1	15
Jain	5.3	0.1	11
Taoism	3.4	0.1	5
Shintoism	2.8	[a]	8
Zoroastrian	.2	[a]	24
Other Religion	1.2	[a]	79

Source: Barrett, Johnson, and Crossing 2008. Reprinted with permission from *Encyclopedia Britannica Almanac 2008.* Copyright © 2008 by Encyclopedia Britannica, Inc.

Note: Numbers add up to more than the six billion people in the world because many people identify themselves with more than one religious tradition. Thus, the percentages will also add up to more than 100%. Percentages are rounded.

a = Less than 0.05%.

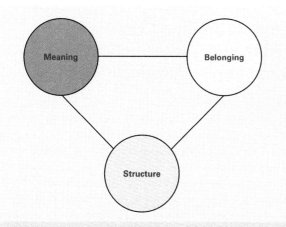

Figure 12.1   Three Components of Religion

Note: Religious commitment can involve any one or more of these dimensions of religion.

explanation about death or injustice or suffering provided by the religious group. They feel comfortable sharing similar feelings and beliefs.

Research on people who switch religious affiliations or join new religious movements (NRMs) indicates that loyalty to a friendship network usually comes first, followed by commitment to the meaning and structural systems. In many cases, accepting a new meaning system is the final stage rather than the initial stage of change (Roberts 2004).

There is more fluidity in religious membership now than at any time of our history. Historically, most people stayed part of the same religious group for a lifetime. A Pew Foundation study released in 2008 found that 44% of Americans will change their religious affiliation in their lifetime, just as a very high percentage will change their place of residence, their jobs, and even their spouses (Pew Forum 2008). In fact, the increase in cross-religious marriages is a

The Bat Mitzvah, shown here, is the initiation ceremony into the faith for Jewish girls.

An Amish family enjoys a trip to the beach. Their faith influences every aspect of their lives—including their beach attire.

frequently try to control the boundaries and protect their members from outside influences. The Amish in the United States have done this by living in their own communities and attempting to limit schooling of their children by outside authorities. To help perpetuate religious beliefs and practices, most religious groups encourage endogamy, marrying within the group. For example, Orthodox Jews have food taboos and food preparation requirements that limit the likelihood they will share a meal with "outsiders."

Religious groups also try to socialize members to make sacrifices of time, energy, and financial resources on behalf of their faith. If one has sacrificed and has devoted one's resources and energy for a cause, one is likely to feel a commitment to the organization—the structural system (Kanter 2005; Sherkat and Ellison 1999). Many young men in the Church of Jesus Christ of the Latter-Day Saints (Mormons) devote two years of their lives to being missionaries, and young women devote one to one-and-a-half years. They must save money in advance to support themselves. This sacrifice of other opportunities and investment of time, energy, and resources in the church creates an intense commitment to the organization. Few of them later feel that they have wasted those years or that the investment was unwise.

The survival of a religious group depends in part on how committed its members are and whether they share freely of their financial and time resources. Most religious groups try, therefore, to socialize their members into commitment to the meaning system, the belonging system, and the structural system of their religion.

Thinking Sociologically

How did you or individuals you know become religious? Did you think about the process as it occurred?

Symbols and the Creation of Meaning: A Symbolic Interactionist Perspective

Dina is appalled as she looks around the Laundromat. The *gaje* (the term Gypsies use to refer to non-Gypsies) just do not seem to understand cleanliness. These middle-class North American neighbors of hers are very concerned about whether their clothes are *melalo*—dirty with dirt. By contrast, they pay no attention to whether they are *marime*—defiled or polluted in a spiritual sense. She watches in disgust as a woman not only places the clothing of men, women, and children in a single washing machine but also includes clothing from the upper and lower halves of bodies together. No respectable Gypsy would allow such mixing, and if it

factor in the religious switching, as 27% of current marriages involve spouses with different religious affiliations (Pew Forum 2008). Change is becoming part of the norm in North America, particularly since World War II, and this is affecting religious affiliation as well. Still, the change is likely to be to a new faction of the same religion rather than to an entirely different religious tradition, and when it does involve a more major shift, it is usually because of the increased diversity of our society so that we know someone personally from the other faith tradition.

Because changing religious groups occurs most often through change of friendship networks, religious groups did occur, the cloth could be used only as rags. The laws of spiritual purity make clear that the lower half of the body is defiled. Anything that comes in contact with the body below the waist or that touches the floor becomes *marime* and can never again be considered *wuzho*—ritually clean. Food that touches the floor becomes filthy and inedible.

Ideally, a Gypsy woman would have separate wash tubs for men's upper-body clothing, men's lower-body clothing, women's upper-body clothing, women's lower-body clothing, and children's clothing. Gypsies know too well that the spirit of Mamioro brings illness to homes that are marime. The lack of spiritual cleanliness of non-Gypsies causes Gypsies to minimize their contact with gaje, to avoid sitting on a chair used by a gaje, and generally to recoil at the thought of assimilation into the larger culture (Southerland 1986; Sway 1988). How we make sense of the world takes place through meaning systems, as illustrated in the above example. For the Gypsies, things have meaning in ways that differ from the ideas that are prominent in the larger society, and the different meanings result in different behaviors and sometimes separation.

Symbolic interaction theory focuses on how people make sense of the meaning of things and how we construct our worlds. In an ambiguous situation, we seek help from others: Is the situation funny, scary, bizarre, normal, or mysterious? Think about how you feel attracted to, or perhaps put off by, someone who wears a cross as a necklace or who has other religious symbolism such as a yarmulke, worn by Orthodox Jewish men to cover the crown of the head, or a Muslim woman with head scarf. Symbols affect the way we feel about people and whether we are inclined to form a relationship. Symbols affect micro-level interaction. Note that a Muslim woman may wear a head scarf, and while she finds it a reassuring reminder of her family's long tradition, others may view it as a symbol of women's oppression or even find it a cause for hatred as "other."

It is the meaning system that most interests symbolic interactionists—the worldview or conceptual framework by which people make sense of life and cope with suffering and injustice. Religious meaning systems are made up of three elements: myths, rituals, and symbols.

Myths are stories embodying ideas about the world. When sociologists of religion use the word *myth*, they are not implying that the story is untrue. A myth may relate historical incidents that actually occurred, it may involve fictional events, or it may communicate abstract ideas such as reincarnation. Regardless of the literal truth or fiction of these stories, myths transmit values and a particular outlook on life. If a story such as the exodus from Egypt by ancient Hebrew people elicits some sense of sacredness, communicates certain attitudes and values, and helps life make sense, then it is a myth. The Netsilik Eskimo myth of the sea goddess Nuliajuk (explained in the chapter opener) reinforces and makes sacred the value of conservation in an environment of scarce resources. It provides messages for appropriate behavior in that group. Thus, whether a myth is

A Romanian Gypsy woman uses different tubs to wash upper- and lower-body clothing and men's and women's apparel separately so they will not become spiritually defiled.

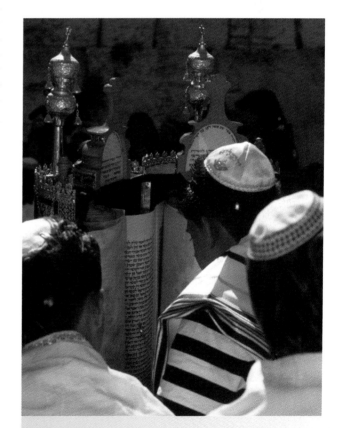

The yarmulke (skullcap or kippah) has been worn by Jewish men since roughly the second century CE. It symbolizes respect for and fear of God and serves to remind the wearer of the need for humility: There is always some distance between himself and God. These caps are also a sign of belonging and commitment to the Jewish community.

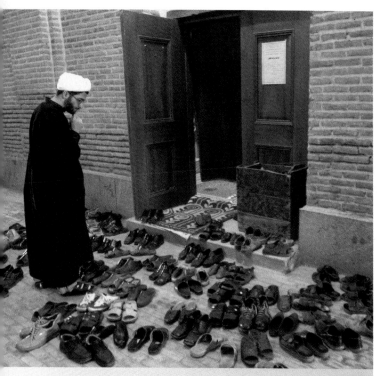

A cleric looks for his shoes outside a mosque. Removal of shoes is an expression of sacred respect for the holy among Muslims.

Muslims pray to God (whom they call Allah) five times a day, removing their shoes and prostrating themselves as they face Mecca. This is an important ritual, and it illustrates that orthopraxy is central for Muslims. Personal devotion, which is expressed in actions, is emphasized in Islam.

factual or not is irrelevant. Myths are always "true" in some deeper metaphorical sense.

Rituals are group activities in which myths are reinforced with music, dancing, kneeling, praying, chanting, storytelling, and other symbolic acts. A number of religions, such as Islam, emphasize devotion to orthopraxy (conformity of behavior) more than orthodoxy (conformity to beliefs or doctrine) (Preston 1988; Tipton 1990). Praying five times a day while facing Mecca, mandated for the Islamic faithful, is an example of orthopraxy.

Often, rituals involve an enactment of myths. In some Christian churches, the symbolic cleansing of the soul is enacted by actually immersing people in water during baptism. Likewise, Christians frequently reenact the last supper of Jesus (Communion or Eucharist) as they accept their role as modern disciples. Among the Navajo, rituals enacted by a medicine man may last as long as five days. An appropriate myth is told, and sand paintings, music, and dramatics lend power and unique reality to the myths.

The group environment of the ritual is important. Ethereal music, communal chants, and group actions such as kneeling or taking off one's shoes when entering the shrine or mosque create an aura of separation from the everyday world and a mood of awe so that the beliefs seem eternal and beyond question. They become sacralized. Rituals also make ample use of symbols, discussed in Chapter 4.

A **symbol** is anything that can stand for something else. Because religion deals with a transcendent realm, a realm that cannot be experienced or proven with the five senses, sacred symbols are a central part of religion. They have a powerful emotional impact on the faithful and reinforce the sacredness of myths.

Sacred symbols have been compared to computer chips, which can store an enormous amount of information and deliver it with force and immediacy (Leach 1979). Seeing a cross can flood a Christian's consciousness with a whole series of images, events, and powerful emotions concerning Jesus and his disciples. Tasting the bitter herb during a Jewish Seder service may likewise elicit memories of the story of slavery in Egypt, recall the escape under the leadership of Moses, and send a moral message to the celebrant to work for freedom and justice in the world today. The mezuzah, a plaque consecrating a house on the doorpost of a Jewish home, is a symbol reminding the occupants of their commitment to obey God's commandments and reaffirming God's commitment to them as a people. Because symbols are often heavily laden with emotion and can elicit strong feelings, they are used extensively in rituals to represent myths.

Myths, rituals, and symbols are usually interrelated and interdependent (see Figure 12.2). Together, they form the meaning system—a set of ideas about life or about the cosmos that seem uniquely realistic and compelling. They reinforce rules of appropriate behavior and even political and economic systems by making them sacred. They can also control social relationships between different groups. The Gypsy revulsion at the filthy *marime* practices of middle-class Americans, like the Kosher rules for food preparation among the Jews, create boundaries between "us" and "them" that nearly eliminate prospects of intermarriage or even of close friendships outside of the religious community. Some scholars think these rituals and symbolic meanings are the key reason why Gypsies and Jews have survived for millennia as distinct groups without being assimilated or absorbed into dominant cultures. The symbols and meanings created barriers that prevented the obliteration of their cultures.

When symbolic interactionists study religion, they tend to focus on how symbols influence people's perception of reality and on the role rituals and myths play in defining what is "really real" for people. Symbolic interactionists stress that humans are always trying to create, determine, and interpret the meaning of events. Clearly, no other institution focuses as explicitly on determining the meaning of life and its events as religion.

Thinking Sociologically

In a tradition with which you are familiar, how do symbols and sacred stories reinforce a particular view of the world or a particular set of values and social norms?

Seeking Eternal Benefits: A Rational Choice Perspective

People with religious freedom make rational choices to belong to a religious group or change to another religion after weighing

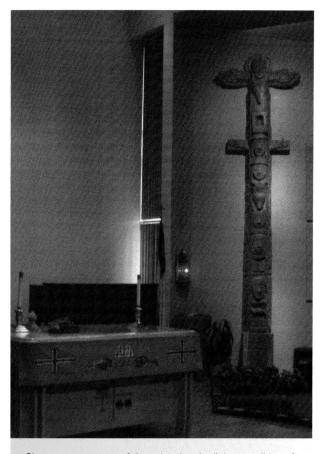

Clan totems are part of the cultural and religious tradition of native peoples in northwest North America, from Oregon to Alaska, and totem poles are used to tell stories. This photo from St. John's United Methodist Church in Anchorage, Alaska, is interesting because it blends local cultural and religious symbols with a Christian symbol (the Cross) in a Christian sanctuary. This one tells the Easter story.

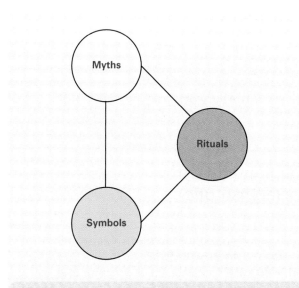

Figure 12.2   The Meaning System of Religion Is Composed of Three Interrelated Elements

the costs (financial contributions, time involved) and benefits of belonging (eternal salvation, a belonging system, and a meaning system) (Finke and Stark 2005; Warner 1993). Rational choice theory is based on an economic model of human behavior. The basic idea is that the process people use to make decisions is at work in religious choices: What are the benefits, and what are the costs? Do the benefits outweigh the costs? The benefits, of course, are nonmaterial when it comes to religious choices—feeling that life has meaning, confidence in an afterlife, sense of communion with God, and so forth. This approach views churchgoers as consumers who are out to meet their needs or obtain a "product." It depicts churches as entrepreneurial establishments, or "franchises," in a competitive market, with "entrepreneurs" (ministers) as leaders. Competition for members leads churches to "market" their religion to consumers. Converts, and religious people generally, are thus regarded as active and rational agents pursuing self-interests, and growing churches are those that meet "consumer demand" (Finke 1997; Finke and Stark 2005; Iannaccone 1994). Religious groups produce religious "commodities" (rituals, meaning systems, sense

This advertisement ran in The Sundial, *the daily paper at the
California State University, Northridge (CSUN). The church is
located only a few miles from the university and hoped to catch,
with their student-friendly service (and their targeted marketing),
the interest of CSUN students.*

of belonging, symbols, and so forth) to meet the "demands" of
consumers (Sherkat and Ellison 1999).

Rational choice theorists believe that aggressive religious
entrepreneurs who seek to produce religious products that
appeal to a target audience will reap the benefits of a large
congregation. Churches, temples, and mosques are competitive enterprises, and each must make investments of effort,
time, and resources to attract and keep potential buyers.
There are many religious entrepreneurs out there seeking
to meet individual needs. The challenge is for the various
groups to beat the competition by meeting the demand of the
current marketplace (Finke and Stark 2005).

For instance, when the United States separated church
from state so that most individuals were not automatically members of a state religion, organized religions had
to offer a product that would sell to consumers (Moore
1995). Indeed, some scholars argue that where religion is
an ascribed identity (adopted based on one's family of birth
or the country's official religion), it is likely to be much
less vigorous than in places where there is a competitive
religious marketplace, and religion is an achieved identity
(chosen freely from many options) (Finke and Stark 2005;
Iannaccone 1995; Sargeant 2000).

When more religious groups compete for the hearts
and minds of members, concern about spiritual matters
is invigorated, and commitment is heightened. Religious
pluralism and spiritual diversity increase rates of religious
activity as each group seeks its market share and as more
individual needs are met in the society (Finke and Stark
2005; Iannaccone 1995).

Not everyone agrees that religion is a competitive enterprise (Stark 2000). This strictly utilitarian economic analysis
of religion seems counter to the way most religious people
understand their own behavior. As one religious scholar
puts it, "It is one thing to describe a person's decision to join
a church *as if* the person were trying to maximize his or her
benefits; it is something different to claim that the person's
actual thought in joining measured his or her potential gains
against potential losses" (McGuire 2002:298–99).

Thinking Sociologically

Does the rational choice approach seem to you to make
sense of religious behavior? Is religious behavior similar to
self-interested economic behavior?

 **RELIGION AND MODERN LIFE:
MESO-LEVEL ANALYSIS**

The Yaqui youth was very ill. He had been bitten by a
rattlesnake in the hot Arizona desert just outside his village.
Although there was a medical clinic staffed by nurses and a
visiting doctor, the family decided to use traditional Yaqui
medicine, a blend of Native American rituals and what is
referred to as *pagan Catholicism*. The medicine man broke
eggs, mixed curative potions, and chanted incantations over
the sick boy. These familiar rituals gave comfort to the family waiting anxiously for signs of the boy's recovery. After the
boy had received the medicine man's treatment, he went to
the clinic as well. He recovered, and the people believe that
what led to the recovery was adherence to their traditional
method of healing. The interaction of traditional religious
practices and modern health care institutions illustrate these
interconnections at the meso level.

In this section, we explore how religion as an institution interacts with other institutions and what kinds of
organizational forms religion takes as it interacts with the
larger social environment.

Religion and Other Social Institutions

In traditional societies, religion is not separated from other
social institutions, as the Yaqui's religious practice was separate from the clinic, but is an integral part of people's social
world. In complex societies, on the other hand, religion is a
distinctive group or organization. The dominant religion(s)
in any complex society generally supports the political
system and ideology of the dominant group. It is closely

related to the economic system, is linked to the education system, and legitimates the family system through sacred rites of passage for marriage, birth, and death. Even the health system, as shown in the Yaqui example, is closely linked to religious beliefs about the healing process, disease, and death.

Religion not only supports other institutions but may also experience support or pressure from these other institutions. The Catholic Church has faced increasing criticism from international organizations, political movements, governments, religious groups, and educational institutions for its ban on birth control. Due to rapid population growth, especially in poor Catholic nations, many interested parties are putting pressure on the Catholic Church to ease its strict ban in these countries. The church cannot ignore these pressures, for they undermine the legitimacy of the church if they are not addressed or countered. Even if the church does not change, it must expend considerable effort to defend its position to keep from losing credibility in the eyes of members and nonmembers alike. Some Catholic clergy and a number of lay members have defected over positions of the church. Let us consider the relationship between religion and three other social institutions: family, politics, and economics.

Religion and Family

Everyone was dressed in colorful finery to welcome the baby into the religious community. The naming ceremony in this Nigerian village takes place when the baby reaches six weeks and is considered a viable human being. After the ceremony, the bonds of religious community are solidified with food, music, and dancing.

Our parents provide our first contacts with religion. They may say prayers, attend worship services, and talk about proper behavior as defined by their religious group. Religious congregations make marriages sacred through ceremonies. Mother's Day, Father's Day, and Grandparents' Day are recognized by many religions and societies, thereby honoring and legitimating parenting. Many of the sacred ceremonies in religion are family affairs: births, christenings or naming of new members, marriages, and funerals. Jews, Muslims, and Latter-Day Saints (Mormons) are especially known for their many ceremonies and gatherings designed specifically for family units, and their moral codes place high value on family loyalty and responsibility.

Religiosity, a person's degree of religious involvement, is positively associated with moral beliefs and behavior in youth and influences interaction with children and support of spouses in marriages (Brody et al. 1994). For instance, young women in the United States who are religious are less likely than other adolescents to become sexually active prior to marriage (Sherkat and Ellison 1999). Some religious groups, such as conservative Protestants, are also involved in childrearing, producing parenting manuals

Yaqui dancers, who blend Christian and indigenous beliefs, appeal to the supernatural for healing.

to guide families. Some of these manuals have created controversy because of their emphasis on hierarchical and authority-centered parenting models (Bartkowski and Ellison 1995). Tensions can arise between family and religion over social control. Among the Amish, if the bishop orders a member of the church to be shunned, the family must comply and must refuse to speak to or associate with that person. If the family does not cooperate with the shunning, members of the community will also shun them. This sometimes leads to intense tension as the church tries to determine communication patterns and interactions within a family (Hostetler 1993).

The New Right and other conservative organizations sometimes argue that if society could reinstitute the family and religious values of the past, today's societal problems would be reduced. They believe that if parents would spend more time instilling proper values in their children, things would be better. However, working parents today often spend more time with their children than parents did in past times. Stereotypes of the families and the religious values of the "good old days" come from a small segment of the total population: those upper middle-class families in which only one parent had to work (Coontz 1997,

Iran's supreme leader, Ayatollah Ali Khamenei, speaks to ethnic Arabs during a visit to Dehlavieh in the southern oil province of Khuzestan on March 25, 2006.

Religion and Politics: Theocracies and Civil Religion

Jan, a Swede, belongs to a state religion: Lutheranism. He was raised a Lutheran and does not really think about the possibility of other religious beliefs, although there is a large Pentecostal movement in Sweden. The Nwankwo family, mentioned in the chapter opening, practices an ancient tribal religion, also with no thought that another religious belief might have something better to offer. Most of us are raised in a particular belief system from childhood and adhere to that religion because it is part of the custom and tradition most familiar to us. We seldom question our "choice."

In a pure **theocracy**, or rule by God, religious leaders rule society in accordance with God's presumed wishes. Iran is one example where religion clearly has a privileged position. In some situations, religion is used as a tool of the state to manipulate the citizenry and to maintain social control. A state religion, on the other hand, has some autonomy but receives support from tax money. Sweden, Britain, and Italy are examples. Some countries, such as the former Soviet Union, outlawed religion altogether so that nothing competed with loyalty to the nation. The continuum in Figure 12.3 shows possible relationships between church and state.

Countries with diverse religious groups experience multiple pressures on their political systems: religious voting blocs, conflicts over definitions of public morality, and lobbying efforts for policies that have moral implications—abortion, euthanasia, rights for homosexuals, care of the poor, war and peace, and so forth. Sometimes religious groups form the basis for political parties and pressure groups lobbying for policies that support their beliefs (Hayes 1995). Even in the United States, which professes separation between church and state matters, religious groups influence policies such as prayer in school, selection of textbooks and reading matter, and abortion. In some countries, religious groups strongly oppose the

2005; Woodberry and Smith 1998). Today, many problems and pressures facing families occur at different levels of analysis and are out of the control of the family or local religious group. However, religiously affiliated organizations and social movements may also attempt to transform or strengthen other institutions. The conservative Christian organization, Focus on the Family, which has a syndicated newspaper column, radio programs, books, DVDs, and a monthly magazine produced by founder James Dobson, is one example of an effort to strengthen families by restoring a traditional model of family life.

Although religion cannot solve all family problems, most religions encourage stable family life and checks and balances for "moral" behavior in other institutions.

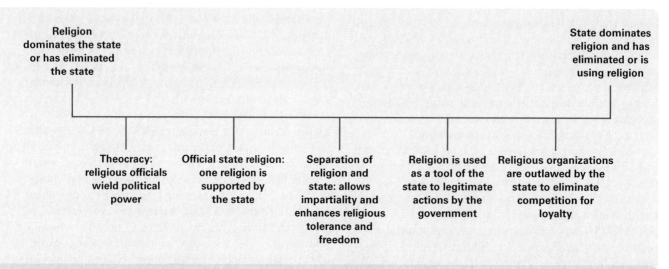

Religion dominates the state or has eliminated the state				State dominates religion and has eliminated or is using religion
Theocracy: religious officials wield political power	Official state religion: one religion is supported by the state	Separation of religion and state: allows impartiality and enhances religious tolerance and freedom	Religion is used as a tool of the state to legitimate actions by the government	Religious organizations are outlawed by the state to eliminate competition for loyalty

Figure 12.3 Links Between Religion and the State

government and seek to undermine the authority and power of political leaders. In Nazi Germany, some church leaders formulated the Barmen Declaration in opposition to Hitler. Many Christian groups in South Africa opposed apartheid. In some parts of Latin America, church leaders work for human rights and more equitable distribution of land and resources. Although religion often reinforces the power of the state, it may also be a source of conflict and tension on issues regarding morality, justice, and legitimate authority. Indeed, depending on the organizational structures, religion can provide a source of authority that offers a real challenge to the power of the state when that government has become oppressive, as shown in the next "Sociology Around the World."

In simple homogeneous societies, religion serves as a kind of glue, sacralizing the current social system by offering it supernatural legitimacy. In complex and heterogeneous societies, on the other hand, no single religion can provide the core values of the culture. In such circumstances, an alternative form of religion called **civil religion** frequently evolves. Civil religion is based on a set of beliefs, symbols, and rituals that pervade many aspects of secular life and institutions. It involves a shared public faith in the nation and what that nation stands for. Although civil religion lacks the structural system of organized religion, it is often supported by various types of patriotic groups. These small voluntary associations develop intense belonging systems, and civil religion also tends to strengthen the sense of belonging of all citizens as members of that society (Bellah 1992; Roberts 2004).

Rituals of civil religion include making the pledge of allegiance, saluting the flag, and singing the national anthem. For example, American civil religion is not explicitly Christian, for it must appeal to those who are non-Christian as well (Bellah 1970), but it involves reference to God in many areas of civilian life and a legitimation of the political system. It attempts to give the nation and the government supernatural blessing and authority. It also calls the nation to a higher standard of justice and may be used by change agents such as Martin Luther King Jr. to make social change more acceptable and compelling.

In Ireland, part of the intense conflict between Protestants and Catholics is over civil religion. Protestants and Catholics not only come from different economic strata and different ethnic backgrounds but also have different visions for the future of the country and different ideas about what gives the country its special place in history. Although civil religion is supposed to unite a country, in Ireland and other divided countries, civil religion can itself be a point of intense conflict (Bellah and Greenspahn 1987; McGuire 2002).

Thinking Sociologically

How does civil religion manifest itself in your country? Give specific examples.

Civil religion blends reverence for the nation with more traditional symbols of faith. Pictured is the chapel at Punchbowl, the Pacific cemetery for U.S. military personnel, located in Hawaii. Note that two U.S. flags are inside the altar area and are more prominent than two of the three religious symbols that also adorn the chancel: the Christian Cross, the Jewish Star of David, and the Buddhist wheel of Dharma.

Religion and the Economy: The Protestant Ethic and Capitalism

Why do most of us study hard, work hard, and strive to get ahead? Why are we sacrificing time and money now—taking this and other college courses—when we might spend that money on an impressive new car? Our answers probably have something to do with our moral attitudes about work, about those who lack ambition, and about convictions regarding the proper way to live. Max Weber ([1904–05] 1958) saw a relationship between the

Sociology Around the World

Transnational Religion: The Catholic Church and Political Systems

The Roman Catholic Church is one of the first complex organizations to be truly transnational, external to any one nation and including representation from many countries. Many religious organizations are autocephalous—that is, the religious hierarchy and membership are contained within a single nation. This type of religious association is not linked to congregations or a denomination in other countries (Roberts 2004).

The Catholic Church is an international body that must be sympathetic to the circumstances of people in many nations, for its membership and its organizational reach spans the globe. It cannot align itself with the economic and political interests of one nation or set of nations without risking the alienation of tens of millions of members in another part of the world.

Multinational religious organizations such as the Catholic Church can have a real impact on the social and economic policies within a nation, sometimes protecting the welfare of the people against a tyrannical state. In Poland during the 1970s and 1980s, the citizenry often felt colonized by a foreign power—the Soviet Union. The Communist government in Poland was extremely unpopular, and the people had no real way to make the government more responsive to their needs. In 1983, only 3% of Poles who were surveyed felt that the government-dominant political hierarchy represented the interests of the Polish people. By contrast, 60% identified the Catholic Church and the Pope as protecting Polish interests (Tamney 1992).

The Catholic Church became a major power broker in negotiations between unions and the government in Poland (Tamney 1992). Catholic bishops sometimes took on a role akin to union leaders and, in so doing,

became major players in the political future of the country. Because those bishops were ultimately responsible to the Pope and had a source of support external to the nation, they experienced a good deal of independence from the Communist party that was in power. Clergy supported by a church financed with tax dollars would not have the same freedom to challenge the government. The global nature of the Catholic Church influenced the role bishops could play in the Polish situation.

Transnationalism can influence the power of religious officials in our complex global environment. It provides an external source of authority that may be seen by citizens as superseding the political authority. In many autocephalous religious denominations, a primary function of churches is to support the political power of the particular state or affirm an ethnic or national identity (Turner 1991b). Poland is an especially intriguing case in that a single religion tended to be identified with national pride and culture, but that religion was global in its power base. That combination provided an exceptionally strong base for challenging governmental policies that were not in the interests of the citizens (Tamney 1992).

Being a religion that crosses over national boundaries can also be a source of suspicion in some circumstances. Roman Catholics were traditionally suspected of lacking national loyalty in the United States. They were derisively called "papists" in the first half of the 20th century. Likewise, Jews have often been accused of maintaining dangerous, subversive ties because of their international networks with others who share their faith. The fact that a religion is more inclusive than just national boundaries can have benefits as well as risks for individuals and the state. This is true for any religious tradition.

---

economic system, particularly capitalism, and ideas about work and sacrifice. He gathered information by studying many documents, including diaries of Calvinists (a branch of Protestantism), sermons and religious teachings, and other historical papers. The following is his argument in a nutshell.

Noting that the areas of Europe where the Calvinists had strong followings were the same areas where capitalism grew fastest, Weber ([1904–05] 1958) argued that four elements in the Calvinist Protestant faith created the moral and value system necessary for the growth of capitalism: predestination, a calling, self-denial, and individualism.

1. *Predestination* meant that one's destiny was predetermined. Nothing anyone could do would change what was to happen. Because God was presumed to be perfect, he was not influenced by human deeds or prayer. Those people who were chosen by God were referred to as the *elect* and were assumed to be a small group. Therefore, people looked for signs of their status—salvation or damnation. High social status was sometimes viewed as a sign of being among the elect, so motivation was high to succeed in *this* life.

2. The *calling* referred to the concept of doing God's work. Each person was put on Earth to serve God, and each had a task to do in God's service. One could be called by God to any occupation, so the key was to work very hard and with the right attitude. Because work was a way to serve God, laziness or lack of ambition came to be viewed as a sin. These ideas helped to create a society in which people's self-worth and their evaluation of others were tied to a work ethic. Protestants became workaholics.

3. *Self-denial* involved living a simple life. If one had a good deal of money, one did not spend it on a lavish home, or expensive clothing, or various forms of entertainment. Such consumption would be offensive to God. Therefore, if people worked hard and began to accumulate resources, they simply saved them or invested them in a business. This self-denial was tied to an idea that we now call *delayed gratification*, postponing the satisfaction of one's present wants and desires in exchange for a future reward. The reward they sought was in the afterlife. Because Calvinists believed in predestination, they did not expect to earn salvation, but they believed that they could demonstrate to themselves and others that they were among the elect.

4. *Individualism* meant that each individual faced his or her destiny alone before God. Previous Christian theology had emphasized group salvation, the idea that an entire community would be saved or damned together. The stark individualism of Calvinistic theology stressed that each individual was on his or her own before God. Likewise, in the economic system that was emerging, individuals were on their own. The person who thrived was an individualist who planned wisely and charted his or her own course. Religious individualism and economic individualism reinforced one another.

The Protestant ethic that resulted from these elements stressed hard work, simple living, and rational decision making by daring individualists. Businesspeople and laborers spent long hours working at their calling, and the profits were reinvested for new equipment or expansion of the company. Individualism allowed people to pursue their own course of action and not to feel guilty for doing so. This combination was ideal for the growth of capitalism. Religion resulted in major changes in cultural values, which, in turn, transformed the economic system. Weber ([1904–05] 1958) saw both the religious and economic systems as dynamic, interrelated, and ever-changing.

Gradually, the capitalistic system, stimulated by the Protestant ethic, spread to other countries and to other religious groups. Many of the attitudes about work and delayed gratification no longer have supernatural focus, but they are part of our larger culture nonetheless. They influence our feelings about people who are not industrious and our ideas about why some people are poor. In fact, some religious sects see individuals as responsible for their own fate, believing the poor and jobless got into their circumstances and should solve their own problems rather than depend on government aid (Davis and Robinson 1999).

Weber recognized that other factors also had to be present for capitalism to arise, but he believed that the particular set of moral values and attitudes that Calvinism instilled in the people was critical. Whereas Marx argued that religion kept workers in their places and allowed the capitalists to exploit the system and maintain their elite positions, Weber focused on the change brought about in the economic system as a result of religious beliefs and values.

Religion interacts with the economy in other ways as well. For one thing, religion is big business. In the United States, at the turn of the 21st century, members donated an average of $440 per year to religious organizations, with contributions to the top 15 denominations topping $18 billion (Sherkat and Ellison 1999). In most countries, religions (1) employ clergy and other people who serve the church, (2) own land and property, and (3) generate millions through collections and fundraising. Some of this money goes to upkeep of the building, some to charitable activities, and some to investments. Religious ventures continue to expand into many areas, from shopping centers to homes and apartment buildings for the elderly. In the United States, televangelism and megachurches (congregations with upward of 10,000 members) are multimillion-dollar industries with sophisticated marketing strategies. The televangelism industry, for example, involves the sale of books and tapes, donations of hundreds of millions of dollars by listeners, establishment of colleges, hospitals, and amusement parks, and provision of jobs in a wide variety of technical electronic areas. These megachurches become corporations and use information from the corporate world to ensure success.

There are other ways in which religion and the economic institutions are linked. When large religious organizations take moral stands on poverty, they may influence the economy. Moreover, when the economy is especially bad, certain kinds of religious movements are more likely

In the high-tech South Barrington, Illinois, Willow Creek Community Church, images of the pastor can be seen projected on several televisions during a worship service. Megachurches, which sometimes draw 20,000 to 30,000 worshippers on a weekend, offer high-entertainment worship and a range of other services. The church is run—and marketed—like a business.

to be spawned: Millenarian movements, which expect the end of the world soon, almost always occur when economic prospects are bleak (Roberts 2004).

Although religion today may not have the power to transform the economy or other social institutions, each institution does affect others. Society also shapes the kind of organization and the relationship to other institutions that the religious group adopts, as discussed in the next section.

Thinking Sociologically

Religion is influenced not only by other institutions in society but also by the media. What messages from the media (movies, TV, music) reflect the state of religion in society?

Types of Religious Associations

From denominations to sects to new religious movements (NRMs), religious organizations take many forms. The following discussion explores *ideal types*, that is, models that summarize the main characteristics of types of religious organizations. Any specific religious group may not fit all of the characteristics exactly. Furthermore, these organizational patterns are particularly relevant to understanding the evolution of Western religious traditions, especially Christianity. The one major world religion that displays a very different pattern is Islam, as is discussed in the next "Sociology in Your Social World."

The Ecclesia

Official state religions are called **ecclesia**, referring to religious groups that claim as members everybody within the boundaries

Sociology in Your Social World

Islam, Mosques, and Organizational Structure

Most mosques in the United States are relatively new, with 87% having been founded since 1970 and 62% since 1980. At the turn of the century, there were 1,209 mosques in the United States (Bagby 2003). Christian congregations tend to be somewhat autonomous entities: supported by members, but linked organizationally to a denomination. According to Islamic scholar Ihsan Bagby (2003:115), "Most of the world's mosques are simply a place to pray. . . . A Muslim cannot be a member of a particular mosque" because mosques belong to God, not to the people. The role of the *imam*—the minister—is simply to lead prayers five times a day and to run the services on the Sabbath, including delivery of a sermon. The imam does not operate an organization and does not need formal training at a seminary—as is true with many Christian and Jewish leaders in the United States. Mosques were historically government supported in other countries, so they had to make major changes in how they operate when they opened in North America. Because they could not depend on government funding, Islamic mosques needed to adapt to the congregational model: members who were loyal to a particular mosque and would support it. They also began to put more emphasis on religious education (which had been done largely by extended families in the "old country"), religious holidays at the mosque rather than with families and dinners at a fellowship hall, and more life-cycle celebrations (birth and marriages solemnized). This is a major change in the role of the mosque and the imam for many Muslims.

Bagby reports that there are two main categories of mosques: those attended primarily by African Americans and those attended primarily by immigrants. African American mosques represent only 27% of the total, and they are in some important ways different in organizational structure from those attended by immigrants (28% of the remaining American Muslims being from South Asia, 15% being Arab, and 30% having a mixture of backgrounds). So even the makeup of mosques is unlike anything most Americans might guess. Only 28% of American mosques depend on an imam as the final authority, whereas the majority are led by an executive committee or board of directors (call the *majlis*), which has authority. More important, 93% of African American mosques are imam-led compared with only 38% of immigrant-attended mosques.

About 33% of all mosques in the United States have a paid, full-time imam, and 16% of those imams have to work a second job. By comparison, 89% of other congregations (Christian and Jewish) have paid ministers. Only 13% of imams have a master's degree in theology, which is the standard expected for most mainstream Christian and Jewish clergy. So despite having exceptionally high levels of adherents in management and the professions, having unusually high incomes, and having 58% of adherents with college degrees, Islamic mosques are less bureaucratized, with less emphasis on professional credentials, membership roles, or denominational connections. It is likely that mosques will begin to assimilate to the religious organizational pattern of the larger society, but at this point, it is important to recognize that the discussion of "denominations" and "sects" is not apt for Islam in America. Islam is less rationalized, bureaucratized, and professionalized, with more stress on family and personal connections.

of a particular society (Roberts 2004). Ecclesia include all members of a society. They try to monopolize religious life in that society, have a close relationship with the power structure, have a formal structure with officially designated full-time clergy, and have membership based on birth into the society.

Many countries have official state religions. Norway and Sweden are Lutheran. Spain, France, Italy, and many Latin American countries are Roman Catholic. Greece is Greek Orthodox. Iran, Egypt, and other Middle Eastern countries are Islamic. England is Anglican. India is predominantly Hindu, although Muslims share power. Because ecclesia represent the interests of the state and those in power, disfranchised groups often seek other religious outlets. In the early 20th century in Britain, 80% of the Welsh

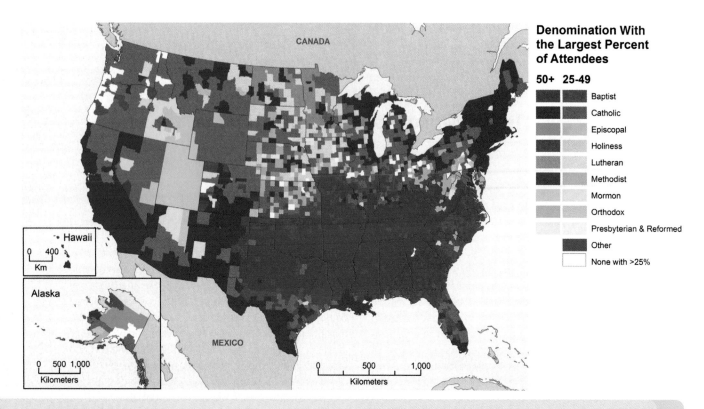

Map 12.2 Denominational Distribution in the United States

Source: Religious Congregations and Membership Study 2000. Map by Anna Versluis.

Note: This map shows the largest religious denomination by attendance for each county. In some cases the largest denomination receives less than a majority of the county's religious adherents. The map thus underrepresents the diversity in any area, but it does demonstrate regional variation. Only one county—in Virginia—has a majority of adherents that are Muslim; in all other counties with a majority, a Christian denomination is the largest religion.

people (Wales is the westernmost of the British Isles) affiliated with nonconformist Christianity, not with the Church of England, in which the queen is officially the head of the church. They explicitly rejected the meshing of religious and national loyalty, feeling that religious bodies should have a free and independent voice that is not compromised by politics or patriotism (Davies 1993; Morgan 1981).

In societies that do not have official religions such as the United States, religion takes several forms: denominations, sects, and NRMs (or cults).

Denominations

In the United States, Congregationalist, Episcopalian, Presbyterian, Lutheran, Baptist, Methodist, and other mainline Christian religious groups are denominations. They all have certain characteristics in common. The denomination is seen as a legitimate form of religious expression but does not have religious dominance or monopoly in the society. Each religious group appeals to a particular segment of the population, often related to class, race, ethnicity, and sometimes regional area. They coexist with and usually are accepting of other denominations (Christiano, Swatos, and Kivisto 2002; Roberts 2004). The largest denominations in the United States are indicated on Map 12.2.

Most denominations have formal bureaucracies with hierarchical positions, specialization of tasks, and official creeds. This hierarchy extends even to the international level in some denominations, such as the Anglicans. The leadership is trained, and there is often a professional church staff. Worship typically involves formal, ritualized, and prescribed ceremonies. Note that the Roman Catholic Church is an ecclesia in Spain because it is the official state religion, but it is a denomination in the United States and Canada, where it is one of many religious groups and is not affiliated with or supported by the state.

Although denominations vary somewhat in the values and beliefs they advocate, they usually support the basic values and social arrangements of the larger society. They may work for moderate changes, but they seldom call for radical or revolutionary restructuring of the society. Thus, the membership tends to be made up of those people who have benefited from the existing social arrangements and who hold positions of power and influence. Most of these denominations are large and financially secure, in part because they attract a middle- and upper-class clientele. This comfortable accommodation between denominations and the existing social order is precisely what made Marx feel that religion was used to keep the social structure from changing.

The key characteristic of a denomination is its accommodation to the state, and thus, disfranchised members of society are more likely to be attracted to sects or cults.

Sects

John Wesley (1703–1791), founder of a movement now known as the Methodist Church, began a renewal movement in the Church of England. He wanted to call people back to the basics of the faith. His evangelical revival called followers to lead Christian lives through a method of strict discipline—prayer, worship, study, and mutual support groups. Hence, the name *Methodists* arose—a term that was originally derogatory. It referred to people whose worship was too "enthusiastic" to be decent and orderly—the standard of worship among Anglicans and Presbyterians of the day. Because church authorities disapproved of Wesley's new methods, he was marginalized and refused an Anglican church to lead. He took his movement to the streets. As a person of deep commitment and a skilled organizer, Wesley formed associations in Great Britain and North America. Today, Methodists have become one of the largest Christian bodies and a mainstream denomination in the United States.

Sects, such as the early Methodists, form in protest against their parent religion. Sometimes they are begun by dissatisfied members who form splinter groups and break away from denominations. Those splitting off do so because of theological concerns or because they feel the church has surrendered to secular authority (Roberts 2004; Stark and Bainbridge 1985). They believe that the true religious doctrines are being abandoned, people are becoming contaminated by worldly ways, and the group must save itself by returning to the true religion. Often, the break has other underlying social dimensions. Sect members may feel the denomination has come to embrace the existing power structure too closely. Part of the membership feels the unjust social arrangements are condemned by God and should be condemned by the faithful. In other instances, the splinter group is simply alienated by the bureaucracy and hierarchical structure of the religious group itself (Niebuhr 1929).

There are more than 400 sects in the United States. Tennessee has the highest sect membership per population. The region with the least sectarianism is New England. By comparison, Africa has six times as many sects as the United States (Stark and Bainbridge 1985).

Sects are characterized by their separation from other religious and even social groups. (See Table 12.2.) There is exclusive commitment to one body of teaching and a claim of monopoly over religious Truth. Sects typically demand total allegiance to the organization (Wilson 1982). An example of

A Tofuni member of the sect of Heavenly Christians kneels in worship during a ceremony. The sect was founded in 1947, in Benin, by Samuel Oshofa and has more than 10 million followers throughout the countries bordering the Gulf of Guinea, Africa.

an extreme isolationist sect—a type of counterculture—is the Old Believers of the Russian Orthodox Church. In the mid-1600s, the Old Believers were so adamant about not adhering to the reforms of the tsar and the head of the Russian Orthodox Church that when troops approached, they barricaded themselves inside their churches and set themselves on fire rather than accommodate to change (Crummey 1970; Pentikänen 1999; Robson 1995).

Table 12.2 Distinguishing Sects From Denominations or Ecclesia

The following are characteristics that distinguish a sect from a denomination or an ecclesia:

1. Exclusive membership policy: Only the saved or those who meet high standards of membership are admitted.

2. Conflict with the host society: The outside secular society is usually viewed as depraved or evil, values of the larger society are rejected, and there is often deep suspicion of the state.

3. Lack of a complex organizational structure: Little or no national organization exists, clergy are often not educated in seminaries and have no formal ordination beyond the local congregation, and there may not be a larger affiliated institution that produces religious education materials.

Source: Yinger 1970.

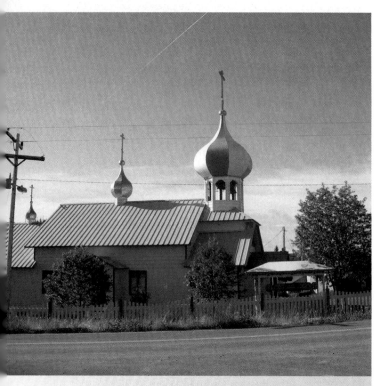

There are now a number of Old Believer communities in the Kenai Peninsula of Alaska, like this Church of St. Nicholas. Some of these Old Believer sects are so isolationist that they are accessible almost entirely by horse or by foot, and they have large "Keep Out" signs as one approaches the community. Commitment to the beliefs of the in-group is intense in this Russian Orthodox sect.

Members of Christian sects in North America are often socially separated from those of higher social classes. As Liston Pope ([1942] 1965) stated, sectarians "substitute religious status for social status." For those who are less well off, a sect gives the feeling that members are among God's chosen, even if they do not have much social prestige in this world. Because most people who join sects feel deprived, there is a high degree of tension between the values of members and those of the larger society (Stark 1985).

As sects grow in membership, coordination becomes necessary, leadership succession occurs, a hierarchy develops, and members become less alienated as social class positions change. Any of these factors can be the catalyst to move the sect toward becoming a denomination. The process of institutionalization occurs and helps survival, but it is fraught with difficulties as the intimacy of a small group is overwhelmed by the impersonality of the emerging large organization.

Sects are often formed because groups split from denominations or individuals feel deprived, but over time, most sects become denominations. Few contemporary groups are pure sect or pure denomination. Instead, they are on a continuum between the two and may be moving toward sectarianism or toward denominationalization.

New Religious Movements (NRMs) or Cults

NRMs, like sects, are protest or splinter groups. However, unlike sects, if NRMs survive for several generations, become established, and gain some legitimacy, they become new religions in the society rather than new denominations of the existing faith. *Cult* was once the common term for this kind of movement, but the media and the public have so completely misused the word that its meaning has become unclear and often negative. The term *cult*, as sociologists have historically used it, is simply descriptive, not evaluative. Most sociologists of religion now prefer NRMs to describe these religious forms (Barker 1989; Christiano et al. 2002).

NRMs are founded on a new revelation (or insight) or on a radical reinterpretation of an old teaching. They are usually out of the mainstream religious system, at least in their early days. Christianity, Buddhism, and Islam all began as NRMs or cults. Either Jesus started a new cult, or else we must conclude that Christianity is a denomination of Judaism—an idea that neither Christians nor Jews would likely accept. The estimated number of NRMs in North America at the turn of the century was between 1,500 and 2,000. The Institute for the Study of American Religion lists 1,667 different religious groups that are nonconventional religions (Melton 1992). There could be 10,000 more NRMs in Africa and an undetermined but large number in Asia. Several scientific research sites discuss major NRMs in North America (Hadden 2006; Religious Worlds 2007).

An NRM is often started by a charismatic leader, someone who claims to have received a new insight, often directly from God. For example, Reverend Sun Myung

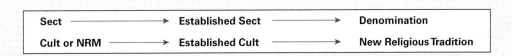

Figure 12.4 The Evolution of Sects and Cults (New Religious Movements: NRMs)
Source: Roberts 2004.

Moon founded an NRM called the Unification Church, the members of which are often referred to as *Moonies*. Some sensational NRMs have ended in tragedy: Reverend Jim Jones led his devoted followers to a retreat in Guyana, South America, and ultimately to their suicides in the belief that heaven was awaiting them (Lacayo 1993; Wright 1995). A group suicide also occurred in 1997 in California by a band called Heaven's Gate, which thought supernatural beings were coming to take them away in a flying saucer (Wessinger 2000).

Most new religious groups are not dangerous to members. Furthermore, most religious groups that are now accepted and established were stigmatized as weird or evil when they started. Early Christians were characterized by Romans as dangerous cannibals, and in the early decades of the 20th century in the United States, Roman Catholics were depicted in the media as dangerous, immoral, and anti-American (Bromley and Shupe 1981). When we encounter media reports about NRMs, we should listen to and read these with a good dose of skepticism and recognize that not all cults are like the sensational ones.

Many NRMs are short lived, lasting only as long as the charismatic leader does. The Jim Jones movement died with him and the cyanide poisoning of its members. Only those groups that institutionalize and prepare for their futures, as did the early Christians, are likely to survive. So both sects and NRMs find that developing a complex organization enhances survival, but in the process, they are usually transformed as religious groups. Figure 12.4 illustrates the parallel evolution of these two types of religious groups.

The social conditions in the late 20th century were ripe for NRMs. Many young people, often from middle-class families in industrialized nations, were attracted to NRMs in their search for who and what they are. These religious communities provide meaning and belonging systems with friendship bonds and clear-cut answers for people seeking meaning and direction in life. This choice has been especially evident in urban areas and on the West Coast of the United States and Canada.

NRMs, however, are hard to study because the members know they might be persecuted for their faith perspective. Witchcraft is one example of a religion that has been forced to remain secretive, and the next "How Do We Know?" explores the strategies of one sociologist to examine this interesting religious community.

Thinking Sociologically

What factors might cause the birth and success of new religious movements (NRMs)?

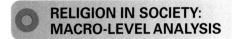

RELIGION IN SOCIETY: MACRO-LEVEL ANALYSIS

As an integral part of society, religion meets the needs of individuals and of the social structure. In this section, we explore functionalist and conflict theories as we consider some functions of religion in society and the role of religion in stratification systems of the society.

The Contribution of Religion to Society: A Functionalist Perspective

Regardless of their personal belief or disbelief in the supernatural, sociologists of religion acknowledge that religion has important social consequences. Functionalists contend that religion has positive consequences—helping people answer questions about the meaning of life and providing part of the glue that helps to hold a society together. Let us look at some of the social functions of religion, keeping in mind that the role of religion varies depending on the structure of the society and the time period.

Social Cohesion

Religion helps individuals feel a sense of belonging and unity with others, a common sense of purpose with those who share the same beliefs. It serves to hold any social unit together and gives the members a sense of camaraderie. Durkheim's ([1897] 1964) widely cited study of suicide stresses the importance of belonging to a group. Research shows that a high rate of congregational membership and religious homogeneity in a community are associated with lower rates of suicide (Ellison, Burr, and McCall 1997). Thus, religion serves society well as long as religious views are consistent with other values of society (Bainbridge and Stark 1981). If there are competing religions,

How Do We Know?

Witchcraft in the United States

In *A Community of Witches: Contemporary Neo-Paganism and Witchcraft in the United States,* Helen Berger (1999) applies sociological analysis to conduct a fascinating study of contemporary Wicca. To study this movement, Berger used several methods of gathering information. First, for two years, she did participant observation in a newly formed coven in New England. A coven is a small congregation of witches, usually having no more than 10 or 12 members. It took considerable effort to establish trust with the members, but this method of gathering data allowed her to experience firsthand the close-knit support group and the actual behaviors and interactions within the group. A national organization provided her with a wealth of printed material produced by Neo-Pagans and allowed her entry to several national Neo-Pagan festivals, where she observed the rituals. She also did in-depth, open-ended interviews with 40 members from a

Rites of the Wiccan religion in Texas: saluting the four cardinal points.

number of covens. By using a variety of methods, Berger was able to gain in-depth information, but she was also able to get an idea of whether her experiences were generalizable to all parts of the country.

Although Berger found Wicca to be a rather healthy and vibrant movement, she also found that it experiences some of the same dilemmas of any other religious congregation. Wicca is feminist, believing in a goddess and involving an emphasis on gender equality. It also celebrates spiritual unity of humans with nature and therefore has a strong ecology ethic. The religion encourages an intuitive approach to decision making (using intuition rather than focusing on logic) and celebrates the senses. This sensuousness embraces sexuality, fertility, and being at one with the universe.

Berger finds that Wicca is a product of the globalized world, for the religion involves bits and pieces selected from religions around the world. It has spread with modern technology, including Internet communication, desktop publishing, and fax machines. Furthermore, it is a religion about self-fulfillment, in keeping with a contemporary obsession with self-awareness and self-transformation.

In a more recent book, *Teenage Witches*, Berger worked with an Australian scholar, Douglas Ezzy (Berger and Ezzy 2007), to explore expansion of witchcraft among teenagers in the English-speaking world. The book is based on interviews that Berger and Ezzy did with 90 young people in the United States, United Kingdom, and Australia (30 in each country). Young people, even more than those of the generation before them, are drawn to the emphasis on self-transformation. Many of the last generation found their politics, particularly their belief in environmentalism and gender equity, mirrored in Wicca. Unlike the last generation, the new generation witches are more likely to practice alone—that is, outside of covens. They learn about the religion in books, magazines, and online. They may interact with others on Web sites, through blogs, or Wiccan chatrooms, but they remain solitary practitioners.

The increase in the number of teenagers becoming witches is in part a product of the growth of positive media representations of witchcraft, such as the movie *The Craft* or television shows such as *Sabrina, the Teenage Witch*. However, Berger and Ezzy found that many more young people search online for information about witchcraft or read books about it than actually become witches. Although the media may stimulate interest, it does not cause young people to join. Those who do become witches tend to find that the religion speaks to their personal needs. They are more likely to already have had an interest in the occult and to have felt themselves to be different than their peers. The influx of young people, particularly because so few of them seek coven training and have the traditional ideas and practices passed on to them, has the potential to significantly change the face of the religion.

cohesion may be reduced and even be a source of conflict and hatred. Societies with competing religions often develop a civil religion—a theology of the nation—that serves to bless the nation and to enhance conformity and loyalty.

Legitimating Social Values and Norms

The values and norms in a culture must not be seen as random or arbitrary if they are to be compelling to members of the society. Religion often sacralizes social norms—grounds them in a supernatural reality or a divine command that makes them larger than life. Whether those norms have to do with care for the vulnerable, the demand to work for peace and justice, the immorality of extramarital sex, the sacredness of a monogamous heterosexual marriage, or proper roles of men and women, foundations of morality from scripture create feelings of absoluteness. This lends stability to the society: Agreement on social control of deviant behavior is easier, and the society can rely less on coercion and force to get citizens to behave themselves. Of course, the absoluteness of the norms also makes it more difficult to change them as the society evolves. This inflexibility is precisely what pleases religious conservatives and distresses theological liberals, the latter often seeking new ways to interpret the old norms.

Social Change

Depending on the time and place, religion can work for or against social change. Some religions fight to maintain the status quo or return to simpler times. This is true of many fundamentalist religions—be they branches of Christian, Jewish, Hindu, or Islamic faiths—that seek to simplify life in the increasingly complex industrial world. Other religious traditions support or encourage change. Japan was able to make tremendous strides in industrialization in a short time following World War II, in part because the Shinto, Confucian, and Buddhist religions provided no obstacles and, in fact, supported the changes. In the United States, the central figures in the civil rights movement were nearly all African American religious leaders. As the first nationwide organizations controlled by black people, African American religious organizations established networks and communication channels that were used by those interested in change (Lincoln and Mamiya 1990; McAdam 1999).

Thinking Sociologically

Which religious groups in your community have a stabilizing influence, sacralizing the existing system? Which groups advocate change in the society, pushing for more social equality and less ethnocentrism toward others? Are there mosques, temples, or churches that oppose the government's policies, or do they foster unquestioning loyalty?

This religious procession in Bolivia (seen from two perspectives) is a community-uniting event. Note that the symbolism represents a synthesis of traditional Christian symbols and local ones from the native religions.

The Link Between Religion and Stratification: A Conflict Perspective

Our religious ideas and values and the way we worship are shaped not only by the society into which we are born but also by our family's position in the stratification system. Religion serves different primary purposes for individuals, depending on their positions in the society. People of various social statuses differ in the type and degree of their involvement in religious groups.

At times, religions reinforce socially defined differences between people, giving sacred legitimacy to racial prejudice, gender bias, and inequality. Conflict theory considers ways in which religion relates to stratification and the status of minority groups.

The Class Base of Religion

Conflict theorist Karl Marx ([1844] 1963) states clearly his view of the relationship between religion and class—that religion helps perpetuate the power structure. For the proletariat or

Table 12.3 Socioeconomic Profiles of American Religious Groups

Religious Group	Educational Level — Percent Having Attained Each Level			Annual Household Income (in $) — Percent Having This Income Range		
	Post-Grad Degree	College Graduate Degree	No High School	% Over 100,000	% Over 75,000	% Under 30,000
Hindu	48	26	4	43	22	9
Jewish	35	24	3	46	12	14
Reformed	35	31	1	55	12	11
Conservative	35	23	4	43	14	12
Episcopal Church in USA	27	30	1	35	8	16
Unitarian	29	22	3	26	13	19
Buddhist	26	22	3	22	17	25
Presbyterian USA	24	23	7	28	8	16
United Church of Christ	21	21	4	18	14	27
Atheist	21	21	8	28	15	21
Orthodox	18	28	6	28	13	20
Disciples of Christ	17	18	10	20	14	31
United Methodist	14	21	8	22	16	23
Evangelical Lutheran in America	11	19	6	17	15	24
Nondenominational Protestant	11	18	6	18	15	24
Latter-Day Saint (Mormon)	10	18	8	15	16	26
Catholic	10	16	17	19	14	31
Muslim	10	14	21	16	10	35
Southern Baptist	7	14	15	15	11	30
Religious but Unaffiliated	6	11	21	12	10	40
Seventh Day Adventist	5	16	24	11	7	46
American Baptist	5	9	23	8	9	46
Assemblies of God	4	8	24	8	11	41
Other Pentecostal	3	8	26	7	8	45
Black Baptist	3	5	19	8	6	50
Jehovah's Witness	3	6	19	9	9	24

Source: Pew Foundation 2008:78–80, 84–86. Published by the Pew Forum on Religion and Public Life, www.pewforum.org.

working class, religion is a sedative, he asserts, a narcotic that dulls people's sensitivity to and understanding of their plight. He calls religion the "opiate of the people." It keeps people in line and provides an escape from reality, from the tedium, if not suffering, of daily life. At the same time, it helps those in power keep other people in line because it promises that if laborers serve well in this life, then life in the hereafter or the next incarnation will be better. Some religions justify the positions of those who are better off by saying they have earned it.

Because the needs and interests of socioeconomic groups differ, religion is class based in most societies. In the United States, different denominations and sects show corresponding differences in social class measures such as education, occupation, and income (Pyle 2006; Smith and Faris 2005).

The specific links between denominational affiliation and socioeconomic measures in the United States at the beginning of the 21st century are indicated in Table 12.3. The sectarian religions (sects) tend to attract lower- and working-class worshippers because they focus on the problems and life situations faced by people in lower social classes. People with higher social status attend worship more regularly and know more about the scriptures than do people with less education and income, but people with lower socioeconomic status are more likely to pray and read the holy scriptures daily (Albrecht and Heaton 1984; Roberts 2004).

Max Weber (1946) referred to this pattern of people belonging to religious groups that espouse values and characteristics compatible with their social status as *elective affinity.*

For example, people in laboring jobs usually find that obeying rules of the workplace and adhering to the instructions of the employer or supervisor are essential for success on the job (Bowles and Gintis 1976; McLeod 2004). The faith communities of the poor and the working class tend to stress obedience, submission to "superiors," and the absoluteness of religious standards. The values of the workplace are reenacted and legitimated in the churches and help to socialize children to adapt to noncreative laboring jobs.

Many people in affluent congregations are paid to be divergent thinkers, to be problem solvers, and to break the mold of conventional thinking. They will not do well professionally if they merely obey rules. Instead, they are expected to be rule makers while trying to solve organizational or management problems (Bowles and Gintis 1976). It is not surprising, then, that the denominations of the affluent are more likely to value tolerance of other perspectives, religions, or values and to view factors that limit individual opportunity (e.g., institutional racism and sexism) as evil. They embrace tolerance of differences and condemn rigidity, absolutism, and conventionalism. Critical thinking, creativity, and even a streak of independence are valuable characteristics. Their religious communities are likely to encourage each member to work out his or her own theology, within limits (Roberts 2004; Roof 1999).

Stratification is found in various world religions, not just Christianity. For example, Hinduism in the upper classes of India conforms much more to the official beliefs of the religion. It is monotheistic and stresses concepts of transmigration of souls (also called reincarnation). The lower castes believe in a sort of Hindu folk religion that is *polytheistic*, having multiple gods. Lower-class Hindus tend to identify Hindu statues as gods in themselves (rather than as symbols), and they believe in heaven and hell rather than in reincarnation (Noss and Noss 1990).

Whatever the particular belief, the relationship between one's religion and one's social status affects everything from life expectancy, likelihood of divorce, and mental health to attitudes regarding sexual behavior, abortion, and stem cell research.

Thinking Sociologically

How do the social class and religious affiliation of people you know relate to the discussion here? How do denominations with higher than average levels of education (Unitarians, Jews, Episcopalians, Presbyterians, and Congregationalists) in your community differ from those with less education?

Racial Bias, Gender Prejudice, and Religion

Most religious groups profess to welcome all comers, yet most have practiced discrimination against some group at some time, often related to political and economic factors in the society. In fact, some studies show positive relationships between religion, prejudice, and discrimination (Hunsberger 1995). It is important to recognize that religion has multiple and even contradictory effects on societies. For example, most Christian denominations have formal statements that reject racial prejudice as un-Christian. The meaning system teaches tolerance. However, informal group norms in a local congregation—the belonging system—may be tolerant of ethnic jokes and may foster distrust of certain races (Woodberry and Smith 1998). Among whites in the United States, for instance, active church members display more prejudice than inactive church members or the unchurched (Chalfant and Peck 1983; Roberts 2004).

Prejudice may be perpetuated because promotions to larger churches are usually awarded to those ministers who are well-liked, who have growing and harmonious churches, and whose churches are financially sound. Ministers are sometimes reluctant to speak out forcefully on controversial issues or for racial equality for fear of offending their parishioners. Bishops may not promote a minister to a larger church if his or her current congregation is racked with dissension and donations have declined. Even though the denomination's meaning system may oppose prejudice, the structural system may reward clergy who do not defend that meaning system (Campbell and Pettigrew 1959; Roberts 2004).

Women have often been the main volunteers and the most faithful attendees in congregations, and in some denominations, they hold leadership positions (Chaves 2004). Yet, they have often been denied entrance into many statuses within religious organizations and are kept separated. In some Christian and conservative Jewish worship services, women must also cover their heads or sit separately. Religious rules regarding attire and hair length also help to reinforce differentiation. Men may enter a Christian cathedral in Europe with very few restrictions, but women must cover their heads so God will not be offended. This symbolizes and communicates the presumed differences between women and men before God (Douglas 1966). Similarly, men within Islam have more power, although women must be treated with respect. Within this faith tradition, many adherents see this stratification as providing protection for both groups to worship without distraction. All worshippers remove their shoes, and women must cover their heads and sometimes their faces, and they cannot enter certain areas of the mosque when men are present. Literal teachings of many religions legitimate treating women differently, often in ways that disallow leadership opportunities and imply inferiority. This is true of all of the Abrahamic religious traditions: Judaism, Christianity, and Islam.

Within Christian groups, women have traditionally played one of two roles: silence and obedience to men in religious authority or specialized subordinate roles within the religious group. Many deeply religious women have been concerned over the lack of significant roles for women and

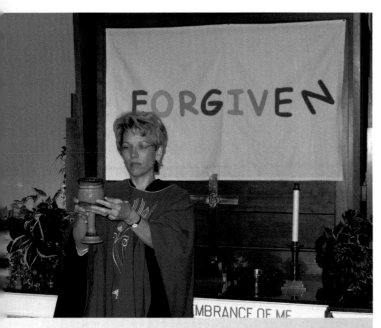

A Methodist minister blesses the cup before offering the sacrament of communion to her congregation.

religions to form new structures in which they can worship as equals, including NRMs. Indeed, women in the Western world have, throughout history, been more likely than men to opt for unconventional forms of religion (McGuire 2002).

In some instances, religion may reinforce and legitimate social prejudices toward racial groups or toward women. In others, religion may be a powerful force for change and for greater equality in a society. Seldom does religion take a passive or entirely disinterested position on these matters. Consider conflicts around the world, many of which are based on religious and class differences. People are fighting and dying for their religious beliefs. In Rwanda, people of the Tutsi and Hutu tribes have slaughtered each other. In Belfast, Ireland, bombs sent civilians to their graves or to hospitals, maimed for life. In India, Muslims and Hindus continue to massacre each other. Protestant against Catholic, Shiite Muslim against Sunni Muslim, Jew against Muslim, Christian against Jew—religion elicits strong emotions and influences people's definition of reality. Ethnocentric attitudes and economically rooted conflicts can be reinforced by religious beliefs. Religion has been the apparent cause of wars and social strife, but it has also been the motivation for altruism and a major contributor to social solidarity.

have fought for reformation within their religions. Ordination of women is a newly won right in several denominations. Moreover, a study of Seventh-Day Adventists found very positive attitudes toward female pastors, and female Anglican clergy in the United Kingdom felt they brought important skills and strengths to their ministries (Robbins 1998).

By the end of the 20th century, 71% of the public in the United States who express a religious preference favor having women as pastors, ministers, priests, or rabbis, compared to 42% in 1977 (Gallup Poll 2000). Still, some religious groups do not ordain women into the ministry or the priesthood. Because such leadership statuses are important symbolic positions, many women feel that this refusal helps sacralize the social stereotype of women as less capable.

While most mainline Christian denominations now have official statements on the equality of women and formal policies against discrimination in ordaining or hiring women pastors, the official meaning system does not tell the whole story. Local congregational search committees who screen and hire new ministers care deeply about the survival and health of the local church. Studies show that such persons are themselves not opposed to women in the pulpit, but they believe that others in their church would be offended and would stop coming and giving money to the church. Thus, local belonging and structural systems of the religion may perpetuate unequal treatment of clergywomen, even if the meaning system says they are equal (Chaves 1999; Lehman 1985; Robbins 1998).

Given these frustrations, some women have been uncomfortable working for reform from within and have left traditional

Thinking Sociologically

From what you know about the status of minority groups and women, how are problems they face in religion and other institutions (education, politics, economics) similar?

Religion in North America

Name almost any religion and a group representing that belief system can probably be found in the United Kingdom, United States, Canada, Kenya, and several other countries where religious diversity is the norm. In the United States, religious pluralism has been a founding principle since Roger Williams settled in Rhode Island. This makes for a complex religious pattern. Sociologists of religion have documented the vitality of American religion with empirical data that track religious trends over time (Finke and Stark 1993; Hadden 1987; Pew Forum 2008; Stark 2000).

Is Religion Dying or Revitalizing in North America?

Although it seemed at times over the last century that society was becoming secular and religion was fading in influence, religion is a fundamental, integral part of culture and individuals' lives (Christiano et al. 2002; Stark 2000). One third of all Americans currently claim no affiliation with any religious tradition, but one third of that unaffiliated group said that religion or spirituality is important in their lives. So we need to be cautious about how we interpret the numbers (Pew Forum 2008).

Religion in North America adjusts to changes in society and takes on new forms. While the number of Protestants in the United States has declined from two thirds of the population in the 1970s to roughly half in 2008, this does not mean that atheism has increased. The latter half of the 20th century saw a wide range of religious groups forming and growing in North America, from the occult and astrology to Moonies and from New Age spirituality to Zen Buddhism. Furthermore, middle-class Catholics and Episcopalians were "speaking in tongues," and "the fervent evangelical culture could not be classified as 'marginal' when successive presidents"—Ford, Carter, Reagan, and Bush—openly affirmed being born-again and claimed membership in the evangelical community (Marty 1983). Polling data indicate that 41% of U.S. Christians identify themselves as born-again or evangelical Christians (Gallup Poll 2006). The religiosity of President George W. Bush was a political factor in his reelection in 2004 (Green and Silk 2005), and religion and race played a role in the 2008 presidential primary—both with Mormon candidate Mitt Romney (a Republican) and with controversies over the church membership of Democrat Barack Obama.

In addition, the makeup of the United States and Canada is changing in many ways. Although two out of every three native-born U.S. citizens are Protestant, two out of every three Christian immigrants are Catholic. Some other religious faiths are represented among those new Americans as well, so the shift in the country may be less a decline in religiosity than a shift in its character (Pew Forum 2008). Religion remains strong as an influence in Canadian life as well. Religious adherence in that country has remained at nearly 90% for the past four decades. Half the population reports having had a personal religious experience, three out of four claim to pray at least occasionally, and overall religious membership in Canada has continued to increase every decade (Bibby 2002).

About 56% of Americans sampled indicate a high confidence in organized religion, more confidence than they have in politics and other institutions, and religious membership has increased over the past three centuries (Gallup Poll 2001). In the "good old days" of American colonialism, only about 17% of the population belonged to a church. Religious membership rose fairly steadily from the 1770s until the 1960s. Although there has been a modest decline in the past 30 years, membership has fluctuated between 64% and 70% since 1992 (Newport 2006). Membership in mosques, synagogues, or churches was reported at 64% of the adult population in 2005 (Newport 2006). Another

Table 12.4a   Leading Religious Indicators

Belief in God	81%[a]
Member of a church	64%[a]
Attended church in past 7 days	35%[a]
Religion *very important* in life	61%[b]
Religion answers problems	65%[c]
High confidence in organized religion	56%[c]

Source: Newport 2006, Bukhari 2003.

a. Gallup Poll 2006.
b. Gallup Poll 2004.
c. Gallup Poll 2001.

Table 12.4b   How Important Is Religion in Your Life?

	(in %)		
	*Very**	*Fairly*	*Not Very*
2005	59	25	16
2000	59	29	12
1995	58	29	12

Source: Newport 2006, Bukhari 2003.

*These figures vary by religious affiliation. Note, for example, that Muslims rate among the highest—at 79% "very important"—in a 2001 survey (Bukhari 2003).

measure of religious strength is belief in God. Gallup Poll results for three decades indicate that 93% of the U.S. population believe in God or a universal spirit or higher power (Newport 2004). Table 12.4a and 12.4b show results from Gallup Polls regarding indicators of the importance of religion in people's lives. Map 12.3 also shows that Americans report high levels of attendance at religious worship services, but as you can see, there are significant geographical variations. Attendance at weekly worship is shown in Figure 12.5.

The relative vibrancy of religion in North America is also seen in the work of Canadian sociologist Reginald Bibby (1987a, 1987b, 2002). He confirms that religion remains strong as an influence in Canadian life. Religious adherence has remained at nearly 90% for the past four decades. Half the population reports having had a personal religious experience, three out of four claim to pray at least occasionally, and overall religious membership in Canada has continued to increase every decade (Bibby 2002). These rates are higher than those in other religiously pluralistic nations and higher than most nations with state religions. In relation to other countries, the United States and Canada are religious. Current trends show mainline denominations losing

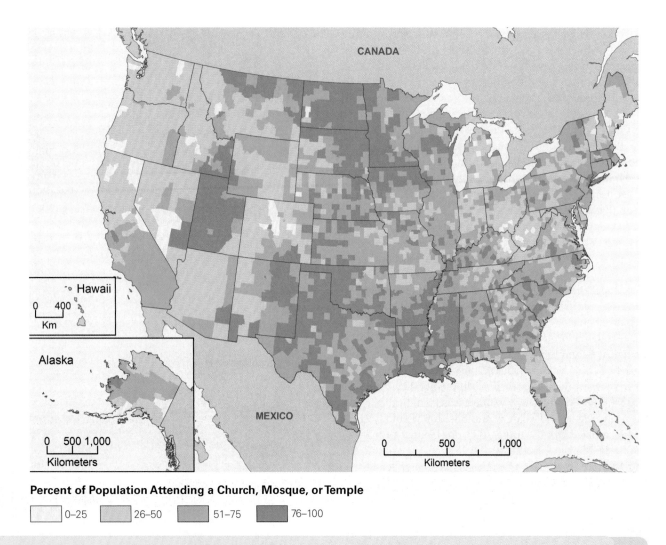

Percent of Population Attending a Church, Mosque, or Temple

☐ 0–25   ☐ 26–50   ☐ 51–75   ☐ 76–100

Map 12.3   Percent of U.S. Population Affiliated With a Church, Mosque, or Temple

Source: Religious Congregations and Membership Study 2000. Map by Anna Versluis.

Note: This map is based on data reported by local congregations and includes both members and other regular attendees; it does not represent weekly attendance. The numbers indicate an over-reporting, but that does not change the overall geographical pattern of religious affiliation.

members while fundamentalist and Pentecostal groups are growing, as are evangelical megachurches (congregations with 10,000 to 40,000 members).

The Process of Secularization

Secularization refers to the diminishing influence and role of religion in everyday life. Instead of religion being the dominant institution, it is but one of many. Secularization involves a movement away from supernatural and sacred interpretations of the world and toward decisions based on empirical evidence and logic. Before modern scientific explanations and technology, religion helped explain the unexplainable.

However, the scientific method, emphasis on logical reasoning, and the belief that there are many different religious interpretations rather than one have challenged religious and spiritual approaches to the world. Although religion is still strong in the lives of individuals, it does not have the extensive control over other institutions of education, health, politics, or family that it once did. It is an institution among others rather than being the dominant one.

Some scholars have argued that secularization is an inevitable and unstoppable force in the modern postindustrial world (Berger 1961; Beyer 2000; Dobbelaere 1981, 2000). Others argue that secularization is far from inevitable and has almost reached its limit (Stark 2000; Swatos and Gissurarson 1997; Warner 1993). Our social world

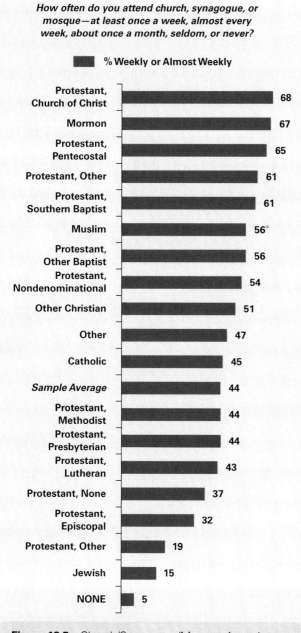

How often do you attend church, synagogue, or mosque—at least once a week, almost every week, about once a month, seldom, or never?

■ **% Weekly or Almost Weekly**

Protestant, Church of Christ	68
Mormon	67
Protestant, Pentecostal	65
Protestant, Other	61
Protestant, Southern Baptist	61
Muslim	56*
Protestant, Other Baptist	56
Protestant, Nondenominational	54
Other Christian	51
Other	47
Catholic	45
Sample Average	44
Protestant, Methodist	44
Protestant, Presbyterian	44
Protestant, Lutheran	43
Protestant, None	37
Protestant, Episcopal	32
Protestant, Other	19
Jewish	15
NONE	5

Figure 12.5 Church/Synagogue/Mosque Attendance

Source: Newport 2006; Bukhari 2003.

*Data on Muslims comes from a difference source (Bukhari) and from an earlier date (2001).

Despite the process of secularization in some parts of the world, the sense of awe before the holy remains strong for many people. This enormous Buddha at the Yungang Buddhist Caves at Wuzhou Mountain in China was built out of a sense of sacredness for Buddha, and it then became a source of veneration for subsequent generations. Secularization may have occurred in many places at the macro level, but religious faith is strong at the micro level.

model helps us understand that, like religion, secularization is a complex phenomenon that occurs at several levels and affects each society differently (Beyer 2000; Chaves and Gorski 2001; Yamane 1997).

Secularization may be occurring at the societal level, but evidence indicates this is not so at the individual level in the United States (Bellah et al.1996; Chaves and Gorski 2001). When religious faith guides guide people's everyday lives—their conduct on the job, in political choices, their

sexual behavior, in the science classroom, or in attitudes toward racial relations—then secularization at the individual level is weak. Many people insist they are "spiritual but not religious" at the micro level. Faith still matters to them (Roof 1999).

Within church-related organizations (Baptist hospitals, Presbyterian colleges, Jewish social service foundations), if the decisions about how to deliver services or who will be hired or fired are based on systematic policies designed for organizational efficiency, then meso-level secularization is present within a religious organization (Chaves 1993). If policies in the society at large are made with little discussion of theological implications, decisions being based on human rights arguments rather than on what is sinful, then society has become secular at the societal level (Chaves

Photo Essay

Prayer in Schools

Burmese students from 5 to 11 years old pray at a school in Myawadi, Myanmar.

First graders share a moment of silent prayer at the start of their school day in a South Carolina school in 1966.

Mongolian children praying at school.

Table 12.5   **The Complexity of Secularization in the Social World**

	Institutional Differentiation	Rational/Utilitarian Decision Making
Macro Level	Institutions in the society, including government, education, and the economy, are functionally independent and autonomous of religious organizations.	Decision making about social policies is based on cost-benefit analyses, using logic and empirical data rather than scripture or proclamations of religious authorities.
Meso Level	Organizations look to other social associations and units that have similar functions and goals for accepted practices of how to operate the organization, and not to religious organizations and authorities.	Decision making about an organization's policies and goals is based on utilitarian analyses and consequences, rather than on scripture, theological arguments, or proclamations of religious authorities.
Micro Level	Individuals emphasize being "spiritual rather than religious," formulate their own meaning system or theology, and may believe that spirituality has little to do with other aspects of their lives.	Decision making about life decisions is based on individual self-interest without concern for the teachings of the religious group or the clergy; calculations of cost and benefit to the individual are foremost in individual decisions.

Source: Roberts 2004. Copyright © 2004 by Wadsworth, a part of Cengage Learning, Inc. Reproduced by permission. www.cengage.com/permissions.

1993; Dobbelaere 2000; Yamane 1997). (See Table 12.5.) Debates about prayer in schools, court decisions about "one nation under God" in the Pledge of Allegiance to the flag, and involvement of religious leaders in political issues suggest that societal-level secularization is a point of controversy in the United States. Still, few will deny that the bureaucratic structures of the United States and virtually every other postindustrial nation are thoroughly secularized. Macro, meso, and micro secularization do not seem to be in harmony, as illustrated in Table 12.5.

The bottom line is that most sociologists of religion believe that religion continues to be a powerful force at the individual level and that it has some influence in the larger culture (the macro level). They maintain there is a macro-level trend toward secularization in most Western societies but that the trend is neither inevitable nor uniform across societies (Dobbelaere 2000; Lambert 2000; Sommerville 2002; Yamane 1997).

At a global level, no particular theological authority has power to define reality or to determine policies, religious authority structures are minimal, and secularization is well established. Perhaps, this is one reason why conservatives of nearly every religious faith are leery of global processes and global organizations, such as the United Nations. Our global organizations are governed by rational-legal (secular) authority, not religious doctrines.

Thinking Sociologically

What might be the results if a society is secularized at the meso and macro levels but not at the micro level? Why?

Religion in the Modern World

Religion and Peace

Can religion bring peace to the world? Most religious systems advocate living in harmony with other humans and with nature, yet often peace is not the reality. Although the meaning system of all the Abrahamic religions—Christianity, Judaism, and Islam—embrace a world of peace and justice, the structural system does not always reward those who pay attention to the meaning system, as we see in cases of racism and sexism. Christian denominations often foster nationalistic loyalty—with displays of the flag and even pledges of allegiance to the flag during worship. This endorsement of national pride can actually foster we/they thinking and can undermine peace. Congregations that take peace activities seriously may decline in membership, whereas those that stir up chauvinistic sentiments attract large numbers. So the structural system may actually undermine the message of the meaning system because growth and financial vitality is a major concern of many local church leaders. Despite rhetoric, fiscal concerns can actually trump claims to worship the "Prince of Peace."

Still, there is movement toward interfaith and transnational cooperation. Christian, Islamic, Jewish, and other world faiths sponsor a variety of programs aimed at health care, hunger relief, and easing of suffering caused by natural disasters. Prior to the 1700s, remarkably few efforts had been made to reach out to people in other cultures. Moreover, from 1700 until well into the 20th century, outreach programs were aimed almost exclusively at trying to convert the "heathen," those with belief systems that differed (Hunter 1983; Lee 1992).

Liberal theologies suggest that God may speak to people through a variety of channels, including the revelations of other religious traditions. While leaders may feel their beliefs provide the fullest and most complete expression of God's Truth, leaders recognize that other beliefs also provide paths to Truth. Many global religious programs today are ecumenical and aimed at humanitarian relief rather than proselytizing.

Some religions that believe they have the only Truth defend themselves or try to spread "the true word" by force. Other religious groups lie at the roots of cultural differences, which cause ethnocentrism and sometimes hatred, and individuals fight and die to defend their belief systems and way of life. Fundamentalist religious groups use strategies to attempt to preserve their distinctive identity as a people or group (Marty and Appleby 1991, 2004). They seldom believe in pluralism or tolerance of other beliefs but rather believe they are the only true religion. Consequently, they resist and defend themselves against modernism, which threatens their beliefs and way of life, or try to spread the "true word," sometimes by force (Billings and Scott 1994; Lamy 1996; Stern 2003; Wessinger 2000). Members of fundamentalist groups—be they Orthodox Jews, traditional Muslims, or born-again Christians—generally believe in a literal interpretation of their holy books and a personal experience with Allah or God. Some fundamentalist groups remove themselves from the secular world, including politics, but other fundamentalist groups are active in politics.

Conflict between religious groups is especially intense if ethnic, economic, and religious differences are present. Consider Ireland, where the main landowners are Protestants of Scottish descent. The laborers are predominantly native Irish in ethnicity and are Roman Catholic. Hatred between Protestants and Catholics is exacerbated by the lack of cross-cutting loyalties or friendships (McGuire 2002). Frustrations of groups not in power lead to ethnocentrism and sometimes hatred against others. Those in power similarly develop stereotypes about those unlike themselves whose ideology and values are different. Cross-cutting social cleavages reduce social hostilities, as Figure 12.6 illustrates.

Religion has the greatest potential for reducing hatred between groups when those groups share some type of common identification. If the conflict is over ethnicity and economics, a common religious heritage can lessen the likelihood of violent confrontation. Some religious groups have joined together in peaceful enterprises such as attempts to ban nuclear weapons or to bring about peace in the Middle East. This common purpose provides for cooperation and collaboration, thus lessening animosity and we-versus-they thinking.

Perhaps the core reason that some countries are secular is because of history. The conflicts in Europe between religions were very brutal, beginning with the bloodletting in the Hundred Years' War. From that time, "religion was the sixteenth century word for nationalism" (Wallerstein 2005:125). The intense religious in-group loyalties led to a willingness to kill those who were Other. The horrific religious conflicts in European societies did not reach closure until the

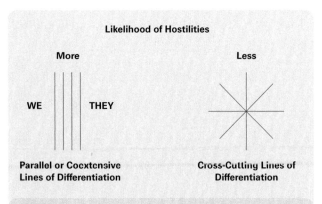

Figure 12.6   Lines of Differentiation Between "We" and "They"

Note: Imagine that each line represents a division in the society between groups based on religion, ethnicity, political party, economic status, language spoken, skin color, or other factors. Parallel lines of differentiation divide people in each conflict along the same lines. *Cross-cutting lines* cut the differences so that people who were part of "they" in a previous antagonism become part of "we" in the present discord. This lessens the likelihood of deep and permanent hostilities within a social unit.

Enlightenment. At this time, tolerance of other religions became dominant and a primary foundation for determining national policy (Dobbelaere 1981, 2000; Lambert 2000).

As we have seen, the disconnect between micro and macro levels—religious passion at the micro level and secular domination at the macro level—has resulted in severe tensions around the world (Wallerstein 2005). For instance, in the United States, the movement is toward increasing religiosity at the micro level and increasing secularism—with its openness to diversity—at the macro level.

The rise of religious fundamentalism in the 20th century, whether Islamic, Buddhist, Hasidic Jewish, evangelical Christian, or Malaysian Dukway, appears to be a reaction against global modernization (Davidman 1990; Robertson and Garrett 1991; Shupe and Hadden 1989; Turner 1991a). Rapid global change has resulted in anomie as people confront change—fear obliteration of their own culture, encroaching secularization of the society as the supernatural realm shrinks, threat to the material self-interests of religious organizations, and fear of interdependence with powerful nations of the Western world. All of these threats have strengthened fundamentalism.

Thinking Sociologically

What specific religious beliefs or behaviors might influence the way in which religions and countries relate to one another? How might religious organizations influence international relations?

Religion, Technology, and the World Wide Web

Technology and the Internet impact not only nations but also religions. From television broadcasts of megachurch services to Muslim chat rooms using technology to communicate, religious messages travel in new ways.

Prior to the wide distribution of religious texts to people who were not ordained ministers, the hierarchies of Christendom controlled what was disseminated as Truth. The common (and typically illiterate) member of the local church did not have any basis for challenging the Pope or other church leaders. Those leaders were the authority. However, Martin Luther used the printed word in many powerful ways. He and other reformers claimed that the Bible alone was the ultimate source of Truth and religious authority. The church leaders were to be believed only insofar as they were faithful to the scriptures. Luther himself used the printed word to spread his version of Christian Truth, and he did so with a vengeance. He not only wrote more than other dissenters, he outpublished the entire legion of Vatican defenders (Brasher 2004). He published in the common languages of the people rather than in Latin, and the Protestant Reformation was launched. It is doubtful that this could have happened without the printing press. The printing press had similar revolutionary effects within Judaism (Brasher 2004).

Today, television and multimedia worship have enhanced the marketing of religion, including the modification of the product to meet "consumer" demand (Frankl 1987; Hadden and Shupe 1988; Roberts 2004; Sargeant 2000). The Internet is the most recent technology with enormous impacts. Brasher (2004) reports that there are more than a million religion Web sites and they cover an extraordinarily wide range of religious beliefs and practices. Even conservative Christians such as Jerry Falwell, who dubbed the Internet an evil Tower of Babel, have used it to spread their message. The panic over whether the turn of the millennium (Y2K) would result in massive crashes in computers around the world was related to the "end of the world" prophesies by some conservative Christians (Brasher 2004; Lamy 1996). The computer, in short, was to be the medium to bring an end to life in this world.

The medium of the Internet is fast-paced and oriented to the now (Brasher 2004). Technology is often outdated in a few years if not in a few months, and the past hardly seems a source of authority or of Truth. Yet, traditional religious communities often excel in maintaining and propagating memories of past events that give meaning to life or that define notions of sacredness and Truth as the world around them changes rapidly. It is too early to tell for sure what impacts these most recent technologies might have on religions around the world, but one thing is clear: The Internet allows instant access to information about religions that otherwise might be obscure or nonexistent for many people.

Social Policy: The Homosexuality Debates

Gays in the church, ordination of gay ministers, same-sex marriage in churches—these issues make for heated debate over church policy and even threaten to split some denominations. Most established religious groups assume the normality of heterosexuality.

Marriage is sanctified by religious ceremony in all major religious groups, but recently, some religious bodies have openly debated the possibility of recognizing officially sanctioned weddings for gays and lesbians. In the Christian tradition, there are six passages in scripture that condemn homosexual relationships, only one of which condemns lesbian relationships (Genesis 19:1–28; Leviticus 18:22, 20:13; Romans 1:26–27; I Corinthians 6:9; I Timothy 1:10). Opposition to homosexuality is especially high among religious fundamentalists. In recent years, there have been strident conflicts in the Presbyterian (U.S.) and United Methodist denominations, but in the most conservative denominations, few questions are even raised about homosexuality because the rightness of absolute heterosexuality is taken for granted.

Thinking Sociologically

The film *Brokeback Mountain,* depicting two gay men struggling with their sexuality and with societal expectations, shows the power of norms, including religious beliefs, to influence the lives of gay and bisexual men and women. How is this conflict depicted in the film, and what role does religion play in the conflict?

Liberals in the churches tend to see this issue as one of prejudice against people for a characteristic that is immutable. They assume that homosexuality is an inborn trait. Conservatives argue that homosexuality is a choice that has moral implications. They tend to see homosexuality as a behavior that is acquired through socialization. Therefore, acceptance of homosexuality will likely increase the numbers of people who engage in this lifestyle, they believe. Conservatives see liberal notions about homosexuality and gender roles as a threat to society and family, a threat to the moral social order, whereas liberals often feel that sexuality within a committed relationship is not a moral issue. The real moral issue for them is bigotry—lack of tolerance of other lifestyles. Thus, the two groups have socially constructed the meaning of morality along different lines.

Some mainstream denominations have developed policies supportive of lesbian, gay, and bisexual persons in local churches: More Light (Presbyterian), Open and Affirming (United Church of Christ and Christian Church), Reconciled in

Christ (Lutheran), and Reconciling Congregations (Methodist). These designations apply to about 300 congregations that wish to be known as "gay and lesbian friendly" (www.mlp .org/resources/history). A new denomination, Universal Fellowship of Metropolitan Community Churches (UFMCC), affirms homosexuality as a legitimate lifestyle for Christians (Rodriguez and Lupfer 2000). It has more than 300 local churches in the United States, with 17 in the conservative state of Texas. There are also congregations on six continents (Metropolitan Community Churches 2008). One study conducted on a UFMCC congregation in New York found that homosexuals affiliated with this church have exceptionally positive personal adjustment. They are more likely to have an integrated self-concept as both a gay person and as a religious person (Rodriguez and Ouellette 2000). At the same time, some religious people who are homosexual and members of traditional congregations struggle with their sense of self-integration.

One of the most controversial issues in several mainline denominations is over ordination of homosexuals as ministers. A Gallup Poll shows an overall shift toward acceptance of homosexual clergy by Americans: Whereas only 36% approved in 1977, 49% approved by 2004 (Gallup and Lindsay 1999:87; Gallup Poll 2004). Still, most denominations do not knowingly ordain homosexuals as ministers and do not allow their ministers to perform marriages or "holy unions" of two gay men or two lesbian women. If ministers do so, they may be defrocked as ministers. In one denomination, the Episcopalian Church in the United States, the election in 2003 of gay clergyman Gene Robinson as bishop created a breach in the international Anglican community, as African churches cut off ties to Episcopalians in the United States. In the summer of 2008, the Presbyterian Church (USA) also officially voted to change its rules and to approve ordination of gay and lesbian pastors. The decision is highly controversial, but the policy shift has been building for many years (Helfand 2008).

Some ministers continue to perform marriage ceremonies as a protest against a policy they think is immoral. They may take a "don't ask, don't tell" position with their bishops. One retired minister estimated that even in his very conservative Midwestern state, there are roughly 50 homosexual holy unions performed by Methodist pastors each year. He stated,

> Back in the 1950s, ministers could lose their ordination and ministerial privileges if they married someone in a church wedding who had been divorced. Performing a marriage of someone who had been divorced was a serious offense in the Methodist church—and in most other Protestant churches, too. If a divorced person wanted to marry a second time, a civil wedding was supposedly the only option. Many of us in the pastorate thought that the policy was inhumane. These were people whom we pastored. They had made a mistake in a previous selection of a spouse and wanted to start again. Many clergy secretly

went against formal policy of the church, but we did not tell our bishops. By the 1960s, if the church purged all of us who had done this, the Methodist church would have lost more than half of its ministers. In another 20 years, the same thing will be true with holy unions. If you have two people in your congregation who really care for each other and want to ritually affirm their lifelong commitment, how can we not honor that commitment and caring? I think it is a matter of time before this will become widely accepted. (Roberts 2004:299)

One study has documented more acceptance of homosexual rights among religiously committed people (Petersen and Donnenwerth 1998). Even where there are strong reservations about marriage of gays or lesbians, there is support for nondiscrimination in other areas such as jobs.

In our social world, religious organizations influence society, and the larger society influences religious groups. Moreover, attitudes in a local community or a region of the country influence attitudes within a congregation, irrespective of the positions of the official denomination (Koch and Curry 2000). Two catalysts are creating tension for change in religious organizations: (1) the emphasis on the equality of all people before God in Christian theology and (2) an impetus in the larger society that legitimates people in leadership roles based on competence and commitment rather than on traits beyond their control (skin color, gender, or sexual orientation).

Thus, the policy issues for all religious communities are (1) whether a homosexual person can ever have the spiritual qualities to lead a congregation as its minister; (2) whether that faith community should or should not endorse and permit same-sex marriages in their churches, mosques, or temples; and (3) whether faith groups should be involved in government policy regarding the right of the state to grant marriage licenses to homosexuals or other civil unions—a secular equivalent to the marriage contract that would allow more than 1,000 rights and privileges that heterosexuals enjoy. One proposed solution is that, because marriage has historically been "owned" by religious communities, the state could grant licenses for civil unions (not marriages) for both homosexuals and heterosexuals. Faith communities alone would decide whether they acknowledge a couple as married. The notion that the state should have any say in the matter of marriage began only with Martin Luther, who insisted that marriage was not a sacrament. These highly contested areas of public policy continue to be contentious.

Thinking Sociologically

How is hostility toward homosexuals similar and different from sexism and racism? Does religion play a role in heterosexism and homophobia? Why?

So What ?

Religion is a powerful force in the lives of people around the world. It typically elicits passions and deep loyalties, and in so doing, it can stimulate people to great acts of self-sacrificing charity, or it can elicit horrible atrocities and intergroup bigotries. People's religious affiliation is strongly related to their nationality, ethnic and racial group, and lifestyle. Religion is the one institution in most societies that consistently professes a desire for peace and goodwill, yet there may be inconsistencies between what people say and what they do. Religion can provide us with hope that the world's problems may be dealt with in humanitarian ways.

Religion provides a sense of meaning in life regarding the big questions, and that is why religious things come to have sacred meaning. They address our spiritual life and our sense of purpose. Humans in the modern world, however, are not just spiritual. They live in states with massive governmental bureaucracies that hold power and resolve conflicts. The next institution we will examine is politics—how power relations are negotiated at each level in the social world.

Key Points

What Have We Learned?

- Religion makes our most important values sacred, operating through three interconnected systems: a meaning system, a belonging system, and a structural system. (See pp. 382–383.)

- We become committed through these three systems, by our attachment to a reference group that becomes a belonging system, by making investments in the organization (the structural system), and by holding as real the system of ideas (the meaning system). (See pp. 383–385.)

- At the micro level, symbolic interaction theory illuminates how the meaning system works, with an interaction of myths, rituals, and symbols coming to define reality and making the values and the meaning system sacred. Rational choice theory focuses on costs and benefits that influence how individuals make decisions about religious commitments, but it also examines how religious organizations go about seeking a "market share" in the competition for members. (See pp. 385–392.)

- At the meso level, religious communities usually have a mutually supportive relationship with other institutions—family, the political system, and the economy. Religious organizations themselves can evolve into

one of several types of structures (or even bureaucracies): ecclesia, denomination, sect, or New Religious Movement (NRM). (See pp. 392–403.)

- At the macro level of analysis, functionalists maintain that religions can serve as a kind of glue to help solidify the country and can meet basic needs of the populace. By contrast, conflict theorists focus on ways that religion reinforces conflicts and inequalities in the society, whether socioeconomic, racial, or gender. (See pp. 403–408.)

- In the United States and Canada, secularization is dominant at the meso and macro levels, but seems not to be happening much at the micro level. This is the source of tension in societies. (See pp. 408–413.)

- At the global level, religion can be involved in issues of war and peace (sometimes undermining peace unwittingly) and is currently experiencing interface with the world of technology and the World Wide Web. (See pp. 413–415.)

- Finally, homosexuality, same-sex marriage, and ordination of gay or lesbian clergy are examples of religious policy issues causing considerable controversy. (See pp. 415–416.)

Contributing to Our Social World: What Can We Do?

At the Local Level: Nearly all colleges and universities have campus religious foundations or ministries, many of which, such as the Newman Foundation (Roman Catholic) and Hillel Foundation (Jewish), are branches of national organizations. Contact a student representative or faculty sponsor of one of these foundations on your campus. Arrange to attend a meeting to learn about the group's activities. If the group is involved in outreach work to other denominations, volunteer to assist in this type of initiative. Most religious organizations sponsor social service outreach in their local communities, including soup kitchens, food pantries, or thrift stores for the poor, and they welcome help. Contact a religious or lay leader of one of these organizations to volunteer in its community work.

At the Organizational or Institutional Level: At the end of Chapter 7, the faith-based Habitat for Humanity (www .habitat.com) was mentioned. This organization makes extensive use of volunteers and would welcome your participation. For a different look at religion in the United States, visit the Web site of the American Atheists at www .atheists.org. "Now in its fourth decade, American Atheists is dedicated to working for the civil rights of Atheists, promoting separation of state and church, and providing information about Atheism." Volunteers assist in this work through contributions, research, and legal support.

At the National and Global Levels: Several religious groups are committed to working for justice and peace at the national and global levels. The following are just two examples of peace and justice organizations. Tikkun Community (www.tikkun.org) is an ecumenical organization, started in the Jewish community to "mend, repair, and transform the world. . . . International community of people of many faiths calling for social justice and political freedom in the context of new structures of work, caring, communities and democratic social and economic arrangements." The American Friends Service Committee (www.afsc.org) is "a Quaker organization which includes people of various faiths who are committed to social justice, peace, and humanitarian service." These and similar faith-based organizations sponsor many relief and peace projects around the world.

Visit **www.pineforge.com/ballantine2study** for online activities, sample tests, and other helpful information. Select "Chapter 12: Religion" for chapter-specific activities.

CHAPTER 13

Politics

Penetrating Power

The sociology of politics is about penetrating power—a term that has a double meaning. First, we try to penetrate the consequences of power and what power means in the lives of people. Second, the phrase in our subtitle also refers to the fact that power penetrates every aspect of our lives.

Think About It . . .

Micro: How does political power penetrate my own life, even in the privacy of my own home?

Micro: How do people in my local community exercise power in constructive or destructive ways?

Meso: How does the political institution interact with the economic institution?

Macro: Who holds power in my government, and why?

Macro: Why do power relations often devolve into war and terrorism?

Macro: Global Community

Macro: Society

Meso: National Organizations, Institutions, and Ethnic Subcultures

Micro: Local Organizations and Community

Micro: Me (and My Political and Workplace Allies)

Micro: Fraternities/ sororities; civil clubs; family life

Meso: State/provincial government; state Supreme Court; political parties

Macro: Federal government; national Supreme Court

Macro: Cross-national political or economic organizations such as the United Nations; global programs to address human rights or poverty at international level (such as Amnesty International)

magine that a nuclear disaster has struck. The mortality rate is stunning. The few survivors gather together for human support and collectively attempt to meet their basic survival needs. They come from varying backgrounds and have diverse skills. Before the disaster some—the stockbroker and the business executive, for instance—earned more money and held higher social status than the others, but that is in the past. Faced with the new and unfamiliar situation, different skills seem more immediately important for survival.

Where should this group begin? Think about the options. Some sort of organization seems essential, a structure that will help the group meet its needs. Food and shelter are paramount. Those with experience in agriculture and building trades are likely to take leadership roles to provide these initial necessities. As time goes on, the need for clear norms and rules emerges. The survivors decide that all members must work—must contribute their share of effort to the collective survival. At first, these norms are unwritten, but gradually some norms and rules are declared more important and are recorded, with sanctions (penalties) attached for noncompliance. Committees are formed to deal with group concerns, and a semblance of a judicial system emerges. Someone is appointed to coordinate work shifts and others to oversee emerging aspects of this small society's life. This scenario could play out in many ways.

Politics is about power and about mobilizing support to lead. The 2008 presidential primaries and November election generated intense interest in the United States. Two senators—Barack Obama and Hillary Rodham Clinton—fought for the Democratic Party nomination. Then Senator Obama (right) and Senator John McCain (left), the Republican Party nominee, battled for the most powerful political office on the planet—the U.S. presidency.

What is happening? A social structure is evolving. Not everyone in the group will agree with the structure, and some people will propose alternatives. Whose ideas are adopted? Leadership roles may fall to the physically strongest, or perhaps the most persuasive, or those with the most skills and knowledge for survival. Those who are most competent at organizing may become the leaders, but that outcome is by no means assured.

Political systems that have developed and been refined over centuries probably went through similar processes, probably under less immediately dire circumstances. However, a war, an invading power, or revolutionary overthrow of an unstable government can change the form of a political system overnight, necessitating rapid reorganization. The daily news brings stories of governments overthrown by military leaders in coups, with new governments emerging to fill the gap.

The opening scenario and the political activity in our modern society share a common element—power. The concept of power is critical to understanding many aspects of our social world. Our primary focus in this chapter is the political dimension of society, although both the political and economic systems enforce the distribution of power in a society. Political systems involve the relationships between individuals and between the individual and larger social institutions.

In this chapter, we will consider the nature of power, power and politics at each level in our social world, theoretical perspectives on power, individuals and power, political systems and the distribution of power, and national and global systems of governance, including international conflicts, war, and terrorism.

Thinking Sociologically

How do you, your family members, your boss, or your professors use power? Why does each of these people have power?

What Is Power?

Power is an age-old theme in many great scholarly discussions. Social philosophers since Plato, Aristotle, and Socrates have addressed the issue of political systems and power. Machiavelli, an early 16th-century Italian political philosopher, is perhaps best known for his observation that "the end justifies the means." His understanding of how power was exercised in the 15th, 16th, and 17th centuries significantly influenced how monarchs used the powers of the state (the means) to obtain wealth, new territories, and trade dominance (the ends).

The most common definition of power used in social sciences today comes from Max Weber (1947), who saw **power** as the ability of people or groups to realize their own will in group action, even against resistance of others who disagreed.

Building on Weber's idea of power, one perspective is that there are various *power arenas*. First, the nation-state (national governments) attempts to control the behavior of individuals through *physical control* (police force) or *outright coercion* (threats and actual violence), through *symbolic control* such as intimidation or manipulation of people, and through *rules of conduct* that channel behavior toward desired patterns, such as workplace rules. For instance, the military in Haiti used torture, rapes, and death to intimidate workers and families, representing physical force as a mechanism of power.

Second, Weber's definition explains power as the ability to influence social life. Wherever people interact or participate in activities or organizations, power is a consequence (Olsen 1970). Therefore, individuals who have an understanding of interorganizational dynamics and can manipulate organization members are likely to have more power than others in organizational settings.

A third perspective focuses on a traditional Marxist approach to class structures, arguing that the control of economic resources and production allows the ruling class to keep ruling (Therborn 1976). People who control economic resources also protect their self-interests by controlling political processes through ideology, economic constraints, and physical coercion or political resources. Among many recent examples, Zimbabwe's leader, Robert Mugabe, used all of these methods of controlling political processes to hold onto power. Thus, power is found in all parts of the social world and is an element of every social situation (Domhoff 1998; Kettl 1993). So how does power work at each level?

Thinking Sociologically

Martin Luther King Jr. argued that, contrary to Machiavelli's ideas, the ends do not justify the means. Instead, the means are the end "in process." The method of attaining power will shape the social trust level and therefore the possibility of having a democratic system. Who is right? Why?

Power and Politics at Various Levels in the Social World

Power operates at the most micro levels of interaction, from individuals to family groups. In family life, husband-wife relations often involve negotiation and sometimes conflict over how to run a household and spend money. Interactions between parents and children also involve power issues as parents socialize their children. Indeed, the controversies over whether spanking is effective discipline or abusive imposition of pain is a question of how parents use their power to teach their children and control their behavior.

At the meso level, power operates in cities, counties, and states and provinces. Governments make decisions about which corporations receive tax breaks to locate their plants within the region. They pass laws that regulate everything from how long one's grass can be before a fine is imposed to how public schools will be funded. State and provincial governments in Western democracies also can control the way people live and make their living. Therefore, people have an interest in influencing governments by selecting their leaders, contributing to political campaigns, and helping to elect the people who support their views. Interest groups such as ethnic or minority groups and national organizations and bureaucracies also wield power and try to influence the political process at the meso level.

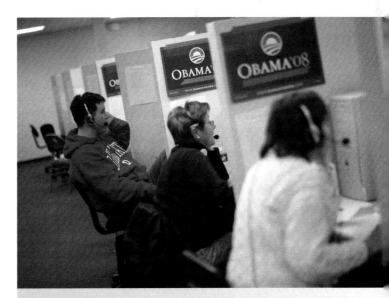

Individuals can work to elect the party—and the candidates—that they think will make their lives better and improve conditions in the world. They work at the micro level to influence the meso and the macro system.

At the macro level, international organizations such as the United Nations and World Bank, nongovernmental organizations (NGOs) such as Doctors without Borders, and military, political, and economic alliances such as the North Atlantic Treaty Organization (NATO) are parts of the global system of power.

Power processes pervade the micro, meso, and macro levels. Locally organized groups can force change that influences politics at the local, state/provincial, national, or global levels. Provincial or state laws shape what can and cannot be done at the local level. Laws at the national level influence state, province, or county politics and policies. Global treaties influence national autonomy.

Power can be studied in political structures such as governments, in political parties, and in different types of national political systems. It can also be understood in terms of the allocation of economic resources in a society and what factors influence patterns of resource distribution. Both economic and political systems are important in the sociologist's consideration of power distribution in any society. Let us first consider the theoretical lenses that help us understand power and politics.

Theoretical Perspectives on Political Systems and Power

Do you and I have any real decision-making power? Can our voices or votes make a difference, or do leaders hold all the power? Many sociologists and political scientists have studied these questions and found several answers to who holds power and the relationship between the rulers and the ruled.

Among the common theoretical perspectives on power are our familiar ones: interaction, functional, and conflict theories. Interaction theorists focus on symbols and constructions of reality that allow some people to assume power. A core concern is the legitimacy of power, or whether power is accepted by those who are ruled. Functionalists believe that citizens legitimize political systems by supporting them through their votes or traditions. They do this because political systems serve important functions, or purposes, in society. They establish and coordinate societal goals—for example, promoting stability, providing law and order, carrying out societal goals, engaging in relations with other countries, providing protection, and meeting social needs. Conflict theorists believe the state protects the privileged position of a few, allowing them to consolidate power and perpetuate inequalities that keep them in power. This power elite theory stems from conflict theory's contention that power is concentrated in the hands of the elite, and the masses have little power.

Micro- and Meso-Level Perspectives: Legitimacy of Power

For symbolic interactionists, a central question is how loyalty to the power of the state is created—a loyalty that is so strong that citizens are willing to die for the state in a war. In the founding years of the United States, loyalty tended to be mostly to individual states. Even as late as the Civil War, northern battalions fought under the flag of their own state rather than that of the United States. The Federalist Party, which stressed centralized government in early U.S. history, faded from the scene. The Democratic Republican Party, which evolved into the current Democratic Party, had downplayed the power of the federal government. This has changed. Today, the Democratic Party generally supports a larger role for the federal government than its rival, although Republican President George W. Bush expanded federal powers substantially.

Most people in the United States now tend to think of themselves as U.S. citizens more than Virginians or Pennsylvanians or Oregonians, and they are willing to defend the whole country. National symbols such as anthems and flags help create loyalty to nations. The treatment of flags is an interesting issue that illustrates the social construction of meaning around national symbols. The next "Sociology in Your Social World" explores this issue.

Thinking Sociologically

First, read "The Flag, Symbolism, and Patriotism" on the facing page. Is wearing a shirt or sweater with the U.S. stars and stripes in some sort of artistic design an act of desecration of the flag or a statement of patriotism? Does flying a Confederate flag symbolize disrespect for the national U.S. flag? Why?

Socialization of individuals at the micro level generally includes instilling a strong sense of the legitimacy and authority of the reigning government in a particular society. This includes loyalty to a flag or a monarch that represents the nation.

Legitimacy, Authority, and Power: Social Constructions

Max Weber (1946) distinguished between legitimate and illegitimate power. Legitimate power, which he referred to as **authority**, is recognized as rightful by those subject to it. Governments are given legitimate power when citizens acknowledge that the government has the right to exercise power over them. This is measured by two factors: whether the state can govern without the use or threat of forceful

Sociology in Your Social World

The Flag, Symbolism, and Patriotism

Flags have become pervasive symbols of nations, creating a national identity (Billig 1995). In some countries, loyalty to the nation is taught with daily pledges to the flag at work or school. National loyalty becomes sacred—as does the flag itself. Indeed, the nation is *reified*—it becomes a concrete material reality through this symbol. Durkheim (1947) maintained that one's larger group elicits sacredness, and thereby becomes *sacralized.* He believed that sacredness actually is a form of respect for that which transcends the individual, in this case the state.

In the United States, the flag and its construction illustrate key ideas in symbolic interaction theory. For many decades after the nation was founded, Americans had more loyalty to their state than to a federal government, but in the aftermath of the Civil War, a sense of nation began to gel (Answers.Com 2006).

Symbolic interactionists sometimes speak of the externalization, objectification, and internalization of important symbols (Berger and Luckmann 1966). In this case, the symbol was created (*externalized* by Betsy Ross in the summer of 1776), it came to have a life of its own separate from its creator (*objectified* by Presidential Order in 1912 when the official arrangement of stars was established), and it came to be incorporated by people as a symbol that was meaningful (*internalized* as a symbol of "us" for Americans) (Independence Hall Association 2008). In places like Britain and India, a national flag does not have the same symbolic power and internal resonance as a national symbol. This is not because those countries are less loyal to the nation or less proud of their heritage. It is that other symbols, such as royal status, work just as well.

Care of the U.S. flag is an interesting example of symbolism and respect for that symbol. Flag etiquette instructions make it clear that flying a flag that is faded, soiled, or dirty is considered an offense to the flag. We are told to either burn or bury a damaged flag as a way to honor and respect it.

Some propose a constitutional amendment prohibiting burning of the U.S. flag to prevent protestors from using the flag as a protest statement against certain American policies. Because protests show disrespect, some patriots have a visceral reaction of outrage. As recently as June 2006, the Senate came within one vote of sending the flag burning amendment to the individual states for ratification (CNN.com 2006). Supporters want flag burners punished and disrespect

for the flag outlawed. For many, the flag is dear and symbolizes all that is good about the United States (Billig 1995).

Those who oppose this amendment feel that only tyrannical countries limit freedom of speech. They feel that the principle of free speech, central to democracy, must be allowed even if a sacred symbol is at stake. Indeed, opponents of the amendment think passing such a law would be a desecration of what that flag stands for. The two sides have each attached different meanings to what is considered desecration of the national symbol. In the meantime, if you have a tattered or fading flag, burning it is the way you honor that flag—as long as you do so in private!

Other aspects of the U.S. Flag Code, which specifies what is considered official respect for or desecration of the flag, are interesting precisely because many people violate this code while they believe themselves to be displaying their patriotism.

1. The flag should *never* be used for advertising in any manner whatsoever. It should not be embroidered on cushions, handkerchiefs, or scarves, nor reproduced on paper napkins, carry-out bags, wrappers, or anything else that will soon be thrown away.

2. No *part* of the flag—depictions of stars and stripes that are in any form other than that approved for the flag design itself—should ever be used as a costume, clothing item, or athletic uniform.

3. Displaying a flag after dark should not be done unless it is illuminated, and it should not be left out when it is raining.

4. The flag should never be represented flat or horizontally (as many marching bands do). It should *always* be aloft and free.

5. The flag should under no circumstances be used as a ceiling covering. (U.S. Flag Code 2008)

According to the standards established by U.S. military representatives and congressional action, any of these forms of display may be considered a desecration of the flag, yet the meaning that common people give to these acts is quite different. Symbolic interactionists are interested in the meaning people give to actions and how symbols themselves inform behavior.

This man no doubt feels he is expressing his patriotism, yet technically he is violating the U.S. Flag Code and "desecrating" the American flag. During the Vietnam War, protesters risked attack for dressing this way, which was viewed as disrespect for the flag and the country.

To Weber, illegitimate power is sustained by brute force or coercion. Authority is granted by the people who are subject to the power, which means that no coercion is needed.

How Do Leaders Gain Legitimate Power?

In constitutional democracies, those with power do not have the right to hold people against their will, to take their property, to demand they make unauthorized payments, or to kill them to protect others. Yet, even in democracies, certain people in power have the right to carry out such duties against people who are determined to be threats to society. How do leaders get these rights? To establish legitimate power or authority, leaders generally gain their positions in one of three ways:

1. *Traditional authority* is passed on through the generations, usually within a family line, so that positions are inherited. Tribal leaders in African societies pass their titles and power to their sons. Japanese and many European royal lines pass from generation to generation. Usually called a monarchy, this has been the most common form of leadership throughout history. Authority is seen as "normal" for a family or a person because of tradition. It has always been done that way, so no one challenges it. When authority is granted based on tradition, authority rests with the position rather than the person. The authority is easily transferred to another heir of that status.

2. *Charismatic authority* is power held by an individual resulting from a claim of extraordinary, even divine, personal characteristics. Charismatic leaders often emerge at times of change when strong, new leadership is needed. The most vivid examples of charismatic leaders are Jesus, Muhammad, and the founder of the Mormon Church, Joseph Smith. Charismatic political leaders include Mao Zedong in China and Mahatma Gandhi in India. Both men led their countries to independence and had respect from citizens that bordered on "awe." Some women have also been recognized as charismatic leaders, such as Burma's (Myanmar) Aung San Suu Kyi, pro-democracy activist, widely recognized prisoner of conscience, leader of the National League for Democracy of Burma, and winner of the Nobel Peace prize.

coercion and the degree to which challenges to state authority are processed through normal channels such as the legal system (Jackman 1993). Citizens of Western societies recognize elected officials and laws made by elected bodies as legitimate authority. They adhere to a judge's rulings because they recognize that court decrees are legitimate. In contrast, illegitimate power, or coercion, includes living under force of a military regime or being kidnapped or imprisoned without charge. (See Figure 13.1.) These distinctions between legitimate and illegitimate power are important to our understanding of how leaders or political institutions establish the right to lead.

Force	+	Consent	=	Power
Force	<	Consent	=	Legitimate Power (Authority)
Force	>	Consent	=	Illegitimate Power (e.g., Dictatorship)

Figure 13.1 Weber's Formula Regarding Power

Other charismatic leaders such as Adolf Hitler, leader of Nazi Germany, and Jim Jones, leader of the Jonestown cult that urged its members toward mass suicide, were charismatic but led their followers to negative ends. The key point is that for charismatic leaders, unlike traditional authority leaders, the right to lead rests with the person, not the position. This is an inherently change-oriented and unstable form of leadership because authority resides in a single person. Ultimately, as stability reemerges, power will become institutionalized—rooted in stable routine patterns of the organization. Charismatic leaders are effective during transitional periods but are often replaced by rational-legal leaders once affairs of state become stable. Most important for our purposes here is that followers believe power is rooted in the personality of a dynamic individual.

3. *Rational-legal authority* is most typical in modern nation-states. Leaders have the expertise to carry out the duties of their positions, and the leadership structure is usually bureaucratic and rule bound. Individuals are granted authority because they have proper training or have proven their merit. This is the form of authority most familiar to individuals living in democracies. The rational-legal form of authority often seems entirely irrational and an invitation to chaos to people in tradition-oriented societies.

The important aspect of rational-legal authority is that it is divided between the position (which establishes criteria and credentials for the position) and the person (who has achieved those credentials for the position). The authority in government is shared and recognized by members of the community.

Each of these three types of authority, according to Weber, is a "legitimate" exercise of power because the people being governed give their consent, at least implicitly. However, on occasion leaders overstep their legitimate bounds and rule by force.

Macro Perspectives: Who Rules?

Pluralist Theory

Pluralist theory holds that power is distributed among various groups so that no one group rules. It is primarily through interest groups that you and I—as part of the masses—influence decision-making processes. Our interests are represented by groups such as unions or environmental organizations that act to keep power from being concentrated in the hands of an elite few (Dahl 1961; Dye and Zeigler 1983:10).

Politics involves negotiation and compromise between competing groups. Interest groups can veto policies that conflict with their own interests by mobilizing large numbers against certain legislative or executive actions. Witness the efforts to influence health care reform in the United

His Royal Highness Charles, Prince of Wales, at his investiture in Caernarvon Castle. Charles is next in line to inherit the throne of England, and his position has legitimacy because the citizenry of England consent to the system. The authority is traditional, passing through a line of succession.

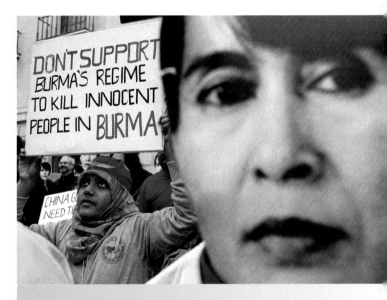

Protesters against the situation in Burma hold masks with the face of Aung San Suu Kyi outside the Chinese Embassy in London, England, on October 24, 2007. That marked the 12th anniversary of the leader's detention by the country's military regime in Myanmar. (The new dictatorship changed the name of the country as part of the effort to delegitimize her right to govern.) She is a charismatic leader, held in high esteem—by those who admire her.

States and to reform government and industry practices. Greenpeace, Nader's Raiders, Common Cause, Earth First!, Bread for the World, the Christian Coalition, Focus on the Family, various labor unions, and other consumer,

Pluralist theories see value in having many sources of power in a society, so that no one group can dominate. For workers, this usually means uniting to have a strong voice through unions. Here we see several hundred ironworkers and their supporters stage a protest against poor pay and working conditions, outside the Hong Kong government's headquarters in 2007.

environmental, religious, and political action groups have had impacts on policy decisions. According to pluralists, shared power is found in each person's ability to join groups and influence policy decisions and outcomes.

National or international nongovernmental organizations (NGOs) can have a major impact on global issues and policy making, as exemplified by the Grameen Bank and other micro-credit organizations (Yunus and Jolis 1999). NGOs exert influence on power holders because of the numbers they represent, the money they control, the issues they address, and the effectiveness of their spokespeople or lobbyists. Sometimes they form coalitions around issues of concern such as the environment, human rights, health care, and women's and children's issues. An example is opposition to the U.S. Patriot Act by Libertarians on the far right and the American Civil Liberties Union on the far left. Although the groups differ on many issues, their opposition to infringements of civil liberties and individualism brought them together to contest many aspects of the Patriot Act, which was intended to fight terrorism.

According to pluralists, multiple power centers offer the best chance to maintain democratic forms of government because no one group dominates, and many citizens are involved. Although an interest group may dominate decision making on a specific issue, no one group dictates all policy.

Another major theory counters the pluralists, arguing that the real power centers at the national level are controlled by an elite few and that most individuals like you and me have little power.

Elite Theory

Power elite theorists believe it is inevitable that a small group of elite will rule societies. They argue that this is the nature of individuals and society and that pluralists are imagining a world that does not exist. Individuals have limited power through interest groups (Domhoff 1998, 2008; Dye 2002b; Mills 1956), but real power is held by the power elite. They wield power through their institutional roles, make decisions about war, peace, the economy, wages, taxes, justice, education, welfare, and health issues—all of which have serious impact on citizens. These powerful elite attempt to maintain, perpetuate, and even strengthen their rule.

Michels ([1911] 1967), a well-known political philosopher, believed that elite rule is inevitable. He described this pattern of elite domination as the *iron law of oligarchy*. In democratic and totalitarian societies alike, leaders have influence over who is elected to succeed them and to whom they give political favors. This influence eventually leads those in elite positions to abuse their power.

The social philosopher Pareto ([1911] 1955) expanded on this idea of abuse of power, pointing out that abuse would cause a counter group to challenge the elite for power. Eventually, as the latter group gains power, its members become corrupt as well, and the cycle—a circulation of the elite—continues. Corruption in many countries illustrates this pattern.

Several recent theorists are critics of the concentration of power idea. Some members of the decision-making elite do not hold the visible top positions, wielding their power instead from behind the scenes. C. Wright Mills argues that there is an invisible but interlocking power elite in U.S. society, consisting of leaders in military, business, and political spheres who make the key political, economic, and social decisions for the nation. This group manipulates what the public hears (Mills 1956). At the turn of the century, the top U.S. elite included 7,314 people from these three spheres (Dye 2002b). For example, in the business sphere, the top corporations control more than half of the nation's industrial assets, transportation, communication, and utilities. They also manage two thirds of the insurance assets. These corporations are controlled by 4,500 presidents and directors. According to the power elite theory, the U.S. upper class provides a cohesive economic/political power structure that represents upper-class interests (Domhoff 1998, 2008).

Private preparatory schools are one example of how elite status is transmitted to the next generation (Howard 2007; Persell and Cookson 1985). Many of those who hold top positions on national committees and boards or in the foreign policy-making agencies of national government attended the same private preparatory schools and Ivy League colleges, for example, Brown, Columbia, Cornell, Harvard, University of Pennsylvania, Princeton, and Yale.

Domhoff analyzed the power elite in domestic and foreign policy decision making (Domhoff 2008) and found that the elite have the strongest impact on national policy decisions because they run large corporations and financial institutions. Their common characteristics promote a network of connections, or "higher circles," and constitute a pool of potential appointees to top government positions. Key government officials come from industry, finance, law, and universities. They are linked with an international elite that helps shape the world economy. According to this theory, Congress ultimately has minimal power. The elected representatives accede to the power elite. Elite theorists believe that government seldom regulates business. Instead, business co-opts politicians to support their interests by providing financial support needed to run political election campaigns.

Pluralist theorists, however, disagree, believing that one reason we have big government is that a very powerful government serves as a balance to the enormous power of the corporate world. Big business and big government are safety checks against tyranny—and each is convinced that the other is too big. Thus, although middle-level white-collar workers make decisions in specialized areas of interest, their decisions have much less influence on our lives than those made at the macro level by the few at the top.

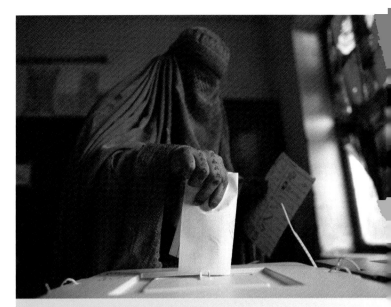

A Pakistani woman casts her ballot in the 2008 Pakistani national and provincial elections. The elections were considered a crucial step in moving Pakistan from military to civilian rule. Voting is viewed as a wonderful privilege and a source of hope in this setting.

Thinking Sociologically

Is your national society controlled by pluralist interest groups or a power elite? Can individuals influence the power elite? What evidence supports your view?

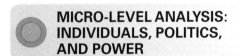
MICRO-LEVEL ANALYSIS: INDIVIDUALS, POLITICS, AND POWER

Whether you have health insurance or are subject to a military draft depends in part on the political and economic decisions made by the government in power. Political systems influence our personal lives in myriad ways, some of which are readily apparent: health and safety regulations, taxation, military draft, regulations on food and drugs that people buy, and even whether the gallon of gas pumped into one's car is really a full gallon. In this section, we explore the impact individuals have on the government and the variables that influence participation in political and economic policy-making processes. A key issue at the micro level is decisions by individuals to vote or otherwise participate in the political system. This private decision is, in turn, affected by where those individuals fall in the stratification system of society, not just by personal choices.

Participation in Democratic Processes

Citizens in democratic countries have the power to vote. Most countries, even dictatorships, have some form of citizen participation. In only a handful of countries are there no elections. Sociologists ask many questions about voting patterns, such as what influences voting and why some individuals do not participate in the political process at all. Social scientists want to know how participation affects (and is affected by) the individual's perception of his or her power in relationship to the state. The following "Applied Sociologist at Work" discusses the world of a political sociologist as he considers the voting patterns of red, blue, and purple states in the United States.

Ideology and Political Attitudes

Political ideology affects how people think about power. Let us consider several ways that our beliefs and attitudes affect our political ideas. First, what do we believe about the power of the individual versus the power of the state? If we believe that individuals are motivated by selfish considerations and desire for power, we may feel as the 17th-century English philosopher Thomas Hobbes did: Humans need to be controlled, and order must be imposed by an all-powerful sovereign. This is more important than individual freedom and liberty. On the other hand, we might believe, as did John Locke, another 17th-century political philosopher, that

The Applied Sociologist at Work— Ruy Teixeira

The Future of Red, Blue, and Purple America: The 2008 Election and Beyond

The election of 2008 was exciting and unusual in the political arena. Prominent among those studying the election period is Dr. Ruy Teixeira, a sociologist and specialist in political demography and geography.

Dr. Teixeira's 2008 research was a joint project of the Brookings and American Enterprise Institutes. It considered the U.S. political scene with its red and blue states, and particularly "purple" or swing states. Dr. Teixeira convened a group of researchers to consider social changes that affected the American political landscape. Each researcher analyzed a specific aspect of the political scene. Dr. Teixeira focused particularly on the purple swing states.

Past elections have been influenced by voters' needs and interests, the advance of suburbanization, the rise of baby boomers, and women's entry into the labor force. In the most recent election, new issues were shaping voter behavior. Seven dominant themes affecting the political landscape emerged from the work of these researchers:

the structure of American suburbs and changes in urban living patterns more generally;

geographic clustering—the idea that people are increasingly likely to live near, and vote like, those who look, act, and think just like them (Bishop and Cushing 2008);

race and immigration factors, including changes in the numbers and voting patterns of blacks, Hispanics, and Asians;

class structure changes, especially the decline of the white working class and the rise of the middle class;

American family modifications, including the decline in the number of married couple households with children and the rise of the proportion of singles;

cultural issues that make the nation more secular, more religious, or both (what these changes in religious belief and practice mean for our politics); and

aging of the baby boomers, the largest generation in American history, and the rise of the millennial generation (Teixeira 2008).

According to Teixeira and colleagues, the American class structure has gone through major social shifts since World War II in education levels (more high school graduates and more college-educated citizens), types of occupations (more white-collar jobs), and income levels. Today there are fewer people in the white working class and a rise in the mass upper middle class. These demographic trends, the themes mentioned above, and geographic movements have resulted in new political alignments.

A reality of the first two presidential elections of the 21st century was political polarization, enhanced by polarized media hype, gerrymandering of political voting boundaries, and cultural "sorting" of people supporting each major party. See Map 13.1 for the political breakdown of states in the 2004 presidential election. The political orientations of various groups shifted over two or three decades, resulting in deadlock on each side of the political spectrum. However, the researchers believe this deadlock is likely to begin to ease by the 2016 elections. Growth in Hispanic and Asian groups, shifts of the population not only to different regions of the country but to suburbs and just beyond the suburbs, changing family structures and shifting women's roles, aging of baby boomers, and the high levels of political engagement by "millennials" (younger people who generally value diversity) combine to suggest major changes by the 2016 election.

Dr. Teixeira predicts that "culture wars"—the polarization and clashes between segments of society over differences in values—will not be as important in the future. Issues such as how to help nontraditional families, improve education, and provide health care will be shared concerns that unite people. Therefore, he predicts that the polarization that has divided some communities will not last.

The range of methodological tools used by sociologists has been essential to Dr. Teixeira's work. Theories that help explain social structure and demographic change guide his research, and working with large data sets results in many of his findings. He is interested in the U.S. government, policy making, and wrestling with issues that face the country. Dr. Teixeira has found that sociology provides exceptionally useful theory and methods to help understand our political world.

Note: Dr. Ruy Teixeira is a Senior Fellow at The Century Foundation and American Progress, a Fellow at the New Politics Institute, and a Visiting Fellow at the Brookings Institution. Being a fellow means you are employed as a scholar to carry out research that meets the goals of the organization or *think tank*.

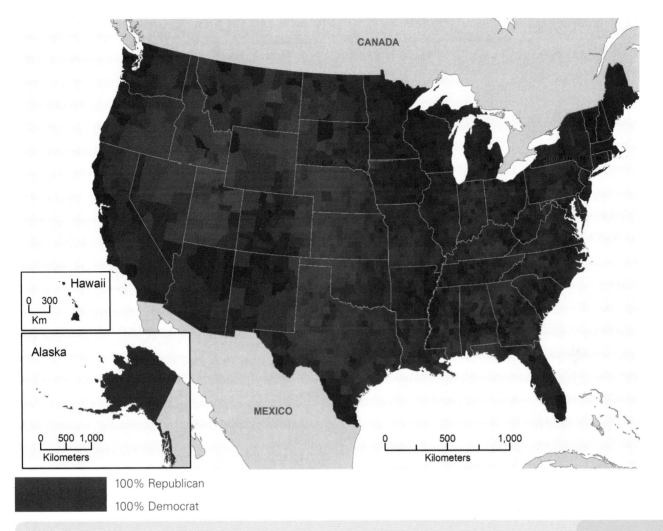

100% Republican

100% Democrat

Map 13.1 Percentage of the Population by County That Voted Republican (Bush/Cheney) and Democrat (Kerry/Edwards) in the U.S. Presidential Election of 2004

Source: USA Today and the GeoVISTA Center at Pennsylvania State University 2008 (http://www.personal.psu.edu/ acr181/election.html). Map by Anna Versluis.

human nature is perfectible and rational, that we are not born selfish but learn selfishness through experience with others. Humans, Locke argued, should have their needs and interests met, and among these needs are liberty, ability to sustain life, and ownership of property. He felt the people should decide who governs them. Thus, we can see that support for democracy is influenced by one's core assumptions about what it means to be human.

Second, do we believe in equal distribution of resources, or do we think that those who are most able or have inherited high status should receive more of the wealth? Some social scientists, politicians, and voters think that individuals have different abilities and are therefore entitled to different rewards. Some are successful, and some are not. (Recall the structural-functional theory discussion in the stratification chapter about the inevitability of inequality.) Others think society should facilitate more equal distribution of resources

simply because all persons are equally deserving of human dignity. Conflict theorists would be most likely to support this view.

In the United States, for example, Republicans (and others on "the right") tend to believe individuals and local communities should take more responsibility for education, health care, welfare, child care, and other areas of common public concern, feeling that this protects rights to local control and prevents creation of a powerful bureaucracy. Democrats (and those on "the left") are more likely to argue for the federal government's social responsibility to the people. For instance, Democrats have been concerned that leaving policies such as school integration to local communities would perpetuate inequality and discriminatory patterns in some communities. National government involvement, they feel, would protect the rights of all citizens. The ongoing debates about the national welfare system and health care policies in the United States reflect these different philosophies. Both parties support government spending and national laws; the question is for what? Military? Social programs? Education? Health care? Abortion? Prisons?

Third, do we believe that change is desirable? Generally, these views fall into two camps: change as a potential threat to stability versus policy change to benefit the general population or segments of the population. Views on change affect how people vote.

Voters in many countries are influenced by issues such as the environment or immigration rather than traditional party ideology. Party affiliation based on ideology is becoming relatively weak in the United States, and an increasing number of people are identifying themselves as independents rather than Democrats or Republicans, either because they do not want to commit themselves to one ideology or because they are more interested in specific issues than in an overriding philosophy of government.

Thinking Sociologically

How might your decision to vote (a micro-level decision) make a difference in your life at the state/provincial, national, or global levels?

Levels of Participation in Politics

The majority of people in the world are uninvolved in the political process because there are few opportunities for them to be meaningfully involved (especially in nondemocratic countries). They feel that involvement can have little relevance for them (apathy), or that they cannot affect the process (alienation from a system that does not value them). However, political decisions may affect people directly, and they may be drawn unwittingly into the political arena. Peasants making a subsistence living may be forced off the land and into refugee camps by wars over issues that have little relevance to them. Their children may be drafted and taken away to fight and be killed in these battles. Religious or ideological factions may force them to help pay for conflicts in which they see no purpose or have no stake. In recent years, such situations have drawn the uninvolved into politics in countries such as Guatemala, Uganda, Cambodia (Kampuchea), Haiti, Rwanda, Somalia, India, Iraq, Lebanon, Gaza, and Darfur (Sudan).

In representative systems, citizens are encouraged to have a voice, although their levels of involvement vary greatly. While some remain uninvolved, some vote in most elections but otherwise do not participate in politics. Others have contact with government representatives only when they have issues of personal concern. Still others are involved in local politics, actively working on issues or local elections that are of concern to them. The most involved

engage in both community affairs and national political campaigns (Verba and Nie 1972).

Political participation is affected by election laws, including those that enfranchise people, that stress voting as a requirement of citizenship, and that structure elections to facilitate representation by historically underrepresented groups. In some countries, voting is an obligation of citizenship and voter turnout is above 90%. In Australia and New Zealand, for example, it is a violation of the law not to vote. One must gain permission to miss a vote—which is extended over many days to ensure that people can get to the polls. Some other countries also make sure that ethnic minorities and women have a voice by structuring elections to ensure broad representation. The next "Sociology Around the World" examines the reasons that an African country—the war-torn nation of Rwanda—emerged early in the 21st century with the highest percentage of women in government of any nation in the world.

In the United States, voter turnout went down from 63% of eligible voters in 1960 to 50% in 1996 to 47.3% in 2000. However, in the 2004 presidential election, turnout was 60% (Bergman 2005). More than 70% of citizens age 45 and older voted in 2004, and 67% of whites voted in 2004 compared to 60% of African Americans, 47% of Hispanics, and 44% of Asian Americans (Bergman 2005).

Participation in elections in the United States is the second-lowest of the Western democracies, as indicated in Table 13.1 on page 434. This means that citizens are not exercising their right to vote. The unusually high number of "inactives" is not an encouraging sign for the vitality of a democracy (Orum 2001). Still, there was a resurgence of interest in politics among those under 30 years old during the 2008 presidential campaign as discussed in the "Sociology in Your Social World" feature on page 435, with the primary elections for nomination of candidates and the November election itself yielding record-breaking turnouts.

Thinking Sociologically

First read "Sociology in Your Social World" on page 435. How important do you think the youth vote was in the most recent election? Were there other voting blocks—women, African Americans, Latinos, the religious right, blue collar families, white males—that were more important in the outcome of this election?

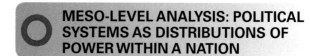

MESO-LEVEL ANALYSIS: POLITICAL SYSTEMS AS DISTRIBUTIONS OF POWER WITHIN A NATION

A village within the Bantu society of southern Africa has lost its chief. Bantu societies provide for heirs to take on leadership when a leader dies. However, there is no male heir to the

Sociology Around the World

Women and Political Change in Post-Genocide Rwanda

By Melanie Hughes

In 2003, Rwanda became the new global leader in women's political representation. Women were elected to 49% of the seats in Rwanda's Chamber of Deputies, making it the most gender balanced of any national legislature in the history of the world (Paxton and Hughes 2007; see also Table 9.1 on page 280). For the first time since 1988, a country outside of Scandinavia garnered the top spot in women's political representation, and for the first time in history, the position was held by an African country. From just 10 years earlier, the number of women serving in Rwanda's parliament almost tripled.

Many were particularly surprised about Rwanda's women's involvement, given the country's recent history of economic upheaval and civil war. The instability culminated in 1994, when during a span of 100 days, about 800,000 Rwandans died at the hands of their countrymen and -women in a horrific ethnic genocide. (Compared to the 58,000 American soldiers who died in Vietnam, this is simply an astounding number.) The economy and the old power structure were decimated. Many political leaders were killed or were among the more than 100,000 Rwandans imprisoned on charges of war crimes. So, how did Rwanda bounce back within a decade to lead the world in women's political representation? What follows is a brief discussion of what happened to catapult women to the top of Rwandan politics.

At the micro level, research suggests that the behavior of individual women during and after the Rwandan genocide generated support for their empowerment (Hughes 2004). During the civil war, women served on the front lines with men, led military actions, and worked as mediators to help end the insurgency. After conflict subsided, women played key roles in the reconstruction effort. Women took on new roles, becoming heads of their households and taking on traditionally male occupations. Women also adopted some 400,000 orphans from the war (UNIFEM 2002). Interviews with Rwandans suggest that the burdens taken on by women during this period generated both the political will and public support necessary to advance women in politics (Mutamba 2005).

Important changes also occurred at the meso level. Immediately after the killing subsided, women's associations, both new and old, began to step into the void (Longman 2005). Women's organizations took action early on to shape the new state. For example, in 1994, an organization of women's associations drafted a document addressing Rwanda's post-conflict problems and suggesting how women could foster reconciliation (Powley 2003). Building up to the adoption of the new constitution in 2003, women's organizations served as a bridge, taking suggestions from women at the grassroots level into meetings with the transitional government. These groups also made specific recommendations to ensure that the constitution provided space for women to participate in the political process.

Women at all levels were supported by international organizations and foreign aid. Rwanda's economic troubles meant that dependence on international funding was unavoidable, and women were well situated to take advantage of foreign monies. The empowerment of women, especially in the Global South, was on the agenda of the United Nations and other global bodies. Therefore, many international organizations helped to advance the idea that women's incorporation into political decision-making positions was essential for sustainable peace. Overall, research suggests that these global-level processes helped generate political change in Rwanda (Hughes 2004).

Action by individual women, native women's associations, and international organizations all helped to encourage the transitional government to adopt female-friendly political institutions. Women's councils and women-only elections were established to guarantee female representation down to the grass-roots level. A Ministry for Gender and Women in Development was established, along with gender posts in all other government and ministerial bodies. The new constitution mandated that women fill 30% of all policy-making posts in Rwanda. These women-friendly political institutions, combined with the politicization of women during and after the war, help to explain the success of Rwandan women in politics.

Rwanda today is not a democratic country, but since their election in 2003, women have still been able to leave their mark on Rwandan politics. Women politicians have helped to revise inheritance laws, pass a law banning discrimination against women, and strengthen rape laws (Longman 2005). Some even argue that "women in government are now perceived by Rwandans as more approachable and trustworthy politicians than their male counterparts" (Remmert 2003:25). Skeptics argue that the focus on women diverts attention from the absence of ethnic diversity within government. Regardless, Rwanda has come a long way since 1994.

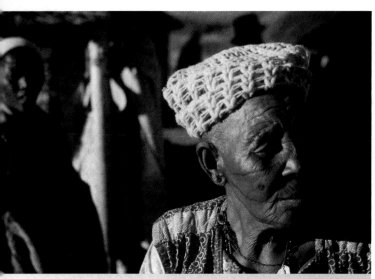

Among the Bantu of Southern Africa, if a chief dies it is possible for a woman within the family lineage to succeed him, but she must take a "wife" and fulfill the leadership role normally established for males.

| Table 13.1 | **Voter Turnout Percentages for Elections Since 1945*** |

Country	Voter Participation %
Italy	92.5
Iceland	89.5
New Zealand	86.2
South Africa	85.5
Austria	85.1
Netherlands	84.8
Australia	84.4
Denmark	83.6
Sweden	83.3
Germany	80.6
Greece	80.3
Guyana	80.3
Israel	80.0
Suriname	77.7
Malta	77.6
United Kingdom	74.9
Republic of Korea	74.8
Turkey	73.5
Argentina	70.6
Uruguay	70.3
Philippines	69.6
Papua New Guinea	69.1
Japan	69.0
Dominican Republic	68.7
Canada	68.4
Costa Rica	68.4
France	67.3
Bolivia	61.4
India	60.7
Bangladesh (6)	56.0
Switzerland	49.3
USA	48.3
Mexico	48.1
Peru	48.0
Brazil	47.9
Thailand	47.4
Chile	45.9
Ecuador	44.7
El Salvador	44.3
Colombia	36.2
Guatemala	29.8

Source: International Institute for Democracy and Electoral Assistance 2008.

*The figures are averages of voter participation for all elections over a 60-year period. Note that enfranchisement of women and various ethnic minorities has changed in some countries during that time, so these should be viewed as very crude overall indicators of voting patterns.

Note: To see the voting participation figures for 172 countries in the world, go to www.idea.int/vt/survey/voter_turnout_pop2.cfm.

position, so a female from the same lineage is appointed. This woman must assume the legal and social roles of a male husband, father, and chief by acting as a male and taking a "wife." The wife is assigned male sexual partners, who become the biological fathers of children. This provides heirs for the lineage, but the female "husband" is their social father because she has socially become a male. This pattern has been common practice in many southern Bantu societies and among many other populations in four separate geographic areas of Africa. Anthropologists interpret this as a means of maintaining public positions of dominance and power in the hands of males in a particular family and community (O'Brien 1977). Ruling groups in society, in this case a meso-level tribal society under jurisdiction of a nation-state, have mechanisms for ensuring a smooth transition of power to keep the controlling structure functioning.

Meso-level political institutions include state or provincial governments, national political parties, and large formal organizations within the nation. Equally important is that meso-level political institutions influence and are influenced by other institutions: family, education, religion, health care, and economics.

What Purposes Do Political Institutions Serve?

Most of us have had an argument over ownership of property, have been in an accident, have met people who needed help to survive, or have been concerned about wars raging around the world. The political institution addresses these issues and serves a variety of other purposes, or functions, in societies.

Sociology in Your Social World

Young Voters and the U.S. Presidential Election of 2008

Young Americans, those under 30 years old, have for four decades been notoriously uninvolved in politics and elections. During the civil rights activism and Vietnam War years of the 1960s, young voters were motivated to vote by idealism and by fear of the military draft. In 1972, 55% of 18- to 29-year-olds in the United States voted. After the Watergate scandal and other events that spawned cynicism, the voting percentage in that age group dropped, bottoming out at 40% in the 2000 general election. Participation was even lower for primary elections. By contrast, in the 2008 primary elections, 18- to 29-year-olds voted at high rates (Marks 2008). There seem to be multiple reasons for the increase: social movements to increase voter registration among this age group, a candidate who focused on mobilizing the youth vote, use of technology that appeals to younger citizens, and a shift in attitudes in this generation regarding citizenship.

In 1990, Rock the Vote was launched. This movement is a nonpartisan effort to stimulate political involvement in young people. Rock the Vote's strategies involved trying to depict the casting of a ballot as "fashionably subversive" and encouraging young adults to register, in recent years by facilitating voter registration online (Rampell 2008). Another nonpartisan movement—Declare Yourself—has used similar strategies. Still, by 2000, only two in five citizens in this age group voted in the presidential election (Marks 2008). Combined with other social factors, however, these voter registration efforts began a shift in young voters. Rock the Vote and Declare Yourself had each registered roughly a million young people, resulting in 4.2 million more people in this age category voting in 2004. In 2008, Rock the Vote had registered half a million new voters by early April and expected to register at least two million in time for the presidential election in 2008 (Smith 2008). In the 2008 presidential primaries, the rate of participation among 18- to 29-year-old voters nearly quadrupled in Tennessee and Missouri (Rampell 2008). In Iowa's caucuses, young adult participants increased from 20,740 in 2004 to 52,580 in 2008. This young adult vote was an astounding 22% of the Iowa total (Mulligan 2008). In South Carolina, the numbers jumped from 26,181 to 74,245 (Bristow 2008), representing an increase from 9% of all voters to 14% (Song 2008). In the most recent elections, according to the Youth Vote Coalition, 64% of young adults were registered to vote (Romano 2008). Still, the increase in actual voting cannot be attributed solely to efforts of Rock the Vote and Declare Yourself, for the number had not increased during the 1990s. Something else has been at work.

The 2008 election cycle also involved candidates who excited many younger voters. Among the Republicans, Ron Paul was an outsider who seemed to offer very different approaches to policies, and Mike Huckabee was liked because he talked to younger citizens in a way that seemed to communicate authenticity (Emerling and Ballantoni 2008). John McCain, although the oldest person ever to be nominated for a first term of the presidency, was deeply admired not only as a war hero but as an independent thinker who stood up against the powerful, even within his own party, when he thought they were wrong. Even early in the primary season, he was drawing hundreds of young supporters to rallies (Powell 2008b). Then he selected Governor Sarah Palin, a relatively young woman—only the second in the history of the country to be nominated for the vice presidency—as his running mate. She brought to the ticket a reputation for being a courageous reformer and for standing up to the "old boy" system in her state.

On the Democratic side, many young women were drawn to Hillary Clinton as the first woman who seemed to have a realistic chance at the presidency. Still, it was Barack Obama who was the big beneficiary of youth participation. Like John Kennedy in 1960 and his brother, Robert Kennedy, in 1968, Obama entered the race as a young candidate and an agent of change—visionary, charismatic, transcending the rhetoric of we/they politics, and exuding a message of hope (Bristow 2008). This generation of voters likes people who are independent, who do not seem to be part of the insider

(Continued)

(Continued)

party machine, and who are willing to cross party lines to solve problems. It should not be surprising that Obama and McCain emerged—with the help of young adult votes—as the two major party nominees.

A third factor has involved technologies used by younger Americans. Obama's "Yes, we can" mantra was a YouTube video created by Will.i.am of the Black Eyed Peas, and many of Obama's speeches were put on YouTube. The Obama channel on YouTube had counted three million hits by February 10, early in the primary season (Geist 2008). The Obama campaign used MySpace and Facebook heavily as well. On MySpace, many personal profiles suddenly spawned campaign signs. In February, the official Obama Facebook page had more than 300,000 supporters, and his MySpace "friends" exceeded 250,000 (Greist 2008; Sarno 2008). Moreover, both MySpace and Facebook held "primary elections"—with Obama winning easily—and many activists used that technology to urge those on their networks to vote. The Obama campaign staff also very intentionally placed young people directly behind him—rather than white-haired politicians—in many speeches covered by the media (Powell 2008a). Even in the first Democratic caucus in Iowa, with a full slate of candidates, Obama won 57% of the under-30 vote (Emerling and Bellantoni 2008).

Finally, after the convention, the Obama staff initiated a contest between young people of the 50 states to see which state could generate the most text-messages to Barack Obama. Having received those messages, the Obama staff then had electronic addresses for millions of young people they could contact on Election Day to urge them to vote. So the Obama campaign, more than any other, was focused on mobilizing the younger vote, using their favored technologies. Finally, the current group of people in their late teens and twenties are more involved in community volunteerism and service, and they are less cynical and less rebellious than twenty-somethings of previous decades (Marks 2008). These young people are more civic-minded than some earlier groups. A report from the Harvard University Institute of Politics says that this is not a one-time phenomenon but represents the "civic reawakening of a new generation" (Cillizza and Murray 2008). The idealism, the desire for national unity, the avoidance of red-state-blue-state polemics, the desire for hope and optimism, and the rejection of explicit racial or gender categories as defining characteristics of leadership have all been traits of this group of younger voters, and those attitudes have matched well with the emphasis of Barack Obama. In any case, the increased involvement is a hopeful sign, not just for one candidate but for the democratic process.

For most people, interaction with the government begins with a record of their birth and ends with a record of their death. In between, the government is the institutional structure that collects taxes, keeps records of the work activities and wages of citizens, and keeps fingerprints and other personal information on file.

We have learned in earlier chapters that each institution has purposes or functions it serves. Just as family, education, medicine, and religion meet certain societal needs, so does the political system. The following six activities are typical purposes (functions) of meso-level political institutions such as political parties. They set the stage for power carried out at the macro level in national and international arenas.

1. *To maintain social control.* We expect to live in safety, to live according to certain "rules," to be employed in meaningful work, and to participate in other activities prescribed or protected by law. Ideally, governments help clarify expectations and customs and implement laws that express societal values. However, in some cases, governments rule with an iron hand and people live in fear because of the social control imposed by government. This has been the case in Afghanistan under the Taliban, when leaders used armed militia to terrorize the country by imprisoning, torturing, and killing suspected dissenters to make sure the population did the Taliban's bidding.

2. *To serve as an arbiter in disputes.* When disputes arise over property or the actions of another individual or group, a judicial branch of government can intervene. In some systems, such as tribal groups mentioned above, a council of elders or powerful individuals performs judicial functions. In other cases, elected or appointed judges have the right to hear disputes, make judgments, and carry out punishment for infractions.

3. *To protect citizens of the group.* Governments are responsible for protecting citizens from takeover by external powers or disruption from internal sources. However, they

are not always successful. Cities are often violent, gangs roam the streets, terrorists threaten lives, minority groups receive unfair treatment, and governments lose territory or even control of their countries to external forces. Venezuelan President Hugo Chavez has nationalized some of the nation's oil and other industries to prevent foreign interests from controlling the country's resources. A similar situation occurred in Guatemala in the 1950s, when the democratically elected president proposed nationalizing certain natural resources and industries (Herman and Peterson 2006; Parenti 2006; Oliver 2003).

4. *To make plans for the future of the group.* As individuals, we have little direct impact on the direction our society takes, but the official governmental body—be it elected, appointed, or imposed through force—shares responsibility with economic institutions for planning in the society. In some socialist societies, this planning dictates what each individual will contribute to the nation: how many engineers, teachers, or nurses they need. They then train people according to these projections. In other societies, power is much less direct. In capitalist systems, for instance, supply and demand is assumed to regulate the system, and there is less governmental planning—especially in economic matters—than in socialist societies.

5. *To provide for the needs of their citizens.* Governments differ greatly in the degree to which they attempt to meet the needs of citizens. Some economic systems provide for most of the health and welfare needs of citizens, whereas others tend to leave this largely to individuals, families, local community agencies, and other institutions such as religion. Not everyone agrees that providing needs is an inherent responsibility of the state. The debates over a health care system and welfare system in the United States point to the conflicts over who should be responsible—the state or private individuals. Should such services be coordinated by the government or left to "the invisible hand" of market forces? Should the economy regulate such things, or should this be in the realm of the political institution?

6. *To represent the group in relations with other groups or societies.* Individuals cannot negotiate agreements with foreign neighbors. Official representatives deal with other officials to negotiate arms and trade agreements, protect the world's airways, determine fishing rights, and establish military bases in foreign lands, among other agreements.

The ways in which governments carry out these six functions is largely determined by their philosophies of power and political structures. Political institutions, like family and religious institutions, come in many forms. In essence, these variations in political institutions reflect variations in human ideas of power. The point is that functionalists focus on the positive role of each institution in the lives of people and for the stability of society.

A boy with a toy rifle sits on his father's shoulders at a pro-Taliban demonstration in late September of 2001 in Pakistan. The protest supported the Taliban movement in Afghanistan. Sometimes animosities toward a feared "other" such as the United States are so strong that people will support even oppressive authoritarian regimes. This is part of the power of vilifying "others."

Thinking Sociologically

How do you think the function to "protect the safety of the citizens" has affected the ability of governments to meet their other functions in an era of terrorist threats?

Meso- and Macro-Level Political Systems in the Modern World

The major political systems in the world range from fascist totalitarianism to democracy. However, each culture puts its own imprint on the system it uses, making for tremendous variation in actual practice. Two broad approaches are discussed below to illustrate the point.

Authoritarian Systems

The government of Kuwait is a hereditary monarchy based on traditional leadership. After the Persian Gulf War of 1991, it brought to trial and condemned to death a number of its citizens, mostly of Palestinian background, who were accused of collaborating with the Iraqis during the takeover of Kuwait. Although the sentences were commuted, this was a lesson to would-be dissenters. The regime has

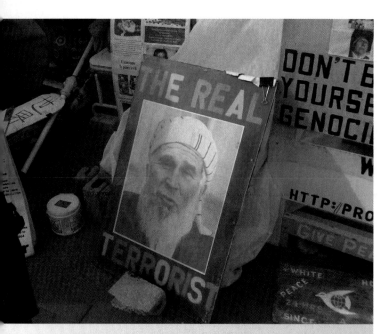

Within a democracy, individuals have a variety of ways they can influence the government such as voting, working for political parties, and protesting policies. Such individual voice is greatly enhanced if one has constitutional guarantees of freedom of speech. This protestor carrying a sign across from the U.S. White House in Washington, D.C., enjoys freedom of speech as he accuses his nation's president of being a terrorist.

absolute power, allows little citizen involvement and no criticism of governmental decisions, and determines much of what happens in individuals' lives.

Authoritarian regimes headed by dictators or military *juntas* with absolute power are and have been common forms in the world. Some of these regimes are helpful to citizens, but most stamp out dissent. Saddam Hussein ruled in Iraq, and Muammar Gaddafi remains in command of Libya. Other examples from the 20th century include Ferdinand Marcos in the Philippines, Idi Amin in Uganda, Benito Mussolini in Italy, Eva (Evita) Peron in Argentina, Robert Mugabe in Zimbabwe, and the military regime in Myanmar (Burma).

Totalitarian political systems are often based on a specific political ideology and run by a single ruling group or party, referred to as an *oligarchy*. Russia under Joseph Stalin and Germany under Adolf Hitler were totalitarian dictatorships that followed strong ideologies and demanded adherence to them. The state often controls the workplace, education, the media, and other aspects of life. All actions revolve around state aims. Dissent and opposition are discouraged or eliminated. Interrogation by secret police, imprisonment, and torture are used to quiet dissenters. Terror is used as a tactic to deal with both internal and external dissent, but when it is used by the state to control

the citizenry or to terrorize those of another nation, it is called *state terrorism*.

Throughout history, most people have lived under authoritarian or totalitarian systems. Under certain conditions, totalitarian regimes can turn into democratic ones, and of course, democratically elected leaders can become self-proclaimed dictators, as was the case of Ferdinand Marcos in the Philippines. The next "Sociology Around the World" provides an example of one totalitarian regime.

Democratic Systems

In contrast to totalitarian regimes, democratic systems are characterized by accountability of the government to the citizens and a large degree of control by individuals over their own lives. Democracies always have at least two political parties that compete in elections for power and that generally accept the outcome of elections. Mechanisms for the smooth transfer of power are laid out in a constitution or other legal document. "Ideal-type" democracies share the following characteristics, although few democracies fit this description exactly:

1. *Citizens participate in selecting the government.* There are free elections with anonymous ballots cast, widespread suffrage (voting rights), and competition between members of different parties running for offices. Those who govern do so by the consent of the majority, but the political minorities have rights and representation.

2. *Civil liberties are guaranteed.* These usually include freedom of association, freedom of the press, freedom of speech, and freedom of religion. Such individual rights ensure dissent, and dissent creates more ideas about how to solve problems. These freedoms are therefore essential for a democracy to thrive.

3. *Constitutional limits are placed on governmental powers.* The government can intrude only into certain areas of individuals' lives. Criminal procedures and police power are clearly defined, thus prohibiting harassment or terrorism by the police. The judicial system helps maintain a balance of power. These limits have caused dissent in the United States in recent years, with debates over whether the Patriot Act inappropriately limits freedoms.

4. *Governmental structure and process are spelled out.* Generally, some officials are elected whereas others are appointed, but all are accountable to the citizens. Representatives are given authority to pass laws, approve budgets, and hold the executive officer accountable for activities.

5. *Written documents such as constitutions are the basis for the development of legal systems.* The constitutions describe activities in which the government must—or must not—engage. Constitutions can provide some protection against tyrants and arbitrary actions by government. The

Sociology Around the World

The Khmer Rouge Revolution: A Totalitarian Regime

When the Khmer Rouge faction took over the government of Cambodia in 1978, they abolished private property, relocated urban dwellers to rural areas, seized personal property, classified some people as peasants, workers, or soldiers—and killed the rest. Their most amazing feat was the total evacuation of the capital city, Phnom Penh. This was done to remove urban civilization and isolate Cambodia from other political influences, such as democracy.

This complete social and economic revolution under the leadership of Pol Pot was planned in Paris by a small group of intellectual revolutionaries. They believed it would allow Kampuchea, their former name for the country, to rebuild from scratch, eliminating all capitalism, private property, and Western culture and influence.

After urban dwellers were resettled in rural camps, the totalitarian regime tried to break down the family system by prohibiting contact between members, including sexual relations between husbands and wives. Many people, including defeated soldiers, bureaucrats, royalty, businesspeople, intellectuals with opposing views, Moslems, and Buddhist monks, were slaughtered for minor offenses—hence the term *the killing fields* to describe the execution sites. The death toll is estimated at more than 1.25 million. However, the Cambodian Genocide Program has uncovered meticulous records kept by Khmer Rouge leaders, and combined with evidence from mass graves, these data may double that number (Crossette 1996; Mydans 1996).

Famine followed the killings, causing many Cambodians to flee their land, traveling by night and hiding by day to reach refugee camps across the border in Thailand. In the camps, life was rough, and crime was widespread.

Today, the economy in Cambodia is growing, especially in the areas of garment work and tourism. Thousands of tourists visit Angkor Wat and the killing fields each year. Despite growth, more than 80% of the citizens work in agriculture, and 90% of poverty is in rural areas (Asian Development Bank 2002).

The economy in Cambodia mostly provides sweatshop employment. More than 200,000 young women work in the 200 export garment factories, making clothes for companies such as The Gap. Their wages were $35 a month in 2002. To keep their jobs, they

These skulls are the remains of people massacred by the government in the Killing Fields of the Khmer Rouge in Cambodia.

must often work overtime, up to 80 hours a week, with no extra pay (Sine 2002).

Cambodia has never been a country at peace (Prasso 1994), and that seems to be true today. Violence still exists. The Human Rights Center reports chaos, corruption, poverty, and a reign of terror in Cambodia, as the military kills and extorts money from citizens. Killings, violence, and intimidation surrounded elections in 2002, with more than 14 killings of political activists and candidates (U.S. Department of State 2002a). The Khmer Rouge is still a threat to any hopes of democracy, but since the United States government officially recognizes the current government in Cambodia, it will not grant political refugee status to any new refugees from Cambodia (Tomsen 1994).

The British system of government is a democracy and parliamentary in form. This is the opening ceremony in 2007 for the Parliament. Note the pomp and circumstance that are used to create a sense of awe for power and authority.

two main forms of democratic constitutional government are the parliamentary and presidential systems. In typical parliamentary governments, the head of state is often a monarch, and the head of government is a prime minister, chancellor, or premier. These are two different people. Belgium, Canada, Denmark, Great Britain, Japan, the Netherlands, Norway, and Sweden have this model. Examples of presidential governments include France, Italy, the United States, and Germany. The presidents in these countries tend to have more autonomy than the heads of parliamentary governments.

Proportional representation means that each party is given a number of seats corresponding to the percentage of votes it received in the election. In winner-take-all systems, the individual with more than 50% of the votes gets the seat. In the United States, the "winner-take-all" system has come under attack because the winner of the popular vote could lose the electoral vote to an opponent who won only several of the most populous states. This actually happened in the presidential election in the United States: Al Gore received the most votes for president in 2000, but because

all but two states (Maine and Nebraska) had a winner-take-all system for electing the Electoral College, George W. Bush became the next president, as elected by the Electoral College. Defenders of this system of choosing the president argue that this protects the voice of each state, even if each individual voice is not given the same weight.

Constitutional governments may have from two to a dozen or more parties, as has been the case in Switzerland. Most have four or five viable ones. In European countries, typical parties include Social Democrats, Christian Democrats, Communists, Liberals, and other parties specific to local or state issues, such as green parties.

Technology and Democracy

In the modern world, there are new challenges and issues that face democracies. Electronic technology—the Internet and other telecommunications technologies—can be a boon to democracy, an opportunity for people around the world to gain information necessary to be an informed electorate, or a burden that hinders thoughtful debate and civic engagement in ideas. The latter are essential ingredients of a functioning democracy (Barber 2006).

The Internet, fax machines, camcorders, and other telecommunications devices have been major instruments for indigenous people, linking them to the outside world and combating oppressive governments. On the other hand, blogs, talk shows, Web pages, and Internet discussions are often known more for sound bites and polemical attacks on opponents than for reasoned debates in which opposing sides express views.

The key contribution that these technologies bring is speed. However, speed is not necessarily good for democracy:

> Democracy takes thought, patience, and reconsideration. That is why parliamentary procedure often requires several readings of a legislative bill prior to passage. The aim is to require time before precipitous action is taken. . . . Both representative and strong democracy are speed-averse, requiring time and patience to implement civic judgment. (Barber 2006:64)

Representative democracy involves citizens electing officials periodically and then letting them make the decisions. In a strong democracy, the voters make major policy decisions, and citizens work in communities to govern their social life, develop civic trust, and create social capital. This, of course, requires a well-informed electorate, which does not always exist.

Rapid communication can help individuals stay in touch with their representatives in a representative democracy—witness the mass text messaging at the 2008 Democratic convention. However, we must be aware of the pros and cons of various technologies for democratic decision making. Several features of technology can produce contradictory outcomes:

1. speed and the need for careful deliberation in democratic process;

2. the tendency of digital media to reduce everything to simplistic binary opposites, as though only two choices are possible;

3. the tendency to isolate individuals behind their own keyboards and monitors, so that collaborative skills may wane;

4. pictorial images that sensationalize issues so decisions are based on emotional responses more than reasoned deliberation;

5. immoderate, impulsive rhetoric, divisive attacks by people who know little or nothing about the history of the problem (as often happens on blogs and talk shows);

6. the tendency for the Internet (and many other media) to be primarily about commerce—creating a consumer mentality rather than a place for debate and problem solving; and

7. a confounding of information (with which we are sometimes overloaded) with wisdom, which is solely needed.

Social policy consideration—careful deliberative reflection—is necessary if we are to have technology benefit and not undermine democratic systems (Barber 2008).

Thinking Sociologically

How can the seven issues of technology be problems for representative democracy? Which are benefits? What effect do they have on strong participatory democracy?

Politics and the Economic Institution

While *politics* refers to the social institution that determines and exercises power relations in society, *economics* is the social institution that deals with production and distribution of goods and services. Both focus on questions related directly to the concept of power and on the power relationships between individuals, organizations, nation-states, and societies. How goods are distributed to the members of society is often determined by who has power.

Government officials have a vested interest in the well-being of the economy, for should the economy fail, the state is likely to fail as well. Recessions, depressions, and high rates of inflation put severe strains on governments that need stable economies to run properly. When problems occur, government officials are inclined to increase their roles in the economic sector. Witness the volatile money markets in 2008 and measures such as bailouts taken by the governments to stabilize the economy.

In many countries, the government is the largest employer, purchaser of goods, controller of exports and imports, and the regulator of industry and of interest rates. In the United States, many government regulatory agencies, such as the Food and Drug Administration, Department of Agriculture, and Justice Department, watch over the economic sector to protect consumers.

Types of Economic Systems

As societies become industrialized, one of two basic economic systems evolves: planned or market systems. **Planned or centralized systems** involve state-based planning and control of property, whereas **market systems** stress individual planning and private ownership of property, with much less governmental coordination or oversight. These basic types vary depending on the peculiarities of the country and its economy. For instance, China has a highly centralized planned economy with strict government control, yet some private property and incentive plans exist, and these

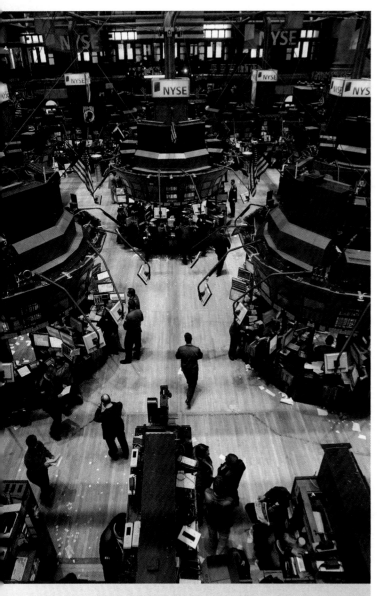

A stable economic system is essential to political stability, and extreme fluctuations in the economy are frightening to those in power. In September 2008, the Dow Jones index dropped an unprecedented 777 points in one day and fell another 782 points one week later. The New York Stock Exchange, usually bustling, is nearly empty, and President Bush, Treasury Secretary Paulson, and Congress immediately began to look for "stimulus packages" to keep the economy from going into a recession or even depression. Turning the economy around is one of the key challenges for the new U.S. president if he is to be successful.

are expanding. The United States is a market system, yet the government puts many limitations on business enterprises and regulates the flow and value of money. Distinctions between the two major types rest on the degree of centralized planning and the ownership of property. In each type of system, decisions must be made concerning which goods (and in what quantity) to produce, what to do in the event

of shortages or surpluses, and how to distribute goods. Who has power to make these decisions helps determine what type of system it is.

Market systems. The goal of capitalism is profit, made through free competition between competitors for the available markets. It assumes that the laws of supply and demand will allow some to profit while others fail. Needed goods will be made, and the best product for the price will win out over the others. No planning is needed by any oversight group because the invisible hand of the market will ensure sufficient quality control, production, and distribution of goods. This system also rewards innovative entrepreneurs who take risks and solve problems in new ways, resulting in potential growth and prosperity.

The goal of capitalist manufacturers is to bring in more money than they pay out to produce goods and services. Because workers are a production cost, getting the maximum labor output for the minimum wage is beneficial to capitalists. Thus, for example, multinational corporations look for the cheapest world sources of labor with the fewest restrictions on employment and operations. Marx predicted that there would be victims in such a system—those whom the system exploited. This potential for exploitation leads most governments to exercise some control over manufacturing and the market, although the degree of control varies widely.

Capitalism was closest to its pure form during the Industrial Revolution, when some entrepreneurs gained control of the capital and resources to manipulate those who needed work and became laborers. Using available labor and mechanical innovations, these entrepreneurs built industries. Craftspeople such as cobblers could not compete with the efficiency of the new machine-run shops, and many were forced to become laborers in new industries to survive.

Marx predicted that capitalism would cause citizens to split into two main classes: the *bourgeoisie,* capitalists who own the means of production (the "haves"), and the *proletariat,* those who sell their labor to capitalists (the "have-nots"). He argued that institutions such as education, politics, laws, and religion would evolve to preserve the privileges of the elite. Religious ideology often stresses hard work and deference to authority, allowing entrepreneurs to increase profits that benefit the owners. Furthermore, members of the economic and political elite usually encourage patriotism to distract the less privileged from their conflicts with the elite. According to Marx, the elite want the masses to draw the line between "us" and "them" based on national loyalty, not based on lines of economic self-interests (Gellner & Breuilly 2008). So in Marxist thought, even patriotism is a tool of the elite to control the workers. However, Marx believed that ultimately the workers would realize their plight, develop political awareness or consciousness, and rebel against their conditions. They would overthrow the "haves" and bring about a new and more egalitarian order.

The revolutions that Marx predicted have not occurred in most countries. Labor unions have protected workers from the severe exploitation that Marx witnessed in the early stages of industrialization in England, and capitalist governments have created and expanded a wide array of measures to protect citizens, including social security systems, unemployment compensation, disability programs, welfare systems, and health care systems. Therefore, workers have not been discontent to the point of revolt, but they have expressed frustrations through union walkouts and strikes followed by compromises between workers and capitalist owners.

Some contend that the largest corporations in the United States have such enormous power that they "own the United States." The largest 635 corporations controlled three quarters of corporate assets in 2000 (U.S. Census Bureau 2001a). Moreover, the combined sales of the 200 largest corporations surpass the combined federal budgets of all but 10 countries in the world (Rothenberg 2006a). A few elite businesspeople control many top companies through a system of interlocking directorates, giving them enormous power (Domhoff 1998, 2008; Rothenberg 2006a).

The capitalist emphasis on market control encourages a close relationship between U.S. corporations and the government's decision-making apparatus. Business interests often argue that government intervention in markets or regulation of commerce discourages competition, encourages mergers, and causes concentration of wealth and power in fewer and fewer hands. Thus, they argue that it is in the best interests of corporate decision makers to have influence in politics and government. According to power elite theorists, they do!

The Chinese system has been a highly centralized economy in which the government does the planning. In recent years, it has permitted more initiatives by entrepreneurs, rewarding those who would take a risk in the market.

Thinking Sociologically

Should we be worried that freedom of the press—and therefore democracy—is threatened when a few corporations own a very large number of the nation's radio stations and newspapers? Why or why not?

One of the major criticisms of pure capitalism is that profit is the only value that drives the system. Human dignity and well-being, environmental protection, rights of ethnic groups, and other social issues are important only as they impact profits. This leaves some people deeply dissatisfied with capitalism.

Planned systems. Communist systems attempt to eliminate private ownership of property and have the government do economic planning. All matters of production and labor are, in theory, governed with the "communal" good in

mind. There is deep suspicion of the exploitation that can occur when individuals all pursue their own self-interests. Those who hold to this philosophy believe that the market system also results in oligarchy—a system run by the financial elite in the pursuit of their own self-interests. According to Marxist analysis, when a true Communist state is achieved, motivating incentives for individuals such as earning more money are not needed. Each individual contributes to the general welfare of the community or society in exchange for benefits from the system, including food, shelter, employment, schooling, and cultural events. The state oversees the total economy. Monotonous, tedious jobs are shared voluntarily by all. The idea is that this frees individuals to concentrate on the humanistic and culturally important aspects of life. Values other than profits can be protected and affirmed. China, Cuba, and about 24 nations in Africa, Asia, and Latin America have planned economies with industry controlled by the state (Freedom House 2002).

In reality, however, no system is a perfect planned state with the complete elimination of private property or exploitation. China, based on a Communist ideology, made rapid progress in tackling hunger, illiteracy, drug addiction, and other problems by using its strong central government to establish five-year economic development plans. Today, however, the government is experimenting with new economic plans including limited private entrepreneurship, more imported goods, and trade and development agreements with other countries. Much of China has moved beyond the survival level and can experiment with modifications to the economic system. China has not, however, granted much political freedom to its citizenry.

One key criticism of Communist systems is that placing economic power and political power in the hands of the leadership can lead to control by a few leaders. Power centers in government, the business world, and the military can balance each other and help to protect against dictatorships and tyranny (Heilbroner and Milberg 2007).

Democratic socialism (welfare states). Democratic socialism refers to collective or group planning of the development of the society, but within a democratic political system. Private profit is less important than in capitalism, and the good of the whole is paramount. Planning may include goals of creating equality, protecting the environment, or supporting families, but individuals' rights to pursue their own self-interests are also allowed within certain parameters. The system seeks checks and balances so that both political and economic decision makers are accountable to the public. Several countries, including Sweden, Great Britain, Norway, Austria, Canada, and France, have incorporated some democratic socialist ideas into their governmental policies, especially in public services (Olsson 1990).

Sometimes these systems are called mixed economies or "welfare states." Many Western European democracies redistribute income through progressive tax plans that tax according to people's ability to pay. The government uses this tax money to nationalize education, health plans and medical care, pensions, maternity leaves, and sometimes housing for its citizens. Although much of industry is privately run, the government provides regulations for the industry and assesses high taxes to pay for government programs. Typically, public service industries such as transportation, communications, and power companies are government controlled.

Such systems are recent experiments in governance, and they remain an idealized vision that has yet to be implemented. In some ways, democratic socialist states outproduce capitalist ones, and in some ways, they can seem cumbersome ways to run a complex society. The bottom line in evaluating which system works best comes down to value priorities: individualism and economic growth for the system versus values such as equality, distribution of wealth, and protection of the environment.

Many Marxists in Europe believe that democratic socialism is what Karl Marx really had in mind, not the bureaucratic system that evolved in the Soviet Union, China, and elsewhere. Marx, after all, felt that the worst of all governments was state capitalism—a system in which the state controlled the economy. His early writings, in particular, put much more emphasis on decentralization and even a withering away of the government (Marx 1963). Few social democrats today think the government will ever wither away, but they think that the public, not just the elite, should have input into economic as well as governmental decisions and planning.

The market system (capitalism) and the planned systems (socialism and communism) both have their advocates, but each system also has its shortcomings. The question, then, is whether there is an economic system that can avoid the dangers of each. More than two centuries ago, it was widely believed, perhaps rightly at that time, that democracy could not work. The notion of self-governance by the citizenry was discredited as a pipedream. Yet this experiment in self-governance is continuing, despite some flaws and problems. In a speech to the British House of Commons in 1947, then-Prime Minister Winston Churchill said that "democracy is the worst form of government, except for all those other forms that have been tried." Some economists and social philosophers have argued that if the people can plan for self-governance, they certainly should be able to plan for economic development in a way that does not put economic power in the hands of a political elite.

The institutions of politics and economics cannot be separated. In the 21st century, new political and economic relationships will emerge as each institution influences the other. Both institutions ultimately have a close connection to power and privilege.

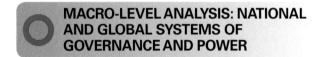

MACRO-LEVEL ANALYSIS: NATIONAL AND GLOBAL SYSTEMS OF GOVERNANCE AND POWER

Power and the Nation-State

A *nation-state* is a political, geographical, and cultural unit with recognizable boundaries and a system of government. Boundaries of nation-states have been established through wars, conquests, negotiations, and treaties. These boundaries change as disputes over territory are resolved by force or negotiation. For example, Russia and the country of Georgia recently had a conflict over whether two breakaway provinces of Georgia, Ossetia and Abkhazia, belonged within the national boundaries of Georgia. There are more than 200 nation-states in the world today, 192 of which are represented in the United Nations (United Nations 2007). This number is increasing as new independent nation-states continue to develop in Europe, Asia, Africa, and other parts of the world.

Within each nation-state, power is exerted by the systems that govern people through leaders, laws, courts, tax structure, the military, and the economic system. Different forms of power dominate at different times in history and in different geographical settings.

The notions of the nation-state and of nationalism are so completely internalized as realities that we do not stop to think of them as social constructions of reality, created by people to meet group needs. In historical terms, nationalism is a rather recent or modern concept, emerging only after the nation-state (Gellner 1983, 1987, 1993).

Medieval Europe, for example, knew no nation-states. One scholar writes that "Throughout the Middle Ages, the mass of inhabitants living in what is now known as France or England did not think of themselves as 'French' or 'English.' They had little conception of a territorial nation (a 'country') to which they owed an allegiance stronger than life itself" (Billig 1995:21). Some argue that the nation-state has "no precedent in history" (Giddens 1987:166) prior to the 16th century and perhaps considerably later than that.

This raises an interesting question: Why did nation-states emerge in Europe and then spread throughout the rest of the world? This is one of the major puzzles of modern history, and it has to do with the change to rational organizational structures (Billig 1995:21–22). It is noteworthy that today every square foot of the Earth's land-space is thought to be under the ownership of a nation-state. Yet, even today, a sense of nationalism or patriotism linking one's personal identity to the welfare of the nation is a foreign idea to many. People have loyalty to their region, their ethnic or tribal group, their religious group, or their local community, but a sense of being Pakistani or Kenyan or Afghani is weak at best. Yet, in places like the United States, having a passionate sense of national loyalty for which one would die is so taken-for-granted that anyone lacking this loyalty is suspect or deviant. Note the earlier discussion of the role of the flag. The nation is largely an imagined reality, something that exists because we choose to believe that it exists (Anderson 2006; McCrone 1998). Indeed, for some people, belonging to the nation has become the substitute for religious faith or local ethnic belonging (Billig 1995; McCrone 1998).

Revolutions and Political Rebellions

From the 1980s to the new century, significant social and political changes have taken place throughout the world. The Berlin Wall was dismantled, leading to unification of East and West Germany. The Baltic states of Estonia, Latvia, and Lithuania became independent. In Eastern Europe, political and social orders established since World War II underwent radical change. When the Soviet Union and Yugoslavia broke apart, national boundaries were redrawn. Internal strife resulted from ethnic divisions formerly kept under check by the strong centralized governments in both areas.

Were these changes revolutions? *Revolution* refers to social and political transformations of a nation that result when states fail to fulfill their expected responsibilities (Skocpol 1979). Revolutions can be violent, and they result in altered distributions of power in the society. Revolutions typically occur when the government does not respond to citizen needs and when leadership emerges to challenge the existing regime. News from around the world frequently reports on nation-states that have been challenged by opposition groups attempting to overthrow the regimes. In 2008, Thailand's

Revolutions can be violent overthrows of governments or nonviolent events such as this Burmese monk protest that was violently suppressed by the government.

prime minister faced threats from opposition forces demanding that he resign due to charges of corruption and lack of action on pressing problems, charges not substantiated in a court of law but compelling to the citizenry.

The Meso-Macro Political Connection

State or provincial governments and national political parties are meso-level organizations that operate beyond the local community, but they are less encompassing in their

Another nonviolent revolution has been the Zapatista movement in southern Mexico (Chiapas). Here we see Zapatista commanders holding a Mexican flag as they attend a mass rally in Mexico City's main square. The Zapatista delegation called for indigenous rights including clean water and schooling for their children through sixth grade. The Zapatistas wore masks so they could not be identified and persecuted by the government. They are a sophisticated movement that is in communication with other human rights movements around the globe.

wins by only a half of a percentage point. One state (Texas) has both a primary election and a party caucus. Still others have a formula by which some delegates are elected in the primary based on proportion of the statewide vote while others are chosen based on who wins each congressional district. (See Table 13.2.)

This means that some state governments decide when the primaries will be held while elsewhere the primaries are "owned" by the political parties. Some states have split primaries, so the Democratic and Republican primaries are not on the same day. New Hampshire has in its state constitution a clause that the state must have the first presidential primary.

Thinking Sociologically

Is it acceptable that some states never get any say in the nomination of candidates because the process is completed before they get to vote? Can one state write into its constitution that it must have the first primary election, or should this be a decision that is somehow made at the national level? Who has the authority to tell a state they cannot put that in their constitution?

influence than national or federal governments or global systems. Still, decisions at the state or provincial government level can have major influences in political processes at the national level. We have already seen some of these debates elsewhere in this book in discussions of state and federal policies on same-sex versus strictly heterosexual marriage. Here we look at another issue: the recent controversies about how to nominate and elect a president within the United States. Although the focus is on the U.S. political system, this discussion should be seen as illustrative of the tensions and peculiarities of the meso-macro link in any complex political system.

In some U.S. states, each political party runs its own caucuses (face-to-face meetings of voters in homes, schools, and other buildings) to discuss policy and to carry out public votes. In caucus states, the political party funds and operates the process of selecting delegates who will nominate the presidential candidate. By contrast, other states have primary elections run by the state government, but even these are not all the same. On the Democratic side, states distribute their delegates based on the proportion of the vote won by a candidate in that state. On the Republican side, the delegate selection may be based on the proportion of the vote for each candidate, whereas in other states, it is a winner-take-all system, even if one candidate

With a contentious U.S. election just completed, several controversial questions were raised. Can a political party tell a state when to have its elections and then punish that state if it does not obey by refusing to seat its delegates at the party convention? This is exactly what happened in Michigan and Florida in 2008. However, it gets even more complicated. In Florida, a Republican-dominated legislature moved the date of the primary election. The Democrats from that state were outvoted in the state legislature, but they still lost the right to represent their state at the convention where a presidential candidate is nominated. Can a state legislature—a meso-level political entity—tell a national political party—another meso-level political entity—how to run its nomination process? The answers to these questions are not clear, yet they can have profound effects on who becomes the next president of the most powerful nation on Earth.

In some states, only members of the party can vote. In other states, citizens who are registered as independents can vote in either primary election and help select the party's candidate. In other states, Democrats and Republicans can cross over and vote in the primary for the other party. What are the implications of having different rules in different states about crossover party voting?

Finally, in some states, the Republican primary is a "beauty contest" with no binding outcome. The results are purely advisory, and the delegates from that state are free to ignore the outcome of the election. The delegates are

Table 13.2 Meso-Level Presidential Nomination Variations in the United States

	State-Run Primary (P) Versus Party-Run Caucus (C)	Split-Party (SP) Versus Co-current (CC)[1]	Closed (CL), Semi-closed (SC), Open (O) Primaries/ Caucuses[2]	Winner-Takes-All (WTA) Versus Proportional (%) Delegates in Primaries[3]	Winner-Takes-All (WTA) Versus Proportional (%) for Electoral College
Alabama[4]	P	CC	O	Republican Combination Democrat %	WTA
Alaska	C	CC	SC	Republican % Democrat %	WTA
Arizona	P	CC	CL	Republican WTA Democrat %	WTA
Arkansas	P	CC	O	Republican % Democrat %	WTA
California	P	CC	SC	Republican % Democrat %	WTA
Colorado	C	CC	CL	Republican % Democrat %	WTA
Connecticut	P	CC	CL	Republican WTA Democrat %	WTA
Delaware	P	CC	CL	Republican WTA Democrat %	WTA
Florida	P	CC	CL	Republican WTA Democrat %	WTA
Georgia	P	CC	SC	Republican WTA Democrat %	WTA
Hawaii	P	SP	CL	Republican % Democrat %	WTA
Idaho	P	SP	O	Republican % Democrat %	WTA
Illinois	P	CC	SC	Republican % Democrat %	WTA
Indiana	P	CC	O	Republican WTA Democrat %	WTA
Iowa	C	CC	SC	Republican % Democrat %	WTA
Kansas	C	SP	SC Democratic CL Republican	Republican % Democrat %	WTA
Kentucky	P	CC	CL	Republican % Democrat %	WTA
Louisiana	P	CC	CL	Republican % Democrat %	WTA
Maine[4]	C	SP	CL	Republican % Democrat %	%
Maryland	P	CC	CL	Republican WTA Democrat %	WTA
Massachusetts	P	CC	SC	Republican % Democrat %	WTA
Michigan	P	CC	O	Republican WTA Democrat %	WTA
Minnesota	C	CC	O	Republican % Democrat %	WTA

(Continued)

Table 13.2 (Continued)

	State-Run Primary (P) Versus Party-Run Caucus (C)	Split-Party (SP) Versus Co-current (CC)[1]	Closed (CL), Semi-closed (SC), Open (O) Primaries/ Caucuses[2]	Winner-Takes-All (WTA) Versus Proportional (%) Delegates in Primaries[3]	Winner-Takes-All (WTA) Versus Proportional (%) for Electoral College
Mississippi	P	CC	O	Republican WTA Democrat %	WTA
Missouri	P	CC	O	Republican WTA Democrat %	WTA
Montana	P	SP	O Democrat CL Republican	Republican Purely Advisory[6] Democrat %	WTA
Nebraska[4]	C	SP	CL	Republican Purely Advisory[6] Democrat %	%
Nevada	C	CC	CL	Republican % Democrat %	WTA
New Hampshire	P	CC	SC	Republican % Democrat %	WTA
New Jersey	P	CC	SC	Republican WTA Democrat %	WTA
New Mexico	P	SP	CL	Republican % Democrat %	WTA
New York	P	CC	CL	Republican WTA Democrat %	WTA
North Carolina	P	CC	CL	Republican % Democrat %	WTA
North Dakota[4]	C	CC	O	Republican WTA Democrat %	WTA
Ohio	P	CC	SC	Republican WTA Democrat %	WTA
Oklahoma	P	CC	CL	Republican WTA Democrat %	WTA
Oregon	P	CC	CL	Republican % Democrat %	WTA
Pennsylvania	P	CC	CL	Republican Purely Advisory[6] Democrat %	WTA
Rhode Island	P	CC	SC	Republican % Democrat %	WTA
South Carolina	P	SP	O	Republican WTA Democrat %	WTA
South Dakota	P	CC	CL	Republican % Democrat %	WTA
Tennessee[4]	P	CC	O	Republican WTA Democrat %	WTA
Texas	P and C[5]	CC	SC Primary CL Caucus	Republican WTA Democrat %	WTA
Utah	P	CC	O Democrat CL Republican	Republican WTA Democrat %	WTA
Vermont	P	CC	O	Republican WTA Democrat %	WTA
Virginia	P	CC	O	Republican % Democrat %	WTA
Washington[4]	C	SP	O	Republican Combination Democrat %	WTA

	State-Run Primary (P) Versus Party-Run Caucus (C)	Split-Party (SP) Versus Co-current (CC)[1]	Closed (CL), Semi-closed (SC), Open (O) Primaries/ Caucuses[2]	Winner-Takes-All (WTA) Versus Proportional (%) Delegates in Primaries[3]	Winner-Takes-All (WTA) Versus Proportional (%) for Electoral College
West Virginia	P	SP	O Democrat CL Republican	Republican District WTA + Statewide % Democrat %	WTA
Wisconsin	P	CC	O	Republican WTA Democrat %	WTA
Wyoming	C	SP	CL	Republican % Democrat %	WTA
Washington DC	P	CC	CL	Republican WTA Democrat %	WTA

Source: BBC News 2008; Bowen 2008; The Center for Voting and Democracy 2008; The Green Papers 2008a; The Green Papers 2008b; National Archives and Records Administration 2008; *The New York Times* 2008; Project Vote Smart 2008; State of Delaware 2008; Voting and Democracy Research Center 2008.

Notes:

1. SP (split party) means primaries or caucuses for the two major political parties occur on two different days In contrast, CC (co-current) means caucuses/primaries occur on the same day.
2. In a closed primary/caucus, only voters registered as party members may vote in that party's election. Semi-closed primary/caucus allows independents to vote in either party primary. Open primary/caucuses allow any voter to vote in any party's primary.
3. Proportional distribution may include division by congressional district and/or percentage of state popular vote.
4. These states have some unique variations that are not elaborated here.
5. Texas has a primary and caucus, giving Democratic voters the opportunity to legally vote twice. Two thirds of the delegates are determined by the primary results, and one third of the delegates are determined by the caucus results.
6. In a Purely Advisory primary (which currently operates only in the Republican Party), the results of the primary are not binding on the delegates, who are chosen by a process different from that of the election. The national Democratic Party only recently banned purely advisory primaries, but they have a system of "super delegates" who are not formally elected and may vote for whomever they wish at the party's convention.

selected by the party insiders in that state, not by the voters. The Democratic Party has only recently passed a national policy banning this kind of primary. On the other hand, the Democratic Party has 915 "super delegates"—party insiders who have not been elected by the populace and who may commit their votes to anyone they please. So both parties allow delegates to vote who are not representing any constituency that elected them. What are the implications for a democracy?

Even selection of the Electoral College, which actually decides who will be president after the general election, is not uniform in policy across the states. Two states have proportional distribution of electors and all the others having winner-take-all. If one additional state with large numbers of electors were to shift to proportional distribution of electors, it could change the outcome of our national elections for a long time to come. Should there be consistency between the states in the way the Electoral College is selected? Should state elections all be proportional or all be winner-take-all?

Because the Constitution grants considerable autonomy to states to make these decisions, how does the nation ever get consistency? At the state (meso) level, legislatures are very protective of their right to make their own decisions.

Yet, governance of the nation and the nation's relationships with the global community may be at stake.

Thinking Sociologically

Is it a problem for a *national* democracy when the delegate selection system is convoluted at the meso level, or does this make elections even more democratic because states can make their own autonomous decisions? Explain your answer.

Global Interdependencies and Politics

Dependency theorists and world systems theorists point out the inequality between rich core countries and developing peripheral countries that are dependent on the core countries for survival. The more dependent a country is, the more inequality is likely to exist between that country and core countries. The physical quality of life for citizens in dependent countries is also likely to be poor. For example, permitting a foreign company to mine resources in a Global South country may produce a short-term gain in employment for the country and may make some leaders wealthy, but when the exhaustible resources are gone, the dependent country is often left with its natural resources destroyed and an even poorer economy (Wallerstein 1979, 1991).

Young democracies are emerging in peripheral countries in eastern Europe, East Asia, and Latin America. In several Central and Latin American countries formerly ruled by civilian and military dictatorships, democratic governments are taking hold, and elected officials are gaining power. In Mexico, President Vincente Fox, a former successful businessman with degrees in business administration and management, ran the government, replacing the six-decade-old ruling party and the military (BBC News 2000).

Despite the movement toward political liberalization, democracy, and market-oriented reforms in countries such as Chile, Mexico, Nigeria, Poland, Senegal, Thailand, and Turkey, not all of these societies are ready to adopt democratic forms of governance. In a study of the experiences of 26 developing Asian, African, and Latin American countries, the conclusion was that several factors were important for these countries to develop stable democracies: political participation, interest groups, economic growth, control of corruption, and maintenance of order without reducing liberty (Diamond 1987, 1992). In addition, literacy is critical for the citizens of a democracy to be informed voters.

Several African nations are looking to the economic success stories in Asia (such as Singapore, Malaysia, Thailand, and South Korea) for models of development. They are finding strong central governments in some of these countries. The most affluent countries in the Global North have democracies, but there is some question about how to create a democratic system in poor countries with different cultures.

What are the chances that the United States or another powerful nation-state will be successful in attempts to create democracies elsewhere? The odds are probably not good, according to a number of political analysts. Foreign powers can do little to alter the social structure and cultural traditions of other societies, and as indicated, these structures are key to the successful development of democracy. If the imposed system is premature or incompatible with the society's level of development and other institutional structures, authoritarian dictatorship rather than democracy may emerge as the traditional authority structure breaks down. Some African and Latin American countries have experienced these breakdowns. However, the United States and other developed societies have influence over political and economic developments through their economic, military and political power, foreign aid, trade, treaties, multinational corporations, and other factors.

Some scholars believe certain preconditions are necessary for the emergence of democracy:

- high levels of economic well-being;
- the absence of extreme inequalities in wealth and income;
- social pluralism, including a particularly strong and autonomous middle class;
- a market-oriented economy;
- influence in the world system of democratic states;
- a culture that is relatively tolerant of diversity and can accommodate compromise; and
- a literate population informed about issues. (Bottomore 1979; Inglehart 1997)

Thinking Sociologically

Why might some analysts believe that Iraq—where the United States is attempting to set up democracy—is not in a position to have a successful democratic government at this time? Which of these conditions are in place and which ones are missing in Iraq?

Socioeconomic development strengthens democracy by contributing to social stability (Diamond 1992). Promoting democracy means offering moral, political, financial, and diplomatic support to efforts to replace authoritarian regimes (Diamond 1992, 2003). Thus, an outside power can help establish the structures necessary to support democracy but is seldom successful trying to impose it. If countries in the Global North want more democracies around the world, an important strategy is to support economic development in less affluent countries.

Some countries see discussions of democracy as a ploy—a cover-up used by dominant affluent nations for advancing their wealth. For example, the Global North nations have combined to form a coalition of nations calling itself the Group of 7 (or the G7—the United States, Japan, Germany, Canada, France, Great Britain, and Italy). Recently, Russia was added, and the group is now the G8. The G8 uses its collective power to regulate global economic policies to ensure stability (and thereby ensure that members' interests are secure). The G8 has the power to control world markets through the World Trade Organization, the World Bank, and the International Monetary Fund. This is discussed further in Chapter 16 (Brecher, Costello, and Smith 2006; Cockburn 2006; Eitzen and Zinn 2006; Stein 2006; Weidenbaum 2006; Weller and Hersh 2006). Global South nations responded to the G8 with an organization of poor countries that they called the G77. They are attempting to create collective unity so they will have some power to determine their own destinies (Brecher et al. 2006; Hayden 2006). Map 13.2 shows where the G8 and G77 nations are located.

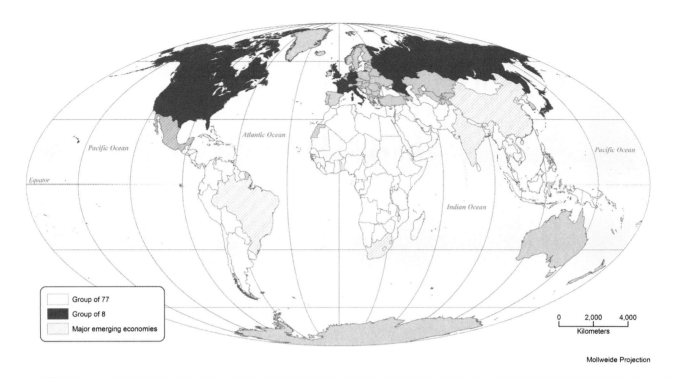

Map 13.2 Countries of the Group of 8, Major Emerging Economies, and Countries of the Group of 77

Source: http://www.g77.org and http://www.g-8.de/Webs/G8/EN/Homepage/home.html, retrieved April 2008.
Map by Anna Versluis.

Political systems can face threats from internal sources such as disaffected citizens, the military, and interest groups vying for power, or they can be challenged by external sources such as other nations wanting land or resources or by coalitions of nations demanding change. This is the situation for North Korea and Iran as coalitions of nations demand that they drop their nuclear enrichment programs. Sometimes these power struggles erupt into violence. The following section discusses how war, terrorism, and rebellion challenge existing systems.

Violence on the Global Level

Once upon a time, gallant knights in shining armor went forth to battle with good luck tokens from their ladies and the cause of their religion or their monarch to spur them on. They seldom died in these battles, and the daily life of the society went on as usual. By contrast, since the invention of modern weaponry, no one has been safe from death and destruction in war. Weapons can destroy whole civilizations. A malfunctioning computer, a miscalculation, a deranged person, a misunderstanding between hostile factions, or a terrorist attack could kill millions of people.

War is armed conflict occurring within, between, or among societies or groups. It is sometimes called

"organized mass violence" (Nolan 2002). War is a frequent but not inevitable condition of human existence. Many countries are now engaged in wars that are debilitating and detrimental to their economies and morale. Some of these wars (between India and Pakistan, in the Sudan, between Palestine and Israel, and between rival factions in the Congo) have lasted for years. Others have been short and decisive, like the "Desert Storm" war with Iraq. Table 13.3 lists ongoing world conflicts as of 2007.

Why Do Nations Go to War?

Leaders use moral, religious, or political ideology to legitimize war, although the cause may be conflicts over economic resources or ethnic tensions. Wars have been waged to support religions through crusades and jihads; to liberate a country from domination by a foreign power; to protect borders, resources, and cultural customs; and to capture resources, including slaves, land, and oil. War can also distract citizens from other problems in their country, and it may therefore be used by politicians intent on staying in power. On the other hand, there are cultures where war is virtually unknown. Groups, often isolated, live in peace and cooperation, with little competition for land and resources. The bottom line is that war is a product of societies, created by societies, and learned in societies.

Palestinian schoolchildren take cover under their desks in their classroom during an emergency drill in Israel. This exercise to prepare for war is stimulated by the government's fear of attacks by neighboring enemies. Children in North America seldom live with such anxieties.

Table 13.3 **Significant Ongoing Armed Conflicts, 2007**	
Main Warring Parties	*Year It Started*[1]
Middle East	
U.S. and UK vs. Iraq	2003
Israel vs. Palestinians	1948
Asia	
Afghanistan: U.S., UK, and Coalition Forces vs. al-Qaeda and Taliban	2001
India vs. Kashmiri separatist groups/Pakistan	1948
India vs. Assam insurgents (various)	1979
Indonesia vs. Papua (Irian Jaya) separatists	1969
Philippines vs. Mindanaoan separatists (MILF/ASG)	1971
Sri Lanka vs. Tamil Eelan[2]	1978
Africa	
Algeria vs. Armed Islamic Group (GIA)	1991
Côte d'Ivoire vs. rebels	2002
Democratic Republic of Congo and allies vs. Rwanda, Uganda, and indigenous rebels	1997
Somalia vs. rival clans and Islamist groups	1991
Sudan vs. Darfur rebel groups	2003
Uganda vs. Lord's Resistance Army (LRA)	1986
Europe	
Russia vs. Chechen separatists	1994
Latin America	
Colombia vs. National Liberation Army (ELN)	1978
Colombia vs. Revolutionary Armed Forces of Colombia (FARC)	1978
Colombia vs. Autodefensas Unidas de Colombia (AUC)	1990

Source: "Significant Ongoing Armed Conflicts" 2007. www.infoplease.com/ipa/A0904550.html, as it appeared on June 3, 2008, Information Please ® Database, © 2007 by Pearson Education, Inc. Reproduced by permission of Pearson Education, Inc. publishing as InfoPlease. All rights reserved.

Note: As of December 2007.

1. Where multiple parties and long-standing but sporadic conflict are concerned, date of first combat deaths is given.
2. 2002 cease-fire collapsed in 2006.

Two familiar sociological theories attempt to explain the social factors that can lead to war. Functional theorists think underlying social problems cause disruptions to the system, including war, terrorism, and revolution. If all parts of the system were working effectively, they contend that these problems would not occur. Agents of social control and a smooth-running system would prevent disruptions. However, some functionalists also argue that war brings a population together behind a cause, resulting in social solidarity.

Conflict theorists see war, terrorism, and revolution as the outcome of oppression by the ruling elite and an attempt to overthrow that oppression. Many businesses profit from wars because their manufacturing power is put to full use. In fact, more money is spent on war than on prevention of disease, illiteracy, hunger, and other human problems. Citizens from the lower classes and racial minorities join the military, fight, and die in disproportionate numbers, since they are more likely to join the military as an avenue to job training and join as enlistees who serve on the front lines. Meanwhile business organizations make profits from war. Often perceived social inequities lead to wars, such as the conflicts in Northern Ireland where Catholics feel Protestants have come to control the land Catholics once called their own.

Some nations are more war-prone than others, and one cannot tell simply by paying attention to the rhetoric about war and peace. U.S. politicians give much vocal support to peace, but the country has been at war 190 of the 230 years since the colonies declared independence. Indeed, during the entire 20th century, there were only six years when the United States was not engaged in some sort of military action around the world (Brandon 2005; Noguera and Cohen 2006).

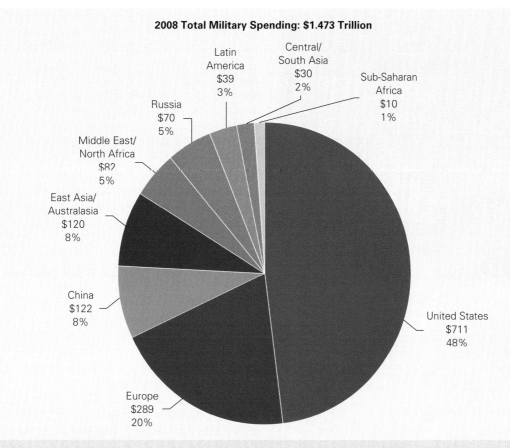

2008 Total Military Spending: $1.473 Trillion

Figure 13.2   U.S. Military Spending Versus the World, 2008 (in billions of U.S. dollars and % of total global)

Source: Sharp 2008. From *The FY 2009 Pentagon Spending Request—Global Military Spending,* by Christopher Hellman and Travis Sharp. Center for Arms Control and Non-Proliferation, February 20, 2008. Reprinted with permission.

The conclusion is that war is not a natural or biological necessity. It is in large part a result of leaderships' decisions. Like incest, slavery, and cannibalism (which at times were thought to be instinctual but have come to be understood as aberrations), some sociologists believe that war can be "unlearned" (Stoessinger 1993), though not all agree.

How Can Nations Avoid War?

Deterrence is one approach to discourage and perhaps avoid war by placing restrictions on others' choices. Some government officials argue that if a nation is militarily strong, no one will dare attack it, and the country will be secure. Leaders can "negotiate from strength." Believers in this approach argue nations should become superior to others or to maintain a balance with other militaristic nations. However, evidence from ongoing statistical analyses of militarization concludes that neither type of deterrence has been effective in reducing the chance of war. The more militarized a country becomes, the more likely the country is to enter into war. Continual buildup of weapons increases mistrust and raises the potential for misunderstandings, mistakes,

or disaster. Furthermore, military personnel often have a vested interest in war—that is what the military is trained to do and what proves its competence. Business interests and economies may also profit from supporting war.

Deterrence is extremely expensive. As countries develop their military power, the spiral toward bigger, more sophisticated, and expensive technological weaponry such as nuclear weapons in North Korea and Iran, and the Strategic Defense Initiative (SDI) in the United States continues. Figure 13.2 shows military spending around the world giving rise to what is often called the military-industrial complex. The question is whether *brinkmanship,* expending money and pushing the potential for conflict to the brink, works to deter others. The question has been applied to many international conflicts including North Korea. Two classic experiments (Deutsch and Kewicki 1970; Deutsch and Krauss 1960) that have been replicated numerous times consider the many possible strategies leading up to brinkmanship and how to reduce threats. The results indicate that parties with similar power or wealth usually do not lock themselves into positions they cannot reverse, especially if they will continue to have

A soldier, just back from Iraq after finishing his service, looks at boots of nearly 2,000 U.S. soldiers and thousands of Iraqi civilians killed during the Iraq war. The display was at a Military Park in Newark, New Jersey, and sponsored by the American Friends Service Committee on the human cost of the Iraq war. Those who have served in war-time know better than anyone the agonies and costs of war that tables and pie charts cannot convey.

interaction with their opponents. Brinkmanship is a high-risk strategy.

World military expenditures in 2006 were $1.204 billion. The United States accounts for 48% of world military spending (Shah 2008). Military expenditures are usually at the expense of social programs such as education and health care. Spending for weapons widens the gap between rich and poor countries and diverts money from social causes at home and abroad (Ayers 2006). Still, many people feel that protection of the citizenry is the government's most essential responsibility.

In 2008, 20% of the U.S. budget went to the Defense Department (Runningen and Faler 2008). How the military budget percentage is calculated varies depending on whether social security trust fund and other programs are figured into the total annual budget. If they are not, the percentage of spending on the military is dramatically higher. Current stockpiles of U.S. weapons include 10,000 long- and short-range nuclear weapons, enough to annihilate the human race many times over (Johnson 2007; Younger 2000). There are an estimated 31,000 nuclear warheads deployed or in the stockpiles of eight nations: China, France, Great Britain, India, Israel, Pakistan, Russia, and the United States. About 13,000 are deployed, and 4,600 are on high alert ready to be launched in minutes (Ware 2008). The debate is over whether such preparations are essential or actually create the possibility for violence as a way to solve problems.

Negotiation is a second approach to avoiding war and resolving conflicts by discussion to reach agreement. For example, diplomacy and treaties have set limits on nuclear weapons and their use. In the 1990s, the superpowers made major efforts to move into a new peaceful era. Peace talks were held in the Middle East, Cambodia, Rwanda, the former Yugoslavia and Bosnia, Ireland, and other countries threatened by tensions and war. Leaders of the United Nations were often involved in diplomatic attempts to resolve conflicts. The inherent problem, however, is that negotiation means a partial win—and a partial loss—for each side. Each gives a little, and each gets a little. Both sides tend to want a win/lose resolution—with the other side losing. Commitment to a win/lose perspective can lead to a lose/lose situation with neither side really winning.

Some citizens are not satisfied to leave peace-keeping efforts to their government leaders. Strong grassroots peace movements in Europe, the Middle East, the United States, South Africa, and other countries are aimed at lessening tensions and conflicts around the world. The widespread demonstrations in many European and U.S. cities by people opposed to the Iraqi war is one such example.

Many peace groups sponsor educational programs and museum displays. The horrors depicted in the Hiroshima Peace Museum in Japan; the Killing Fields in Cambodia; the Holocaust Museum in Washington, D.C.; the Anne Frank Museum in Amsterdam, Netherlands; and the Korean and Vietnam War Memorials in Washington all help sensitize the public and politicians to the effects of war. Interestingly, most war memorials in the United States glorify the war and lionize the heroes who fought in those wars. In Europe, many memorials stress the pathos and agony of war. However, the Vietnam Memorial in Washington, D.C., sends a different message about the sorrows of war. Peace advocates and veterans of the war often stand and weep together in front of that memorial.

Scholars draw several conclusions from studies of war in the past century: (1) no nation that began a major war in the 20th century emerged a clear winner; (2) in the nuclear age, war between nuclear powers could be suicidal; and (3) a victor's peace plan is seldom lasting. Those peace settlements that are negotiated on the basis of equality are much more permanent and durable. War is often stimulated by inequitable distribution of resources. Therefore, peace that is lasting also requires attention to at least semi-equitable distribution of resources.

In the long run, people around the world would seem to benefit from peace, yet many leaders and citizens hold bitter hatred against their neighbors. Obviously, this is not a climate for peace. As long as there is discrimination, hunger, and poverty in the world, the roots of violence are present. The world is a complex interdependent system. When the linkages between peoples are based on ideologies that stress we/they polarities and power differentials that alienate people, then war, terrorism, and violence will not disappear from the globe.

Terrorism

On September 11, 2001, three commercial airplanes became the missiles of terrorists, two crashing into the twin towers of the World Trade Center in New York City and one into the Pentagon in Washington, D.C., killing over 3,025 people from 68 nations, and injuring countless others. This was an act of terrorists. Why did they do it?

Terrorism refers to the use of indiscriminate violence, which can cause mass fear and panic, intimidate citizens, and advance a group's political goals (Nolan 2002). Terrorism usually refers to acts of violence by private nonstate groups to advance revolutionary political goals, but *state terrorism* is government use of terror to control people. Terrorists are found at all points on the political continuum: anarchists, nationalists, religious fundamentalists, and members of ethnic groups. In 2006, terrorist attacks were up 25% from 2005, with half of the attacks (14,000) and two thirds of the fatalities in Iraq (CNN.com 2007).

What makes terrorism effective? Terrorists strike randomly and change tactics so that governments have no clear or effective way of dealing with them. This unpredictability causes public confidence in the ability of government to protect citizens and deal with crises to waver. Terrorists seldom attack targets in oligarchic or dictatorial societies because these countries ignore their demands despite the risk to innocent civilians and hostages' lives (Frey 2004).

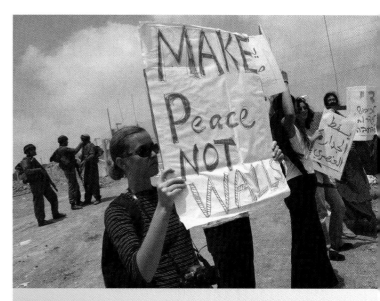

Activists of the International Solidarity Movement (ISM) protest against the construction of the Israeli security fence near a Palestinian village. Dozens of people from many nations have put their own bodies on the line to prevent bulldozing of Palestinian homes and construction of the fence. American Rachel Corrie, a member of the ISM, was run over and killed by an Israeli bulldozer March 16, 2003, when she tried to stop it from destroying a family's home. People like Rachel believe so strongly in peace that they sometimes place their own bodies between the military and the targets of military action.

Why do terrorists commit hostile acts? In our anger against terrorists, we sometimes fail to look at why they commit these atrocities. Who are the terrorists, and what have they to gain? Without understanding the underlying causes of terrorism, we can do little to prevent it.

One person's terrorist may be someone else's freedom fighter. In other words, terrorism is in the eye of the beholder. Few terrorists act alone. They are members of groups that are highly committed to an ideology or cause— religious, political, or both. Terrorists are willing to die to support their groups' cause. Class, ethnic, racial, or religious alienation often lie at the roots of terrorism. The ideology of terrorist groups stresses *we* versus *they* perceptions of the world, with *they* being "evil." Those committing terrorist acts often feel they are the victims of more powerful forces, and sometimes, they see their only weapon to fight back as the ultimate sacrifice—their lives.

Ahmad is a terrorist. All his life, his family has been on the move, forced to work for others for hardly a living wage, controlled by rules made up by other people—ones that he feels are hostile to his group. When he was very young, his family's home was taken away and the residents of his town scattered to other locations. Resentment resulted in an environment hostile to the forces that dislocated his family, put some in jail, and separated him from friends and relatives.

Ahmad sees little future for himself or his people, little hope for education or a career of his choosing. He feels he has nothing to lose by joining a resistance organization to fight for what he sees as justice. This organization cannot be publicly known because it is surrounded by stronger enemies. Its members keep their identities secret. They are not powerful enough to mount an army to fight, so they rely on terrorist tactics against those they see as oppressors.

Ahmad puts the "greater good" of his religious and political beliefs and his group above his individual well-being. When he agrees to commit a terrorist act, he truly believes it is right and is the only way he can retaliate and bring attention to the suffering of his people. If killed, he will be praised and become a martyr within his group.

Continued frustration by those who are alienated is illustrated by ongoing current events: militants setting off bombs in London, Madrid, Pakistan, and Mumbai, India; suicide bombers in Iraq; and terrorist attacks by Palestinian suicide bombers in Israel. These examples are terrorist incidents in a long string of violent, sophisticated, bloody acts. Those who are attacked feel that they are the real victims and have done nothing to deserve the brutality.

Religious and political beliefs lead some terrorists to commit violent acts. Timothy McVeigh and Terry Nichols were charged with bombing the Alfred P. Murrah Federal Building in Oklahoma City, Oklahoma. Research on their backgrounds shows connections to paramilitary, antigovernment militia groups, many of which opposed government intervention in the private lives of Americans. These patriot groups are antigovernment (despite their fanatic pro-Americanism) and white supremacist. Most patriot paramilitary groups consider themselves to be devoutly Christian, and they believe their acts are justified by their religion and their "good intentions." They are scattered throughout the United States as shown in Map 8.4 on page 248. Structural explanations help predict when conditions are right for terrorism. Terrorism and war are unlikely to exist unless there is conflict and strife within and between societal systems. Ahmad learned his attitudes, hatreds, and stereotypes from his family and friends and through the media. These beliefs were reinforced by his leaders, religious beliefs, and schools.

Conflict theory explanations of terrorism lie in the unequal distribution of world resources and the oppression of groups in the social world. Wealthy countries such as Germany, Japan, and the United States control resources and capital and have considerable economic influence and power over peripheral nations. Citizens of poor countries work for multinational corporations, often for very low wages, and the profits are returned to wealthy countries, helping to perpetuate their elite status. The result is that the rich get richer, and the poor get poorer. This inequity results in feelings of alienation, hostilities, and sometimes terrorism against the more powerful country. The attack on the New York City World Trade Center was carried out in part to terrorize and punish the United States.

Reactions to terrorism range from demands for immediate retaliation to frustration with the lack of power and control to fight a "hidden" enemy. People disagree over whether governments should negotiate with the terrorists and try to understand their demands or hold firm by not negotiating or giving in to such coercion. Terrorism, then, is the means by which the powerless can attempt to receive attention to their cause and gain some power in the global system, even if it involves hijackings, bombings, suicides, kidnappings, and political assassinations. The victims of these acts are understandably outraged.

So What ?

The most direct source of power is the political system, with the ability to influence decisions about how society is run. Perhaps that is why it is the first venue for those interested in changing aspects of the society. There is no one right way to organize a political system, for each structure has shortcomings. However, some systems do a better job of distributing power, ensuring accountability, and providing checks on abuses of power.

Democracy comes in many forms and structures. If you want to live in a society where you have a voice, get involved in the political system and stay well informed about the policies that your government is considering or has recently enacted. Healthy political systems need diverse voices and critics—regardless of what party is currently in power—to create vibrant societies that represent the citizens.

There have been many debates about how closely linked the political system should be with health care. We turn to the health care system in the next chapter.

Key Points

What Have We Learned?

- The study of political processes and systems involves penetrating power—in the sense that we try to penetrate the meanings and consequences of power and that power penetrates every aspect of our lives. Power involves ability to realize one's will, despite resistance. (See pp. 422–424.)

- Power penetrates our intimate (micro-level) lives, our (meso-level) organizations and institutions, and our (macro-level) national and global structures and policies. (See p. 424.)

- Leadership facilitates getting things done in any social group. It can be accomplished through raw power (coercion) or through authority (granted by the populace). Different types of leadership invest authority in the person, the position, or both. (See pp. 424–427.)

- Various theories illuminate different aspects of political power and view the nation's policy-making processes very differently—as power-elite dominance or as pluralistic centers of power. (See pp. 427–429.)

- At the micro level, a key issue is each citizen's decision to vote or participate in politics. These decisions are not just individualist choices but are shaped by culture and structures of the society. (See pp. 429–432.)

- At the meso level, the political institution (when it functions well) works to resolve conflicts and to address social needs within the political system. It is also highly interactive with other institutions, especially the economic system, which determines who has the power to plan the future and who has access to resources. Within nations, meso-level policies have major implications for national elections. (See pp. 432–444.)

- At the macro level, nation-states have emerged only in the past four or five centuries as part of modernity. (See pp. 444–449.)

- At the global level, issues of power, access to resources, alienation, and ideology shape economic policies, war, terrorism, and the prospects for lives of peace and prosperity for citizens around the planet. (See pp. 449–456.)

Contributing to Our Social World: What Can We Do?

Local Level: Learn about student government on your campus. Contact a member or officer and arrange to attend a meeting. Consider running for office. There is no better or more convenient way to learn the basic principles of the democratic process. If your campus has a model legislature or Model U.N. program, often administered through the department of political science, learn about it and get involved. Consider arranging a campus visit by a local political candidate or office holder. If this can be done through a sociology club, it would be especially appropriate to have the visitor discuss the political system as a social institution.

At the Organizational or Institutional Level: Many groups influence the political process. Consider working for a nongovernmental organization or volunteering for a political cause such as MADD (Mothers Against Drunk Driving). Consider an internship with a member of your state/provincial legislature or with the governor's office. Although the two major parties in the United States receive nearly all of the votes and media attention, there are several smaller, special-interest parties that are worth learning about. These include The Green Party (www.gp.org), the Libertarians (www.lp.org), and the Socialist Party (www.sp-usa.org). Contact one of these parties and discuss its programs and

strategies with members. Ask, especially, how the party views its role in the larger political system.

At the National and Global Levels: Contact the local office of your congressional representative or senator to explore the possibility of volunteer work in that office. Each representative and senator has a Web site that provides local contact information. Congressional internships are much-sought-after appointments, but a good way to learn about how they are assigned is to begin as a local volunteer. Several agencies of the United Nations use interns. The general contact for relevant information is www.un.org/Depts/OHRM/sds/interns/index.htm. An agency that uses interns with social science backgrounds is the U.N. Development Program. Contact it at www.undp.org/internships.

Visit **www.pineforge.com/ballantine2study** for online activities, sample tests, and other helpful information. Select "Chapter 13: Politics" for chapter-specific activities.

CHAPTER 14

Medicine

An Anatomy of Health and Illness

Health and illness are social matters, influenced by social interactions, affected by complex organizations intended to provide health care, and shaped by social policies at national and global levels. A true anatomy of health and illness involves comprehension of the social parts of medicine.

Think About It . . .

Micro: What does it mean for you to be sick or healthy? Why is this a social state and not solely individual?

Micro: How does health or illness affect the functioning of your local community?

Meso: Which health care systems keep people healthiest?

Macro: Is health care a right for all citizens within a nation or a privilege for those who can afford it?

Macro: What are variations in health care around the world?

Macro: Global Community

Macro: Society

Meso: National Organizations, Institutions, and Ethnic Subcultures

Micro: Local Organizations and Community

Micro: Me (and My Doctor)

Micro: Local health care providers; health influences; religious organizations; community, schools, and the local business world

Meso: State governments regulate health care; economy influences who gets health care; government deals with epidemics and medical research world

Macro: National governments develop policies to support those with serious illnesses; federal governments fund research to cure diseases

Macro: International organizations (e.g., United Nations, Doctors Without Borders) establish programs to help countries and continents with pandemics such as AIDS or cholera

Debbie, a 20-year-old woman in Portland, Oregon, lay in pain, dying from ovarian cancer. She had not eaten or slept in two days and was struggling for air. Her words to the physician were, "Let's get this over with." In this case of medical futility, in which treatment "fails to end total dependence on intensive medical care," the physician relieved her suffering with a syringe of morphine sulfate. She began breathing normally and shortly thereafter died as a result of the physician-assisted suicide. This case and others like it raise great controversy in medical, legal, and religious communities. Oregon is the only state where euthanasia suicide is legal.

Allowing individuals to choose death to relieve the irreversible suffering of an incurable disease and allowing physicians to hasten the death of terminally ill patients are actions accepted by proponents of active euthanasia ("good death"). This involves aiding the dying individual by prescribing or administering a lethal dose of drugs to patients who request it, usually under legally controlled conditions. Most deaths of terminally ill individuals are planned and sometimes hastened by medical interventions (American Psychological Association 2008). In addition, anyone can sign a living will or right-to-die form requesting that no extraordinary efforts be made to help keep one alive when death would naturally occur (passive euthanasia). However, opponents see aiding death as a sin or even as murder.

Those who favor euthanasia argue that (1) physicians should be able to create comfortable environments for death to occur; (2) terminally ill individuals have a right—without interference by the state—to determine how they die and to make the decision to die; (3) legal safeguards are available to prevent abuse of physician-assisted suicide; (4) high rates of self-induced suicide already exist among terminally ill patients; (5) a majority of the public favors legalization of physician-assisted suicides; and (6) extending life with no hope of recovery is costly to families, as well as to the medical care system.

Those opposed to euthanasia argue that (1) physicians are responsible to sustain life and relieve suffering; (2) medical measures are available to relieve pain, so few have to suffer; (3) religious beliefs affirm the sanctity of life, which means supporting life at every turn; (4) terminally ill individuals who request to die are often acting out of depression, or they may feel pressured to accept a facilitated death to save the family's resources; and (5) a terminally ill patient's acceptance of active euthanasia may make suicide a more acceptable option for those people who are depressed, disabled, elderly, or retarded (Weiss and Lonnquist 2008).

Some countries and states have passed laws legalizing and controlling euthanasia. In the Netherlands, doctors can assist patients in dying, but with very strict regulations. In Oregon, a law that has been challenged in the courts requires that two or more doctors must agree that the patient has six or fewer months to live, and the patient must also ask to die at three different times, the last time in writing, before doctors can act on the request. Doctors have to wait 15 days before complying with the patient's wishes (Werth et al. 2002).

The cost of dying differs tremendously, from nothing in many poor Global South countries with no health care for the dying, to an estimated $35,838 for the last six months of life in Manhattan, New York. About 27% of the budget for the U.S. government's Medicare program goes toward the final year of life. In about 12 years, the number of people who are sick, old, and frail will double, and the Medicare system will be under great strain to cover expenses at the current rate due to increased medical costs and increasing numbers of people living longer (Appleby 2006).

Whereas in the past people died from heart attacks and bad infections, today people who are afflicted with these problems can be kept alive. Policy analysts point out that cost for elder care could be reduced and quality of care improved by providing more in-home services to allow people to die at home rather than in an intensive care unit of a hospital. Some medical ethicists raise questions about large expenses for efforts to prolong life of elderly people with heart failure, provide chemotherapy for advanced cancer, or do expensive procedures for complications from diabetes and other chronic ailments. In a public survey of attitudes toward end-of-life issues, 48% of respondents advocated weighing the costs of keeping a person alive as long as possible, versus 40% who argued to keep the person alive as long as possible regardless of cost (Appleby 2006).

Dying is not something that just happens. How we die, where we die, who is with us when we die, and whether

Dr. Kevorkian (left) is accompanied to court in Michigan. He was tried and found guilty of helping people who were in severe pain and who no longer wanted to live to commit suicide.

we have a choice about when to die are decisions bound in cultural values, beliefs, and laws. Death and its various issues are but one aspect of the interrelationship between our physical condition and our social system. This chapter illustrates that events surrounding health, illness, and death are social events governed by rules of the social world. In this chapter, we will consider why health is a social issue, and we will examine theoretical perspectives on health and illness, the status and roles of sick people, modern health care systems, and health care policy issues at the national and global levels.

Why Is Health a Social Issue?

In the West African country of Nigeria, fundamentalist religious leaders in the northern part of the country refused to allow international medical teams to immunize children against polio, and there was an outbreak of this crippling disease that had almost been eradicated elsewhere. The religious leaders had little trust in the motives of Western medical teams. When the epidemic broke out, however, and children began dying, the leadership relented and allowed the immunization programs to take place. This illustration of health at the global level points out how individual decisions have an effect on health of a community and shows the importance of medical organizations and their efforts to control world pandemics such as polio, AIDS, SARS, bird flu, and other illnesses.

Health is a state of physical, mental, and social well-being, or the absence of disease. **Illness**, or lack of health, affects the way we perform our individual responsibilities in the social world. Like any key social issue, effective health care affects individuals and groups at the micro, meso, and macro levels.

Health at the Micro Level

Sociologists are concerned with how our state of health affects our individual ability to carry out social responsibilities. Everyday lives are shaped by our own state of health or illness and that of our loved ones and close associates. If a roommate, significant other, or child is ill, it affects our lives in a number of ways. It alters our schedules, takes time as we deal with the illness, causes us to worry, and costs us in terms of medical care and lost work time. If a parent is dying of cancer or a child has epilepsy, our lives are influenced in profound and disruptive ways.

Communities are responsible for providing adequate health care, sanitation, and clean drinking water to citizens, services that affect the health of citizens. The health of citizens also affects community activities. A serious case of influenza

Other institutions, like schools, interact with health care systems in a variety of ways. The Chinese school toilet facility shown here indicates a different standard of sanitation and health than many of us are accustomed to seeing.

in the public schools may force schools to close for several days, causing repercussions in workplaces throughout the community as parents struggle to deal with child care issues. Thus, health status affects other institutions in the community, from family to schools to the workplace.

Health at the Meso Level

The institution of health care provides for the physical, mental, and social well-being of citizens. This includes prevention, diagnosis, and treatment of illness and regulation of the dispensing of medicine. The health care institution works in conjunction with families, education, religion, politics, and economics. What happens in the system of health care affects every part of the social world, as shown in the example of assisted suicide. The economic well-being of individuals in a society relates to health care access and who can pay. This often determines who lives, who dies, who is healthy, and who is not. Education about health care influences health and life expectancy. Well-educated citizens are more likely to develop health-enhancing lifestyles. Families attempt to prevent illness and care for sick individuals and often have responsibility to care for the ill and ailing. Political systems determine standards for health care and regulate medicinal drugs. Religious organizations establish support systems and health services, sometimes offer faith-healing alternatives to supplement the established medical system, and offer solace in times of illness and death. At the meso level, institutions are interconnected.

Health at the Macro Level

Each society has a vested interest in the health of its citizenry because the general state of health affects the quality of life of the people and the state of the economy. Imagine the society in which citizens had "permission" to be sick frequently. How would that society continue to function? Societies have social policies that influence the way medicine is organized and health services are delivered. Beliefs about who is ill with what kinds of illness and for how long vary by society.

Consider the case of the now-dissolved Soviet Union. After the Soviet victory over Czarist Russia in 1917, the new revolutionary government was faced with an underdeveloped nation that essentially still produced its food with human-powered plows and simple hoes. The task of leading the country out of the 16th century and into the 20th was formidable. It called for a total effort from the nation's workforce. Confronted with a severe shortage of labor, the new government determined that absenteeism at work, regardless of excuse, had to be kept very low. Accordingly, they instituted rules that required workers to obtain a certificate allowing them to be absent from work because of illness (Weiss and Lonnquist 2008). These certificates could be obtained only from government clinics, and each clinic could issue a limited number of permits. In some cases, physicians were actively encouraged to compete with one another to see how few certificates they could issue. Thus, absence due to illness

was controlled, and the human resources needed for rebuilding the nation were augmented.

Global health focuses on several issues, including possible pandemics such as highly contagious diseases, which have become worldwide threats as global travel increases. A pandemic is a disease that is prevalent throughout an entire country and may infect a continent or reach around the world. The global nature of the pandemic of AIDS is illustrated in Map 14.1. To control such diseases requires cooperation across national boundaries by organizations such as the United Nations. For instance, smallpox remained a serious global threat from the Middle Ages until the mid-20th century. The World Health Organization of the United Nations eliminated the disease completely in the 1960s. River Blindness afflicted thousands of West Africans but has been eradicated due to international cooperation. Funding by organizations such as the Bill and Melinda Gates Foundation provides for research, treatment, and eradication of killer diseases such as malaria, AIDS, and tuberculosis. However, the threat of bioterrorism has raised the specter of other diseases such as smallpox and polio reappearing.

Illness may seem like an individual problem, but as shown in the above examples, it is far more than that. It is a national and global issue. This chapter examines health care at each level of analysis, from individual behaviors and decisions, to religious, political, and economic aspects, to the effect of stratification and ethnic status on the quality

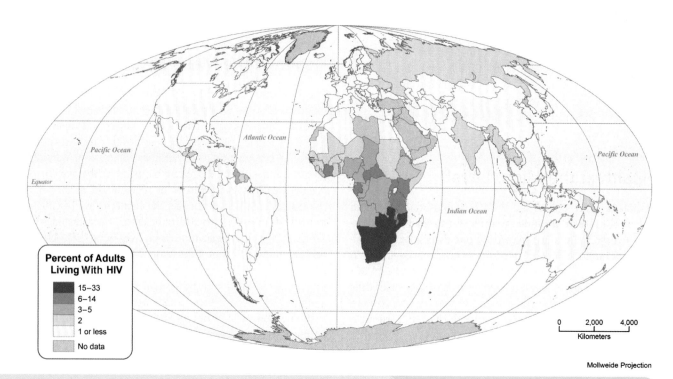

Map 14.1 Estimated Percentage of Adults Living With HIV in 2005

Source: World Health Organization and UNAIDS. Map by Anna Versluis.

of health care one receives. Keep the social world model in mind as you read about health, illness, and medical care.

Thinking Sociologically

Why do pandemic diseases that affect a local community require international solutions?

Theoretical Perspectives on Health and Illness

As in the analysis of each institution, it is important to understand how each of the major paradigms or perspectives in sociology approaches the analysis of medicine and health care. Each offers a lens for seeing or noticing different aspects of health and illness in a given society and within the global system.

Micro-Level Theoretical Perspectives

Unruly school children were once considered ill mannered or ill behaved. Now, they are often labeled as hyperkinetic or having attention deficit disorder (ADD), suffering from conditions that can be controlled by appropriate medication. Heavy gamblers, alcoholics, and drug abusers are now defined as addicts rather than as people lacking self-discipline. How conditions are labeled can result in social stigma of varying degrees (Freund and McGuire 1999) and lead to different policies to treat problems.

The Symbolic Interaction Perspective and Labeling Theory

To symbolic interactionists, illness is whatever powerful individuals in society, such as doctors, define or label it to be. In recent years, the definition of illness has expanded to encompass substance abuse and some forms of deviant behavior, giving physicians even more power and authority over broad areas of social life. Illness used to be viewed as a physical condition—germs, viruses, bacteria—causing the body to malfunction. Through the labeling process, behaviors that were once seen as criminal or "bad" are now defined as illness.

Medicalization and Labeling

Medicalization refers to the shift in handling of some forms of deviance as well as some normal human functions (such as pregnancy and childbirth) from the familial, legal, or religious arenas to the health care system. In some cases, the shift

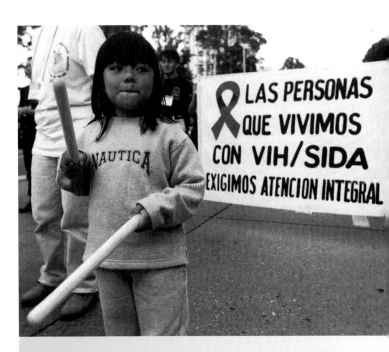

A Guatemalan child infected with the HIV-AIDS virus marches outside an AIDS conference in Guatemala City. Hundreds of people from different countries marched to bring attention to the problems of poor medical assistance and lack of government attention for infected people.

is away from the issue of individual self-control and toward medical diagnosis and treatment. Consider addictive behaviors such as alcoholism and drug abuse. There is considerable debate about how we define alcoholism because this influences the interpretation of the problem, the physician's role in treatment, whether we hold the patient to blame for the problem, and how it will be treated (Cockerham 2007; Keller 1991). Symbolic interactionists emphasize the social definitions or labels such as *alcoholic* or *drug addict* and examine the effect such labels have on the life of the individual. Medical conditions can be treated, and less stigma may be attached to these illnesses if they are not labeled as moral degeneracy (White 2002). On the other hand, labeling the alcoholic as sick creates another type of stigma that may never be erased, and seeing alcoholism as a medical condition takes away individual responsibility, putting control in the hands of the health care system. The next "Sociology in Your Social World" explores the issue of policy toward alcoholism.

Thinking Sociologically

First, read "Sociology in Your Social World" on page 464. Many of us have friends or relatives who consciously or unconsciously struggle with alcohol problems. Do you see that person being labeled by others? What might you do to help the person?

Sociology in Your Social World

Alcoholism, Medicalization, and Policy

Perhaps you know someone who struggles with an alcohol problem. A hotly contested debate in the medical, sociological, and psychological fields is how to define *alcoholism,* for that definition affects everything from treatment procedures to who has responsibility for rehabilitation. Is the alcoholic to be held responsible, or is this a condition beyond the individual's control? The classic disease conception of alcoholism, for instance, was first proposed in the 1930s by two reformed drinkers and given scientific support in the work of E. M. Jellinek (1960). In the aftermath of social and political debates (Acker 1993), key professional groups officially labeled alcoholism a disease.

Through this process, referred to as "the medicalization of alcoholism" (Conrad and Schneider 1992), alcoholism was added to the list of behaviors that were formerly considered morally reprehensible—bad, something sinners did, or a result of weakness—but now considered medical problems over which the individual had little control. The individual became "sick" rather than "bad." Alcoholism was being defined as a medical problem with medical solutions. In fact, many detoxification clinics use medical interventions and drugs to treat alcoholics. The medical definition of alcoholism now includes three dimensions: biophysical, psychological, and social:

> Alcoholism is a primary, chronic disease with genetic, psycho-social, and environmental factors influencing its development and manifestations. The disease is often progressive and fatal. It is characterized by impaired control over drinking, preoccupation with the drug alcohol, use of alcohol despite adverse consequences, and distortions in thinking, mostly denial. Each of these symptoms may be continuous or periodic. (Meyer 1996:163)

The medical view of alcoholism has several implications: Unless there is intervention, alcoholics suffer physical and emotional breakdown and an early death. Schoeman (1991) writes about those who are vulnerable. They are characterized by

1. having a physiological predisposition in the way their bodies process alcohol
2. taking up drinking and thus becoming ill
3. drinking resulting in consumption of ever greater amounts with increasingly severe consequences
4. drinking that results in distinctive disability, including the loss of ability to choose when it comes to alcohol consumption
5. progressing through a predictable sequence of stages, independent of individual characteristics

The label alcoholic *has a number of implications, including the fact that the stigma associated with the term may prevent some people from seeking help. This is one reason many alcohol treatment centers have recast alcoholism as a disease, hoping that the redefinition would remove stigma. Other problems arise when the issue is medicalized.*

Many health care professionals, however, are reluctant to treat alcoholism as a problem drug (Meyer 1996). Some argue that the disease concept is the wrong approach, that what is really at stake is "heavy drinking" as a way of life. Rather than treating a "disease," they feel that professionals should be concerned with approaches that will change the way in which individuals organize their behaviors. These researchers and practitioners argue that heavy drinkers can become nondrinkers or moderate drinkers and can control their drinking. Some critical sociological theorists see medicalization as one more form of social control. By labeling alcoholism as a medical disease, the medical profession becomes an agent of social control for the state (Conrad and Schneider 1992). Changing the alcoholic by altering perceptions, routines, attitudes, and habits of behavior gives the individual responsibility in a context of supportive family or friends, economic opportunities, and alternative role models.

A third possibility exists—that there is truth in both models based on individual differences. Treatment programs can be found based on both of these models, and the debate is still going strong. Recent approaches to alcoholism often combine medical and social-behavioral treatments. Key in approaches to alcoholism is to help alcoholics recognize that they need help.

Some "problems" may not be problems at all. As a result of movements to "demedicalize" various social behaviors, homosexuality has been removed from the American Psychiatric Association's list of mental disorders. Furthermore, social critics argue that once conditions are medicalized, they come to be controlled and exploited by powerful experts. However, some scholars see medicalization of health issues as part of a healthy social system because with stigma removed, the issues can be more effectively addressed.

Having some sense of the issues raised by the symbolic interactionists, we turn now to how the experience of illness or health at the micro level is shaped by forces at the meso and macro levels in our social world.

Meso- and Macro-Level Theoretical Perspectives

The institution of health care in Western culture differs dramatically from that of many other cultures around the world. Consider the conflicting ideas of illness between the Hmong culture in the United States, made up of immigrants from Vietnamese hill tribes, and the medical community. In the book *The Spirit Catches You and You Fall Down*, Anne Fadiman (1997) describes the contrasts between how an immigrant Hmong family views an epileptic child and how the hospital in their U.S. community sees the situation. When the parents take their child for treatment of her epileptic seizures, everything from the concepts of what causes the problem, to the cures, to communication about the disease are problematic. The medical staff treats the epileptic seizures with Western medical techniques, whereas the Hmong family attributes the seizures to spirits (Fadiman 1997). Concepts of health and disease vary greatly in different ethnic groups. Theories and cross-cultural knowledge help to understand this and other cultural differences in approaches to health care.

The Functionalist Perspective

Functional theorists focus primarily on the macro level of the health care system. Studies of suicide, carried out by the early French sociologist Émile Durkheim, illustrate that social conditions and events in the larger society and people's group affiliations affected inclinations to commit suicide. Other studies have linked illnesses such as heart disease, kidney failure, stroke, mental illness, and infant mortality to macro-level processes and trends in societies. For example, economic recessions cause social stress and disruption in lifestyles, which can activate mental problems. These, in turn, can result in health problems.

According to functionalists, social norms define what counts as illness and how to treat it. The purpose of the health care system in society is to maintain the social structure and a harmonious balance between individuals and institutions in society. Illness is potentially disruptive to the balanced social world. The sick role is sometimes considered a deviant one

because it "robs" the so
we saw in the Soviet exa
sick role at the same time, t
society cannot be performed
of the medical profession is
individuals from being unable t

Despite the harmonious
ambivalence does exist in his d
Paul Starr (1982), in his award-w
Transformation of American Medicine, ...physicians
hold power over patients in the docto... ...t relationship,
and patients may have contradictory expectations for their
treatment. We turn to conflict theory for a different perspective on the health care system.

Thinking Sociologically

What duties and responsibilities do you relinquish when you occupy a sick role? Which ones do you continue during your illness?

The Conflict Perspective

Poverty, unemployment, low wages, malnutrition, and a host of other economic conditions affect people's access and ability to compete for health care and medicines in many countries. Differential access is a key theme in conflict theorists' approach to health issues. Consider the case of Nkosi, a four-year-old boy in a rural Ghanaian village. He came down with an infection from the polluted water, causing diarrhea and vomiting. Nkosi was already weakened by malnutrition and parasites, and by the time help came, dehydration was so extensive that he died, one of millions of similar casualties. Why was health care not available?

Nkosi had less access to medical treatment, immunizations, antibiotics, vitamins, and a balanced diet than children in major Global North countries or even in urban areas of the Global South. Children in poor countries around the world suffer from malnutrition and chronic disease before succumbing to pneumonia or other infections, normally curable diseases. The explosion in new "emerging infectious diseases" such as AIDS, Brazilian Purpuric fever, new strains of Ebola, and various insect- and bird-transported diseases such as SARS and bird flu add to the problems faced by health care workers in the Global South (Farmer 1999). In fact, life expectancy (average length of life) is as low as 35 years in some drought-ridden and war-torn countries, such as regions of Sudan where disease has ideal conditions to spread.

In the world system of rich and poor countries, individuals suffer different illnesses depending on the level of development of their society and their position in it. Poor people in

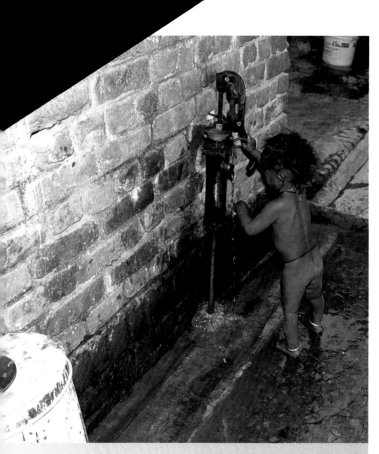

One way to combat diarrhea diseases in Ghana or here in India is through provision of safe drinking water by the government. This is a primary concern of the World Health Organization. However, the World Bank and International Monetary Fund have been pushing for privatization of water, meaning that water is not affordable for many.

government has built clinics called *Mission Barrio Adentro* to serve those living in urban and rural poverty. Before the Chavez government revolutionized the health delivery system, many poor had no access to care. Today, each clinic serves a community for free. In the four-tiered system, Tier 1 provides basic care; Tier 2 has some beds, does small surgeries, and treats asthma and similar illnesses; Tier 3 includes small hospitals that accept referrals from the clinics for medical tests such as MRIs and X-rays; and Tier 4 is a hospital for surgeries and other procedures (Witness for Peace 2008). One result of these changes has been that the infant mortality rate has been cut in half, and life expectancy has risen. Cuba has also developed a system to reach all of its citizens, as explained in the next "Sociology Around the World." However, many poor countries do not have oil or other natural resources to help pay for health care.

At the global level, multinational companies that build plants in the poor Global South provide examples of the profit motive's influence on health conditions. These businesses are looking for large profit margins and cost-cutting opportunities, so they may seek countries where health and safety standards are lower than those in the Global North, which has more stringent health regulations. Although many multinational companies provide health clinics for workers, lower safety standards can lead to long-term illnesses, eye problems, lung disease, and other debilitating health problems. Moreover, multinational pharmaceutical companies have resisted generic drugs or inexpensive vaccines that are crucial to combating disease in the Global South. Poor countries are places to save money in manufacturing labor costs and raw materials but are not places to provide services because people there can afford little, with the result of insignificant profit. A few countries such as India are developing their own cheaper versions of drugs for AIDS and other diseases, bypassing pharmaceutical companies.

A consistent theme in Parsons's (1975) functional model of the sick status is the physician's need for total authority in the relationship in order to meet the health needs of clients. Some conflict theorists argue that physicians seek this power so that they can decide who they will treat. Some physicians prefer not to locate in poor or rural areas or countries, to treat elderly patients, or to spend time on those with AIDS. The most lucrative positions with the most prestige are generally located in major global urban areas and at well-known clinics, treating people who can pay for private care. This leads some conflict theorists to discuss the doctor-patient relationship as an association in which the doctor exercises social control and loyalty of the doctor to the patient depends in part on the social status of the patient (White 2002).

Feminist Theory

For feminist theorists, gender is a key variable that affects health and illness. Feminist theorists argue that the patriarchal control of women carries over to health care systems

poor countries die from ailments that are curable infectious diseases in rich countries. Consider the case of Swaziland in sub-Saharan Africa, a country of 1,032,000 people. Weakened from poor nutrition and hungry because their land has been ravaged by drought, many people in Swaziland die of treatable diseases. However, the real killer is AIDS. About 40% of parents are infected by AIDS. Life expectancy in Swaziland is 38 years for men and 37 years for women and dropping rapidly (World Health Organization 2007). By 2010, it is expected to be 30 years. What little governmental health care system exists cannot cope with the crisis. The numbers of orphans, now at 40 million, is growing rapidly. Forget education. Children are concerned with trying to survive on the little food available and to raise their younger siblings. International aid organizations provide most of the meager food they consume (Senate Democratic Policy Committee Hearing 2004).

At the national level, many governments officially proclaim that health care is a basic right of all citizens, although many do not have the means to meet the health needs of citizens. One country that has revolutionized its health care system under the revolutionary government of Hugo Chavez is Venezuela. With oil revenues and tax dollars, the

Sociology Around the World

Health Care: Cuba's Pride

One thing all Cubans were promised under the Communist regime of Fidel Castro was access to good health care, which he viewed as a basic right of all people. When Cuba had trading partners and support from the former Soviet Union and allied nations in Europe's eastern bloc, its system was considered a model, especially for a Global South country. Now, the country has lost external support due to the collapse of the Soviet system. Cuba has fallen on hard economic times primarily because of the U.S.-imposed embargo on goods going to Cuba, with the health care system being one victim. Shortages of drugs, diagnostic equipment, and medical supplies have forced Cuba's well-trained doctors to be creative. They use herbal remedies, hypnosis, and acupuncture in place of needed supplies and equipment.

The health care system still has an ample supply of doctors (58.2 for every 10,000 inhabitants). Hospitals and clinics are spread throughout the country. Infant mortality and life expectancy rates are comparable to those of developed countries (Pan American Health Organization 2000). However, because of economic hardships and lack of medicine and equipment that could easily control some illnesses and diseases, some experts fear these numbers will begin to slip. Cuba experienced a typhoid fever and tuberculosis outbreak in the early 1990s, even though these diseases were once almost nonexistent in the country. Water contamination in Cuba is increasing. These problems illustrate the interrelationship between health, economic resources, and global links between countries (Golden 1994).

Health statistics have a human face; diary entries of a recent visitor to Cuba tell of the impact economic sanctions have on the health of ordinary citizens:

I visited Dr. Barbara, a young family doctor, in her neighborhood *consultorio* in Havana, Cuba. Her waiting room was full of young mothers holding plump and healthy babies, sitting against a wall covered with a hand-painted wall mural. A portrait of Fidel Castro (Cuba's head of government) hung next to a painted caricature of Mickey Mouse on the wall behind her desk. Her eyes bright, her long

A Ukrainian boy jokes while surrounded by friends at a pediatric hospital near Havana, Cuba. This child is one of thousands Cuba has treated since 1990—free of charge—for loss of hair, skin disorders, cancer, leukemia, and other illnesses attributed to the radioactivity unleashed by the Chernobyl nuclear power plant reactor meltdown in Ukraine in 1986, years before they were born.

hair bouncing against her shoulders, she said she was very proud to be a Cuban physician and to care for a patient community of 200 families.

However, she added with a pause, sometimes she felt helpless to provide the care that her patients needed. She explained that diagnostic tests were often missed or delayed because of shortages of X-ray film or replacement parts for equipment. Blood work was limited by lack of reagents needed in the labs. Her prescription choices were restricted to the medicines available at the time, a situation that she found very frustrating when her patient had multiple medical problems that dictated the use of one medicine rather than another. Prozac and other state-of-the-art antidepressants were unheard of, and only a few drugs for treating depressive and anxiety disorders were available. Many anticancer medicines were difficult or impossible to get. She said that people were dying sooner than necessary because of these scarcities. (Lemkau 2006) and reinforces dependence, submission, and definitions of what is illness for women. Western women are profitable for the health care system because they are seen more often and have more expensive procedures, such as hysterectomies (White 2002). Controlling women's reproductive health and defining women's normal biological experiences as medical problems are strategies rooted in Western society's class interests and in maintaining patriarchal authority. However, in some countries, women are important and respected healers and doctors. Consider one example, Gujarat, India, where women medical practitioners hold significant and autonomous places in the medical establishment, giving women power and a voice in their health care.

Feminist theorists contend that women have been kept in inferior social positions through much of history because powerful members of society said that their bodies limited them (Shorter 1991). This is especially true in Western societies. For instance, drugs to control depression keep women in situations that cause the depression in the first place. Menopause is treated as an illness or is brushed aside. Women, then, are defined in the medical profession by their reproductive life cycle (White 2002). One result is that more women than men are patients because of medicalization of women's normal life cycles.

To regain control of women's health, some feminists have formed health organizations concerned with reproductive health: midwifery, natural childbirth, home deliveries, and menopause (Clarke and Olesen 1999). With increasing numbers of women physicians, attitudes toward women's health and communication practices between women and physicians are changing.

Conflict theorists argue that the institution of health care creates the conditions that contribute to sickness through low employment opportunities, stress, health hazards at work, poor living conditions, and lack of access to medical care. We now consider the sick role and being sick.

Thinking Sociologically

How might each of the theoretical perspectives deal with conditions such as attention deficit disorder (ADD) or addictions such as gambling, sex, or drugs?

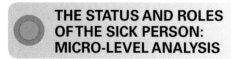

THE STATUS AND ROLES OF THE SICK PERSON: MICRO-LEVEL ANALYSIS

What constitutes illness behavior rests on the signs, symptoms, and circumstances defined by our social group rather than on a set of universally recognized bodily malfunctions. Cultural definitions combined with physical symptoms help us understand illness (Weiss and Lonnquist 2008). A poor Central American woman, asked if she has been sick, illustrates this point by commenting that she wished she knew what it meant to be sick. Sometimes she felt so bad she could curl up and die, but she kept going because the kids needed her, and she didn't have money to spend on a doctor. She didn't have time to be sick. She asks, how does one know when someone is sick? Some of us can go to bed almost any time with anything, but many of the world's people can't be sick, not even when they need to be (Koos 1954).

To this woman, being sick was not just a physical condition or how she felt or any physical symptoms she displayed. From a cultural perspective, she had responsibilities that could not be ignored, little access to health care, and no money to buy medicine or care. So who defines the poor woman above as sick? She herself? Her friends and family? Her employer? A health care professional? What is necessary before we can say, from the sociological point of view, that someone is sick?

Illness, or being sick, is a complex matter resulting from changes in the body. Try comparing illness to an iceberg: We do not see the whole iceberg. Similarly, most illness lies under the surface and may never come to public attention unless it forces the person to alter routines or fail in carrying out responsibilities. Generally, physical disorders can be identified, and a health professional can relieve pain or discomfort and return individuals to a healthy state (Kurtz and Chalfant 1991).

However, for the sociologist, the view of illness as only a physical disorder is too limited. A society's definitions influence who is considered sick and under what conditions. Illness, then, is in part socially constructed. The health establishment, schools, and workplaces acknowledge illness only if certain society-defined conditions are present.

Surveys of health in populations around the world indicate that few people are totally free from some degree of physical disorder. Yet, the presence of such disorders does not mean that individuals will seek treatment or that the illness will be recognized and treated. Both individual (micro) and structural (meso or macro) factors are important in health care decisions and treatment. The political and economic environment, access to the health care system that provides services, and the predisposition by an individual to seek medical care all enter into health care decisions.

Thinking Sociologically

The Central American woman felt like she could "curl up and die," but she survived. Was she sick? Would you be sick if you felt the way she did? Why might your definition of your situation be different from hers?

The Sick Role

Think of all the social relationships, engagements, and responsibilities that are affected when you are sick. You miss class, have to cancel other engagements, avoid your friends so that you do not infect them with your germs, and cannot carry out your usual responsibilities. Most people are sympathetic for a couple of days, but then, they expect you to get back to your usual routines and responsibilities. Let us consider this "role" of being sick.

Those who are ill occupy a special position or status in society—the **sick role** (Parsons 1975). They are deviant in that they are not carrying out their role expectations. Other members must pick up those responsibilities. Unlike other deviance, however, the sick role is not punished but is tolerated as long as the sick individual cooperates and acts to overcome illness, returning as soon as possible to fulfill his or her usual social roles.

In an early contribution to the sociology of health, Parsons (1951a) presented a functional theoretical model of the "sick role," outlining four interrelated behavioral expectations—two rights and two obligations:

Right 1: The sick person has the right to be excused from normal social responsibility as needed to be restored to normal functioning in the society. For example, sick students expect to receive permission to miss class or to make up a missed exam.

Right 2: The sickness is not the individual's fault. The sick person did not mean to deviate from normal social expectations and cannot become well by self-decision or by willing it so.

Obligation 1: The sick person should define being sick as undesirable. To avoid the accusation of laziness or malingering, the sick person must not prolong illness unnecessarily to avoid social obligations.

Obligation 2: Those in the sick status are expected to seek technically competent help and cooperate in getting well. In Western countries, the help is most often a medical doctor.

Parsons (1951a) describes the physicians' roles as complementing the "sick role"—to restore routine behavior and "orderliness" in patients. The models presented by Parsons are clearly related to functionalist thought. They focus on integrating all aspects of medical care into a working social system.

One problem is that some individuals might like being excused from tasks and allowed to deviate from social responsibility (such as taking tests or doing an arduous task). Certainly, being sick can be a less demanding lifestyle than going to work or school or taking care of a family. The sick role can also legitimize failure by providing a ready excuse for poor performance at some task (Cole and

Many people in industrialized societies, especially in the United States, are extremely overweight, a serious health hazard that brings with it many risks. This is a concern to the society as a whole because it means lowered productivity and increased health care costs.

Lejeune 1972). People who believe they are permanently unable to fulfill their normal social roles may be motivated to define themselves as sick. Yet, an excess of sick people could be disruptive to the social fabric, so it is necessary to develop means to control who enters the sick status, as did the Soviet regime, and to guard against misuse of illness as an excuse for avoiding social responsibility.

Individuals make choices about their own health and lifestyles—decisions about leisure time activities; exercise; the amount and type of food they consume; use of alcohol, drugs, and tobacco; and sexual behavior. All of these choices affect health. Any of these taken to extremes can result in illness. Health and lifestyle choices are influenced by socialization patterns, family backgrounds, peers, jobs, and cultural expectations.

Eating patterns are a concern for U.S. public health officials. Both children and adults fall into the couch potato syndrome of a sedentary life as flab accumulates into excess weight, a recipe for certain illnesses. Fast food has become a convenient

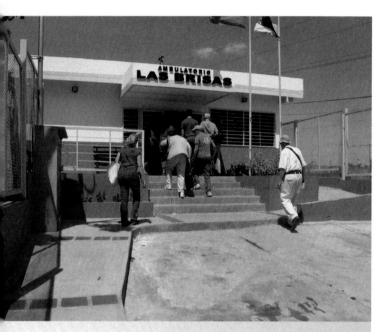

Being sick is more than a physical problem of fever, aches and pains, loss of energy, and other symptoms. Being sick changes relationships, how other people spend their time, and how other people respond to the sick person, including lowered expectations of what that person can do and taking on a new role. The experience of being sick differs across countries. Shown is a health clinic for the poor in Venezuela, where they can obtain free care.

time-saver and a recipe for gaining weight. Health care workers have developed education campaigns to change eating patterns, and schools are removing pop machines from cafeterias. Another concern is the millions of people with negative body images that result in health problems as some men and women abuse their bodies with excessive and unhealthy eating and behavior patterns, such as extreme diets and steroid use.

Thinking Sociologically

Do you feel the problems of eating unhealthy food and becoming obese, depicted in the film *Super Size Me*, are serious ones related to the health of a nation? Should this be an individual problem or a national problem? Do changes in eating patterns need to be made, and if so, what would you recommend to policymakers?

Determining who is sick goes beyond physical symptoms and feelings of discomfort. Symptoms such as distress, anxiety, or perceived seriousness of the symptoms often result in seeking health care. Individuals may postpone health action or not seek health care because of lack of availability and affordability or because they deny the existence of the ailment.

Social Factors in Illness and Health

An American Peace Corps volunteer in a South American village could not understand the resigned attitude of the mother, Mónica, as she held her dying baby. He offered to help Mónica get the baby to the clinic 15 miles away, but she seemed resigned to its death. The expectations that shaped Mónica's behavior were learned in her cultural setting. Three of her seven children had died. In this rural Global South setting, as many as half of the babies born will die in infancy because of illness, poor sanitation, lack of clean water, and lack of health care and medicine. People come to accept infant deaths, often easily preventable, as normal. Many children are not even named until their parents determine that they are likely to live.

Individual beliefs, experiences, and decisions about health and illness may be deeply rooted in meso- and macro-level structural factors that shape availability of medicines and health services as well as factors that shape one's lifestyle and attitudes toward health care. Consider some of the social dimensions that affect our individual health.

Cultural Belief Systems and Health

Western scientific medicine centers on physicians who use medical technology to heal those who are sick and return them to society as contributing members. In non-Western parts of the world, quite different healing approaches are used. In North Africa, for example, members of the Azande tribe believe in a spiritual system of healing centered on the activities of the local shaman. Illness occurs, they believe, when an offended individual arranges for a "sickness pellet" to be placed in the body of the offender. Through spiritual ceremonies, the sorcerer sees that the pellet is withdrawn from the body and restores the person to health.

Some Hispanic cultures practice a unique ancient complex of healing known as *curanderismo*. The origins are found in indigenous herbal medicine, indigenous religious belief systems, witchcraft, and Spanish Catholicism. Good health and a strong body are viewed as God's blessing for the faithful. Illness comes either when one has sinned or as a message from God to help the person learn to be good. The relationship between the curandero, or healer, and the patient is close, relying on psychological and spiritual as well as physical treatment. Many Hispanics combine Western medicine and *curanderismo*. For "non-Hispanic illnesses," the physician is the healer of choice. However, for culture-specific conditions such as *susto* (characterized by extreme fright), the *curandero* may be consulted because many believe that such conditions are impervious to even the highest technology of the scientific physician (Weiss and Lonnquist 2008). The role of the curandero combines elements of psychologist and healer.

Definitions of who is considered mentally ill and who is put away for their own and society's protection vary greatly

Gerardo Queupukura, a renowned shaman of the Mapuche tribe in Chile, attends to the line of patients and looks at the urine samples to determine patients' health status. The medicine man holds consultations twice a week.

across societies (Basaglia 1992). Manuel is a schizophrenic who "goes crazy" when the moon is full (the concept of lunacy) and is put in a Nicaraguan mental hospital during that time. Otherwise, he lives a relatively normal life with his parents. In another culture, he might be put in long-term hospital care or given drugs to control the condition. His mental instability might be given a different definition (Fernando 2002).

Pain is a universal experience, yet how it is perceived, experienced, and reacted to varies by cultural background, ethnic group membership, and socialization experience (Showalter 2002). In a U.S. hospital-based study of reactions to pain, researchers observed that patients' responses fell into two main categories: stoic and emotive. Patients with Jewish and Italian cultural backgrounds responded to pain emotionally, while patients of Yankee background were stoical and tried to bravely endure pain. Those of Irish descent denied pain altogether. Although the Jewish American and Italian American patients exhibited similar reactions to pain, their reasons for these reactions were different. The Jewish American patients took a long-term view toward pain. They were concerned about its meaning for their future, and their reactions did not subside when pain-relieving drugs were

administered. The Italian American patients, on the other hand, were mainly concerned with the pain itself, and drugs both relieved the pain and their complaints (Thomas and Rose 1991; Zborowski 1952).

Other studies have linked expressive, emotive responses to Hispanic, Middle Eastern, and Mediterranean patients, while stoic patients were more often from Northern European and Asian backgrounds (Davidhizar, Shearer, and Giger 1997; Thomas and Rose 1991). Decisions we make and experiences we have are directly related to our socialization, culture, and definition of reality.

Group Factors in Health Care

Individual micro-level variables such as age, gender, ethnicity, economic factors, social status, and urban or rural residence are important in determining patterns of health and illness as well. For example, age affects health in several ways. People age 65 and older need medical intervention and hospitalization more often than any other age group. They also receive more preventative care than other age groups. As the size of the world's senior population has grown, this age cohort has increased as the population most

Figure 14.1 Number of Visits per Year by U.S. Females and Males to Physicians, 1996–2003

Source: National Center for Health Statistics 2007.

using the health care system. In the United States, of those citizens 65 and older, 26.5% had 10 or more visits to the doctor in 2005, 36.7% had 4 to 9 visits, 31% had 1 to 3 visits, and 5.7% had no visits (National Center for Health Statistics 2007). Figure 14.1 shows the number of visits by females and males to physicians between 1997 and 2005.

Gender patterns are clear, too: In Western cultures, women report more health problems than do men. They use more physician services on a regular basis and receive more preventive and reproductive care, take more medications, and are more likely to be hospitalized (Anson 1998; Weiss and Lonnquist 2008). By contrast, men use emergency services more.

Ethnic groups, meso-level groups, impact the micro level through socialization of individuals into health behaviors and experiences. Consider the cases of Hispanic *curanderismo,* the Hmong concepts of illness, and different experiences of pain. Socialization into possible health care options ranges from modern medical practitioners to alternative medical practitioners (from traditional folk healers to modern chiropractors who are not part of the medical establishment), nonmedical professions (e.g., social workers and clergy), lay advisers, and self-care (Pescosolido 1992).

As we saw in Chapter 8, racial privilege and disprivilege are often rooted in discrimination in organizations and are often not a result of individual prejudice. In the United States, African Americans are less likely to have regular health care providers and more likely to use hospital emergency rooms and health clinics than the majority of the population. Health care is less available in inner cities and rural

areas, where there are concentrations of minority residents. Minority women are less likely to receive prenatal care than other women, and the infant mortality gap between whites, African Americans, and other minorities in the United States (i.e., the number of live-born infants who die in their first year) is shown in Table 14.1 (National Center for Health Statistics 2007). The high infant-mortality rate of the United States compared with other affluent countries is due largely to social class differentials between minorities and whites in the United States. African Americans also have higher rates of cancers and shorter survival times than whites at all stages of cancer diagnosis (American Cancer Society 2006; Ries et al. 2000).

Social status affects health because wealthier individuals are more likely to seek professional help early for physical or

Table 14.1 **Infant Deaths per 1,000 Live Births by Race of Mother, 2004**

Race or Ethnic Origin	Number per 1,000
All races	6.8
White	5.7
American Indian	8.4
Asian or Pacific Islander	4.7
Black	13.6
Puerto Rican	7.8

Source: National Center for Health Statistics 2007.

psychological distress, partly because they can afford treatment. However, contact with physicians is highest among the lowest income categories (7.6 doctor visits per year compared to an average of 6 for the entire population) (Weiss and Lonnquist 2008). Lower income citizens' perceptions of necessary health consultation often involve response to crises. The "working poor" who do not qualify for Medicaid but cannot afford private insurance or medical care delay care (Weiss and Lonnquist 2008). About 20% of adults did not receive needed health-related services in the 2007 because they could not afford a physician visit (National Center for Health Statistics:Table 79). Without universal access to health care, income affects health status.

Thinking Sociologically

Why do some people in the world have more access to health care than others? What does this mean for health and productivity of individuals supporting their families and for societies as a whole?

Differences in access to health care relate to meso and macro levels of the social system, discussed in the next sections.

MODERN HEALTH CARE SYSTEMS: MESO-LEVEL ANALYSIS

At one time, health care was largely an issue addressed in homes by families. Today, in wealthy countries, health care has become institutionalized. The bustling hospital, the efficient nurses and nurse's aides, and the technically proficient physicians have replaced home care, visiting doctors, folk remedies, and homes as the setting for births, deaths, and many health issues in between. Much of the treatment of diseases depends on research that is funded by governments or foundations, and health delivery is performed by

organizations that are bureaucratized corporations. This section explores the institution of medicine: organization of health care systems, hospitals as complex organizations, and changes of professional status for physicians.

The Organization of Health Care Systems

Citizens' access to health care depends on several factors: the cultural values concerning the government's role in providing health care, whether health care is seen as a human right for all citizens or a privilege for those who can pay, the amount and source of funding to provide health care, and the type of health care available. Societies around the world struggle with issues of cost, quality and access to care, and medical technology (Gallagher, Stewart, and Stratton 2000). In the Global North, these struggles result from aging populations with more health needs and smaller numbers of citizens in the taxpaying working population to support health care programs. Nations in the Global South struggle with problems that result in high death rates from curable diseases and from epidemics. Nations develop health care philosophies and systems based on population needs and their ability to address them.

Types of National Health Care Systems

The two most common national models for providing health care—socialized medicine and decentralized national health care programs—are based on the philosophy of health care as a human right. Add to that the U.S. fee-for-service plan. Table 14.2 summarizes key aspects of these three most common national models for health care.

Socialized medicine programs provide a government-supported consumer service with equal access to health care for all citizens of a country (Cockerham 2007). The political system controls the organization and financing of health services and owns most facilities, pays providers directly, and allows private care for an extra fee. There are variations in systems. Developed countries that have socialized medicine systems include Canada, Great Britain, Israel, Norway, Sweden, and several other European countries.

Table 14.2 **Types of Health Care Delivery Systems Around the World**			
Role of Government	*Fee-for-Service*	*Socialized Medicine*	*Decentralized National Health*
Regulation	Limited	Direct	Indirect
Payment to providers	Limited	Direct	Indirect
Ownership of facilities	Private and public	Private and public	Private and public
Public access	Not guaranteed	Guaranteed	Guaranteed
Private care	Dominant	Limited	Limited

Source: Cockerham 2007.

High-tech medical equipment is expensive (top photo), but in places like Ghana (bottom photo), physicians must use what little technology they have available.

Countries with decentralized national health programs have many of the same characteristics, but the government's role is different. The government has less direct control over health care systems and acts to regulate the system, not operate it (Cockerham 2007). Countries with decentralized systems include France, Germany, Japan, and

the Netherlands. The United States, unique among Global North countries, has a fee-for-service system, financed by a mix of private and public purchasers.

Most governments in Europe decided to support health care as a human right for all citizens and put these systems into place in the late 1800s and early 1900s. Their motivations were to develop healthier populations, to strengthen their military forces and their economic systems, and to reduce the possibility of revolution by the poor and working classes by providing for basic health care needs. By providing health insurance and protection for the injured or unemployed, financial security in case of illness was increased.

Health care systems in poor countries are often patterned after former colonial systems. However, most countries struggle to provide for basic health care needs, to ensure access to health care for citizens living in rural areas, and to deal with costly diseases such as AIDS. Because of the lack of physicians, especially in rural areas, most countries in the Global South rely on a combination of Western and indigenous medical practices using herbs and other local remedies. Trained midwives deliver babies, and health education workers travel to villages to teach about the spread of diseases such as AIDS, sometimes making condoms available. In Ugandan villages, where a high percentage of the adult working population has been infected with or died from AIDS, social workers visit regularly to be sure orphaned children are eating and sowing crops.

The World Health Organization and other international organizations help provide immunizations and treatment for epidemics but not for ongoing health needs. For example, Kenya, in East Africa, has a rapidly growing population, 85% of which lives in rural areas. Kenya has a socialized health care system based on the British model, with a national health service that employs doctors and owns hospitals. However, these services are available primarily in the largest cities of Nairobi and Mombasa. In fact, 80% to 85% of the health care budget goes to these urban areas. Rural areas are served by only 10% of the doctors in the national health system, and citizens in remote areas rely on folk healers and herbalists for care (Cockerham 2007).

Hospitals as Complex Organizations

Hospitals are places for the care and treatment of the sick and injured, providing centralized medical knowledge and technology for treatment of illnesses and accidents. The Industrial Revolution in Western Europe and the United States caused population shifts to urban areas. These shifts, in turn, precipitated new and threatening environmental and health conditions from crowding and lack of sanitation. Rational, systematic approaches to health care replaced individual folk remedies. In the late 1800s, there was an explosive growth in the number of hospitals, many of which were sponsored by religious organizations. The focus of these early hospitals was on segregating the destitute and terminally ill, who might be contagious and were likely to die. At this time, most hospitals were still small, but improvements in medical knowledge and competency were changing the old system.

The status of the hospital shifted dramatically in the early 1900s due to advances in medical science. Trained staff, sterile conditions, and more advanced techniques and technology changed hospitals from being the last resort of the urban poor and the dying to places of healing for all classes. Small community hospitals were an essential element of town life. As hospital care has become more available, the structure of hospitals also changed.

The post–World War II period produced huge growth in health care facilities and numbers of employees in the health care system. Medicines and vaccines controlled many infectious diseases that had formerly killed and disabled individuals. This period also saw the growth and funding of medical schools and large medical facilities that provided not only patient care but also education and research. Thus began the dominance of the hospital in providing medical care. Today, many hospitals are centers of medical knowledge and technology, housing not only patients and surgical units but laboratories and diagnostic centers, specialty clinics, and rehabilitation centers.

Although medical health systems differ across societies, hospitals exhibit many characteristics similar to other large, bureaucratic organizations: hierarchical structures, rules and regulations, positions (doctors, nurses) based on competency and training, hiring and promotion based on merit, and contracts for work performed. Primary-care physicians and other gatekeepers control client access to hospitals.

Historically, hospitals were designed for the convenience of physicians. However, today two rather independent bureaucracies function within modern large-scale hospital organizations. Physicians dominate the medical operations, while lay administrators operate the everyday functioning.

Health care systems are major employers in most affluent nations. In the United States, for instance, more than four million people are employed in a variety of hospital jobs as nurses, hospital administrators, pharmacists, physical therapists, physician's assistants, and imaging specialists (those who do X-rays). Nurses are the largest group of health care workers: licensed registered nurses (at 2,449,000), licensed practical nurses (at 531,000), and physicians (at 819,000) (U.S. Census Bureau 2005h). About 75% work in hospitals and nursing homes (U.S. Census Bureau 2001a). In the hospital, the nurse manages the patient care team under the authority of the physician, who is the prime decision maker. Under the nurse's authority in this hierarchical structure come increasing numbers of ancillary personnel.

As hospitals and other medical facilities in the United States are increasingly owned and operated by for-profit corporations, the overwhelming power of the professional or medical line is giving way to powerful corporate management—the lay or administrative line. Physicians have become the customers of the hospital, buying space and time to carry out their functions. Sometimes, the physician's orders contradict those of the administrative line, especially with regard to medical decisions versus cost-saving decisions.

Thinking Sociologically

Who controls the medical facilities in your community? Do you see evidence of hospitals' corporate structures being geared to efficiency and profit? What effect, if any, has this had on service and commitment to clients?

Changing Professional Status of Employees in the Health Care System

Special features distinguish the hospital from other large-scale organizations or bureaucracies. The division of labor in the hospital is extensive and more highly specialized than other formal organizations. The hospital has a hierarchical pecking order based on prestige and power, and hospitals depend on the cooperation of highly skilled people whose work must be coordinated. Not only are patterns of authority rigidly followed, but the clothing and symbols peculiar to particular positions are recognizable and, as in the army, serve as status badges. The physicians, at the top of the stratification ladder, exercise the most power and receive the highest financial and prestige rewards. Signs of their superior status include wearing long white coats or not wearing special uniforms at all.

The physician's position is changing in modern societies. Physicians rank among the most respected professionals in most societies. Although trust and prestige seem to decline each year for all professions, physicians continue to command great respect, based on an assumption that they have special esoteric knowledge and humanitarian intent (Starr 1982; Weiss and Lonnquist 2008).

The widespread acceptance of physician authority is relatively recent. Before the 19th century, too little medical knowledge was established, and too few means of practice were successful to command such recognition. Physicians gained status from the discovery that some diseases were caused by bacteria and could be treated with antiseptics, from the introduction of anesthesia, and from the idea that specially trained people could treat illnesses. Coupled with scientific advances and more sophisticated diagnostic tools, these beliefs began to elevate the status of physicians and scientific medicine (Pescosolido and Boyer 2001).

The transformation of physicians to a position of professional recognition in the United States came when some 250 physicians meeting in Philadelphia in May 1847 established the American Medical Association (AMA). This umbrella organization became the means to gain legitimacy and power over health care practice (Cockerham 2007). The predominantly female health care areas such as midwifery and other holistic approaches such as osteopathy, chiropractic medicine, and homeopathy were delegitimized by the powerful new AMA. Only one approach was granted credibility: **allopathy,** the

Photo Essay

Clothing and Status in the Hospital

Note the difference in how each of these people dresses. The outfits they wear are not insignificant, for they distinguish status, authority, and rights to certain prerogatives within the hospital or clinic.

approach involving counter-symptomatic treatment used by the dominant groups of physicians in the West.

Physicians entering practice in the United States today are faced with several major changes. First, health care is now a system shaped by the purchasers of care and the competition for profits where it was once run by doctors who knew their patients and were committed to the Hippocratic oath of healing. Second, there has simultaneously been a decline in the public's trust of physicians, with greater willingness to question them and even outright distrust by some people. Third, an emphasis on specialization and subspecialization has arisen where previously there had been prestige and rewards in primary care (family doctors). Fourth, outpatient care in homes and doctors' offices is once again becoming more common, where the middle part of the 20th century saw an emphasis on hospitalization. Finally, there is a demand by payers (especially insurance companies) for detailed accounts of medical decision making, fixed prepayment rates established by insurers, and less willingness to pay doctors based solely on their decisions about patients' needs (Cockerham 2007).

Deprofessionalization means that the work of physicians is increasingly controlled by nonprofessional outside forces—financial concerns, government regulation, technological changes, new medical administrators, and a more knowledgeable public. Many physicians now work for managed care systems (Hafferty 2000; Waitzkin 2000), so their own autonomy is limited by bureaucrats for whom they work. Moreover, bureaucratization of hospitals and controls by insurance companies on doctors' decisions have reduced the autonomy of physicians to make decisions they think are best for the patient, another element of deprofessionalization.

We have explored issues of health care at the micro level (the role of sick people) and at the meso level (organization of health care and hospitals as complex organizations). We now move to macro-level policy issues at national and global levels.

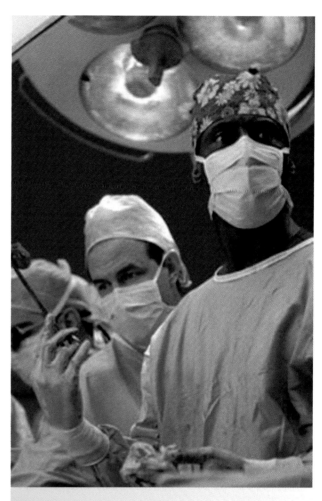

Television shows such as Grey's Anatomy *depict doctors as highly autonomous and respected professionals. Although there is some truth to this, physicians are increasingly working in bureaucratic settings in which the bureaucracy governs many of their decisions, causing deprofessionalization.*

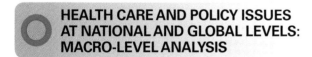

HEALTH CARE AND POLICY ISSUES AT NATIONAL AND GLOBAL LEVELS: MACRO-LEVEL ANALYSIS

Eloise knew something was seriously wrong when she lost her appetite, vomited when she ate more than a few bites, and lost her usually abundant energy. Without health insurance and fearing to lose her job if she missed work to sit in the outpatient waiting room of the hospital to see a doctor, she tried home remedies and hoped the symptoms would go away. When she finally did go to the hospital, she was in serious condition. Eloise spent a few days in intensive care and is now on treatments, but without income from her job, she cannot pay the bills for herself and her child. Similar medical emergencies occur across the United States for more than 46 million people who lack medical insurance (Quinn 2006).

Thinking Sociologically

Doctors have been depicted in many television shows over the past five decades. How might these depictions affect people's expectations of doctors and hospitals? In what ways are TV doctors and nurses different from real-life doctors and nurses?

The Health Care System in the United States

The United States has the best system—and the worst. It is one of the best in the world in terms of quality medical care, trained practitioners, facilities, and advanced medical

How Do We Know?

Historical Content Analysis in Sociology:
The Social Transformation of American Medicine

In this Pulitzer Prize–winning book, Paul Starr (1982) documents and analyzes the development of medicine in America from the 1700s to the 1980s. The research was a massive undertaking. Starr consulted books, journals, historical documents and accounts of medical practice, government reports, public health documents and records of specific diseases, hospital records, medical cost reports, medical school histories and catalogs, information on medical organizations, biographies and autobiographies, and other documents that shed light on the history and development of medicine in the United States. By doing content analysis on each historical period—that is, systematically studying the written materials available about medicine—he pieced together a picture of the themes and trends at different time periods. Starr used many sociological concepts and theories throughout his research to give his analysis depth.

His book represents two long movements: (1) the rise of medical profession sovereignty and (2) the transformation of medicine into an industry with the expansion of corporate influence and state control. Starr examines a number of issues about the institution of medicine. Why, for example, did Americans change from being wary of medicine to being devoted to it? Doctors who were previously deeply divided became united—and prosperous. Why was that? Hospitals, medical schools, clinics, and other medical organizations assumed forms in the United States that were unlike those institutions in other countries, an intriguing difference. In the process, hospitals became the central institutions in medical care while public health became marginalized, unlike other places in the world. Similarly, there is no national health insurance in the United States, and commercial indemnity insurance now dominates the private health insurance market. In an interesting twist, some physicians are now taking part in the creation of corporate health care systems, a new development. Why did they evolve the way they did? Medicine is now a business as well as a cultural phenomenon in the United States, and Starr's investigation helps us understand that reality.

During the early years of U.S. history, the medical profession was not yet established. Many doctors were educated people who had no coursework in the sciences, and hospitals were places where people went to die, not to be healed. With the advent of modern medicine—sanitation and sterilization, understanding of disease, medicines, and vaccines—medicine grew in stature and people turned to doctors and hospitals for their medical needs. Starr documents the changing trends in medicine and ends with a discussion of recent problems with insurance systems and the debates between private insurance, medical systems, and public programs. Concerns today center around privatization of health care, hospital and physician services, insurance, and containment of costs.

By using historical analysis, Starr was able to give both an overview of trends and a detailed account of medicine throughout U.S. history. Only such a long-term perspective could help us to deeply understand many of the issues regarding medical care, the status of physicians, and the institutionalization of medicine.

technology. People from around the world seek training and care in the United States. It is also the worst system: It requires the highest cost per capita in the world to provide care (discussed in more detail later), does not provide equal access to citizens, is inefficient, has competing interests, and is fragmented. Some critics claim that the U.S. health care system is a social problem. It developed without specific direction and responded to demands piecemeal, allowing practitioners, medical facilities, and insurance and drug companies to establish themselves and then protect their self-interests, sometimes at the expense of citizens. In a discussion of the development of the U.S. health care system (see "How Do We Know?" above), Starr uses historical analysis to determine key elements in its transformation.

Health Care Achievements

Medical research into gene therapy, understanding of the human genome, and research into new drug and technological therapies makes research one of the most rapidly advancing medical fields. New therapies will help people live longer, more comfortable, and productive lives—if they can afford the care. As science moves rapidly, ethical questions about use of fetal tissue in experiments and treatments, cloning, prolonging life, and other issues challenge ethicists and lawmakers (Mike 2003).

In addition to advances in medical science, there have been achievements in public health and education that prolong lives: motor vehicle safety, safer workplaces, control

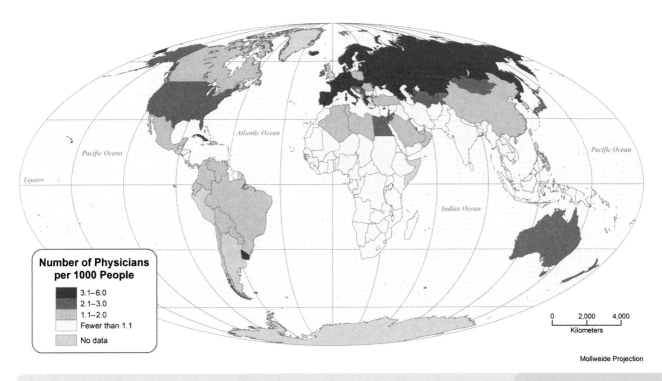

Map 14.2 Number of Physicians per 1,000 People
Source: World Health Organization, most recent data from 2000–2007. Map by Anna Versluis.

of infectious diseases, decline in heart problems, healthier foods, healthier mothers and babies, family planning, clean drinking water, and education of citizens about the dangers of tobacco and other substances as health hazards (Morbidity and Mortality Weekly Report 1999).

Problems in the U.S. Health Care System

The fragmented way in which the U.S. health care system has developed has led to two major problems: lack of universal access to health care and constantly escalating health care costs along with a sizeable uninsured population, resulting in lack of health care security (LeBow 2004; Oberlander 2002).

Access to health care. No matter how advanced technical-medical skills may be, they are of little use to society if they are not available to those who need them. In the United States, services are not necessarily distributed according to the needs of the people (Andersen, Rice, and Kominski 2001).

First, there is a maldistribution of services. The shortage of physicians in rural areas in the United States and many other countries is particularly serious (White 2002), and there is no indication that this will change soon. See Map 14.2 for an illustration of the maldistribution of physicians globally. Some free-enterprise advocates contend that an oversupply of physicians will lead to a trickle-down to rural areas, but data analysis shows that this is not occurring. The expectation that family or primary-care physicians would gravitate to rural areas is not occurring either. The United States has

followed the lead of some other countries, which cover physician education costs in exchange for a commitment to work in poor or rural areas for a set time period. Called the National Health Service Corps (NHSC), this strategy encourages better distribution of health services but also brings less experienced and nonpermanent physicians to poor and rural locations (Gallagher and Johnson 2001; Ginsberg 1999).

Within cities, physicians are concentrated in certain neighborhoods—and outside certain neighborhoods. As a hospital's service area becomes increasingly populated by poorer residents, the facility faces a higher demand for free care. Closure and relocation to more profitable areas are particularly common among for-profit hospitals, and poor minority populations suffer.

Another aspect of maldistribution is the lack of family practice physicians. Many physicians choose to enter one of more than 30 specialty areas in medicine. The reward system of medicine in terms of prestige, income, and lifestyle makes specialty practice more appealing than general medicine. Moreover, most specialists are found in urban areas. The result of lack of access in rural areas and urban poor areas, especially for the poor and uninsured, is less frequent care, fewer regular physician visits and procedures, and a higher chance of serious costly illness and of dying in a hospital once they do get admitted.

Health care cost and funding. Perhaps the most serious problem for health care systems and consumers in the United States, however, is the escalating cost of health care. Since 1947, expenditures for health care (now at 16% of the

Dr. Nilda Soto, director of the Open Door Health Center in Homestead, Florida, walks with a patient along a hallway. The Open Door Health Center is a free health clinic that assists the uninsured poor. Doctors and other medical personnel in the United States who work at facilities that serve the poor often do so with very poor financial compensation for their training. In other countries, governments generally do not expect health care to be provided by altruistic people. Insurance helps pay for medical care in developed countries.

Thinking Sociologically

Develop several hypotheses to explain why health care costs are rising rapidly. How would you test these hypotheses?

The United States is now the only developed country in the world that does not have a national health insurance program providing health care coverage for all citizens. Proposals for universal coverage plans have failed primarily because of philosophical differences between politicians and opposition from private insurance companies, physicians, and drug companies. The medical profession fought against the first proposed government medical insurance programs—Medicare and Medicaid (Marmor 1999). The programs passed mainly because they allowed physicians to retain their autonomy and to control their financial rewards (McKinlay and Marceau 1998). More recent attempts to nationalize health care have failed due in part to lobbying from physician advocates such as the AMA, insurance companies, and drug companies.

Managed health care plans developed quickly to fill the gap after the 1994 national health plan failed to pass in Congress ("Why Comprehensive Health" 1994). About 61% of insured patients are in managed health care plans. Health care companies control costs by limiting visits to specific physicians in their network, requiring referrals for specialists, and demanding preauthorization for hospital stays. Each insured individual is guaranteed care in exchange for a monthly sum paid by the employer and employee.

As health care costs rise, employers are shifting more of the cost to employees by charging higher deductibles, using mail-order and generic prescription programs, and increasing patient co-pays. Workers are now paying an average of $1,400 more in premiums annually than they did in 2000 (National Coalition on Health Care 2008). The problem is that these strategies cannot keep up with the rising costs (Weatherly 2004). These recent developments

gross national product) have increased more rapidly than expenditures for other areas of the economy, and the United States spends twice as much per year on health care as other countries. For example, Switzerland spends 10.9% of the GDP and Canada 9.7% (National Coalition on Health Care 2008). About 30% of health care costs in the United States go to administration. This cost is much lower in other countries (for example, it is 16% in Canada) (Woolhandler, Campbell, and Himmelstein 2004). Table 14.3 shows the increases in costs of health care over time in the United States.

Table 14.3   **National Health Expenditures: United States**

Year	In Billion Dollars	Percentage of Gross Domestic Product	Yearly Amount per Capita (in $)
1960	26.9	5.1	141
1970	73.2	7.1	341
1980	247.2	8.9	1,051
1990	699.5	12.2	2,689
2000	1,309.4	13.3	4,670
2002	1,553.0	14.9	5,440
2007	$2,300.0	16	7,600

Source: Centers for Medical and Medicaid Services 2004; National Coalition on Health Care 2008.

in administration and cost containment have controlled but not reduced costs because of increased demand for care, rising numbers of senior citizens who need more health care, and expensive new technologies.

Managed care tries to integrate two goals—efficiency and high-quality care—with two means—financing and health care delivery (Gold et al. 1998). Evidence indicates that managed health care plans are making profits. Although surveys indicate that 43% of consumers have been satisfied with their health care (Burda 2001; Health Confidence Survey 2001; Vandenburgh 2001), 80% are dissatisfied or very dissatisfied with how much it costs. Almost all other Global North countries have national health care systems that cover all citizens, but citizens pay higher taxes for the coverage. However, the cost structure for administration is much less, saving money overall. Michael Moore's 2007 documentary, *Sicko,* compares the high profitability of the U.S. health care industries to the free universal health care offered at lower overall cost in countries such as Canada, United Kingdom, and France. Table 14.4 shows sources of funding for health care.

Managed care has its critics who argue that for-profit corporations do not belong in the business of health care because health is a human right. Costs of for-profit care are high and rising, leading to demands for a national health plan that would provide universal coverage at less expense, such as the plan the Clinton administration hoped to develop. Meanwhile, the federal government is passing piecemeal legislation to deal with problems.

For clients who cannot pay for health care, options are to use the shrinking numbers of public hospitals, county and state facilities, and free clinics. Paying for health care was the number 1 economic concern of 50% of U.S. citizens (National Coalition on Health Care 2008), and many uninsured

citizens delay health care. Nearly 47 million U.S. citizens are uninsured because of cost or preexisting conditions that cause insurance companies to deny them health insurance. Those who had reduced access to health care because of cost included more women than men, more African Americans than other ethnic groups, those with lower education levels, those below the poverty line, and those between 18 and 44 years of age (National Coalition on Health Care 2008). By the time the uninsured seek help, the situation is often an emergency, costing much more than early intervention. Who pays? Public hospitals rely on tax dollars from you and me to foot the bill for those who do not have insurance or cash. Not only are there more emergencies, but health care for the poor costs more because it has been delayed. Poor people cannot afford the time off from work to get to a public facility for themselves or their children. Each government administration tries to work on the problem, but solutions are difficult with conflicting philosophies of health care. In any case, we end up paying whether we have an official health plan or not

Controversies such as extending health benefits to domestic partners—unmarried cohabiting heterosexual and homosexual couples—have further clouded the issues of insurance coverage. However, some city and state government employees do receive partner benefits. New York City granted benefits to its employees' domestic partners, but in 1999, Pennsylvania voted to deny such benefits to homosexual partners.

Thinking Sociologically

What are the benefits of the U.S. managed health care systems? What are the benefits of national health care systems? What are the problems with each? What is your solution to the health care problems faced by the United States?

Lack of health care security. The biggest criticism of the U.S. system is that 47 million Americans, including 11.2% of U.S. children and 18.9% of children in poverty, remain uninsured (National Coalition on Health Care 2008; Quinn 2006; U.S. Census Bureau 2005g). This figure was up from 45 million people in 2003. About 15.7% of citizens had no insurance coverage in 2004, compared to 13.6% in 2001, and the numbers of uninsured keep rising (U.S. Census Bureau 2005g). Even those who rely on Medicaid (45 million) and Medicare are likely to see reductions in benefits in insurance coverage. Of the poor people with no insurance, a disproportionate number are unmarried women, often with children, or members of ethnic groups (Mills 2001). During recessions, the number of uninsured grows. Even in the best of times,

Table 14.4	**Sources of Payment for Health Services, 2007 (in billions of dollars)**
National health expenditures	$2.3 trillion dollars
Annual percentage change	6.9 percent higher
Percentage of gross domestic product	16 percent
Private expenditures	$913.2 (about 54.1%) (2004)
Private insurance	$600.6 (35.4%)
Out-of-pocket	$230.5 (13.7%)
Other	$61.5 (5.0%)
Paid by the government	$765.7 (about 45.9%) (2004)
Medicare	$283.1

Source: U.S. Census Bureau 2006e: Table 119; National Coalition on Health Care 2008.

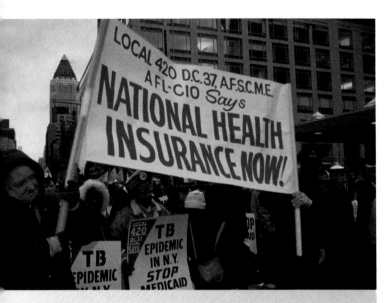

Union members and health care workers demonstrate for national health care and Medicaid. This demonstration in New York City was stimulated by federal cuts in Medicaid that left many people without health care.

limits (National Center for Health Statistics 2002a). Whatever the medical profession charged was what the government paid. Since the original legislation, Congress has had some success in regulating and limiting charges and the length of hospital stays, but "creative billing" has thwarted government attempts to control the costs of the services. Thus, efforts to reform the system and control costs continue.

Lack of universal access and escalating costs are adversely affecting the quality of care offered to some citizens. For example, many uninsured clients such as Eloise, the woman discussed at the beginning of this section, defer care due to unaffordable fees. This compounds their health risks, increasing the likelihood of more expensive emergencies later. Financial considerations may also affect the type of services offered to clients. Socioeconomic status influences the decision to perform some surgical procedures, such as Caesarian deliveries.

When government money is supporting health care programs, evaluation is required to be sure that dollars are being spent effectively. "The Applied Sociologist at Work" describes the role sociologists can play in this process.

Policy Issues and Social Reforms in the U.S. System

We return to this question: Is medical care a right or a privilege? Some argue it is a human right that cannot be bought and sold to the highest bidder or richest segments of society. Others argue that it is a privilege, a commodity to be purchased in a free market and that competition will both improve quality and reduce costs. The human rights argument provides the model for most of the Global North, whereas the market-driven system is the main model in the United States for all but the elderly and poor, who qualify for some government insurance (Harrington and Estes 2004).

Current proposals for reform of the U.S. health care system take several forms:

1. Revise the partly public, partly private system with a mix of governmental and private insurers. This model would be the simplest reform because it is most compatible with the current system.

roughly 6% of people applying for coverage are refused, and roughly an equal number are charged significantly higher rates if they have preexisting medical conditions. Insurance companies can deny medical claims to reduce their costs if they deem a procedure unnecessary (Levinson 1993).

Barriers to health care and lack of health insurance keep many from using services, even with the payments of Medicare and Medicaid. Table 14.5 shows the differences and disparities in health insurance coverage between groups in the United States. Note the numbers of uninsured, lowest for white citizens at 12.5%, and the number of privately insured, highest for whites at 79.3%. All of this has resulted in a call for universal health coverage, a major issue in the 2008 presidential election.

Medicare and Medicaid—services for the growing percentage of citizens 65 and older (estimated to be one in five by 2050) and for the poor—were legislated without cost

Insurance Type	Total U.S.	White Non-Hisp.	Black Non-Hisp.	Mexican	Puerto Rican American	Cuban American
Private	71.7%	79.3%	57.0%	46.6%	52.6%	63.6%
Medicaid	9.4	6.3	19.3	12.5	27.6	9.7
Other Public	2.1	1.9	3.7	1.0	3.4	1.5
Uninsured	16.8	12.5	20.0	39.9	16.4	25.2

Table 14.5   **Health Insurance Coverage for Persons Under Age 65, Hispanic Origin and Race, U.S. 2000**

Source: National Center for Health Statistics 2002a.

The Applied Sociologist at Work— Harry Perlstadt

Evaluating and Improving Health Services

When organizations or communities receive money from government or foundations for health care projects, some form of accountability is required. Grant recipients must show that they have used the money effectively and for the intended purpose. Thus, grant applications have checks for evaluating the project. This is where Dr. Harry Perlstadt comes in. As a faculty member affiliated with the Michigan State University Institute for Public Policy and Social Research, he has conducted many evaluation studies, mostly in the area of medical sociology. Below are three examples of Dr. Perlstadt's research.

- The Kellogg Foundation gives grants to local health projects, and Professor Perlstadt has helped to keep these projects on track. For instance, in the Comprehensive Community Health Models of the Michigan project, three communities were given funds to increase access to health insurance. Perlstadt met biweekly to advise those involved in carrying out the project. He looked at each of the three sites independently and at the overall project, working with a local director at each site. In many cases, coordinating between grantors (Kellogg Foundation), project directors at each site, and evaluators required careful balancing as each participant in the project had different goals.
- The federal Centers for Disease Control and the Michigan Department of Community Health asked Perlstadt and fellow sociologists Stan Kaplowitz and Lori Post to develop a better method to tell health care providers whether or not to screen young children for elevated blood lead levels. At the time, five standard questions were used in diagnosis, but these questions did not provide the right data to allow physicians to predict the child's need for the test. The researchers first developed an extensive survey that was given to parents at the time that blood was drawn from their child. It turned out that having the street address enabled the researchers to draw on census data on housing conditions and neighborhood poverty levels that was more accurate than what the parents were reporting. The researchers then developed a Web site where health providers could type in the street address and answer a few questions about ethnicity, income, and insurance. The Web site quickly reported the probability of the child having elevated blood lead levels, which was an excellent assessment tool for the physicians to be able to test the at-risk children.
- The World Health Organization has organized ministerial (Cabinet-level) conferences to develop programs to improve environmental health in European countries. The World Health Organization hired Perlstadt as an adviser to assess the work of the conference planning committee. Perlstadt worked with a small group to develop a pilot study and then conduct a survey of people who had served or worked with the conference planning committee. The instruments contained both quantitative items and many opportunities for respondents to write in their opinions and suggestions. Perlstadt analyzed the data using a computer statistical program and in his reports illustrated the numerical findings with quotes from the written comments. The quantitative data made his findings applicable to a broad range of situations, but the qualitative reports from respondents gave a human dimension and made the report more convincing.

In his work, Perlstadt uses multiple research tools and draws on extensive knowledge and experience about medical sociology. He travels frequently to meet with involved parties to solve perplexing issues. Each project has its challenges; Perlstadt points out that that is part of the fun—learning new information on each new project and looking at the evaluation as a puzzle to be solved. His job is rather like being a detective discovering information to solve problems.

Note: Dr. Harry Perlstadt received his doctorate in sociology from the University of Chicago and his master's in public health from the University of Michigan. He directs the Program in Bioethics, Humanities, and Society at Michigan State University.

2. Vote in reforms one at a time. This is currently happening.

3. Pass a comprehensive reform package that would provide national health insurance and government oversight and administration. Some states have passed programs to provide access and contain costs for their residents.

Thinking Sociologically

What are the advantages and disadvantages of each proposal mentioned? What effect would each proposal have on different groups of people in a society?

A significant problem for state and federal governments and for individuals is the high cost of drug prescriptions. The pharmaceutical industry does not cap costs in the United States as it does in many other countries, as required by governments, partly due to what they argue are research costs connected with developing new drugs. For this reason also, only brand-label drugs can be sold in the United States for a certain period before similar but cheaper generic drugs can be sold. Many individuals and even states have turned to Canada and other countries for cheaper drugs to control costs. However, the U.S. administration opposes purchases outside of the United States, pointing out possible problems with quality control.

Social scientists say that three factors must be present for a major social initiative such as universal health insurance to pass the U.S. Congress: common understanding of the problem, general agreement on the approach to solving the problem, and positive political ramifications for legislators taking a position on the problem. The last major attempt to pass a comprehensive reform plan in the United States during the Clinton presidency failed in 1994 (Oberlander 2002). Although there was agreement on the problem, the policy issues—how to approach and solve the problem—never coalesced. Thus, the crisis in U.S. health care continues, and there are likely to be continuing efforts to reform the system. Many reformers look to Canada's system as a possible model. (See "Sociology Around the World.")

Experts in health care predict that several trends will affect the future direction of U.S. health care (Coile 2002; Weber 2003):

1. Response to the threat of bioterrorism means hospitals must be prepared to be first responders in emergency, and public health officials and the Centers for Disease Control have taken on new importance with the national threats from terrorism.

2. Hospitals are growing to meet increased demand for services, advertising their services, and changing their images to please clients.

3. Use of computer technology for record keeping and medical tests is growing.

4. Medical advances are changing the way physicians and hospitals treat clients. For example, gene testing and therapy, stem-cell therapy, and individualized drugs are imminent.

5. Employers are fighting the rapid increases in health care insurance costs. Many are dropping managed health programs and shifting more cost for health care to employees.

6. Growing numbers of citizens without health insurance and reformers are reviving debates about national health insurance. Several organizations have plans ready to present to Congress (Physicians' Working Group 2003).

Although it is difficult to predict whether change will mean dramatic restructuring or tinkering with the current system, change is inevitable. The health care system of the United States faces three main challenges: (1) what to do about the rising uninsured population; (2) how to control costs, especially in a managed care system; and (3) what the physician-client relationship will be under new structures of health care (Pescosolido and Boyer 2001). The next section looks at change in health care at the global level of the social world.

Thinking Sociologically

Do profit motive and competition create higher quality in a service field such as health care, as they seem to in production of products? Why or why not? What are some positive and some negative consequences of a competitive system with the "winners" rewarded by higher profits?

Health Care Around the Globe

During a year-long sabbatical in England, the Ballantine family was signed up with a local surgeon, as the British call family physicians. Their sore throats, upset tummies, and bruised feet were taken to the doctor at no direct cost. The school referred their daughter to the hospital eye clinic for glasses at no cost. Their son was diagnosed and treated for "glandular fever" (mononucleosis), again at no cost. In Great Britain, all citizens have access to treatment by family physicians and dentists, to the dispensing of prescribed drugs, to eye care, and to community nursing and health visitor services. Universal health care is covered by taxes.

The demographic makeup, value systems, and financial status of each country will have an effect on how health care is delivered. Global North societies, with a high proportion of elderly and a low proportion of young people, have very different needs from Global South societies with many dependent children. In societies with many elders, special care for chronic illness is more necessary, whereas societies with many children must deal with childhood illnesses.

Each society organizes its health care system in ways congruous with its culture. Although societies have developed different ways of dealing with illness, Western scientific medicine is spreading throughout the world. Yet, ideas about health and medicine are moving in more than one direction. Some of the ideas from other parts of the world are now influencing Western approaches to health and illness, as the following example from China illustrates. China mixes traditional with Western medicine.

Sociology Around the World

Comparing Health Care Systems: The Canadian Model

Two principles underlie Canada's system: All Canadians should have the right to health care, and financial barriers to care should be eliminated. After World War II, the Canadian government established universal health insurance to improve the health of all Canadians, with costs shared 50–50 by federal and provincial governments. Rather than a government salary, physicians are paid by the national health insurance in a fee-for-service or per-patient-fee plan. The plan has led to improved productivity and prosperity (Bolaria and Dickinson 2001).

As a publicly funded insurance plan in a privately controlled system, physicians are not government employees. They maintain autonomy, are well-paid, and have high prestige, in contrast to doctors in other nations' socialized health care systems. The government, in consultation with the medical professionals, sets prices for services. This plan contains costs by determining the level of reimbursement for services, controlling the number of physicians entering medical schools, and limiting private insurance to supplemental plans for vision, dental, and drug coverage.

Comparing major health indicators in Canada and the United States, Canada has lower infant mortality (4.6 deaths per 1,000 live births in Canada versus 6.4 in the United States) and higher life expectancy (80.3 years in Canada versus 78.0 years in the United States) (United North America 2008). Canada pays for the system with taxes that are 10% to 15% higher than the United States, but at .33% less cost per capita for health care than the United States. Canada spent 10.6% of its GDP in 2007 on health expenditures, while the United States commits 16.1% of its GDP (Canadian Institute for Health Information 2007; National Coalition on Health Care 2008). Comparing Canada and the United States with 16 developed countries, the United States spent the most per capita ($5,635 in 2003). Norway, Switzerland, and Canada follow with $3,807 to $3,001 per capita (Canadian Institute for Health Information 2007). The Canadian system is the one most often mentioned as a model for a future U.S. system (Cockerham 2007).

Problems of care denied because of lack of insurance, discrimination, and geographic maldistribution—major issues in the U.S. system—have been largely solved. In a comparison of access in the U.S. and Canadian systems, 13% of Americans are unable to get needed

An intensive care nurse checks the monitors for a patient at Lion's Gate Hospital in Vancouver, Canada. In Canada, medical care is guaranteed by citizenship.

care, many for financial reasons. In Canada, 3.7% cannot get care, almost none for financial reasons.

In addition, controls by corporations result in hospital stays in the United States that are 20% to 40% shorter than in most other countries for similar procedures. Some attribute this to the profit motive, which undermines attention to services and to client needs as foremost. Yet, in Canada, waiting periods for nonessential procedures are longer, and tests such as MRIs are given less often.

Fewer people in the United States report being satisfied with their health system than in Canada. A comparison of public opinion regarding the health care systems resulted in the following: Because the Canadian system has many positive qualities, why have Americans not adopted it? A proposal for a similar system has been put before Congress, but controversy continues. Concern among conservatives in the United States about government control—combined with lobbying by physicians, insurance companies, and drug companies—has helped to keep the U.S. system in private hands. Other concerns raised about the Canadian system have to do with access to some types of care, waiting periods for nonessential surgeries, and rationing of care for some procedures (Cockerham 2007; Schiff, Bindman, and Brennan 1994). No system is perfect, including the Canadian one. The issue of how to provide better and affordable care to citizenry is shaping key political debates and was a central issue in the 2008 U.S. presidential election.

This acupuncturist is inserting needles on the back of his patient. This is an ancient and highly respected medical technique in China, and it has gained adherents in the United States and other Western countries.

The People's Republic of China: Medicine in a Communist State

Jeanne, one of the coauthors, met Xi (pronounced "She") on a train in China. He was returning to his village after completing a medical training course that covered first aid treatment, immunizations, and recognition of serious symptoms. He is one of more than 1.8 million barefoot doctors or *countryside doctors,* paramedics trained in basic medicine who provide health care for rural residents in China's villages.

Barefoot doctors are generally local peasants selected by fellow members of their agricultural communes. They continue to work on the farm but, after some training, take responsibility for preventive medicine and some aspects of primary care in the local neighborhood. Their income is determined in the same manner as other agricultural workers. The barefoot doctor is the only medical practitioner that many of the 800 million people living in rural China ever see. From a sociological perspective, a strength of these practitioners is their within-culture socialization. Given the homogeneity of peasant neighborhoods, the barefoot doctor should have little difficulty understanding the local culture.

Little was known outside China about its health care system until the 1970s, when Western visitors, including health observers, were welcomed by the government. When the "bamboo curtain" was raised in 1971, the outside world learned that, against a background of poverty, a primary network of health services had been established. However, health care delivery faced major problems because the country was so large and the population so spread out and rural. In addition, the political leaders were determined to bring industrialization and a modern lifestyle to the country in a very short time. This put severe pressures on all of China's institutions, including the health care system.

Western-style medicine expanded rapidly in China. From 1978 to 1980, the number of traditional Chinese medical personnel increased slightly, but the number of higher level medical personnel increased significantly. Today, clinics for preventive care, birth control, and first aid are scattered throughout rural areas, and the very sick go to regional hospitals. Although the number of barefoot doctors has declined, there seems to be no government plan to eliminate these practitioners. On the contrary, the government is attempting to upgrade their training with formal educational programs such as the one Xi attended. Participants are tested and licensed under close supervision by local departments of public health. Today, these practitioners take formal training for a minimum of six months. Many have taken courses in specific areas of Western medicine, such as minor surgery, as well as Chinese practices. So although Western medicine is not supplanting the old system, it is being integrated into traditional medicine. Doctors are trained in both. Doctors known as "worker doctors" function in similar capacities in urban factories.

Chinese medical practices are also influencing medicine around the world. Consider the example of acupuncture, an ancient Chinese method for treating certain physical problems and relieving pain. It is part of a healing system that understands health and the human body in relation to nature. The body seeks a balance between itself and the world around it; when imbalance occurs, disease results. Thus, the goal of Chinese medicine is to restore internal balance to the body.

Acupuncture, along with related treatments, is based on the idea that the body has certain points that ease and control pain and stimulate body functions. The process of inserting fine sharp needles into selected points (there are 700 possible points) related to affected organs in the body is essentially painless, and doctors have even done operations without chemical anesthesia using acupuncture to block pain. The procedures are widely practiced in Asia and are gaining popularity in many Western countries.

Although acupuncture has been practiced for more than 5,000 years in China, only in the 1970s, when relations with China improved, did this treatment become known and practiced in the West. Many Western doctors reject the practice as unscientific and ineffective, and some regulating agencies have put limits on its practice. However, many patients feel otherwise. An increasing number of acupuncture pain clinics are opening around the world, and about 8.2 million U.S. adults have used acupuncture (Barnes et al. 2004). Some insurance companies also cover the costs of acupuncture, and the World Health Organization recognizes more than 40 conditions that can be effectively treated by acupuncture (Weiss and Lonnquist 2008). In Australia, 15% of general practitioners offer acupuncture (Lupton

These two women are of similar age, both in their thirties. Health facilities make an enormous difference in one's life chances, health, and how one ages. The woman on the left lives in North America; the woman on the right raises a family in Senegal, West Africa.

2001). Thus, we see that diffusion of medical knowledge throughout the world brings new practices to all countries.

The Chinese health care system does face problems. In rural areas, many people practice traditional folk medicine. Disease, poor sanitation, pollution, ignorance, and smoking result in lowered life expectancy. Chinese account for about 30% of the world's tobacco consumption, with 300 million smokers. About 70% of China's male population smokes. Smoking-related deaths are increasing, with lung cancer deaths increasing 4.5% a year (Lin et al. 1998). Government efforts to control smoking have been uneven because the government receives money from foreign tobacco sales.

Today, China's health care system is financed by the government, patient fees, and health insurance. Health care expenditures amount to 4.7% of the gross domestic product (World Health Organization 2007). Although only 155 million of 1.2 billion people are covered by health insurance, with the increasingly comprehensive health care network, China has brought down the death rate. Average life expectancy is now 70.9 years (compared to Japan at more than 80 years), whereas just after the Chinese Cultural Revolution in 1955, it was 40.8 years (U.S. Census Bureau 2006b). Most significant for the rest of the world is the impact Chinese traditional medical techniques and remedies are having around the world.

Health care systems around the world illustrate the impact of national and global political and economic factors on the health care available to citizens. The political systems of countries and their economic status influence the philosophy toward health care and the money they have to put into health care. International policies such as embargoes between countries influence availability of health care *within* countries. International organizations, such as the World Health Organization, focus on epidemics and pandemics throughout the world.

Globalization of Medical Problems

A dramatic worldwide health problem illustrating the interconnectedness between countries is the international sale of body parts. In some countries, people at the bottom of the stratification system are so desperately poor that they sell their body parts to help their families survive. For example, mothers and fathers in some poor slums of Mumbai and other cities in India sell their kidneys for money to pay for housing, food, education for their children, and dowries to marry off daughters. In the process, their health often deteriorates, and when the money is gone, life is even more difficult. Although laws were passed in India in 1994 banning the sale of human organs, few violators are caught and punished (Kumar 2001).

Wealthy individuals in need of kidneys buy these body parts to improve their chances of survival and a normal life. For example, the transplant trade attracts medical tourists from Europe, who visit impoverished countries in Latin America and Asia for transplants and other "cheap" treatments. This is a dramatic illustration of world stratification of health care, effects of government policies, the differences in health attitudes, and behavior between rich and poor.

The black market in body parts is spreading to many countries. For example, an international "transplant Mafia" (based in Moldova, which was once part of the Soviet Union) smuggles live donors to the United States to sell their lungs and kidneys because the market for body parts exceeds the supply (Kates 2002). Even officials in coroners' offices have been apprehended harvesting body parts without consent of family members, often making a profit from the sales (Mashberg 2002). Reports from Nigeria indicate that mortuary and cemetery workers are selling body parts at markets (Ananova 2001), and a survey of students in the United Kingdom found that one in four would sell a kidney to help pay for their education (Ananova 2002). This issue emphasizes the global differences between rich and poor people and countries. Where there is a need and a market for goods, those in need will step in to fill the gap, and many sick individuals will pay handsomely for body parts.

The status of a nation's health and medical care are often measured by key international markers—decrease in infant mortality and increase in life expectancy. **Infant mortality** refers to the number of deaths within the first year of life divided by the number of live births in the same year times 1,000. The rate for each country is a good indicator of the availability of and access to prenatal care and care for infants. **Life expectancy** refers to the average number of years people live in a particular society. It shows the overall health conditions in a country. These basic data tell us a great deal about the health and health care of a nation. Consider the health statistics in Tables 14.6 and 14.7.

Table 14.6 **Infant Mortality Rates in 2006 in Countries With 5+ Million Persons**

Number of Deaths Under 1 Year per 1,000 Live Births

Lowest		Highest	
Sweden	2.8	Angola	185.4
Japan	3.2	Sierra Leone	160.4
Finland	3.6	Afghanistan	160.2
Czech Republic	3.9	Mozambique	129.2
Germany	4.1	Niger	118.3
France	4.2	Somalia	114.9
Switzerland	4.3	Mali	107.6
Spain	4.4	Tajikistan	106.5
Denmark	4.5	Tanzania	96.5
Austria	4.6	Malawi	94.4
United States	6.6 (21st)		

Source: U.S. Census Bureau 2006b.

Table 14.7 **Life Expectancy in the Year 2006 in Countries With 5+ Million Persons**

Highest		Lowest	
Japan	81.3	Angola	37.5
Australia	80.5	Mozambique	39.8
Switzerland	80.5	Zambia	40.0
Sweden	80.5	Zimbabwe	40.4
Canada	80.2	Malawi	41.7
Italy	79.8	Niger	43.8
France	79.7	Rwanda	47.3
Spain	79.7	Cote d'Ivoirie	48.8
Israel	79.5	Ethiopia	49.0
Greece	79.2	Uganda	52.7
United States	77.9		

Source: U.S. Census Bureau 2006b.

Thinking Sociologically

First examine Tables 14.6 and 14.7. Select several countries with the highest and lowest infant mortality and life expectancy. What do the figures tell you? That is, what might one conclude about health care or quality of life from these figures?

Globalization and the Mobility of Disease

In December 2007, a man boarded an international flight bound for the United States. The passengers and crew did not know that he was carrying a deadly strain of tuberculosis, one that is very difficult to treat with current medicines. The Centers for Disease Control knew he carried the strain, tracked him down, and brought him in for testing. They needed to know if he was contagious. If so, they would need to contact all people on the flight and start preventative measures to reduce the possibility of a pandemic. The media picked up this story, and it blanketed the front pages of newspapers for several days, showing the concern about uncontrollable diseases spreading around the globe.

When the West Nile virus—a deadly mosquito-borne disease—was first discovered in New York City in 1999, it killed seven people before any action could be taken. Within a year, it had spread to 12 states, and within two years, it was found in not only in mosquitoes but in 60 species of birds and a dozen different types of mammals (Wilson 2006). Although health officials acted rapidly to stem the spread of this disease, other pandemics are a constant threat. The world is highly connected, and diseases anywhere in the world can quickly spread to other continents, overpowering the medical communities' ability to diagnose, isolate, and treat diseases. Because both people and infection are highly mobile today, the problem is global.

Global change and interconnectedness facilitate the spread of diseases and require countries and world organizations working together to attack health problems. The density and mobility of the world's population (discussed in Chapter 15) affects human health. For example, use of land and space determines the number of rodents and insects, the water supplies, and the direct contact people have with one another. Currently, about half of the world's people live in urban areas, many in slums surrounding major cities. Problems such as open sewers, inadequate sanitation, lack of electricity, and polluted water pervade these slums. Most infections spread more readily where there is a population of at least 150,000, although more than one million is even more favorable for infectious germs by increasing the chances that the germs will find hosts that are not already immune (Wilson 2006). Our globe has increasing numbers of cities that exceed one million people.

Other factors that help the spread of disease are the growing numbers of settings with shared circulated air (airplanes, domed stadiums, air-conditioned office buildings and hotels). In addition, most diseases travel by direct contact with other infected people. A World Health Organization study indicates that of the infections leading to death, 65% are due to person-to-person contact. Another 22% come from food, water, or soil contamination; 13% are transmitted by insects; and just 0.3% are acquired directly from animals (bird flu, rabies, etc.) (Wilson 2006). Because people are moving around the globe for business and tourism much more today than in the past, they are exposed to more people in more environments. More than 5,000 airports now host international travelers, and more than one million people cross international borders each day, counting only commercial airline travel (Wilson 2006).

Examples of contagious diseases spread by world travelers include SARS, bird flu, tuberculosis, and HIV/AIDS. In 2005, the HIV/AIDS pandemic took the lives of two million people in sub-Saharan Africa alone, and an additional 2.7 million people in the region became infected with HIV (UNAIDS-Joint United Nations Programme on HIV/AIDS 2006). In South Africa, the HIV-infected population grew to 18.8% of the total population in 2007, with 5.5 million people infected. In 2005, 320,000 people died of AIDS, and there are an estimated 1,200,000 AIDS orphans (Centers for Disease Control 2007).

AIDS is spread in part due to local traditions. In sub-Saharan Africa, where AIDS is rampant and some villages have only children and elderly people remaining, cultural practices have men traveling from their rural villages to urban areas for work, where they are infected with AIDS by prostitutes. When they return, they infect their wives. A major problem is the lack of resources for medications.

When the South African government passed a law that would make life-saving HIV/AID medicines available to the

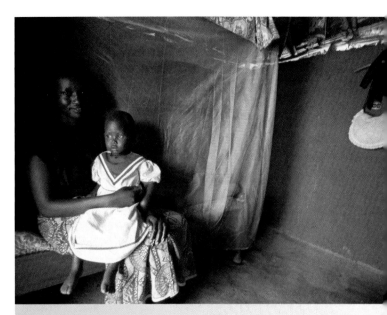

This woman has just acquired new bed nets, which her family will use to protect themselves from malaria-causing mosquitoes. Often, people are bitten and infected while they sleep.

4 million people suffering from the disease in that country, the pharmaceutical giants from the Global North united and used their clout to crush the law. Only intense negative publicity caused them to relent. Many places in the world have diseases that are not being controlled due to lack of resources to buy needed medications (Booker and Minter 2006). Some funding comes from international organizations and foundations such as the Bill and Melinda Gates Foundation, which in 2006 funded a new initiative to help combat AIDS and malaria in poor countries. To rephrase Martin Luther King Jr.'s statement about injustice, disease anywhere is disease everywhere.

The issue of global health is not limited to diseases and their treatment. Use of tobacco is a major issue, with perhaps a trillion "sticks"—mostly American made—being sold to and smuggled into countries around the world. Mark Schapiro (2006) documents the active involvement of a number of American tobacco companies in illegal smuggling activity, and the top U.S. tobacco companies now earn more from cigarette sales abroad than at home. These companies have a vested interest in the globalization of their product, which is made difficult if countries bar or severely limit the importation of tobacco products. The World Health Organization considers smuggling tobacco products a major world health issue, and the nations involved also see it as a major health issue. Governments have mixed reactions: They gain tremendous revenue from taxes and tariffs on tobacco products, but health care costs also increase due to diseases. Criminal justice systems have little leverage over companies that operate abroad, so it is rare that action to curb illegal sales of tobacco products abroad is ever taken (Schapiro 2006).

Depicted here is the process of creating traditional medicines, from start to finish, in Ethiopia. First the plants are cultivated or picked from wild herbs. Then the medicine is extracted from the plants. This is sold in the equivalent of pharmacies or prescribed by traditional healers.

Indigenous Medicine: Traditional and Modern Medical Practices

In India, an ancient Hindu approach to medical care focuses on the link between mind and body. It suggests that health can be achieved if there is an adequate balance between the two and that balance can be brought about through meditation and medication, a combination of Western medicines and appropriate relaxation and exercise. Such beliefs are consistent with the overall pattern of Indian culture and religion.

In a rural Mexican–Native American village in Arizona, a gravely ill young boy named Yas is being treated by the shaman of the village for a rattlesnake bite. Prayers are chanted by all present as the shaman pours a mixture of herbs and other ingredients over Yas's head. After this procedure, Yas is taken to a local health care clinic for additional Western-style treatment.

An elderly Nicaraguan woman, Lucia, comes to a rural clinic with the complaint of "sadness in my body and fear in my chest." Was this a heart problem? Arthritis? Some other sickness? Knowing the cultural context of the woman's description, the doctor determines her problem. After checking her physical condition, he finds that her complaint is not symptomatic of a heart attack, but rather of missing her children, who have all left to work in foreign countries. For a modest fee based on her income, and with limited access to psychological care, she had found what help she could.

In an African village in Ghana, the local shaman, Kofa, grows his own herbal garden, which produces many of the medicinal plants that he uses for treatment, using recipes passed down through the generations. There are herbal mixtures for infection, impotence, infertility, asthma, stomach ailments, and numerous other problems. Using combinations of traditional and Western treatments, he gains legitimacy. He points out that the herbal medicines he uses are very effective and, in fact, form the basic substances of many Western medicines. Down the road from this shaman, patients can seek treatment from Amma, the priestess, in exchange for a small contribution. The closest role in Western medicine to Amma's services would be a psychologist or psychiatrist. Her visitors include the lovesick, the lonely, the hypochondriacs, and the bereaved. She sings

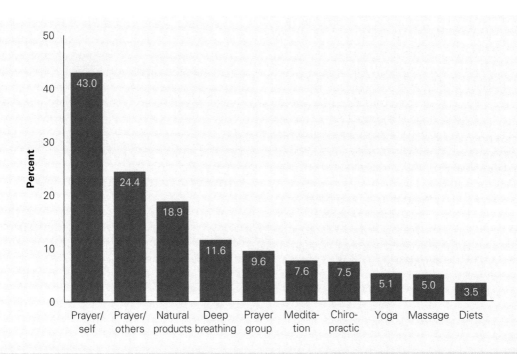

Figure 14.2 Most Commonly Used Practices in Ten Complementary and Alternative Medicine

Source: National Institute of Health 2007.

chants, prescribes potions (mixtures of herbs, often sedatives), and gives advice.

People around the world rely on a variety of medical models and practitioners to meet their needs. As migrations occur, practices spread. Western medicine has borrowed from folk medicine traditions; tested many of the traditional herbal remedies; incorporated acupuncture, pressure point, and massage therapies; and used other procedures adopted from traditional medicine. *Allopathy* (medicine based on remedies that simply reverse one's symptoms) retains dominance over alternative medical practices—homeopathy, chiropractic, acupuncture, and other types of medical practices that Western medical practitioners sometimes label quackery. Yet, folk medicines in many societies, often combined with Western medicine, effectively treat people's illnesses in their social contexts. Medicine itself has become globally informed, delivered with awareness of local social settings.

One result of the spread of medical ideas around the world is the "Complementary and Alternative Medicines" movement (CAM) in the United States and other Western countries. CAM includes health care systems, practices, and products that are used to complement conventional medicine or as alternative medicine used in place of conventional medicine. CAM therapies include acupuncture and chiropractic, natural products, special diets, and megavitamin therapy. Of interest to sociologists is the spread of practices, along with who accepts alternative practices and who resists them.

In a major survey of U.S. health practices, 62% of adults said they use some form of CAM, including megavitamins and prayer, for health reasons. The profile of CAM users looks like this: more women than men, those with higher education, those who have been hospitalized, and former smokers. About 12% of the study population sought care from a CAM practitioner such as an acupuncturist or chiropractor (National Institutes of Health 2007; Sherman 2005).

Pressures for change in the health care system come from consumers, health care financing, and competition to keep medical practices profitable. As the population ages and people live longer, as patients look for alternative ways to deal with chronic illness, and as alternative health providers set up shop, more doctors are adding aspects of holistic medicine and CAM to meet consumer demands (Winnick 2006). The medical establishment has incorporated some of these practices, especially if scientific study finds them effective, but others lie outside accepted Western medicine at this time. The most prevalent CAM practices that have been imported to Western countries from traditional medical practices are acupuncture, ayurveda, biofeedback, chelation therapy, chiropractic care, deep breathing exercises, diet-based therapies, energy healing therapy, folk medicine, guided imagery, homeopathic treatment, hypnosis, massage, meditation, megavitamin therapy, natural products, neuropathy, prayer for health reasons, progressive relaxation, Qi gong, Reiki, Tai chi, and Yoga. Figure 14.2 shows the percentages using the 10 most common CAM practices.

Because of the uneven distribution of health care, doctors, and medicines around the world, many preventable and curable diseases go untreated. When the average life expectancy in countries is in the 30s, we know that medical help is not available for common medical problems. For example, dehydration from diarrhea caused by water-borne diseases such as cholera, blindness caused by vitamin A deficiency, malaria cause by infected mosquitoes, and other preventable diseases are unnecessary afflictions in today's world. Yet, many nations in the Global South have few physicians per capita. For instance, in Malawi, there is one doctor for every 100,000 people, in Ethiopia and Niger, three doctors for every 100,000 citizens, and in Mali, four doctors per 100,000 citizens. The few doctors in these countries are located mostly in urban areas (United Nations Development Programme 2005a). Folk remedies are the only health care most of these citizens have.

As long as there is inequality in our social world, adequate health care is unlikely to reach all people and all countries (Garrett 2000). In spite of increasingly sophisticated medical technology and medicines, availability, cost, distribution, and policies of governments are the determinants of who receives health care around the world.

Thinking Sociologically

We live in a global world, yet our most immediate experiences are local. What are benefits you and your family might receive if international agencies resolve health problems in Africa, Asia, and South America?

So What ?

When you are sick and when you are diagnosed and cared for, the norms that allow you to be sick and the expectations of you in the sick role may differ from the expectations placed on others around the world. Although health is a private, personal concern, it is also a public concern, delivered through organizations dispensing health care and government practices determining access and funding of health care. Distant from your daily life but important to your well-being are the global health organizations that concern themselves with global epidemics. In addition, whether you have insurance or money to pay doctors depends in part on the economic conditions in society and the global marketplace of health care delivery.

Our social institutions—from family, education, and religion to politics, economics, and health—maintain stability in societies. However, the world in which we live is a dynamic one. In the final two chapters, we turn to an examination of how change occurs. First, we examine two forces that have changed exponentially in the past two centuries—population patterns and urbanization. We close with an examination of social change in its many manifestations.

Key Points

What Have We Learned?

- Sociology looks at the anatomy of medicine by examining the social implications of health and illness—from the micro level of individual coping with illness to the meso level of institutional interactions and complex organizations that manage health and illness, to the global issues of controlling spread of diseases around the world. (See pp. 460–461.)

- Whether looking at the medicalization of social problems through labeling or examining functions and socioeconomic conflicts regarding health care in society, various social theories offer alternative lenses for our sociological anatomy of medicine. (See pp. 461–468.)

- At the micro level, we can look at issues of the "sick role," how social and cultural factors affect our responses to pain and ill health, or how our age, gender, and other personal aspects of identity are related to our responses to health and illness. (See pp. 468–473.)

- Hospitals and other elements of organizational complexity, the issues of professionalism and of deprofessionalization of medical personnel, and the linkages between institutions like the economy, politics, education, and family are all aspects of health care at the meso level. (See pp. 473–477.)

- The national level is often linked to access to health care, the cost as a proportion of the nation's resources, the issues of security of citizens, and questions of reform of health-care delivery. (See pp. 477–479.)

- Questions of policy are also highly controversial, with countries approaching the responsibilities of the individual versus the nation with different philosophies. This is a particularly contentious issue right now in the United States. (See pp. 479–484.)

- Globally, we find not only that diseases spread around the planet much faster in our age of rapid travel and migrations but also that curing philosophies and techniques from around the globe are influencing the approaches we each choose in our own local communities. (See pp. 484–492.)

- In summary, the study of anatomy is at the core of preparation for a career in medicine, but sociologists would argue that understanding the anatomy of the social processes that affect health, illness, and the delivery of health care are necessary for a full comprehension of medicine in the modern world.

Contributing to Our Social World: What Can We Do?

At the Local Level: Obesity is one of the most serious health issues among young people today. Does your campus have obesity support groups or awareness programs, possibly administered through the student health service? If so, make contact with the people involved and arrange to attend meetings and explore opportunities to volunteer. If not, contact the student health service and see if it is feasible to establish a program to assist students who are struggling with obesity. Obesity in America is an organization that maintains a Web site (www.obesityinamerica.org/support.html) with information on a wide range of resources, much of which is directly applicable to problems faced by students.

At the Organizational or Institutional Level: Every community has free or low-cost clinics that provide health screening and other services to uninsured individuals and families. The U.S. Department of Health and Human Services has a locator Web site at http://ask.hrsa.gov/pc/ that searches for free clinics by state and city. United Way and larger hospitals have the names and contact persons of these clinics in your community. Most have volunteer and internship opportunities that afford interesting and valuable experiences, especially if you are considering a career in the health care field.

At the National and Global Levels: HIV/AIDS is now the world's most serious epidemic disease. The Joint United Nations Program on HIV/AIDS, whose Web site is at www.unaids.org/en/, is seeking volunteer and professional help to conduct research, participate in educational outreach, and raise funds to fight this epidemic. According to the World Vision Web site, www.worldvision.org, 6,000 children are orphaned daily by HIV/AIDS throughout the world, and especially in the poorer countries in Africa and Asia. The organization's Hope Child program lists several suggestions for getting involved, including sponsorship of a child. AVERT, an international AIDS charity (www.avert.org/worldaid.htm), has designated December 1 as International AIDS Awareness Day. Visit the site for suggestions on getting involved, including organizing AIDS Awareness Day activities on your campus or in your community.

Visit **www.pineforge.com/ballantine2study** for online activities, sample tests, and other helpful information. Select "Chapter 14: Medicine" for chapter-specific activities.

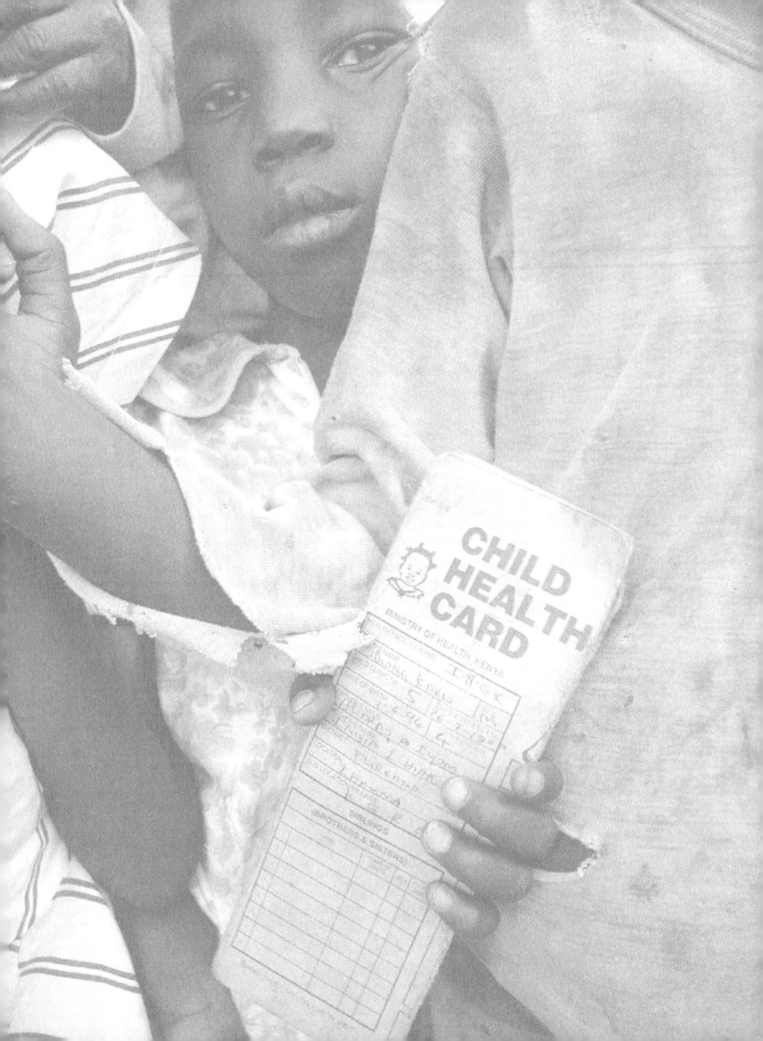

PART V

Social Dynamics

Social structures such as institutions—family, education, religion, health, politics, and economics—tend to resist change. Yet, this entire book shows that societies are dynamic and changing. Institutions and organizations come alive with processes that are fluid and vibrant. Globalization itself, a major theme in this book, is a process bringing transformation to our social world. We do not live in the same sort of world our grandparents inhabited. The macro- and meso-level dimensions of the world have become increasingly powerful, which is exactly why we need a sociological imagination to understand how the events in our own micro worlds are influenced by the larger society.

This section looks at some of those processes that are dynamic, fluid, and vibrant—population changes, urbanization, expansion of technology, social movements, and more. We live in exciting and challenging times, and we will thrive best if we understand the micro-, meso-, and macro-level dimensions of change in our lives and the linkages between parts of our social world. We turn next to population dynamics and urbanization.

CHAPTER 15

Population and Urbanization

Living on Spaceship Earth

The human population is limited to this one moderately sized sphere, on which it depends for survival. The question is whether human groups can cooperate with each other and use the resources of the planet responsibly. In the meantime, humans are concentrated in dense urban areas, illustrated by the night shot in the background of this page, in which bright lights beam from urban areas in Europe but from fewer places in Africa.

Think About It . . .

Micro: Why is your family the size it is?

Micro: What characterizes the population composition of your hometown or city? What makes you feel comfortable or uncomfortable there?

Meso: Why do people move from rural areas to urban areas? What problems does this urbanization trend create?

Macro: How might immigration affect the makeup of a nation, and what effect could this have on a nation's policies?

Macro: How do global issues relating to urbanization, the environment, and technology affect your family and your local community?

Macro: Global Community

Macro: Society

Meso: National Organizations, Institutions, and Ethnic Subcultures

Micro: Local Organizations and Community

Micro: Me (and My Neighbors)

Micro: Population trends affect schools, churches, businesses, and communities

Meso: Family, education, religion, health, politics, and economics all affect and are affected by population growth and movement

Macro: National policies on population—birth incentives, birth control, abortion

Macro: Global migrations, epidemics, wars; United Nations policies that affect population magine that we are looking down from our satellite at a spherical object drifting through space. It appears to be a beautiful mix of greens and blues, and at night, parts of the sphere glows with lights while other parts are dark. That is home—our little (relatively speaking) planet. The controlling inhabitants of the planet are humans, all 6.7 billion of them (U.S. Census Bureau 2008a), increasing by 211,090 people daily (World Factbook 2008). The topic of this chapter is the spread and distribution of those humans living on spaceship Earth (Diamond 1999, 2005).

Since the emergence of *Homo sapiens* in East Africa, human populations have grown in uneven surges and declines due to births, deaths, and migrations. The World Population Data Sheet (see Table 15.1) illustrates the process.

The world's human population has grown sporadically over the millennia, so the explosion of human beings on the planet in the past two and a half centuries is stunning. If we collapsed all of human history into one 24-hour day, the time period since 1750 would consume one minute. Yet, 25% of all humans have lived during this one-minute time period. In the 200 years between 1750 and 1950, the world's population mushroomed from 800 million to 2.5 billion. On October 12, 1999, the global population reached 6 billion. It has now expanded to more than 6.7 billion, growing by 74.2 million in 2006. Estimates put the world population at 9 billion by 2050 (World Factbook 2008). This means the world is growing each year by the number of people in the country of Germany, Philippines, or Vietnam. Every minute, 249 children are born and 108 people die around the world, resulting in a net increase of 141 people per minute (U.S. Census Bureau 2006c).

Between 2000 and 2050, virtually all of the world's growth will occur in Africa, Asia, and Latin America, where 81% of the world's population lives and 90% of each year's births occur (Population Reference Bureau 2008).

Let us start by focusing on one area of our world, Kenya in East Africa. We focus here partly because East Africa, where Kenya and Tanzania are located, was—according to many scientists—home to spaceship Earth's earliest human inhabitants. Scientists believe bones found in the dry Olduvai Gorge area are the oldest remains of *Homo sapiens* ever found. We also focus here because today Kenya is making human history for another reason. With a population of nearly 38 million people and a natural increase of 2.78% annually (World Fact Book 2008), Kenya has one of the most rapidly growing populations on Earth. Let us transport ourselves to this country and attempt to understand the situation of the Kenyan to see if that holds some explanation for Kenya's ballooning population. Kenya is made up of many tribal groups of people. With different religions and value systems, they have clashed in power struggles in recent years. Still, there are several themes that pervade most Kenyan subcultures.

Wengari, like Kenyan girls of most tribal affiliations, married in her teens. She has been socialized to believe that her main purpose in life is to bear children, to help with the farming, and to care for parents in their old age. Children are seen as an asset in Kenya. Religious beliefs and cultural value systems encourage large families. However, the population of Kenya is 44% dependent: people under 15 or over 65, who rely on working-age citizens to support them (Population Reference Bureau 2007a). The working-age population is becoming scarce and cannot continue

Table 15.1 **World Population Data Sheet: World, Global North and Global South Countries, 2008**

	World	More Developed (Global North)	Less Developed (Global South)	(without China)
Population (millions)	6,705	1,227	5,479	4,154
Births per 1,000 Pop.	21	2	23	26
Deaths per 1,000 Pop.	8	10	8	9
Rate of Natural Increase	1.2%	0.2%	1.5%	1.8%
Infant Mortality Rate	49	6	54	59
Total Fertility Rate	2.6	1.6	2.8	3.2
Percentage of population < 15	28	17	30	34
Percentage of population 65+	7	16	6	5
Life Expectancy at birth	68	77	67	65
Life Expectancy—Males	67	74	65	63
Life Expectancy—Females	70	81	68	66

Source: Population Reference Bureau 2008.

to feed the growing population. Added to that are severe droughts in parts of the country—droughts that are killing animal herds and preventing growth of crops. These facts, however, have little meaning to young women like Wengari, who have been socialized to conform to the female role within their society.

By contrast, to the north, in many of the industrialized, urbanized countries of Europe, birth rates are below population replacement levels, meaning population size eventually may begin to drop. Germany, Hungary, and Latvia, for instance, are losing population.

> While Asia's share of world population may continue to hover around 55 percent through the next century, Europe's portion has declined sharply and could drop even more during the twenty-first century. Africa and Latin America each will gain part of Europe's portion. By 2100, Africa is expected to capture the greatest share. Countries growing by less than 1 percent annually include Japan, Australia, New Zealand, Russia, and much of Europe. (Population Reference Bureau 2006)

In industrialized societies, children in the middle class and above are dependent until they leave home. Typical European young people often wait until their late 20s or even 30s to start a family, postponing children until their education is complete and a job is in hand. Many limit their family size because societal values support small families. It is difficult to house large families in small urban apartments where the majority of the population live. Workers must support and feed their families on earned wages rather than through farming. Both mother and father often work, and unlike many children in the Global South, most children born in Europe will survive to old age. Life expectancy, the average age at death, is 47 years in Kenya. In some European countries, it is older than 80 years.

On yet another continent, China, the country with the largest population in the world (1.31 billion people), had the greatest drop in population growth in the late 20th century due to strict governmental family planning practices (*Time Almanac* 2008). India, the second-largest country, has a population growth rate (increase in a country's population during a specified period of time) of 1.58% a year, just over replacement level (World Factbook 2008).

Although some countries have birth rates below population replacement levels, the world's population continues to grow because of the skyrocketing growth rate in other countries and because of population momentum caused by the large number of individuals of childbearing age having children. Even though birth rates per couple drop, the number of women of childbearing age is still very high, resulting in continued growth in population size. Unfortunately, most of the countries with the highest growth rates are in the Global South, where there are fewer resources to support the additional population.

Changes in the environment and in the global economy make it difficult for this Kenyan family to provide for itself. Some of these children and their cousins may find it necessary to move to urban centers, a worldwide migration trend. Much of the socialization they received in villages will not be relevant to their adult urban lives.

What we have been discussing is the study of human populations, called **demography**. All permanent societies, states, communities, adherents of a common religious faith, racial or ethnic groups, kinship or clan groups, professions, and other identifiable categories of people can be referred to as **populations**. The size, geographical location, and spatial movement of the population, its concentration in certain geographical areas, and changing characteristics of the population are important elements in the study of demography and constitute a core subfield within sociology.

With growing populations and limited farmland to support the population, hungry people move to cities in hopes of finding jobs. This pattern of movement is called **urbanization**. The second half of this chapter will consider the evolution, growth, and development of populated areas, including movements from rural areas to cities, the organization of urban life, the relationship between individuals and the city, and some problems facing cities.

The previous chapters have been organized by moving from micro- to macro-level analysis. Because demographic work has focused on societies and global trends, we will reverse the order in the first section and discuss macro-level patterns in world population growth first, followed by meso-level institutional influences on population, and micro-level population patterns. We then move to a discussion of a major factor in population, urbanization—movement from rural to urban areas. Our topics include cities as micro-level living environments, the evolution of cities, and macro-level urban problems, the environment, and social policy.

Hanoi, Vietnam, is a crowded Asian city. The overcrowding in some cities means that one cannot even walk easily down a street, as this photograph shows.

Thinking Sociologically

Do you have choice in how many children you have? What factors go into your decision? How might your decision differ if you were in a different country? Should global patterns—which include food shortages and climate change—be a consideration in the size of your family and those of your neighbors? Why or why not?

MACRO-LEVEL PATTERNS IN WORLD POPULATION GROWTH

For thousands of years, early humans roamed the plains of Africa, their survival and growth depending on the environment in which they lived. They mastered fire and tools, then domesticated animals and invented agriculture, and with these skills slowly increased control over the environment, allowing their numbers to expand. This evolution in the growth patterns of human populations is worth closer examination.

Patterns of Population Growth Over Time

Members of the small band of early *Homo sapiens* who inhabited the Olduvai Gorge moved gradually, haltingly,

from this habitat into what are now other parts of Africa, Asia, and Europe. The process took thousands of years. At times, births outnumbered deaths and populations grew, but at other times, plagues, famines, droughts, and wars decimated populations. From the beginning of human existence, estimated from perhaps one million years ago until modern times, the number of births and deaths balanced each other over the centuries (Diamond 2005). The large population we see today results from population evolution that consisted of three phases:

1. Humans, because of their thinking ability, competed satisfactorily in the animal kingdom to obtain the basic necessities for survival of the species.

2. With the agricultural revolution that occurred about 10,000 years ago and the resulting food surplus, mortality rates declined, and the population grew as more infants survived and people lived longer.

3. The biggest increase came with the Industrial Revolution, beginning about 300 years ago. Improved medical knowledge and sanitation helped bring the death rate down.

When industrialization made its debut, it brought the social and economic changes discussed in Chapter 3 (e.g., machines replacing human labor and mass production using resources in new ways), but it also augmented urbanization of societies. The population explosion began with industrialization in Europe and spread to widely scattered areas of the globe. With trade and migrations came the diffusion of ideas and better medical care, influencing population growth rates in all parts of the world by keeping people alive longer. Figure 15.1 shows population growth throughout history.

The worldwide *rate* of population growth reached its peak in the 1960s and has decreased to a current rate of about 1.16% per year, resulting in a leveling off of increases in world population (World Factbook 2008). (See Figure 15.2.)

Predictors of Population Growth

Children in some sub-Saharan and East African countries, which have the highest rates of HIV/AIDS in the world, are forced to fend for themselves. With large percentages of the working-age population dead (or dying) from AIDS, orphaned children take care of their younger siblings. In some villages in Uganda, for instance, social workers visit periodically to bring limited food for survival and see that children are planting crops. These children must learn survival skills and gender roles at a very young age. They have little chance to experience a childhood typical in other places.

Think for a moment about the impact that your age and sex have on your position in society and your activities. Are you of childbearing age? Are you dependent on others

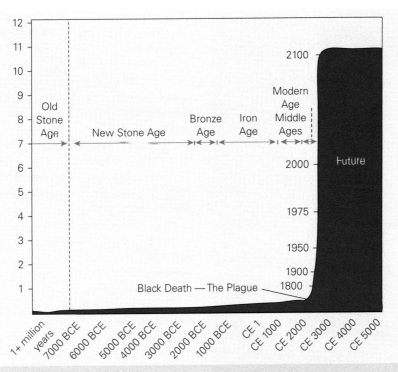

Figure 15.1 The Exponential World Population Growth From About 8000 BCE to 21st Century

Source: Abu-Lughod 2001:50.

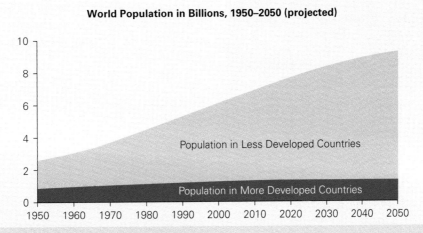

World Population in Billions, 1950–2050 (projected)

Figure 15.2   World Population Growth Rate, 1950–2050

Source: Population Reference Bureau 2007a. "Global Population Growth Is Driven by Developing Countries," from Population Reference Bureau, "World Population Highlights," *Population Bulletin 62*, no. 3 (2007). Reprinted with permission.

Note: Global population growth is driven by poor Global South countries.

for most of your needs or are you supporting others? Your status is largely due to your age and what that age means in your society. These matters greatly influence your behavior and that of others like you, and collectively, they shape the population patterns of an entire society. In analyzing the impact of age and sex on human behavior, three sets of concepts can be very useful: dependency ratios, sex ratios, and age-sex population pyramids.

The *youth dependency ratio* is the number of children under age 15 compared to the number between 15 and 64. The number of those older than 64 compared to those between 15 and 64 is called the *aged dependency ratio*. Although many of the world's young people under 15 help support themselves and their families, and many over 64 are likewise economically independent, these figures have been taken as the general ages when individuals are not

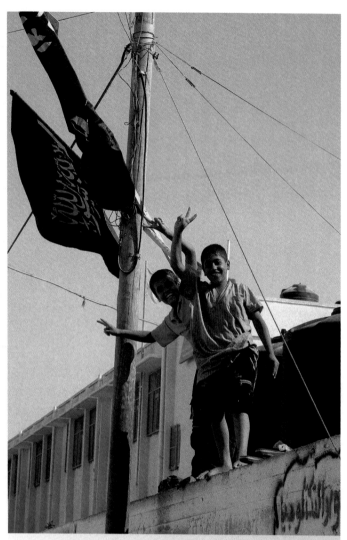

Palestinian children attempt to fly the flag of a Palestinian group. With half of the Palestinian population under age 15, younger Palestinians are taking active roles in politics, and many are responsible for helping to support their families.

contributing to the labor force. They represent the economic burden (especially in wealthy countries) of people in the population who must be supported by the working-age population. The **dependency ratio**, then, is the ratio of those in both the young and aged groups compared to the number of people in the productive age groups between 15 and 64 years old.

In several resource-poor countries about 9 out of every 20 people are under 15 years of age. These include Benin (43.6%), Rwanda (41.9%), Gaza (47.1%), Liberia (44%), and Ethiopia (43.1%) (World Factbook 2008). Working adults in less privileged countries have a tremendous burden to support the dependent population, especially if a high percentage of the population is urban and not able to be self-supporting through farming.

Similarly, high percentages of older dependent people over 64 are found in most Global North countries. In the European countries of Norway, Sweden, Denmark, the United Kingdom, and Germany, between 15% and 20% of the population is in the age group 65 and older. These countries have low death rates, resulting in the average life expectancy at birth being as high as 80 years (World Factbook 2008).

The percentage of dependent elderly people is growing, especially in affluent countries. Consider the case of Japan, which faces the problem of its "graying" or aging population. In 2008, 21.6% of its population was 65 or older, and the average life expectancy was over 82 years (World Factbook 2008). The Japanese population is graying nearly twice as fast as the population in many other nations, in large part because the birth rate is very low, only 1.2 children per woman. There simply are not enough replacement workers to support the aging population. Japan provides a glimpse into the future for other rapidly aging societies, including Germany, the United States, and China (Moffett 2003). (See Figure 15.3.)

The sex ratio refers to the ratio of males to females in the population. For instance, the more females, especially females in or soon to be in the fertile years, the more potential there is for population growth. The sex ratio also affects population growth patterns by determining the supply of eligible spouses. Marriage patterns are affected by economic cycles, wars in which the proportion of males to females may decrease, and migrations that generally take males from one area and add them to another. **Population**

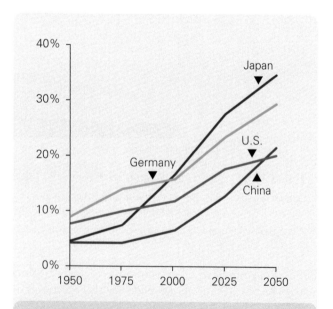

Figure 15.3 Japan Grows Old

Source: Moffett 2003.

Note: Japan's percentage of population over 65 is growing faster than any other nation.

pyramids illustrate sex ratios and dependency ratios (see Figure 15.4).

The graphic presentation of the age and sex distribution of a population tells us a great deal about that population. The structures are called pyramids because that is the shape they took until several decades ago. By looking up and down the pyramid, we can see the proportion of population at each age level. Looking to the right and left of the centerline tells us the balance of males to females at each age. The bottom line shows us the total population at each age.

The first pyramid shows populations that have fairly low birth and death rates, typical of Global North countries. The second pyramid illustrates populations with high birth rates and large dependent youth populations, typical of the Global South. The world population has been getting both younger (the Global South) *and* older (the Global North), resulting in large numbers of dependent people.

As Global South nations have more and more children, they are creating more potential parents in later years, adding momentum to the world's population growth. Because today young children survive their early years, whereas in the past they might have died of disease and malnutrition, they are likely to reproduce, adding to the population size. Fewer deaths of infants and children, which can be credited to immunizations and disease control, lower mortality rates, resulting in younger populations and higher potential numbers of births in the future.

Japan is an aging society, with life expectancy exceeding 81 and more than 20% of the population over age 65. Ninety-two-year-old Toshi Uechi practices her traditional Okinawan dance with some other men and women at a senior center on Okinawa, Japan. An active lifestyle and Spartan diet have helped make Okinawa home to one of the highest percentages of centenarians in the world—39.5 per 100,000 residents. How might societies differ if they have a young versus old population?

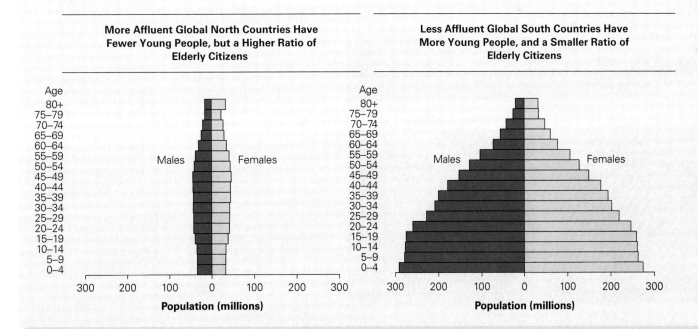

Figure 15.4 Population Pyramids, by Level of Affluence, 2008

Source: Population Reference Bureau 2008. From Population Reference Bureau, "World Population Highlights," *Population Bulletin 62,* no. 3 (2007). Reprinted with permission.

Thinking Sociologically

Consider your own country's population pyramid. What can you tell about your country's level of development by studying the population pyramid?

Population Patterns: Theoretical Explanations

From the earliest historical writings, we find evidence of interest in population size and growth. Scriptures such as the Quran and the Bible have supported population growth to increase the ranks of the faithful. Of course, population expansion made sense at the time these holy tracts were written. Government leaders throughout the ages have adopted various philosophies about the best size of populations. The ancient Greek philosopher Plato (350 BCE/1960) argued that the city-state should have 5,040 citizens and that measures should be taken to increase or decrease the population to bring it in line with this figure. However, the first significant scholarly analysis that addressed global population issues came from Thomas Malthus (1766–1834), an English clergyman and social philosopher.

Malthus's Theory of Population

In his "Essay on the Principle of Population," Malthus ([1798] 1926) argued that humans are driven to reproduce

Malthus predicted that if left unchecked, population increases would result in massive famine and disease. This is exactly what has happened in Ethiopia, as this gathering of famished people at a relief camp shows.

and will multiply without limits if no checks are imposed. An unchecked population increases geometrically: 2 parents could have 4 children, 16 grandchildren, 64 great-grandchildren, and so forth—and that is simply with a continuous average family size of 4 children. Because the means of subsistence (food) increases at best only arithmetically or lineally (5, 10, 15, 20, 25), the end result is a food shortage and possible famine.

Malthus recognized several positive checks on populations, factors that would keep populations from excessive growth, including wars, diseases and epidemics, and food shortages leading to famine (a drastic, wide-reaching shortage of food). Malthus held strong political views based in part on his population theory. He suggested preventive checks on rapid population growth, primarily in the form of delayed marriage and practice of sexual abstinence until one could afford a family. Contraception technology was crude and unrealistic in his day, and therefore, he did not present it as an option for population control.

Looking at historical factors and at the world today, we see examples of these population checks. War decimated the populations of several countries during the world war and has taken its toll on other countries in Eastern Europe, Africa, and the Middle East since then. The AIDS virus, SARS, Ebola, and bird flu have raised fears of new plagues (epidemics of often fatal diseases). Waterborne diseases such as cholera and typhus strike after floods, and the floods themselves are often caused by environmental destruction resulting from too many humans in a geographic area. Famine in Ethiopia and countries in the horn of Africa during the latter part of the 20th century resulted in massive relief efforts, but too little and too late to save thousands who died of starvation. More than 20 million people are experiencing famines in East Africa ("Millions Vulnerable to Famine in Africa" 2006) and part of Sudan and Niger in West Africa. Famines are caused in part by erosion and stripping the Earth of natural protections such as forests and grasslands by people in need of more land to grow food and graze animals and of more firewood to cook. Today, there are also economic factors in checks on population. For example, imported cheap food is driving local farmers out of business in some areas.

Four main criticisms have been raised about Malthus's theory. First, although we see evidence of Malthus's population checks today, his ideas stemmed from ethnocentric attitudes that blamed the victims for creating their own suffering. This ignored the role capitalism plays in the process, exploiting raw materials and laborers and encouraging excessive consumption patterns in wealthy industrial nations. In fact, having large families made sense to many, who believed having more children provided more workers and more economic security (Robbins 2005).

Second, Malthus's idea that food production would grow arithmetically and could not keep up with population growth must be modified in light of current agricultural techniques, at least in some parts of the world. Third, Malthus saw abstinence from sex, even among the married, as the main method of preventing births and did not recognize the potential for contraception. Fourth, poverty has not always proven to be an inevitable result of population growth.

Two neo-Malthusians, scientists who accept much of his theory but make modifications based on current realities, are Garrett Hardin and Paul Ehrlich. Hardin (1968), a biologist, argues that individuals' personal goals are not always consistent with societal goals for population growth. An individual may decide to have many children, but this could be detrimental to the whole society. If many people act solely on their own individual interests, social tragedy may well ensue.

Ehrlich and Ehrlich (1990) add to the formula of "too many people and too little food" the problem of a "dying planet" caused by environmental damage. To hold on to economic gains, population must be checked, and to check population, family planning is necessary, they assert. Ehrlichs' ideas can be summed up as follows:

> America and other rich nations have a clear choice today. They can continue to ignore the population problem and their own massive contributions to it. Then they will be trapped in a downward spiral that may well lead to the end of civilization in a few decades. More frequent droughts, more damaged crops and famines, more dying forests, more smog, more international conflicts, more epidemics . . . will mark our course. (p. 23)

The neo-Malthusians favor contraception rather than simple reliance on the moral restraint that Malthus proposed (Weeks 2005). They also acknowledge that much of the environmental damage is caused by corporate pollution and excessive consumption habits in affluent areas such as the United States, Canada, and Europe.

Near Alem Kitmama in Ethiopia, scarcity of fresh water and other resources threatens survival. In the 19th century, Thomas Malthus predicted such shortages due to population increases.

Thinking Sociologically

What are contemporary examples of Malthus's checks on population growth—war, disease, famine? Are family planning and contraception sufficient to solve the problem of global overpopulation by humans? Can you think of any other alternatives?

Demographic Transition: Explaining Population Growth and Expansion

Why should a change in the economic structure such as industrialization and movement from rural agricultural areas to urban cities have an impact on population size? One explanation is found in the **demographic transition theory**.

The idea of demographic transition involves comparing countries' stages of economic development with trends in birth and death rates. Three stages of development are identified in this theory:

Stage 1: These populations have high birth and death rates that tend to balance each other over time. Births may outpace deaths until some disaster diminishes the increase. This has been the pattern for most of human history.

Stage 2: Populations still have high birth rates, but death rates decline (i.e., more people live longer) because of improvements in health care and sanitation, establishment of public health programs, disease control and immunizations, and food availability and distribution. These factors are especially important in declining death rates of less poor countries today. This imbalance between continuing high births and declining deaths means that the population growth rate is very high.

Stage 3: Populations level off at the bottom of the chart (see Figure 15.5) with low birth rates and low death rates. Most industrial and postindustrial societies are in this stage. Population growth rates in these countries are very low because nuclear families are small.

These stages are illustrated in Figure 15.5.

Demographic transition theory helps explain the developmental stage and population trends in countries around the world, but it does not consider some important factors that affect the size of populations: (1) people's age at marriage determines how many childbearing years they have (late marriage means fewer years until menopause); (2) contraceptive availability determines whether families can control their number of children; (3) a country's resources and land may determine how much population a country can support; (4) the economic structure of a country, religious beliefs, and political philosophies affect attitudes toward birth control and family size; and (5) economic expansion rates influence a country's need for labor.

Not all societies go through the same time frame in transition from one stage to another. For example, demographic transition occurred rapidly in Europe, where notions of modernization, urbanization, and progress evolved naturally from the cultural values. People generally married later, and the value of having children varied with resources available. In addition, many deadly diseases that at one time kept population growth in check were under control.

Critics argue that there is a built-in assumption that modernization in the second and third stages will result in rational choices about family size. Yet, unless women gain status by having smaller families, they are likely to continue to have large families (Robbins 2005).

Economic development generally results in a decline in the birth rate. The process of modernization that parallels economic development puts pressure on extended families to break apart into smaller nuclear family units, especially as families move to crowded urban areas. Urban families tend to have fewer children because children are a liability and cannot help support the family. Economic development, modernization, and urbanization did not occur together in all parts of the world, so the outcome of the three-stage transition has not always occurred as predicted in the theory.

The wealth flow theory suggests that two strategies are operating in couples' personal decisions about their family size. When wealth flows from children to parents, that is, when children are an asset working on the family farm or laboring, parents have larger families. When wealth flows

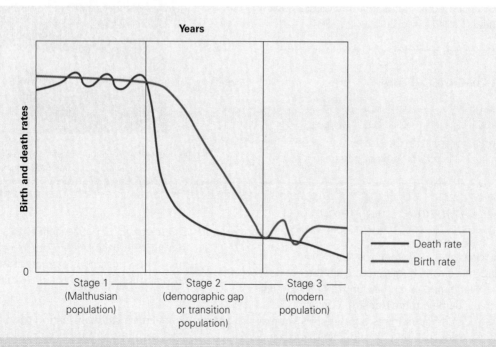

Figure 15.5   The Demographic Transition

from parents to children, families are likely to have fewer children (Caldwell 1982). To raise a child to 17 years in the United States, for instance, costs on average more than $200,000 (Robbins 2005).

Conflict Theorists' Explanations of Population Growth

Karl Marx and Fredrick Engels did not agree with Malthus's idea that population growth outstrips food and resources because of people's fertility rates, resulting in poverty. They felt that social and structural factors built into the economic system were the cause of poverty. Capitalist structures resulted in wealth for the capitalists and created overpopulation and poverty for those not absorbed into the system. Workers were expendable, kept in competition for low wages, used when needed, and let go when unprofitable to capitalists. In short, for conflict theorists, inequitable distribution and control of resources are at the heart of the problem.

Socialist societies, Marx argued, could absorb the growth in population so the problem of overpopulation would not exist. In a classless society, all would be able to find jobs, and the system would expand to include everyone. Engels asserted that population growth in socialist societies could be controlled by the central government. This regulation is, in fact, what is happening in most present-day socialist countries through such methods as strict family planning and liberal abortion policies. In China, for instance, a couple is not supposed to marry until their combined age is 50, and they may have only one child without penalty. Exceptions are made for rural citizens and some ethnic minorities. Those who exceed the state birth limits in planned societies may receive fewer state benefits and be ostracized.

Policy Implications: Population Patterns and Economic Development

Does rapid population growth retard the economic development of a country? This question has been a subject of debate among demographers and policymakers in recent years. It is an important issue because the beliefs of decision makers affect the policies and solutions they advocate. For instance, if policymakers feel population growth does not retard economic development, then they are less inclined to curb population growth. On the other hand, if they feel population growth does retard economic development, family planning efforts are more likely because economic prosperity is of more immediate concern to political office holders (Solow 2000).

This issue of population growth has caused heated debate at several World Population Conferences. Some socialist and Catholic countries argue that capitalistic

Overpopulation presents a challenge to food and water resources, and large populations damage the environment and provide little ecological recovery time. This creates a cycle that is hard to reverse. This photo shows pollution of a stream in Yunnan, China.

This billboard in Shanghai is advertising the Chinese government's "One Child Only" policy. The government decided three decades ago that the nation's rate of population growth was a threat to its viability.

economic exploitation and political control, not population growth, cause poverty in Global South countries. Multinational companies and foreign countries exploit poor countries' resources, sometimes with payoffs to government officials, leaving the citizens with no gains. In most nations,

In an urban area in Cambodia (Kampuchia), residents crowd onto this truck, a common form of transportation. With a high fertility rate and migration from rural to urban areas, crowded transportation is common.

policymakers and demographers agree, high population growth contributes to poverty. Rapid population growth is bad for economic growth because countries cannot adjust quickly enough to provide the infrastructure (housing, health care, sanitation, education) for so many additional people (United Nations Population Division 2005). Better sex education, access to contraceptives, and birth control advice help reduce population growth and spread of disease. Also important to limiting population growth is providing opportunities for citizens, especially women, to obtain education and jobs.

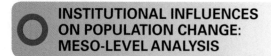

INSTITUTIONAL INFLUENCES ON POPULATION CHANGE: MESO-LEVEL ANALYSIS

Populations change in size (overall number of people), composition (the makeup of the population, including sex ratio, age distribution, and religious or ethnic representation in the population), and distribution (density or concentration in various portions of the land). The key variables that cause changes in the size, composition, or distribution are major population processes. Populations change when births and deaths are not evenly balanced or when significant numbers of people move from one area to another. So the most important demographic processes are **fertility** (the birth rate), **mortality** (the death rate),

and **migration** (movement of people from one place to another). Although migration does not change the size or composition of the world as a whole, it can affect size or makeup in a local micro-level or national macro-level population. The most unpredictable yet controllable population factor in the world or in a nation is fertility.

Factors Affecting Fertility Rates

Jeanne, one of the coauthors, was riding in the back of a "mammy wagon," a common means of transport in Africa. Crowded in with the chickens and pigs and people, she did not expect the conversation that ensued. The man in his late 20s asked if she was married and for how long. Jeanne responded, "Yes, for three years." The man continued, "How many children do you have?" Jeanne answered, "None." The man commented, "Oh, I'm sorry!" Jeanne replied, "No, don't be sorry. We planned it that way!" This man had been married for 10 years to a woman three years younger than he and had eight children. The ninth was on the way. In answer to his pointed questions, Jeanne explained that she was not being cruel to her husband and that birth control was what prevented children, and no, it did not make sex less enjoyable. He expressed surprise that limiting the number of children was possible and rather liked the idea. He jumped at the suggestion that he visit the family planning clinic in the city. With his meager income, he and his wife were finding it hard to feed all the little mouths. Knowledge of available family planning options is not always available.

Demographers consider micro-, meso-, and macro-level factors in attempting to understand fertility rates around the world. We know that individuals' personal decisions are key. People deciding to marry, couples' decisions to use contraception, their ideas about the acceptability of abortion, and whether they choose to remain childless can have an impact on national and global rates of population change. So choices at the micro level do make a difference at the macro level.

Fertility also fluctuates with what is happening in meso-level institutions such as economic, political, and family systems. During depressions, for example, the rate of fertility tends to drop. However, macro-level structural factors also affect fertility: (1) level of economic prosperity within the nation, (2) the government's commitment to providing (or restricting) contraception, (3) changes in norms and values about sexuality within a society, and (4) health care factors, including the availability of food and water.

Economic Factors

Poverty, the status of women, and exploitation of resources and labor by wealthy individuals and countries are some factors that contribute to overpopulation. Note the cyclical nature of the problem—overpopulation leads to poverty, which leads to overpopulation. The relationship between poverty and population reduction is very complex, which makes agreement about a solution difficult.

We know that one of the most significant distinguishing characteristics between rich Global North and poor Global South countries is their fertility rates. The worldwide fertility rate has fallen in every major world region, but some still remain very high. In sub-Saharan Africa, the average number of children per woman is 5.4, which is high, but that number is actually reduced since 1950, when the average was 6.7. Worldwide, the number of children per woman fell from 5.0 in 1950 to 2.6 by 2008 (Population Reference Bureau 2008). Figure 15.6, below, compares Global North regions of the world with the poorest Global South regions.

Thinking Sociologically

What does Figure 15.6 (fertility rates by development levels) tell you about the lives of individuals in these different regions of the world?

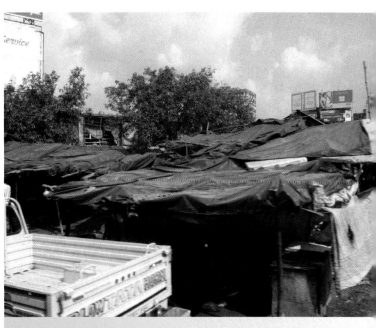

Extremely dense populations are often found in poverty-stricken areas. This slum in Kolkatta (Calcutta), India, is very overpopulated.

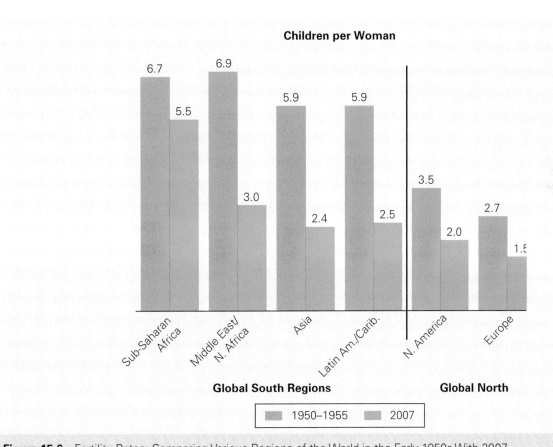

Figure 15.6   Fertility Rates: Comparing Various Regions of the World in the Early 1950s With 2007

Source: Population Reference Bureau 2007a. From Population Reference Bureau, "World Population Highlights," *Population Bulletin 62,* no. 3 (2007). Reprinted with permission.

Note: Fertility rates have fallen in every major world region but are still highest in sub-Saharan Africa.

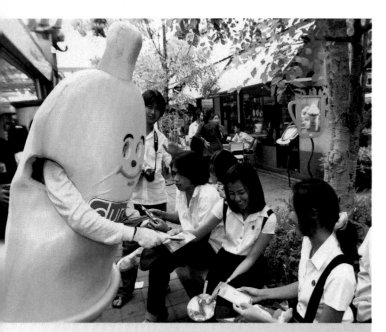

A condom mascot offers leaflets to teenagers in Bangkok, Thailand, during a promotional campaign to educate Thai youths on how to use condoms. The issue is partially related to birth control and partially to AIDS.

Although women's fertile years are roughly from 15 to 44, women in Global South countries have 80% of their children between the ages of 20 and 35, with a few below age 20 (United Nations 2006). Still, close to 20% of births in developing regions occur at age 35 or older, ages when there is greater risk in pregnancy, labor, and delivery. An important point in this section, however, is how various organizations and institutions affect fertility rates.

Government Influence

Some governments provide incentives for having children, whereas others discourage high fertility. Thus, meso- and macro-level social policies shape decisions of families at the micro level. Pronatalist policies (those that encourage fertility) or antinatalist policies (those that discourage fertility) may be expressed in several ways: by manipulating contraceptive availability; by promoting change in factors that affect fertility such as the status of women, education, and degree of economic development; through propaganda for or against having children; by creating incentives (maternity leaves, benefits, and tax breaks) or penalties (such as fines); and by passing laws governing age of marriage, size of family, contraception, and abortion.

Antinatalist policies arise out of concern over available resources and differences in birth rates among population subgroups. Singapore, a country in Asia located off the Malay peninsula, consists of one main island and many smaller

islands. It is one of the most crowded places on Earth, with 17,496 people per square mile. This is compared to 80 in the United States, 8 in Canada, and 876 in Japan (Population Reference Bureau 2005). The entire population of Singapore is urban, and 90% live in the capital city. The country has little unemployment and one of the highest per capita incomes in Asia. However, it is dependent on imports from other countries for most of its raw materials and food.

Some years ago, the central government in Singapore started an aggressive antinatalist plan. Birth control was made available, and residents of Singapore who had more than one or two children were penalized with less health care, smaller housing, and higher costs for services such as education. Singapore now claims one of the lowest natural increase rates (the birth rate minus the death rate) in Southeast Asia, at 0.8% a year, just behind China. Governmental policies really can affect the natural increase rate.

China's antinatalist policy has been in effect since 1962. The government discourages traditional preferences for early marriage, large families, and many sons by using group pressure, privileges for small families, and easy availability of birth control and abortion. The government has reduced the natural increase rate in China, the most populous nation on earth, to only 0.5% annually (Population Reference Bureau 2008). Unfortunately, there are side effects to such a stringent policy among a people who value male children. There has been an increase in selective abortions by couples hoping to have sons, and there are instances of female infanticide—killing of female infants when they are born—so that families can try for a male child.

An example of pronatalist government policies can be seen in Romania. Many Romanian men were killed in World War II, creating a sex imbalance. Marriage and birth rates plummeted. Concerned about the low birth rate, in 1966, the government banned abortions and the importation of most contraceptives. Within eight months, the birth rate doubled, and within 11 months it tripled.

In the United States, citizens like to think that decisions about fertility are entirely a private matter left to the couple. Indeed, it is sometimes hard to pin a simple label of antinatalist or pronatalist on the administration in power. President George W. Bush reinstated the "gag rule" that Presidents Ronald Reagan and George H. W. Bush had implemented, limiting the availability of birth control for teens in the United States unless parents are informed that the teen has applied for contraception. Many experts argue that this policy has contributed to the increased teen pregnancy rates in the United States. The Bush administration also blocked U.S. funding to international family planning groups that offer abortion and abortion counseling (Blackman 2001) and proposed a 19% cut in international family planning contributions for 2006 ("Overseas Population Spending Threatened" 2006). Both limits to contraceptive availability and prohibitions on abortion are pronatalist because they encourage fertility. Many conservatives who oppose birth control measures and abortion may not intentionally be pronatalist. While promoting births may not be their rationale, the policy still has the latent consequence of encouraging population increases. On the other hand, pronatalist governmental policies that might encourage larger families, such as family tax breaks or access to day care centers, are much less available. U.S. government policies have a mixed effect on domestic fertility rates, in part because there is no clear philosophy.

Other U.S. policies in effect well into the 20th century encouraged sterilization of black women. While white women were being encouraged to have large families in the 1950s, poor women of color were being discouraged from reproducing. Legal scholar Dorothy Roberts has found a continuing legacy of dual treatment of black and white fertility and motherhood in the United States. This has led to a continuing distrust of governmental family policies in some parts of the African American community (Roberts 1997, 2002).

Thinking Sociologically

Is it appropriate for governments to use enticements or penalties to encourage or discourage fertility? Why or why not? What are positive factors and problems with different policies?

Religious and Cultural Norms

A primary shaper of morality and values in most societies is religion. Norms and customs of a society or subculture also influence fertility. In some cultures, pronatalist norms support a woman having a child before she is married so she can prove her fertility. In other societies, a woman can be stoned to death for having a child or even sex out of wedlock.

Some religious groups oppose any intervention, such as birth control or abortion, in the natural processes of conception and birth. Roman Catholicism, for example, teaches that large families are a blessing from God and that birth control is a sin. The Roman Catholic Church officially advocates the rhythm method to regulate conception, a less reliable method in lessening birth rates than contraception technology. It might be noted, however, that a great many Catholics in the Western world are not following these teachings and are little different from their neighbors in use of contraception. Islam also encourages births. Large family size increases the likelihood that the faithful will multiply to carry the religion into future generations. These policies were created when population growth was kept in check by high death rates.

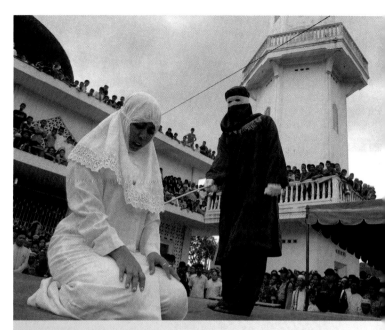

In Indonesia, Nur Azizah binti Hanafiah, 22, receives a caning, having been found by a citizen having illegal sex with her boyfriend at her house. This Aceh region of Indonesia has practiced Islamic Sharia law since 2001. In some societies, she would have been stoned to death for having premarital sex.

Nonreligious cultural customs affect fertility as well. Couples may be pressured to delay marriage until they are in their late 20s or even 30s when they are economically secure. In Ireland, the mean age at first marriage for men was 32.9 and for women 30.3 years in 2000 (Council of Europe 2001, 2004). Although Ireland is a predominantly Catholic country, delayed marriage helps to keep the birth rate down. Another antinatalist custom in some groups is sexual abstinence after birth of a child, usually during the lactating (breast-feeding) period, which lasts anywhere from one to five years.

Education

The higher women's status in society as measured by education level and job opportunities, the lower their fertility. "Women with at least a secondary-level education give birth to one-third to one-half as many children as women with no formal education" (Population Reference Bureau 2007a:4). If a country wants to control population growth, raising the status of women is key. Figure 15.7 shows the relationship between education and family size in eight Global South countries (Population Reference Bureau 2007a). Note that the higher the educational level, the lower the fertility rate and population growth. So, again, education and reduction of poverty are major variables contributing to moderation in population size.

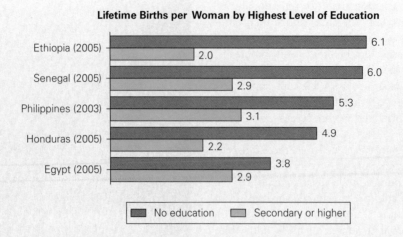

Figure 15.7 Women's Education and Family Size in Selected Countries, 2007

Source: ORC Macro, MEASURE DHS STATcompiler (www.measuredhs.com, accessed June 15, 2007). From Population Reference Bureau, "World Population Highlights," *Population Bulletin 62*, no. 3 (2007). Reprinted with permission.

Note: Among women in developing countries, more education often leads to lower fertility.

Studies repeatedly show that investing in education of girls and women raises every index of a country's progress toward economic growth and development. Yet, 300 million children are without access to education, two thirds of them girls. Of 771 million illiterate adults in the world, two thirds are women. Although this gender gap has narrowed, it persists in sub-Saharan Africa, Arab states, and South and West Asia where only 6 in 10 adults are literate (Institute for Statistics 2005). Two thirds of the world's illiterate adults live in nine countries, and 45% live in India and China.

Family planning programs and contraceptive availability have resulted in a significant decline in global fertility rates, over and above such factors as education (Rama Rao and Mohanam 2003). Availability of contraception may determine a woman's ability to control the number of children she has during the fertile years. For instance, worldwide use of contraception increased from 10% in the 1960s to 62% in 2007, with sharp contrasts between regions (Population Reference Bureau 2007a). Usage doubled in Global South countries, resulting in a decline of fertility in all regions and a total world decline from 3.2% to 2.7%. However, availability of contraception is spotty. In Africa, only 27% of married women are using any method of contraception, and only 20% are relying on modern methods. In some parts of Africa, fewer than 5% use modern methods. As a result, the region has the highest levels of fertility (and AIDS) in the world. Globally, 201 million women lack access to effective contraceptives, but many would practice family planning if given the option (United Nations Population Fund 2005).

As seen above, many factors affect fertility rates and have important consequences for individuals and societies. Increases in numbers of humans and consumption patterns

of citizens in wealthy Global North countries deplete the environmental resources and cause more pollution. Lower population growth means less pressure on governments to provide emergency services for booming populations and means more attention given to services such as schools, health care, and jobs. Most population experts are concerned about these consequences, and they encourage governments and other meso-level institutions in fast-growing countries to act aggressively to control population size. Critics argue that wealthy countries need to curb excesses as well.

There are consequences of population fluctuations in affluent parts of the world as well as for poor parts. The impact of the baby boom in the United States illustrates this, as discussed in the next "Sociology in Your Social World."

Thinking Sociologically

First, read about the baby boom on the facing page. What impact have the baby boom and baby boomlet had on your opportunities for education and a career? How will retirement of baby boomers affect your opportunities?

Mortality Rates and National Health Care Organizations

Imagine living in Sierra Leone, West Africa, where the life expectancy at birth is 41.8 years (United Nations Development Programme 2007/2008) and women have an

Sociology in Your Social World

The Significance of the Baby Boom

At the end of World War II, the birth rate shot up temporarily in most countries involved in the war, as many young people who had been forced to delay marriage made up for lost time. The postwar economy was growing, people were employed in relatively well-paying positions, and the norms supported large families. While this baby boom lasted about only 3 years after World War II in Britain, it lasted 17 years in the United States, from 1946 to 1963.

The baby boom phenomenon has had many impacts. During the late 1960s, school boards and contractors were busy building schools to educate the growing number of children. By the 1980s, student numbers declined, and towns were consolidating schools and closing buildings. When the baby boomers entered the job market starting in the mid-1960s, there were great numbers of applicants for jobs, and employers could pay less. The supply was so great they were assured that someone would take the job.

Two decades later, it was much easier for young people to find jobs because there were fewer of them in that age range looking for starting-level positions. However, that generation is finding it hard to get promotions because the baby boomers have dominated so many of the high-level positions. In addition, trends in marketing and advertising have, for years, been dictated by the baby boom generation because they are such a large segment of the consumer public.

By the 1960s, changes in people's views of the ideal family size and the proper age for marriage changed. Zero population growth movements and environmental concerns slowed the rate of growth. The period from the late 1960s to early 1970s has been referred to as a "baby bust" or the "birth dearth." (This fluctuation resulted in a population structure that did not look very much like a pyramid, as shown in Figure 15.8a, page 519.)

In the mid-1970s and into the 1980s, when the baby boom generation started having babies, there was another baby boom—or "baby boomlet"—but it was much smaller because the baby boomers had smaller families. The result is that population growth in many developed countries has remained below the

The 1950s was the era of the baby boom.

replacement level, or the number of births or migrants a location needs to maintain its population. Growth in the overall size of populations in Global North at this point is due largely to immigration. Otherwise, many populations would be declining more significantly.

Population growth also triggers cultural and social change. Generation Xers (or the children of the baby boomers) now look at careers as transient, and they often move from job to job to advance instead of working up the internal labor market of one firm or organization. Similarly, Generation Xers are experiencing "delayed adulthood" (Furstenburg et al. 2003). Unlike their parents, who saw having a family as the major rite of passage for growing up, Gen Xers spend longer attaining education and have delayed partnering and parenting until they achieve fiscal security. These are two strategies societies have made to adapt to population shifts. The point is that extreme fluctuations in fertility rates can affect societies in a number of ways.

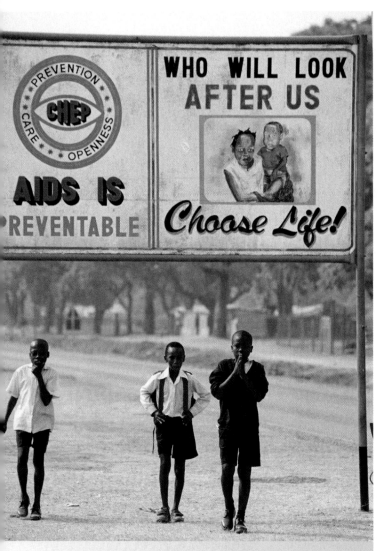

AIDS is a huge problem in Africa. This roadside billboard in Kitwa, Zambia, is part of an educational campaign to help get control of the pandemic.

Table 15.2	**Infant Mortality Rates Around the World**	
Region		Infant Mortality Rate
World		49
More affluent (Global North) countries		6
Less affluent (Global South) countries		54
Least affluent (the very poor Global South)		85
Africa		82
Northern America		7
Latin America		23
Asia		45
Europe		6
Oceania		25

Source: Population Reference Bureau 2008.

average of 6.5 children. Those who survive to adulthood may well live longer, but of every 1,000 babies born alive, 258 will die within the first year (World Factbook 2007b). A majority of the population lives on less than $2 a day (United Nations Development Programme 2007/2008). At 20, life would be almost half over. Close to 70% of men and women are subsistence farmers, working small plots that may not provide enough food to keep their families from starving. When one plot is overfarmed and the soil depleted so that plants will no longer grow, the family moves to another and clears the land, depleting more arable land. What medical care is available is mostly in urban areas.

Some other African countries face similar situations. Life expectancy in Swaziland is 33 years, Lesotho 36 years, Zimbabwe 40 years, and Zambia 38 years (Population Reference Bureau 2008). Average life expectancy for sub-Saharan Africa as

a whole is 49 years. The low life expectancy is due to epidemics such as AIDS, as well as wars, malnutrition, and resulting susceptibility to diseases. Table 15.2 shows the infant mortality rate around the world, meaning the number of infant deaths (children under one year) per 1,000 births. This is a key indicator of a country's overall prosperity.

What causes the stark contrast in life expectancy and infant mortality rates between Global South and North countries? This is a complex issue involving the world economic system, exploitation of natural resources by foreign companies, corruption, lack of access to basic resources, poverty, malnutrition, and lack of opportunity. Access to health care, discussed in Chapter 14, is one key factor accounting for the difference. For instance, in many poor countries, rural families have no access to doctors or medicine such as antibiotics. They rely on local healers and herbal remedies that are effective for some illnesses but cannot cure other medical problems. People frequently die from problems that are easily cured in affluent countries. Note the different causes of death in affluent/Global North versus poor/Global South countries in Table 15.3 (World Health Organization 2002).

Even in technological Global North countries such as the United States, some groups have less access to health care and are less likely than others to receive prenatal care. These are also the groups at highest risk for problem births and infant deaths: those under 18, the unmarried, African Americans, Hispanics, people of low socioeconomic status, and women with little education and lack of prenatal care (Saenz 2008). Infants born to minority teenage mothers living in poverty are of particular concern in the United States. These infants come into the world with many strikes against them, and their mortality rate is especially high. They often have low birth weight, the most common direct or indirect

Table 15.3 **Leading Causes of Death in 2001**			
Poor Countries' Deaths		*Affluent Countries' Deaths*	
Coronary heart disease	10.8%	Coronary heart disease	17.1%
Lower respiratory infections	10.0%	Stroke/Cerebrovascular disease	9.8%
HIV/AIDS	7.5%	Trachea/bronchus/lung cancers	5.8%
Perinatal diseases	6.4%	Lower respiratory infections	4.3%
Stroke/cerebrovascular diseases	6.0%	Chronic obstructive pulmonary disease	3.9%
Diarrhoeal diseases	5.4%	Colon and rectal cancers	3.3%
Malaria	4.4%	Alzheimer and other dementias	2.7%
Tuberculosis	3.8%	Diabetes mellitus	2.7%
Chronic obstructive pulmonary disease	3.1%	Breast cancer	1.9%
Road traffic accidents	1.9%	Stomach cancer	1.8%

Source: World Health Organization 2007.

cause of infant mortality. The U.S. infant mortality rate improved from 12.5 deaths per 1,000 births in 1980 to 10.0 in 1990 to 6.6 in 2008, but it is still higher than many other Global North countries. For example, Canada's rate in 2008 was 5.5 per 1,000 births (Population Reference Bureau 2008).

Migration: Why and Where People Move

Most of us have moved one or more times in our lives. Perhaps, we have moved to a larger house down the block, maybe to another area of the United States for a job opportunity or school, or even to another country altogether. If we have changed our residence, we have been part of the process called **geographic mobility**.

Over the history of the human race, people have migrated to the far reaches of the globe. Because of adaptability to climatic and geographic barriers, humans have dispersed to more areas of the globe than any other species. Even inhospitable locations such as the Arctic North and the South pole and have human settlements.

The *push-pull* model points out that some people are pushed from their original locations by wars, plagues, famine, political or religious conflicts, economic crises, or other factors and pulled to new locations by economic opportunities or political and religious tolerance. Most people do not leave a location unless they have been forced out or they have a viable alternative in the new location and the benefits of moving outweigh the costs (Weeks 2005). In some cases, the push factors are especially strong; in others, the pull factors dominate.

When we are young, we go where our parents go. If a parent receives a lucrative job offer in another location, the family moves. If the family grows and the dwelling becomes too small, the family moves. If a relative needs help or a family member's health requires a different climate, the family moves. Migration is often initiated at the micro level—by an individual's personal traits (such as the willingness to take risks) or by an individual's perception that living in a different place is advantageous. If an opportunity is present, the individual may move. However, if the risks are high, if the information about migration is scarce, or if negative factors such as leaving family behind are present, individuals may decide not to move.

Although the decision to move is often a personal or family one, it is also influenced by the sociocultural environment. History is replete with examples of large groups of people who left an area because of aspirations to improve their life chances, hopes of retaining a way of life, or expulsion by political, economic, or religious forces. Chinese workers came to the United States for economic reasons, to help build the railroad. Amish and Mennonite settlers from Europe sought religious freedom and preservation of their way of life. The Amish, a group originating in Germany, left Germany *en masse*, and the members of this group now live entirely in North America. Italian immigration to the United States took place in a collective manner. When a family left Italy, they would usually move to a U.S. city where a relative or a previous acquaintance lived. Thus, residents of entire apartment buildings in the North End of Boston were from the same extended family, or entire city blocks of people came from the same town or region of southern Italy (Gans 1962). Also, former colonial powers have numerous immigrants from colonized countries. This has helped make many European cities, such as London and Paris, the multicultural environments they are today.

Migrations can be international, from one country to another, or internal, within a single nation. Moves from rural farm communities to urban areas are a common internal migration pattern found around the world. International

This ship containing more than 300 immigrants from Eritrea, East Africa, was spotted by an Italian customs police helicopter. Every year, thousands of illegal immigrants departing from the Mediterranean coasts of Africa try to reach Europe through Sicily. The commute is dangerous, and many immigrants are found dead on the Sicilian shoreline, but the desire for a better future keeps the masses coming.

moves are often influenced by political unrest or discrimination against a group of people such as the Nazi persecutions of the Jewish population. For people who depend on the land, drought and other adverse environmental conditions force movement.

International Migration

An amazing 3% of the world's population is "on the go" each year. That is 191 million international migrants in 2005 alone. These migrants change the size and characteristics of populations around the world, from those being expanded to those being left behind (Population Reference Bureau 2007b). From 1995 to 2000, 2.6 million migrants left the Global South for Global North countries, and more than half of them entered the United States or Canada. An entirely new phenomenon—previously unknown in human history—is also occurring: cyber-migration is a process by

which the Internet creates global connections across physical and cultural boarders, allowing for new opportunities for migration (http://cybermigration.com/).

In the contemporary world situation, international migration is especially common where political turmoil, wars, famines, or natural disasters ravage a country. *Refugees,* that is, those "who flee in search of refuge as in times of war, political oppression, or religious persecution" (www.answers.com/topic/refugee), numbered 9.9 million during 2006. Many citizens are also "internally displaced, forcibly relocated within their own countries by violent conflict or environmental disaster" (Population Reference Bureau 2007b:9). The tsunami in Indonesia and the hurricane that hit New Orleans and the Gulf coastal areas are examples of natural disaster displacement. People from war-torn Darfur seek refuge in neighboring Chad. In the 1970s and 1980s, refugees from Kampuchea (Cambodia) fled military offensives and moved to refugee camps on the Thailand border. Israelis worked secretly to transport Ethiopian Jews to Israel. Tamils from northern Sri Lanka fled to India to escape war. Indigenous Central American refugees fleeing guerilla warfare have entered Mexico and the United States. Hindu and Muslim hostilities in India have led to mass migrations among the countries of India, Pakistan, and Bangladesh as residents look for safe havens. The list of international population movements due to internal crises is extensive and constantly changing. These are not just irrelevant events occurring elsewhere in the world. They involve human beings who are seeking a place to live and may end up as your neighbors.

International migrations in modern times are also motivated by economic opportunities abroad or by fluctuations in the local and world economy. Demand for cheap labor has brought many guest workers from the Global South to European nations and the Persian Gulf states, where foreign workers make up the majority of the labor force. Other economic refugees seek opportunities such as those fleeing Zimbabwe's economic crisis to enter South Africa. Women, who make up a growing proportion of those seeking economic opportunities, total 55% of legal immigrants to the United States. This high percentage has to do with the demand for specific types of work, creating available jobs (Population Reference Bureau 2007b). In some cases, women enter countries due to illegal human trafficking, usually involving both women and children.

Prior to 1914, when World War I began, it was not standard practice for nations to require a passport to enter a country (Friedman 2005). Because most people could not afford intercontinental travel, controlling the flow of people was not an issue. During most of the past century— until the 1980s—there was a more restrictive stance in the United States than in Canada or most European countries regarding immigration (Farley 2005). Strict policies did not entirely stem the tide, however. The number of foreign-born people in the United States was 31 million in 2000 and is expected to rise to 48 million by 2025, resulting in 14% of the U.S. population being foreign-born. First- and second-generation residents will constitute about one third of the U.S. population by 2025 (Population Reference Bureau 2007b:8). About 11 million illegal migrants from Mexico and other South and Central American countries now live in the United States, and half a million illegal immigrants enter the country each year. Some people are so desperate to cross over to the United States that they risk everything. Four hundred Mexicans died in 2005 trying to cross the desert to the U.S. border (*The Economist* 2006a, 2006b).

Two factors curb migrations: restrictive immigration laws of receiving countries and economic depressions. During recessions, many countries restrict immigration by passing strict immigration quotas, even for political refugees from war-torn countries.

Thinking Sociologically

Think about your own grandparents or great-grandparents. How long have your ancestors occupied the same land or lived in the same community? Do they go back more than one generation on the same property? If they have been mobile, what factors were critical to their mobility? How has their mobility or stability influenced your family's experiences?

Since the terrorist attacks of September 11, 2001, the idea that the U.S. borders are porous has been highly divisive as the U.S. Congress and state legislatures struggle to find appropriate policies. The lack of agreement stems from conflicts over how the country feels about immigrants. Some favor the diversity and new ideas brought by skilled, highly educated immigrants, as well as the labor brought by low-skilled immigrants, who work at jobs not filled by U.S. citizens. Conflicts focus on who the migrants are, their religions, economic impact of immigrants, settlement patterns, whether immigrants bring crime, political loyalties of immigrants, moral values, and work habits. Research finds that, for the most part, immigrants are industrious, innovating, and hard working. They pay taxes and contribute to their communities. However, 9/11 affected attitudes about immigration, with a 20% increase in U.S. citizens favoring policies restricting immigration. One such policy that is in progress, for example, is a fence along a length of the Mexican-U.S. border (Inhofe 2008).

There is no agreement on a comprehensive nationwide policy. As of July 2007, more than 1,404 bills related to immigration had been introduced in the 50 state legislatures; 170 of these bills had been proposed in 2007 alone. In addition, 182 different bills became laws in 43 states. The laws relate to employment eligibility, health care, acceptable identification,

Two women refugees from Eritrea walk past their refugee camp in east Sudan. Ethnic cleansing and political turmoil have left many people around the world not only homeless but without a country.

drivers' licenses, public benefits, and human trafficking (National Conference of State Legislatures 2007). Many laws protect the rights of immigrant workers and their families to education and health care. Most immigrants are of working age and accounted for 60% of the labor force increase between 2000 and 2004, and they will account for all of the increase within 5 to 25 years (Population Reference Bureau 2007b).

A bill that passed in the House of Representatives would make all illegal aliens felons and would make it a crime (akin to smuggling) for U.S. citizens (including church and social workers who help immigrants) to help anyone who is in the United States illegally. This bill led to protest marches in many cities, including a 500,000-person demonstration in Los Angeles. In contrast to the House bill, some leading senators favor giving some long-term illegal residents a path to citizenship. President Bush has endorsed a guest worker program for people who work at jobs that other Americans are not willing to do, at least for the wages currently being paid, yet many people fear job competition by illegal immigrants who will work for very little and flood the job market.

The debate is intense, and the solutions will not be easy (*The Economist* 2006a, 2006b). What the new president of the United States will do remains to be seen, but whatever the outcome of the election, the new policy is unlikely to be as restrictive as many against immigration would like.

Internal Migration

The rate of internal migration in the United States is high compared with most places in the world. Patterns

Table 15.4 **Reasons for Moving by Type of Move, 2006 (in percentages)**

Reasons for Mobility	All Movers	Type of Mobility		
		Intracounty	Intercounty	From Abroad
Family-related reasons	11,025	6,894	3,759	372
Change in marital status	2,395	1,547	786	62
To establish own household	3,389	2,617	753	19
Other family reasons	5,241	2,730	2,220	290
Work-related reasons	7,328	2,160	4,491	677
New job/job transfer	3,481	538	2,641	302
To look for work/lost job	638	153	319	166
Closer to work/easier commute	1,440	737	701	2
Retired	170	9	159	2
Total	39,837	24,851	13,690	1,296

Source: U.S. Census Bureau 2006b, 2006d.

Note: Reported in thousands.

have primarily involved individual "pull" migration to economic opportunities and better housing. Almost half report housing as the main reason for their relocation: a better apartment or house, owning rather than renting, cheaper housing, and better neighborhood with less crime are primary reasons for moving (U.S. Census Bureau 2006b, 2006d). Table 15.4 provides reasons for moving that fall into several categories.

During different historical periods, movement directions have varied. For many years, rural residents in the United States moved to higher income urban areas. Until the 1950s, people moved out of the southern states and into northern states, especially north central states. Then the pattern reversed, and the flow started south and west. Movement since the 1960s has been toward the Sunbelt, especially to California, Arizona, Texas, and Florida. Movement to the Pacific Coast and even Alaska has also increased due to economic opportunities in these locations.

Although decisions about family size and migration are individual ones, they are influenced by what happens at the meso and macro levels.

Thinking Sociologically

What are the benefits and costs for individuals and governments of extensive internal migration? What are the advantages and disadvantages of having large numbers of immigrants?

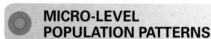

MICRO-LEVEL POPULATION PATTERNS

You might get the impression that population studies are mostly about other places and problems that do not affect your country. However, understanding demography can be extremely important for comprehending social processes very close to your everyday life. While most Global North countries do not have massive famines or population explosions, population fluctuations influence us in many ways.

In 1969, Keith, one of your coauthors, lived in Boston, and his wife taught in a suburban school system there. The elementary school where she taught had four first-grade classrooms, with 28 children per room—112 first graders in the school. By the next year, the decline in the fertility rate six years earlier was being felt, and the number of first graders declined. Within four years, the number of first graders in her school was reduced to 40, with two classrooms and only 20 students per class. Some school systems lost half of their student population in a short time. One year, first-grade teachers were losing their jobs or having to move to another grade, and the next year, it was second-grade teachers who were scrambling. The third year, third-grade teachers were in oversupply, and so forth. With low demand, these were not times for college students to be pursuing teaching careers.

We have already mentioned the impact of the baby boom (the high fertility rates from 1946 to about 1963) and the following baby bust (the drop in fertility for more than a decade following the baby boom). The impact on the population is graphically represented in the population pyramid

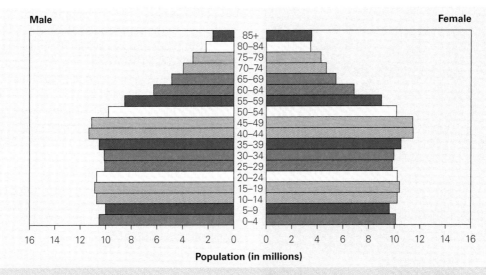

Figure 15.8a   United States, 2005

Source: U.S. Census Bureau 2006c.

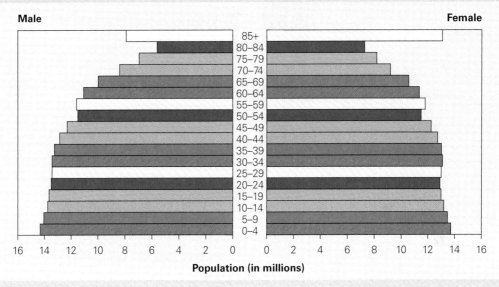

Figure 15.8b   United States, 2050

Source: U.S. Census Bureau 2006c.

of the United States (see Figure 15.8a). As you can see, the U.S. population no longer looks anything like a pyramid, and this odd population pattern affects job prospects, retirement security, career decisions, and deviance rates, to name only a few of the outcomes. Note the projected implications for 2050 in Figure 15.8b.

The decision about your career is a deeply personal decision, but population trends also shape that decision. For example, if a business that produces children's products expands its production shortly after a dip in fertility rates, the timing of the business expansion may cause severe financial hardships or even bankruptcy for the company. Smart businesspeople pay a great deal of attention to characteristics of the population. That same information might be relevant to an individual deciding on a career. For example, this is an incredibly good time for students who enjoy working with older people (gerontology) or in the medical field to think about a career in gerontology or health care.

Retirement is another topic for which population patterns are critical. Most countries in the Global North are struggling with how young working people are going to support the nonworking aging populations. The number of working people contributing to pensions compared to retirees who depend on support is changing dramatically. Systems in many countries are in trouble because of low birth rates and increasing numbers of nonworking elderly people.

For example, when social security was established in the United States in the 1930s, life expectancy was 59.

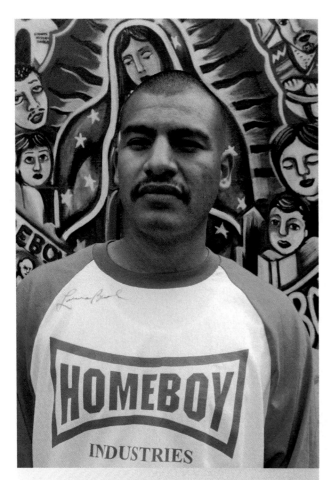

This former gang member is like many teenage delinquents. He eventually accepted the Global South roles and responsibilities of adulthood and began to work within the system. He now helps young men change their lives. When a large percentage of the population is between 16 and 24, the deviance rates in the society increase.

been mismanaged. They are pointing to problems created by changes in the composition of the U.S. population.

In the 1980s, the U.S. administration and Congress saw the problem coming and for the first time began to save funds in a social security account for the baby boomers. They also passed laws requiring baby boomers to work longer before they qualify for social security. That there are so many baby boomers—and that an extremely high percentage of citizens over the age of 65 vote—makes it unlikely that Congress or the president would cut back on benefits to this group, once they have retired. Still, with the federal budget squeezed by war and natural disasters (such as Hurricane Katrina) causing the deficit to grow, some members of Congress have voiced interest in "borrowing" from the social security reserves. Members of the younger generations will be the ones to pay if insufficient funds are available for the baby boomers, and their future pensions may be in jeopardy.

Thinking Sociologically

You have probably not thought much about economic security after retirement. What plans can you make now for this long period of life after work? Why is this planning important?

The number of people in the age-dependent categories of under 15 or over 65 was low. For each person who received social security, 20 paid into the federal coffers. Twenty people each paying $500 a year could easily support a retired person, who might receive $10,000 per year. However, the average life expectancy has shifted, and the age-dependent population increased. Currently in the United States, roughly 12.7% of the population is over the age of 65 (World Factbook 2008), as opposed to 4% in the 1930s. Moreover, predictions are that by 2035, 20% of the population will be over 65. When the baby boomers are collecting social security, the people born during the birth dearth will be the ones in their prime earning years, but there are far fewer of them paying into the system. When commentators and politicians say social security is in trouble, therefore, they are not generally saying it has

Rates of deviance and juvenile delinquency are also influenced by population patterns. In the 1960s and 1970s, these rates climbed precipitously. When the rates of juvenile delinquency began to decline in the 1980s and 1990s, members of both major U.S. political parties claimed it was their policies that made the difference. However, most deviant acts are committed by young people in their mid-teens to early twenties. Thus, when the baby boom generation was in their teens and early twenties, the overall rates of deviance were higher. Many of those same delinquents became upright citizens—even law-and-order conservatives—once they had families and careers. When the birth dearth group was in their teens, overall rates of crime dropped because there were fewer teenagers.

Understanding how immigration and internal migration patterns affect individuals can help you make location decisions. Enhanced or weakened economic prospects of certain countries or regions change the demand for workers. For example, representation in the U.S. Congress is based on the census done every 10 years. If a state loses population, it may have fewer representatives to Congress the following year. Shifts in the distribution of the population, therefore, can mean shifts in the amount of power a state holds in national policy making.

Demography is relevant to job prospects and career planning, to policy decisions about pension plans such as social security, to market research for businesses, and to understanding political power and influence within a country. Because population trends will shape your life, understanding those trends can help you use that knowledge to your advantage.

To illustrate the power of demographic trends on individual decisions, the above "Sociology in Your Social World" provides an exercise in problem solving using information from population pyramids of U.S. cities.

Our next topic continues the discussion of population trends by focusing on growth of urban areas.

Urbanization: Movement From Rural to Urban Areas

Mumbai (Bombay), India; Caracas, Venezuela; Lagos, Nigeria; Shanghai, China; and New York City, United States, are all bustling megacities (cities with more than 10 million people) with traffic congestion and people rushing to their destinations.

Sociology in Your Social World

Population Pyramids and Predicting Community Needs and Services

Study these three Population Pyramid graphs. Based on what you see, answer the following questions:

1. Which community would be likely to have the lowest crime rate? Explain.

2. Which would be likely to have the most cultural amenities (theaters, art galleries, concert halls, and so forth)? Explain.

3. Imagine you were an entrepreneur planning on starting a business in one of these communities.
   a. Name three businesses that you think would be likely to succeed in each community. Explain.
   b. Name one business that you think would be unlikely to succeed in each community. Explain.

Bloomington, Indiana, 2000

(Hint: Bloomington is a town of about 65,000 and is the home of Indiana University, a Big Ten university.)

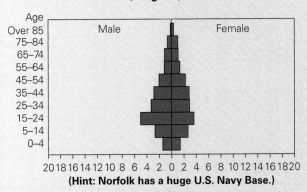

Norfolk, Virginia, 2000

(Hint: Norfolk has a huge U.S. Navy Base.)

Naples, Florida, 2000

(Hint: Naples is a major retirement location.)

Photo Essay

World Cities

Cities are vibrant places: rich in cultural diversity, artistic creativity, fine cuisine, high-paying jobs, and exciting nightlife for young people—and also poverty. The world cities pictured here illustrate variations and similarities (clockwise, from top left, New York City; Singapore; Hong Kong; Agra-Delhi, India; Saigon, Vietnam; and Guanajuato, Mexico).

Carts, bicycles, and taxis weave in and out of traffic jams. The local spices and other aromas scent the air. Sidewalk merchants display vegetables and fruits unique to the country. Beggars and the homeless, often migrants from rural areas, dot the sidewalks, while merchants sell colorful wares. Cities are vibrant places with diversity and contributions of a variety of ethnic traditions coming together. The amazing sights, sounds, smells, tastes, and cultural activities—from art and theater, to music and night clubs—mean there is always excitement. There is also the draw of exciting and high-paying jobs. These options and opportunities lure people to cities.

These megacities around the world are part of a global trend that has gained momentum over several centuries—urbanization. The "Sociology Around the World" feature below outlines major urbanization trends in the world (Brunn et al. 2003; United Nations Population Division 2003).

Sociology Around the World

World Urbanization Trends

World Urbanization Prospects are reports published by the United Nations Population Division. They provide a valuable data set on past, present, and future urbanization trends in regions and subregions of the world. They also provide data on individual cities and urban areas. The major findings of the most recent edition are as follows:

1. During 2008, for the first time in history, the proportion of the population living in urban areas will reach 50 percent. While in the more developed regions, the proportion urban was already nearly 53 percent in 1950, in the less developed regions the 50 percent level will likely be reached around 2019.

2. The world urban population is expected to nearly double by 2050, increasing from 3.3 billion in 2007 to 6.4 billion in 2050. By mid-century the world urban population will likely be absorbed by the urban areas of the less developed regions, whose population is projected to increase from 2.4 billion in 2007 to 5.3 billion in 2050. The urban population of the more developed regions is projected to increase modestly, from 0.9 billion in 2007 to 1.1 billion in 2050.

3. The world rural population is expected to reach a maximum of 3.5 billion in 2018 or 2019 and to decline slowly thereafter, to reach 2.8 billion in 2050. . . . The rural population of the less developed regions more than doubled since 1950 and will likely continue to grow until 2021 before a long-term decline sets in.

4. The rate of growth of the world urban population is slowing down. Between 1950 and 2007, the world urban population grew at an average rate of 2.6 percent per year and more than quadrupled over the period, passing from 0.7 billion to 3.3 billion. . . .

5. Among the less developed regions, Latin America and the Caribbean have an exceptionally high level of urbanization (78 percent), higher than that of Europe. Africa and Asia, in contrast, remain mostly rural, with 38 percent and 41 percent, respectively, of their populations living in urban areas. Over the coming decades, the level of urbanization is expected to increase in all major areas of the developing world. . . .

6. Despite its low level of urbanization in 2007, Asia was home to about half of the urban population in the world. Europe had the second highest share, at 16 percent. Over the next four decades, African and Asia will experience a marked increase in their urban populations. . . .

7. . . . In 2007, three-quarters of the 3.3 billion urban dwellers on Earth lived in 25 countries, whose urban populations ranged from 29 million in South Africa to 561 million in China. China, India and the United States accounted for 35 percent of the world's urban population. . . . Most countries have small urban populations.

(Continued)

(Continued)

Table 15.5   **Total, Urban and Rural Populations by Development Group, Selected Periods, 1950–2050**

Development Group	Population (billions)					Average Annual Rate of Change (percentage)			
	1950	1975	2007	2025	2050	1950–1975	1975–2007	2007–2025	2025–2050
Total population									
World	2.54	4.08	6.67	8.01	9.19	1.90	1.54	1.02	0.55
More developed regions	0.81	1.05	1.22	1.26	1.25	1.01	0.48	0.16	−0.04
Less developed regions	1.72	3.03	5.45	6.75	7.95	2.26	1.84	1.19	0.65
Urban population									
World	0.74	1.52	3.29	4.58	6.40	2.89	2.42	1.84	1.33
More developed regions	0.43	0.70	0.91	0.99	1.07	1.98	0.81	0.49	0.30
Less developed regions	0.31	0.82	2.38	3.59	5.33	3.88	3.35	2.27	1.58
Rural population									
World	1.80	2.56	3.38	3.43	2.79	1.41	0.87	0.08	−0.82
More developed regions	0.39	0.35	0.31	0.26	0.17	−0.44	−0.32	−0.94	−1.67
Less developed regions	1.41	2.21	3.06	3.16	2.62	1.80	1.02	0.17	−0.75

Development Group	Percentage urban					Rate of Urbanization (percentage)			
	1950	1975	2007	2025	2050	1950–1975	1975–2007	2007–2025	2025–2050
World	29.1	37.3	49.4	57.2	69.6	0.99	0.88	0.82	0.59
More developed regions	52.5	67.0	74.4	79.0	86.0	0.97	0.33	0.33	0.24
Less developed regions	18.0	27.0	43.8	53.2	67.0	1.62	1.51	1.08	0.78

Source: Quoted from United Nations Population Division. 2008. *World Urbanization Prospects: The 2007 Revision.* Department of Economic and Social Affairs.

This urbanization process involves "1. the movement of people from rural to urban places, where they engage in primarily non-rural occupations, and 2. the change in lifestyle that results from living in cities" (Brunn, Williams, and Zeigler 2003:5). Urbanization accompanies (1) modernization—transformation from traditional, mostly agrarian societies, to contemporary bureaucratized states, and (2) industrialization—transformation from an agricultural base and handmade goods to manufacturing industries. We explore urbanization in this chapter as a very specific demographic trend that has major social implications for how people live and interact.

Most people live their lives in communities: locations that provide dwellings, a sense of identity and belonging, neighbors and friends, social involvements, and access to basic necessities. Our most intimate micro-level interactions take place in these communities. Yet, we are connected through our communities to larger meso- and macro-level social structures, such as political and religious organizations, world health organizations, and international relief agencies (e.g., UNICEF). In this section, we consider the development of communities—from rural areas and small towns to urban areas such as megacities.

Thinking Sociologically

First, read the "World Urbanization Trends" feature that begins on page 523. How might global urbanization affect you? How might the trend affect people from Global South countries?

The second half of this chapter is a continuation of the discussion of demographic patterns. However, we will return here to the pattern used in previous chapters of discussing micro-level analysis first, followed by meso- and macro-level analyses. First, how do urban environments affect us as individuals?

CITIES AS MICRO-LEVEL LIVING ENVIRONMENTS

In the 17th and 18th centuries, when Europe was undergoing dramatic changes, small, bucolic villages contrasted sharply with the rapidly growing urban centers. Tonnies (1855–1936) described these two extreme types on a continuum from **Gemeinschaft**, a German word indicating a small traditional community, to **Gesellschaft**, meaning a large, impersonal urban area. He saw social life as an evolution from family units to rural villages, towns, cities, nations, and finally cosmopolitan urban life (Tonnies [1887] 1963). Family, friendship, relations to the land, common values, traditions, and experiences are key elements of Gemeinschaft. Gesellschaft, a product of urban industrial society, is characterized by formal relations, contracts, laws, and economies built on money. People in urban areas do not necessarily know one another or share common values. They tend to be employees of bureaucratic organizations, and they tend to be more isolated as individuals rather than members of a collectivity.

A number of other theorists living in the Europe of the 19th century suggested similar contrasts. Durkheim (1858–1917) described the social bonds that held society together and the changes that arose from industrialization and urbanization. **Mechanical solidarity** was his term for the glue that held a society together through shared beliefs, values, and traditions typical of rural areas and simple societies. In mechanical solidarity, social bonds were formed by homogeneity of thought.

Think of any large business in which each employee has a specific task to perform in the division of labor. The social glue that holds modern industrial and postindustrial societies and people together is **organic solidarity**, a division of labor with each member playing a highly specialized role in the society. Each person is dependent on others with interrelated, interdependent tasks. This interdependence of specialized tasks is the key to unity in more complex societies with organic solidarity.

The ways in which order is maintained in society illustrate the differences between the two types of societies. In mechanical solidarity, legal systems are concerned with moral order, upheld by shared beliefs and values and a desire to be well regarded in the community. Organic solidarity stresses making amends for a wrongdoing by paying fines or spending time in jail (Durkheim [1893] 1947). So even the notion of how to maintain social order varies as this transformation in the society occurs.

For most of human history, humans lived in small population centers. Rural areas dominated. *Rural sociology*, which refers to the study of social life in nonmetropolitan areas, considers patterns and behaviors among people at a distance from population centers. In the United States, **rural areas** have fewer than 1,000 people per square mile. According to the 2000 U.S. census, this constituted 21% of the U.S. population. Some rural residents are in farming or agribusiness and are concerned with the economics of farm production, ranching, and mining. Others live in resort towns or cater to tourists. Popular rural destinations are mountain areas, the Ozarks, coastal regions, and some Midwestern areas in Nebraska, Kansas, and surrounding states.

As the years pass, agriculture occupies many fewer citizens, and a rural exodus has been under way, with movement to cities that have more economic opportunities and better health care and education. Rural areas face problems just as cities do: environmental degradation from overfarming, overuse of water resources, toxic dumps, and poverty due to reductions in economic opportunities and selling of family farms.

Major population shifts from rural to urban areas came with industrialization in Europe and North America, followed by the same process in other areas of the world. As urbanization continues to sweep the world, many rural areas are disappearing, and those that remain are taking on aspects of metropolitan life as they move away from mechanical and toward organic solidarity. Even the remotest villages are influenced by urban and global concerns. For instance, decisions about what crops to grow are often tied to nonlocal demand. Poor farmers in South America and Afghanistan make more money growing poppies for drug suppliers in big cities than from food crops to feed the local population, making them food dependent.

The early interpretations of urbanization, especially by European sociologists, were made through a rather pessimistic lens. The trend was seen largely as a decline of civil society. However, there are pluses as well as minuses in quality of life as people inhabit more densely populated areas.

Life in the City

On warm evenings, the residents come out of their oppressive apartments to sit on the front steps. Children play ball in the street or splash in front of open fire hydrants. Neighbors chat about work and politics and other things neighbors share. Across the interstate highway, the professional couple is having cocktails with friends from work in their renovated, air-conditioned Victorian home. In a nearby suburb, families are returning from sports practices, mowing their lawns, and preparing dinner. Political, economic, and cultural factors help to shape these different scenarios in the inner city and its surrounding area, as described by urban residential patterns and suburbanization.

While life in urban areas of North America is typically individualistic and bureaucratic, life in small towns, such as Bhakatapur, Nepal (top), and a Tibetan village (bottom) is more communal and personal, but one has much less privacy.

Urban Residential Patterns

Neighborhoods are identifiable areas within the larger metropolitan area. Four characteristics help define neighborhoods:

1. A neighborhood can meet most of the needs of residents: food, schools, religions.

2. Neighborhoods are "natural areas"; that is, to a great degree, residents are homogeneous with respect to income, interests, ethnicity or race, and other shared characteristics.

3. There is a high degree of social interaction among the residents of a neighborhood.

4. There is substantial symbolic commitment, the feeling of belonging to a meaningful sociogeographic area.

Some neighborhoods in cities, especially in ethnic immigrant concentrations, are close-knit. This is especially true when members of extended families live in the same area and provide support for one another (Guest and Stamm 1993; Logan and Spitze 1994). In major cities around the world, ethnic enclaves offer security, familiarity, and protection. For new migrants to cities, neighborhoods provide gradual adaptation to the strange new society and the dominant group. Immigrant groups often attempt to re-create their former, more intimate village-type settings within their urban neighborhood (Gans 1962). Ethnic communities can provide job opportunities and gradual acculturation into language and customs.

Supportive ethnic enclaves are also found in African American inner-city neighborhoods of predominantly single mothers and children. Stack (1998) found that women created support networks—sustaining each other through sharing of child care and resources. However, in some low-income tenement areas, little interaction has been found because of high turnover of residents and fear of violence (Renzetti 2003).

Homogeneous middle-class city and suburban dwellers often have an active neighborhood life as well. A suburb is an area immediately adjacent to a city, extending outward beyond the city limits or the core of the city (Flanagan 2001). The variables that create a sense of community are complex, and generalizations that apply to all types of communities are difficult to make.

City dwellers become accustomed to the fast pace of life, the danger of stepping off the curb to cross the street, the crowds jostling and pushing them along as they rush to work, the impersonal attitudes of clerks, and the impatience with inconveniences. The thrill of city life outweighs the problems for many residents, who are sentimentally attached to the unique nature of life in cities. Let us look at some of the variables that affect how people experience city life.

Human Relationships in Cities

Sociologist Georg Simmel ([1902–17] 1950) was concerned with the experience of urban life, with what it does to people's thoughts and behavior. He argued that two factors—the intensity and stimulation of city life and the market effects on urban relations—cause people to have different attitudes, beliefs, and values from those in rural areas. City dwellers have no choice but to be somewhat insensitive, to avoid intense relationships, and to keep social relationships superficial to protect their privacy. However, he did not feel this was necessarily negative. Cities free people from the social constraints of close relationships in small towns. Erving Goffman ([1959] 2001) called behaviors of urban dwellers *civil inattention,* elaborate modes of pretending that we do not look, make eye contact, bump into others, pay attention, or listen to what others are doing. Residents show an awareness of others without being conspicuous, threatening, or overly friendly. To visitors or strangers to city life, these behaviors seem callous and cold. However, they offer anonymity and freedom in a crowded environment.

Sociologist Louis Wirth (1964) also argued that because urban residents live in heterogeneous, high-density areas, they develop coping mechanisms for dealing with the situation. They become sophisticated, removed from others to insulate themselves from too many personal claims and expectations of others. The depersonalization that results from lower commitment to a common community "goal" also leads to a higher tolerance for nonconformity in cities, resulting in more individual freedom—and as a result more deviance.

Urban sociologist Claude Fischer (1984) argues that urbanism shapes social life rather than leaving residents as alienated individuals in a sea of traffic, noise, and pollution. City life strengthens social groups, promotes diverse subcultures, and encourages intimate social circles. These urban groups share similar activities or traits. The larger numbers of people make it possible for individuals with similar interests—from ethnic subcultures to gay communities to artist groups—to draw together as clubs, organizations, or neighborhoods. These little social worlds "touch but do not interpenetrate" (Fischer 1984:37). As long as there are enough members of a group, each can maintain its own identity. When different groups come in contact with each other, the result may be positive sharing of cultures, or it may be conflict, causing members to associate all the more closely with their own group. Gangs fall into this latter category. So rather than creating isolated individuals who interact defensively with others, urban life may create choices about lifestyle and enhance a different kind of community base, intensifying the interactions.

Despite these benefits of urban life in countries where cities have substantial resources to provide services, urbanization can have very different consequences, especially in poor regions of the world. Rapidly growing cities in impoverished countries often face challenges to provide services—shelter, water, electricity, sanitation, schools, health care—for the increasing numbers of residents.

Thinking Sociologically

What do you see as the most important consequences for individuals or groups living in urban areas?

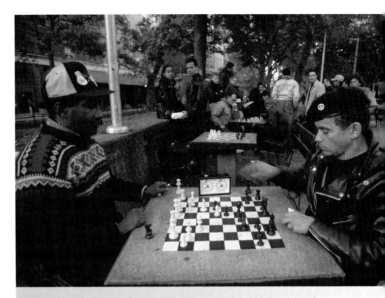

Despite the sometimes impersonal environment of cities, local neighborhoods in urban areas often have a sense of community and local traditions. Here we see people playing chess at Washington Square in New York City. This is enough of a community event that it attracts interested spectators.

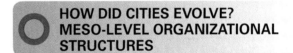

HOW DID CITIES EVOLVE? MESO-LEVEL ORGANIZATIONAL STRUCTURES

Human settlements have gone through massive transitions over the past 10,000 years, from small agricultural settlements to bustling crowded metropolises with millions of people. The first step in the development of urban life came when those living nomadic lives became more settled. Archeological evidence indicates that there may have been early settlements in southern Russia as early as 15,000 years ago (Zimolzak and Stansfield 1983). Starting about 10,000 years ago with the advent of agriculture, domestication of animals, and the shift from food gathering to food production, small groups established permanent settlements. Among the first was Eridu in Iraq, a settlement of some 25 permanent compounds with a population of up to 200 in each compound and a grain storage facility in the center (see Figure 15.9). The people grew wheat and barley and domesticated dogs, goats, and sheep.

These settlements were not cities as we think of them today, however, because they had different cultural and economic structures, and there was little division of labor. Everyone shared roles, worked the land to support the population, and banded together for protection. Cities, by contrast, are large permanent settlements with nonagricultural specialists, a literate elite, and surplus food to support the social classes that are not involved in food production. They have been the source of intense fascination for many social science theorists.

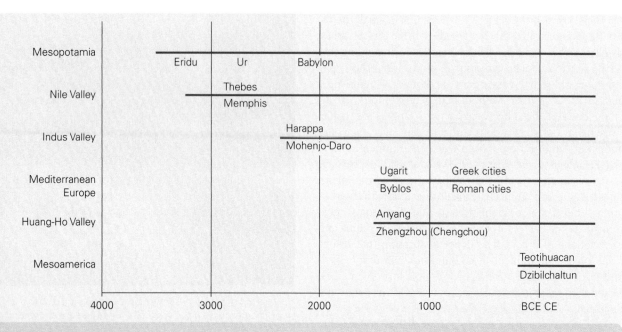

Figure 15.9   Cities in Antiquity

Source: Sjoberg 1965:56–57.

Theories of Urban Development

Among the first sociologists in the United States were urban scholars, dubbed the Chicago School, who studied problems in the city of Chicago. Their studies of urban ecology focused on the patterns of land use and residential distribution of people in urban areas. These theorists pictured the city's growth pattern as a series of circles. Moving out from the center, each circle was dominated by a particular type of activity and residential pattern, from central city ghettoes and rooming houses to working-class apartments and bungalows, to middle-class housing, to upper-class suburbs (Park, Burgess, and McKenzie [1925] 1967). See Figure 15.10 for an illustration of this pattern.

Urban ecologists further refined the Chicago School's original ideas by exploring social, economic, political, and technological systems of cities' spatial patterns (Abu-Lughod 1991). Several processes constantly take place in urban areas: residential segregation; invasion by a new ethnic, religious, or socioeconomic group; and succession by that group. These processes are part of dynamic city life (Berry and Kasarda 1977).

Racial and ethnic segregation is a continuing and troubling issue in many urban areas of the United States. Despite some reductions in racism in the nation, American cities—especially northern cities—have high levels of residential segregation. This segregation affects networking, school segregation, and access to community resources. Figure 15.11 illustrates the likelihood that someone of a given race will have contacts in their neighborhood that cross racial lines. This figure is based on one city—Chicago, Illinois—but you can easily check the residential patterns in your city by going to www.censusscope.org/segregation.html.

In the past three decades, very new and different theories of urban development have emerged, spurred in part by the decay, riots, and disturbances in cities around the world that dramatized inequalities and prompted sociologists to find new explanations for urban problems. The idea is that urban space is both socially defined and in scarce supply. Therefore, political-economic conflict will arise over how space gets allocated and by whom. Any effective solution to urban problems must address inequalities between groups and allocations of resources in urban areas (Castells 1977; Harvey 1973).

Some conflict theorists see growing city problems as a result of domination by elites, creating poverty and exploitation of the poor (Flanagan 2001; Gottdiener and Hutchison 2006). Cities produce profits for those who buy and sell property and for investors and politicians who redevelop urban areas. Sometimes, poor urban residents are displaced in the process (Hannigan 1998). In short, conflict theorists see urbanization and modernization as a cause of poverty among city residents around the world.

Types of Cities

Although organizational structures of cities have changed and evolved over time, in the following section, we will focus on industrial and several variants of postindustrial cities.

Industrial Cities

The onset of industrialization in 17th- and 18th-century Europe started the trend toward urbanized nations, countries in which more than half of the population live in

Figure 15.10   Burgess's Theory of City Growth: The Chicago School envisioned urban growth as a series of concentric circles, with ethnicity, class, residential patterns, and types of activity evolving with each ring removed from the central city.

Source: Park, Burgess, and McKenzie (1925) 1967:55.

urban areas. Rural peasants migrated to the cities in search of opportunities and to escape the tedium and poverty of agricultural existence and shortage of available farmland. Often, this resulted in a rapid influx of migrants and an unplanned urbanization process. Cities served the rapidly advancing industrial sector, but crowded conditions, poor sanitation, polluted water supplies, and poor working conditions all contributed to the misery of poor urban residents and to their short life expectancy compared to those living in the countryside. Urban systems became overwhelmed by the large numbers of migrants, and conditions became as desperate as those the people had tried to escape in the rural areas. Today, Global North countries are more than 75% urban, and Global South countries are on average 40% urban. By 2030, this imbalance will be even greater.

Industrial cities became primarily commercial centers motivated by competition, a characteristic that differentiated

them from preindustrial cities. The advent of power-driven machinery and the new capitalist factory system transformed and replaced the former craft and cottage industries and guild structures (Abu-Lughod 1991). Roads, waterways, and railroads made travel and communication between towns and cities easier and faster. Cities became fast-paced as mechanical vehicles took to the streets.

By 1850, profound changes began taking place in many European countries and in the United States. A shift from predominantly rural to urban living was under way. In about 1870, Great Britain became the first truly urban nation with more than 50% of the population in urban areas. Economically changing conditions in the British Isles were conducive to urbanization and industrialization. Parliament had passed "reorganization of land acts" that pushed many rural citizens from the countryside to cities. In addition, raw materials were available from colonies; new technology was

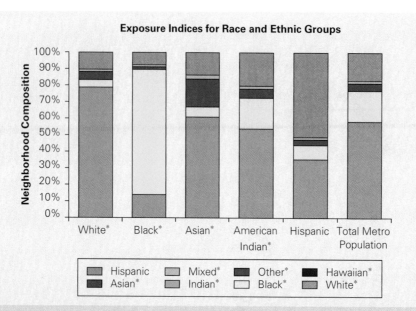

Figure 15.11 Residential Segregation and Cross-Race Contact: Chicago, Illinois

Source: Residential Segregation and Cross-Race Contact: Chicago, Illinois. www.census.org/segregation.html.

Note: Unless there is complete integration, the racial composition of neighborhoods where most whites live differs from the composition of neighborhoods lived in by blacks, Hispanics, or other groups. To examine this, the Census Bureau calculates exposure indices—the average racial composition of neighborhoods experienced by members of each racial group. This bar graph illustrates the typical contact of most residents with members of their own and other races in a metropolitan area. In this graph, the first five columns represent the average racial composition of the neighborhood of a person of a given race as a person of a given race would experience it. The rightmost column shows the racial composition of the metro area as a whole.

Despite the many jobs created, one of the downsides of industrialized cities is phenomenal pollution.

rapidly advancing manufacturing techniques; and the banking facilities, credit, stock and other financing for industry were falling into place (Benevolo 1995; Mumford 1961).

Residential population patterns in the United States are illustrative. About 90% of the U.S. population lived on farms in the 1790s. Today, agricultural workers hold only about 859,000 jobs, and this number, including farmers, those who work with animals, agricultural inspectors, and other related workers, is unlikely to change in the next decade (U.S. Bureau of Labor Statistics 2008–09). Only 1.84% of the population works in farming and related work in 2002, and only 6.5% of rural households are working farms (U.S. Department of Agriculture 2002). Agribusiness conglomerates have bought out family farmers who could not compete with these large businesses. Young people have moved from farms, leaving the population in rural areas older than that in urban areas.

Between 1940 and 2000, the number of urban areas in the United States increased from 33 to 453 (The Federal Register 2002), and many cities have become global economic centers (Abu-Lughod 2001). Urban growth was aided by an increase in agricultural productivity, which made food available to support urban dwellers, and by the development of an adequate distribution system to get the produce to markets to feed those in urban areas.

With the advent of public transportation in the late 1800s, people in many countries began to escape crowded city conditions by moving out into emerging suburbs. Private automobiles and telephones aided movement to the suburbs. Road systems were developed to accommodate the growing numbers of autos, and more businesses and services relocated to suburban areas.

Since the 1990s, the U.S. Census shows that some rural areas are once again gaining population. This is especially the case in recreation areas, where urban residents relocate to exurbs (rural areas within commuting distance of city jobs), and retired people look for new locations with clean air, space, interpersonal civility, and a slower pace than the city (Johnson and Fuguitt 2000).

Postindustrial Cities

Postindustrial cities (Bell [1976] 1999) have a high percentage of employees in the service sector—business headquarters, government and intergovernmental organizations, research and development, tourism, finance, health, education, and telecommunications. They are found in the most technologically advanced, wealthy nations. Washington, D.C., fits most of these characteristics, as does La Defense, an urban center on the outskirts of Paris, built as a commercial, service, and information exchange center to serve France.

Postindustrial cities are closely tied to the economic structures of capitalism, with global production systems and instant exchanges of information (Abu-Lughod 2001; Friedman 2005). In the transformation from industrial to postindustrial economies, from manufacturing to service economies, some people get left behind. There are often severe income disparities between those trained for the new economies and those with less training and in lower level positions. Cities such as Bangalore, India, illustrate the disparities between high-tech industries and poor agricultural peasants in the surrounding areas. These high-tech centers attract business from around the world. This book would have been produced in the United States a few years ago, but with the tightening publication market, publishers find it economically prudent to outsource and save on costs.

Some urban areas are carefully planned. *New towns*, for example, are cities built from scratch as economically self-sufficient entities with all the needed urban amenities. Urban planners believed that these cities could relieve the congestion of urban areas, provide new economic bases and residences near jobs, and solve many problems faced by older cities. Some new towns have been success stories: Columbia, Maryland; Brasilia, Brazil (the relatively new capital); Canberra, Australia. However, cities around the world have experienced influxes of poor migrants who squat (set up shelter) in any location available—abandoned buildings, cemetery mausoleums, hillsides surrounding cities. "Sociology Around the World" on page 532 discusses archeological research indicating that large planned cities existed in North America before white Europeans even knew the continent existed.

As people move to the suburbs, and manufacturing firms, services, commerce, and retail trade follow (Meltzer 1999), these movements lock cities and suburbs into competition over jobs and tax revenues (Stanback 1991). When this happens, farmland and open lands disappear; quality of construction is often shoddy because builders want to

While these men may look impoverished by North American standards, they are relatively well off in comparison to many urban neighbors in India, for they own a method of transportation that can earn a cash income, providing food and shelter for their families. For them, this is life in a postindustrial city.

make big profits; energy and water demands increase, often straining public utilities; and sprawl leads to vast, crowded freeway systems. Such a suburbanization of industry took place between 1970 and 1990, as many industries relocated out of central city areas, looking for favorable tax rates.

In some urban areas, neatly manicured lawns and freshly painted exteriors reflect new directions away from either suburbanization or deterioration of inner-city neighborhoods. The process of **gentrification** refers to members of the middle and upper class, mostly young white professionals, buying and renovating rundown properties in central-city neighborhoods. The process begins when affluent urban residents leave their stylish homes and move to suburbs. Poorer residents are left behind to rent once-fashionable homes from absentee owners. Later, affluent professionals buy the rundown homes at bargain rates, renovate them, and live in these newly gentrified areas (Feagin 1983).

In recent years, these neighborhoods, which are often adjacent to the central business districts, have become the "fashionable" residential areas. Georgetown in Washington, D.C., and German Village in Columbus, Ohio, are examples. Beautiful old classic homes have become affordable to mostly young upper-middle-class professionals who decide they want ready access to the cultural opportunities of the city. Relocating downtown makes this possible. This brings consumers, leadership, and a tax base to the city. On the other hand, the new residents also force poor people to leave the area as rents soar and landlords can make more profit by selling the properties.

Sociology Around the World

City Planning in Prehistoric Central America: Teotihuacan

Teotihuacan was a Mesoamerican city (between the American continents) created by a society that had no metal tools, had not invented the wheel, and had no pack animals. At its height, Teotihuacan covered 8 square miles (20 square kilometers), which made it larger than imperial Rome. Its central religious monument, the Temple of the Sun, was as broad at its base as the great pyramid of Cheops in Egypt. Its population may have reached 100,000.

Strategically located astride a valley that was the gateway to the lowlands of Mexico, Teotihuacan flourished for 500 years as a great urban commercial center. Yet, it was more than that. It was the mecca of the New World, a religious and cultural capital that probably housed pilgrims from as far away as Guatemala. Perhaps most startling, Teotihuacan was a totally planned city. Its two great pyramids, its citadel, its hundred lesser religious structures, and its 4,000 other dwellings were laid out according to an exact design. Streets (and many of its buildings) were organized on a perfect grid aligned with the city center. Even the shape of the river that divided the city was changed to fit the grid pattern.

Planning for the construction of Teotihuacan's major temples must have been an incredible undertaking. The Temple of the Sun, for instance, rises to a height of 215 feet and has a base of 725 square feet. These dimensions mean that it took about one million tons of sun-baked mud bricks to build the temple. When the Spaniards conquered Mexico in the 16th century,

Teotihuacan was a pre-European city in the heart of Central America, a city of 100,000 people.

they were amazed to find Teotihuacan's ruined temples. Local inhabitants claimed that the temples had been built by giants. They showed the Spaniards the bones of giant elephants (which had lived there in prehistoric times) to prove their point.

Small buildings as well as large ones were cleverly conceived in Teotihuacan. Houses were apparently planned for maximum space and privacy. Apartments were constructed around central patios, with each patio designed to give dwellers light and air, as well as an efficient drainage system. In a Teotihuacan housing complex, a person could indeed have lived in relative comfort (Jordan-Bychkov and Domoch 1998).

If professional people are taking over the low-rent districts and fixing them up, where are the low-income people to turn for housing? The poor are pushed into less attractive parts of town with fewer services and recreational areas and often pay higher rents for less adequate housing. Alternative housing for displaced residents may be difficult to find, contributing to problems of homelessness. Conflict theorists view gentrification and other urban developments that favor the wealthy and displace or exclude the poor to be exploited by real estate capitalists. By contrast, others argue that wealthy residents who

choose the lifestyle of the city over suburbia are helping to support viable, livable cities (Caulfield 1994).

Thinking Sociologically

What are some positive and negative aspects of gentrification for individuals and cities? Explain.

Table 15.6   Ten Largest Population Centers (population in millions)

2000 Rank	Center and Country	Population	2008 Rank	Center and Country	Population
1	Tokyo, Japan	34,450	1	Tokyo, Japan	33,600
2	Mexico City, Mexico	18,066	2	Seoul,Korea	23,400
3	New York/Newark, U.S.	17,846	3	Mexico City, Mexico	22,400
4	Sao Paulo, Brazil	17,099	4	New York/Newark, U.S.	21,900
5	Mumbai (Bombay), India	16,086	5	Mumbai (Bombay), India	21,600
6	Calcutta, India	13,058	6	Delhi, India	21,500
7	Shanghai, China	12,887	7	Sao Paulo, Brazil	20,600
8	Buenos Aires, Argentina	12,583	8	Los Angeles, U.S.	18,000
9	Delhi, India	12,441	9	Shanghai, China	17,500
10	Los Angeles area, U.S.	11,814	10	Osaka, Japan	16,700

Source: United Nations Population Division 2003; AmO Life 2008.

Megacities

As we look at Earth from space, some areas glow. These urban areas of 10 million or more residents, called megacities, dot the globe. In the 1950s, New York City was the only place in the world that had 10 million people. At that time, there were 75 cities in the world with 1 to 5 million residents, mostly in the Global South. Table 15.6 shows the rapid change in this pattern with the 10 largest population centers in 2000 and 2008.

As the world becomes more congested and cities continue to attract residents, cities start to merge or to become continuous urban areas without rural areas between them. Those who have driven from Boston to Washington, D.C., an area sometimes called Boswash, know the meaning of *megalopolis*, a spatial merging of two or more cities along major transportation corridors (Brunn et al. 2003).

Global Urban Variations

Many people around the globe live in cities with long, often glorious histories. Some live in relatively new suburbs surrounding central cities, and others live in new urban areas, recently planned and constructed. Cities' spatial arrangements vary by their histories, as the following examples illustrate.

Kabul, Afghanistan, is an example of a traditional, indigenous city in the Global South. Indigenous cities usually predate European cities. Kabul dates back to between 500 and 300 BCE, and it became the capital of Afghanistan in 1776. In the old section, bazaars and flat-roofed houses crowd the narrow winding streets, which were designed for foot and cart traffic. The newer sections have wide, tree-lined streets. Land use is mixed, with small businesses and residences sharing the same dwellings. In many indigenous cities, certain occupational types occupy distinctive

areas. The centers of indigenous cities usually include a market or bazaar, monuments, government buildings, and a religious mosque, church, or temple. Some of the elite live in the heart of these cities, whereas the poor live on the periphery of the city or on the city streets, a pattern vastly different from affluent North America. Global South countries often have dual cities such as Delhi–New Delhi, India, and Abidjan, Ivory Coast, in which a modern Westernized colonial central city is located next to a traditional indigenous city.

From cities built on ancient foundations to new urban centers, cities are a main organizational structure in modern life. How do these urban areas develop? This leads us to a discussion of macro-level issues.

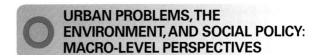

URBAN PROBLEMS, THE ENVIRONMENT, AND SOCIAL POLICY: MACRO-LEVEL PERSPECTIVES

The mountains rise from the sea, dotted with pastel-colored shanties. On the drive from the port city of Guaira up into the mountains to the capital city of Caracas, Venezuela, one sees settlements nestled into the hillsides. The poor, who have come from throughout the country to find opportunities in the capital, make shelters in the hills surrounding Caracas, often living with no running water, electricity, or sewage disposal. The laundry list of urban problems is overwhelming: excessive size and overcrowding; shortages of services, education, and health care; slums and squatters; traffic congestion; unemployment; and effects of global restructuring, including loss of agricultural land, environmental degradation, and resettlement of immigrants and refugees (Brunn et al. 2003). This section considers several of the many problems facing urban areas such as Caracas.

The hills surrounding Caracas, the capital of Venezuela, are densely packed with migrants from rural areas looking for opportunities in the urban area. Many of these areas lack the most basic services.

Rural Migrants and Overcrowding

Barriadas surround the outskirts of Caracas, a situation in many cities where migrants find any available space within or around the city to squat. For example, in Cairo, Egypt, a huge, sprawling graveyard full of large mausoleums, the City of the Dead, has become home to thousands of families transplanted from rural areas. In cities in India such as Chennai (Madras), Mumbai (Bombay), and Kolkatta (Calcutta), thousands of homeless migrants live on the sidewalks, on highway medians, and in river channels, which can flood.

Overcrowding exists in cities throughout the world but causes special problems in the Global South, where rural residents seek opportunities in urban areas. Squatters with hopes for a better future set up shacks of any material available —tin, cardboard, leaves, mud, and sticks—in settlements known as *barriadas* in Spanish, *shantytowns* in English, *bidonvilles* in French, *favelas* in Portuguese-speaking Brazil, and *bustees* in India. The majority of migrants to the city are young. They are pulled to the city in hopes of finding jobs and often have been pushed from the rural areas because of limited land on which to farm.

In the past three decades, the urban populations in Africa, Asia, and Latin America have begun to grow rapidly, and as Map 15.1 shows, many of the largest cities in the world are now in the Global South. Rural-to-urban migration and development of megacities dominate the economic and political considerations in many countries. The newcomers spill out into the countryside, engulfing towns along the way. Figure 15.12 shows the population living in urban and rural areas by more or less developed regions of the world, indicating trends from 1950 to 2007 and making projections through 2030 (United Nations Population Division 2008).

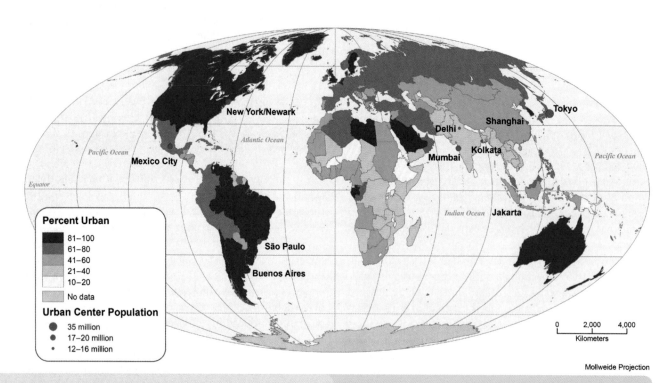

Map 15.1 Percent Urban Population by Country in 2006

Source: World Bank. Map by Anna Versluis.

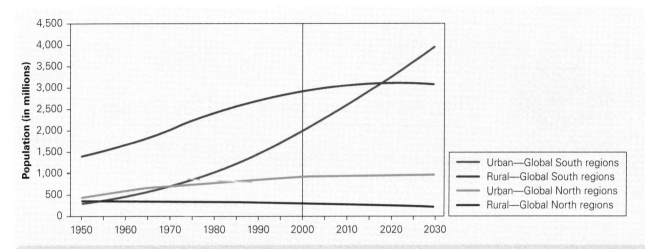

Figure 15.12 Urban and Rural Populations, 1950–2030

Source: United Nations Population Division 2008.

Countries have little time or money to prepare infrastructures and provide services for the rapidly increasing numbers of urban residents. Technological development, job opportunities, and basic services have not kept up with the large migrations of would-be laborers. Providing services such as water, electricity, sanitation, schools, transportation, and health services to these people has become a major problem—even impossible for some poor governments. Health and disease, especially contagious diseases, cause deadly epidemics due to the lack of services and poor sanitary conditions. The next "Sociology in Your Social World" describes one plague that ravaged much of Europe.

Lack of adequate housing is a worldwide problem. It is not helped by high birth rates and lower death rates in resource-poor countries, which cause population increases that are greater than the rate of economic growth or the capacity of society to absorb the migrants into urban areas. Because residents of the squatter settlements hold traditional rural values, adaptation to urban bureaucracy and overcrowding become even more difficult, resulting in *anomie* (normlessness) and exacerbating urban problems. Planning and social policy have failed poor migrants in rapidly growing slums of many world cities.

Environment, Infrastructure, and Urban Ecosystems

"Life on Earth in 2050 will be marked by struggles for food, water, and energy security," according to a recent study of the link between human well-being and health of the planet ("Ecosystems Report Links Human Well-Being with Health of Planet" 2006). The study, involving 1,360 scientists from 95 nations, asserts, "Sixty percent of the ecological systems that sustain life on Earth are being degraded or used unsustainably"

("Ecosystems Report Links Human Well-Being with Health of Planet" 2006). Extinction of species, lack of water and water pollution, resource exploitation, collapse of some global fisheries, and new diseases are the likely results of this breakdown. Urbanization by 2050 will stretch resources to their limits. Cities will have no way to dispose of wastes, resulting in epidemics. We cannot address environmental problems in detail here, but humans are contributing to the problems that are killing people now and will kill many in the future. The problems are exacerbated by an increase in natural disasters (e.g., hurricanes), which scientists believe to be a result of global warming. We can ignore the problems or call them nonexistent because life has improved for many people, but this is a shortsighted response. This increase in quality of life is actually magnifying the problems and hastening the demise of cities and the environments that support cities ("Ecosystems Report Links Human Well-Being with Health of Planet" 2006).

Additional infrastructure problems threaten to immobilize cities in the Global South. Traffic congestion and pollution are so intense in some cities that the slow movement of people and goods reduces productivity, jobs, health, and vital services. Pollution of the streets and air are chronic problems, especially with expansion of automobile use around the world. Older cities face deteriorating infrastructures, with water, gas, and sewage lines in need of replacement. In Global South countries, concern for these problems has brought some action and relief, but in impoverished countries where survival issues are pressing, environmental contamination is a low priority. Thus, the worst air pollution is now found in major cities in the Global South—such as Mexico City; Sao Paulo, Brazil; and several Chinese cities, including Beijing, host to the 2008 Olympics.

Water, an essential resource for survival, illustrates the complex urban ecosystem. Cities pipe in millions of gallons of water each day to residents from lakes, rivers, or reservoirs,

Sociology in Your Social World

"Ring Around the Rosey" and the Plague

Ring around the Rosey, Pockets full of posies, Ashes, Ashes, We all fall down!

Remember this nursery school rhyme? You probably did not understand the meaning of the rhyme as a child. It refers to the bubonic plague, which ravaged England and Europe in the early to mid-1600s, leaving dead and dying people in its wake. One account says that people infected with the plague got red circular sores that smelled very bad. People would put flowers (posies) in their pockets or on their bodies somewhere to cover up the smell. Because people were dying so rapidly, it was difficult to keep up with burials, and the dead were burned to reduce the spread of the disease (ashes, ashes). So many people were sick and dying that "we all fall down." Although there are variations on this story, it is probably true that the rhyme was related to the plague.

From 1603 to 1849, the clergy had the task of recording the deaths, burials, and the cause of deaths that occurred. These were circulated weekly, with a summary put out before Christmas. This process is one of the earliest records of vital statistics. In 1662, John Graunt from London analyzed the records for the first known statistical analysis of demographic data. Among his findings was that "for every 100 people born in London, only 16 were still alive at age 36 and only 3 at age 66" (Weeks 1999:61). The plague had an impact on social relationships, too. Many citizens avoided anyone who was a stranger, and some who contracted the disease died miserable lonely deaths because of others' fears of the disease. As the Industrial Revolution advanced, so did income, housing, sanitation, and nutrition. All of these improvements in people's lives reduced the incidence of plague and increased life expectancy. Today, cases of the plague can be found in several places, including India and the rural southwest United States. Antibiotics are effective treatment for people who have access to them, but many poor people cannot afford expensive medications from affluent countries.

Modern plagues, such as Avian Influenza (bird flu) and Severe Acute Respiratory Syndrome (SARS), have claimed hundreds of lives this decade, but both have significantly smaller impact than the bubonic plague. The World Health Organization is monitoring bird flu and SARS throughout the world to make sure the impact never reaches the tragic levels of the bubonic plague.

---

sometimes located at a distance from the city. Through a complex network of pipes, the water is connected to each establishment. After use—cooking, cleaning, showering, disposing of wastes—the water is discarded and becomes an output. Some of the water is used in products or for industrial uses and some is stored, but most waste water—about 95%—is piped out to sewer plants, rivers, or other disposal sites. Among other plans, environmental scientists are working on methods to purify and recycle greywater (non-toilet waste water) for reuse. External strains from floods, droughts, or various contaminants can cause water supplies to be less than safe (Jordan-Bychkov and Domoch 1998). Water is but one example of the complex urban ecosystem with its interdependent parts.

To understand the urban ecosystem, its growth and its decay, we must understand that there are pressures on the city from both external sources and internal dynamics, as illustrated in the next topic.

Poverty in the World's Cities

Poor people are often invisible. Around the world, they are tucked away in enclaves most affluent people do not see. Until something brings attention to the poor, leaders and most of the citizenry can ignore them. Invisibility of urban poverty results because these residents have little power to make their problems public and little energy beyond that needed for survival. Earlier chapters addressed reasons for poverty and the groups who fall disproportionately into poverty. Urban residential patterns generally reflect the same patterns of poverty.

The *permanent underclass* refers to the poor worldwide, people who do not have education or skills to become part of the local or world economy. Children leave school at young ages to help support their families, reducing their opportunities to get out of poverty. However, modernizing economies have little need for unskilled labor.

The *feminization of poverty* refers to the increase of women and their children in the ranks of the impoverished. This is a growing problem in rich and poor countries. The increasing numbers of teenage mothers who have little education, are unemployed, and have few prospects to get out of poverty result in their disproportionate representation among the homeless. (See "How Do We Know?" for a discussion of the circumstances and coping strategies of homeless people.) One cause of feminization of poverty is divorces, which may leave women with small children and poor job prospects. Single-parent homes with a woman as the breadwinner are far more likely than other types of households to be in economic trouble, with poor housing, lack of education, and scant job opportunities.

In some cities, residents are working collectively for survival and improvement in their conditions. In Harlem, New York, some residents live in cooperatives and rental buildings that they manage, taken over after landlords abandoned the buildings. The "community household model" in which residents control their own housing may provide a new method of organization and leadership by tenants and community activists (Leavitt and Saegert 1990).

Crime and Delinquency in the City

Social disruption and crime are not intrinsic to cities. One can walk through many areas of Toronto, London, or Paris at night with little likelihood of problems. Traditional African cities had very low crime rates, but today, they are much less safe because of high numbers of new migrants. When people are transient, when they move frequently, they are more likely to experience *anomie*, to have less commitment to community norms, and to lack a sense of commitment to the norms and the well-being of the local community. Add to that the desperate situation of the very poor, and you have a recipe for crime.

As young people move from rural to urban life, juvenile delinquency becomes a problem. In rural communities and tribal cultures, strict norms govern behavior, but in

Many children sleep on the streets of Bombay each night.

Thinking Sociologically

Some scholars argue that crime and delinquency are not a natural part of city life but that crime is shaped by anomie, migrations, changing neighborhoods, and lack of connectedness. How might we begin to build a sense of community, belonging, and attachment in urban areas?

urban areas, cohesiveness of families and ties with tribal groups are lessened. When education, economic security, and social services increase, conformity again becomes a

How Do We Know?

Understanding Urban Homeless People

Immigration to urban areas can result in homeless people sleeping under bridges, in parks, in vacant lots, in unused subway tunnels, or even on the sidewalks of main thoroughfares. Although homelessness was frequently observed in Third World countries, it was uncommon in North American and European cities until the early 1980s. Two sociologists, David Snow and Leon Anderson, undertook a study at the macro, meso, and micro levels of analysis to understand the processes of homelessness in America.

Because any one source of data might not provide the whole picture and understanding contributing factors at each level of analysis would help, Snow and Anderson (1993) used triangulation by collecting several forms of data. First, they did an ethnographic study, making friends and becoming "buddy-researchers" with the homeless people they came to know in Austin, Texas. They did interviews, made extensive observations, listened in on conversations, and asked homeless people to help them understand the implications and the processes of homeless living in a modern American city. Second, they used "tracking data" by contacting homeless people through a variety of organizations and institutions in the city and state. This provided them with access to official files and data, allowed them to confirm stories, enabled them to identify how homeless people drew on resources, and provided information on how street people related to social service and religious agencies.

The Department of Housing and Urban Development (HUD) and the Urban Institute use similar methods to estimate the number of homeless individuals in the United States. In 2007, the most recent year for which data are available, there were an estimated 123,833 chronically homeless individuals living in the United States compared to 155,623 in 2006 and 175,914 in 2005. This does not include those who are temporarily homeless. HUD officials measure overall homelessness via funding applications for housing services and state that even this number is a large underestimation of the total number of people who experience homelessness (HUD 2008).

In trying to make sense of homelessness, the researchers identified key variables that distinguished different types of homelessness, uncovering a wide range of causes, circumstances, and coping methods. Clarifying eight key variables helped them to identify several types of homeless people and to prevent overgeneralization about any one kind of homelessness.

Snow and Anderson's (1993) work was a form of detective work—sorting through information and trying to understand the many dimensions of homelessness. Using macro-level perspectives, they looked at employment trends and wage labor issues in the larger society, social policies of the government designed to address poverty and homelessness. Meso-level issues involved study of family life and caregiving organizations. The researchers also considered the micro culture of street people, how they lend each other support and help each other make sense of their circumstances. They point to many forces at work on the homeless, from global economic trends to the way their families relate to them.

Perhaps the most intriguing findings of this study involved how people affirmed a sense of self in this humiliating situation. After all, to be a person of worth in American society is to (1) own some property, (2) have someone who cares about you enough to take you in if you are really desperate, and (3) occupy a significant status in society by earning some money and having a career or position deserving of respect. The homeless not only lack all of these, their master status—"homeless person"—is one that elicits disrespect. "Dignity and worth are not primarily individual characteristics, but instead flow from the roles we play," write the authors (Snow and Anderson 1993:9). To be homeless, then, is far more than to be without a residence or shelter. It is to be without a place to restore one's dignity. So how did the homeless cope?

This research showed a number of coping strategies, only a few of which can be reported here. Sometimes, the homeless people explained away their circumstances as temporary "bad luck" or part of a normal cycle in which they just happened to be on the down end for a while. Sometimes, they would distance themselves from the role of homelessness, pointing out that they were "different" than other homeless people, "didn't really belong," and did not really deserve to be seen as homeless at all. Some people coped by fictive storytelling, pointing to pronounced achievements in the past (often fictionalized or embellished) or creating stories of their phenomenal accomplishments when they finally do get on their feet. By affirming another identity in the past or the future, their self-esteem was salvaged. However, perhaps the most surprising strategy to preserve self-worth was to embrace the role of being homeless with pride—to boast about how one was the best at being a survivor, the best at being a friend to the homeless, or the best at rejecting shallow values of materialism in our commercial society. They could thus affirm themselves for coping skills, for caring qualities, or for deep spirituality. They had defined reality in a way that allowed them to see themselves in a positive light. They had changed the social construction of reality, at least among themselves.

This research not only used multiple methods to check accuracy of findings and insights but also explored social interaction and processes at more than one level of analysis in the social world.

norm for these newcomers, replacing the anomie of the transition.

A key message from the study of urbanization is that people's lives are influenced by the environment in which they live. Applied sociologists can play a role in improving the conditions of urban areas, as described in "The Applied Sociologist at Work" on page 540.

Urban Planners and Social Policy in the Global Social World

Try planning an ideal city. First, list everything you need to consider. Now think of organization: Who will handle what? Consider services, maintenance, financing, and leadership. This would be quite a task. The problem is that most urban planners do not have the luxury of starting from scratch. They must work with decaying areas, being cognizant of the meaningful landmarks and treasured sites. Planners may also have to undo hasty or inadequate planning from previous actions. Among other things, they attempt to maximize technical efficiency such as getting water from Point A to Point B.

Planners must meet needs for housing, sanitation, education, food distribution, jobs, family life, and recreation. Planning efforts need to take into consideration what will happen to various groups, including the poor, elderly, women, children, and homeless populations.

In the early 21st century, a number of global trends affect urban planning (Brunn et al. 2003):

1. The process of urbanization—people migrating to cities—will continue, exacerbating the already difficult situation of providing services for many of the world's crowded urban areas.

2. Information and transportation technologies allow people in any part of the globe to be in contact. However, this may also reduce the feelings of belonging to a specific place, reducing commitment to work on city problems.

3. International boundaries will diminish in importance as the flow of information, goods, services, labor, and capital increasingly ignores national boundaries. For example, migration of Asians to cities around the world will continue and will have an impact on these cities.

4. Economies will increasingly rely on brain work, including invention of new technologies, rather than on the brawn work of older manufacturing. Thus, the gap between haves and have-nots is likely to continue.

In the urban Global South, many homeless people must bathe every day in public in whatever water supply they can find. Here in Kolkatta (Calcutta), India, even some people with homes would not have their own water supply and would have to use fire hydrants on the streets, as this family is doing.

Although cities have many problems, they are exciting bustling places to live or to visit. Some of the liveliness of urban neighborhoods is depicted in this Chinese street scene.

The Applied Sociologist at Work— Jay Weinstein

Improving Quality of Life by Transforming Community Structure

As is true of many urban centers, Detroit, Michigan, has its share of distressed neighborhoods. Dr. Jay Weinstein has been director of an interdisciplinary team attempting to bring about economic, social, and physical restructuring of some of these areas. By developing long-term relationships in several urban neighborhoods, the team has had success working with residents and others to improve conditions. Weinstein calls this approach *relationship brokering*—bringing people together to share perspectives and to clear up misperceptions between residents, local officials, service providers, and police. These efforts have helped to empower residents to take action and improve their neighborhoods.

A major project along these lines, which began in 1990 and continues to the present, is in the Detroit suburb of Taylor, Michigan. For decades, residents of Taylor and the surrounding Down River area were painfully aware of the problems of their neighborhood, known by uncomplimentary names such as "Crack Ridge," "Hooker Heaven," and "Sin City." With about 7,500 people packed into an area of one-half square mile, most residents were living in rental units controlled by the U.S. Department of Housing and Urban Development Section 8 program (subsidized private housing).

In 1989, an influential local newspaper published a series of articles showing that the neighborhood had earned the labels applied to it. The series exposed the high incidences of drug trafficking and use, prostitution, alcoholism, and violent crimes in the neighborhood. The people living in Down River were only too familiar with the situation. Nevertheless, the articles inspired local and federal political leaders to demand action.

In the spring of 1990, Weinstein and his colleagues were awarded an applied research grant by the City of Taylor Department of Community Development. The purposes of the work were to assess the problems by providing reliable data and to make recommendations to improve the community. The fact-finding stage revealed that the problems of "Crack Ridge" were every bit as serious as portrayed by the media. However, it was also shown that the residents of the neighborhood were not the main perpetrators. Instead, for as long as anyone could remember, the area had been under siege by nonresidents who came and went, drifted from apartment to apartment, or illegally occupied residences after threatening to harm the rightful owners.

Based on these and other findings, the research team recommended a plan for a thorough physical, economic, social, and political reconstruction of the neighborhood. Fortunately, city and federal officials understood the value of such sociological expertise. With few reservations, they accepted the recommendations of the sociological team and set out on a 10-year program of implementation. Working with residents of the neighborhood and other citizens of the city, Taylor's mayor, city council, Department of Human Resources, police department, and many others tackled the problem. Weinstein and his colleagues helped to guide the rebirth of this community.

Today, the neighborhood has a new name (The Villages of Taylor), a new human services center, a new residential owner (a private nonprofit corporation established by the city), and many new or redesigned buildings. The population density has been reduced by more than 20% and all this without one person being displaced against his or her will, other than drug dealers. The average median income of Taylor is now higher than the national average, and this has led to several new housing developments.

In 1998, after receiving national attention, Taylor was called "a model for the nation" by the secretary of Housing and Urban Development. Many communities have looked to Taylor to see their plans for redevelopment. In fall 2001, in one of the most treasured moments of his life, Weinstein attended the official dedication of The Villages of Taylor.

For Weinstein, sociological theory is at the root of his neighborhood work. He tries to identify the "definitions of reality" held by the residents and then helps residents examine those definitions, a symbolic interaction approach. Only by understanding their definitions can residents begin to act to change the situation.

In his work, Weinstein uses a multiple-methods approach: surveys, participant observation, census data, and other large data sets. Each technique has strengths and limitations. Using a variety of approaches in combination brings him closer to the elusive truths of social life.

Note: Dr. Jay Weinstein, a professor at Eastern Michigan University, specializes in urban sociology, demography, and social change. He received his doctorate from the University of Illinois, Champaign-Urbana. He has been doing private consulting for more than 20 years, with contracts from international and local governments and nonprofit organizations. His studies have included analysis of demographic trends and changes in India, Albania, Bulgaria, and Jamaica.

5. Conflicts between cultural and political groups, including religious and political extremists, will continue to affect urban life.

6. *McDonaldization*—creation of a consumer world dominated by major Western food, music, fashion, and entertainment—will continue, even as we see an increasing diversity of people within Western nations and communities.

Awareness of these trends can help urban planners in their efforts to design cities to meet the needs of the future (Friedman 2006).

In the past, men were designers of cities, but women also experience them. Some analysts believe that women's experiences in the city are quite different from men's. Spaces that have been designed with women in mind emphasize opportunities for participation, involvement in community development, and leisure activities such as informal places for meeting (Renzetti 2003; Wilson 1993a). Unfortunately,

profit is often the motivation in planning models, and few planning efforts consider cities in a holistic fashion. Urban planners in socialist countries with centralized national plans for urban areas may find it easier to consider the needs of all residents (Flanagan 2001).

Millions of people live satisfying lives in cities, but for others, life is misery. Whether the economic base and urban planners can keep up with the demands for even basic services in the Global South remains to be seen. This is especially true in areas of the world where population is outstripping the amount of land available, and people are flocking to cities for survival. This basic population pattern—urbanization—has consequences at the most global levels and at the most micro levels of human life. Our social world model—which looks at the connections of micro, meso, and macro levels of the social system—makes us cognizant of the consequences of decisions made by millions of individuals and families. It also makes us mindful of the consequences for individuals and for cities of global trends and forces.

So What?

Population trends, including migration resulting in urbanization, provide a dynamic force for change in societies. Whether one is interested in understanding social problems, social policy, or factors that may affect one's own career, demographic processes are critical forces. We ignore them at our peril—as individuals and as a society. Family businesses can be destroyed, retirement plans obliterated, and the health of communities sabotaged by population factors if they are overlooked. If they are considered, however, they can enhance planning that leads to prosperity and enjoyment of our communities. Urban living creates problems, but it can have enormous benefits as well, and this is but a single example of a population trend.

Many other factors create change in a society, and the factors contributing to social dynamics are interactive, some of them contributing to change in a particular direction and others retarding change. The next chapter examines the larger picture of social transformation in our complex and multileveled social world.

Key Points

What Have We Learned?

- Population analysis (called demography) looks at the composition, distribution, and size of a population as the society is affected by variables of fertility, mortality, and migration. (See pp. 498–500.)

- The planet-wide increase in the human population has been stunning in the past century, and it has serious implications for adequate resources to support life. (See pp. 500–504.)

- Various theories explain causes of the rapid growth, ranging from medical technology to cultural factors. (See pp. 504–508.)

- Many institutions affect and are affected by fertility and mortality rates at the meso level—political policies, religious beliefs, economic factors, education, and health care. (See pp. 508–515.)

- Migration is also an important issue for the society—whether the migration be international or internal—for it can change the size, distribution, and composition of a nation's citizenry. (See pp. 515–518.)

- Population patterns can also affect individual decisions at the micro level, from career choices to business decisions to programs that will affect retirement possibilities. (See pp. 518–521.)

- A major element of population migration has been urbanization. As populations become more densely concentrated, this creates a series of opportunities and problems for meeting human needs. (See pp. 521–525.)

- At the micro level, human relationships are affected by having widespread or dense population concentration. In urban areas, social relations may be less closely knit. On the negative side, this creates anomie and alienation. On the positive side, it provides more choices for people about their social relationships and lifestyles. (See pp. 525–527.)

- Cities themselves are extremely complex meso-level social settings that vary in size and operations. (See pp. 527–533.)

- At the macro level, urban environments must be understood as ecosystems that have dense poverty and homelessness, major pollution issues, and higher crime rates. These are the focus of urban planners, who try to use sociological knowledge to plan for a better future. (See pp. 533–541.)

Contributing to Our Social World: What Can We Do?

At the Local Level: At the end of Chapter 2, a suggestion was made to invite an official of the U.S. Census Bureau to your campus—possibly through your sociology club—to discuss the bureau's activities. You can also contact someone from your local department of urban planning, urban and regional development, or community development for a similar discussion. It would be especially relevant to have them discuss how population information is used in planning and service delivery contexts. Your community probably has neighborhood recreation departments, crime watch, or community-organizing agencies that need volunteers to provide services or to help neighbors solve problems and work with local government. Such volunteers are especially needed in minority and poor neighborhoods.

At the Organizational or Institutional Level: Urban planning, urban and regional development, community development, and similar municipal, regional, and state departments often use volunteers and hire interns. Contact one of these organizations and explore the possibility of making a contribution and/or exploring interest in this field.

At the National and Global Levels: Planned Parenthood (www.plannedparenthood.org) is a national organization that promotes family planning education and outreach programs throughout the United States. Founded in the early 20th century by feminist activist and nurse Margaret Sanger, the organization uses volunteers and interns, as well as providing long-term employment opportunities. The Population Council, www.popcouncil.org, conducts research worldwide to improve policies, programs, and products in three areas: HIV and AIDS; poverty, gender, and youth; and reproductive health. Its Web site discusses several ways to get involved, locally as well as globally.

Visit **www.pineforge.com/ballantine2study** for online activities, sample tests, and other helpful information. Select "Chapter 15: Population and Urbanization" for chapter-specific activities.

CHAPTER 16

The Process of Change

Can We Make a Difference?

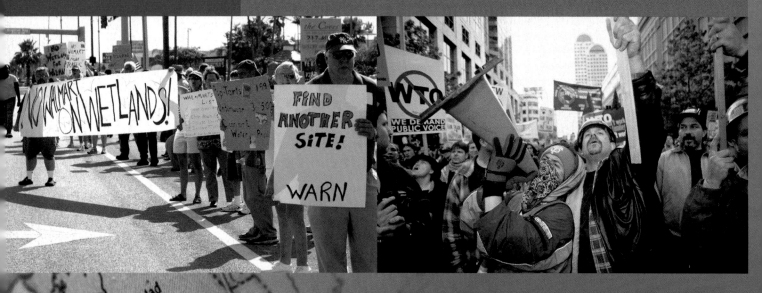

Humans are profoundly influenced by the macro structures around them, but people are also capable of creating change, especially if they band together with others and approach change in an organized way. Social movements such as those depicted in the pictures are one powerful way to bring about change.

Think About It . . .

Micro: Can you as an individual bring about change in the world?

Micro: How does change at the micro level of the social world affect change at other levels?

Meso: What organizational or ethnic community factors enhance or retard social change?

Macro: How does the training and support for technological innovation in a nation affect the process of change in that country?

Macro: How do global changes—such as climate change—impact people and societies at each level?

Macro: Global Community

Macro: Society

Meso: National Organizations, Institutions, and Ethnic Subcultures

Micro: Local Organizations and Community

Micro: Me (and My Inner Circle)

Micro: Unemployment due to plant closings; hate crimes; and business scandals, causing personal losses

Meso: Family instability from economic recessions; church scandals; failures of schools to provide quality education

Macro: National government decisions about going to war, trade agreements, or tariffs

Macro: Global actions by United Nations, the World Court, or the International Monetary Fund; agreements by international alliances; business decisions of multinational corporations

There is a movement afoot—a social reform movement! It has come on gradually, stirred by increasing indications around the world that we have a crisis that is related to the population dilemma explored in the previous chapter. From the Asian subcontinent to the Arctic and from Africa to the Americas, there are symptoms of a planet in peril (Intergovernmental Panel on Climate Change 2007). A major part of this problem is the waste humans create.

Wet, dry, smelly, and sometimes recyclable—garbage is a problem. We are running out of space to dispose of our refuse. We dump it in the ocean and see garbage surfacing on beaches and killing fish. We bury it in land fills and the surrounding land becomes toxic. We sort and recycle it, creating other problems (Pellow 2002). Perhaps your community or campus has separate bins for glass, cans, paper, and garbage. Recycling is a relatively new movement in response to the urgent pleas from environmentalists about our garbage and trash: polluted water sources, dying areas of the oceans from trash dumping, and depletion of renewable resources.

Recycling, salvaging items that can be reused, is part of a social reform movement—the environmental movement. However, few issues have simple solutions. The dumping and recycling have to take place somewhere. Many of the recycling plants and trash dumps are located in areas where poor people and minorities live. Some have referred to this as *environmental racism*, in which ethnic minorities are put at risk by the diseases and pollutants that recycling entails (Pellow 2002). This illustrates the complexity of solving global problems: While we may help solve one issue, others may be created. Such issues need to be approached at the micro, meso, and macro levels. At the micro level, each of us can do our part in the environmental movement to save the planet through responsible personal actions. At the meso level, the environmental movement can help local and regional governments enact policies and plans to reduce the garbage problem, and at the macro level, world leaders need to find responsible ways to dispose of environmental wastes. Yet, the solution to this macro-level issue of protecting the Earth's resources may have micro implications for local minority families. Our social world is, indeed, complex.

Turn on the morning or evening news, and there are lessons about other aspects of our changing social world. We see headlines of medical advances and cures for disease; biological breakthroughs in cloning and the DNA code; terrorist bombings in Israel, Iraq, Pakistan, Chechnya, and other parts of the world; famine in drought-afflicted sub-Saharan Africa; disasters such as earthquakes, hurricanes, tsunamis, and floods; and social activists calling for boycotts of Wal-Mart, chocolate, coffee, oil companies, or other multinational corporations. The world's problems bombard us, depress us. They also point out that social, political, environmental, and biological events bring change into the personal lives of people and that individuals can change events. Some events seem far away and hard to imagine: thousands killed by a tidal wave in India or hundreds swept away by mud

from an erupting volcano in Colombia. Some of these are natural events. Others are due to human actions: a rise in terrorism reflecting divisions in world economic, political, and religious ideologies; or biological advances that revolutionize the meaning of life—cloning, stem cell therapies, and DNA testing. Regardless of the source, these events bring about change, and the changes themselves have implications for other aspects of this complex social world.

Social change is defined as variations or alterations over time in the behavior patterns, culture (including norms and values), and structure of society. Some change is controllable, and some is out of our hands, but change is inevitable and ubiquitous. Change can be rapid, caused by some disruption to the existing system, or it can be gradual and evolutionary. Very often, change at one level in the social world occurs because of change at another level. Micro, meso, and macro levels of society often work together in the change process, but are sometimes out of sync.

In this chapter, we explore the process of change, causes of change, and some strategies for bringing about desired change. We consider the complexity of change in our social world; explanations and theories of social change; the role of collective behavior in bringing about change; planned change in organizations; and macro-level social movements, technology, and environment as they affect and are affected by change.

Our social world model is based on the assumption that change, whether evolutionary or revolutionary, is inevitable and ever present in the social world. The impetus for change may begin at the micro, meso, or macro level of analysis. Studies of the change process are not complete, however, until the level under study is understood in relation to other levels in the model, for each level affects the others in a multiplicity of ways.

Thinking Sociologically

In what ways do you participate in recycling or seek other ways to lessen your impact on the environment? Might your activities be linked to worsening conditions for ethnic minorities?

The Complexity of Change in Our Social World

The Yir Yorant, a group of Australian aborigines, have long believed that if their own ancestors did not do something, then they must not do it. It would be wrong and might cause evil to befall the group (Sharp 1990). Obviously, this is not a people who favor change or innovation. By contrast,

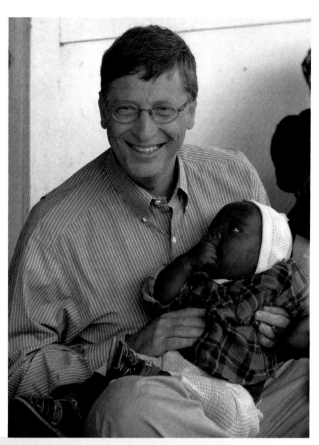

Mother Teresa, an Italian nun, who devoted her life to helping the dying and destitute in India, established the orphanage shown here in Kolkatta (Calcutta). In the other photo, Bill Gates holds a child who is receiving a trial malaria vaccine at a medical research center in Mozambique. Gates announced a grant of $168 million to fight malaria, a disease that kills more than one million people a year, 90% of them children in Africa. Sometimes, social change occurs because of individual initiatives.

progress is a positive word in much of Australia and in other countries where change is seen as normal, even desirable. The traditions, cultural beliefs of a society, and internal and external pressures all affect the degree and rate of change in society.

Change at the Individual Level: Micro-Level Analysis

One of the nation's top entrepreneurs, Microsoft's Bill Gates, combines intelligence, business acumen, and philanthropy, qualities that appeal to American individualism. Gates has power to influence others because of his fame, wealth, and personal charisma. He is able to bring about change in organizations through his ability to motivate people and set wheels in motion. Many people have persuasive power to influence decision making, but it is not always based on charisma. For some, it is due to expertise, wealth or privileged positions, and information—or even the ability to use coercive force.

Most organizations—schools, businesses, volunteer organizations—use one or more of the following strategies to persuade individuals to accept change: They appeal to individuals' values, they use persuasion by presenting hard data and logic, they convince individuals that the existing benefits of change outweigh the costs, they remove uncooperative individuals from the organization, they provide rewards or sanctions for acceptance of change to alter the cost-benefit ratio, or they compel individuals to change by an order from authority figures. Thus, individuals are active agents who initiate and bring about change.

Change at the Institutional Level: Meso-Level Analysis

The terrorist attacks of September 11, 2001, which killed 3,025 innocent people from 68 nations, resulted in repercussions in many U.S. institutions. Local, state, and national governments responded by putting in place measures to deter any further attacks and to seek out and punish the

Revolutionary groups with terrorist tactics operate at the meso level, trying to change the society by intimidating the citizens and government so they will change policies. In this photo, we see the memorial site for victims of the bombing of a federal building in Oklahoma City—a terrorist act by members of a "patriot group" that was opposed to governmental policies. The small chairs are for deceased children who were in a day care center in the destroyed building.

guilty parties. Religious services had high attendance in the weeks that followed the attacks as religious leaders and members tried to make sense of the brutal attacks. Some families lost loved ones. Other families were soon separated as the military and the National Guard were called into action. Security measures were stepped up at airports and other transportation centers. These institutions at the meso level—government, religion, family, the military—guided the response to the attacks.

Terrorism refers to "the use of indiscriminate violence to cause mass fear and panic to intimidate a population and advance one's political goals, whatever they may be" (Nolan 2002:1648). This usually refers to acts of violence by private nonstate groups to advance revolutionary political goals. In 2006, there were 14,000 terrorist attacks around the world, which killed 20,000 people. These figures were up 25% from 2005, boosted by the insurgencies in Iraq (CNN.com 2007). Contemporary terrorism is a meso-level phenomenon, even though it has both personal and global ramifications. Most modern terrorist organizations are not nations. They are ethnic, political, or religious subgroups that have elicited passionate loyalty from followers—even to the point of suicide on behalf of the group and its ideology.

Terrorism also has consequences for economies. Not only do terrorist acts destabilize economies, but they change the kinds of jobs that are available. Consider the new jobs created in airport and seaport security. In addition to new

jobs, investors hesitate to invest if they think the economy will be negatively affected, and this lack of investment can spawn a recession. However, it is not only the economic systems of Global North nations that are important when we discuss terrorism. The ripple effects have repercussions in all countries. Economic disruptions are a core motivating factor for terrorists who commit horrific acts.

After 9/11, health care professionals began to make plans for biological and chemical terrorist attacks, changing the way monies are allocated in the health care industry. Despite this, the United States has done very little to protect against the threats of bioterrorism (O'Toole and Henderson 2006). Most resources have gone to airport security and to fighting terrorists in other parts of the world (Flynn 2006). Unfortunately, analysts point out that North America would be an easy target, where medical response capacity could easily be swamped by having to deal with biological or chemical attacks on water supplies, subways, or high-density population areas (Flynn 2006; O'Toole and Henderson 2006). Thus, terrorism is a concern of the medical institution as well.

Change at the National and Global Levels: Macro-Level Analysis

To understand why terrorism occurs around the world, we must look at some of the driving forces. The unequal distribution of world resources has inspired deep anger toward affluent countries among those poor who believe the rich are using their power to maintain the inequities. High-income countries consume $22,187 billion in resources. That amounts to 80% of the world's resources for one billion people. Middle-income countries with three billion people consume $4,537 billion in resources, and low-income countries with 2.3 billion people consume $783 billion in resources. U.S. citizens make up only 4.6% of the total world population, yet the United States accounted for 33% of the consumed resources in the world in 2004 (World Resources Institute 2007). This was 30% more than it produced (World Almanac Education Group 2001). The average U.S. citizen consumes six times more energy than the world average (U.S. Department of Energy 2006). This seems grossly unfair to people who can barely feed their families and who have limited electricity, water, and sanitation and minimal shelter for their children. Furthermore, wealthy countries have considerable economic influence over nations of the Global South because poor countries are dependent on the income, employment, and loans from the core of affluent countries. Citizens of poor countries may work for multinational corporations, often for very low wages. However, the profits are returned to wealthy countries, helping to perpetuate the gross inequity in distribution of resources. Whether or not we think it is justified, this inequity leads to hostilities—and sometimes terrorism—against more powerful countries.

The 9/11 attack was partially motivated by Middle Easterners intensely pro-Palestinian and anti-Israeli. From the terrorist perspective, the attack on the New York City World Trade Center was an effort to strike out at the United States. September 11 was a symbolic date for Palestinians, the date when Britain declared control of Palestine. This set off a chain of events leading to the United Nations' granting the land to Jews to establish Israel. Many Middle Easterners felt this was unjust because the Palestinians lost the country in which they had been living. Moreover, the Camp David Accords, which established Israel's right to exist in the Middle East, were signed on September 11, 1979. So on two counts, this date had powerful symbolic meaning to the people who were displaced from Palestine, just as the date has new and powerful meaning today for Americans. Political acts, mostly those supported and implemented by the United States, undergirded the rage of terrorists who saw the United States and its supporters as evil.

The events of September 11 changed the United States as a nation and the core issues, priorities, and spending of the Bush presidency. George W. Bush's administration proposed, and Congress approved, a Patriot Act that channeled resources into heightened security and military preparedness. The provisions of the bill also greatly restricted civil liberties and allowed the government to snoop into the private lives of citizens in ways that had never before been tolerated, from monitoring home telephone connections of Americans to scrutinizing the books they checked out of the library. Fear for their security meant that many U.S. citizens welcomed efforts to prevent further attacks, although the root causes of terrorism were not addressed.

Following September 11, many state governments mandated more intense patriotism training and rituals in the schools, with additions to the curriculum and daily loyalty ceremonies. In Wisconsin, for example, every classroom was required to either recite the Pledge of Allegiance or listen to the national anthem (Ladson-Billings 2006). The No Child Left Behind education bill, which was passed by Congress in 2002, also mandated that school personnel turn over personal information about students to military recruiters, including private information that had previously not been available to anyone but the student and school personnel (Ayers 2006; Westheimer 2006).

Thinking Sociologically

How has terrorism affected institutions and countries with which you are familiar? How is your life being changed by threats of terrorism?

Societal Level Change

Our social world becomes increasingly more complex and more biologically interdependent. Pollution of the environment by any one country now threatens other countries. Carcinogens, acid rain, and other airborne chemicals carry across national boundaries (Brecher, Costello, and Smith 2006). About 5% of the world's population emits 25% of the heat-trapping gases (Lindsay 2006). Pollutants can also pollute the air that surrounds the entire planet, destroying the ozone that protects us from intense sun rays and warming the planet in ways that could threaten all of us. In the past century, scientists claim, the Earth's surface has warmed by one degree. That does not sound like much until one considers that during the last ice age, the Earth's surface was only seven degrees cooler than today. Small variations can make a huge difference, and we do not know what all of those consequences might be if the Earth's surface temperature increases by another two or three degrees. Currently, sea ice is melting each year at a rate that equals the size of Maryland and Delaware combined (Cousteau 2008; Lindsay 2006). It is alarming to visit the glaciers on the South Island of New Zealand (closest to Antarctica) and realize that glaciers there are melting so fast that they have receded by as much as 10 or 12 miles in just a couple of decades. In a warmer world, there is less snowfall, smaller mountain icecaps, and a resultant smaller runoff in the spring (Barnett, Adam, and Lettenmaier 2005; Cyranoski 2005; Struck 2008). This causes major water shortages, which will be discussed later. While some of the environmental change may be rooted in natural causes, the preponderance of the evidence suggests that human activity—the way we consume and the way we live our lives—is the primary cause (Gore 2006). Even if humans were not a significant cause, the global climate change has consequences that mean change. What happens when people do not have enough water in their current location to survive? What happens when they try to move into someone else's territory?

Obviously, this is a global issue with implications for nations that must work together for change. Yet, some nations do not want to change because they feel controls will impede progress. U.S. President Bush rejected the Kyoto Treaty on global warming because it "does not make economic sense," and his trusted adviser, Condoleezza Rice, bluntly asserted, "Kyoto is dead" (Lindsay 2006).

Fixing the environmental issues will be expensive, it may hinder the economy and slow the rate of growth, and it may even stimulate a recession. Because recessions are terrifying for any elected politician, who aims to keep the public happy, change is not easy. Still, most of the rest of the world's nations have signed the Kyoto Treaty, and there is continuing pressure on the United States to concede. Because nations are still the most powerful units for allocating resources and for setting policy, changes in national policies that address the issues of a shared environment are of critical importance. The two big quandaries are (1) the costs and benefits to various nations of participating in a solution and (2) the matter of time—will nations respond before it is too late to make a difference? Currently, most of the cost of pollution is accruing to impoverished countries, while rich nations benefit from the status quo.

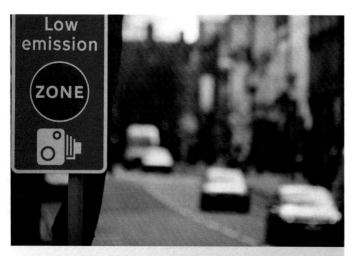

Environmental destruction and global climate change are problems that cannot be solved by individual nations. If nations do not cooperate, the problems will only worsen. This low emission zone sign in London, England, signals new legislation that will charge operators of lorries, buses, and coaches that do not meet the Low Emission Zone standards. Drivers of the highest greenhouse carbon-emitting cars will pay a stiff tax for not complying.

Global Systems and Change

As the world becomes increasingly interconnected and interdependent, impetus for change comes from global organizations, national and international organizations and governments, and multinational corporations. New and shifting alliances between international organizations and countries link together nations, form international liaisons, and create changing economic and political systems. The following international alliances between countries, for example, are based primarily on economic ties:

- SADC: Southern African Development Community
- NAFTA: North American Free Trade Agreement
- CEFTA: Central European Free Trade Agreement
- CAFTA: Central American Free Trade Agreement
- ASEAN: Association of Southeast Asian Nations
- WIPO: World Intellectual Property Organization
- G8: Group of Eight
- OPEC: Organization of Petroleum Exporting Countries
- ADP: Asian Development Bank
- EFTA: European Free Trade Association
- EEA: European Economic Area
- APEC: Asia-Pacific Economic Cooperation
- EU: European Union
- SEATO: Southeast Asian Treaty Organization

Consider NAFTA, which was initiated in 1993 to establish a free trade area between Canada, the United States, and Mexico to facilitate trade in the region. Promoters, including many global corporations, promised the agreement

would create thousands of new high-wage jobs, raise living standards in each of the countries, improve environmental conditions, and transform Mexico from a poor developing country into a booming new market. Opponents (including labor unions, environmental organizations, consumer groups, and religious groups) argued the opposite—that NATFA would reduce wages; destroy jobs, especially in the United States; undermine democratic policy making in North America by giving corporations free rein; and threaten health, environment, and food safety (American Cultural Center Resource Service 2004; Public Citizen's Global Trade Watch 2003; U.S. Trade Representative 2003).

Analyses of the agreement show mixed results. There is some indication that tariffs are down and U.S. exports have increased. Some Mexican markets are doing well and have weathered global economic crises, and there is growth in manufacturing in Mexico. There is also improvement in some areas of environmental protection and labor rights. On the other hand, it appears that regulations on product quality and environmental pollution have been reduced, U.S. trade deficits have increased, immigration from poorer to wealthier countries has resulted in tensions, income inequality has increased, and perhaps as many as three million—one in six—manufacturing jobs in the United States have been lost. It is clear that NAFTA has resulted in change at all levels in the social world, from restructuring of economies at the national and global levels to affecting individual job security and availability. The overall verdict on NAFTA's effect is still out.

The principle is that change at one level of the social world leads to change in other levels as it did in the global example of NAFTA and the societal, community, and individual example of terrorism and climate change. Changes at the macro level affect individuals, just as change at the micro level has repercussions at the meso and macro levels.

Thinking Sociologically

How have you or others in your community been affected by global agreements such as NAFTA?

Social Change: Process and Theories

The Process of Social Change

Something always triggers a social change. The impetus may come from within the organization, the source known as **strain**. Sometimes, it comes from outside the organization, in what sociologists call **stress**. Two examples of strain are conflicting goals and different belief systems within the organization.

Conflicting goals are seen in the case of the steel industry and its workers. Individual workers' goals are to meet their basic needs for food and shelter for their families by holding jobs. In Pittsburgh and Cleveland, many steel companies have closed down or moved to less costly sites due to lack of profits from changing economic demands and competition. Their profit goals led to decisions to downsize or move to other less costly production sites, creating massive unemployment in Cleveland and Pittsburgh. People who had created hopeful futures for themselves and their families were left without jobs.

Different belief systems (political, religious, economic, and social) within a society can also have a major effect on the type and rate of change that takes place. For example, some religious groups expect their members to obey moral dictates of their belief system, yet the values of the surrounding society stress individual freedoms, often in ways disapproved of by the religion. These conflicting goals create strain. Some religious groups oppose stem cell research, which uses cells of fetuses, most of which were created in test tubes. Others within the same congregation believe this research will alleviate suffering of loved ones and save lives. Although both sides believe they are pro-life, the internal strain in the religious group emanates from events and forces in science, medicine, and other institutions.

Stresses, those pressures for change that come from the organization's external environment, can be traced to several sources: the natural environment, population dynamics, actions of leaders, technologies, other institutions, and major historical events.

The natural environment can bring about either slow or dramatic change in a society. Natural disasters such as floods, hurricanes, tsunamis, heavy snows, earthquakes, volcanic eruptions, mud slides, tornadoes, and other sudden events are not planned occurrences, but they can have dramatic consequences. Disease epidemics, such as the SARS (Severe Acute Respiratory Syndrome) outbreak in 2002 or the potential bird flu epidemic, are often unpredictable.

SARS is the first severe transmissible disease to emerge in the 21st century. The first case occurred in Guangdong Province, China, in November 2002, and the outbreak, affecting 305 people, caused five deaths. Many of the cases involved medical staff treating patients with SARS. The outbreak, which was reported to the World Health Organization in February 2003, began spreading around the world along international air travel routes, several of which became hot spots. In May 2003, half a year after the first case was discovered, 7,761 probable cases in 30 countries on six continents had been reported, with 623 deaths from the disease (Wilson 2006; World Health Organization 2003).

The SARS threat brought about change in the World Health Organization, global medical reporting systems, and response networks. For instance, the Global Public Health Intelligence Network scans Internet communications for rumors and reports of suspicious diseases. This way, health organizations from the local to global levels can act quickly to contain the spread of deadly epidemics.

Natural disasters—floods, hurricanes, tornadoes, earthquakes, volcanic eruptions—can be the cause of major social changes in a community. As shown in this photo from a community on Lake Pontchartrain near New Orleans, Hurricane Katrina took its toll on Mississippi and Louisiana.

Less rapid natural changes also can have incremental but dramatic effects. For example, most scientists predict that the climatic changes resulting from the greenhouse effect are warming our atmosphere, transforming agricultural land areas into deserts, raising sea levels about one meter in this century, causing ice sheets to melt, increasing rainfall in currently dry areas, and intensifying the strength of hurricanes. This warming of the Earth's atmosphere results from a buildup of carbon dioxide or other gases (Environmental Protection Agency 2004). The majority of scientists are convinced that global warming is a human-generated problem and is a genuine threat to our survival. However, policy change is the responsibility of political powers (Lindsay 2006).

Without human intervention to address the causes, change in the climate will affect habitable land areas, very possibly create disasters that cost great amounts of money, and increase the cost of living for ordinary people, thus changing their lifestyles. In the film *An Inconvenient Truth*, former U.S. vice president and presidential candidate Al Gore (2006) addresses the threat and what the world needs to do to save the environment. Natural disasters are so important that the sociology of disasters has become a specialty field within the discipline, as indicated by one of the classic sociological studies of disasters, reported in the next "How Do We Know?"

Thinking Sociologically

First, read the "How Do We Know?" feature on pages 552–553. What lessons can we take from Erikson's (1976) findings to shed light on the Hurricane Katrina disaster in New Orleans in 2005?

How Do We Know?

Research on Disasters and Their Aftermath

A series of small villages were settled along a mountain creek of West Virginia known as Buffalo Creek. This was mining country, and at the top of the creek, there was a substantial bank of land that held in a reservoir of wastewater. A coal company had poured more than one million tons of wastewater and coal waste into this company created basin. The restraining embankment of shale, clay, slag, and low-quality coal that created the reservoir was referred to by the coal company as an "impoundment," but the people themselves referred to it as a "dam."

Whatever one calls it, this restraining wall was weakened by heavy rains in the winter of 1972, and on February 26, it broke, setting forth a massive flood of black sludge and oily, slag-filled wastewater down the valley toward the homes of 5,000 residents in the mountain villages. The first village hit was not just crushed, it disappeared entirely. This meant that the villages farther down the creek-bed had not just filthy water coming at them but the remains of homes, churches, stores, vehicles, and bodies descending on them. By the time the water subsided, the flood had taken with it almost everything in its path.

Newspapers reported on the economic loss and the staggering death toll, but lawyers, psychologists, and sociologists were interested in the human cost to survivors—costs to their sense of self, their mental and emotional well-being, and their family and friendship ties. Yale sociologist Kai Erikson's (1976) research is one of the classic pieces of investigation regarding the human and social toll of disasters. Here was a community that had an extraordinarily close-knit social network, where crime was virtually nonexistent, divorces were extraordinary, chemical abuse and mental problems were far below national norms, and neighborhoods were like extended families. Yet, the community had been ripped apart by the flood. Time had not healed the social and emotional wounds, even years after the flood: Few marriages remained intact, problems of deviance and delinquency were rife, and more than 90% of the people interviewed were judged to be in need of psychological counseling.

Erikson used several methods to gather data. He read depositions and other existing materials gathered by a law firm that was engaged in litigation against the coal company, he conducted extensive interviews with many of the survivors, and he did observations in the devastated communities.

The federal government's response to the flood in Buffalo Creek dealt mostly with immediate needs for survival. Thus, mobile homes were brought in and emergency food was provided, but people were placed in these shelters with no attentiveness to neighborhoods or preexisting kinship ties. Thus, people found themselves surrounded by strangers at a time when they desperately needed support and when they also had few interpersonal resources needed to forge new relationships.

The mental health symptoms tied to individual trauma include psychic numbness (feeling mentally blank and emotionally limp), constant death anxiety, feeling of guilt for having survived when so many members of one's family have not, experiencing guilt for not having saved people who were seen being swept down the river, losing the "furniture of self" (the symbols of one's life that might include one's home, family heirlooms, photographs of loved ones, and other artifacts that connect one to others and to a personal history), and loss of trust in the order of the universe or a loving God that people believed was in control of life's events.

Erikson (1976) argued that the "collective trauma" was more important to understand than the individual trauma: "People find it difficult to recover from the effects of individual trauma so long as the community around them remains in shreds. It is a general theory in psychiatry that time heals . . . wounds, but . . . time can work its special therapy only if it acts in concert with a nurturing communal setting" (p. 155). The collective trauma included five dimensions:

1. Disorientation: Erikson (1976) found that many persons were so socially displaced that they could hardly orient themselves in time and space, even two or three years after the flood.

2. Loss of morale and morality: Following the flood, people were more likely to commit deviant acts and to think they were surrounded by immoral people.

3. Loss of connection: Marriages began to disintegrate, and people lost their sense of connection to others. "Members of a family find that intimacy and gentleness are hard to sustain in an emotional atmosphere as dry as this one. The general community validated . . . bonds and gave them shape," reports Erikson (1976:221).

4. Illness and identity: The people seemed to feel that the land was polluted and untrustworthy, with some people being afraid to till the soil lest they find a body part of a family member or a neighbor buried there. Because the land was polluted, many people felt their own bodies were polluted, too.

5. Lost sense of safety: People slept in their clothes and boots, and whenever it rained, many residents would run to the creek every hour to check on the water levels.

This disaster at Buffalo Creek indicates how much of our personal mental health rests in the health of the larger community. It helps us understand how anomie (normlessness) can create anxiety and disorientation. Most of all, it helps us understand that natural disasters and human catastrophes, such as the September 11 terrorist attacks and devastating storms such as Hurricane Katrina and the daily killings in Iraq, can have pervasive consequences on individuals and communities. Although Erikson has been a leading figure in outlining what steps to take after disasters, his work is not always considered when larger policies are made. Particularly with Hurricane Katrina, Erikson went to numerous public and media forums and created a Task Force on Katrina with the Social Science Research Council. However, his influence on addressing the trauma and rebuilding has not been as strong as his experience might warrant.

Work on collective trauma forces us to be aware of the extent to which we depend on a larger community to regain our footing when a disaster disrupts our lives. We humans are, indeed, profoundly social beings. Changes that disrupt our social ties can have severe and wide-ranging consequences.

Population dynamics—birth and death rates, size of populations, age distribution, and migration patterns—can be important contributors to external stress on organizations. Where populations are growing at extremely rapid rates, strains on government systems result in inability to meet basic needs of the people. Values and beliefs regarding childbearing, knowledge of birth control, and the position of women in society are some of the crucial social variables in addressing the ability to meet needs. Immigration due to political upheavals or motivated by anticipated economic opportunities creates stress on the societies that receive the newcomers as they attempt to meet the immigrants' needs. For example, many refugees from the Darfur region in Sudan are fleeing to camps in the nearby country of Chad. Maps 16.1 and 16.2 show visually the hot spots globally for refugees and others who have been uprooted or displaced from their homelands. Refugees from war-torn countries are dependent on international aid and are separated from their families and neighbors.

Leaders or dominant individuals influence change through their policy decisions or social movements they help generate. Mohandas K. (Mahatma) Gandhi in India taught the modern world ways of bringing about change in political systems through nonviolent methods. Mikhail Gorbachev created new relations between the United States and the Soviet Union through *glasnost*—open communication and thawing tense relations. Policies of

New arrivals at Al Salaam camp, in Sudan's Darfur region, make temporary shelters out of household goods they were able to carry with them. A USAID-supported program at this one site is helping register more than 10,000 people who were displaced by violence in their home regions. Migration is a major factor in social change, and in cases like this, it is associated with great suffering and hardship.

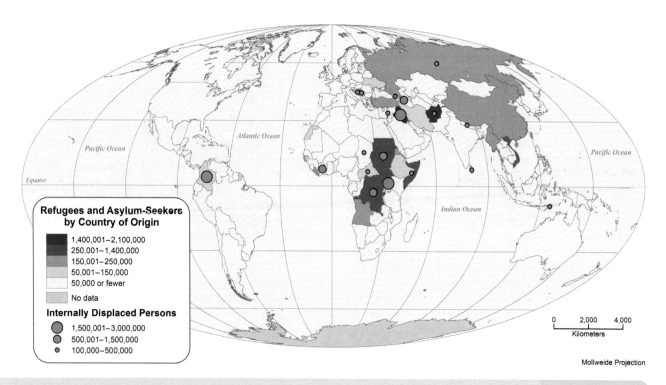

Map 16.1   Refugees, Asylum Seekers, and Internally Displaced People by Their Country of Origin, 2006

Source: UNHCR. Map by Anna Versluis.

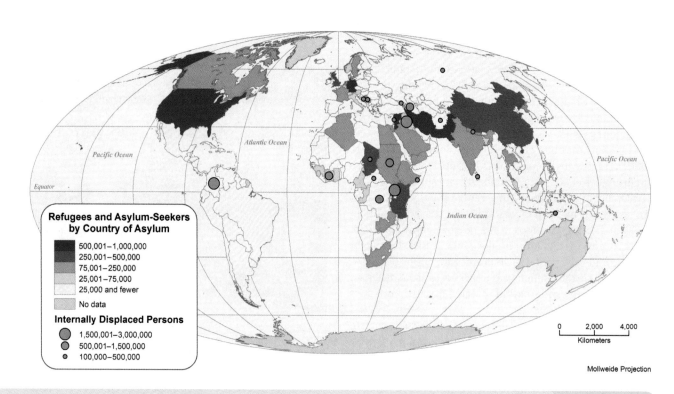

Map 16.2   Refugees, Asylum Seekers, and Internally Displaced People by Their Country of Asylum, 2006

Source: UNHCR. Map by Anna Versluis.

Charles Taylor, former military dictator of Liberia, created long-term war and resulted in thousands of deaths. These leaders' actions created internal strains in their own countries and external stressors resulting in change in the international community.

Technology has been a strong influence on societal change. For example, the invention of the plow allowed more land to be used for agriculture, creating greater food surpluses and allowing for new classes of people to move off of farms and into towns and urban areas. The invention of the steam engine resulted in looms and spinning jennies that helped develop factories and the cities around those factories. The computer makes possible the management of worldwide production, investments, and banking systems.

Consider one example: William F. Ogburn compiled a list of 150 social changes in the United States that resulted from the invention of the radio, such as instant access to information (Ogburn 1933). Other lists could be compiled for the telephone, automobile, television, and computers. Some of these changes give rise to secondary changes. For example, automobile use led to the development of paved highways, complex systems of traffic patterns and rules, and need for gasoline stations. The next "Sociology in Your Social World" explores several issues involving the automobile and change.

The diffusion or spread of the technology throughout the world is likely to be uneven, especially in the early stages of the new technology. For example, computer technology is advancing rapidly, but those advances began in corporate boardrooms, military bases, and university laboratories. Policies of governments and leaders, such as funding for school computers, determine the rate of public access. Thus, only gradually are computers reaching the world's citizenry through schools, libraries, and eventually private homes.

The social environment includes the institutionalized patterns of relationships that develop in organizations and nations. For example, historically Timbuktu in northwest Africa developed a strong interdependent relationship with England. The two nations exchanged gold and slaves for woven cotton cloth. As can be imagined, these interdependencies were also sources of stress. In Timbuktu, bolts of cloth became symbols of prestige. Greater conflicts were created as more people from Timbuktu sought to enslave others and to exchange humans for cloth. In England, greater separation developed between those with access to gold and slaves and those without such resources. Both situations resulted in changes in the social structure of society.

Major historical events—wars, economic crises, assassinations, political scandals, and catastrophes—can change the course of world events. For instance, the triggering event that actually started World War I was the assassination of Archduke Franz Ferdinand of the Austro-Hungarian empire. This assassination resulted in the German invasion of several other countries and the beginning of the war. So a micro-level act, the murder of an individual, had global ramifications. Clearly, internal

These Ugandan children are also refugees. Most have survived without their parents and must now cope with life as best they can. They were forced to flee from their homes or they would have been killed.

strains and external stressors give impetus to the processes of change. The question is: How do these processes take place?

Thinking Sociologically

First, read "Sociology in Your Social World," which begins on the next page. What might be some long-term social consequences for our individual lives and societies of the expanded use of the computer, the microwave oven, or the cell phone?

Theories of Social Change

Social scientists seek to explain the causes and consequences of social change, sometimes with the hope that change can be controlled or guided. Theories of change often reflect the events and belief systems of particular historical time periods. Conflict theory, developed during periods of change in Europe, began to gain adherents in the United States

Sociology in Your Social World

Technology and Change: The Automobile

When we think of technology and its impact on society, the innovation of the past two decades that is especially prominent is the computer and accompanying Internet. However, only a century ago, a newfangled novelty was spreading quickly from urban areas to the countryside: the automobile. At the turn of the 20th century, this strange horseless carriage was often referred to as the "devil wagon" in rural areas. The introduction of this self-propelled vehicle was controversial, and it sent ripples through the society in a number of ways. In the 1890s and early 1900s, some cities and counties had rules forbidding motorized vehicles. In Vermont, a walking escort had to precede the car by an eighth of a mile with a red warning flag, and in Iowa, motorists were required to telephone ahead to a town they planned to drive through to warn the community. This was so people could take action lest their horses be alarmed (Berger 1979; Clymer 1953; Glasscock 1937; Morris 1949). In most rural areas, motorists were expected to pull their cars to a stop or even to shut down the motor when a horse-drawn buggy came near. Legislation known as "pig and chicken clauses" meant that in most states, the automobilist was liable for any accident that occurred when passing an animal on or near the road, even if the injury was due to the animal having run away in fright (Scott-Montagu 1904). Such norms were considered the decent way to conduct oneself only a hundred years ago.

Automobiles were restricted to cities for nearly a decade after their invention because roads were inadequate outside of the urban areas. Owen G. Roberts invented a seatbelt in about 1915 because on a day-long 80-mile drive westward from Columbus, Ohio, Mary Roberts was knocked unconscious when the rough roads caused her head to hit the roof of the car with great force. Cars in the first decade of the 20th century often slid off muddy roads into ditches or got caught in deep tracks. These conditions had not deterred horses. Paving of roads became a necessity for automobile travel and, of course, made automobile travel much faster and more common. The expansion was stunning. An estimated 85,000 motored vehicles were in use in

Automobiles brought major changes to the modern world, many of them unanticipated. In the 19th century, in rural areas of the United States, they were actually called "Devil's Wagons" because they were viewed as an evil influence on American life. Clearly, automobiles have affected both the environment and social life in many ways. People often adopt technology without understanding the full social consequences of that technology.

In the early days, when laws required that an automobile have a flagman walk ahead of the car to warn people or call to the next town that a car was coming through, it would have been inconceivable how traffic now contributes to gridlock, smog, and even socioeconomic and ethnic segregation.

rural America in 1911. By 1930, the number was nearly 10 million (Berger 1979).

Forms of entertainment began to change when people were able to go longer distances in shorter periods of time. As the Model T made cars affordable, families no longer had only each other for socializing. Thus, the complete dependence on family was lessened, possibly weakening familial bonds (Berger 1979). Furthermore, entertainment gradually became available virtually any night of the week, not just on Saturdays and at special events such as the county fair (Berger 1979; McKelvie 1926). Even courting was substantially changed, as individuals could go farther afield to find a possible life partner, couples could go more places on dates, and two people could find more privacy.

Transportation that made traversing distances more possible changed how people related to a number of other institutions as well. Because people could drive farther to churches, they often chose to go to city churches, where the preachers were more skilled as public speakers and where the music was of higher quality. Small country churches began to consolidate or to close. However, many people found that a country drive was a more interesting way to spend Sunday mornings, and preachers often condemned cars for leading people away from church (Berger 1979). Still, once pastors could afford cars, many people received services such as pastoral calls that had previously been unknown in rural areas (Wilson 1924). Likewise,

motorized buses made transportation to schools possible, and attendance rates of rural children increased substantially (U.S. Department of Interior 1930). In addition, small rural hospitals began to close, so even the delivery of medical services was changed. Moreover, one of the banes of life for farm women was isolation, sometimes becoming so severe in the Western states as to lead to "madness" (Berger 1979; McNall and McNall 1983). The automobile was a boon to mental health by helping to solve this problem.

As people could live in less congested areas but still get to work in a reasonable amount of time via an automobile, the suburbs began to develop around major cities. No longer did people locate homes close to shopping, schools, and places of worship. Yet, a dispersed population needs to use more gasoline, thereby creating pollution. As the wealthy moved to expensive suburbs and paid higher taxes to support outstanding schools, socioeconomic and ethnic stratification between communities increased.

When Owen G. Roberts built one of the first automobiles in Ohio and established a large automobile dealership in Columbus, it was not his intent to heighten segregation, to create funding problems for poor inner-city areas, or to pollute the environment. Yet, these are some of the unintended consequences of the spread of the automobile. It sometimes takes decades before we can identify the consequences of the technologies we develop and adopt.

---

during the 1960s when intense conflict over issues of race and ethnic relations, the morality of the Vietnam War, and changes in social values peaked. Theories that focused on social harmony were of little help.

Major social change theories fall into micro level (symbolic interaction and rational choice) and overlapping meso and macro level (evolutionary, functional, conflict, and world systems theories). As we review these theories, some will be familiar from previous chapters.

Micro-Level Theories of Change

Symbolic interactionism. According to symbolic interaction theory, human beings are always trying to make sense of the things they experience, figure out what an event or interaction means, and determine what action is required of them. Humans construct meanings that agree with or diverge from what others around them think. This capacity to define one's situation, such as concluding that one is

oppressed, even though others have accepted the circumstances as normal, can be a powerful impetus to change. It can be the starting point of social movements, cultural changes, and revolutions.

Some sociologists believe that individuals are always at the core of any social trends or movements, even if those movements are national or global (Blumer 1986; Giddens 1986; Simmel [1902–17] 1950). After all, it is individuals who act, make decisions, and take action. Neither corporations, nor nations, nor bureaucracies make decisions—people do. The way in which an individual defines the reality he or she is experiencing makes a huge difference in how that person will respond.

Social institutions and structures are always subject to maverick individuals "thinking outside the box" and changing how others see things. Individual actions can cause riots, social movements, planned change in organizations, and a host of other actions that have the potential to transform the society. That people may construct reality in new ways can be a serious threat to the status quo, and those who want to protect the status quo try to ensure people will see the world the same way they do. If change feels threatening to some members who have a vested interest in the current arrangements, those individuals who advocate change may face resistance.

Leaders often provide opportunities for group members to participate in suggesting, planning, and implementing change to help create acceptance and positive attitudes toward change. This collaborative process is often used when a firm or a public agency is planning a major project, such as the development of a shopping mall or a waste disposal site, and cooperation and support by other parts of the community become essential. Symbolic interactionists would see this as an effort to build a consensus about what the social changes mean and to implement change in a way that is not perceived as threatening to the members.

Rational choice. To rational choice theorists, behaviors are largely driven by individuals seeking rewards and limiting costs. Because of this, most individuals engage in those activities that bring positive rewards and try to avoid the negative. A group seeking change can attempt to set up a situation in which desired behavior is rewarded. The typology presented in Figure 16.1 shows the relationship between behaviors and sanctions.

Bringing about change may not require a change in costs or rewards. It may be sufficient simply to change the people's perception of the advantages and disadvantages of certain actions. Sometimes, people do not know all the rewards, or they have failed to accurately assess the expenditures. For example, few citizens in the United States realize all the benefits of marriage. To change marriage rates, we may not need more benefits to encourage marriage. We may do just as well to change the population's appraisal of the benefits already available.

Change, according to this perspective, is enhanced through doing a force-field analysis. What are the forces or payoffs in favor of change, and what are the forces rewarding no change? These are the issues that influence an individual's support for, or opposition to, change.

Meso- and Macro-Level Theories of Change

Social evolutionary theories. Social evolutionary theories assume that societies move slowly from simple to more complex forms. Early unilinear theories maintained that all societies moved through the same steps and that advancement or progress was desirable and would lead to a better society. These theories came to prominence during the Industrial Revolution when European social scientists sought to interpret the differences between their own societies and the "primitive societies" of other continents. Europe was being stimulated by travel, exposure to new cultures, and a spawning of new philosophies, a period called the Enlightenment. Europeans witnessed the developments of mines, railroads, cities, educational systems, and rising industries, which they defined as "progress" or "civilization." World travelers reported that other peoples and societies did not seem to have these developments. These reports provided the empirical evidence that early sociologist Auguste Comte used in proposing his theory of unilinear development from simple to complex societies. Unilinear theories came to legitimate colonial expansion and exploitation of other people and lands that were seen as "inferior."

In a more recent version of evolutionary theory, the authors discuss five stages through which societies progress: hunter-gatherer, horticultural, agrarian, industrial, and postindustrial (see Chapter 3) (Nolan and Lenski 2008). This does not mean that some stages are "higher" or "better" than others but that this is the typical pattern of development due to expansion of technology and more efficient harnessing of energy sources. Despite their claim that this theory is not judging some as "better," the authors do use the term *progress*. This phrase refers to greater technological sophistication rather than to moral superiority. Still, in terms of technology, they do think the later stages are more advanced.

Many modern cases do not fit this pattern because they skip steps or are selective about what aspects of technology they wish to adopt. Less developed countries such as India and China are largely agricultural but are importing and developing the latest technology. Furthermore, advocates of

		Sanction	
		Formal	**Informal**
Behavior	**Positive**	Bonuses, advances, fringe benefits, recognition	Praise, smile, pat on the back
	Negative	Demotion, loss of salary	Ridicule, exclusion, talk behind back

Figure 16.1 Relationship Between Behaviors and Sanctions

some religious, social, and political ideologies question the assumption that "material progress" (which is what technology fosters) is desirable.

Even the phrase "developing countries" has been controversial with some scholars because it might imply that all societies are moving toward the type of social system characterized by the affluent or developed societies. Many now use the term *Global South* because poor countries are disproportionately south of the 20th latitude north whereas affluent nations are typically north of that line. Note that the term is a metaphor for all poor countries. Some prosperous countries are in the south, and some poor ones in the north, but the term is meant to avoid an assumption of inevitable evolution toward Western cultures.

Contemporary evolutionary theories are multilinear, acknowledging variations in the way change takes place. Simple societies go through a process of change to become large, complex, technologically advanced societies. The rapid spread of ideas and technologies means that societies today may move quickly from simple to complex, creating modern states with pockets of previous states of the cultures. Consider the mass of contradictions of the Middle East today. Due to the world demand for their oil, several countries in this region have among the highest per capita incomes in the world. In 2002, average per capita income for the entire world was $6,328. Saudi Arabia had a per capita income of $10,140, Kuwait $22,470, and the United Arab Emirates $23,770 (World Bank 2006). Especially the urban elite have access to modern conveniences such as computers, jets, and cell phones. Yet other Middle Eastern people still live traditional lives as nomads or herders in small villages or earn their living from the desert. Not all segments of society change at the same rate. This makes it nearly impossible to categorize some societies as being in one stage.

Functionalist theories. Functional theorists assume that societies are basically stable systems held together by the shared norms and values of their members. The interdependent parts work together to make the society function smoothly. A change in one part of the society affects all the other parts, each changing in turn until the system resumes a state of equilibrium. Change can come from external or internal sources, from contact with other societies, or from strains within. Slow, nondisruptive change occurs as societies become more complex, but any change may be seen as a threat to the equilibrium of a system. Rapid change is seen as especially dysfunctional or disruptive for the system. For example, the downfall of the former Soviet Union resulted in economic chaos that is still unresolved. Because sudden, disruptive change is difficult to explain using functional theory and because any change is viewed with some suspicion, some sociologists have turned to conflict theories to help explain change, especially rapid or violent changes.

Modes of transportation for goods and people vary around the world. The efficiency and speed of these modes often reflects the level of development of the region or country. "Pre-modern" modes of transportation leave less pollution and sometimes move more easily through congested streets than trucks. Sometimes, technological progress has a high cost, and resistance to that "progress" makes sense.

Conflict theories. Conflict theorists assume that societies are dynamic and that change and conflict are inevitable. According to Karl Marx, socioeconomic class conflict is the major source of tension leading to change in any society. Karl Marx and Friedrich Engels ([1848] 1969) argued that the antagonistic relationship they saw developing between the workers (proletariat) and the owners of the production systems (bourgeoisie) in 19th-century England would lead to social revolution. From this, they thought a new world order would emerge in which the workers themselves would own the means of production. Thus, conflict between the owners and the workers would be the central factor driving social change.

Other conflict theorists study variables such as gender, religion, politics, and ethnic and interest group problems in their analyses, feeling that these factors can also be the grounds for oppression and "we" versus "they" differences (Dahrendorf 1959). Some see conflict as useful for society because it forces societies to adapt to new conditions and leads to healthy change (Coser 1956). Conflict over slavery or over gender inequality are examples of problems that cause stresses and strains, eventually resulting in improved society. The current conflict over health care in the United States may also eventually lead to a better system.

World systems theory of global change. World systems theorists focus on the historical development of the whole

In this typical situation, these South African miners are all black, whereas the supervisors and managers are white. These gold miners are part of a multinational corporation and the larger world economic system, with stockholders from around the globe.

world and how that development has influenced individual countries today. Capitalist economies first appeared about 1500. Since then, except for a few isolated tribal groupings, almost all societies have been at least indirectly influenced by dominant capitalist world economic and political systems (Wallerstein 1974).

This theory divided the world system into three main parts: the core, semiperipheral, and peripheral areas (see Figure 16.2). The core areas are economically and

politically powerful. Core countries include European states, Australia and New Zealand, Japan, Canada, the United States, and a few others (Wallerstein 1974). Historically, they have controlled global decision making, received the largest share of the profits from the world economic system, and dominated peripheral areas politically, economically, and culturally by controlling the flow of technology and capital into those countries. Peripheral countries, many of which are in Africa and Asia, provide cheap labor and raw materials for the core countries' needs. The semiperipheral countries are in an intermediate position, trading with both the core and the peripheral countries. Former republics of the Soviet Union generally are considered semiperipheral. Because most semiperipheral countries are industrializing, they serve as areas to which core-country businesses and multinational corporations can move for continued growth, often in partnerships, as semiperipheral states aspire to join the core countries. The core and semiperipheral countries process raw materials, often from peripheral countries, and may sell the final products back to the peripheral countries. The semiperipheral countries and the peripheral countries need the trade and the resources of the core countries, but they are also at a severe disadvantage in competition and are exploited by those at the core, resulting in an uneasy relationship.

These basic relationships between the core, semiperipheral, and peripheral countries have endured since the 1700s. However, several small, rapidly developing "Asian tigers" (South Korea, Thailand, Taiwan), along with China, may challenge the existing relationships with their expanding economies.

Since the 1960s, however, these relationships have been dramatically modified. Changes in technology and

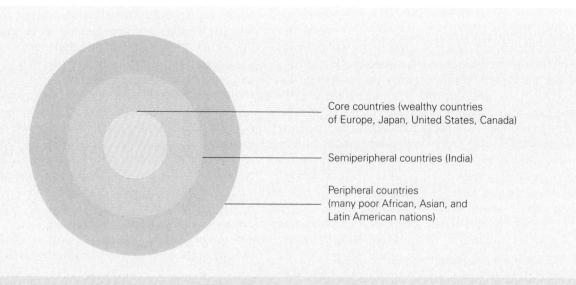

Core countries (wealthy countries of Europe, Japan, United States, Canada)

Semiperipheral countries (India)

Peripheral countries (many poor African, Asian, and Latin American nations)

Figure 16.2 World Systems Theory

in international global institutions have allowed corporations to break their production processes into smaller segments. These segments are then scattered over the world to take advantage of the lower manufacturing costs in the periphery. This process creates commodity chains—worldwide networks of labor resources and production processes that create a product. The 2008 contract awarded to Northrop Grumman for military refueling planes caused controversy in the United States with the debate about whether Northrop or its competitor, Boeing, was more "American." Both companies planned to produce parts of the new plane in several different world locations. Each piece of the chain can be located in a core, semiperipheral, or peripheral country. Because manufacturing processes are often performed in semiperipheral countries, their share of the world's manufacturing and trade production has risen sharply. By contrast, the distribution of profits from multinational corporations still benefits the core countries.

The core countries have been a major force in the development of global institutions, such as the International Monetary Fund (IMF), that facilitate and attempt to control international capital flow. By increasing frameworks for debt restructuring for peripheral countries, the IMF attempts to restore sustainability and growth to countries that default on their loans. At least 30 countries have restructured their debt under IMF guidelines (International Monetary Fund 2003).

However, the IMF leaves countries little economic autonomy. The restructuring plans control what countries do even within their own national boundaries, creating debt dependencies on core countries that the poorer countries can never overcome. For example, the IMF has demanded and instituted freezes on salaries and minimum wages in places such as Brazil and Argentina, has mandated opening of borders to imports, and has unintentionally undermined the economies of some very poor countries. The problem has been one of insisting on application of economic theories that work in affluent counties but not always in poor ones (The Dollars and Sense Collective 2006; Friedman 2006; Weidenbaum 2006; Weller and Hersh 2006).

In one sense, world systems theory is a conflict theory that is global in nature, with core countries exploiting the poor countries. As we might expect from conflict theory, some groups of noncore countries have increased their collective power by forming alliances such as OPEC (Organization of Petroleum Exporting Countries), OAS (Organization of African States), and SEATO (Southeast Asia Treaty Organization). These alliances present challenges to the historically core countries of the world system because of their combined economic and political power. For example, the price we pay at the gas pump reflects the power of OPEC to set prices. Other types of alliances such as NAFTA (North American Free Trade Agreement) are being forged between core countries and their neighbors. When we understand international treaties and alliances as part of larger issues of conflict over resources and economic

self-interests, the animosity by noncore countries toward core countries such as the United States begins to make sense. Likewise, the mistrust of the United States toward countries that seem to be getting U.S. jobs is not entirely unfounded. The problem is an extraordinarily complex system that always leaves the most vulnerable more at risk and the wealthiest even richer.

Not all scholars think that conflict theory is the most useful approach to globalization, and one of the leaders in globalization theory, Roland Robertson, focuses on matters of culture, consciousness, and values that world systems theory ignores. Globalization is more than macro-level changes in national and international social systems. It also has to do with a change in individual and group consciousness, so that the world really becomes a single sociocultural place for people living their everyday lives. Robertson examines some of these issues in the next "Sociology Around the World" on page 562.

Sometimes behavior that results in change is unplanned, even spontaneous as described in the following section.

Thinking Sociologically

Where is your clothing made? Did a multinational corporation have it assembled in the Global South? Who benefits from companies buying cheap labor from the Global South: You? The workers? Governments? The companies that manufacture the products? Who, if anyone, is hurt?

COLLECTIVE BEHAVIOR: MICRO-LEVEL BEHAVIOR AND CHANGE

The following incident occurred in Chicago during riots in the 1960s and provides an example of collective behavior, a form of unplanned action that can be understood at a micro level.

On Saturday, July 15, [Director of Police Dominick] Spina received a report of snipers in a housing project. When he arrived he saw approximately 100 National Guardsmen and police officers crouching behind vehicles, hiding in corners and lying on the ground around the edge of the courtyard.

Since everything appeared quiet and it was broad daylight, Spina walked directly down the middle of the street. Nothing happened. As he came to the last building of the complex, he heard a shot. All around him the troopers jumped, believing themselves to be under sniper fire. A moment later a young guardsman ran from behind a building.

Sociology Around the World

Globalization: Top Down and Bottom Up

By Roland Robertson

Globalization has become one of the most prominent concepts in contemporary social sciences. Globalization refers to two master processes, ones that have been continuing throughout the history of humanity. The first of these is increasing connectivity (sometimes called interconnectedness) between peoples of the world, and the other is increasing global consciousness. Whereas increasing connectivity has been accorded a vast amount of recent attention, the issue of global consciousness has been relatively neglected. However, the increasing significance of such worldwide problems as global warming and climate change, controversial attempts to substitute fossil fuel with biofuel, and a widespread sense of the planet being poised on the brink of potential disaster, bring consciousness of global citizenship into view. Global consciousness is the rapidly increasing sense of all human beings being "in the same boat"—indeed, in peril. This does not mean there is a global consensus concerning possible solutions to our present predicaments. Rapidly increasing globalization has led to numerous and violent conflicts over access to basic necessities, including food and water, and to assumptions about the purpose and fate of humankind. The clash between Islam and Christianity is a major example of the latter.

The overall process of globalization can be divided into four primary dimensions: the cultural, the social, the political, and the economic. The economic dimension has received the most attention since the early 1990s. In this respect, globalization has come to mean, for many, the worldwide expansion of capitalism and advocacy of the opening of economic markets.

Nevertheless, well before communism began to collapse in the late 1980s, a few social scientists, particularly sociologists, had begun to use *globalization* in a multidimensional manner, with the focus on the world becoming a single sociocultural place. Specifically, this involved *equal* attention to cultural, social, political, and economic factors.

One of the main concerns in the study of globalization has been its form. Globalization over the past five centuries or so has had four major, increasingly concrete, components: the nation-state, the international system, individual selves, and humanity. In fact, the United Nations, founded in the mid-1940s, is organized precisely in these terms. For example, even though religions and ideologies have played a role in accelerating consciousness of the world as a whole, they have by no means been the truly pivotal forces of world formation. Instead, the critical organizing forces have been nations and international alliances at the macro level and individuals and human rights issues at the micro level.

A major and increasingly important concern is the degree to which globalization overwhelms local traditions and customs, creating sameness or homogeneity everywhere. This is often the way globalization is discussed. However, the contemporary world is characterized by a mixture of sameness and difference. The thing that makes life interesting is our differences, such as local traditions, and often there is a primary loyalty to local cultural idiosyncrasies. This idea that local traditions and customs are valuable empowers localities to be increasingly assertive in protecting their distinctiveness. A currently popular phrase is "globalization from below" (that is, local control of the direction of globalization). This phrase came into existence in tandem with the antiglobalization movement at the end of the 1990s. This movement was initially directed at global capitalism and the dominating institutions that supported it (such as the World Bank, the International Monetary Fund, and the World Trade Organization). Resistance to this top-down globalization is a more recent and interesting social movement. This is what I call "glocalization"—with global trends and forces being modified and even remade by local customs and traditions. So a movement toward homogenizing traditional cultures is real, but it is not the only force at work, as local cultures exert themselves and modify the global trends. The process is truly complex and incredibly interesting.

The Director of Police went over and asked him if he had fired the shot. The soldier said yes, he had fired to scare a man away from a window; his orders were to keep everyone away from windows. Spina said: "Do you know what you just did? You have now created a state of hysteria. Every guardsman up and down this street and every state policeman and every city policeman that is present thinks that somebody just fired a shot and that it is probably a sniper."

A short time later more "gunshots" were heard. Investigating, Spina came upon a Puerto Rican sitting on a wall. In reply to a question as to whether he knew "where the firing is coming from?" the man said: "That's no firing. That's fireworks. If you look up to the fourth floor, you will see the people who are throwing down these cherry bombs."

By this time four truckloads of National Guardsmen had arrived and troopers and policemen were again crouched everywhere looking for a sniper. The Director of Police remained at the scene for three hours, and the only shot fired was the one by the guardsman. However, at six o'clock that evening two columns of National Guardsmen and state troopers were directing mass fire at the Hayes Housing Project in response to what they believed were snipers. (Report of the National Advisory Commission on Civil Disorders 1968:3–4)

Collective behavior refers to unplanned, spontaneous, unstructured, disorganized actions that often violate norms. It arises when people are trying to cope with stressful situations and unclear or uncertain conditions (Goode 1992; Smelser 1963, 1988). Collective behavior falls into two main types: crowd behavior and mass behavior. It often starts as a response to an event or stimulus as in the perceived threat from snipers in the above example. It could begin with a shooting or beating, a speech, a sports event, or a rumor. The key is that as individuals try to make sense of the situations they are in and respond based on their perceptions, collective social actions emerge.

Crowd behaviors—mobs, panics, riots, and demonstrations—are all forms of collective behavior in which a crowd acts, at least temporarily, as a unified group (LeBon [1895] 1960). Crowds are often made up of individuals who see themselves as supporting a just cause. Because the protesters are in such a large group, they may not feel bound by the normal social controls—either internal (normal moral standards) or external (fear of police sanctions).

Mass behavior occurs when individual people communicate or respond in a similar manner to ambiguous or uncertain situations, often based on common information from the news or on the Internet. Examples include public opinion, rumors, fads, and fashions. Unlike social movements, these forms of collective behavior generally lack a hierarchy of authority and clear leadership, a division of labor, and a sense of group action.

Crowds can stimulate change in a society, but they can also become unruly and unpredictable. Government officials spend a good deal of money and time equipping and training officers in how to control angry and radicalized members of crowds.

Theories of Collective Behavior

Social scientists studying disruptions in the social world have looked at group and crowd dynamics, finding that most members of crowds are respectable, law-abiding citizens, but faced with specific situations, they act out (Berk 1974; Turner and Killian 1993). Several explanations of individual involvement dominate the modern collective behavior literature.

The minimax strategy (Berk 1974) is based on principles of rational choice theory. It suggests that individuals try to minimize their losses or costs and maximize their benefits. People are more likely to engage in behavior if they feel the rewards outweigh the costs. Individuals may become involved in a riot if they feel the outcome—drawing attention to their plight, the possibility of improving conditions, solidarity with neighbors and friends, looting goods—will be more rewarding than the status quo or the possible negative sanctions.

Emergent norm theory (Turner and Killian 1993) points out that individuals in crowds do have different emotions and attitudes that guide their decisions and behaviors than

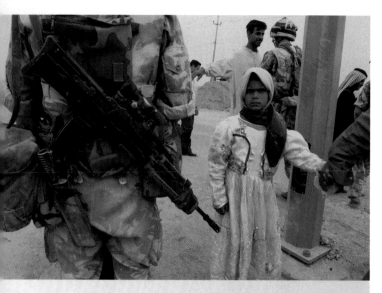

On the southern outskirts of Basra in Iraq, British soldiers monitor a checkpoint leading into the city, checking people for weapons. A young Iraqi girl experiences the tense and hostile realities of war as her relative is checked by British soldiers. This kind of military presence is often scary for residents and is very dangerous work for soldiers.

if they act alone. The theory addresses the unusual situations and breakdown of norms in which most collective behavior takes place. Unusual situations may call for the development of new norms and even new definitions of what is acceptable behavior. The implication of this theory is that in ambiguous situations, people look to others for clues about what is happening or what is acceptable, and norms emerge in ambiguous contexts that may be considered inappropriate in other contexts.

The value-added theory describes conditions for crowd behavior and social movements. Key elements are necessary, with each new variable adding to the total situation until conditions are sufficient for individuals to begin to act in common, and collective behavior emerges (Smelser 1963). These are the six factors Smelser (1963) identified:

1. *Structural conduciveness:* Existing problems create a climate that is ripe for change (such as tensions between religious and ethnic groups in Iraq).

2. *Structural strain:* The social structure is not meeting the needs and expectations of the citizens, which creates widespread dissatisfaction with the status quo—the current arrangements (the Iraqi government is unable to control violence and provide basic services).

3. *Spread of a generalized belief:* Common beliefs about the cause, effect, and solution of the problem evolve, develop, and spread (U.S. troops may leave; militias are killing members of other groups).

4. *Precipitating factor:* A dramatic event or incident occurs to incite people to action (groups of men from different religious groups are kidnapped, bound, and shot).

5. *Mobilization for action:* Leaders emerge and set out a path of action, or an emergent norm develops that stimulates common action (citizens gather to protest the killings and lack of security and services).

6. *Social controls are weak:* If police, military, or strong political or religious leaders are unable to counter the mobilization, a social movement or other crowd behavior (e.g., a riot or mob) is likely to develop. (Some analysts have argued that Iraq has erupted into a civil war because of lack of social controls.)

When all six factors are present, some sort of collective behavior will emerge. Those interested in controlling crowds that are volatile must intervene in one or more of these conditions (Kendall 2004; Smelser 1963).

Thinking Sociologically

Think of an example of crowd behavior or a social movement, preferably one in which you have been involved. Try to identify each of the six factors from Smelser's theory as they operate in your example.

Types of Collective Behavior

Collective behavior ranges from spontaneous violent mobs to temporary fads and fashions. Figure 16.3 shows the range of actions.

Mobs are emotional crowds that engage in violence against a specific target. Examples include lynchings, killings, and hate crimes. Near the end of the U.S. Civil War, self-appointed vigilante groups roamed the countryside in the South looking for army deserters, torturing and killing both those who harbored deserters and the deserters themselves. There were no courts and no laws, just "justice" in the eyes of the vigilantes. Members of these groups constituted mobs. The film *Cold Mountain* (Frazier 1997) depicts these scenes vividly. Unless curbed, mobs often damage or destroy their target.

Riots—an outbreak of illegal violence committed by individuals expressing frustration or anger against people, property, or both—begin when certain conditions occur. Often, a sense of deprivation sets the stage for a riot—hunger, poverty, poor housing, lack of jobs, discrimination, poor education, or an unresponsive or unfair judicial system. If the conditions for collective behavior are present, many types of incidents

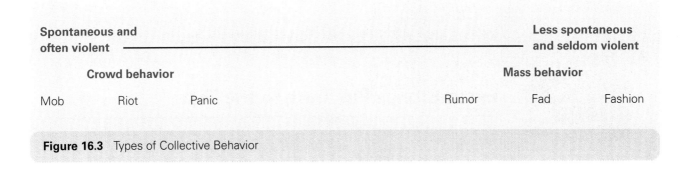

Figure 16.3   Types of Collective Behavior

Riots involve dispersed actions expressing frustration
(e.g., urban riots over poor conditions).

Mobs involve a group collectively focusing their
action on a single individual or location
(e.g., a lynch mob).

Figure 16.4   The Difference Between Riots and Mobs

can be the precipitating factor setting off a riot. Participants may come not only from poor neighborhoods but also from middle-class areas in which residents feel frustrated with an emotionally charged issue that is not being solved by the leaders of the city or nation. For example, residents of many towns in Iraq have been rioting over lack of jobs, poor pay, and the limited resources available to sustain a decent life.

In 1969, when the police raided a New York gay bar, Stonewall Inn, they were seeking arrests on immorality charges. The frustration of being under attack for their sexuality finally led homosexuals at the bar to erupt. A three-day riot ensued. Eventually, this angry energy was transformed into a social movement for change, the international Stonewall Movement for gay, lesbian, and bisexual rights. The distinction between riots and mobs is illustrated in Figure 16.4.

Panic occurs when a large number of individuals become fearful or try to flee threatening situations that are beyond their control, sometimes putting their lives in danger. Panic can occur in a crowd situation, such as a restaurant or theater in which someone yells "fire," or it can occur following rumors or information spread by the media. Panic started by rumors set off the run on the stock market in October 1929. A large number of actions by individuals caused the stock market crash in the United States and repercussions around the world. In 2008, the collapse of global investment banking and securities trader Bear, Stearns and Co. resulted in turmoil

in the financial markets. Only with radical intervention by the federal government was the immediate crisis abated. When panics have subsided, collapse, death, or destruction can be the result of the group action.

Rumors are a form of mass behavior in which unsupported or unproven reports about a problem, issue, or concern circulate widely throughout the public. Rumors may spread only in a local area, but with electronic means available, rumors are spreading more widely and rapidly. Without authoritative information, ambiguous situations can produce faulty information on which decisions are made and actions are based. *Urban legends*, one example of widely spread but unverified messages, are unsubstantiated stories that sound plausible and become widely circulated. People telling them usually believe them (Henslin 2005). The next "Sociology in Your Social World" provides an example.

Thinking Sociologically

What role is the Internet playing in spread of information and rumors? How is e-mail changing the way we communicate and our interpersonal relationships?

Sociology in Your Social World

Exam Stories Put Truth to the Test

College exams are quickly approaching, so it is a good time to take a look at the latest chapter in the tome of teacher-student legend and rumors.

The first one was reported from Calgary, Alberta, by a civil engineering student at the University of Manitoba. This tale says a professor announced an open-book final examination in which the students could "use anything they are able to carry into the exam room." One innovative undergraduate, it is reported, carried in a graduate student who wrote his exam for him.

Another legend came from North Carolina. Supposedly, on the day before the final exam, the professor left his office unattended, leaving the door open and the examinations left sitting on his desk. A student who came by to ask a question found the room empty and quickly left with one of the exams. However, the professor had printed the exact number of exams that he needed, and the next morning, he counted them again before going to the classroom. Discovering that he was one short, he suspected that it had been stolen, so he trimmed one-half inch from the bottom of the remaining exams. When the exam papers were turned in, the student whose paper was longer than the others received a failing grade.

Another classic exam story was about a philosophy professor who was wrapping up a class in metaphysics. For the final exam, the teacher placed a chair on the desk in front of the room. "Prove that this chair exists," he said. "You have two hours." One student was purported to have written, "What chair?" and left the room while classmates frantically composed elaborate essays. As the story goes, the student who wrote the two-word challenge got the A.

A student procrastinated on writing a paper. Twenty-four hours before the paper was due, he went to the university library and found an old paper on the topic. He copied it and turned it in. A few weeks later, the professor returned the papers and he stopped by the student's desk. He supposedly said to the student: "Twenty-five years ago, when I wrote this paper, it got a B. I always thought it deserved an A." There was an A on the cover, but the professor added: "Try anything like this again, and I'll have you thrown out of school."

Another college legend goes like this: Jack, a less than industrious student, was taking an examination with two blue books, a pen, and a question that had him baffled. Being naturally bright, even if lazy, he solved the problem in the following way. In one of the blue books, he wrote a letter to his mother, telling her that he had finished his exam early but was waiting for a friend to finish and was taking the opportunity to write her a note. He said he had been studying very hard for this instructor, who was a nice guy but had pretty high standards. When the time was up, he handed in one blue book and quickly left with the unused one. When he got to his room, he opened his text, wrote an answer, and mailed the blue book to his mother. When the instructor found the letter, he called Jack, who explained that he had written in two blue books and must have gotten them mixed up. The examination essay must be in the mail on the way to Boston where his mother lived. He offered to call his mother and have her send the envelope back as soon as she got it. He did, she did, and the blue book was returned, with the inner envelope postmarked the day of the test and outer envelope postmarked Boston.

Campus legends such as these help reduce the strains of college life and spread the reputations of legendary professors. Furthermore, they keep alive hopes of someday outfoxing the professors—or the students, depending on which side you are on.

Note: These and other urban legends about exams and college experience can be reviewed at http://www.snopes.com.

Fads are temporary items or activities that spread rapidly and are copied enthusiastically by large numbers of people. Body modification, especially tattooing, appeals mostly to young people of all social classes. Tattoo artists emblazon IDs, secret society and organization emblems, fraternity symbols, and decorations to order on all parts of the customers' bodies. Body modification has taken place for centuries, but it goes through fads (University of Pennsylvania 2007). Sometimes, fads become institutionalized—that is, they gain a permanent place in the culture. Other fads die out, replaced by the next hot item.

Fashions refer to a social pattern favored by a large number of people for a limited period of time. Here today, gone tomorrow. Examples would include clothing styles, music genres, color schemes in home decor, types of automobiles, and architectural designs. Fashions typically last longer than fads but sometimes survive only a season, as can be seen in the clothing industry. Music styles such as "post hard core," "conscious hip hop," and "UK 2-step garage" were popular among some groups as this book was being written but may be passé by the time you read this, replaced by new styles resulting from change in mass behavior.

Thinking Sociologically

Why did body adornments and piercings become so popular with today's younger generation? Does this influence or is it influenced by change in the larger society?

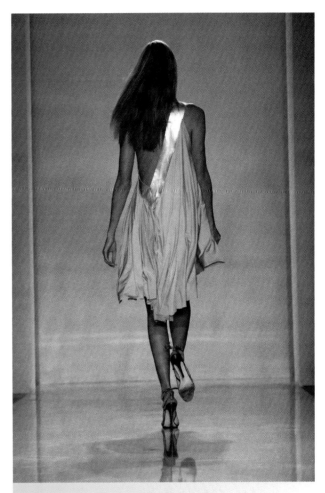

Fashions are established largely at fashion shows, where designers introduce new clothing styles. Fashions cannot occur unless there is a very high level of affluence, where people can afford to throw away perfectly good clothing for something more stylish. For many in the Global South, it is a gift just to have clean, warm clothing, and the very existence of such displays of consumerism is both amazing and appalling.

Each of these forms of collective behavior involves micro-level individual actions that cumulatively become collective responses to certain circumstances. However, ripples are felt in other levels of the social world. Insofar as these various types of collective activity upset the standard routines of the society and the accepted norms, they can unsettle the entire social system and cause lasting change.

The separation of each of the forms of change into levels is somewhat artificial, of course, for individuals are also acting in organizations and in national social movements. However, when we move to meso- and macro-level analyses, the established structures and processes of the society become increasingly important. Much of the change at these levels is planned change.

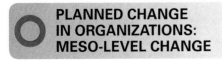

PLANNED CHANGE IN ORGANIZATIONS: MESO-LEVEL CHANGE

The board of trustees of a small liberal arts college has witnessed recent drops in student enrollments that could cause the college to go out of business, but the college has a long tradition of fine education and devoted alumni. How does the college continue to serve future students and current alumni? The problem is how to plan change to keep the college solvent.

A company manufactures silicon chips for computers. Recently, the market has been flooded with inexpensive chips, primarily from Asia, where they are made more cheaply than this North American firm can possibly make them. Does the company succumb to the competition, figure out ways to meet it, or diversify its products? What steps should be taken to facilitate the change? Many companies in Silicon Valley, California, face exactly this challenge.

A nonprofit organization concerned with research into a rare disease has held fundraising drives for many years to support research regarding the causes of and cures for this disease. However, the breakthrough has come, and vaccines are now being produced to prevent the disease. Does the nonprofit agency close shop or find another cause to support? The March of Dimes collected money for poliomyelitis research and helped support the discovery of a cure, effectively eradicating the disease. Should it just fold up the charity and lay off its employees or redirect its energies?

A Native American nation within the United States faces unemployment among its people due in large measure to discrimination by Anglos in the local community. Should the elders focus their energies and resources on electing sympathetic politicians, boycotting racist businesses, filing lawsuits, becoming entrepreneurs as a nation so they can hire their own people, or beginning a local radio station so they will have a communication network for a social movement? What is the best strategy to help this proud nation recover from centuries of disadvantage?

All these are real problems faced by real organizations. Anywhere we turn, organizations face questions involving change, questions that arise because of internal strains and external stresses. How organizational leaders and applied sociologists deal with change will determine the survival and well-being of the organizations.

How Organizations Plan for Change

If you work for an organization during your lifetime, you will engage in the process of planning for change. Some organizations are well prepared to meet the challenge of change. They spend time and money writing long-range strategic plans and doing self-studies to determine areas for ongoing change. Other organizations may not be prepared. Sometimes, change is desired, and sometimes, it is forced on the organization by stresses from society, more powerful organizations, or individuals (Kanter 1983, 2001a, 2001b; Olsen 1968). Change in one part of an organization can send ripples through the rest of the organization. A problem solved in one area creates unanticipated problems someplace else. The speed of change due to our modern communication and transportation technologies makes the unexpected outcomes of minor changes even more complex.

Planned change such as strategic planning is the dream of every organizational leader. It involves deliberate, structured attempts, guided by stated goals, to alter the status quo of the social unit (Bennis, Benne, and Chin 1985). Some applied sociologists devote their careers to combining research and advocacy of change, as illustrated in the "Applied Sociologist at Work" feature on the facing page.

There are several important considerations as we think about planned change: How can we identify what needs to be changed? How can we plan or manage the change process successfully? What kind of systems adapt well to change? Here, we briefly touch on the topic and outline three approaches advocated by experts to plan change. Keep in mind the levels of analysis as you read about change models.

Models for Planning Organizational Change

Change models fall into two main categories: closed system models, which deal with the internal dynamics of the organization, and open system models (such as our social world model), which consider the organization and its environment. Let us sample a couple of these models.

Closed system models, often called classical or mechanistic models, focus on the internal dynamics of the organization. The goal of change using closed models is to move the organization closer to the ideal of bureaucratic efficiency and effectiveness. An example is time and motion studies, which analyze how much time it takes a worker to do a certain task and how it can be accomplished more efficiently. Each step in the McDonald's process of getting a hamburger to you, the customer, has been planned and timed for greatest efficiency. In some closed system models, change is often legislated from the top executives and filters down to workers.

The human relations approach or "Theory Y," and the organizational development (OD) movement state that participants in the organization should be involved in decision making leading to change. The leadership is more democratic and supportive of workers, and the atmosphere is transparent—open, honest, and accountable to workers and investors. This model emphasizes that change comes about through adjusting workers' values, beliefs, and attitudes regarding new demands on the organization. Many variations on this theme have evolved, with current efforts including team building and change of the organizational culture to improve worker morale. Closed-system models tend to focus on group change that occurs from within the organization.

Open system models combine both internal processes and the external environment. The latter provides the organization with inputs (workers and raw materials) and feedback (acceptability of the product or result). In turn, the organization has outputs (products) that affect the larger society. There are several implications of this model: (1) change is an ever present and ongoing process, (2) all parts of the organization and its immediate environment are linked, and (3) change in one part has an effect on other parts. The model in Figure 16.5 illustrates the open system.

Thinking Sociologically

Using the model in Figure 16.5, fill in the parts as they relate to your educational institution. For example, inputs might include faculty members and students.

The Process of Planned Change

Nongovernmental organizations (NGOs) plan ways to improve the lives of individuals in many parts of the world.

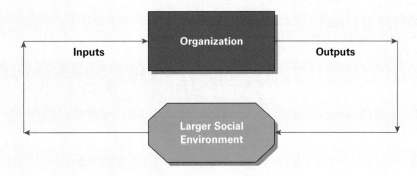

Figure 16.5 Open Systems Model

The Applied Sociologist at Work— Stephen Steele   Local Community Research Center

Dr. Stephen Steele started using sociology to help a business he was working for solve a problem and bring about needed change. He has been in the business of helping organizations solve problems with sociological knowledge ever since.

"If someone has knowledge and fails to use it, that is a terrible waste," comments Steele. The idea of being involved in social betterment and making a difference were guiding principles that led Steele to a life of sociological research. In 1978, he used his research skills to help set up a Community Research Center at the local community college. The goals were for the nonprofit center to help community organizations solve their problems, train students to use research skills, help bring about needed change, and provide a service to all. In 1982, he became director, a position he still holds.

Many students have developed sophisticated analytical and research skills by working on projects in the community, and the center has supported itself by contracting its high-quality, low-cost research services to community organizations. Although the range of the center's research is broad, the main foci have been community change, economic development, and county government issues. For instance, Steele's company, Applied Data Associates, received one federal grant to evaluate an antidrug project and another to evaluate ways to increase the active involvement of Hispanic Americans in community civic organizations.

The interaction between theory and research is crucial in his work. Consider the four basic sociological theories: He looks for systems of interaction (functionalism), for power centers (conflict), for interaction patterns and definitions of reality within corporate cultures (symbolic interactionism), and for costs and benefits of various choices (rational choice).

Steele likens applied sociology to being a "social plumber"—there is a specific problem, so he uses his tools to fix it. He finds being a social plumber rewarding and exciting, using sociological knowledge and tools to change groups, organizations, and environments, and in the process improving the quality of life for people.

Note: Dr. Stephen Steele received his bachelor's and master's degrees from Eastern Michigan University and his doctorate from Catholic University of America. He teaches sociology at Ann Arundel Community College in Maryland and runs his own research center. His students gain practical experience working in the center.

One big issue in the Global South is the availability of clean drinking water (discussed in Chapter 11). For example, in parts of Africa, women must spend as much as six hours a day carrying water to the home. Because daughters are needed to care for younger siblings while the mother is away, many girls are unable to attend school. This, in turn, has implications for the continuation of poverty. If estimates are correct—that 443 million school days are lost each year due to water-related diseases—this adds even more to the crisis of continuing poverty (WaterAid 2008).

Clean water is essential for life and for health, but one out of six people—more than a billion humans on this planet—do not have access to it. This and poor sanitation result in annual deaths of more than two million people, but the lack of clean water close to home also affects how people use time, how they make their livelihoods, and the quality of their lives. Furthermore, with global climate change, the glaciers on top of mountains like Mount Kenya are melting. Although that mountain peak has been snow-covered for more than 10,000 years, the glaciers are expected to be completely gone in perhaps 20 years (Cousteau 2008). When that snow source disappears, the water supply for hundreds of thousands of people and animals in Kenya will disappear. This problem is by no means limited to Africa (Barnett et al. 2005; Cyranoski 2005; Struck 2007). Some organizations have formed to respond to the current and anticipated crisis.

An example of one British organization that is bringing about change is WaterAid, launched in 1981. It has grown to become an international NGO that focuses entirely on water and sanitation issues, including hygiene. Communities in Zambia and Sri Lanka were the first to receive support, with other projects following in Ethiopia, Tanzania, Uganda, Sierra Leone, Ghana, Kenya, Bangladesh, Nepal, India, Gambia, Nigeria, Mozambique, Zambia, Madagascar, and Malawi. Communities in those countries were assisted in developing the most appropriate technologies for clean water, given the geographical features and resources of the area.

Prince Charles of England became the president of the organization for several years in the early 1990s, which enhanced the visibility of the cause. WaterAid has helped more than eight and a half million people in the poorest parts of the world gain access to one of the most fundamental of human requirements (WaterAid 2008). In 2006, the organization was voted Britain's most admired charity. It all started with a group of people with a vision, some organizational skills, and passionate commitment to improving the quality of life for people. Some other organizations, also working on this issue, have employed the skills of sociologists who use their understanding of social processes that exacerbate or can lessen this problem. This is illustrated by the work of Ruth Meinzen-Dick, which is explained in the next "Applied Sociologist at Work."

For our understanding of change, this example shows one of the many types of organizations that both changes within itself to meet new conditions and brings about change in the world. The process of planned change is like a puzzle with a number of pieces that differ for each organization but must fit together for the smooth operation of the organization. The goal of most organizations is to stay balanced and avoid threats or conflict. Change is generally perceived as desirable if it is evolutionary or planned. Unplanned change can be disruptive to the system.

At the societal and global macro levels, change is often stimulated by individuals and events outside the chambers of power, and there is much less control over how the change evolves. We turn next to an exploration of change at the macro level.

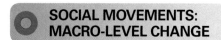

SOCIAL MOVEMENTS: MACRO-LEVEL CHANGE

Beijing, China, hosted the prestigious summer 2008 Olympics, athletic games that promote peace and goodwill around the globe. The Olympic torch traversed the globe to prepare for and celebrate the event. However, its travels and the opening of the games were far from peaceful and full of goodwill. Protests dogged the torch, and major political leaders refused to attend the opening ceremonies. A social movement was spurred by an uprising in Tibet, a region that was an independent country until the 1950s and is now part of China. The issue—human rights violations by China and autonomy of Tibet—created protests and demonstrations around the world. Will this social movement bring about change in the status of Tibetans? Worldwide attention may aid the cause of those in Tibet seeking improved life conditions, or it may not. However, those people who are making an issue of the games in China are hoping to change more serious life and death policies for people. A social movement tries to bring change, but questions arise: What is a social movement, what brings it about, and what might be the results?

What Is a Social Movement?

From human rights and women's rights to animal rights and environmental protection, individuals seek ways to express their concerns and frustrations. **Social movements** are consciously organized attempts outside of established institutions to enhance or resist change through group action. Movements focus on a common interest of members, such as human rights. They have an organization, a leader, and one or more goals that aim to correct some perceived wrongs existing in the society or even around the globe. Social movements are most often found in industrial or postindustrial societies made up of diverse groups that advocate for their own goals and interests.

Movements are usually begun by individuals outside the power structure who might not otherwise have an opportunity to express their opinions (Greenberg 1999). The problems leading to social movements often result from the way resources—human rights, jobs, income, housing, money for education and health care, and power—are distributed. In turn, they may stimulate the formation of countermovements—social movements against the goals of the original movement (McCarthy and Zald 1977).

Many individuals join social movements to change the world or their part of the world and affect the direction of history. In fact, social movements have been successful

What does a sociologist have to say about natural resource management? This is a question Dr. Ruth Meinzen-Dick has often been asked during her career. For 19 years, she has been showing the importance of understanding how farmers are organized and relate to government and other organizations as part of her work at the International Food Policy Research Institute (IFPRI), part of a larger network of international agricultural research organizations.

Her interests came from growing up in a dry part of India, where water was critical. She returned to India to study how small-scale irrigation systems were operated and found that farmers' organizations played an important role, even though the systems were formally under government management. Other students and faculty from different fields at Cornell University were finding similar patterns of farmer-managed irrigation systems in other parts of the world, so Dr. Meinzen-Dick was able to be part of a larger effort to understand the human side of water management. This was not just an academic exercise, as the Cornell program advised USAID. Even while still in graduate school, Dr. Meinzen-Dick had a consultancy with the World Bank to review the extent of farmer participation in their irrigation programs.

During her work at IFPRI, Dr. Meinzen-Dick has been able to continue studying what brings people together to manage water systems in developing countries and to compare this with factors that encourage collective action for managing forests, rangelands, and other natural resources. This has involved field research in countries such as India, Pakistan, Zimbabwe, Kenya, and Uganda. She has been able to bring all this together by coordinating an international network on Collective Action and Property Rights (CAPRi), which helps people working on different aspects of agricultural research and natural resource management in developing countries to understand that the social institutions of property rights and collective action play a major role in shaping how people use and share resources. Understanding these institutions requires looking beyond simple indicators like title deeds (for property rights) or formal organizations (for collective action)—it requires a combination of qualitative and quantitative research methods to understand how people in different societies relate to each other and to their natural resources. The CAPRi program, therefore, provides training to researchers and practitioners from many countries on the importance of collective action and property rights and on the research methods to study them.

Much of Dr. Meinzen-Dick's professional life has involved working across disciplines. At times, this has been frustrating, especially when it seemed that more quantitative fields like economics or engineering were seen as more "rigorous." Still it has also been deeply satisfying when people from other backgrounds see the relevance of social institutions, or when principles from economics, political science, or the natural sciences give her insights into why people do (or don't) work together. To achieve this, it has been especially important for her to communicate the findings of sociological research clearly to nonsociologists. Institutional economics and a strong background in quantitative analysis have been especially helpful for her in communicating with her colleagues, who are mostly economists. To achieve impact in terms of changes in government policies or development programs (e.g., to allow farmers to have more voice in water management), it has been important to use sound research methods and then explain the results clearly to policymakers, not just in academic publications but also in research briefs and presentations.

Note: Dr. Ruth Meinzen-Dick received her master's and PhD degrees in development sociology at Cornell University, with minors in agricultural economics and international agriculture. Her training stressed qualitative and quantitative methods and a strong emphasis on interdisciplinary work, both in terms of coursework in other fields and work with economists, political scientists, and engineers researching water management, which helped prepared her to work across fields in international development.

in doing just that. Consider movements around the world that have protected lands, forests, rivers, and oceans, seeking environmental protection for the people whose survival depends on those natural resources. For example, the Chipko Movement (meaning "embrace") in a number of areas of

India has been fighting the logging of forests by commercial industries. Villagers, mostly women, use Gandhi-style nonviolent methods to oppose the deforestation. A movement by local peasants in Bihar, India, fought efforts to control their fishing rights in the Ganges River.

Stages of Social Movements

What would mobilize you to become involved in an issue that concerns you? Why do people become involved in PETA (People for Ethical Treatment of Animals), pro-choice or pro-life movements, or political demonstrations against policies such as war? Social movements begin because of cultural conflicts in society and because people come together who want to create—or to resist—social change. Movements take the time and energy of individual volunteers, and these human resources must be focused as the movement evolves. In the preliminary stage, the purpose for a movement is set. Long-standing problems or very recent events may create dissatisfaction and discontent in the general public or a part of the public. This discontent can galvanize people through a single event.

Sociologists have identified several conditions that give rise to the preliminary stage. First, individuals must share some basic values and ideals. They often occupy similar social statuses or positions and share concerns. Second, social movements need to have a "preexisting communication network" that allows alienated or dissatisfied people to share their discontent (Farley 2005). Several recent political movements, such as MoveOn.org and TrueMajority.com, were carried out primarily on the Internet. Third, a strain and a precipitating event galvanize the people around the issue. Fourth, effective leadership emerges—leaders who can mobilize people, organize the movement, and garner resources to fund the movement. Finally, the people in the movement develop a sense of efficacy, a sense that they actually can be successful and change the system. Sometimes, as in the case of the civil rights movement, a sense of confidence in success comes from a religious conviction that God will not let the movement fail (Farley 2005).

In the popularization stage, individuals coalesce their efforts, define their goals and strategies, develop recruitment tactics, and identify leaders. The social movement enters the public arena. The leaders present the social problems and solutions as seen by the members of the social movement. Now the social movement enters the institutionalized stage, becoming a formal organization. This organized effort generates the resources and members for the social change efforts.

In some movements, the final stage is fragmentation and demise. The group may or may not have achieved its goals, but fragmentation breaks apart the organization because the resources may be exhausted, the leadership may be inept or may have lost legitimacy, or the leaders may be co-opted by powerful mainline organizations. In this latter case, radical renewal movements may arise among those still strongly committed to the original cause (Mauss 1975).

In the case of the women's movement, interested women were linked into "preexisting communication networks" by serving on state Commissions on the Status of Women (Ferree and Merrill 2000). The refusal of the Equal Employment Opportunities Commission to consider women's rights as equal to those of racial minorities became the strain and precipitating event that led women to form the National Organization for Women (NOW), a group that continues to fight for women's rights today (Freeman 1975). The Equal Rights Amendment (ERA) provided a major issue around which women's groups rallied. Many women spent tremendous time and effort in attempts to have the ERA ratified by the necessary number of states. Spokespersons emerged, and fundraiser events provided resources. For a long time, advocates were convinced that the campaign would be successful. However, when the realization of failure came, an era in the women's movement ended. Some women's organizations fragmented and faded from the scene, while others revised their goals and strategies and moved on to new efforts to support women's empowerment.

Social movements sometimes focus on regional or even organizational modification, but typically, their focus is on national or global issues. For example, Amnesty International's primary interest is human rights violations by nations, and the organization publishes information on violations around the world. Another way to classify social movements is by their purpose or goals.

Thinking Sociologically

What evidence can you see in your local area, your country, or the world of stages in a social movement such as the women's movement?

Types of Social Movements

Stonewall is a gay, lesbian, and bisexual rights movement that began when patrons fought back against a police raid of a gay bar in New York in 1969. After that incident, the concern about gay rights erupted from a small number of activists into a widespread movement for rights and acceptance. Stonewall now has gone global, with chapters in other countries and continents. Proactive social movements, such as the gay rights movement, promote change. Reactive social movements, such as Focus on the Family, resist change. James Dobson's Focus on the Family has organized lobbying efforts and rallies fighting against the acceptance of homosexuality or giving gays equal status to heterosexual married relationships, although this is not the organization's only concern. Within the proactive and reactive social movements, there are four main types.

Expressive movements are group phenomena, but they focus on changing individuals and saving people from corrupt lifestyles. Many expressive movements are religious, such as the born-again Christian movements, Zen Buddhism, Scientology, the Christian Science Church, and

Transcendental Meditation. Expressive movements also include secular psychotherapy movements and self-help or self-actualization groups.

Social reform movements seek to change some aspect of society, but members generally support the society as a whole. These movements focus on a major issue such as environmental protection, women's rights, same-sex marriage, "noncorporate" and "just" globalization, gay rights, or civil rights. Typically, these movements use nonviolent, legislative means or appeals to the courts to accomplish their goals, although splinter groups may resort to more aggressive methods.

Social reform labor movements around the globe fight for workers rights. In Cambodia, garment workers, who sew many of the clothes sold in the Global North, are experiencing better working conditions through a joint effort of the International Labor Organization and the U.S. government. The project started in 2001 to alleviate problems in sweatshops. Periodic unannounced visits by inspectors, interviews with workers, and new training opportunities for workers are all part of the agreement that guarantees Cambodia access to U.S. markets (Better Factories Movement in Cambodia 2006).

Another social reform movement is ACORN (Association of Community Organizations for Reform Now), a grassroots neighborhood-based antipoverty group. Started in each community by concerned residents, the movement now has offices in more than 100 U.S. cities and more than 200,000 members—and it is still growing. Community members knock on doors to register voters, get petitions signed, and get people on the streets to protest against the severe inequality in society. They are funded by foundations, private donations, and organizations working jointly to bring about change. In Gary, Indiana, this group paid its utility bills in pennies to protest the quick shutoff of power to financially strapped customers. In Chicago, members gathered signatures for a law requiring Wal-Mart to pay employees $10 per hour plus benefits. Each community's issues involve populist organizing that can affect policies and bring about change in society. ACORN combines local projects with national action on larger issues. This type of grassroots organizing has the potential to be a major force for change in many communities (Eckholm 2006).

Revolutionary movements attempt to transform society, to bring about total change in a society by overthrowing existing power structures and replacing them with new ones. These movements often resort to violent means to achieve their goals, as has been the case with many revolutions throughout history. When we read in the paper that there has been a coup, we may be looking at a revolutionary movement that has ousted the government in power. Although it was not violent, Nelson Mandela's African National Congress succeeded in taking power in South Africa in 1994, rewriting the constitution, and purging a racially segregated apartheid social system that had oppressed four fifths of the South African population.

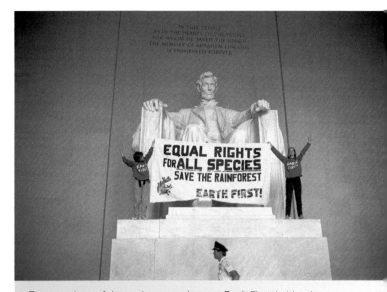

Two members of the environmental group, Earth First, hold a sign in front of the Lincoln Memorial in Washington, D.C., to protest the destruction of the Earth's rainforests and to advocate for the rights of various species that are endangered. Such movements use nonviolent protest, legislative means, and appeals to the public or to the courts to accomplish their goals.

Some social movements are regressive; they seek to reverse social trends and return to a previous set of social arrangements. Here, veiled women and children in Lebanon march in support of the Iranian leader, Ayatollah Khomeini. They hope to restore traditional values and modest roles and images for women, and to counter Western influences.

Resistance or regressive movements try to protect an existing system or part of a system or return to what a system had been by overthrowing current laws and practices. They see societal change as a threat to values or practices and wish to maintain the status quo or return to a former status by reversing the change process (Inglehart and Baker 2001). The American Family Association seeks to preserve functions and structure of the family as it was in the middle of the 20th century. The movement to pass a referendum in California to ban gay marriage is one of the association's recent efforts. The Islamic movement under the Ayatollah Khomeini in Iran sought to restore fundamentalist Islam and eliminate Western influences.

Global transnational movements focus on large-scale, often global issues and take place across societies as international organizations seek change in the status of women, child labor, rights of indigenous peoples, global warming, and animal rights around the world. Examples include any movement to improve the working conditions and environmental conditions resulting from actions of multinational corporations (The Durban Accord 2003; Flavin 2001; World Resources Institute 2003). Another example is Free the Slaves, a global antislavery organization started by sociologist Kevin Bales (2000, 2004). Figure 16.6 summarizes the types of movements and focus of each, from the micro to the macro level.

Thinking Sociologically

Consider a social movement with which you are familiar. What type of movement is it, and what was or is it trying to accomplish?

	Proactive	Reactive
Macro level	*Social Reform Revolutionary Global Transnational*	**Resistance or Regressive**
Micro level	*Expressive*	*Expressive*

Figure 16.6 Types of Movements

Globalization and Social Movements

Social movements are about people trying to improve their situations within society or their societies. They are intriguing because they provide compelling evidence that humans make choices and are capable of countering macro- and meso-level forces. As Eitzen and Zinn (2006) put it,

> Social structures constrain what we do, but they do not determine what we do. While these structures are powerful, human beings are not totally controlled. . . . Individuals acting alone, or with others, can shape, resist, challenge, and sometimes change the social structures that impinge on them. These actions constitute *human agency*. (p. 322)

Since World War II, power in the global system has been dominated by a group of industrial giants called the Group of 8 (or the "G8"). These nations control world markets and regulate economic and trading policies (Henslin 2005). Included among this elite are the dominant three (Japan representing the East, Germany representing central Europe, and the United States representing the Western Hemisphere) and five other important but less dominating powers (Canada, France, Great Britain, Italy, and now Russia). The G8 (called the G7 until Russia was added) are the core countries that have the most power in the World Trade Organization, the World Bank, the IMF, and other regulatory agencies that preside over the global economy. These agencies have often demanded that poor countries adhere to their demands or lose the right to loans and other support. Yet, the policies imposed from above have often been disastrous for poor countries, creating situations in which a debt burden is created that can never be paid off due to World Bank and IMF policies. If these were individuals rather than countries, we would call them indentured servants or slaves (Brecher et al. 2006; Cockburn 2007; Weller and Hersh 2006). This creates nations where hopelessness would seem to reign supreme, yet, social movements are arising in precisely these places and are often joining forces across

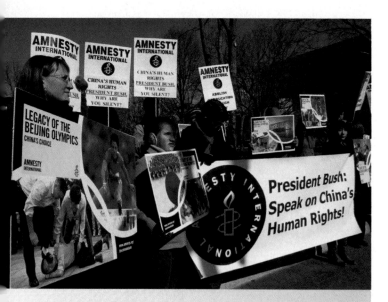

Protestors hold signs outside the White House in Washington, D.C., in 2008 during a demonstration organized by Amnesty International. The group was calling on China to respect human rights, using the Olympic Games in Beijing as an occasion to pressure China by affecting their international reputation. This is an example of a global transnational movement.

national boundaries (Stein 2006; Weidenbaum 2006). Even some groups within the G8 nations—labor unions, college student groups, and religious bodies concerned about social justice—are joining the movements.

Some of the most interesting social movements in the 21st century have created networks with other groups around the world, using the Internet to communicate and to find common ground. Moreover, some of the poorest nations have now formed their own organization to counter what was then called the G7 (now G8). Calling themselves the G77, the alliance has existed since the 1970s, but the first meeting of the heads of state of these poor nations occurred in 2000. The countries are now uniting, rather like a labor union seeking collective unity among workers, in attempts to gain some power and determine their own destinies by challenging what they experience as the tyranny of the G8 (Brecher et al. 2006; Hayden 2006). Map 13.2 on page 451 displays the location of G8 and G77 countries.

Globalization as it now exists—with corporate profits as the ruling principle of most decision making—has lowered environmental standards, lessened consumer protection, decreased national sovereignty and local control of decisions, and reduced safety and other protections for workers. However, in the competition to find cheaper labor for higher profits, there is a "race to the bottom," as communities must lower standards or else lose jobs to some other part of the world that is even more impoverished. When jobs move elsewhere, the people who had come to depend on those jobs are devastated and often thrust into poverty and homelessness, and the country loses tax revenue. Unemployed workers often migrate, becoming either illegal aliens in another country or squatters in slums of cities in their own countries.

Although workers risk losing jobs by participating, one result of globalization has been a rise in countermovements. Globalization from below refers to the efforts by common people in small groups and protest movements to fight back. Rather than globalization being controlled solely by the pursuit of profits, these countermovements seek to protect workers, to defend the environment, and to combat the bone-crunching poverty that plagues so much of the Global South, where poverty has increased in the past 30 years and continues to rise. The argument goes like this:

> It is the activity of people—going to work, paying taxes, buying products, obeying government officials, staying off private property—that continually re-creates the power of the powerful. . . . [The system, for all its power and resources, is dependent on common people to do the basic jobs that keep the society running.] This dependency gives people a potential power over the society—but one that can be realized only if they are prepared to reverse their acquiescence. . . . Social movements can be understood as the collective withdrawal of consent to established institutions. The movement against globalization can be understood as the withdrawal of consent from such globalization (Brecher et al. 2006:337).

Nelson Mandela voted for the first time in his life in South Africa on April 27, 1994. This was the first democratic election open to all races in South Africa after segregation was abolished. A political prisoner for 26 years, Nelson Mandela was held by the apartheid-based government as a dangerous revolutionary for his beliefs in racial equality. He was elected president of the country in this election and was co-recipient of the Nobel Peace Prize for his work for democracy and equality. His nonviolent movement brought revolutionary change, but it did so with the help of pressures from other countries and movements that advocated for racial justice.

The authors of this argument describe the Lilliputian strategy, named after the tiny Lilliputians who, in the book *Gulliver's Travels,* captured Gulliver by tying him up with hundreds of tiny threads. The tiny threads in this case are thousands of small resistance actions to the oppressive policies of G8 transnational corporations. Consider the following three examples:

> Under heavy pressure from the World Bank, the Bolivian government sold off the public water system of its third-largest city, Cochabamba, to a subsidiary of the San Francisco–based Bechtel Corporation, which promptly doubled the price of water for people's homes. Early in

Protesters sitting on the ground are confronted by riot police during a World Trade Organization's (WTO) conference in Seattle. There were more than 500 arrests at this protest in Seattle, most of people from G-8 countries. The protesters oppose policies sponsored by the G-8 and the International Monetary Fund that they feel are harmful to common citizens who are not wealthy—whether they be in the Global North or South. This is another example of a global transnational movement.

like The Gap and Nike to establish acceptable labor and human rights conditions in their factories around the world. Their efforts gradually grew into an anti-sweatshop movement with strong labor and religious support and tens of thousands of active participants. In the U.S., college students took up the anti-sweatshop cause on hundreds of campuses, ultimately holding sit-ins on many campuses to force their colleges to ban the use of college logos on products not produced under acceptable labor conditions. (Brecher et al. 2006:333)

Many concerned citizens in the Global North now buy Fair Trade goods such as coffee, cocao, and fruits.

Individuals in G8 countries have been extremely generous in donating to international organizations helping victims of disasters and in joining in solidarity with those in dire straits in the poor Global South. However, governments have often been unsympathetic. The United States spends 0.13% of 1% of its gross national product on United Nations programs that address poverty, famine, illiteracy, and disease. That represents a decrease of 90% from the Kennedy administration era, more than 40 years ago. However, many activists believe that actions by individuals and small groups, the Lilliputian strategy, can have a real impact.

Thinking Sociologically

What are cases in which the Lilliputian strategy has made a difference in local, national, or international events with which you are familiar?

In summary, some social change is planned by organizations, some is initiated by groups that are outside the organizational structure (social movements), and some is unplanned and spontaneous (collective behavior). The most important point, however, is that actions by individuals affect the larger social world, sometimes even having global ramifications. Likewise, national and international changes and social movements influence the lives of individuals.

Technology, Environment, and Change

2000, the people of Cochabamba rebelled, shutting down the city with general strikes and blockades. The government declared a state of siege, and a young protester was shot and killed. Word spread all over the world from the remote Bolivian highlands via the Internet. Hundreds of e-mail messages poured into Bechtel from all over the world, demanding that it leave Cochabamba. In the midst of local and global protests, the Bolivian government, which had said that Bechtel must not leave, suddenly reversed itself and signed an accord accepting every demand of the protestors. (Brecher et al. 2006:341–42)

In April 2000, AIDS activists, unions, and religious groups were poised to begin a lawsuit and picketing campaign denouncing the Pfizer Corporation as an AIDS profiteer for the high price it charges for AIDS drugs in Africa. Pfizer suddenly announced that it would supply the drug fluconazole, used to control AIDS side effects, for free to any South African with AIDS who could not afford it. (Brecher et al. 2006:342)

Groups in Europe, Japan, and the U.S. that had been involved in support for development and popular movements in third world countries found that those developing countries were increasingly being used as production platforms by global corporations. They began calling attention to the growth of sweatshops and pressuring companies

At the edge of the town of Bhopal, India, looms a subsidiary plant of the American-based Union Carbide Company. The plant provides work for many of the town's inhabitants. However, on December 3, 1984, things did not go as normal. A storage tank from the plant, filled with the toxic chemical liquid methyl isocyanate, overheated and turned to gas, which began to escape through a pressure-relief valve. The gas formed a cloud and drifted away from the plant. By the time the sirens were sounded, it was too late for many people. The deadly gas had done its devastating work: More than 3,000 were dead and thousands ill, many with permanent injuries from the effects of the gas. Put in perspective, the number of casualties was about equal to the number in the terrorist attack on the Twin Towers of New York City on September 11, 2001.

The legal systems became tangled in battles that prevented many of the victims from receiving any needed compensation for their injuries or the deaths of wage earners. The company settled with the government of India for a fraction of the claims put forth by individuals, and many people were never compensated for their medical expenses or their losses. (Not all multinational companies have been such poor citizens.)

This example illustrates change at multiple levels of analysis. We see a global multinational company (Union Carbide) in a society (India) that welcomed the jobs for its citizens. A community within that larger society benefited from the jobs until many residents were killed or disabled, leaving shattered families and devastated individual lives. The accident also spawned a number of forms of collective behavior. The immediate aftermath of the accident at Bhopal included panic, as people tried to flee the deadly gas. Like many environmental and nuclear crises, this one later resulted in several social movements as activists demanded accountability and safety measures. The disaster also brought about planned change in the way Union Carbide does business and protects workers and citizens.

Technology refers to the practical application of tools, skills, and knowledge to meet human needs and extend human abilities. However, nuclear disasters also make clear that technology and environment cannot be separated. The raw products that fuel technology come from the environment, the wastes resulting from technology return to the environment, and technological mistakes affect the environment. This section discusses briefly the development and process of technology, the relationship between technology and environment, and the implications for change at each level of analysis.

Human abilities enable scientists to invent new and better ways to make life more comfortable and safe. Throughout human history, there have been major transition periods or waves when changes in the material culture brought about revolutions in human social structures and cultures (Toffler and Toffler 1980). The agricultural revolution used technology in the form of a plow to till the soil, establishing new social arrangements, and eventually resulting in food surpluses that allowed cities to flourish. The Industrial Revolution brought machines powered by steam and petrol, resulting in mass society, divisions of labor in manufacturing, and socialist and capitalist political-economic systems. Today, postindustrial technology, based on the microchip, is fueling the spread

Global protests often focus on actions of Western multinational corporations. Women demonstrators, including Bhopal Gas victims in India, hold a "Wanted" poster of former Union Carbide Chairman Warren Anderson, arguing that he should be tried for crimes. More than 3,000 people were killed and tens of thousands injured when a tank at the Union Carbide pesticide plant leaked five tons of poisonous gas.

of information, communication, and transportation on a global level. This postindustrial revolution is producing new technologies that can move information and people rapidly around the globe; explore space; and analyze, store, and retrieve masses of information in seconds. Exploration of Mars is under way as this chapter is being written. However, each wave affects only a portion of the world, leaving other people and countries behind and creating divisions between the Global North and Global South.

Scientists have developed technologies to ease the looming energy crisis and climate change. Solar panels on this restaurant in Portugal provide independence from other sources of energy.

According to sociologist William Ogburn ([1922] 1938, 1961, 1964), change is brought about through three processes: discovery, invention, and diffusion. Discovery is a new way of seeing reality. The material objects or ideas have been present, but they are seen in a new light when the need arises or conditions are conducive to the discovery. It is usually accomplished by an individual or small group, a micro-level activity.

Invention refers to combining existing parts, materials, or ideas to form new ones. There was no light bulb or combustion engine lying in the forest waiting to be discovered. Human ingenuity was required to put together something that had not previously existed. Social inventions of the past 300 years include democracy, capitalism, bureaucracy, and the right to privacy. Technological innovations often result from research institutes and the expansion of science, increasingly generated at the meso level of the social system.

Diffusion is the spread of an invention or discovery from one place to another. The spread of ideas such as capitalism, democracy, and religious beliefs has brought changes in human relationships around the world. Likewise, the spread of various types of music, film technology, telephone systems, and computer hardware and software across the globe have had important ramifications for global interconnectedness. Diffusion often involves expansion of ideas across the globe, but it also requires individuals to adopt ideas at the micro level.

Technology and Science

Science is the systematic process of producing human knowledge. The question, "How do we know what we know?" is often answered, "It's science." Whether social, biological, or physical, science provides a systematic way to approach the world and its mysteries. It uses empirical research methods to discover facts and test theories. Technology applies scientific knowledge to solve problems. Early human technology was largely a result of trial and error, not scientific knowledge or principles. Humans did not understand why boats floated or fires burned. Since the Industrial Revolution, many inventors and capitalists have seen science and technology as routes to human betterment and happiness. With the emphasis on science, the scientific process is a major social institution in 21st-century industrial and postindustrial societies, providing the bases of information and knowledge for sophisticated technology.

Indeed, one of the major transformations in modern society is due to science becoming an institution. Prior to the 18th century, science was an avocation. People like Benjamin Franklin experimented in their backyards with whatever spare cash they had to satisfy their own curiosity. Franklin discovered that lightning was actually electricity by flying a kite in a thunderstorm. It was impossible then to imagine that we would now have a vehicle exploring Mars or that a human would walk on the moon.

Institutionalization means creating a stable pattern of roles, statuses, and groups that address some basic societal need—in this case, science and the need for new resources and new ways of understanding the natural world. Science in the contemporary world is a social process. It involves mobilizing financial resources and employing the most highly trained people (which in turn required the development of educational institutions).

Social conditions can be conducive or deleterious to scientific or technological innovation. Innovation resulting in change will be very slow until a society has institutionalized science and accepted change. Innovation involves providing extensive training, paying some people simply to do research, and funding the investigations. Specialization in science speeds up the rates of discovery. A researcher focuses in one area and gets much more in-depth understanding. Effective methods of communication across the globe mean that we do not need to wait six years for a research manuscript to cross the ocean and to be translated into another language. Competition in science means that researchers move quickly on their findings. Delaying findings may mean that the slowpoke does not get tenure at his or her university, promotion in the research laboratory, or awards for innovation.

We would not have automobiles, planes, missiles, space stations, computers, the Internet, and many of our modern conveniences without the institutionalization of science and without scientific application (technology). Science is big business, funded by industry and political leaders. University researchers and some government-funded science institutes engage in *basic research* designed to discover new knowledge, often on topics that receive funding. Industry and some governmental agencies such as the military and the Department of Agriculture employ scientists to do *applied research* and to discover practical uses for existing knowledge.

Scientific knowledge is usually cumulative, with each study adding to the existing body of research. However, radical new ideas can result in scientific revolutions (Kuhn 1970). Galileo's finding that the Earth revolves around the sun and Darwin's theory of evolution are two examples of radical new ideas that changed history. More recently, cumulative scientific knowledge has resulted in engines that power cars and machines and computer technology, which has revolutionized communication.

Thinking Sociologically

Imagine what your life would have been like before computers, e-mail, and the Internet. What would be different? (Note that you are imagining the world from only 10 to 20 years ago.) Ask your parents or grandparents what this past world was like.

Technology and Change

The G8, discussed earlier, holds yearly meetings to determine the world's markets and regulate global economic policy, including interest and currency rates and tariffs. The group's power enables those eight countries to control technology by obtaining cheap raw products, especially oil. In the process, they profoundly influence which countries will be rich or poor. Although politicians like to tell us they believe in a free market economy, uninhibited by governmental interference, they actually intervene regularly in the global market.

New technological developments can be a force for world integration but also for economic and political disintegration (Schaeffer 2003). The technological revolution in communications has resulted in fiber optic cable and wireless microwave cell phones and satellite technologies that make it easier to communicate with people around the world. We now live in a global village, a great boon for those fortunate enough to have the education and means to take advantage of it (Drori 2006; Howard and Jones 2004; Salzman and Matathia 2000).

However, the changes in technology do not always have a positive effect on less affluent countries. For example, by substituting fiber optic cable for old technologies,

Technology has had some unexpected consequences, including a staggering increase in the amount of trash generated in the society. Depicted here is trash from the fast-food industry in Egypt. The volume of trash has created problems regarding disposal.

the demand for copper, used for more than 100 years to carry electrical impulses for telephones and telegraphs, has bottomed out. Countries such as Zambia and Chile, which depended on the copper trade, have seen major negative impacts on their economies. New developments resulting in artificial sweeteners reduced demand for sugar, the major source of income for 50 million people who work in the beet and cane sugar industries around the globe. As new technologies bring substantial benefits to many in the world, those benefits actually harm people in other parts of the interconnected world.

Some societies are attempting to replace the old economies with new service industries such as tourism. However, with violence and terrorist threats, many potential tourists prefer not

Sociology in Your Social World

Making a Difference

To develop sociological interventions that will bring about change, applied sociologists and individuals like you can take certain steps (Glass 2004). Because bringing about change requires cooperation, working in a group context is often essential. Flexibility, openness to new ideas, and willingness to entertain alternative suggestions are also key factors in successful change. The following steps provide a useful strategy for planning change:

1. *Identify the issue:* Be specific and focus on what is to be changed. Without clear focus, your target for change can get muddied or lost in the attempt.

2. *Research the issue and use those findings:* Learn as much as you can about the situation or problem to be changed. Use informants, interviews, written materials, observation, existing data (such as Census Bureau statistics), or anything that helps you understand the issues. That will enable you to find the most effective strategies to bring about change.

3. *Find out what has already been done and by whom:* Other individuals or groups may be working on the same issue. Be sure you know what intervention has already taken place. This can also help determine whether attempts at change have been tried, what has been successful, and whether further change is needed.

4. *Change must take into account each level of analysis:* When planning a strategy, you may focus on one level of analysis, but be sure to consider what interventions are needed at other levels to make the change effective or to anticipate the effects of change on other levels.

5. *Determine the intervention strategy:* Map out the intervention and the steps to carry it out. Identify resources needed, and plan each step in detail.

6. *Evaluate the plan:* Get feedback on the plan from those involved in the issue and from unbiased colleagues. If possible, involve those who will be affected by the intervention in the planning and evaluation of the change. When feasible, test the intervention plan before implementing it.

7. *Implement the intervention:* Put the plan into effect, watching for any unintended consequences. Ask for regular feedback from those affected by the change.

8. *Evaluate the results:* Assess what is working, what is not, and how the constituents that experience the change are reacting. Sociological knowledge and skills should help guide this process.

to travel to peripheral countries. Money spent on travel often goes to airlines, first-class hotels, and cruise ship lines based in core countries, rather than to local businesses in the peripheral countries (Schaeffer 2003). Changes in technology and the economy have forced many individuals to leave their native villages in search of paid labor positions in the urban factories and the tourism industry, disrupting family lives.

With the changes brought about by technology come changes in the nonmaterial culture—the values, political ideologies, and human relationships. Note that the social world is interdependent as functionalists have claimed. However, relations are not necessarily harmonious, and people are often exploited based on competition over resources, as conflict theories point out.

In the opening questions, we asked whether you as an individual can make a difference. In closing, we present the final "Sociology in Your Social World," a plan you can follow to make a difference, on the facing page.

Thinking Sociologically

First, read "Making a Difference" on the facing page. Then use the steps to plan how you would bring about a change that would make a difference in your community, region, nation, or world.

So What ?

Can you change the world? The underlying message of this chapter and the text is that choices we as individuals make facilitate change at each level in our social world. Understanding sociology provides knowledge and tools to make informed decisions and allows us to work with groups to make a difference.

As you face individual challenges to bring about change in your social world, keep in mind this message: Change at one level affects all others. Sociology as a discipline is focused on gathering accurate information about the society in which we live. Still, sociologists as citizens often use their knowledge to advocate for changes that they think will make a better society, and applied sociologists help organizations bring about change. Although you are not yet a sociologist, we hope you have gained important insights that will help you to contribute to the dialogue about how to make our social world a better, more humane, place.

Key Points

What Have We Learned?

- Social change—variation or alteration over time in behavior patterns, culture, or structure in a society—typically involves change at one level of the social system that ripples through the other levels, micro, meso, and macro. (See pp. 546–550.)

- Strains within an organization or group can induce change—as can stress that is imposed from the outside environment. (See pp. 550–555.)

- Sociological theories—whether micro or macro—offer explanations for the causes of change. (See pp. 555–561.)

- At the micro level, change is often initiated through collective behavior, which can take several forms: crowds, mobs, riots, rumors, fads, and fashions. (See pp. 561–567.)

- At the meso level, change of organizations is often managed through a planned process. (See pp. 567–570.)

- Social movements often provide impetus for change at the macro level. Social changes can be induced at the micro level, but they have implications even at the global level. (See pp. 570–576.)

- Science and technology can also stimulate change, but science has its greatest impact for change when it is institutionalized. (See pp. 576–581.)

- Social structures constrain what we do, but individuals, especially when acting in concert with others, can challenge, resist, and change the social systems that constrain them. We can change our society because of *human agency*. (See pp. 574–576.)

Contributing to Our Social World: What Can We Do?

At the Local Level: Students on all campuses are involved in a wide range of social movements, including international peace, environmental issues, human rights, and specific student concerns such as campus safety and rising costs of higher education. Identify a cause that interests you for which a campuswide movement organization exists. Contact the participants, arrange to attend a meeting, and consider participating in its activities. If you feel strongly about an issue for which no movement exists on your campus, consider organizing one with a few like-minded students.

At the Organizational or Institutional Level: Numerous social movement organizations are active in every community and state. Consider inviting movement leaders at the state or regional level to your campus for a lecture, or organize a conference that features several experts in a particular field. Environment, civil rights, and alternative health care are topics that have wide appeal. Consider getting involved with one of these groups so you can be proactive in shaping the society in which you live.

Volunteer Match is an organization that seeks to connect individuals with movements of interest to them. Its Web site (www.VolunteerMatch.org) has suggestions for getting involved in your local area.

At the National and Global Levels: Among the many social movements that focus on globalization and its impacts, perhaps none is as dramatic (or as urgent) as that dealing with the international debt burden. A major obstacle to improvement in living conditions in the less-developed countries is the enormous amount of money they owe to banks and governments in the industrialized nations for past-due development-oriented loans. The interest on these loans alone often exceeds the gross domestic product of the poorest nations. The leading organization in the promotion of debt forgiveness—a solution that the U.S. government has embraced in principle—is Jubilee. Named for the commandment in the Old Testament that every Jubilee Year (the seventh cycle of seven "sabbatical" years), people are to cancel all debt owed to them, the organization has legislative programs, research work, and educational outreach activities throughout the world. The Web site of the U.S. branch of Jubilee (www.jubileeusa.org) provides information on ways in which you can get involved, and the international Web site includes information about international debt, activities, and a history of the movement. It is at www.jubileeresearch.org/jubilee2000.

Visit **www.pineforge.com/ballantine2study** for online activities, sample tests, and other helpful information. Select "Chapter 16: The Process of Change" for chapter-specific activities.

References

Abbott, Carl. 1993. *The Metropolitan Frontier: Cities in the Modern American West.* Tucson: University of Arizona Press.

Abma, J. C., G. M. Martinez, W. D. Mosher, and B. S. Dawson. 2004. "Teenagers in the United States: Sexual Activity, Contraceptive Use, and Childbearing, 2002." *Vital Health Statistics* 23(24). Atlanta, GA: National Center for Health Statistics.

Abu-Lughod, Janet L. 1991. *Changing Cities: Urban Sociology.* New York: Harper Collins.

———. 2001. *New York, Chicago, Los Angeles: America's Global Cities.* Minneapolis: University of Minnesota Press.

Acker, C. 1993. "Stigma or Legitimation? A Historical Examination of the Social Potentials of Addition Disease Models." *Journal of Psychoactive Drugs* 25:13–23.

Acker, Joan. 1990. "Hierarchies, Jobs, Bodies: A Theory of Gendered Organizations." *Gender and Society* 4:139–58.

———. 1992. "Gendered Institutions: From Sex Roles to Gendered Institutions." *Contemporary Sociology* 21:565–69.

Adams, Mike S. 1996. "Labeling and Differential Association: Towards a General Social Learning Theory of Crime and Deviance." *American Journal of Criminal Justice* 20(2):147–64.

Ad Hoc Committee on Environmental Stewardship. 2000. "Green Facts for the U.S. and the World at Large." Atlanta, GA: Emory University.

Adler, Emily Stier and Roger Clark. 2003. *How It's Done: An Invitation to Social Research,* 2nd ed. Belmont, CA: Wadsworth.

Adler, Freda, Gerhard O. W. Mueller, William S. Laufer, and E. Mavis Hetherington. 2004. *Criminology,* 5th ed. New York: McGraw-Hill.

Adler, Patricia A. and Peter Adler. 1991. *Backboards and Blackboards: College Athletes and Role Engulfment.* New York: Columbia University Press.

———. 2004. "The Gloried Self." Pp. 117–26 in *Inside Social Life,* 4th ed., edited by Spencer E. Cahill. Los Angeles: Roxbury.

Adler, Roy D. 2001. "Women in the Executive Suite Correlate to High Profits." *Harvard Business Review* 79(November 16):3.

Agrell, Siri 2008. "Youth Vote Goes Solidly to Obama." *The Globe and Mail* (January 5):A15

Aguirre, Adalberto and David V. Baker. 2007. *Structured Inequality in the United States,* 2nd ed. Englewood Cliffs, NJ: Prentice Hall.

Aguirre, Adalberto, Jr., and Jonathan H. Turner. 2006. *American Ethnicity: The Dynamics and Consequences of Discrimination,* 5th ed. Boston: McGraw-Hill.

Ahrons, Constance. 2004. *We're Still Family.* New York: Harper Collins.

Akbar, Imran. 2006. "Internet Users Currently Spend More on Online Dating Than Music." Retrieved March 13, 2008 (www.news wiretoday.com/news/5114/).

Akers, Ronald. 1992. *Deviant Behavior: A Social Learning Approach,* 3rd ed. Belmont, CA: Wadsworth.

———.1998. *Social Learning and Social Structure: A General Theory of Crime and Deviance.* Boston: Northeastern University Press.

Akers, Ronald L., Marvin D. Krohn, Lonn Lanza-Kaduce, and Marcia Radosevich. 1979. "Social Learning and Deviant Behavior." *American Sociological Review* 44(August):635–54.

Albrecht, Gary. 2002. *The Disability Business: Rehabilitation in America.* Thousand Oaks, CA: Sage.

Albrecht, Stan L. and Tim B. Heaton. 1984. "Secularization, High Education, and Religiosity." *Review of Religious Research* 26(September):43–58.

Alexander, Victoria D. 2003. *Sociology of the Arts: Exploring Fine and Popular Forms.* Malden, MA: Blackwell.

Alldritt, Leslie D. 2000. "The Burakumin: The Complicity of Japanese Buddhism in Oppression and an Opportunity for Liberation." *Journal of Buddhist Ethics* 7(July).

Altbach, Philip G. and Todd M. Davis. 1999. "Global Challenge and National Response: Note for an International Dialogue on International Higher Education." *International Higher Education* 14:2–5.

Altheide, David, Patricia A. Adler, Peter Adler, and Duane Altheide. 1978. "The Social Meanings of Employee Theft." P. 90 in *Crime at the Top,* edited by John M. Johnson and Jack D. Douglas. Philadelphia: Lippincott.

Amato, Paul R. 2000. "The Consequences of Divorce for Adults and Children." *Journal of Marriage and the Family* 62(November):1269–87.

Amato, Paul R. and Bruce Keith. 1991. "Parental Divorce and the Well- Being of Children: A Meta-Analysis." *Psychological Bulletin* 110(1):26–46.

Amato, Paul R. and Juliana M. Sobolewski. 2001. "The Effects of Divorce and Marital Discord on Adult Children's Psychological Well-Being." *American Sociological Review* 63(December):697–713.

American Association of University Women Educational Foundation. 2001. "Hostile Hallways: Bullying, Teasing, and Sexual Harassment in School." Retrieved August 26, 2006 (http://www.aauw.org/research/hostile.cfm).

American Cancer Society. 2006. *Cancer Facts and Figures for African Americans 2005–2006.* Atlanta, GA: Author.

American Cultural Center Resource Service. 2004. "North American Free Trade Agreement." Retrieved September 29, 2006 (http://usinfo.org/law/nafta/chap-01.stm.html).

American Library Association. 2008. "The Most Frequently Challenged Books of 2007" (Office of Intellectual Freedom). Retrieved August 12, 2008 (http://www.ala.org/ala/of/bannedbooks/challengedbanned/challengedbanned.htm).

American Medical Association. 1988. "It's Over, Debbie." *Journal of the American Medical Association* 259(14):2094–98.

American Psychological Association. 2008. "Report From: Working Group on Assisted Suicide and End-of-Life Decisions." Retrieved August 16, 2008 (http://www.apa.org/pi/aseol/introduction.html).

American Sociological Association. 2002. *Careers in Sociology,* 6th ed. Washington, DC: American Sociological Association.

———.2006. "Trend Data on the Profession." Retrieved July 28, 2006 (www.asanet.org/page.ww?section=Profession+Trend+Data&name=Trend+Data+on+the+Profession).

Ammerman, Nancy Tatom. 1988. *Bible Believers: Fundamentalists in the Modern World.* New Brunswick, NJ: Rutgers University Press.

———. 1990. *Baptist Battles: Social Change and Religious Conflict in the Southern Baptist Convention.* New Brunswick, NJ: Rutgers University Press.

Amnesty International. 2005. "Abolish the Death Penalty: The Death Penalty Is Racially Biased." Retrieved August 4, 2006 (http://www.amnestyusa.org/abolish/factsheets/racialprejudices.html).

————. 2006. "Facts and Figures on the Death Penalty." Retrieved August 8, 2006 (http://web.amnesty.org/pages/deathpenalty-facts-eng), (http://web.amnesty.org/pages/deathpenaltycountries-eng).

————.2007. "Stop the Death Penalty: The World Decides." Retrieved July 6, 2008 (www.amnesty.org/en/news-and-updates/news/stop-the-death-penalty-the-world-decides)

Amodeo, Karrin. 1999. "Japan Nuke Update" (Federation of American Scientists). Retrieved September 29, 2006 (www.fas.org/news/japan/990930-jpn.htm).

AmO Life. 2008. "Top 10 Largest Cities in the World." Retrieved April 12, 2008 (http://amolife.com/great-places/top-10-largest-cities-in-the-world.html).

Ananova. 2001. "Death Workers Sell Body Parts for Extra Christmas Cash." Retrieved December 4, 2005 (www.ananova.com/news/sm_465113.html).

————. 2002. "Students Willing to Sell Body Parts to Fund Education." April 8. Retrieved August 26, 2006 (www.ananova.com).

Andersen, Ronald M. 1995. "Revisiting the Behavioral Model and Access to Medical Care: Does it Matter?" Journal of Health and Social Behavior 36(1):1–10.

Andersen, Ronald M., Thomas H. Rice, and Gerald F. Kominski. 2001. Changing the U.S. Health Care System: Issues in Health Services, Policy and Management, 2nd ed. San Francisco: Jossey-Bass.

Anderson, Benedict. 2006. Imagined Communities: Reflections on the Origin and Spread of Nationalism, Rev. ed. London: Verso

Anderson, David A. and Mykol Hamilton. 2005. "Gender Role Stereotyping of Parents in Children's Picture Books: The Invisible Father." Sex Roles: A Journal of Research 52(3/4):145.

Anderson, Elijah. 2000. Code of the Street: Decency, Violence, and the Moral Life of the Inner City. New York: W. W. Norton.

Anderson, Margaret L. 2006. Thinking About Women: Sociological Perspectives on Sex and Gender, 7th ed. Boston: Allyn & Bacon.

Anderson, Michael. 1994. "What Is New About the Modern Family?" Pp. 67–90 in Time, Family, and Community: Perspectives on Family and Community History, edited by Michael Drake. Oxford, UK: The Open University.

Andrew, Caroline and Beth Moore Milroy, eds. 1991. Life Spaces: Gender, Household, Employment. Vancouver: University of British Columbia Press.

ANRED (Anorexia Nervosa and Related Eating Disorders, Inc.). 2007. "Statistics: How Many People Have Eating Disorders?" Retrieved March 7, 2008 (www.anred.com/stats.html).

Anson, Ofra. 1998. "Gender Difference(s) in Health Perceptions and Their Predictors." Social Science and Medicine 36(4):419–27.

Answers.com. 2006. "Flag." Retrieved July 15, 2006 (http://www.answers.com/flag&r=67).

Anti-Defamation League. 2007. "2006 Audit of Anti-Semitic Incidents." Retrieved January 27, 2008 (www.adl.org/PresRele/ASUS_12/4993-12.htm).

Antoun, Richard T. 2001. Understanding Fundamentalism: Christian, Islamic, and Jewish Movements. Walnut Creek, CA: AltaMira.

Anyon, Jean. 1980. "Social Class and the Hidden Curriculum of Work." Journal of Education 162(1):67–92.

Appleby, Julie. 2006. "Debate Surrounds End-Of-Life Health Care Costs." USA Today (October 18). Retrieved April 4, 2008 (http://www.usatoday.com/money/industries/heaslth/2006-10-18-end-of-life-costs_x.htm).

Armstrong, Karen. 2000. The Battle for God. New York: Knopf.

Arnold, David O., ed. 1970. The Sociology of Subcultures. Berkeley, CA: Glendessary.

Aronson, Ronald. 1978. "Is Busing the Real Issue?" Dissent 25(Fall):409.

Arrighi, Barbara A. 2000. Understanding Inequality: The Intersection of Race, Ethnicity, Class, and Gender. Lanham, MD: Rowman & Littlefield.

Aseltine, Robert H., Jr. 1995. "A Reconsideration of Parental and Peer Influences on Adolescent Deviance." Journal of Health and Social Behavior 36(2):103–21.

Ashley, David and David Michael Orenstein. 2009. Sociological Theory, 7th ed. Boston: Allyn & Bacon.

Asian Development Bank. 2002. "Cambodia's Economy Continues to Gain Ground" (News Release No. 042/02, April 9).

Astone, Nan Marie and Sara S. McLanahan. 1991. "Family Structure, Parental Practices and High School Completion." American Sociological Review 56(3):318–19.

Attewell, Paul. 2001. "The First and Second Digital Divides." Sociology of Education 74(3):252–59.

Aulette, Judy Root. 2002. Changing American Families. Boston: Allyn & Bacon.

Ayalon, Hanna and Yossi Shavit. 2004. "Educational Reforms and Inequalities in Israel: The MMI Hypothesis Revisited." Sociology of Education 77(2):103–20.

Ayers, William. 2006. "Hearts and Minds: Military Recruitment and the High School Battlefield." Phi Delta Kappan 87(8):594–99.

Ayers, William and Michael Klonsky. 2006. "Chicago's Renaissance 2010: The Small Schools Movement Meets the Ownership Society." Phi Delta Kappan (February):453–56.

Azumi, Koya. 1977. "Japan's Changing World of Work." The Wilson Quarterly. (Summer):72-80.

Bagby, Ihsan A. 2003. "Imams and Mosque Organization in the United States: A Study of Mosque Leadership and Organizational Structure in American Mosques." Pp. 113–34 in Muslims in the United States, edited by Philippa Strum and Danielle Tarantolo. Washington, DC: Woodrow Wilson International Center for Scholars.

Bainbridge, William S. and Rodney Stark. 1981. "Suicide, Homicide, and Religion: Durkheim Reassessed." Annual Review of the Social Sciences of Religion 5:33–56.

Baker, David P. 2002. "International Competition and Education Crises: Cross-National Studies of School Outcomes." Pp. 393–98 in Education and Sociology: An Encyclopedia, edited by David L. Levinson, Peter W. Cookson, Jr., and Alan R. Sadovnik. New York: RoutledgeFalmer.

Balch, Robert W. 1982. "Bo and Peep: A Case Study of the Origins of Messianic Leadership." Pp. 13–72 in Millennialism and Charisma, edited by Roy Wallis. Belfast, Northern Ireland: The Queen's University.

————. 1995. "Waiting for the Ships: Disillusionment and the Revitalization of Faith in Bo and Peep's UFO Cult." Pp. 137–66 in The Gods Have Landed: New Religions from Other Worlds, edited by James R. Lewis. Albany: State University of New York Press.

Bales, Kevin. 2000. New Slavery: A Reference Handbook, 2nd ed. Santa Barbara, CA: ABC-CLIO.

————. 2002. "Because She Looks Like a Child." Pp. 207–29 in Global Woman: Nannies, Maids, and Sex Workers in the New Economy, edited by Barbara Ehrenreich and Arlie Russell Hochschild. New York: Henry Holt.

————. 2004. Disposable People: New Slavery in the Global Economy, Rev. ed. Berkeley: University of California Press.

Ballantine, Jeanne H. 1991. "Market Needs and Program Products: The Articulation Between Undergraduate Applied Programs and the Market Place." Journal of Applied Sociology 8(3/4):1–19.

————. 2001. "Education." Pp. 277–93 In Social Problems: A Case Study Approach, edited by Norman A. Dolch and Linda Deutschmann. Dix Hills, NY: General Hall.

Ballantine, Jeanne H. and Floyd M. Hammack. 2009. The Sociology of Education: A Systematic Analysis, 6th ed. Upper Saddle River, NJ: Prentice Hall.

Ballantine, Jeanne H. and Joan Z. Spade. 2008. Schools and Society, 4th ed. Belmont, CA: Cengage/Wadsworth.

Banbury, Samantha. 2004. "Coercive Sexual Behavior in British Prisons as Reported by Adult Ex-Prisoners." The Howard Journal 43(2):113–30.

Bankston, Carl L., III. 2004. "Social Capital, Cultural Values, Immigration, and Academic Achievement: The Host Country Context and Contradictory Consequences." Sociology of Education 77(2):176–80.

Barash, David. 2002. "Evolution, Males, and Violence." *The Chronicle Review* (May 24):B7.

Barber, Benjamin R. 2006. "The Uncertainty of Digital Politics: Democracy's Relationship with Information Technology" Pp. 61–69 in *Globalization: The Transformation of Social Worlds*, edited by D. Stanley Eitzen and Maxine Baca Zinn. Belmont, CA: Wadsworth.

Barber, Bonnie L., Jacquelynne S. Eccles, and Margaret R. Stone. 2001. "Whatever Happened to the Jock, the Brain, and the Princes? Young Adult Pathways Linked to Adolescent Activity Involvement and Social Identity." *Journal of Adolescent Research* 16(5):429–55.

Barefoot, Coy. 2003. "Our Childhood Memories." *U.S. Airways* (November).

Barker, Eileen. 1989. *New Religious Movements: A Practical Introduction.* London: HMSO.

Barnes, Patricia M., Eve Powell-Griner, Kim McFann, and Richard L. Nahin. 2004. "Complementary and Alternative Medicine Use among Adults: United States, 2002." *CDC Advance Data Report*, No. 343.

Barnett, T. P., J. C. Adam, and D. P. Lettenmaier. 2005. "Potential Impacts of a Warming Climate on Water Availability in Snow-Dominated Regions." *Nature* 438(November 17):303–9.

Barraclough, Geoffrey, ed. 1986. *The Times Concise Atlas of World History*, Rev. ed. London: Times Books Limited.

Barrett, David B., Todd M. Johnson, and Peter F. Crossing. 2008. "The 2007 Annual Megacensus of Religions." In *Time Almanac 2008.* Chicago: Encyclopaedia Britannica.

Bartkowski, John P. and Christopher G. Ellison. 1995. "Divergent Models of Childrearing in Popular Manuals: Conservative Protestants vs. the Mainstream Experts." *Sociology of Religion* 56(1):21–34.

Bartlett, Donald L. and James B. Steele. "How the Little Guy Gets Crunched." *Time* (February 7):38–41.

Basaglia, Franca Ongaro. 1992. "Politics and Mental Health." *International Journal of Social Psychiatry* 38(1):36–39.

Basow, Susan A. 1992. *Gender: Stereotypes and Roles,* 3rd ed. Belmont, CA: Wadsworth.

———. 2000. "Gender Stereotypes and Roles." Pp. 101–15 in *The Meaning of Difference: American Constructions of Race, Sex and Gender, Social Class, and Sexual Orientation*, 2nd ed., edited by Karen E. Rosenblum and Toni-Michelle C. Travis. New York: McGraw-Hill.

Basso, Keith H. 1979. *Portraits of the Whiteman: Linguistic Play and Cultural Symbols Among the Western Apache.* Cambridge, UK: Cambridge University Press.

Batavia, A. I. 2000. *So Far So Good: Observations on the First Year of Oregon's Death with Dignity Act.* Washington, DC: American Psychological Association.

Bayley, David. 1991. *Forces of Order: Policing Modern Japan.* Berkeley: University of California Press.

BBC News. 2000. "Profile: Vicente Fox." *World News* (July 3).

———. 2004. "Q and A: Muslim Headscarves." Retrieved March 6, 2008 (www.news.bbc.co.uk/2/hi/europe/3328277.stm).

———. 2005. "Mukhtar Mai—History of a Rape Case." Retrieved July 13, 2008 (http://news.bbc.co.uk/2/hi/south_asia/4620065.stm).

———. 2008. "US Elections Map: State-by-State Guide" (March 5). Retrieved March 21, 2008 (http://news.bbc.co.uk/2/hi/in_depth/629/629/7223461.stm).

Beckwith, Carol. 1983. "Niger's Wodaabe: People of the Taboo." *National Geographic* 164(4):483–509.

———. 1993. *Nomads of Niger.* New York: Harry N. Abrams.

Belding, Theodore C. 2004. "Nobility and Stupidity: Modeling the Evolution of Class Endogamy." Retrieved August 7, 2008 (http://arxiv.org/abs/nlin.AO/0405048).

Bell, Daniel. 1973. *The Coming of Post-Industrial Society: A Venture in Social Forecasting.* New York: Basic Books.

———. [1976] 1999. *The Coming of Post-Industrial Society: A Venture in Social Forecasting,* Special anniversary edition. New York: Basic Books.

Bellah, Robert N. 1970. "Civil Religion in America." Pp. 168–215 in *Beyond Belief: Essays on Religion in a Post-Traditionalist World.* New York: Harper & Row.

Bellah, Robert N. 1992. *The Broken Covenant: American Civil Religion in Time of Trial.* Chicago: University of Chicago Press.

Bellah, Robert N., and Frederick E. Greenspahn, eds. 1987. *Uncivil Religion: Interreligious Hostility in America.* New York: Crossroad.

Bellah, Robert N., Richard Madsen, William M. Sullivan, Ann Swidler, and Steven M. Tipton. 1996. *Habits of the Heart: Individualism and Commitment in American Life,* Updated edition. Berkeley: University of California Press.

Bellisari, Anna. 1990. "Biological Bases of Sex Differences in Cognitive Ability and Brain Function." Unpublished paper.

Bem, Sandra L. 1974. "The Measurement of Psychological Androgyny." *Journal of Consulting and Clinical Psychology* 42(2):155–62.

———.1983. "Gender Schema Theory and Its Implications for Child Development: Raising Gender-Aschematic Children in a Gender-Schematic Society." *Signs: Journal of Women in Culture and Society* 8(Summer):598–616.

Benavot, Aaron. 1992. "Curricular Content, Educational Expansion, and Economic Growth." *Comparative Education Review* 36(2):150–74.

Benavot, Aaron, John Meyer, and David Kamens. 1991. "Knowledge for the Masses: World Models and National Curricula: 1920–1986." *American Sociological Review* 56(1):85–100.

Benderly, Beryl Lieff. 1982. "Rape Free or Rape Prone." *Science* 82(3):40–43.

Benevolo, Leonardo. 1995. *The European City.* Cambridge, MA: Blackwell.

Benguigui, Yamina. 2000. *The Perfumed Garden.* Brooklyn, NY: First Run Icarus Films.

Bennett, Neil, Ann Blanc, and David Bloom. 1988. "Commitment and the Modern Union: Assessing the Link between Premarital Cohabitation and Subsequent Marital Stability." *American Sociological Review* 53(1):127–38.

Bennis, Warren G., Kenneth D. Benne, and Robert Chin. 1985. *The Planning of Change,* 4th ed. New York: Holt, Rinehart and Winston.

Benokraitis, Nijole V. 2004. *Marriages and Families: Changes, Choices, and Constraints,* 5th ed. Englewood Cliffs, NJ: Prentice Hall.

Benokraitis, Nijole V. and Joe R. Feagin. 1995. *Modern Sexism: Blatant, Subtle, and Covert Discrimination,* 2nd ed. Englewood Cliffs, NJ: Prentice Hall.

Berger, Helen A. 1999. *A Community of Witches: Contemporary Neo-Paganism and Witchcraft in the United States.* Columbia: University of South Carolina Press.

Berger, Helen A. and Douglas Ezzy. 2007. *Teenage Witches: Magical Youth and the Search for the Self.* New Brunswick, NJ: Rutgers University Press.

Berger, Michael L. 1979. *The Devil Wagon in God's Country: The Automobile and Social Change in Rural America, 1893–1929.* Hamden, CT: Archon.

Berger, Peter L. 1961. *The Noise of Solemn Assemblies.* Garden City, NY: Doubleday.

———. 1990. *The Sacred Canopy.* Garden City, NY: Anchor Books.

Berger, Peter L. and Thomas Luckmann. 1966. *The Social Construction of Reality.* Garden City, NY: Doubleday.

Bergman, Mike. 2005. "U.S. Voter Turnout Up in 2004." *U.S. Census Bureau News.* Retrieved March 26, 2008 (www.census.gov/Press_Release/www/releases/archives/voting).

Berk, Richard A. 1974. *Collective Behavior.* Dubuque, IA: Brown.

Berry, Brian J. L. and John Kasarda. 1977. *Contemporary Urban Ecology.* New York: Macmillan.

Bertman, Stephen. 1998. *Hyperculture: The Human Cost of Speed.* Westport, CT: Praeger.

Better Factories Movement in Cambodia. 2006. Retrieved September 29, 2006 (www.betterfactories.com).

Bettie, Julie. 2003. *Women Without Class: Girls, Race, and Identity.* Berkeley: University of California Press.

Beyer, Peter. 2000. "Secularization from the Perspective of Globalization." Pp. 81–93 in *The Secularization Debate*, edited by William H. Swatos, Jr., and Daniel V. A. Olson. Lanham, MD: Rowman and Littlefield.

Bianci, Suzanne M., Melissa A. Milkie, Liana C. Sayer, and John P. Robinson. 2000. "Is Anyone Doing the Housework? Trends in the Gender Division of Household Labor," *Social Forces* 79(1):191–228.

Bibby, Reginald W. 1987a. *Fragmented Gods: The Poverty and Potential of Religion in Canada.* Toronto, Canada: Irwin.

———. 1987b. "Religion in Canada: A Late Twentieth Century Reading." Pp. 263–67 in *Yearbook of American and Canadian Churches*, edited by Constant H. Jacquet, Jr. Nashville, TN: Abington.

———. 2002. *Restless Gods: The Renaissance of Religion in Canada.* Toronto, Canada: Stoddard.

Billig, Michael. 1995. *Banal Nationalism.* Thousand Oaks, CA: Sage.

Billings, Dwight B. and Shaunna L. Scott 1994. "Religion and Political Legitimation." *Annual Review of Sociology* 20:173–202.

Birdwhistell, Raymond L. 1970. *Kinesics and Context: Essays on Body Motion Communication.* Philadelphia: University of Pennsylvania Press.

Blackman, Ann. 2001. "Bush Acts on Abortion 'Gag Rule.'" *Time* (January 22). Retrieved September 20, 2006 (http://www.time.com/time/nation/article/0,8599,96275,00.html).

Blank, Rebecca M. 2002. "Evaluating Welfare Reform in the United States." *Journal of Economic Literature* 40(4):1105–1166.

Blasi, Joseph Raphael and Douglas Lynn Kruse. 1991. *The New Owners: The Mass Emergence of Employee Ownership in Public Companies and What it Means to American Business.* New York: Harper Collins.

Blasi, Joseph, Douglas Kruse, and Aaron Bernstein. 2003. *In the Company of Owners.* New York: Basic Books.

Blau, Peter M. 1956. *Bureaucracy in Modern Society.* New York: Random House.

———. 1964. *Exchange and Power in Social Life.* New York: John Wiley.

Blau, Peter and Otis Dudley Duncan. 1967. *The American Occupational Structure.* New York: John Wiley.

Blauner, Robert. 1964. *Alienation and Freedom.* Chicago: University of Chicago Press.

———. 1972. *Racial Oppression in America.* New York: Harper & Row.

Blee, Kathleen M. 2008. "White Supremacy as Extreme Deviance." Pp. 108–17 in *Extreme Deviance*, edited by Erich Goode and D. Angus Vail. Thousand Oaks, CA: Pine Forge Press.

Blendon, Robert J., Cathy Schoen, Catherine M. DesRoches, Robin Osborn, Kimberly L. Scoles, and Kinga Zapert. 2002. "Inequities in Health Care: A Five-Country Survey." *Health Affairs* 21(3):182–91.

Blumer, Herbert. 1969. *Symbolic Interactionism: Perspective and Method.* Englewood Cliffs, NJ: Prentice Hall.

———. 1986. *Symbolic Interactionism: Perspective and Method.* Berkeley: University of California Press.

Blumstein, Philip and Pepper Schwartz. 1985. *American Couples: Money, Work, Sex.* New York: Pocket Books.

Bobo, Lawrence and Ryan A. Smith. 1998. "From Jim Crow Racism to Laissez-Faire Racism: An Essay on the Transformation of Racial Attitudes in America." Pp. 182–220 in *Beyond Pluralism: Essays on the Conceptions of Groups and Identities in America*, edited by Wendy Freedman Katkin, Ned C. Landsman, and Andrea Tyree. Urbana: University of Illinois Press.

Bohannan, Paul. 1959. "The Impact of Money on an African Subsistence Economy." *Journal of Economic History* 19:491–503.

Bolaria, Singh and Harley D. Dickinson. 2001. "The Evolution of Health Care in Canada: Toward Community or Corporate Control?" Pp. 199–213 in *The Blackwell Companion to Medical Sociology*, edited by William C. Cockerham. Malden, MA: Blackwell.

Boli, John. 2002. "Globalization." Pp. 307–13 in *Education and Sociology: An Encyclopedia*, edited by David L. Levinson, Peter W. Cookson, Jr., and Alan R. Sadovnik. New York: RoutledgeFalmer.

Bonacich, Edna. 1972. "A Theory of Ethnic Antagonism: The Split Labor Market." *American Sociological Review* 37(October):547–59.

———. 1976. "Advanced Capitalism and Black White Race Relations in the United States: A Split Labor Market Interpretation." *American Sociological Review* 41(February):34–51.

Bonacich, Edna and Jake B. Wilson. 2005. "Hoisted by Its Own Petard: Organizing Wal-Mart's Logistics Workers." *New Labor Forum* 14:67–75.

Bonczar, Thomas P. and Tracy L. Snell. 2005. "Capital Punishment, 2004." *Bureau of Justice Statistics Bulletin* (NCJ 211349). Washington, DC: U.S. Department of Justice.

Booker, Salih and William Minter. 2006. "Global Apartheid: AIDS and Murder by Patient." Pp. 517–22 in *Beyond Borders: Thinking Critically about Global Issues*, edited by Paula S. Rothenberg. New York: Worth.

Booth, Alan and Paul R. Amato. 2001. "Parental Predivorce Relations and Offspring Postdivorce Well-Being." *Journal of Marriage and the Family* 63(February):197–212.

Borg, Marcus J. 1994. *Meeting Jesus Again for the First Time.* San Francisco: Harper San Francisco.

Bottomore, Tom. 1979. *Political Sociology.* New York: Harper & Row.

Boulding, Elise with Jennifer Dye. 2002. "Women and Development." In *Introducing Global Issues*, 2nd ed., edited by Michael T. Snarr and D. Neil Snarr. Boulder, CO: Lynne Rienner.

Bourdieu, P. and J. C. Passeron. 1977. *Reproduction in Education, Society and Culture.* London: Sage.

Bowen, Debra. 2008. "History Behind California's Primary Election System." Retrieved March 21, 2008 (http://www.sos.ca.gov/elections/elections_decline.htm).

Bowler, I. R., C. R. Bryant, and M. D. Nellis, eds. 1992. *Contemporary Rural Systems in Transition, Volume 1: Agriculture and Environment, Volume 2: Economy and Society.* Wallingford, Oxfordshire, UK: C.A.B. International.

Bowles, Samuel. 1977. "Unequal Education and the Reproduction of the Social Division of Labor. P. 137 in *Power and Ideology in Education*, edited by Jerome Karabel and A. H. Halsey. New York: Oxford University Press.

Bowles, Samuel and Herbert Gintis. 1976. *Schooling in Capitalist America.* New York: Basic Books.

———. 2002. "Schooling in Capitalist America Revisited." *Sociology of Education* 75(1):1–18.

Boy, Angie and Andrzej Kulczycki. 2008. "What We Know About Intimate Partner Violence in the Middle East and North Africa." *Violence against Women* 14(1):53–70.

Bracey, Gerald W. 2003. "April Foolishness: The 20th Anniversary of A Nation at Risk." *Phi Delta Kappan* (April):616–21.

———. 2005. "The 15th Bracey Report on the Condition of Public Education." *Phi Delta Kappan* (October):138–53.

Brady, Henry E., Sidney Verba, and Kay Lehman Schlozman. 1995. "Beyond SES: A Resource Model of Political Participation." *American Political Science Review* 89(2):271–285.

Brandon, Mark E. 2005. "War and American Constitutional Order." In *The Constitution in Wartime: Beyond Alarmism and Complacency*, edited by Mark Tushner. Durham, NC: Duke University Press.

Brasher, Brenda E. 2004. *Give Me That On-Line Religion.* New Brunswick, NJ: Rutgers University Press.

Brecher, Jeremy, Tim Costello, and Brendan Smith. 2006. "Globalization and Social Movements." Pp. 330–47 in *Globalization: The Transformation of Social Worlds*, edited by D. Stanley Eitzen and Maxine Baca Zinn. Belmont, CA: Wadsworth.

Brettell, Caroline B. and Carolyn F. Sargent. 2001. *Gender in Cross-Cultural Perspective*, 3rd ed. Englewood Cliffs, NJ: Prentice Hall.

———. 2005. *Gender in Cross-cultural Perspective*. 4th ed. Englewood Cliffs, NJ: Prentice Hall.

Brier, Noah Rubin. 2004. "Coming of Age." *American Demographics* 26(9):16.

Brint, Steven, Mary F. Contreras, and Michael T. Matthews. 2001. "Socialization Messages in Primary Schools: An Organizational Analysis." *Sociology of Education* 74(July):157–80.

Bristow, Jason. 2008. "Can Canadian Youth Be Inspired to Vote?" *The Toronto Sun* (March 6):17

Britton, Dana M. 2000. "The Epistemology of the Gendered Organization." *Gender and Society* 14(3):418–34.

Britz, Jennifer Delahunty. 2006. "Are Today's Girls Too Successful?" *Dayton Daily News* (March 31):A7.

Brody, Gene H., Zolinda Stoneman, Douglas Flor, and Chris McCrary. 1994. "Religion's Role in Organizing Family Relationships: Family Process in Rural, Two-Parent African American Families." *Journal of Marriage and the Family* 56(November):878–88.

Bromley, David G. and Anson D. Shupe, Jr. 1981. *Strange Gods: The Great American Cult Scare*. Boston: Beacon.

Brookover, Wilbur B., C. Beady, P. Flood, J. Schweitzer, and J. Wisenbaker. 1979. *School Social Systems and Student Achievement: Schools Can Make a Difference*. New York: Praeger.

Brookover, Wilbur B. and Edsel L. Erickson. 1975. *Sociology of Education*. Homewood, IL: Dorsey.

Brookover, Wilbur B., Edsel L. Erickson, and Alan McEvoy. 1996. *Creating Effective Schools: An In-Service Program*. Holmes Beach, FL: Learning Publications.

Brooks, Clem and Jeff Manza. 1997. "Social Cleavages and Political Alignments: U.S. Presidential Elections, 1960–1992." *American Sociological Review* 62(December):937–46.

Broom, Leonard and Philip Selznick. 1963. *Sociology: A Text with Adapted Readings*, 3rd ed. New York: Harper & Row.

Brophy, Jere E. 1983. "Research on the Self-Fulfilling Prophesy and Teacher Expectations." *Journal of Educational Psychology* 75:631–61.

Brown, Dee. 2001. *Bury My Heart at Wounded Knee: An Indian History of the American West*, 30th anniversary ed. New York: Holt.

Brown, Donald E. 1991. *Human Universals*. Philadelphia: Temple University Press.

Brown, Louise. 2001. *Sex Slaves: The Trafficking of Women in Asia*. London: Virago/Little, Brown.

Bruner, Jerome. 1996. *The Culture of Education*. Cambridge, MA: Harvard University Press.

Brunn, Stanley D., Jack F. Williams, and Donald J. Zeigler. 2003. *Cities of the World: World Regional Urban Development*, 3rd ed. Lanham, MD: Rowman and Littlefield.

Bryant, A. L. 1993. "Hostile Hallways: The AAUW Survey on Sexual Harassment in America's Schools." Washington, DC: AAUW Foundation.

Brym, Robert J. and John Lie. 2007. *Sociology: Your Compass for a New World*, 3rd ed. Belmont, CA: Wadsworth.

Buchmann, Claudia and Thomas A. DiPrete. 2006. "Gender Specific Trends in the Value of Education and the Emerging Gender Gap in College Completion." *Demography* 43:1–24.

Buechler, Steven. 2008. "What Is Critical about Sociology?" *Teaching Sociology* 36(4).

Bukhari, Zahid H. 2003. "Demography, Identity, Space: Defining American Muslims." Pp. 7–18 in *Muslims in the United States*, edited by Philippa Strum and Danielle Tarantolo. Washington DC: Woodrow Wilson International Center for Scholars.

Bumiller, Elisabeth. 1990. *May You Be the Mother of a Hundred Sons: A Journey Among the Women of India*. New York: Fawcett Columbine.

Bumpass, Larry L. and Hsien-Hen Lu. 2000. "Trends in Cohabitation and Implications for Children's Family Contexts in the United States." *Population Studies* 51(1):29–41.

Bumpass, Larry L., James A. Sweet, and Andrew Cherlin. 1991. "The Role of Cohabitation in Declining Rates of Marriage." *Journal of Marriage and the Family* 53 (November): 913–27.

Burda, D. 2001. "Hospital Operating Margins Hit 5.2%." *Modern Healthcare* 31(45):10.

Burgess, Robert and Ronald L. Akers. 1966. "A Differential Association-Reinforcement Theory of Criminal Behavior." *Social Problems* 14:363–83.

Burgos-Debray, Elisabeth, ed. 1984. *I, Rigoberta Menchu: An Indian Woman in Guatemala*, translated by Ann Wright. London: Verso.

Burn, Shawn Meghan. 2000. *Women Across Cultures: A Global Perspective*. Mountain View, CA: Mayfield.

———.2005. *Women Across Cultures: A Global Perspective*. 2nd ed. New York: McGraw-Hill.

Burt, Ronald S. 1992. *Structural Holes: The Structure of Competition*. Cambridge, MA: Harvard University Press.

CALCASA (California Coalition against Sexual Assault). 2006. "Statistics about Rape and Sexual Assault, 2006." Retrieved September 15, 2006 (www.denimdayinla.org/documents/RapeSexualStats2006.doc).

Caldwell, John C. 1982. *Theory of Fertility Decline*. New York: Academic Press.

"Cambodia Labor Protest" 2002. "Gap Worker Shot and Killed in Cambodia Labor Protest." (www.nlcnet.org/campaigns/gapcambodia/)

Campbell, A., P. Converse, W. Miller, and D. Stokes. 1960. *The American Voter*. New York: Wiley.

Campbell, Ernest Q. and Thomas F. Pettigrew. 1959. *Christians in Racial Crisis*. Washington, DC: Public Affairs Press.

Canadian Institute for Health Information. 2007. "National Health Expenditure Trends, 1975–2007." Retrieved August 26, 2008 (http://secure.cihi.ca/cihiweb/dispPage.jsp?cw_page=PG_876_E&cw_topic=876&cw_rel=AR_31_E)

Cancian, Francesca M. 1992. "Feminist Science: Methodologies that Challenge Inequality." *Gender and Society* 6(4):623–42.

Carrothers, Robert M. and Denzel E. Benson. 2003. "Symbolic Interactionism in Introductory Textbooks: Coverage and Pedagogical Implications." *Teaching Sociology* 31(2):162–81.

Cashell, Brian W. 2007. "CRS Report for Congress: "Who Are the Middle Class?" Retrieved February 28, 2008 (http://opencrs.cdt.org/rpts/RS22627_20070320.pdf)

Cashmore, Ellis and Barry Troyna. 1990. *Introduction to Race Relations*. London: Routledge.

Casper, Lynne M., Sara S. McLanahan, and Irwin Garfinkel. 1994. "The Gender-Poverty Gap: What We Can Learn from Other Countries." *American Sociological Review* 59(August):594–605.

Castells, Manuel. 1977. *The Urban Question: A Marxist Approach*. Cambridge, MA: MIT Press.

———. 1989. *The Informational City: Information Technology, Economic Restructuring and the Urban-Regional Process*. Cambridge, MA: Basil Blackwell.

Caulfield, Jon. 1994. *City Form and Everyday Life: Toronto's Gentrification and Critical Social Practice*. Toronto: University of Toronto Press.

CBS News. (2003). "Hispanics Now Largest U.S. Minority" (January 21). Retrieved March 3, 2008 (www. CBSNews.com/stories/2003/01/21/national/main537369.shtml).

———.2008. "Big Cities Battle Dismal Graduation Rates" (August 18). Retrieved August 23, 2008 (www.cbsnews.com/stories/2008/04/01/national/main3985714.shtml).

"Cell Phone Use Booming Worldwide." 2007. Retrieved September 15, 2007 (http://www.sunherald.com/business/story/134849.html).

Center for Defense Information. 2002. "Military Almanac 2001-2002." Retrieved September 15, 2007 (www.cdi.org/projects/almanac0102.pdf)

Center for Education Policy. 2006. *Survey on Hours Spent on Subjects*. Menlo Park, CA: SRI International.

Center for Voting and Democracy. 2008. "Understanding Super Tuesday: State Rules on February 5 and Lessons for Reform."

Retrieved March 21, 2008 (http://www.fairvote.org/?page=27& pressmode=showspecific&showarticle=185).

Center on Budget and Policy Priorities. 2006. "The Number of Uninsured Americans Is at an All-Time High" (August 29). Retrieved March 2, 2008 (www.cbpp.org/8-29-06health.htm).

Centers for Disease Control and Prevention. 2006a. "Average Life Expectancy 2006." Retrieved July 20, 2006 (www.voanews.com/english/2006– 04–27-voa32.cfm).

————.2006b. "Survey of Childless People Ages 15 to 44." *Dayton Daily News* (June 1):1A.

————. 2007. "CDC Global HIV/AIDS Activities—South Africa." *Global HIV/AIDS.* (www.cdc.gov/nchstp/od/gap/countries/SouthAfrica/) Retrieved April 3. 2008.

Centers for Medical and Medicaid Services. 2004. *Health Care Indicators.* Baltimore, MD: Office of the Actuary, Office of National Health Statistics.

Chabbott, Colette and Francisco O. Ramirez. 2000. "Development and Education." Pp. 163–87 in *Handbook of Sociology of Education,* edited by Maureen T. Hallinan. New York: Kluwer Academic Publishers/Plenum.

Chaffins, Stephanie, Mary Forbes, and Harold E. Fuqua, Jr. 1995. "The Glass Ceiling: Are Women Where They Should Be?" *Education* 115(3):380–87.

Chalfant, H. Paul, Robert E. Beckley, and C. Eddie Palmer. 1994. *Religion in Contemporary Society,* 3rd ed. Palo Alto, CA: Mayfield.

Chalfant, H. Paul and Charles W. Peck. 1983. "Religious Affiliation, Religiosity, and Racial Prejudice: A New Look at Old Relationships." *Review of Religious Research* 25(December):155–61.

Chambliss, William J. 1973. "The Saints and the Roughnecks." *Society* 11(December):24–31.

Charles, Camille Z., Vincent J. Roscigno, and Kimberly C. Torres. 2007. "Racial Inequality and College Attendance: The Mediating Role of Parental Investments." *Social Science Research* 36(1):329–52.

Charon, Joel M. 2007. *Symbolic Interactionism: An Introduction, an Interpretation,* 9th ed. Upper Saddle River, NJ: Prentice Hall.

Chase, Cheryl. 2000. "Genital Surgery on Children Below the Age of Consent: Intersex Genital Mutilation." In *Psychological Perspectives on Human Sexuality,* edited by L. Szuchman and F. Muscarella. New York: John Wiley.

Chase-Dunn, Christopher and E. N. Anderson. 2006. *The Historical Evolution of World-Systems.* New York: Palgrave Macmillan.

Chase-Lansdale, P. Lindsay, Andrew J. Cherlin, and Kathleen E. Kiernan. 1995. "The Long-Term Effects of Parental Divorce on the Mental Health of Young Adults: A Developmental Perspective." *Child Development* 66(6):1614–34.

Chaves, Mark. 1993. "Denominations as Dual Structures: An Organizational Analysis." *Sociology of Religion* 54(20): 147–69.

————. 1999. *Ordaining Women: Culture and Conflict in Religious Organizations.* Cambridge, MA: Harvard University Press.

————. 2004. *Congregations in America.* Cambridge, MA: Harvard University Press.

Chaves, Mark and Philip S. Gorski. 2001. "Religious Pluralism and Religious Participation." *Annual Review of Sociology* 27:261–81.

Chen, Zeng-Yin and Howard B. Kaplan. 2003. "School Failure in Early Adolescence and Status Attainment in Middle Adulthood: A Longitudinal Study." *Sociology of Education* 76(2):110–27.

Cherlin, Andrew J. 2005. *Public and Private Families: An Introduction,* 4th ed. Boston: McGraw-Hill.

Child Trends Data Bank. 2005. "Percentage of Births to Unmarried Women." Retrieved August 22, 2006 (http://www.childtrends databank.org/pdf/75_PDF.pdf).

Chivers, M. L., M. C. Seto, and R. Blanchard, R. (2007). "Gender and Sexual Orientation Differences in Sexual Response to Sexual Activities Versus Gender of Actors in Sexual Films." *Journal of Personality and Social Psychology* 93(6):1108–21.

Christiano, Kevin J., William H. Swatos, Jr., and Peter Kivisto. 2002. *Sociology of Religion: Contemporary Developments.* Walnut Creek, CA: AltaMira.

Chubb, John E. and Terry M. Moe. 1990. *Politics, Markets, and America's Schools.* Washington, DC: Brookings Institution.

Cillizza, Chris and Shailagh Murray. 2008. "This Time We Mean It: The Youth Vote Matters." *The Washington Post* (April 27):A8.

Clark, Burton R. 1985. "The High School and the University: What Went Wrong in America?" *Phi Delta Kappan* (February): 391–97.

Clarke, Adele E. and Virginia L. Olesen. 1999. *Revisioning Women, Health, and Healing.* London: Routledge.

Clausen, John A. 1986. *The Life Course: A Sociological Perspective.* Englewood Cliffs, NJ: Prentice Hall.

Clawson, Dan, Alan Newstadt, and Denise Scott. 1992. *Money Talks: Corporate PACs and Political Influence.* New York: Basic Books.

Clinard, Marshall B. and Robert F. Meier. 2004. *Sociology of Deviant Behavior,* 12th ed. Belmont, CA: Wadsworth/Thomson Learning.

Clymer, Floyd. 1953. *Those Wonderful Old Automobiles.* New York: Bonanza.

CNN.com. 2006. "Flag-Burning Amendment Fails by a Vote" (June 28). Retrieved August 16, 2008 (http://www.cnn.com/2006/POLITICS/06/27/flag.burning/).

————. 2007. "Report: Global Terrorism Up More Than 25 Percent" (April 30). Retrieved April 14, 2008 (www.cnn.com/2007/US/04/30/terror.report/index.html).

Cockburn, Andrew. 2006. "21st Century Slaves." Pp. 299–307 in *Globalization: The Transformation of Social Worlds,* edited by D. Stanley Eitzen and Maxine Baca Zinn. Belmont, CA: Wadsworth.

Cockerham, William C. 2007. *Medical Sociology,* 10th ed. Englewood Cliffs, NJ: Prentice Hall.

Cohen, Elizabeth G. 1997. "Equitable Classrooms in a Changing Society." Chapter 1 in *Working for Equity in Heterogeneous Classroom: Sociological Theory in Practice,* edited by E. Cohen and R. Lotan. New York: Columbia University Press.

Coile, Russell C., Jr. 2002. "Top 10 Trends in Health Care for 2002." *Health Trends* 14(3):2–12.

Cole, Stephen and Robert Lejeune. 1972. "Illness and the Legitimation of Failure." *American Sociological Review* 37(3):347–56.

Coleman, James S. 1968. "The Concept of Equality of Educational Opportunity." *Harvard Education Review* 38(Winter):7–22.

————. 1990. *Equality and Achievement in Education.* Boulder, CO: Westview.

Coleman, James S., Ernest Q. Campbell, Carol J. Hobson, James McPartland, Alexander M. Mood, Frederic D. Weinfeld, and Robert L. York. 1966. *Equality of Educational Opportunity.* Washington, DC: Government Printing Office.

Coleman, James William. 2006. *The Criminal Elite: Understanding White Collar Crime,* 6th ed. New York: Worth.

Colligan, S. 2004. "Why the Intersexed Shouldn't Be Fixed: Insights from Queer Theory and Disability Studies." Pp. 45–60 in *Gendering Disability,* edited by B. G. Smith and B. Hutchinson. New Brunswick, NJ: Rutgers University Press.

Collins, Patricia Hill. 2000. *Black Feminist Thought: Knowledge, Consciousness, and the Politics of Empowerment,* 2nd ed. New York: Routledge.

Collins, Randall. 1971. "A Conflict Theory of Sexual Stratification." *Social Problems* 19(Summer):2–21.

————. 2004. "Conflict Theory of Educational Stratification." *American Sociological Review* 36:47–54.

Collins, Randall and Scott L. Coltrane. 2001. *Sociology of Marriage and the Family: Gender, Love, and Property,* 5th ed. Belmont, CA: Wadsworth.

Coltrane, Scott. 2000. "Research on Household Labor: Modeling and Measuring the Social Embeddedness of Routine Family Work." *Journal of Marriage and the Family* 62(November):1208–233.

Comarow, Murray. 1993. "Point of View: Are Sociologists above the Law?" *The Chronicle of Higher Education* (December 15):A44.

Committee for the Study of the American Electorate. 2000. *Participation in Elections for President and U.S. Representatives, 1968–2000.* Washington, DC: Author.

Common Sense for Drug Policy. 2006. "Estimating the Illicit Drug Market." Retrieved February 10, 2008 (www.drugwardistortions.org/distortion19.htm)

Condron, Dennis J and Vincent J. Roscigno. 2003. "Disparities Within: Unequal Spending and Achievement in an Urban School District." *Sociology of Education* 76(January):18–36.

Conrad, Peter and Joseph Schneider. 1992. *Deviance and Medicalization: From Badness to Sickness.* Philadelphia: Temple University Press.

Cook, Karen S., Jodi O'Brien, and Peter Kollock. 1990. "Exchange Theory: A Blueprint for Structure and Process." Pp. 158–81 in *Frontiers of Social Theory: The New Syntheses,* edited by George Ritzer. New York: Columbia University Press.

Cookson, Peter W., Jr., and Caroline Hodges Persell. 1985. *Preparing for Power: America's Elite Boarding Schools.* New York: Basic Books.

Cooley, Charles Horton. 1902. *Human Nature and the Social Order.* New York: Scribner.

———.[1909] 1983. *Social Organization: A Study of the Larger Mind.* New York: Schocken Books.

Coontz, Stephanie. 1997. *The Way We Really Are: Coming to Terms with America's Changing Families.* New York: Basic Books.

———. 2005. *Marriage, a History: From Obedience to Intimacy, or How Love Conquered Marriage.* New York: Viking.

Corbett, Thomas. 1994–95. "Changing the Culture of Welfare." *Focus* 16(2):12–22.

CorpWatch. 1999. "Maquiladoras at a Glance." Retrieved March 7, 2008 (www.corpwatch.org/article.php?id=1528#wages).

Corsaro, William A. and Donna Eder. 1990. "Children's Peer Cultures." *Annual Review of Sociology* 16:197–220.

Coser, Lewis A. 1956. *The Functions of Social Conflict.* New York: The Free Press.

Council for a Livable World. 1998. *Nuclear Weapons: Still High Costs and Huge Stockpiles.* Washington, DC: Author.

Council of Europe. 2001, 2004. *Recent Demographic Developments in Europe 2001, 2004.* Strasbourg, France: Council of Europe Publishing.

"Cousin Marriages in the United States." 2008. Retrieved January 20, 2008 (www.marriage.about.com/cs/marriagelicenses/a/cousin.htm).

Cousteau, Jacques-Yves. 2008. "The Great Ocean Adventure." Lecture at Hanover College, January 15.

Crafts, William A. 1876. *Pioneers in the Settlement of America,* Vol. 1. Boston: Samuel Walker.

Creswell, John W. 2003. *Research Design: Qualitative, Quantitative, and Mixed Methods Approaches,* 2nd ed. Thousand Oaks, CA: Sage.

Crosby, Faye J. 2004. *Affirmative Action Is Dead; Long Live Affirmative Action.* New Haven, CT: Yale University Press.

Crossette, Barbara. 1996. "Angkor Emerges From the Jungle." *The New York Times* (January 28). Retrieved September 9, 2008 (http://query.nytimes.com/gst/fullpage.html?res=9500e0d91139f93ba1 5752c0a960958260&sec=travel&spon=&page wanted=1).

Crummey, Robert O. 1970. *The Old Believers and the World of Antichrist: The Vyg Community and the Russian State, 1694–1855.* Madison: University of Wisconsin Press.

Curtiss, S. 1977. *Genie: A Psycholinguistic Study of a Modern-Day "Wild Child."* New York: Academic Press.

Cushman, Thomas and Stjepan G. Mestrovic. 1996. *This Time We Knew: Western Responses to Genocide in Bosnia.* New York: New York University Press.

Cuzzort, R. P. and Edith W. King. 2002. *Social Thought into the Twenty-First Century,* 6th ed. Belmont, CA: Wadsworth.

Cyranoski, David 2005. "The Long-Range Forecast." *Nature* 438(November 17):275–76.

DaCosta, Kimberly McClain. 2007. *Making Multiracials: State, Family, and Market in the Redrawing of the Color Line.* Stanford, CA: Stanford University Press.

Dahl, Robert A. 1961. *Who Governs?* New Haven, CT: Yale University Press.

Dahlberg, Frances. 1981. *Woman the Gatherer.* New Haven, CT: Yale University Press.

Dahrendorf, Ralf. 1959. *Class and Class Conflict in Industrial Societies.* Palo Alto, CA: Stanford University Press.

Dalit Liberation Education Trust. 1995. *10th Anniversary Newsletter* (May). Madras: Human Rights Education Movement of India.

Danesi, Marcel. 2008. *Popular Culture.* Lanham, MD: Rowman and Littlefield.

Daniel, John, Asha Kanwar, and Stamenka Uvalic-Trumbic. 2006. "A Tectonic Shift in Global Higher Education." *Change* (July/August).

Darr, Kurt. 2007. "Assistance in Dying: Part II. Assisted Suicide in the U.S." *Hospital Topics* 85(2):31–36.

Darwin, Charles. [1858] 1909. *The Origin of Species.* New York: P. F. Collier.

da Silva, Marina. 2004. "France: Outsider Women." *Le Monde Diplomatique* (October). Retrieved July 4, 2006 (http://mondediplo.com/2004/10/12women).

Davidhizar, R., R. Shearer, and J. N. Giger. 1997. "Pain and the Culturally Diverse Patient." *Today's Surgical Nurse* 19(6):36–39.

Davidman, Lynn. 1990. "Accommodation and Resistance to Modernity: A Comparison of Two Contemporary Orthodox Jewish Groups." *Sociological Analysis* (Spring):35–51.

Davies, James C. 1962. "Toward a Theory of Revolution." *American Sociological Review* 27(1):5–19.

———. 1974. "The J-Curve and Power Struggle Theories of Collective Violence." *American Sociological Review* 39(August): 607–619.

Davies, John. 1993. *A History of Wales.* London: Penguin.

Davis, Kingsley. 1940. "Extreme Social Isolation of a Child." *American Journal of Sociology* 45:554–65.

———. 1947. "A Final Note on a Case of Extreme Isolation." *American Journal of Sociology* 52:432–37.

———.1960. "Legitimacy and the Incest Taboo." Pp. 398–402 in *A Modern Introduction to the Family,* edited by Norman W. Bell and Ezra F. Vogel. Glencoe, IL: The Free Press.

Davis, Kingsley and Wilbert Moore. 1945. "Some Principles of Stratification." *American Sociological Review* 10(April): 242–45.

Davis, Nancy J. and Robert V. Robinson 1999. "Their Brothers' Keepers? Orthodox Religionists, Modernists, and Economic Justice in Europe." *American Journal of Sociology* 104(6):1631–65.

Death Penalty Information Center. 2006. "Nationwide Murder Rates." Retrieved August 4, 2006 (www.deathpenalty info.org).

Degenova, Mary Kay and Philip F. Rice. 2002. *Intimate Relationships, Marriages, and Families,* 5th ed. New York: McGraw-Hill.

Delfattore, Joan. 1992. *What Johnny Shouldn't Read: Textbook Censorship in America.* New Haven, CT: Yale University Press.

———.2004. "Romeo and Juliet Were Just Good Friends." Pp. 177–83 in *Schools and Society,* 2nd ed., edited by Jeanne H. Ballantine and Joan Z. Spade. Belmont, CA: Wadsworth.

DeMaris, Alfred and K. Vaninadha Rao. 1992. "Premarital Cohabitation and Subsequent Marital Stability in the United States: A Reassessment." *Journal of Marriage and the Family* 54(February):178–90.

DeMartini, Joseph R. 1982. "Basic and Applied Sociological Work: Divergence, Convergence, or Peaceful Coexistence?" *The Journal of Applied Behavioral Science* 18(2):205–6.

Deming, W. E. 2000. *Out of the Crisis.* Cambridge, MA: MIT Press.

DeMitchell, Todd A. and John J. Carney. 2005. "Harry Potter and the Public School Library." *Phi Delta Kappan* (October):159–65.

Denali Commission. 2001. "Telecommunications Inventory Survey." Retrieved June 29, 2006 (www.commonwealth.north.org/tran scripts/denalicom.html).

Denzin, Norman K. 1992. *Symbolic Interactionism and Cultural Studies: The Politics of Interpretation.* Cambridge, MA: Blackwell.

DePalma, Anthony. 1995. "Racism? Mexico's in Denial." *The New York Times* (June 11):E4.

Deutsch, M. and R. M. Krauss. 1960. "The Effect of Threat on Interpersonal Bargaining." *Journal of Abnormal and Social Psychology* 61:181–89.

Deutsch, Morton and Roy J. Lewicki. 1970. "'Locking-In' Effects During a Game of Chicken." *Journal of Conflict Resolution* 14(3):367–78.

Diamond, Jared. 1999. *Guns, Germs, and Steel: The Fates of Human Societies.* New York: W. W. Norton.

———.2005. *Collapse: How Societies Choose to Fail or Succeed.* New York: Viking.

Diamond, Larry. 1987. "Ethnicity and Ethnic Conflict." *Journal of Modern African Studies* 25(3)(March):117–28.

———. 1992. "Introduction: Civil Society and the Struggle for Democracy." Pp. 1–28 in *The Democratic Revolution: Struggles for Freedom and Pluralism in the Developing World,* edited by Larry Diamond. New York: Freedom House.

———. 1994. "The Global Imperative: Building a Democratic World Order." *Current History* 93(January):1–7.

———.2003. "Universal Democracy?" *Policy Review* (June/July). Retrieved August 28, 2008 (www.hoover.org/publications/poicyreview/3448571.html).

Dickens, Charles. 1948. *Bleak House.* London: Oxford University Press.

Diekman, Amanda B. and Sarah K. Murmen. 2004. "Learning to Be Little Women and Little Men: The Inequitable Gender Equality of Nonsexist Children's Literature." *Sex Roles: A Journal of Research* 50(5/6):373.

Dieter, Richard C. 2004. *Innocence and the Crisis in the American Death Penalty.* Retrieved July 6, 2008 (www.deathpenaltyinfo.org/article.php?scid=45&did=1149).

Divorce Magazine. 2008 "U.S. Divorce Statistics." Retrieved March 14, 2008 (www.divorcemag.com/statistics/statsUS.shtml).

Dobbelaere, Karel. 1981. *Secularization: A Multidimensional Concept.* Beverly Hills, CA: Sage.

———.2000. "Toward an Integrated Perspective of the Processes Related to the Descriptive Concept of Secularization." Pp. 21–39 in *The Secularization Debate,* edited by William H. Swatos, Jr., and Daniel V. A. Olson. Lanham, MD: Rowman and Littlefield.

Dobriansky, Paula. 2006. *The Education of Girls in the Developing World.* Washington, DC: U.S. Department of State.

Dodds, Peter Sheridan, Roby Muhamad, and Duncan J. Watts. 2003. "An Experimental Study of Search in Global Social Networks." *Science* 301(5634):827–29.

Dolan, Maura. 2008. "California Supreme Court Overturns Gay Marriage Ban." *Los Angeles Times.* Retrieved August 9, 2008 (www.latimes.com/news/local/la-me-gaymarriage16-2008 may16,0,6182317.story).

The Dollars and Sense Collective. 2006. "The ABCs of the Global Economy." Pp. 82–92 in *Globalization: The Transformation of Social Worlds,* edited by D. Stanley Eitzen and Maxine Baca Zinn. Belmont, CA: Wadsworth.

Domhoff, G. William. 1967. *Who Rules America.* New Jersey: Prentice Hall.

———. 1971. *Higher Circles: The Governing Class in America.* New York: Random House.

———. 1983. *Who Rules America Now? A View for the Eighties.* Englewood Cliffs, New Jersey: Prentice-Hall.

———. 1998. *Who Rules America? Power and Politics in the Year 2000,* 3rd ed. Mountain View, CA: Mayfield.

———. 2001. *Who Rules America? Power, Politics, and Social Change,* 4th ed. New York: McGraw-Hill.

———. 2005. *Who Rules America? Power, Politics, and Social Change,* 5th ed. New York: McGraw-Hill.

———. 2008. *Who Rules America.net: Power, Politics, and Social Change.* Retrieved March 24, 2008 (http://sociology.ucsc.edu/whoruleeesamerica).

Domina, Thurston. 2005. "Leveling the Home Advantage: Assessing the Effectiveness of Parental Involvement in Elementary School." *Sociology of Education* 78(3):233–49.

Dotzler, Robert J. and Ross Koppel. 1999. "What Sociologists Do and Where They Do It—The NSF Survey on Sociologists' Work Activities and Work Places." *Sociological Practice: A Journal of Clinical and Applied Sociology* 1(1):71–83.

Douglas, Mary. 1966. *Purity and Danger.* London: Routledge and Kegan Paul.

Drafke, Michael and Stan Kossen. 2002. *The Human Side of Organizations,* 8th ed. Englewood Cliffs, NJ: Prentice Hall.

Drori, Gili S. 2006. *Global E-Litism: Digital Technology, Social Inequality, and Transnationality.* New York: Worth.

DuBois, W.E.B. [1899] 1967. *The Philadelphia Negro: A Social Study.* New York: Schocken.

Dudley, R. L. 1996. "How Seventh-Day Adventist Lay Members View Women Pastors." *Review of Religious Research* 38(2): 133–41.

Dufur, Mikaela J. and Seth L. Feinberg. 2007. "Artificially Restricted Labor Markets and Worker Dignity in Professional Football." *Journal of Contemporary Ethnography* 36(5):505–36.

Duncan, Arne. 2006. "Chicago's Renaissance 2010: Building on School Reform in the Age of Accountability." *Phi Delta Kappan* (February):457–58.

The Durban Accord. 2003. "Our Global Commitment for People and Earth's Protected Areas" (World Commission on Protected Areas). Retrieved September 16, 2006 (www.iun.org/themes/wcpa/wpc2003/pdfs/outputs/wpc/durbanaccord.doc).

Durkheim, Émile. [1893] 1947. *The Division of Labor in Society,* translated by George Simpson. New York: The Free Press.

———. 1947. *Elementary Forms of Religious Life.* Glencoe, IL: The Free Press.

———.1956. *Education and Society,* translated by Sherwood D. Fox. Glencoe, IL: The Free Press.

———. [1897] 1964. *Suicide.* Glencoe, IL: The Free Press.

———.[1915] 2002. *Classical Sociological Theory,* edited by Craig Calhoun. Malden, MA: Blackwell.

Dworkin, Anthony Gary. 2001. "Perspectives on Teacher Burnout and School Reform." *International Education Journal* 2(2):69–78.

———.2007. "School Reform and Teacher Burnout: Issues of Gender and Gender Tokenism." Pp. 69–78 in *Gender and Education: An Encyclopedia,* edited by Barbara Banks, Sara Delamont, and Catherine Marshall. New York: Greenwood.

Dworkin, Anthony Gary and Rosalind J. Dworkin. 1999. *The Minority Report: An Introduction to Racial, Ethnic, and Gender Relations,* 3rd ed. Fort Worth, TX: Harcourt Brace.

Dworkin, Anthony Gary, Lawrence J. Saha, and Antwanette N. Hill. 2003. "Teacher Burnout and Perceptions of a Democratic School Environment." *International Education Journal* 4(2):108–20.

Dye, Thomas R. 2002a. *Who's Running America? The Bush Restoration.* Englewood Cliffs, NJ: Prentice Hall.

Dye, Thomas R. 2002b. *Who's Running America? The Clinton Years.* Upper Saddle River, NJ: Prentice Hall.

Dye, Thomas and Harmon Zeigler. 1983. *The Irony of Democracy.* Massachusetts: Duxbury Press.

Ebaugh, Helen Rose Fuchs. 1988. *Becoming an Ex: The Process of Role Exit.* Chicago: University of Chicago Press.

Eckert, Penelope. 1989. *Jocks and Burnouts: Social Categories and Identity in High School.* New York: Teacher's College Press.

Eckholm, Erik. 2006. "City by City, an Antipoverty Group Plants Seeds of Change." *The New York Times* (June 26):A12.

The Economist. 2006a. "Immigration: Don't Fence Us Out" (April 1–7):41.

The Economist. 2006b. "The United States and Mexico: Sense, Not Sensenbrenner." (April 1–7):10.

"Ecosystems Report Links Human Well-Being with Health of Planet." 2006. *Popline* 28(January/February):1.

Eder, Donna, Catherine Colleen Evans, and Stephen Parker. 1995. *School Talk: Gender and Adolescent Culture.* New Brunswick, NJ: Rutgers University Press.

Edwards, Harry. 1994. "Black Youth's Commitment to Sports Achievement: A Virtue-Turned-Tragic-Turned-Virtue." *Sport* 85(7):86.

———. 2000. "Crisis of the Black Athlete on the Eve of the 21st Century." *Society* 37(3):9–13.

Ehrenreich, Barbara. 2001. *Nickel and Dimed: On (Not) Getting By in America.* New York: Henry Holt.

———. 2005. *Bait and Switch. The (Futile) Pursuit of the American Dream.* New York: Henry Holt.

Ehrlich, Paul and Ann Ehrlich. 1990. *The Population Explosion.* New York: Simon and Schuster.

Eitzen, D. Stanley and George H. Sage. 2003. *Sociology of North American Sport.* Boston: McGraw-Hill.

Eitzen, D. Stanley and Maxine Baca Zinn, eds. 2006. *Globalization: The Transformation of Social Worlds.* Belmont, CA: Wadsworth.

Ellens, G. F. S. 1971. "The Ranting Ranters: Reflections on a Ranting Counter-Culture." *Church History* 40(March):91–107.

Ellison, Christopher G., John P. Bartkowski, and Michelle L. Segal. 1996. "Do Conservative Protestant Parents Spank More Often?" *Social Science Quarterly* 77(3):663–73.

Ellison, Christopher G., J. A. Burr, and P. L. McCall 1997. "Religious Homogeneity and Metropolitan Suicide Rates." *Social Forces* 76(1):273–99.

Ellison, Christopher G. and Daniel A. Powers. 1994. "The Contact Hypothesis and Racial Attitudes among Black Americans." *Social Science Quarterly* 75(2):385–400.

EM-DAT: The OFDA/CRED International Disaster Database. 2006. Brussels, Belgium: Université Catholique de Louvain. Retrieved August 12, 2006 (http://www.em-dat.net).

Emerling, Gary and Christina Bellantoni. 2008. "Youth Enthusiastic for Voice in Primary." *The Washington Times* (February 12):A1.

"Endogamy." 2007. University of Michigan. Retrieved November 2007 (http://www.personal.umich.edu).

Engels, Friedrich. 1902. *The Origin of the Family, Private Property, and the State.* Chicago: Charles H. Kerr.

———. [1884] 1942. *The Origin of the Family, Private Property, and the State.* New York: International Publishing.

Enloe, Cynthia. 2006. "Daughters and Generals in the Politics of the Globalized Sneaker." In *Beyond Borders: Thinking Critically about Global Issues,* edited by Paula S. Rothenberg. New York: Worth.

Environmental Protection Agency. 2004. "Terms of Environment." Retrieved (www.epa.gov/OCEPAterms/gterms.html).

Erikson, Erik H. 1950. *Childhood and Society.* New York: W. W. Norton.

Erikson, Kai T. 1976. *Everything in Its Path: Destruction of Community in the Buffalo Creek Flood.* New York: Simon & Schuster.

———. 1987. "Notes on the Sociology of Deviance." Pp. 9–21 in *Deviance: The Interactionist Perspective,* 5th ed., edited by Earl Rubington and Martin S. Weinberg. New York: Macmillan.

———. [1966] 2005. *Wayward Puritans: A Study in the Sociology of Deviance.* Boston: Pearson Education.

Eshleman, J. Ross and Richard A. Bulcroft. 2006. *The Family,* 11th ed. Boston: Allyn & Bacon.

Esperitu, Yen Le. 1992. *Asian American Panethnicity: Bridging Institutions and Identities.* Philadelphia: Temple University Press.

Esposito, L. and J. W. Murphy. 2000. "Another Step in the Study of Race Relations." *The Sociological Quarterly* 41(2):171–87.

Esquivel, Laura. 2001. *Like Water for Chocolate.* New York: Anchor.

Etzioni, Amitai. 1975. *A Comparative Analysis of Complex Organizations.* New York: The Free Press.

Europa World Year Book. 2005. London: Europa Publications Limited.

Evans, Peter and John Stephens. 1988. "Development and the World Economy." Pp. 739-773 in *Handbook of Sociology,* edited by Neil Smelser. Newbury Park, CA: Sage Publications.

Fadiman, Anne. 1997. *The Spirit Catches You and You Fall Down.* New York: Noonday.

Fainstein, Susan S., Ian Gordon, and Michael Harloe, eds. 1992. *Divided Cities: New York and London in the Contemporary World.* Oxford, UK: Blackwell.

Fallows, Deborah. 2005. "How Women and Men Use the Internet." Washington, DC: Pew Internet and American Life Project.

Faludi, Susan. 1993. *Backlash: The Undeclared War Against American Women.* New York: Anchor.

Farley, John E. 2005. *Majority-Minority Relations,* 5th ed. Englewood Cliffs, NJ: Prentice Hall.

Farley, Reynolds. 2000. *Strangers to these Shores,* 6th ed. Boston: Allyn & Bacon.

Farmer, Paul. 1999. *Infections and Inequalities: The Modern Plagues.* Berkeley: University of California Press.

Farrer, Claire R. 1996. *Thunder Rides a Black Horse: Mescalero Apaches and the Mythic Present,* 2nd ed. Prospect Heights, IL: Waveland.

Faulkner, James B. 2006. "Social Capital, Social Services, and Recidivism." Thesis for Applied Behavioral Science Program, Wright State University.

Fausto-Sterling, Anne. 1992. *Myths of Gender: Biological Theories About Women and Men,* 2nd ed. New York: Basic Books.

———.1993. "The Five Sexes: Why Male and Female Are Not Enough." *The Sciences* (March/April): 20–24.

———. 2000. *Sexing the Body: Gender Politics and the Construction of Sexuality.* New York: Basic Books.

Feagin, Joe R. 1983. *The Urban Real Estate Game: Playing Monopoly with Real Money.* Englewood Cliffs, NJ: Prentice Hall.

Feagin, Joe R. and Clairece Booher Feagin. 1986. *Discrimination American Style: Institutional Racism and Sexism.* Malabar, FL: Krieger.

———.2007. *Racial and Ethnic Relations,* 8th ed. Englewood Cliffs, NJ: Prentice Hall.

Feagin, Joe R. and Hernan Vera. 2001. *Liberation Sociology.* Boulder, CO: Westview.

Feagin, Joe R., Hernan Vera, and Pinar Batur. 2001. *White Racism: The Basics.* New York: Routledge.

Featherman, David L. and Robert Hauser. 1978. *Opportunity and Change.* New York: Academic Press.

Federal Bureau of Investigation. 2005. *Fact Sheet for Hate Crime Statistics (2004 Uniform Crime Reports).* Washington, DC: Author.

———. 2006a. "Innocent Images International Task Force." Retrieved February 10, 2008 (www.fbi.gov/publications/innocent.htm).

———. 2006b. "2006 Financial Crime Report." Retrieved February 8, 2008 (www.fbi.gov/publications/financial/fcs_report2006/financial_crime_2006.htm).

———. 2006c. "Crime Clock." Retrieved February 8, 2008 (www.fbi.gov/ucr/cius2006/about/crime_clock.html).

———. 2006d. "Crime in the United States." Retrieved February 8, 2008 (www.fbi.gov/ucr/cius2006/data/table_01.html).

Federal Register. 2002. Office of the Federal Register, National Archives and Records Vol. 67.

Federation of American Scientists. 2007. "Estimates of U.S. Nuclear Weapons Stockpile, 2007 and 2012." Retrieved April 16, 2008 (www.fas.org/blog/ssp/2007/05/estimates_of_us_nuclear_weapon.php).

Felson, Richard B. 2002. *Violence and Gender Reexamined.* Washington, DC: American Psychological Association.

Fernando, Suman. 2002. *Mental Health, Race and Culture,* 2nd ed. New York: Palgrave.

Ferree, Myra Marx. 1991. "The Gender Division of Labor in Two-Earner Marriages: Dimensions of Variability and Change." *Journal of Family Issues* 12(2):158–80.

Ferree, Myra Marx and David A. Merrill. 2000. "Hot Movements, Cold Cognition: Thinking about Social Movements in Gendered Frames." *Contemporary Sociology: A Journal of Reviews* 12:626–48.

Field, Mark. 1953. "Structured Strain in the Role of the Soviet Physician." *American Journal of Sociology* 58(5):493–502.

———.1957. *Doctor and Patient in Soviet Russia.* Cambridge, MA: Harvard University Press.

Fields, Jason and Lynne Casper. 2001. "America's Family and Living Arrangements: March 2000." *Current Population Reports*. Washington, DC: U.S. Census Bureau.

Fine, Gary Alan. 1990. "Symbolic Interactionism in the Post-Blumerian Age." Pp. 117–57 in *Frontiers of Social Theory: The New Synthesis*, edited by George Ritzer. New York: Columbia University Press.

Finfacts. 2005. "From World Bank Development Indicators 2005." Retrieved August 21, 2006 (http://www.finfacts.com/biz10/globalworldincomepercapita.htm).

Fingarette, Herbert. 1988. *Heavy Drinking: The Myth of Alcoholism as a Disease*. Berkeley: University of California Press.

Finke, Roger. 1997. "The Consequences of Religious Competition: Supply-Side Explanations for Religious Change." Pp. 45–64 in *Rational Choice Theory and Religion: Summary and Assessment*, edited by L. A. Young. New York: Routledge.

Finke, Roger and Rodney Stark. 1993. *The Churching of America, 1776–1990: Winners and Losers in Our Religious Economy*. New Brunswick, NJ: Rutgers University Press.

———. 2005. *The Churching of America, 1776–2005: Winners and Losers in Our Religious Economy*. New Brunswick, NJ: Rutgers University Press.

Finkelhor, David. 2008. *Childhood Victimization: Violence, Crime, and Abuse in the Lives of Young People*. New York: Oxford University Press.

"First Born Children." 2008. Retrieved June 29, 2008 (http://social.jrank.org/pages/261/Firstborn-children.html).

Fischer, Claude S. 1984. *The Urban Experience*, 2nd ed. San Diego: Harcourt Brace Jovanovich.

Fish, Virginia Kemp. 1986. "The Hull House Circle: Women's Friendships and Achievements." Pp. 185–227 in *Gender, Ideology, and Action: Historical Perspectives on Women's Public Lives*, edited by Janet Sharistanian. Westport, CT: Greenwood.

Fishbein, H. D. 1996. "Experimenting on Social Issues: The Case of School Desegregation." *American Psychologist* 40:452–60.

Fiske, Alan Page. 1991. *Structures of Social Life: The Four Elementary Forms of Human Relations*. New York: The Free Press.

"Five Rules for Online Networking." 2005, April 1. CNN. Retrieved July 25, 2006 (www.cnn.com/2005/US/Careers/03/31/online.networking).

Flanagan, William G. 1993. *Contemporary Urban Sociology*. New York: Cambridge University Press.

———. 2001. *Urban Sociology: Images and Structure*, 4th ed. Boston: Allyn & Bacon.

Flavin, Christopher. 2001. "Rich Planet, Poor Planet." Pp. 1–410 in *State of the World 2001*, edited by Lester R. Brown, Christopher Flavin, and Hilary French. New York: W. W. Norton.

Flavin, Jeanne. 2004. "Employment, Counseling, Housing Assistance . . . and Aunt Yolanda? How Strengthening Families' Social Capital Can Reduce Recidivism." *Fordham Urban Law Journal* 3(2):209–16.

Florida, Richard. 2002. *The Rise of the Creative Class*. New York: Basic Books.

———. 2004. *Cities and the Creative Class*. New York: Routledge.

Flynn, Stephen. 2006. "Why America Is Still an Easy Target." Pp. 246–52 in *Globalization: The Transformation of Social Worlds*, edited by D. Stanley Eitzen and Maxine Baca Zinn. Belmont, CA: Wadsworth.

Ford, Clennan S. 1970. *Human Relations Area Files: 1949–1969—A Twenty Year Report*. New Haven, CT: Human Relations Area Files.

Fox, Mary F. 1995. "Women and Higher Education: Gender Differences in the Status of Students and Scholars." Pp. 220–37 in *Women: A Feminist Perspective*, 5th ed., edited by Jo Freeman. Mountain View, CA: Mayfield.

Frank, Kenneth A., Yong Zhao, and Kathryn Borman. 2004. "Social Capital and the Diffusion of Innovation within Organizations: The Case of Computer Technology in School." *Sociology of Education* 77(2):148–71.

Frank, Mark G. and Thomas Gilovich. 1988. "The Dark Side of Self- and Social Perception: Black Uniforms and Aggression in Professional Sports." *Journal of Personality and Social Psychology* 54(1):74–85.

Frankl, Razelle. 1987. *Televangelism: The Marketing of Popular Religion*. Carbondale: Southern Illinois University Press.

Frazier, Charles. 1997. *Cold Mountain*. New York: Atlantic Monthly Press.

Free the Slaves. 2005. "Modern Slavery." Retrieved June 29, 2006 (www.freetheslaves.net).

———. 2008. Retrieved March 1, 2008 (www.freetheslaves.net/NETCOMMUNITY/Page).

Freedom House. 2002. *Freedom in the World 2001–2002*. New York: Freedom House.

Freeman, Jo. 1975. *The Politics of Women's Liberation: A Case Study of an Emerging Social Movement and Its Relation to the Policy Process*. New York: McKay.

Freese, J., B. Powell, and L. C. Steelman. 1999. *Rebel without a Cause or Effect: Birth Order and Social Attitudes*. Washington, DC: American Sociological Association.

French, Howard W. 2003. "Challenges for Japan: The Glass Ceiling Starts at the Floor." *International Herald Tribune* (June 25):1, 4.

Freud, Sigmund. [1923] 1960. *The Ego and the Id*. New York: W. W. Norton.

Freund, Peter E. S. and Meredith B. McGuire. 1999. *Health, Illness, and the Social Body*, 3rd ed. Englewood Cliffs, NJ: Prentice Hall.

Frey, Bruno S. 2004. *Dealing With Terrorism—Stick or Carrot?* Cheltenham, UK: Edward Elgar.

Friedman, Thomas L. 2005. *The World Is Flat: A Brief History of the Twenty-First Century*. New York: Farrar, Straus, and Giroux.

———. 2006. "Opening Scene: The World Is Ten Years Old." Pp. 21–29 in *Globalization: The Transformation of Social Worlds*, edited by D. Stanley Eitzen and Maxine Baca Zinn. Belmont, CA: Wadsworth.

Fuentes, Annette and Barbara Ehrenreich. 1983. *Women in the Global Factory*. Institute for New Communications; South End Press, INC Pamphlet No. 2.

Furnham, Adrian. 1994. "Explaining Health and Illness: Lay Perceptions on Current and Future Health, The Causes of Illness, and the Nature of Recovery." *Social Science and Medicine* 39(5):715–25.

Furstenberg, F. F. 2003. "Growing Up in American Society: Income, Opportunities, and Outcomes." Pp. 211–33 in *Social Dynamics of the Life Course: Transitions, Institutions, and Interrelations*, edited by W. R. Heinz and V. W. Marshall. New York: A. deGruyter

Future for All. 2008. "Future Technology and Society." Retrieved January 14, 2008 (www.futureforall.org/).

Gallagher, Charles. 2004. "Transforming Racial Identity Through Affirmative Action." Pp. 153–70 in *Race and Ethnicity: Across Time, Space and Discipline*, edited by Rodney D. Coates. Leiden, Holland: Brill.

Gallagher, Eugene B. and Janardan Subedi, eds. 1995. *Global Perspectives on Health Care*. Englewood Cliffs, NJ: Prentice Hall.

Gallagher, Eugene B., Thomas J. Stewart, and Terry D. Stratton. 2000. "The Sociology of Health in Developing Counties." Pp. 389–97 in *Handbook of Medical Sociology*, 5th ed., edited by C. Bird, P. Conrad, and A. Fremont. Englewood Cliffs, NJ: Prentice Hall.

Gallagher, Timothy J. and Robert J. Johnson. 2001. "A Model for Unmet Medical Care Needs." Paper presented at the American Sociological Association meetings, August, Anaheim, CA.

Gallaway, Brad. 2003. "Dead or Alive: Xtreme Beach Volleyball (Review). Retrieved August 5, 2008 (http://www.gamecritics.com/review/doaxvolleyball/main.php).

Gallup, George, Jr., and D. Michael Lindsay. 1999. *Surveying the Religious Landscape: Trends in U.S. Beliefs*. Harrisburg, PA: Morehouse.

Gallup Poll. 1999. "Work Satisfaction: Employed Full-time- Part-time." *The Gallup Poll Monthly*. No. 408(September).

————. 2000. Retrieved February 15, 2003 (http://www.gallup.com/poll/indicators/indreligion.asp).

————.2001. "Gallup Poll Topics: Religion." Retrieved July 10, 2006 (http://www.gallup.com/poll/indicators/indreligion4.asp).

————. 2004. "Gallup Poll Social Series: Values and Beliefs." Retrieved July 10, 2006 (http://brain.gallup.com/documents/question.aspx?question=152992&Advanced=0&SearchConType=1&SearchTypeAll=homo sexual%20clergy).

————. 2006. "Gallup Poll Topics: A-Z." Retrieved July 10, 2006 (http://poll.gallup.com/content/default/aspx?ci=1690&pg=2).

GameSpy 2002. "Top Ten Shameful Games." Retrieved July 9, 2007 (http://archive.gamespy.com/top10/december02/shame/index4.shtml).

Gamoran, Adam. 1987. "The Stratification of High School Learning Opportunities." Sociology of Education 37:19–35.

————. 2001. "American Schooling and Educational Inequality: A Forecast for the 21st Century." Sociology of Education (Extra Issue: Currents of Thought: Sociology of Education at the Dawn of the 21st Century) 60(3):135–55.

Gamson, Zelda F. 1998. "The Stratification of the Academy." Pp. 67–73 in Chalk Lines: The Politics of Work in the Managed University, edited by Randy Martin. Raleigh, NC: Duke University Press.

Gans, Herbert J. 1962. The Urban Villagers: Group and Class in the Life of Italian-Americans. New York: The Free Press.

————. 1971. "The Uses of Poverty: The Poor Pay All." Social Policy 2(2):20–24.

————. 1991. People, Plans, and Policies: Essays on Poverty, Racism, and Other National Urban Problems. New York: Columbia University Press.

Gans, Herbert J. 1994. "Positive Functions of the Undeserving Poor: Uses of the Underclass in America." Politics and Society 22(3):269–83.

————. 1995. The War Against the Poor. New York: Basic Books.

————. 2007. "No, Poverty Has Not Disappeared." Reprinted in Sociological Footprints, edited by Leonard Cargan and Jeanne Ballantine. Belmont, CA: Wadsworth.

Gardner, Howard. 1987. "The Theory of Multiple Intelligences." Annual Dyslexia 37:19–35.

————. 1999. Intelligence Reframed: Multiple Intelligences for the 21st Century. New York: Basic Books.

Garfield, Richard, and Glen Williams. 1992. Health Care in Nicaragua: Primary Care Under Changing Regimes. New York: Oxford University Press.

Garner, Catherine L. and Stephen W. Raudenbush. 1991. "Neighborhood Effects on Educational Attainment: A Multilevel Analysis." Sociology of Education 64(4):251–60.

Garreau, Joel. 1991. Edge City: Life on the New Frontier. New York: Doubleday.

Garrett, Laurie. 2000. Betrayal of Trust: The Collapse of Global Public Health. New York: Hyperion.

Gaustad, E. S. and Phillip L. Barlow. 2001. New Historical Atlas of Religion in America. Oxford, UK: Oxford University Press.

Gay, Lesbian, and Straight Education Network (GLSEN). 2006. "GLSEN's 2005 National School Climate Survey Sheds New Light on Experiences of Lesbian, Gay, Bisexual and Transgendered (LGBT) Students." Retrieved August 8, 2008 (http://www.glsen.org/cgi-bin/iowa/all/library/record/1927.html).

Gehrig, Gail. 1981. "The American Civil Religion Debate: A Source of Theory Construction." Journal for the Scientific Study of Religion 20(1):51–63.

Geist, Michael. 2008. "How Obama's Using Tech to Triumph." The Toronto Star (February 4):B1.

Gelles, Richard J. 1995. Contemporary Families: A Sociological View. Thousand Oaks, CA: Sage.

Gellner, Ernest. 1983. Culture, Identity, and Politics. Cambridge: Cambridge University Press.

————.1993. "Nationalism." Pp 409–11 in Blackwell Dictionary of Twentieth Century Thought, edited by William Outhwaite and Tom Bottomore. Oxford, UK: Basil Blackwell.

Gellner, Ernest and John Breuilly. 2008. Nations and Nationalism, 2nd ed. Ithaca, NY: Cornell University Press

"Getting Married in Japan." 2007. About.com. Retrieved November 2007 (http://japanese.about.com/library/weekly/aa080999.htm).

Gettleman, Jeffery. 2008. "Mob Sets Kenya Church on Fire, Killing Dozens" The New York Times (January 2). Retrieved June 3, 2008 (www.nytimes.com/2008/01/02/world/africa/02kenya.html?pagewanted=1&ref=africa).

Gibbs, Jack P. 1989. Control: Sociology's Central Notion. Urbana: University of Illinois Press.

Gibson, William. 1999. "Science and Science Fiction." Talk of the Nation, National Public Radio, November 30.

Giddens, Anthony. 1986. The Constitution of Society. Berkeley: University of California Press.

————. 1987. Social Theory and Modern Sociology. Cambridge, UK: Polity Press

Gilbert, Dennis. 2008. The American Class Structure in an Age of Growing Inequality, 7th ed. Thousand Oaks, CA: Pine Forge Press.

Gilbert, Dennis and Joseph A. Kahl. 2003. The American Class Structure in an Age of Inequality: A New Synthesis, 6th ed. Belmont, CA: Wadsworth.

Gilchrist, John. 2003. Anderson's Ohio Family Law. Cincinnati, OH: Anderson.

Gilligan, Carol. 1982. In a Different Voice: Psychological Theory and Women's Development. Cambridge, MA: Harvard University Press.

Ginsberg, E. 1999. "U.S. Health Care: A Look Ahead to 2025." Annual Review of Public Health 20(1):55–67.

Gitelson, Alan, Margaret Conway, and Frank Feigert. 1984. American Political Parties: Stability and Change. Boston: Houghton Mifflin.

Glaser, James M. 1994. "Back to the Black Belt: Racial Environment and White Racial Attitudes in the South." The Journal of Politics 56(1):21–41.

Glass, John. 2003. "Hunting for Bambi. Hoax? Reality? Does It Matter?" Common Dreams (online journal). Retrieved August 5, 2008 (http://www.commondreams.org/views03/0801-05.htm).

————. 2004. "Developing Sociological Interventions." Retrieved September 29, 2006 (www.geocities.com/solviolence/frame.htm).

Glasscock, C. B. 1937. The Gasoline Age: The Story of the Men Who Made It. Indianapolis, IN: Bobbs-Merrill.

Glasser, Susan B. 2005. "U.S. Figures Show Sharp Global Rise in Terrorism." The Washington Post (April 25):A01.

Glenn, Evelyn Nakano. 1999. "The Social Construction and Institutionalization of Gender and Race: An Integrative Framework." Pp. 3–43 in Revisioning Gender, edited by Myra Marx Ferree, Judith Lorber, and Beth B. Hess. Thousand Oaks, CA: Sage.

Globalis Interactive World Map. 2006. Retrieved August 30, 2006 (http://globalis.gvu.unu.edu/indicator_detail.cfm?Country=CN@IndicatorID=18).

Globe Women's Business Network. 2006. "Corporate Women Directors International." Retrieved August 21, 2006 (http://www.globewomen.com).

Goffman, Erving. [1959] 2001. Presentation of Self in Everyday Life. New York: Harmondsworth: Penguin.

————. 1961. Asylums: Essays on the Social Situation of Mental Patients and Other Inmates. New York: Anchor.

————. 1967. Interaction Ritual. New York: Anchor.

Gold, Marsha R. 1999. "The Changing U.S. Health Care System: Challenges for Responsible Public Policy." Milbank Quarterly 77(1):3–37.

Gold, Marsha R., L. Nelson, T. Lake, R. Hurley, and R. Berenson. 1998. "Behind the Curve: A Critical Assessment of How Little Is Known About Arrangements between Managed Care Plans and Physicians." Pp. 67–100 in Contemporary Managed Care: Readings in Structure, Operations, and Public Policy, edited by M. R. Gold. Chicago: Health Administration Press.

Goldberg, David Theo, ed. 1990. *Anatomy of Racism*. Minneapolis: University of Minnesota Press.

Goldberg, Gertrude Schaffner and Eleanor Kremen. 1990. *The Feminization of Poverty*. New York: Praeger.

Golden, Tim. 1994. "Health Care, Cuba's Pride, Falls on Hard Times." *The New York Times* (October 30):1.

Goode, Erich. 1992. *Collective Behavior*. New York: Harcourt Brace Jovanovich.

Goode, Erich. 1997. *Between Politics and Reason: The Drug Legalization Debate*. New York: St. Martin's.

———. 2005. *Drugs in American Society*, 6th ed. Boston: McGraw-Hill

Goode, William J. 1970. *World Revolution and Family Patterns*. New York: The Free Press.

———. 1990. "Encroachment, Charlatanism, and the Emerging Profession: Psychiatry, Sociology, and Medicine." *American Sociological Review* 25(6):902–14.

Goodman, Marc D. and Susan W. Brenner. 2002. "The Emerging Consensus on Criminal Conduct in Cyberspace." *International Journal of Law and Information Technology* 10(2):139–223.

Gordon, Milton. 1970. "The Subsociety and the Subculture." Pp. 150–63 in *The Sociology of Subcultures*, edited by David O. Arnold. Berkeley, CA: Glendessary.

Gore, Al. 2006. *An Inconvenient Truth*. Emmaus, PA: Rodale.

Gottdiener, Mark. 1987. *The Decline of Urban Politics: Political Theory and the Crisis of the Local State*. Newbury Park, CA: Sage.

Gottdiener, Mark and Ray Hutchison. 2006. *The New Urban Sociology*, 3rd ed. Boston: McGraw-Hill.

Gottfredson, Michael R. and Travis Hirschi. 1990. *A General Theory of Crime*. Palo Alto, CA: Stanford University Press.

Gottlieb, Lori. 2006. "How Do I Love Thee?" *The Atlantic* 297(2):58–70.

Gould, Stephen J. 1997. *The Mismeasure of Man*. New York: W. W. Norton.

Gracey, Harry L. 1967. "Learning the Student Role: Kindergarten as Academic Boot Camp." Pp. 215–226 in *Readings in Introductory Sociology*, 3rd ed., edited by Dennis Wrong and Harry L. Gracey. New York: Macmillan.

Grandpa Junior. 2006. "If You Were Born before 1945." Retrieved July 20, 2006 (www.grandpajunior.com/1945.shtml).

Granovetter, Mark. 2007. "Introduction for the French Reader." *Sociologica* 1, S, 1–10.

Grant, Gerald and Christine E. Murray. 1999. *Teaching in America: The Slow Revolution*. Cambridge, MA: Harvard University Press.

Grant, Linda. 2004. "Everyday Schooling and the Elaboration of Race-Gender Stratification." Pp. 296–308 in *Schools and Society: A Sociological Approach to Education*, 2nd ed., edited by Jeanne H. Ballantine and Joan Z. Spade. Belmont, CA: Wadsworth.

Greeley, Andrew M. 1972. *The Denominational Society*. Glenview, IL: Scott, Foresman.

———.1989. *Religious Change in America*. Cambridge, MA: Harvard University Press.

Green, John C. and Mark Silk. 2005. "Why Moral Values Did Count." *Religion in the News* 8(1):5–8.

Greenberg, Edward S. 1999. *The Struggle for Democracy*, 3rd ed. New York: Addison-Wesley.

The Green Papers. 2008a. "Presidential Primaries, Caucuses, and Conventions." Retrieved March 21, 2008 (http://www.thegreen papers.com/P08/CO-R.phtml).

———. 2008b. "Presidential Primaries 2008: Republican Delegate Selection and Voter Eligibility." Retrieved March 21, 2008 (http://www.thegreenpapers.com/P08/R-DSVE.phtml? sort=a).

Greensboro Justice Fund. 2005. "Courage from the Past." *GJF Newsletter* (17, Summer):1.

Greimel, Hans. 2007. "Outbreak of Violent Crime Unnerves Japan." *Associated Press*. Retrieved July 6, 2008 (www.breitbart.com/article.php?id=D8P6V7B80)

Guest, Avery M. and Keith R. Stamm. 1993. "Paths of Community Integration." *Sociological Quarterly* 34(4):581–95.

Gumpers, John J. and Stephen C. Levinson. 1991. "Rethinking Linguistic Relativity." *Current Anthropology* 32(5):613–23.

Hadden, Jeffrey K. 1987. "Toward Desacralizing Secularization Theory." *Social Forces* 65:587–611.

———. 2006. "New Religious Movements." Retrieved August 14, 2008 (http://www.hirr.hartsem.edu/denom/new_religious_movements .html).

Hadden, Jeffrey K. and Anson Shupe. 1988. *Televangelism: Power and Politics on God's Frontier*. New York: Henry Holt.

Hafferty, Frederic. 2000. "Reconfiguring the Sociology of Medical Education: Emerging Topics and Pressing Issues." Pp. 238–57 in *Handbook of Medical Sociology*, 5th ed., edited by C. Bird, P. Conrad, and A. Fremond. Englewood Cliffs, NJ: Prentice Hall.

Hagan, Frank E. 2002. *Introduction to Criminology*, 5th ed. Belmont, CA: Wadsworth.

Hagan, John L. 1993. "The Social Embeddedness of Crime and Unemployment." *Criminology* 31:465–91.

———. 1994. *Crime and Disrepute*. Thousand Oaks, CA: Pine Forge Press.

Hagan, John, Edward T. Silva, and John H. Simpson. 1977. "Conflict and Consensus in the Designation of Deviance." *Social Forces* 56(2):320–40.

Hagopian, Mark N. 1984. *Regimes, Movements, and Ideologies*, 2nd ed. New York: Longman.

Hall, Edward T. 1959. *The Silent Language*. New York: Doubleday.

———. 1983. *The Dance of Life*. Garden City, NY: Anchor Books/ Doubleday.

Hall, Edward T. and Mildred Reed Hall. 1992. *An Anthropology of Everyday Life*. New York: Doubleday.

Hall, Richard H. 2002. *Organizations: Structures, Processes, and Outcomes*, 7th ed. Englewood Cliffs, NJ: Prentice Hall.

Hallinan, Maureen T. 1994. "Tracking: From Theory to Practice." *Sociology of Education* 67(2):79–91.

Hallinan, Maureen T. and Richard A. Williams. 1989. "Interracial Friendship Choices in Secondary Schools." *American Sociological Review* 54(February):67–78.

———. 1990. "Students' Characteristics and the Peer-Influence Process." *Sociology of Education* 63(2):122–32.

Hamilton, Brady E., Stephanie J. Ventura, Joyce A. Martin, and Paul D. Sutton. 2006. "Final Births for 2004." (National Center for Health Statistics). Retrieved September 15, 2006 (www.cdc.gov/nchs/products/pubs/pubd/hestats/finalbirths04/finalbirths04 .htm).

Hammersley, Martyn and Glenn Turner. 1980. "Conformist Pupils." In *Pupil Strategies: Explorations in the Sociology of the School*, edited by Peter Woods. London: Croom Helm.

Handel, Gerald, Spencer Cahill, and Frederick Elkin. 2007. *Children and Society: The Sociology of Children and Childhood Socialization*. New York: Oxford University Press USA.

Handwerk, Brian. 2004. "Female Suicide Bombers: Dying to Kill." *National Geographic News* (December 13). Retrieved July 5, 2008 (http://news .nationalgeographic.com/news/2004/12/1213_041213_tv_suicide_ bombers.html)

Hannigan, John. 1998. *Fantasy City: Pleasure and Profit in the Postmodern Metropolis*. London: Routledge.

Hansen, Randall and Katharine Hansen. 2003. "What Do Employers Really Want? Top Skills and Values Employers Seek From Job-Seekers" (Quintessential Careers). Retrieved June 23, 2008 (www .quintcareers.com/job_skills_values.html).

Hanser, Robert D. 2002. "Labeling Theory as a Paradigm for the Etiology of Prison Rape: Implications for Understanding and Intervention." *Professional Issues in Counseling On-line Journal* (April). Retrieved August 4, 2006 (http://www.shsu.edu/~piic/ summer2002Hanser.htm).

Hardin, Garrett. 1968. "The Tragedy of the Commons." *Science* 162(3859)(December):1243–48.

Hargreaves, D. H. 1978. "The Two Curricula and the Community." *Westminster Studies in Education* 1: 31–41.

Harms, William. 2000. "Research Looks at Cohabitation's Negative Effects." *University of Chicago Chronicle* 19(11).

Harrington, Charlene and Carroll L. Estes. 2004. *Health Policy: Crisis and Reform in the U.S. Health Care Delivery System,* 2nd ed. Sudbury, MA: Jones and Bartlett.

Harris, Judith Rich. 1998. *The Nurture Assumption: Why Children Turn Out the Way They Do.* New York: The Free Press.

Harris, Marvin. 1989. *Cows, Pigs, War, and Witches: The Riddles of Culture.* New York: Random House.

Harrison, P. M. and J. C. Karberg. 2003. *Prison and Jail Inmates at Midyear 2002.* Washington, DC: U.S. Bureau of Justice Statistics.

Harvey, David. 1973. *Social Justice and the City.* London: Edward Arnold.

Haskins, Ron. 2006. *Work Over Welfare: The Inside Story of the 1996 Welfare Reform Law.* Washington, DC: Brookings Institution Press.

Haupt, Arthur and Thomas T. Kane. 2003. *Population Reference Bureau Report, 2003.* Washington, DC: U.S. Population Bureau.

Hayden, Tom. 2006. "Seeking a New Capitalism in Chiapas." Pp. 348–54 in *Globalization: The Transformation of Social Worlds,* edited by D. Stanley Eitzen and Maxine Baca Zinn. Belmont, CA: Wadsworth.

Hayes, Bernadette C. 1995. "The Impact of Religious Identification on Political Attitudes: An International Comparison." *Sociology of Religion* 56(2):177–94.

Haynie, Dana L. 2001. "Delinquent Peers Revisited: Does Network Structure Matter?" *American Journal of Sociology* 106(4):1013–57.

Headlam, Bruce. 2000. "Barbie PC: Fashion over Logic." *The New York Times* (January 20):G4.

Healey, Joseph F. 2006. *Race, Ethnicity, Gender and Class: The Sociology of Group Conflict and Change,* 4th ed. Thousand Oaks, CA: Pine Forge.

Health Confidence Survey. 2001. "2001 Health Confidence Survey: Summary of Findings" (pp. 1–9). Washington, DC: Health Confidence Survey/Employee Benefit Research.

Health in Schools. 2002. "Annual Summary of Vital Statistics Shows Continued Decline in Teen Pregnancies." *Health and Healthcare in Schools* 3(10). Retrieved August 22, 2006 (www.healthinschools.org/ejournal/2002/dec02_2.htm).

Heaton, Tim B. 1990. "Religious Group Characteristics, Endogamy, and Interfaith Marriages." *Sociological Analysis* 51(4):363–76.

Heilbroner, Robert L. and William Milberg. 2007. *The Making of Economic Society,* 12th ed. Englewood Cliffs, NJ: Prentice Hall.

Heilbroner, Robert L. and Lester C. Thurow. 1981. *The Economic Problem,* 6th ed. New Jersey: Prentice Hall.

Heilman, Samuel. 2000. *Defenders of the Faith: Inside Ultra-Orthodox Jewry.* Berkeley: University of California Press.

Helfand, Duke. 2008. "Presbyterian Leaders OK Gay Clergy." *Los Angeles Times* (June 28). Retrieved August 18, 2008 (www.latimes.com/news/local/la-me-ordain28-2008jun28,0,7679148.story).

Helgesen, Sally. 1995. *The Female Advantage: Women's Ways of Leadership.* New York: Doubleday.

Hendry, Joy. 1987. *Becoming Japanese: The World of the Preschool Child.* Honolulu: University of Hawaii Press.

———. 1995. *Understanding Japanese Society,* 2nd ed. New York: Routledge.

Henley, Nancy, Mykol Hamilton, and Barrie Thorne. 2000. "Womanspeak and Manspeak: Sex Differences in Communication, Verbal and Nonverbal." Pp. 111–15 in *Sociological Footprints,* edited by Leonard Cargan and Jeanne Ballantine. Belmont, CA: Wadsworth.

Hensley, Christopher, M. Koscheski, and Richard Tewksbury. 2005. "Examining the Characteristics of Male Sexual Assault Targets in a Southern Maximum-Security Prison." *Journal of Interpersonal Violence* 20(6):667–79.

Henslin, James M. 2005. *Sociology: A Down-to-Earth Approach,* 8th ed. Boston: Allyn & Bacon.

Heritage House '76. 1998. "Adoption or Abortion: Decision of a Lifetime." Retrieved April 3, 2008 (www.abortionfacts.com/literature/literature_9338aa.asp).

Herman, Edward S. and David Peterson. 2006. "The Threat of Global State Terrorism: Retail vs Wholesale Terror." Pp. 252–57 in *Globalization: The Transformation of Social Worlds,* edited by D. Stanley Eitzen and Maxine Baca Zinn. Belmont, CA: Wadsworth.

Hertsgaard, Mark. 2003. *The Eagle's Shadow: Why America Fascinates and Infuriates the World.* New York: Picador.

Hess-Biber, Sharlene Nagy and Patricia Lina Leavey. 2007. *Feminist Research Practice: A Primer.* Thousand Oaks, CA: Sage.

Hewitt, John P. 2007. *Self and Society: A Symbolic Interactionism Social Psychology,* 10th ed. Boston: Allyn & Bacon.

Hill, Christopher. 1991. *The World Turned Upside Down: Radical Ideas During the English Revolution.* New York: Penguin.

Himmelstein, David U. and Steffie Woodhandler. 1992. *National Health Program Chartbook.* Cambridge, MA: Center for National Health Program Studies.

Hirschi, Travis. [1969] 2002. *Causes of Delinquency.* New Brunswick, NJ: Transaction Publishers.

Hitler, Adolf. 1939. *Mein Kampf.* New York: Reynal and Hitchcock.

Hochschild, Arlie. 1989. *The Second Shift: Working Parents and the Revolution at Home.* New York: Viking.

———. 1997. *The Time Bind: When Work Becomes Home and Home Becomes Work.* New York: Metropolitan Books.

Hoffer, Thomas, Andrew M. Greeley, and James S. Coleman. 1987. "Catholic High School Effects on Achievement Growth." Pp. 67–88 in *Comparing Public and Private Schools, Vol. 2, Student Achievement,* edited by Edward H. Haertel, Thomas James, and Henry M. Levin. New York: Falmer.

Hogeland, Lisa Maria. 2004. "Fear of Feminism: Why Young Women Get the Willies." Pp. 565–68 in *Women's Voices, Feminist Visions,* 2nd ed., edited by Susan M. Shaw and Janet Lee. Boston: McGraw-Hill.

Homans, George C. 1974. *Social Behavior: Its Elementary Forms.* New York: Harcourt, Brace Javanovich.

Hood, Roger. 2002. *The Death Penalty: A World-wide Perspective,* 3rd ed. Oxford, UK: Clarendon Press.

Horrigan, John B. and Aaron Smith. 2007. "Home Broadband Adoption 2007 Report" (Pew Internet and American Life Project). Retrieved July 7, 2008 (http://222.pewinternet.org/pdfs/PIP_Broadband%202007.pdf)

Hossfeld, Karen J. 2006. "Gender, Race, and Class in Silicon Valley." Pp. 264–70 in *Beyond Borders: Thinking Critically About Global Issues,* edited by Paula S. Rothenberg. New York: Worth.

Hostetler, John A. 1993. *Amish Society,* 4th ed. Baltimore: John Hopkins University Press.

Houlihan, G. Thomas. 2005. "The Importance of International Benchmarking for U.S. Educational Leaders." *Phi Delta Kappan* (November):217–18.

House, James S. 1994. "Social Structure and Personality: Past, Present, and Future." Pp. 77–102 in *Sociological Perspectives on Social Psychology,* edited by Karen Cook, Gary Fine, and James S. House. Boston: Allyn & Bacon.

Housing and Urban Development. 2008. "HUD Reports Drop in the Number of Chronically Homeless Persons" (News Release No. 08-113). Retrieved August 23, 2008 (www.hud.gov/news/)

Howard, Adam. 2007. *Learning Privilege: Lessons of Power and Identity in Affluent Schooling.* New York: Taylor and Francis.

Howard, Philip N. and Steve Jones, eds. 2004. *Society On-Line: The Internet in Context.* Thousand Oaks, CA: Sage.

Hu, Winnie. 1999. "Woman Fearing Mutilation Savors Freedom." *The New York Times* (August 20):A21.

Hughes, David and Lesley Griffiths. 1999. "On Penalties and the Patient's Charter: Centralism V. De-centralised Governance in the NHS." *Sociology of Health and Illness* 21(1):71–94.

Hughes, Melanie M. 2004. "Armed Conflict, International Linkages, and Women's Parliamentary Representation in Developing Nations." Master's Thesis, Department of Sociology, The Ohio State University.

Huizinga, David, Rolf Loeber, and Terence P. Thornberry. 1994. "Urban Delinquency and Substance Abuse: Initial Findings." *OJJDP Research Summary.* Washington, DC: Government Printing Office.

Human Rights Campaign. 2003. *Answers to Questions About Marriage Equality.* Washington, DC: Human Rights Campaign, Family Net Project.

———. 2008. "Questions About Same Sex Marriage" Retrieved February 20, 2008 (http://www.hrc.org/issues/5517.htm).

Hunsberger, B. 1995. "The Role of Religious Fundamentalism, Quest, and Right-Wing Authoritarianism." *Journal of Social Issues* 51(2):113–29.

Hunter College Women's Studies Collective. 2005. *Women's Realities, Women's Choices: An Introduction to Women's Studies,* 3rd ed. New York: Oxford University Press.

Hunter, James Davidson. 1983. *American Evangelicalism.* New Brunswick, NJ: Rutgers University Press.

Hurst, Charles E. 2006. *Social Inequality: Forms, Causes and Consequences,* 6th ed. Boston: Allyn & Bacon.

Iannaccone, Laurence R. 1994. "Why Strict Churches Are Strong." *American Journal of Sociology* 59(5):1180–211.

———. 1995. "Voodoo Economics? Reviewing the Rational Choice Approach to Religion." *Journal for the Scientific Study of Religion* 34(1):76–88.

Independence Hall Association. 2008. "Betsy Ross and the American Flag." Retrieved August 16, 2008 (http://www.ushistory.org/betsy/flagtale.html).

Information Please Almanac. 2008. "Languages." Retrieved January 20, 2008 (www.infoplease.com/ipa/A0775272.html).

Ingersoll, Richard M. 2004. "The Status of Teaching as a Profession." Pp. 102–18 in *Schools and Society: A Sociological Approach to Education,* 2nd ed., edited by Jeanne H. Ballantine and Joan Z. Spade. Belmont, CA: Wadsworth.

———. 2005. "The Problem of Underqualified Teachers: A Sociological Perspective." *Sociology of Education* 78(2):175–79.

Inglehart, Ronald. 1997. *Modernization and Postmodernization: Cultural, Economic, and Political Change in 43 Societies.* Princeton, NJ: Princeton University Press.

Inglehart, Ronald and Wayne E. Baker. 2001. "Modernization's Challenge to Traditional Values: Who's Afraid of Ronald McDonald?" *The Futurist* 35(2):16–22.

Inhofe, James M. 2008. "Senate Republicans Introduce Package of Immigration Enforcement Bills." Retrieved April 9, 2008 (www.imhofe.senate.gov/public/index.cfm?FuseAction=PresRoom.PressReleases&Co).

Inside Higher Ed. 2007. "More Students and Higher Scores for ACT" (August 15). Retrieved April 2, 2008 (www.insidehighered.com/news/2007/08/15/act).

Inside Higher Ed. 2008. "The SAT's Growing Gaps" (August 27). Retrieved October 14, 2008 (www.insidehighered.com/news/2008/08/27/sat).

Institute for Statistics. 2003. "Pupil-Teacher Ratio: Primary." New York: UNESCO. Retrieved August 26, 2006 (http://education/en/ev.phb-URL_ID=13602&URL).

———. 2005. *Fact Sheet: International Literacy Day 2005.* New York: United Nations.

———. 2006a. "Global Education Digest 2006: Comparing Education Statistics across the World." New York: UNESCO. Retrieved July 28, 2006 (www.uis.unesco.org/TEMPLATE/pdf/ged/2006/GED2006.pdf).

———. 2006b. "The State of the World's Children 2007." Retrieved August 23, 2008 (http://www.unicef.org/sowc07/report/report.php).

Intergovernmental Panel on Climate Change. 2007. *Climate Change 2007. Synthesis Report.* Retrieved August 29, 2008 (www.ipcc.ch/pdf/assessment-report/ar4/syr/ar4_syr_spm.pdf).

International Association for the Evaluation of Educational Achievement. 2007. "Trends in International Math and Science Studies." Retrieved August 23, 2008 (http://www.iea.nl/timss2007.html).

International Centre for Prison Studies. 2006. "Entire World: Prison Population Rates per 100,000 of the National Population" (King's College, London). Retrieved August 4, 2006 (www.kcl.ac.uk.depsta/rel/icps/worldbrief/highest_to_lowest_rates.php).

International Forum on Globalization. 2006. "A Critical Look at Measures of Economic Progress" Pp. 346–55 in *Beyond Borders: Thinking Critically about Global Issues,* edited by Paula S. Rothenberg. New York: Worth.

International Institute for Democracy and Electoral Assistance. 2008. "Turnout in the World—Country by Country Performance." Retrieved June 13, 2008 (www.idea.int/vt/survey/voter_turnout_pop2.cfm).

International Monetary Fund. 2003. "Proposal for a Sovereign Debt Restructuring Mechanism: A Factsheet." Retrieved September 29, 2006 (www.imf.org/external/np/exr/facts/sdrm.htm).

Inter-Parliamentary Union. 2008. "Women in National Parliaments." Retrieved August 5, 2008 (http://www.ipu.org/wmn-e/classif.htm).

Interpol. 2003. "Drugs and Criminal Organizations." Retrieved August 4, 2006 (www.interpol.int/public/drugs).

———. 2007. "Interpol Funds Recovery Scam." Retrieved February 18, 2008 (http://www.interpol.int/default.asp).

Irvine, Leslie. 2004. *If You Tame Me: Understanding Our Connection with Animals.* Philadelphia: Temple University Press.

Irwin, John. 1985. *The Jail: Managing the Underclass in American Society.* Berkeley: University of California Press.

———. 2005. *The Warehouse Prison: Disposal of the New Dangerous Class.* Los Angeles: Roxbury.

Jackman, Robert W. 1993. *Power Without Force: The Political Capacity of Nation-States.* Ann Arbor: University of Michigan Press.

Jackson, Philip W. 1968. *Life in Classrooms.* New York: Holt, Rinehart & Winston.

Jacobs, Jane. 1961. *Life and Death of Great American Cities.* New York: Random House.

———. 1969. *Economy of Cities.* New York: Random House.

James, William. [1890] 1934. *The Principles of Psychology.* Mineola, NY: Dover.

Jao, Jui-Chang and Matthew McKeever. 2006. "Ethnic Inequalities and Educational Attainment in Taiwan." *Sociology of Education* 79(2):131–52.

Japan Institute of Labor. 2002. "Women's Work Patterns and the M-Shaped Curve." Retrieved August 22, 2006 (http://www.jil.go.jp/index-e.htm).

Jarrett, R. L., P. J. Sullivan, and N. D. Watkins. 2005. "Developing Social Capital Through Participation in Organized Youth Programs: Qualitative Insights From Three Programs." *Journal of Community Psychology* 33(1):41–55.

Jayson, Sharon. 2005a. "Cohabitation Is Replacing Dating." *USA Today* (July 17). Retrieved April 3, 2008 (www.usatoday.com/life/lifestyle/2005-07-17-cohabitation_x.htm).

————.2005b. "Divorce Declining, But So Is Marriage." *USA Today* (July 18):3A.

Jellinek, E. M. 1960. *The Disease Concept of Alcoholism.* New Haven, CT: Hillhouse.

Jencks, Christopher. 1972. *Inequality: A Reassessment of the Effects of Family and Schooling in America.* New York: Basic Books.

————, ed. 1979. *Who Gets Ahead? The Determinants of Economic Success in America.* New York: Harper & Row.

————. 1992. *Rethinking Social Policy: Race, Poverty, and the Underclass.* Cambridge, MA: Harvard University Press.

Jenkins, Patricia H. 1995. "School Delinquency and School Commitment." *Sociology of Education* 68(July):221–39.

Jenness, Valerie and Kendal Broad. 1997. *Hate Crimes.* New York: Aldine de Gruyter.

Jennings, Jerry T. 1992. "Voting and Registration in the Election of November 1992." *Current Population Reports* (P-20–466). Washington, DC: U.S. Department of Commerce, Economics and Statistics Administration, U.S. Bureau of the Census.

Jensen, Robert and Emily Oster. 2007. *The Power of TV: Cable Television and Women's Status in India* (NBER Working Paper No. 13305). Cambridge, MA: National Bureau of Economic Research.

Johnson, David W. and Frank P. Johnson. 2006. *Joining Together: Group Theory and Group Skills,* 9th ed. Boston: Allyn & Bacon.

Johnson, Jeff. 2007. "U.S. Presses for New Nuclear Weapons." *Chemical and Engineering News* 85(12):34–37.

Johnson, Kenneth M. and Glenn V. Fuguitt. 2000. "Continuity and Change in Rural Migration Patterns, 1950–1995." *Rural Sociology* 65(1):27–49.

Johnson, Paul. 2005. "Majority of Americans Believe Homosexuality Should Not Be Illegal, Support Partner Rights: Gallup Poll." Retrieved August 22, 2006 (www.sodomylaws.org/usa/usnews 141.htm).

Johnson, Robert. 2002. *Hard Time: Understanding and Reforming the Prison.* Belmont, CA: Wadsworth/Thompson Learning.

Jones, Jacqueline. 1992. *The Dispossessed: America's Underclasses from the Civil War to the Present.* New York: Basic.

Jordan-Bychkov, Terry G. and Mono Domoch. 1998. *The Human Mosaic,* 8th ed. New York: W. H. Freeman.

Kagan, Sharon Lynn and Vivien Stewart. 2005. "A New World View: Education in a Global Era." *Phi Delta Kappan* (November):185–87.

Kain, Edward L. 1990. *The Myth of Family Decline: Understanding Families in a World of Rapid Social Change.* Lanham, MD: Lexington.

Kaiser Family Foundation. 2005a. *Generation M: Media in the Lives of 8 to 18 Year-Olds—Report.* Retrieved July 20, 2006 (www.kff.org/entmedia/7251.cfm).

————. 2005b. "U.S. Teen Sexual Activity." Retrieved August 7, 2008 (http://www.kff.org/youthhivstds/upload/U-S-Teen-Sexual-Activity-Fact-Sheet.pdf).

Kalmijn, Matthijs. 1991. "Shifting Boundaries: Trends in Religious and Educational Homogamy." *American Sociological Review* 56(December):786–800.

Kalmijn, Matthijs, and Gerbert Kraaykamp. 1996. "Race, Cultural Capital, and Schooling: An Analysis of Trends in the United States." *Sociology of Education* 69(1):22–34.

Kamens, David H. and Aaron Benavot. 1991. "Elite Knowledge for the Masses: The Origins and Spread of Mathematics and Science Education in National Curricula." *American Journal of Education* 99:2 (February) 137–180.

Kanter, Rosabeth Moss. 1977. *Men and Women of the Corporation.* New York: Basic Books.

————. 1983. *The Change Masters: Innovation for Productivity in the American Corporation.* New York: Simon and Schuster.

————. 2001a. "Creating the Culture for Innovation." In *Leading for Innovation: Managing for Results,* edited by Frances Hesselbein, Marshall Goldsmith, and Iain Somerville. San Francisco: Jossey-Bass.

————. 2001b. "From Spare Change to Real Change: The Social Sector as Beta Site for Business Innovation." *Harvard Business Review on Innovation:*153–178.

————. 2005. *Commitment and Community.* Cambridge, MA: Harvard University Press.

Kantrowitz, Barbara and Pat Wingert. 2003. "What's at Stake?" *Newsweek* (January 27):30–37.

Kao, Grace. 2004. "Social Capital and Its Relevance to Minority and Immigrant Populations." *Sociology of Education* 77:172–76.

Kaplan, Howard B. and Robert J. Johnson. 1991. "Negative Social Sanctions and Juvenile Delinquency: Effects of Labeling in a Model of Deviant Behavior." *Social Science Quarterly* 72(1):117.

Karen, David. 2005. "No Child Left Behind? Sociology Ignored!" *Sociology of Education* 78(2):165–82.

Karraker, Katherine Hildebrant. 1995. "Parent's Gender-Stereotyped Perceptions of Newborns: The Eye of the Beholder Revisited." *Sex Roles* 33(9/10):687–701.

Kates, Brian. 2002. "Black Market in Transplant Organs." *New York Daily News* (August 25).

Katz, Jackson. 2006. *The Macho Paradox: Why Some Men Hurt Women and How All Men Can Help.* Naperville, IL: Sourcebooks

Kaufman, Bel. 1964. *Up the Down Staircase.* Englewood Cliffs, NJ: Prentice Hall.

KBYU-TV, producer. 2005. *Small Fortunes: Microcredit and the Future of Poverty.* Provo, Utah: Author.

Keith, Verna M. and Cedric Herring. 1991. "Skin Tone and Stratification in the Black Community." *American Journal of Sociology* 97(3):760–78.

Keller, Mark. 1991. "On Defining Alcoholism." *Alcohol Health and Research World* 15(4):253–59.

Kemmis, S. and R. McTaggart. 2000. "Participatory Action Research." Pp. 567–606 in *Handbook of Qualitative Research,* 2nd ed., edited by Norman K. Denzin and Yvonna S. Lincoln. Thousand Oaks, CA: Sage.

Kendall, Diane. 2004. *Sociology in Our Times: The Essentials,* 4th ed. Belmont, CA: Wadsworth.

Kerbo, Harold R. 2008. *Social Stratification and Inequality,* 7th ed. Boston: McGraw Hill.

Kerckhoff, Alan C. 2001. "Education and Social Stratification Processes in Comparative Perspective." *Sociology of Education* (Extra Issue: Currents of Thought: Sociology of Education at the Dawn of the 21st Century):3–18.

Kerckhoff, Alan C. and Lorraine Bell. 1998. "Hidden Capital: Vocational Credentials and Attainment in the United States." *Sociology of Education* 71(2): 152–74.

Kettl, Donald F. 1993. *Sharing Power: Public Governance and Private Markets.* Washington, DC: Brookings.

Kilbourne, Jean. 1999. *Deadly Persuasion: Why Women and Girls Must Fight the Additive Power of Advertising.* New York: The Free Press.

————. 2000. *Killing Us Softly, III* (Video). Northampton, MA: Media Education Foundation.

Kilgore, Sally B. 1991. "The Organizational Context of Tracking in Schools." *American Sociological Review* 56(2):201–2.

Killian, Caitlin. 2006. *North African Women in France: Gender, Culture, and Identity.* Palo Alto, CA: Stanford University Press.

Kimmel, Michael S. 2003. *The Gendered Society,* 2nd ed. New York: Oxford University Press.

Kimmel, Michael S. and Michael A. Messner. 2004. *Men's Lives,* 6th ed. Boston: Allyn & Bacon.

King, Edith W. 2006. *Meeting the Challenges of Teaching in an Era of Terrorism.* Belmont, CA: Thomson.

King, Jacqueline E. 2000. *Gender Equity in Higher Education.* Washington, DC: American Council on Education, Center for Policy Analysis.

Kinsey, Alfred E., Wardell B. Pomeroy, and Clyde E. Martin. 1948. *Sexual Behavior in the Human Male.* Philadelphia: Saunders.

Kinsey, Alfred E., Wardell B. Pomeroy, Clyde E. Martin, and H. Gephard. 1953. *Sexual Behavior in the Human Female.* Philadelphia: Saunders.

Kirk, Gwyn and Margo Okazawa-Rey. 2007. *Women's Lives: Multicultural Perspectives,* 4th ed. Boston: McGraw-Hill.

Kitano, Harry H. L. 2001. *Asian Americans: Emerging Minorities,* 3rd ed. Englewood Cliffs, NJ: Prentice Hall.

Kitano, Harry H., Pauline Aqbayani, and Diane de Anda. 2005. *Race Relations,* 6th edition. Englewood Cliffs, NJ: Prentice Hall.

Klaus, Patsy. 2007. *Crime and the Nation's Households, 2005* (National Crime Victimization Survey, NCJ 217198). Washington, DC: U.S. Department of Justice, Bureau of Justice Statistics.

Knapp, Mark L. and Judith A. Hall. 1997. *Nonverbal Communication in Human Interaction,* 4th ed. Fort Worth: Harcourt Brace College.

Knickmeyer, Ellen. 2008. "Turkey's Gul Signs Head Scarf Measure" (February 23). Retrieved March 6, 2008 (www.washingtonpost.com/wp-dyn/content/article/2008/02/22).

Knox, Paul L. and Peter J. Taylor, eds. 1995. *World Cities in a World-System.* Cambridge, UK: Cambridge University Press.

Koch, Jerome R. and Evans W. Curry. 2000. "Social Context and the Presbyterian Gay/Lesbian Debate: Testing Open Systems Theory." *Review of Religious Research* 42(2):206–14.

Kodish, Bruce I. 2003. "What We Do with Language—What It Does with Us." *ETC: A Review of General Semantics* 60:383–95.

Kohlberg, Lawrence. 1971. "From Is to Ought." Pp. 151–284 in *Cognitive Development and Epistemology,* edited by T. Mischel. New York: Academic Press.

Kohn, Melvin. 1989. *Class and Conformity: A Study of Values,* 2nd ed. Chicago: University of Chicago Press.

Kollock, Peter, Philip Blumstein, and Pepper Schwartz. 1985. "Sex and Power in Interaction: Conversational Privilege and Duties." *American Sociological Review* 50(February):34–66.

Koos, Earl. 1954. *The Health of Regionville.* New York: Columbia University Press.

Korte, Charles and Stanley Milgram. 1970. "Acquaintance Networks Between Racial Groups." *Journal of Personality and Social Psychology* 15:101–08.

Kosmin, Barry A. and Seymour P. Lackman. 1993. *One Nation Under God: Religion in Contemporary American Society.* New York: Harmony Books.

Kozol, Jonathan. 1991. *Savage Inequalities: Children in America's Schools.* New York: Crown.

———. 2005. "Confections of Apartheid: A Stick-and-Carrot Pedagogy for the Children of Our Inner-City Poor." *Phi Delta Kappan* (December):265–75.

———. 2006. *The Shame of the Nation: The Restoration of Apartheid Schooling in America.* New York: Crown.

Kramer, Laura. 2005. *The Sociology of Gender: A Brief Introduction,* 2nd ed. Los Angeles: Roxbury.

Krieger, Nancy. 1994. "Epidemiology and the Web of Causation: Has Anyone Seen the Spider?" *Social Science and Medicine* 39(7):887–903.

Kristof, Nicholas D. 1995. "Japan's Invisible Minority: Better Off than in Past, but Still Outcasts." *The New York Times* International (November 30):A18.

Krug, E., L. Dahlberg, J. Mercy, A. Zwi, and R. Lozano. 2002. *World Report on Violence and Health.* Geneva, Switzerland: World Health Organization.

Kübler-Ross, Elizabeth. 1997. *Death, the Final Stage of Growth,* Rev. ed. New York: Scribner.

Kuhn, Manford. 1964. "Major Trends in Symbolic Interaction Theory in the Past Twenty-Five Years." *Sociological Quarterly* 5:61–84.

Kuhn, Thomas. 1970. *The Structure of Scientific Revolutions,* 2nd ed. Chicago: University of Chicago Press.

Kumar, Sanjay. 2001. "Despite Ban, Organs Still Sold in India." *Reuters Health* (March 9). Retrieved September 20, 2006 (http://www.geocities.com/somewhereal/bodyparts.html).

Kurtz, Richard A. and H. Paul Chalfant. 1991. *The Sociology of Medicine and Illness.* Boston: Allyn & Bacon.

Kyle, David and Rey Koslowski, eds. 2001. *Global Human Smuggling: Comparative Perspectives.* Baltimore, MD: Johns Hopkins University Press.

Lacayo, Richard. 1993. "Cult of Death." *Time* (March 15):36.

Laconte, Joe. 1998. "I'll Stand Bayou: Louisiana Couples Choose a More Muscular Marriage Contract." *Policy Review* 89:30–35.

Ladson-Billings, Gloria. 2006. "Once Upon a Time When Patriotism Was What You Did." *Phi Delta Kappan* 87(8):585–88.

Laird, J. S. Lew, M. DeBell, and C. Chapman. 2006. *Dropout Rates in the United States: 2002 and 2003* (NCES 2006–062). Washington, DC: U.S. Department of Education, National Center for Education Statistics.

Lake, Robert. 1990. "An Indian Father's Plea." *Teacher Magazine* 2(September):48–53.

Lamanna, Mary Ann and Agnes Riedmann. 2003. *Marriages and Families: Making Choices throughout the Life Cycle,* 8th ed. Belmont, CA: Wadsworth.

Lambert, Lisa. 2006. "Half of Teachers Quit in Five Years: Working Conditions, Low Salaries Cited." *Washington Post* (May 9):A7.

Lambert, Yves. 2000. "Religion in Modernity as a New Axial Age: Secularization or New Religious Forms?" Pp. 95–125 in *The Secularization Debate,* edited by William H. Swatos, Jr., and Daniel V. A. Olson. Lanham, MD: Rowman and Littlefield.

Lamy, Philip. 1996. *Millennium Rage.* New York: Plenum.

Lareau, Annette. 2003. *Unequal Childhoods: Class, Race, and Family Life.* Berkeley: University of California Press

Lareau, Annette and Erin McNamara Horvat. 1999. "Moments of Social Inclusion and Exclusion: Race, Class, and Cultural Capital in Family-School Relationships." *Sociology of Education* 72(1):37–53.

Larimer, Tim. 1999. "The Japan Syndrome." *Time* (October 11):50–51.

Lassey, Marie L., William R. Lassey, and Martin J. Jinks. 1997. *Health Care Systems Around the World.* Englewood Cliffs, NJ: Prentice Hall.

Lawson, Carol. 1991. "Sheltering Children of the Vietnam War." *The New York Times* (April 18). Retrieved June 24, 2008 (http://query.nytimes.com/gst/fullpage.html?res=9D0CE7D61538F93BA25757C0A967958)

Laythe, Brian, Deborah Finkel, and Lee A. Kirkpatrick. 2001. "Predicting Prejudice From the Religious Fundamentalism and Right–Wing Authoritarianism." *Journal for the Scientific Study of Religion* 41(1):1–10.

Leach, Edmund R. 1979. "Ritualization in Man in Relation to Conceptual and Social Development." Pp. 333–37 in *Reader in Comparative Religion,* 3rd ed., edited by William A Lessa and Evon Z. Vogt. New York: Harper & Row.

Leavitt, Jacqueline and Susan Saegert. 1990. From *Abandonment to Hope: Community-Households in Harlem* (Columbia History of Urban Life). New York: Columbia University Press.

LeBon, Gustave. [1895] 1960. *The Crowd: A Study of the Popular Mind.* New York: Viking.

LeBow, Bob. 2004. *Health Care Meltdown: Confronting the Myths and Fixing Our Failing System.* Chambersburg, PA: Alan C. Hood.

Lechner, Frank J. and John Boli. 2005. *World Culture: Origins and Consequences.* Malden, MA: Blackwell.

Lee, B. C. and J. L. Werth. 2000. *Observations on the First Year of Oregon's Death with Dignity Act.* Washington, DC: American Psychological Association.

Lee, Gang, Ronald L. Akers, and Marian J. Borg. 2004. "Social Learning and Structural Factors in Adolescent Substance Use." *Western Criminology Review* 5(1):17.

Lee, Jennifer and Frank D. Bean. 2004. "America's Changing Color Lines: Immigration, Race/Ethnicity, and Multiracial Identification." *Annual Review of Sociology* 30(August):222–42.

———. 2007. "Redrawing the Color Line?" *City and Community* 6(1):49–62.

Lee, Richard B. 1984. *The Dobe!Kung*. New York: Holt, Rinehart & Winston.

Lee, Richard Wayne. 1992. "Christianity and the Other Religions: Interreligious Relations in a Shrinking World." *Sociological Analysis* (Summer):125–39.

Lee, Seh-Ahn. 1991. "Family Structure Effects on Student Outcomes." In *Resources and Actions: Parents, Their Children, and Schools*. Washington, DC: National Science Foundation and National Center for Educational Statistics.

Lee, Sharon M. and Barry Edmonston. 2005. "New Marriages, New Families: U.S. Racial and Hispanic Intermarriage." *Population Bulletin* 60(2). Retrieved August 7, 2008 (http://www.prb.org/pdf05/60.2NewMarriages.pdf).

Leeder, Elaine J. 2004. *The Family in Global Perspective: A Gendered Journey*. Thousand Oaks, CA: Sage.

Legters, Nettie E. 2001. "Teachers as Workers in the World System." Pp. 417–26 in *Schools and Society: A Sociological Approach to Education*, edited by Jeanne H. Ballantine and Joan Z. Spade. Belmont, CA: Wadsworth.

Lehman, Edward C., Jr. 1980. "Patterns of Lay Resistance to Women in Ministry." *Sociological Analysis* 41(4):317–38.

———. 1981. "Organizational Resistance to Women in Ministry." *Sociological Analysis* 42(2):101–18.

———. 1985. *Women Clergy: Breaking Through Gender Barriers*. New Brunswick, NJ: Transaction.

Lehne, Gregory K. 1995. "Homophobia Among Men: Supporting and Defining the Male Role." Pp. 325–36 in *Men's Lives*, 3rd ed., edited by Michael Kimmel and Michael Messner. Boston: Allyn & Bacon.

LeMay, Michael L. 2000. *The Perennial Struggle: Race, Ethnicity, and Minority Group Politics in the United States*. Upper Saddle River, NJ: Prentice Hall.

Lemert, Edwin M. 1951. *Social Pathology*. New York: McGraw-Hill.

———.1972. *Human Deviance, Social Problems, and Social Control*, 2nd ed. Englewood Cliffs, NJ: Prentice Hall.

Lemkau, Jeanne Parr. 2006. "Fences, Volcanoes, and Embargoes." Unpublished Manuscript.

Lemkin, Raphael. 1933. "Akte der Barbarei und des Vandalismus als *delicta juris gentium*" (Acts of Barbarism and Vandalism under the Law of Nations). *Anwaltsblatt Internationales* 19(6):117–19.

Lengermann, Patricia M. and Jill Niebrugge-Brantley. 1990. "Feminist Sociological Theory: The Near-Future Prospects." Pp. 316–44 in *Frontiers of Social Theory: The New Synthesis*, edited by George Ritzer. New York: Columbia University Press.

Lenski, Gerhard E. 1966. *Human Societies*. New York: McGraw-Hill.

Lerner, Richard M. 1992. "Sociobiology and Human Development: Arguments and Evidence." *Human Development* 35(1): 12–51.

Lesko, Nancy. 2001. *Act Your Age*. London: Routledge/Taylor and Francis.

Leslie, Gerald R. and Sheila K. Korman. 1989. *The Family in Social Context*, 7th ed. New York: Oxford University Press.

Leung, K., S. Lau, and W. L. Lam. 1998. *Parenting Styles and Academic Achievement: A Cross-Cultural Study*. Detroit, MI: Wayne State University Press.

Levin, Jack and Jack McDevitt. 2003. *Hate Crimes Revisited: America's War on Those Who Are Different*. Boulder, CO: Westview.

Levine, Leslie. 2004. *If You Tame Me: Understanding Our Connection with Animals*. Philadelphia: Temple University Press.

Levine, Michael H. 2005. "Take a Giant Step: Investing in Preschool Education in Emerging Nations." *Phi Delta Kappan* (November):196–200.

Levine, Robert, Suguru Sato, Tsukasa Hashimoto, and Jyoti Verma. 1995. "Love and Marriage in Eleven Cultures." *Journal of Cross-Cultural Psychology* 26(5):554–71.

Levinson, Arnold R. 1993. "Outcomes Assessment." *National Law Journal* 16(6):S8.

Levitt, Peggy. 2001. *The Transnational Villagers*. Berkeley: University of California Press.

Levy, Howard S. 1990. *Chinese Footbinding: The History of a Curious Erotic Custom*. Taipei, Taiwan: SMC.

Levy, Howard S., Arthur Waley, and Wolfram Eberhard. 1992. *The Lotus Lovers: The Complete History of the Curious Erotic Custom of Footbinding in China*. New York: Prometheus.

Lewin, Tamar. 2006. "At Colleges, Women Are Leaving Men in the Dust." *The New York Times* (July 9):A1, 18.

Lewis, Oscar. 1961. *The Children of Sánchez: Autobiography of a Mexican Family*. New York: Random House.

———. 1986. *La Vida: A Puerto Rican Family in the Culture of Poverty*. New York: Irvington.

Lieberson, Stanley. 1980. *A Piece of the Pie: Blacks and White Immigrants Since 1880*. Berkeley: University of California Press.

Lieberson, Stanley, Susan Dumais, and Shyon Bauman. 2000. "The Instability of Androgynous Names: The Symbolic Maintenance of Gender Boundaries." *American Journal of Sociology* 105(5):1249–87.

Lin, BoQi, Richard Peto, Zheng-Ming Chen, Jillian Boreham, Ya-Ping Wu, Jun-Yao Li, T. Colin Campbell, and Jun-Shi Chen. 1998. "Emerging Tobacco Hazards in China: Retrospective Proportional Mortality Study of One Million Deaths." *British Medical Journal* 317(7170):1411–22.

Lincoln, Erik and Laurence Mamiya. 1990. *The Black Church in the African American Experience*. Durham, NC: Duke University Press.

Lindberg, Richard and Vesna Markovic. n.d. "Organized Crime Outlook in the New Russia: Russia Is Paying the Price of a Market Economy in Blood." Retrieved January 4, 2001 (www.search-international.com/Articles/crime/russiacrime.htm).

Lindsay, James M. 2006. "Global Warming Heats Up." Pp. 307–313 in *Globalization: The Transformation of Social Worlds*, edited by D. Stanley Eitzen and Maxine Baca Zinn. Belmont, CA: Wadsworth.

Lindsey, Linda L. 2005. *Gender Roles: A Sociological Perspective*, 4th ed. Englewood Cliffs, NJ: Prentice Hall.

Linton, Ralph. 1937. *The Study of Man*. New York: D. Appleton-Century.

Lips, Hilary M. 1991. *Women, Men, and Power*. Mountain View, CA: Mayfield.

———. 2005. *Sex and Gender: An Introduction*, 5th ed. Boston: McGraw-Hill.

Lipset, Seymour Martin. 1959. *Political Man*. New York: Doubleday.

———. 1963. "The Value Patterns of Democracy: A Case Study on Comparative Analysis." *American Sociological Review* 28(August):515–31.

———. 1993. "Racial and Ethnic Conflicts: A Global Perspective." *Political Science Quarterly* 107:585–606.

Lipset, Seymour Martin and Stein Rokkan. 1967. *Party Systems and Voter Alignments: Cross-National Perspectives*. New York: Free Press.

Liska, Allen E. 1999. *Perspectives in Deviance*, 3rd ed. Englewood Cliffs, NJ: Prentice Hall.

Lofland, John and Norman Skonovd. 1981. "Conversion Motifs." *Journal for the Scientific Study of Religion* 20(4):373–85.

Logan, John and Harvey Molotch. 1987. *Urban Fortunes: The Political Economy of Place*. Berkeley: University of California Press.

Logan, John R. and Glenna D. Spitze. 1994. "Family Neighbors." *American Journal of Sociology* 100(2):453–76.

Longman, Timothy. 2005. "Rwanda: Achieving Equality or Serving an Authoritarian State?" In *Women in African Parliaments*, edited by Gretchen Bauer and Hannah Britton. Boulder, CO: Lynne Reinner.

Lopez, Ian F. Haney. 1996. *White by Law*. New York: New York University Press.

Lopez-Garza, Marta. 2002. "Convergence of the Public and Private Spheres: Women in the Informal Economy." *Race, Gender, and Class* 9(3):175–92.

Lorber, Judith. 1998. "Reinventing the Sexes: The Biomedical Construction of Femininity and Masculinity." *Contemporary Society* 27(5):498–99.

Lorber, Judith and Lisa Jean Moore. 2007. *Gendered Bodies.* Los Angeles, CA: Roxbury.

Los Angeles Times. 2008. "Kenyans Recall the Screams of the Dying in Burning Church" (January 3). Retrieved June 3, 2008 (http://articles.latimes.com/2008/jan/03/world/fg- church3).

Lubeck, Sally. 1985. *Sandbox Society: Early Education in Black and White America.* London: Falmer.

Luby, Dianne. 2007. "Getting Real with Sex Education." *Boston Globe* (December 27). Retrieved March 17, 2008 (www.boston.com/bostonglobe/editorial_opinion/oped/articles/2007/12/27/getting_).

Lucas, Samuel R. 1999. *Tracking Inequality: Stratification and Mobility in American High Schools.* New York: Teachers College Press.

Lucas, Samuel R. and Mark Berends. 2002. "Sociodemographic Diversity, Correlated Achievement, and De Facto Tracking." *Sociology of Education* 75(4):328–48.

Luhman, Reid and Stuart Gilman. 1980. *Race and Ethnic Relations: The Social and Political Experience of Minority Groups.* Belmont, CA: Wadsworth.

Lumsden, Charles J. and Edward O. Wilson. 1981. *Genes, Mind, and Culture: The Coevolutionary Process.* Cambridge, MA: Harvard University Press.

Lundt, John C. 2004. "Learning for Ourselves: A New Paradigm for Education." *The Futurist* (November-December):22.

Lupton, Deborah. 2001. "Medicine and Health Care in Australia." Pp. 429–40 in *The Blackwell Companion to Medical Sociology*, edited by William C. Cockerham. Malden, MA: Blackwell.

Macaulay, David. 1978. *Underground.* Boston: Houghton Mifflin.

MacDougal, Gary. 2005. *Make a Difference: A Spectacular Breakthrough in the Fight Against Poverty.* New York: St. Martin's Press.

MacFarlane, Ann G. 1994. "Racial Education Values." *America* 17(9):10–12.

Macionis, John. 2007. *Sociology,* 11th ed. Upper Saddle River, NJ: Prentice Hall.

Mackey, Richard A. and Bernard A. O'Brien. 1995. *Lasting Marriages: Men and Women Growing Together.* Westport, CT: Praeger.

MacLeod, Jay. 1995. *Ain't No Makin' It: Aspirations and Attainment in a Low-Income Neighborhood.* Boulder, CO: Westview.

Made in Mexico, Inc. 2005. "What Are Maquiladoras? The Maquiladora Industry." Retrieved March 7, 2008 (www.madeinmexicoinc.com/maquiladoras_industry.htm).

Makhmalbaf, Mohsen, producer. 2003. *Kandahar: The Sun behind the Moon* (Film).

Malthus, Thomas R. [1798] 1926. *First Essay on Population 1798.* London: Macmillan.

Mann, Michael. 1993. *Sources of Social Power,* Vol. II. Cambridge: Cambridge University Press.

Manning, Wendy D. and Pamela J. Smock. 1995. "Why Marry? Race and the Transition to Marriage Among Cohabitors." *Demography* 32(4):509–20.

Manza, Jeff, Michael Hout, and Clem Brooks. 1995. "Class Voting in Democratic Capitalist Societies Since World War II: Dealignment, Realignment, or Trendless Fluctuation?" *Annual Review of Sociology* 21:137–63.

Marcus, Richard R. 2008. "Kenya's Conflict Isn't 'Tribal.'" *Los Angles Times* (January 24). Retrieved June 3, 2008 (www.latimes.com/news/opinion/la-oew-marcus24jan24,0,4231203.story).

Marger, Martin N. 2006. *Race and Ethnic Relations: American and Global Perspectives,* 7th ed. Belmont, CA: Wadsworth.

Marks, Alexandra. 2008 "For Election 08, Youth Voter Turnout Swells." *Christian Science Monitor* (January 16):1

Marmor, Theodore R. 1999. *The Politics of Medicare,* 2nd ed. Hawthorne, NY: Aldine de Gruyter.

Marsden, Peter V. 1987, February. "Core Discussion Networks of Americans." *American Sociological Review*:122–31.

Martin, Patricia Yancey and Robert A. Hummer. 1989. "Fraternities and Rape on Campus." *Gender and Society* 3(4):457–73.

Marty, Martin E. 1983. "Religion in America Since Mid-Century." Pp. 273–87 in *Religion and America*, edited by Mary Douglas and Stephen Tipton. Boston: Beacon.

———. 2001. "The Logic of Fundamentalism." *Boston College Magazine* (Fall):44–46.

Marty, Martin E. and R. Scott Appleby, eds. 1991. *Fundamentalism Observed.* Chicago: University of Chicago Press.

———. 1992. *The Glory and the Power: The Fundamentalist Challenge to the Modern Age.* Boston: Beacon.

———. 2004. *Accounting for Fundamentalism: The Dynamic Character of Movements.* Chicago: University of Chicago Press.

Marx, Karl. [1844] 1963. "Contribution to the Critique of Hegel's Philosophy of Right." Pp. 43–59 in *Karl Marx: Early Writings,* translated and edited by T. B. Bottomore. New York: McGraw-Hill.

———. [1844] 1964. *The Economic and Philosophical Manuscripts of 1844.* New York: International Publishers.

———. 1963. *Early Writings,* translated by Thomas B. Bottomore. New York: McGraw-Hill

Marx, Karl and Friedrich Engels. 1955. *Selected Work in Two Volumes.* Moscow: Foreign Language Publishing House.

———. [1848] 1969. *The Communist Manifesto.* Baltimore: Penguin.

Mashberg, Tom. 2002. "Med Examiner's Office Has Secret Body-Parts Deal." *Boston Herald* (May 20):1.

Mason-Schrock, Douglas. 1996. "Transsexual's Narrative Construction of the 'True Self.'" *Social Psychology Quarterly* 59(3):176–92.

Massey, Douglas S. 2007. *Categorically Unequal: The American Stratification System.* New York: Russell Sage Foundation.

Massey, Douglas S. and Nancy A. Denton. 1998. *American Apartheid: Segregation and the Making of the Underclass.* Cambridge, MA: Harvard University Press.

Masters, William H. and Virginia Johnson. 1966. *Human Sexual Response.* Boston: Little, Brown.

———. 1970. *Human Sexual Inadequacy.* Boston: Little, Brown.

Mauksch, Hans. 1993. "Teaching of Applied Sociology: Opportunities and Obstacles." Pp. 1–7 in *Teaching Applied Sociology: A Resource Book,* edited by C. Howery. Washington, DC: American Sociological Association Teaching Resources Center.

Mauss, Armand. 1975. *Social Problems as Social Movements.* Philadelphia: Lippincott.

Mayo Clinic. 2007. "Domestic Violence Toward Women: Recognize the Patterns and Seek Help." Retrieved August 7, 2008 (http://www.mayoclinic.com/health/domestic-violence/WO00044).

Mayoux, Linda. 2002. "Women's Empowerment or Feminisation of Debt? Towards a New Agenda in African Microfinance." Report at the One World Action Conference in London, March 21–22.

———, ed. 2008. *Sustainable Learning for Women's Empowerment: Ways Forward in Micro-Finance.* UK: ITDG Publishing.

McAdam, Doug. 1999. *Political Process and the Development of Black Insurgency, 1930–1970,* 2nd ed. Chicago: University of Chicago Press.

McCaghy, Charles H., Timothy A. Capron, J. D. Jamieson, and Sandra Harley Carey. 2006. *Deviant Behavior: Crime, Conflict, and Interest Groups,* 7th ed. Boston: Allyn & Bacon.

McCarthy, John D. and Mayer N. Zald. 1977. "Resource Mobilization and Social Movements: A Partial Theory." *American Journal of Sociology* 82(6):1212–41.

McConnell, E. D. and E. Delgado-Romero. 2004. "Latinos, Panethnicity, and Census 2000: Reality or Methodological Construction." Retrieved February 24, 2008 (www.allacademic.com/meta/p109991_index.html).

McCormick, John. 1992. "A Housing Program That Actually Works." *Newsweek* (June 22):61.

McCrone, David. 1998. *The Sociology of Nationalism*. London: Routledge.

McEneaney, Elizabeth H. and John W. Meyer. 2000. "The Content of the Curriculum: An Institutionalist Perspective." Pp. 189–211 in *Handbook of the Sociology of Education*, edited by Maureen T. Hallinan. New York: Kluwer Academic/Plenum.

McEvoy, Alan W. 1990. "Confronting Gangs." *School Intervention Report* (Learning Publications) 3/4 (February/March): 1–20.

McEvoy, Alan W. and Jeff B. Brookings. 2008. *If She Is Raped: A Guidebook for the Men in Her Life*, 4th ed., abridged. Tampa, FL: Teal Ribbon Books.

McGuire, Meredith. 2002. *Religion: The Social Context,* 5th ed. Belmont, CA: Wadsworth.

McIntosh, Peggy. 1992. "White Privilege and Male Privilege: A Personal Account of Coming to See Correspondences Through Work in Women's Studies." Pp. 70–81 in *Race, Class, and Gender: An Anthology*, edited by Margaret L. Anderson and Patricia Hill Collins. Belmont, CA: Wadsworth.

———.2002. "White Privilege: Unpacking the Invisible Knapsack." Pp. 97–101 in *White Privilege: Essential Readings on the Other Side of Racism*, edited by Paula S. Rothenberg. New York: Worth.

McKelvie, Samuel R. 1926. "What the Movies Meant to the Farmer." *Annals of the American Academy of Political and Social Science* 128(November):131.

McKinlay, John B. and L. D. Marceau. 1998. "The End of the Golden Age of Doctoring." Presented at the American Public Health Association, November, Washington, DC.

McLemore, S. Dale, Harriett Romo, and Susan Gonzalez Baker. 2001. *Racial and Ethnic Relations in America,* 6th ed. Boston: Allyn & Bacon.

McLeod, Jay. 2004. *Ain't No Makin' It: Aspirations and Attainment in a Low-Income Neighborhood,* 2nd ed. Boulder, CO: Westview.

McLuhan, Marshall, and Bruce R. Powers. 1992. *The Global Village: Transformations in World Life and Media in the 21st Century*. New York: Oxford University Press.

McManus, Patricia A. and Thomas A DiPrete. 2001. "Losers and Winners: The Financial Consequences of Separation and Divorce for Men." *American Sociological Review* 66(April):246–68.

McNall, Scott G. and Sally Allen McNall. 1983. *Plains Families: Exploring Sociology Through Social History*. New York: St. Martin's.

McNeal, Ralph B. 1995. "Extracurricular Activities and High School Dropouts." *Sociology of Education* 68(January):62–81.

McNeil, John J. 1993. *The Church and the Homosexual*, 4th ed. Boston: Beacon.

McTaggart, R. 1997. *Participatory Action Research: International Contexts and Consequences*. Albany: SUNY Press.

Mead, George Herbert. [1934] 1962. *Mind, Self, and Society*. Chicago: University of Chicago Press.

Mead, Margaret. [1935] 1963. *Sex and Temperament in Three Primitive Societies*. New York: William Morrow.

———. 1973. *Coming of Age in Samoa*. New York: Morrow Quill.

Mehan, Hugh. 1992. "Understanding Inequality in Schools: The Contribution of Interpretive Studies." *Sociology of Education* 65(1):1–20.

Mehra, Bharat, Cecelia Merkel, and Ann P. Bishop. 2004. "The Internet for Empowerment of Minority and Marginalized Users." *New Media and Society* 6:781–802.

Melton, J. Gordon. 1992. *Encyclopedic Handbook of Cults in America,* Revised and Updated Edition. London: Routledge.

Meltzer, B. 1978. "Mead's Social Psychology." Pp. 15–27 in *Symbolic Interactionism: A Reader in Social Psychology*, 3rd ed., edited by J. Manis and B. Meltzer. Boston: Allyn & Bacon.

Meltzer, Bernard N., John W. Petras, and Larry T. Reynolds. 1975. *Symbolic Interactionism: Genesis, Varieties and Criticism*. London: Routledge and Kegan Paul.

Meltzer, Jack. 1999. *Metropolis to Metroplex: The Social and Spatial Planning of Cities*. Baltimore: Johns Hopkins University Press.

Merrill Lynch and Capgemini. 2007. "World Wealth Report 2007." Retrieved July 7, 2008 (http://www.ml.com/media/79882.pdf).

Merton, Robert K. 1938. "Social Structure and Anomie." *American Sociological Review* 3(October):672–82.

———.1949. "Discrimination and the American Creed." Pp. 99–126 in *Discrimination and National Welfare*, edited by Robert M. MacIver. New York: Harper.

———. 1968a. "Social Structure and Anomie." *American Sociological Review* 3(October):672–82.

———. 1968b. *Social Theory and Social Structure,* 2nd ed. New York: The Free Press.

Metropolitan Community Churches. 2008. "Churches." Retrieved March 1, 2008 (http://www.mcchurch.org/AM/Template.cfm?Section=Find_an_MCC).

Metz, Mary Haywood. 1986. *Different by Design: The Context and Character of Three Magnet Schools*. New York: Routledge & Kegan Paul.

Meyer, John W., David Kamens, Aaron Benavot, Yun-Kyung Cha, and Suk-Ying Wong. 1992. *School Knowledge for the Masses: World Models and National Primary Curriculum Categories in the Twentieth Century*. London: Falmer.

Meyer, Madonna H. and Eliza K. Pavalko. 1996. "Family, Work, and Access to Health Insurance among Mature Women." *Journal of Health and Social Behavior* 37(4):311–25.

Meyer, R. 1996. "The Disease Called Addiction: Emerging Evidence in a Two Hundred Year Debate." *The Lancet* 347(8995):162–66.

Michels, Robert. [1911] 1967. *Political Parties*. New York: The Free Press.

Mickelson, Roslyn Arlin. 1990. "The Attitude-Achievement Paradox Among Black Adolescents." *Sociology of Education* 63(January):44–61.

Mike, Valerie. 2003. "Evidence and the Future of Medicine." *Evaluation and the Health Professions* 26(2):127–52.

Milgram, Stanley. 1967. "The Small World Problem." *Psychology Today* 1:61–67.

Miller, Donald E. 1997. *Reinventing American Protestantism*. Berkeley: University of California Press.

"Millions Vulnerable to Famine in Africa." 2006. *Popline* 29(March/April):1–2.

Mills, C. Wright. 1956. *The Power Elite*. New York: Oxford University Press.

———.1959. *The Sociological Imagination*. New York: Oxford University Press.

Mills, Robert J. 2001. "Health Insurance Coverage 2000." *Current Populations Reports*. Washington, DC: U.S. Census Bureau.

Mills, Theodore M. 1984. *The Sociology of Small Groups,* 2nd ed. Englewood Cliffs, NJ: Prentice Hall.

Mincy, Ronald B. 2006. *Black Males Left Behind*. Washington, DC: The Urban Institute Press.

Miniwatts Marketing Group. 2008. "Internet World Stats." Retrieved July 7, 2008 (http://www.internetworldstats.com/stats.htm).

Minkoff, Debra C. 1995. *Organizing for Equality*. New Brunswick, NJ: Rutgers University Press.

Mintz, Morton and Harry Cohen. 1971. *America, Inc*. New York: Dial Presses.

Misztal, Bronislaw and Anson D. Shupe. 1998. *Fundamentalism and Globalization: Fundamentalist Movements at the Twilight of the Twentieth Century*. Westport, CT: Praeger.

Moffett, Sebastian. 2003. "Going Gray: For Ailing Japan, Longevity Begins to Take Its Toll." *The Wall Street Journal* (February 11): A1, 12.

Mohanty, Chandra Talpade. 1988. "Under Western Eyes: Feminist Scholarship and Colonial Discourses." *Feminist Review* 30 (Autumn):61–88.

Molotch, Harvey. 2003. *Where Stuff Comes From: How Toasters, Toilets, Cars, Computers, and Many Other Things Come to Be as They Are*. London: Routledge.

Moore, Laurence. 1995. *Selling God: American Religion in the Marketplace of Culture.* New York: Oxford University Press.

Moore, Valerie Ann. 2001. "Doing Racialized and Gendered Age to Organize Peer Relations: Observing Kids in Summer Camp." *Gender and Society* 15(6):835–58.

Morbidity and Mortality Weekly Report. 1999. "Ten Great Public Health Achievements—United States, 1900–1999." *Journal of the American Medical Association* 281(16):1481–84.

Morgan, Kenneth O. 1981. *Rebirth of a Nation: Wales, 1880–1980.* Oxford, UK: University of Oxford Press.

Morgan, Stephen L. 2001. "Counterfactuals, Causal Effect Heterogeneity, and the Catholic School Effect on Learning." *Sociology of Education* 74(4):341–73.

Moritz, Owen. 2001. "Trafficking in Humans Is Thriving Business in Africa." *New York Daily News* (April 17):4.

Morris, Edward W. 2005. "From 'Middle Class' to 'Trailer Trash': Teachers' Perceptions of White Students in a Predominately Minority School." *Sociology of Education* 78(2):99–121.

Morris, Lloyd R. 1949. *Not So Long Ago.* New York: Random House.

Morrison, J. Ian. 2000. *Health Care in the New Millennium.* San Francisco: Jossey-Bass.

Mother Jones. 2007. "Aftermath: Long-Term Thinking." (www.motherjones.com/news/features/2007/03/aftermath.html) Retrieved April 16, 2008.

Mulkey, Lynn M., Robert L. Crain, and Alexander J. C. Harrington. 1992. "One-Parent Households and Achievement: Economic and Behavioral Explanations of a Small Effect." *Sociology of Education* 65(January):48–65.

Mulligan, Susan. 2008 "Young People Make Voices Heard in Iowa." *The Boston Globe* (January 5):A9.

Mumford, Lewis. 1961. *The City in History: Its Origins, Transformations, and Prospects.* New York: Harcourt, Brace, and World.

Murphy, Cullen. 1993. "Women and the Bible." *Atlantic Monthly* 272(2):39–64.

Murstein, Bernard I. 1987. "A Clarification and Extension of the SVR Theory of Dyadic Pairing." *Journal of Marriage and the Family* 49(November):929–33.

Mutamba, John. 2005. "Strategies for Increasing Women's Participation in Government." Expert Group Meeting on Democratic Governance in Africa, Nairobi, Kenya, December 6–8.

Mydans, Seth. 2002. "In Pakistan, Rape Victims Are the 'Criminals.'" *The New York Times* (May 17):A3.

Myers, John P. 2003. *Dominant-Minority Relations in America: Linking Personal History With the Convergence in the New World.* Boston: Allyn & Bacon.

Myrdal, Gunnar. 1964. *An American Dilemma.* New York: McGraw-Hill.

Nagel, Joane. 1994. "Constructing Ethnicity: Creating and Recreating Ethnic Identity and Culture." *Social Problems* 41(1):152–176.

Nakamura, Lisa. 2004. "Interrogating the Digital Divide: The Political Economy of Race and Commerce in the New Media." Pp. 71–83 in *Society On-Line: The Internet in Context,* edited by Philip N. Howard and Steve Jones. Thousand Oaks, CA: Sage.

Nanda, Serena and Richard L. Warms. 2007. *Cultural Anthropology,* 9th ed. Belmont, CA: Wadsworth.

Nardi, Peter M., ed. 1992. *Men's Friendships.* Newbury Park, CA: Sage.

National Archives and Records Administration. 2008. "What Is the Electoral College?" Retrieved March 21, 2008 (http://www.archives.gov/federal-register/electoral-college/about.html).

National Center for Education Statistics. 2000. *Distribution of Undergraduate Enrollment Among Students Aged 24 or Younger, by Race/Ethnicity, Gender, and Income.* Washington, DC: U.S. Department of Education. Retrieved August 26, 2006 (nces.ed.gov/fastfacts/dailyarchive.asp?StatCat).

———. 2002. *Digest of Education Statistics 2002.* Table 207. Washington, DC: U.S. Department of Education.

———. 2004. "Trends in Educational Equity of Girls and Women: 2004" (November). Retrieved August 25, 2006 (http://nces.ed.gov/pubsearch/pubsinfo.asp?pubid=2005016).

———. 2005a. *The Condition of Education.* Washington, DC: U.S. Department of Education.

———. 2005b. *Digest of Education Statistics Tables and Figures 2005.* Washington, DC: U.S. Department of Education.

———. 2006a. "A First Look at the Literacy of America's Adults in the 21st Century: National Assessment of Adult Literacy (NAAL)" (U.S. Department of Education). Retrieved April 1, 2008 (http://nces.ed.gov/naal/).

———. 2006b. 2004 Integrated Postsecondary Education Data System (IPEDS), previously unpublished tabulation.

National Center for Health Statistics. 2002a. *Health: United States 2002.* Washington, DC: Government Printing Office.

———. 2002b. "Physician Visits Increase for Older Patients" (News Release). Retrieved August 26, 2006. (www.cdc.gov/nchs/releases/01news/olderpat.htm).

———. 2005. *Health: United States, 2005.* Washington, DC: U.S. Government Printing Office.

———. 2007. *Health, United States, 2007: With Chartbook on Trends in the Health of Americans.* Hyattsville, MD: Author. Retrieved August 16, 2008 (http://www.cdc.gov/nchs/data/hus/hus07.pdf).

National Center for Policy Analysis. 2001. "Crime and Gun Control." Retrieved August 4, 2006 (http://www.ncpa.org/pi/crime/pd042501e.html), (http://www.ncpa.org/iss/cri/2002/pd060302c.html).

National Coalition on Health Care. 2008. "Health Insurance Cost." Retrieved April 3, 2008 (http://www.nchc.org/facts/cost.shtml).

National Conference of State Legislatures. 2007. "2007 Enacted State Legislation Related to Immigrants and Immigration." Retrieved April 9, 2008 (www.ncsl.org/programs/immig/2007Immigration831.htm).

National Institutes of Health. 2007. "The Use of Complementary and Alternative Medicine in the United States." Retrieved April 4, 2008 (http://nccam.nih.gov/news/camsurvey_fs1.htm).

National Labor Committee. 2002. "School Uniforms Made in El Salvador: The Case of Elder Manufacturing." Retrieved April 4, 2008 (www.nlcnet.org/campaigns/uniforms/elsalvador/report.shtml).

National Parent Information Network. 2000, May-June. "Kids and Media at the New Millennium." *Parents News.*

National Postsecondary Education Cooperative. 2004. *How Does Technology Affect Access in Postsecondary Education? What Do We Really Know?* (NPEC 2004–831). Washington, DC: Author.

National Public Radio. "Poppy Growing in Afghanistan." *Morning Edition,* February 9, 2008.

National Science Foundation. 2005. *Children, TV, Computers and More Media: New Research Shows Pluses, Minuses.* Retrieved July 20, 2006 (http://www.eurekalert.org/pub_releases/2005–02/nsf-ctc021005.php).

National Urban League. 2006. *The State of Black America.* New York: Author.

National Vital Statistics Report. 2001. *Infant Mortality Rates by Race: United States, 1940–1999* 69(8).

Navarro, Vicente.1996. "Why Congress Did Not Enact Health Reform." *Journal of Health Politics, Policy and Law* 20:455–62.

Neuman, Michelle J. 2005. "Global Early Care and Education: Challenges, Responses, and Lessons." *Phi Delta Kappan* (November):188–92.

Newman, Andy. 2008. "What Women Want (Maybe)." *The New York Times* (June 12):E6.

Newman, David M. and Liz Grauerholz. 2002. *Sociology of Families,* 2nd ed. Thousand Oaks, CA: Pine Forge.

Newport, Frank. 2004. "A Look at Americans and Religion Today." Retrieved July 7, 2006 (http://speakingoffaith.publicradio.org/programs/godsofbusiness/galluppoll.shtml).

———.2006. "Mormons, Evangelical Protestants, Baptists Top Church Attendance List" (Gallup Poll). Retrieved April 14, 2006 (http://brain.gallup.com/content/?ci=22414).

News of Future. 2007. "Future News in Technology." Retrieved January 14, 2008 (www.newsoffuture.com/technology).

New York Times. 2008. "Primary Calendar: Democratic Nominating Contests." Retrieved March 30, 2008 (http://politics.nytimes.com/election-guide/2008/primaries/democraticprimaries/index.html).

Nguyen, Nathalie Huynh Chau. 2005. "Eurasian/Amerasian Perspectives: Kim Lefevre's *Metisse blanche,* and Kien Nguyen's *The Unwanted.*" *Asian Studies Review* 29(June):107–22.

Niebuhr, H. Richard. 1929. *The Social Sources of Denominationalism.* New York: Henry Holt.

———. 1932. *Moral Man and Immoral Society.* New York: Scribner.

Nightingale Alliance. 2007. "Fast Facts." Retrieved January 20, 2008 (www.nightingalealliance.org/cgi-bin/home.pl?section=3).

Nock, Steven L. 1999. "The Problem with Marriage." *Society* 36(5):20–27.

Nock, Steven L., James D. Wright, and Laura Sanchez. 1999. "America's Divorce Problem." *Society* 36(4):43–52.

Noel, Donald. 1968. "A Theory of the Origin of Ethnic Stratification." *Social Problems* 16(Fall):157–72.

Noguera, Pedro A. 1996. "Preventing and Producing Violence: A Critical Analysis of Responses to School Violence." *Sociology of Education* 56(3):189–212.

———. 2004. "Social Capital and the Education of Immigrant Students: Categories and Generalizations." *Sociology of Education* 77(2):180–84.

Noguera, Pedro and Robby Cohen. 2006. "Patriotism and Accountability: The Role of Educators in the War on Terrorism." *Phi Delta Kappan* 87(8):573–78.

Nolan, Cathal J. 2002. "Terrorism." Pp. 1648–49 and "War" in *The Greenwood Encyclopedia of International Relations.* London: Greenwood.

Nolan, Patrick and Gerhard Lenski. 2008. *Human Societies.* Boulder, CO: Paradigm.

Noss, David S. and John B. Noss. 1990. *A History of the World's Religions.* New York: Macmillan.

The Nuclear Information Project. 2008. "Status of World Nuclear Forces." Retrieved April 16, 2008 (www.nukestrat.com/nukestatus.htm).

Nyden, Philip W. 1984. *Steelworkers Rank and File: The Political Economy of a Union Reform Movement.* New York: Praeger.

Oakes, Jeannie. 1985. *Keeping Track: How High Schools Structure Inequality.* New Haven, CT: Yale University Press.

———. 1990. *Multiplying Inequalities: The Effects of Race, Social Class, and Tracking on Opportunities to Learn Mathematics and Science.* Santa Monica, CA: The Rand Corporation.

Oakes, Jeannie, Amy Stuart Wells, Makeba Jones, and Amanda Datnow. 1997. "Detracking: The Social Construction of Ability, Cultural Politics, and Resistance to Reform." *Teacher's College Record* 98(3):482–510.

Oberlander, Jonathan. 2002. "The U.S. Health Care System: On a Road to Nowhere?" *Canadian Medical Association Journal* 167(2):163–69.

O'Brien, Denise. 1977. "Female Husbands in Southern Bantu Societies." In *Sexual Stratification: A Cross-Cultural View,* edited by Alice Schlegel. New York: Columbia University Press.

O'Brien, Jody. 2006. *The Production of Reality,* 4th ed. Thousand Oaks, CA: Pine Forge.

O'Brien, Patrick K., ed. 1999. *Atlas of World History.* New York: Oxford University Press.

"O Come All Ye Faithful: Special Report on Religion and Public Life." 2007. *The Economist* (November 3):6.

O'Connel, Sanjida. 1993 "Meet My Two Husbands." *Guardian* (March 4, Sec. 2):12.

Ogbu, John U. 1998. "Understanding Cultural Diversity and Learning." *Educational Researcher* 21(8):5–14.

Ogburn, William F. 1933. *Recent Social Trends.* New York: McGraw-Hill.

———.[1922] 1938. *Social Change, with Respect to Culture and Original Nature.* New York: Viking.

———. 1950. *Social Change.* New York: Viking.

———. 1961. "The Hypothesis of Cultural Lag." Pp. 1270–73 in *Theories of Society: Foundations of Modern Sociological Theory,* Vol. 2, edited by Talcott Parsons, Edward Shils, Kaspar D. Naegele, and Jesse R. Pitts. New York: The Free Press.

———. 1964. *On Culture and Social Change: Selected Papers,* edited by Otis Dudley Duncan. Chicago: University of Chicago Press.

Olin, Susan Moller. 1996. "Families and Feminist Theory: Some Past and Present Issues." Pp. 13–26 in *Feminism and Families,* edited by Hilde Lindemann Nelson. New York: Routledge.

Oliver, Arnold. 2003 "Iran and the Forgotten Anniversary." *Foreign Policy in Focus* (August 29).

Oller, Kimbrough. 2006. "Development and Evolution in Human Vocal Communication." *Biological Theory* 1(4):349–51.

Olsen, Marvin E. 1968. *The Process of Social Organization.* New York: Holt, Rinehart, and Winston.

———.1970. "Power as a Social Process." Pp. 2–10 in *Power in Societies,* edited by Marvin Olsen. New York: Macmillan.

Olson, C. L., H. D. Schumaker, and B. P. Yawn. 1994. "Overweight Women Delay Medical Care." *Archives of Family Medicine* 3(10).

Olsson, Sven E. 1990. *Social Policy and the Welfare State in Sweden.* Stockholm: Swedish Institute for Social Research.

Omi, Michael and Howard Winant. 1989. *Racial Formation in the United States: From the 1960s to the 1980s.* New York: Routledge.

"Omiai and Miai-gekkon, Arranged Marriages in Japan." Hanami Web 2007. Retrieved November 2007 (www.hanamiweb.com/omiai.html).

Ontario Consultants on Religious Tolerance. 2004. "'Fundamentalism' in Christianity and Islam." Retrieved July 5, 2008 (www.religioustolerance.org/reac_ter9.htm).

———. 2005. "Homsexuality and Bisexuality." Retrieved August 23, 2008 (http://www.religioustolerance.org/hom_mar6.htm).

———. 2008. "Prohibiting Same-Sex Marriages in the U.S.: Federal and State 'Doma' Legislation." Retrieved August 7, 2008 (http://www.religioustolerance.org/hom_mar6.htm).

Orfield, Gary, Mark D. Brachmeier, David R. James, and Tamela Eitle. 1997. "Deepening Segregation in American Public Schools." *Equity and Excellence in Education* 30(2):5–24.

Orum, Anthony M. 2001. *Introduction to Political Sociology,* 4th ed. Upper Saddle River, NJ: Prentice Hall.

Oswald, Ramona Faith. 2000. "A Member of the Wedding? Heterosexism and Family Ritual." *Journal of Social and Personal Relationships* 17(June):349–68.

———. 2001. "Religion, Family, and Ritual: The Production of Gay, Lesbian, and Transgendered Outsiders-Within." *Review of Religious Research* 43(December):39–50.

O'Toole, Tara and Donald A. Henderson. 2006. "A Clear and Present Danger: Confronting the Threat of Bioterrorism." Pp. 239–45 in *Globalization: The Transformation of Social Worlds,* edited by D. Stanley Eitzen and Maxine Baca Zinn. Belmont, CA: Wadsworth.

Ottenheimer, Martin. 1996. *Forbidden Relatives: The American Myth of Cousin Marriages.* Urbana: University of Illinois Press.

"Overseas Population Spending Threatened." 2006. *Popline* 29(March/April):1.

Page, Ann L. and Donald A. Clelland. 1978. "The Kanawha County Textbook Controversy: A Study of the Politics of Life Style Concern." *Social Forces* 57(September):265–81.

"A Painful Tradition." 1999. *Newsweek* (July 5):32–33.

Pan American Health Organization. 2000. *Physicians per 10,000 Inhabitants Ratio for Year 1999.* Washington, DC: Division of Health Systems and Services Development, Human Resources Development Program.

———. 2003. *Violence Against Women: The Health Sector Responds.* Washington, DC: Author.

Papalia, Diane E., Sally Wendkos Olds, and Ruth Duskin Feldman. 2006. *A Child's World: Infancy Through Adolescence,* 10th ed. Boston: McGraw-Hill.

Parenti, Michael. 2006. "Mass Media: For the Many, by the Few" Pp. 60–72 in *Beyond Borders: Thinking Critically about Global Issues,* edited by Paula S. Rothenberg. New York: Worth.

Pareto, Vilfredo. [1911] 1955. "Mathematical Economics." In *Encyclopedie des Sciences Mathematique.* New York: Macmillan.

Parish, Thomas S. and Joycelyn G. Parish. 1991. "The Effect of Family Configuration and Support System Failures during Childhood and Adolescence on College Students' Self-Concepts and Social Skills." *Adolescence* 26(102):441–47.

Park, Ken. 2006. *World Almanac and Book of Facts.* Mahway, NJ: World Almanac.

Park, Robert Ezra, Ernest W. Burgess, and Roderick D. McKenzie. [1925] 1967. *The City.* Chicago: University of Chicago Press.

Parkinson, C. Northcote. 1957. *Parkinson's Law.* Boston: Houghton Mifflin.

Parrillo, Vincent N. 2005. *Understanding Race and Ethnic Relations,* 2nd ed. Boston: Pearson Allyn and Bacon.

Parsons, Talcott. 1951a. *The Social System.* New York: The Free Press.

———. 1951b. *Toward a General Theory of Action.* New York: Harper & Row.

———. 1975. "The Sick Role and Role of the Physician Reconsidered." *Milbank Memorial Fund Quarterly* 53(3):257–78.

Parsons, Talcott and Robert F. Bales. 1953. *Family, Socialization, and Interaction Process.* Glencoe, IL: The Free Press.

Passeron, Jean Claude and Pierre Bourdieu. 1990. *Reproduction in Education, Society, and Culture,* 2nd ed. Newbury Park, CA: Sage.

Paulhus, D. L., P. D. Trapnell, and D. Chen. 1999. *Birth Order Effects on Personality and Achievement Within Families.* Malden, MA: Blackwell.

Paxton, Pamela and Melanie M. Hughes. 2007. *Women, Politics, and Power: A Global Perspective.* Thousand Oaks, CA: Pine Forge Press.

Pellow, David Naguib. 2002. *Garbage Wars: The Struggle for Environmental Justice in Chicago.* Cambridge, MA: MIT Press.

Pennington, Bill. 2006. "Small Colleges, Short of Men, Embrace Football." *The New York Times* (July 12):A1.

Pentikänen, Juha. 1999. *"Silent as Waters We Live": Old Believers in Russia and Abroad.* Helsinki, Finland: Finnish Literature Society.

Perrucci, Robert and Earl Wysong. 1999. *The New Class Society.* Lanham, MD: Rowman & Littlefield.

Persell, Caroline Hodges. 2005. "Race, Education, and Inequality." Pp. 286–24 in *Blackwell Companion to Social Inequalities,* edited by M. Romero and E. Margolis. Oxford, UK: Blackwell.

Persell, Caroline Hodges and Peter W. Cookson, Jr. 1985. "Chartering and Bartering: Elite Education and Social Reproduction." *Social Problems* 33(2):114–129.

Pescosolido, Bernice A. 1992. "Beyond Rational Choice: The Social Dynamics of How People Seek Help." *American Journal of Sociology* 97(4):1113.

Pescosolido, Bernice A. and Carol A. Boyer. 2001. "The American Health Care System: Entering the Twenty-first Century with High Risk, Major Challenges, and Great Opportunities." Pp. 180–98 in *The Blackwell Companion to Medical Sociology,* edited by William C. Cockerham. Malden, MA: Blackwell.

Pescosolido, Bernice A. and Sharon Georgianna. 1989. "Durkheim, Suicide, and Religion: Toward a Network Theory of Suicide," *American Sociological Review* 54(February):33–48.

Peters, William. [1972] 1987. *A Class Divided.* New York: Doubleday.

Petersen, Larry R. and Gregory V. Donnenwerth. 1998. "Religion and Declining Support for Religious Beliefs about Gender Roles and Homosexual Rights." *Sociology of Religion* 59(4):353–71.

Peterson, Richard R. 1996. "A Re-evaluation of the Economic Consequences of Divorce." *American Sociological Review* 61 (June):528–36.

Pew Forum on Religion and Public Life. 2008. "U.S. Religious Landscape Survey, 2008." Retrieved March 2, 2008 (http://religions.pewforum.org/pdf/report-religious-landscape-study-full.pdf).

Pew Internet and American Life Project. 2004. "Tracking Survey, February 3 to March 1, 2004." Retrieved January 9, 2008 (www.infoplease.com/ipa/A0921872.html).

———. 2007. "Home Broadband Adoption 2007." Retrieved July 11, 2008 (www.pewinternet.org/pdfs/PIP_Broadband%202007.pdf).

Pharr, Suzanne. 1997. *Homophobia: A Weapon of Sexism,* Expanded ed. Berkeley, CA: Chardon.

Phi Delta Kappa/Gallup Poll. 2001. "The 33rd Annual Phi Delta Kappa/Gallup Poll of the Public's Attitudes toward the Public Schools." Retrieved August 26, 2006 (www.pdkintl.org/kappan).

———. 2005. "The 37th Annual Phi Delta Kappa/Gallup Poll of the Public's Attitudes Toward the Public Schools." *Phi Delta Kappan* (September):41–57.

Phipher, Mary. 1994. *Reviving Ophelia: Saving the Selves of Adolescent Girls.* New York: Ballantine Books.

PHNIP Country Health Statistical Report: Nicaragua. 2002. Retrieved October 4, 2006 (www.constellafutures.com/abstract.cfm/2830).

Physicians' Working Group for Single-Payer National Health Insurance. 2003. "Proposal of the Physicians' Working Group for Single-Payer National Health Insurance." *Journal of the American Medical Association* 290(13):798–805.

Piaget, Jean. 1989. *The Child's Conception of the World.* Savage, MD: Littlefield, Adams Quality Paperbacks.

Piaget, Jean and Barbel Inhelder. [1955] 1999. *Growth of Logical Thinking.* London: Routledge and Kegan Paul.

Pickard, Ruth and Daryl Poole. 2007. "The Study of Society and the Practice of Sociology." Previously unpublished essay.

Pieterse, Jan Nederveen. 2004. *Globalization and Culture.* Lanham, MD: Rowman and Littlefield.

Pinker, Steven. 2002. *The Blank Slate: The Denial of Human Nature.* New York: Viking.

Piven, Frances Fox and Richard Cloward. 1988. *Why Americans Don't Vote.* New York: Pantheon Books.

Plato. [circa 350 BCE] 1960. *The Laws.* New York: Dutton.

Polgreen, Lydia. 2008. "Scorched-Earth Strategy Returns to Darfur." *The New York Times.* (March 2):1A, 10A.

Pollack, William. 1999. *Real Boys: Rescuing Our Sons From the Myths of Boyhood.* New York: Owl Books.

Pope, Liston. [1942] 1965. *Millhands and Preachers.* New Haven, CT: Yale University Press.

Popenoe, David, Jean Bethke Elshtain, and David Blankenhorn. 1996. *Promises to Keep: Decline and Renewal of Marriage in America.* Lanham, MD: Rowman and Littlefield.

Population Action International. 1993. *Closing the Gender Gap: Educating Girls: Report on Progress Toward World Population Stabilization.* Washington, DC: Population Action International.

Population Reference Bureau. 2001. "World Population Data Sheet." Retrieved September 29, 2006 (www.prb.org/pdf05/05WorldDataSheet_Eng.pdf).

———.2005. "World Population Data Sheet." Retrieved September 29, 2006 (www.prb.org/pdf05/05WorldDataSheet_Eng.pdf).

———. 2006. "Human Population: Fundamentals of Growth: Population Growth and Distribution." Retrieved September 29, 2006 (www.prb.org/Content/NavigationMenu/PRB/Educators/Human_Population/Population_Growth).

———. 2007a. "World Population Data Sheet." Retrieved April 9, 2008 (www.prb.org).

———. 2007b. "Migration." *Population Bulletin* 62:3.

———. 2008. "World Population Data Sheet." Retrieved August 23, 2008 (http://www.prb.org/Publications/Datasheets/2008/2008wpds.aspx).

Porter, Eduardo. 2007. "More Than Ever, It Pays to Be the Top Executive." *The New York Times* (May 25). Retrieved July 7, 2008 (http://www.nytimes.com/2007/05/25/business/25execs.html?scp=3&sq=Porter%20%22more%20than%20ever%22&st=cse).

Portes, Alejandro and Ruben G. Rumbaut. 2001. *Legacies: The Story of the Immigrant Second Generation.* Berkeley: University of California Press.

Poverty Research News. 2002. Retrieved August 22, 2006 (www.jcpr.org/newsletters/index.html).

Povik, Fili. 1994. *Zlata's Diary: A Child's Life in Sarajevo.* New York: Viking.

Powell, Andrea D. and Arnold S. Kahn. 1995. "Racial Differences in Women's Desires to Be Thin." *International Journal of Eating Disorders* 17(2):191–95.

Powell, Michael. 2008a. "Campaigns Try to Lure the Facebook Generation." *International Herald Tribune* (January 9):5

———. 2008b. "Tidal Wave of Youth Buoys 2 Campaigns." *International Herald Tribune* (January 9):2

Powell, Walter W. 1990. "Neither Market nor Hierarchy: Network Forms of Organization." *Research in Organizational Behavior* 12:295–336.

Powley, Elizabeth. 2003. "Strengthening Governance: The Role of Women in Rwanda's Transition." In *Women Waging Peace,* edited by S. N. Anderlini. Washington, DC: Hunt Alternatives Fund.

Prasso, S. 1994. "Cambodia: A Heritage of Violence." *World Policy Journal* 11(3).

Preston, David L. 1988. *The Social Organization of Zen Practice: Constructing Transcultural Reality.* Cambridge, UK: Cambridge University Press.

Prime Time. 1991. "Dignity for Sale: Selling Kidneys in India." August 1.

Project Vote Smart. 2008. "State Presidential Primary and Caucus Dates." Retrieved March 21, 2008 (http://www.votesmart.org/election_president_state_primary_dates.php).

Public Citizen's Global Trade Watch. 2003. "The Ten Year Track Record of the North American Free Trade Agreement: U.S. Workers' Jobs, Wages and Economic Security." Retrieved September 29, 2006 (http://www.citizen.org/documents/NAFTA_10_jobs.pdf).

Purcell, Piper and Lara Stewart. 1990. "Dick and Jane in 1989." *Sex Roles* 22(3/4):177–85.

Putnam, Robert D. 1995. "Bowling Alone, Revisited." *The Responsive Community* (Spring):18–33.

———. 2001. *Bowling Alone: The Collapse and Revival of American Community.* New York: Simon and Schuster.

Pyle, Ralph E. 2006. "Trends in Religious Stratification: Have Religious Group Socioeconomic Distinctions Declined in Recent Decades?" *Sociology of Religion* 67(Spring):61–79.

Quinley, Harold. 1974. *The Prophetic Clergy.* New York: John Wiley.

Quinn, Jane Bryant. 2006. "Health Care's New Lottery." *Newsweek* (February 27):47.

Quinney, Richard. 2002. *Critique of Legal Order: Crime Control in Capitalist Society.* New Brunswick, NJ: Transaction Publishers.

Radcliffe-Brown, A. R. 1935. "On the Concept of Functional in Social Science." *American Anthropologist* 37(3):394–402.

Rama Rao, Saumya and Raji Mohanam. 2003. "The Quality of Family Planning Programs: Concepts, Measurements, Interventions, and Effects." *Studies in Family Planning* 34(4)(December):227–48.

Rampell, Catherine. 2008. "Why Obama Rocks the Vote." *The Washington Post* (March 30):B7

Randerson, James. 2008. "Cutting TV Time Makes Children Healthier, Says U.S. Study." *The Guardian* (March 4).

Rankin, Bruce H. and Işik A. Aytaç. 2006. "Gender Inequality in Schooling: The Case of Turkey." *Sociology of Education* 79(1):25–43.

Reiman, Jeffrey. 1998. *The Rich Get Richer and the Poor Get Prison,* 5th ed. Boston: Allyn & Bacon.

Relethford, John H. 2008. *The Human Species: An Introduction to Biological Anthropology,* 7th ed. Boston: McGraw Hill.

Religious Worlds 2007. "New Religious Movements." Retrieved August 14, 2008 (www.religiousworlds.com/newreligions.html).

Remmert, Consuelo. 2003. "Women in Reconstruction: Rwanda Promotes Women Decision-makers." *UN Chronicle* 4(3):25.

Renzetti, Claire. 2003. "Urban Violence Against Women." Speech, September 30, Dayton, Ohio, Wright State University.

Renzetti, Claire M. and Daniel J. Curran. 2003. *Women, Men, and Society,* 5th ed. Boston: Allyn & Bacon.

Report of the National Advisory Commission on Civil Disorders. 1968. New York: Bantam.

Residents of Hull House. [c. 1895] 1970. *Hull House Maps and Papers.* New York: Arno.

Richardson, James T. 1985. "Active Versus Passive Converts: Paradigm Conflict in Conversion/Recruitment Research." *Journal for the Scientific Study of Religion* 24(2):163–79.

Riehl, Carolyn. 2001. "Bridges to the Future: Contributions of Qualitative Research to the Sociology of Education." *Sociology of Education* (Extra Issue):115–34.

Ries, L. A. G., M. P. Eisner, C. L. Kossary, B. F. Hankey, B. A. Miller, and B. K. Edwards, eds. 2000. *SEER Cancer Statistics Review, 1973–1997.* Bethesda, MD: National Cancer Institute.

Riesman, David. 1961. *The Lonely Crowd: A Study of the Changing American Character.* New Haven, CT: Yale University Press.

Riley, Glenda. 1997. *Divorce: An American Tradition.* Lincoln: University of Nebraska Press.

Riordan, Cornelius. 2004. *Equality and Achievement: An Introduction to the Sociology of Education.* Upper Saddle River, NJ: Prentice Hall.

Ritzer, George. 1998. *The McDonaldization Thesis: Explorations and Extensions.* Thousand Oaks, CA: Pine Forge.

———. 2004a. *The Globalization of Nothing.* Thousand Oaks, CA: Pine Forge.

———. 2004b. *The McDonaldization of Society* (New Century edition). Thousand Oaks, CA: Pine Forge.

Ritzer, George and Douglas J. Goodman. 2004. *Sociological Theory,* 6th ed. New York: McGraw-Hill.

Roach, Ronald. 2004. "Survey Reveals 10 Biggest Trends in Internet Use." *Black Issues in Higher Education* (October 21).

Robbins, Mandy. 1998. "A Different Voice: A Different View." *Review of Religious Research* 40(1):75–80.

Robbins, Richard H. 2005. *Global Problems and the Culture of Capitalism,* 3rd ed. Boston: Allyn & Bacon.

Robbins, Thomas. 1988. *Cults, Converts, and Charisma: The Sociology of New Religious Movements.* London and Newbury Park, CA: Sage.

Roberts, Dorothy. 1997. *Killing the Black Body: Race, Reproduction, and the Meaning of Liberty.* New York: Pantheon.

———. 2002. *Shattered Bonds: The Color of Child Welfare.* New York: Basic Books.

Roberts, Keith A. 2003. Interviews with Ohio residents in communities considering tax levies. Unpublished.

———. 2004. *Religion in Sociological Perspective,* 4th ed. Belmont, CA: Wadsworth.

Roberts, Keith A. and Karen A. Donahue. 2000. "Professing Professionalism: Bureaucratization and Deprofessionalization in the Academy." *Sociological Focus* 33(4):365–83.

Robertson, Roland. 1989. "Globalization, Politics, and Religion." Pp. 1–9 in *The Changing Face of Religion*, edited by James A. Beckford and Thomas Luchmann. London: Sage.

———. 1992. *Globalization: Social Theory and Global Culture*. London: Sage.

———. 1997. "Social Theory, Cultural Relativity and the Problem of Globality." Pp. 69–90 in *Culture, Globalization and the World System*, edited by Anthony King. Minneapolis: University of Minnesota Press.

Robertson, Roland and William R. Garrett, eds. 1991 *Religion and Global Order*. New York: Paragon.

Robertson, Roland, and H. H. Khondker. 1998. "Comparative Sociology, Global Sociology and Social Theory." *Sociology* 13(1):25–40.

Robson, Roy R. 1995. *Old Believers in Modern Russia*. DeKalb: Northern Illinois University Press.

Rodriguez, Eric M. and Michael B. Lupfer. 2000. "Gay and Lesbian Christians: Homosexual and Religious Identity Integration in the Members of a Gay-Positive Church." *Journal for the Scientific Study of Religion* 39(3):333–47.

Roethlisberger, Fritz J. and William J. Dickson. 1939. *Management and the Worker*. Cambridge: Harvard University Press.

Romano, Lois. 2008 "Generation Y: Ready to Rock the 2008 Election." *The Washington Post* (January 10):C1.

Roof, Wade Clark. 1999. *Spiritual Marketplace: Baby Boomers and the Remaking of American Religion*. Princeton, NJ: Princeton University Press.

Rose, Stephen. 2000. *Social Stratification in the United States*. New York: The New Press.

Rosen, Karen. 2007. "Women Still Lag in College Sports" (June 6). Retrieved March 7, 2008 (www.oxfordpress.com/sports/content/shared/sports/stories/2007/WOMEN_SPORTS_0606_COX.html).

Rosenbaum, James E. 1999. "If Tracking Is Bad, Is Detracking Better? A Study of a Detracked High School." *American Schools* (Winter):24–47.

Rosenthal, Robert and Lenore Jacobson. 1968. *Pygmalion in the Classroom*. New York: Holt, Rinehart & Winston.

Rossi, Alice S. 1984. "Gender and Parenthood." *American Sociological Review* 49(February):1–19.

Rossides, Daniel W. 1997. *Social Stratification: The Interplay of Class, Race, and Gender*. Englewood Cliffs, NJ: Prentice Hall.

Rossman, Parker. 2005. "Beyond the Book: Electronic Textbooks Will Bring Worldwide Learning." *The Futurist* 39(January/February):18–23.

Rothbard, Nancy P. and Jeanne M. Brett. 2000. "Promote Equal Opportunity by Recognizing Gender Differences in the Experience of Work and Family." In *The Blackwell Handbook of Principles of Organizational Behavior*, edited by Edwin A.Locke. Malden, MA: Blackwell.

Rothenberg, Paula S. 2006a. *Beyond Borders: Thinking Critically About Global Issues*. New York: Worth.

———. 2006b. "Transnational Institutions and the Global Economy" Pp. 411–18 in *Beyond Borders: Thinking Critically about Global Issues*. Edited by Paula S. Rothenberg. New York: Worth.

———. 2007. *Race, Class, and Gender in the United States: An Integrated Study*, 7th ed. New York: Worth.

———. 2008. *White Privilege: Essential Readings on the Other Side of Racism*, 3rd ed. New York: Worth Publishers.

Rothman, Robert A. 2005. *Inequality and Stratification: Race, Class, and Gender*, 5th ed. Englewood Cliffs, NJ: Prentice Hall.

Rothman, Stanley and Amy E. Black. 1998. "Who Rules Now? American Elites in the 1990s." *Society* 35(6):17–20.

Rubin, Jeffrey Z. 1974. "The Eye of the Beholder: Parents' Views on Sex of Newborns." *American Journal of Orthopsychiatry* 44(4):512–19.

Rugh, Andrea B. 1997. *Within the Circle: Parents and Children in an Arab Village*. New York: Colmbia University Press.

Rumbaut, Ruben G. and Alejandro Portes. 2001. *Ethnicities: Children of Immigrants in America*. Los Angeles: University of California Press.

Runningen, Roger and Brian Faler. 2008. "Bush Boosts Defense Spending in $3.1 Trillion Budget" (February 4). Retrieved September 2, 2008 (www.bloomberg.com/apps/news?pid=20601103&sid=azGB.29vVkzA8&refer=us).

Sabol, William J. 2007. *Prisoners in 2006*. Washington, DC: U.S. Department of Justice, Bureau of Justice Statistics.

Sack, Kevin. 1996. "Burnings of Dozens of Black Churches across the South Are Investigated." *The New York Times* (May 21):A6.

Sadker, Myra and David Sadker. 1995. *Failing at Fairness: How Our Schools Cheat Girls*. New York: Touchstone.

———. 2005. *Teachers, Schools, and Society*, 7th ed. New York: McGraw-Hill.

Sado, Stephanie and Angela Bayer. 2001. "Executive Summary: The Changing American Family" (Population Resource Center). Retrieved August 22, 2002 (www.prcdc.org/summaries/family/family/html).

Sadovnik, Alan R. 2004. "Theories in the Sociology of Education." Pp. 7–26 in *Schools and Society: A Sociological Approach to Education*, 2nd ed., edited by Jeanne H. Ballantine and Joan Z. Spade. Belmont, CA: Wadsworth.

Saenz, Rogelio. 2008. "The Growing Color Divide in U.S. Infant Mortality." Retrieved April 9, 2008 (www.prb.org/Articles/2007/ColorDivideinInfantMortality.aspx).

Sage, George H. 2005. "Racial Inequality and Sport." Pp. 266–75 in *Sport in Contemporary Society*, 7th ed., edited by Stanley D. Eitzen. Boulder, CO: Paradigm.

Sager, Ira, Ben Elgin, Peter Elstrom, Faith Keenan, and Pallavi Gogoi. 2006. "The Underground Web." Pp. 261–70 in *Globalization: The Transformation of Social Worlds*, edited by D. Stanley Eitzen and Maxine Baca Zinn. Belmont, CA: Wadsworth.

Saha, Lawrence and A. Gary Dworkin. 2006. "Educational Attainment and Job Status: The Role of Status Inconsistency on Occupational Burnout." Paper presented at the International Sociological Association, July 23–29, Durban, South Africa.

Salzman, Marian and Ira Matathia. 2000. "Lifestyles of the Next Millennium: 65 Forecasts." Pp. 466–71 in *Sociological Footprints*, edited by Leonard Cargan and Jeanne Ballantine. Belmont, CA: Wadsworth.

Samovar, Larry A. and Richard E. Porter. 2003. *Intercultural Communication*. Belmont, CA: Wadsworth.

Sanday, Peggy Reeves. 1981. "The Socio-Cultural Context of Rape: A Cross-Cultural Study." *Journal of Social Issues* 37(4):5–27.

———. 1996. *A Woman Scorned: Acquaintance Rape on Trial*. Berkeley: University of California Press.

———. 2007. *Fraternity Gang Rape: Sex, Brotherhood, and Privilege on Campus*. New York: New York University Press.

Sanday, Peggy and Ruth Gallagher Goodenough, eds. 1990. *Beyond the Second Sex*. Philadelphia: University of Pennsylvania Press.

Sander, William. 1993. "Catholicism and Intermarriage in the United States." *Journal of Marriage and the Family* 55(November):1037–41.

Sapir, Edward. 1929. "The Status of Linguistics as a Science." *Language* 5:207–14.

———. 1949. *Selected Writings of Edward Sapir in Language, Culture, and Personality*, edited by David G. Mandelbaum. Berkeley: University of California Press.

Sapiro, Virginia. 2003. *Women in American Society: An Introduction to Women's Studies*, 5th ed. Mountain View, CA: Mayfield.

Sarat, Austin. 2001. *When the State Kills: Capital Punishment and the American Condition*. Princeton, NJ: Princeton University Press.

Sargeant, Kimon Howland. 2000. *Seeker Churches: Promoting Traditional Religion in a Nontraditional Way*. New Brunswick, NJ: Rutgers University Press.

Sarno, David. 2008. "Looking for the Youth Vote? It's Online." *Los Angeles Times* (January 13):E42.

Sassler, Sharon and Amanda Miller. (forthcoming). "Waiting to Be Asked: Gender, Power, and Relationship Progression among Cohabiting Couples." *Journal of Marriage and Family*.

Sax, Leonard. 2005. *Why Gender Matters: What Parents and Teachers Need to Know About the Emerging Science of Sex Differences*. New York: Doubleday.

Scarce, Rik. 1999. "Good Faith, Bad Ethics: When Scholars Go the Distance and Scholarly Associations Do Not." *Law and Social Inquiry* 24(4):977–86.

Schaefer, Richard T. 2008. *Racial and Ethnic Groups*, 11th ed. Englewood Cliffs, NJ: Prentice Hall.

Schaefer, Richard T. and Jenifer Kunz. 2007. *Racial and Ethnic Groups*. Upper Saddle River, NJ: Pearson/Prentice Hall.

Schaeffer, Robert K. 2003. *Understanding Globalization: The Social Consequences of Political, Economic, and Environmental Change*, 2nd ed. Lanham, MD: Rowman and Littlefield.

Schapiro, Mark. 2006. "Big Tobacco." Pp. 271–84 in *Globalization: The Transformation of Social Worlds*, edited by D. Stanley Eitzen and Maxine Baca Zinn. Belmont, CA: Wadsworth.

Schemo, Diana Jean. 2006. "Public Schools Close to Private in U.S. Study." *The New York Times* (July 15):A1, 10.

Schieber, George and Akiko Maeda. 1999. "Health Care Financing and Delivery in Developing Countries." *Health Affairs* 18(3): 193–206.

Schienberg, Jonathan. 2006. "Firefighters, Doctors and Nurses Considered Most Prestigious Occupations." *CNNMoney.com* (July 31). Retrieved July 7, 2008 (http://money.cnn.com/2006/07/26/news/economy/prestigious_professions/).

Schiff, Gordon D., Andrew B. Bindman, and Troyen A. Brennan. 1994. "A Better-Quality Alternative: Single-payer National Health System Reform." *Journal of the American Medical Association* 272(10):803–7.

Schleuter, Albert. 2006. Personal interview, July.

Schmalleger, Frank. 2006. *Criminology Today*, 4th ed. Englewood Cliffs, NJ: Prentice Hall.

Schneider, Barbara and James S. Coleman. 1993. *Parents, Their Children, and Schools*. Boulder, CO: Westview.

Schneider, Barbara and David Stevenson. 1999. *The Ambitious Generation: Imagining the Future*. New Haven, CT: Yale University Press.

Schneider, Barbara and Linda J. Waite. 2005. *Being Together, Working Apart: Dual-Career Families and the Work-Life Balance*. Cambridge University Press.

Schneider, Linda and Arnold Silverman. 2006. *Global Sociology*, 4th ed. Boston: McGraw-Hill.

Schoeman, Ferdinand. 1991. "Book Review: Heavy Drinking: The Myth of Alcoholism as a Disease." *The Philosophical Review* 100(3):493–98.

Schoen, Robert and Robin M. Weinick. 1993. "Partner Choice in Marriages and Cohabitations." *Journal of Marriage and the Family* 55(May):408–14.

Schweinhart, Lawrence J. 1997. "Child-Initiated Learning Activities for Young Children Living in Poverty." *ERIC Digest* (October). Washington, DC: Office of Educational Research and Improvement.

Scott, Ellen K., Andrew S. London, and Nancy A. Myers. 2002. "Dangerous Dependencies: The Intersection of Welfare Reform and Domestic Violence." *Gender and Society* 16(6):878–97.

Scott-Montagu, John. 1904. "Automobile Legislation: A Criticism and Review." *North American Review* 179(573):168–77.

Senate Democratic Policy Committee Hearing. 2004. "America's Uninsured: Myths, Realities and Solutions." Retrieved September 29, 2006 (democrats.senate.gov/dpc/hearings/hearing9/Pollack.pdf).

The Sentencing Project. 2006. "International Rates of Incarceration 2003." Retrieved August 4, 2006 (http://www.sentencing project.org/pdfs/pub9036.pdf).

Sernau, Scott. 2005. *Worlds Apart: Social Inequalities in a New Century*, 2nd ed. Thousand Oaks, CA: Pine Forge.

Shade, Leslie Regan. 2004. "Bending Gender into the Net: Feminizing Content, Corporate Interests, and Research Strategy." Pp. 57–70 in *Society On-Line: The Internet in Context*, edited by Philip N. Howard and Steve Jones. Thousand Oaks, CA: Sage.

Shaffer, David Williamson, Kurt R. Squire, Richard Haverson, and James P. Gee. 2005. "Video Games and the Future of Learning." *Phi Delta Kappan* (October):95–112.

Shah, Anup. 2008. "World Military Spending." Retrieved April 16, 2008 (www.globalissues.org/Geopolitics/Armstrade/Spending/asp).

Sharp, Henry S. 1991. "Memory, Meaning, and Imaginary Time: The Construction of Knowledge in White and Chipewayan Cultures." *Ethnohistory* 38(2):149–73.

Sharp, Lauriston. 1990. "Steel Axes for Stone-Age Australians." Pp. 410–24 in *Conformity and Conflict*, 7th ed., edited by James P. Spradley and David W. McCurdy. Glenview IL: Scott Foresman.

Sharp, Travis. 2008. "U.S. Military Spending vs. the World in 2008" (Center for Arms Control and Non-Proliferation, February 20). Retrieved September 3, 2008 (www.armscontrolcenter.org/policy/securityspending/articles/us_vs_world.gif).

Shaw, Clifford R. and Henry D. McKay. 1929. *Delinquency Areas*. Chicago: University of Chicago Press.

Shaw, Susan M. and Janet Lee. 2005. *Women's Voices, Feminist Visions: Classic and Contemporary Readings*, 3rd ed. Boston: McGraw-Hill.

Shepherd, William R. 1964. *Historical Atlas*, 9th ed. New York: Barnes & Noble.

Sherif, Muzafer and Carolyn Sherif. 1953. *Groups in Harmony and Tension*. New York: Harper & Row.

Sherkat, Darren E. and Christopher G. Ellison. 1999. "Recent Developments and Current Controversies in the Sociology of Religion." *Annual Review of Sociology* 25:363–94.

Sherman, Karen J. 2005. *Complementary and Alternative Medicine in the United States*. Washington, DC: National Academies Press.

Shore, Cris. 2008. "Corruption Scandals in America and Europe: Enron and EU Fraud in Comparative Perspective." Pp. 191–98 in *Deviance Across Cultures*, edited by Robert Heiner. New York: Oxford University Press.

Shorter, Edward. 1991. *Women's Bodies: A Social History of Women's Encounter With Health, Ill-Health and Medicine*. New Brunswick, NJ: Transaction Publishers.

Showalter, Shari. 2002. "Culture and Pain" (College of Nursing, University of Iowa). Retrieved March 19, 2003 (www.nursing.uiowa.edu).

Shu, Xiaoling. 2004. "Education and Gender Egalitarianism: The Case of China." *Sociology of Education* 77(4):311–36.

Shupe, Anson and Jeffrey K. Hadden. 1989. "Is There Such a Thing as Global Fundamentalism?" Pp. 109–22 in *Secularization and Fundamentalism Reconsidered*, edited by Jeffrey K. Hadden and Anson Shupe. New York: Paragon.

Siegel, Dina and Hans Nelen, eds. 2008. *Organized Crime: Culture, Markets, and Policies. Series: Studies in Organized Crime*, Vol. 7. New York: Springer.

Siegel, Larry J. 2000. *Criminology*, 7th ed. St. Paul, MN: West.

———. 2006. *Criminology*, 9th ed. Belmont, CA: Wadsworth.

"Significant Ongoing Armed Conflicts 2007." Retrieved March 26, 2008 (www.infoplease.com/ipa/A0904550.html).

Simmel, Georg. [1902–17] 1950. *The Sociology of Georg Simmel*, translated by Kurt Wolff. Glencoe, IL: The Free Press.

———. 1955. *Conflict and the Web of Group Affiliation*, translated by Kurt H. Wolff. New York: The Free Press.

Simmons, Rachel. 2002. *Odd Girl Out: The Hidden Culture of Aggression in Girls*. Orlando, FL: Harcourt.

Simon, David R. 2006. *Elite Deviance,* 8th ed. Boston: Allyn & Bacon.

Sine, Richard. 2002. "Garment Workers Say Gap Aided in Cambodian Strife." Retrieved September 2, 2008 (http://laborcenter.berkeley.edu/press/sfchronicle_dec02.shtml).

Sizer, Theodore R. 1984. *Horace's Compromise: The Dilemma of the American High School.* Boston: Houghton Mifflin.

Sjoberg, Gideon. 1960. *The Preindustrial City: Past and Present.* Glencoe, IL: The Free Press.

———. 1965. "The Origin and Evolution of Cities." *Scientific American* 213(September):56–57.

Skocpol, Theda. 1979. *States and Social Revolutions: A Comparative Analysis of France, Russia, and China.* Cambridge, UK: Cambridge University Press.

Smelser, Neil J. 1963. *Theory of Collective Behavior.* New York: The Free Press.

———. 1988. "Social Structure." Pp. 103–29 in *Handbook of Sociology,* edited by Neil J. Smelser. Newbury Park, CA: Sage.

Smerdon, Becky A. 2002. "Students' Perceptions of Membership in their High Schools." *Sociology of Education* 75(4):287–305.

Smith, Barbara Ellen. 1999. "The Social Relations of Southern Women." Pp. 13–31 in *Neither Separate Nor Equal,* edited by B. E. Smith. Philadelphia: Temple University Press.

Smith, Brent L. 1994. *Terrorism in America: Pipe Bombs and Pipe Dreams.* New York: State University of New York Press.

Smith, Christian and Robert Faris. 2005. "Socioeconomic Inequality in the American Religious System: An Update and Assessment." *Journal for the Scientific Study of Religion* 44(1):95–104.

Smith, Daniel R. and David F. Ayers. 2006. "Culturally Responsive Pedagogy and Online Learning: Implications for the Globalized Community College." *Community College Journal of Research and Practice* 30.

Smith, David M. and Gary J. Gates. 2001. *Gay and Lesbian Families in the United States: Same-Sex Unmarried Partner Households: A Preliminary Analysis of 2000 United States Census Data.* Washington, DC: Human Rights Campaign.

Smith, Heather. 2008. "Galvanizing Young Voters." *The Washington Post* (April 5):A13.

Smith, Russell. 2005. "How Many Have Died in Darfur?" *BBC News* (February 16). Retrieved February 16, 2005 (http://news.bbc.co.uk/2/hi/africa/4268733.stm).

Smock, Pamela J. 2004. "The Wax and Wane of Marriage: Prospects for Marriage in the 21st Century." *Journal of Marriage and Family* 66(November):966–73.

Snarr, Michael T. and D. Neil Snarr, eds. 2002. *Introducing Global Issues,* 2nd ed. Boulder, CO: Lynne Rienner.

Snow, David A. and L. Anderson 1993. *Down on Their Luck: A Study of Homeless Street People.* Berkeley: University of California Press.

Snow, David A., Louis A. Zurcher, Jr., and Sheldon Ekland-Olson. 1980. "Social Networks and Social Movements: A Microstructural Approach to Differential Recruitment." *American Sociological Review* 45(5):787–801.

Snyder, Benson R. 1970. *The Hidden Curriculum.* New York: Alfred A. Knopf.

Social Security Online. 2008. "Popular Baby Names." Retrieved March 6, 2008 (www.ssa.gov/cgi-bin/popularnames.cgi).

Solow, Robert M. 2000. *Growth Theory: An Exposition,* 2nd ed. New York: Oxford University Press.

Sommerfeld, Julia. 2002. "U.S. Lags Behind in Cutting Teen Births." *MSNBC News.* Retrieved January 10, 2002 (www.msnbc.com/news/664476.asp?0si).

Sommerville, C. John. 2002. "Stark's Age of Faith Argument and the Secularization of Things: A Commentary." *Review of Religious Research* (Fall):361–72.

Son, Young-ho. 1992. "Korean Response to the 'Yellow Peril' and Search for Racial Accommodation in the United States." *Korean Journal* 32(2):58–74.

Song, Jason. 2008. "Return of the Youth Vote." *Los Angeles Times* (February 5):B1

Southerland, Anne. 1986. *Gypsies: The Hidden Americans.* Prospect Heights, IL: Waveland.

Southern Poverty Law Center. "Active U.S. Hate Groups in 2002" (Intelligence Project). Retrieved September 9, 2008 (web1.splcenter.org/intel/map/hate.jsp).

Sowell, Thomas. 1994. *Race and Culture: A World View.* New York: Basic Books.

Spade, Joan Z. 2004. "Gender in Education in the United States." Pp. 287–95 in *Schools and Society: A Sociological Approach to Education,* 2nd ed., edited by Jeanne H. Ballantine and Joan Z. Spade. Belmont, CA: Wadsworth.

Spade, Joan Z., Lynn Columba, and Beth E. Vanfossen. 1997. "Tracking in Mathematics and Science: Courses and Course Selection Procedures." *Sociology of Education* 70(2):108–27.

Sperling, Gene B. 2005. "The Case for Universal Basic Education for the World's Poorest Boys and Girls." *Phi Delta Kappan* (November):213–16.

Sperling, Gene and Barbara Herz. 2004. *What Works in Girls' Education: Evidence and Policies from the Developing World.* Washington, DC: Council on Foreign Relations.

Stack, Carol B. 1974. *All Our Kin: Strategies for Survival in a Black Community.* New York: Harper and Row.

———. 1998. *All Our Kin: Strategies for Survival in a Black Community.* New York: Harper & Row.

Stallings, Jane A. 1995. "Ensuring Teaching and Learning in the 21st Century." *Educational Researcher* 24(6):4.

Stanback, Thomas M. 1991. *The New Suburbanization: Challenge to the Central City.* Boulder, CO: Westview.

Staples, Brent. 1992. "Black Men and Public Space." Pp. 29–32 in *Life Studies,* edited by D. Cavitch. Boston: Bedford.

Staples, Robert. 1999. *The Black Family: Essays and Studies,* 6th ed. Belmont, CA: Wadsworth.

Stark, Rodney. 1985. "Church and Sect." Pp. 139–49 in *The Sacred in a Secular Age,* edited by P. Hammond. Berkeley: University of California Press.

———. 2000. "Secularization, R.P.I." Pp. 41–66 in *The Secularization Debate,* edited by William H. Swatos, Jr., and Daniel V. A. Olson. Lanham, MD: Rowman and Littlefield.

Stark, Rodney and William Sims Bainbridge. 1985. *The Future of Religion: Secularization, Revival, and Cult Formation.* Berkeley: University of California Press.

Stark, Rodney, Daniel P. Doyle, and Jesse Lynn Rushing. 1983. "Beyond Durkheim: Religion and Suicide." *Journal for the Scientific Study of Religion* 22(March):120–31.

Starnes, Bobby Ann. 2006. "What We Don't Know Can Hurt Them: White Teachers, Indian Children." *Phi Delta Kappan* (January):384–92.

Starr, Paul D. 1982. *The Social Transformation of American Medicine.* New York: Basic Books.

State of Alaska. 2006. "Workplace Alaska: How to Apply." Retrieved July 5, 2006 (http://notes3.state.ak.us/WA/MainEntry.nsf/WebData/HTMLHow+to+Apply/?open).

State of Delaware. 2008. "Presidential Primary Election." Retrieved March 21, 2008 (http://elections.delaware.gov/information/elections/presidential_2008.shtml).

Steele, Stephen F. and Jammie Price. 2004. *Applied Sociology: Terms, Topics, Tools, and Tasks.* Belmont, CA: Wadsworth.

Steele, Tracey L. 2005. *Sex, Self, and Society: The Social Context of Sexuality.* Belmont, CA: Thomson Wadsworth.

Steele, Tracey and Norma Wilcox. 2003. "A View from the Inside: The Role of Redemption, Deterrence, and Masculinity on Inmate Support for the Death Penalty." *Crime and Delinquency* 49(2):285–313.

Stein, Nicholas. 2006. "No Way Out." Pp. 293–99 in *Globalization: The Transformation of Social Worlds*, edited by D. Stanley Eitzen and Maxine Baca Zinn. Belmont, CA: Wadsworth.

Stephen Roth Institute for the Study of Contemporary Antisemitism and Racism. 2006. *Antisemitism Worldwide 2006: General Analysis*. Israel: Tel Aviv University.

Stern, Jessica. 2003. *Terror in the Name of God: Why Religious Militants Kill*. New York: HarperCollins.

Stevens, Daphne, Gary Kiger, and Pamela J. Riley. 2001. "Working Hard and Hardly Working: Domestic Labor and Marital Satisfaction Among Dual-Earner Families." *Journal of Marriage and the Family* 63(May):514–26.

Stevenson, Mark. 2003. "Mexico Finishes Repaying Restructuring Debt." *Laredo Morning Times* (June 13):14A.

Stewart, Vivien. 2005. "A World Transformed: How Other Countries Are Preparing Students for the Interconnected World of the 21st Century." *Phi Delta Kappan* (November):229–32.

Stoessinger, John. 1993. *Why Nations Go to War*. New York: St. Martin's Press.

Stoltenberg, John. 1993. *The End of Manhood: A Book for Men of Conscience*. New York: Dutton.

Stolzenberg, Ross M., Mary Blair-Loy, and Linda J. Waite. 1995. "Religious Participation in Early Adulthood: Age and Family Life Cycle Effects on Church Membership." *American Sociological Review* 60(February):84–103.

Stone, Norman, ed. 1991. *The Times Atlas of World History*, 3rd ed. Maplewood, NJ: Hammond.

Straus, Murray and Richard J. Gelles. 1990. *Physical Violence in American Families*. New Brunswick, NJ: Transaction Publishers.

Straus, Murray A., Richard J. Gelles, and Suzanne K. Steinmetz. 2006. *Behind Closed Doors: Violence in the American Family*. New Brunswick, NJ: Transaction Publishers.

Stringer, Donna M. 2006. "Let Me Count the Ways: African American/European American Marriages." Pp. 170–76 in *Intercultural Communication: A Reader*, edited by Larry A. Samovar, Richard E. Porter, and Edwin R. McDaniel. Belmont, CA: Wadsworth.

Stritof, Sheri and Bob Stritof. 2008. "Same Sex Marriage License Laws." Retrieved March 7, 2008 (http://marriage.about.com/cs/marriagelicenses/a/samesexcomp.htp).

Struck, Doug. 2007. "Warming Will Exacerbate Global Water Conflicts." *Washington Post* (August 20). Retrieved August 21, 2008 (www.washingtonpost.com/wp-dyn/content/article/2007/08/19/AR2007081900967.html).

Stryker, Sheldon. 1980. *Symbolic Interactionism: A Social Structural Version*. Menlo Park, CA: Benjamin Cummings.

———. 2000. "Identity Competition: Key to Differential Social Involvement." Pp. 21–40 in *Identity, Self, and Social Movements*, edited by Sheldon Stryker, Timothy Owens, and Robert White. Minneapolis: University of Minnesota Press.

Stryker, Sheldon and Anne Stratham. 1985. "Symbolic Interaction and Role Theory." Pp. 311–78 in *Handbook of Social Psychology*, edited by Gardiner Lindsey and Eliot Aronson. New York: Random House.

Stutz, Fredrick P. and Barney Warf. 2005. *The World Economy*. Upper Saddle River, NJ: Prentice Hall.

Suarez-Orozco, Marcelo M. 2005. "Rethinking Education in the Global Era." *Phi Delta Kappan* (November):209–12.

Sun, Yongmin. 2001. "Family Environment and Adolescents' Well-Being Before and After Parents' Disruption: A Longitudinal Analysis." *Journal of Marriage and the Family* 63(August):697–713.

Sutherland, Edwin H., Donald R. Cressey, and David Luckenbil. 1992. *Criminology*. Dix Hills, NY: General Hall.

Swatos, William H., Jr., and Luftur Reimur Gissurarson. 1997. *Icelandic Spiritualism: Mediumship and Modernity in Iceland*. New Brunswick, NJ: Transaction.

Sway, Marlene. 1988. *Familiar Strangers: Gypsy Life in America*. Urbana: University of Illinois Press.

Sweatshop Watch Newsletter. 1996. "Average Hourly Wages for Garment Workers." 2(1) Fall.

Sweet, Stephen. 2001. *College and Society: An Introduction to the Sociological Imagination*. Boston: Allyn and Bacon.

Swivel. 2007. "Infant Mortality." Retrieved February 26, 2008 (www.swivel.com/data_sets/spreadsheet/1006156).

Szymanski, Linda A., Ann Sloan Devlin, Joan C. Chrisler, and Stuart A. Vyse. 1993. "Gender Role and Attitude toward Rape in Male and Female College Students." *Sex Roles* 29:37–55.

Tamney, Joseph B. 1992. *The Resilience of Christianity in the Modern World*. Albany: State University of New York Press.

Tapscott, Don. 1998. *Growing Up Digital: The Rise of the Net Generation*. New York: McGraw-Hill.

Taub, Diane E., and Penelope A. McLorg. 2007. "Influences of Gender Socialization and Athletic Involvement on the Occurrence of Eating Disorders." Pp. 81–90 in *Sociological Footprints*, 10th ed., edited by Leonard Cargan and Jeanne Ballantine. Belmont, CA: Wadsworth.

Tavris, Carol and Carol Wade. 1984. *The Longest War*, 2nd ed. San Diego: Harcourt Brace Jovanovich.

Taylor, Humphrey. 2002. "Scientists, Doctors, Teachers, and Military Officers Top the List of Prestigious Occupations." *The Harris Poll* (October 16). Retrieved August 22, 2006 (Harrisinteractive.com/harris_poll/index.asp?Pollyear=2002).

Teixeira, Ruy. 2008. "The Decline of the White Working Class and the Rise of a Mass Upper Middle Class" (Brookings Institution). Retrieved June 27, 2008 (www.brookings.edu/experts.aspx).

Terkel, Studs. 1974. *Working*. New York: Pantheon Books.

Therborn, Goran. 1976. "What Does the Ruling Class Do When it Rules?" *Insurgent Sociologist* 6:3–16.

Thiagaraj, Henry. 2006. *Minority and Human Rights from the Dalit Perspective*. Chennai, India: Oneworld Educational Trust.

Thiagaraj, Henry. 2007. *Human Rights From the Dalits' Perspective*. New Delhi, India: Gyan Publications.

Thio, Alex. 2007. *Deviant Behavior*, 9th ed. Boston: Allyn and Bacon.

Thoits, Peggy A. and Lyndi N. Hewitt. 2001. "Volunteer Work and Well-Being." *Journal of Health and Social Behavior* 42(June):115–31.

Thomas, Charles B. 1985. "Clergy in Racial Controversy: A Replication of the Campbell and Pettigrew Study." *Review of Religious Research* (June):379–90.

Thomas, V. J. and F. D. Rose. 1991. "Ethnic Differences in the Experience of Pain." *Social Science and Medicine* 32(9):1063–66.

Thorne, Barrie. 1993. *Gender Play: Girls and Boys in School*. New Brunswick, NJ: Rutgers University Press.

Thumma, Scott and Dave Travis. 2007. *Beyond Megachurch Myths: What We Can Learn From America's Largest Churches*. Hoboken, NJ: Jossey-Bass.

Tichenor, Veronica Jaris. 1999. "Status and Income as Gendered Resources: The Case of Marital Power." *Journal of Marriage and the Family* 61(August):638–50.

Time Almanac. 2008. "China" (pp. 277–80). Chicago: Encyclopedia Britannica.

Tipton, Steven M. 1990. "The Social Organization of Zen Practice: Constructing Transcultural Reality." *American Journal of Sociology* 96(2):488–90.

Tjaden, Patricia and Nancy Thoennes. 2000. "Full Report of the Prevalence, Incidence and Consequences of Violence Against Women: Findings from the National Violence Against Women Survey." Washington, DC: National Institute of Justice.

Toffler, Alvin and Heidi Toffler. 1980. *The Third Wave*. New York: Morrow.

Tomsen, Peter. 1994. "Cambodia Recent Developments." U.S. Department of State Dispatch (May 23).

Tonnies, Ferdinand. [1887] 1963. *Community and Society*. New York: Harper & Row.

Torche, Florencia. 2005. "Privatization Reform and Inequality of Educational Opportunity: The Case of Chile." *Sociology of Education* 78(4):316–43.

Toynbee, Arnold and D. C. Somervell. [1934–61] 1988. *The Study of History*. Oxford, UK: Oxford University Press.

Transparency International. 2003. "Corruption Perceptions Index, 2003." Retrieved August 4, 2006 (http://www.transparencyinternational.org).

———. 2007. "Global Corruption Report 2007." Retrieved February 10, 2008 (http://www.transparency.org/publications/gcr/download_gcr/download_gcr_2007).

Travers, Jeffrey and Stanley Milgram. 1969. "An Experimental Study of the Small World Problem." *Sociometry* 32:425–43.

Tuchman, Gaye. 1996. "Women's Depiction by the Mass Media." Pp. 11–15 in *Turning It On: A Reader on Women and Media*, edited by Helen Baehr and Ann Gray. London: Arnold.

Tumin, Melvin M. 1953. "Some Principles of Social Stratification: A Critical Analysis." *American Sociological Review* 18(August): 387–94.

Turnbull, Colin M. 1962. *The Forest People*. New York: Simon & Schuster.

Turner, Bryan S. 1991a. "Politics and Culture in Islamic Globalism." Pp. 161–81 in *Religion and Global Order*, edited by Roland Robertson and William R. Garrett. New York: Paragon.

Turner, Bryan S. 1991b. *Religion and Social Theory*. London: Sage.

Turner, Jonathan H. 2003. *The Structure of Sociological Theory*, 7th ed. Belmont, CA: Wadsworth.

Turner, Ralph H. and Lewis M. Killian. 1993. "The Field of Collective Behavior." Pp. 5–20 in *Collective Behavior and Social Movements*, edited by Russell L. Curtis, Jr., and Benigno E. Aguirre. Boston: Allyn & Bacon.

Tyler, Sir Edward B. [1871] 1958. *Primitive Culture: Researches Into the Development of Mythology, Philosophy, Religion, Art and Custom*, Vol. 1. London: John Murray.

UNAIDS–Joint United Nations Programme on HIV/AIDS. "Fact Sheet 2006: Sub-Saharan Africa." Retrieved September 8, 2008 (http://data.unaids.org/pub/GlobalReport/2006/200605-FS_SubSaharanAfrica_en.pdf).

UNESCO. 2005. *Education for All Global Monitoring Report 2005: The Quality Imperative*. Paris: UNESCO.

———. 2006a. *Education for All Global Monitoring Report 2006: The Quality Imperative*. Paris: UNESCO.

———. 2006b. "Worldwide Shortage of Teachers." Retrieved April 1, 2008 (http://portal.unesco.org/education/en/ev.php-URL_ID=8674&URL).

UNHCR. 2006. "2005 Global Refugee Trends: Statistical Overview of Populations of Refugees, Asylum-Seekers, Internally Displaced Persons, Stateless Persons, and Other Persons of Concern to UNHCR." Retrieved August 15, 2006 (http://www.unhcr.org/cgi-bin/texis/vtx/statistics).

UNHCR Statistical Yearbook. 2006. "Asylum and Refugee Status Determination" (Chapter 5). Retrieved March 2, 2008 (www.unhcr.org/doclist/statistics/4148094d4.html).

UNICEF. 2004. *Progress for Children: A Child Survival Report Card, No. 1*. New York: UNICEF.

UNIFEM. 2002. "Report of the Learning Oriented Assessment of Gender Mainstreaming and Women's Empowerment Strategies in Rwanda." Retrieved April 7, 2008 (http://www.unifem.org/attachments/products/rwanda_assessment_report_eng.pdf).

United Nations. 2000. *The World's Women: Trends and Statistics*. New York: United Nations.

———.2002. *World Urbanization Prospects, 2001 Revision*. New York: United Nations Population Division. Retrieved September 29, 2006 (www.unpopulation.org).

———. 2003. "Demographic Yearbook: 2003." Retrieved August 22, 2006 (http://unstats.un.org/unsd/demographic/products/dyb/dyb2.htm).

———. 2006. "Demographic Yearbook: 2006." Retrieved August 23, 2008 (www.unstats.un.org/unsd/demographic/products/dyb/dyb2006/notestab04.pdf).

———. 2007. "UN Member States." Retrieved March 26, 2008 (www.un.org/members/list.shtml).

United Nations, Department of Economic and Social Affairs, Population Division. 2005. *World Population Prospects: The 2004 Revision. Vol. 3: Analytical Report*. New York: Author.

United Nations, Development Programme. 2005a. "Human Development Indicators." *Human Development Report.* Retrieved September 20, 2006 (http://hdr.undp.org/reports/global/2005).

United Nations, Development Programme.. 2005b. United Nations Office on Drugs and Crime. 2005. *World Drug Report 2005*. Retrieved August 4, 2006 (http://www.unodc.org/unodc/world_drug_report.html).

United Nations, Development Programme. 2007/2008. *Human Development Report: Country Fact Sheets*. New York: Author.

United Nations, International Telecommunication Union. 2004. "Internet Indicators by Country for 2004." Retrieved August 9, 2006 (http://www.itu.int/ITU-D/ict/statistics/at_glance/Internet 04.pdf).

United Nations, Millennium Project (http://unmillenniumproject.org/reports/)

United Nations, Office on Drugs and Crime. 2003. *Global Illicit Drug Trends 2003*. New York: Author.

———. 2006a. "Annual Reports Questionnaire Data/DELTA." Retrieved September 20, 2006 (www.unodc.org/pdf/WDR_2006/wdr2006_ex_summary.pdf).

———. 2006b. "World Drug Report 2006, Volume 1." Retrieved September 20, 2006 (http://www.unodc.org/pdf/WDR_2006/wdr2006_volume1.pdf).

United Nations, Population Division. 2001. *World Urbanization Prospects: The 2001 Revision*. New York: Author.

———. 2003. "World Urbanization Prospects: The 2003 Revision." Retrieved September 29, 2006 (www.un.org/esa/population/publications/wup2003/WUP2003Report.pdf).

———. 2005. "World Urbanization Prospects: The 2005 Revision." Retrieved September 29, 2006 (http://esa.un.org/unup).

United Nations, Population Fund. 2005. "State of the World Population 2005." Retrieved September 29, 2006 (www.unfpa.org/swp/2005/pdf/en_swp05.pdf).

United North America. 2008. "Similarities and Differences Between Canada & United States." Retrieved August 26, 2008 (www.unitednorthamerica.org/simdiff.htm).

U.S. Bureau of Justice Statistics. 2001. *National Crime Victimization Survey Report*. Washington, DC: U.S. Department of Justice.

———. 2002, 2003, 2004, 2005, 2006. *Sourcebook of Criminal Justice Statistics*. Washington, DC: U.S. Department of Justice.

U.S. Bureau of Labor Statistics. 2008–09. "Occupational Outlook Handbook, 2008–09 Edition." Retrieved April 9, 2008 (www.bls.gov/oco/ocos285.htm).

U.S. Census Bureau. 2001a. *Current Population Survey, 2001*. Washington, DC: U.S. Government Printing Office.

———.2001b. "9-in-10 School-Age Children Have Computer Access; Internet Use Pervasive Census Bureau Reports." Retrieved July 20, 2006 (http://www.census.gov/Press- Release/www/2001/cb01-147.html).

———. 2001c. "The Hispanic Population. Census 2000 Brief." Retrieved March 2, 2008 (www.census.gov/prod/2001 pubs).

———. 2003a. "2001 Annual Report: The Status of Equal Employment Opportunity and Affirmative Action in Alaska State Government." Retrieved September 29, 2006 (http://factfinder.census.gov/servlet/ACSSAFFFacts?_event=&geo_id=04000US02&_geoContext=01000US%7C04000US02&_street=&_county=&_cityTown=&_state=04000US02&_zip=&_lang=en&_sse=on&ActiveGeoDiv=&_useEV=&pctxt=fph&pgsl=040).

————. 2003b. "International Database." Retrieved August 26, 2006 (www.census.gov/ipc/www/idbnew.html).

————. 2003c. "Statistical Abstract of the United States: 2007, Table 77." Retrieved February 9, 2008 (www.census.gov/compendia/statab/tables/08s0077.xls) Table 10.

U.S. Census Bureau. 2004. "Geographical Mobility: 2002–2003." *Current Population Reports*. Retrieved September 29, 2006 (www.census.gov/prod/2004pubs/p20-549.pdf).

————. 2005a. "Annual Demographic Supplements." *Current Population Survey 2005*. Washington, DC: Author.

————. 2005b. "Computer and Internet Use in the United States: 2003." *Current Population Reports*. Washington, DC: Author.

————. 2005c. "Educational Attainment in the United States: 2004." *Current Population Survey*. Washington, DC: Author.

————. 2005d. "Housing Vacancies and Housing Ownership." *Annual Statistics 2005*. Retrieved September 15, 2006 (http://www.census.gov/hhes/www/housing/hvs/annua105/ann05def.html).

————. 2005e. "Income, Poverty, and Health Insurance Coverage in the United States: 2004." *Current Population Reports*. Washington, DC: Author.

————. 2005f. "National Population Estimates: Characteristics." Retrieved August 22, 2006 (http://www.census.gov/popest/national/asrh/NC-EST2005-srh.html).

————. 2005g. "Number of Uninsured Americans." Retrieved August 26, 2006 (www.census.gov/Press-Release/www/2005).

————. 2005h. *Statistical Abstracts of the United States: 2004–2005*, 124th ed. Washington, DC: Government Printing Office. Retrieved August 26, 2006 (www.census.gov/Press-Release/www/releases/archives/labor_table597.pdf).

————. 2005i. *U.S. Citizens over 65*. Washington, DC: U.S. Department of Commerce.

————. 2006a. "America's Families and Living Arrangements 2006." Retrieved February 20, 2008 (http://www.census.gov/population/www/socdemo/hh-fam/cps2005.html).

————. 2006b. "Geographical Mobility Between 2004 and 2005." *Population Profile of the United States*. Washington, DC: Author.

————. 2006c. "International Database." Retrieved September 29, 2006 (www.census.gov/ipc/www/idbnew.html).

————. 2006d. "Movers by Type of Move and Reason for Moving 2006." *Statistical Abstracts 2008* (Table 0031). Retrieved August 23, 2008 (infochimps.org/dataset/statab2008_0031_moversbytypeofmoveandreasonfor movin).

————. 2006e. "Poverty Thresholds." Retrieved August 22, 2006 (www.census.gov/hhes/www/poverty/threshld).

————. 2006f. "Quickfacts." Retrieved Augsut 22, 2006 (www.quickfacts.census.gov/qfd/states).

————. 2006g. *Statistical Abstracts of the United States, 2006*. Washington, DC: Author.

————. 2006h. "The 2006 Statistical Abstract, The National Data Book, Table 18." Retrieved August 6, 2006 (http://www.census.gov/compendia/statab/education/educational_attainment/).

————. 2007a. "Median Earnings in the Past 12 Months of Workers by Sex and Women's Earnings as a Percentage of Men's Earnings" (Table 5). *Income, Earnings, and Poverty Data from the 2005 American Community Survey*. Washington, DC: Author.

————. 2007b. "National Population Estimates: Characteristics." Retrieved August 11, 2008 (http://www.census.gov/popest/national/asrh/NC-EST2007-srh.html).

————. 2008a. "Mean Earnings by Highest Degree Earned: 2005." *Statistical Abstracts of the United States, 2008* (Table 220). Washington, DC: Author.

U.S. Census Bureau. 2008b. "Statistical Abstract of the United States: 2007 (Table 77)." Retrieved February 9, 2008 (www.census.gov/compendia/statab/tables/08s0077.xls).

————. 2008c. World POPClock Projections. Retrieved April 4, 2008 (www.census.gov/ipc/www/popclockworld/html).

U.S. Department of Agriculture. 2002. *Economic Research Service: Data set of United States Farm and Farm-Related Employment, 2002*. Washington, DC: Author.

————.2005a. *Characteristics of Food Stamp Households: Fiscal Year 2004 Summary*. Washington, DC: Author

————. 2005b. "Household Food Security in the United States, 2004." *Economic Report Vol. 11*. Washington, DC: Author.

U.S. Department of Energy. 2006. "Energy Consumption: Energy Kids Page." Retrieved November 8, 2006 (www.eia.doe.gov/kids/energyfacts/saving/efficiency/savingenergysecondary.html).

U.S. Department of Interior, Office of Education. 1930. *Availability of Public School Education in Rural Communities* (Bulletin No. 34, edited by Walter H. Gaummitz). Washington, DC: Government Printing Office.

U.S. Department of Justice. 2002. *National Crime Victimization Survey*. Washington, DC: Bureau of Justice Statistics.

————. 2004. *2004 National Crime Victimization Survey*. Washington, DC: Bureau of Justice Statistics.

————. 2006. *National Crime Victimization Survey*. Washington, DC: Bureau of Justice Statistics.

U.S. Department of Labor. 2005. *Current Population Survey*. Washington, DC: Bureau of Labor Statistics.

U.S. Department of State. 2001. "Patterns of Global Terrorism 2001 Report." Retrieved September 29, 2006 (http://www.state.gov/s/ct/rls/pgtrpt/2001.pdf).

————. 2002a. "Curbing Violence against Political Activists in Cambodia" (Press release). Retrieved September 9, 2008 (www.state.gov/r/pa/prs/ps/2002/15978.htm).

————. 2002b. *Patterns of Global Terrorism, 2001*. Washington, DC: Government Printing Office.

U.S. Executive Office of the President. 2001. *Budget of the U.S. Government*. Washington, DC: Author.

U.S. Flag Code. 2008. "U.S. Flag Code (4 US Code 1)" Retrieved August 28, 2008 (http://suvcw.org/flag.htm).

U.S. General Accounting Office. 2003. "Defense of Marriage Act—Update to Prior Report." Retrieved August 18, 2006 (www.gao.gov/new.items/d04353r.pdf).

U.S. Office of Personnel Management. 2007. "Family Leave Policies." Retrieved April 4, 2008 (www.opm.gov/OCA/LEAVE/).

U.S. Trade Representative. 2003. "North American Free Trade Agreement: Overview." Retrieved September 29, 2006 (www.ustr.gov/regions/whemisphere/overview.shtml).

University of Michigan. 2002. *Demographic Transition: An Historical Sociological Perspective. Online*. Ann Arbor: Author.

University of Michigan Documents Center. 2003. "Documents in the News—1997/2003." Retrieved June 29, 2006 (www.lib.umich.edu/govdocs/affirm.html).

University of Pennsylvania. 2007. "Bodies of Cultures: A World Tour of Body Modification." Retrieved April 14, 2008 (www.museum.upenn.edu/new/exhibits/online_exhibits/body_modification/querypublic.shtml).

UPI. 2008. "Annan Says Kenyan Conflict 'Evolving'" (January 27). Retrieved June 3, 2008 (www.upi.com/NewsTrack/Top_News/2008/01/27/annan_says_kenyan_conflict_evolving/1912/).

The Urban Institute. 2004. "Family Support, Substance Abuse Help, and Work Release Programs Are Essential as Ex-Prisoners Restart Lives in Baltimore." Retrieved September 9, 2008 (http://www.urban.org/publications/900688.html).

Vandell, Deborah Lowe and Sheri E. Hembree. 1994. "Peer Social Status and Friendship: Independent Contributors to Children's Social and Academic Adjustment." *Merrill-Palmer Quarterly* 40(4):461–75.

Vandenburgh, Henry. 2001. "Emerging Trends in the Provision and Consumption of Health Services." *Sociological Spectrum* 21(3):279–92.

Veblen, Thorstein. 1902. *The Theory of the Leisure Class: An Economic Study of Institutions.* New York: Macmillan.

Verba, Sidney and Norman H. Nie. 1972. *Participation in America: Political Democracy and Social Equality.* New York: Harper & Row.

Victor, Barbara. 2003. *Army of Roses: Inside the World of Palestinian Women Suicide Bombers.* Emmaus, PA: Rodale Books.

Von Holzen, Roger. 2005. "The Emergence of a Learning Society." *The Futurist* 39(January-February):24–25.

Voting and Democracy Research Center. 2008. "Primaries: Open and Closed." Retrieved March 21, 2008 (http://www.fairvote.org/?page=1801).

Wagmiller Robert, Jr., Li Kuang, J. Lawrence Aber., Mary Clare Lennon, and Philip Alberti. 2006. "The Dynamics of Economic Disadvantage and Children's Life Chances" *American Sociological Review* 71(5):847–66.

Waite, Linda J. and Maggie Gallagher. 2000. *The Case for Marriage: Why Married People Are Happier, Healthier, and Better off Financially.* New York: Doubleday.

Waitzkin, Howard. 2000. "Changing Patient-Physician Relationships in the Changing Health-Policy Environment." Pp. 271–83 in *Handbook of Medical Sociology,* 5th ed., edited by C. Bird, P. Conrad, and A. Fremont. Englewood Cliffs, NJ: Prentice Hall.

Walby, Sylvia. 1990. "The Historical Roots of Materialist Feminism." Paper presented at the International Sociological Association, Madrid, Spain.

Walker, Henry A. and Jennifer A. Karas 1993. "The Declining Significance of Color: Race, Color, and Status Attainment." Paper presented at the annual meeting of the American Sociological Association, Miami, FL.

Wallenstein, Peter. 2002. *Tell the Court I Love My Wife: Race, Marriage, and Law—An American History.* New York: Macmillan.

Waller, Willard. [1932] 1965. *Sociology of Teaching.* New York: Russell & Russell.

Wallerstein, Immanuel. 1974. *The Modern World System.* New York: Academic Press.

———. 1979. *The Capitalist World Economy.* London: Cambridge University Press.

———. 1991. *Geopolitics and Geoculture: Essays on the Changing World-system.* Cambridge, MA: Cambridge University Press.

———. 2004. *World Systems Analysis: An Introduction.* Durham, NC: Duke University Press.

———. 2005. "Render Unto Caesar? The Dilemmas of a Multicultural World." *Sociology of Religion* 66(2):121–33.

Wallerstein, Judith. 1996. *Surviving the Breakup: How Children and Parents Cope with Divorce.* New York: Basic Books.

Wallerstein, Judith S. and Sarah Blakeslee. 1996. *The Good Marriage: How and Why Love Lasts.* New York: Warner Books.

Wallerstein, Judith S. and Sarah Blakeslee. 2004. *Second Chances: Men, Women and Children a Decade After Divorce,* 15th ed. Boston: Houghton Mifflin.

Walsh, Edward J. and Rex H. Warland. 1983. "Social Movement Involvement in the Wake of a Nuclear Accident: Activists and Free Riders in the IMI Area." *American Sociological Review* 48(December):764–80.

Walsh, Mark. 1991. "Students at Private Schools for Blacks Post Above-Average Scores, Study Finds." *Education Week* (October 16).

Walum, Laurel Richardson. 1974. "The Changing Door Ceremony: Some Notes on the Operation of Sex Roles in Everyday Life." *Urban Life and Culture* 2(4):506–15.

Ward, Martha C. 1996. *A World Full of Women.* Boston: Allyn & Bacon.

Ward, Martha C. and Monica Edelstein. 2006. *A World Full of Women,* 4th ed. Boston: Allyn & Bacon.

Ware, Alyn. 2008. "Nuclear Stockpiles" (Project of the Nuclear Age Peace Foundation). Retrieved September 3, 2008 (www.nuclearfiles.org/menu/key-issues/nuclear-weapons/basics/nuclear-stockpiles.htm).

Warner, R. Stephen. 1993. "Work in Progress Toward a New Paradigm for the Sociological Study of Religion in the United States." *American Journal of Sociology* 98(5):1044–93.

Warren, Jennifer. 1990. "Schoolbook Furor Rends Rural Town." *Los Angeles Times* (August 20):A3.

War Resisters League. 2008. "Where Your Income Tax Money Really Goes." (www.warresisters.org/pages/piechart.htm) Retrieved April 16, 2008.

WaterAid. 2004 "No Water, No School." *Oasis* (Spring/Summer). Retrieved February 25, 2008 (http://www.wateraid.org/international/about_us/oasis/springsummer_04/1465.asp).

———. 2008 "WaterAid's Key Facts and Statistics." Retrieved February 25, 2008 (http://www.wateraid.org/international/what_we_do/statistics/default.asp).

Waters, Melissa S., Will Carrington Heath, and John Keith Watson. 1995. "A Positive Model of the Determination of Religious Affiliation." *Social Science Quarterly* 76(1):105–23.

Weatherly, Leslie A. 2004. "The Rising Cost of Health Care: Strategic and Societal Considerations for Employers." *HR Magazine* (September). Retrieved April 4, 2008 (http://findarticles.com/p/articles/mi_m3495/is_9_49/ai_n6206615).

Weber, B. J. and L. M. Omotani. 1994. "The Power of Believing." *The Executive Educator* 19(September):35–38.

Weber, David. 2003. "25 Health Care Trends: What's Hot, What's Not, and What Does the Future Hold." *Physician Executive* 29(1):6–14.

Weber, Max. 1946. *From Max Weber: Essays in Sociology,* translated and edited by Hans H. Gerth and C. Wright Mills. New York: Oxford University Press.

———. 1947. *The Theory of Social and Economic Organization,* translated and edited by A. M. Henderson and Talcott Parsons. New York: Oxford University Press.

———. [1904–1905] 1958. *The Protestant Ethic and the Spirit of Capitalism,* translated by Talcott Parsons. New York: Scribner.

Weeks, John R. 1999. *Population: An Introduction to Concepts and Issues,* 7th ed. Belmont, CA: Wadsworth.

———. 2005. *Population: An Introduction to Concepts and Issues,* 9th ed. Belmont, CA: Wadsworth.

Weidenbaum, Murray. 2006. "Globalization: Wonderland or Waste Land?" Pp. 53–60 in *Globalization: The Transformation of Social Worlds,* edited by D. Stanley Eitzen and Maxine Baca Zinn. Belmont, CA: Wadsworth.

Weil, Elizabeth. 2008. "Teaching to the Testosterone." *The New York Times Magazine* (March 2):38+.

Weisenberg, Faye and Elizabeth Stacey. 2005. "Reflections on Teaching and Learning Online: Quality Program Design, Delivery, and Support Issues from a Cross-Global Perspective." *Distance Education,* 26(3).

Weiss, Gregory L. and Lynne E. Lonnquist. 2008. *The Sociology of Health, Healing, and Illness,* 6th ed. Englewood Cliffs, NJ: Prentice Hall.

Weitz, Rose. 1995. "What Price Independence? Social Reactions to Lesbians, Spinsters, Widows and Nuns." Pp. 448–57 in *Women: A Feminist Perspective,* edited by Jo Freeman. Mountain View, CA: Mayfield.

Weitzman, Lenore J., Deborah Eifler, Elizabeth Hokada, and Catherine Ross. 1972. "Sex-role Socialization in Picture Books for Preschool Children." *American Journal of Sociology* 77(May):1125–50.

Welch, Michael. 1996. *Corrections: A Critical Approach.* St. Louis, MO: McGraw-Hill.

Weller, Christian E. and Adam Hersh. 2006. "Free Markets and Poverty." Pp. 69–73 in *Globalization: The Transformation of Social Worlds,* edited by D. Stanley Eitzen and Maxine Baca Zinn. Belmont, CA: Wadsworth.

Wells, Amy Stuart and Jeannie Oakes. 1996. "Potential Pitfalls of Systemic Reform: Early Lessons from Research on Detracking." *Sociology of Education* 69(Extra Issue):135–43.

Wenglinsky, Harold. 1997. "How Money Matters: The Effect of School District Spending on Academic Achievement." *Sociology of Education* 70(3):221–37.

Werner International Management Consultants. 2005. *Primary Textiles Labor Cost Comparisons.* Herndon, VA: Author.

Werth, James L., Dean Blevins, Karine L. Toussaint, and Martha R. Durham. 2002. "The Influence of Cultural Diversity on End-of-Life Care and Decisions." *American Behavioral Scientist* 46(2):204–19.

Wessinger, Catherine. 2000. *How the Millennium Comes Violently: From Jonestown to Heaven's Gate.* New York: Seven Bridges.

West, Candace and Don H. Zimmerman. 1987. "Doing Gender." *Gender and Society* 1(2):125–51.

Westermann, Ted D. and James W. Burfeind. 1991. *Crime and Justice in Two Societies: Japan and the United States.* Pacific Grove, CA: Brooks/Cole.

Westheimer, Joel. 2006. "Patriotism and Education: An Introduction." *Phi Delta Kappan* 87(8):569–72.

Wheeler, David L. 1995. "A Growing Number of Scientists Reject the Concept of Race." *The Chronicle of Higher Education* (February 17):A15.

White, Kevin. 2002. *An Introduction to the Sociology of Health and Illness.* London: Sage.

White, Merry I. 1987. *The Japanese Educational Challenge: A Commitment to Children.* New York: The Free Press.

Whorf, Benjamin Lee. 1956. *Language, Thought, and Reality.* New York: John Wiley.

"Why Comprehensive Health System Reform Failed" (Editorial). 1994. *American Family Physician* 50(5):919–20.

Whyte, William H. 1956. *The Organization Man.* New York: Simon and Schuster.

Wilcox, Norma and Tracey Steele. 2003. "Just the Facts: A Descriptive Analysis of Inmate Attitudes toward Capital Punishment." *The Prison Journal* 83(4):464–82.

Williams, Brian K., Stacey C. Sawyer, and Carl M. Wahlstrom. 2006. *Marriages, Families, and Intimate Relationships.* Boston: Allyn & Bacon.

Williams, Catrina. 2000. *Internet Access in U.S. Public Schools and Classrooms 1994–1999.* Washington, DC: National Center for Education Statistics.

Williams, Christine L. 1992. "The Glass Escalator: Hidden Advantages for Men in the 'Female' Professions." *Social Problems* 39(3):253–66.

Williams, D. R. and C. Collins. 1995. "U.S. Socioeconomic and Racial Differences in Health: Patterns and Explanations." *Annual Review of Sociology* 21:349–86.

Williams, Gregory H. 1996. *Life on the Color Line: The True Story of a White Boy Who Discovered He Was Black.* New York: Dutton.

Williams, Robin Murphy, Jr. 1970. *American Society: A Sociological Interpretation,* 3rd ed. New York: Alfred Knopf.

Williams, Terry and William Kornblum. 1985. *Growing Up Poor.* Lexington, MA: Lexington.

Willie, Charles Vert. 2003. *A New Look at Black Families,* 5th ed. Walnut Creek, CA: AltaMira.

Willis, Paul. 1979. *Learning to Labor: How Working Class Kids Get Working Class Jobs.* Aldershot, Hampshire, England: Saxon House.

Wilmore, Gayraud S. 1973. *Black Religion and Black Radicalism.* Garden City, NY: Doubleday.

Wilson, Bryan. 1982. *Religion in Sociological Perspective.* Oxford, UK: Oxford University Press.

Wilson, Edward O. 1980. *Sociobiology.* Cambridge, MA: Belknap.

———. 1987. *The Coevolution of Biology and Culture.* Cambridge, MA: Harvard University Press.

Wilson, Edward O., Michael S. Gregory, Anita Silvers, and Diane Sutch. 1978. "What Is Sociobiology?" *Society* 15(6):1–12.

Wilson, K. 1993. *Dialectics of Consciousness: Problems of Development, the Indian Reality.* Madras: Oneworld Educational Trust.

Wilson, Mary E. 2006. "Infectious Concerns: Modern Factors in the Spread of Disease." Pp. 313–19 in *Globalization: The Transformation of Social Worlds,* edited by D. Stanley Eitzen and Maxine Baca Zinn. Belmont, CA: Wadsworth.

Wilson, Warren H. 1924. "What the Automobile Has Done to and for the Country Church." *Annals of the American Academy of Political and Social Science* 116(November):85–86.

Wilson, William Julius. 1978. *The Declining Significance of Race: Blacks and Changing American Institutions.* Chicago: University of Chicago Press.

———. 1984. "The Black Underclass." *The Wilson Quarterly* (Spring): 88–89.

———. 1987. *The Truly Disadvantaged: The Inner City, the Underclass, and Public Policy.* Chicago: University of Chicago Press.

———. 1993a. *The Ghetto Underclass: Social Science Perspectives.* Newbury Park, CA: Sage.

———. 1993b. "The New Urban Poverty and the Problem of Race." *The Tanner Lecture on Human Values,* October 22 (printed in *Michigan Quarterly Review,* 247–73).

———. 1996. *When Work Disappears.* New York: Alfred A. Knopf.

Winders, Bill. 2004. "Changing Racial Inequality: The Rise and Fall of Systems of Racial Inequality in the U.S." Paper presented at the Annual Meeting of the American Sociological Association, San Francisco.

Winkler, Karen J. 1991. "Revisiting the Nature vs. Nurture Debate: Historian Looks Anew at Influence of Biology on Behavior." *Chronicle of Higher Education* (May 22):A5, 8.

Winnick, Terri A. 2006. "Medical Doctors and Complementary and Alternative Medicine: The Context of Holistic Practice." *Health: An Interdisciplinary Journal for the Social Study of Health, Illness and Medicine* (10:2):149–73.

Wirth, Louis. 1964. "Urbanism as a Way of Life." *American Journal of Sociology* 44(1):1–24.

Witness for Peace. March 2008. Venezuelan Delegation on Health Care. (Personal communication; interviews with members of the delegation).

Witte, John F. and Christopher A. Thorn. 1996. "Who Chooses? Voucher and Interdistrict Choice Programs in Milwaukee." *American Journal of Education* 104(May):186–217.

Witzig, Ritchie. 1996. "The Medicalization of Race: Scientific Legitimation of a Flawed Social Construct." *Annals of Internal Medicine: American College of Physicians* 125(8):675–76.

Women's Sports Foundation. 2005. "Women's Sports: Title IX Q and A" (May). Retrieved March 7, 2008 (www.org/cgi-bin/iowa/issues/rights/article).

Wong, Sandra L. 1991. "Evaluating the Content of Textbooks: Public Interests and Professional Authority." *Sociology of Education* 64(January):11–18.

Wood, Julia T. 2003. *Gendered Lives: Communication, Gender, and Culture,* 5th ed. Belmont, CA: Wadsworth.

———. 2005. *Gendered Lives: Communication, Gender, and Culture,* 6th ed. Belmont, CA: Wadsworth.

Wood, Julia T. and Nina M. Reich. 2006. "Gendered Communication Styles." Pp. 177–86 in *Intercultural Communication,* 11th ed., edited by Larry A. Samovar, Richard E. Porter, and Edwin R. McDaniel. Belmont, CA: Wadsworth.

Woodberry, Robert D. and Christian S. Smith. 1998. "Fundamentalism et al: Conservative Protestants in America." *Annual Review of Sociology* 24:25–26.

Woolhandler, Steffie, Terry Campbell, and David U. Himmelstein. 2004. "Health Care Administration in the United States and Canada: Micromanagement, Macro Costs." *International Journal of Health Services* 34(1):65–78.

World Almanac Education Group. 2001. *The World Almanac and Book of Facts 2001*. Mahwah, NJ: World Almanac Books.

World Bank. 2006. "Per Capital Income-World" (World Bank Development Indicators). Retrieved February 26, 2008 (www.finfacts.com/biz10).

World Factbook. 2003. "SARS: Status of the Outbreak and Lessons for the Immediate Future." Retrieved September 29, 2006 (www.who.int/csr/media/sars_who.pdf).

World Factbook. 2004. "Explaining Women's Legislative Representation in Sub-Saharan Africa." *Legislative Studies Quarterly* 29(3):447–68.

———. 2005. "Sub-Saharan Africa." Chapter 7 in *Sharing Power: Women, Parliament, Democracy,* edited by Manon Tremblay and Yvonne Galligan. Aldershot, UK: Ashgate.

———. 2006a. "The Current State of Global Health." Pp. 356–63 in *Beyond Borders: Thinking Critically about Global Issues,* edited by Paula S. Rothenberg. New York: Worth.

———. 2006b. "World Health Statistics 2006" and "The World Health Report, 2006 Edition." Retrieved August 14, 2006 (http://www.who.int/statistics/en/).

———. 2007a. "Literacy." Retrieved December 13, 2007 (www.cia.gov/library/publications/the-world-factbook/html).

———. 2007b. "World Health Statistics 2007." Retrieved April 4, 2008 (http://www.who.int/countries/swz/en/) and (http://www.who.int/whosis/database/core/core_elect_process.cfm?country=chn&indicators).

———. 2008. "World." Retrieved August 23, 2008 (https://www.cia.gov/library/publications/the-world-factbook/geos/xx.html).

World Health Organization. 1999. "World Health Report." Retrieved February 28, 2008 (www.who.int/whr/1999).

———. 2002. "The World Health Report: Reducing Risks, Promoting Healthy Life." *The World Health Report 2002.* Retrieved September 29, 2006 (www.who.int/whr/2002/en/whr02_en.pdf).

World Resources Institute. 2003. "Coalition of Twelve Major U.S. Corporations and WRI Announce Largest Corporate Green Power Purchases in U.S." Retrieved September 17, 2006 (www.thegreenpowergroup.org/groupevents.html).

———. 2007. "Ask Earth Trends: How Much of the World's Resource Consumption Occurs in Rich Countries?" *EarthTrends.* Retrieved April 14, 2008 (http://earthtrends.wri.org/updates/node/236).

WorldWideLearn. 2007. "Guide to College Majors in Sociology." Retrieved June 23, 2008 (www.worldwidelearn.com/online-education-guide/social-science/sociology-major.htm).

Wright, Erik Olin. 2000. *Class Counts: Comparative Studies in Class Analysis,* Student ed. Cambridge, MA: Cambridge University Press.

Wright, Stuart A. 1995. *Armageddon in Waco: Critical Perspectives on the Branch Davidian Conflict.* Chicago: University of Chicago Press.

Wuthnow, Robert, ed. 1994. *"I Come away Stronger:" How Small Groups Are Shaping American Religion.* Grand Rapids, MI: William B. Eerdmans.

Yablonski, Lewis. 1959. "The Gang as a Near-Group." *Social Problems* 7(Fall):108–17.

Yamane, David. 1997. "Secularization on Trial: In Defense of a Neosecularization Paradigm." *Journal for the Scientific Study of Religion* 36(1):109–22.

Yinger, J. Milton. 1960. "Contraculture and Subculture." *American Sociological Review* 25(October):625–35.

———.1970. *The Scientific Study of Religion.* New York: Macmillan.

Yoon, Mi Yung. 2001. "Democratization and Women's Legislative Representation in Sub-Saharan Africa." *Democratization* 8(2):169–90.

Younger, Stephen M. 2000. "Nuclear Weapons in the Twenty-first Century." Los Alamos National Laboratory, June 27. Retrieved September 2, 2008 (www.fas.org/nuke/guide/usa/doctrine/doe/younger.htm).

youthxchange 2007. "Women's Literacy." Youthxchange.net/main/b138_population_literacy.

Yung, Judith. 1995. *Unbound Feet: From China to San Francisco's Chinatown.* Berkeley: University of California Press.

Yunus, Muhammad and Alan Jolis. 1999. *Banker to the Poor: Micro-Lending and the Battle against World Poverty.* New York: Public Affairs.

Zborowski, Mark. 1952. "Cultural Components in Response to Pain." *Journal of Social Issues* 8(4):16–30.

Zelizer, Viviana A. 1985. *Pricing the Priceless Child: The Changing Social Value of Children.* New York: Basic Books.

———. 1994. *The Social Meaning of Money.* New York: Basic Books.

Zhao, Yong. 2005. "Increasing Math and Science Achievement: The Best and Worst of the East and West." *Phi Delta Kappan* (November):219–22.

Zigler, Edward, Sally J. Styfco, and Elizabeth Gilman. 1993. *Headstart and Beyond.* New Haven, CT: Yale University Press.

Zimbardo, Philip C. 2004. "Power Turns Good Soldiers Into 'Bad Apples.'" *Boston Globe* (May 9). Retrieved July 5, 2008 (http://www.boston.com/news/globe/editorial_opinion/oped/articles/2004/05/09/power_turns_good_soldiers_into_bad_apples/).

———. 2007. "You Can't Be a Sweet Cucumber in a Vinegar Barrel." Pp. 122–25 in *Sociological Footprints,* edited by Leonard Cargan and Jeanne Ballantine. Belmont, CA: Wadsworth.

Zimbardo, Philip C., Craig Haney, Curtis Banks, and David Jaffe. 1973. "The Mind Is a Formidable Jailer: A Pirandellian Prison." *The New York Times* (April 8):38–60.

Zimmer, Hans. 1992. *Millenium: Tribal Wisdom and the Modern World.* Milwaukee, WI: Narada Productions.

Zimolzak, Chester E. and Charles A. Stansfield, Jr. 1983. *Human Landscape,* 2nd ed. Columbus, OH: Merrill.

Credits

Image, "How Do We Know?" features.
© iStockphoto.com.

Image, "Key Points: What Have We Learned?"
features. © iStockphoto.com.

Image, "Sociology Around the World" features.
© iStockphoto.com.

Image, "Sociology In Your Social World" features.
© iStockphoto.com.

Chapter 1

Photo, page 2 (background). © iStockphoto.com.

Photo, page 2 (upper left). © Mansir Petrie.

Photo, page 2 (upper middle). © iStockphoto.com/
Judy Foldetta.

Photo, page 2 (upper right). © Keith Roberts.

Photo, page 2 (bottom). © Juan Collado/
iStockphoto.com.

Photo, page 4. © iStockphoto.com.

Photo, page 5. © Peter Turnley/Corbis.

Photo, page 6. © Tony Tremblay/iStockphoto.com.

Photo, page 7. © Peter Turnley/CORBIS.

Photo, page 8. © M. ou Me. Desjeux, Bernard/
CORBIS.

Photo, page 9. © Jessica Liu/iStockphoto.com.

"Sociology in Your Social World: How Will You
Spend the 21st Century?" page 11. Reprinted with
permission of Peter Dreier.

Photo, page 12 (top). © Pascal Genest/iStockphoto
.com.

Photo, page 12 (bottom). © Image Source/Corbis.

Photo, page 13. © Alain Le Garsmeur/CORBIS.

Photo, page 15. © Paul Prescott/iStockphoto.com.

Photo, page 18. © United Nations Watch.

Photo, page 22. © U.S. Navy photo by Petty Officer
2nd Class Philip A. McDaniel.

Photo, page 24. © Sylvie Fourgeot/iStockphoto.com.

Chapter 2

Photo, page 28 (background and lower left).
© Victkor Pryymachuk/iStockphoto.com.

Photo, page 28 (upper left). © iStockphoto.com.

Photo, page 28 (upper, second from left). © Mansir
Petrie.

Photo, page 28 (upper, second from right).
© iStockphoto.com.

Photo, page 28 (upper right). © James McDivitt,
Gemini 4, NASA.

Photo, page 28 (lower right). © Laurence Gough/
iStockphoto.com.

Photo, page 30. © Sean Sprague/The Image Works.

Photo, page 31. © Hulton-Deutsch Collection/
CORBIS.

Photo, page 33. Public domain.

Photo, page 34. © Alessandro Della Bella/epa/Corbis.

Photo, page 36. © Sean Sprague/The Image Works.

Photo, page 41. © Ed Quinn/Corbis.

Photo, page 43. © Bettmann/CORBIS.

Photo, page 44. © Sion Touhig/Corbis.

Photo, page 50. © Kurt Gordon/iStockphoto.com.

Photo, page 52. © Karen Porter.

Photo, page 53. © Jeanne Ballantine.

Photo, page 54. © Bettmann/CORBIS.

Photo, page 55. © Bettmann/CORBIS.

Photo, page 57. © Bettmann/CORBIS.

Chapter 3

Photo, page 62 (background and upper left).
© 2005 Peter Menzel from "Hungry Planet: What
the World Eats."

Photo, page 62 (upper middle). © 2005 Peter
Menzel from "Hungry Planet: What the World Eats."

Photo, page 62 (upper right). © 2005 Peter Menzel
from "Hungry Planet: What the World Eats."

Photo, page 62 (bottom). © 2005 Peter Menzel from
"Hungry Planet: What the World Eats."

Photo, page 64. © Peeter Viisimaa/Istockphoto.com.

Photo, page 65 (top). © Lawrence Manning/Corbis.

Photo, page 65 (bottom). © John Henley/CORBIS.

Photo, page 66 (top). © Bettmann/CORBIS.

Photo, page 66 (second from top). Public domain.

Photo, page 66 (second from bottom). Public
domain.

Photo, page 66 (bottom left). Public domain.

Photo, page 66 (bottom right). Public domain.

Photo, page 67. © Olivier Martel/Corbis.

Photo, page 68. © DLILLC/Corbis.

Photo, page 69. © iStockphoto.com.

Photo, page 70. © Fritz Hoffmann/Corbis.

Photo, page 71 (left). © Richard Stamper/
iStockphoto.

Photo, page 71 (right). © Keith Roberts.

"Sociology in Your Social World: Pop Culture and
Technology," page 74. Summarized from Danesi
(2008).

Photo, page 75. © Karen Kasmauski/Corbis.

Photo, page 76. © Bettmann/CORBIS.

Photo, page 77 (left). © Paige Falk.

Photo, page 77 (right). © Elise Roberts.

"Sociology Around the World: Evolutionary
Cuisine," page 78. Ward (1996).

Photo, page 79. © Vasiliy Koval/iStockphoto.com.

Photo, page 81. © Andy Aitchison/Corbis.

Photo, page 82. © Diane Diederich/iStockphoto.com.

Photo, page 85. © Steve Raymer/Corbis.

"Sociology Around the World: Life and Death in
a Guatemalan Village," page 86. Summarized from
Burgos-Debray (1984).

Photo, page 88. © BRUNO DOMINGOS/Reuters/
Corbis.

Photo, page 91 (top left). © www.istockphoto.com.

Photo, page 91 (top right). © Sarah Jolly.

Photo, page 91 (bottom). © www.istockphoto.com.

Photo, page 92. © Kim Kulish/Corbis.

Photo, page 94. © Shannon Stapleton/Reuters/
Corbis.

Chapter 4

Photo, page 98 (background and bottom). © Yang
Liu/Corbis.

Photo, page 98 (upper left). © Sean Locke/
iStockphoto.com.

Photo, page 98 (upper middle). © J. B. Russell/
Corbis Sygma.

Photo, page 98 (upper right). © Ariel Skelley.

Photo, page 100. © Ben German/iStockphoto.com.

Photo, page 101. © Peeter Viisimaa/iStockphoto
.com.

Photo, page 104. © www.123rf.com.

"Sociology in Your Social World: Black Men and
Public Space," page 106. Staples (1992). Reprinted
by permission of the author.

Photo, page 108. © Jose Luis Pelaez, Inc./CORBIS.

Photo, page 109. © Christopher Knittel/iStockphoto
.com.

Photo, page 110 (left). © Matt Matthews/
iStockphoto.com.

Photo, page 110 (right). © Lindsay Hebberd/Corbis.

Photo, page 111 (top). © Harish Tyagi/epa/Corbis.

Photo, page 111 (bottom). © Jehad Nga/Corbis.

Photo, page 112. © Alan Eisen/iStockphoto.com.

Photo, page 114. © Max Whittaker/Corbis.

Photo, page 116 (top). © Everett Kennedy Brown/
epa/Corbis.

Photo, page 116 (bottom). © Tibor Bognar/Corbis.

"Sociology Around the World: Socialization in
Japan: The Family and Early Schooling," page 117.
This text summarizes work by Hendry (1995).

Photo, page 118. © Keith Roberts.

Photo, page 119. © Ryan Pyle/Corbis.

Chapter 5

Photo, page 126 (background). © Caitriona Dwyer/iStockphoto.com.

Photo, page 126 (top left). © Tim Pannell/Corbis.

Photo, page 126 (top middle). © iStockphoto.com.

Photo, page 126 (top right). © Aaron Kohr/iStockphoto.com.

Photo, page 126 (bottom). © Sean Locke/iStockphoto.com.

Photo, page 128. © Michael DeLeon/iStockphoto.com.

Photo, page 131. Public domain.

Photo, page 132 (top). © Jim Jurica/iStockphoto.com.

Photo, page 132 (bottom). © Jacob Wackerhausen/iStockphoto.com.

Photo, page 133 (top left). © Mark Coffey/iStockphoto.com.

Photo, page 133 (top right). © iStockphoto.com.

Photo, page 133 (bottom left). © Julie Deshaies/iStockphoto.com.

Photo, page 133 (bottom right). © Michael Westhoff/iStockphoto.com.

Photo, page 134 (top). © Stephanie Phillips/iStockphoto.com.

Photo, page 134 (bottom). © Larry Hirshowitz/CORBIS.

Photo, page 135. © Jim Winstead.

Photo, page 139 (top left). © Jeanne Ballantine.

Photo, page 139 (top right). © Kate Ballantine.

Photo, page 139 (middle left). © Jeanne Ballantine.

Photo, page 139 (middle right). © Virginia Caudill.

Photo, page 139 (bottom left). © Jeanne Ballantine.

Photo, page 139 (bottom middle). © Jeanne Ballantine.

Photo, page 139 (bottom right). © Kate Ballantine.

Photo, page 140. © Nancy Louie/iStockphoto.com.

Photo, page 142. © Bettmann/CORBIS.

Photo, page 143 (top). © Elise Roberts.

Photo, page 143 (bottom). © Jeanne Ballantine.

Photo, page 144. © Mansir Petrie.

Photo, page 145. © Steve Starr/Corbis.

Photo, page 147. © Sean Locke/iStockphoto.com.

Photo, page 148. © Fred de Noyelle/Godong/Corbis.

Photo, page 150. © NILSEN ALAN BRIAN/CORBIS SYGMA.

Photo, page 152. © USAID.

Photo, page 155 (left). © Clay Ballantine.

Photo, page 155 (right). © Clay Ballantine.

Chapter 6

Photo, page 158 (background). © Peter Chen/istockphoto.

Photo, page 158 (top left). © Scott Houston/Corbis.

Photo, page 158 (top, second from left). © Mark Goddard/iStockphoto.com.

Photo, page 158 (top, second from right). © Jose Fuste Raga/Corbis.

Photo, page 158 (top right). © Stephanie Phillips/iStockphoto.com.

Photo, page 158 (bottom). © Corbis.

Photo, page 160. © Kim Kulish/Corbis.

Photo, page 162 (top left). © Jennifer Matthews/iStockphoto.com.

Photo, page 162 (top middle). © Viviane Moos/CORBIS.

Photo, page 162 (top right). © Eva Serrabassa/iStockphoto.com.

Photo, page 162 (middle left). © Philip James Corwin/CORBIS.

Photo, page 162 (bottom left). © DAVE MARTIN/Associated Press.

Photo, page 162 (bottom right). ©Fritz Hoffmann/The Image Works.

Photo, page 163 (top). © Jerry Koch/iStockphoto.com.

Photo, page 163 (bottom). © Frances Twitty/iStockphoto.com.

Photo, page 165. © Kathye Killer/iStockphoto.com.

Photo, page 168. © JLP/Sylvia Torres/CORBIS.

Photo, page 169. © Topham/The Image Works.

Photo, page 170. © Simon Marcus/Corbis.

Photo, page 173. © Peter Turnley/Corbis.

Photo, page 175. © Reuters/CORBIS.

Photo, page 176. © Warrick Page/Corbis.

Photo, page 180. © Jeffrey L. Rotman/Corbis.

Photo, page 181 (left). © Ed Kashi/CORBIS.

Photo, page 181 (right). © Adam Mastoon/CORBIS.

Photo, page 183. © Ryan Tacay/iStockphoto.com.

Photo, page 185. © Ron Sachs/CNP/Corbis.

Photo, page 189. © Brandon Laufenberg/iStockphoto.com.

Chapter 7

Photo 7.1, page 198 (background). © Skip O'Donnell/istockphoto.com.

Photo, page 198 (top left). © Elise Roberts.

Photo, page 198 (top, second from left). © Jeanne Ballantine.

Photo, page 98 (top, second from right). © Juan Collado/istockphoto.com.

Photo, page 198 (top right). © Jeanne Ballantine.

Photo, page 198 (bottom left). © Fergus O'Brien.

Photo, page 198 (bottom right). © Bob Ainsworth/istockphoto.com.

Photo, page 201 (top). © Pool Photograph/Corbis.

Photo, page 201 (bottom). © USAID.

Photo, page 202 (top). © USAID.

Photo, page 202 (bottom). © Thania Navarro/iStockphoto.com.

Photo, page 204. © Elise Roberts.

Photo, page 205 (top). © Jeff Kravitz /FilmMagic/Getty Images.

Photo, page 205 (bottom). © Paul Almasy/CORBIS.

Photo, page 209 (top). © Wendy Stone/CORBIS.

Photo, page 209 (bottom). © Artiga Photo/Corbis.

Photo, page 210. © Dave Bartruff/CORBIS.

Photo, page 213 (left). © Jeanne Ballantine.

Photo, page 213 (right). © Ben Blankenburg/iStockphoto.com.

Photo, page 214. © Keith Roberts.

"Sociology in Your Social World: Nickel-and-Dimed," page 216. Based on Ehrenreich (2001).

Photo, page 217. © Elise Roberts.

Photo, page 218. © Kate Ballantine.

Photo, page 223 (left). © istockphoto.com.

Photo, page 223 (right). © Emma Rian/zefa/Corbis.

"Sociology in Your Social World: The Functions of Poverty," page 226. Based on Gans (1995) and Eglitis (2004).

Photo, page 227 (left). © Elise Roberts.

Photo, page 227 (right). © iStockphoto.com.

Chapter 8

Photo, page 232 (background). © iStockphoto.com.

Photo, page 232 (top left). © Jiang Dao Hua/iStockphoto.com.

Photo, page 232 (top middle). © Elise Roberts.

Photo, page 232 (top right). © Jeanne Ballantine.

Photo, page 232 (middle). © Robert A. Sabo/Getty Images.

Photo, page 232 (bottom). © Jeanne Ballantine.

Photo, page 234. © Zana Briski and Kids with Cameras.

Photo, page 235 (top). © Sophie Elbaz/Sygma/Corbis.

Photo, page 235 (bottom). Public domain.

"Sociology in Your Social World: Historical Attempts to Define Race," page 238. Much of this entry is drawn from www .aaanet.org/press/an/cfp_race05.htm (retrieved July 5, 2006).

Photo, page 240. © Bettmann/CORBIS.

Photo, page 241. © Elise Roberts.

Photo, page 246 (top left). © Bettmann/Corbis.

Photo, page 246 (top right). © Corbis.

Photo, page 246 (bottom). © Corbis.

Photo, page 247. © Andrew Holbrooke/Corbis.

Photo, page 250. © Bettmann/CORBIS.

Photo , page 251. © Phil Schermeister/CORBIS.

Photo, page 254. © David Turnley/Corbis.

Photo, page 255 (top). © Ed Lallo//Time Life Pictures/Getty Images.

Photo, page 255 (bottom). © Josef Scaylea/CORBIS.

Photo, page 258. © Jeanne Ballantine.

Photo, page 259. © William Campbell/Sygma/Corbis.

Photo, page 262. © Bettmann/CORBIS.

Photo, page 263. © istockphoto.com.

Photo, page 264. © Ken Chambers.

"Sociology in Your Social World: Preference Policies at the University of Michigan," page 266. Includes a summary of Kantrowitz and Wingert (2003).

Photo, page 267. © TOUHIG SION/CORBIS SYGMA.

Chapter 9

Photo, page 270 (background). © Kazuyoshi Nomachi/Corbis.

Photo, page 270 (top left). © Zsolt Nyulaszi/iStockphoto.com.

Photo, page 270 (top, second from left). © David Van Der Veen/epa/Corbis.

Photo, page 270 (top, second from right). © Jo Ann Snover/iStockphoto.com.

Photo, page 270 (top right). © Jeanne Ballantine.

Photo, page 270 (bottom left). © Mansir Petrie.

Photo, page 270 (bottom right). © Mansir Petrie.

Photo, page 273. © Atlantide Phototravel/Corbis.

Photo, page 274. © Thomas Strange/iStockphoto.com.

Photo, page 276 (top left). © Matthew Cavanaugh/epa/Corbis.

Photo, page 276 (top right). © epa/Corbis.

Photo, page 276 (bottom). © Lynsey Addario/Corbis.

Photo, page 277. © Jeanne Ballantine.

Photo, page 282. © Jostein Hauge/iStockphoto.com.

Photo, page 283. © Robert Cumming/iStockphoto.com.

Photo, page 284 (left). © Lynn Goldsmith/CORBIS.

Photo, page 284 (right). © Lynn Goldsmith/CORBIS.

Photo, page 285 (left). © Hubert Boesl/dpa/Corbis.

Photo, page 285 (right). © Lawrence Lucier/FilmMagic.

Photo, page 287 (top). © Greg Fiume/NewSport/Corbis.

Photo, page 287 (bottom). © S. Carmona/CORBIS.

Photo, page 289. © Pathathai Chungyam/iStockphoto.com.

Photo, page 291. © USAID.

Photo, page 292. © Trinette Reed/Brand X/Corbis.

Photo, page 293. © Adrian Weinbrecht/Getty Images.

Photo, page 294. © Jeanne Ballantine.

Photo, page 296. © Nadeem Khawer/epa/Corbis.

Photo, page 297. © Kate Ballantine.

Photo, page 300. © BAUMGARTNER OLIVIA/CORBIS SYGMA.

Photo, page 301. © UNESCO, photo by Dominique Rogers.

Photo, page 302. © Narendra Shrestha/epa/Corbis.

Photo, page 303. © Lynette Osborne.

Chapter 10

Photo, page 308 (background and bottom). © Akram Saleh/Reuters/Corbis.

Photo, page 308 (top left). © Sandra Gligorijevic/iStockphoto.com.

Photo, page 308 (top middle). © Nancy Louie/iStockphoto.com.

Photo, page 308 (top right). © Radu Razvan/iStockphoto.com.

Photo, page 308 (middle left). © SAUL LOEB/AFP/Getty Images.

Photo, page 308 (middle right). © Fred Palmieri/istockphoto.com.

Photo, page 310. © Tomas van Houtryve/Corbis.

"Sociology in Your Social World: The Ideal Family," page 311. Adapted from a classroom questionnaire created by Charles Green, University of Wisconsin, Whitewater.

Photo, page 312. © Kate Ballantine.

Photo, page 313 (top left). © Jelani Memory/iStockphoto.com.

Photo, page 313 (top middle). © Jaren Wicklund/iStockphoto.com.

Photo, page 313 (top right). © Glenda Powers/istockphoto.

Photo, page 313 (middle left). © Kate Ballantine.

Photo, page 313 (middle right). © Creatas Images / Jupiter Images.

Photo, page 313 (bottom left). © Kate Ballantine.

Photo, page 313 (bottom right). © Andrew Sacks/Corbis.

Photo, page 314 (left). © Kate Ballantine.

Photo, page 314 (right). © Joshua Black/iStockphoto.

Photo, page 315. © Wolfgang Kaehler/CORBIS.

Photo, page 316. © Carla Howery.

Photo, page 318. © Kazuyoshi Nomachi/Corbis.

Photo, page 325. © China Photos/Getty Images.

Photo, page 326. © Mark Peterson/Corbis.

Photo, page 327. © Jacques M. Chenet/Corbis.

Photo, page 330. © Karen Kasmauski/Corbis.

Photo, page 333. © Justin Sullivan/Getty Images.

Photo, page 334. © David Adame/Getty Images.

Photo, page 336. © Mansir Petrie.

Chapter 11

Photo, page 342 (background). © iStockphoto.com.

Photo, page 342 (top left). © Jeanne Ballantine.

Photo, page 342 (top middle). © Keith Roberts.

Photo, page 342 (top right). © Elise Roberts.

Photo, page 342 (bottom left). Courtesy of Hanover College.

Photo, page 342 (bottom right). © Jeanne Ballantine.

Photo, page 344. © Earl & Nazima Kowall/CORBIS.

Photo, page 346. © Daniel O. Conkle.

Photo, page 347. © Brandon Laufenberg/iStockphoto.com.

Photo, page 348. © Elise Roberts.

Photo, page 352 (top left). © iStockphoto.com.

Photo, page 352 (top right). © Bonnie Jacobs/iStockphoto.com.

Photo, page 352 (middle left). © iStockphoto.com.

Photo, page 352 (middle right). © Charles Silvey/iStockphoto.com.

Photo, page 352 (bottom left). © Friedman Wagner-Dobler/iStockphoto.com.

Photo, page 352 (bottom right). © Jason Andras.

Photo, page 353. © Gideon Mendel/Corbis.

Photo, page 354. © Kevin Russ/iStockphoto.com.

Photo. Page 356 (top left). © TWPhoto/Corbis.

Photo, page 356 (top right). © Jamie Wilson/iStockphoto.com.

Photo, page 356 (middle left). © Keith Dannemiller/D70s/Corbis.

Photo, page 356 (middle right). © Keith Roberts.

Photo, page 356 (bottom left). Courtesy of Hanover College.

Photo, page 356 (bottom right). © USAID.

Photo, page 357. © Najlah Feanny/Corbis.

Photo, page 361. © Bonnie Jacobs/iStockphoto.com.

Photo, page 363. © Keith Roberts.

Photo, page 364. © USAID.

Photo, page 370. © Gideon Mendel/Corbis.

Photo, page 371 (top). © Karen Kasmauski/Corbis.

Photo, page 371 (bottom). © Karen Kasmauski/Corbis.

Photo, page 373. © Najlah Feanny/Corbis.

Photo, page 374 (top). © Alain Nogues/Corbis.

Photo, page 374 (bottom). © Anthony Bannister/Corbis.

Photo, page 375. Courtesy of Hanover College.

Chapter 12

Photo, page 380 (background and top left). © Steven Allen/istockphoto.com.

Photo, page 380 (top middle). © iStockphoto.com.

Photo, page 380 (top right). © Nancy Louie/iStockphoto.com.

Photo, page 380 (bottom). © Elise Roberts.

Photo, page 383. © Jeanne Ballantine.

Photo, page 384. © Christophe Boisvieux/Corbis.

Photo, page 386. © Corbis.

Photo, page 388 (top). © Corbis.

Photo, page 388 (bottom). © Kevin Fleming/Corbis.

Photo, page 389 (top). © Peter Turnley/CORBIS.

Photo, page 389 (bottom). © Matthias Wassermann/iStockphoto.com.

Photo, page 390 (top). © Kaveh Kazemi/Corbis.

Photo, page 390 (bottom). © Antoine Gyori/CORBIS SYGMA.

Photo, page 391. © Keith Roberts.

Photo, page 392. Used with permission from the First Presbyterian Church of Granada Hills.

Photo, page 393. Ken Matesich, photographer. Courtesy of the Arizona State Museum and the University of Arizona.

Photo, page 394. © AFP/Getty.

Photo, page 395. © Keith Roberts.

Photo, page 398. © JOHN GRESS/Reuters/Corbis.

Photo, page 401. © Juan Echeverria/Corbis.

Photo, page 402. © Keith Roberts

Photo, page 404. © Rebecca McEntee/Corbis Sygma.

Photo, page 405 (top). © Virginia Caudill.

Photo, page 405 (bottom). © Virginia Caudill.

Photo, page 408. Photo courtesy of Reverend Vickie Perkins. © Keith Roberts.

Photo, page 411. © Elise Roberts.

Photo, page 412 (top left). © Paula Bronstein/Getty Images.

Photo, page 412 (top right). © Bettmann/Corbis.

Photo, page 412 (bottom). © Setboun/Corbis.

Chapter 13

Photo, page 420 (background). © Mark Poprocki.

Photo, page 420 (top left). © Ann Steer/istockphoto.com.

Photo, page 420 (top right). © Tony Tremblay/iStockphoto.com.

Photo, page 420 (bottom). © USAID.

Photo, page 422. © Larry W. Smith/epa/Corbis.

Photo, page 423. © Eric Thayer/Getty Images.

Photo, page 426. © iStockphoto.com.

Photo, page 427 (top). © Anwar Hussein/Getty Images.

Photo, page 427 (bottom). © Cate Gillon/Getty Images.

Photo, page 428. © ANDREW ROSS/AFP/Getty Images.

Photo, page 429. © Paula Bronstein/Getty Images.

Photo, page 434. © Ernst Haas/Ernst Haas/Getty Images.

Photo, page 437. © Per-Anders Pettersson/Getty Images.

Photo, page 438. © Elise Caffee.

Photo, page 439. © Elise Roberts.

Photo, page 440. © Steve Parsons/AFP/Getty Images.

Photo, page 442. © Mario Tama/Getty Images.

Photo, page 443. © TEH ENG KOON/AFP/Getty Images.

Photo, page 445. © AFP/AFP/Getty Images.

Photo, page 446. © JORGE UZON/AFP/Getty Images.

Photo, page 452. © AHMAD GHARABLI/AFP/Getty Images.

Photo, page 454. © Mia Song/Star Ledger/Corbis.

Photo, page 455. © David Silverman/Getty Images.

Chapter 14

Photo, page 458 (background). © Andreej Tokarski/iStockphoto.com.

Photo, page 458 (top left). © Tony Arruza/CORBIS.

Photo, page 458 (top, second from left). © Luis Enrique Ascui/Reuters/Corbis.

Photo, page 458 (top, second from right). © Macduff Everton/CORBIS.

Photo, page 458 (top right). © Silvia Morara/Corbis.

Photo, page 458 (bottom). © Matthew Rambo/iStockphoto.com.

Photo, page 460. © Thomas Pidgeon/Sygma/Corbis.

Photo, page 461. © Kate Ballantine.

Photo, page 463. © Reuters/CORBIS.

Photo, page 464. © William Casey/iStockphoto.com.

Photo, page 466. © World Health Organization 2006.

Photo, page 467. © Claudia Daut/Reuters/Corbis.

Photo, page 469. © Luis Pedrosa.

Photo, page 470. © Jeanne Lemkau.

Photo, page 471. © Erwin Patzelt/dpa/Corbis.

Photo, page 474 (top). © David Elfstrom/iStockphoto.com.

Photo, page 474 (bottom). © Mika/zefa/Corbis.

Photo, page 476 (top left). © Leah-Anne Thompson/iStockphoto.com.

Photo, page 476 (top right). © Sean Locke/iStockphoto.com.

Photo, page 476 (bottom left). © Rich Legg/iStockphoto.com.

Photo, page 476 (bottom right). © Joseph Abbot/iStockphoto.com.

Photo, page 477. © 2006 CNET Networks, Inc.

"How Do We Know? Historical Content Analysis in Sociology: *The Social Transformation of American Medicine*," page 478. Starr (1982).

Photo, page 480. © Ed Kashi/CORBIS.

Chapter 15

Photo, page 496 (background). © NASA.

Photo, page 496. © NASA.

Photo, page 499. © USAID.

Photo, page 500. © Elise Roberts.

Photo, page 502. © Micah Walter/Corbis.

Photo, page 503. © Reuters/CORBIS.

Photo, page 504. © Alain Keler/Sygma/Corbis.

Photo, page 505 (top). © 2006 World Health Organization.

Photo, page 505 (bottom). © 2006 World Health Organization.

Photo, page 507 (top). © Kate Ballantine.

Photo, page 507 (bottom). © Wolfgang Kaehler/CORBIS.

Photo, page 508. © www.downtheroad.org.

Photo, page 509. © Jeanne Ballantine.

Photo, page 510. © PORNCHAI KITTIWONGSAKUL/AFP/Getty Images.

Photo, page 511. © Nani Afrida/epa/Corbis.

Photo, page 513. © Ted Streshinsky/CORBIS.

Photo, page 514. © Louise Gubb/CORBIS SABA.

Photo, page 516. © Mimi Mollica/Corbis.

Photo, page 517. © Peter Turnley/CORBIS.

Photo, page 520. © Rob DeLorenzo/ZUMA/Corbis.

Photo, page 522 (top left). © Timothy Babasade/istockphoto.com.

Photo, page 522 (top right). © Jeannette Meir Kamer/istockphoto.com.

Photo, page 522 (middle left). © Ralph Paprzycki.

Photo, page 522 (middle right). © Jeanne Ballantine.

Photo, page 522 (bottom left). © Jeanne Ballantine.

Photo, page 522 (bottom right). © Elise Roberts.

Photo, page 526 (top). © Elise Roberts.

Photo, page 526 (bottom). © Kate Ballantine.

Photo, page 527. © Michael S. Yamashita/CORBIS.

Photo, page 482. © Najlah Feanny/CORBIS SABA.

Photo, page 485. © Christopher J. Morris/Corbis.

Photo, page 486. © Havard Saebo/iStockphoto.com.

Photo, page 487 (left). © Noriko Coop.

Photo, page 487 (right). © USAID Dakar, Senegal.

Photo, page 489. © USAID.

Photo, page 490 (top left). © 2006 World Health Organization. All Rights Reserved.

Photo , page 490 (top right). © 2006 World Health Organization. All Rights Reserved.

Photo, page 490 (bottom). © 2006 World Health Organization. All Rights Reserved.

Chapter 16

Photo, page 544 (background). © Bart Sadowski/iStockphoto.com.

Photo, page 544 (left). © Brave New Films.

Photo, page 544 (right). © Christopher J. Morris/CORBIS.

Photo, page 547 (left). © Jeanne Ballantine.

Photo, page 547 (right). © Jon Hrusa/epa/Corbis.

Photo, page 548. © Keith Roberts.

Photo, page 550. © Daniel Berehulak/Getty Images.

Photo, page 551. © iStockphoto.com.

Photo, page 553. © USAID.

Photo, page 555. © USAID.

Photo, page 556 (top). © Sharon Meredith/iStockphoto.com.

Photo, page 556 (bottom). © Philippe Renault/istockphoto.com.

Photo, page 559. © Jeanne Ballantine.

Photo, page 560. © Gideon Mendel/Corbis.

Photo, page 563. © Xuan Busto/iStockphoto.com.

Photo, page 564. © Peter Turnley/The Denver Post/Corbis.

Photo, page 567. © Juan Monino/iStockphoto.com.

Photo, page 571. © Ruth Meinzen-Dick.

Photo, page 573 (top). © Bettmann/Corbis.

Photo, page 573 (bottom). © Francoise de Mulder/Corbis.

Photo, page 574. © Nicholas Kamm/AFP/Getty Images.

Photo, page 575. © WALTER DHLADHLA/AFP/Getty Images.

Photo, page 576. © Christopher J. Morris/CORBIS.

Photo, page 577. © TEKEE TANWAR/AFP/Getty Images.

Photo, page 578. © Jeanne Ballantine.

Photo, page 579. © Jeanne Ballantine.

Photo, page 530. © iStockphoto.com.

Photo, page 531. © Jeanne Ballantine.

Photo, page 532. © Steven Allen/iStockphoto.com.

Photo, page 534. © Loic Bernard/iStockphoto.com.

"Sociology Around the World: 'Ring Around the Rosey' and the Plague," page 536. Summarized from Barefoot (2003).

Photo, page 537. © Louie Psihoyos/CORBIS.

Photo, page 539 (top). © Elise Roberts.

Photo, page 539 (bottom). © Jeanne Ballantine.

Glossary/Index

Drug traffic/abuse, 180, 181, 182, 188, 284, 463, 469
Dual-career families, 327–328
Du Bois, W. E. B., 33, 55
Durkheim, É., 33, 37, 53, 67, 142, 173, 292, 403, 465, 525
Dyads, 6, 17, 18, 81 (table)
Dysfunctions. Actions that undermine the stability or equilibrium of society, 53, 257

Earth First!, 427
Eastern Europe, 7, 467, 504
Eating disorders, 172, 299–300, 469
Eating patterns, 469–470
Eavesdropping, 184
eBay, 187
Ebola, 465, 504
Ecclesia. Official state religions; refers to religious groups that claim as members everybody within the boundaries of a particular society, 398–400
Eckert, P., 15
Economic recession, 465, 549
Economics, 13
Economic systems, 6, 17
    bailouts, volatile money markets and, 441
    capitalist systems, support of, 103
    conflict theory and, 204–206
    debt bondage, 234–235
    democratic socialist/welfare states, 444
    economic institutions, politics and, 441–444
    estate systems and, 217, 219
    family structure and, 316, 325–328, 326 (tables), 327 (figure)
    fertility rates and, 508–510, 509 (figure)
    five-year development plans, 443
    globalized economies, 70, 214, 230, 574
    health of citizens and, 462
    inequalities, crime and, 186
    instability in, 18, 20
    Internet technology and, 229
    market systems, 441, 442–443
    mass education and, 345
    micro-lending organizations, 156, 231, 235, 278
    mixed economies, 444
    nickel-and-dimed individuals, 215–216
    planned/centralized systems, 441, 443–444
    population growth, economic development and, 506, 507–508
    power and, 54, 55, 220
    prosperity, creativity/local culture and, 71, 72
    Protestant ethic, capitalism and, 395–398
    recession and, 174
    resource distribution and, 11, 95, 204–207
    scientific knowledge, economic purposes and, 70
    social mobility and, 213
    socioeconomic status, deviance and, 170
    technologically-based societies, 70–71
    terrorism and, 548
    types of, 441–444
    unemployment, trauma of, 9–10
    See also Capitalism; Social mobility; Stratification system
Educational systems, 6, 17, 344
    access to, 8, 207
    achievement gap, 367
    administrators/managers, 357, 362
    book banning and, 364, 365 (table)
    bureaucratic school structure, 362–363
    choice/voucher programs, 371
    conflict perspective, stratification systems and, 350–351
    correctional facilities and, 193–194
    distance education and, 375, 376

dropouts, 169, 351, 354
early childhood education programs, 373
education-based social class, 71, 118
education gaps, 344, 367, 369, 369 (table), 373–374, 512
elite education organizations, 350–351, 358, 367
equality issues and, 366, 367, 369–371, 369 (table)
family institution and, 363–364
formal education, 110, 113, 344, 347, 362, 362 (table)
functionalist perspective on, 347–350, 348 (figure), 349 (map)
funding sources and, 370
future of global education system, 374–375
gender socialization and, 115, 275, 286, 300
girls' education, developing nations and, 373–374, 512
global education systems, 344–345, 345 (table)
government policy and, 18, 225
higher education, rape and, 295
high schools, environment of, 15
ideal-type bureaucracy and, 150
individualism/achievement ethic and, 103
individuals, micro-level theories and, 346–347
informal education, 347
informal system of schooling, 357–361, 358–359 (tables)
learning disabilities, 282
literacy development, 124, 345, 345 (table)
local-level influences on, 364, 365 (table)
macro-level theories on, 347–351, 366–371
magnet schools, 368
mass education, 345
meso-level analysis and, 21, 362–366
microcultures in, 79, 83 (figure)
micro-level theories on, 346–347, 351–361
multicultural education, 263, 349–350
national-level influences on, 364–366
peer culture of schools and, 351–355
personal/social development and, 350
power elite and, 95, 350, 351
private schools, 350–351, 370–371
public schools, 370–371
rational choice theory and, 346–347
religious practice and, 406, 406 (table), 412, 413
school-to-work transition, 375
secondary groups and, 143
sex education, 364
sexual harassment and, 353, 355
skilled laborers and, 33
social change and, 349–350
socialization process and, 18, 103, 115, 117, 118–121, 203, 316, 344, 348–349
social mobility and, 212–213, 213 (table), 366, 367
social policy issues and, 371–376
sports programs and, 286, 317
standardized testing, 355, 363, 366, 367, 369, 369 (table)
STEM initiative and, 303
stratification systems and, 350–351, 366–371
student associations for equity issues, 269
student-teacher ratios, 345
symbolic interaction perspective on, 346
teacher roles and, 355–357, 358–360, 359 (table)
technical institutes, 70
tracking in, 213, 249, 369
violence in schools, 355
See also Formal education; Head Start program; Life chances
Egalitarianism, 322, 323, 353, 442
Egoistic suicide, 142
Egypt, 219, 389, 399, 534

Ehrlich, A., 505
Ehrlich, P., 505
Eitzen, D. S., 574
Elderly population, 110–112, 119, 222
    dependency and, 502
    medical care for, 460–461, 471–472, 473
    retirement issues, 519–520
Election politics:
    Constitution and, 449
    election laws, 279, 432, 438
    super delegates, 449
    United States, 446–449, 447–449 (table)
    See also Electoral College; Voter participation
Electoral College, 440, 449
Electronic media. *See* Computers; Media effects
Elite theory, 428–429
Elrod, L., 172
El Salvador, 262, 279, 300
Embarrassment, 108, 172, 287, 288
Embezzlement, 182
Emergent norm theory, 563–564
Emotional support, 316
Empathy, 57, 291
Empirical knowledge. Collection of facts and observations that can be objectively observed and carefully measured using the five senses (sometimes enhanced by scientific instruments); the reality of what is being measured should be the same for all people who observe it, 28, 34
Employee-employer contracts, 52
Employee-owned companies, 153, 205
Endogamy. Norms that require individuals to marry inside certain human boundaries, whatever the societal members see as protecting the homogeneity of the group, 320, 321
Energy harnessing, 69, 71, 72
Engels, Friedrich, 293, 294, 317, 507, 559
Enlightenment, 414, 558
Enron Corporation scandal, 152–153
Entertainment, 557
Entrepreneurial enterprise, 205–206, 442, 443
Environment. The setting in which the social unit operates, including everything that influences the social unit, such as its physical surroundings and technological innovations, 19
    human agency and, 50
    human culture and, 73
    religious organizations and, 19
    social change and, 551
    symbols, naming objects and, 107
    technology, change and, 576–581
    urban ecosystems and, 535–536
Environmental conservation, 86–87, 175, 186, 546
Environmental degradation, 78, 183
    Bhopal disaster, 577
    corporate pollution and, 505
    dying planet scenario, 505
    famine and, 504, 514
    global warming, 71, 122, 535, 549
    overpopulation and, 507, 512
    recycling and, 546
    urbanization and, 533, 535–536
Environmental Protection Agency (EPA), 183
Environmental racism, 546
Epidemics, 500, 504, 506, 535, 536
Epilepsy, 461, 465
Equal Employment Opportunity Commission, 264
Equality issues, 32, 33, 55, 57, 444
    See also Educational systems; Feminist theory; Inequality issues
Equal opportunity, 57, 288, 294, 366, 367
Equal Rights Amendment (ERA), 572
Erikson, K. T., 552